The Context

Forsaken histories

&

Prophecies

End of The Beginning

Baxter Todd

Copyright © 2022 D. Baxter Todd.

ISBN: 979-8986636313

Written by D. Baxter Todd.

The Context: End of the Beginning

Table of Contents

Chapters		Page
Introduction		iii
Prologue		iii
Peering from the Ice Age		1
Divergence at Olduvai		3
Foothills of Rwenzori:	The Proto-Anu-BaTwa	6
The Southern Sphere		11
• Wetlands of the Kalahari	The Proto-Khoisan	11
Primal Migrations:		17
The Big Freeze:	Ice Age Glaciations	20
Emergence of the Nilotics		24
The Glacial Maximum		24
Ascendance of the Anu		25
• The Prescient Kings		29
• Path of Ptah:	The Awakening	30
• Destiny of Bes:	The Eternal War	53
• Eponymous An:	The Guiding Light	109
Emergence of the Nagas		165
• Nascent Nagu-Naro	The Proto-Naga	166
Dawn of the Eon		173
The Kumari Peninsula		176
Rise of Nagu-Noro		178
The Allerød Warming		185
• Excursions of the Khoisan:	Naga-Sunda	186
• Exodus of the Adi-Dasas:	Kumari Kandam	187
Northward Push of the Nagas		190
• First Neolithic War		191
• Rise of Nagu-Punt		195
Foreshadowers of Empire		199
The Vela X Supernova		201
• The Great Floods		202
• Deluge at Sunda		202
• Inundation at Kumari		203

Chapters		Page
Prosperity at Nagu-Punt		205
The Final Inundations		206
• Isles of Sunda	Sunda Archipelago	207
• Isles of Kamari	Kumari Nadu	209
The Northern Sphere		211
• The Saharan Pump		211
• Central Saharan Seas		212
• The Northward Migrations		213
Kwa of the Niger		217
• Emergence of the Manding		218
• Western Inland Sea:	The Mauritanian Sea	220
• Rise of the Manding-Si (Xi)		221
Northern Inland Sea:	The Fabled Triton Sea	224
• Shrouds of the Si (Xi)		226
• Highland Sanctuaries		227
Tropic of Cancer	The First Pluvial	234
• The Triton River Valley		236
• Legendary Lake Tritonis		239
Watergate at Gabes		241
• Rise of the Atlas		244
• Coalescence of Fire:	The Inter-Pluvial	247
. Return of the Rains:	The Second Pluvial	251
Ascendance at the Atlas:	Rise of Atlatia	256
• The Holocene:	Neolithic Sub-Pluvial	261
• Islands in the Sahara		263
• Atlatian Archipelago		267
Height of Atlatia	Plato's Atlantis	269
• Traces of the Fall		281
• Revenge of Ra:	Return of the Sun	285
Rise of the Sahel:	Ancient Land of Kush	287
• Tribes of Kush		290
• Kushite Migrations		293

Chapters		Page
Encountering the Nagas		294
• Second Neolithic War		297
• Allies at Kumari Nadu		305
The Asian Excursion:	Crossing the Straits	306
• Yves of Yemen		307
• Sunrise at Sumer		308
• Enter Elam		312
Sea of Knowledge:	Island City of Shambhala	317
Naga-Mandla:	Realm of Shiva (Shambo)	322
• Into India		324
Kusha-Dwipa:	Nascent Kushite Empire	336
Return to Sumer		339
• Rescuing Nimrod		340
On to Kánaán:	Eastern Mediterranean	346
• Port City of Gubal:	Old Byblos	348
• Island City of Tyre		348
• Island City of Sidon		349
• Early Ancient Ugarit	The Kena-Anu	350
Kushites at Kánaán		352
Plying the Northern Seas		356
• Voyage to the Isle of Crete		357
• The Cyclades Archipelago		364
• Voyage to the Isle of Naxos		365
Excursion into Eurasia:	Earliest Thrace	371
• Old Kavala City		373
• Early Ancient Athens		375
• Early Ancient Thrace		376
Proto-Black Sea:	The Euxine Sea	380
• Early Ancient Troy		381
• The Prometheus Paradox		385

Chapters		**Page**
The Phrygian League	Old Phrygia	389
• Kingdom of Troas	Old Troy	392
• Early Ancient Lykia		395
• Isle of Cypress		399
Return to Khemet:	House of Khem	401
• Island City of Hēráclĕŏpŏlis		404
• Isle of Khmunu: Hermopolis	"City of Eight"	407
• Return to Ancient Thebes		414
Wisdoms of Isis		415
• Shadow of Atlatia		415
• Encountering Het-Heru (Aphrodite)		418
• Reunion and Solace with Ausar		440
Endeavor for Accord with Seteth (Set)		442
• Assassination of Ausar (Osiris, Kush)		443

Introduction

It has been said, with a degree of empirical authority, that history, and by extension pre-history, is, in essence, a continuing debate about the past, what happened, and what it means; that it is an ongoing debate because it is understood that the past can never be recovered in full.[i] While new evidence and new perspectives will inevitably shift interpretations, it must be acknowledged that some aspects of the past will be known imperfectly and sadly, there are some things that will never be known. By definition, the reconstructed past is contested terrain. It proceeds from great skepticism. Nothing is taken for granted. Everything is contingent. Everyone lied ---- at least as a presumption.[1]

History is a clock that people use to tell their political and cultural time of day. It is also a compass that people use to find themselves on the map of human geography. The role of history is to tell people what they have been, where they have been, what they are and where they are. Yet the most important role that history plays is to tell a people what they still must be, and where they still must belong."[ii] There are no people without history and traditions; traditions are the lifeblood of a people. A people who refuse to express their love and appreciation for their ancestors will die because, in traditions, if you are not expressing your own, you are expressing faith in someone else's ancestors.[iii]

People unfamiliar with their true history are people with amnesia, who have forgotten their historic timeline and the timeline of our planet, a timeline ignored by mainstream historians. Historical thought is essentially timelessness in the sense that *time* is not *duration,* as it affects the fate of individuals. It marks the *rhythm* of the collective evolution of a people. It is not a river flowing in one direction from a known source to a known outlet; it incorporates eternity in both directions. Bygone generations are not lost to the present. In their own way, they remain as influential as they were during their lifetimes, if not more so. The social nature of the "African" conception of time lends it a historical dimension, for history in full context is the story of the evolution and development of humankind in time.[iv]

During the inhuman *Atlantic Slave Trade* and the centuries after that, corrupted and false histories were forged into "mainstream" history books. However, indelible ancient sources continued to reveal the true origins and history of Africa and peoples of African descent. As of late, people have been able to trace their ancestry with access to historical, archeological, and other information, which has allowed the victims of historical deceit to put accurate historical knowledge and perspective in present-day historical cannons. A process that is ongoing, with newly discovered evidence presented each year supporting discussion and reconstruction of the "forsaken histories". [v]

---

[1] From American Slavery in History and Memory, by Ira Berlin

Where no written records or inscriptions are preserved, archaeology and oral tradition assume the tasks of transmitters of the social and cultural creations of ancient peoples said to have no written records. Written history merely brushes the fringes of Africa's past; much of the continent's recorded history is only a century or two old. As a result, prehistoric archaeology is the main key to unlocking Africa's ancient past, a key to revealing aspects of earliest antiquity that have been imperfectly known until recently. Africa's archaeological heritage is both ancient and rich; peoples have emerged and migrated, a multitude of cultures have emerged, and empires have risen and fallen. Archaeologists are painting an increasingly complex and vivid picture depicting much of Africa's known and recently discovered ancient past.

Archaeology can be divided into two basic categories. Historic archaeology deals with periods that have written records produced either by local people or outsiders. Prehistoric archaeology studies the nuances of ancient cultures or periods without written records.[vi] Notwithstanding, archaeology alone is insufficient to capture a full spectrum picture. Thus other tools are also employed, such as historical linguistics, which provides clues about past migrations and the relationships of ethnic groups. Ethnography, another useful tool, is the study of present-day ethnic groups and their immediate ancestors. Accordingly, it helps archaeologists trace connections between the past and the present.[vii] Geography and geology, in turn, offer insights into the physical landscapes people inhabited from the earliest antiquity through the much later ancient historical age.

Of course, artifacts are the most familiar objects of archaeological research; studying early ancient tools and other material allows archaeologists to discover clues about the way people lived during antiquity through the ancient historical age. While much has been looted and is forever lost, much has been discovered and much more awaits excavation. Objects of study range from simple stone tools to the ruins of great prehistoric civilizations. What evidence is now uncovered or discovered must usually first be reconstructed from slim and elusive clues, an example of which is the thousands of ancient parchments saved when the Alexandrian library was destroyed – amounting to many thousands of volumes of early ancient African history, philosophy and spiritual belief that had long passed out of the reach of profane hands.[viii] [ix]

Before history became legend and legend became myth, the oral traditions of "pre-history" were maintained for thousands of years, preserved, and handed down throughout the generations since the dawn of civilization. These were ancient traditions weakened by the vagaries of the victors of man's incessant wars, who readily recast and corrupted ancient and contemporary history to fit their own image. Thus, truth has been sacrificed and lost to the hubris of the victors of man's wars, who, in turn, distorted and readily recast it to serve their own purposes. Advents that have, over time, fragmented, supplanted, and buried the true context of historical evolution and development within the false narratives and half-truths of past and present regimes. A central theme of this work is the reconciliation of global history by placing the long and evident history of Africa at its center, like the missing piece of a puzzle that, when added, provides true historical context.[x] [xi]

1

History is not linear; the fabric of human history is adorned with confusing and sometimes confounding patterns. Notwithstanding, throughout the ages, through myth, allegory, parables, iconography and symbolism, the fragmented remains of ancient civilizations have preserved key aspects of true history down to the present day.[xii] What is needed is an effort to weave the various threads provided into a coherent, prismatic tapestry revealing the reconciled truth of prehistory and global history. Fortunately, there is no need to spin and weave thread at the same time; the threads of the earliest antiquity, as well as the starting pattern of the fabric of human history itself, are irrefutably African. Accordingly, what follows is premised on a conceptual framework in which ancient African history is deemed the central *missing aspect* needed to coherently reconcile and contextualize true history.[xiii]

It is pertinent to note that this book is written in the "creative nonfiction genre" to allow optimal facility and flexibility in contextualizing African prehistory within the era spanning the emergence of civilization through the dawn of early antiquity. Relatedly, because ancient African mythology has been pillaged of fantasy and romanticism or subjected to deliberate usurpation and appropriation by others (an example of which is the fairytale of "Snow White and the Seven Dwarves", whose formative character structure is eerily similar to that of "Ptah and the Seven Dwarves" (described as wooly-haired pygmies)), and further, because for the literary use of "parables" has been limited in accentuating and animating early ancient African mythos, a liberal literary license is used in the *parables* presented in the book.[xiv]

Last but certainly not least, it must be acknowledged that this book has been written from the vantage point of having stood on the shoulders of giants of African historical research and thought. Giants such as Chancellor Williams, Cheikh Anta Diop, John Henric Clark, Yosef Ben-Jochannan, John G. Jackson, Runoko Rashidi, Dr. Frances Cress Welsing, Dr. Frantz Fanon, Ivan Van Sertima, Dr. Jacob H. Carruthers, Drusilla D. Houston, Dr. Vamos-Toth Bator, Professor Molefi Kete Asante, Ra Un Nefer Amen, Paul Alfred Barton, Dr. B. R. Ambedkar, Dr. Clyde A. Winters and many others whose names are included in the "End Notes" to the book, which have been set forth as a sort of compendium to the research and information presented. I have acknowledged the scholarship of all those whose work I draw on here.

Prologue

If, as is often said, history is prologue, then "prologue" must surely have been the beginning, which, for purposes of this work, appears to have been somewhere between 130,000 to 110,000 years ago,[xv] when the climate of the Earth was much like that of today, though somewhat warmer and moister in southern hemispheric and equatorial regions.[xvi] When the period ended is uncertain. However, sediment records suggest it was a sudden rather than a gradual progression to colder conditions over thousands of years.[xvii] As the cold grew more severe, the climate became drier because the "global weather machine" that evaporates water from the oceans and drops it on the land operates less effectively at colder temperatures, particularly when the polar ice is extensive.

The era between 130,000-110,000 years ago is known as the Eemian interglacial period, and though the time at which the Eemian interglacial ended is subject to some uncertainty, what seems evident from sediment records that cross this boundary is that it was a relatively sudden event. Following this initial cooling event, conditions often changed in sudden leaps and bounds, followed by thousands of years of relatively stable climate or even a temporary reversal to warmth. Still, overall, there was a continued decline in global temperature. The northern forest ultimately gave way, retreating and fragmenting as the summer and winter months grew dryer and colder.

Large ice sheets began to grow in the northern latitudes when the snow that fell in winter failed to melt and instead piled up from one year to the next until it reached thousands of feet in thickness. Even in areas that were not directly affected by the ice sheets, aridity began to cause forests to die and give way to dry grassland, which required less water to survive. Eventually, much of the grassland retreated and gave way to semi-deserts and deserts as global conditions reached a cold, dry low point around 70,000 years ago (known as the "Lower Pleniglacial"). By this time, most of Northern Asia, Eurasia and North America were covered by thick ice sheets. The last "Great Ice Age" started during the Lower Pleniglacial, in the Middle Paleolithic period.

The Earth was much colder at the onset, as great ice sheets miles think formed in the highlands and northern regions and gradually blanketed increasingly larger areas of land, locking up huge amounts of water in the thick glacial ice-pact, an advent resulting in a simultaneous lowering global sea levels. The onset and progression of these phenomena changed the surface of the earth, altering global waterways and landscapes. By roughly 60,000 years ago, global conditions gradually became warmer, though still generally colder than today. Then around 30,000 years ago, the earth entered another big freeze, called the "Glacial Maximum"; temperatures fell, deserts expanded, and ice sheets spread across the northern latitudes. Climate during the Glacial Maximum was arid, with semi-desert and desert occupying huge areas of the continents as forests shrunk back into refugia.

Peering from The Ice Age

Around 14,000 years ago, there was a rapid global warming and moistening of climates, occurring within the span of only a few years or decades when the enormous ice sheets and gigantic glaciers began to withdraw under the gradual global warming. During this period, the huge icecaps and deep cold temperatures in the northern hemisphere functioned as a sort of global 'cap', under which a temperate climate was maintained in the southern hemisphere. However, after only a few thousand years of recovery, the Earth was suddenly plunged back into a new and very short-lived ice age known as the "Younger Dryas" though it did not affect everywhere, it destroyed the returning forests in the north. It led to a brief resurgence of the great ice sheets.[xviii][xix]

The end of the Great Ice Age occurred about 11,600 years ago, just after the *Vela X Supernova* was seen on earth; the ensuing rise in temperatures marked the start of the Holocene. According to the ancient Khemetan (Egyptian) Priest *Manetho*, a student at the *Ancient Mystery School* before the invasion of Alexander (ca 330 B.C.), 11,600 years ago marked the beginning of the *Rule of Mortal Humans* on Earth. According to *Manetho's* chronology, the 11,000 years preceding the end of the Great Ice Age marked the closing phase of an early ancient *Ice Age Civilization* which spanned from 65,000 B.C. to 12,000 B.C. During this period, Ice Age peoples of Africa, Southern Asia and the warm lands were building, developing, and refining the foundations of the first civilizations, while the peoples of Europe, Northern Asia, and the cold lands were trapped in a bitter struggle for survival.

Glaciers of Africa

Contrary to popular belief, there were significant glaciations in Africa during the Ice Age, when massive sheets of ice covered the continent's highest peaks. In the north, glaciers covered the highest peaks of the Atlas Mountains in present-day Morocco and Mount Atakor in present-day Algeria. In Central Africa, glaciers covered the highest peaks of the Rwenzori Mountains, between Uganda and Zaire. To the east, they covered the peaks of the Ras Dashen and Simen Mountains in northern Ethiopia and the Bale Mountains in the Ethiopian south. Glaciers also covered the peaks of Mt Kenya, Mt Kilimanjaro, and Mt Meru in east Africa. Like in the north, they expanded and receded from the highest elevations.

The second highest peak, *Mount Kenya,* is just north of *Kilimanjaro* in central Kenya, followed by the third highest peak, *Mt Margherita* in the *Ruwenzori Mountain Range,* the fabled "Mountains of the Moon", situated along the border between Uganda and Zaire. The *Ras Dashen* range in the highlands of northern Ethiopia is the next highest mountain, followed by *Mt Elgon* on the border of Uganda and Kenya. Finally, there is the *Atlas* range in the north, stretching across Morocco, Algeria, and Tunisia, parallel to the Mediterranean coast. The highest peak is *Mt. Toubkal* in the west. To the west, the Atlas separated into two lower parallel ranges, the *Tell Atlas* to the north and the *Saharan Atlas* to the south.[xx]

The temperature spectrum in central Africa during the era ranged from the bitter cold emanating from the glaciers covering the highest peaks to the thick heat blanketing the lowlands of the Great Rift Valley. The temperature spectrum appears to have played a unique role in fomenting the divergence and emergence of the ancient ancestral ethnicities and ethnocentric cultures of the earliest prehistory. Compounding this, the ancient geographical landscape contributed two essential characteristics that, over time, played decisive roles in intra-continental and outbound migrations: first, the higher tablelands in the east and south of the continent, together with the progressive diminution in altitude towards the west and north. Secondly, the Great Rift Valley itself is a significant feature originally formed by the separation of the African and Arabian tectonic plates.[xxi]

The Great Rift Valley

The Great Rift Valley is one of the most distinctive features of African topography; in its middle section, the Great Rift Valley splits into two major branches, the Eastern and Western Rift Valleys (the latter known as the "Albertine Rift"). The Great Rift Valley is flanked by towering escarpments (up to 4,900 feet high) along the Eastern Rift Valley in central Kenya, and in the northern part of the Western Rift Valley (up to 4,300 feet high) along the Congo border with Uganda, Rwanda, and Burundi.[xxii] Mountains, canyons, and rivers, fed by rains, which anciently formed a series of great lakes along the floor of the valley, fill the lower depressions within the Rift Valley.

The Olduvai Gorge forms part of the Great Rift Valley; the gorge is actually an ancient canyon carved by the descending waters of the southern Serengeti. The Olduvai Gorge drains the slopes of nearby mountains, in addition to the Serengeti Plain; by the dawn of the Age of Man, the waters had carved much of the 30-mile long, 295-foot deep, steep-sided Gorge in the eastern Plains of the Serengeti, where, in remote times the Gorge was occupied by a shallow lake. Olduvai first garnered archeological interest in 1911 when a German Professor found some fossil bones in the Gorge. Upon examination of exposed deposits, they found many ancient human remains. The fossil remains found in the Gorge provide the most continuous known record of early ancient humanity during the past two million years.

Archaeological evidence suggests that the area of the Olduvai Gorge, situated in present-day northern Tanzania, was the place of origin of the early ancient *Alkebu* ("Africans"), among the earliest fully modern humans, short in stature, with dark brownish black smooth, hairless skin and complexions, and dark brown or black curly to wavy hair. The early ancient *Alkebu* were hunter-gathers who migrated throughout the Gorge and from there into the highlands of the *Serengeti*. This land is among the longest-inhabited places on earth. Ancestral Alkebu settlements have been found along the highland channels of rivers and streams descending into the lake. Archaeological finds in the settlement areas reflect a functioning human population inhabiting the region over 35,000 years *before* the beginning phases of the *Last Great Ice Age*.[xxiii]

Divergence of Olduvai

The *Olduvai Gorge* has provided the longest known archeological record of the development of the stone-tool industries of ancient man; items belonging to one of the oldest stone tool technologies of remote antiquity, referred to by Archaeologists as the *Olduwan Tool Industry*, including tools and hand axes fashioned from stones and bones. Skeletal remains at campsites and what is believed to have been temporary hunting butchery sites have been excavated in the gorge. The main sites are near the ancient lake basin, with permanent living sites found some distance away, mainly where streams from the highlands carry fresh water into *Olduvai Lake*. It has been discovered that cultures inhabiting the Gorge manufactured rudimentary tools for use in a wide range of functions.[xxiv]

Because of their relatively small numbers, *Ancestral Alkebu* clans in *Olduvai* each lived in comparative isolation. With their broader range of habitation and settlement, their environments gradually came to differ greatly as life varied somewhat from region to region. However, it had a common basic pattern. Except for short periods in good seasons, large groups were unsustainable. Therefore clans generally consisted of several families and hunting and food-gathering hands. Each clan had its own recognized territory and consisted of several generations. The clans probably never numbered more than about fifty, but in good times, several clans might band together for considerable periods. However, each clan would normally maintain its small parentage group as its nucleus.

Although they all shared common features, over the millennium, regional characteristics gained gradual prominence. Over time, the differentiation would become most distinct between early ancient highlanders and lowlanders, the latter being descendants of those who migrated along the rivers and streams flowing into the Gorge from the *Serengeti* highlands. With altitudes ranging from 3,000 to 6,000 feet, the Serengeti is higher than most of Europe, with temperatures among the coolest in *Alkebu-lan* (the original and true name of "Africa"). Over the ages, the Serengeti's sheer size (20,000 square miles) and climate encouraged the emergence of two distinct ethno-groups within the *Alkebu*, *Primordial-Negroids* in the lowlands and *Primordial-Sudroids* in the highlands.

When the first *Primordial-Sudroids* emerged in the highlands, sometime before 150,000 BCE, they were not much differentiated from the parent stock from which they arose. Adaptation to the cooler environment of the highlands over the long millennium, aided by reproductive isolation of the nascent population, gave rise to unique Sudroid traits, such as straight wavy hair texture, which evolved to protect and insolate against the colder temperatures on the highland plains during the Ice Age.[xxv][xxvi] The varied terrain of the eastern highlands, one of the oldest on earth, encouraged the growth of closely related clans in the highlands.

East African Highlands: Primordial Sudroids

Accustomed to the open highland plains, over time *Primordial-Sudroids* extended their range southward into the highlands plains and valleys of present-day Southern Tanzania. When the highland population expanded, the size of clan territories became more distinct and guarded, with smaller provinces ranging from a few square miles to much larger provinces, each with relatively well-defined borderlands and boundaries. They exploited their territories with routines determined by the seasons and seasonal availability of foods and water, taking care not to waste precious or scarce resources.

Food was obtained by the hunters, gatherers, and cultivators (or agriculturists) with deliberate and well-coordinated effort. Both men and women had to spend from half to two-thirds of each day hunting, collecting or foraging for food. Hunting was organized by the men on co-operative lines, while the women went into the forests with wooden digging sticks and dug up yams and edible roots and collected fruits, berries, seeds, vegetables and insects; and killed lizards and other small creatures, while the men went hunting. There was a clear division of labor in food collection, but this was not rigidly maintained; the main concern was gathering and storing the food.

In certain parts of the highlands, particularly in the well-watered, fertile regions, clan territorial divisions and borders were less 'hardened' and not so clear-cut, allowing a greater degree of social inter-mixing between groups. Much of this would be seasonal, centered upon the harvest seasons when there was great excitement and activity; there was usually feasting, trading, exchanging new methods and techniques, meeting old friends, settling old scores, inter-mixing, and a general harmonization of customs and gene pools between the clans in the region. An advent reinforcing emergent and growing diversity among *Primordial-Sudroids* in the Ice Age highlands.

Forested Coastal Plains: Primordial Veddoids (the "Veddäs)

The East African coastal plains south of the Horn were then a far more extensive expanse than exist today; a broad, varied coastal expanse with a diverse range of habitat. Here a miscegenated (or "missing link") ethno-group arose between the *Primordial-Sudroids and Primordial-Negroids*, an early ancient ethno-group called *Primordial-Veddoids*. The *Veddas* emerged in the forested foothills along the east African coastal plains (east of the Serengeti), where, over time, they diverged from their ancestral parentage in adaptation to their environment and a measure of reproductive isolation. The passage of time accentuated the ethno-cultural distinctions between the *Primordial-Veddoids, Sudroids, and Negroids* from their ancient ancestral stock.

The *Primordial-Veddas* expanded as a somewhat homogenous population of hunters and gatherers concentrated in the forested foothills of the coastal belt, from where they expanded along the coastal plains. The *Väddoids* were of diminutive stature with dark brown skin, curly or wavy hair, broad faces, flat noses, deeply set eyes, and full lips. They were a semi-nomadic people who inhabited the caves along the coastal foothills in remote times, where they crafted stone implements, like arrow points used for hunting, and cutting stones and scrapers used to carve meat and prepare animal skins for clothing. From the foothills, the *Primordial-Veddas* expanded into the then-broad coastal plains, where they lived in early hunting, gathering, and fishing villages.

East African Lowlands: Primordial Negroids

Like *Primordial-Sudroids*, when *Primordial-Negroids* emerged, they were not much differentiated from the stock of their common parentage. *Primordial-Sudroid*s differentiated in the highlands, while *Primordial-Negroid*s differentiated in the lowlands.[xxvii] Temperatures in the Rift Valley made it one of the hottest and driest places on earth, culminating in the main observable difference between *Sudroids* and *Negroids,* hair texture. Negroid hair texture developed a tighter curl, providing a woolly texture, better shielding against the heat and harsh sunlight of the lowlands. In contrast, *Sudroid* hair texture developed a wavy texture, better shielding against the frigid cold of the highlands Like their parent stock, *Primordial Negroids* were small in stature, similar in appearance to the *Ba-Twa* still found in Africa (those Europeans disparagingly called "Pygmies").

Primordial-Negroids expanded throughout and inhabited the whole of the Rift Valley, occupying the vast region for thousands upon thousands of years, from the habitable lands below the glaciers atop the Rwenzori Mountains to the varied floor of the valley. The *Great Rift Valley* runs in two north–south-trending branches; the *Eastern Rift Valley,* which stretches from Ethiopia in the north through the Kenyan border region and western Tanzania to the border with Mozambique at its southern extent. The *Western Rift Valley*, known as the *Albertine Rift*, stretches from Uganda in the north, southward through the present-day Congo, U-Rwanda, Burundi and finally Tanzania in the south, where it joins the eastern arm of the Rift Valley.

A central plateau lies between the two arms of the *Great Rift Valley*, with the Rwenzori Mountains situated in the Western (or *Albertine)* Rift Valley. The Rwenzori stretch some eighty miles long and are about thirty miles wide, straddling the border between the present-day Congo and Uganda. Lakes Tanganyika created a fertile environment with abundant vegetation, fruit, and wild game of various sizes and varieties along the floor of the valley. In has been found that as early as 100,000 BC *Primordial-Negroids* were creating sophisticated tools of stone and bone in the *Semlike River Valley* of Congo; writing by the etching of stone was also found.

The fertile Western Rift attracted large groups, over time leading to settlements spreading along the foothills of the valley and centered around the numerous large lakes stretching across the floor of the valley. Several huge ancient lakes stretch across the floor of the Western and Eastern Rift Valleys, each providing vast lowland settlement areas, attracting *Primordial-Negroid* clans mobilized and migrating as territorial assertions became an issue. A chain of ancient lakes and waterways along the valley floor assisted the spread of *Primordial-Negroids* throughout and beyond the forests of the *Rift Valley* into the wetlands of the *Kalahari* in the *Southern Sphere*.

A further divergence within the *Primordial-Negroid* group occurred during the start of the third interglacial period of the *Last Great Ice Age,* a phase known as the *Würm Glaciation,* occurring perhaps as early as 250,000 BC. Temperature changes in the *Southern Sphere* (between glacial-interglacial transitions), and a shift in atmospheric heat exchange between the tropics and the southern latitudes, culminated in the emergence of two distinct early Negroid groups: the *Ba-Twa* (or "Twa:") who emerged in the tropics of the *Great Rift Valley* in the *Central Sphere*, and the *Sarwa* (San) who emerged in the warmer confines of the *Kalahari* and the *Southern Sphere*.[xxviii]

To the south, at the southern extent of the Rift Valley, inter-marriage between the *BaTwa* (Twa) and *Sarwa* (also known as the "San") gave birth to another ancient indigenous people known as the *"KhoiKhoi"*, who appears to have emerged in the region of Botswana during the latter part of the third interglacial period. It was nonetheless a definitive group of *Ba-Twa* who expanded along the forested foothills of the *Rwenzori,* the fabled *"Mountains of the Moon"*; a definitive subset whose early ancient progeny would lay the foundation for one of the earliest coherent forms of human civilization; those best described as the *"Proto-Anu"*.

Foothills of the Rwenzoris: Proto-Anu-BaTwa

The *Rwenzori* range is about eighty miles long and thirty miles wide, reaching heights of over sixteen thousand feet. Steep-sided ravines, forming six massifs, link the mountain range: *Mount Baker*, *Mount Emin*, *Mount Gessi*, *Mount Luigi di Savoia*, *Mount Speke*, and *Mount Stanley*. Dense clouds and mists almost perpetually cover these peaks. A continual rain and an abundance of vegetation and game in the foothills and forested lower river valleys made the *Rwenzori* an ideal environment for the *Proto-Anu* subset of the *Ba-Twa* to emerge. They lived in communities of extended family clans, forming small villages and clusters in the forested foothills and river valleys of the *Rwenzori*. The *Rwenzori* (meaning "the one who brings the rain") are snowcap mountains, an alpine island surrounded by dry plains, less than thirty miles from the equator.

The Proto-Anu spread throughout the foothills and river valleys of large tributaries descending the highlands through the foothills to the chain of great lakes occupying the depressions along the floor of the Western Rift Valley (the *"Albertine Rift"*). A permanent fog creates an atmosphere of the sauna, favoring the appearance of unique plant-life in the Rwenzori; the highland forests down into the forested foothills were and are home to thousands of unique plant species. The highlands are home to extraordinary ancient plant species, with giant versions of plants whose closest relatives grow as small herbs in temperate zones. Giant Lobelias and Senecios, which grow like enormous candelabra below the jagged peaks, create an otherworldly scene. Plants reach unnatural dimensions, surrounded by dripping water and the smell of wet moss and mushrooms. The term "mushrooms" generally refers to a broad category of macro fungus with a distinctive fruiting body, large enough to be seen with the naked eye and to be picked by hand.[2]

---

[2] Chang and Miles (1992)

Highland mushrooms were treasured as a source of food and medicinal treatment for thousands of years. Many mushroom fruit bodies contain biologically active polysaccharides, and complex carbohydrates in the form of starch, glycogen, and dextran, stored in the liver and muscles and readily converted to energy. Prompting widespread use of mushrooms as a food source, and for medicinal treatments, throughout the foothills and river valleys. Mushrooms, herbs and aromatic plants played important roles in the socio-cultural and spiritual awakening of the Proto-Anu in the foothills, river valleys, and highlands of the *Ruwenzori*. Medicinal herbs and plants provided remedies for common diseases such as diarrhea, dysentery, liver diseases, malaria, gastritis, leucorrhoea, and tapeworm infestations. They gathered specific herbs, roots, and mushrooms for identifiable medicinal properties. Early practitioners acquired knowledge through observation, experience, and training; knowledge further enriched as it passed from generation to generation.

The fabled "Mountains of the Moon" are among the largest mountains on the African continent; its vegetation cover includes tropical rain forests, bamboo, and alpine meadows. The steep mountain slopes were anciently covered by thick vegetation and trees which reached forty feet in height. All plants here overcame the crowns of trees, and plants reached enormous dimensions. The *Rwenzori* is crossed by numerous waterfalls, and everywhere there was immense fertility due to nearly year around rainfall above the mid-highlands. The lower parts of Ruwenzori were covered with dense tropical rain forests, separated by powerful rivers. For hunter-gatherers foraging in the river valleys for wild honey, yams, and particularly wild mushrooms, the gathering must have come quite easily. Mushroom fruit was literally lying on the ground; the fruit first emerges as a white "egg" shape, then grows to maturity, with the cap eventually inverting so that its margins are higher than its center.

Nearly two hundred species of psilocybin-containing mushrooms thrive in humus-rich soils of the forests and meadows of tropical and sub-tropical places like the highland valleys of the Rwenzoris. Psychoactive alkaloids found in some of these species produce some of the most amazingly potent plants on earth. The ingestion of these psychoactive substances is said to have provided the spark that lifted the mind and imagination of these early humans above the mundane to contemplations of existence, the cosmos, and man's place in the cosmos, propelling the Proto-Anu to the forefront of the evolutionary race. Human-mushroom interaction is not a static symbiotic relationship but rather a dynamic one; the experience is subjective and different for each user and at each instance of use.[xxix] Psilocybin mushrooms are said to carry with them a message from nature about the health of the planet and its place in the Cosmos.

For Paleolithic humans, the effects of ingesting psilocybin mushrooms precipitated one of the most phenomenal events ever experienced: a virtual cascade of consciousness, such as the awakening of the spiritual and intellectual self and the introduction to other realms of thought and dimension. Certain mushrooms were ceremonially eaten to induce psychoactive (hallucinogenic), prophetic, and revelatory states, with transcendent "Dreamtime" experiences awakening one's "since of self", the environment, and the Cosmos. It made such a big impression that many believed the mushrooms to be divinely inspired and incorporated them into religious rituals ..the ancients used honey to preserve these sacred mushrooms. The shared revelations and pronouncements of the early "Seers" attuned community-wide perceptions of the cycles of nature, the planet, and cosmic forces.

Oddly enough, mushrooms grow on a lunar cycle, and many primitive spiritual beliefs revolve around such a cycle, apparently corresponding to mushroom availability. Widespread harvesting, storing, and ingestion of psilocybin proved to be a competitive evolutionary advantage for the *Proto-Anu*. While the compounds in the "ritual mushrooms" did not necessarily catalyze the immune system into higher states of activity (although this may have been a secondary effect), they catalyzed consciousness, that peculiar self-reflecting ability that has reached the greatest apparent expression in human beings. Consciousness, like the ability to resist disease, confers an immense adaptive advantage on any who possesses it.

Consciousness has been called the "awareness of awareness", a so-called "mirror of self-recognition" thought to indicate self-awareness, which is required to understand "selfhood"" in others, and ultimately to be empathic. The Proto-Anu discovered a new application for their acquired abilities and capacities, the learned to adeptly relocate whole villages during sustained periods of higher temperatures, increased aridity, and reduced food source availability. When they found they could simply relocate to higher inclines along the river valleys, to regions of more moderate climate, to preserve their access to abundant and diverse food sources and preserve the comfort and life-styles to which they had become accustomed, they became ready adaptors. Ancient Seers of the Proto-Anu studied the cycles of the stars from the highlands, particularly in relation to seasonal and climatic changes, to first understand and later predict the severe climatic changes affecting their world.

The earliest features of the deity were associated with functions of the Sky, originally recognized and defined by attributes of day and night, symbolized by the Sun and Moon. This, until their observance and witness of the *Celestial Serpent* (the mythological cosmic "*Hydra*" with the given name of "*Heru*" (later called "*Horus the Elder*")), believed to traverse the *Cosmos*, streaking across and illuminating the midnight skies.[xxx] The Obliquity (the "degree of tilt") of the Earth relative to the Sun during the Last Great Ice Age allowed the "Southern Lights" (the "*Aurora Australis*"), anciently deemed the "*Celestial Serpent*", to be observed in latitudes as far north as the *Lands of Yam* in the Great Rift Valley.[xxxi,xxxii] When the winds of the solar cycle were at their optimum, the "Southern Lights" could be seen from anywhere in the southern hemisphere.

The Parables

In the earliest periods of human differentiation, man was incapable of self-government but was ruled, instead, by those appointed by *Nature* to preserve and unfold him to the point when he would be capable of governing himself.[3] As soon as man was capable of thought, his mind turned upon himself. He sought to find a solution to the mystery of existence, which his unfolding intelligence was revealing in greater fullness each day. Mother-earth was seen as the womb of life, the producer and provider of nourishment in various kinds, and much like a mighty tree, the source of life and nourishment to its branches, leaves and blossoms. Thus was the mythical great "*Tree of Life*" envisioned as the progenitor and provider of nourishment to all living beings, deemed its offspring.

---

[3] Metu Neter, Nefer Amen 1990

The *Tree of Life* permitted diagramed imagery of the processes through which an unknowable Creator endows the world …and Man's sojourn in the world. The "Baobab" tree, also called the "upside-down tree" because its branches appear to be rooted, provided an apt image of the *Tree of Life*; with even greater affinities in that the Baobab is capable of providing shelter, food, and water for human inhabitation where it grows. Like the "upside-down tree", early seers believed that in the beginning, there arose a sacred *Tree of Life* from which the cosmos and all flowers blossom. The deity was first defined by reference to the functional attributes of the *Tree of Life,* manifested by a divine life force, a serpentine-like fire emanating from the tree, forming the functions and creative works of an unknowable, hidden, and all-powerful Creator.[4]

The oldest story of the *Celestial Serpent* translates as the arrival of a "multiplicity of beings" at the time of earth's greatest darkness. Perceived as *divine fire* emanating, in serpentine-like fashion, from the sacred *Celestial Tree of Life,* this was the *Celestial Serpent*, the mythological "*Hydra*", with the given name of "*Heru*", who symbolized self-determined, creative energy and immortality.[5] Thus, the *Winged Serpent,* anciently symbolized as the "*Winged Sun Disc*", became the earliest symbol of the incipient faith and the culture that would then develop. A faith whose followers, adherents, and sages would become anciently known as "*Followers of Heru*".

The most ancient of legends whisper of enlightened *Proto-Anu* seers who, having witnessed the Celestial Serpent illuminate the midnight skies, became the first to elucidate and proselytize reverence for "Heru" (the "Cosmic Hydra"). Heru was portrayed as a giver of life through direct connection with the Creator and was thus believed to have mystical powers. As the *Proto-Anu* migrated and expanded, adherents of the faith, the "Followers of Heru", proselytized its reverence throughout and beyond the ancient *Lands of Yam* in the Great Rift Valley. *Proto-Anu* prophets viewed man's day-to-day activities to secure a living and provide for his family, clan and village as acts in harmony with the creation unfolding before them. Enlightened Seers divined that man must approach these tasks in the same manner in which the Creator endows and maintains creation.

The Proto-Anu took note of major climatic changes and dislocations affecting their lives, retaining the wisdom attained through oral traditions. When vast areas became desserts separated by large lakes that existed for 1,000 years in a given area, the phenomenon left an indelible impression on the Proto-Anu, who rationally sought to learn from what they experienced, including the cyclical nature of the seasons and the patterns inherent in the oscillating climatic conditions of the era. Over time, migrating and expanding Proto-Anu clans spread throughout suitable areas of the Western and Eastern Rift Valleys. Migrations were slow and continuous, covering many centuries and generations, moving from place to place. They lived by hunting and gathering and built only semi-permanent dwellings, migrating as resources and needs required.

---

[4] Metu Neter, Nefer Amen 1990
[5] Metu Neter, Nefer Amen 1990

The Proto-Anu tended to be semi-sedentary, settling in an area where food could be obtained for a time and then moving on. Archaeologists have located settlement sites spread from the Rwenzoris, on the border of the present-day Republic of the Congo and Uganda, to the *Olduvai Gorge* in Tanzania, to the edge of *Lake Naivasha* in present-day Kenya, in their early eastward expansion.[xxxiii] The severity of the drought in the *Albertine Rift Valley* led to population concentrations around available sources of water, leading to an early form of urbanization as villages clustered along the foothills and river valleys. The lower parts of *Ruwenzori* were covered with dense tropical rain forests, with food still reasonably available due to the nearly all-year-round rainfall in the mountains. At the higher altitudes, the vegetation became less dense, and the rain forests were gradually replaced by forests of giant moss-covered heather trees.

At the snow lines were forest of giant Senecio and lobelia trees, rendering the Rwenzori an alpine island surrounded by dry plains. The *Ruwenzori* trapped the humid air rising from the Congo basin at a higher altitude; consequently, the mountains remained wet, with rain falling most days, even in the dryer months. Though not as high as Mount Kilimanjaro and slightly lower than Mount Kenya, the Rwenzori have a larger alpine area than either, and at high elevations temperatures swing from above to below freezing, alternating between freezing nights and warm days.[6][7] In addition, leaching rocks at the higher altitudes produced acidic soils of low fertility, except on parts of the northern ridge, where ancient volcanic ash is deposited,[8] foreclosing the high-altitude river valleys as suitable habitats for the ever-growing and concentrated populations.

When the sustained warm climate in the lowlands caused evaporation levels to exceed precipitation levels, water levels dropped, and vast areas of the Rift Valley became dry and barren, with the population increasingly concentrated along the rivers flowing from the highlands. This led to increased urbanization in the foothills and suitable plateaus of the highland river valleys. As the heightening aridity ravaged lowland forests and the dwindling of the forest spread into the foothills, astute *Proto-Anu* clans moved into the upper river valleys and still well-watered terrain of the lower-highlands of the fabled "Mountains of the Moon".

---

[6] Butynski, 1992
[7] Yeoman,1985; Howard,1991; Lush,1993
[8] Loefler 1997

The Southern Sphere

At its southern reaches, the Great Rift Valley cuts through the center of the northern Kalahari, forming the Okavango Delta. The Kalahari is situated on a plateau connecting Botswana, Southwest Africa, Namibia, and the Northern Cape. It extends from the Okavango River in the north, encompassing large portions of five present-day nation-states in Southern Africa: Botswana, Namibia, South Africa, Zimbabwe, Zambia and Angola. The Kalahari has been largely shaped by the pluvial and inter-pluvial around the last *Great Ice Age*, which re-shaped the ancient landscape and river drainage patterns. The region had its last major wet-phase during the pluvial of the Pleistocene when its rivers and large basins were often flooded beyond capacity. [xxxiv]

The Okavango Delta is situated between two parallel fault lines, with elongated shallow basins between the faults flooded by the Okavango River. The river flows into the Kalahari from the northwest, with its floodwaters fanning out to form and give shape to the huge Okavango Delta. These northern Kalahari wetlands provided the *Proto-Anu* with a welcome respite from the long hot droughts of the central Rift Valley; the waters of the delta flowed through a maze of lagoons, channels, meandering waterways, islands, and lush grassy plains, making the habitat an ideal terrain for *Proto-Anu* settling in the region. Yet, predictably, the Southern Sphere was not devoid of others; here, they would encounter an indigenous people known as the *Khoisan*.[xxxv]

Wetlands of the Kalahari: The Proto-Khoisan

Before and during the last Great Ice Age, a huge ancient lake known as *Paleo-Lake Makgadikgadi* covered a large area of present-day northern Botswana. The lake was fed by the *Nata* and *Boteti Rivers* and initially had no natural outlet. With the passage of time, the huge basin of the lake filled to capacity, overflowing into valleys below. The massive waters from the overflowing lake drained northwards and then eastward, forcing the middle and lower *Zambezi Rivers* to connect, forging the mighty *Victoria Falls* into existence. However, with the onset of the aridity of the *Ice Age*, coupled with the huge lake having developed a viable outlet, the pre-ice age iteration of the massive lake slowly began to disappear, draining over thousands of years until it eventually dried up, leaving behind a series of salt pans covering over almost 10,000 square miles.[xxxvi] Over the long millennium, as water levels in the paleo-lake fluctuated seasonally, wild animals congregated around the water holes on the lakebed, providing fertile hunting grounds. Early *Khoi* and *San* populations of the era viewed the area as a prolific hunting ground, with food resources in the region more concentrated than at times when the climate was wetter, and the lake was full.

It was in the ancient convergence zone of *Paleo-Lake Makgadikgadi* that ancestors of the ancient *Khoi* and *San* intermixed to the point and extent were drawing a clear line of distinction often became nearly impossible, prompting common use of the contracted term '*Khoisan*'. Descendent *Khoisan* clans gradually spread, stretching their settlement range throughout large portions of the broader Southern African Sphere; in the lands of the present-day countries of Angola, Botswana, Namibia, South Africa, Zimbabwe, and Zambia.[xxxvii] The whole of ancient Zambia was inhabited by the *Khoisan* by the time the *Proto-Anu* migrated into the region.[xxxviii] The *Proto-Anu* were nominally familiar with the *Proto-Khoisan* from interactions in the region of present-day *Angola*. When the *Proto-Khoisan* extended into the region of present-day Zambia, it opened a second point of contact and cultural transmission between them and the *Proto-Anu*.

Proto-Anu clans settled in the forests of northern Zambia, from where they expanded southward, establishing closer cultural relationships, discourse and philosophical transmission between them and the Proto-Khoisan. The Proto-Khoisan made sophisticated tools from wood and animal products which increased hunting efficiency and allowed for further innovation. In the course of their interactions, the Proto-Khoisan taught the Proto-Anu of their arts of survival in the Wet Kalahari. The Proto-Anu, in turn, informed the Proto-Khoisan of their knowledge of navigation using the stars; in reciprocation, the Proto-Khoisan familiarized the Proto-Anu with the cycle of the seasons in the Southern Sphere. *Proto-Khoisan* were an admixture of *Khoi* and *San,* a miscegenated, multifaceted ethno-cultural group that spread throughout the terrain of their ancestral parentage, a far from broadly shared outcome between the theretofore often contentious oldest peoples of the *Southern Sphere*. The *San* were the indigenous people of the region, though the term "San" was the first use by the *Khoikhoi*.[xxxix]

The *Khoi* called themselves the "Khoikhoi" to set themselves apart from those who were not; proud, perhaps to the point of arrogance, they presumed control over any area into which they might migrate. The *Khoikhoi* were the first of the early ancient herders, at first using strategic hunting, then tracking, and finally herding of wild humped cattle and sheep and goats that grazed on vegetation and did not require the herders to feed them. The early ancient *Khoi* guided, protected, and created near symbiotic relationships with the herd animals they tended, allowing them to hunt on the periphery of the herds, culling the old and weak, and in so doing, aiding the long-term health and strength of their herds. In early ancient *Khoi* society, the larger the herds a family tended, the wealthier they were, thus distinguishing between those who possessed much and those who didn't. This was in stark contrast with *San*, who believed in communal sharing; for the San, land could not be owned, only shared, preserved, and used for necessity.[xl]

The *Khoi* moved from place-to-place seasonally to ensure their herds' sufficient grazing, a nomadic existence in which they slept on reed mats in dome-shaped huts made from stripped branches, which could be taken apart easily to facilitate moving. Though they lived in villages, which consisted primarily of members of the same patrilineal clan, *Khoi* society was strictly hierarchical. They lived in larger groups than the *San*, with those who tended the largest herds regarded as 'wealthy', as herd animals were sources of food, clothing, and materials for tools. In *Khoi* society, men routinely culled their herds by hunting. At the same time, the women would gather wild plants and herbs, an ethos that gave them a stable, balanced diet and a competitive advantage over the rival *San* of the region.[xli]

The *Khoi* migrated into *San* territory following their large herds, bring with them an ethos that, in many ways, was in opposition to the way of life of the *San*. In the ethos of the *San,* land could not be possessed, only shared, preserved, and used for necessity. As a loose guideline, the territory of a *San* clan could stretch to a twenty-mile circle. If there are no other bordering clans, their territory could stretch as far as needed to ensure adequate food and water sources. *San* social structure was not tribal because they had no paramount leader, and their ties of kinship were relaxed. They were a loosely knit family culture where decisions were made by discussion and agreement by consensus; theirs was a culture in which an individual's opinion was weighted according to their level of skill and experience in the particular field of discussion.

The *San* were inherent pacifists with an informal economy and a nonhierarchical leadership system based on their age-old tradition of consensus. In contrast to the *Khoi*, they lived in caves or huts made of branches built near waterholes so that drinking water would be near. The men of the *San* were skilled trackers who hunted with spears, wooden bows, and if necessary, poison arrows on hunts that could last days or even weeks. The *San* were generally nomadic, within boundaries limited by the proximity of the other families and clans; a culture intruded upon them as the Khoi migrated more-and-more into their territory. The *Khoi's* culture of herding, and possession of large tracks of land, came into direct opposition with the nomadic way of life of the *San,* differences that led to misunderstandings and unfortunate conflict between the clans.

The *San* were inherently more spiritual than the *Khoi* and, as such, were initially more open and receptive to the explanations of the ontological connection and spiritual dimension of the great *Southern Lights.* A phenomenon viewed more frequently and with greater radiance in the *Kalahari* and the *Southern Sphere*, at latitudes far more southern than those of the *Lands of Yam* and the more northern confines of the *Great* Rift *Valley*. Though perhaps less spiritual than the *San*, the *Khoi* found resonance in their own celestial observations; the Khoi drew an association between the "Southern Lights" phenomena, which they called the "Great Rainbow Serpent", and the seemingly more than coincidental arrival of rain and fertility in its wake. Fertility meant better grazing for their herds and an abundance of food. Though less spiritual than the ancient *San*, the early ancient *Khoi* revered a shape-shifting divine being said to reside in the heavens. The belief that the "Great Rainbow Serpent" was an instrument of this unknowable Deity was central to early ancient Khoi ontological thought.

The Legends

The *Rainbow Serpent*, or the "*Naga*" as it would later come to be known, was said to be a massive flying ethereal being of the cosmos, renowned for its shinning, multicolored, translucent body, which glowed in the dark; it was said to have been the first being into the world, and, by establishing order from chaos, was believed to have aided in the very creation of the universe. Residing as a "Serpent of Light" in the heart of the cluster of stars, observable in both northern and southern hemispheres, the celestial *Naga* was said to have descended to earth, revealing itself as the radiant *Great Rainbow Serpent*, illuminating and streaking across and against the darkness of the midnight heavens.[xlii]

The *Great Rainbow Serpent* was said to be so huge that it encircled the entire cosmos with the radiant coils of its long, majestic, multicolored, translucent tail. The celestial Naga was said to have mystical powers, and it was by those cosmic powers that all life survives.[xliii] It was thus that the *Great Rainbow Serpent* was portrayed as the protector, often linked to guardianship, of the human race, sustaining them with rain, waterways, and fertile lands. Indeed, the *Naga* was revered as the ancient divine transformer of the land and creator of the huge ridges, mountains, lakes, rivers, and gorges that came to define the landscape.

Wherever and whenever it appeared, life and water were said to be in abundance; when the *Great Rainbow Serpent* (or "Naga") was sighted, it was considered a sign of immensely good fortune. Yet early ancient legends whisper of the great Serpent manipulating weather to create massive, destructive rainstorms and floods when angered. The *Great Rainbow Serpent* was said to be an unpredictable and destructive force if not properly respected.

The *Naga* was known to have a dual nature, one of both creation and destruction, with a transformative significance; it was said to play a role in the "Transmigration of Souls", with its tail regarded as the 'bridge-of-souls', transporting souls to a band of stars viewed as the 'river of spiritual light' known as the "Road of Souls"; the path by which souls were conducted to the afterlife. Thus, the Great Rainbow Serpent, the eminent *Naga*, became a symbol of spiritual creation, destruction, renewal, and immortality.

It was the mystical ability of the *Cosmic Serpent* to move between worlds and dimensions that granted it such wisdom in the ways of knowing and being and power in the ways of spiritual and physical transformation and regeneration. Inuring a reverence, by some subsets of the early faith, for the similar physical and transformational qualities of 'earthly serpents'. The early *San,* in particular, has left an invaluable legacy of rock art depicting this as an aspect of their early ethos.[xliv] Those inhabiting the Tsodilo Hills in northwestern Botswana, west of the Okavango Delta, created an ancient ritual site in what is known as the "*Serpent Cave,*"; a small cave on the northern side of the Tsodilo Hills, explicitly for Ophiolatry (Serpent reverence).[xlv] The four massifs that form the Tsodilo Hills are a small area of massive quartzite rock formations, rising dramatically from an otherwise flat Kalahari. Anointing the hills as a mausoleum for ancestral spirits, the San covered them with ancient rock art, which testifies to their long, continuous habitation of the area. The Tsodilo Hills are considered one of the greatest concentrations of rock art in the world, with over 4,500 paintings and dozens of archeological sites.

This is where you will find the oldest ritual worship site ever found, with some ancient artwork in the area estimated to be over 70 000 years old.[xlvi] The Serpent Cave presents a clear picture of an early "serpent-worshiping" culture that existed long ago; a people who worshiped and held reverence for a serpentine life force in the agency of an unknown deity. Perhaps it was the passion of the rituals of the *San*, or perhaps it was the perception of the intercedence of those rituals in invoking the appearance of the *Rainbow Serpent*, bestower of rain, fertility and rich pastures for grazing for their herds, that first and most attracted the somewhat more reserved *Khoi* to the eccentricities of the faith. Trance Chanting was the most prominent and impressive of the *San* rituals of the era and was usually an all-night affair incorporating every member of the Clan who wished to participate. The ritual took place every couple of weeks or so and was a regular event the members of the clan looked forward to as an opportunity to be together, chanting, singing, dancing, and celebrating their bond.

Only the most charismatic of Sages were accepted to guide the *Chant*, one who could best invoke and employ the spiritual energies enlivened by the *Chant,* enabling the Sage and Chanters to commune with cosmic forces. The Sage began by improvising a line of *call and response*, with the women the first to reply, in a melodic high-tone chorus, followed by the men, echoing the chorus in harmonized low bass tones, resulting in a layered rhythmic refrain, cadenced by the reverberating beat of the drums.[xlvii] The Sage cycled through praise, devotion and invocation chants, with the women in the inner circle, and men of the outer circle swaying in opposing directions, all chanting and clapping in rhythm around the fire for hours. Beginning with the 'praise chant', the chanters began in a low melodic whisper reverberating from the inner to the outer circle, in cadence with the rhythm of the drums. As the drum beat deepened, so too did the breath of the chanters, with the chorus of the chant becoming surer, stronger, rhythmically vibrating in ever-heightening spiritual harmony.

At the height of the Chant, when the atmosphere is most charged, the trance state is attained, and the Sage and Chanters seem to co-exist in the domain of the mind. The spirit is then one, and the rich sound of the Chant takes on the soulful quality of the vibrational energy that connects all living things.[xlviii] Some say that chanting alone, the repetitive use of sound is the lone tool used to induce trance, while others say that trance states are the result of drumming's effects on the central nervous system.[xlix] Rhythm-induced trance is one of the many documented modes of altered states of consciousness. The rhythms in such ceremonies are often slowly increased, eventually matching everyone's individual brain frequencies, increasing the release of adrenaline, and decreasing blood glucose, resulting in the release of adrenochrome, a substance chemically related to hallucinogens.[l]

The peak of the *Chant* is a moment of intense energy and communal rhythm, where there is the sensation of total peace as exhalation stops, silence ensues, as the Sage and Chanters enter a trance that grants them admission to the spiritual realm. A vibrating wall of energy, created by the series of repeated sounds and resounding rhythms, is said to surround the physical body, elevating and transporting the spirit of the Chanter to the depths of his or her being, where one's soul is said to be in touch with all of creation. The Chant would last for hours, sometimes throughout the night until dawn, with the melodic tones and rhythms of chanters and drums echoing from the quartzite chambers of the *Serpent Cave* throughout and beyond the Tsodilo Hills (called the "Mountain of the Gods"), to be carried upon the wind and faintly heard in the distant Okavango Delta.

Perhaps it was curiosity about the source and nature of the rhythmic chanting and drumming emanating from the *Serpent Cave* that first attracted the *Khoi*, who often lurked in the night, just beyond the glow of firelight radiating from the cave's mouth, observing and listening intently to the ritual. What they observed, in time, was presumed to be a connection between the invocation of the *Chant* and the coincidental appearance of the *Rainbow Serpent,* a linkage that brought their collective interest to a peak. Traditions of early barter soon grew into traditions of broader cooperation between the *Khoi* and *San* in the ancient Okavango region of Botswana, prompted by the *Khoi's* intrigue with the mystical powers of the *Chant*. Clans of the early ancient pastoral *Khoi* were inherently insular, moving from place-to-place seasonally, not staying in the same area for more than a few weeks; primarily to ensure their animals had sufficient grazing.

At the base of Khoikhoi society was also the nuclear family. The *Khoi* had no centralized system of government, yet, they did have a political system that aided in managing their affairs. A group of related clans made up a tribe or village; each village operated as an independent political unit, which usually recognized the most prosperous of the Clan Elders as head of the village (the "Village Elder"). Though similarly, the society of the *San* was built on the nuclear family, men and women had equal status, although the male head of the main family usually took a leading role in decision-making. The *San* developed their society over thousands of years in isolation, moving about the countryside, hunting and gathering sometimes for long periods in particularly productive environments; sometimes splitting apart and joining other groups when food was scarce. Their social structure had no paramount leader; their ties of kinship were relaxed with a loosely knit family culture where decisions were made by universal consensus.

The San generally lived within limited boundaries, with very loose guidelines; the territory of a family might stretch twenty miles or more as far as is needed to ensure adequate food and water sources. San lived by gathering edible plants, berries, and shellfish and by hunting game and fishing. The gathering was primarily the task of women, while men hunted, made tools and weapons from wood and stone, and produced clothing from animal hides. San also created vast numbers of rock paintings--South Africa contains the bulk of the world's prehistoric art still extant--which both express an extraordinary esthetic sensibility and documents San hunting techniques and religious beliefs.

The Khoi, in turn, held their political meetings in public and ordinary members were free to attend the proceedings. This kind of political organization was better than that of the San. The Khoi brought pastoralism to the San – with their sheep and cattle contributing to a balanced diet. Unlike the San, who did not live in a hierarchical society, the Khoi had a complex social structure. They believed in an unknown deity who was said to be the first being and creator of the cosmos, a deity who resides in the heavens. Early ancient Khoi seekers proffered that it was the unknown deity in whose service the *Rainbow Serpent* was in agency. Mutual curiosity and trade drew the two groups into regular contact, with eventually intermarriage and miscegenation culminating in the peoples known as the "Khoisan".

Notwithstanding, subsets of the two groups remained culturally distinct, as the Khoikhoi continued to move seasonally in search of good grazing areas for their livestock, and the San continued to subsist on hunting and gathering. Descendent Khoisan became semi-nomadic pastoralists, herding cattle and sheep, staying in one area until their herds had eaten the good grass and then moving on. They usually moved in a cyclical pattern that followed the seasons and stayed within the same region. Added to this, like their ancestral San, who hunted antelope using bows and arrows smeared with poison, the Khoisan became expert hunters, earning a now more diversified living by hunting animals, which in turn would be used for food, clothing, trade, and a way to show how much men, families and clans could earn.

The land area remained important to the emergent Khoisan because they now needed good secure places to graze their animals and areas in which to hunt.[li] The Khoisan had a more diverse and stronger economy and thus lived in larger political groups (than either the Khoi or the San). Early Khoisan clans included between 600 to 2,000 people, with their social organization ultimately influencing the nature of their economy, imbuing a more distinct since of territory or regency within the early or "*Proto-Khoisan*", as they would come to be known. Like the *Khoi*, the *Proto-Khoisan* initially moved from place-to-place seasonally to ensure their herd's sufficient grazing, while like the *San,* they lived within distinct boundaries governed by proximity to other clans. They moved in cyclical patterns that followed the seasons, and though they had no centralized system of government, theirs was an inherited system in which related clans made up village-clusters, operating as independent socio-economic groups.

Over time the *Khoisan* became more rigidly orthodox, evolving into a well-adapted, disciplined, reverent early civilization. They were even then largely a spiritually guided people who held reverence for their interpretive observations of the unfolding and changing world. In their precept, the *Cosmic Serpent* symbolized fertility, procreation, wisdom, death, and resurrection; the Serpent (whom they called the "Naga") was the symbol of the "Word". Proto-Khoisan ontology drew on the spiritual beliefs of the early San, heavily influenced by a subset of the San known as the *Naro-San*.

Like the *Naro-San,* the Proto-Khoisan used Trance Chanting in pursuit of altered states of consciousness to open entry into the spiritual realms, realms in which one can commune in the spiritual realm in an out-of-body experience. For the less ceremonially demonstrative *Proto-Khoisan*, attainment of the "Trans State" was a personally transformative experience that promoted spiritual awakening, mental clarity, physical stamina, and emotional well-being, which were hallmarks of their early ancient civilization. Theirs was an antediluvian civilization, with the *Serpent Cave* alone as clear evidence linking the *Khoisan* to the origin and inception of the *Nagas*, whose early influence, correspondent with that of the *Khoisan,* spread across the greater ancient world. [liii]

Primal Migrations

The tropical heartland of Alkebu-lan (ancient name of Africa) became extraordinarily arid and dry around 100,000 B.C., as documented by researchers who reported long and intermittent periods of drought affecting the region around that time. The persistence of drought-like conditions prompted a series of early out bound migrations from the lowlands of the Rift Valley, among the first region to be impacted. *Proto-Anu* clans from the lowlands around the Mountains of the Moon gradually moved eastward and northeastward, ultimately breaching the tablelands of Ethiopia and Somalia, from where they expanded into northern Sudan and beyond along the corridors of the ancient Nile. Others migrated through the Kenyan leg of the Rift Valley to the lakes and highlands of the Horn, which were cooler year around, in contrast to the hot, arid floor of the Rift Valley.

The eastern Rift Valley and central highlands form the backbone of present-day Kenya and the theretofore northern extent of the territorial terrain of the Proto-Anu. The Rift valley stretches through Kenya to Lake Turkana in the north, running southward through the Kenyan Highlands into Tanzania. The *Proto-Anu* migrated from around *Great Lake Nyanza* (colonial *"Lake Victoria"*) in western *Kenya*, and gradually but eventually pushed into the highlands where Kenya's two major rivers, the *Tana* and the *Galana,* originate and ultimately flow through eastern Kenya to reach the Indian Ocean. *Proto-Anu* clans at the northern end of this range pressed further northward, while those clustered at the southern end pressed southward toward *Mount Meru* and *Mount Kilimanjaro*.

To the south, the highlands of Tanzania are covered by lakes, including the portion of *Great Lake Nyanza* ("Lake Victoria") in Tanzania and Lake Tanganyika, where Proto-Anu (BaTwa) settlements were established along the lakeshores and forested areas of the western, northern and central foothills and mid-highlands. The main rivers flowing through the Tanzanian highlands to the Indian Ocean are the Pangani, Wami, Mkondoa, Ruvu, Rufiji, Ruaha, Kilombero, Mbarangandu, Matandu, Mbwemkulu, Lukuledi and Ruvuma, with the descending courses of large rivers, like the Pangani, marking the migratory path to the Tanzanian coast, where the coastline's geographical location made it ideal for outbound migrations.

The Tanzanian coastline runs mostly north-south and is dominated by three large offshore islands, Pemba, Zanzibar and Mafia. Close to the mainland, there are reefs along much of the coast north of the Pangani River, with a wide lagoon and only occasional patch reefs further south, around *Dar es Salaam*.[liii] The mouth of the Pangani River is located between the Zanzibar Channel to the south and the Pemba River Channel to the north, which defines the broad settlement area of Proto-Anu on the Tanzanian coast. The lower Pangani Basin and the flanking lowlands of northeastern Tanzania are critical geographical spaces for understanding aspects of the East African past. Yet, despite the urgings of archaeologists who discovered numerous sites along the coast, the lowlands remain a virtual archaeological terra incognita.

The East African coast has a relatively uniform and stable topography but has been subjected to a complex mosaic of geological and climatic influences. In consequence, deep-water lagoons and natural harbors characterized early configurations of the ancient shoreline, configurations providing the Proto-Anu access to the sea and coastal settlement areas. A major cluster of settlements was centered on the central Tanzanian coast, between *Dar Es Salaam* and the *Rufiji Delta*, while others were clustered on the coastal plain north of *Mombasa*. Still, others pushed beyond the shore to the coastal islands; the earliest migrants made sea crossings on fishing boats, as more sophisticated watercraft with sails were later developed. The first incursions beyond the seasonal fishing grounds were expeditionary but ultimately led to colonies, using the islands as stepping-stones in migrations across the seas.

The Vedda Vanguard: Proto-Veddas

Along the coast to the north, *Väddoids* inhabiting the forested coastal foothills and plains east of the Serengeti had, over time, expanded across the vast coastal plains, coastal plains which were then a far more extensive expanse than exist today, providing a broad and diverse range of habitat into which the Veddas spread. The *Veddas* were a semi-nomadic people who, in the remotest times, first lived in caves along the coastal foothills, where they crafted stone implements, like arrow points used for hunting, and cutting stones and scrapers used to carve meat and prepare animal skins for clothing. From the forested coastal foothills, the *Veddas* spread into the coastal plains, where they lived in hunting, gathering, and fishing villages. In their fishing villages, the *Veddas* used large hollowed-out tree-trunk canoes along the coast for both greater mobility and fishing. Early functional organization within the coastal villages of the *Veddas* aided their eventual expansion beyond the shoreline.

The men hunted and fished, while women gathered fruits, nuts, roots and herbs, and in some cases, seeds for planting and cultivation. The men constructed the villages, and the women maintained them and prepared and stored the food. Using their simple form of watercraft to cross between mainland and coastal islands, the *Veddas* were able to undertake longer and longer fishing voyages. The *Veddas* would set-up seasonal fishing and hunting encampments on favorable coastal islands as they ventured further into the ancient Indian Ocean. Like the *Sudroids* ("*Sudra*") of the East African inland foothills and mid-highlands, the *Veddas* of the coastal plains were pressed into migration by incursions of the *Proto-Anu*, sometime before 100,000 B.C. As *Proto-Anu* coastal settlements increased in size and number, *Proto-Vedda* clans were compelled to convert offshore seasonal settlements into permanent settlements, an advent that began their migrations across the Indian Ocean. Expanding drought-like conditions further prompted the *Veddas* to join the ongoing outbound migrations of the *Proto-Anu*.

Ancient adaptations to the great inland lakes provided the *Proto-Anu* with sufficient boating and maritime skills to cross the seas between the coast and then larger island-landmasses intervening and guiding the migrations and aiding early settlement of the islands across the Indian Ocean and Southern Seas. The rudimentary boats of the *Veddas* predisposed their eastward migrations and migratory path to the major offshore landmasses, most notably, ancient *Seychelles*, then a single large landmass comprised of the contiguous islands of the present-day archipelago. Ancient *Seychelles* extended from the present-day Seychelles isles, then the northern most mountain range of the ancient island landmass, to the southeast, where ancient *Seychelles* fully encompassed the present-day *Mauritius* isles, then the southernmost mountains of the ancient island landmass.

From ancient Seychelles, the *Veddas* moved slightly northeastward to the western coasts of the ancient *Kumari* peninsula, then a long, relatively narrow extension of the Indian sub-continent, extending southwestward from present-day Sri Lanka to the peninsula's southern extent, south of the equator, just beyond the present day Chagos Archipelago, then the southernmost mountains of the peninsula. At reaching the western coasts of *Kumari*, the *Veddas* pushed into the interior of the peninsula, where settlements and villages were established throughout the lowlands plains stretching from the central highlands of the peninsula, marked by the present-day Maldives Islands, to the foothills of the southern mountains, marked by the present day *Chagos Archipelago*.

Majesty at Mount Meru: Proto-Dasas

Negroid, Veddoid, and Sudroid peoples are, of course, genetically closely related, the most evident similarity being their black skin, which often approaches deep black. The Adi Dravidas (or "pure" Dravidians, or "Dasas") of South India are Sudroids with a slightly different hair texture than Veddoids or Negroids. The broad noses of Adi-Dasas closely resemble that of Negroids; in both the pure Negroid and Adi-Dasas, it is often broad in contrast to Caucasians, who are thin-nosed.[liv] The hair of Adi-Dasas is wavy and often curly, while that of Negroids is curly and often frizzy. Though the word "Sudra" is attested from the Vedic Dark Ages, this word is of African origin, whilst the term "Dravida" is of Sanskrit origin. The term "Sudra" and "Adi-Sudra" are now more in vogue for this very reason.

The Dravidian word "Sudra" is, in fact, derived from the lands of present-day Sudan. The Adi-Sudra (or "pure" Sudra) settlement range anciently stretched southward both along the highland corridor and coastal plains; their settlements formed around suitable habitation areas, anciently scattered across the expanse between the plains of the Serengeti. And the foothills of Mounts Kilimanjaro ("Kilima Njaro"), the highest point in Africa, just south of the equator. Kilimanjaro is the crown of Africa, rising abruptly from the open planes to form the snow-capped peaks, often fringed by clouds.[lv] However, it was in the highlands and foothills of Mount Meru, Kilimanjaro's smaller sister, just a few miles to the wes, that became home terrain to the *Proto-Dasas,* an emergent ethno-group of the Sudra arising in the highlands between Meru and Kilimanjaro, where the temperate climate and lush vegetation below the glacier belt provided a uniquely nurturing environment.

Mount Meru reaches 14,980 feet in height, with a landscape that gets noticeably lusher at a higher elevation. The highland fields at about 6,000 feet were anciently lush, green, and semi-isolated, the environment into which the Proto-Dasas clans first spread. Proto-Dasas anciently spread throughout the highlands of Meru, which descend through a variety of landscapes, plains, forests, moorlands, and lava-desert terrain, then into the rich, lush area of Arusha. Situated between the great Serengeti plains and Kilimanjaro, nestled between the peaks of Kilimanjaro and Meru, at the southern base of Meru, Arusha became an early ancient nucleus for the Proto-Dasas.

Arusha was (and is) situated in the shadow of Mount Meru amid rolling green foothills, divided into two sections by the Naura River Valley. Proto-Dasas clans migrated into the broad highlands and anciently expanded throughout the region. It was during this period that the lush inclines of Mount Meru became densely populated along the southern and eastern slopes, which, exposed prevailing winds, were well watered, and this, combined with the fertile volcanic soil, provided an abundant and bountiful habitat. Archaeological discoveries have found rings and bowls made from obsidian flakes, which were found on the western slopes.[lvi]

Reverence at Rwenzori: Proto-Anu

The Proto-Anu (BaTwa) were part of a wider group of equatorial forest-dwelling *BaTwa* peoples originating in the fabled "Lands of Yam" in the Great Rift Valley. They were among the original diminutive Negroids, disdainfully called "Pygmies"(due to their short stature, an inherent trait of each of the first peoples in the epoch of man) to cross the ancient seas. They stood around 4'3" on average, with typically roundish faces, very little body hair, and skin of a melanic hue. Their time of dominance is said to have extended from 250,000 years ago to about 17,000 years ago. [lvii] The legendary Rwenzori Mountains (the fabled "Mountains of the Moon") and the nearby Great Lakes along the floor of the Western Rift Valley were anciently known as the "Hapi Valley", the fabled "Land of Man.[9] The Proto-Anu (BaTwa) considered themselves guardians of the forests. From the dawn of humanity, their Sages proselytized that the forests, with all that they contain, belonged first to the "first people", and they, as the "first people", accordingly sought to guard, protect and nuture the forest.

A daunting task as the glaciers of Mount Kenya, Mount Kilimanjaro, and the Ruwenzori grew larger; most records indicate that drier ensued and intensified in the lowlands of the Rift Valley. Evidence exists of multiyear droughts, as the largest lake in the Rift Valley, Lake Victoria, slowly shriveled, and the surface level of far deeper Lake Tanganyika fell nearly one thousand feet. Lake Albert also declined, all of which eventually pressed the Proto-Anu into migration. The extreme aridity during the progression of the glacial build-up of the Last Last Great Ice Age (some 120,000 years ago) led to retreat and fragmentation of the equatorial forests of the tropics. Most rain forests had the best chance of survival in the highlands, where drought stresses were lowest due to moisture at the upper elevations; with the cloud shrouded *Mountains of the Moon* once again becoming the refuge of choice.

The Big Freeze: Ice Age Glaciations

The progression of the Last Great Ice Age encouraged and eventually prompted clans of the Proto-Anu to migrate beyond the shores of Africa and to settle throughout and beyond the lands of the east. The first incursions were expeditionary but ultimately led to the temporary and then permanent settlements, which, in turn, became colonies. The same series of events that followed using the islands of the Ice Age Indian Ocean as stepping-stones into and beyond southern and western Asia. To the south, migrations of the *Proto-Khoisan* were among the first series of outbound migrations to reach *Madagascar* and the then more prominent *Andaman Islands,* in the middle of the Indian Ocean, arriving not long after the *Proto-Anu,* who colonized the islands as early as 98,000 B.C.

---

[9] Book of the Dead CVII-CVL." Source: Richard King, M.D. African Origin of Biological Psychiatry. 1990

The initial period of glaciation caused a tremendous accumulation of ice over landmasses in the northern hemisphere and over the mountain peaks at the higher latitudes in the south. As the moisture accumulated over land, sea levels fell dramatically, falling over 300 feet (roughly one hundred meters) during the last glacial episode alone. As sea levels fell, ensuing weather patterns leach-out the sea bottom, adversely affecting coastal plains and swamps, converting large swaths into savanna or desert as coastal land areas expanded. Offshore islands within a roughly fifty-fathom contour became part of the continental landmasses during the last glacial episode. Present-day islands, including Zanzibar, Pemba, and the Dahlak Archipelago, became nothing more than unobtrusive hills among the coastal lowlands during the height of the early glacial episode.

During the build-up phase of the initial glaciations, conditions in the tropics were far drier than at present; however, several millenniums after the height of the initial glaciations, conditions gradually became moister, with drought and near drought conditions prevalent only in the lowland areas not privy to a network of rivers and lakes fed by the glacial melt. The long period of aridity associated with the initial build-up and sustained period of glaciation resulted in severe draughts in the impacted greater lowlands, causing species extinctions and mass population dislocations, prompting waves of outbound migrations. The pace of the outbound migrations of *Proto-Anu* and *Proto-Khoisan* increased with the intensity of the droughts.

The Ice Age Migrations

Major migrations of the *Khoisan* occurred after tropical Africa's climate became wetter (around 70,000 B.C.), dramatically increasing the flow of inland rivers and expanding the wetlands and estuaries of the Kalahari. The inundation of large areas of fertile land and the dramatic expansion of the wetlands ultimately gave impetus to ensuing waves of migrations by both the *Khoisan*, in the western Kalahari, who pressed further northward, and the *Khoisan* in the eastern Kalahari, who spread southward beyond the shores of Southern Africa to and beyond the shores of ancient *Sahul*. The outbound migrations by the *Proto-Sudra* returned with the return of lower temperatures and sea levels. With the sea-surface temperature higher than that of the continent, strong offshore winds reduced the flow of moist sea air onto the continent; consequently, draining aridity ensued, blanketing tropical Africa.

After decades of droughts, the continent suffered an extinction of more than thirty-percent of its wildlife, prompting waves of outbound migration. Full-statured *Proto-Sudra* has been traced along the eastern coast during this era, reaching the Cape sometime prior to 50,000 years ago. Their migrations across the southern seas were aided by lower sea levels during the Ice Age. For thousands of years, enormous volumes of water were withdrawn from the world's oceans, frozen primarily in the polar ice-caps and massive glaciers across the northern hemisphere, exposing vast tracts of coastal and island landmasses. Islands archipelagos, now separated by water, were then connected by lands exposed to the lower sea levels. A virtual southern land bridge made of a chain of such islands stretched eastward, across the Indian Ocean Ridges from Southern Africa, directing the path of migrations into lands of the southern seas.

When sea levels were near their lowest, southern island groups like the *Crozet Archipelago*, situated along the *Ninetyeast Ridge*, were transformed into mountain ranges of what became a chain of islands. These islands made-up the *land bridge* between southern *Africa* and ancient *Sahul*. Lower sea levels allowed short voyages between the islands, permitting early migrants greater ease of migration. The lower seas exposed a chain of islands extending eastward from the Southern African Cape, along the Indian Ocean Ridge to points just off the coasts of present-day Australia. Lower sea levels exposed an ancient Australian coastline that extended halfway towards present-day *Timor,* and fully encompassed present-day *New Guinea* in the north, and *Tasmania* in the south, resulting in an Ice Age continental landmass known as ancient *"Sahul"*.

At the height of the first glaciation, lower sea-levels exposed broad coastal planes and the interconnecting lowlands, giving full effect to Ice Age *Sahul*. It is believed that the first people to settle in *Sahul* crossed no more than 80 miles of contiguous open water to reach its shores. The migrants took full advantage of the low-lying islands bridging Southern Africa and Sahul, with groups settling in the suitable areas of the intersecting islands, while others pushed on to *Sahul*. Present-day Australia, New Guinea and Tasmania were then highlands connected by the lowlands of Sahul, offering the migrants a broad diversity of terrain. Archaeological findings indicate full-statured *Proto-Sudra,* those who anciently called themselves "*Blackfellas*", reached *Sahul* as early as 52, 000 years ago.

Lands of the Southern Seas: Shores of Sahul

There were five major waves of migration of ancient peoples who arrived at *Sahul* from Africa during the Last Great Ice Age; the first to arrive was a slightly-built people of pygmoid stature with dark skin and very frizzy hair, the ancestral *San* (whom later Europeans would call "Negritos"), followed by the *Proto-Anu*. The third group to reach *Sahul* were the *Veddas,* who migrated southward from the then-existent Sunda Sub-Continent; the fourth group to arrive was the full-statured *Proto-Sudra,* who anciently called themselves the '*Blackfellas*', whom the far later Europeans would call "*Aborigines*". The *Veddas* and *Proto-Anu* each settled in the forested river valleys of the tropical north, with predominantly the Proto-Anu settling in the eastern rainforest, while the *Proto-Sudra* opted for the grasslands in the central and western regions. The *San* inhabited the south of present-day Tasmania.

The *San* reached the shores of southern *Sahul*, present-day Tasmania, as early as 57,000 years ago, having migrated through the southern route from the present-day Cape of Good Hope. They migrated northward from southern *Sahul* along the then forested eastern coastal belt to northern *Sahul,* present day *New Guinea,* where they joined the earlier arriving *Veddas.* To the north of *Sahul*, the islands of the present-day Indonesian archipelago were then a huge single sub-continental landmass connected to southeastern Asia.[lviii] The huge *Sunda Sub-Continent* was a prominent peninsula during the low sea levels of the *Last Great Ice Age*.[lix] The *Proto-Anu* and *San* each expanded their settlement ranges northward into the ancient Sunda Sub-continent, on what present day geologists refer to as the Sunda Shelf, an exposed Ice Age landmass situated south of present-day Southeast Asia, which connects the present-day islands of the Indonesian archipelago with Indochina.

Southeast Asian Sub-Continent: Sunda Peninsula

During the Last Great Ice Age, the Sunda sub-continent separated the south China Sea from the Indian Ocean (in the region of the present-day Indonesian archipelago). Today the Sunda Shelf lies mostly submerged off the coasts of present-day Indonesia, Malaysia and Indo-China; during and immediately after the Last Great Ice Age, this low-lying region comprised the gigantic central plain of Sunda, forming the heart of the sub-continent. The gigantic Sunda Sub-continent was twice the size and landmass of the present-day Indian sub-continent. Sunda had thick-forested mountains in the west, in the regions of present-day Sumatra and Java; the mountain system ran northeast to southwest along the western coast, presenting a formidable highland shield for the vast Sunda plain in the central region of the sub-continent.

The present-day island of Borneo then comprised the mountain heights situated in the southeast of the Sunda sub-continent, mountains to the east and northeast of the great central plain, which extended to the southern shoreline in a broad valley between the western (Sumatra and Java) highlands, and the eastern (Borneo) highlands, just north of Sahul. Sunda was in the subtropical zone, and near the plain, in the centre of the sub-continent was a mountain of moderate statue, not very high on any side, which influenced weather patterns. Sunda had loftier mountains at Sumatra, Java and Borneo, and rivers flowed from their highlands throughout the sub-continent.

Underwater mapping of the Sunda Shelf reveals that the largest of these rivers, the "North Sunda River", was well-defined by a set of long winding valleys joining in the center to form a huge north-running channel'.[10] The North Sunda River ran north from the eastern coast of Sumatra to join the large "Kapuas River" from Borneo before entering the sea northeast of Natuna Island.[11] Most researchers agree on the course of the North Sunda River, and some of its river valleys have been located and mapped in detail.[12] The ancient North Sunda River joined many rivers of Borneo and Sumatra and had a major influence on the dispersal of freshwater fish in the region.[13]

The Siam River system, another major river, included Sumatra's Sungai Kampar that ran north through the Singapore Straits, where it was joined by the Johore River and ran north over a large expanse of the Sunda Shelf. At the time of the last glacial maxima, the Siam River was approximately equal in length to the present-day Mekong River.[14] Further east, the East Sunda River entered the sea near Bali.[15] This river system included virtually all the present-day rivers of the north coast of Java, the south coast of Borneo, and the northeast coast of Sumatra. A much smaller river, with tributaries in southeast Sumatra and the Thousand Islands (Seribu'Islands) area of the Java Sea, flowed south through the Sunda Straits to enter the Indian Ocean.[16] [17] Another major river, the Malacca Straits River flowed between the Malay Peninsula and Sumatra, running northwest to the Andaman Sea. .

---

[10] Kuenen, 1950
[11] Dickerson 1941
[12] Molengraaff, 1921
[13] Inger & Chin, 1962
[14] Fairbanks, 1989
[15] van Bemmelen, 1949; Tjia, 1980
[16] Umbgrove, 1949
[17] Verstappeh, 1975; Olliel; 1985; Rainboth, 1991; 1996a, b

Situated on the equator, well-watered Sunda enjoyed a warm climate for thousands of years during the Last Great Ice Age. In those days, the huge sub-continent was blessed with lush vegetation and a large variety of animals and wild game. *Proto-Anu* and *San* hunting and gathering clans were thus attracted to the region, generally migrating in small groups. The immigrants organized into extended family village clusters to best benefit from the vast abundance and resources of the virgin sub-continent. Over the ensuing millennium, they spread throughout the region, from the Andaman Islands off the west coast of Burma to the tropical highlands of New Guinea, from the central mountains of Malaysia to the rainforests of the Philippines.

Emergence of the Nilotics

In East Africa, the Proto-Nilotics, full-statured Negroids, first emerged during rains of the interglacial, in the abundance of the wetlands in the *East African* lowlands, with Nilotic affinities clearly identifiable as early as 55,000 years ago. Much of the data at our disposal suggests that the process of Nilotic adaptation favored partial sedentism and encouraged food storage. Oral tradition and linguistic affinities suggest that the Nilotics first emerged around Lake Nyanza (colonial Lake Victoria), from where they expanded northward along the main southern tributaries of the Nile, but no historical records exist. Great Lake Nyanza (Lake Victoria) dominated the Eastern lowlands in the great lakes region, her deep blue waters funneling into the Nile River.

In full extent, the *Nile River*, an early thoroughfare of the Nilotics, stretches from the Great Lakes region through the highlands, from where it descends into Sudan and the Nile River Valley. Proto-Nilotic clans migrated along the river tributaries into what would over time become the core Nilotic area, northwest of *Lake Turkana* in the northwestern rift valley in Kenya, between the northeastern region of *Lake Victoria* and *Mt. Elgon*. From there, the Nilotics fragmented and moved in and around *Lake Nyanza*, as well as numerous rivers in the region. As the aridity and drought-like conditions of the *Glacial Maximum* became pronounced, it began to decimate and transform the terrain of the East African forest belt, prompting the *Nilotics* into northward migration.[18]

The Glacial Maximum

Around 28,000 BC, the climate entered another big freeze; temperatures fell, and ice sheets spread across the northern latitudes, just as they had done 40,000 years earlier. Once again, glaciation build-up resulted in a tremendous accumulation of ice over land at the higher latitudes. Climatic conditions at the lower altitudes were arid almost everywhere, with semi-deserts and deserts occupying huge areas of the continental landmass, as forests shrunk back into refugia, announcing the onset of the Glacial Maximum. The Glacial Maximum was the period ice sheets were at their greatest extent; the massive ice sheets locked-up water, lowering sea levels, exposing continental shelves, connecting adjoining landmasses, and creating broad coastal plains. During the Glacial Maximum much of the world was cold, dry, and inhospitable; during this period the great African rain forests were at their smallest.

---

[18] Descendants of the 'Early Nilotics'

During the height of the Last Glacial Maximum, the African rain forest was smaller in surface area than today and fragmented because the climate was cooler, but, more importantly, also drier. This new cold and arid phase reached its extreme point around 21,000-17,000 years ago, a period is known as the Late Glacial Cold Stage.[19] This period has been recognized as one of the most arid on records, characterized by extended and severe aridity when East African Rivers and Great Lake levels were reduced by at least fifty-percent. Under these cold, dry conditions, people and trees had the best chance of survival in the highlands, where drought stresses were lowest due to constant cloud cover over the highland forests.[20]

The Rwenzori (the fabled "Mountains of the moon") rises from the floor of the Western Rift Valley, towering above the Albertine Rift, making the famed mountains visible from great distances. The majestic mastiffs of the Rwenzori present a unique and pristine landscape of alpine vegetation studded with giant lobelias, groundsels, and heathers, which have been called "Africa's botanical big game". The combination of spectacular snow-capped peaks, glaciers, V-shaped valleys, fast-flowing rivers with magnificent waterfalls, clear blue lakes and unique flora must have made the mountains appear as an oasis to those migrating from the lowlands amid the heightening aridity blanketing the floor of the *Great Rift Valley*.[lx]

As the highest source of the ancient *Nile River* and a vital water catchment area with a multitude of fast-flowing rivers, waterfalls, and lakes, the mist-covered Rwenzori beaconed beleaguered migrants from the surrounding arid lowlands. The six massifs of the Rwenzori are higher than the European Alps, with permanent snow lines and then still-existent glaciers on each of the six peaks. The landscape of the Rwenzori has been sculptured over time by the growth and contraction of the ancient glaciers, culminating in the numerous lakes, rivers and river valleys that characterize the mountains. The foothills were anciently covered by tropical rain forests, which dwindled during the progression of the Last Glacial Maximum, an advent prompting clans in the foothills to migrate into highland river valleys and the habitable-highlands.

Ascendance of the Anu

The heightening aridity of the Glacial Maximum prompted clans to migrate into the habitable-highland forests, with many, if not most, migrating through the river valleys toward the well-watered and lush rain forests of the mid-highlands. The Rwenzoris massifs are separated by rugged terrain, mountain passes, and deeply cut river valleys, with five main rivers descending from large fresh water lakes and glaciers in the upper highlands. Proto-Anu clans migrated through the fertile river valleys, where many settled, while most continued onward to the lush mid-highlands. These were hunter-gatherer-foraging clans that migrated separately and together along the ascending river valleys. Some settled in the more secluded river valleys of the larger tributaries of the era, while most continued onward to the lush, well-watered rain forests of the mid-highlands. These clans were originally egalitarian, with no one clan more powerful than another. Traditionally they were divided into clans who were territorially separate, and in their view they did not "own" land, but had guardianship and use of the land.

---

[19] 18,000-15,000 radiocarbon years ago
[20] Maley, 1987

Though they strived to maintain this type of 'open' society – a boundary-less, flexible social system that emphasized the equality of all, with no basis for excluding anyone; clans which became very powerful were deemed to have "proprietary rights" to the areas they inhabited and controlled. Although Proto-Anu clans freely traveled in each other's areas, most people stayed within their own territories, where they knew the resources best. *Clan* villages were populated by lineal and extended family members, with each *clan* headed by a "hereditary elder" (or "*Clan Leader*"), answerable to a "*Council of Elders*"; comprised of the Elders heading each family and extended family making up the clan. Clan Leaders were responsible for and held great power over the prosperity, security and territory of the Clan. Each *Clan* claimed a distinctive territory, with natural boundaries, including ridges, rocky outcroppings, and ravines, defining the borders between the land of one clan and another.

Following the Hunter-Gatherer-Forager clans came the Aquatic Foragers, the "Fishing Clans", mobilized into migration by the dwindling water levels of the Great Lakes. The Ruwenzori is situated between *Lake Rutanzige* (colonial Lake Edward) to the south and *Lake Mwitanzige* (colonial Lake Albert) to the north, with *Lake Rutanzige* discharging northward, via the Semliki River, into *Lake Mwitanzige*. Nonetheless, the level of *Lake Mwitanzige* fell over 150 feet between 20,000 and 18,000 B.C., prompting the Fishing Clans to migrate into the river valleys and around highland lakes for sanctuary. Compounding the situation, the surface level of the largest lake, *Lake Nyanza*, located between the Eastern and Western Rift Valleys, fell by an astounding fifty percent, mobilizing clans along its western coastal belt into joining the migrations into the Ruwenzori.

Similarly, the surface level of Lake Tanganyika, the second largest and deepest freshwater lake in the world, fell by nearly one thousand feet, mobilizing the clans along its northern coasts and abutting forests into joining the stream of migrations into the Ruwenzori for refuge.[lxi] As aquatic foragers, these clans focused on freshwater fish, mollusks, crabs, turtles, and small mammals such as Otters; subsistence activities that required the creation of specialized tools like fishing nets, hooks and harpoons; tools that would serve them well in adapting to settlement along the shores of the rivers and lakes of the highlands.[lxii] Like the Hunter-Gatherer Clans before them, the Fishing Clans migrated separately and together along the ascending river valleys, where many settled along the banks of the rivers while others continued onward to the ancient lakes of the era, each of which occupied large basins in the highlands, around which several clans would settle.

The fishing clans around the highland lakes evolved specialized subsistence patterns, focusing their aquatic foraging efforts on a limited range of species, allowing them to become more efficient at harvesting them. As a result, they usually had abundant food supplies, with many residing in larger communities than the hunter-gather clans.[lxiii] Early fishing clan settlements were the first to become permanent in the highlands. The economies of the Aquatic Foregoers (the "Fishing Clans") were the first to promote inter-clan trade; once settled, they eagerly sought to trade fish for bush meats and other forest products from the Hunter-Gatherers. The economies of the Hunter-Gatherer Clans were based on the wild animal meats they hunted and the wild yams, herbs, mushrooms, berries, fruits, nuts, eggs, and honey they collected.[lxiv] To these activities, the Hunter Gatherers then added barter with the Fishing Clans; routinely and regularly trading wild herbs, yams, fruits, nuts, animal hides, meats and medicinal herbs for freshwater fish, crabs, and turtles.

Over time, inter-marriage and cohesion led to clan integrations, with fully integrated clans ("Complex Clans") employing hunting, gathering and fishing, as well as early forms of plant cultivation, for sustenance. Thus emerged the eldest structures of evolved society beyond the limits of lineages, where the bonds of kinship and clan are extended and transformed into broader group solidarity by a union of a common culture, heritage, and communal values and interests. The *Complex Clans* used fishing traps and nets along the banks and shores of highland rivers and lakes. They developed the skills and capabilities to harvest and use wild grains, exploit water resources, and cultivate and facilitate the growth of desirable plant species beyond their natural range[lxv]. Complex Clans developed subsistence, economic and social organizations far more interdependent than the independent Hunter-Gatherer-Foraging or Aquatic-Foraging clans. The *Complex Clans* no-longer lived in small and mobile villages but in long-term, organized permanent villages; these are clearly visible archaeologically. They also did not harvest only what was available around them. They focused on gathering specific and very productive food products and combining them with other secondary resources.

Other themes that emerged were greater assemblage diversity and an elaboration of the skills and technologies required to adapt to particular environments, including experiments in resource intensification. It was in this way that "Complex Clans" paved the way for complex societies with mixed economies. The rise of such complex societies brought with it the subtle nuances of status and hierarchy, as hierarchical structures were formed to maximize efficiencies. With their larger, permanent and more internally differentiated villages, greater amounts of available food, the distribution of the economic surplus, and the increased division of labor in these clanic societies evolved the first form of non-egalitarian allocation of wealth. Status and authority became influenced, if not determined, by prominent hereditary ranks and associations, culminating in the emergence of incipient class structures and wealth distinctions.[lxvi] Lost were the egalitarian ideals of the past, at least for the most prosperous of the emergent highland clanic societies.

Proto-Anu clans migrating from the lowlands into the Rwenzori highlands followed winding, rugged, and often steep old ancient pathways, ascending up amenable river valleys, where they eventually encountered the first vestiges of the prominent "hereditary" (or "dynastic") clans of the mid-highland river valleys. Here they encountered an ancient highland civilization and complex societies with mixed economies, more interdependent than any they had theretofore experienced; an early civilization far more complex than the primitive "hunter-gatherer" and "fishing clan" form of "pre-civilization" prevailing in the lowlands". The new immigrants also encountered the strong since of territoriality, made evident by the closely guarded forests of the hereditary (or "dynastic") clans. It was a time when immigrants from the lowlands were met with hostility and prompted onward to the habitable highlands by the powerful dynastic clans along the forested river valleys of the mid-highlands.

The dynastic clans claimed dominion over large areas of fertile forest, both within and outside their province, with migrating clans were often driven to intrusion as they foraged to replenish their food supplies along their journey to the habitable upper highlands. Reports of such intrusion traveled quickly and brought an equally quick response, with elders of the dynastic clans quickly assembling warriors to ward off the intruders, usually in an unexpected, asymmetrical response, driving the intruding clans from claimed lands. The migrants found traditional "hunter-gatherer" societies more like themselves in the habitable upper highlands, those pressed to the higher altitude by the dynastic clans of the mid-highlands. The habitable upper highland rain forests were notoriously wet, with the new immigrants learning the rigors of survival from the older inhabitants.

But most poignantly, they learned of the provinces and asserted prerogatives of the dynastic clans of the mid-highlands and of the mounting tension between these abundantly resourced kingdoms and the clans of the upper highlands. With shorter seasonality at the higher altitude, the habitable upper highland rain forests were naturally less bountiful than the mid-highland rain forests, creating conflict as forays into the mid-highland rain forests invoked hostile response. Enlightened leaders of the earlier inhabiting dynastic clans had long prior directed cultivation of forest gardens to enhance food availability within their asserted provinces, an age-old tradition by which they identified the most useful plants, protected them and worked to exclude unwanted competing plants around them. Over time, preferred species were selected in favor of inferior varieties; other useful plants were introduced from neighboring areas, creating the mature forest gardens the new migrants relished in mid-highlands.

Forest gardens of the era were essentially ancient agroforestry systems comprised of layers of plant varieties, with large trees at the apex and small, ground-covering herbs at the base, with not an inch of growing space wasted. Unlike present-day monoculture techniques, ancient forest garden systems promoted polyculture, that is, a large number of species represented by multiple varieties. It was during the era of Ptah that the Proto-Anu first began to shape the highland forests into cultural landscapes. The period's population expansion and wild plant introduction within the various clan territories contributed, in no small way, to the trajectories that culminated in many of the prime ancient forests in the highlands today. Because Proto-Anu managed and expanded these "Forest Gardens" and tropical woodlands as "Sacred Forests" and hunting and fishing sanctuaries …for an untold millennium, the natural history of the forests cannot be completely disentangled from this early human intervention.

While the forests clearly evolved in concert with the continent's geological and climatic history, the ecology of the forests is undeniably reflective of ancient agro-forestry patterns and the pulsations of climate change.[lxvii] For over twenty thousand years, African foragers have domesticated prime forested lands to produce wild foods such as legumes, tubers and grains. Consequently, many present-day forests are botanical mosaics, reflective of the long legacy of human-nature interaction. The first of the old forest kingdoms arose around the "Sacred Forests" surrounding the villages of the dynastic clans. Each early forest kingdom expanded over the ages, optimizing its terrain using hills, ravines, rivers, lakes and other natural boundaries to demarcate its territory.

Forest fortifications of the dynastic clans were often miles in circumference, with thick belts of nearly impenetrable forest surrounding hillsides, grasslands, woodlands and well-tended sacred forest and forest gardens, interspersed with scattered extended family clan villages at the periphery. Villages of the lineal or hereditary clans were at the heart of the forest fortresses. Villages of the era were distinctive by their circular arrangements and round mud-plastered houses, encircling the village centers used for food preparation and gatherings. Yet the most impressive structures within the forest fortresses were the mud-plastered long houses, with their distinctive pitched-roof halls where elders of the hereditary clans presided. Elder councils were at the heart of the governance of the forest kingdoms, with the elders council at the epicenter of the power dynamic.

In vying for survival during the extreme aridity and dwindling forests of the Glacial Maximum, the kingdoms of the dynastic clans wantingly exploited all the natural resources around them, even if there was only one abundant resource, and even if it was only seasonally abundant. In order to exploit the natural resources, the craftsmen of the mid-highland clans developed specific tools (sickles, mortars, fishnets, fish traps, dugout canoes), and built dams and water ponds, and more intensively by incurring these investments shifted from "immediate-return" based economies, to economies based on "delayed-return". Migrants from the dwindling forests habitats of the lowlands, seeking suitable refuge in the highlands during the hyper-arid phases of the glacial maximum, would, out of desperation, inevitably raid the food storage facilities of the dynastic clan en route to the habitable upper highlands.

Such raids inevitably elicited conflict not only with the migrating clans but also with the clans of the habitable upper highlands. The powerful dynastic clans asserted sovereignty over broad swaths of the forest beyond the confines of their forest fortresses and thus found themselves in constant conflict with clans of the habitable upper highlands. Clans of the upper highlands were predictably prompted into the forests of the mid-highlands by the shorter seasons of the upper rain forests, culminating in conflict over lands the dynastic clans considered their exclusive province. Yet in the midst of the conflict, a peculiar nexus existed a tacit code of warfare delimiting weaponry such as poison darts and acts of conquest such as rape and the kidnapping of the women of the conquered clans. The peculiar nexus involved medicinal mushrooms not available at the mid-highland inclines and medicinal and psychoactive plants of unusual potency and effect.

The Prescient Kings

The Rwenzori upper highlands are among the strongest on earth. Due to the mists that enshroud them, the flora is characterized by exotic and unusually giant plants. Though the upper rainforest was smaller during the glacial maximum, near the peaks of the Ruwenzori were the most wondrous forests, dream gorges, and fairy-tale highland panoramas. Due to its configuration and height, the mountain range acts as a large condenser, drawing up hot moist air from the surrounding plains and precipitating it as snow, rain and mist. In consequence, the Ruwenzori were wetter than other East African Massifs, creating an ideal environment during the Glacial Maximum for the growth of unique and potent varieties of medicinal and psychoactive mushrooms native exclusively to the uplands. Medicinal and psychoactive mushrooms were broadly used in the maintenance of health and for ritual purposes. Therein was the "peculiar nexus" for the powerful dynastic clans of the mid-highlands to gain access to the most potent herbs they needed to trade with the clans in the uplands.

Progression of the Glacial Maximum brought with it a renewed retreat of lowland equatorial forests; surrounding lake levels fell throughout the floor of the rift valley, with the mounting aridity even consuming the foothills of neighboring Mt Kenya, which experienced a drier climate and widespread suppression of the forests. Though periods of intense aridity during the Last Glacial Maximum were considered shorter than those that formerly subsumed the region, they were nonetheless the most intense in 20,000 years. Most rain forests had the best chance of survival in the still well-watered uplands, where drought stresses were lowest due to cloud-blankets of moisture at the upper elevations. The flow of clan migrations into the cloud-shrouded uplands of the *Ruwenzori* ensued in earnest as the existential crisis that was the Last Glacial Maximum became more pronounced. Nonetheless, as providence and fate would have it, the clans of Proto-Anu were guided to sanctuary and attainment by the first of three prescient kings, each of whom arose during a time of crisis, when most needed. Each of whom would be deified in death.[lxviii]

Path of Ptah: The Awakening

Whilst the earth's beginnings are far more ancient than even the most ancient of legends, suggest, the timeframe quoted for the reign of the first of the prescient kings reflected time far beyond the memory and legends of early-civilized man. This period also represented the memory of the migrations and settlements from the lowlands of the Great Rift Valley, from whence most of the ancient ancestors came during the various progressions of the Last Great Ice Age. The first of the prescient kings was Ptah, whose rise to prominence began when he became hereditary head of his ancient highland clan, whose totem was the *Winged Serpent*; the start of his reign is said to have begun during Ice Age. [lxix] Ptah was a profoundly wise and gifted seer who is said to have illuminated every subject he touched. He was held in high esteem by the most respected elders of all the other clans. It was he, together with his consort, the highland Sage and mystic Sekhmet (Sakhmet), who first led the clans into the refuge of the highlands.

The massifs of the Rwenzoris are separated by rugged terrain, mountain passes, and deeply cut river valleys, crafting the five main rivers descending the upper highlands. Ptah's s dominion could be seen in the upper mountains, where great canyons and plateaus, rich upper highland rainforests, glacial lakes, rivers teaming with fish, arched mesas, and many other wondrous sights could be seen. Constructed in the heart of the Rwenzori, nearly impervious to invasion, were the boundaries of Ptah's highland dominion, fashioned by optimizing local terrain, using hills, ravines, rivers, lakes and other natural defenses provided by the landscape. Forest fortification of the kingdom was in the highland rainforest just below, where the fortification was over several miles in circumference, with thick belts of impenetrable tropical forest surrounding grasslands, hillsides, and well-tended woodlands, interspersed by lineal clan villages, with access into the interior limited to two paths.

A prescient, charismatic leader of the type endowed with special gifts of the spirit that conferred upon him extraordinary or supernatural intuition, Ptah avidly pursued the spiritual path, which is often symbolized as a great "mountain". When treading the spiritual path, one seeks entry into what was referred to as the realm where spiritual masters reside; one endeavors to attain a higher form of consciousness as one undertakes a journey leading to the source of their being, an "Unknowable Creator". He proselytized that at Creation, "Netjer" (the "Unknowable Creator") shaped, conditioned, structured, and prepared the Cosmos so that it be receptive to life, dispatching his divine messenger "Heru", the Great Cosmic Serpent, to animate the cosmos and set it in motion.[21]

First to pontificate the mysteries of creation beyond notions of the "Cosmic Serpent" (the mythological "Hydra"), Ptah proselytized that in the earliest ages, the man was incapable of self-rule and was ruled instead by those appointed by Nature to preserve and unfold him to the point where he would be capable of taking care of himself. A philosophy reflected a profound respect for the seen and unseen forces of Nature and a belief in "higher powers", the "spiritual-realm," and an afterlife.[22] A nascent priesthood formed around Ptah and his beliefs, anchored at his upland Sanctuary, where aspirants brought offerings from the seven dominions surrounding his own in pursuit of personal enlightenment.

---

[21] The Secret Teachings of All Ages: Manly Palmer Hall
[22] What the Ancient Wisdom Expects of Its Disciples, by Manly Hall.

The "Divine Serpentine Fire" emanating from the tail of the "Cosmic Serpent" (the mythological "Hydra", with the given name of "Heru") was believed to be the animating the forces of life; those forces animating Nature and Man. Through careful observance of such forces, Ptah first gained insight and began to make practical use of Nature's secrets. He came to understand the nature of the *"lodestone"* and *"mineral magnetism"*, which revealed a sympathy between the *visible* and *invisible* aspects of Nature. Enlightenment constituted a large portion of his *theurgic practices*, those enabling him to focus divine forces upon inferior natures and, in so doing, change courses of events in the physical realm. The spiritualistic nature of the practices of *Ptah* was fundamental, with *"Animism"* best defining that spiritualism. Animism is, in essence, the belief that everything is alive and imbued with that "vital life forces" known as "spirit"; that everything in the Cosmos that is *animate* has life, energy, and a quality which makes it unique, with its own place in Nature and Creation.

It is a belief system that requires developing a greater degree of sensitivity, perception, and understanding of the world, life, and our relationship with other beings, allows the Cosmos to be seen from an entirely different perspective, one that may only be attained through a metamorphosis of consciousness. In his metamorphosis, Ptah discovered the verity that the visible and invisible, or seen and unseen worlds, together constitute the whole of Nature; that "Nature" is as much an invisible world as it is a visible world, and that there are many powers of Nature that lie beyond our physical sense perceptions. In "Nature," there is a cause for every effect. Still, there are many causes that elude our perception, and there are many effects that elude our understanding. Nonetheless, the Divine Cause seemingly remained shrouded, *Ptah* discovered that its manifold actions could be traced through its effects in Nature, actions comprehensible, if not manifest, to Humankind.

For *Ptah*, it was enlightenment accentuated by their union with his wife and consort, the highland Sage and Mystic *Sekhmet*. In the spiritual traditions of the earliest antiquity, such women were keepers of the ancient wisdom; it was believed they maintained harmony and balance and were especially attuned to walk in both the natural and spiritual worlds. *Sekhmet's* mystic ability to tap into higher wisdom was highly revered; she was the first of the Great Sages to learn to awaken Nurture. Hers was the illumination that Nature is "Deity" manifest and ever becoming; "ever becoming" is the process of spiritual growth and achievement through which all living forms, comprising all the kingdoms of Nature, pass in an eons-long evolutionary journey.[lxx] With "ever becoming" described as a process of progression, subject to the laws of cause and effect, whereby everything that is, is the result of what came before. It is logical that all things and events have antecedents, which themselves become causes of later effects. The chain is continuous, unbroken, unbreakable, irreversible, and inexorable.

Sekhmet propounded that the chain also has a moral aspect with the consequences of *motive* brought into effect, where the consequences of an act are inherent in the act itself. Under this law, the process of "ever becoming" is beautifully and harmoniously ordered and manifests equilibrium. If anything gets out of line, it is inevitably put back to fulfill whatever purpose it has in the scheme of things. It was with the enlightenment that *Ptah* discovered and came to appreciate the multifaceted duality of Nature; that there is a material and a spiritual aspect, as there is a moral and ethical aspect, but moreover, that the surrounding invisible world constantly acts on the visible world as one of the forces of *Nature*. When *Ptah* grasped the idea that influences affecting one's life could work both ways and that through the exercise of *will,* he could influence the natural world, thus began the ancient art of "Natural Magick". Magick was believed to be one of the forces of creation used by the Creator, and every act (of magick) was considered a continuation of that creative process.

There are three essential kinds of magick; divine magick, working through the purely spiritual; alchemy, working through "transmutation" and vibration. And natural magick, working through the reciprocal attraction of bodies to one another. Natural magick requires a knowledge of Nature; that one searches out her secrets and comes to understand the component parts, qualities, virtues, and secrets of plants, animals, metals, and stones. It was through such pursuit that *Ptah* discovered the innermost secrets of the Laws of Nature; that the visible world (the "physical realm") and the invisible world (the "spiritual realm") are linked, and that the invisible world can influence the visible world as easily as the visible world can the invisible world. The study of Magick was the study of the 'hidden' relationships, interacting energies and correspondences within Nature, and how one may influence and direct these energies and activities.[lxxi]. As a power that flows through *Nature*, the ancient art and practice of *Natural Magick* was, of necessity, based on and confined to imitation of the laws and secret powers of Nature.[lxxii]

Beginning with the revelation that - not only in the manifested matter of our phenomenal plane, in the visible (material) world, but also in the psychic plane of the invisible (spiritual) world – there is no rest or cessation of motion in *Nature*; Ptah came to understand that its secrets would need to be resolutely pursued. In his quest for further illumination and enlightenment, Ptah sought and pursued the more subtle powers of Nature through meditation and meditative pathways to higher consciousness. It was an undertaking for which the mystic *Sekhmet* made careful and astute preparation, for at the gateway of such knowledge are the guardians of the moral threshold; where the motive is assessed, and the essence of the seeker's pursuit is determined from its (prospective) consequences. It was in such preparation that *Ptah* began the earliest practices of asceticism in Africa, which were viewed as a journey towards higher consciousness and spiritual transformation, a higher consciousness that *Ptah* sought for both himself and those of his highland kingdom.

The sanctuary of his mountain monarchy was built deep in the seclusion of the upper highlands, where steps leading to the sanctuary were said to have been carved into the steepest part of the highest hill in the mountains surrounding the mountain kingdom. Near the base of the hill was said to be a path that forked in two directions; to the left, it turned to the south, sloping downward into the highland rainforest in the valley below; to the right, it turned to the north, ascending the steps leading to the Sanctuary. Well above the Sanctuary, on the eastern side of the hill, just below the peak of the mountain-like hill, was a cave with four small caverns surrounding a large central cavern of sufficient size to retain and evenly distribute the warmth of a modest fire, at its center, in the midsts of the cold, frigid temperatures of the upper highlands.

The Mountains of the Moon were the legendary mountains from where early Seers watched the ancient skies and observed the cycles of the stars moving against a seemingly infinite dome of bluish hue, a hue the Seers believed emanated from the surrounding "Primordial Chaos". Faint mythos holds that it was here, in the main cavern of the cave revered as the "Cave of the Ascetics," that Ptah first journeyed into the spiritual realm, the unseen world behind our material or physical realm, the invisible ethereal world wherein the spirits of the plants and elements of the earth are said to dwell. The spiritual realm was a once-believed mythical world of nature spirits and elemental beings who animate the forces of nature; however, the idea of such myths containing hidden elements of truth is finally gaining greater understanding and appreciation.

The earliest knowledge of the ancients' was expressed and passed down through the ages in the form of well-crafted tales, poems and allegories as the best means of explaining creation, life, the soul, humankind's place in the cosmos, and the need to evolve to higher levels of consciousness. Allegories were the chosen means of communicating deep spiritual knowledge and were used to dramatize cosmic principles, relationships, and processes and express them in easy-to-understand ways. Once the inner meanings of the allegories are revealed, they become part of the listener's consciousness and completeness. The more they are studied, the richer they become, with the 'inner teachings' of each story capable of revealing several layers of knowledge, according to the development of the listener, with greater "secrets" revealed as one evolves higher. It was thus with the tales of Ptah, who, in the midst of a looming complacency in the uplands, is said to have set a personal example by renouncing the caste imperatives and hereditary hierarchies of the powerful clanic kingdoms, resisting their drift away from ancient egalitarian tradition and guardianship of the forests.

Through *asceticism,* Ptah and his cohorts sought not only to reject the drift toward materialism, but they were also pursuit of spiritual enlightenment. The original ban included Ptah, Sekhmet, his wife; Kontomble, Initiate of the Sanctuary from the clanic sovereignties to the northwest; Luruya, Initiate of the Sanctuary and gifted ritual drummer from Ptah's own dominion; Tellem, Initiate from the clanic sovereignties to the east, and the twin Sage Wadjet, from Ptah's own clan and dominion. Wadjet and her twin sister Nekhebet were the first to cultivate giant sacred mushrooms in the upper highlands and were renowned for their unique expertise in preparing and administering ritual herbs, potions, and elixirs. Wadjet provided each of the ascetics with the smallest piece of the sacred herb to relax, open the mind, and prepare the spirit. A spiritual quest was not something to be undertaken lightly; such a journey might last several minutes or several days in the physical world. A spiritual endeavor for which the physical body requires a place or setting that provides solitude, modest comfort, and security.

The Cave of the Ascetics, high on the mountain well above the Sanctuary, was a secure, spiritual place where meditating in the cavern around a small fire somehow deepened the experience. The fire at the center of the central cavern was seen as an emanation of the divine energies of creation, aiding in creating a meditative state of mind. The temperature in the cave, even without the fire, was warm even with the bitter coldness of the highlands, leaving it quite comfortable. All external sounds were shut out of the cave, allowing near absolute solitude and uninterrupted meditation. *Ptah* and *Kontomble* were the first among the band to undertake the journey, aided by an ancient form of guided meditation led by *Sekhmet*, accompanied by *Luruya*. As *Ptah* and *Kontomble* meditated, the resonance of *Sekhmet's* chant against the rhythmic tempo and ritual drumming of *Luruya,* induced the states of altered consciousness to need to facilitate their journeys into the spiritual realm.

Similar to coming out of a dream, nearly twenty minutes later, when Ptah again opened his eyes, it was as if has had truly been on a journey and now found himself again sitting around the fire in the main cavern of the Cave of Ascetics. To his right sat Sekhmet, with the drummer Luruya to his left. Directly across the fire sat the Initiate Kontomble, with the twin Sage Wadjet tending the fire and the initiate Tellem guarding the entrance of the cave. Sekhmet then prompted both Ptah and Kontomble to relate their experiences in the spiritual realm while they were still fresh in their minds, with Ptah deferring to Kontomble to first relate the experience of his journey into the spiritual realm. Because it is a personal quest, with each arriving by differing paths, one may easily ascend to the spiritual realm, while for another, it may be more arduous.

Such was the experience of Kontomble, who related that he "spent what seemed like hours in meditation" before he awoke to find himself "in a dreamlike forest, where the season was no longer winter". "It appeared or seemed similar to the forests of the northwest", he continued, "yet the vibrance of the plants and trees, and even the air and water, was somehow different; somehow more alive". Kontomble related that he wandered in the forest for what again seemed like hours, encountering no one, until off in the distance, he saw what appeared to be a beautiful woman whom he attempted to hail. "She appeared some distance away, standing on the bank of a small river, Kontomble explained, noting that "as I sought to get closer, she walked away along the bank of the river, leading me further into the forest. Until, finally, we reached a small waterfall at the end of the river, where she turned, made eye contact, and with the most alluring smile, slowly walked into and seemed to disappear under the waterfall".

Kontomble confessed that he "followed her into the waterfall", where he searched the entire area behind the fall; "but to no avail, she was nowhere to be found". Believing there to have been more to her eye contact and smile, Kontomble confessed he remained at the waterfall awaiting her return for again what seemed like hours. "Until", he noted, "the faint sound of drumming and the voice of Sekhmet instructing that I retrace my steps back to where I entered the spiritual realm became evermore present in my mind. During the long walk back along the riverbank, as Sekhmet's guidance became increasingly predominant, the spiritual realm itself began to fade; but not before a vivid reflection of the mysterious woman appeared in the river, with her standing on the opposite bank. Somehow, Kontomble surmised, she seemed to be beckoning my return".

Ptah, in turn, told of his encounter with the Nature Spirits that ensoul the plants, flowers and trees that make-up the forests of the highlands and of their ability to manifest and communicate in human-like form. Ptah told of Pixie-like beings that ensoul the individual plants and flowers and of the Fauns and Nymphs that ensoul the trees of the forests. He told of their ability to manifest individually as Pixies, Fauns and Nymphs and collectively as powerful Fairy-like beings, possessing the cumulative wisdom and powers of all those comprising their being. "A Fairy", Ptah propounded, "may represent a species of plant or tree or an entire area of the forest; as such, they are powerful Beings." "Yet it is the respective powers of the Nature Spirits themselves that appear most fundamental", Ptah proffered, illuminating that "it is they who transmute the divine energy bestowed through *Heru*, the celestial messenger (the "Great Cosmic Serpent")".[lxxiii] " Nature Spirits somehow convert this invisible energy into visible energy", Ptah propounded, illuminating that "pixies transmute this energy for forest foliage, while tree fauns and nymphs transmute it for the trees of the forests.

Trees made of wood, sap, leaves, and branches are physical manifestations of invisible energy transmuted by fauns or nymphs inhabiting and giving manifestation to the trees". "However, for all their powers", Ptah continued, "*Nature Spirits* are themselves interdependent and mutually reliant upon the powers of the *Elemental Beings* within their realm, beings whom I have yet to encounter; an encounter for which, like Kontombo, I am beseeched to return". Ptah further illuminated that the *Nature Spirits* he encountered "share the strife we in the physical realm now experience; it is anguish they in the spiritual realm also experience and seek relief. They thus offer the use of their powers on our behalf in the physical realm, provided we work in harmony and in service of Nature in our endeavors to ease and eventually resolve our distress" The six Ascetics absorbed, contemplated, and discussed all that had been said well into the evening; Kontomble made mention of the strange familiarity of the forest in the spiritual realm, which, though somehow more vibrant, seemed strikingly similar to the forest of his kingdom.

In light of Ptah's revelations, Kontomble surmised that the mysterious woman he followed into the forest must have also been some sort of Nature Spirit. However, she did not seem to fit any of the descriptions alluded to by Ptah, not that of the small-winged pixie-like beings, nor the tree fauns, or the fairy-like beings. Instead, Kontomble noted, "she appeared simply as a beautiful, full-bodied woman". Ptah, in turn, revealed the curious familiarity he shared with the Nature Spirits he encountered. "A familiarity undergirding a sense of mutual understanding and trust," he noted, illuminating that "greater powers can be made accessible, provided those now availed are effectively used". Ptah propounded that how they use the powers thus far availed is itself a test of their integrity and capability.

A test that must be past before attaining greater wisdom and access to greater powers; a test that must be completed by the first day of the Spring Equinox, when he is to return to the spiritual realm to engage the Elemental Beings. Word of Ptah's encounters in the spiritual realm spread first throughout the highland Sanctuary, as Kontomble, from the clanic dominions to the northwest, Tellem from the dominions to the east, and Luruya from Ptah's own dominion, related their stories to the other Initiates of the Sanctuary. The Initiates were each from one of the seven clanic dominions bridging the highlands; the tale of Ptah's journey in the spiritual realm was directly related to Perniankhu, from the dominions to the north, Ogriwabibikwa, from the dominions to the southwest, Khnum, from the south, Mmortia, from the southeast, and Seneb, from the northeast.

Word spread quickly from the Sanctuary to the dominions of the seven sovereignties, with legend growing and spreading throughout and beyond the highlands of the Mountains of the Moon. Informed by his enlightenment, Ptah proselytized the need to not only work in harmony with Nature and guardianship of the forests but to practice conservation as a means of preserving the vitality of the forests, particularly in the face of the mounting aridity of the Glacial Maximum. It became a simple matter of economics; if they had the opportunity to get by with less, he advocated they take it. *Ptah* was the first to instruct that the clans erect permanent dwellings and villages where food could be stored, with seasonal abundances to be spread and used throughout the year ...and his kingdom prospered.

Word of Ptah's successes spread quickly throughout the highlands, with the sovereignties of the other six clanic dominions striving to emulate him but, alas, falling short. Until finally, at the behest of a majority of the elders within the greater realm, the sovereigns of the other clanic kingdoms were pressed to anoint him "High-King". A position, in the view of the other sovereigns, that was to be somewhat of a "symbolic" ruler of an *informal federation* of the sovereignties; a federation that was, in essence, to be ruled together with the six sovereigns ...with whom Ptah was to collaborate. However, when Ptah became "High King," he viewed the title differently and unified the clans bridging the uplands with the edict of returning to their rightful role as inheritors and *guardians of the forests*.

Mystical Reign of Ptah (Pëtāh)

Thus began the reign of Ptah, with the dominions of his mountain kingdoms entering a prolonged period of prosperity, where the upland clanic dominions became centers of trade. While traditional hunter-gatherer-clans beyond the realm continued to consume their food as soon as they harvested it, the clans of the mountain kingdom subsistence incorporated a large amount of food storage, as Ptah prompted clans elders to develop and use food storage and logistics, combining food storage-networks with the networks of villages, for distribution and trading. With temperature seasonality more prevalent in the highlands, meaning shorter periods in which to gather, harvest and collect food, the shift to stocking storable surplus food provided a viable solution, lessening the need for seasonal migrations. Enlightened clan elders were prompted to more broadly use and expand forest gardens to enhance food production within their provinces, identifying and protecting the most useful plants while working to exclude unwanted competing vegetation.

Eventually, useful plants from neighboring areas were introduced into the forest gardens in the highlands. The forest gardens were essentially ancient agroforestry systems comprised of planted layers, with large trees at the apex and small, ground-covering herbs at the base, with not an inch of growing space wasted. Unlike western monoculture techniques, the ancient forest garden systems promoted polyculture, that is, a large number of species represented by multiple varieties. It was during this era that the ancients first began to shape the highland forests into cultural landscapes in the mountains. The period's population expansion and wild plant introduction into new areas contributed, in no small way, to forest history trajectories that culminated in many of the prime ancient forests of the highlands today.[lxxiv] It is an untold story of forest transformation tied to the history of foraging and ancient early agriculture in the rain forests.

It is a story of early ancient settlement areas where inhabitants enriched and even created a forested landscape. Because for an untold millennium, the clans managed the tropical woodlands as "Sacred Forests", the natural history of the forests cannot be completely disentangled from human intervention. Sacred groves cultivated by the clans in the rainforests and habitable highlands were, in essence, mini forests populated by sacred trees with rich varieties of rare and medicinal plants cultivated in the fertile soil beneath them. The sacred trees of the groves were regarded as temples (and expressions) of the unknown creator and as such, were worshipped not for themselves but for what was revealed through them and for the medicinal and spiritual powers they possessed.[23]: Beyond the trees, the groves contained a variety of medicinally important plants, most unique to each grove, and some species only found in certain groves; all tended to and controlled by local Sages.

With their knowledge of local flora and fungi, the Sages discovered the secrets of the natural distributions of psychoactive fungi species in their locale and developed an ancient knowledge of mushroom habitats, morphology, and seasons. The upland Sages learned to distinguish between edible and toxic species and were able to identify, collect and process a variety of differing species of varying potencies and effects. There were strictly enforced clan rules about by whom, when, and how plants in the Sacred Groves could be harvested, with the adept local Sages, in many ways holding the gateways. A tacit tradition that extended the Sage is the additional role of opening the pathway to enlightenment, obtained through meditation.

---

[23] Eliade 1958: 268; Zahan 1979; Millar et al. 1999: 35; Hamilton 2002

As the mountain kingdoms prospered, they constructed the foundation of an early ancient civilization whose influence radiated well beyond the fabled seven kingdoms of the Mountains of the Moon, with the highland citadel of Ptah as its recognized seat of power. From the rainforests of the Congo Basin in the west to the plateaus of present-day Ethiopia in the east, the kingdom of Ptah became the personification of order and learning, with many of those in the surrounding regions striving, often fruitlessly, to emulate its successes. So began the repute and mystique of Ptah as one of the most enigmatic of early ancient kings; word of his spiritual quest and encounters and rumors of his "mysterious powers" spread well beyond the realm of the highlands.

With the arrival of the Spring Equinox, Ptah and the ban of ascetics again gathered in the seclusion of the cave high above the Sanctuary. Once again, the twin Sage Wadjet prepared the herbs to open and prepare the mind for a journey into the spiritual realm. A fire at the center of the central cavern aided in creating a meditative atmosphere. Ptah and Kontomble were again first to undertake the journey, once again aided by the guided meditation Sekhmet, accompanied by the ritual drumming of Luruya. Yet, to avoid the seemingly rude abruptness at which their last sessions ended, Sekhmet advised that "when you hear the change in drumming, find closure in the spiritual realm"; she then commenced the chant, inducing the altered states of consciousness needed to facilitate a journey into the spiritual realm.

This time Kontomble again awoke first, and slightly over half an hour later, Ptah opened his eyes and again seemed to have returned from a true journey. Again, Sekhmet prompted that he and Kontomble relate their experiences while they were still fresh in their minds, and again Ptah deferred to Kontomble, who seemed somehow transformed by the experience. "We met again immediately upon my arrival in the spiritual realm", Kontomble slowly began, speaking of the mysterious woman-like being who last appeared standing on the opposite bank of the small river in the mystical forest where he once again found himself. "This time, however", he noted, "she was on my side of the river, indeed standing right before me; clearly the most beautiful woman I've ever seen. I actually felt entranced as she held out her hand, allowing me to touch and grasp it as we slowly walked along the riverbank, each without saying a word".

When we reached the place alongside the river which she conveyed, with a slight glance, was our destination;. However, the surrounding plants and trees, and even the water and air appeared more vibrant, the area seemed curiously familiar; a place I played alone as a child, and often sought as refuge as a young man. As we sat alongside the riverbank, I broke the silence by telling her that my name, Kontomble, and that I am an Initiate of the Order from the kingdom of the Clans of the northwestern forests. To which she smiled and replied that she is Ipæcia, a fairy of the lake and river nymphs of the northwestern forest …through whose eyes, she confessed, she has seen me before.

We spent what seemed like hours talking and getting to know each other; she told of Nature's Spirits and Elemental Beings of the forests and of the evolution of souls. That a soul is an incarnating spirit, and each such spirit has evolved from the smallest, most insignificant abstract force of nature to its current incarnation, and how she has thus incarnated as a fairy of the water elementals of the northwestern forests. It was as if we had always known each other; I related how as a withdrawn child, ostracized for lack of hunting ability, under the tutelage of my mother, an honored Sage, I became the first male Sage. An aptitude noticed by a wise old mystic of the clans, who, for some reason, took an interest in cultivating and developing my abilities.

A story to which I at first found her response somewhat surprising, as she, in turn, related her own story about the wise old mystic to whom I had alluded. Her story recalled that one day as a young man and clan herbalist, he met a very beautiful girl under a tree in the forest near his home and immediately married her. However, her past had remained a mystery. After years of blissful marriage, one day, he decided to cut down the tree under which the two had met to make room for the growth of additional herbs. Upon learning of this, his wife told him not to cut it down because she was the spirit of the tree, a warning he unwisely took lightly. When he cut the tree down, his wife disappeared as it fell to the ground. Over time, in his relentless endeavor to find her, he became a wise mystic.

We lay together alongside the riverbank, talking for much of the rest of the day and well into the evening; she told of how when two water spirits approach, their auras blend so that everything one feels, the other feels; an aptitude, she confessed, that inures within her the ability to merge her vibration and aura with my own. A sharing permitted purely by mutual attraction, and earnest emotional attachment, such as she rightfully sensed in me; an intimate and mutually pleasurable confluence, she informed, permitted only to the extent of one earnest emotion; a sharing, she held-out, that I ponder in earnest, so that should I desire, our spirits may touch. It was then I detected Sekhmet's faint voice, beckoning me to return to my physical body.

Ptah, in turn, told of the spiritual realm being the true archetype of their world, with familiar features and landmarks. He told of his encounter with those multitudes who ensoul and care for the energy of the undergrowth of the forest, the "Pixies" who work hand-in-hand with the Elemental Beings. He told how water spirits convey ether into the plants, which would otherwise wither and die. He then told of his encounter with "Oshün", a High Fairy of the water elementals with a surprisingly familiar face. Finally, he told of the enigma of the Gnomes and of the Dark Elf who the prospect of higher enlightenment. And lastly, he told of his charge to apply all that he has thus far learned for the betterment of the two worlds, the two that are one.

The bone-chilling coldness and the unrelenting aridity of the Glacial Maximum blanketing the central African lowlands gradually rosed above the foothills, resulting in the foothill rainforests becoming fragmented and perceptibly smaller in surface area. An advent prompted more clans from the foothills to migrate into the highlands for refuge. However, it was a time when vegetation in the mid-highlands was depressed, and grasslands had become more widespread; the formerly lush mid-highland forests were, alas, becoming increasingly less yielding and abundant.[24] Temperatures during the approaching Glacial Optimum were far lower than at present. This, coupled with the intensive aridity and regression of river flows and lakes levels, eventually resulted in a growing sense of food insecurity among the clans of the mountain kingdom.[lxxv]

The unrelenting coldness and rising aridity synchronous with the Glacial Optimum was at the crux of what was essentially an evolving existential crisis where, in the arid and semi-arid climates advancing into the mid-highlands, water abundance quickly became more important than the temperature for plants, animals, and the clans themselves to survive.[lxxvi] The clanic dominions and societies of the mountain kingdom depended on the ebb and flow of seasonal rains and melting glaciers as ample sources of water from the rivers and lakes. These formed the conditions for the accumulation of excess food; when these conditions declined due the weaker monsoons and stronger dry trade winds, many of the clanic villages and societies teetered upon virtual collapse.

---

[24] Flohn and Nicholson, 1980

With less vegetation and plant availability, most of the available food in the uplands was in the form of animal prey, leading the clans to increase their reliance on hunting and food storage techniques. An adaptation that resulted in greater territorial behavior and the creation of inter-clan social bonds prompted hunter-gatherer clans to increase trade with the aquatic-foraging clans around the upper lakes. The hunter-gatherer clans traded for fish in exchange for the meat they hunted, with the clans using desiccation to store both meat and fish. There were more than thirty freshwater lakes in the uplands, all of glacial origin, with heavier rainfall in the upper highlands recharging the still substantial upper lakes, each with one or more clans in residence.[lxxvii]

Infrequent rains below the upper highlands, caused by the weaker monsoons and stronger dry trade winds of the era, were nonetheless substantial. When joined with the runoff from the heavier rains of the upper highlands, the combined waters caused rapid flooding throughout the whole of the highland watershed. Inundated river tributaries and rivers overflowing their banks quickly flooded low-lying areas of the highland river valleys and occupied a majority of the clans of the mountain kingdom. Compounding the catastrophes, while the monsoonal rain-driven floods caused massive damage, destroying many of the clan villages, the hastened runoff of the rapidly moving floodwaters left much of the adjacent forests along the floor of the highland river valleys nearly barren for want of water.

The forest gardens along the valley floors located nearest the overflowing rivers and those near and around water-pans and catchments along the forested floor of the valleys were those that recovered best in the wake of the floods. This while those farthest away from such water sources fared worst. Having observed the effectiveness of transitory streams in re-charging ephemeral water-pans from floodwaters, along with the effectiveness of naturally occurring levies in slowing river waters, aiding in diverting some of the water through those transitory streams and channels into the water-pans and catchments, Ptah was first to foment the ancient technique of accentuating natural levies to divert a portion of lower "non-flood level" water through the natural streams into the catchments; extending the lives and usefulness of both the streams and water pans.[lxxviii]

After testing and witnessing the success of the technique, Ptah encouraged the other clans of the mountain kingdom to use soil and rocks to reinforce and lengthen those natural levees immediately next to and downstream of water-channels flowing into the catchment areas where their Forest Gardens and Sacred Groves are located. Word of his latest journey and enlightenment in the spiritual realm had once again been spread by Initiates of the Sanctuary, those from the prominent clanic provinces who, upon returning to their dominions and clans, imparted the illuminations related by Ptah to their eagerly awaiting clans and clan elders. The Initiates told of how, as denizens of the water, water spirits carry ether into plants, without which plants eventually wither and die; a verity to which enlightened clan Sages professed self-witness.

Sages of the highland clans had taken notice that the soil around water-pans remained damp for a considerable length of time after each rainfall and that plants around these catchments remained healthier and more fruitful. As "Guardians of the Forest," clan elders felt compelled to come to the aid of the forest, knowing that in so doing, they aid themselves; it is thus that the highland campaign to enlist the aid of the water spirits was undertaken with both intent and reverence, throughout the mountain kingdom,. Each clan within each of the petty kingdoms sought to use soil, debris and rock to reinforce and elongate the downstream levees immediately next to water-channels through which floodwaters usually flow into the catchments surrounded by their Sacred Groves and Forest Gardens.

When successful, the levees were reinforced and lengthened to divert a measure of lower, non-flood level river current through the otherwise transitory inlet-channels flowing through the forest into interior catchments along the river corridors, where the water pooled, seeping through the earth, irrigating the forest gardens and sacred groves around the periphery of the water-pans. Clans planted shrubs and grasses to bind and preserve the embankments against erosion and placed stones on the sides of the levies to reinforce and stabilize the walls. While erosion from strong river currents was a greater threat to the integrity of the levees than strong rainfall, the clans found that the planting of suitable vegetation over the reinforced embankments withstood the effects of both types of erosion.

The transformed permanent nature of the inlet-channels and streams flowing through the riverine highland forests into the then permanently filled water-pans along the floor of the forests permitted water infiltration and replenishment of soil moisture all along the courses inlet channels; particularly around the water-pans along the floor of the interior of the highland forests. The replenishment of soil moisture fomented plant recovery and growth all along the courses and corridors of the inlet channels and streams, most notably around the water-pans, with the areas once again blossoming with abundant and fruitful plant growth of every variety; particularly in the carefully cultivated forests gardens of the clans.

Once clans successfully cultivated a wild plant harvested for food within the forest gardens, they expanded to other wild plants harvested for food. This form of forest gardening was used throughout the river valleys of the mountain kingdom. As they learned in the lowlands, with their cultivations of wild yam patches in the early forest gardens, even though a multiple year interval is required to produce sustainable a harvest, producing food patches could be used for many years. They identified the most useful plants in the forests, and then worked to exclude unwanted competing vegetation from around them. Over time, as the most productive forms of each plant came to light, these were cultivated in favor of inferior varieties. Eventually, useful plants from neighboring areas were similarly introduced into the forest gardens, for greater food variety.

The highland clans found that by altering the shape of the water-pans, the surface area and capacity could be increased with time, further enhancing overall food production. A somewhat serendipitous advancement, as the infrequent but heavier monsoonal rains, returned with a vengeance, causing flash floods and rapid river flooding, resulting in the overwhelming destruction of some levies. Nonetheless, for the most part, most of the reinforced levies held, diverting portions of the flood waters through the inlet channels, quickly inundating and overflowing even the largest of the enlarged catchments, giving rise to networks of naturally occurring water-channels flowing into and transforming small depressions on the forests floor into scattered ponds and water-pans along the interior of the highland forests.

Having learned from earlier floods, enlightened clans built their villages in elevated areas or atop mounds protected by the levies they reinforced and maintained, with most villages avoiding severe damage from the floods. The irrigation of the parched soil of the highlands by the monsoonal floods caused the river valleys to again blossom into luxurious tropical evergreen forests with abundant and fruitful plant growth. However, this time, rather than waning as before, as non-flood level waters continued to flow through the expanded network of water channels, re-charging the old, enlarged water-pans and the newly created catchments and ponds along the forest floor, water infiltration maintained vital soil moisture throughout the broader network of water-channels and catchments, allowing the forests to continue to blossom and flourish.

The forest gardens around the enlarged water-pans blossomed with wild plants of every variety to harvest for food. The sacred groves and forest gardens of the era were essentially ancient agroforestry systems comprised of planted layers, with large trees at the apex and small, ground-covering plants and herbs at the base, with not an inch of growing space wasted. Unlike western monoculture techniques, ancient forest garden systems promoted polyculture, that is, a large number of species represented by multiple varieties. During this era, they first began to shape the highland forests into cultural landscapes. The period's wild plant introduction into new areas within the various clanic provinces significantly contributed to forest history trajectories that culminated in many of the prime ancient forests of the highlands today.

Because the ancient clans managed the tropical woodlands as "Sacred Forests" and hunting and fishing sanctuaries for the untold millennium, the natural history of the forests cannot be completely disentangled from human intervention. While the highland forests were clearly preserved and evolved in concert with the continent's geological and climatic history, the ecology of the forests is undeniably reflective of ancient agroforestry patterns and the pulsations of climate change. African foragers domesticated prime forested lands for over twenty thousand years; in consequence, many of the present-day forests are botanical mosaics, reflective of the long legacy of human-nature interaction.

The success of the natural levies and naturally occurring inlet water-channels inspired additional innovative techniques by enlightened clans and clan leaders; perhaps the most successful of such early techniques was the diversion dam, an earthen structure built across the bed of an intermittent stream; such dams diverted water into water pans and catchments, without having to master the technique of diverting noon-flood level river flow through naturally occurring inlet channels. With these, together with the other sources of natural irrigation, the forest of the highland river valleys responded with vibrant growth and rich abundances to be gathered, and large surpluses to be stored for leaner months.

The newly achieved abundance, together with the development of durable food storage networks and increased use of logistics, ushered in a new era of sustainable self-sufficiency and perhaps the first real since of food security and social wealth creation; this while working in harmony with nature and preserving the vitality of the forests. It was only then, legend holds, that Ptah would permit himself to return to the spiritual realm; it had been nearly two years since his last return; he deferred to Kontomble, Initiate Adept from the clanic dominions to the northwest, and Tellem, Initiate from the dominions to the east, during the first of the three intervening sojourns of the ascetics, and to Kontomble and Khnum, gifted young Initiate Adept from the central lands of the present day Nile-Congo Divide, on the remaining two of the three sojourns.

Granting or perhaps awarding the vanguard in the spiritual exploration of the Ascetics to the foremost Initiates of the Sanctuary, Ptah opted instead for a form of contemplative meditation, focusing the mind on illuminating and gaining a greater understanding of some experience or teaching. As the twin, Sage Wadjet gave the ritual herbs used for a journey into the spiritual realm to Kontomble, Tellem, and Khnum, while they again sat around a small fire at the center of the central cavern of the Cave of the Ascetics, Ptah sat alone in a small cavern to the side, but within view, focused on harnessing and channeling his emotional and mental activity toward attainment of that abiding state of stillness, silence and inner peace in which contemplative activity shifts away from cognitive intellect to subliminal insight.

As the ritual drumming of Luruya rendered the spiritual voyagers more amenable to the entrancement of the guided chants by the Mystic Sekhmet, Ptah focused on the connectedness of all things and the attraction of his own spiritual awakening. While the combination of guided meditation chants, rhythmic drumming, and ritual herbs was employed to induce the entrancement required for the journey of the spiritual voyagers, contemplative meditation required self-mastery over the ability to enter trance state, as a channel for higher consciousness. Contemplative meditation focuses on illuminating inner vision and understanding rather than on the experiential aspects of the meditation. Thus, as the chosen Initiates were transported into the spiritual realm, Ptah was transported to the threshold of inner enlightenment.

Contemplative meditation begins in the intellect, concentrating on a particular theme and focusing on an inner object, such as visualization, while internally chanting a short evoking phrase as a catalyst to transport the conscious mind through a visual journey of the experiences to be contemplated. It is an ancient form of visualization meditation that permitted Ptah to become immersed in the object of his contemplation, to gain a better understanding of his teachings in the (invisible) spiritual realm and the dual effects of applying that knowledge in the (visible) material realm. Ptah sought to better understand the duality and interconnection between the archetype (invisible) spiritual realm and the archetype of its (visible) physical manifestation in the material realm.

A contemplation that led to the revelation of what would later become two of the early ancient laws of magick; the first being the ancient Law of Unity, that is, that all things are interconnected in a pattern of actions and potentiality; that every phenomenon in Nature is linked directly or indirectly to every other, past, present, or future phenomenon. These interconnections are both subtle and obvious, but there is always a connection, and this interconnectedness allows all things to affect or be affected by all other things. A second epiphany would later be known as the Law of Association, that if any two or more archetypes have elements in common, the archetypes interact "through" those common elements, and control of one archetype facilitates control over the other(s). A reciprocating principle seemed partly to define the dynamic between the (invisible) spiritual realm, which is said to be the archetype of the physical reality that is the (visible) material realm.

For Ptah, the revelations heightened his curiosity, and with this enlightened curiosity, he resumed his position at the vanguard of spiritual exploration …in the Cave of the Ascetics. Thus, once again, the original ban of ascetics, Ptah, Sekhmet, Kontomble, Tellem, Luruya, and the twin Sage Wadjet assembled in the central cavern of the cave. However, this time, realizing the importance and significance of this Ptah's third journey into the spiritual realm, Sekhmet informed that the journey would be permitted to last longer for deeper exploration and resolution. In keeping with their custom, Ptah, Kontomble, Sekhmet, and Luruya sat around the small fire at the center of the cavern as Luruya's rhythmic drumming relaxed and rendered the spiritual explorers amenable to the entrancement of Sekhmet's soft, resonating guided meditation chants. Soon the two were once again transported on their separate journeys into the spiritual realm.

Again, Kontomble awoke, returning first from the spiritual realm ...after nearly a full day, Ptah awoke many hours later to find himself sitting once again around the fire in the cavern of the Cave of Ascetics, together with Sekhmet, Kontomble and Luruya, with Tellem and the twin Sage Wadjet gathered around the periphery. Sekhmet's eyes expressed tearful relief at the safe return of Ptah as she explained that he had been on his journey, in deep meditation, for over a full day and night, with little sign of tire or desire to return. Until he uttered, "there is more to accomplish", Sekhmet recounted, she and Wadjet had been concerned that he was somehow unable to return. "Kontomble also had a long journey", she informed, "and returned exhausted and had immediately fallen and remained asleep".

However, once Ptah had safely returned, Sekhmet instructed Wadjet to awaken Kontomble, and, in keeping with their tradition, she encouraged both he and Ptah relate their experiences while they were still fresh in their minds. And again, as has been his custom, Ptah deferred to Kontomble, who told of how he again arrived in the spiritual realm in the dreamlike forest similar to the forests of the northwestern clanic dominion in which he grew to majority ...and presently resides. "Again", Kontomble related, "I arrived along the bank of a small pond, similar to a place I played as a child and later sought as refuge as a young man; it was the pond at the base of the small waterfall where I last left my spirit guide, and where she often appeared.

"As in my last two journeys and sojourns in the spiritual realm, Kontomble continued, "Pæcia, my spirit guide, met me almost immediately upon arrival; but this time she manifested standing right before me. She personifies as an enchantingly beautiful woman, and, as has become her way, she first spoke to me subconsciously. Water fairies such as she that is, "Mermaids", feel the feelings of others; for them, it is a natural way to interact with those they feel are closest to them. During our many sojourns together over the past two years, she has become far more to me than a mere spirit guide, Kontomble confessed, revealing that "we have become far more to each other".

"A Mermaid can adjoin her aura with that of another so that the two combine into a single aura", Kontombo explained, describing it as "perhaps as close two Beings can come to be a single entity. It is a spiritual connection that enables Mermaids and those with whom they bond to share thoughts and emotions, as well as personal histories and dreams. It is a form of trust and bonding, an eternal bonding that provides me a clear vision and understanding of parts of their realm. Pæcia is a "Prime Fairy"', he continued, "a Prime Fairy of the shape-shifting water nymphēs and fãwns who guard the rivers, lakes and ponds of the northwestern forests; those who watch over and govern the flow of the lesser evolved water elementals on their journeys to the Sea".

There are secondary and tertiary fairies of the lesser domain within her province; prime fairies exist only within the dominions of Fire, Air and Water Elementals. Fairies of the equal station in the *Order of Nature Spirits* are "Species Fairies", that is, fairies of the Nymphs and Fauns of tree and plant species in a given region. The unique fairies of Earth Elementals arise from the collective consciousness of differing types of Gnomes. The Spiritual Realm is thus governed by an ordered society of intricate inter-connection", Kontombo explained, "all are inter-related and inter-dependent. The water element", he further explained, "evolved from the aether, air, and fire; aether provides water the space to exist within, while air provides water with the ability to move and flow".

"The relationship between fire and water is a bit more esoteric", Kontombo opined, explaining that "as nature becomes denser from one element to the next, the first, "fire", becomes denser as it cools, taking a greater flowing form: a fluidic form first of air, then (gasses), (mist), and water. The water element in turn protects against the dissolution of the aether element, the rough motion of the air element, and the heat of the fire element. In its denseness the water element takes the form of fluidic matter, announcing its inter-relationship with the earth element". It is thus that from the perspective of those of the spiritual realm", Kontombo propounded, "we of the physical realm suffer a vain misconception about the illusion and meaning of individuality".

"The Earth is encompassed by a (magnetic) field that unites everyone, everywhere, in every moment", Kontombo propounded, explaining that "in the view of those who inhabit the spiritual realm, all are truly indivisible. Therefore, for an empathic *Water Fairy* such as Pæcia, endowed with the ability to feel my emotions and experience my stresses as intensely she feels and experiences her own, she was first rendered deeply saddened and reduced to tears at the feelings of separation, isolation and what she called the unbearable loneliness of human individuality. She was then left perplexed by the nature and need of human emotional bonding. Water Elementals do not emotionally bond with their mate; however, their emotional detachment is far from being unloving.

Their detachment stems largely from the indivisible nature of their *Being*, autonomous indivisibles with coherent identities, inescapably cognizant of the inter-related and non-independent nature of their existence. For Pæcia, the allure of human emotional bonding eventually overcame her reservations, as the allure of her beauty and manner overcame mine. Mermaids are *Beings* of both refined and untamed feminine sensuality; while they feel what their lover feels and desires, they have a way of stimulating and feeding those emotions and impulses. We lay together, Kontombo confessed, we lay together on my two previous sojourns in the spiritual realm as well, and though they do not normally participate in human bonding, we are so bonded.

"My query", Kontombo asked of Sekhmet, "is regarding the offspring of such a mating", to which Sekhmet responded that "if the offspring is a product of procreation in the physical realm, the offspring will be born of and into the physical realm, as a being of this realm; if however, the offspring is a product of procreation in the spiritual realm, the offspring will be born into and of the spiritual realm, as a being of that realm". An answer that seemed to both fascinate and satisfy Kontombo as he pondered its prospects before then turning and directing his unexpected gratitude to Ptah, whom he then referred to as 'Pëtāh', in whose sole companionship he was "endowed with an early and enduring trust by Pæcia, and through her, many others in the spiritual realm".

Ptah told of how his quest for enlightenment ultimately led to recognition, realization, reconciliation, and spiritual empowerment, with each step along the path, in its own fashion, unlocking the illusions that bind. He told of his spiritual guide, Möura, the staidly Matriarch of the Baobabs with whom he shared much of his journey, and of his rendezvous and journey with the elf Tröm, and of the ability of such Gnomes to raise and extend their vibratory rate to interior transit corridors of the earth. Ptah told of his journey through the subterranean valley and kingdom of the Gnomes, and of the subterranean river and forest, along with the huge pyramidal mountains, giant megaliths, and the Palace of the Queen, in the heart of the Sacred City.

Ptah told of how he learned that everything in the Cosmos vibrates and that the low rate of vibrations in the physical realm creates the illusion and reality of solidity. He then told of the mystical fifth element of Æther, the mysterious angelic-like beings who ensoul that element, and how their element is the medium in which the Cosmos exists and through which vibrational waves, the invisible force of the Cosmos, travel. Ptah told of how their hierarchy presides as a catalyst, giving form, shape, and dimension to the archetypes, and how all magick is based on Nature and the invisible forces of the Cosmos, and that much of magick is theurgic, requiring the accord of the archetypes; accord which he has been granted, From these legends arose the theurgic arts, the power of adapting mystical forces to physical ends, through which legend holds that Ptah was able to perform feats of magick. The ancient Art of Natural Magick he practiced was a technique of harnessing the secret powers of Nature to influence events to aid humankind.

Ptah employed and taught techniques of imitating Nature in activities such as plant cultivation, metallurgy, and distillation. But most significantly, he is closely associated with the earliest encounters with the Netjeru, the divine forces that created the Cosmos; thus, over the ages, he became known by some as the "Creator God".[lxxix] However, through the early ancient priesthood he fomented, Ptah was more aptly associated with some of the most philosophical and metaphysical of all the ancient belief systems.[lxxx] The people were inspired to productive works and righteous karma under the spiritual guidance and moral authority of Ptah, with the belief that future events in their lives had their roots in the causes of the present, binding their destinies to good works.[lxxxi] Microlithic technologies became widespread as the complex clanic societies adapted and transitioned towards a social structure that practiced special crafts and occupations. Ptah was known as a great engineer and master artifice, the greatest of the early master artisans, always most revered for his own creative efforts, in particular stone-based crafts.

A patron of craftsmen as they came to be understood, Ptah was the first to organize stonemasons, sculptors, blacksmiths, and craftsmen. He extolled those who produced works of great quality and assured they received the due recognition warranted.[lxxxii] One of the traditions he instituted was that all the best artisans and craftsmen were to be trained in the Sanctuary; all other artisans and craftsmen were trained by graduates of the Sanctuary. These artists and craftsmen included architects, draftsmen and stone workers. It was through the graduates, journeymen, and apprentices of the graduates of the Sanctuary that Ptah invented masonry and directed the hewing and erecting of early ancient rock-cut architecture, sculpting rock-cut shrines, and the building of the earliest cities. He brought forth cities, towns, religious shrines, and chapels and established ceremonies for the worship of the "One" who makes Himself into millions.[lxxxiii] Most of the chapels and rock shrines are now ruins.

As the ethos and influence of the kingdom of Ptah spread from within the heart of the Mountains of the Moon to the clanic kingdoms throughout the range, the splendors of his mountain empire could be seen firsthand across the highlands in the great canyons and fertile plateaus carved into urban designs, and the majestic mountains and well-watered mesas too high to see their apexes, as well as many other wondrous sights. Cities of the highland kingdoms could be seen built into the mountainsides, constructed upon huge plateaus, or hidden in enormous cave-like cities deep in the mountainsides. There were two magnificent cave-like cities in the highlands, each consisting of a network of caves and shafts, with a series of pyramidal hypogeum dug into the bedrock, all connected by a network of manmade corridors and passageways.

The ancient cities of the highland kingdom remain shrouded in mystery, some say, because none have been able to locate them yet. However, according to the account of the first European to enter this particular region of eastern Africa, the Scottish geologist, naturalist, and explorer Joseph Thomson discovered large rock-cut buildings in both Mount Elgami and Mount Elgon, the largest of the Mountains of the Moon; he reported he found singular cave structures, which led him to conjecture that ages ago a civilized people had labored there. Thomson found great rock-cut buildings in Mount Elgon, which, according to his description, none but a civilized nation could have produced, leading him to further remark, "what a historical past has once run its course on this marvelous scene". There were no large urban centers with tens of thousands of inhabitants in the ancient highland cities; however, there were small cities with nonetheless important urban functions, even though they may have lacked large populations. Urban settlements with different levels of settlement and diverse sets of urban functions are typically called cities.

Smaller settlements with fewer levels of settlement and urban functions are generally called towns, with townships being the smaller version.[lxxxiv] Cities, towns and townships arose and prospered in the highlands as the vestiges of early state-level societies began to emerge. The complex clans expanded and became better socially and politically organized to contend with the ever-looming prospect of drought and scarcity, such as that that oppressed the lowlands , as the long era of the Glacial Optimum progressed.[lxxxv] By some mysterious immense power, the highland rainforest of the Rwenzoris, and indeed the whole of the Rwenzoris range, the legendary Mountains of the Moon, were somehow oddly sheltered from the progressing stages of the glacial maximum, with the Rwenzori serving as a refuge for several vital plant species of the era, with several species of trees migrating into the foothills and mid highlands. The clanic societies of the highlands became more diverse in their social structures with the passage of time. As considerable surpluses were obtained and stored, they developed and accumulated the first forms of assessable and tradable wealth.

Even as the glacial optimum progressed, under the enlightened leadership of Ptah, the highlands of the mountain kingdom continued to prosper and grow for several generations, though now they have largely been relegated to myth. It is nonetheless well known that in the account of British American explorer Henry Morton Stanley, regarding the 'Mountains of the Moon', like Thompson, he too elaborated about seeing "great buildings and refined caves" in the Ruwenzori".[lxxxvi] But alas, at the death and ascension of Ptah, hereditary secession to the House of Ptah, and rule over his Mountain Kingdom, was passed to his eldest son, Nefertum. The coupling of Ptah and Sekhmet had produced two sons, the eldest, Nefertum, and his younger brother Maahes; with the death of Ptah, Nefertem, whom many considered the 'favored son', inherited the throne by birthright, but only the throne of Ptah's native clanic kingdom, which he ruled under the watchful eye of Sekhmet, his mother, the Queen.

Worthy hereditary successors of clanic sovereigns ascend only to the leadership of their native clans; High Kings, such as Ptah, were selected by a vote of the council of elders representing the sovereigns of constituent clanic societies of the kingdom, sovereigns each aspiring and conspiring in their own ways to become the "new Ptah", the new "High King". Thus for 'favored son Nefertem, the task of ascending to his father's old throne over the Grand Kingdom was all but immediately fraught with a challenge; only the revere of Sekhmet by the sovereigns of the other clans held their challenges to his presumed authority at bay. As the hereditary sovereign of his father's native clans, whose totem was the serpent and were thus collectively known as the 'Serpent Clan', Nefertem's first challenge was to protect and defend their territorial domain.

Sekhmet's reputation as a defender of the realm was well deserved, as she had in an earlier age once prompted the Serpent Clan to war to dramatic effect, under the reign of Ptah, in defense against those seeking to supplant his domain. Sekhmet's name comes from the ancient word sekhem, which means "power or might,"; a name that has been fully translated as the "Powerful One" or "She who is Powerful". She was also often called epithets such as the "One Before Whom Evil Trembles". If aggression were ever asserted against Nefertem, the response would be carried out under the aegis of Sekhmet, and her's and Ptah's youngest son Maahes, who was usually referred to by his most common epithet," the lord of Massacre". It would be Maahes who would lead them against any who would seek to usurp their domain.

Thus, though no longer the 'House of the High King', the House of Ptah continued to be a symbol of strength and retained significant influence in the highlands. It was an influence further augmented by the character of Nefertem himself, who shared his mother's intuitive abilities. Under the auspices of the Kontomble, then High Priest of the Sanctuary, he gained a measure of his father's prescience. Through continued spiritual exploration of the ascetics, it was revealed that, like Ptah (Pëtāh), unbeknownst to her, at least on a cognitive level, Sekhmet ('Ŝækmĩs') herself had descended from the spiritual realm. It was a revelation of Kontombo, through his bond with Pæcia, that 'Ŝækmĩs' had been a fairy of the celestial æthereals, the most mysterious Beings of the spiritual realm, from where it is said she devotedly accompanied Pëtāh through the 'Great Forgetting', into the physical realm. [lxxxvii]

With knowledge of such revelation and under the spiritual guidance of Queen Sekhmet ('Ŝækmĩs') and High Priest Kontomble, Nefertem cultivated his own intuitive abilities, becoming adept at the art of reading the innermost sentiments of the other clanic sovereigns, winning over the susceptible by enchantment and his abilities in the art of healing. As the son of Ptah and Sekhmet, he was a patron of the healing arts derived from plants and flowers and was the first to use aromatherapy in healing. Perfume then was not like present-day perfume, perfume then was holistic, and its narcotic qualities were used for medicinal purposes. Nefertem was most closely associated with the blue lotus, a flower with narcotic properties; it was claimed he could cure any disease of men, a reputation which enhanced his influence among the clans of the uplands.

Queen Sekhmet died less than a generation following the ascendance of Ptah, leaving Nefertem to rule in his own right. As a vindicator of his father, defender and guardian of the social order, as well as the lands of the realm, Nefertem appointed his brother, Maahes, as Vizier, an appointment signaling his conviction to maintain order and prosperity. The highland Sanctuary, crucial to the remaining influence of the House of Ptah, as led by the well-regarded High Priest Kontomble, was still broadly celebrated and held in reverence throughout the clanic dominions of the highlands. Though, at the time, the aging Kontomble spent much if not all of his time in meditation, presumably in the spiritual realm with Pæcia and their progeny, whose distant descendants are the water spirits commonly known as the "*Kontomble*" in present-day West Africa.

The Rwenzori, the fabled 'Mountains of the Moon', somehow mysteriously remained sheltered from the oppressive phases of the glacial maximum and the aridity blanketing the surrounding lands. Though Kontomble died in the sixth year of the reign of Nefertem, there was continued goodwill and prosperity throughout the clanic dominions of the highlands, a feeling of continued peace and prosperity that finally led to Nefertem's selection as 'High King'. A mantle Nefertem wore proudly during the generations he reigned before his death. Nefertem's son 'Ihmos' preceded him in death, leaving the line of the session to Maahes. But alas, the rise of the less spiritually inclined Mashes was greeted by a waning of moisture that had so long sheltered the highlands from the heightening aridity of the Glacial Maximum, ushering in a period of creeping food insecurity.

As the aridity of the Glacial Maximum blanketed the foothills of the Rwenzori, gradual displacement of those who had re-occupied the once again fertile foothills once again led to an ever-increasing stream of migration into the highlands, disrupting and destabilizing the clanic dominions of the Great Mountain Kingdom. Like his brother Nefertem, Maahes saw himself as the 'son' of the divine admixture of Ptah and Sekhmet. They desperately sought to be worthy of such parentage by maintaining social order and enforcing peace. Maahes endeavored to promote moral guidance by punishing those who violated the tacit ethical code Ptah established. Yet, as the result of a rebellious youth, he had little understanding of the significance of the ethical structure nor the way his enforcement violated its imperatives.

Headstrong and rebellious as a young man, unlike Nefertem, Maahes rejected the spiritual teachings and promptings of his mother, Sekhmet and resisted being cast in the image of his father, Ptah. Thus, with the loss of most of Ptah's original ban on ascetics, Maahes and the Greater Mountain Kingdom lost much of their connection with the spiritual realm. The gifted ritual drummer, Luruya, preceded Ptah in death, and the Initiate Adepts Tellem and Khnum had long ago returned to their distant homelands. The twin Sage Nekhebet preceded both Sekhmet and her twin sister Wadjet in death, leaving only the elderly Wadjet available from the surviving members of Ptah's original ban of Ascetics. The aged Wadjet was held in high esteem throughout the clanic dominions of the highlands, prompting Maahes to anoint her 'High Priestess of the Sanctuary' in an endeavor to preserve the waning influence of the House of Ptah.

Inter-relationships between the clanic dominions of the highlands were nonetheless strained and tested as the sovereigns of each of the other dominions again vied to become the next 'High King". A short-lived exercise interrupted by the increasingly destabilizing impact and effect of the Glacial Maximum, not merely the mounting disruption from the migrations into the highlands and conflicts over territory but the dwindling resources. A confluence of events led the stronger clans to not only assert greater autonomy but to assert extended dominion over the territories and resources of weaker neighboring clans. An advent prompting Maahes to abandon his quest to become 'High King' and instead rally the forces of the Serpent Clan to defend their dominion.

Maahes's war-like response only served to heighten tensions, leading to increased instances of open conflict as the clanic dominions of the old Mountain Kingdom prepared for Civil War. Maahes endeavored to promote order and unity, but the crisis deepened, and the old Mountain Kingdom fell into disarray as food shortages and hunger emerged, prompting outbreaks of social disorder. With the spread of starvation, the authority of rulers dwindled, and the highlands clans began to openly raid, plunder, and severely attack and defend against one another. As vestiges of the old Mountain Kingdom seem to disintegrate before his eyes, Maahes finally retreated to the sanctum of the upper highlands, a scarcely penetrable realm of fog, laced with streams and ponds, covered in heather and colossal plants; for Maahes, a place of peace.

Maahes permanently returned to reside in the old Sanctuary in his later years, a time when he and a select group of Initiates would again gather each solstice and trek up the mountain to the 'Cave of the Ascetics' in pursuit of enlightenment. It is thus that Maahes became the last 'High Priest' of the Sanctuary, a time when he proselytized that the most important illumination of Ptah was that of the representations of Netjer …through his Netjeru'. It was in his effort to preserve this orthodoxy that Maahes was given the epithet "Maahes the Righteous", and it was also in this effort that he inaugurated and anointed the revered Hydra Priesthood and the first of its warrior priests, those ordained to defend and preserve the prefecture and prerogatives of the orthodoxy. Yet, as the rise in open conflict shifted to the eastern Rwenzoris, where the dynastic clans were concentrated, the final fate of the old Sanctuary was lost to the sands of time.

The ascendancy of a culture of domination and accumulation, alas transformed the charismatic egalitarian ethos of the old Mountain Monarchy into the harsh territorially obsessed imperatives and sovereignties of the latter-day hereditary clans. Competition and conflict over territories struggle to regain control of lost lands, and ongoing disputes over new boundaries characterized relationships between the former clanic dominions. All semblance of social cohesion was lost with the rupture and fragmenting of the old priesthood that formed around the teachings at the Mountain Sanctuary. Yet through the height of the renewed existential crisis, and the depths of despair, the laity were sustained by their belief in Netjer, a belief buoyed by the rare appearance of his messenger, the celestial serpent and mythological cosmic "Hydra". When searching the night skies, the ancient Seers, Sages, Prophets, Fetish Priests, and laity alike were each unavoidably reminded of the oldest prophecies, which alluded to the arrival of the Celestial Serpent at times of earth's greatest despair, bestowing the curative grace of the unknown god.

Best observed around midnight, on clear highland nights, when it was darkest, the rare and abrupt arrival of 'Heru', the "Hydra", was unambiguously announced by its brilliant auroral displays of luminescent blue and purplish-red colored lights, pulsating across and fully illuminating the midnight highland skies. An impressive display of the awe-inspiring power of Netjer, leaving one with absolute reverence for the immense power of Netjeru, such as Heru, through whom Netjer manifests. It was a time when the obliquity of the earth and the position of the southern magnetic pole, on rare occasions, allowed auroral displays of the southern lights, deemed the 'celestial serpent' (the mythological 'Hydra') to be seen as far north as the Equator.[lxxxviii] Perceived as divine fire emanating, in serpentine like fashion, the Hydra was believed to be a messenger of the unknown creator, bestowing sacred energies that give life to mother Earth and all that springs from her womb.

Though fragmented, the old priesthood symbolized many things; to most, it was a symbol of wisdom; the vestiges of the old priesthood preserved the ideals undergirding the complex societies in which the clans now found themselves. The hereditary clans formed around core familial clans, buttressed surrounded by extended family clans, forming autonomous clanic societies. The hereditary clans with the most enlightened leadership became most prosperous and prominent over time, with their long familial reigns maturing into dynasties, with these "Dynastic Clans" holding sway over key river valleys. There was nonetheless a nobleness in the *Dynastic Clans* in that it was they who preserved the crafts and adapted tools for the blooming of later ancient civilization.

Unfortunately, in adapting to their environments, the Dynastic Clans exploited the natural resources of the forests around them, even if there were only a few abundant resources and even if they were only seasonally abundant. Increased sedentism, food storage, logistics, the emergence of status hierarchies, and creeping social inequality were characteristic themes of the era. In order to fully exploit available resources, the Dynastic Clans led the way in developing and modifying specific and custom tools. In response to the rising aridity, Dynastic Clans built levies and water ponds to nourish their sacred gardens and groves; by incurring these "investments," they shifted from "immediate-return" based economies to "delayed-return" based economies. They maintained large food storage networks, requiring more organization, logistics and management, culminating in further social stratification, hierarchies, and inequalities.

Intrusions by the Dynastic Clans into the territories of smaller, weaker clans served to forge confederacies between such clans, though most were less than permanent and mired by infighting for status within their alliance. Thus, began a long era of inter-clan dispute and conflict, punctuated by instances of open warfare. The race for sovereignty over the dwindling resources of the highlands was a race for survival, as the progression of the Glacial Maximum increasingly made much of central Africa uninhabitable. Looming starvation was widespread, except in refuge areas such as the highland rainforests and river valleys, where people were able to survive. Mountain glaciers were at their maximum during this Glacial Maximum, when the stifling aridity blanketing the lowlands and creeping into mid highlands was most heightened. Migrating lowland clans sought refuge in the rainforest and river valleys of the highlands, territories protected by the powerful clans residing in those areas.

The Dynastic Clans jealously guarded their territories, marshaling their considerable collective forces of young warriors to defend against any who might intrude, while the clans of the upper highland confederacies would join together, but more often than not be forced to independently defend against intruders into their territory. It was a period stained by instances of open conflict between migrants, and those asserting sovereignty over lands deemed to have been bestowed to them by Nature. The obsession with ownership rather than guardianship of the forests thus became a point of harsh contention between the sovereignties and the influential vestiges of the old priesthood. Aspirants to the mantle of the old priesthood were the Seers, Sages and Prophets who practiced the ancient traditions of asceticism, ritual meditation, and spiritual exploration. They were the first of the ancient *Fetish Priests* who pondered the causal relationship between the nature of what transpires in the physical realm and events in the spiritual realm.

Opposition of the Fetish Priests to the harsh aggressions of the sovereigns toward the clans immigrating into the uplands became manifest in the disposition of the people and their adherence to the spiritual beliefs and dictums propounded by the priests. Thus, a moral dilemma was created when resources became strained to the extent that clans competed for food and things vital to their existence. As inbound migrations pressed more fully into the rainforest and river valleys of the uplands, asymmetrical responses ensued from the haughty Dynastic Clans, compared to the firm yet more congenial response of the upland confederacies, presenting a clear distinction between the creeping materialism of the Dynastic Clans and the spiritual idealism of the old priesthood.[25] Assertions of greater territorial control by the Dynastic Clans led to open conflict across the uplands. Advents leading to further strife and dispossession, prompting many of the clans of the uplands to join the flow of immigration northward, along the tributaries of the Nile River.

The northward migrations may not have begun with highland clans migrating from the Mountains of the Moon, but they were fully joined by an increasing flow of clans from the Ruwenzori uplands. Ruwenzori is situated in the central part of a great riverine region presently known as the 'Congo-Nile Divide'. In this area, the sources of the Congo and Nile rivers flow from the uplands of present-day Rwanda and Burundi. It is a region where the dominant feature is mountain chains extending along a north-south axis, where the terrain is reminiscent of tropical Switzerland.[lxxxix] The interior highlands are comprised of rolling hills and valleys, yielding to a low-lying depression west of the Congo-Nile divide along the ancient shores of Lake Kivu.

---

[25] Woodburn, J. (1982)

The Congo-Nile divide, or more aptly the 'Congo-Nile Watershed', is a continental divide that separates the drainage basins of the Nile and Congo rivers, with the rivers flowing to the west forming the tributaries of the Congo River and the rivers flowing to the east eventually entering Lake Nyanza (colonial Lake Victoria), and ultimately the Nile River.[xc] These are the vast lands and dominions into which Khnum, the gifted Initiate Adept of the Highland Sanctuary, returned and spread the spiritual beliefs and ethos of Ptah. As he had previously revealed to the original ban of Ascetics of the Sanctuary after his spiritual journeys, in forming his own school, Khnum revealed his encounters in the spiritual realm with the overarching Water Elemental of the vast riverine region in which he and his students resided.

Khnum taught of a great Water Elemental, a High Fairy known as 'Häpï', whom he described as the 'embodiment of the water spirits ensouling and personifying the rivers forming the tributaries east of the continental divide' separating the Nile and Congo River drainage basins; specifically, the rivers flowing through Lake Victoria into the Nile. It was in honor of this great Netjer that the vast riverine region assumed its name, the "Hapi River Valley" (though the name is somewhat of a misnomer, given the vast riverine region is composed of not one but numerous river valleys). Khnum revealed that the Netjer Häpï 'is the personification of the tributaries forming the mighty Nile River, and indeed the Nile itself, and further illuminated that his counterpart, west of the divide, is a High Fairy known as 'Mämbä Müntü' (colloquially called 'Mami Wata'), who personified the tributaries forming the Congo River, and indeed the Congo River itself. Mämbä Müntü (Mami Wata) was the embodiment of the Mami and Papi Wata spirits, ensouling and personifying the rivers forming the tributaries flowing westward into the ancient Congo River.

The central Congo-Nile Divide was an interlacustrine area mixed with clans and divergent groups interconnecting the clans and cultures in the Nile and Congo basins.[xci] It is a region of untold early innovations and advances of civilization, such as the inception of mathematics and what is believed to be the first primitive form of calculator; the early ancient Ishango Bone, dated to 25,000 BCE, considered to be the first evidence of a calculator in the world. The Ishango Bone was discovered in 1960 near the Semliki River and the headwaters of the Nile at Lake Rwicanzige (colonial Lake Edward). Part of Rwicanzige empties into the Semliki, which forms the headwaters of the Nile River.[xcii] The Ishango Bone is actually two bones, with several incisions on the faces of each. The first bone has groupings of notches scientists confirm are indicative of mathematical understanding beyond simple counting. Mathematicians conclude the notches on the larger bones follow a mathematical succession they interpret as a form of prehistoric calculator.[xciii][xciv]

The early ancient civilizations of the Hapi River Valley and those of the Congo basin west of the central divide were foundational to the later ancient highland civilization fomented by Ptah; it was in these ancient domains that the Early Anu first mastered new technologies such as pottery, stone-tool assemblages, and fabrication of polished stone. The Proto-Anu of the region were potters and jacks-of-all-trades, who, as first of the early ancient metal smiths, were accordingly the first to develop metal smelting. Evidence of their intensive iron-ore mining and smelting in the forested regions of the northern Congo Basin date to the late Holocene; however, the Ishango Bones, discovered at the headwaters of the Nile, are dated to 25,000 BC, fully seven thousand years before the rise of the highland civilization fomented by Ptah.[xcv]

As the Glacial Maximum approached its Optimum, one of the effects of the climatic change was the shriveling of the rivers and forest of the Congo Basin and the Hapi River Valley. These were formerly moist forested areas where a large number of lowland clans gathered for refuge against the stifling aridity blanketing the surrounding regions. This fragmentation and dwindling of the forests of the central divide finally prompted clans from the Hapi River Valley to join the flow of migration northward from the foothills of the Mountains of the Moon. Thus began the waves of northern migrations, with the clans migrating separately and together, the larger clans migrating separately, and the smaller clans migrating together. The flow of migration proceeded along the tributaries and corridors of the Nile into the ancient lands that thousands of years later would be known as Ancient Khemet. The flow of migrating clans reached the lands of early ancient upper Khemet (Egypt) by 17,000 BC, establishing a cultural continuum extending from the Hapi River Valley and the Mountains of the Moon to what would later become ancient Khemet.[xcvi]

These were the ancestral Proto- Anu of the ancient lands of Khemet, whose descendants would later enshrine, "we came from the beginning of the Nile where God Hapi dwells, at the foothills of The Mountains of the Moon." They bought the earliest forms of irrigation, agriculture, mathematics, science, and culture down the Nile, where legend reports they arrived not as immigrants but as inheritors of lands bestowed by Netjer; therefore, they rightly are called autochthonous is almost universally accepted.[xcvii] The highlands of the legendary Mountains of the Moon, the Rwenzori, nonetheless remained a core province of the Proto-Anu after the early colonization of Nile Valley. There was a nobleness to the old "dynastic clans" in which complex clanic society had developed; it was they who developed the crafts and adapted the tools for the emergence of early ancient civilization. It was they who had maintained the use of forest gardens to enhance food production, and it was they who identified the most useful plants in the forest, protected them, and then worked to exclude unwanted competing vegetation around them.

The forest gardens of the era were again essentially ancient agroforestry systems comprised of planted layers, with large trees at the apex and small, ground-covering herbs at the base, with not an inch of growing space wasted. Again, unlike western monoculture techniques, the forest garden systems promoted polyculture; that is, a large number of species represented by multiple varieties. It was during this era that they first began to shape the highland forests into cultural landscapes in the mountains. While the forests clearly evolved in concert with the continent's geological and climatic history, the ecology of the forests is undeniably reflective of ancient agroforestry patterns, as well as the pulsations of climate change.[xcviii] Africans domesticated prime forested lands for over twenty thousand years to produce wild foods such as legumes, tubers, grains, and fish. Consequently, many present-day forests are botanical mosaics, reflective of the long legacy of human-nature interaction.

Temperatures rose as the Glacial Maximum waned, combining with the hyperaridity blanketing the lowlands, further exacerbating the contraction and loss of lowland forests. But as the glaciers retreated and the monsoonal rains ensued, new grasslands and forests began to spread; but then something happened, and there was a sharp drop in temperatures and a return to glacial conditions for almost another fourteen hundred years. The gradual warming began around 20,000 BC but was interrupted four thousand years later by the first of three cold periods present day scientists refer to the "Oldest, Older and Younger Dryases".[xcix] The Oldest Dryas was the coldest period after the Glacial Maximum, bringing a return a glaciation around 16,000 BC.[c]

The Oldest Dryas lasted for three thousand years, until around 13,000 BC, but was interrupted by an intervening warm period called the "Bølling oscillation,"; a warm temperate period that began around 14,650 BC, bringing welcomed respite for roughly six hundred fifty years, until about 14,000 BC.[ci] The following Older Dryas was a briefer return to glacial conditions, lasting roughly a hundred years until around 13,900 BC. A second intervening warm period called the "Allerød oscillation" followed the Older Dryas, beginning at 13,900 BC and lasting one thousand years until 12,900 BC.[cii] The Younger Dryas cold period then followed with a return to glaciations, reversing the warming of the Allerød oscillation.

These three distinct cold periods were each anciently and successively known in the highlands as the "times of great turmoil"; the Younger Dryas, the "third time of great turmoil," was among the longest of the three Dryas cold periods, beginning around 12,900 BC, and lasting roughly twelve hundred years, until around 11,700 BC.[ciii] The ensuing change of the Younger Dryas was relatively sudden, taking place in decades rather than centuries, with advances of glaciers in the upper highlands and hyperaridity in the lowlands the central theme of an era characterized by a sharp decline in temperature, a return to hyperaridity and contraction of the forests and grasslands, with fierce and intense inter-clan rivalry over the dwindling resources.

Destiny of Bes: The Eternal War

The second of the prescient kings, Bes (or Bisu), arose in the Ethiopian highlands, slightly northeast of the Rwenzori, on what is known as the "Horn of Africa" during the "third time of great turmoil".[civ] The Ethiopian highlands are divided into northwestern and southeastern plateaus by the Great Rift Valley. The larger northwestern side is known as the "Ethiopian Plateau," and the smaller southeastern side is the "Eastern Plateau". Bes (Bisu, Aha) arose in the eastern uplands, where his clan, whose totem was the 'Black Leopard,' had been forced to relocate after having been displaced by a more powerful clan on the Ethiopian Plateau. Like *Ptah*, Bes (Bisu) rose to prominence as a young man, guided by the belief that he was destined to be a great leader; but unlike Ptah, he rose to prominence as a warrior.Each clan was anciently represented by a totem, usually an animal or reptile, a tradition started by the Ancestral BaTwa sometime during the Ice Age. By the Glacial Maximum the tradition had spread throughout East Africa and beyond.

In the ancient tradition, those who shared the same totem regarded each other as related, even though they may not have actually been blood relatives; kinship was established by both bloodlines and totem. The concept behind totemism is that the Clan formed a spiritual bond with an animal they deeply admire, of which the totem is then a symbolic representation. The essence of totemism is the bonding of the animal spirit with that of the Clan, in order that the Clan may associate with the powers of the animal spirit.The animal represented by the totem is seen to spiritually represents the clan and its identity and is closely associated with the inherent cultural disposition clan. Black Leopards (Panthera pardus, also known as "Black Panthers"), for instance, are nocturnal, hunting by night, and can hunt in various habitats. Black Leopards are highly intuitive, stealth-like, incredibly patient, fast, agile and powerful, aspects emulated by warriors of the Black Leopard Clan. If you combine all of these attributes and refine them through practice and focused dedication, you end up with a revered warrior such as Bes (Bisu).[cv]

Bes (Bisu) reached the majority in the uplands during the end of the third "time of great turmoil,"; an era spanning several centuries when clans in the highlands fought in open conflict over the dwindling resources of the once abundantly rich highlands. Prior to the Glacial Maximum, there were lush, expansive rainforests covering large areas of the ancient Ethiopian highlands, rainforests devastated by the long cool aridity of the Younger Dryas. As the Last Glacial Maximum (LGM) waned, the highlands of Ethiopia remained hyper-arid until interrupted by the "Bølling oscillation", a warm temperate period beginning around 14,650 BC. Before this the hyperaridity had been so pronounced that sedimentary core segment recovered from Lake Tana, source of the Blue Nile, indicates a complete drying of the lake by 17,000 B.P.

But for the drying of Lake Tana, northward migration along the corridors of the Blue Nile might have relieved tensions, as large areas of rainforest covering the Ethiopian highlands gradually turned into savannas. During the long cool, dry seasons, rainfall ceased completely, and the sky was permanently overcast. Conditions under which lush rain forests only survived in the foothills and highlands, where most frequently occurred, compensating for the absence of rainfall. It was a time when the Ethiopian highlands were also affected by growth in population, encroachment and expropriation of the lands of weaker clans, beginning a long era of conflict and open warfare. A period when clans could be reduced to starvation after a raid or surprise attack.

Fear of the dwindling of the forests and their natural resources, rather than actual shortages, served to heighten tensions in the highlands, with most clans maintaining a cautionary preparedness for war so that in the event they ran short of food, they could readily raid the supplies of neighboring clans, and thus stave-off starvation. Under such circumstances, war was deemed vital to survival, a matter of life or death, and skilled warriors such as Bes (Bisu) were much in demand and highly extolled. He was called "Aha" (the "fighter") because of his ferocity – legend holds that he was a fierce fighter able to do battle with man or beasts alike; it is said that he was able to best and strangle beasts with his bare hands.

Adept martial skills, which led to his early rise to leadership of the clan of the Black Leopard, predisposed his leadership toward conquests. Like Ptah, Bes (Bisu, Aha (the "fighter")) assumed the role while still a fairly young man, yet he was nonetheless a skilled warrior and military commander who saw war as a necessity grounded in preservation. This is reflected in the many depictions of Bes (Bisu) during late antiquity; he is usually depicted with a regalia of swords, knives, daggers, and other amazing weapons such as maces and boomerangs. As a product of his time, Bes saw war as part of the nature of life, a life of "conquer or be conquered", and he stood ready to meet any foe head-on. Yet, as clan leader, he was now called upon to be more than a protector and defender, but also a provider.

With large once fertile areas of the highlands in full retreat and basic life remaining difficult and harsh for most if not all of the clans in the highlands, a brutal realization enabling clan leaders with thirst avarice and power to use the reality of the dwindling forests, to assert distinct rights of sovereignty over "traditional lands". An advent fomenting inter-clan rivalries and, ultimately, the necessity of war. This was the existential crisis during the time Bes was born, times in which the inherent predisposition of man to struggle for sheer survival was on full display. Inter-clan warfare and a "survival of the fittest" basis to defined life during the time of the rise of Bes (Bisu, Aha (the "Fighter")). Given the parity of weaponry, it was a time when strength was measured by clan size and the number of able-bodied warriors. A time when larger clans imposed their will by assailing and dispossessing smaller clans.

In surveying the territory, resources, and vulnerabilities of the Black Leopard Clan, Bes (Bisu, Aha) keenly observed that their territories bordered and were surrounded by those of five separate clans. Two of the five clans, the *Oryx Clan* to their southeast and the *Catbird Clan* to their southwest, were about the same size and strength in terms of warriors as the *Black Leopard Clan*. One of the five clans, the *Raven Clan* to their south, was larger. The remaining two clans, the *Crocodile Clan*, on the southeastern edge of the plateau, and the clans of the *Ibis*, on the northeastern edge of the plateau, were each even larger and more powerful, with the *Ravens* often forcing smaller clans to cede territory. After assessing the strengths of the five clans and the nature of their territories, Bes (Bisu, Aha) convened a meeting of his Council of Elders.

Standing before and addressing the Council, Bes is said to have taken a moment to maintain eye contact with each elder of the council, as if studying the depth of their courage, before finally proclaiming, in a whisper loud enough for all to hear, that 'it is better to eliminate the very possibility of threat than to wait for the threat to fully develop, and then take losses in defense against that threat'. Bes (Bisu, Aha) saw that the clanic kingdoms of the central-eastern plateau had been weakened by their antagonisms. He has formulated a plan for conquering five of the other six clans, unifying the eastern plateau. With his own unique form of charisma, Bes (Bisu, Aha) propounded that 'a compulsion of necessity creates the imperatives for war', emphasizing, in full-throated voice, that 'before you is the choice to survive, or perish.'

It was a time when the primary motivation for war was the threat of invasion by a hostile clan; clans were forced by their own dire circumstances to violently invade the territory of a weaker neighbor, driving out its inhabitants. A time when large clans went to war to seize the lands of their weaker neighbors, and small clans went to war against other small clans after having been displaced or dispossessed of a portion of their lands. Bes (Bisu, Aha) rose to leadership of one of the midsized clans, whose territories had been invaded and displaced long before his ascendance. As a young warrior, he fought with valor in numerous battles in which his clan had fought other clans …to defend against being forced to cede vital parts of their lands. It was a period marked and characterized by raids and assaults by one clan against another, as each vying for survival

Bes (Bisu, Aha) explained his belief to the Council that the powerful clans of the Ibis, on the northeastern edge of the plateau, and the powerful Crocodile Clan, on the southeastern edge of the plateau, would eventually conquer and dispossess each of the midsize and small clans in the midlands. A dilemma for which Bes (Bisu, Aha) prescribed an alliance between the clans of the midlands, noting, however, that 'given the high level of suspicion and mistrust between the clans, the first will have to be an alliance of immediate convenience. After a crisis, when one of the other clans is most in need, he contended, adding that "until such time, we ourselves remain at risk lest we prepare in a fashion others have not." Bes propounded that they prepare for war against each of the clans in the midlands and ally with a distant clan to aid in defense against those nearby.

Bes then again took his seat among the Elders of the Council, imploring that in their deliberations and final decision-making, they affirm his plan and adopt a "warrior ethos" and a permanent warfare footing. For Bes (Bisu, Aha), warfare was seen as a necessary evil of the human struggle for survival; "the vast rewards of war", he contended, "often outweighed the costs in lives and resources". Bes (Bisu, Aha) was the first to imbue the notion of a "warrior caste" within each clan; he proclaimed that all the young, single men were the natural cadre of the clan's warriors. Men with families and older men were warriors of the rear guard (defense forces

Bes (Bisu, Aha ("The Fighter")) proclaimed that they must be more valiant, better skilled, and shrewder in their tactics than the warriors of the larger clans. He contended that 'if they outnumber us by three to one, we must be more than three times better; for every one of our warriors that falls, three of theirs must fall, for every slight, they cast against us, three-fold must be cast back against them. Bes (Bisu, Aha) valued courage and honor above all, and he believed that all men must instinctively be warriors; indeed, he considered war a rite of passage for men. Discipline and innovation in weaponry in warfare are two of his greatest achievements, as perhaps the first to organize for war with standardized weaponry among his warriors, equipping each with a short bow, long knife and round shield for use in close combat.

In imbuing the ethos of the warrior caste, Bes (Bisu, Aha) set apart those most adept at crafting weapons and assigned to them the apprentices of their choice, with the charge that they are each warrior with a strong short spear and well-crafted long knife, and each warrior charged with crafting his own study "short bow", for use in combat; a technique and skill Bisu had honed and used to deadly effect in battle. Large game hunting bans were formed and enlisted to both augment food supplies …and train young warriors of the clan in coordinated hunting and attacking techniques, in addition to refining their archery skills. Skilled elders trained the young warriors in the ways of their totem, the "Black Leopard", who are excellent at stalking prey; they are silent and inconspicuous hunters, able to move in and out of situations without being seen.

The Black Leopard Clan was comprised of three sub-clans, with Bes (Bisu, Aha) holding the most proven and martially adept warriors of each accountable to both themselves and the security of the entire clan. A mighty warrior known as "Kherau", whose skills were second only to those of Bes (Bisu Aha) himself and was a trusted member of their same sub-clan, was the natural choice to represent their own clan. As was a famed warrior name, "Menew," of the second sub-clan, and a revered warrior name, "Amam," of the third sub-clan. Each of these adept warriors was chosen by their elders and appointed by (Bisu Aha) to train and sharpen the skills and martial abilities of the young warriors of their sub-clans, appointments which would mature into positions of command.

A key aspect of their inculcating the spirit of the *Black Leopard* was in adapting the powers of the clan's totem. Black leopards are smaller but fiercer than lions and tigers, with greater speed; however, because black leopards are solitary hunters, during generations past, the clan adopted certain of the useful traits of the distantly related *Black Lion Clan*. Lions hunt cooperatively, allowing them to tackle prey that would otherwise prove too large, too fast or too elusive. Their hunts are well organized, with normally several lions circling around the herd they are attacking, slowly driving their victims towards fellow lions hiding in tall grass. Lions lying in wait then attack their prey from the sides or the rear; skills Bes insisted young warriors perfect, and for which he held elder warriors accountable, to both themselves and the entire clan.

These were the teachings, techniques, skills and abilities Bes (Bisu, Aha) employed to train and select the most able-bodied warriors of the clan, those who, having attained the instincts and skills of superiors warriors, lack only the unique mixture of courage and fearlessness a superior warrior must have. Bes (Bisu, Aha) viewed true courage, the highest form of courage, as the wisdom, bravery, and unrelenting determination to prevail. Fearlessness did not mean, literally, "to have no fear", nor did it mean that the warrior must somehow be deficient in the instincts and tools that are sensibly trying to keep him alive. Fear was considered a useful response and was, instinctually, to further heighten the abilities of the warrior.

Fear is a powerful force. It entwines itself through our entire existence in so many ways, though the conquest of one's fears is necessary for Spiritual Growth. Bes (Bisu, Aha) proselytized that it is necessary to face our fears head-on; that one may reduce their fear by meditating on the cause of the fear, which is usually "the unknown". The "unknown" was then attacked and conquered through guided visualization, in which the warrior envisions the battle that lay ahead and sees and portrays himself as victorious in every phase, every aspect and every prospective difficulty or challenge that lay before him, carefully working through effective and superior offensive and defensive tactics, decidedly transcending his fear.

When fear was transmuted in this manner, it enlightened and bestowed the highest form of courage upon the warrior.[cvi] It was believed that this form of fearless ability could be tapped and used for benevolent purposes; it created a special aura around the warriors who acquired it, imbuing them with supernatural abilities. Bes (Bisu, Aha) affirmed that 'once you have accessed this state and become firmly anchored in it, you no longer worry about your fate in the fight. He contended that warfare was the perfect opportunity for a warrior to display his manliness and excellence in battle. If one is to perish, he queried, 'is it not better to perish on the battlefield?' Bes (Bisu, Aha) proclaimed that 'with war came the possibility of conquest, and the opportunity for territorial expansion and access to better lands'; he emphasized that "conquest rewards those who prevail".

In keeping with the nature of the totem of his clan, Bes (Bisu) patiently waited for the right moment. Then finally, the opportunity he awaited presented itself; the Raven Clan, a somewhat larger clan to the south, had launched an attack on the Catbird Clan to the southwest, killing many Catbird warriors and abducting several of their women. The Ravens raided and confiscated much of the food storage supply of the Catbirds, no doubt their primary objective, leaving the defeated clan with little to survive on. The Catbird Clan were known more for their music, singing, and festivity than for their fighting aptitude; howsoever, once recuperated, they gathered themselves and responded in a series of attacks that, alas, left them further weakened.[cvii]

Bes (Bisu, Aha ("The Fighter")) grasped the opportunity by inviting an alliance between his formidable Black Leopard Clan and a Catbird Clan with little other option. In the assessment of Bes (Bisu), the warfare between the Raven and Catbird clans had weakened and rendered both clans somewhat vulnerable. The collective forces of the Black Leopard, together with the remaining warriors of the Catbird clans, then outnumbered those of the Raven. In keeping with the nocturnal spirit of their totem, the warriors of the Black Leopard, who were at the lead of the attack against the Raven Clan, opted to attack at night. Like their totem, the warriors of the Black Leopard clans were masters at camouflage, making use of natural cover as they positioned themselves and the warriors of the Catbird clan to surround the encampment of the Raven clans on three sides.

They purposefully left a visible opening for escape, a trap, with the archers of the Black Leopard warriors, led by the trusted warrior Kherau, awaiting in silent ambush. Bes (Bisu, Aha (the "Fighter")) himself launched the assault by silent gestures, which signaled a coordinated barrage from the arrows by the warriors of the Black Leopard and Catbird clans surrounding the encampment, causing a state of pure panic. The guards of the Raven clans were the first to fall, causing more panic and chaos than ever as the arrows rained down from the sky, striking warriors but also women and the elderly. The chaos within the encampment made it difficult, if not impossible, to assemble warriors for defense, or for that matter, to simply see their attackers.

Arrows rained down on the interior of the Raven encampment with increasing intensity, with many members of the Raven clan falling in their panic as the others of the clan finally discovered a route of escape. As the mass of the clan stampeded through the opening, the archers of the Black Leopard lying in wait remained still and patient, with Kherau instinctively sensing the precise moment to attack. Kherau and the Black Leopard warriors waited until the panicked horde were within range of their bows, and then launched a series of barrages, falling the warriors at the front of the panicked peoples of the clans, prompting the horde to then scatter into the forest to escape. Throughout the entire affair Bes maintained the presence of mind to capture the leader and several elders of the Raven clans.

In assembling the elders of the Ravens clan before he and the leader of the Catbird clan, Bes (Bisu) informed them that the women of the Catbird clan must be returned, as must three-fourths of the food supplies taken from them. Bes (Bisu) informed that they shall render to the alliance no more than one-fourth of their remaining food supply. He then advised the elders of the Raven clans that under the right of conquest, rather than dispossess them of their lands, he presented them with a choice; they may either submit to his sovereignty or join the alliance. Thus, like the Catbird clans before them, the Raven clans were left with little option other than joining the alliance led by the Bes (Bisu, Aha (the "fighter")).

Once word spread of the swift defeat of the larger Raven clan, by what became known as a defeat solely by the Black Leopard clan, and the alliance being formed by the Black Leopard, the smallest clan on the plateau, the clans of the Red Fox, opted to freely join the alliance. With the addition of the Red Fox, the alliance was in control of the entire midlands, and their combined forces were nearly comparable to those of the two largest clans on the plateau. True to his nature, Bes opted to confront the largest clan, the totemic clan of the Ibis, represented by two clusters of clans on the plateau: with the largest, most warlike of the two based near the central foot of the Ahmar Mountains. It was here that Bes launched the second aspect of his plan, alliance with a once crucial ally, the Black Lion Clan; a moderate size clan on the plateau comprised of four sub-clans; perhaps the fifth largest clan on the southeastern plateau. Their village was at the ancient site of Harar on the north of the plateau.

The territories of the clans of the Black Lion extended beyond the southeastern plateau, northwestward into and beyond the Ethiopian leg of the Great Rift Valley, the divides the southeastern and northwestern plateaus. The territories of the third largest totemic clan of the Black Lion were spread between three sub-clans, at the ancient villages at the sites of present-day Gewane, Erer, and Dire Dawa, in the Ethiopian leg of the Great Rift Valley separating the northwestern and southeastern plateaus defining the region. The largest by far of the clans of the Black Lion resided on the northwestern plateau, at an ancient village at present-day Dese, near the western edge of the central Ethiopian Rift Valley. It was this distantly kindred totem clan who came to the aid of the fleeing clans of the Leopard in their time of greatest need. The ancestral Leopard clan anciently resided in the most fertile lands on the northwestern plateau, lands desired by the most dominant clan on the plateau.

What began as minor clan rivalry soon evolved into open warfare, a period in which the ancestral clans of the Leopard were first forced to cede large swaths of their lands and then to fully relocate to preserve the peace, a peace that never came. Years of warfare followed, during which the Leopard clans acquitted themselves well but were alas outmatched by sheer force of size. In a final decisive battle, the Leopard clans were forced to flee their homeland, with half the clans fleeing southward and half fleeing eastward into the Great Rift Valley, where the clans of the Black Lion aided in ending the enemy's pursuit. The clans of the Black Lion were more than a kindred totem. They had been a formative influence on the ancestral Leopard clan. When contingents of the dominant clan from the northwestern plateau pursued the fleeing Leopard clans who sought refuge with the Black Lion clans at Gewane (in the Ethiopian leg of the Great Rift Valley), the determined invaders were repulsed on three separate occasions as they sought to raise the village.

Though the warriors of the Black Lion and Leopard clans acquitted themselves well, the continued attacks by the aggressors provoked intervention by the Black Lion clans of Erer and Dire Dawa in the Rift Valley. The combined warriors of the Black Lion and Leopard clans were soundly defeated and drove the invading clan back onto the northwestern plateau, driving them back into the highlands. The elders of the Black Lion clans in the Rift Valley prompted the Leopard clans to relocate to the northeastern Plateau, where they might recover under the protection of the Black Lion clan on the plateau. Advice the elders of the remnant Leopard clan took to heart, relocating and renaming the clan the "Black Leopard" in tribute to the Black Lion clan. Remnants of the ancestral clan of the Leopard that remained on the northwestern plateau are known as the "Spotted Leopard" clan, who resettled well south of their old homeland.

Generations later, as a young warrior, Bisu (Bes) twice led Black Leopard clan contingents to aid in defense of the territory of the Black Lion in the far north. Bes fought side-by-side with the most valiant of warriors among the main clan of the Black Lion on the southeastern plateau, "Segeb", now their clan leader. As young men, the two long dreamed of an alliance to enforce an era of peace. Such was the alliance Bes now proposed, with the added benefit of revenge against the totem clan of the Ibis who had sought to encroach in Black Lion terrain. There was a smaller Ibis clan in the northeast, near the eastern foot of the Ahmar Mountains. Pressing the advantage of the alliance, Bes positioned his forces between the two clans of the Ibis, first isolating and attacking the larger clan, near the central base of the Mountains, where they were ultimately defeated.

After the conquest of the larger Ibis clan on the plateau, Bes turned his attention toward the village of the smaller Ibis clan to the east, where, upon arrival, he and his warriors were taken total by surprise …as they were joyously greeted and received, like liberators, by members of the clan as they walked through the center of their village. As Bes walked through the village whispers referring to him as the "*Postulant of the Prophecy*" echoed behind him. Standing before the elders of the minor Ibis clan Bes (Bisu) was told of a premonition foretelling his rise and unification of the clans and "Lands of the Plateaus", and notably, that the Ibis clan was far larger than first appeared. The Ibis were divided into five clans, two on the "middle" (southeastern Ethiopian) plateau, and three on the "eastern" (Somalian) plateau.

The main clans were further east, in present-day northwestern Somaliland, on the eastern plateau, from where the clans of the Ibis had long ago migrated. When pressed by Bes regarding the origin of their premonition, a fetish priest of the smaller Ibis clan, known as "Apu-t'", related an ancient tale told by the *High Priestess* of the main clan of the Ibis in the east, a *Prophetess* from the totem clan of the Hippopotamus, a priestly clan; from the sacred land of *Ta Netjeru* ("Land of the Gods") to the south.[cviii] The Fetish Priest Apu-t' explained that the "Hypothalamus clan" from which the High Priestess came, the clanic family of "Tellem", lineal descendants of the ancient ascetic "Tellem", a member of Ptah's inner circle.

Apu-t' told of the migration of the priestly Hippopotamus clan from the foothills of the Rwenzori and of their re-settlement at Ta Netjeru (the "Land of the Gods"). The Fetish Priest explained that the ancient legend related by the Prophetess arose from a vision shared or granted her renowned ancient ancestor in the time of Ptah, a vision granted to him during his sojourn in the spiritual realm. The legend and its prophecy, the Fetish Priest explained, has been passed down through the ages, preparing each generation, and, according to its omen regarding the "Postulant of the Prophecy", "we shall know him by his deeds"; among the first being his arrival amidst unifying the clans and the *Lands of the Plateaus*.

The Postulant shall be recognized only by those attuned to the omen, the Fetish Priest explained, noting that, according to legend, the next sign is that the Postulant consent to being brought before the Prophetess, who shall affirm his authenticity. Having been so anointed, the Postulant shall be transformed, becoming the "Initiant", he who brings forth the destiny of the prophecy; fully uniting the clans of the Lands of the Plateaus, and in so doing, become the prophesized "Archon", an exalted leader.[cix] The legend is the "Vessel of the Prophecy", the Fetish Priest intoned, explaining that it instructs that those who recognize the Postulant accept and aid his effort to stand before the Prophetess. A tale that left Bes wary yet intrigued; prompting his consent to stand before their Prophetess, and, for his purposes, gain the allegiance of the elders of the Ibis clans.

Apu-t explained that the legend foretells the unification of the clans of the eastern plateau, a peaceful unification through coalescence rather than conquests, a coalescence prompted by his authentication and anointment by the High Priestess. Turning to the leader of the minor Ibis clan on the middle plateau, the Fetish Priest informed that the legend instructs he allot the clans' most capable warriors, as "Guardians of the Prophecy", to guide, accompany and spread the word of the arrival of the Postulant, and the Initiant once anointed. The "Guardians of the Prophecy" are to be of the clan's most capable guides and its most able warriors, those most familiar with the travails of the journey ahead, and lastly, that he himself introduce the Postulant before the Prophetess.

A still wary Bes (Bisu, Aha (the ("Fighter")) gathered a third of his forces for the journey east, leaving the remaining two-thirds of his forces under the trusted command of Segeb, revered leader of the Black Lion clan, with his confidant Kherau, revered warrior of his own sub-clan of the Black Leopard, as second in command. Bes then placed Amam, revered warrior of the third of the three clans of the Black Leopard, in command for the eastern campaign, with Menew, revered warrior of the second of the three clans of the Black Leopard, as second in command. In so doing, Bes granted himself an opportunity to fully grasp the "Legend" and its "Prophesy", inquiring and learning what he could from the Fetish Priest Apu-t during their journey eastward. A journey that would take them through the northern "Haud", from the lands of present-day Ethiopia into the lands of present-day Somaliland.

The Haud is situated between the northern highlands of the southeastern Ethiopian plateau and the northern Somali Mountains; it stretches south from the foothills of the mountains, with its southern portions merging with the Ogaden plateau. In the north, the Haud extends eastward from southeastern Ethiopia into northwestern Somalia, crossed by natural depressions that, during the heavy rains of the early Holocene, became ephemeral lakes and ponds across a landscape characterized by thick woodlands and broad well-watered grasslands. The northern Haud was within the territory of the Ibis clans. However, it bordered the northernmost extent of the lands of the totem clans of the Grey Owl, whose villages lay just to the south, a clan who jealously guarded and protected their territory and borderlands against all intruders and interlopers.

The Grey Owl was comprised of four totemic clans whose provinces were spread throughout the north, central and southern Haud. The route taken by Bes (Bisu, Aha (the "Fighter")) and his men, following the guides provisioned by the smaller clan of the Ibis, led from the middle plateau into the northern Haud, through the borderlands of the northernmost clan of the Grey Owl. Once detected, the formidable procession would surely cause alarm and prompt the Grey Owl clans to prepare their defenses and perhaps even attack the procession. A prospect defused by a detachment of the "Guardians of the Prophecy", dispatched by Apu-t to inform the elders of the northernmost clan of the Grey Owl of the recognition of the Postulant of the Prophecy and of his mission through their borderlands, to stand before the Prophetess.

The clans of the Grey Owl shared the spiritual beliefs inherent in the mysteries revealed by Ptah, as delivered through the ages and generations by the priestly Hippopotamus Clan of the sacred land of Ta Netjeru (the "Land of the Gods"). Leaders and elders of the Grey Owl clans held the far larger Ibis clan in high regard. Like many of the clans of the eastern plateau, their spiritual leaders were initiates of the "House of Tellem" and devout adherents to its portending legends and prophecies. The slow progression of the large entourage through the northern Haud into the northwestern region of the eastern plateau provided Bes (Bisu, Aha) ample opportunity to commit hours upon hours in discourse with the Fetish Priest, learning of the mysteries revealed by Ptah, as delivered through the generations of the House of Tellem.

The Fetish Priest dispatched a second detachment of 'Guardians of the Prophecy' only a day after the first, a detachment tasked to apprise the Prophetess of the recognition and affirmation of the Postulant …to stand before her for authentication and anointment. The village of the main clan of the Ibis was located in present-day northwestern Somaliland, in an enclosed highland valley in the northwestern Ogo Mountains, where the ancient village cluster was surrounded by the thick woodlands and grasslands in the highlands during the era. As Bes and his men followed Apu-t and his guides along the narrow corridors leading into the highlands, Bes took notice of warriors appearing in the forest at a distance.

Ancient Sanctuary at Laas Geel

Warriors were aligned on each side of the narrow path upon which Bes (Bisu, Aha) and his cadre were slowly filing into the highlands, prompting Bes to gesture that his commander Amam signal his sub-commanders to spread their warriors as they move through the forest. Disarming tensions, the Fetish Priest Apu-t called out to several of the warriors in the forest by name, with warm greetings and waves returned as Bes and his men finally entered the village of the main clan of the Ibis. True to his warrior spirit, Bes (Bisu, Aha) could not help but notice the large number of warriors in the village, a force, he thought, perhaps larger than his own. A concern was laid to rest after Apu-t introduced the leader of the main clan of the Ibis, Metes-ab, de facto leader of the whole of the totem clans of the Ibis.[cx]

Metes-ab is said to have warmly welcomed and received Bes (Bisu, Aha) as 'the "Postulant of the Prophecy" who shall usher in the new era'. Having received advance word of his impending arrival, Metes-ab arranged that a large feast and adequate accommodations for Bes and the huge cadre that was his entourage be prepared; a feast in which the warriors and villagers alike took part, as he, Bes (Bisu, Aha), Apu-t, and Abu lead warrior and commander of the warriors of the main Ibis clan, gathered for private discussion.[cxi] In a rather forthwith manor Metes-ab informed Bes of the Ibis being the largest clan on the eastern or middle plateau, yet not a clan of single lineage; a clan forged from a unity principle and ideal; precepts imbued by the Prophecy of the House of Tellem'.

"That you are a mighty warrior and great leader is evident in your accomplishment of near unity on the middle plateau, a region that emerged in wars and clan rivalries for untold generations", Abu opined. "Howsoever", Metes-ab propounded, "whether you are the "One" who can initiate and usher in the era of peace and prosperity envisioned by the prophecy can only be ascertained by the hierophant and Prophetess at the Sanctuary of the House of Tellem, in the north of the plateau." "Let this then be so determined", a now somewhat impatient Bes retorted, with the Fetish Priest Apu-t assuaging the situation by advising that they shall stand before the Prophetess, in the Sanctuary, at first light in the morrow'. The Sanctuary was outside the village, situated in a complex of cave-like shelters, famous for the earliest known rock art on the Horn of Africa.[cxii]

The ancient rock art in the region (present-day Somaliland) is perhaps the most impressive archaeological find on the Horn of Africa. During the neolithic age, inhabitants of the region decorated cave and rock shelter walls with engravings and paintings of themselves and animals of the era, including domesticated animals, all of which are depicted at a site called the "Laas Geel" complex in northwestern Somaliland. Laas Geel is situated near the union of two ancient rivers that once channeled the heavy rains of the Holocene. Lass Geel contains approximately twenty rock shelters or caves made of naturally occurring rock formations of different sizes, the largest being over thirty feet long, with a depth of about fifteen feet.

The rock art at Laas Geel is distributed throughout the twenty caves or rock alcoves of the complex.[cxiii] The Laas Geel cave paintings and petroglyphs are thought to be some of the most vivid prehistoric rock art in Africa. The cave paintings and rock art date between 15,000 B.C. to 8,000 B.C. and, among other scenes, depict inhabitants of the era wearing ceremonial robes, some with their hands raised in worship.[cxiv] Human figures are represented with a rather standardized shape, frontally depicted, wearing a kind of shirt, usually white; heads are small and sometimes surrounded by a halo. In some cases, they carry a bow or a shield. The cave walls are covered in old hieroglyphic scripture, with undeciphered inscriptions beneath each of the cave paintings depicting people with their hands extended in a worshipping posture.[cxv]

The Legends

The caves of Laas Geel were anciently the sanctuary abode of a sect of the House of Tellem in the north of the eastern plateau, a sect of sages, artisans, craftsmen and seers headed by Prophetess Ta-Urt. The cave settlement and sanctuary were located just outside the village of the main clan of the Ibis, near the Naasa Hablood hills, where it overlooked a countryside of vast grasslands where wild bovine, goats, and antelopes roamed and grazed.[cxvi] Three of the twenty caves in the settlement complex were exclusively dedicated and used for the purposes of the Sanctuary; the first, home to the largest number of ancient paintings, was the creative center of the ancient settlement.

The second cave or cavern was the largest and was used as a meeting room. In the third cavern, there was a large flat stone, bringing to mind an ancient throne; the cavern was thus called and used as the "Throne Room" of the Prophetess. A cavern in close proximity was partitioned off into smaller spaces with little window-like openings; the rest of the caverns were used as living quarters. After first conferring with the elders of the three clans of the Ibis on the eastern plateau, Bes, accompanied only by the Fetish Priest Apu-t, was escorted before the Prophetess at Laas Geel, where she stood upon the stone of the throne, flanked by guards at each side, as Bes and Apu-t were led into the cavern.

Standing before Ta-Urt, her eyes transfixed firmly upon those of Bisu, she inquired of the Fetish Priest, 'is he an "Aspirant of the Prophecy"?' To which Apu-t replied, 'yes, he spent much time with me inquiring and seeking to resolve the riddle of the legend and its prophecy. To his credit, he appointed a second in command for our long journey, allowing himself ample opportunity to grasp an understanding of the significance of the legend'. With her eyes still transfixed upon those of Bisu, Ta-Urt then inquired of him, 'what does thou seek of me?' to which Bes replied without hesitation, 'I aspire to comprehend the riddle of the legend, and how a prophecy thousands of years old could possibly foretell my destiny'.

'Tell me of the destiny of which you speak ?,' Ta-Urt inquired, to which Bes replied that 'it is my destiny to unite the "clans of the lands of the plateau"'. A reply prompting Ta-Urt to then inquire, "in your heart, did this become your destiny before or after your knowledge of the legend." to which Bes replied, in all honesty, it became the focus of my destiny after my awareness of your legend'. The legend is the *vessel of the prophecy*, Ta-Urt intoned, illuminating that 'the legend portends the prophecy; portending a specific potentiality from a spectrum of potentialities …this through a vision granted the Prophet Tellem, during his sojourn in the spiritual realm, during the time of Ptah.

'As a recipient of the vision,' Ta-Urt explained, 'Tellem witnessed the prophecy in the fullness of its culmination …the telling of which became the story of the legend. Thus, the legend became the vessel of the prophecy; it is, in essence …a legend foreshadowing and guiding the prophecy to fruition'. As to the alignment of your destiny with that of the prophecy, according to legend, we must look first to the tenets of Natural Magick, Ta-Urt propounded. As a disciple of Ptah's highland Sanctuary, she explained, the Prophet Tellem became proficient in Natural Magick and its Laws, such as the *Law of Sympathy,* which informs the greater the affinity, the greater the sympathetic link. [cxvii]

The linkage is strengthened when the *Postulant* is a true believer in the Prophecy" and is enhanced as the *Postulant* comes to accept all that the Prophecy holds. That being said, with his eyes firmly transfixed upon those of Ta-Urt, Bisu finally inquired, 'am I the 'One?'" to which Ta-Urt asked in response, "are you the 'One?'" upon which Bes (Bisu, Aha) reflected for more than a moment as he pondered all that had been said, and, in keeping with his nature, then replied, 'I believe I might be,' to which Ta-Urt revealed, 'I feel you *will* be, but it is not solely a simple matter of being the "One"; there is much you need learn, things we will discuss when we meet next, in the morrow'. Though visibly unaccustomed to being dismissed, Bes nonetheless joined the Fetish Priest in taking his leave.

En route back to the village of the main clan of the Ibis, sensing a growing impatience within the warrior spirit of Bes (Bisu, Aha), Apu-t revealed to him that the 'Anointment has begun'. It is not a single event, but a series of three acts, the Fetish Priest explained. The first act was that of the revelation that the Prophetess feels you will be the "One"; the second act is the affirmation of the first, by those whom the legend terms, "aspirants of the priesthood." That you stand before them is no small thing, they are the foremost Sages, Shaman and of the clans of the Eastern Plateau; 'Prelates' of the House of Tellem, students of the Mysteries of the School of Ptah, aspirants of the prophesied priesthood of the east.[cxviii]

Bes (Bisu, Aha) is said to have then protested that he is neither priest nor spiritual leader, to which Apu-t replied that the legend requires only that he is a warrior; in the end, a spiritual warrior in pursuit of truth in the form of Netjer. The Prophetess herself suffices as Hierophant of the Order. The third Act of the anointment is the illumination of the first and the second Acts when you appear before the Prophetess in the morrow when she shall reveal the Dualities and Trials of the Prophecy, imbuing you with its mission and anointing you as its "Initiant." It is the coalescence of the formative priesthood brought about by this anointment that, according to the legend, shall inspire and give impetus to the unification of the clans of the eastern plateau.

The appearance of Bisu before the "aspirants of the Priesthood" accorded him the affirmation needed for the final Act of the "anointment." The following morning, he and Apu-t were again brought before the Ta-Urt, in the throne room of the Sanctuary, where she again stood upon the stone of the throne, but this time alone, as Bes and Apu-t entered the cavern. Again, with her eyes transfixed firmly upon those of Bisu, Ta-Urt inquired of Apu-t, 'does the *Postulant* possess the temperament of spirit required of the Initiant?' to which the Priest replied, 'he does'. Dismissing Apu-t to dispatch the Guardians of the Prophecy to spread the word of the anointment, Ta-Urt stepped down from the throne to inform Bes of the *Dualities of the Prophecy*.

The first duality is that of the "Initiant", Ta-Urt illuminated, explaining that 'the Initiant is simultaneously Initiator and Initiate of the reverence he fosters'. The second duality is that of the "Archon", she explained, advising that 'the Archon is both "First to Rule", as you will be upon completion of the three trials, and more significantly, icon and intermediary on behalf his people before Netjer. It will take a true warrior to accomplish each of the trials, Ta-Urt cautioned, explaining that 'the first trial is unification and enlightenment of this, the eastern (Somalian) plateau; the second to complete unification and cultivate enlightenment on the "middle" plateau. The third, perhaps the most daunting, she noted, is unification of the huge northwestern plateau.

The fourth trial is without question the most challenging, Ta-Urt cautioned, explaining that it is 'the trial of fulfilling the second duality; that of becoming intermediary between the reverent clans of the realm, and the hierarchical forces of Netjer. To accomplish this aspect of the prophecy, she propounded, you must be more than a warrior, you must be a spiritual warrior; one who will not give up his journey ahead the forces of Netjer, which manifests in myriad forms, called "Netjeru." For this you need become adept in the arts of Spiritual Warriorship, and the transcendent abilities you will need for your quest and sojourn in the spiritual realm; much of such adeptness you will acquire here, upon completion of the trials.

Drawn now to both the Prophecy and the Prophetess, Bes (Bisu) requested of Ta Urt that she tell him more of this notion of "Spiritual Warriorship", with Ta Urt illuminating that Spiritual Warriorship is a Spiritual Path of Wisdom, Self-Knowledge, and Self-Discipline; abilities needed for mastery of the ability to travel and battle within the spiritual realm. The Spiritual Warrior faces this challenge with the awareness that this war is fought within himself. Guided meditation helps assuage the fear, and in this way, I shall be of assistance. To which Bes replied, 'a true warrior's first conquest is that of his own fears, to which Ta Urt replied, 'true fearlessness is full enlightenment when you realize that you are far more than a physical being'.

There is much I have to teach you, and much we have to learn together, Ta Urt proffered, reminding of the 'ominous darkness that has long shrouded the Lands of the Plateaus and the vast lands beyond. During the time of Ptah, it was first he and then the Initiates of his sanctuary which once held this looming chaos at bay. The darkness has shrouded the lands since the decline and disappearance of the Great Sanctuary and Initiates of the House of Ptah. Beyond the Prophecy of the House of Tellem, what has been passed down over the ages are mere vestiges of the tenets of that Sacred Order; what survives among them are oral legends of the celestial observations of the ancient Initiates of the Order. These observations inform and form much of what we know of the Cosmos.

The observations of the Ancients inform us that the rhythm of the Cosmos is seen in its cyclical nature and the celestial cycles that mark the passage of each Cosmic Age. It is through the observations of these celestial cycles that the ancient Initiates were able to visualize and predict distant future events; one such prediction, which comports with the Prophecy of the House of Tellem, is that we are in the midst of a "Great Synchronicity" which avails an alternate future. Through the House of Tellem, and indeed Tellem himself, we are informed that such synchronicities unveil hidden alignments between the spiritual and physical realms, projecting what is inside on the outside.

Such synchronicities foreshadow ensuing change or the prospect of change in the physical realm. The challenge of the Fourth Trial is to attain the duality of the "Archon", icon and intermediary of the reverent before *Netjer,* indeed leading the hierarchies of the Netjeru, the "Forces of Light" in their campaign against the "Forces of Darkness." A metaphor of the internal battle within the spiritual warrior the prophecy portends, Bes presumed. A notion not unnoticed by Ta Urt, who then emphasized, "the trials must be completed well before lapse of the Great Synchronicity. Know that the hardships and challenges of the Fourth Trial embody those of the first three,' she continued, explaining that 'it is only with the collective reverence of the clans that the Netjeru maybe influenced and persuaded to your aid.

There is much you still need to know, Ta-Urt confessed, 'however,' she conceded, 'time simply does not permit; we do not know the length of the Great Synchronicity, or how long we may avail ourselves of it. The newly ordained High Priest Apu-t will assist in all that you must know of the Prophecy as you proceed from here to unite your kingdom Lord Bes,' Ta-Urt informed, assuming a more formal tone. The prophecy instructs she remain at Laas Geel; where, she advised, she shall 'await the return of a "King", an "Archon"'.

Leaving Laas Geel, Bes (Bisu, Aha) joined Apu-t in the village of the clan of the Ibis, where the priest apprised him and his general Amam of what they might expect ahead. 'Spiritual leaders of the clans of the lands of the eastern plateau who are Initiates of Laas Geel will be instrumental in preparing your way,' Apu-t advised, explaining that 'it is they, or , more aptly, "we" before whom you stood in "Affirmation." "Aspirants of the formative Priesthood" ordained into its prophesied Eastern Order by your anointment, Apu-t explained; noting that 'in realizing the prominence of the eastern plateau in the prophecy of the House of Tellem, throughout the ages their lineage has proselytized the rise of an Archon, signaling the dawning of a new era.

The formative fetish priesthood,' Apu-t elucidated, 'accepts that greater avail of Netjer is achievable only through greater coalescence and reverence and that it is the collective reverence imbued by them, the formative priesthood, that shall strengthen the availing facility of the Archon'. It is the "Guardians of the Prophesy" who shall be at your avail to dispatch and apprise the clans of the eastern plateau of your impending plans and arrival, Apu-t informed, advising that 'the clans whose spiritual leaders are Initiates of the Sanctuary will welcome and be prepared to join your cause'. However, Apu-t cautioned not all clans on the eastern plateau are so spiritually guided; there are warlike clans among those of different beliefs.

Rather than mere conquest of their lands and physical being, the prophecy requires opening of their hearts so that they may again awaken the powers of their spiritual being, Apu-t Illuminated, explaining that, for our purposes, we do not require an alignment of belief, but an alignment of reverence. Though called different names by differing creeds, all acknowledge and give homage to that creative force that animates the Cosmos. However, homage fades with the harshness of this life, a life that brings into question and challenges the strength of one's beliefs. Apu-t further explained, 'it is this collective "fading of reverence" in man that has strengthened the Forces of Darkness that ply against the forces who contend on behalf of Netjer. This is nothing less than the eternal battle between the Forces of Chaos and Darkness and the Forces of Order and Light.

It is a spiritual war that lies before you, Lord Bes. Apu-t apprised, the "Guardians of the Prophesy shall aid in opening the hearts and minds of the clans with differing beliefs, conferring and informing their spiritual leaders of the legend and enlightenment of the unfolding prophecy. They shall inform of the struggle between the Forces of Chaos and Darkness that so oppress the land and the Forces of Order and Light that seek to restore the land and its peoples. The Guardians of the Prophesy shall confer with the spiritual leaders of the clans of differing belief that they may aid and guide in the flow of reverence achieved through the enlightenment they imbue. Reverence is much deeper than outward behavior, although appropriate behavior flows from true reverence, Apu-t explained. It is more than an attitude of deep respect tinged with awe and veneration; reverence recognizes and honors the divine presence existent in all manifestations of creation.

Reverence for the plants, animals, trees, rivers, grasses, stones, hills, and forests who, in many respects, possess a right to life equal to that of man. Reverence involves a humbling of the self in respectful recognition of an ideal that transcends the self; reverence promotes balance, harmony, and dynamic equilibrium between humankind and their environments. Reverence is one of the greatest manifestations of spirituality. Without it, enlightenment can never be attained. The object of reverence is recognition of the ideal and oneness of *Netjer*, both as a divine source and medium through which all existence resides. In many ways, Reverence is the essence of Spirituality. Apu-t illuminated, viewed in its true perspective, its sacred powers are said to manifest as luminous energies, a flowing spiritual force that shall aid the "Archon" in the final trial.

The Prophesy says that sacred reciprocity is called into service through deep reverence, mutuality, and alignment; this then is the mission of the "Guardians of the Prophesy." Through their work, it is said the Archon shall be imbued with great strength and power during the fourth and final trial. Though in appearance their work may seem mundane, Apu-t opined, theirs is the task of reviving the casual rituals of Reverence… which shall aid in the battle for Renewal. As Bes pondered this and the challenges ahead, Amam took the opportunity to inform him that a messenger had arrived from Segeb with word of affairs on the eastern Ethiopian Plateau since his departure. Segeb informed that word of their conquest of the Ibis clan on the plateau has spread, and the Kudu clans have joined them in a common cause; now only the Crocodile Clan in the southern Ogaden remain defiant; adding that Kherau awaits only his command to bring them to submission.

With a now more informed perspective, in his return message, Bes instructed that Segeb conscript a third of the able-bodied warriors of the Ibis on the middle plateau to their combined forces and that he retain command of one-half of the forces in the north and that Kherau proceeds southward with the balance of the force to await further word at the village of Kudu, at (present-day) Imi in the southern borderlands of the Ogaden. Bes (Bisu, Aha) then instructed that Amam conscript a third of the able-bodied warriors of the main clan of the Ibis to his forces, and, with permission of Metes-ab, that Abu command their contingent, along those to follow from the other Ibis clans. Bes then instructed that Amam prepare all for the upcoming campaign. Apu-t reminded that 'the Ibis is divided into three sub-clans on the eastern plateau,' and that 'the second largest clan is at the coastal village of Berbara, on the seaboard of the Gulf of Aden.

Apu-t advised that the coastal village was several days northwest of that of the main Ibis clan, a journey that would take them through Daallo mountains, where the Frankincense Forest lies.[cxix] Apu-t advised that while the third clan of the Ibis was located just a few days east, at the village of Burao, the prophecy foresees his first triumph at Berbara. Apu-t explained that the unification of the three clans of the Ibis, while largely ceremonial, would add warriors and strength to his forces, forces he would need for the campaign in the south. A sentiment with which Bes concurred. The journey through the Daallo forest was itself illuminating; it is the forest that contains the richest and densest fauna of the region. The most enchanting part is the Daallo Frankincense Forest; there is no other forest in the world with such fragrance. After the rains one can feel the sweet, unusual fragrance produced by trees which grow only here.[cxx]

In the cliffs and along the steep mountainsides are caves where extended families of frankincense collectors have resided for hundreds of years; they inherit the trees of the forests from their fathers and, over the ages, have learned to harvest the resin without adversely affecting the trees. The oil and resin from the trees were anciently used medicinally as salves to heal wounds and relieve pain and for their anti-inflammatory properties. Frankincense oil was used to treat asthma and other inflammatory diseases and also as an incense in religious and aromatherapeutic rituals; the oil has mysterious rejuvenating properties, and its smoke produces a psychoactive substance (trahydrocannabinole) which aids in expanding one's consciousness.[cxxi] 'Though truly the smallest clans within the province of the Ibis, Apu-t explained, 'the clans of the caves along the mountainsides are accepted as fully part of the totem clan of the Ibis, sharing an ancient relationship where all mutually benefit and prosper'.

Over the ages, the trees of the great forests have been allotted among the families and extended families of the clans throughout the highlands; they, Apu-t emphasized, 'who are most adept at cultivating and harvesting the vital resin of the trees. Harvesting the resin is done two to three times a year, spaced out so the trees can recover; it is the clans of these highlands who protect and maintain the frankincense forests'. Although somewhat mesmerized by the captivating fragrance and sheer beauty of the frankincense forests and rugged mountainsides, Bes (Bisu, Aha) took measures to ensure the cliffside clans of the forest that the large force of warriors moving through their domain represented no threat to the nor the main villages of their clans at Berbera. Bes (Bisu, Aha) dispatched messengers to inform the mountainside clans, together with traders, to trade fresh fruit and dried meats and vegetables for pounds of valuable frankincense resin, which Bes (Bisu, Aha (the "Fighter")) then transported to ancient Berbera.

Early ancient Berbera was then a coastal village cluster along the southern shore of the present-day Gulf of Aden (a Gulf that would become anciently known as the "Gulf of Berbera"). Bes (Bisu, Aha) entered the heart of the ancient village cluster striding aside the Fetish Priest Apu-t (Aput), ahead of his entourage and army of warriors led by Amam. Bes was ceremonially received and extolled, first by the newly anointed priest of the clan, followed by the elders and finally the clan leader who bestowed his allegiance. A huge feast was arranged in celebration, with festivities spread throughout the village cluster as Bes was given a tour of the nearby fishing and trading villages later known as the ports of "Berbera" and "Bulhar."[cxxii] Elders of the coastal villages told of their trade in frankincense with villages as far south as the coast of Ta-Netjeru (present day Kenya and Tanzania), and as far across the sea as the then ancient off-shore island-landmass comprised of the present-day Seychelles archipelago.

During the Glacial Maximum, the present-day Seychelles Isles comprised a large single-island land mass whose name is lost to posterity and is thus called "ancient Seychelle." It was by way of ancient Seychelle that mariners of Berbera and Bulhar traded with villages as far away as Kumari, a large peninsular landmass extending from the Indian subcontinent. The Indian sub-continent was a far more extensive landmass during the lower sea level of the Glacial Maximum; the Kumari peninsula fully encompassed the Isle of Sri Lanka, from where the Kumari peninsula began and stretched southward, just beyond the Equator. Kumari fully encompassed the present-day Maldives islands, then its central mountain range, from where the peninsula extended southward, in a slight westerly direction, encompassing the Chagos Archipelago, then the Kumari peninsula's southernmost mountain range.

The ancient mariners of early Berbera and Bulhar traded and exchanged herbs for spices with villages along the western coast of Kumari by way of trading settlements on the coasts of ancient Seychelle. Traders from Berbera also traded with villages along the coast of Ta Netjeru, who traded with villages on the southern coast of Kumari through offshore islands and trading settlements then existed beyond the southern tip of the peninsula. Traders of Berbera and Bulhar traded frankincense for cinnamon and other spices, which the Ibis clans then traded throughout and beyond the Lands of the Plateaus. The Fetish Priest Apu-t (Aput) opined that the early frankincense trade provided the Ibis clans with much prosperity and great influence before reminding Bes (Bisu, Aha) of the huge tasks before them and the lapsing of time.

Apu-t advised that Berbera was the largest of two such villages of the Ibis clan on the seaboard; to the east of Berbera was the ancient coastal village cluster of Karin, where Bes and his entourage and formidable army arrived on the fifth day of their sojourn on the coast.[cxxiii] Again, Bes (Bisu) was ceremonially received and extolled, first by the anointed priest of the clan, followed by the elders and finally the minor clan leader, who bestowed his allegiance. Arising before dawn on the sixth day, Bes instructed Amam prepare their ever-growing army for the long southward trek to Burao, third and final stronghold of the clans of the Ibis on the eastern plateau. The route southward took them through the ancient region of Dhambalin, where the rock shelters contain ancient polychrome pictographs depicting people, animals, and scenes of life during the Neolithic era.

Pictographs at Dhambalin

Dhambalin (meaning "half-cut mountain") is a unique archaeological site with some of the best polychrome paintings in the Horn of Africa.[cxxiv] There are depictions of men, usually as part of hunting scenes, armed with bows and arrows, surrounded by wildlife, with leaping antelopes, prancing giraffes, and snakes poised to strike. The animals and reptiles depicted in other paintings are portrayed with astonishing clarity; some animals have distinctive bands around their backs and bellies, suggesting ancient farming traditions. Several of the paintings include types of giraffes that are now extinct, evidencing the extreme antiquity of the artwork.[cxxv]

The Dhambalin site also includes paintings of hunters armed with bows and arrows and features one of the earliest known depictions of a warrior or hunter on horseback. Ancient Burao (meaning the "Sandy Place") is located in a flat semi-desert; the ancient village arose at its site due to the availability of water along the dry valley in which it is located, as well as its position on the trade routes between the villages on the coast and those of the interior. The *Togdheer River* ran through the heart of the village, dividing it in half, crossed only by a makeshift bridge. Bes (Bisu) entered the village, again, aside from the priest Apu-t (Aput) ahead of what was by then an awe-inspiring assemblage of warriors led by Amam, who conscribed a third of the able-bodied warriors of each clan.

Ancient Burao was a small inland marketplace connecting the coastal villages with the interior; the ancient village was a trading center for clans throughout the region. Burao brought together traders from as far as Ta Netjeru in the south and Djibouti in the north. As before, Bes (Bisu, Aha) entered the ancient village aside from the priest Apu-t, just ahead of his entourage, who was then followed by the army led by Amam. While there were those of the Ibis clan in Burao who had received word from the Guardians of the Prophecy regarding the arrival of the Initiate, there were many in the village from the southern provinces and others from far away as Djibouti who were both intimidated by the size of the army of warriors and perplexed by the formality and ceremony.

Most in the village were pressed alongside its main thoroughfare as Apu-t guided Bes and his army through the center of the village to the bridge at its heart. Bes then walked to the center of the bridge where he was ceremonially received before all, first by the priest of the clan, followed by the clan elders and clan leader, who bestowed their allegiance. Again, a feast was arranged, but this time with an array of exotic herbs and spices brought from far and wide, together with an assortment of wild meats and fruits and vegetables from the hunting and gathering of Bes and his warriors en route to Burao. The festivities went into the evening, but Bes nonetheless rose early the following morning to discuss the upcoming campaign with Amam, Abu and Apu-t.

Apu-t informed that of the six prominent clans to the south, 'the first we shall encounter in the central Haud, province of the main clan of the Grey Owl. The totem clan of the Grey Owl, he reminded, is comprised of four clans whose provinces are in the north, central, and southern Haud, into the central Ogaden. He noted that two of the clans are in the north, with the largest being the northernmost clan to whom we dispatched "Guardians of the Prophecy" to inform of your mission. The main clan of the Grey Owl is the largest and most influential, Apu-t advised, with the smallest of the four clans to their south. The Grey Owl, he reiterated, shares a belief in the mysteries revealed by the House of Tellem; we will be well received in their villages.

"Beyond the provinces of the Grey Owl,' Apu-t further informed, 'are the lands of the totem clans of the Spotted Hyena …in Southern Ogaden. The Spotted Hyena is divided into four totemic clans, whose province is just south of that of the Grey Owl", Apu-t informed, advising that "the clans of the Spotted Hyena are only in the *Southern Ogaden*, where they are at constant war'. 'Those with whom the Spotted Hyena is mostly at war are the clans of the Cobra. Though the Cobra is divided into five sub-clans, Apu-t advised, "they are but slightly larger in size and strength than the more warlike Spotted Hyena.

Even though the collective clans of the Spotted Hyena are smaller than the collective clans of the Grey Owl who are known for notoriously guarding their territory", Apu-t recounted, it was the fierceness of the clans of the Spotted Hyena that forced the Grey Owl northward into the central Ogaden.[cxxvi] The main clan of the Cobra is centered at the eastern edge of the Ogaden, Apu-t informed, noting that "it is they who gave rise to the village at Beledweyne in the Shebelle Valley; from where their sub-clans spread westward along the Shebelle River into the Southern Ogaden. The smaller of the two clans began the village at K'ellafo, on the river, while the largest of the clans settled further west on the river, where they formed the village at Gode.

Gode is a village that has since become a trading marketplace, attracting clans throughout the region; an advent that invited the ire of the Spotted Hyena, Apu-t recounted, noting that they eventually launched an all-out attack that raised Gode and forced the Cobra to retreat eastward, to K'ellafo." "But for intervention of the Crocodile clans, who sent large contingents of warriors from their villages at Doolow, Dolo, Bandera and Belad Hawo in the south,' Apu-t continued, 'the Spotted Hyena would have pursued the Cobra eastward and raised K'ellafo."[cxxvii] "The Crocodile and Cobra are kindred totem of the *Serpent*, and together they ultimately drove the Spotted Hyena from Gode."

"The province of the Hippopotamus clan is to the south of that of the Cobra at Beledweyne; their main village is in the plains between the Jubba and Shebelle rivers at Baidoa."[cxxviii] "The totem clans of the Hippopotamus", Apu-t noted, "are eight in total, spread from as far south as *Ta Netjeru* to these, the highlands of the *Lands of the Plateaus*." The Hippopotamus clan at Baidoa migrated onto the plateau in the midst of the heightened aridity in the lowlands… this was during the "third time of great turmoil", Apu-t intoned, noting that they "permanently settled at Baidoa, where their villages are clustered around an ancient spring that has provided water to the area for untold centuries."

"As the influence of the Hippopotamus Clan spreads beyond the plains between the Jubba and Shebelle rivers,' Apu-t recounted, 'it raised the ire of the fierce Crocodile clan, who has long dominated the region from their stronghold around Doolow to the east." "The Crocodile clan gained control over much of the region through the dominance of its water during the heightening aridity now blanketing the lowlands", Apu-t noted. "The Crocodile are divided into five totemic clans", he advised, "with the main clan spread between the villages of Dolo, bordering the Ogaden, and nearby Doolow on the Jubba River. Three of the clans are at the nearby villages of Mandera, Bandera and Belad Hawo, with the fifth clan at the village of Bu'ale, in the southern Jubba River valley'.[cxxix]

"The main clan of the Cobra at Beledweyne, where they and the entire Cobra clan were ancient vassals of the Crocodile clan", Apu-t further informed, noting, 'at least, until the intrusion of the Hippopotamus Clan, whose spreading influence has lessened that of the Crocodile clan in the region. It is a mystery that the warlike Crocodile clan did not attack, and seek to raise Baidoa, when their former vassals, the clans of the Dugong, at the villages of Kismayo near the mouth of the Jubba River, became followers and adherents of the House of Tellem,' Apu-t pondered. "With Initiation of the spiritual leaders of the Dugong at the Sanctuary at Buur Heybe, near Baidoa,' Apu-t opined, 'particularly given the ensuing reverence and affinity the Dugong openly display for the precepts of the House of Tellem …and the Hippopotamus Clan, it must surely be an affront to the prideful Crocodile clan'.

'The Dugong is comprised of four sub-clans,' Apu-t informed, advising that 'their main clan is at the village of Kismayo; the other four clans are on the largest of six islands, which, with several smaller islands, make-up an (ancient) offshore archipelago'. 'The Dugong were anciently fishing clans who built sturdy sea-going vessels and relied upon their fleets,' Apu-t noted, advising that, 'over the centuries, the old maritime clans eventually became involved in transporting cargo for other clans along the coasts, as far south as the coasts of Ta Netjeru, and southeast across the open sea, as far as ancient Seychelles. 'Though they have not forbidden participation of the Crocodile clan at their market at Baidoa, Apu-t continued, the Hippopotamus Clan has inadvertently usurped control of the eastern spice trade'. Bes then raised his hand, indicating that he had heard enough, and instructed them to proceed to the village of the main clan of the Grey Owl, in the Central Haud, that they may 'conclude the pomp and ceremony, and begin the true crusade.'

Finally, after having garnered the allegiance of the Grey Owl clans, and conscripting a third of their able-bodied warriors, in a departure from the prophecy, Bes instructed Apu-t to dispatch a detachment of Guardians of the Prophecy to Baidoa to inform the Hippopotamus Clan of his impending arrival and collect intelligence regarding warfare between the Spotted Hyena and Cobra clans. Bes (Bisu, Aha (the "Fighter")) then instructed Amam, Menew and Abu to use the ensuing weeks to prepare and sharpen the skills of their warriors for the upcoming campaign, ensuring each is adequately armed and proficient in all the necessary aspects of field warfare.

Bes then informed his Generals of his daring plan to subdue the region in a single campaign, advising and instructing that Amam and his forces assail and subdue the main village of the Cobra at Beledweyne as Abu and his forces assail and subdue the Cobra village at K'ellafo. Menew and his forces assail and subdue the village of the Cobra at Gode. Bes (Bisu, Aha (the "Fighter")) explained that he and his forces shall rendezvous with Kherau and his forces above the bend in the Shebelle River between Ima and Gode. Bes then advised and instructed that Apu-t (Aput) and his Guardians of the Prophecy proceed forthwith to Baidoa and inform the elders of the Hippopotamus clan of their campaign.

Bes (Bisu, Aha ("The Fighter")) instructed that Apu-t advise that the Hippopotamus prepare against possible attack by the Crocodile clan, should they connect the fall of Beledweyne, K'ellafo, and Gode to the *House of Tellem*. He then instructed that Amam dispatch his a detachment forthwith to the village of Ima, with the message that Kherau and his forces rendezvous with Bes (Bisu, Aha) above the bend in the Shebelle River …in six days. Lastly, Bes informed that the next new moon was in a little more than two weeks away and instructed that the attacks on Beledweyne and K'ellafo by Amam and Abu be launched just before dawn …following the night of the new moon.

Bes (Bisu, Aha) informed that after their conquest, he and Kherau would lead their armies to Gode, where he shall meet with the elders of the Cobra clan and solicit their allegiance. Execution of his plan and strategy went almost as expected, with the warrior-depleted villages of K'ellafo and Beledweyne falling in a matter of hours, but the fight at Gode turned into a protracted two-day battle before the battle-hardened village was fully subdued. Bes and Kherau joined forces at their rendezvous point above the Shebelle River bend, with Bes and his forces attacking the exhausted warriors of the Spotted Hyena, while Kherau and his forces assailed the exhausted warriors of the Crowned Vulture; this only hours after the Spotted Hyena and Crowned Vulture had returned to their lairs following their own joint attack on Gode.

When the Spotted Hyena fell in battle, and their warriors were finally subdued, the elders of their clans wisely opted for surrender over annihilation. The Crowned Vulture clans, however, fought until finally subdued, for which their clan leaders were summarily executed, as were several of their elders. Like those of the Spotted Hyena, surviving elders of the Crowned Vulture wisely chose allegiance over annihilation. Nonetheless, as a condition of their surrender, Bes required absolute support for his mission to unite the clans and Lands of the Plateaus. Standing before and making direct eye contact with each surviving or newly appointed elder of each clan, Bes extracted a pledge of dedication to his broader mission of ushering in a new era of harmony, an era in which they may craft a more reverent future.

Bes (Bisu, Aha) informed those elders of the Spotted Hyena and Crowned Vulture clans that a key element of their support was the immediate conscription of half of their able-bodied warriors to aid in his campaign. He then advised that his next campaign shall be against their old nemesis, the Crocodile clans, the last on the eastern plateau to be brought into the alliance. An irresistible, if thinly veiled, enticement, to which the elders of the Hyena and Vulture clans enthusiastically responded by assembling their most able-bodied warriors to be added to Bes's forces. After several days, as promised, Bes then led his huge force to Gode, K'ellafo, and Beledweyne, obtaining allegiances of the elders of the clans of the Cobra inhabiting each village and conscripting a third of their able-bodied warriors to the commands of Amam, Abu and Menew, as he moved east.

Believing the villages of the Hippopotamus clan to be under imminent threat of reprisal by the fierce and vengeful Crocodile clan, after no more than a day of rest, Bes (Bisu, Aha) mobilized his armies for a rapid trek southward from Beledweyne to defend Baidoa. He ordered Abu to lead his army fully around Baidoa and make his encampment south of the village. Amam also led his army around the village and made his encampment to the southwest. Kherau, in turn, was ordered to make the encampment of his huge army due west of Baidoa, and Menew to make his encampment northwest of the village. Forces under the direct command of Bes (Bisu, Aha (the "Fighter")) were then instructed to make their encampment due north of the village, creating a defensive arc between Baidoa and the stronghold of the Crocodile clans around Dolo …to the east.

Sanctuary at Gogollis Qabe

Bes entered the villages at Baidoa, accompanied only by a small band from his own clan, with whom he was met by none other than Apu-t, who took his place beside Bisu and directed the entourage follow as the two entered the village, striding together toward its center.[cxxx] The village corridors were lined with onlookers as they made their way through the outer village. Apu-t sought to explain the celebrative and festive atmosphere. The Fetish Priest explained that "nowhere on the plateau is belief in the *Prophecy* stronger than here, and your accomplishment and arrival are viewed as nothing less than confirmation of its vision'. To which Bes inquired, 'have they not heeded your warning of possible attack by the Crocodile clans?

Apu-t then advised that "the Crocodile clans will stay their hand", explaining that the *Prophetess Ipet* (affectionately called "Ipy") of the Hippopotamus clan not long ago sent tribute to *Medjed*, (de facto) leader of the Crocodile clans at their main village at Doolow. This she sent along with an invitation to their esteemed High Priest, called Shai, to confer at the Sanctuary at Buur Heybe near Baidoa. Buur Heybe is the largest of several small granitic mountains, known as "inselbergs," which abruptly rise above the flat alluvial plains of the inter-riverine region of the Lower Shebelle and Jubba Rivers in the southeastern confines of the plateau.[cxxxi] The ancient Sanctuary was at "Gogollis Qabe" ("the furnished place"), the largest of the rock shelters on Buur Heybe.

Buur Heybe was over a half day southwest of Baidoa. As such, was the province of three small sub-clans of the Hippopotamus clans, ardent adherents of faith residing in the villages on the small mountain. The largest of the clans resided in the main village at Berdaale. In contrast, the others two resided in the mountain villages of Muuney and Howaal Dheeri. The Sanctuary at Gogollis Qabe was near the main village at Berdaale, headed by an affable clan elder known as Athpi, with whom the Prophetess Ipet had previously conferred. Ipy had also conferred with the leader of the main clan of the Hippopotamus at Baidoa before extending an invitation to the Fetish Priest Shai of the main clan of the Crocodile. Shai arrived at Buur Heybe several days later, accompanied by three minor priests of his Order.

The esteemed High Priest was met and received by a small delegation of elders from the main village at Berdaale, together with an Initiate from the Sanctuary at Gogollis Qabe and six warriors, two from each of the clans at Buur Heybe. The High Priest and those of his sect were brought to the Sanctuary at Gogollis Qabe, where he alone met with the *Priestess Shepset* of the Sanctuary, who prepared him for an audience with the Prophetess. It is said the Priestess Shepset first told of the origin of the *House of Tellem*, its descendants from the *House of Ptah*, and its emergence from a vision granted to the *Prophet Tellem* during his sojourn in the spiritual realm in the time of Ptah.

The Priestess is said to have then recited the poem that is the story of the *Legend* that is the *Vessel of the Prophecy*. A revelation that is said to have resonated within the very being of the Fetish Priest Shai, not so much for the Prophecy, but for the Legend, which Shai disclosed provides insight into the early history of his own Order. He revealed that their Order, the "Hydra cult" is descendent from the ladder day *House of Ptah,* an Order ordained and anointed by "Maahes *the Righteous"* youngest son and last High Priest of the Sanctuary of the House of Ptah. Shai revealed that they know little of the ascendant era of the House of Ptah, little beyond the "Songs of Nefertem", which, according to Shai, are but strung-together fragments and remnants of poems chronicling the later era by the "Poet King Nefertem", the oldest son of Ptah, whose reign preceded that of Maahes.

Shai informed that the Fetish Priesthood aligned to preserve the prefecture and prerogatives of an orthodoxy derived from mysteries first illuminated by the House of Ptah. The Fetish Priesthood of the cult is symbolized by the celestial Serpent, the fabled "Hydra", with its heads represented by the High Priest of the reverent totem clans of the Crocodile. The legends as we know them have been passed down through the ages, but beyond them, we know little. The "*Songs of Nefertem*" list Tellem among the venerated Initiates of the House of Ptah. They name him among those who sojourned in the spiritual realm. The Prophetess Ipet then revealed that instruction for her invitation to Shai came from Upàst, a great Seer at *Ta Netjeru*, by whose insistence she shares the *Legend of the House of Tellem*.

Ipet was tasked by Upàst to inform the priests of the Crocodile clans that the "House of Tellem" and the "Songs of Nefertem" are each composed of fragments from the House of Ptah. These fragments form vital parts of lost enlightenment. Upàst informed that this revelation has fomented cohesion between the clans of the House of Tellem at Ta Netjeru and the totem serpent clans from the uplands of the "Mountains of the Heavens" as well as those in the lowlands and around the southern shores of Lake Turkana, with whom the Crocodile clans of the plateaus have long traded. A revelation surprising the Shai, who resolved to reciprocate the graciousness granted him at Gogollis Qabe by then and there reciting the "Songs of Nefertem", after which he advised that he shall duly inform his clan elders of the Prophecy of Tellem.

Apu-t informed that "there have since been exchanges of clerics, and that the Priestess Shepset, whom Shai has since taken as his wife, now recites the poem that is the story of the Legend to Initiates of the *Hydra cult* at Doolow. Medjed ("the Smiter"), feared warrior and leader of the Crocodile clans, had sought on several occasions to meet and reach an accord with Ur-henu, leader of the main clan of the Hippopotamus on the plateau, a capable warrior in his own right. However, Ur-henu deferred to the Prophecy, as interpreted by Ipet, requiring that such accord be the judgment of the *Initiant*. "Here in Baidoa, you shall first meet with Ur-henu, with whom Medjed and other matters shall be discussed", Apu-t advised, noting that "you will receive his allegiance before continuing to Buur Heybe. Baidoa was a large village of the Hippopotamus clans, with minor clan leaders joining Ur-henu warmly and receiving Bes (Bisu, Aha) upon his arrival.

Once introductions were out of the way, Bes apprised Ur-henu that Kherau, his closest confidant, had not long ago informed of a defiant Crocodile clan, leaving him to cause for concern. Bisu advised that he shall nonetheless seek to meet with Medjed and instructed invitation be sent forthwith to the revered leader of the Crocodile clans, inviting him to meet and confer at week's end at Berdaale, the main village near the Sanctuary at Gogollis Qabe. Upon return to Berdaale, Bes found the village prepared to receive Medjed, with its warriors lined along the pathway leading toward the village center. Ahead of being met by Athpi, the clan leader of Berdaale, Bes (Bisu, Aha) was instead met by a messenger from Amam, advising that Medjed had arrived ahead of two fairly large armies of warriors, which together form a substantial but still smaller force than the armies shielding Buur Hebye. Bes instructed Apu-t to dispatch messengers to his commanders in the lowlands and informed them that, despite all that had been said, his meeting with Medjed would go ahead. Bes then instructed he and Medjed first be left alone so that he may take the measure of the man.

Medjed arrived at Berdaale accompanied by the High Priest Shai and his most trusted General, Khente-Khtai, leader of the Crocodile clan at Mandera, and two warriors, along with a small delegation from the village. All of whom were intercepted in route to the village by Athpi, who informed and accompanied Medjed, alone, to the entrance of the House of the Elders, where he then posted two guards, as Medjed ('the Smiter') finally found himself face-to-face with Bes (Bisu, Aha ('The Fighter')). After a moment of silence as the two sized each other up, characteristically, without further hesitation, Bes (Bisu) stepped to within inches of the nose of Medjed, and staring eye-to-eye, he asked, 'so what is your decision regarding alliance …are we enemies or allies'? To which the slightly older, cold, steely-eyed Medjed unflinchingly replied, "it appears destiny has decided that for us Bes, and upon my word, then we shall be among your most ardent allies …one day you shall count me among your most trusted generals."

The two leaders spoke alone for hours, bonding around previously suspected similarities. They were each skilled warriors who grew up and lived in violent times, leading each to early idealized warrior culture; each believing it honorable to die valiantly on the battlefield for what one believes. Medjed told of the long migrations that brought the Crocodile clans eastward to the well-watered southern Lands of the Plateaus; he told of the legends of the pitched battles against well-entrenched clans over suitable lands in which to settle. It was a time when clans were forced into migration and conflict by the dwindling forests, rivers and lakes in the lowlands, a time when only spiritual reverence and belief separated us from those who had descended into barbarism. 'Vestiges of the old priesthood still survived among clans discernable by their kindred serpent totem,' Medjed then told of assistance granted the Crocodile clans by kindred serpent clans during their migrations and of the kindred clans aiding in their defense against attacks through the lowlands.

He told of how each of the kindred clans encountered during their migration contributed an ancient verse or two in the composition of the Songs of Nefertem'. An act harmonizing the beliefs and culture of the kindred clans, and more than this, an act causing a thirst for further enlightenment. Bes (Bisu, Aha) revealed that it is only by the Prophecy of the House of Tellem that he has come to understand his destiny, a destiny is vaguely known since childhood, though admittedly not truly understood. Bes told of the pitched battles and dispossession of his own clan and their ancient migrations to the middle (or "Eastern Ethiopian") plateau and of the warrior ethos that has since come to define the totem clans of the Black Leopard. Like many, if not most, the Seers and Sages of the Black Leopard clans are "Followers of Heru", with only faint remembrance of the ancient "Legends of Ptah." "Like many, if not most", Bes informed, "our faith long ago devolved into mere star gazing, awaiting the return of the celestial serpent (with the given name of "Heru") for salvation, absolving ourselves of responsibility and role in pursuing and extolling the will of Netjer."

For me, Bes revealed, 'the Prophecy of the House of Tellem has illuminated the path to a more sacrosanct destiny; a destiny felt since childhood'. Medjed, in turn, told of how the Crocodile clans gained early control over much of the region through the dominance of its water during the onset of the heightening aridity now blanketing the Lands of the Plateaus'. He told of how the Crocodile clans held sway and monopolized the water resources of the Jubba and Shebelle Rivers, and how the Juba River has three main tributaries in its upper catchment in Ethiopia, the Dawa, the Genale and the Weyb, all of which flow south-eastwards. Medjed explained that the Weyb and the Genale unite, forming the Juba River just north of Doolow. At the same time, the Dawa tributary joins the Juba River at Dolo, just beyond the borderlands of the eastern and middle plateaus, in the heart of the stronghold of the totem clans of the Crocodile.

Medjed told of how for untold generations, the Crocodile clans held uncontested sway over the fertile lands between the Jubba and Shebelle Rivers, that is until the arrival of the totem clans of the Hippopotamus. After but a single generation, the clans of the Hippopotamus gained control of the middle and lower Jubba and Shebelle Rivers. Added to this, from our then vantage point, Medjed explained, it appeared they usurped the dominion and overlordship of the Crocodile Clan over our former vassals, the totem clans of the Dugong, along the coast and islands of the offshore archipelago'. Only three of the five clans of the Crocodile were prompted to war by such intrusion into the rich middle lands; the brazen interposition of the Hippopotamus clans with the clans of the Dugong served to arouse the final two clans. A petition of war requires unanimity among the councils of the five totem clans of the Crocodile, and the unanimity at last attained was to a petition presented for the incessant incursions of the Hippopotamus clans into our dominion.

We were thus surprised, and word spread quickly when we received tribute and invitation from the *Prophetess Ipet*, inviting our High Priest Shai to confer at the Sanctuary at Buur Heybe. There he was intrigued to discover the spiritual order at the core of the clans of the Hippopotamus, but more than this, in keeping with our warrior ethos, he was more drawn to the prospect of discovering the weaknesses of our prospective adversary. This was the spirit in which the High Priest Shai was first permitted entrance to the Sanctuary at Buur Heybe, where he learned of the Legend and Prophecy of the House of Tellem. Equally as significant, it was where he learned that the House of Tellem and the Order of the Hydra cult each sprang from the House of Ptah, and that, though fragmented, the Songs of Nefertem affirm parts of the "Legend", like the times in which they now live affirm parts of the "Prophecy."

It was perhaps divine providence, Medjed opined, cautioning Bes that 'though you have accomplished a great feat in uniting the clans and lands of the central and eastern plateaus, know that maintaining that which you have united shall be a separate task altogether'. It will not be as easy as the alliance we have affirmed here today. Medjed illuminated that 'the long, cold, suffocating dryness that has long shrouded and suppressed the fertility and rich abundance of the land, driving men and their clans to extreme lengths for survival, has alas led to a highland culture of dissension, discord, and retribution. The clans of the lands of the eastern and middle plateaus have warred, killed, and supplanted one another as each strived to survive for untold generations. What survives with them is a long tradition of revenge killings, one of the foremost obstacles to true reconciliation and unity.

Victims carry forward grudges which in turn lead to an endless cycle of revenge, with clans generally refusing to admit their past wrongs, provoking and fueling further conflict. Such revenge killings routinely reach across several generations in search of reprisal and rectitude'. When Bes (Bisu, Aha) and Medjed finally emerged from the House of Elders together, it is said the alliance that had been sewn was apparent to all; Medjed would head the sixth grand army of the Initiant and, in time, become one his most trusted Generals. An advent that found impetus in Medjed's haunting admonition about the incivility and revenge-driven disunity that had come to plague the clans of the lands of the plateaus. In seeking the perspectives of his generals regarding the incivility plaguing the land, it is said Bes first opined that 'while there is no doubt military force under strong leadership will be necessary to hold the kingdom together; rather than rule by war, it is our charge to rule by divine reverence'.

Bes (Bisu, Aha (the "Fighter")) nonetheless made it clear that he would keep the united kingdom strong by using force whenever and wherever necessary. In accord with the Legend and its Prophesy, Bisu then instructed his generals ready their armies for the upcoming unification war on the northern plateau. Bisu informed that he himself would lead the first of six armies, with the second led by his closest confidant Kherau, and the third by equally reliable Menew. Abu would continue to lead the fourth army, and Medjed would lead the fifth, but more than this, Bes imbued him with authority to form the six armies, effectively making him second only to himself. Finally, Bes appointed his faithful confidant Amam "Viceroy" of the southeastern plateau, instructing he establish a royal residence at Berbera, above the eastern seaboard, with Khente-Khtai of the Crocodile clan to lead the sixth army.[26] Bes then awaited the just right moment to mount his assault on the great northwestern plateau, and as the moment arrived, like the winds of change, the six armies swept into the Omo river valley in the southern confines of the plateau, quickly vanquishing the vaunted totem clans of the Buffalo.

It was a campaign in which Bes rescued the *Matriarch Mafdet* of the Spotted Leopard clan and recaptured her province within the Great Western Bend. Together with the warriors of the Spotted Leopard under their valiant leader, Dedun, the six armies made a stronghold of the uplands of Jiren. Chosen for its strategic position and elevation, the Citadel Bes could observe the enemy in the surrounding lowlands. Though it had been generations since the fall of the ancestral Leopard Clan, Bes and Dedun knew well the history of their clans and that beyond the battle with the Buffalo, the real test would be against the dreaded Great Rhino. At the behest of his totem kin, the Matriarch Mafdet and Dedun, Bisu assumed leadership of the Leopard clans, adding the warriors of the Spotted Leopard to his forces, over whom he astutely placed Dedun. Bes (Bisu, Aha) then planned to gain an advantage by attacking the range of control of the totem clans of the Great Rhino on the plateau, forcing them to spread their defenses.

Bes (Bisu, Aha (the "Fighter")) dispatched over half his forces, the three armies led by Medjed, Abu and Menew, to locate and assail the strongholds of the Great Rhino in the upper midlands, contesting their control of the central plateau. At his behest, the Matriarch assigned knowledgeable scouts to Medjed so that he might readily find the hidden strongholds and place the Great Rhino on defense in the central plateau. Bes (Bisu, Aha) then turned to Khente-Khtai and Kherau. They instructed that during the days it takes Medjed to reach the central midlands, they aligned their forces and launched a coordinated surprise attack on Adaama. Ever the shrewd and tactical Bes (Bisu, Aha) sought to seize the initiative, placing the enemy at a disadvantage, striking at times and places for which they were unprepared.

Ever thorough, Bes then asked the Matriarch Mafdet to tell of what she knew of the enemy's strengths and weakness; a mystic of sorts, the Matriarch proffered that "though the forces of the Rhino are great, their weakness rest in the heart of their strength, which is their perception of their own preeminence." The Matriarch Mafdet assessed that "this advantage would be in question against the three armies, of course", but she cautioned, "the three armies will be severely tested", adding that "only by piercing their aura of invincibility can the Great Rhino expect to be bested." Yet, as Bes would soon learn, it wasn't the Rhino alone with whom he would first be concerned. It was the realigned clans of the Buffalo. After their humiliating defeat and disastrous retreat, the Buffalo clans had fled east; in a fleeting effort to thwart the invaders, they sought refuge with their old ancient nemesis, the dreaded Black Rhino, provided asylum and offered alliance in exchange for their submission and vassalage.

---

[26] Anciently known as the "Gulf of Berbera"

It was a time of giants among leaders of the clans, referring not only to Bes himself but equally so Mer-wer (the "great black"), exalted leader of the totem clans of the Great Rhino, who ruled from his stronghold at Adaama.[cxxxii] Too far north of Adaama, at Bahir Dar (ancient "Bahir Giyorgis"), was the valiant Ḥun-sāḫu, leader of the clans of the Great Rhino that controlled the northern midlands as far south as the southern highlands of Gojjam. To the northwest of this was the shrewd Sed, leader of the vassal clans of the Jackal, who controlled much of the northern highlands of Gojjam.[cxxxiii] To the east was the crafty leader of the vassal clans of the wolf, who, from their stronghold, controlled the southern highlands of Wollo. To the northeast at Dese was the revered warrior Anhur, leader of the totem clans of the Black Lion, who controlled much of the northeast.[cxxxiv] The rule of Anhur was augmented at length by the Warrior Queen Pakhet ("Pakhet the Great"), whose Black Lion clans ruled much of the northern Wollo highlands south of Gondar. It was thus that the Black Lion held sway over the northeast and central north, under the rule of Anhur.[cxxxv].

Peering from the highlands of Jiren, Bes (Bisu, Aha), Khente-Khtai, and the Matriarch carefully watched the warriors of the Buffalo clans as they amassed to the north, just beyond the distant wetlands. And this, as Dedun and Kherau watched the gathering of warriors of the Rhino amass just beyond the wetlands to the south. At the head of the Rhino clans were their revered leader, Mer-wer (the "great black"), directing not only the Rhino but also the Buffalo, as each form for the attack. Never one to allow an enemy to claim the initiative, Bes (Bisu, Aha ("the fighter")) seize the advantage, first by dispatching Khente-Khtai and his warriors to the wetlands to counter-attack the Buffalo …in the midst of their charge. From what Bisu knew of the totem of the Buffalo, he presumed they would launch a retaliatory attack, a battle, he felt, would be best waged in the wetlands …to the benefit of Khente-Khtai. Those led by Khente-Khtai were from the Crocodile, Cobra, Viper and Hippopotamus clans, who then took a position in the wetlands awaiting the charge of the Buffalo, on the terrain in which the serpent clans would have a decided advantage.

Bisu (Bes, Aha (the "Fighter")) secondly dispatched Dedun and Kherau and their forces to the wetlands to the south. Bes surmised that the well-known "attack is the best defense" strategy of the Rhino could make them both dangerous, and quite vulnerable; understanding that, like their totem, the Great Rhino could be easily provoked into attack; an attack that could be shaped and fought on favorable ground for a counterattack. Like the Buffalo, the vaunted charge of the Rhino would be both predictable and muted in the shallow wetlands, where the more fleet-footed warriors of the Leopard, Hippopotamus, Ibis, Grey Owl, Oryx, and Raven clans would have the advantage. Bes (Bisu, Aha ("the fighter")) showed off his own tactical skills, together with his ability to readily assess the strengths and capabilities of his own commanders …in relation to his opponent's weaknesses. The warriors of the Buffalo were predictably provoked into a full-scale attack by the mere audacity of Khente-Khtai and his warriors assuming the position in the wetlands.

A provocation frustrating the Buffalo's part in the closely coordinated plan of attack directed by Mer-wer (the "great black"), a frustration prompting the Rhino to react by attacking the threat posed by the forces of Kherau and Dedun in the shallow wetlands. As the Buffalo sought to join the attack, their vaunted charge was muted. It became mired in the wetlands, with Khente-Khtai and the warriors of the Crocodile, Viper, Cobra, and Hippopotamus clans inflicting a serious defeat …in which the Buffalo lost many warriors. But true to their totem, the Buffalo regrouped for yet another charge, in which they were again repulsed and lost many warriors. To the north, the confrontation between the warriors of the Rhino and those of Kherau and Dedun had come to hand-to-hand combat in the midst of the northern wetlands. After a series of bloody clashes in which each side took serious losses, Bes (Bisu, Aha ("the fighter")) and Mer-wer ("the great black") each pulled backed and reinforced their forces.

It was the Matriarch Mafdet who advised Bes (Bisu, Aha) that, frustrated with having taken such losses, Mer-wer would now surely summon additional forces ..." he will seek warriors from the clans of the midlands in a bid to regain his usual advantage. It was for this that Bes sent word instructing that Medjed forthwith engage the Rhino clans of the central midlands. Upon word of this, Medjed ("the Smiter") first sent Abu and his warriors to engage Ḥun-sāḫu and Rhino clans of the north in their stronghold at Bahir Dar. Medjed then took it upon himself to assail the elusive Rhino clans of the central midlands ...and left it to Menew to contend with the Rhino clans in the lower midlands, whom Menew attacked in a series of skillful assaults, upending them each in a devastating rout. For a time, the battle at Bahir Dar to the north led by the shrewd Jackal leader Sed, the warriors of the Topi and the Jackal forced Abu and his warriors to fight long into the night just to survive until, mercifully, under the darkness,, they were able to take flight.

This while at the *Citadel at Jeren*, Mer-wer re-grouped his warriors for a renewed round of attacks. Having summoned the vassal clans of the Wolf and Buffalo, he now aligned their formations with those of the Rhino in preparation for an all-assault. To Bes, it appeared an obvious attack across the northern wetlands through the lowlands into the highlands to topple the Citadel. As he watched the Rhino and their vassal from above, Bisu adjusted his own forces to counter the attack. From the south, he brought the able forces of Khente-Khtai to the shallow wetlands in the north, reinforcing the battle-tested forces of Dedun and Kherau. Bisu then summoned Apu-t, whom he dispatched with a cadre of his most adept 'Guardians of the Prophecy' to instruct Segeb, his Viceroy on the Southeastern Plateau, to lead the balance of his forces on the southeastern plateau against the Rhino stronghold at Adaama. Bisu knew Segeb was head of the easternmost clan of the Black Lion. By the arrival of Apu-t, Segeb would understand and seek to enlist the full might of the Black Lion clan.

Turning again to the defense of the Citadel, Bes (Bisu, Aha ("the fighter")) stood atop the highest hill in view of his own forces, beckoning and provoking Mer-wer to bring forth his worst. But this time, less inclined to abandon his plan, Mer-wer held fast, awaiting just the right moment to unleash his forces, a moment that came in the haze just before nightfall. Warriors of the Wolf and Buffalo clans, and those of the Great Rhino slowly entered the wetlands in the north, not in a rage, but in silent stealth. When they suddenly arose in the mid shallows, in near surprise, they were nonetheless countered and repelled by the warriors of Khente-Khtai. The shallow wetlands were familiar terrain for the warriors of the totem clans of the Crocodile, Viper, Cobra, and Hippopotamus, and they punished and drove the Rhino back in the direction from which they came.

Mer-wer ("the great black") then led a second attack, again in stealth, in the haze just before dawn. But this time, they caught none by surprise, as Khente-Khtai led the warriors of the Crocodile, Viper and Cobra into the fight, warriors who were soon joined by the archers of the Grey Owl and Ibis clans led by Dedun and Kherau who attacked the rear flanks of the Rhino, leaving the warriors of the Buffalo and Wolf clans vulnerable in the midst of the shallows; a battle that ended when the warriors of the Rhino were again repelled from the wetlands. In his third effort, Mer-wer again led the attack, this time using the able archers of his own clans, who rained down indiscriminate arrows on those in the wetlands for what seemed like an hour. A tactic that drove Khente-Khtai and his warriors back, abandoning the advantageous ground to the then-advancing warriors of the Rhino.

Mer-wer took the lowlands surrounding Jiren as his first victory, as Bes (Bisu, Aha) was forced to withdraw his warriors to defend the Citadel. With the warriors of the dreaded Rhino then in control of the lowland, Mer-wer ordered forward the warriors of the clans of the vassals, as he awaited the right time for his attack on the citadel …just before dawn the following morning. Never one to await, Bes (Bisu, Aha ("the fighter")) himself led the warriors of the Leopard clans in an attack upon the vassal clans in the still dead of night, the Buffalo clans were panicked, and the warriors of the Wolf clans took flight. When the Rhino finally arrived at their support, as suddenly the Black Leopard had appeared, it was gone, leaving the Rhino little recourse but to await the dawn.

After his masterful rout in the upper southern midlands, rather than pursue the Rhino fleeing to the south, Menew instead chose to join Medjed in his pursuit of the elusive Rhino clans of the central midlands. Upon his arrival, Medjed told Menew of the fateful plight of Abu after a surprise attack by the vassal clans of the Topi and Jackal, whom Medjed deemed his forces better configured to handle. And so it was that in the midst of the long battle, Menew was granted the task of pursuing the Rhino clans of the central midlands, while Medjed joined common cause with Abu, assuming the lead in assailing the vassals and northernmost clans of the Rhino. In his opening campaign, Medjed sought first to weaken the northern Rhino by first defeating their vassals.

The vassal clans of the Topi clans occupied the northern lands below the southern wetlands of ancient Lake Tana, the lands west of the Blue Nile before the river entered its deep canyon and plunged over the Blue Nile Falls. While the lands of the Jackal were in the northern uplands of Gojjam to the west. The Topi was a clan comprised of five sub-clans, whose villages were in the lands south of Lake Tana, west of the Blue Nile and ancient Bahir Dar (Bahir Giyorgis), a stronghold of the northern clans of the Rhino led by Ḥun-sāḥu. Thus began the campaign for the north, as Medjed and his warriors assailed and, one-by-one forced the clans of the Topi to both submit, renounce their vassalage to the Rhino, and declare their allegiance to Bisu and the 'Prophesy of Tellem'.

Hard-fought losses prompted the Jackal into flight as they sought refuge at the Rhino stronghold at Bahir Dar; once there, Sed forewarned Ḥun-sāḥu to prepare for an enormous fight. The wily Sed warned of the enormity of the approaching force, a force he thought greater than that of the Rhino at Bahir Dar. Thus the age-old Rhino advantage of asymmetrical warfare would be lost. In the south, in response to an imminent attack on the Citadel at Jiren, Bes launched a preemptive attack just before dawn, finding the warriors of the Buffalo and Rhino clans on guard but unprepared for the fullness of the onslaught to come. Despite being forced to abandon their position and fall back, Mer-wer gathered his forces and nonetheless attacked the Citadel just before dusk that evening.

Bes rallied his forces, unleashing the power of his archers, who launched a series of volleys into the front ranks of the Rhino as well as over their heads into the ranks of the warriors behind them. Bisu then unleashed a full-scale downhill charge that broke through the front lines of Buffalo and Rhino, prompting Mer-wer to retreat to avoid being routed. The Citadel at Jiren, by all appearances, was impregnable. Its heart could only be reached by a single pathway. In re-forming for another round of attacks, instead of seeking to assault the citadel from the sides and front simultaneously, Mer-wer consolidated forces for a series of frontal assaults, one after another, while guarding his flanks, with Bes, in response, launching a third counterattack, again with warriors charging downhill driving the attackers back to the lowlands.

There is no clear-cut legend describing the actual strategies and tactics Mer-wer used to advance his forces through the lower highlands to within view and striking distance of the citadel. What is known is that the tactics of Mer-wer ("the great black") originated on the battlefield and that the battle opened with archers shooting uphill at the forces of Bisu, with most overshooting their targets as arrows flew over the heads of the warriors atop the hill. Bes then commanded a full fledge attack, and with his warriors still in command of the uplands, they again took position and launched a downhill charge, but this time directly into the ranks of Rhino and Buffalo in the midst of their uphill assault on the pathway leading to the citadel. They fought fiercely, and for the assailants, it was literally an uphill fight as they fought their way up the mountainside.

The fight raged for hours, with Bes (Bisu, Aha ("the fighter")) himself entering the fray to encourage his warriors to fight with fierce fury and abandon. With Bes's inspiration, his warriors began to push Rhino forces back. Bes's forces suffered several minor losses as the Rhino continued to retreat downhill until Bes launched what at first appeared to be a decisive attack, turning the tide of the battle, with Mer-wer withdrawing his forces in full retreat, drawing the forces of Bes into full pursuit. When the Rhino and Buffalo warriors again reached the lower highlands, they were utterly exhausted; for all of Mer-wer's tactical brilliance, the terrain proved to be the greatest obstacle for the warriors of the Rhino, and Buffalo

The two armies met again in the lowlands just before the wetlands, with the two colliding in a ferocious melee that again forced Mer-wer to withdraw in retreat. Mer-wer didn't panic but instead personally assumed command of his warriors, withdrawing to the suitable ground, at first, using the deliberate tactic of feigned flight to draw the forces of Bes into pursuit. A tactic allowing Bes and his forces to believe they were winning by yielding ground, with Bes and his forces confident of the momentum of their charge as they advanced. However, their push through the middle of the Rhino lines allowed Mer-wer to form a formation that enveloped his attackers on both flanks and then have his archers shoot into their ranks, forcing Bes to withdraw as the Mer-wer resumed his retreat.

After such a defeat, Bes avoided direct confrontation with the retreating Mer-wer but instead used his own tactical brilliance to mount lightning-fast hit-and-run attacks against the retreating Rhino and Buffalo warriors. Nonetheless, at great risk, Mer-wer and his forces outmaneuvered Bes by sneaking across the lowlands during a lull in the action at dusk, and once across, they pushed on well into the night to reach their stronghold at Adaama. Once at the stronghold, Mer-wer assigned a rearguard to delay the forces of Bes until they could reinforce Adaama, which was under separate attack from the north, defended by the clans from the southern midlands who had been routed by Menew …Adaama had thus far held its own.

When Bes (Bisu, Aha ("the fighter")) and his forces finally arrived, they not only advanced on Adaama but sought to surround the stronghold …when they were met by the most surprising reinforcement, the Priest Apu-t and his Guardians of the Prophesy. Apu-t informed that he had been dispatched by Segeb, whose forces assail Adaama from the north, and further that, rather than leave the southeastern plateau undefended, Segeb left the army Bisu had allotted him to defend the realm and instead has rallied the warriors of his own clans of the Black Lion on the southeastern plateau, as well as the four clans from the Rift Valley to aid in the offensive.

Howsoever, Apu-t informed, in pursuit of the concurrence of Anhur, revered (de facto) leader of the Black Lion clans, from his stronghold at Dese, Segeb sent Apu-t himself to explain the Legend and the Prophesy it portends. After due consideration, the venerable Anhur consented to no more than a short period of support by the clans of the Black Lion …without the Legend and its Prophesy being blessed by the spiritual leaders on the great plateau …to whom all clans have anciently looked for guidance, even the clans of the Great Rhino. Apu-t informed that Anhur requested Bes to seek the blessing of the renowned *Seers of Gondar* …blessing with which you shall then be able to unite the great plateau. Apu-t further informed that Anhur has accordingly provided knowledgeable guides to aid in the journey.

Unaware of the success of the campaigns to seize control of the upper and northern midlands by the three armies led by Medjed, after due consideration Bes (Bisu, Aha ("the fighter")) consented to meet and pursue the blessing of the Seers of Gondar, in the hope that it would provide an expeditious end to the war. Faint legend reports he placed his closest confidant, Kherau, in command of the armies who, together with the forces led by Segeb, had the Rhino stronghold at Adaama completely under siege.

The Blind Seer of Gondar

The clans of the Eland resided in the highlands of the Gondar, to the northeast; gateway to an almost mystical world even then anciently known as the "Mystic North", a land of spirituality and mysticism. There were three sub-clans of the Eland in the highlands of Gondar; so ancient was the origin of the clan that its beginning was even then long lost in the mists of early antiquity. The totem of the clan, the regal "Eland," is a large and powerful Antelope, regarded as brave but gentle; the Eland was anciently believed to have powerful spiritual significance.[cxxxvi] The Eland was an animal that many, if not most, of the ancient peoples of central-eastern and southern Africa regarded as sacred; it is represented and found in many early ancient cave paintings and rock engraving throughout the greater region and is well represented in ancient African folklore, known as "the animal of a thousand legends."

Flanked by twin mountain streams at an elevation of about 7,500 feet, Gondar commands spectacular views over the intervening lands and gleaming waters of Lake Tana in the distance to the south. Having ascended through the highlands, Bes, Apu-t and a small cadre of Guardians of the Prophesy, led by the Black Lion guides provided by Anhur, Bisu and his party then descended through a spectacular mountain passé studded with inhabited domed inselbergs, into the ancient valley of the inselbergs. An inselberg is essentially a small isolated mountain that rises abruptly from a sloping or virtually flat surrounding plain; three of the five clans of the Eland resided around and in the largest inselberg in the midst of the floor of the valley.

The Legends

As Bes and his party traversed the floor of the valley toward the village of the main clan of the Eland at the base of the inselberg, Apu-t informed Bisu of what he had learned of the *Seers of Gondar*, that 'they are diviners of the heavens, and as such are ardent ancient adherents and followers of the (Celestial Serpent) "Heru".' Yet, Apu-t noted, 'though they are the fount spiritual wisdom here on the great plateau, more than reverence earns their respect from the vassals and clans of the Black Rhino; they are allied with their most rent adherents, the nine clans of the Ibex of Ras Dejen, as well as the clans of the Black Lion itself.' Apu-t relayed the sentiment of Anhur, who opined that with the siege upon Adaama, the undecided campaigns in the midlands, the dreaded Rhino will be left with little option but to yield.

Apu-t noted that it is 'Anhur's belief that 'with the blessing of the "Prophesy" by the Seers of Gondar and the very real prospect of the Black Lion and Ibex joining the battle in pursuit of the vision of the Prophesy, the dreaded Rhino will concede to the unity you seek. Yet, at what cost, Anhur pondered,' Apu-t recounted, noting that Anhur assumed a somewhat solemn tone as he suggested Bisu seek the council of the mystic *Blind Seer of Gondar*, whose blessing will surely transform those relationships he will need to pursue the Prophesy."

Welcomed in the accompaniment of the guides of the Black Lion, Bisu and Apu-t were met by a small group as they approached the village at the base of the largest inselberg on the floor of the valley. Informed that Anhur had sent a message advising of their arrival after a shared meal and discourse with the village leader, Nebti, and a woman known as the "Grand Sage", Thmei, from the village atop the mountain, Bes and his companions were invited to take a well-deserved nights rest.[cxxxvii] The following morning Bes and Apu-t were invited to accompany Nebti and Thmei on a nearly a full days trek up the mountain to a small village just below its peak to confer with the most knowledgeable Seer of their clans, an elder known as "Septu ."

On the trek, up the mountain, Thmei took the occasion to inform Bes of the traditions of the totem clans of the Eland, 'that among the clans every man is a Seerer and every woman a Sage, by skills cultivated from childhood'. Though by necessity, Nebti added, 'every man is also a hunter and warrior, by skills cultivated from childhood.' 'Our is a culture,' Thmei explained, in which leaders are not rulers and have no direct control over the lives of their clans; they possess only the authority which their wisdom or spiritual influence grants them. Thus, the Seer Septu, whom we now en route to see, is and has been the true (de facto) leader of the five clans of the Eland for nearly seventy years. Though he is aged and all but completely blind, his internal vision of the celestial heavens is unsurpassed.

Although the name of the early ancient village near the top of the huge inselberg has been lost in the midst of time, ancient lore describes the mountainside village as centered around a multi-cavern cave near the top of the inselberg. The cave was the abode of the Seer Septu and those invited to learn at his side. After cordialities traditional to the Eland, Bes and Apu-t were invited to join *Nebti* and *Thmei* around a small, robust fire at the center of the central cavern of the abode of the elder Seer Septu. Not long after they were seated, the Seer himself was ushered in and assisted in taking place around the fire, after which, once informed of who sat where he stared intently as if into the spirit of the fire as he softly advised that the arrival of Bisu had been foreshadowed by a confluence in the celestial heavens.

Then, at the subtle behest of Bes (Bisu), Apu-t seized the moment to formally introduce himself and Lord Bes and with the consent of his hosts, to tell of the Legend of the House of Tellem and the Prophesy it portends. Apu-t spoke of the 'ominous darkness that had long shrouded the lands and of how during the time of Ptah, it was first he and then the Initiates of his Sanctuary who once held this looming darkness at bay. Apu-t told of how Ptah ascended into the spiritual realm and enlisted the support of powerful forces to hold back the darkness, ominous darkness that has shrouded the lands since the fall of the Great Sanctuary and its Initiates. It was one such Initiate, known as "Tellem", whose vision is the story of the Legend, Apu-t informed, and whose descendants form the House of Tellem that has, through the ages, passed down the Legend and Prophesy it portends.

Apu-t told of the twelve configurations (the "constellations") of the celestial stars in the heavens and that the rhythm of the Cosmos is seen in the cyclical nature of these celestial bodies, cycles that mark the passage of the Ages. Through these observations, the Seers of the Sanctuary were able to predict future events, Apu-t further informed; one such prediction foreshadowing the Prophecy informs that we are in the midst of a "Great Synchronicity" availing humankind an alternate destiny. It is through the House of Tellem we are informed that such Synchronicities unveil hidden alignments between the spiritual and physical realms, foreshadowing the prospect of change in the physical realm. We do not know the length of the Synchronicity or how long we may avail ourselves of it, only that it approaches.

The Prophetess Ta Urt of the House of Tellem, Apu-t continued, advises that the Forces of Chaos equally threaten heavenly places, such as the Celestial Palace, the abode of Ptah, whom Upȧst, a great Seer of the House of Tellem, says battles against these forces even now in the spiritual realm. Echoes of these battles are what we experience here in the physical realm …most notably in the form of the ominous darkness that has long shrouded the land and pervades the very spirit of man. The "Great Synchronicity", Apu-t concluded, avails the next true Archon an opportunity to intervene in the eternal battle on behalf of humankind. This endeavor may be man's last best chance to prevail.

With this, it is said, the Grand Sage Thmei intervened to explain the ritual of conferring through a shared vision with Sepṭu, whom she said was among the 'Mystic Seers of Gondar'; Thmei illuminated that 'just as the twelve "constellations" are configurations of the countless celestial stars in the heavens, so too are their constellations of diverse plants within the realm of Nature. There are a small number of constellations of sacred plants which, because of their great power, are known amongst knowledgeable Sages as the "Twelve Fruit of the Tree of Life." Each constellation represents a collection of species with a particular (psychoactive) effect to induce visionary or mystical (trance) states.

The ancient recipes used by the Sages of Gondar induce a powerful but natural stimulation of the imagination. She illuminated, 'the mystical experience evoked involves first overcoming the doubts of the lower self, the Grand Sage advised, "this is needed to be a fully receptive participant in the shared vision availed by the Seer." "It involves perception", she informed, "mystical experiences are perceived only according to the perceiver's ability to see. What the individual sees in the vision is dependent on the mental state of the participant, and, above all, his own repository of beliefs."

Thmei then cautioned, 'the authority of the Seer is paramount in this experience; his role is pivotal. It is he who must interpret and skillfully balance the forces of the cosmos to safely guide the participant. It is he who places the protective cloak about the participant during their shared vision, at which juncture a young Sage ("Ḥebit") who attends to the needs of the blind Seer Sepṭu, entered the cavern, accompanied by two younger Sages, each holding and handing a small bowl, only slightly filled, to the participants sitting around the fire. The young Sage Ḥebit retained her bowl as she sat beside and assisted Sepṭu. As Thmei explained, 'in ritual, we all sip from our bowls together, led by Sepṭu, who will alternately speak, then sip, then speak, and sip, and so on.

The Parables

Unlike Ptah, Thmei explained, 'there will be no ascendance into the spiritual realm; yet, for the fully receptive, a shared vision is made manifest by Sepṭu as he recalls aspects of the Cosmos as he witnessed as a younger man and came to better understand as an older man. The herbal recipes used by Sages here in the upper village allow a relaxing of the lower-self-sufficient to effect a special (psychic) connection, a link permitting a shared vision among the receptive. According to ancient lore, Sepṭu was said to be capable of psychically projecting images of his thoughts and imprinted memories of the cosmos. To the fully receptive, these projections are said to have appeared both corporeal and dynamic as the Seer guided them through the heavens and his understanding of the Cosmos.

With all then readied, and the attention of each firmly upon Sepṭu as he gazed intently into the fire and began the telling of how the lineage and lore of the clans of the Eland extended sufficiently back through the ages to have witnessed and recited several occasions of the arrival of Heru (the celestial serpent and mythological "Hydra"), steaking across the celestial heavens to spreading his restorative serpentine fires. Sepṭu then took a sip from his bowl and went on to describe the abode of Heru in the celestial heavens, describing the longest of the ancient constellations still recognized in the present day, the "Hydra" constellation. As the mental vision Sepṭu described gained greater clarity in the minds of Bisu and the other participants, Sepṭu spoke of the dynamic interaction of the constellations.

The Blind Seer explained that 'once the ancient architects of old gave symbol to the clusters of stars (sometime before 24,000 BCE) by naming the constellations; it, in effect, mapped the celestial heavens, revealing the cosmic tempo and grand cycles governing the processes of eternal change. Sepṭu described it as a major cycle subsuming lesser cycles. However, the actual duration of such cycles has been a matter of diverse opinion. Sepṭu explained that "the Seers of Gondar believe the duration of a given age is indirectly influenced by both seen and unseen events in the Cosmos. Many disagree on the exact beginning or end of a given Age, he noted, opining that 'often we only see things as they appear, yet there is much more to reality than meets the eye; one must look beneath the surface in order to see the inner-workings at play."

We are surrounded by a spiritual realm, teeming with spirits that show us there is a connection between the 'inner' and 'outer worlds'; that the two are not separate realities but one and the same. The truth is, there are myriad events taking place in the spiritual realm – in the background, so to speak – that underlie or are somehow otherwise related to many of the ills of our world. The cosmos passes through endless repetitive cycles of destruction and rebirth, reflective of the eternal cosmic battle, a battle in which the faithful must embrace the Light, Septu opined.[cxxxviii] While most people have the impression that nothing is changing in our world, an eternal war between the dark and light forces is being fought over this great prize.

Septu then paused but a moment, took another sip from his bowl, and illuminated that 'the Cosmos is alive and growing, constantly changing as can be seen in the uniqueness of the Great Ages. As our world moves through the celestial heavens, it traverses twelve great constellations of the stars, whom the ancient ones named after the twelve Netjeru. The number of years in any given "Great Age" (as seen from our world) is based on the movement of our world through each such constellation.[cxxxix] Each Age is somehow different in duration, one from the other and from earlier Ages; the Great Ages also overlap, making it difficult to determine when one Great Age ends and the next begins.[cxl] It is nonetheless a cosmic tempo that governs the unfolding of the ages and the rise and fall of things within each Great Age. The Blind See then further illuminated that the 'constellations mutually influence the constellations by which they are surrounded and that with no constellation, this is truer than the constellation "Hydra."

Like a living creature, the Hydra constellation winds its coils from afar, with its head tucked beneath the middle of the Crab constellation (Cancer) and its coils winding beneath the body of the Lion constellation (Leo) as its tail hovers above the Centaur constellation (Centaurus). The Hydra constellation (also known as "Draco") is a fulfilling constellation that almost spans the length of the night sky; like the whole of the Cosmos, Septu elucidated, 'the celestial bodies comprising Hydra are but reflections, manifestations in the physical realm, of heavenly bodies in the spiritual realm. 'It is there,' Septu noted pointedly, 'there in the expanse of the celestial heavens of the constellation Hydra in the spiritual realm …that the cosmic battle between the forces of Darkness and Chaos and the forces of Light and Order ensues.

Though it is a battle beyond our vision,' Septu illuminated, 'know that it is a battle between the forces of Netjer and the forces of Khaos, an eternal struggle that makes our reality and our world what it is.' Though the cosmic battle happens on a battlefield in the spiritual realm, Septu propounded that it is also a battle within the minds and souls of all in the physical realm. The avarice and evil we experience here are things that pervade Khaos, who seeks to assail the Celestial Palace after the conquest of Hydra.' In ancient mythology, it was Hydra who guarded the entrance to the spiritual realm (the so-called "underworld"), the world upon which the material realm (and its physical manifestations) is based.

The Hydra constellation is the largest of the eighty-eight (88) modern constellations, winding over a quarter of the way around the night sky, snaking its way between the neighboring constellations whose borders it shares; the constellations Leo, Cancer, Canis Minor, Monoceros, Puppis, Pyxis, Antlia, Centaurus, Libra, Virgo, Corvus, Crater, and Sextans. The images that ancient Seers associated with the constellations have always been coherently imaginative, recognizing progressive distortions from the slow drift in the constellations from the processional movement of the earth's axis.

Yet, it is said, over only a shortage, certain of the constellations bordering Hydra appeared subtly but unusually distorted. To the mystic Seers of Gondar, this betrayed influences beyond the physical realm. The ancient Seers were raised at the foot of their fathers, as their fathers had been raised at the foot of their fathers century after century. The ancient Seers of Gondar had observed and divined the celestial heavens for generations and, in so doing, had meticulously traced the cycles and influences of the constellations, detecting even the slightest of anomalies. It is thus, Sepṭu revealed, that 'even though the eternal battle is beyond our vision …in the spiritual realm, it is a battle the consequences of which we are nonetheless able to perceive.

Sepṭu revealed further that 'through cosmic voyages undertaken in deep states of meditation, the Seers of Gondar have over the ages gained great knowledge and understanding of the cycles and influences of the constellations …this by projecting their spirits into the celestial heavens for closer witness. The Hydra constellation is a pathway to understanding the Cosmos (even for present-day astronomers).[cxli]. Hydra is host to numerous galaxies, such as the Spiral Galaxy, a smaller sister to the Milky Way, and a galaxy present-day astronomers call the "Southern Pinwheel Galaxy", together with one of the more mysterious galaxies, containing numerous blue spirals and a strange yellow elliptical, only partial paint massive the celestial landscape of the Hydra constellation.[cxlii]

Strengthening his psychic connection with the participants in his shared past vision of the Hydra constellation, Sepṭu availed them of the view approaching the constellation, informing that 'there is a cluster of Galaxies within Hydra that (as termed by present-day astronomers) span over ten million light years; there are over one hundred fifty Galaxies in Hydra, Sepṭu noted, explaining that 'the largest of which are two elliptical galaxies, and the Spiral Galaxy.[cxliii] Sepṭu then solemnly noted that 'the "Hydra Constellation" is notable for having a high proportion of "Dark Matter", pausing for effect before pointing out other notable objects as he surveyed the body of the constellation; objects such as the dying Star present-day astronomers call the "Ghost of Jupiter." [cxliv]

The Ghost of Jupiter is a planetary nebula located in the Hydra constellation. When a Star with a mass up to eight times that of our own Sun runs out of energy, it blows off its outer shells at the end of its life and begins to lose mass. This occurrence allows the hot inner core of the dying star (as it collapses from a red giant to a white dwarf) to radiate strongly, causing this outward-moving cocoon of gases to glow brightly. Such phenomena are called "planetary nebulae" because early observers thought they looked like planets, but in actuality, they didn't have anything to do with planets. The Ghost of Jupiter appears as an oval disk, bearing a close resemblance to the huge planet Jupiter within our own solar system, hence its name. The central white dwarf star within the Ghost of Jupiter is visible at the center of the elongated inner ring, completing what is known as the "Eye"; a central nebula is embedded in a much larger faint halo.[cxlv]

Sepṭu illuminated that it is phenomena such as the Ghost of Jupiter that betray the stresses of the battle between the forces of light (Netjer) and those of darkness (Khaos) upon the celestial bodies in the heavens of the spiritual realm …those which underpin their existence of such bodies in the physical realm. It is a cosmic expanse, nay, a celestial battlefield in which the shadow of the combatants and the consequence of their contest is made manifest by celestial ruins evident in the physical realm. Underscoring his point, Sepṭu pointed out the "Southern Owl" nebula in Hydra, noting that "it may look like a supernatural apparition, but the mysterious blue bubble is actually the ghost of a dying star …describing it as 'a "planetary nebula" created by the dying star.'

Sepṭu then pointed out another such seemingly supernatural apparition, an apparition present-day astronomers call the "Diamond Ring" nebula, a spherical planetary nebula with features similar to those of the Owl nebula. Sepṭu then informed that "the lives of stars with masses greater than eight-fold that of our own Sun are ended in far more spectacular fashion than a mere planetary nebula; the lives of such stars are ended by supernova, an eruption of immense proportion." The Blind Seeker then solemnly and softly advised that "the Hydra constellation, province of Heru …is littered with such supernovae."

"Hydra is clearly the battleground of the cosmic struggle between the Forces of Light and those of Darkness, betraying a struggle between two opposing forces of immeasurable power", Sepṭu propounded; "immense contesting powers of strength sufficient to subtly distort and alter the celestial cycles, and lay waste to celestial bodies in the spiritual and physical realms of the cosmos. Clues to understanding the story of the battle can be derived by examining the destruction and ruins of old celestial bodies and the appearance of new celestial bodies, and their negated and new influences on the cycles of the constellations and the Great Ages."

"While the forces of Light (Netjer) seek to create and sustain life, the forces of Darkness (Khoas) seek to destroy what has been created and ordered; each leaving signs through which we gain insight into the meaning and purpose of the eternal battle", the Blind Seer illuminated. "You can detect the subtle shadows of the adversaries between the great stars and certain of the galaxies within the Hydra constellation; shadows that betray the adversaries and their struggles; though we cannot see their struggles, by this, we know they are very real …and portend the unfolding of each Age.

This is the eternal struggle between the Forces of Light and the Forces of Darkness …and souls are at stake. You, too, Lord Bes (Bisu), have been fighting this very battle …here in the physical realm, where you have fought against greed, deceit, corruption and rule through force of violence; weapons used by the forces of Khaos (Chaos) here in the Lands of the Plateaus. The Blind Seer illuminated that "the supernatural powers an "Archon" attains are obtained purely by virtue of the strength and piety of the faithful that constitutes his station." Sepṭu paused again before taking a final sip, then, gazing up from the fire for the first time, he stated pointedly that we are about to enter a new age, whether it is characterized by chaos and darkness or the divine order and light shall be determined by the collective reverence of the faithful.

"The forces of darkness are nefarious, he cautioned, advising that 'one must not underestimate how completely they have penetrated and deluded the minds of men …you shall know them by their deeds," Sepṭu opined. The Blind Seer then implored that there is no task of greater importance than unifying the faithful and dispelling the delusions that have held humankind in bondage for so long. Such is the destiny of an Archon, Sepṭu propounded, opining that each Great Age has been characterized by great leaders who have intuitively aided the forces of the Light. For the first time pointedly addressing Bes (Bisu Aha (the "Fighter")), Sepṭu propounded that "such Spiritual Warriors and Seekers of the Way are often called upon to confront the demons of their time, …yet the warrior must first overcome the demons within himself."

"If one is to imbue reverence for the Forces of the Light, one must be truly reverent himself; it is such reverence that aligns the spirit, and it is by the Law of Attraction that such alignment channels the collective will and reverence of the faithful constituting the station of the Archon." Sepṭu further informed that 'the supernatural powers an Archon attains are obtained by virtue of the exalted piety of the faithful." And Lord Bes, Sepṭu appended, "by vision of the disruption portending the passing of the present Age and arrival of the next, heed that you shall indeed need the reverence of *all* the faithful."

A now visibly tired Sepṭu again appeared to gaze deeply into the fire, as the young Sage again aided him in grasping the small bowl before him …as he extended his blessing to the Prophesy of the House of Tellem and to its aspiring "Archon, Bes (Bisu, Aha (the "Fighter"))¸ ritually binding the blessing with the last sip from a small bowl taken first by Sepṭu, then by each of the others in unison. With this, the old Seer gradually slumped into a sound sleep as the ever-attendant young Sage rescued the small bowl from his slipping grasp. The Grand Sage Thmei gestured that it was time they departed the abode of the Mystic Seer.

In their return journey down the small mountain, Thmei affirmed the blessing bestowed by Sepṭu and sought to affirm the understanding of his message regarding the need to align all the clans, whom he termed "*all* the faithful"'. Thmei opined that to convert, rather than conquer, is an act of the highest sovereignty, advising that "for this one must transcend the dualities of right and wrong, and notions of good and bad, and gravitate to that which is most effective. A feat best achieved through harmonization,' the Grand Sage resolved, as she recalled the faint auras they witnessed around the celestial bodies during their shared vision with Sepṭu, noting that 'the "auras" are emanations of the life forces within the celestial bodies. By the tone of voice, Thmei emphasized that everything in the Cosmos, both visible and invisible, vibrates with the resonating forces of "life"' for there to be peace, there must be harmony, then there is order.

"It is important to know that the life force of every being resonates at its own unique rate (or frequency), as does every distinct group", Thmei illuminated. "Nothing is more powerful than the cultivation of life force through the strengthening of the inner spirit," she propounded. Know that by the 'Law of Attraction,' similar (vibrating) frequencies tend to align, with the stronger frequency dominating and the weaker. In the clans of man, this is manifested as harmony", the Grand Sage illuminated; "only chaos and discord are fomented by war, peaceful interaction foments mutual accord and harmony." "As Sepṭu alluded", Thmei further explained, "the supernatural powers imbued in an Archon are availed through the channeling of the collective reverence, piety and determination of the faithful, and his blessing was indeed based on the hope that by your shared vision, you will heed the need for reverence by the *all* the faithful of the land'.

The Grand Sage then illuminated that "in many ways, your adversaries, the totem clans of the Great Rhino and their allies …are much like you; to destroy rather than cultivate their reverence seems self-defeating …for an aspiring Archon. "The Great Rhino and their allies are not without reverence", added Nebti, leader of the main clan of the Eland in the village at the base of the maintain" Most, like most, he continued, "they are "Followers of Heru". However, they ascribe to a different interpretation of the blessings of Heru. Their Sages believe the blessing bestowed by Heru is the source of all abundance. During this period of darkness, as the abundance has waned, they have come to believe it is the will of Heru that the fittest, those most capable, be most prominent and rule. This has fostered an ethos that has served them well as scarcity spread over the lands; it is an ethos that has allowed them to survive and prosper."

"An ethos that by your very presence you threaten", Thmei noted, "you have left your adversaries little choice but to fight and defend. The Seers of Gondar have for generations propagated the notion that a great leader would arise to usher in the change that the next Great Age portends; this is the reason the clans of the Great Rhino so quickly aligned their allies against you and any such force that threatens their existing order. It is harmonizing", the Grand Sage opined, "to view things from your adversary's perspective; the Seers among the Great Rhino proselytize that Heru is a living emanation of the Celestial Tree of Life; embodiment of the divine fire emanating, in serpentine-like fashion, from the *Sacred Tree*.

"The Fetish Priest of the Great Rhino propounds that the energy coursing through nature, and each man, woman, and child, is a serpentine force that each must master to transcend normal human limits and attain the powers needed to survive in a world of dwindling abundance. It is a belief at the very heart of the warrior ethos of the clans of the Great Rhino. The Seers of the Rhino are not unaware of the approaching new age …nor the change it surely portends", the Grand Sage informed, advising that "it is their inherent fear of this change that you must disarm; you must disarm the forces of fear, rage, and resistance." You must cast aside the use of crude strategies of conquest, Nebti proffered, propounding that, "animosity begets animosity; if you continue acting adversarial, they'll continue to resist …no matter what clever strategies you employ."

"Every evil thought, word or action foments a bad vibration and does harm," Thmei reminded, adding that "conversely, every good thought, word or action produces a good vibration and does good. To break the cycles of negativity, Lord Bes, Thmei advised, you need to harmonize with their beliefs; the change will emerge as a result. It is often harmonizing, the Grand Sage then coyly informed, 'if you can find something that you both are able to unite against, a common enemy, such as the looming Chaos'. Thmei opined that the Great Rhino must come to know that Chaos and Darkness were the primordial state before creation, the first thing to exist, complete opposite of the emergent divine forces of Order and Light. That the cosmic battle between these two infinite forces began at the beginning of time, and that, as part of the Divine Order, it is incumbent upon man to resist and overcome the power of the Dark.

That the Dark uses fear, limitation, privilege, punishment, deceit, violence, repression, and struggle over basic needs to turn people and clans against one another, weakening the brotherhood of man. They must come to know that Divine Light is stronger than the Dark; that the reach of the Light is boundless, as is its purpose. The utmost the Dark can achieve is winning people over to their detriment, destroying their contact with the higher self. An ally needs to see that the benefits of supporting you outweigh the benefits of going against you, the Grand Sage propounded, paraphrasing the point made by Septu, that 'we are about to enter a new Age, whether it is characterized by the forces of Chaos and Darkness, or forces of Divine Order and Light shall be determined by the harmonized reverence and collective will of the faithful'.

At this stage of his enlightenment Bes (Bisu Aha) no longer sought the absolute defeat and acquiescence of each enemy, coming to understand that at this stage of his trial, violence for its own sake was self-defeating; he rather sought to tactically position and contrast his overwhelming forces and allies with the weakening position of the Great Rhino, as their vassals, one by one, abandons them upon hearing the word of the Seers of Gondar. Nebti advised that the Eland will dispatch emissaries to inform of the blessing of Septu upon *Prophesy of the House of Tellem* and the mission of Bes (Bisu) as its Prophet. He then explained that the clans of the Eland are revered for more than their spiritual wisdom. The formidable totem clans of the Ibex of Ras Dejen are self-ascribed guardians of the Eland.

To the Ibex, Nebti explained, such is the path to ascendance for the unanointed. They have taken as their mission to protect and project the influence of the Eland, whom they view as anointed. Nebti informed that a small emissary delegation, protected by the redoubtable warriors of the Ibex, will accompany you on your return Lord Bes; it is a configuration that will be recognizable to the clans of the great (northwestern) plateau; all will have by then been well informed by our earlier emissaries. After a well-deserved night's rest at the village at the base of the large inselberg, Bes (Bisu), Nebti, Apu-t and his small cadre, together with emissaries of the Eland, began their (return) journey across the floor of the Valley of the Inselbergs.

The procession emerged from mystic north, where they were joined at the top of the pass by warriors of the clans of the Ibex of Ras Dejen, who positioned themselves to shield and protect the mission of the procession. According to faint lore Bes (Bisu, Aha (the "Fighter")) walked before the procession onto the battlefield west of Bahir Dar (Bahir Giyorgis), flanked by Nebti to his left and Apu-t to his right, where they then summoned and were then joined in the center of the battlefield by Ḥun-sāḥu, leader of the northernmost clans of the Great Rhino, together with the leader of the vassal totem clan of the Jackal, Sed, as well as Abu and Medjed

After Nebti affirmed the blessing of Sepṭu upon the Prophesy and the mission of Bes (Bisu) as its prophet, Bes advised a still wary Ḥun-sāḥu that there would be no dispossession, pillage or plunder; that what is needed and what they seek is an abiding peace in which all shall align in the battle against the chaos and darkness that oppresses the land and the clans who depend upon the land. Bisu told of the great cosmic battle between the forces of Chaos and Darkness and the forces of Order and Light he witnessed by shared vision with the Blind Seer, a vision alerting that the fate of the battle, indeed fate itself, shall verily be determined by the harmonized reverence of the faithful among the clans of man. It is said that Bisu extolled the warrior spirit of the clans of the Great Rhino, emphasizing that the battle ahead could not be won without them.

Appealing to the beliefs of the clans of the Rhino, Bes (Bisu) propounded that the battle they join is in defense of the Celestial Tree of Life itself. He called upon Ḥun-sāḥu, as leader of the northernmost clans of the Great Rhino, to join the Eland in declaring their allegiance to the Prophesy and the battle ahead by harmonizing the reverence of the faithful, an objective that can only be achieved in true peace. Bisu advised that this is the message he shall deliver to the clans of the central midlands in route to the south, where he shall then lift the siege at Adaama and deliver the same message to Mer-wer (de facto) leader of the totem clans of the Great Rhino; with this Ḥun-sāḥu assented and agreed to provide Bes (Bisu) a small delegation to affirm such to Mer-wer.

In the central midlands, Bisu arrived with a procession thrice its original size; this with the additions of the huge armies of Abu and Medjed. The Great Rhino clans of the central midlands were largely independent and elusive but would nonetheless coalesce to fight together on a larger scale when forced to do so, coming together in a sudden coordinated fashion to all at once overwhelm an unsuspecting adversary, then just as suddenly disband, disappearing in all directions at once, confounding an enemies pursuit. Such was the plight of Menew as he and his army sought to subdue and weaken the control of the Rhino over the central midlands. By the time Bes (Bisu, Aha (the "Fighter")) and his huge force arrived, the Warrior Queen Pakhet (known as "Pakhet the Great") of the Black Lion clans of the Northern Wollo highlands, south of Gondar, had joined the battle.

For this reason, the Rhino clans of the central midlands had separately fled to the refuge of their northeastern lair by the time of the arrival of Bes. Once there, what occurred next must have seemed a curious twist of fate, for they immediately found themselves surrounded by the warriors of the Black Lion led by the Warrior Queen Pakhet. Having received an emissary from the Seers of Gondar, as well as a messenger from Anhur instructing that she aid in the campaign for the central midlands, the ever-astute warrior queen observed the discrete retreat by the clans of the Rhino and, familiar with their northeastern lair, set a trap, and awaited in ambush. Once sprung, Pakhet's warriors held fast the Rhino, as she then sent a message, summoning and directing Menew and his forces to the hidden lair.

Menew he and his forces joined those of Pakhet, fully encircling the Rhino northeastern stronghold, with ultimatums of force and death, lest they capitulate and accede to allegiance. Upon arrival, like at the battlefield at Bahir Dar, Bes met with the leaders of the Rhino clans of the midlands and informed them there would be no dispossession, pillage or plunder, that what is needed and what is being achieved is an abiding peace in which all shall align in a great battle against the chaos and darkness that has long oppressed the land and the clans who depend upon the land. Bisu then again told of the great cosmic battle between the forces of Darkness and the forces of Light he witnessed by shared vision with Septu and that the fate of the battle, indeed fate itself, shall verily be determined by the reverence and will of the faithful among the clans of man.

Bisu (Bes, Aha (the fighter)) informed of the accord and allegiance of Ḥun-sāḥu, again propounding that the battle to be joined is in defense of the Celestial Tree of Life itself. Bisu called upon the noble leaders of the midland clans of the Rhino to declare their allegiance to the 'Prophesy,' as it has been blessed by Septu, most exalted of the Seers of Gondar, and join him in the battle ahead by strengthening and focusing the reverence among their clans. Bisu extolled the warrior spirit of the great clans of the Rhino and again emphasized that the battle ahead could not be won without them. Bisu informed once again that this is the message he shall also deliver to Mer-wer ("the great black") upon lifting the siege at Adaama, to which each leader of the Rhino clans of the midlands acceded, assenting to allegiance to the 'Prophesy and Bes (Bisu) as its prophet.

At Adaama, when Bisu and his procession finally arrived, they found the warriors of the Black Lion clans of Anhur had joined those led by Segeb and, together with the forces of Khente-Khtai, Dedun and Kherau, had further tightened the siege. Bisu summoned Segeb and Kherau, instructing they unconditionally lift the siege, after which he dispatched a trio of messengers to Mer-wer; one from the contingent allotted by Ḥun-sāḥu, one from the reverent clans of the Eland, and one from the Guardians of the Prophesy. The message they carried was of the story and blessing of the Prophesy of the House of Tellem and Bes (Bisu) as its prophet by Septu, most exalted of the Seers of Gondar …with an offer of reconciliation. The message requested Mer-wer join Bisu, alone in the center of the battlefield, where Bisu affirmed the fullness of the message that had been given.

Though the sheer size of his force was now clearly superior, Bisu again affirmed there would be no dispossession, pillage, or plunder and again told of the great cosmic battle between the forces of Chaos and Darkness, which oppress the lands and all who depend upon the lands, and the forces of Order and Light which foment the good things of life. Bisu again told of how the battle to be joined is in defense of the Celestial Tree of Life itself and how the fate of the battle, and indeed fate itself, shall be determined by the reverence and will of the faithful among the clans of man. Bisu again extolled the warrior spirit of the great clans of the Rhino and again emphasized that the battle ahead could not be won without them. To which a still wary Mer-wer inquired as to how would one channel reverence?' Which Bes relied on that "it will take strong and inspired leadership, such as that Mer-wer (the "Great Black") provides."

"Such a grand leader", Bisu opined, "will be needed to head a Grand Council of Elders on the great plateau; as the largest of the clans, the (de facto) leader of the clans of the Great Rhino would seem the most appropriate choice,' he then openly resolved. To this, Mer-wer took a moment of pause, then replied, "I know little of such spiritual endeavors", to which Bisu assured, there shall be elders from the reverent clans of the Eland, as well as the spiritual warriors of the clans of the Ibex of Ras Dejen to aid you, and, given his acceptance, Bisu revealed, I shall appoint the noble Anhur as Viceroy to guide your hand. As Mer-wer took another pause for thought, Bisu reiterated that the battle to be joined is in defense of the Celestial Tree of Life, and indeed fate itself, to which Mer-wer (the "Great Black") then acceded, assenting to allegiance with the mission of Bisu.

The accord at Adaama was marked with several days of great celebration at the Rhino stronghold, as clans from across the lands of the great (northwestern) plateau sent envoys and gifts of homage to the prophecy and "Lord Bes" as its prophet. After a deserved celebration and needed rest, the Eland and Ibex returned to Gondar, Bisu, Apu-t, and a small cadre journeyed north to Dese to meet and seek the accord of Anhur to become Viceroy of the Great (northwestern) Plateau. Bes (Bisu) and his entourage were met at Dese with pageantry worthy of all he had achieved. The Anhur "Lion of the North" made clear his allegiance to Bisu as sovereign of the 'Lands of the Plateaus'. Having previously spent hours under the tutelage of the ever-faithful Apu-t, Anhur understood well the challenge of his undertaking and its importance to the task still ahead.

Upon request of Bes (Bisu), Anhur graciously accepted his appointment as Viceroy, permitting Bisu (Bes, Aha (the fighter)), upon his return to Adaama, to apprise the Generals of the six Armies, Dedun, Kherau, Medjed, Abu, Khente-Khtai and Menew that they and their warriors are to return to their home provinces, not to disband, but rather be transformed into an "Army of the Faithful", disseminating and holding fast to the vision of the Prophesy. Thus did the long struggle of the third trial end, as subtly as it began, as Bisu, along with Kherau and Menew, first returned to the province of the clans of the Black Leopard on the Southeastern (or middle) Plateau, where Bes and the clan elders anointed Kherau as (de facto) leader of the clans in his place.

It is thus that Bisu (Bes, Aha (the fighter)) then returned victoriously to the *Sanctuary at Laas Geel* on the Somalian Plateau, where Apu-t had arranged a fitting reception. He was once again united with the Prophetess Ta-Urt, whom, in accordance with the Prophesy, he then took as his wife. As sovereign, Bisu established residence at the ancient royal city of Berbera, on the northeastern coast, prepared by his faithful Viceroy, Amam. Upon proclamation of Berbera as the royal city of the sovereign, he also gave the first name to ancient "Lands of the Plateaus", collectively declaring them the "Land of Punt", and he its first true Sovereign. Faint legends hold that Bes (Bisu) and Ta-Urt resided at Berbera for three years, preparing for the fourth and final trial of his ascension to Archon.

Mystical Reign of Bes (Bisu)

The fourth and final trial of Bes was that of fulfilling the duality of the Archon, that is, becoming a liaison between those who constitute his station and Netjer through the personages of the Divine Netjeru. The fourth trial is without question the most challenging, Ta-Urt reminded, explaining again to Bisu that to accomplish this aspect of the Prophesy, like Ptah, you must travel into the spiritual realm and enlist the support of the Netjeru. In preparation for this, the Prophetess Ta-Urt diligently instructed Bisu. Over the following weeks, months and years, she instructed them in refining his abilities in meditation. They sojourned at Laas Geel twice each year, during the summer and winter solstice, when the Bes (Bisu) spent hours in meditation, awaiting the right time for his pilgrimage to sacred Ta Netjeru (the "Land of the Gods")

In the third year of his reign, after ritual morning meditation with Apu-t and Ta-Urt at Laas Geel, the Prophetess, at last, revealed that the time for the pilgrimage had arrived. The Prophetess recounted that there are twelve Celestial Ages based on the precession of the equinoxes, a cycle depicted as our world passes through each of these Celestial Ages along its path through the night sky and greater Cosmos. Ancient Seers, long before Ptah discovered the "Secret of the Precession." They divined that after the completion of the cycle of twelve ages, the cycle repeats itself. Ta-Urt illuminated that it is a cycle said to last 25,968 years, a time span the ancient Seers called the "Great Year."[cxlvi]

As the trio emerged from Laas Geel in the dead of night, Ta-Urt instructed, "look up to the night sky", noting that "over the long ages, great Seers have traced and depicted the movement of our world through the celestial totems assigned the twelve great ages." The Prophetess illuminated that each Age lasts 2,000 to 2,500 years, depending on the breadth of the constellation (among other factors). Ta-Urt explained that the Great Ages are measured by the Pleiades, the cluster of stars nearest our world and most obvious to the naked eye in the night sky, as our world can be seen to move through each constellation.[cxlvii] The Pleiades have been used as celestial timekeepers by knowledgeable Seers for untold ages; it is through the understanding of the cycle of the "Great Year" that such Seers divined the Ages.[cxlviii]

Ta-Urt added, 'that such Seers have been in a long quandary over what appears a hindrance in the arrival of the Age of Leo. It is a postulation of many, led by the Great Seer Upast of the House of Tellem, that the hindrance in the progression of the celestial cycle is caused by the advent of the "Great Synchronicity." Such synchronicities are said to disclose ephemeral disjuncture in the spiritual and physical realms, portending what is inside on the outside. According to the Prophet Tellem, all things are interconnected, and this interconnectedness allows all things to affect or be affected by all other things. A reciprocating principle that, in part, defines the dynamic between the spiritual realm archetype of the physical realm.

"The physical realm is reflexively informed through its reciprocal connection to the spiritual realm", Ta-Urt illuminated, "it is in this way that spirit shapes matter and matter affects the spirit. It is thus that the consequences and effects of human deeds affect fate and destiny", the Prophetess noted, connoting that "the intended role of man is one of guardianship, harmonizing with nature through reverence and enlightenment. A world in which the righteous are prosperous and happy, however", she noted solemnly, "in a world of darkness and chaos, it is the wicked that are prosperous and happy", noting further that, "it is the wicked that have been prosperous and happy in our world for many generations. It is thus that the Great Seers surmised that chaos prevails in the eternal battle between the forces of Darkness and Light.

Ta-Urt informed us that the journey ahead is long but less than arduous; we must travel across the lowlands to the lands of the totem clans of the Hippopotamus at the foot of Ta Netjeru (Mt Kenya). The Hippopotamus clans reside in the forests and foothills of *Ta Netjeru*, the "Land of the God," where the Netjeru are said to reside in the upper highlands. In the caverns at the foot of Ta Netjeru is where we will meet Upast, Ta-Urt informed. Metni, a leader among the Hippopotamus clans of the forests, met Bes (Bisu) and Ta-Urt and their small cadre at the edge of the forest approaching Ta Netjeru. Metni had known the Prophetess Ta-Urt since her youth and warmly welcomed her return with the Bisu, advising them that Upast would be their arrival. The Queen Mother of the House of Tellem shall duly join them.[cxlix]

They then traversed the fascinating landscape of continuous forest tree stands, with interlocking canopies extending for miles; *Ta Netjeru*, which can be seen from miles away, was (and is) itself surrounded by such forests. There is much history preserved there that might otherwise have been lost, Ta-Urt informed, before then advising that they will first encounter the ancient clans who guard the sacred forests, those who have inhabited and for untold centuries used the hidden caves in the forests as a refuge. Descendants of the old ancestral clans expanded into these forests and hidden caves during the earliest of times; caves are often interconnecting networks, allowing the warriors of these clans to seemingly appear from nowhere in the forest and disappear just as mysteriously.[cl]

The landscape ahead has an array of such caves, Ta-Urt further informed, explaining that most are uninhabited, and many are left unexplored. However, this was not the case with the network of caves at the base of Ta Netjeru, inhabited by the main totem clan of the Hippopotamus, descendants of the House of Tellem. Theirs was a spectacular interconnecting cave network, extending through the Naro Moru forest and foothills to the base of Ta Netjeru. Metni himself was the (de facto) leader of the clans in the Naro Moru forest. It was his charge to guide the Prophetess and aspiring Archon to the abode of the Queen Mother of the main clan at Ta-Netjeru. It was in the mysterious cavern village at the base of Ta Netjeru that Queen Mother Ahti awaited and prepared for the fourth and final trial.[cli]

Mount Kenya (Ta Netjeru) is the second-highest mountain in Africa and the main water catchment area for the two largest rivers in Kenya, the Tana and Ewaso Ng'iso. The serenity of the Mountain has appealed to the spiritual imagination of ancient Seers, Sages and Prophets throughout the Ages. Since the earliest of time, the sacred mountain has been known as "Ta Netjeru" (the "Land of the Gods"). While the mountain straddles the equator, it is usually capped with ice and snow, with ancient glaciers nestled in its rugged peaks. For many during the early ages, the most symbolic aspect of the sacred mountain was its twin peaks because it was believed they were closest to the heavens, where the Netjeru resided.

The mountain actually has three peaks; Batian is the highest peak. Nelion the second-highest peak. And lastly, Point Lenana. Its two highest peaks called the great "Twin Peaks", Batian and Nelion, are located near the center of the mountain range and have a somewhat Alpine appearance, with the two peaks within three hundred yards of each other. Batian and Nelion are separated by a space anciently known as the "Gate of the Mists," …which was deemed a highly spiritual place. The Gate of the Mists is where the night sky is filled with constellations and galaxies most have never seen; a sacred place where on a clear night, the shimmering in the heavens seems to outshine the darkness.

Bestriding the equator, Mount Kenya is not only the geographic heartland of the wider region, but the great Twin Peaks of the Gate of the Mists are at the center of it all.[clii] Majestic Mount Kenya (Ta Netjeru) erupts from the plains like a vast pyramid with a base forty (40) miles in diameter until, at 14,000 feet in elevation, it narrows and makes a spectacular, jagged leap toward the heavens. Above the rain forests of its lower slopes is what is known as the "Bamboo Forests", a thicket where bamboo stands are so dense that passage is only possible along elephant paths. The bamboo is over thirty feet tall, growing from massive rootstocks, with new shoots developing almost continuously, while older ones die, but remain standing for years. Higher up the mountain, the Bamboo Forests give way to the upper montane forests, where a few tree species of the lower rainforest have reached.[cliii][cliv]

Covered in mist and mystery, the legend of the cloud-shrouded Twin Peaks of Batian and Nelion, as they soar over 17,000 feet into a tapestry of clouds, is that here is where the unknowable creator (Netjer) dispenses his blessings. There are countless stories, legends and myths to this account, the most ancient being that this is the earthly abode of the Netjeru, the many faces and aspects of Netjer; that here, the *Terrestrial Netjeru* represent the mystical, transformative forces of Netjer (the "Netjeru") that interact, maintain and synchronize existence. While Celestial Netjeru, with whom Terrestrial Netjeru interact, are the forces and energies through which Netjer created the Cosmos and the order through which it is protected and maintained.

Faint legend alludes to the "Gate of the Mists" as both the portal and abode of the divine Netjeru. A place of sheer, undeniable beauty where they are close to heaven at the top of the mountain; where, according to legend, they employ their magical powers and divine abilities. The oldest of oral legends hold that it was the eldest of the Celestial Netjeru, the "Paut Netjeru", the Nine who are One; those who are sometimes portrayed together as a single composite entity, and sometimes separately, and sometimes in binary form, who gave shape to chaos through their will, and whose powerful vibrational energy can be felt by those so attuned as they approach the Gate.[clv] The ancient Seers intuitively knew that wherever the earth's energy appeared to gather into a vortex was a sacred place of spiritual power.[clvi]

Contemporary theorists hypothesize that such vortexes are areas of high-energy concentrations originating from magnetic, spiritual, or unknown sources; they are also considered gateways or portals to the spiritual realms. Vortexes are detectable in the physical realm as areas of high energy concentrations, often with faint halos of lights emanating and observed hovering well above them. Theorists postulate that such vortexes are a feature of the spiritual realm that form of necessity to regulate, balance and stabilize the electromagnetic field of the physical realm. Researchers have been able to show that there is such a helical vortex of energy emanating from the Twin Peaks of Mount Kenya (Ta-Netjeru); however, the vortex appears more subtle than most and depends on the coming together of certain unexplained conditions.

Well below this, in the upper timberline forest, within the lower reaches of the province of the Netjeru, were said to be the mysterious caves of the mystical clans and brotherhood of the "Nōmmo"; most orthodox of the ancient sects of the House of Tellem. Legend holds that the little-known ancient sect inhabited a network of caves with a central chamber over a thousand square feet in size. The entrance to the secretive cave was said to be nondescript and barely noticeable. Yet, from the interior of its main chamber, it was a refuge to behold. The main chamber was a rounded, high-ceiling, multilevel cave complex consisting of three levels, with two narrow passageways leading from the main chamber to the two upper chambers. The main chamber was the most extensive, with a gallery of pillars supporting a high ceiling and passageways leading to chambers where the esoteric sect resided. Ancient Seers of the Nōmmo were said to regularly ascend to the Gate of Mists, below which, on a clear night, they tracked the cycles associated with the Pleiades, those of the precession of the Ages.

As they finally arrived, Metni led Bes (Bisu) and Ta-Urt and their cadre to a small waterfall partially hidden by thickets, with the entrance to the caves visible beneath the waterfall. The bridge brought them to a path leading behind the waterfall to the entrance, where Metni then led the way down a few steps and through a narrow passageway to a cavern of the village, where they were met by a young Seeker known as Ur-pehti, an escort sent by the Queen Mother. Ur-pehti, in turn, led Bisu and Ta-Urt through the narrow entrance of a separate cave network where, in a cavern near the interior entrance, the Queen Mother Ahti patiently awaited their arrival. Ahti first warmly welcomed the return of Ta-Urt, in whose training she had participated during her adolescence. The Queen Mother then warmly greeted and welcomed Bes (Bisu), whom she revered as the "aspirant Archon."

Then turning to Ur-pehti, the Queen Mother requested he guide the couple to comfortable accommodations to eat, rest and recuperate and that Metni guide their cadre to accommodations where they might eat, rest, recuperate and await the return of Bes (Bisu) and Ta-Urt after completion of the fourth trial. Yet, after the briefest rest, the Queen Mother sent Ur-pehti to request Bisu and the Prophetess join her in the cavern in which they first greeted. There they found Ahti seated near a small fire at the center of the cavern. Ahti apologized for interrupting their rest but informed them that "time itself is of the essence, and "the opportunity presented by the Great Synchronicity is fleeting." Queen Mother informed that not in the morrow, but the following day the Great Seer, Upàst, last of only four such Prophets of the House of Tellem, including Tellem himself, to journey into the spiritual realm …shall arrive here, from his village in the highlands, to fulfill his role in the Prophesy.

Of the four prophets to have journeyed to the spiritual realm, Ahti informed, you, Lord Bisu, have auspiciously arrived at a time when you shall be aided by two such experienced voyagers, the esteemed Upàst and myself. There is much to discuss and far more to actually do and experience in order that you be fully prepared upon his arrival; let us begin with the great celestial timekeepers. The Queen Mother then told of the Pleiades, a prominent star cluster visible in the night sky; this as Ur-pehti discretely joined the group away from the fire, alongside the cavern wall, with a very old ritual drum. Ahti noted that Ur-pehti was a ritual drummer in the oldest of traditions, interrupting herself before she went on to explain that the Pleiades actually contains hundreds of stars, with only a handful visible to the unaided eye. The Queen Mother illuminated that the brightest stars in the cluster are known as the "Seven Sisters", an important time-marker for great Seers throughout the Ages.

Ahti informed that the Pleiades have been observed to have four major processional points, one when they disappear from the sky (conjunct with the sun), another when they are at the eastern horizon just before dawn (the "heliacal" rising), yet another when they are on the eastern horizon just after sunset (the "acronychal" rising), and finally when they appear directly overhead at midnight (the "culmination").[clvii]. The heliacal rising has, for many if not most, anciently marked the beginning of each new year.[27] In contrast, the acronychal rising period through the culmination was considered a time when the gateways to the spiritual realm were open, gateways between the physical realm and the spiritual realm.

'The spiritual realm is verily all around us, and though we cannot touch, taste, smell, hear or see it,' the Queen Mother illuminated, explaining that 'it is in many ways more real than the physical realm, which is our world. Ahti knowledge that, under due tutelage of the Prophetess Ta-Urt, Bisu had, for the past three years, diligently endeavored to cultivate, enhance and refine his personal powers of meditation, the Queen Mother granted that such skills require adept self-mastery, yet focused on inner-vision, rather than the experiential aspects of the meditation. The Queen Mother informed that the meditation of the ancients guides your journey to the experiential aspects of the spiritual realm. Recognizing their long tiring journey, the Queen Mother then graciously bid goodnight, requesting arise to meet in the early hours of dawn in the morrow.

The earliest ancient legends of Ta Netjeru ("Mount Kenya") are intertwined with the tales of Archons in roles of demigods, coalescing the faithful and rallying the sons of men during the long dawn of the Age of Man. "Archon" means "to stand between the people and a transcendent Creator; the Archon as demigod would lead legions of Netjeru in the battle between the forces of Order and Light and those of Chaos and Darkness. The Ancient Prophets honored one thing above all else, the emergence of Order from Chaos; the spheres of the Celestial Heavens themselves were said to manifest order among the realms of the Cosmos. The Prophets believed that causally related events in the spiritual and physical realms occur within a narrow window. Such synchronicities foreshadow the prospect of change, which can be positively affected, indeed altered, by pious spiritual intervention.

The Legends

They reconvened in the same cavern early hours of dawn the morning, with Ahti informing that they shall begin forthwith, advising that the ancient ritual begins with a traditional libation, as she motioned that her young protégé Seshat, who stood just beyond the cavern, enter the cavern and place a small bowl of the libation before Bisu who found it reminiscent of the ritual at Gondar. With Ta-Urt sitting to his right and Ahti to her right, the three triangulated the small fire at the center of the cavern as Bisu slowly and solely partook of the libation. This is Ur-pehti began a rhythmic ritual drumming that resonated throughout the cavern, rendering Bisu amenable to the guidance of Ahti, who directed him 'enter within, relax and allow yourself to journey and awaken in the spiritual realm'.[clviii]

---

[27] Maunder, 1906; Sparavigna, 2008; White, 2016

While still seemingly listening to the guidance of the Queen Mother, Bes is said to have suddenly startled, opening his eyes. . Astutely grasping the still somewhat shaken look in the eyes of Bisu, before he could utter a word, Ahti asked that he first describe what he saw about him …when first he opened his eyes. Bisu is said to have told of how he found himself sitting alone in the cavern and that they (Ta-Urt, Ahti and Ur-pehti) were each gone, to which Ahti is said to have replied, 'no Bisu, it is you who were gone.

To our eyes, you sat relaxed, undisturbed, until your sudden startle when you wiped your eyes as if clearing them and, as I suppose, found yourself again here in the physical realm'. Rising to her feet, signaling that Ur-pehti ceases drumming, Ahti is said to have instructed that after a good night's rest, they reconvene in the morrow and try again. Retiring to their cavern, where they lay together Ta-Urt sought to comfort and strengthen Bisu, softly stroking his brow as she soothingly advised, the only way to overcome the sudden fear of the unknown is to step into it and thoroughly experience it; for when one experiences the unknown, it transforms and becomes the known.

The Prophetess counseled that he must transform his fear 'with the serenity and single-pointedness of purpose and focus his consciousness on the center of his Being and the connectedness of all things. With this, the two slept until just before dawn, awakened by the young Sage Seshat, who brought a variety of foods that they might eat before reconvening with Ahti and Ur-pehti. After the briefest of meals, they reconvened at the cavern in which they first greeted the Queen Mother.

In the early hours just after dawn the next morning, they again found themselves seated and triangulated around a small fire in the center of the cavern; Bisu again partook of the libation as the rhythmic sound and vibrations of the drumming again resonated throughout the cavern. Yet this time, Ahti advised that, as time itself is of the essence, she too shall seek to journey into the spiritual realm, and the High Priestess Ta-Urt shall provide guidance. The Prophetess explained that when Ptah journeyed into the spiritual realm, it was by the guidance of his trusted spouse, the Mystic Sekhmet, in whose voice and words he comforted; so too shall you be comforted by the resonance, voice and words of your spouse, the Prophetess Ta-Urt.

Ahti now joined Bisu in partaking of the libation as they again sat around a small fire at the center of the cavern. The rhythmic sound and vibrations of drumming again resonated throughout, with her and Bisu each becoming amenable to the entrancement of Ta-Urt. The Prophetess directed that each 'close your eyes, as she then intoned, 'relax evermore deeply, feel the connectedness of all things, yet maintain your awareness; find your center, enter within and allow yourself to journey, and awaken in the spiritual realm'. Less than an hour later, with the guidance of Ta-Urt, Bisu and Ahti slowly awoke to find themselves again seated around the fire in the center of the cavern. In the tradition of Ptah, Ta-Urt prompted each of the voyagers to relate their experiences while still fresh in their minds.

Bes (Bisu) told of how when he cautiously opened his eyes, he again found himself in the cavern. However, he sensed he was not alone, and when he lifted his gaze before were three short human-like Beings of a kind not seen before witnessed, peering from perches within the cavern. As Bes told of how when he rose to his feet for a closer look, a voice not from one of the Beings echoed throughout the cavern. The Being seemed to appear from within a recess in the cavern wall, from where he approached and stood before me, and without altering his eye contact, implored, "you must gain an immediate understanding of our plight; the moment is wasting, know that the spiritual and physical realms are but aspects of a single realm, the "Two that are One." The Being further informed that "we of the spiritual and physical realms each battle a common adversary, Chaos.

The Queen Mother told of arriving in the spiritual realm in the ancestral lands of the Tellem, in the wooded foothills at the eastern base of Ta Netjeru, where, among the flora of the foothills, she found herself, amongst Nature Spirits amid the flowers, plants and trees they ensoul. Ahti explained how she found herself drawn to her spiritual guide, a Tree Nymph of a Baobab tree in the woodlands who cautioned of an approaching peril and a growing fear. Ahti further explained that this was an awareness shared with her spiritual guide by a High Fairy of the Baobab Trees, a High Fairy of mythic proportion whom it is said once critically aided Ptah himself,

Ahti explained that the spiritual realm is inhabited by Nature Spirits and Elemental Beings, the latter ensouling the four fundamental elements: each belonging to a separate element, while the former are those who ensoul plants and trees. Ahti further explained that Nature Spirits and Elemental Beings show themselves in forms associated with what they ensoul, a form the observer will readily recognize. To the imagination of humankind, Nature Spirits and Elemental Beings manifest as Gnomes, Pixies, Sirens, Fairies, Elves, Sprites and Trolls; personifications in human-like form, Ahti noted, adding that the Beings first encountered by Bes, by his description, were Gnomes, Elemental Beings who ensoul living stone. However, the Being encountered second appears to have been one of the most mysterious of Beings …a Troll, those who ensoul the molten core of our world.

Early ancient African spiritual beliefs and practices were embodied by generations upon generations of handed-down oral tradition rather than scripture, including belief in higher and lower "attributes" of the unknowable creator. The most fundamental of early ancient precepts propounded that the Cosmos came into being during a titanic struggle between two opposing forces, one the forces of Light and Order and the Forces of Darkness and Chaos. Out of this battle, fought since the beginning of time, all of creation was said to have come into being. Early ancient spiritual traditions held that the forces of Chaos and Order are opposites of the same dialectic and so strive against each other; that existence is a phenomenon of the equilibrium between these two forces.

This Cosmic dialectic was deemed an important aspect of the Divine Order and something which was manifest not only throughout the World around us but also within our lives …in an all-pervading and ubiquitous manner. The eternal Cosmic Battle is an essential feature of the transcendent template of the Divine Order; it portends a dynamic kind of equilibrium, representing the ultimate unity of the Cosmos. The struggle between the Forces of Chaos and Darkness and the Forces of Order and Light is, in essence, the dynamic equilibrium underlying the unity of the Cosmos. There is unity in their separation and separation in their unity. There is chaos in order and order in chaos. That chaos exists in order, and order in chaos is both mechanism and impetus of change; there is no permanent chaos or order. Both are transitory because everything changes.

Thus, life without struggle was deemed impossible in the physical or the spiritual realms; the eternal struggle against ever-enduring chaos was deemed "the Way of Netjer" (the unknowable creator); this was deemed the essence of the contest between the diametrically opposed forces, and its purpose. Ancient prophets described this dialectic as happening throughout the realms of the Cosmos, as well as transcendentally within each individual. The cosmic battle was depicted as occurring on a scale that literally encompassed the entire Cosmos and all of Creation. A battle said to have begun at the beginning of time, upon the emergence of the Forces of Order and Light from Chaos and Darkness. The earliest ancient legends allude to the many great feats of Bes (Bisu) in the spiritual realm.

To an extent, the ancient oral legends and myths reflect an underlying truth, the celestial sphere is more than mere physical existence. The Cosmos is partitioned into "separate" planes or dimensions, which function as parallel realms of reality. Early ancient spiritual belief espoused that the hierarchy of realms is interrelated, with each plane sustained by the others and all subject to a milieu of natural laws, both metaphysical and physical. Theoretical astrophysicists purport that the "matrix of energies" that fomented the hierarchy of realms came into being as a result of the initial act of creation and the subsequent effects of the Big Bang that created the Cosmos. During early antiquity, the Seers and Sages recognized and identified this "matrix of energies", and indeed the presence of energy in everything, with the divine Netjeru, personifying the attributes of Netjer.

The ancient conception of the Cosmos as a hierarchical order began during the dawn of early antiquity. It is reflected in their concept of the "dialectic" of Cosmos and Chaos, a dialectic said to have given rise and impetus to the hierarchy of the Divine Netjeru. The cosmic battle between these metaphysical forces is both metaphorical and very real; an eternal battle between two opposed forces in a struggle that is said to have presaged creation in stages, the first stage being Chaos and Darkness, the last being the emergence of Order and Light. The eternal battle is said to have begun upon the emergence of Order and Light (and the "Cosmos"), and it is this dynamic that the ancient prophets believe gives impetus to the unfolding of creation.[clix] The ancients' saw it as an eternal cosmic drama, a dance between Order and Chaos, Light and Darkness, Good and Evil.

The Legends

In the upper reaches of the upper timberline forest, within the lower of the province of the Netjeru, are the mysterious caves of the Seers of the ancient sect of the "Nōmmo,"; most mystic of the clans of the House of Tellem. The little-known sect inhabited a sprawling network of caves, with a majestic central chamber over one thousand square feet in size. The entrance to the secretive cave was said to be nondescript and barely noticeable. Yet, from the interior, its main chamber was said to be a mountain refuge to behold. The huge main chamber was a rounded, a high-ceiling, multilevel cave with three levels and interconnecting passageways leading to the upper chambers.

The main chamber was said to be the most extensive, with a gallery of pillars the color of supporting a high rounded ceiling and passageways interconnecting the chambers where the families of the esoteric sect resided. The ancient Seers of the Nōmmo were said to regularly ascend the heights to the Gate of Mists, below which, on a clear night, legend holds, they tracked the main cycles associated with the Pleiades; those of the precession of the equinox. Ahti informed that it was not far below the "Gate of the Mists", where, according to lore, the founder of the sect, the Mystic known as Nōmmo, encountered an apparition professing to be the Netjeru who granted Tellem the vision of the Prophesy.

The apparition informed Nōmmo he stood before the portal and abode of the Divine Netjeru of Tr-Netjeru (the "Land of the Gods"), Terrestrial Netjeru, earthly Celestial Æthereals who inhabit the upper highlands of Ta Netjeru. The apparition then availed Nōmmo of a vision that further affirmed the Prophesy and enhanced his understanding of the peril foreshadowed by the omen in the celestial heavens. It was a vision illuminating the motion of the stars that mark the passage of time and that the stars do not rise or set, as do the Sun and Moon, but instead slowly turn counterclockwise around the Northern Star of the era, "Vega."[clx]

But be not misled, the Apparition is said to have apprised Nōmmo as he gazed at the array of constellations and stars comprising the Milky Way Galaxy, which the Apparition called the "Celestial Palace", that 'our world lies within the precincts of the far outer provinces of the Celestial Palace.[clxi] 'Our world,' the Apparition explained, 'has its place at the edge of the Celestial Palace (the "Milky Way Galaxy"), aligning first with our Sun, and ultimately the Great Sun at the center of the Celestial Palace; the brightest star in the ancient night sky.[clxii]

From the perspective of the Seers of the earliest antiquity, it appeared, over the ages, that all the stars in the night sky slowly turn around to the brightest star at the center of the Celestial Palace.[clxiii] Ahti added that "the Apparition informed that the brightest star at the center of the Celestial Palace is itself held in place as it slowly revolves (counterclockwise) around a great void near the center of the Celestial Palace'; this in concordance with the dynamics and equilibrium of the opposing forces of the Cosmos.[clxiv] It is by this Nōmmo observed the precession and antagonisms to the precession of the twelve ages, and by this that he affirmed the advent of the Great Synchronicity and the veracity of the Prophesy'.

The Queen Mother concluded her tale, affirming that 'since the world was young, there have been Netjeru living at the heights of the sacred mountain; it is, for this reason, the ascetic sect of the Nōmmo made their permanent abode in the highlands. Ahti further informed that it is from the cavern villages in the highlands of the Mountains of the Heavens ("Mt Elgon") that Upāst originally descended to pursue the Prophesy. Upāst rarely, if ever, now, descends from the heights of Ta Netjeru, acknowledging that 'it is indeed a perilous journey for one of his great age …which bespeaks the importance he places on the Prophesy. He shall arrive accompanied by a throng of young Seers who regularly trade in obsidian from the heights.

Ahti explained that, like Nōmmo, the great Seer Upāst was permitted through the "Celestial Gate of the Netjeru", where he was granted a vision that took him on a cosmic journey through time and space, not unlike Nōmmo. As it is said, Upāst beheld heavenly bodies in the spiritual realm and the influence they presage on the celestial bodies in the physical realm. It is said that Upāst beheld heavenly bodies under duress in the spiritual realm and witnessed the cosmic battle hindering the procession of the Ages …from the present Age (of Virgo) to the new Age (of Leo), portending alternate eventualities.[clxv]

Although there remains ongoing debate as to the exact beginning of each new age, as measured by the boundaries of the constellations, ancient Seers viewed any overlaps as cycles counter-influenced by the adverse forces. Ancient Seers diligently followed the astronomical traditions of remotest antiquity as passed down through the generations. Seers such as Upāst inherited an intimate knowledge of the night sky and its phenomena; for highland sects such as his, on a clear night, the Milky Way was an animate show …high overhead, animated as a diffuse but cohesive band of celestial lights spanning the length of the night sky.

The great Seers of distant antiquity not only divined the heavens and were first to map and track the cycles of the "Firmament", but they also sought to interpret the anomalies and the change they portend. The ancient Seers tracked the constellations for generations and, by the word of Ahti, were alarmed at a hindrance in the arrival of the new Age (of Leo). The great Seers believed causally related events in the spiritual and physical realms were at the crux of such hindrance; causal events which occur within a narrow window and that such synchronicities can be affected, indeed altered, by pious spiritual intervention.

From an ancient cosmological perspective, all the galaxies were said to converge at a single point ...in the Antares solar system. The huge star "Antares" at the center of the system was seen as the embodiment of sinister, even diabolical powers. Ancient Seers viewed the red star and its solar system as a gateway from the dark sector, the realm of the anti-cosmos (to the degree the anti-cosmos becomes manifest at all).[clxvi]. While most ancient myths are metaphorical, they always reflect an element of truth.[clxvii] In the mythology of the era, Antares was cast as the portal of darkness, where Erebus ("Chaos"), the "Prince of Darkness," and his minions, the dark opposites of the Netjeru, were often found lurking in the shadows.[clxviii] Neither the sun nor any other heavenly bodies are visible from motionless.

In the celestial heavens of the physical realm, massive Antares appears infrared and thus is rarely visible to the naked eye; this is what the ancient Seers asserted to be the cavity to timeless darkness of the Anti-Cosmos that is most often concealed.[clxix] The early ancient Seer Nōmmo first raised alert regarding the Forces of Darkness, alas availing themselves of the "open door" to invade and pursue their mission of destruction in the physical realm. According to Nōmmo, they emerged not only at Antares but also at weak points along certain galactic lines extending from Antares, those intersecting the cosmos and anti-cosmos.

Ancient lore describes our Sun (and solar system) as orbiting around "Alcyone", called the "Great Central Sun,"; the brightest star in the Pleiades" (the "Seven Sisters"), of which our world is a part. Ancient Seers recognized the "Great Year" as the orbit of our world around Alcyone.[clxx] They observed that Alcyone (and all that orbit around it) orbits around a star they called the "Greater Central Sun", a star present-day astronomers call "Sirius A." Sirius was originally composed of two bright bluish stars, the more massive of which exhausted its energy and collapsed into a white dwarf star astronomers call "Sirius B."[clxxi]. Sirius A, the "Greater Central Sun" (and the stars in our galaxy that orbit around it), orbits around a massive black-hole astrophysicists call "Sagittarius A" ...at the galactic center.

The "Greater Central Sun" (Sirius A) was anciently said to dance around a vortex emanating from the Anti-Cosmos (the "black hole") at the galactic center. The ancients' knew that our solar system takes nearly 26 million years to complete its orbit around Alcyone (the "Great Central Sun"), and Alcyone (together with all that orbit around it) takes roughly 225 million years to complete its orbit around the duality of Sirius A (the "Greater Central Sun"), and Sagittarius A (the Black-Hole).[clxxii] How the Seers of earliest antiquity were aware of the Black-Hole at the center of the Galaxy remains a mystery to the scientific community; however, some astute theorists are finally considering the possibility that ancient mystics discovered it through cosmic voyages undertaken in deep states of meditation.

The Great Seer Upāst arrived at the cavern village well after dawn, accompanied and aided by a small group who regularly traded obsidian on behalf of the sect in the heights. Though exhausted from his journey, a stout but somewhat prematurely-aged Upāst insisted upon hearing of the preparation thus far for the journey into the spiritual realm. Convening in the cavern near the entrance of the cavern-villages, the Queen Mother quickly introduced all after a painfully tired Upāst insisted that, rather than rest, he immediately heard of the journeys of she and Bes into the spiritual realm. In the tradition of Ptah and the old mountain sanctuary, Ahti told of arriving in the spiritual realm where she interacted with Pixies, Tree Nymphs, and Fairies.

The Queen Mother told of arriving in the spiritual realm in the wooded foothills of the eastern base of Ta Netjeru, where she found herself amongst the Nature Spirits of the flowers, plants and trees they ensoul in the foothills. Ahti explained that she found herself drawn to her spiritual guide, a Tree Nymph of an ancient Baobab tree in the forests of the foothills, who cautioned of an approaching great peril …and growing fear. Ahti further explained that her spiritual guide gained this awareness through a High Fairy of mythic proportions of the Baobab Trees, a renowned High Fairy whom it is said once lent guidance to Ptah himself. Bes, in turn, told of his encounter with the Gnomes …and a Being Ahti surmised to have been a Troll, who stood before warning that "the moment is wasting", informing that "the spiritual and physical realms battle a common adversary, Chaos."

With this, Ahti insisted on adjourning until a visibly tired Upāst had taken the opportunity to rest and fully recuperate in preparation for the arduous task ahead. It was not until the third day after the arrival of Upāst that all felt sufficiently readied for the final trial of the Prophesy. In was an interim during which Bes, at the behest of Ta-Urt and the abet of Upāst, spent hours in meditation, strengthening the "eye of the mind" (the "imagination") to master the ways of the spiritual warrior. On the night of the third day after the arrival of Upāst, Ahti reconvened all in the small cavern. Once again, with a small fire at the center of the cavern, Bes sitting across the fire from Ta-Urt, with Upāst to his right and Ahti again to his left. It was then the Queen Mother summoned her protégé, Seshat, who again entered and placed separate small bowls of libation before Bes and Upāst, respectively.

Seshat then left, only to return a moment later with Ur-pehti, who assumed his place along the wall of the cavern, as Seshat placed bowls of libation before Ta-Urt and Ahti. The Queen Mother then informed Bes that he and Upāst shall journey together separately into the spiritual realm, where you shall later meet. Ahti informed that the libation before she and Ta-Urt differed from that before Bes and Upāst in that its purpose is to enhance empathic abilities so that they may readily "feel" the emotional state of their charge, which, for Ahti, was Upāst, and for Ta-Urt, Bisu (Bes). The Queen Mother then explained they shall harmonize the verses of guided meditation, facilitating the journey to the spiritual realm. Once there, she instructed, focus only on the voice of your guide; she for Upāst, and Ta-Urt for Bes (Bisu).

As he sipped from his bowl of libation, gesturing that Bes do the same, Upāst explained that among their first tasks shall be to meet at the Threshold of the Duat, where there is no sense of time, only the eternal moment. Upāst further explained we are to meet at the far end of the "Great Crossing:, the interface between the outer celestial sphere and the ethereal plane of the spiritual realm. At the far end of the 'Great Crossing" lies the Threshold, Upāst advised, explaining that, at the end nearest the outer celestial sphere is where you will encounter of the combined legions of the Divine Multiplicity Lord Bes; it is here that you must instill your strategy and battle-plan.

You shall be aided by a High Fairy of the Guardian Netjeru of our world, whom you shall meet at the "Celestial Gate" atop Ta Netjeru ("Mount Kenya"), a place known in the physical realm as the "Gate of Mists"; there, Upāst informed, "you shall meet the High Fairy of the Guardian Netjeru, in her assumed role as senior commander and warlord of the legions of our world." Know that the hierarchy of the legions flows through the succession of ranks and that in the spiritual realm, thought and action can be all but immediate; it is thus crucial that, as Archon, you form to sound a bond with your senior commander.

Ahti then intervened to remind them that the period between the acronychal rising of the Pleiades through its culmination, the time when the gates to the spiritual realm are opened, was upon them and that the Forces o Darkness were surely further availing themselves of the "Open Door" to buttress and further their attack. 'Yes, the challenge of the Prophesy approaches, Upāst concurred, and with a bit of levity, but in all sincerity, the Queen Mother mused aloud, we can little afford to lose your resource Upāst and shall be quite stringent about your safe return; you have been a valiant warrior, now we depend vitally on your sage advice. With a knowing nod, Upāst agreed. All then fell silent as Bisu (Bes, Aha (the "Fighter")) and Upāst again partook in the libation before them.

As the rhythmic drumming of Ur-pehti reverberated throughout the cavern, the Prophetess Ta-Urt began softly intoning and harmonizing the ancient ritual verses of guided meditation with the Queen Mother Ahti, creating a soothing harmonic effect, inducing the needed entrancement for Bes and Upāst to journey into the spiritual realm. This time, unlike before, the minutes turned into hours. The hours turned into days and nights, which turned into slightly more than a week when Ahti felt heightening anxiety from the normally staid Upāst, who was not unfamiliar with warfare in the spiritual realm; out of concern for the aging Seer, the Queen began to prompt his return to his physical body …a prompting for which she felt clear and stubborn resistance from Upāst.

Witnessing what appeared to be his weakening physical state, Ahti requested Ta-Urt appeal to Lord Bes (Bisu) to direct the return of Upāst. As it is told, Upāst awoke moments later, slumped over in front of the fire at the center of the cavern, but surprisingly, when he lifted his head and looked around the cavern …by the features of his face, and indeed his very physical appearance he somehow now appeared slighter younger and more vibrant. Sitting directly across the fire from him was again the Queen Mother, with the Prophetess Ta-Urt sitting to his right and Bes (Bisu), still in sound meditation, sitting to his left. In a whispering tone, Upāst told of his rendezvous with Bisu at the Great Crossing and of the forces of the Divine Multiplicity aligned along the borderlands of the Threshold.

Upāst told of witnessing the invasion of the Threshold by the demonic hordes of the forces of darkness, who battled against Ptah and his legions of Guardian and Warrior Netjeru, who fought valiantly in defense of the Threshold. Upāst told of the divine radiance of the auras of the Archons, not merely Lord Bes, but the Archons all the Divine Multiplicity as they aligned their forces along the borderlands in defense of the Physical Realm. Upāst then told of Bes's invocation of a mystical *Imbuing* by which the radiance of his aura was shared with his forces, an act reflexively enhancing the auras and vital life forces of him and his forces three-fold. An act then emulated by the Archons of the Devine Multiplicity, with the collective radiance expanding until merging into a luminous aura, culminating in a fleeting flash of radiance that spread amongst the rank and file of the Devine Multiplicity.

Having pondered all that had been said, Upāst continued, Lord Bisu then all at once commanded his forces to arms, and as exuberance swept through their ranks, the luminance of the auras of the legions grew ever brighter, as their confidence and enthusiasm mounted. An exuberance that consumed even me, Upāst added, it was thus that I resisted the promptings of Ahti until Lord Bes insisted upon my return. That Lord Bes included me in the *Imbuing* was a parting gift, revitalizing my life force a bit ...for which I shall be forever in his debt.

The ancient African notion of "life force" is one that affirmed the ontological interrelatedness and interdependence underpinning all life.[clxxiii] This concept of vital life force (interconnectedness and interrelatedness) is fundamental to African thought. While it alludes to the Creator as giver and source which pervades all of life, its substance is understood as a somewhat fluid force availed to each in due proportion, weakened by irreverence yet enhanced in greater proportion by reverence for the divine source, Netjer (the unknowable Creator); the latter is what it means to have a strong spiritual core. In ancient African lore, one vital life force reacts and adjusts to every stimulus to which it is exposed within the body, mind, emotions, and spirit of each individual.

In early Ancient African lore, a vital life force was said to flow from non-physical reality to physical reality along its continuum to express itself in the only manner it can manifest, the Aura. Ancient Seers learned that, when properly channeled, this continuum could be availed, from physical to non-physical reality, enhancing one's aura while exploring the spiritual realm. In present-day terms, to grasp this, we first need to understand that our ethereal bodies are literally three-dimensional vibration fields; it is a mystery of earliest antiquity exactly how the ancient Seers came to understand this during such an early age in man's development. The ancient ones postulated that true reverence enhanced one vital-life force, and thus one aura; an enrichment by the sources of such reverence (the laity); spiritual energy channeled through the interconnectedness of all beings and directed and attracted by the vibrational signature of its due recipient.

Though there was no single "Theology" on which the formative faith would craft an early foundation, every clan agreed upon and accepted the validity of the traditional creed that the world and cosmos were created, ordered, and governed by an unknowable creator. A fundamental belief homogenized by the nascent Fetish Priesthood, whose priests and monks prompted and practiced rituals of reverence three times a day, morning, noon and dusk after the evening meal. Evidence of the forms of spiritual observance during earliest antiquity is sparse. Nonetheless, with this early worship came an advancement in the formative priesthood, setting apart some members of the clinic communities to perform rituals of reverence.

There were rituals of reverence performed three times each day, morning, noon and dusk, at the Sanctuary at Laas Geel and the Sanctuary at Gogoshiis Qabe, as well as by the Grand Sage Thmei and the Seers of Gondar. So too, were they performed by Fetish Priests and led by Monks throughout the Land of Punt and surrounding lands far beyond. It was believed their spiritual energy flowed to strengthen and empower its due recipient, Lord Bes, in his battle against the looming Forces of Chaos and Darkness.

The Legends

Bes ever so gradually awoke to find himself again in his physical body, sitting slumped over around the waning fire in the center of the cavern in the cavern-village (the "Mau Mau Caves") at the base of Mt Kenya ("Ta Netjeru"). As Bisu fully awoke, Ta-Urt leaned to his side. With a gesture, Upāst dispatched the Sage Seshat to inform the Queen Mother of his awakening. Ahti arrived shortly after that, together with the Seshat and Ur-pehti, who brought water and a variety of foods for all recuperation. As Ahti took her place around the fire, in a whisper, Ta-Urt inquired whether Bes was okay. With a slight turn of his head and brief eye contact, in a moment in which it seemed only the two of them existed, the strength in his eyes assured her he was just fine.

The Prophetess then reminded Bes and all of the erstwhile tradition of Ptah, that of immediately relating one's experience in the spiritual realm before the clarity of its memory is lost. Partaking of both food and water, Bisu asked exactly how long he had been in meditation, with Upast informing that somewhat of a distortion exists between "time" as we know and experience it here in the physical realm and how the "eternal moment" experienced in the spiritual realm. Upast informed that an hour experienced in deepest meditation here in the physical realm is experienced as several days or more in the spiritual realm,' advising Bisu further that you have been in deepest meditation for many days, which were surely experienced as months in the spiritual realm, my friend.

Ahti then informed Bes that Upast's return, he told of your rendezvous at the *Great Crossing*, where he witnessed the invasion of the Threshold by the Forces of Darkness. An account Bisu acknowledged and then told of the intervention of the forces of the Devine Multiplicity in turning the tide of battle. Bes told of their resounding victory in the 'Battle of the Threshold" and of how they pursued the Forces of Darkness across *Forbidding Field*s into the Valley of Delusions and of their victory in the 'Battle of the Forelands and of their greater victory in the 'Battle of the Shadow Mountain' by which they drove the Forces of Darkness from the Duat. Bisu (Bes) then told of the pursuit and battles with the Forces of Darkness as they fled for refuge and reinforcement at Antares and of their early victories on the battlefield at Antares, nonetheless.

In a recitation lasting well into the night, Bisu told of the final Battle at Antares and of the intervention of Erebus ("Khaos", the "Evil One") himself. Bisu told of how their early victories at Antares invoked direct confrontation with Erebus in battles both seen and unseen. Bes told of how Erebus first unleashed an unseen power from the Anti-Cosmos, burdening every effort of the warriors of the Forces of Light while aiding every effort of the warriors of the Forces of Darkness. An observable unseen ("dark energy") force, Bisu propounded, nullified through my very own person by my spiritual guide, an Ark Fairy of the Divine Brotherhood of the Troll (the "Guardians of Gravity"'). With his unseen force nullified, the Evil One unleashed. We fell into direct combat against a cadre of his Evil Imps, those second in power only to Erebus himself.

It was a fight to behold in which we acquitted ourselves well, Bisu opined, recounting that "the Evil Imps eventually fell to defeat and retreated to the side of Erebus, who had already begun to resign the field, descending back into the portal of the Nether World. Mesmerized by Bes's story but weary after a long day and night, Ahti then suggested, and all agreed they retire for the night. For five days and nights after that, Bisu recuperated, regaining his strength, exploring the secret corridors and mysteries of the Mau Mau Caves with Ta-Urt during the day and spending long evenings in discourse with Upast and Ahti in the evenings. On the morning of the sixth day, Bisu and Ta-Urt departed the caves at the base of Ta-Netjeru for the 'Land of Punt and home.

Metni, leader of the Hippopotamus clans at the foothills of Ta Netjeru (Mt Kenya) who had met accompanied the pair and their entourage upon their arrival, now met Bisu and Ta-Urt, reuniting them with the cadre that had accompanied them from the 'Land of the Plateaus." Metni met and reunited Bisu with his entourage at a hidden opening to the Mau Mau caves in the foothills of Ta Netjeru (Mt Kenya). Surprisingly Metni was also accompanied by Upast, who insisted upon accompanying Bisu and his entourage to the edge of the forest. Though they walked in silence during the early part of the trek, as the journey stretched on, Upāst revealed that the purpose of his accompanying Bisu on this their last trek together was to disclose the final verse in the Prophesy.

As they made their way through the forest, Upāst asserted that there is no greater diviner of the Prophesy than he and that just as he came to understand that there would be one more suited that he to become Archon; he has seen that Bes himself shall not fully harvest all the fruits of his great achievement. Upāst divined that a *Greater King* would rise in the *West*, a King, Upāst opined, that Bes himself will somehow come to recognize and to whom he shall then pledge his allegiance. Upāst further divined that while Bes shall reap the early fruits of his endeavor, it is the *Greater King* who shall reap the greater proportion. The *Prophesy* is a cruel master, Upāst opined, recounting that, after a life of dedication, it had been difficult for him to accept he would not become Archon as it may perhaps be difficult to accept the rise of a Greater King.

As they reached the edge of the forest, Upāst warmly embraced Bes, advising that, though their paths may never cross again, for the time they have spent together, he shall remain eternally grateful. With this, after the long return journey across the lowlands and into the southern highlands of the "Lands of the Plateaus", Bes (Bisu) and Ta-Urt arrived at the Royal Palace, at early ancient Berbera, on the coast of the present-day Gulf of Aden, anciently known as the Gulf of Berbera. The two arrived unannounced and understated, as Bisu preferred. However, as news of their return spread, over the following days, envoys arrived from his Provincial Viceroys reaffirming their allegiance, and gifts arrived from the kingdoms throughout the land. [clxxiv]

Before his departure, Bisu proclaimed ancient *Berbera* his royal city, making the de facto capital of the "Lands of the Plateaus", which Bisu anointed the "Land of Punt", the first and oldest city on the eastern coast of Africa.[clxxv] Together with his queen and his old friend and Viceroy of the Province, Amam, Bisu transformed Berbera into a majestic ancient city with magnificent natural harbors, from which the city's mariners traded with villages as far away as the Kumari peninsula, then an ancient elongation of the Indian subcontinent. The Indian sub-continent was a far more extensive landmass during the prolonged low sea level era of the Ice Age, particularly during the Glacial Maximum when the Kumari peninsula stretched southward from the sub-continent well into and partially across the ancient Indian Sea of the era.

The Kumari Peninsula of earliest antiquity extended southward from the Indian sub-continent, fully encompassing the present-day Island of Sri Lanka in the north, from where the ancient peninsula extended southward beyond the Equator, fully encompassing the present-day Maldives Islands, then the central mountain range of the Kumari peninsula. From its central mountain range, the ancient peninsula stretched southward in a slightly westerly direction, fully encompassing the present-day Chagos Archipelago, then the southernmost mountain range of Kumari. Mariners from early ancient Berbera actively traded and exchanged valuable frankincense, from the Land of Punt, for cinnamon and other herbs and spices from the lands along the western coast of Kumari and as far away as the Sunda Sub-continent further east.

It was under the auspices of Bisu that the Proto-Anu pushed their settlement range across the sea and around the then-broad southern coastal planes of the present-day Arabian Peninsula, advancing their frontier well beyond the lands of present-day Oman. One of Bes's most significant achievements was the inculcation of a social order that altered and, in some cases, completely replaced the older, fragmented and more contentious social of the Proto-Anu. His was a messianic replacement for the old contentious and rivalrous societies of the Proto-Anu; Bes re-instilled a belief in the connectedness of all to the divine source and that all the people had a responsibility to remain in reverence and do good work for themselves, their families, their clans and the Lands of Punt. Everyone—men, women, and even children.[clxxvi]

In contrast, to the southeast of the newly enshrined "Land of Punt", in the fabled "Mountains of the Moon," the stresses of the ages had only seen mounting tension, contention and rivalry between the haughty Dynastic Clans and kingdoms of the mid-highlands, and the Clans and nascent kingdoms of the upper highlands. Though the kingdoms of the upper highlands were generally smaller and more crudely organized than their mid-highland counterparts, they were no less formidable. The kingdoms of the mid-highlands recognized no claim of province or sovereignty purported clans and kingdoms of the upper highlands; the Dynastic clans instead asserted that the treasured *Sacred Groves* in the upper highlands were available to all.

The haughty Kingdoms of the mid-highlands viewed themselves as "ancient guardians of the highland forest, absolved from any claim of territoriality by the "late coming clans and their purported "kingdoms" in the highlands. Essentially a tacit assertion of territorial right over the *Sacred Groves* of the upper highlands, an assertion rightly viewed as a proclamation of control over the forests of the upper highlands, a self-serving proclamation that swept across the Mountains of the Moon as a more powerful clans of the mid-highlands adopted the stance. An advent that soon resulted in open conflict, mostly in the eastern Rwenzori, where the Dynastic clans were concentrated, a state of affairs exacerbated by in waning years of the existential crisis that was the Glacial Maximum.

Eponymous An: The Guiding Light

The third of the Prescient Kings was born in the time of the second. Yet, his story actually began before his birth, during the reign of his father. Still, it is not a story that began with his father. His story began with a young seer who, in time, would become the High Priest of his father's realm and, in turn, inform the vision of the third of the Prescient Kings. The story began with a gifted young Seer known as Khonsu, from the totem clan of the Winged Serpent in the highlands of the western Ruwenzori, the fabled "Mountains of the Moon." The Winged Serpent Clan in the western highlands was part of the diaspora of the old Serpent clan of Ptah, which spread across and beyond the Mountains of the Moon.

The Ruwenzori, the "Mountains of the Moon", cross the western arm of the Great Rift Valley, the arm known as the "Albertine Rift", a region where the arc of the foothills anciently aided in cultural transmission across the interlacustrine *"Lands of Yam."* Thus, Khonsu was influenced not only by legends of Ptah but also by a figure of renown and repute among the clans of the Proto-Kwa.[clxxvii] Like the (Ba-twa) Proto-Anu, the (A-kwa) Proto-Kwa were among the original peoples of the ancient Lands of Yam. Like the Proto-Anu, as the cold arid phase blanketing central Africa reached its height, the Proto-Kwa migrated into the highlands for sanctuary. For the most part, the Proto-Anu sought refuge in the Ruwenzori, while most Proto-Kwa sought sanctuary in the Virunga to the south.

The Ba-twa and A-kwa were among the first to mobilize at the onset of the mounting aridity and droughts spreading across the lowlands around 20,000 BC. A second wave of heightening aridity prompted increased waves of migrations into the highlands over two thousand years later, when huge Lake Nyanza (colonial Great Lake Victoria) is said to have dried out altogether around 17,500 BC. As populations abandoned the surrounding lands and shores of Great Lake Nyanza, the Ba-Twa first concentrated around Lake Mwitanzige (colonial "Lake Albert"), Lake Dweru (colonial "Lake George"), the Kazinga channel, and the Rutanzige (colonial "Lake Edward"), while the A-Kwa were mostly concentrated around the Rutanzige (colonial "Lake Edward") and Lake Kivu.

The Rwenzori is higher than the Alps (the highest mountain range in Europe), with landscapes sculptured over the ages by ancient glaciers, highland lakes, and networks of winding rivers descending through its ancient highland river valleys. The cold, arid phase blanketing the region reached its most extreme extent around 17,500 BCE when the rain forests in the lowlands were further fragmented and rendered even smaller in surface area, an advent prompting renewed rounds of migrations into the well-watered river valleys and highlands for sanctuary. As the foothills, river valleys and lower highlands became populated, later-arriving clans made their way through the long river valleys to settle in the upper elevations.

The Mountains of the Moon cross from the western to the eastern side of the Albertine Rift, with the arc of the foothills of the mountains part of what was known as the "Great Crossing" from the "Land of Man" at the fount of the Hapi Valley in the heart of the interlacustrine Lands of Yam, to Ta-Netjeru (the "Land of the Gods") in present-day Kenya.[clxxviii] A land bridge later anciently ascribed the epithet "Ta-Nebiru" (the "Great Crossing"), an epithet calling to mind the spiritual crossing from the Land of Man on "Earth" to the Land of the Gods in "Heaven."

Part and parcel of the long journey through Ta-Nebiru were the highland Sages of the Rwenzori who had mastered the powers of plants within their domains and bartered in herbs and their mastery of herbology with travelers traversing the crossing. The ancient Sages of the highlands were adept in the uses of the plants and mushrooms within their domains, granting them leverage in the assertions of open access to the sacred groves and gardens of the highlands by the dynastic clans of the lower highlands and river valleys. While the powerful dynastic kingdoms amassed huge territorial land areas by subsuming or aligning with clanic fiefdoms on their periphery, the loosely federated clans of the highlands grew by inbound migration and though formidable, were far less powerful than the dynastic kingdoms during the era in which Khonsu grew to the majority.

The tension between the clans of the highlands and the dynastic clans of the lower highlands and river valleys, and the emergence and growth of the ancient herb trade by nomadic clans traversing the Rwenzori, defined the era in which Khonsu reached the majority. Shorter seasons in the highlands invariably pressed upper highland clans into the lower inclines for subsistence. Forests are usually self-ascribed as the territory of one of the dynastic clans, creating a climate of seasonal contention. The highland Sages further facilitated the ancient herb trade, their keen knowledge of mushroom species in their areas, and their barter with the nomadic clans. An advent that opened new channels of communications as the nomadic clans adopted trade as a strategy to gain subsistence privileges en route through the forests of the Dynastic Kingdoms.

The highland Sages possessed a deep understanding of mushroom species, habitats, and medicinal attributes, as well as the unique states of mind they bestow, stimulating the early ancient herb trade.[clxxix] While psilocybin mushrooms grow worldwide, there has long been folklore about a highly coveted, rare, ancient ultra-potent psychoactive mushroom species, the fabled "Black Mushroom", native to the highlands of the "Mountains of the Moon." Some believe it is only a tale, while others take such mushroom lore quite seriously. The highland Sages were early ancient keepers of the secrets of Black Mushroom habitats and harvests.[clxxx] As a gifted young Seerer, Khonsu was raised to prophesy under the tutelage of such ancient mycologists.

Khonsu was descended from a prestigious lineage among the old totem clans of the *Winged-Serpent* in the western highlands of the Rwenzori since his grandfather, a renowned elder and descendent from the diaspora of Ptah's own totem clan in the old central highlands, a leader known as "Mehen", who led several latter-day clans to the western highlands. Mehen was Khonsu's mother's father and the longest-standing leader of the Winged-Serpent clans in the western highlands. His mother, "Upit, " was a respected Sage with whom Khonsu had a close relationship, as testified by his early mastery of the arts of mycology under her tutelage. Khonsu was the product of a unique mixed parentage, his father, called "Iah", was a prominent leader of the totem clans of the *Roan*. This semi-nomadic clan seasonally traversed the Rwenzori.

Like in the lowlands, nomadic hunting and gathering clans in Rwenzori followed seasonally available wild plants and game, mankind's oldest method of subsistence. The Roan had been a lowland nomadic clan who, like the sedentary clans, abandoned the dwindling forests of the lowlands for the well-watered terrain of the Rwenzori. True to their totem, their nomadic terrain ranged from thick forests to wooded grasslands.[clxxxi]. The men of the clan were apt and able hunters, using blowguns, poison darts and javelins to fell even large prey; there was a proud warrior tradition around which much of their social life and status revolved.

The women of the totem clans of the Roan clan were astute and able gatherers, with the Sages of the clan inheriting and retaining near encyclopedic knowledge of the edible and medicinal plants within their nomadic terrain. An interdependence occurred between the Roan and certain of the sedentary clans within their nomadic arc across the Mountains of the Moon. The Roan provided protein-rich bush meats, along with honey, wild fruit and medicinal herbs and mushrooms, while the sedentary clans provided much-needed starch and vegetable protein, such as potatoes, millet, yams, and assorted beans, to the nomadic traders. When the sedentary clans migrated into the highlands, abandoning the harsh lowlands, so too did the semi-nomadic Roan, altering their nomadic trek to traverse the Mountains of the Moon, ascending and descending inhabited river valleys to the highlands, to sojourn and barter with the clans and Sages of the highlands.

The Rwenzori form a narrow mountain range within the western branch of the Great Rift Valley (the "Albertine Rift"), with the famed mountains forming a promontory on the eastern shoulder of the "Albertine Rift." The ancient seasonal nomadic trek of the Roan traced and traversed the arc of the fabled "Mountains of the Moon", beginning from the western highlands overlooking the Albertine Rift (on the border of the present-day Democratic Republic of the Congo). The Roan departed the western highlands through a large forested descending river valley to the east, proceeding from there across the forested foothills of the western Rwenzori to those of the central Rwenzori.

The clan traversed the forested foothills of the central Ruwenzori to a then heavily inhabited river valley ascending into the central highlands, where, in keeping with their tradition, the Roan sojourned with the clans with whom they bartered and exchanged knowledge. The Rwenzori was home to potent mushroom species only known to grow in the highlands of the six massifs, each of which was home to its own unique strains.[clxxxii] The terminus of the nomadic trek of the Roan was in the highlands of the eastern Rwenzori, in present-day Uganda, below what was then known as the "Land of Eight Lakes."[clxxxiii].

Like most nomadic clans, the Roan followed a fixed seasonal pattern of movements, with the clan's keen knowledge of medicinal and psychoactive herbs and mushrooms and their habitats across the Mountains of the Moon, an eccentricity that, in time, redefined and became synonymous with their very identity. In their evolution, the Roan had become specialized in several procurement strategies (sometimes called multi-resource nomadism); Roan hunters specialized in big game bush meat, while Sages of the clan traded in their knowledge of medicinal and ritual herbs.[28] The roans were forerunners and functionaries in the development of early ancient trade routes across the Rwenzori, well-traveled routes connecting the disparate clans and dominions across the ancient Mountains of the Moon, giving effect to a web of social and economic trade and cultural exchange.

Trade inherently requires mobility, and nomadic clans, such as the Roan, were the ancient architects of the long-distance trade networks that helped spur the coalescence of the greater mountain kingdom. During his early manhood, Khonsu unfailingly accompanied his aging father in their annual nomadic journeys and sojourns across the Rwenzori. Each year the clan would launch their seasonal nomadic journey from the western highlands, through the river valleys descending and ascending the Mountains of the Moon, west to east and back again. While traces of their actual trade routes have been lost in the winds of early antiquity, faint legend holds that the ancient herbs traders bartered across the forested foothills and along the main descending and ascending river valleys of the Rwenzori.

In the descending and ascending river valleys, the Roan traded with the large, prosperous hereditary (or "dynastic") clans and kingdoms whose villages adorned the corridors of the valleys, no doubt among the Roan's primary patrons. Nonetheless, the herb traders sojourned only briefly in the river valleys each year, opting for longer sojourns with the clans of the highlands. Extended sojourns were reserved for the old clans of the highlands. These extended stays facilitated an exchange of rare and potent strains cultivated and harvested by famed highland Sages. Such extended sojourns also permitted long days and nights of discourse, debate and mutual enlightenment between the herb traders and sages of the highlands; exchanges leaving each better for the encounter.

---

[28] Salzman 1972

It was through this and his inimitable curiosity that Khonsu became an early repository of the collective wisdom of the highland Sages. This wisdom brought notoriety and fame to the ancient herb traders' but a notoriety and fame that brought with it the threat of violent theft and robbery as the clan traversed their ancient trade routes. Though renowned for their peacefulness and neutrality, the widely traveled Roan herb traders were apt and able warriors, more than capable of protecting their highly prized merchandise.

Khonsu's fame grew after his father grew older, and he assumed leadership of the annual nomadic journeys across the Rwenzori. After Khonsu assumed leadership of the nomadic journey, each year they spent their longest sojourn with the clans of the central highlands, where he and others so inclined would often spend days in quest of remnants of Ptah's legendary Sanctuary. On one such occasion, as it is told, after a particularly arduous search, an exhausted Khonsu and his cohorts rested in an upper highland valley, with most lying about the ground around the shade of an ancient Baobab Tree, while Khonsu sat with his head down, and his back resting against the old tree. Faint legend holds that it is there Khonsu had a most curious dream, a dream that would shape the path of his life.

Though it was clearly a dream, Khonsu surmised once he fully awoke, without revealing the dream to his cohorts, he led them into the upper inclines, where they found the frail remnants of the old steps carved into the mountainside that once led to Ptah's highland sanctuary. As they sat about the remnants of the old steps, Khonsu finally revealed the dream that had led them there; he told of his life-like dream in which an old man set just beyond his reach …resting next to him with his back against the tree" and of the old man's recollection and direction to the remnants of the steps that once led to Ptah's sanctuary. Khonsu further told of the old man's tale of a great queen in the highlands of the third-highest mountain south of the Mountains of the Moon. A Queen, the old man called Ala (Alla, Ælāta), Khonsu recounted, whose lineage was said to have direct knowledge of the "Arts of Natural Magick" performed by Ptah.

Upon the telling of his dream and of the mysterious queen, Khonsu found there were those among his cohorts who were vaguely familiar with her name and more than vaguely familiar with her domain; there were those among them who had either traded or known others who had traded in the southern domains. Khonsu was told that the peak of which the old man spoke could only be Mt Muhabura in the Virunga mountains to the south, a range perpendicular to the Albertine Rift. There are eight major mountains in the Virunga range, with Mount Muhabura being the third highest and most prominent of the eight. Mount Muhabura was inhabited early on, with water from a crater lake near its summit facilitating the rise of complex clanic societies in its highlands. Knowledgeable traders of the Roan, those most familiar with the southern highlands, affirmed that the renowned Queen presided over the largest kingdom in the southern highlands.[clxxxiv]

The Western Rift Valley (the "Albertine Rift") is crossed by the Rwenzori mountain range, between Lake Mwitanzige (colonial Lake Albert) and Lake Rutanzige (colonial Lake Edward), and the Virunga mountain range, between Lake Rutanzige and Lake Kivu.[clxxxv][clxxxvi] The Virunga separates the basins of the Nile and Congo rivers and are the only mountains in East Africa to form a divide of such continental stature.[clxxxvii] Just south of the Virunga is Lake Kivu, which was a zone where interlacustrine peoples intermixed with peoples of the Congo basin. Upon inquiry, Khonsu's father, Iah, informed him two of the five clans of the Roan seasonally traverse the foothills of the Virunga, clans who trade at the same marketplaces each year, marketplaces that are centers of trade.[clxxxviii]

Sedentism arose gradually during the predawn of the earliest antiquity in central Africa. Since non-agricultural sedentism required year-round, easily accessible natural resources, sedentism first arose in areas of diverse abundance. It was only in areas where the natural resources of several major ecosystems overlapped that early sedentism was sustainable. Thus clans settled in forested foothills with rivers or along or near forested river valleys, lakes and tributaries. Non-agricultural sedentism also required good preservation techniques, such as smoking, drying, and fermentation, and sound storage technologies, such as pottery and special pits, to securely store food while making it available.[clxxxix] Specialization increased and found greater purpose among the sedentary clans as they adopted new subsistence strategies, such as intense cultivation, animal herding, and domestication.

Before this, people had no active roles in their food production and used whatever nature provided. Trade, typically barter and trade through trade-oriented nomadic clans such as the Roan, improved the ability to procure food. Khonsu's father, Iah, explained that the Virunga form a barrier between the Nile and the Congo Basins. Thus, the trade centers around Lake Kivu attract a diverse array of peoples and commodities.[cxc] Archaeological evidence supports that ancient peoples seasonally gathered at such resource-rich locations bridging two ecospheres, bartering and trading commodities before dispersing, with merchants of the sedentary clans returning to their villages and the traders of the nomadic clans continuing the seasonal journeys across their domains.[cxci]

Highland traders from the Virunga, most notably those from renowned Mount Muhabura (Mount Muhavura), where the Queen you seek is said to reside, Khonsu's father advised, will surely be present at the trading centers and open markets around Lake Kivu; many may indeed be familiar with members of the Roan who trade there seasonally. Mt Muhabura is along the route between the Western Rwenzori and Lake Kivu. Iah informed and suggested to Khonsu that merchants and traders from Mount Muhabura with whom he barters and trades ... might aid in arranging a personal presentation of medicinal herbs and sacred mushrooms and their potencies uses before Queen Ala.[cxcii]

Iah reminded his son that the western highlands of the Rwenzori had long been home to both (Ba-Twa) Proto-Anu and (A-Kwa) Proto-Kwa and that the Proto-Kwa was thus not a people or culture unknown to him. The following season, Khonsu and his small cohort of highland herb traders joined the southward journey of the clans of the Roan, who regularly traded at the markets around Lake Kivu. What they found upon arrival was the heart of the ancient "Hapi Valley" civilization.[cxciii] In these ancient domains, diverse peoples such as the Ba-Twa, A-Kwa, Mbuti, and Bak (or Baka) intermixed, exchanged and long ago mastered early ancient technologies such as pottery, stone-tool assemblages and fabrication of polished stone.

Ancient toolmakers of the era used quartz to manufacture scrapers and other flake tools and rarer chert and obsidian lithic materials to manufacture microliths. Obsidian from the Virunga highlands and objects featuring high-quality workmanship were traded. The wares of the ancient toolmakers and craftsmen were readily traded for fish, bush meats, vegetables, fruit, and grains. Gathering grains from the grasslands was among the era's most sustainable, organized food production systems, especially in the drylands prevalent during the waning years of the glacial maximum. The interlacustrine Proto-Kwa and Proto-Anu were differentiated from non-centralized Ba-Twa and A-Kwa by their early organization into kingly states. In contrast, the non-centralized Ba-Twa and A-Kwa formed their own interlacustrine societies organized into patrilineal clans.

In keeping with the advice of Iah, when trading with Proto-Kwa merchants from Mt. Muhabura, Khonsu inquired and sought opportunity to present and explain the potencies and uses of the herbs and sacred mushrooms in which he traded before their esteemed Queen, whom he learned was a Sage in her own right. It is said that when word of his endeavor reached Queen Ala, she welcomed and invited his presentation. Mount Muhabura is the third highest and steepest among the eight peaks of the Virunga; it is located at the rim of present-day Uganda and Rwanda and can be seen from many parts of both nation-states. Giant heather thrives on the cloud-covered slopes of the mountainside as it ascends to the mid-highlands, where the clouds part to reveal an enchanted forest with massive old trees dripping with vines.

As Khonsu and his cohorts followed the A-Kwa highland traders who served as their guides, they pressed through high grasses that gave way to a series of uneven and somewhat cleared meadowlands, separated and surrounded by moss-laden trees on a blanket of dense ground-hugging plants.[cxciv] There were villages at the center of each of the sectioned meadows; distinct yet seemingly identical villages of a rounded, single entrance, reddish-brown earthen domed homes, aligned along three or four pathways, each leading to spacious circular clearings at the center of each village. At heart, each circular clearing, without exception, were large, square structures with open sides, which Khonsu presumed were "village centers."

As the procession progressed along on a path between the trees bordering the meadowlands, an elder, perhaps the oldest of the A-Kwa traders, lagged and trailed behind the brisk pace of his younger cohorts, eventually finding himself striding aside Khonsu, who walked just ahead his small band of herb traders. As it is told, the old trader first informed Khonsu of the grander and majesty of the Queen who awaited his audience; the old trader related that "Queen Ala's influence and rule extended far beyond Mt Muhabura, to the whole of the Virunga." As the procession made its way along the path between the trees bordering the meadowlands, the old trader explained that the meadowlands had once been the sole province of the totem clans of the Python, now led by Queen Ala.

Queen Ala rose to prominence, the old trader informed, nearly four generations ago, when the clans in the lands of the eight peaks were still plagued by turmoil, strife and constant warfare.[cxcv] Like in the north, the rising aridity and dwindling forests and animal life in the lowlands prompted the people to seek refuge in the moist, forested highlands of the Virunga. As in the Rwenzori to the north, the old trader expounded, those who arrived earliest staked broad claims to large swaths of highland forest, which they violently defended. As desperate clans continued to flow into the highlands and struggle for their place and survival for countless generations, the Virunga highlands were plagued with incessant warfare.

The totem clans of the Python were among the earliest to arrive in the meadowlands of Muhabura; they were adept and capable warriors who, over the generations, proved themselves against the most formidable of opponents. Thus, they became among the most powerful and influential of the clans in the highlands, an informality that gained greater credence under their first true "King", a legendary leader known as "Chukwu", who aligned the clans in a distinct federation. The reign of Chukwu was the longest and most powerful of any of the constituent clan leaders. Over the generations of his rule, essentially all of the clans of the Python dissolved his federation into a true kingdom under his rule.

When Chukwu ascended to the world beyond, his throne passed to his beloved daughter, whom the leaders of the former federation deemed emblematic and capable of preserving the kingdom. In this, they gained far more than they had hoped, for with the acknowledgment of Ala as Queen came tacit acceptance of her husband and defender, Amadioha, among the most revered and feared warriors of his era, as *Viceroy*. Queen Ala proclaimed, first and foremost, that all land is 'sacredly endowed by the unknowable creator to provide all that life requires." The Queen proclaimed that if all lived in peace, there would be sufficient harvests from the earth for all. Proclamations were readily accepted by the totem clans of the Python, whose warriors fell under the command of the Viceroy, *Amadioha*, a realization that brought many non-aligned clans into an alliance with the kingdom.

As the alliance grew to encompass clans in the highlands beyond Mt. Muhabura, so too did the reach of their influence on the kingdom; thus, when the Queen promulgated laws emphasizing the importance of honesty, respect, loyalty, the old traditions guiding morality, and there were those among the unaligned clans who at first resisted, their resistance was confronted and ended by the will of Amadioha. The old trader explained that under their combined rule, the gentle matriarchal hand of Queen Ala was the giver of the law. In contrast, the resolute hand of Amadioha, as ever-present Viceroy, is the enforcer of the law. While most laws begin with the Elders Councils and are debated before the Queen, "Ala the Wise" sanctions or deny the laws of the land. [cxcvi]

Queen Ala is said to be "wise beyond her eye", that she sees and knows what others cannot the old trader opined. It was "Ala the Wise" who enshrined in the ancient belief that "we generate our future by the way we act in the present", the old trader informed, calling it "a disposition aiding in the spread of peace and harmony throughout the land. The clans of the Virunga gradually redeployed the efforts theretofore wasted on war. Energies the clans poured into constructive endeavors as they adapted to an ever-narrowing pool of resources during the era. The old trader explained that this and far more has preserved peace and prosperity, so much so that the clans of Mt. Muhabura and the other seven massifs have been able to absorb migrations into their highlands without warfare; it is only required that they bring benefit to the settlement areas.

As the long procession of traders proceeded through the meadowlands, group after group gradually departed, one after the other, as they reached and returned to their villages along the route. Only a handful of Proto-Kwa traders remained as they approached and entered what appeared to be the last village amidst a large mid-highland cul-de-sac. The old trader advised that they had finally arrived, alluding to the village of the main clan. In this village, the enigmatic Queen "Ala the Wise" presided alongside Amadioha. As they entered the village, the old trader took it upon himself to lead Khonsu and his band to the open side of the village center at the heart of the village, where Ala awaited with a court of attendants.

A feast, with a variety of prepared meats, wild yams, succulent vegetables, tubers, mushrooms and assorted fruits spread atop a long table at the center of the room, lay before their eyes as they stood peering into the large room from the opening at the far side of the building from where Ala and Amadioha sat. The Queen and Viceroy sat side-by-side in oversized raised earthen chairs, modeling the archaic thrones of the earliest antiquity, situated and centered against the only wall with no opening at the opposite side of the building from where the tired, motley group of traders stood peering. Warriors and guards stood just inside each opening to the village center, blocking the entrance while allowing the traders to peer into the room …when Ala rose to her feet in recognition of the old trader, whom she then called by name, the guards slightly parted.

"Agwu Nsi," you have at last returned, the Queen is said to have intoned as she motioned for the guards to step aside and permit the entrance of Khonsu and his cohorts. The old trader, Agwu Nsi, motioned that Khonsu and his friends be seated around a long table as he simultaneously waved off the accompanying Proto-Kwa traders, releasing them to return to their homes in the village. An elderly, intransigent Amadioha is said to have then leaned forward and commented that those before him were the first "traders" from the war-ridden lands of the five peaks of the north to be welcomed into the southern highlands. Amadioha then pointedly added that "from the thick shielding of their attire and the lack of wares carried by the northerners, they appear less like traders and more like warriors."

A provocation prompting the charismatic and intuitively diplomatic Khonsu to rise to their feet, not in protest, but in faint agreement, as he conceded and explained that "though the lands of the northern five peaks are plagued with incessant strife and warfare, we nonetheless seasonally trade and collect the most potent and unique of herbs and mushrooms from across the highlands of the five peaks. We carry the valuable wares we collect in animal-skin satchels about our persons. Our shielded attire and weapons are so worn to defend and protect our goods and our very lives. Ours is not a trade for the faint at heart", Khonsu noted, "we survive and prosper in part because, to the man, we are indeed adept and able warriors." An old warrior himself, Amadioha is said to have nodded in understanding and acceptance as he settled back on his throne.

Grasping the moment, matronly Ala is said to have then subtlety prompted Agwu Nsi to introduce the brash young leader of the northern traders, at which juncture, realizing they had forgone formal introduction, Khonsu again rose to his feet; this time in the rescue of Agwu Nsi as he introduced himself and his cohorts. So began the first of three encounters between Ala and Khonsu, an encounter in which she revealed that the ever-modest Agwu Nsi was the most knowledgeable and accomplished of the ancient herbalists and mycologists in the southern highlands. To his slight embarrassment, Ala further revealed that Agwu Nsi first brought the uniqueness and potency of the northern medicinal and psychoactive herbs and mushrooms to her attention.

An adept Sage in her own right, speaking pointedly of the potency of the northern highland medicinal and psychoactive mushrooms, Ala informed that 'we of the southern highlands are familiar with only three of the six northern species of which we are aware. Until now,' she explained, 'the other three species have been shrouded in mystery. At this juncture, Agwu Nsi added that three similarly potent species are endemic to the southern (Virunga) highlands. Over the ages, they encountered the three species endemic to the northern highlands. He attests that the other three northern species were somehow unknown to us; until now, all we have known of them have been mere legend and myth.[cxcvii]

Faint legend tells the tale of Ala the Wise, informing that 'on the (taxonomic) tree of life, mushrooms are actually more closely related to the *animal kingdom* than the *plant kingdom*. She illuminated that mushrooms are acutely aware of their environment and readily adapt to changes in their surroundings, further informing that their mycelium networks are the great connectors of the forests, allowing the forest to act as one big organism. Ala noted that a single mycelium colony may encompass thousands of acres of forest. She informed me that mushrooms are the decayers of the forest, breaking down dead plants and allowing for new vegetative growth. They heal scarred landscapes, Ala advised; regarding our use of these *sacred plants*, she opined, it is as if the *mushrooms* plant spores in our souls and grow their *mycelium* inside us, allowing *us* to connect with the *Divine*.

Humans appear to have a symbiotic relationship with plants, specifically psychoactive mushrooms; it is purported by some researchers that psilocybin mushrooms had a fundamental influence in teaching humans about the nature of the Devine.[cxcviii] Ala propounded that just as mushroom fungi act as a great connector of the forest, mushroom mycelium enables the spirit to transcend ego and recognize our connection with the forest …and the divine source of all. In so doing, sacred mushrooms awaken and foment transformation of the self, an eventuality later masters would call "spiritual alchemy." Though "physical alchemy", the transmutation of elements and base metals, is the form most commonly known, "spiritual alchemy", that is, the transmutation of the self. Spiritual alchemy, Ala intoned, imbues a realization of the "pure self" in commune with the divine source of all.

True "spiritual" and "physical" alchemy" is distinctly different, though, in ancient times, the two were deemed to be the same.[cxcix] Though the processes and objectives of spiritual and physical alchemy were anciently deemed the same, with the essence of each being purification, in spiritual alchemy, which came first, purification is about refining and transforming oneself through enlightenment.[cc] Alchemy began with the early ethnomedicinal uses and cultivation of psilocybin mushrooms and the concomitant enlightenments and transformations derived from the use of psychoactive plants. *Ala the Wise* propounded that "the purpose of spiritual alchemy is enlightenment and mastery, recognizing that you are not separate from the higher aspects of your being, nor are you separate from the divine source of all."

This was the ending lesson of the first of the three encounters between *Khonsu* and *Queen Ala*. This lesson set the stage for the second encounter and lesson. The second excursion to the trading centers and open markets around Lake Kivu and later sojourn in the meadowlands of Mount Muhabura was in lieu of the seasonal nomadic excursion across the Rwenzori, seemingly signaling the incipient change to follow. Whether Agwu-Nsi was truly unavoidably called away or whether his absence was at the behest of Ala, the second encounter and series of meetings between the grandmotherly Ala and Khonsu, whom she had come to view as the grandson she never had, was solely between the two.

The third and last sojourn was far longer than the first and second combined, lasting not days but weeks when many, if not most, of his cohorts had opted to return to the Rwenzori. Thus was Khonsu left with a cadre of only his most ardent followers, who, inspired by his vision and adeptness, sought to cultivate their own skills and abilities in the refinement of minerals and metals. At the behest and guidance of Ala, Khonsu and his cadre spent their days in the upper highlands, around the crater lake atop Mount Muhabura, foraging and collecting rocks, either directly from the ground or by excavating into shallow cave walls in the waning week of their sojourn in the meadowlands.

Early evenings, before meals, were spent with Ala and the entire group discerning and assessing the collected rocks for prospective minerals and metals; at the behest of Amadioha, Khonsu joined him and Ala for evening meals, during which the grand-fatherly Amadioha would impart his own wisdom regarding prudence in the use of all that had been learned and mastered. It is with this wisdom and guidance that Khonsu returned home to the upper highlands of the Western Rwenzoris, where he mesmerized the great Sages and, most notably, the noble Fetish Priests, with his seemingly mystic powers and magical feats; powers he proclaimed were endowed by Netjer and directly derived from the numinous forces of Nature itself.

As before attested, the "Sages" of early ancient clanic society arose first among the women of the clans, the 'gatherers' most intimately involved with the foliage and trees of the forest, and thus the first to discover the secret powers of the plants. Young men, in turn, were decidedly first raised as 'hunters,' yet among each generation of hunters, there are always those more intuitive and spiritually sensitive than the lot, those with an innate understanding of nature and animal behavior' it is young men of this ilk who first rose to fill the ancient ranks of the *Fetish Priests*; those who, in pursuit and development of their aptitude, came to first be called "*Seekers*"; empaths anointed through years of quest, purge, and acquisition of sufficient enlightenment to attain the mantle.

A prestigious position for which many are called, but few are chosen. Young Seekers of the "Path" begin as young men, well before reaching majority, and must learn an assortment of cultural elements, personal creeds, and inherited practices, including an ethos of ethics and medical practices (comprising age-old proverbs, stories, songs, and folklore) transmitted across generations; a skill crafted amongst the Sages. To acquire such skills as Seekers, know the student does not find the teacher. The teacher finds the student, who then must prove himself worthy. Thus, it became incumbent upon true students and "Seekers of the Way" by their pursuits and enlightenment to attract the attention of worthy teachers. Because the Fetish Priests have been so maligned throughout present times, it is important that their contribution to what underscores many of today's "Priesthood" be placed into proper context.

The Fetish Priesthood was compelled by a life-affirming practice that encouraged its participants to better understand the natural processes of life and the spiritual nature of life. It is they who first propounded that all creation is considered divine and therefore contains the power of the divine, and thus that every element of nature, animal, tree, plant, fruit or vegetable is sacred. Such ancient African indigenous epistemology has been impugned, despised, and denigrated since the advent of European colonialism. The eurocentric view has consistently and widely used pejorative terms such as "witchdoctor" and "superstition" when referring to, and in the majority of cases dismissing indigenous African worldview. The term "Witch Doctor" was coined in England, during the height of the slave trade, in the 1700s, part and parcel of Eurocentric efforts to disrupt and destroy recognizable African institutions.[cci]

Similarly, "Voudon", a principal tenet of the Fetish Priests, was so thoroughly demonized as "'Voodoo" (human sacrifices, vampires, and devil worship all make up the stuff of spooky novels and Hollywood movies; while none of this nonsense was ever true of Voudon, it was so demonized), that it permitted the encroachment of foreign faiths and beliefs in foreign concepts and images of "God."[29] Much like later-day ancient Buddhists, Fetish Priests had no central authority but availed themselves of a mutual repository of knowledge. Theirs was an ancient amorphous order in which a rich and deep body of age-old mythology, allegory, songs and tales existed, attesting to their amazing memories and poetic abilities to orally pass it on from generation to generation over the long ages. The Fetish Priests propagated and proselytized belief in the existence of a very abstract, omnipotent yet unknowable force; "Netjer" is the name these distant assertors used before titles like God, Allah and Yahweh were created.

---

[29] "*Voodoo*," is a *term* that is a Euro-American corruption of the *word* "Vodou."

Below Netjer, it said, are the "Netjeru", divine attributes of Netjer, who are said to preside over the affairs of the Cosmos. The Fetish Priests thus act as healers and holy men, availing themselves of the wisdom of the "Way of Nature" in ascertaining medicinal and mystical acuity. Thus, when *Khonsu* informed that the mystical powers they witnessed him perform emanate from forces of *Nature* endowed by Netjer, animated by the *Netjeru*, it struck a familiar cord with the Fetish Priests.[30] Khonsu illuminated that "Magick" was one of the forces used in creation itself and that such mystical powers are bestowed upon the worthy in proportion to their reverence and abilities. Word of the practices of Magick by Khonsu soon spread, attracting *Seekers* from across the Mountains of the Moon.

Khonsu was the first of the ancient magicians of old, during a time when Magick and spiritual belief enjoyed a symbiotic relationship, with no clear line of demarcation separating physicians, priests, and magicians. "Seekers" from across the highlands came to witness the feats of the master, but true tutelage was first preserved for Serq, fatherly Priest of the totem clans of the Winged-Serpent in the western highlands, and secondly for inimitable *Nemur*, Priest of the nomadic totem clan of the Roan, who, together with the Sages across the highlands, aided in raising Khonsu to early prophecy. The Fetish Priest Serq guided Khonsu's growth from early youth, while Nemur guided his growth from adolescence, the latter on the nomadic journeys across the Rwenzori.

Khonsu was the first of the old Alchemist, an artistry reminiscent of ancient herbology that promised no miracles but instead crafted formulations to improve the efficacy of herbal potions and remedies; added to this, he was the first of the true Magicians of old, during a time when magick and religion enjoyed a symbiotic relationship, with no clear line of demarcation. Khonsu proselytized the sacred arts of spiritual and physical transmutation and that "Magick" merely reveals the relationships between causes and effects. In recognition that such abilities would enhance the formative powers of the Fetish Priesthood, in separate counsel, Serq and Nemur each beseech Khonsu to join the fraternity of the priesthood and proselytize the sacred arts.

The Legends

Faint legends whisper of the tasks of initiating the worthy Khonsu into the amorphous fraternity of the Fetish Priesthood …this in exchange for tutelage in the Arts of Natural Magick. As it is told, it was during this era that "true initiations" were first brought into practice; initiations which, in essence, are trials of an initiants ability to transcend (leave) the physical body. The purpose of initiation was for the "Initiated" to witness the fact that he or she is "spirit" and not merely "physical body." By initiation, the initiate would also realize that we continue to live after death and that we do survive departure from the physical body.

The ancient concept of "twice-born" comes from this clinical death experience; when an initiate successfully leaves their physical body consciously and then returns, the initiate essentially performs a rebirth.[ccii] This initiation was one of the most profound and guarded secrets of the later Ancient Khemetan Mystery Schools.[cciii] This "twice-born" is what the Priest alluded to when told Khonsu "you must die before you die", and in so doing, you attain the ability to take spiritual control of your physical body. At this point, the physical body becomes a "slave" rather than a "master". When this level of consciousness has been attained, one becomes truly free.[cciv]

---

[30] Neter means Nature, simply put that before vowels(the corruption) existed it was Ntr. The Khemetan word 'neter' (or nature or 'netjer') means a power that is able to generate life and to maintain it when generated.

The fatherly Fetish Priest Serq, who had guided Khonsu's early youth, instructed him in meditation and the innate ability to transcend the physical body. Though now realized and recognized as a skill anyone willing to practice can learn, meditation was anciently viewed as a purely spiritual practice, a tool for communion with the infinite deemed the exclusive province of Sages and Fetish Priests.[ccv] It was Serq who first instructed Khonsu in mastering the ability to focus his consciousness and project his ethereal body, transcending the constraints of the physical body.[ccvi] During the following weeks, Serq instructed Khonsu in using the subtle sense of discernment. The effect of intent in the spiritual realm informs that 'when projecting the ethereal body, you will disconnect not only from the confines of the physical body but from the physical realm itself, enabling relocation by intent.

Serq instructed that by 'focusing the mind's eye, with the intent of transporting your consciousness to what early Fetish Priest referred to as the "Alcove at the Heights", a cathedral-like high mountain alcove near the apex of the numinous-mountains overlooking the provinces of the Ancestors in the spiritual realm, you will so arrive. It is said that upon ascendance, *Khonsu* first perceived himself outside his body, then just as suddenly found himself amid the *Alcove at the Heights.* Khonsu accordingly told of the fullness of his experience, after which he inquired about the realm of the ancestors he vaguely viewed from the heights, which Serq described as a transitional realm of the Duat. A realm in which all reside to overcome an inherent disease, an infection of the spirit that transcends the death of the physical body. It is the disease of "doubt", Serq explained, a disorder inherited from the physical body which restrains the spirit from ascending to higher realms.

It is "doubt" that pulls you back into your physical body, Serq informed, instructing that "to enter the spiritual realm requires comfort and familiarity with the ethereal-self, a comfort attained through recognition and familiarity with the unique vibrations of one's ethereal body. To which the ever so clever Fetish Priest *Nemur* of the Roan proffered that noble Serq had informed Khonsu of the "how" but not the "why." Nemur opined that the wisdom acquired from Serq are but the mundane traditions of the Fetish Priest of the western highlands. The Fetish Priest of the Roan explained that greater perspective is found in the fullness of the traditions spanning the Mountains of the Moon, adding that it is from the more orthodox tradition of Ptah's own central highlands that all came to understand the self-realization inherent in the anointment into the priesthood.

As you have experienced, Nemur propounded, the spirit departs the physical body and the physical realm, just as it does in the "final release" of death. Thus, in the anointment of each Fetish Priest, it is said, "you die before you die", awakening to the realization that we are far more than our physical bodies. We are indeed seeds of the infinite spirit. As Fetish Priest of the Roan, like the fetish priest of each nomadic clan, Nemur opined, we are the corridors through which such traditions are disseminated across the Mountains of the Moon. Nemur then alluded to a greater depth of perspective to be gained from initiation into the tradition of the eastern highlands, whose wisdoms are informed by of Ta-Netjeru (the "Land of the Gods. Nemur opined that 'there exists a potential to empower and transform the fraternity of the fetish priesthood.

The ever so clever elder Fetish Priest then unveiled the fullness of his proposition, which entailed Khonsu being anointed into each of the three traditions spanning the Mountains of the Moon, thereby uniting the amorphous fraternity of the priesthood.[ccvii] Nemur proffered that by anointing into the three traditions, Khonsu will reconcile the fissures within the priesthood and be the first to do so since Ptah himself. Nemur explained that because he is acquainted with the eastern, central, and western traditions, none is better suited to aid in such an anointment. Nemur then shared his deepest suspicion regarding the legitimacy of many who fraudulently profess to be true Fetish Priest,' noting that there are those who, by dint of description, have clearly been anointed at the "Alcove at the Heights", while there are others who are clearly imposters.

The elder fetish priest opined that they do immeasurable harm to the fraternity through their fraudulent representations in professing intermediation with the ancestors. Nemur explained that in the ethos of the nomadic clans of the Roan, the possibility of such fraudulence and impurities in the priesthood is purged by a tradition of anointment requiring Fetish Priests of each of the clans to assemble at the celestial cathedral and stand in the witness of the "anointment of each new priest. Thus, if an aspirant is incapable of ascending into the spiritual realm, they are incapable of being anointed. Nemur lastly proposed that his tutelage in Natural Magick be in exchange for his tutelage of Khonsu in the three spiritual traditions of the Mountains of the Moon, the Mundane, Esoteric and Mystic traditions.[ccviii]

Ascension into the spiritual realm is considered a "skill" in the Mundane tradition. Nemur noted it is viewed as a natural ability strengthened through practice and visualization.[ccix] The Mundane tradition is a purely meditative tradition, Nemur continued, aided at the onset by herbs of which you Khonsu are more familiar than most; herbs used in ever-decreasing portions until an Initiate achieves attainment without such aid. Like *Seekers* in the other traditions, *Seekers* in the Mundane tradition pursue ascension as evidence of the spirit and spiritual realm that transcend human existence. The Esoteric tradition of the central highlands also uses herbs and a form of guided meditation, overlaying rhythmic ritual drumming, altogether facilitating ascension into the spiritual realm.

Nemur noted that as Fetish Priest of the Roan, a renowned trader of ritual herbs, he has attained appreciation for each of the traditions. However, none are better suited to train in their ways than the practitioners themselves. Revealing the subtlety of his plan, Nemur divulged that after gaining mutual respect within each tradition, Khonsu shall invite the prominent priests in each massif to stand witness at his grand anointment at the celestial cathedral.[ccx] Nemur envisioned that in fulfillment of his anointment, Khonsu would appear before a panel of such *High Priests*, with the truly unanointed, of course, incapable of attending, cleansing the fraternity of its fraudulence and impurities.

Such a 'grand anointment' will strengthen the formative priesthood, Nemur propounded, explaining that 'it will unite the priesthood like none have done since the time of Ptah. In his deliberation, it was then Khonsu chose to disclose his intent to pursue the word of *Ala the Wise,* who advised he re-settle in the eastern highlands and, further, that he settles amongst the clans below the Land of Eight Lakes, where he is to take himself a wife. Yet, most poignantly, Khonsu informed his mentor that in acceptance of his *Grand Anointment*, his forthcoming journey to the eastern highlands may be his last. All of which Nemur deemed to be ultimately auspicious, with his inimitable influence emanating from the west and the exalted influence of *Khonsu* emanating from the east.

In the weeks and months of preparation preceding the departure of the Roan, as word of Khonsu's decision and intention to relocate spread throughout the western highlands, the number of followers and extended family members choosing to join his re-settlement in the well-watered highlands of the east significantly increased. An advent nearly doubling the normal size of the nomadic Roan, who nonetheless prepared and timely commenced their trek to the eastern highlands. Thus began Khonsu's initiation into each of the spiritual traditions practiced throughout and across the river valleys and highlands of the fabled *Mountains of the Moon*.

Khonsu was the first of the old alchemist. His reputation spread quickly along the well-traveled corridors linking the ancient Rwenzori. When the Roan departed and traversed the river valleys and uplands bridging the Mountains of the Moon, in keeping with their tradition, they sojourned only briefly among the dynastic clans with whom they customarily traded in the ascending and descending river valleys. In keeping with their age-old tradition, the Roan reserved their longer sojourns for the upland clans who maintained the sacred gardens, with whom they traded potent strains of medicinal herbs and psychoactive mushrooms.

As Nemur foresaw, the influence of each fetish priest whom Khonsu tutored quickly spread, raising each to higher levels of esteem and authority. In furtherance of the scheme, each fetish priest so tutored was asked to nominate, from among their rank, the foremost fetish priest of their province to attend the grand anointment of Khonsu. An anointment to take place at dawn following the second full moon at the numinous Alcove at the Heights. And though their journey across the Mountains of Moon took longer than usual, the Roan nonetheless arrived timely at their seasonal village below the "Land of Eight Lakes", in the upper Nyamwamba River Valley, on the eastern slopes of the eastern Ruwenzori.

The Nyamwamba River originates from glaciers in the upper Ruwenzori's, from where the ancient river cascaded down the eastern slopes, with a succession of glacial moraine dams formed along its path, each dam creating and giving shape to one of the eight lakes. The Nyamwamba River descends the mountain through the upper and lower Nyamwamba River Valley, snaking its way along before spilling into Lake Dweru (colonial Lake George) at its terminus. A powerful dynastic kingdom existed in the Nyamwamba River Valley during the time of Khonsu, a kingdom stretching from the *Land of Eight Lakes* in the highlands to Lake Dweru in the lowlands. A kingdom that fully annexed the neighboring Mubuku and Ruimi River Valleys, whose rivers also discharge into Lake Dweru, rendering the ancient kingdom the dominant power in the region.

During the time of Khonsu, a sovereign known as Anšar, ruling in a succession of ten generations of his ancestors, presided over the *Nyamwamba River Valley Kingdom*: ruling over this vast kingdom through a hierarchy of lesser kings. Anšar's lineage was said to go back nineteen generations or more. However, it had only been during the ten generations preceding Anšar's rule that the dynasty had been the clear predominant power in the region. There were clans who maintained their independence on the periphery of the vast kingdom, like the clans on the periphery in the lower highlands, below the "Land of Eight Lakes." Three of the clans below the "Land of Eight Lakes" were the totem clans of the "Winged Serpent" of the eastern highlands, whose villages were in proximity to the seasonal village of the Roan, where Khonsu and the migrants from the west initially settled.

Serpent clans were among a cluster of highland clans of various totems surviving by their wits and skills on the highland periphery of the Nyamwamba River Valley kingdom. Relationships were decidedly mutually beneficial, with hardy highland clans, such as the totem clans of the Crowned Eagle, adroit gatherers of minerals and medicinal herbs unique to the land and soil surrounding the upper-most lakes in the 'Land of Eight Lakes'. In contrast, like their counterparts in the central and western highlands, the totem clans of the Winged Serpent in the eastern highlands were adept mycologists, knowledgeable of which plants took only months to be ready for harvest and which took six months to a year before they could be used medicinally; plants cultivated and harvested in the moist atmosphere of the lower lakes in the 'Land of Eight Lakes'.

Faint legend holds that it was through the accord between Nemur and Biluda, fetish priest of the ruling clan in the Nyamwamba River Valley, that the presiding monarch, a King known as Anšar, became aware of the powers and particularly growing influence of Khonsu across the fabled "Mountains of the Moon." Biluda explained the accord between him and Nemur that availed him of personal instruction in "Arts of Natural Magick" in exchange for instructing Khonsu in their tradition of spiritual ascension …and participating in his "Grand Anointment." Biluda told Anšar of his personal witness of feats performed by Khonsu, "Arts of Natural Magick," not seen since the time of Ptah. Biluda then told of his participation in the "Grand Anointment" of Khonsu.[ccxi]

The Fetish Priest intrigued his Sovereign with the tale of Khonsu's anointment at a numinous highland cathedral in the spiritual realm, a tale told to him by Nemur, fetish priest of the Roan, who rightly opined it as an anointment which, for the first time assembled true High Priests from across the Mountains of the Moon. Biluda explained that Khonsu's anointment was in the tradition of the Roan, which seeks to cleanse the priesthood of fraudulence by summoning true High Priests to stand witness at the anointment of each new priest. A ceremony overlooking the provinces of the ancestors in the highlands of the numinous mountains along the borderlands of the *Duat,* Biluda illuminated a highland cathedral known to informed fetish priests as the *"Alcove at the Heights."*

Biluda advised his Sovereign that the Fetish Priest of the Roan informed that he and Khonsu had entered into an accord with no less than eleven of the most influential fetish priests across the Mountains of the Moon, including Biluda himself. Further, only five High Priests aptly ascended and arrived in the *Alcove at the Heights*. Biluda explained that the five who arrived, together with the fetish priest Nemur himself, comprised an "Assembly of Six" who then stood witness to the anointment of Khonsu, an anointment by *presence* demonstrating the abilities all to duly ascend into the spiritual realm, affirming the nascent fraternity of the Fetish Priesthood.

But more than this, Biluda noted, Nemur told of Khonsu revealing a "hidden force" in the *Art of Natural Magick* to those in attendance, illuminating that it was one of the forces used in creation itself. Biluda informed his Sovereign that Khonsu is now held in the highest esteem by the most prominent fetish priest across the Mountains of the Moon.[ccxii] A point not lost on Anšar, though his attention and curiosity were more immediately piqued by the conflict between the clans below the 'Land of Eight Lakes' …on the periphery of his own kingdom. It was a conflict emanating from the intrusion of the totem clans of the Crowned Eagle into the Bujuku valley, home of Lake Bujuku, the second closest of the 'Eight Lakes' to the highland borderlands of Anšar's kingdom.

The fertile Bujuku valley had been the traditional province of the totem clans of the Winged-Serpent, who, until the arrival and settlement of Khonsu and the migrants from the west, had sought to avoid conflict with the larger and thus seemingly more powerful clans of the Crowned Eagle. But alas, for the Crowned Eagle, their intrusion met the full wrath of Khonsu and the warriors of the Roan, who, in a single campaign, fully expelled the Crowned Eagle from the lower Bujuku valley …in a victory so resounding it reordered the power-hierarchy of the nonaligned clans below the 'Land of Eight Lakes'.

Among Anšar's foremost concerns was the emerging power dynamic among the unaligned clans in the high borderlands, but Anšar had a deeper interest in the growing influence of Khonsu over the regional kingdoms across the Mountains of the Moon. Anšar's father, Lahmu, grandfather Apšu, and the eight generations before them were those Patriarchs who had expanded the ancient kingdom beyond the *Nyamwamba River Valley,* each generation vying for greater prominence than the last. Expansion to Lake Dweru ("Lake George"), an ancient delta within Lake Rutanzige ("Lake Edward"), was the accomplishment of the earlier generations, yet it was Anšar's grandfather who annexed the neighboring Mubuku and Ruimi River Valleys, and his father who expanded through the Kazinga Channel to the southern shores of Lake Rutanzige.

And Anšar now sought greater prominence through the prospect of uniting the fabled mountain kingdom of the Rwenzori, a feat not achieved since the time of Ptah. Anšar also believed this would gain him parity in contending with the rising influence of the powerful eastern kingdom of Punt. Thus, Khonsu was summoned to the audience before perhaps the most powerful sovereign in the ancient Mountains of the Moon. When he arrived, he found a vast royal "City of Villages", with partially earthen and partially forested fortifications surrounding the villages of the nine totem clans of the Golden Lion who originally settled and populated the ancient borough. Like other totemic clans, the totem clans of the Golden Lion sought in every way to embody the spirit and essence of their totem.

Lions were anciently a regal symbol of power and pride. In some legends, the lion's mane symbolized boldness and authority, reflecting their strength and majesty. For the totem clans of the Golden Lion, the mane also represented the sun. It was seen to resemble the aura depicting the sun's power. In the earliest days of its prominence, the ancient borough was known as the "Nine Villages" in deference to the villages of the nine clans of the Golden Lion inhabiting the borough. However, with the passage of the generations, the borough came to be known as the "City of Villages." The "Great House", situated atop a small mound near the center of the borough, was the royal abode of Anšar and the place of assembly for the borough's 'Council of Elders'.

Anšar and his court had a near-panoramic view of the nine precincts from the Great House. The villages within the precincts were a tapestry of adobe-like mud-brick dwellings, lining irregular corridors and pathways, through which only the inhabitants and the otherwise well-informed could quickly make their way to the Great House. Khonsu and a small accompanying band of Roan warriors were received at what would today be called a "courtyard" between the royal residence of the Great House and the assembly hall of the Council of Elders. There, in the royal courtyard, is where Khonsu was first introduced to Anšar. On that occasion, it is said, the two seem to have an all but immediate affinity. The Roan warriors were provided a private feast in the central courtyard, while Anšar and Khonsu sat isolated in a far corner of the courtyard, engrossed in mutual discovery and discussion.

Khonsu was enthralled by the self-contained industry of the borough, a unique sort of quasi-autonomy which became more apparent from the vantage point and panoramic view from the courtyard of the "Great House; from there one could see the thick tree-lined forests and sacred groves in between the village-precincts and grasp a full appreciation for the vast size of the borough. Anšar, in turn, found himself fascinated with the charismatic Warrior-Priest, as he inquired into the conflict in the Land of Eight Lakes between the clans of the Winged Serpent and those of the Crowned Eagle. Anšar informed that he is the arbiter of peace within the realm. Though the Land of Eight Lakes is on the periphery, their proximity places them within the scope of his dominion; conflict and warfare there, he propounded, affects stability and peace here.

In this, Khonsu saw reflections of the strength and authority of King Amadioha of the Virunga, reminding him of the personal prophecy of Ala the Wise, who had advised that he re-settle and pursue his destiny there in the western highlands. While Khonsu pondered whether this was the destiny foreseen by Queen Ala, Anšar pondered the prospect of embracing Khonsu to bring the Land of Eight Lakes into the dominion of the nascent empire of the 'City of Villages' and, in so doing, align his own aspirations with those of Khonsu. Errantly believing that the endeavor to cleanse and unify the informal fraternity of the fetish priesthood was an intent and aspiration of Khonsu rather than a machination of Nemur, Anšar believed their aspirations for the unity of the ancient mountain kingdom (the fabled 'Mountains of the Moon') very much coincided.

Over the following weeks and months, the affinity and friendship grew between Anšar and Khonsu. A mutual admiration ultimately prompted Anšar to solicit that Khonsu becomes High Priest of the Realm. Tacitly acknowledging the deference lauded Khonsu by influential fetish priests throughout the 'Mountains of the Moon' and their influence upon their congregations, Elder Councils, and those who rule. The wily Anšar envisioned that by surmounting his stature above that of Khonsu as his sovereign, his own majesty would spread across the 'Mountains of the Moon'. In so doing, in Anšar's view, he would lay the foreground for the unification of the mountain kingdom. A proposition Khonsu perceived as confirmation of the vision of Ala the Wise, who advised he would find his destiny in the eastern highlands.

In an effort to further entice Khonsu's interest, Anšar gave history and survey of the whole of the Kingdom over which Khonsu would be High Priest, explaining that in the heightening aridity and shrinking forests that prevailed some twenty generations past, the totem clans of the Golden Lion sought refuge here, in the Nyamwamba River Valley. The original eight clans settled in the region between the rainforest and the uplands, on the opposite side of the river from this, a distance below the 'Land of Eight Lakes,' where they first built villages of sun-dried clay brick (a kind of adobe) dwellings to sustain in the welcomed rains of the lower highlands. In time the villages grew together and were combined by an open marketplace and a 'House of Elders' its heart, in the central area where the eight-village met.

This was the origin of what Anšar called "Old Town," which rose to prominence along the upper Nyamwamba River Valley after a mere twelve generations. The emergent and nascent kingdom took shape under the auspice of the "Old Town", who ruled the kingdom for seven generations. Anšar explained that the clanic-villages that would become known as the "City of Villages" were founded by strident descendants of the elders at the "Old Town"; succeeding generations who brazenly settled in the lower uplands once the aridity had receded, and the forests fully recovered. The kingdom had been greatly expanded by the generations who ruled from "Old Town"; it is they who expanded beyond Nyamwamba River Valley, embracing the townships the clans maintained at the ancient delta where the Nyamwamba River empties into Lake Dweru ("Lake George").

Growth around the ancient delta (present-day Lake Dweru) led to the eventual subsumption of the clans and villages around its shores and eventually the neighboring river valleys emptying into Great Lake Rutanzige ("Lake Edward"). Anšar explained that his own father, Lahmu, expanded the kingdom through the Kazinga Channel to the eastern shores of Lake Rutanzige. Khonsu, of course, graciously accepted the overture, conditioned upon the fetish priest Biluda remaining High Priest of the Nyamwamba River Valley province, and that Anšar agrees to build a sanctuary to affirmed priest of the realm, first of the ancient temples. Thus, the 'Sanctuary" rose aside the courtyard, giving effect to the fabled triadic structural layout of the compound that was the "Great House." In time, Khonsu assumed residence at the Sanctuary.

In the midst of a time that followed, the fetish priest of the realm made a pilgrimage to the sanctuary at the "City of Villages" for edification and anointment. The transformation began with anointment by Khonsu himself, the "Sage Illuminator", who transformed the priesthood in which the newly anointed were, for the first time, called *Priests of the Mysteries*. An early form of the Mysteries was held by its initiates to inviolable secrecy, with certain death avenging any betrayal of their sacred trusts. Though the emergent Academy at the Sanctuary contributed to the ancient doctrines promulgated by earlier spiritual leaders, the fountainhead of those doctrines was never revealed to the profane for their own protection. The *Mysteries* were guardians of a transcendental knowledge so profound as to be stupefying and so potent as to be revealed safely only to the truly anointed.

It was a time of transformation of the priesthood and the nascent empire of the City of Villages. Advents heightening Anšar's admiration for Khonsu, with the two becoming particularly close, and Khonsu taking many evening meals with Anšar and his wife Kišar and their son An. Like Anšar, his son An held hold Khonsu in high regard. Given the distraction of Anšar's rule of the realm, his wife Kišar one evening requested, with Anšar agreeing, that their young son An study and train at the Sanctuary, under the auspice and tutelage of Khonsu himself. An overture Khonsu accepted with honor, as he found the young An wise beyond his age. Khonsu discerned certain natural abilities within his young charge, an inexplicable aptitude and adeptness with a sword, with the grace and audacity of an experienced warrior.

Recalling his own youth as a young warrior, Anšar admired the discipline and warrior ethos of the Roan and the disposition of pride and confidence it inured in its adherents, important traits for a future king. Thus began the ascendance of An, a journey with Khonsu through late youth and early manhood that was all at once adventurous, challenging, and an earnest study of the ancient teachings of the "Mysteries", as they were then understood. Khonsu was the first of the ancient Warrior Priest, referred to by epithets such as the "Defender", who few could dispute as de facto 'High Priest" of the nascent empire of the City of Villages, and indeed the whole of the fabled "Mountains of the Moon."

Due to his dutiful guardianship of his young charge, Prince An, Khonsu also became known as a benevolent. Yet, when needed, a fierce warrior priest willingly defended his charge and the king against their enemies.[ccxiii] A protective predisposition found favor with Anšar, granting him sufficient comfort to permit An to accompany Khonsu, his entourage, and a royal contingent from the City of Villages in their semi-annual patronage mission to the provincial kingdoms of the realm. Like those that preceded him, Anšar practiced an early ancient form of patronage, where the relationship was hierarchical, but obligations were mutual; a relationship wherein the "patron-protector" bestows privileges and favors and, most importantly, protection to subordinate sovereigns, in exchange for loyalty, service and tribute.

An alliance and allegiance that brought with it protection against the encroachment of any type or manner and also brought trade and access to goods and wares otherwise beyond the reach of the subordinate sovereignties. Tribute was regularly collected twice a year. In essence, the purpose of the patronage mission was that Khonsu and his cadre accompanied what were essentially the royal tax collectors as emissaries of the "Great House." A perception buttressed by the presence of young Prince An. It was an excursion that emerged the young prince in the peaceful yet warrior ethos of the Roan, who made up Khonsu's entourage. The expedition began in delta townships and kingdoms around Lake Dweru ("Lake George"), the Kazinga Channel, and the shores of Great Lake Rutanzige ("Lake Edward")

It was not an undertaking without challenge or peril, expelling and standing fast against intruders and encroachers and projecting an aura of strength in affirming the defense of the provincial sovereignties of the realm. It was a journey of several months that caused a determined transformation in young An, who departed the City of Villages a young lad and returned in every way a young man, a consequence that made Anšar proud. Anšar then turned to his long-held aspiration to unite the kingdoms spanning the fabled "Mountains of the Moon." Through those before Anšar incented the earliest of the northern migrations into the Nile River Valley (around 17,000 BC.), it was Anšar who launched the second wave of migrations, and amid this lot were those who bought the earliest forms of cultivation and culture down the Nile.[ccxiv]

A land anciently known as Ta-Nebiru ("the "Great Pass") arose from the existential crisis that was the Glacial Maximum. A crisis prompted outbound migrations across the uplands above and around a then huge ancient desolate area surrounding and spanning Lake Kyoga and Lake Nyanza ("Lake Victoria"), a surface area of over 25,000 square miles, which dried up completely around 17,300 BC. The arc of the "Mountains of the Moon" in the west, conjoined with the arc of the southern foothills of the Imatong Mountains, anciently called the *"Lesser Mountains of the Heavens"*, leading eastward to the arc of the five peaks of Mount Elgon, called the *"Greater Mountains of the Heavens"*, together formed the arc of Ta-Nebiru (the "Great Pass"); guiding those traversing its course from the fount of the *Land of Man* (in early ancient the "Hapi Valley") to the periphery of the *Land of the Gods* (Ta-Netjeru).[ccxv]

For thousands of years, Ta-Nebiru was a main corridor linking the "Land of Man" to the "Land of the Gods." The arc of the uplands leading eastward to the "Mountains of the Heavens" was deemed the heartlands of Ta-Nebiru.[ccxvi] Anšar harbored what he believed to be a greater vision for the growth and glory of his kingdom through his ambition and vision to extend his kingdom to the eastern arc of Ta-Nebiru, a feat not seen even in the time of Ptah. Anšar knew such a feat would far exceed the accomplishments and glory of all who came before him, elevating his stature to that of the "Greatest King" of the ancient kingdom.[ccxvii] Thus, with enthusiasm, he dispatched his son *An* and a small cadre to accompany *Khonsu* on the seasonal nomadic journey of the *Roan* across the Rwenzori to the western highlands.

Anšar must surely have surmised what better emissaries, particularly given that Khonsu himself had informed that the sojourns of the Roan across the Rwenzori would be with the most influential ancient kingdoms within the Mountains of the Moon. He explained that their sojourns would be exclusive to the kingdoms of the anointed priests, the de facto 'High Priest" of the formative priesthood, whose influence held sway over their sovereigns and dominions. To the west, Khonsu advised they would first arrive at the dominions of the clans of the eastern highlands, noting that there are greater and lesser clans inhabiting highlands and foothills, with the Bujuku Valley at the center, where Mount Ngaliema ("Mount Stanley"), Mount Kiyanja ("Mount Baker") and Mount Ngomwimbi ("Mount Speke") form the heart of the upper valley.

Khonsu explained that the route of the Roan proceeds along the Bujuku valley, beneath the peaks of Mount Ngaliema and Ngomwimbi, southward through the valley between the mountains, to then descend into the lower western highlands. The Roan traditionally sojourned for several months in the western highlands, Khonsu informed, near the village of the clan of the Winged-Serpent, my native clan. The return route, Khonsu explained, will be circuitous rather than direct, first traversing the western forested foothills leading northward around the base of Mount Ngomwimbi toward the lower reaches of the Mugusu valley, through which the clan will then ascend into the lower northern highlands, toward the domain of the totem clans of the Royal Crane. The Roan will again sojourn there, yet only for a few days, as they trade and confer the wisdom of the herbs they exchange.

They will then retrace their route southwards, along the forested foothills of the southern mountains, ascending into the uplands through the southern valleys to trade, sojourn, and confer with the clans of the heights. From there, the Roan shall return to their seasonal village below the "Land of Eight Lakes", and we shall return to the City of Villages, Khonsu concluded. So successful was the first nomadic journey and mission at enhancing recognition of the Nyamwamba Valley Kingdom and the prestige of Anšar that at his behest, Khonsu and An accompanied the Roan every third year as emissaries of the kingdom. The second and third such emissarial missions strengthened relations across the highlands during the Holocene as the glaciers retreated up the Bujuku valley.

The Vela supernova, which signaled the onset of the Holocene, was seen from earth in 14,000 B.C., with the planet then gradually warming. As the glaciers slowly melted, all the valleys across the Rwenzori exploded in an abundance of wild cereal, edible plants and mushroom types. Thus began the era in which the *City of Villages* rose to true prominence, a fortuitous time of lessening strife, scarcity and turmoil, a time that eased the way for the alliances underlying the growth and expansion of the Nyamwamba Valley Kingdom. The nomadic journeys of the Roan, who had come to be seen as agents of the royal house, facilitated broader awareness and affinities across the ancient expanse of the Mountains of the Moon.

By the fourth such nomadic journey and emissary mission by Khonsu and An, the kingdoms across the land with whom the Roan customarily sojourned had come to anticipate, welcome, and celebrate the arrival and stay of the esteemed (de facto) *High Priest* and charismatic *Prince*. As the Holocene progressed, the recovery of the forests brought greater prosperity and trade to the realm, an advent translating into an exceedingly successful trade mission for the emissaries. Yet it was on the return route from the fifth such mission that a messenger from the "*City of Villages*" found and informed *An* and *Khonsu* of the death of *Anšar* and that the Queen requested their immediate return.

The news was distressing but unsurprising, as the aging Anšar had been in waning health for several years. At that very moment, *Prince An*, a prodigy in spiritual guidance and leadership, assumed the tasks of governing the realm. Upon return to the "Great House", the Queen informed *An* that the *Elder's Council* of the city and *Grand Council* of the Kingdom had each sanctioned his succession. As word of Anšar's death spread across the greater mountain kingdom, sympathies in the form of gifts and patronage to the new king arrived from disparate clanic kingdoms of the Mountains of the Moon.

In an interesting irony, it seems what Anšar was unable to actually accomplish during his lifetime. His death somewhat served as a catalyst for that accomplishment in the reign of his son, An (On, Anon). Although granted the advantage of a personal prodigy of the King and High Priest, it was nonetheless his charisma and a disarming mixture of wisdom and humility that best served An in inspiring coalescence and unity across the fabled mountain kingdom. An adept *An* adroitly reciprocated each offering of patronage, not in kind, but in time of most need; those under distress of disease received medicinal herbs, and those in want of wild cereals and dried meats were accorded these in times of need.

This ancient form of patronage and reciprocity under the auspice of An soon assumed a cadence of its own, with patronage flowing into the 'City of Villages' in all forms each year at the anniversary of his coronation. It was an evolution in ancient patronage that gave birth to the first semblance of governing authority over repositories of perishables and non-perishable goods, an advent that facilitated refinement in uses of ancient preservatives, such as diatomaceous earth, smoking, drying, salting, spicing, fermenting, pickling, freezing in cold areas, along with improvements in storage and logistic techniques. The rise of An thus imbued a greater sense of security and well-being across the Ruwenzoris, further facilitating coalescence and feelings of unity among and between the emergent clanic societies within provinces of the fabled mountain kingdom.

With the abundance of wild cereals, grains, fruit, nuts, highland mushrooms, and ample river and lake water resources, the villages and mountain towns in the lower highlands and foothills were readily transformed into early Neolithic farming societies, cultivating varieties of wild edible plants. Gatherers who had harvested wild edible plants and grains sowed some of their seeds in the moist and fertile soils along or in proximity to nearby rivers and lakes, which enabled them to collect the wild plants on a more systematic basis. They began to select the plant types that most readily lent themselves to domestication, eventually establishing regular crops; the regular harvesting of wild roots led to the refinement of specialized digging tools, such as stone hoes grounded to a finer polish than the chipped cutting tools of the earlier age.

Archaeologists have had to grapple with the identification of Holocene agricultural sites from those of erstwhile hunter-gatherers in central Africa because, in many cases, they exhibit similar assemblages. The earliest archaeological evidence found throughout central Africa suggests there was rapid and large-scale domestication of plants and animals around 12,800 BC, an era coinciding with the intense humid phase and equable climate observed in numerous paleo records across the region.[ccxviii] A growing number of sites and sequences are now coming together to paint a more complete picture of early Neolithic agriculture and farming throughout central Africa during the early Holocene.

The emergence of Neolithic agriculture involved a complex interplay of plants, animals, topography, climate, and human ingenuity, techniques and tools, a dynamic prompting further development and evolution of ancient civilization. The generation's earlier dissemination and adaption of the arts of alchemy, particularly the transmutation of elements and metals, aided the transmission of iron-ore mining and smelting techniques from the interlacustrine kingdoms at the front of the fabled "Hapi Valley."[ccxix] The Proto-Anu developed metal smelting abilities and mastered the use of metals, at least elementary metals; they became the smiths, potters, and craftsmen of early ancient civilization… and the early ancient trades.

Khonsu organized the craftsmen and established the guilds that controlled the recruitment of apprentices, organized education and established security funds for their members.[31] These artists and craftsmen included architects, draftsmen, stone workers (large stones and small), jewelers, painters, dyers, and eventually glass workers; these were industrious smiths and potters, mass-producing and trading all manner of goods. All of the best artisans and craftsmen were trained in one place, and all other artists and craftsmen were then trained by the expert artisan and craftsmen who were trained there. Agriculture also allowed the birth rate to become significantly higher than the death rate, with the population exploding during the era.

As political and economic power becomes more centralized, societies increase their ability to organize and control more complex activities, such as operating copper and gold mines. For millennia the Proto-Anu congregated and formed villages and townships, which expanded into small-fortified cities as a way to ensure protection, access to food and water, and fulfill the communities' social needs. These early-fortified cities include agriculture, industry, villages, townships and areas of urbanization. Construction of the early ancient earthen fortifications once intermittently found along the foothills of the fabled mountain kingdom was attributed to these most ancient of ancestors; early ancient cities with remnants of moated villages enclosed by circular earthen walls, some hundreds of yards in circumference.

As the cities grew in vitality and prowess, so did the sovereign provinces and, indeed, the whole of the fabled mountain kingdoms. It was an auspicious time for An to be King; prosperity abounded from every quarter, with the "City of Villages" one of its prime beneficiaries. Scholars see long-distance trade as the first direct stimulus of State formation, requiring the development of centralized authority for administrative purposes and to control sources of trade and protect trade routes.[ccxx] In addition, once you start broadly trading, it is not long before you are building roads, bridges, and irrigation and drainage systems. Though the transition was gradual, the switch to a broadly settled way of life was marked by the appearance of small-fortified Neolithic cities and urban townships with homes equipped with grinding stones for processing grain.

It was an idyllic time, but not a time without dissension. As prosperity and power became more evenly distributed, a competitive environment created an opportunity for ambitious sovereign provinces to contemplate and develop their own strategies +to amass influence and power. Patronage ties were more informal and their obligations less precise than those of feudal vassalage; ancient Patronage was a system of personal ties and networks in which a patron or superior power offered protection and support to an inferior sovereignty, who then owed his patron loyalty and service in return. In emulation of the 'City of Villages' itself, the hand full of larger, more prosperous, and influential ancient cities across the fabled mountain kingdom first vied for prominence through patronage from the smaller clanic kingdoms within their domains.

---

[31] Christiansen 1997

Patronage and its many forms allowed for a minimal form of administration bound by personal relations between parties, yet nonetheless served as the earliest model for a ruling. Patronage, informal networks of influence, factions, corruption, and favoritism 'oiled' the everyday functioning of power in early ancient states to the point that all these elements could simultaneously complete, counterbalance, and menace the authority of the central power. The patronage relationship was not a discrete one, but a network since a patron might be obligated to a higher or greater power, and a patronee might have more than one patron whose interests could conflict. The relationship was hierarchical, but obligations were mutual.

The patron was the protector and benefactor of the patroness; the technical term for this protection was patrocinium. Typically, the patronee was of inferior status. The patron possessed greater wealth, power, and prestige, enabling the patron to aid or defend the patronee. In return, patronee were expected to serve their patron as needed. As the influential and powerful rose to prominence, an air of contention pervaded as control over trade routes and trade flows became symbols of power and prestige. Obsidian was traded long-distance, primarily from the Virunga highlands, imbuing power and prestige in the eastern kingdoms that controlled those trade flows.

The advent of early Neolithic farming had been part of a continuum of socio-economic change over thousands of years, not an abrupt or rapid adaptive shift, yet an eventual shift that nonetheless inspired innovation and advancement in tooling and techniques. Though microlithic tools originated earlier than the Holocene, the advent of early Neolithic farming created the need not just for tooling, but more efficient tooling, sawing the use of new materials such as quartz to manufacture scrapers and other flake tools and the use of rarer chert and obsidian lithic materials to manufacture microliths. Undue control of southeastern trade flows soon distorted and, in many ways, came to challenge the power and authority dynamic across the nascent mountain kingdom. A challenge the inimitable An instinctively knew should not go uncomforted.

Thus, with a serendipitous nudge and an intuitive stroke of genius, An cast his vision eastward, toward the eastern arc of *Ta-Nebiru* (the "Great Pass") and the *Mountains of the Heavens* (majestic "Mount Elgon"). Serendipitous was An's audience with a minor king from the northeastern territories of the Rwenzori. A king of the totem clans of Horned Chameleon, seeking greater status for his minor kingdom at the northeastern extent of the Mountains of the Moon. In his endeavor to curry favor, the king, named *Meni* (euphemistically called the "Chameleon King"), arranged an audience for himself and the leader of a trade-oriented nomadic clan, the totemic clan of the Oryx; a clan much like the Roan, whose territorial domain extended through the crest of Ta-Nebiru (the "Great Pass"), embracing the southern foothills of the Imatong Mountains, leading to the Mountains of the Heavens, overlooking *Ta-Netjeru* (the "Land of the Gods").[ccxxi]

The Chameleon King arrived timely at the 'Great House' with the leader of the Oryx, each bestowing gifts to honor An. Gifts were essentially samples of goods traded by the Oryx, who would serve as a conduit for the royal city and the Mountain Kingdom. A proposition An found of particular interest, given that it offered a northern source of obsidian and quartz from ("Mount Elgon") the *Mountains of the Heavens*. Yet perhaps more significantly, it provided a source of frankincense and myrrh, highly valued and prized commodities across the Mountains of the Moon. Frankincense was used as incense in rituals and ceremonies. In contrast, myrrh was used medicinally for the treatment of diseases and for pain relief and wound healing.

The leader of the Oryx told of the clans along the foothills of the Imatong, with whom they trade and source obsidian and quartz. Yet he most earnestly emphasized that Frankincense and Myrrh are sourced all but exclusively from the totem clans of the Elephant ...who reside in the *Cavern Cities of the Mountains of the Heavens*. On the slopes of Mount Elgon lie some of the most unique caves on earth; the caverns were formed as lava tubes by lava flows from Mt Elgon long ago, some of them extending unknown distances into the mountain.[32]. Near the base Mt. Elgon, but a distance up its slopes, at mid-level elevation, are the large caverns anciently used as villages in which hundreds of people resided; where they built stone houses and corrals into which they herded cattle at night.

The cavern villages of the Elephant clans occupied several multi-level interior caverns so refined by their ancient inhabitants that when discovered by the first European explorer, he deduced that the caves must have been of artificial origin.[ccxxii] The village dwellers made their residences in the upper interior caverns. Legends report they built homes with ample food storage. As part of their livelihood, they maintained cattle, which were kept in corrals in the lower interior caverns at night. The *cavern villages* were spread across an enormous settlement area that archaeologists first described as an *"ancient metropolis"*; a metropolis a comfortable distance above the large caves on the lower slopes, where elephants and buffalo visited each night to eat mineral salts they craved and mined from the cavern walls with their tusks and horns.[ccxxiii]

The Oryx leader affirmed as he had been told by the Elephant clan that Frankincense and Myrrh came from the powerful kingdom of Punt, a kingdom headed by one so legendary his shadow is cast even over *Ta-Netjeru* (the "Land of the Gods"). It is the powerful kingdom of Lord Bes himself, the Oryx leader related, noting that "his kingdom has come to be called "Ta-Netjer" ("God's Land"), an epithet interpreted by the clans of the *Mountains of the Heavens* as the subtle subsumption of *Ta-Netjeru* ...the sacrosanct "Land of the Gods." The prospect of further expansion by Punt has inspired an alliance amongst the Mountains of the Heavens clans, an alliance extending westward to the pastoral clans along the southern foothills of the Imatong Mountains.

The clan leader of the Oryx then told of the often-perilous journey across the western lowlands approaching the crest of Ta-Nebiru. Whilst these lands are largely the dominions of pastoral Nilotic clans, the Oryx leader noted, they are nonetheless lands plagued by bandits and rogues, accosting not only the pastoralists but also accost traders as they traverse the terrain. *An* listened intently and then sat before his guest in what was surely a prolonged uncomfortable silence as he pondered all that had been said, particularly the part about alliance across the *Mountains of Heaven* in response to the ominous power of the Kingdom of Punt. His father, Anšar, shared such concerns that "a great power must be dealt with from a position of great strength."

In the proposition before him, An assessed his opportunity to secure sources of obsidian and quartz, counterbalancing the sources from the west but, more significantly, securing all but exclusive sources of Frankincense and Myrrh. Realizing he would eventually have to pacify the lowlands of the "Great Pass" to ensure reliable trade routes across of Ta-Nebiru, An informed the leader of the Oryx that he would indeed barter for all they have available to trade now and in the foreseeable future. However, the permanence of their agreement would require the concurrence of his Council of Elders. Thus began the first organized trade flows across the arc of Ta-Nebiru; trade flows in Obsidian and Quartz aided in rebalancing the power dynamic in the 'Mountains of the Moon'.

---

[32] Mt. Elgon first eruption more than 24 million years ago

The Legends

As envisioned by *An*, trade in Frankincense and Myrrh stretching beyond the kingdoms of the "Mountains of the Moon" to the Virunga, Hapi Valley, and points beyond will enhance the stature of his mountain kingdom. Yet the vital trade flows need to be protected from intermittent disruption by the bandits of the lowlands. An's plan began with an eastward expedition headed by Khonsu, who, together with his usual cadre from the Roan and a contingent of the totem clans of the Golden Lion, joined the Oryx in their fifth return journey eastward across the arc of Ta-Nebiru (the "Great Pass"). The destination of the expedition was majestic Mount Elgon at the eastern extent of Ta-Nebiru.

According to plan, with the aid of the *Chameleon King*, Khonsu arranged gatherings with elders of the pastoral clans of the grasslands of Ta-Nebiru to solicit and enlist support for an alliance to protect and defend their lands; this as Khonsu and his cohorts traversed the varied terrain en route to the *Cavern Metropolis* at Mount Elgon. The grasslands of *Ta-Nebiru* were an area where *Proto-Anu* and emergent *Proto-Nilotics* had intermixed for thousands of years. The totem clans of the Horned Chameleon were very much products of this admixture, making their king, *Meni*, a recognizable personage among the clans of the Nilotics, a valuable affinity in arranging gatherings of *Proto-Nilotics* elders to meet with Khonsu.

And so it went until Khonsu, and his entourage reached the greater *Mountains of the Heavens*, Mount Elgon. The Oryx led the way to the *cavern cities* on the slopes of Elgon overlooking Ta-Netjeru ("Land of the Gods"). Majestic Mount Elgon boasts five peaks (Wagagai, Mubiyi and Masaba in Uganda, Sudek on the Kenya / Uganda border, and Koitobos, a flat-topped basalt column that is the third highest peak and the only one solely in and facing Ta Netjeru). When Khonsu and his entourage arrived at the entrance of the *cavern cities*, though the clan leader of the Oryx was readily recognized, the unexpected group accompanying him gave cause for caution by the ever-wary guards at the obscure entrance to the cavernous metropolis.[ccxxiv]

The clan leader of the Oryx, with several members of his ban, together with Khonsu and a few members of his cadre, were allowed entrance, bringing with them samples of the goods they brought to barter. Most particularly, Khonsu brought samples of highly valued *Black Mushrooms* cultivated in the uplands of the *Mountains of the Moon*, an ultra-potent species renowned even amongst the distant clans of the *Mountains of the Heavens*. Word of the availability of the rare herb attracted a fetish priest from the villages of the Elephant clans, a priest known as *Ḥeb* who, once introduced to Khonsu as a *High Priest* from the Mountains of the Moon, advised that there are no such "high priests" in the *Mountains of the Heavens*. However, there are those more revered than others.

Ḥeb informed that the Elephant clans occupy twenty or more of the villages in the *cavern cities*, advising that the village uses Frankincense as currency in bartering for necessities not provided within the cavern metropolis. Ḥeb further informed that the metropolis was otherwise self-contained, with wells, livestock enclosures, and homes, some with dry-stone-walls around them. The Fetish Priest explained that the caverns go deep into the heart of the mountain, with several villages connected by a network of passageways. The Elephant clans are the predominant occupants within the metropolis, though not its only occupants. Heb then told of the other main occupants, the totem clans of the *Winged Serpent*.

Be not misled by their priestly posture, Ḥeb counseled, the totem clans of the *Winged Serpent* are self-described "warrior-priests" whose legends boast of their having stood in defense of the *Duat* against an onslaught of Chaos that once threatened not only our world but every world within creation. Beyond this, Heb continued, through their trade with kindred Serpent Clans across the lowlands, they source Frankincense and Myrrh from the kingdom of Punt. Heb then again noted that each village of the cavern metropolis acquires and maintains its own stores of Frankincense and Myrrh for use as currency in bartering for other necessities from the outer mountain clans.

It has become customary for Oryx traders to hire knowledgeable elders to guide them through the labyrinth of corridors connecting the villages of the metropolis, Heb noted, a somewhat nomadic undertaking that typically takes several days as they trade to acquire Frankincense, Myrrh and Salt throughout the caver metropolis. Then, seizing the opportunity at hand, the ever-astute Heb propounded that surely the proportions needed to feed the appetite of the Mountains of the Moon will exceed that readily attainable from the cavern metropolis alone. Heb proposed that in exchange for access to *Black Mushrooms*, he guide Khonsu through the corridors to the precincts of the clans of the Winged Serpent, who acquire and provide Frankincense & Myrrh to the cavern metropolis.

The wily Fetish Priest assured that though the serpent clan is highly secretive and selective with whom they barter, his reputation and long-standing relations with them will position Khonsu in good stead. Thus, they journey through the passageways and inter-connecting corridors to the precincts of the totem clans of the Winged Serpent in the cavern villages at majestic Mount Elgon. True to his word, soon after arrival, Heb was warmly received by a highly regarded fetish priest known as "Åmi-ta", who, upon examining samples of the coveted Black Mushrooms offered in barter, summoned those more knowledgeable than himself. A priest of presumably higher rank, introduced as Meṭu-ta, accompanied by an equally elderly Sage, introduced as Pesi, soon joined them, each carefully examining the rare, dried herb.

Shortly after that arrived one who appeared to be the defacto High Priest of the totem clans of the Winged Serpent at Elgon, a priest known as Seta-ta, who, after a brief word with Pepsi, sat to negotiate the terms of barter with Khonsu. Seta-ta explained that their stores of Frankincense & Myrrh are acquired from a kindred Serpent Clan in the southeastern lands of the kingdom Punt, the totem clans of the Crocodile, who, though they are a powerful force in their own right, must themselves acquire Frankincense & Myrrh from the clans of the Frankincense forests in the northeastern confines of the land.

Though the rare and highly sought-after Black Mushrooms you offer are worth many times their weight in Frankincense & Myrrh, Seta-ta opined, it would nonetheless require significant amounts of the rare black herb …to acquire sufficient quantities of Frankincense & Myrrh to satisfy the needs of a kingdom as vast as the *Mountains of the Moon*. It was then that Khonsu told the tale of the cultivation of the ultra-potent ebony mushroom in the highlands of the Mountains of the Moon; he told of how the damp, moist climate across the mid-highlands was ideal for the cultivation and accentuation of ultra-potent strains of gigantic "Black Mushrooms." Khonsu explained that many, if not most, of the plants and mushrooms in the highlands of the 'Mountains of the Moon' are of gigantic size and proportion.

A peculiarity of the highland habitat, where ancient Sages, most notably those of the totem clans of the 'Winged-Serpent,' my native clan in the western highlands, Khonsu revealed, gained keen knowledge of the medicinal attributes and unique states of mind the herbs bestow. That Khonsu was a native son of the kindred clan of the *Winged-Serpent* was revelatory to Heb and Seta-ta, and most certainly grasped the attention of Ămi-ta", Pesi and Meṭu-ta. At hearing Khonsu was of a kindred serpent clan, the defacto high priest *Seta-Ta*, seeking further clarification, inquired of Khonsu, 'are you and your clan "Followers of Heru ?" by which it is meant, are you "Pursuers of Heru'?.

The ancient ones viewed "Heru", the fabled "Winged or Luminous Serpent", the mythological "Celestial Hydra" (an early ancient interpretation of the "Southern Borealis" (the "Aurora Australis")) as an instrument of creation, the pursuit and pursuant enlightenment of which would grant one greater understanding of creation and the Creator. Khonsu, in turn, affirmed that the clans of the *Winged-Serpent* in the highlands of the 'Mountains of the Moon", from whence the *Diaspora* of the serpent clans began, are indeed "Followers of Heru." A revelation and affirmation all at once, changing the tenor and palpable level of trust between kindred clansmen.

Khonsu explained that the coveted Black Mushroom is native to the highlands of the Mountains of the Moon, where the ancient Sages seized upon them as both a medicinal panacea and, for the true adept, a portal to the spiritual realm. The ancient art of cultivation in the highlands goes back over generation, after generation, beyond memory, with the highland Sages acquiring ever-greater knowledge of the ideal habitats, morphology, and seasonality of the coveted ebony herb. Ultra potent strains of the black mushroom were spread throughout the vast highlands of the "Mountains of the Moon,' primarily through barter and trade over the centuries, Khonsu further explained, assuring that the harvests they shall render to barter will be more than sufficient to accommodate the Frankincense & Myrrh they seek to acquire.

An assurance satisfying Seta-ta, as well as Meṭu-ta, Ămi-ta and the Sage Pesi, thus established the accord and pursuant trade relationship between *Lord An*, on behalf of the kingdoms of the Mountains of the Moon, and *Seta-ta*, on behalf of the cavern cities of the Mountains of the Heavens; one of the earliest fairly long-distance trade pacts. That being settled, Khonsu used the opportunity before him to delve more deeply into the ethos of the priestly class of the clans of the "Celestial Serpent." Khonsu specifically inquired into the legend shared by Heb, which tells the tale of the warrior priests of the serpent clans who posit themselves as the "Sons of Heru", those who stood in defense of the Duat amidst an onslaught of the forces of Chaos that threatened our world.

To this, Seta-ta noted, "the monk-like Order appropriated the "Winged Serpent" as its totem at the behest of a great Seer known as Upāst, who insisted it would necessarily focus and conjoin energies of the auras of the priestly clan, which would better serve them in the spiritual realm. The Sage Pesi explained that Upāst understood that the Creator prevailed over the forces of Chaos through the creation of the Cosmos and relied upon humanity's help to maintain it. Pesi added, speaking of Upāst, he was a restless sort, restless due to intuitive abilities that ultimately prompted his pilgrimage to Ta Netjeru (the "Land of the Gods"). It was a pilgrimage he began as a young man, whom we did not see again until he was middle-aged.

Upāst returned with tales of a clan of Mystic Seers with whom he enlisted in the heights of Ta Netjeru, Pesi mused, noting that it was he who first informed of the rise of the forces of Chaos and the assault on the Duat. Upāst told of battles beyond the borderland provinces of the ancestors, battles well beyond the *Threshold*, and a struggle to save the *Duat* itself. We were admonished to heighten our preparedness, Pesi recounted, noting that she was very young at the time. From then on, young men adhered to the protocols provided to us. The de facto high priest Seta-ta added that "when the warrior priests of the totem clans of the Winged Serpent were called to defend the Duat, they were an ardent but paltry lot, yet when aligned with those from other worlds, they were all at once many and formidable.

Legend holds, Seta-ta continued that they formed their lines of defense along the mountain tops at the far side of the provinces of the ancestors in the borderlands of the Duat, where it is sad they held fast… awaiting an onslaught by the forces of chaos that thankfully never arrived. According to legend, Seta-ta recounted, the battle was fought and won by great armies beyond the Duat. A fascinated *Khonsu* vowed to soon return, that he might train and become adept enough in their protocols to train others in the kingdoms, the Mountains of the Moon. There was a clear air of mutual appreciation and respect between Seta-ta and Khonsu, an advent leaving Heb a bit unnerved and uncertain, as he wondered if the service of he and those of his clan would be needed in a lasting sense between the kindred clansmen.

A concern, once expressed, Khonsu immediately put to rest, informing Heb they shall rely on and compensate his clan for the internal transport of the bartered goods within the Cavern Metropolis. Khonsu further informed that he hoped Heb would be instrumental in his efforts to bring the kingdom spanning the 'Mountains of the Moon' into the grand alliance to protect and defend the clans and lands of Ta-Nebiru, which he deemed to be essential to unmolested trade across the trade routes of the 'Great Crossing'. Revealing that he was one the three most influential of the Elephant clans, Heb expressed assurance that the kingdom of the 'Mountains of the Moon' would be warmly welcomed into the 'Grand Alliance'.

Such an arrangement, Heb mused, would fulfill the vision shared by the ruling clans of a unified Ta Nebiru in counterbalance to the power and prowess of Punt. Thus, it was that Khonsu returned triumphantly to the *City of Villages* and the Great House, where he affirmed the availability of obsidian and quartz from clans of the Mountains of Heavens and told of the accord at the Cavern Metropolis to trade Black Mushrooms for Frankincense & Myrrh. Lastly, Khonsu apprised of the Grand Alliance and their presumed role and responsibility in pacifying the western lowlands of Ta-Nebiru. It was then that Khonsu learned of the campaigns while he was away at Elgon.

It seems that in the wake of Khonsu's efforts to recruit the pastoral clans into a "grand alliance", the same clans had sought the aid of Meni, the Chameleon King, to protect and defend them against the bands of marauders plaguing the grasslands and lives of the docile pastoralist. A complaint and request that Meni brought forthright to *An*; ever the Roan, *An* organized contingent of warriors from each of the clans in the Mountains of the Moon, informing each that reliable access to Frankincense & Myrrh depended upon defending and protecting the trade routes across Ta-Nebiru.

The brash An, ever the Roan, personally had led four separate campaigns into the western lowlands while Khonsu was gone, each at the behest of victimized pastoral clans who accepted Khonsu's solicitation to join the alliance; they thus committed allotments of their own warriors to An's forces. During each of the first three campaigns, the adept acuity of the Roan and Oryx enabled them to easily track the marauders, while the greater familiarity with the terrain possessed by the warriors of the pastoral clans allowed them to outmaneuver and trap the intruders. Under An's command, each direct encounter began with volleys from the eagle-eye archers of the totem clans of the Bat-Hawk, followed by purposely ruckus charges by resolute warriors of the Golden Lion, Horned Chameleon, Mountain Cheetah, and Royal Crane, among others.

The marauders were vanquished at each encounter, with their survivors left fleeing for their very lives; yet, after a time, the marauders would always nonetheless return. Thus the mission of the fourth campaign was solely to construct a network of four permanent fortifications along the forests-line north of the pastoral lowlands. The forts were permanently staffed and provisioned by lowland and highland clans, on a revolving basis, with An himself inspecting and, on occasion, randomly staying at and leading assaults against remaining intruders from each fortress, gaining him the epithet, "the Lion-Hearted." And so, with the trade routes unmolested, and Obsidian, Quartz and Frankincense Myrrh flowing from the 'Mountains of the Heavens,' prosperity abound, with An extolled and exalted as the "Dawn of a New Day."

Thus, it was, for the better part of a generation, a time and prosperity during which the daughters and sons of Khonsu and An grew into the majority. An had one wife, Uraš, by whom he had two sons, the first being Enlil, who was only slightly older than his brother Enki, and one daughter, Bau (or Baba), the youngest of her siblings.[ccxxv]. Khonsu, in turn, had two wives, the first was Ruia, who gave him three children, a daughter, Uiay, and two sons, User and Tjay, with Tjay being the youngest of the lot. His second wife, Mutia (or Maiay, or Maay), came a bit later, and she gave him seven children. However, it was the two sons and daughters of An and the two sons and daughters of Khonsu by Ruia who grew to majority during a time of great prosperity.

It was an idyllic time of peace and contentment across the land, which many felt would never end until it did, with the first in a sequence of three existential crises, each worst than the last. The era of peace and contentment was during the "warm" climatic optimum hallmarking the Holocene and the first in a series of super floods. The great rains and warmer climate ushered at the onset of Holocene, over time, facilitated the melt of the great glaciers, whose water filled the highlands lakes formed by the then weakening the ice-dams until, alas, the upper highland dams gave way, causing a cascading effect. The lower dams soon gave way as well, causing devastating floods and destruction throughout the valleys and foothills. Whole communities were literally destroyed and displaced, as was the case in the Nyamwamba River Valley.[ccxxvi]

The villages below the Land of Eight Lakes were all but completely destroyed, as was much of Old Town and virtually all of the City of Villages. Displacement was rampant across the Mountains of the Moon, with many villages and lives lost; yet resilient as ever, having absorbed the trauma, the Proto-Anu began the long, tedious tasks of rebuilding. Intermittent torrential rains made the tasks of rebuilding all the more challenging. Still, with determination, vision and native grit, the mountain kingdom rose from the destruction like the mythical phoenix. Yet only to be revisited by devastation within three short years when the torrential rains came again, causing even great destruction, displacement, and loss of life. And once again, with *An* standing tall throughout the turmoil, imparting vision, and exemplifying faith and fortitude, the clans banded together to raise their ancient civilization from the ashes.

Again, they rebuilt, and as they had before, and then, as fate would have, another truly second existential crisis arose …at first disguised as a blessing. The rains became less torrential and less frequent, allowing ample opportunity to rebuild the village communities in the valleys and foothills. For a time, it seemed as if life had returned to "normal", and needed trade resumed across Ta-Nebiru as the clans rebuilt …they were so enraptured by the grace granted them between the rains that few took notice of the increasingly cooler climate and that the rains had all but ceased. Roughly around 13,000 B.C., seemingly inexplicably, the planet plunged into a massive global cooling, spreading southward from the Northern Hemisphere, returning abruptly to near-glacial temperatures …for more than a thousand years; a climatic event known as "The Younger Dryas."

The Younger Dryas marked a return to the drier times of the Great Ice Age, bringing with it an aridity that blanked the lowlands and rapidly rose into the lower highlands. Once again, the forests were weakened, and sources of sustenance diminished, bringing with them the extinction of some thirty-five different animal species.[ccxxvii] A present-day "Younger Dryas Hypothesis" postulates that fragments of the "Vela Supernova" hit the Earth about 13,000 BC, causing rapid climatic changes and megafaunal extinctions. This hypothesis focuses on the impact of the Vela Supernova fragment as a triggering mechanism for the abrupt, rapid cooling amid the theretofore global trend of natural warming and ice sheet melting (evidenced by the fossil and sediment record).[ccxxviii]

The torrential rains during the initial phase of the Holocene interlude gradually recharged massive Lake Nyanza (Lake Victoria), which had all but completely dried up in the wake of the Glacial Maximum. The massive shallow lake recovered to some degree from the heavy opening rains of the Holocene, transforming it from a desolate, mostly dry, mosquito-plagued land of scattered swamps. After the Younger Dryas ushered in a new era of global cooling and a return to the dry, arid conditions of the last Ice Age as moisture was again increasingly locked up in the growing glaciers. The huge land areas encompassing Lake Kyoga and Lake Nyanza, a surface of over 25,000 square miles, were again transformed into a desolate, dry, mosquito-ridden land of scattered swamps.

Ta-Nebiru (the "Great Pass" or "Crossing") once again became all the more important as a trade and transit route, bridging the "Land of Man" with Ta-Netjeru, the "Land of the Gods." And alas, as "Lake Nyanza" (Lake Victoria) and Lake Kyoga were again transformed into huge desolate, mosquito-ridden lands; once again, the clans of the lowlands migrated into the highlands fomenting harsh territoriality and increased conflict. A culmination that again became particularly heightened in the wake of the dwindling forests and food resources, an advent that called upon the tutelary head of the ancient mountain kingdom for a solution. Lord An did not disappoint, invoking an old solution, for a new problem.

Intermittent trickles of northbound migrations towards the well-watered and fertile lands of the ancient Nile River Valley had never truly ceased. Once An began to promote it as a solution to the scarcity, overcrowding and conflict in the foothills and highlands, the flow of migrations began to increase. Lord An prompted and encouraged "follow the water to the rich fertile lands of the northern river valley", but it wasn't until the ceremonial coronation of his youngest son Enki to lead and represent the kingdom in the precincts of the northern river valley that the migrations re-ensued in earnest, lessening the crisis in the highlands. Much like An himself, Enki reached the majority be benefited from the direct tutelage of Khonsu and the warrior ethos of the Roan, whom he accompanied on seasonal nomadic journeys across the Mountains of the Moon.

Like An before him, the several years of seasonal nomadic journeys across the mountain kingdom served to familiarize and ingratiate the young prince with the clans and kingdoms of the realm. As he reached the age of majority, Enki accompanied and joined An in leading his third and fourth campaigns to pacify the western lowlands of Ta-Nebiru, with Enki, ever the Roan, acquitting himself well in each battle of the campaign, driven to prove himself a worthy progeny of "*An the Lion-Hearted*." And prove himself he did. Indeed it was a mature and proven *Enki* whom An placed in charge of managing and completing construction of the fourth fortification, in the heart of what was deemed the "Crest of Ta-Nebiru"; an undertaking in which he again acquitted himself well.

The challenge "the coronation" now presented to Enki was not only one of leadership but of providing a vision for a journey into the unknown. The illustrious Nile Valley was not then as it is today; the modern discharge regime of the river can be traced back to the beginning of the Holocene wet phase, around 12 000 BC. During the preceding millennium, the Nile carved a deep, wide "Grand Canyon" size gorge (the "Nile Valley Canyon") through the granite tablelands on its way to the Delta. In consequence, at the mouth of the river, the valley floor reaches depths similar to the Grand Canyon (in Arizona); as one travels southward upstream, the ancient canyon becomes less entrenched. Over the ensuing millennium, the river has infilled the canyon with untold volumes of silt and sediments brought down from the highlands, with the build-up eventually forming the floor of the Nile River Valley. [ccxxix]

In addition, it is clear and evident (from geological studies) that the Nile River has, over thousands of years, significantly altered its course, as well as its location. Although present-day geologists continue to debate the precise dates of the shift in the course, they do not dispute that the Nile River once flowed about ten miles west of its present-day course and may have been over three hundred feet higher than its present water level. Evidence has also been found indicating that the Proto-Anu who formed the earliest Nile Valley civilization actually drew their water from west of the course of the present-day Nile River. Ancient ruins west of Nile Valley have yielded remains of early ancient aqueducts which flowed from west to east, from what present-day Geologists refer to as the "*Proto-Nile.*"

The "Proto-Nile" flowed out of the Central African highlands, much as the *Ancient Nile* does today; however, instead of flowing to the Mediterranean Sea at the Delta in northern Nile Valley, as the present day *Ancient Nile* does, the *Proto-Nile* continued its course through the floor of the valley, and then turned westward, flowing towards and into the deepest part of the northeastern Sahara, a depression later known as the "Faiyum", where it created a huge lake west of the *Nile Valley* during remotest antiquity known as Lake Moeris.[ccxxx] The present-day Faiyum depression is still below the average elevation of the desert and well below sea level, occupying the seven hundred square mile bed of early ancient *Lake Moeris*.[ccxxxi]

Early Proto-Anu migrations moved sporadically along the *Proto-Nile*, establishing settlements as they pushed northward through the Sudan corridor until ultimately reaching the fertile lands of the *Fayoum* surrounding the shores of *Lake Moeris*. The *Proto-Anu* spread first into the Fayoum as the present-day delta was then covered with water beyond what would later become the province of Waset (Thebes). Ancient legends hold that no part of the land north of *Lake Moeris* was then above water, legends corroborated by the configuration and composition of the lowlands of the region, which leave no room for doubt that the sea once washed against the base of the rocks on which the pyramids of *Memphis* would later stand.[ccxxxii]

In final preparation for Enki's northward migrations, An convenes a meeting with his eldest son Enlil. Khonsu, along with Khonsu's eldest son, User, advises all of the concurrences of the Elders Councils to provision the northern migrations. And further, to reveal that, with the inbound migrations, rising aridity, and the further retreat of the forests …soon the "City of Villages" itself will no longer be sustainable. An informed that he and Khonsu considered relocation to "Old Town", as the rising aridity was well below the elevation of the villages, but alas, they resolved that this would be but a temporary solution, as the inbound migrations would soon overwhelm the limited seasonal resources of the highlands. Khonsu then added that an equally important consideration …is the preservation of the unity and sovereignty of Ta-Nebiru.

An then revealed that after much consideration and after long hours of deliberation in the Council of Elders, it has been decided that the "Royal City" shall be relocated to the heart of the still well-watered lands at the "Crest of Ta-Nebiru." An informed that simultaneous to the departure of Enki and User to the northern river valley, Khonsu, Enlil and Tjay shall depart to the "Crest of Ta-Nebiru" to plan the relocation of the "Royal City" to the site of the fourth fortification, which shall be used as the "Citadel of the Great House." An advised that he and Biluda shall remain behind to prepare for the eastward migration across the western lowlands to the "Crest of Ta-Nebiru." An then opined that they are living in perilous times, times have unseen in a millennium and that the tasks before them shall be no small undertaking and will require both fortitude and vision.

Then, as if speaking only to his eldest son, Lord An intoned that 'fortitude is reinvigorated by vision', propounding that "without vision, the people shall perish." He then urged that his youngest son Enki "follow the wisdom of the water", which shall lead him to the fertile and abundant lands of the northern river valley, where the aridity is arrested. None live under pain of duress." Advice that Enki and User each took to heart as they set out on the long journey of their migrations into the river valley of the north. It was this lot, those of the third great northward migrations, that bought agriculture, science and culture down the Nile, where legend holds they did not arrive as immigrants but are natives of the country and are therefore rightly called autochthonous. [ccxxxiii]

This was the aboriginal race of Anu (or Aunu, written with three pillars), who became a part of the historic inhabitants of the Nile Valley; the Anu whose initial home range extended from the land that would later become Nubia (Ta-Nehisi) into the Southern (or "Upper") Nile River Valley. From the perspective of the Proto-Anu of the era, their settlements were merely extensions of the small-enchanted village communities that anciently settled along the Nile River Valley, which, from their perspective, extended from the "Land of Man", through the lakes region of the middle Africa, into the lands of the northern river valley. Enki's (first) base of operations, according to legend, was on the island of Abu (now called Elephantine on account of its shape), located just above the first cataract of the Hapi (Nile) River at Aswan.

These Anu were agricultural people, raising cattle on a large scale along the Nile and shutting themselves up in walled cities for defensive purposes.[ccxxxiv] The development of stone buildings was based on earlier crafts and the carvings in wood and ivory, a translation that is seen in the stone copies of wooden doorways and wooden doors. They built the beginnings of major cities and complex societies in the Nile River Valley. All those early ancient cities (Ant, Annu Menti, Aunti, and Aunyt-Seni, today called Esneh, Erment, Quoch, and Heliopolis) bare symbols which denote the name Anu. Theocentric in nature, spirituality played a central role in the lives of the Anu; the esoteric knowledge of the priesthood formed the people's ontological, cosmological, astronomical, cosmographic and horticultural knowledge, guiding their aspirations and achievements.

Arithmetic, geometry, astronomy, geology, philosophy, chemistry, medicine, and other physical and metaphysical sciences were all gifts from the Anu to an unfolding world. They developed metal smelting and mastered the other crafts necessary for the rise of early Nile Valley civilization and were familiar with the tools those trades required. This explains the emergence of a well-organized civilization possessing knowledge of the celestial bodies, capable of navigation on the lakes, rivers, and of the earth. And further, how they came to know the circumference of the planet, the length of the year, the length of the Earth's orbit around the sun, the 25,920-year cycle of the equinoxes, and the speed of light in order to build the Great Sphinx at Giza.

The Legends

The Nile River flows south to north just east of the Giza Limestone Rock Plateau on earth, analogous to the celestial Milky Way spanning the length of our galaxy just east of the Constellation Orion in the sky, along a south to north course, is where the Anu carved and gave life and stature to the Great Sphinx. At nearly 240 feet long—almost the length of a football field—and almost 70 feet tall—the height of the White House—the Sphinx is the largest statue in all of Khemet, an ancient land renowned for its oversized monuments.

However, the Sphinx is more than just a lion. It's also part human; when you put the human head on the lion's body, you have all the strength and power of the lion. You have the human head, which is a symbol of intelligence and control. And so, it is an image of power under control. The giant paws of the Sphinx are longer than a city bus. Its whipping tail wraps around its back, with its enormous body, about the weight of fifty 747 jumbo jets, on haunches, poised to pounce.

There were originally two sphinxes at Giza, each carved right out of the natural mother rock of the Giza Plateau.[ccxxxv] A close examination has revealed that the upper body and heads of the sphinxes were carved out of one huge rock; even closer inspection reveals the Sphinxes were made and formed of limestone. All the limestone at Giza, including the body of the Sphinxes, was once the floor of the sea, as the Great Sphinx once stood at the shore of the sea; so you have frozen into the stone, various elements of seafloor life.[ccxxxvi]

The Great Sphinxes is an equinoctial marker, with their gazes directed precisely at the point of sunrise and sunset on the vernal equinox, symbols of eternity.[ccxxxvii] The carving and building of the Sphinxes began at the end of the last Ice Age, beginning about 12,000 BC, with the objective of completing the multi-generational project by the dawn of the Age of Leo, in 10,500 BC, when the alignment of the heavens would line up with the Giza Plateau.[ccxxxviii] In the pre-dawn on the vernal equinox in 10,500 BC, with the sun twelve degrees below the horizon, the Great Sphinx would gaze directly at his own celestial counterpart, the constellation of Leo, which experienced its helical rising at that moment.

The modern discharge regime of the Ancient Nile can be traced back to the Holocene wet phase, around 12 000 BC; over the ensuing millennium, the river carved a deep, wide, "Grand Canyon" size gorge (the "Ancient Nile Valley Canyon") through the hard granite bedrock tablelands of the Nile Valley floor on its journey to the delta. Toward the mouth of the river, the "Nile Valley Canyon" reaches depths similar to that of the Grand Canyon in Arizona. As it progresses southward, the canyon becomes less entrenched. The powerful Holocene-driven currents of the "Ancient Nile" deposited and infilled the Nile Valley Canyon with volumes of silt and sediments from the highlands; a gradual build-up eventually formed the Nile floor River Valley.[ccxxxix]

Enki and User-led the northward migrations through the gorges, descending valleys, and thick forests of the midlands, transporting the ancient ethos of the Anu into the northern river valley.[ccxl] The Anu were a spiritual people who studied and were guided by the consistency of the celestial heavens; a people who demarcated the seasons purely by the stars, an aptitude that aided the emergence of a well-organized civilization, possessing knowledge of the celestial bodies, and capable of navigation on the great lakes and seas. The new province in the upper river valley began as a federation of the five early ancient cities of Ant, Annu Menti, Aunti, and Aunyt-Seni, a federation founded on fundamental solidarity protected against the hazards of life, fomenting the growth of an early market economy.

With an inherent mastery of basic commerce and trading between the five early cities via both the river and its tributaries and several overland trade routes, the establishment of far-reaching south-north trade connected the cities of the northern river valley with the clanic kingdoms of the fabled Mountains of the Moon, the Hapi Valley (heart of the "Land of Man"), and most significantly, the kingdom of Ta-Nebiru. It is commonly acknowledged that at least rudimentary political structures existed along the course of the Upper Nile at this and the earlier phases of the northern migrations. That such long-distance trade was a primary cause of "State" formation and growth is a well-founded perspective shared by many historians and present-day archaeologists. Oliver Page 1962 Vansina 1966 Wilson 1972 Huffman 1970 Summers 1969

A number of scholars see long-distance trade as a direct stimulus of State formation, first by requiring the development of centralized authority for administrative purposes, second as the mechanism through which ideas of hierarchical political organization were transmitted, and third by stimulating territorial expansion into control resources and protect trade routes. From this perspective, long-distance trading activities not only were the chief cause of central African States' formation but also exerted a strong influence on the particular organization of African States and their territorial goals. The culmination of early state formation was brought about by the recognition of the first sovereign assigned the epithet "King of King", a king whose prescience facilitated needed transformation during a time of existential crisis, eponymous Lord An Ta-Nebiru

There exists a question in the deepest recesses of early antiquity, and that is simply this... 'did the fabled and mythical lands of Ta-Nebiru really exist? There has always been great confusion as to exactly where this powerful kingdom of earliest antiquity was located. According to ancient oral legend, this remarkable kingdom was said to be vast, proud, and powerful, a legendary or perhaps merely mythological paradise that symbolized purity, abundance and magic. In the faint whispers of the earliest antiquity, it was said to be the oldest recognizable monarchy in human history, a monarchy in which the tributary kings across the vast lands of Ta-Nebiru (the "Great Pass") were united under Lord An, the first true "King of Kings." [ccxli]

As discussed and planned, Khonsu transformed, prepared, and led the eight clans of the Golden Lion from the eastern highlands of the Mountains of the Moon north-eastward through the western uplands to Ta-Nebiru' to the "Crest." As word spread of the prosperity of the vast land of the nascent "City of An" itself, clans from the increasingly desolate lowlands and shores around Lake Kyoga and Great Lake Nyanza soon added their numbers to the migrations into the ancient Crest of Ta-Nebiru.

The Legends

The "City of An" was an ancient walled city nestled in the fertile crest of Ta-Nebiru, a land crossed by crystal blue rivers flowing from the Mountains of the Heavens. Atop a grass-laden mound at the center of the city was the "Great House", in effect an early ancient royal palace consisting of four long-house structures constructed of sun-dried (adobe-like) bricks, with the four structures enclosing an interior courtyard. The Royal Residence faced the entrance of the city, with the Hall of Elders to its left as one entered the city, the Royal Storage and Administrative building to its right, and the Royal Temple enclosing the interior courtyard at the rear.

The Great House atop the grass-laden mound at the center of the city was itself surrounded by grasslands and isolated tree stands. The villages and townships of the original eight clans from the 'City of Villages' occupied the grasslands surrounding the Great House. Their precincts formed what became known as the "Eight Houses" of the walled city. The city itself was surrounded by large walls, with the inhabitants within the walls self-sufficiently sustaining themselves with a form of early agriculture. The precincts of the city were home to cultivated groves, with gardens amid the grasslands and tree stands.

Beyond the grasslands and tree stands were the forestlands, crossed by the crystal blue rivers flowing from the Mountains of the Heavens. The wall surrounding the city divided the grasslands in half, with half forming the inner precincts of the city and the other half forming the exterior periphery. The clans migrating from the desolate lands around the drying great lakes to the south settled on the periphery, forming an outer suburb of the city where they erected earthen dams along river tributaries and built artificial ponds as fish farms.

The city was bound by a bond of a spiritual nature, with the Temple and its allusions to cosmological illumination at the center of spiritual belief, science, philosophy, mathematics, and astronomy. It was where Khonsu first proselytized that the path to wisdom, though fraught with peril, is the path to greater understanding and harmony with the creative force that is the "Creator." He propounded that participation in a virtuous life through well-meaning thoughts and deeds, with a tenacity to prevail against ever-looming chaos, strengthens and aligns the spirit with that of the "Creator."

Sacred aspects of "the Mysteries" were first illuminated at the Temple, where initiates came to refer to Khonsu as the "Sage Illuminator", master teacher of the "Mystic Arts"; a necessarily secretive society. Initiants were seen as guardians of sacred knowledge, such as the "Transmutations of Elements and Metals", which Khonsu taught must occur in harmony with the primal forces of creation. Khonsu proselytized that magical powers are bestowed upon the worthy …in proportion to their reverence, wisdom, and intuitive abilities to partake in the ongoing unfolding of creation.[ccxlii]

Khonsu taught Initiants of the seven primary metals of alchemy: gold, silver, copper, tin, iron, lead and mercury, and of the mysterious eighth element, the Quintessence (the "Devine Ether"), the element beyond the four foundational elements of fire, air, water and earth; a subject in which a young Prince An excelled, with a seemingly instinctive understanding and aptitude. Aspirants came from all over Ta-Nebiru, and from as far away as the Mountains of the Moon and the Mountains of the Heavens to study with scholars at the Temple. Others came attracted by a rumor of a city of promise, commerce, music, and pleasure, a fabled city in a vast land teeming with potential riches.

There is no shortage of mythology surrounding the ancient lost "City of An" and its place in the ancient coalescence and governance of Ta-Nebiru. The prosperity of the city was enhanced by its geopolitical and geographical position at the nexus of trade between the Mountains of the Moon in the west, the Mountains of the Heavens in the east, and the early cities of the Nile River Valley in the north. Word of the prosperous city and exaggeration of its richness attracted masses of migrants to the fertile crest of Ta-Nebiru, an advent that, in less than a generation, shifted the impending crisis of overpopulation in the Mountains of the Moon, to the crest of Ta-Nebiru …and the original ancient City of An (On).

In addressing the impending crisis of the increasing population, An availed himself of an old solution to a new yet familiar problem. Just as prompting, promoting, and provisioning the earlier flow of migrations into the fertile northern river valley aided in relieving the crisis of overpopulation in the Mountains of the Moon, so too would promoting and provisioning migrations to the distant lands of the Mesopotamian River Valley aid in alleviating crisis of overpopulation in the fertile Crest of Ta-Nebiru. Yet, as An knew the well, free and open passage to the coast, where they need launch the journey to the Lower Mesopotamian River Valley, would require crossing the powerful kingdom of Punt, and thus the accord of Lord Bes.

In deliberations with the Elders of the Nine Houses of the City of An, Lord An was reminded of encounters and vital assistance the earliest migrants from the Mountains of the Moon received from the more warlike clans from Punt as they met en route to the fertile northern river valley. An was reminded that at the juncture of the ancient "Nile" and the (former) "Yellow Nile," the migrations of the clans from the Mountains of the Moon were forestalled by territorial assertions by a people known as the Si (Xi), whose professed ancient realm extended from the highlands of the Ennedi Mountains, in the heart of the Sahara, along the course of the ancient Yellow Nile River.[33]

They called themselves the Si (Xi) or Shi people, who were the northernmost and earliest of the ancient clans of Yam to reach and, in time, became the autochthonous peoples of the Great Sahara. During the height of the Glacial Maximum, when conditions across the Great Saharan lowlands became oppressive and desert-like, the primordial Si (Xi) of the lowlands en masse joined their ancestral brothers in the well-watered and fertile valleys of the Ennedi highlands. The ancient Si (Xi) of the era transformed the Ennedi highlands into a vast territorial realm that, in time, extended eastward along the course and corridor of the ancient "Yellow Nile River", a territorial proclamation that extended to the Yellow Nile's juncture with the ancient "Hapi/Nile River", near the southern part of the "Great Bend."

It was there, at the southern part of the Great Bend, that the migrating clans from the Mountains of the Moon encountered the territorial proclamations of the Si (Xi), who, in no uncertain terms, warned the migrating Anu to not only proceed no further but rather to retreat back up the corridors of the early ancient "Hapi / Nile River Valley. Though the clans from the Mountains of the Moon were unprepared and ill-suited for such confrontation, not so for the more war-like clans from the highlands of Punt. The Si (Xi) had, alas, grown wary of the continued migrations of the Anu and the Proto-Anu before them. Though the later migrating Anu had not ventured into the Yellow Nile province of the Si, the Si (Xi) was nonetheless wary of the growing population and force of the Anu in the ancient upper Nile River Valley.

---

[33] The Ennedi Mountains are in present day north-western Sudan and north-eastern Chad.

The arrival of the war-like clans from Punt added to the forces and defensive profile. Posture of the clans from the Mountains of the Moon, a reinforced defensive force the warlike clans from Punt quickly transformed into an aggressive offensive, which, through a series of sustained and determined battles, eventually forced the Si (*Xi*) back up the corridor of the Yellow Nile, opening the way for the further flow of the northern migrations of the Anu. In counseling An, the Elders of the High Council propounded that though Lord Bes of Punt had responded in kind to the northward migrations launched by An's father (Ansar), unlike Ansar's worst fears, it was not an endeavor launched in competition, but in cooperation.

That being said, it was then that the Elders of the Ninth House, the house divided between the totem clans of the Oryx and the Roan, informed that the proposed migration route would require crossing the hostile terrain of the clans of the intervening lowlands. To this, Khonsu added that 'it would also no doubt require the accord of Lord Bes …for the migrants from Ta-Nebiru to traverse his domain to reach the seacoast, from where they need launch their journey to the distant Mesopotamian River Valley'. Khonsu suggested a solution to problems by telling the tale of how the Winged-Serpent Clans of Elgon use their affinity with the network of Serpent Clans across the intervening lowlands to access and bring Frankincense and Myrrh to the uplands.

Khonsu reminded that he himself is of the Winged-Serpent Clan of the Western Rwenzoris (the "Mountains of the Moon"), and with the assistance of the totem Clans of the Celestial Serpent at Elgon (the greater "Mountains of the Heavens"), with whom he had by then cultivated a trusting and close relationship. He shall avail himself of the protection of the network of Serpent Clans spanning the intervening lowlands for safe passage to the highlands of Punt. Which An then insisted it shall require a fully provisioned and well-armed force, expressing his concern for the aging Khonsu, to which Khonsu opined that a somewhat smaller, discrete, yet astute cadre would be less likely to elicit a reflexive response.

Thus, it was set, with the sole exception of the inclusion of Enlil, at his own insistence. Feeling somewhat slighted that his younger brother had been chosen to head the colonies in the northern river valley, Enlil saw the mission to Punt as an opportunity to prove himself, noting that he could best protect and serve his aging mentor, Khonsu, standing as his second in command. A proposition An readily consented to, realizing his eldest son had failed to grasp that he was being groomed to one day assume the throne of Ta-Nebiru. In consenting that Enlil joins in opening passage to the eastern lands, An informed that while the eastern lands are visible across a narrow sea strait from the northern coast of Punt, the lands of Mesopotamian River Valley are still some distance away.

An resolved that those migrating to the eastern lands would need to build boats to cross the narrow sea strait, and once across, they would need the best route to the Lower Mesopotamian River Valley; that being said, An then requested that should accord and opportunity permit, Enlil cross into the eastern lands and survey the best and most opportune route. A charge that reaffirmed a father's confidence in his son, more so for the son than the father, but for An's purposes, it re-instilled in Enlil that sense of certainty leadership requires. Then, as planned, Khonsu and his entourage began their mission at the Cavern Cities of Elgon, where word of the objective of their mission was well received by the Elders of the totem clans of the Cosmic Serpent, whose assistance Khonsu sought.

Though the Elders of the totem clans of the Cosmic Serpent viewed the plan advanced by Khonsu as a bold one, they realized that similar problems of migrations into the highlands, and resulting territorial disputes, were plaguing the outer-mountain clans of Mt. Elgon itself. And though the powerful Elephant clans of the Cavern Cities had held fast in thwarting intrusion or invasion of the Cavern Metropolis, they felt the prospect was still a real threat. Thus did the Elders of the Celestial Serpent Clans at Elgon agree to commit Men and recourses to Khonsu, availing him of a cadre of warriors and able guides, led by the Fetish Priest Ámi-ta, who was familiar to the serpent clans of the intermittent lowlands, on whom the mission would rely for support and assistance.

All appeared to be falling perfectly into place, but Khonsu knew it would be to little avail without a better grasp of the enigmatic Lord Bes, for which he sought a private audience with his now old friend and confidant, Seta-ta, defacto High Priest of the Celestial Serpent Clans of the Cavern Cities, and his equally close and trusted friend, the Grand Sage Pesi. The three met separately in a small cavern in the province of Seta-ta's clan, where the defacto High Priest admonished that Lord Bes was far more than merely a powerful warrior and renowned Sovereign. Seta-ta emphasized that Lord Bes is a powerful spiritual warrior who has not only fought alongside the Devine Netjeru, he has led them in battle.

The Sage Pesi attested that 'by the words of Upāst, who stood at the side of Lord Bes as they prepared for battle against the forces of Chaos'. Pesi then noted that 'the veracity of the words of Upāst is affirmed by the most curious of things'. As told before, she continued, I was a very young girl, a child really, when Upāst first departed from us for the highlands of Ta-Netjeru (Mount Kenya, the "Land of the Gods"). He returned to briefly sojourn with us on five separate memorable occasions over the span of many years, years in which I grew past majority and into aged maturity, and noticeably, after his second return to us, he seemed aged beyond his years. Then when Upāst returned for the fourth time, he appeared clearly aged far beyond his years; yet when he returned for his fifth and final visit, he appeared younger, as though he were my age.

In response to our inquiry, Pesi continued, Upāst told the tale of the occurrence of a mystical spiritual invigoration, which he called an "Imbuing", which heightened the collective and individual brilliance of the auras of the "Forces of Light", those amassed to defend the Cosmos against the Forces of Chaos. Upāst explained that the "Imbuing" is a thing used to strengthen the "Forces of Light" for battle against the demonic hordes of Chaos, a battle in which each encounter exhausts a bit of one life force. The "Imbuing", Upāst explained, invigorates and strengthens one's the life force and vitality. Upāst further explained that it was Lord Bes himself, whom he called "", that invoked the "Imbuing" as he and the forces under the command of Bisu prepared to join the battle against the forces of Chaos.

But alas, Pesi continued, Upāst related that he had fought many earlier battles in defense of the Duat and had thus lost much of the vital energies of his life force, aging him beyond his years. It had been agreed, between him and Bisu, that he would return rather than join the "Forces of Light" in the battle before them… For him, Upāst explained, the "Imbuing" was a parting gift from Bisu, returning many of his lost years, so that he may live a long and fulfilling life. His youthful appearance was a testament to the truth of his tale, Pesi submitted, his fifth final sojourn here, among those with whom he was reared. However, he is a much older man. By the witness of all, he appeared as though he were near my age, which all interpreted as a testament to the veracity of his tale.

So, know that you go to meet with one who is more than merely a renowned Sovereign, Un-tȧ illuminated, Lord Bes, is the one who proved himself Archon of the Prophesy of Tellem. However, you may be strengthened by this, Seta-ta reminded Khonsu, the Prophesy at its end foretells the rise of a great king in the West, a king of kings of such towering achievement and personage. He shall be duly recognized and acknowledged, even by the Archon. By his own account, Seta-ta recounted, the rise of this "king of kings", portending the dawn of a new day, was the last thing spoken of between Upȧst and Lord Bes. 'We know little of the personage of your Lord An,' Un-tȧ confessed, 'but none can refute his towing achievement in uniting and breathing life into Ta-Nebiru'.

The journey ahead was long and arduous, particularly given that it was over unfamiliar and uncertain terrain, yet with the aid and assistance of the serpent clans across the intermittent lowlands. Khonsu, Enlil and the entourage of the mission were safely guided to the province of the most prominent of the kindred serpent clan of Punt, the totem clans of the Crocodile, on the southeastern plateau, at their ancient city of Doolow. It was here that Ȧmi-ta and the monk-like "Sons of Heru", self-described defenders of the Duat (in the spiritual realm), first encountered the monastic order of the "Hydra", self-described defenders of the prefecture and prerogatives of an orthodoxy derived from "Songs of Nefertem", last sovereign of the House of Ptah, led by High Priest, called Neb-Un.

Once duly informed of the Emissaries from Ta-Nebiru, and at the behest of Neb-Un, the Elders of the City of Doolow put on a festive ceremonial welcome that evening, honoring distinguished Emissaries and celebrating their entourage from Ta-Nebiru, a grand ceremony with all the pomp and circumstance deserving of Prince Enlil and the High Priest Khonsu. Though the aurous journey across the intermittent lowlands was certainly worthy of such a celebration and brief sojourn at DooLow, Khonsu was intent on continuing on to Berbera to meet forthwith with Lord Bes. An intent tempered by the diplomacy protocols of Punt, which, as advised by Neb-Un, required word of their pending arrival to be sent in advance to Lord Bes that he may appropriately prepare.

Neb-Un explained that just a few days would be sufficient and advised that Prince Enlil, High Priest Khonsu, and their entire emissarial entourage would be guests of the Clans of Doolow. This Khonsu would use as an opportunity to delve into the seemingly similar ethos and missions of the two monastic sects, the "Sons of Heru" from Elgon, and the order of the "Hydra" at DooLow, in Punt. Neb-Un explained that totem clans of the Crocodile are largely informed by pieced-together fragments of the "old knowledge" preserved during and after the migrations which brought them to the "Lands of the Plateaus." The preserved knowledge is embodied in the fragmented songs of the last King of the House of Ptah, Neb-Un noted, the "Poet King", his youngest son Nefertem.

These are what we refer to as the "Songs of Nefertem", Neb-Un continued, noting, however, that they inform only of the consequences of rising and rampant chaos here, in our world, the physical realm, but not of its cause, which is inferred to emanate from the spiritual realm. Beyond this, we know little of the spiritual realm, Neb-Un confessed, adding only that 'we are aware that our world, the physical realm, is affected by events transpiring in the spiritual realm, and that the spiritual realm is somehow informed by the reverence and order within our world. The latter, Neb-Un advised, informs the mission of the order of the "Hydra", a monastic warrior caste who model and inspire eternal reverence, vigilance, virtue, vision and discipline among the laity.

The " Hydra " monastic order defends the sacred "Mysteries" by preserving and recital of its tenets, Neb-Un informed. The irony is that each is a professed "Order of Spiritual Warriors", Khonsu observed, probing for further insight from the Fetish Priest Ȧmi-ta regarding the Sons of Heru in the "Mountains of the Heavens." To which Ȧmi-ta informed that the "Mysteries" illuminated by Ptah, first and foremost, reveal the existence of the Spiritual Realm and that by their interpretation, Ptah was and remains the "Opener of the Way." The "Mysteries" further reveal the duality of the Cosmos ("creation") and Chaos (the "abyss") and the eternal struggle between the two, Ȧmi-ta further explained.

In pondering the "Mysteries", the monastic order of the "Sons of Heru" came to understand that the Creator prevailed over the forces of Chaos through the very creation of the Cosmos and that the Creator relies upon humankind, here on the physical plane, to so actualize, maintain and defend it against the tenets of Chaos. It is the latter, Ȧmi-ta noted, that informs the missionary fervor of the "Sons of Heru", a monastic warrior caste so informed and called to defend the borderlands of the Duat, the province of the Ancestors, against the loom threats of the forces of Chaos. These forces ultimately threaten our own world. Monks within the Order arise to their aptitude between the ages 12 to 24, and all undergo training during this period.

Individual training culminates with a series of initiation rites, allowing passage through the "warrior archetypes", each warrior maturing from archetype to archetype. In their discipline and reverence, Ȧmi-ta propounded, like "Hydra", the "Sons of Heru," are a monastic order that models and inspires eternal reverence, vigilance, virtue, vision, and discipline among the laity. But how, Neb-Un inquired, do the "Sons of Heru" ascend and defend all together in the spiritual realm? Explaining that, while on rare occasions, there exists an exceptionably gifted priest capable of ascending to interface with Ancestors in the spiritual realm, in their practice, such interface more commonly occurs in the ceremonial audience, with the priest using a form of "spiritual hearing" ("clairaudience").

It is a ritual in which the family seeking advice from their ancestors gather and informs the priest of their family history. He may gain experience in recognizing, distinguishing and interfacing with the voices of their ancestors emanating from the spiritual realm. Because family history is a spiritual work, opportunities for spiritual promptings are plentiful, Neb-Un noted, explaining in further detail that ritual "spiritual hearing" is employed only when the priest can tune in to the spiritual realm and receive messages by actually hearing the identifiable voices of the petitioner's ancestors, and bring evidence, with no doubt, as to who is coming through and speaking. This is the broader practice among most of the clans of the 'Lands of the Plateaus."

Still, the gifted priest capable of ascending into the spiritual realm, of whom I am among the few, Neb-Un revealed, are incapable of ascending in joint mission together. For us, such ascendance is a rather personal endeavor and experience, but one that nonetheless requires irrefutable evidence as to with which ancestor and ancestors one has been speaking. To this, a patient, Khonsu intervened to respond and inform Neb-Un that 'it is the root (mycelium) of the "Black Mushroom" that facilitates, harmonizes and focuses the ability to ascend together into the spiritual realm. Though we are unfamiliar with its use, Neb-Un confessed, we are aware of its use by the Hippopotamus clans to the southeast, the keepers of the Legend of Tellem.

The Hippopotamus clan is the native clan of the Queen Mother and Prophetess Ta-Urt, wife of Lord Bes, in residence at Berbera on the northern coast, Neb-Un informed, noting that the Hippopotamus clans of the north and south originally migrated on the "Lands of the Plateau" from Ta-Netjeru (the "Land of the Gods"), bringing with them the legend that was the vessel of the Prophesy of Tellem. It is tacitly acknowledged that the heightened mysticism and powers of clairvoyance of the High Priestess, and perhaps even Lord Bes himself, Neb-Un noted, is aided by regular ritual use of the sacred and potent "Black Herb." That you, too, Khonsu, are adept in its use and enjoy its benefits will serve you well in your discourse with Lord Bes, Neb-Un opined.

Khonsu, in turn, informed Neb-Un of his Temple at the Great House in the City of An, where they endeavor to unify and strengthen the formative priesthood, an endeavor, he advised, that is greatly fortified by the participation and sharing of an esteemed High Priest such as himself. A gesture and invitation appreciated and accepted by Neb-Un, on behalf of the Elders of the Crocodile clans of Doolow, who provisioned, arranged and instructed experienced guides from the clans to lead and usher to the northern coastal city of Berbera, capital of Punt, and the home of Lord Bes. With ample time to prepare, Khonsu, Enlil, and their entourage arrived at a festive affair and welcoming by Lord Bes and Queen Ta-Urt, a ceremony befitting the Prince and High Priest of Ta-Nebiru.

Granted audience the next morning, Khonsu and Enlil first met promptly and privately with Lord Bes (Bisu) and Queen Ta-Urt over breakfast, where Khonsu explained the purpose of their mission, informing them of the migrations and dislocations, overcrowding and mounting strife in the highlands of the heartland. Khonsu reminded me of how migrations into the northern river valley had relieved similar crises of the past for both the kingdoms of the Mountains of the Moon and those of Punt. Propounding that renewed northward migrations, perhaps of greater proportions than those of the past, would only destabilize the fledgling provinces of the north, to which Bes agreed, Khonsu then requested passage through Punt to allow eastward migrations to the Mesopotamian River Valley.

An affable Lord Bes (Bisu) first informed that Punt itself had colonies and provinces in the eastern lands across the sea, colonies specifically arising around the Frankincense forests of the eastern peninsula, securing Punt's position as the primary source of the highly sought-after herb and incense. The colonies are each in the "Land of Incense", along the southeastern and eastern coasts of the peninsula, a province ending at a natural port known as the "Incense Harbor." Beyond this is the Mesopotamian River Valley, Bisu informed, noting that Anu (or more aptly, the "Proto-Anu") have migrated into these lands for generations upon generations. For generations upon generations, they have inter-mixed with the Vedda, who entered the land at an early age.

This ancient admixture that of Vedda and Anu (called the "Eastern Anu") is unique to the lands of the huge peninsula. Still, Anu nonetheless, Lord Bes affirmed., further informing Khonsu that this is the lot the immigrants will encounter and join in the broad and fertile lands of the Mesopotamian River Valley. Then, after allowing Khonsu to absorb all he had said for a moment, he Conditioned upon agreement that the migrations were to be singularly and solely from Ta-Nebiru to the Mesopotamian River Valley. Thus, forbidding settlement or colonies along the coast or within the "Land of Incense", Bisu readily and surprisingly agreed to permit the passage of the migration through the land and ports of Punt without other condition, advising further that he would avail them of the ports of both northern and southern Punt.

Though the swiftness and certitude of the agreement counter-proposed by Bisu left Khonsu momentarily stunned, after but a moment of consideration, he wholeheartedly agreed, an agreement opening passage for the eastern migrations from Ta-Nebiru to the Mesopotamian River Valley. It was Queen Ta-Urt who cautioned that the journey to the Mesopotamian River Valley is a particularly perilous one for those not informed of its challenges. It is a journey that shall require knowledge of seamanship, to which replied, advising that there shall be those within the migrations whose clans have sailed upon and plied the waters of the "Great Lakes" for untold generations, their skills may have waned, but their knowledge is keen.

A perfect opportunity for Enlil to interject that he had hope, with the accord of Lord Bes and time permitting, that he would be able to briefly survey the lands into which the migrants would journey. Which Bisu then informed that, using their knowledge of seasonal tides. The pattern of prevailing winds and currents, maritime time traders from the northern and southern ports of Punt have established regular trade along the southeastern and eastern coasts, as far as the "Incense Harbor"; a voyage the traders make several times a year.[ccxliii]. They prepare for this seasons voyage as we speak, Bisu noted, specifically advising Prince Enlil that the traders and vessels leaving from the Port of Berbera would be led by his own son, Prince Ba-tau, whom Prince Enlil was welcomed to join on the voyage.

An invitation Enlil readily accepted, prompting Bisu to summon and send word advising Prince Ba-tau that he should prepare for at least three guests, Prince Enlil and his two closest associates. Lord Bes further grasped the opportunity to request Queen Ta-Urt take the priest Ami-ta for a tour of the Sanctuary at Laas Geel so that he may learn and come to understand the tenets of the Legend and Prophesy of the House of Tellem. With these accommodations, Lord Bes had provided an opportunity for him and Khonsu, the renowned High Priest of Ta-Nebiru, to become better acquainted. They met over dinner each evening after the departure of Prince Ba-tau and Prince Enlil on their voyage to the eastern lands and the departure of the High Priestess Ta-Urt and the Fetish Priest Ami-ta for the Sanctuary at Laas Geel.

In the days and weeks to follow, Lord Bes and Khonsu each took the opportunity to get to know and better understand the other. An anxious Khonsu was first to truly probe by inquiring into the legends told by the Grand Sage and (defacto) High Priest in the Cavern Cities of the Mountains of the Heavens, inquiring specifically into the lofty legends of Bisu's journeys beyond the "Threshold" with one known as Upāst. Bisu modestly acknowledged, replying, "it is far more than legend, and there is much to tell, but let us begin with your story Khonsu of Ta-Nebiru. What can you share of this?." Momentarily taken aback, Khonsu pondered for a moment or two before finally deciding to begin at the beginning, explaining himself to have been a Sage at a very young age.

Khonsu told of the Winged Serpent Clans of the Mountains of the Moon, a diaspora of the native clan of Ptah, into which Khonsu himself was born and among whom he was raised until approaching majority. He then told of the warrior ethos of the nomadic clans of the Roan, amongst whom he was then reared and trained until and after reaching the majority. He told of the annual nomadic journeys across the mountains, of his quest to discover the mystic arts mastered by Ptah, and further, about his dreamlike encounter with the mysterious Tree Faun, "Obrüm", in the central highlands native to Ptah. Khonsu told of how Obrüm proved himself by directing him to the precise location of the remnants of the old Sanctuary in the highlands.

Khonsu emphasized that the remnants of the old sanctuary, though mostly reclaimed by the ages, were found precisely where the Tree Faun Obrüm said they would be, affirming his truth and authenticity. He then told of how Obrüm advised that he seek the council of a great Queen by the given name of Ala but known as "Ala the Wise,"; whose lineage had known Ptah (Pëtāh) and still retained knowledge of his "Mystic Arts." It was from "Ala the Wise." Khonsu revealed he learned and cultivated talents in the Arts of Natural Magick. It was under her tutelage and guidance that he discovered his path, a path that led him to the 'House of An. To which Bisu then inquired, 'it is said that you have known and tutored your Lord An since infancy. What of this can you share?

Khonsu replied without ponder that it was fully true; he has known and tutored the gifted Lord An since the youngest of ages, to which Bisu then quizzically inquired, 'did the child have any unique or unusual birthmarks?' To which Khonsu, again taken somewhat aback, first pondered for more than a moment before affirming that indeed, as an infant and through much of his childhood, young An did bear an unusual birthmark. A dual birthmark really, which could best be described as short, incised wound-like markings at his right side, with matching markings front and back, appearing as though the child had once been pierced clear through. But the wound-like birthmarks faded with time, Khonsu advised, and Lord An was free of them well before he reached majority.

Lord Bes then began, like yourself, Khonsu of Ta-Nebiru, a great sense of destiny ran strong through my veins, yet for me, at first, it was more about revenge than prophecy. Bisu recounted that during the desolate times, the great 'Time of Turmoil,' clans in the 'Lands of the Plateaus' warred one against another, with the victor dispossessing the fallen, and that it was these times that his clan, the totem clan of the Black Leopard, had been dispossessed and driven from their homeland on the northern plateau. It was an event that shaped and motivated much of my early development, Bisu revealed, noting that the feeling of destiny that ran strong in his veins was destiny to first and foremost reclaim the lost homelands of his clan.

Once rising to leadership, Bisu recounted, a campaign was launched unifying the western regions of the southern plateau, in which pursuit we first encountered the 'Prophesy of Tellem'. We came as conquers, and admittedly, Bisu conceded, at the first encounter, of the fullness of the "Legend that is the Vessel of the Prophesy." A legend that foretold of one loosely fitting my discretion who would unite the 'Lands of the Plateaus,' with a growing understanding of how broadly its tenets were shared by the clans in the eastern regions of the southern plateau, we felt given the sameness of the goals, we could use the legend and its prophecy to achieve common ends. Through my shrewdness, I planned to bend the legend and prophesy to my will; instead, they transformed me.

Under the guidance of the "Legend and Prophesy", Bisu continued, we subdued the remainder of the Southern Plateau. We went on to subdue the whole of the Northern Plateau. By your story Khonsu of Ta-Nebiru, the illuminator of your path, was the one known as "Ala the Wise", Bisu mused, to which Khonsu nodded in agreement; Bisu then informed that for him it was a mystic seer name "Sepṭu", known as the "Blind Seer of Gondar", whose council was seeking to fulfill the destiny of the Prophesy. It was through the eyes of the "Blind Seer" that the vision of the greater spiritual battle, the true battle of causation, that between the forces of light and the forces of darkness, that eternal struggle between Creation and Chaos, and the power of reverence among men in this.

It was with the enlightenment and guidance of the "Blind Seer" that we subdued the Northern plateau, ushering in a new era of unity, peace and reverence among men, Bisu recounted, a reverence foreseen by the Prophesy of Tellem. You asked of Upāst; Bisu then reminded, yes, I knew him. Yet, it was not until after I saw him last that I came to understand that, for his time, he was the keeper of the 'Prophesy of Tellem,' the pursuit of which came to define the path that has delivered me here before you. The legend of which you make mention, Bisu continued, is in large part the story of the pursuit of the prophecy, which foretold of the forces joining the forces of the Divine Netjeru to defeat and drive back the forces of Chaos … those fomenting the 'Times of Turmoil' oppressing our world.

Your Lord An is undoubtedly the "Great King of the West" alluded to in the prophesy, Bisu added, and from what I know of him, he is a more than worthy king. It is befitting that he fulfill the final verses of the prophesy, Bisu agreed, cautioning that 'nonetheless the distractions in this world are many, and he shall need to remain true, and be held accountable. Though perhaps unaware of the fullness of his destiny, Bisu resolved that your Lord An is the sum of all he has ever been. I say again, it is worthily a king to fulfill the final verses of the prophecy. Pondering all that had been said for a moment, Khonsu then informed that "Ala the Wise" had advised that as the "Age of the Gods" ends, so then begins the "Age of Man,"; to which Bisu then propounded, by the prophecy your Lord An then shall be the last to descend, the one the prophesy aptly calls the "Guiding Light."

Thus, did Lord Bes and Khonsu find both affinity and accord in the days and weeks before the return of Ta-Urt and the Åmi-ta from the Sanctuary at Laas Geel, only days before the return of Prince Ba-tau and Prince Enlil from their voyage to and along the eastern coast of the eastern lands. And with the accord between Punt and Ta-Nebiru arranged, Khonsu, Enlil, Åmi-ta and their entourage prepared for the long journey home.

In parting, Bisu privately admonished Khonsu to hold fast to "what has been said of Än, lest you interfere in his destiny. With that, Lord Bes arranged guides from the City of Berbera to aid in their path southward to the ancient City of Doolow in the province of the Crocodile clans. In route to Doolow, an enthusiastic Enlil informed Khonsu of great promise in the broad, fertile lands of the Mesopotamian River Valley, advising that the migrations will require a revolving armada, part of which, according to Prince Ba-tau, will be available for hire by barter at the ports of Punt. The larger number needs to be built, Enlil informed, further advising that the migrations must be carefully planned to both allow time to build seaworthy craft and accommodate the seasons.

It was a thoroughness that left Khonsu impressed yet somewhat suspicious that the prince was entertaining notions of perhaps leading the migrations himself. A thought momentarily dismissed as the fetish priest Åmi-ta told of his enlightenment at the Sanctuary at Laas Geel and of the repository and preservation of sacred tenets by recitals at the nearby monastery. It was an enlightenment that transported the ethos of the Hydra cult to the cavern cities in the Mountains of the Heavens, where it transformed the "Sons of Heru" into its monasterial counterpart. It was an enlightenment by proxy that transported the monasterial ethos to the Temple at the ancient *City of An*.

They returned to the city with little fanfare, with groups and members of the entourage returning to their clans and families with tales of their journey. Khonsu and Enlil first meeting briefly with Lord An in the residence of the "Great House" before retiring to share the tales of their adventures with their own families. Early the next morning, Khonsu and Enlil again met briefly and privately with An and several Elders of the Counsel. There Khonsu informed of the accord with Lord Bes. Enlil explained that migrations by land, from Ta-Nebiru to the coast and ports of Punt, and across the sea straits to the coast of the present-day Arabian Peninsula, and around and up the coast to the well-watered and fertile lands in the broad ancient delta of the Mesopotamian River Valley.

As Khonsu had earlier suspected, after emphasizing that the journey is not one to be led by leaders unfamiliar with its challenges, Enlil propounded that, 'by that or any other measure, he is best qualified to lead the migrations …and settlements in the Mesopatamian plain. Given that he hadn't brought it up the night before, he placed all in an awkward position, so all sat in silence, awaiting Lord An's decision. Though Lord An had planned that it would be his elder son Enlil who would inherit his throne, he could see that, like his brother, it was more apt that he build his own kingdom. So, the planning began, along with dissemination and coordination with the mobilized clans migrating from the lowlands.

Dissemination, planning and preparation filled the better part of a year as they awaited the approach of the season best for their voyage around and along the coast of the eastern land, a period Khonsu used to bring the monasterial tenets of the Hydra priesthood to the Temple of the City of An. At the monastery, he established they explored the existing "truths" and understanding of the universal soul (the "Creator"). Initiants who became proficient and properly prepared in the curriculum at the Monastery in the City of An were said to become immortal. When you become immortal, your memory is said to remain intact, and you are wholly conscious from then on; this was the earliest definition of eternal life – continuous unbroken memory.

Though Lord An often found himself occupied with overlordship of the city-state and kingdom of Ta-Nebiru, Khonsu encouraged him to play a role in the Monastery. Lord An thus taught that the acquisition of knowledge enhanced a person's control over his destiny and that every act in one's life is examined, not for its material effect, but for its influence in furthering the evolution of his spirit …and the unfolding of creation. He proselytized that Chaos is ever looming and contends against every effort of Creation, but that even this is by the design of the Unknowable Creator, for it is in the eternal balance between the expanding Cosmos that is the unfolding of "Creation" and the unrelenting Chaos, that is the "Abyss", that life abounds… if it is worthy to exist.

It was after one such provocative session of enlightenment that word was received of the death of Lord Bes, who it was said ascended peacefully in his sleep. Khonsu presumed and advised that though Lord Ba-tau would ascend to the throne, Queen Ta-Urt would most certainly be the true tutelary head; a sentiment expanded upon at the evening meal with Queen Ta-Urt and Prince Enlil, where Enlil apprised of the lasting friendship formed between him and Prince Ba-tau during their voyage along the coast of the eastern lands. Enlil informed that Ba-tau offered to avail both Punts' northern and southern ports to those migrating to the Mesopotamian River Valley. With Khonsu further assuring that Lord Bes held Lord An in great esteem, a disposition shared by Lord Ba-tau

With his initial concerns set aside, Lord An turned his attention and the discussion to progress in preparation, coordination and the onset of the migrations, to which Enlil informed that the season approaches, and the onset is but weeks away. To which Lord An then informed that while they, Khonsu and Enlil, were away, Tjay (the youngest son of Khonsu) solicited the Chameleon King Meni to aid in establishing trade and a compact with the Nilotic clans in the southern borderlands of Ta-Nehesi; this with the dual intent of opening a more direct and shorter route to the northern ports of Punt.[ccxliv] Enlil departed to coordinate with the Elders of the migrating clans. This feat left all impressed, granting Khonsu a moment he had hoped for with Lord An.

Feeling his own mortality, particularly with the death of Lord Bes, Khonsu informed Lord An of his desire for a personal pilgrimage to Ta Netjeru (the "Lands of the Gods") so that he may walk the path of Upāst, a revered warrior priest from the serpent clans of the "Mountains of the Heavens." Upāst studied with the mystic seers of Ta Netjeru, attaining enlightenment and aiding in his right ascendance to the spiritual realm. A sympathetic Lord An, a bit concerned for his aging master, advised that he would, of course, arrange a fitting entourage to ease the burdens and difficulties of the journey. Khonsu then opined that it would nonetheless be a pilgrimage lasting nearly a full year, a far longer period than the Temple and Monastery should be again absent its High Priest.

Khonsu informed that as he has aged and his vigor has waned, he has given great thought to who might replace him and could think of none better suited than Lord An himself. A statement leaving An momentarily speechless as Khonsu explained that none across the land are as prepared as Lord An himself to assume the mantle. Others would require months, if not years, to attain the needed acceptance. Lord An, he noted, requires only anointment. For which you can be readied in a matter of weeks. The two sat in silence for more than a moment as An pondered all that had been said before tacitly agreeing by inquiring into preparation exercises for anointment in the Alcove at the Heights'; exercises which he mastered as a young man

The anointment of An was both unique and pivotal, marking an ending and a beginning; unique in that for the first time, there was said to be a council of nine who stood witness to his anointment, including Khonsu himself, with An appearing directly before him, completing the circle and fulfilling the "anointment by presence." The anointment of An was also said to be particularly unique because it was at his appointment informed An that he would not be returning to the physical realm, that time had come for him to join the ancestors and that his physical body shall appear to have died in his sleep. Faint legend holds that Khonsu and An stood facing each other alone in the sanctum until, alas, Khonsu gradually faded away, leaving only An to ponder the way forward for the first time ...alone.

It was thus that Lord An became the first of the "Priest-Kings", and it was thus, that in honor of Khonsu, he changed the totem of the city to that of the "Winged Lion", a hybrid of the "Golden Lion" of his heritage, and the "Winged-Serpent" of Khonsu's heritage. Lord An, secondly, vowed to undertake the pilgrimage to Ta-Netjeru, in honor of Khonsu. Though An called for a month of mourning, the time arrived for the eastern migrations, which availed themselves of the northern and southern ports of Punt, from where they launched the first migrations along the ancient coastal plains of the Arabian Peninsula. This was several millennia after the Vädda, with whom earlier Proto-Anu migrants had long intermixed along the broad coastal plains of the Peninsula leading to the Southern Mesopotamian River Valley, leading to the emergence of the "Eastern Anu." [ccxlv]

The Legends

The second major Anu migrations crossed the Red Sea between Africa and Asia from natural harbors on the "Horn of Africa" to what was then the broad coastal plains of the Arabian Peninsula.[ccxlvi] The route around the coast of the Arabian Peninsula was due south, through the straits and gulf to the Arabian Sea. Though the straits were never completely closed, it was narrower during and after the end of the last Ice Age, narrowing the distance between the "Horn of Africa" and the coastal plains of the Peninsula. Geographically, the Arabian Peninsula was broad coastal plains bordered by mountains, with a central plateau, each comprising about a third of the Peninsula's landmass.

Along the vast coastal plains, earlier Proto-Anu migrations joined the Vädda in establishing the first villages on the Peninsula. Dozens of archaeological sites mark the Proto-Anu settlements and migrations around the Arabian Peninsular coastal plain. They formed small mound villages, eventually expanding into the small township and village cluster networks, with the migrations progressing around and along the peninsula's eastern "incense coast." The second major Anu migrations were accomplished by boat, along the coastal route, specifically to the broad fertile delta of the southern Mesopotamian River Valley. During the ice age in Mesopotamia, when sea levels were low, the combined Tigris-Euphrates rivers flowed through a wide flat plain-like landscape.

Sea levels dropped over 400 feet during the Ice Age, rendering the bed of the Persian Gulf a swampy freshwater floodplain with small lakes where water was retained in the hollows. This is the land that would become ancient Sumer. This region was, essentially, a swamp-like freshwater extension of the ancient coastal plain of southern Mesopotamia, a floodplain bounded by the Euphrates River on the west and the Tigris River on the east. The glacial era drainage of the Tigris and Euphrates rivers made its way down the marshes of this plain.[ccxlvii]. This was land that would be called "Ancient Sumer," founded by those who called themselves the "black-headed ones," those who established the first ancient townships and later city-states in present-day southern Iraq and Kuwait.[ccxlviii]

The Anu arrived in the plains of Southern Mesopotamia. Like the Proto-Anu before them, they intermixed with Väddic clans adding to the stock of the Eastern Anu who gave the first rise to Ancient Sumer. The heartland of early Sumer lay between the Euphrates and Tigris rivers, in what the Greeks later called Mesopotamia, "the land between two rivers." This territory, once skillfully irrigated, proved very fertile and gave rise to major cities long before the period archaeologists first identified as Sumerian. According to Sumerian history, the very first city ever built was named Eridu, the first royal capital, which Enlil dedicated to his brother Enki in a gesture of unity and familial homage to the greater sovereignty of Lord An.

Ancient Eridu was an immense oval mound in the wetlands of the ancient Euphrates, rising to an elevation of 23 feet. Archaeological evidence suggests that during the era of the second migration, Eridu covered an area of 100 acres. The initial economic foundation of the earliest settlement at Eridu was fishing. Fishing nets, weights, and whole bales of dried fish have been found at the site: models of reed boats, the earliest physical evidence we have for constructed boats anywhere, are also known from Eridu. Notwithstanding, the Anu were the earliest agricultural people, herding and raising livestock. Like their counterparts in the *Hapi Valley*, they shut themselves up in walled village encampments for security.

The *Anu* took with them their spiritual beliefs, rituals, and expertise in early agriculture and how to build dams; their migration brought us the first examples of irrigation architecture, which was to make great cities possible. Although Eurocentric historians falsely assert that ancient Sumer is where agriculture began, it remains evident that Enlil and the Anu arrived with a pre-existing knowledge of agriculture.[ccxlix] From its beginnings as a collection of farming villages, the earliest settlements in the southern alluvial flood plain developed as a result of sophistication in agricultural and irrigation techniques. The Anu / Sumerians practiced the same irrigation techniques as those used in Khemet (Egypt).[ccl]

The early ancient city of Nippur, logographically recorded as "Enlil City," was home to Enlil. Nippur was built upon a great complex of mounds situated on both sides of one of the earliest courses of the Euphrates, between the present bed of that river and the Tigris, with the highest point, a conical hill, rising nearly 100 feet above the level of the surrounding plain. A prominent feature of the city was a midtown canal, which flowed through the middle of the city. It was maybe the original course of the Euphrates, dividing the ancient city into clearly defined eastern and western sectors. Though the exact form of the Temple at that period cannot be determined, the city's Temple was believed to have been built by Enlil himself.[ccli]

Nippur (Sumerian: Nibru) was one of the most ancient and sacred of all the Sumerian cities. Tens of thousands of Sumerian tablets have been found in Nippur, and it was at Nipper we found the name Tel-Anu.[cclii] In further homage to Lord Anu, Enlil adopted the fabled winged lion (a hybrid between the "Golden Lion" and the "Winged Serpent") as the totem symbol of his kingdom, a symbol that later became synonymous with mysticism, and was featured broadly throughout ancient Sumer.

Mesopotamia is the ancient region north of the Arabian Peninsula. It is historically divided into two parts: northern or "Upper Mesopotamia" and southern or "Lower Mesopotamia,"; with the latter formerly known as ancient "Sumer." Early Sumer was largely defined by the *Mesopotamian basin,* a long trough of land between the mountain ranges and the Tigris and Euphrates Rivers that slopes downward, from northwest to southeast, and empties into the Persian Gulf. Early settlements were located on slight rises within aquatic habitats resulting from seasonal monsoonal rains or in the upper wetlands at the head of the Persian Gulf.[34] From here, the earliest settlers moved further inland. Whether they relocated to evade the erratic flooding of the alluvial plains or were pushed from the south as sea levels rose remains unresolved.[ccliii]

The glacial retreat of the last Ice Age (from c. 13,000 BC) and the rains of the Holocene (beginning about 12,000 BC) released huge amounts of water along the Tigris and Euphrates River systems, resulting in violent and long-lasting floods in Southern Mesopotamia. The Tigris and Euphrates Rivers each arise and descend from the highlands of the Taurus Mountains of southern Turkey in the north, each winding their respective long courses to the Persian Gulf on the coast of present-day Kuwait in the south. Due to the constant flooding of the Tigris and Euphrates, the Southern Mesopotamian alluvial plain gradually formed and, over time, expanded between the two rivers. As these rivers moved out of their positions, the floods brought fertile topsoil down from the mountains, which, together with the sediment and silt left behind, made the area very fertile.

---

[34] Pournelle, 2003

Eridu was the southernmost of the early Sumerian settlements; built on the shoreline of an ancient north Arabian lake, the city acted as a prime entrepot. Settlements then expanded along the major rivers, with settlers irrigating the land along the banks to grow crops. Since they did not have local access to many natural resources, contact, and trade, first primarily with Ta-Nebiru and Punt and then with neighboring lands, became important. In many respects, early Sumer was a twin to the early Hapi / Nile Valley civilization, spawned by the same progenitors; in the names of cities and towns, there was Anu. Another group of Africans related to the Anu who migrated to Mesopotamia was the Bak groups, first from the interlacustrine ("between lakes") region of the Hapi River Valley, the font of the "Land of Man" in Central Africa.

The first migration of the Bak occurred about 10,000 BC., roughly two thousand years after the second major migration of the Anu, a migration from the "Land of Man" through Ta-Nebiru to the "Land of the Gods" across East Africa and the Red Sea; around the coastal plains of the Arabian Peninsula to the fertile plains of Southern Mesopotamia. The Bak migrated further into Asia about 2800 BC, when Hu Na Kunte settled the Loh River Valley with a number of Black Mesopotamian families.[ccliv] Early ancient history reports that the "Eastern Anu" expanded northeastward into Asia themselves, with their history recorded in the earliest Indian treatise, the Rig-Veda, as well as the later Puranas, where the names of the Anu tribes are clearly identified. [cclv]

Recently there has been clarification regarding the similarities and direct ancient linkages between the Anu found in Asia and those found in Central and Eastern Africa across the late Pleistocene and early Holocene boundary. It has been broadly acknowledged that the founders of civilization in Southwest Asia were the Anu (archaeologists call them "Natufians"), who is given credit for being the first farmers in Asia, around 11,500 B.C. The Mesolithic period (between the Paleolithic and the Neolithic) started around 12,000 B.C. It ended a few centuries later with the introduction of the earliest forms of agriculture around 11,500 B.C.

It started with the transition from the Pleistocene to the Holocene, marking the end of the Last Great Ice Age. Early agriculture revolutionized human life and was an enormous catalyst for change. People learned how to mark out fields, plant seeds, harvest crops, and make bread. Early settlements in southern Mesopotamia required complicated irrigation methods to replicate the traditions of plant cultivation built up first in Central Africa as a precursor to the development of early farming. The Anu at Eridu brought plant cultivation and early farming traditions with them from the Ta-Nebiru, modifying their techniques to fit the terrain.[cclvi]

Because of irrigation, the early settlements in southern Mesopotamia became rich in agricultural products, including a variety of wild cereals, fruits, vegetables, nuts, and other edible parts of plants. For most other essential goods, such as metal ores and timber, Mesopotamia needed trade. To solve that issue, Anu obtained those natural resources through early trading with ancient Punt and Ta-Nebiru. Evidence of maritime trade between civilizations dates back at least 10 millennia. One of the vital instruments which facilitated maritime trade was portage and the early development of coastal cargo-ships.

Maritime trade began with safer coastal trade and evolved with the manipulation of the monsoon winds, soon resulting in trade crossing boundaries such as the Arabian Sea and the Bay of Bengal. Ancient Punt had trade links with Kumari and the long-distance trade in spices, importing spices from as far away as the Sunda Peninsula. Sumer exported agricultural products such as grains, barley, flax, pearls, carnelian, and reeds, in exchange for Camphor or Sandalwood and Spices from Punt and a variety of trade goods from Ta-Nebiru

The Parables

The ancient "City of An" was the original "City of *On*," not its later successor name-sake in the Lower Nile River Valley. The "City of An" was an early ancient walled city governed from a hilltop at its center, upon which rest the citadel of governance, a walled citadel atop a majestic mound surrounded by the nine houses (or precincts) comprising the urban center of the city. The surrounding suburbs were comprised of townships and villages amid the grasslands and tree stands beyond the walls of the city. In the city's urban center were dwellings of inner luxury amid gardens and groves along well-planned avenues.

Neighboring mountains were a source of year-round rivers. The nine houses in the urban core used a network of aqueducts to pull and store water in a network of cisterns (made of gypsum and lime mortar).[cclvii] Irrigation in the urban core of the early ancient city allowed the people to cultivate sorghum, groundnuts, simsim, telebun, and sweet potatoes. At the same time, those in the open lands of the suburbs lived in less dense villages and townships, where they also cultivated millet, melons, sweet potatoes, and beans, butalso, kept large herds of cattle, sheep, and goats.

The gleaming City of An arose at a unique nexus, with triangulated trade flows between the fledgling cities along the banks of the Nile River Valley and the fledgling cities that arose in early ancient Sumer (via Punt). The reverent city also intermediated trade flow between the "Mountains of the Moon" and the "Mountains of the Heavens." However, the city's greatest treasures were its Temple, a sanctuary of spiritual excellence where priests were mystically anointed, and its monastery, a repository of the early ancient *Mysteries*.

This was the beginning of the ancient mystery schools that passed on secrets to initiates who had shown discipline of mind, body, and spirit. It began the ethos of keeping esoteric knowledge strictly hidden amongst only a few initiates who had proven themselves worthy. The monastery monks were taught how to use metals, at least elementary metals, and scribes were taught the earliest form of proto-writing. Africa has the world's oldest and largest collection of ancient writing systems and is home to the world's first identifiable proto-writing.[cclviii] Writing is essentially a symbol system with linguistic links, an ideographic system used to convey observations and inform. Language started in symbolism over 100,000 years prior, with early proto-writing first emerging around 40,000 BC.[cclix]

The power of symbols to convey much by minimal means was central to the growth and dissemination of early knowledge; representational and abstract images of the sort began to appear about 30,000 BC in Africa.[35] Scribes at the monastery memorialized the earliest teaching of the Mysteries by etchings on ochre tablets. It is such engravings that later evolved into so-called proto-writing.[cclx] It was Khonsu who first engraved ochre tablets containing the wisdom accumulated (and debated) that produced the first ochre tablets of the Alchemical texts and the ancient Mysteries.

Lord An proselytized that through the ancient Mysteries, individual souls evolved from lower to higher states and entered into rapport with the essence of the highest attainable order. An illuminated that the cosmos is an immense spiritual organism that is evolving…eternally unfolding its infinite possibilities of expression.

In the third year of his reign after the ascendance of Khonsu, Lord An undertook the proposed Pilgrimage to Ta-Netjeru, the "Land of the Gods," Sacred Mount Kenya.[cclxi] Unlike other mountains, which formed over millions of years, this mountain formed in just seconds when a large meteorite crashed into modern-day Kenya millions of years ago, an impact culminating in the formation of the now-extinct volcano, which originally erupted and arose an estimated 3 million years ago.[cclxii] Mount Kenya is situated in one of the most remarkable landscapes in Kenya, where the majestic mountain is an awe-inspiring sight, with its ragged series of peaks crowned with snow and its slopes thick with forest.

Ta Netjeru could be seen from miles away, surrounded by rich, thick forest, with continuous tree stands and interlocking canopies, extending for miles; a fascinating landscape traversed by Lord An and his guides and entourage en route to the cavern villages at the base of Ta Netjeru; villages anciently inhabited by the totem clans of the Hippopotamus. Theirs was a spectacular cavern network in the foothills of Ta Netjeru, in the ancient Naro Moru Forest, where Lord Bes himself had once famously pilgrimaged. Like Lord Bes before him, as An and his entourage approached the ancient Naro Moru Forest, they encountered the guardian clans who inhabited the hidden caves in the forests; cave networks allowing warriors of clans to seemingly appear in the forest from nowhere and disappear just as mysteriously.

Word of the arrival of Lord An and his entourage had been sent weeks earlier. Thus, the warriors of the guardian clans had been awaiting their arrival and led the way to the cavern village at the foothills of Ta Netjeru (Mount Kenya). As they made their way over an ancient bridge to a waterfall, the opening to the caves slowly came into view behind the waterfall. The bridge brought them to a path leading behind the waterfall to the entrance to the cavern villages, where they were then met by a small group of Seers, the leader of whom, an elder called "Zuab" informed that "the inner sanctums of Ta-Neteru are only availed to a chosen few, such as you Lord An, and if you must," Zuab allowed, "two of your most trusted companions."

---

[35] See "Handbook of Human Symbolic Evolution," by David Barton and Mary Hamilton

Ever the Roan, An informed that he would continue on alone, to which Zuab then advised and instructed that his entourage shall be given worthy accommodations in the cavern villages of guardian clans, father informing the leaders of the entourage that Lord An shall meet them here again, where they stand, at dawn, on the fifth day from this. With that, Zuab and the small cadre of Seekers ushered Lord An through a network of tunnels to what Zuab explained to be a precisely positioned cavern to avail An of the spiritual energies of Ta-Netjeru during his meditations and hopeful transcendence. The ancients recognized and were somehow sensitive to the swirling spiritual vortex within Sacred Mount Kenya; like mystic gateways, these vortexes allow one to harmonize with the ebb and flow of the Cosmos.[cclxiii]

As they proceeded along the corridors, Zuab explained that in the inner sanctums of Ta-Neteru, the Initiate-Adept is figuratively put to "death" for three days, where in the three days, the Initiate-Adept ascends to the spiritual realm and endeavors to achieve the fullness of his or her 'Ka,' a divine generative force, the fullness of which transforms the Adept through theogony. Like your traditions of initiation in the Mountains of the Moon, and from what is said, across all of Ta-Nebiru, Zuab opined, further explaining that the first purpose of our tradition is for the "Initiated" to experience and witness the fact that he or she is a "spirit," and not merely a "physical body." The second purpose is that the initiate discovers and realizes we live and survive the departure after the death of the physical body, understanding that we are eternal Beings.[cclxiv]

Reaching their destination, a small cavern with a large, flat, table-like, black obsidian stone at its center; as the group entered the cavern, the small cadre of Seers sat around the base of the surrounding walls of the small cavern. Zuab then took his place at the center of the cavern, sitting at one side of the table-like obsidian stone; this as he gestured that Lord An join him by taking his place, directly opposite him, at the other side of the obsidian table. The third purpose of our tradition, Zuab then continued, is for the Initiate to discover and forever retain the ability to ascend the physical body. At this point, the physical body becomes a "slave" rather than a "master," and the spirit is then and forevermore freed from its chains. Zuab opined that one has taken the first steps to true immortality when this level of consciousness has been attained.

Our tradition begins with a traditional libation, Zuab advised, as he motioned that a young Sage name Urit, who stood just beyond the cavern, enter and place a small bowl of the libation before Lord An. He, which he did promptly.[cclxv] Zuab described the young Sage as a protégé of the Queen Mother Seshat, who patiently awaits to anoint your resurrection.[cclxvi] Zuab explained that theirs is a tradition of guided meditation aided by the resonance of ritual drumming. Still, given that Lord An has passed ascended and is intuitively acquainted with the path of transcendence, we dispense with unnecessary ritual. That being so, Zuab continued, we are informed that in the ascendance of fetish priests, the destination is the province of the ancestors in the spiritual realm.

The destination under our tradition is quite different," Zuab propounded. "Under our tradition," Zuab explained as he sipped from his bowl of libation …gesturing that Lord An join him, "the destination is decidedly beyond this, explaining that, in their tradition, one destination is the abode of one *Ka* (the "higher self") in the spiritual realm. Zuab explained that as the *Ba* (the "soul") enters the physical body at birth, it is guided and accompanied by an aspect of the eternal self, the inner Being, and indwelling consciousness known as the Ka (the "Spirit"). All living things have a *Ka,* Zuab illuminated, from plants to animals up to the Netjeru themselves, which is evident in that all are simply *alive*.

The Ka is inherently different from the Ba, Zuab explained, in that the Ka is that part of each individual that is directly shared by the Divine (the "Creator"). The destination of your journey is the lower, attainable abode of your Ka, Zuab elaborated, an aspect anciently known as the "Seat of your Ka."[cclxvii] To aid in your transcendence and transit, Zuab advised, in keeping with our tradition of guidance and resonance, you are first prepared by informing you of your destination in the spiritual realm …this is as the libation begins to loosen your physical bonds. Gesturing then that An sip again from his bowl and closed his eyes, Zuab intoned, "we know you are weary after your long journey Lord An. Let it be a weariness used to further loosen your physical bonds."

You are second prepared by distinction and alertness to the vibration of the ethereal-self.. It facilitates the meditative state needed to free one from the physical body.[cclxviii] As *An* felt himself drifting into a deep state of trance, he could nonetheless hear the reassuring voice of *Zuab* guiding him, "follow the path of your consciousness," assuring that "the path leads to the abode of your *Ka* in the spiritual realm."

An awoke to again find himself in the small cavern within the cavern village of Ta-Netjeru. Yet, this time he sat alone, granting him the opportunity to absorb all he had just experienced. It was only a moment or two later that the young Sage Urit entered the cavern carrying a small bowl of warm libation, which she placed before Lord An, informing them that it would awaken and revitalize him. The young Sage further informed that, once she noticed Lord An begin to stir and re-awaken, she summoned the Seer Zuab, who, in turn, advised the Queen Mother Seshat, upon whose arrival, in the tradition of Ptah, An gave testimony of his journey to the spiritual realm.

When the tradition of Ptah, when all were in attendance, An told of his experience in the spiritual realm, while still fresh in his memory; he told of ascending to the Psi-om, the Isle of Wisdom in the vast Astral Sea, and of the guiding enlightenment he attained from discourse with his KA. Even in defeat, Chaos has spread seeds of dissension in this physical realm, seeds finding fertile ground among those unaware of the purpose and intent of reverence and truth. An informed that it is thus prophesied that from the lands east of the shores of Alkebu-lan will come envy and greed, evils that shall assail the southern kingdoms of the east when the peoples of the lands below the (Ural) central mountains are driven south by great floods issuing from the highlands.

From the lands north of the shores of Alkebu-lan will come cunning and deceit, evils that will pervade the northern kingdoms, aided by a great betrayal of one of the royal sons of great northern power of Alkebu-lan, a misguided royal son who shall errantly empower and mobilize the peoples of the caverns of the (Caucasus) northeastern mountains; people that will assail and invade the northern and north-eastern kingdoms. Theirs is a pervasive evilness that will eventually assail and subdue Alkebu-lan itself. There then shall be a "spell" cast upon the peoples of Alkebu-lan, a spell of spiritual ignorance and indifference fomented by the agency of cunning and deceit.

Spiritual truth shall be corrupted and perverted in service of this agency. The people of Alkebu-lan will be hypnotized by its magic powers, hypnosis sealed with spiritual ignorance and indifference. The only way the spell will be broken, and the peoples of Alkebu-lan free again is that the ignorance into which they shall have been plunged need be destroyed by spiritual enlightenment.[36] So know that preservation of the Sacred Mysteries shall be key to reversing the evil spell; indeed, the magic formula to destroy the evil spell is to be found in the Sacred Mysteries, for which reason it's tenets must be held in secrecy and forever guarded and protected from the eyes of the profane.

The "Mystery Schools" must become "Secret Orders," with membership gained only by apt initiation and pledge to secrecy …to preserve the ancient wisdom. When the destruction of the evil spell is complete, the peoples of Alkebu-lan will again have a free, right, and united mind. As each Initiate, who shall become teacher, ascends to comprehend the essence of the Divine Mysteries, the whispering voice illuminated, they shall come to grasp and align with creation itself and the very purpose of the Creator, the "Divine Dividual" of which all "Individuals" consists.[cclxix] This is the knowledge that will again allow the truly reverent to live for centuries and the adept at traversing the spiritual realms, for it is this knowledge that separates man from the Gods.

This sacred knowledge will be fought over, lost, hidden, and stolen many times through-out the histories of mankind, the whispering voice (the *Ka (*the "*Spirit*") the "Higher-Self") prophesized, propounding that this should serve to clarify and affirm the purpose and path of (the *Ba* (the "*Soul*") the "*Lower-Self*"), of An himself. Upon completion of his testimony, An was anointed by Queen Mother Seshat. Yet unlike other worthy Aspirants, Lord An was not merely anointed into the priestly Order at Ta-Netjeru. He was recognized as the first of the true "Priest-Kings" and, as such, the first true "King of Kings."

After his pilgrimage and sojourn at Ta-Netjeru, Lord An became the source of all legitimate power and the one who bestowed the right to rule upon other kings. The first true "King of Kings." The influence of An extended from the "Land of Man" across Ta Nebiru to the Mountains of the Heavens and beyond this to Punt, Sumer, and the early ancient Nile River Valley. But most significantly, to Ta-Netjeru, the "Land of the Gods" was anciently seen as the abode of *Netjer* and entry to the very gates of heaven. As has been recently written, the identification of *Mount Kenya* as biblical *Mount Zion* has to be one of the most astounding of all geographical discoveries in Africa.[cclxx] The implications are far-reaching when we consider that the land known today as Israel is believed to be the true site of Mount Zion.[cclxxi]

As a geographical area, Mount Zion is currently the center of much controversy. According to ancient scriptures, Mount Zion was said to be at the center of the navel of the earth …east of the Garden of Eden. The equator in central Africa is the center of the navel of the earth, not Jerusalem. It is there we find the Garden of Eden (the "Land of Man"), along with Mount Zion to the east. The true Mount Zion has always been Mount Kenya, which sits just below the equatorial line in east Africa, where the "River Zion" (now called the "River Tana") still flows from the heights of Mount Kenya (Ta-Netjeru).

---

[36]. Bible Interpretations and Explanations (by Amun Nubi Re Akh Ptah (1967))

Mount Kenya, Ta-Netjeru ("Land of the Gods") is the true Holy Mountain of God, "Mount Zion," a term used interchangeably for "His land," "His people," and "His Mountain."[cclxxii] The present-day realization that Mount Kenya is biblical Mount Zion should not be too surprising. The name "Kenya" means *"God's Resting Place"* in all three of the original languages of the indigenous peoples of the area (even in the present day). Mount Zion anciently became a province in the "incidental empire" anchored by the ancient "City of An, "; an informal empire whose influence extended to the Nile Delta in the north and the extent of the ancient "Lands of Yam" in the south.[cclxxiii]

The "postglacial pluvial" brought five hundred years of persistent, heavy rains that transformed the lowlands, highlands, and great lakes of the *Lands of Yam* and lands well beyond. Torrential rains caused the overflow of *Lake Nyanza* (colonial era Lake Victoria) northwards into the Nile, transforming it into the "Wild Nile," which carved gorges a mile deep. *Lake Mwitanzige* (colonial Lake Albert) overflowed into the White Nile, as did Lake Tsana (colonial Lake Tana) into the Blue Nile. Widespread flooding by the *Wild Nile* inundated many of the early townships and fledgling cities along the banks of the river, an event still reported as the largest flood (the "Great Floods") ever recorded on the Nile River.[cclxxiv]

Harnessing of the Nile was crucial. Crops could be planted after the annual inundation, and management of the inundation to improve its coverage over the land-increased yields.[cclxxv] The Neolithic Sub-pluvial (the Holocene Wet Phase) was an extended period in which for two or three thousand years before and about a thousand years after it rained and rained. Then, as though marking an ecological turning point, the floods came. The Nile valley and delta are the results of thousands of years of such floods, with the river overflowing its banks and depositing sediment from the highlands across the landscape. In addition, the Nile delta itself slowly expanded northward towards the Mediterranean Sea as its sediments were deposited. Meanwhile, many, if not most, of the flooded townships and fledging cities along the banks of the upper river were the first to adapt and recover.

An ancient continuum extended from the early Nile River Valley complex, through the lands of Ta-Nebiru, to the ancient civilization in the Hapi Valley; a continuum extending through the ancient City of An (On) via Punt to early ancient Sumer. This was a time when early agriculture was well under way in the Hapi Valley, the Nile River Valley, and early Sumer, between the Tigris and Euphrates rivers. In early ancient Sumer, regular flooding along the Tigris and Euphrates made the land especially ideal for growing crops, the impetus for the expansion of the early Sumerian complex. All of these constituted the Neolithic Revolution, the so-called Agricultural Revolution that began about 12,000 B.C. It wasn't long after that trade networks inextricably linked the incidental empire of the Anu.

Thus was the rise and height of the fabled original ancient City of An (On), prominently and prosperously poised at the nexus of early ancient trade and the emergence and rise of the early ancient city-states. The "Great House" of the ancient city was an apt example of early ancient monotheistic governance, guided by the first of the ancient Priest-Kings, Lord An himself. Yet, alas, like at its inception, in its foreseeable future, the city would face two existential crises, the second worst than the first. The first existential crisis would arise from the very forces that lifted the City to early ancient prosperity, the rains of the Sub pluvial (the early "Holocene"). However, the second existential crisis will arise from an encounter and eventual conflict with a rising power, a power perhaps greater than that of the early ancient "Incidental Empire of the Anu."

Emergence of the Nagas

The closing era of the last Great Ice Age was a period of incredible climatic change as the gigantic ice sheets that covered much of the northern hemisphere and higher elevations in the south began to retreat. The winters shortened while the summers lengthened. While temperatures in southern Africa were several degrees colder than at present, there were no major ice sheets covering the land, notwithstanding the high mountains of Lesotho, which had small glaciers on some of the south-facing mountains. The seas were generally colder, and the cold "Benguela Current" then extended much further north than at present. The amount of moisture reaching the interior was lower, and the climate arider, especially in the Kalahari, northern Botswana, and western Zambia regions.

The low rainfall reduced vegetation cover over much of the Kalahari, where the prevailing winds shaped the sand into long, linear dunes that can still be seen today. Taken as a whole, the pattern of the dunes seems to suggest a large anti-cyclone, probably reflecting stable, high-pressure atmospheric circulation over the region. The dunes provide some indication of just how arid the region was because dunes of this type only form if annual rainfall is less than about 150 mm per annum. The Kalahari at that time was thus a true sand-desert, devoid of vegetation; the sand-sea in the interior extended to a latitude north of the Equator, forming what is still today the most extensive sand body on Earth.

Western historians are generally divided about the true history of Southern Africa, where the interior has usually been seen as devoid of significant archaeology. However, there is an overwhelming and undeniable amount of evidence to be found indicating that history, as we have been taught, is, in fact, false. Many ancient ruins and artifacts have been found, indicating that an ancient civilization lived and thrived in Southern Africa long before any recorded civilizations are known to have existed. Much historical evidence suggests that an advanced civilization inhabited Southern Africa in the earliest antiquity, from a time pre-dating any known civilization on Earth.

These discoveries will undoubtedly be a catalyst for rewriting ancient human history; however, much controversy surrounds these ancient discoveries, as "mainstream history" taught in "Western" schools and universities does not account for industrial civilizations existing before 12,000 B.C. Notwithstanding, an antediluvian city of unprecedented antiquity was discovered near the apex of the northern Kalahari in the late 19th century. It was an unprecedented archaeological discovery in which the ruins of the early ancient city were said to be quite extensive, partly buried beneath the sand at some points, and fully exposed to view in others.[cclxxvi] They carved detailed images into the hardest rock and were the first to carve an image of the Khemetan Ankh – the key of life and universal knowledge, over 75,000 years before Khemet arose.

The report indicated that the ruins could be traced for nearly a mile and consisted of huge hewn stones. In some places, the cement was said to be in perfect condition and plainly visible between the various layers of the walls. The top row of stones was weathered and abraded by the drifting sand. Some of the uppermost stones were grotesquely worn away on the underside, resembling a small center table supported by a short leg.[cclxxvii] The surrounding geology was also found interesting due to the number of ancient gold mines located in the vicinity of the ante-diluvial city. Prospectors of the era left evidence of their search not only in the form of alluvial diggings and ore processing plants but also in agricultural terraces and spiritual structures built of dry stone. [cclxxviii]

Ancient legends report the existence of an ancient city in the northern confines of the "Wet Kalahari" during and after the Ice Age. According to those living in the region, there was an ancient city built by early civilization. Though the building of the city was said to have never been completed, it was possible to unearth relics from the debris. What makes this even more remarkable is that this civilization and early ancient city is thought to be over 70,000 years old. Mainstream historians and anthropologists would have us believe that civilized man is no more than 13 000 years old. However, the time scale given to us by the historical view of mainstream academia is false; civilization began much further back than has been "officially" recognized.

The present-day Kalahari is a large semi-arid sandy desert in southern Africa extending 900,000 square kilometers, covering much of the present-day nation-states of Botswana, parts of Namibia, and South Africa. During most of the earliest antiquity, the *Kalahari* was a vast wetland where huge inland lakes, lagoons, rivers, and waterways provided both sustenance and a means of transport.[cclxxix] The Khoisan spread throughout the Kalahari, where they became the dominant group, expanding along the network of inland waterways. Inter-connecting waterways of the era flowed through a maze of lagoons, channels, and a mix of wetlands and grassy plains. Settlements spread along major river tributaries, reaching as far as the coast of the Indian Ocean, with the riverine acuity of the *Khoisan* aiding their early expansions throughout the region.[cclxxx]

Nascent Nagu-Naro: The Proto-Naga

Faint legends whisper of the past existence of advanced, pre-diluvial civilization in the "Wet Kalahari." Legends supported by recent discoveries of the infrastructure of the pre-ice age civilization in the Kalahari …said to be one of the "oldest man-made structures that can be seen from a satellite." The agricultural aspect of the infrastructure appears to reflect an innovative technology for food production comprised of an integrated 300-miles-long grid formed by growing agricultural lanes, separated by water canals, with presumed food production capabilities sufficient to supply most of the region.[cclxxxi] These were green, well-watered areas, with ancient "crop circles" now often encountered by local farmers who report they were made in the distant past. Oddly, no one ever bothered to inquire about who made them or how old they were.[cclxxxii]

The Legends

The present-day Kalahari is a large semi-arid sandy savanna in Southern Africa, extending for some 350,000 square miles, covering much of present-day Botswana, parts of Namibia, and South Africa. The very word Kalahari, or Kgalagadi (meaning "Land of the thirst") as it is now known, means "dry, waterless place," presently one of the most desolate places on Earth. It is believed that the ruins of very old ancient cities lie beneath the desert sands of the Kalahari. According to those living in the vast northeastern Kalahari, once upon a time, there was a large antediluvial city there, a city built by an early ancient civilization, which present-day locals say was never truly completed.

A Megalithic City over 70,000 years old with ancient ruins consisting of stone walls constructed of large stones held together by cement, forming an array of semi-circular structures. The ruins are partly buried beneath the sand at some points and fully exposed to view in others but are nonetheless quite extensive. The ruins can be traced for nearly a mile, consisting mainly of huge flat-sided stone; in some places, the cement is in perfect condition and plainly visible between the various layers of the ancient walls.[cclxxxiii] The antediluvial city was said to be west of the present-day Khoti Pan, constructed of ancient stones described as cyclopean or megalithic.

The early ancient Megalithic City was home to those whom the present-day inhabitants call the "Old Race', whose early ancient maritime civilization arose on the banks of the Makgadikgadi–Okavango paleo-wetlands at the distal end of the Okavango River, which flows from the Angolan highlands into northern Botswana.[cclxxxiv] A southern branch of the Great Rift Valley forms the Okavango Delta, where the southern reaches of the rift cut through the center of the Kalahari, with the Okavango Delta lying between two parallel fault lines at the southern extent of the Great Rift Valley. The Okavango Delta is a feature of the pre-ice age pluvial, formed in northeastern Botswana, where the river is dammed by the southern fault lines of the rift, causing its waters to form the huge ancient Makgadikgadi–Okavango paleo-wetlands.

The *Delta* was northeast of Holocene era *Paleo-Lake Makgadikgadi* and consisted of a multitude of main channels, small tributaries, and lagoons, as well as floodplains, islands, and mainland areas. The first settlements were established in the lush, green environment surrounding the wetlands. The founder populations of the pre-diluvial civilization coalesced along the banks of the Makgadikgadi–Okavango delta, giving rise to an early ancient Megalithic City, which survived for at least 70,000 years.[cclxxxv]

The surrounding geology has been found intriguing due to a number of early ancient gold mines located in the vicinity of the Megalithic City. Researchers have propounded that a vanished civilization from the distant past lived and prospered in that part of the world while mining gold. These ancient prospectors left evidence of their search in the form of alluvial diggings, reef workings, and ore processing plants, evidence of an advanced ante-diluvial mining community that lived and thrived in southern Africa long before any recorded civilizations are known to have existed. With the discovery of gold, ancient man moved from the age of stone to the age of metals. This transition clearly began in southern Africa.

They also left remnants of ancient agricultural terraces and religious structures built of dry stone. The agricultural infrastructure, on close examination, proved to be an innovative pre-diluvial technology for producing sufficient food to feed millions of people. The ancient inhabitants possessed an ancient crop-circle science-like technology and constructed over a hundred of these spirals across the landscape. The spirals range in diameter from 20 meters up to 250 meters, with various zigzags between spirals. The circular formations of the ruins are spiral markings, not concentric circles, and were ancient irrigation circles comprising an integrated 300-miles-long grid (1-kilometer-wide agricultural growing lanes, separated by 100-meter-wide water canals) that have long been abandoned.

One theory is that this 300-mile-long agricultural smart grid was powered by the array of crop circle-like spirals that generate a "Tesla-like" crop circle science energy (as a multiplier effect), amplifying the quantity and nutritional value of the food produced, such that this giant agricultural grid could produce sufficient food to feed millions of people. This intensive farming system was unique and the largest in southern and eastern Africa. It included massive investment in stone terracing, which allowed for the cultivation of rich soils on the sides of the escarpments. It was also connected to long-distance trade, which spanned the interior and linked to the east coast and the ancient Indian Ocean trading system.[37]

---

[37] Quote from Professor Delius, see "Past Horizons article."

So, this was not an isolated society. It was part of a much bigger regional system. These incredible ruins mostly consist of stone circles, with most buried in the sand and only observable by aircraft or satellites. Some have been exposed to climate change that has removed some of the sand, revealing walls and foundations. Circular stone ruins are connected by ancient roads, agricultural terraces, and thousands of ancient mines left behind by the antediluvian civilization. Other minor lost cities and ancient ruins have been discovered throughout southern Africa, such as the so-called ancient "Bakoni Ruins" situated on the hills above the present-day town of Machadodorp, west of Maputo harbor, on the southern coast of present-day Mozambique.

The hills around the town are terraced with thousands of stone walls which form part of a vast complex of settlements, fields, and roads; the slopes are covered with terraces made from stone walls, forming a large complex that also consists of suburban settlements. The "Bakoni Ruins" are constructed stonewalls located in mostly grassy pasture areas; they are maze-like ruins that form circular enclosures as well as linear pathways. "Among the maze of stonewalling, there are three main elements visible today: the homesteads, the terraced fields, and the road networks." These stonewalls are spread all throughout the province. To the present-day (at this writing), the site has yet to be excavated and has earned the title of one of South Africa's "Lost Cities" for its mysterious past.

What little we do know about the site comes from interpretations of the site as well as oral histories and written documents that have existed for thousands of years. While oral histories and written documents give us more knowledge, it is still somewhat limited. The extensive number of ruins in the region suggests agriculture was a large part of the lifestyle. Some of the stone walls were used to create terraces, with others surrounding small fields used to cultivate. It is clear the terraces were not built all at once; the process of creating the stone walls and the movement of the soil to create the raised edge of the terraces would have taken a great number of years, indeed decades, if not centuries, to build.[cclxxxvi]

Another minor lost city has been discovered at Lekhubu, a rocky hill in the middle of the Makgadikgadi inland sea, once covering over 10,000 square kilometers in central Botswana. Lekhubu Island, colloquially called "Kubu Island," is situated on the southern periphery of the Sowa Pan, the largest of the Makgadikgadi Salt Pans. Ancient Kubu Island was an amazing place of granite outcrops and baobab trees, with evidence of ante-diluvial occupation, when central Botswana was a vast inland lake, and Kubu was an island paradise. About 10 000 years ago, Lake Makgadikgadi dried up, and Lekhubu left an island surrounded by miles and miles of white salt. Kubu Island, nonetheless, is rich in archaeological remains that chronicle its early human habitation [cclxxxvii]

Ancient legends support that the Makgadikgadi-Okavango paleo-wetlands were central to the emergence of the Khoisan and that they were the founder population of the great pre-diluvial civilization.[cclxxxviii] The deltaic-lacustrine ecosystem of the paleo-wetlands provided an ideal geographical locality for the sustained existence and expansion of the Khoisan, as that population emerged from its two ancestral groups. There were anciently two groups of peoples (in the same language family) in the region, the Khoi-Khoi, meaning the "men of men" or "the real people," who were pastoralists, and the San, who were hunter-gatherers. Archaeological evidence indicates the Khoi-Khoi entered present-day Botswana through two distinct routes, intermixing with the San who entered the region earlier, giving rise to the descendent Khoisan. [cclxxxix]

The emergent Khoisan were indigenous to the region stretching from present-day Botswana to present-day Namibia; notwithstanding, the ancient population of the Khoisan once came to comprise the majority of living humans on the planet for much of the past 150,000 years. They, of course, first expanded throughout and beyond the ancient Kalahari, spreading their civilization and culture throughout much of Southern Africa, a postulate corroborated and supported by the discovery of a second major ante-diluvial city on the coastal south of Southern Africa, around 93 miles west of port Maputo, in present-day Mozambique.

The remains of the huge southern Metropolis, like the northern Megalithic City, according to tests, measured around 1500 square kilometers and were the core of an even larger community of about 10,000 square kilometers. This southern ante-diluvial city is believed to have been constructed well over 70,000 years before Christ and is near the great natural harbor of Maputo, which lies in the sheltered Rio Espirito Santo estuary in southern Mozambique. The ancient city had roads adjoining the complex circular structures with agricultural areas, which indicates that it belonged to the highly advanced Khoisan civilization. Again, the geology of the site is found interesting due to the numerous gold mines in proximity to the city. [ccxc]

The founder population of Northern Khoisan was represented in the northern Megalithic City and throughout the region of western Botswana and north-eastern Namibia. Central Khoisan was in the central Kalahari, while Southern Khoisan populated the southern and coastal regions.[38] For tens of thousands of years, the Khoisan and their subsets expanded throughout southern Africa; one significant ancestral subset was the Naro-San, who spoke a unique "Naro" dialect, which was an important feature of their identity; language loyalty among Naro-San was the strongest of all Khoisan communities.[ccxci] But the greatest contribution of the Naro was the influence of their spiritual beliefs upon the Khoisan.

One of the more interesting parts of nonwestern Botswana, which forms part of the Okavango, is the Tsodilo Hills, where the antediluvial "Serpent Cave" is located, the oldest ritual worship site ever found; by some estimates older than the antediluvial northern megalithic city itself. The ancient Naro who inhabited the Tsodilo Hills referred to them as the "Mountain of the Gods"; the only uplifted hill-like area for over fifty miles in all directions.[ccxcii] Another interesting feature of the Tsodilo Hills is the vast amount of ancient artwork found there; there are over 4 500 rock paintings, some dating back over 25 000 years, making it one of the densest collections of ancient rock art to have been found and possibly the oldest ancient artworks ever discovered.[ccxciii]

When one view rock art in terms of the shamanistic beliefs and experiences of the Naro-San, one is faced with the specific elements of Naro's spiritual belief. Decades of research have shown that the rock art of the Naro is deeply spiritual in nature, situated conceptually in a multilevel cosmos. Their tradition remained oral and was passed down for untold generations until being anciently depicted in rock art, from which it is clear that the Naro believed in a cosmos with spiritual realms above and below this, our own physical realm. The myths of the Naro emphasize processes of change that continually transforms everything in life, a philosophy that stresses the importance of being in accordance with the flow of nature and accepting things of a consequential nature that happen in life.

---

[38] Batibo, 1998

In the teachings and practices of the Naro, the "Creator" is "power," and it is this power that controls and sustains life. Though the Khoi were part of the San religion, they believed in a supreme being who presides over daily life and controls elements of the environment. Traditional Khoi belief included numerous mythic tales of gods and ancestor heroes whose lives provided examples of ways to cope with social conflicts and personal problems. The beliefs of the Khoi incorporated acceptance of good, evil, and ambiguity in the world, a philosophy imbuing a need for personal growth, evolution, and enlightenment …to meet and overcome the ever-present challenges of life.

In bringing the two belief systems together, spiritual leaders of the emergent Khoisan added "Transition Rites," that is, the idea of transformation, or transition from one state to another, as part of the social process to address the duality of acceptance and nonacceptance of the challenges of life; a dichotomy resolved by the inception of "Transition Rites" that formed and marked critical periods of change in each person's life. Emphasis on such rituals to mark an individual's development, preparation, growth, and change in status reflected how important development was in defining maturity and status in ancient Khoisan society. The key elements of all such ceremonial rites involved periods of seclusion and minimalist living associated with self-denial, hardship, and personal attainment.

Thus was the inception and evolution of what became known as "the Path" …to become conscious of one's own mind power and to become awake. Through a legacy of seeking and obtaining enlightenment by minimalist living and self-denial (in terms of postponing gratification), "the Path" to personal attainment was said to lead to the right effort, livelihood, mindfulness, and right concentration, and thus a cessation of suffering. Theirs was an advanced antediluvian civilization for which the "Serpent Cave" in the Tsodilo Hills is clear evidence of the early *Khoisan* inception of the *Naga* cult, whose influence spread across the ancient world with migrations and expansions of the *Khoisan*. [ccxciv]

It was with the emergence of the *Khoisan* that the *Rainbow Serpent* became referred to as the "Naga" (the "*Ng ai*" who serves the Creator), who was said to encircle the entire Cosmos with the radiant coils of its long, majestic, multicolored, translucent tail. The word "Naga" is actually the origin of the word Nega, Negusa, Nagast, Niger, or "NGR," meaning King, Lord, Glory, Black, and Instrument of the Creator, respectively. The priestly class among the early ancient Khoisan was accorded the title and called "Nagas." In their mythology, the ancient priestly class of the Nagas was said to have fearlessly arisen from the primeval waters to defend and protect their realm and were said to have mystical powers by which they aid in the advancement of life.

Khoisan epistemology drew from their own natural history and the spiritual influences of the Naro, through which the name "Nagu-Naro" (the "followers of the Naga in the land of the Naro") originally ascribed solely to the northern city, in time came to be ascribed to the entire antediluvian civilization extending from the northern confines of the ancient Kalahari to the coast of Southern Africa. Inter-connecting waterways of the era enabled the spread and expansion of the ancient culture of the Khoisan, which, in time, became synonymous with the ethos of the Naga. The Nagas anciently spread through the maze of lagoons, channels, and wetlands then, characterizing much of the lowlands of Southern Africa.

Historians are generally divided about the true history of Southern Africa. There is much ancient evidence to suggest an advanced civilization inhabited Southern Africa well before and during the Last Great Ice Age, pre-dating any known civilization on Earth. Much controversy surrounds these ancient discoveries, specifically because "mainstream" (Euro-centric) history taught in schools and universities do not account for mining or industrial civilizations existing until around 12 000 years ago. Notwithstanding, there has been an overwhelming and undeniable amount of early ancient evidence discovered indicating that history, as it has been taught, is, in fact, completely false. There have been ancient ruins and artifacts found which indicate the Naga developed a powerful ante-diluvial civilization in Southern Africa …during the last Great Ice Age. [ccxcv]

Khoisan of the Naga ethos constructed stone pyramids based on the belief that inexplicable or unknown energy was peculiar to properly aligned pyramid structures; that spiritual energies and perceptions were stimulated or heightened by such energies, facilitating spiritual and physical healing. Initially, only the priestly class was called the "Nagas," They were accorded entrance into the inner sanctums by the laity. Among other things, the Nagas used the inner sanctums of the pyramids as meditation areas; faint legend holds that those who meditated in the pyramids in this fashion achieved altered states of consciousness enabling higher levels of spiritual communion. The Nagas, who had become adept in the perception and use of subtle energies, believed that subtle celestial energies were focused within properly aligned pyramids which, during meditation, opened portals to varying dimensions of the spiritual realm.

There is evidence of pyramid-shaped structures and terraces all over the vast terrain of Southern Africa, with the most distinct of these (to date) known as "Adams Pyramid', a name derived from its location at an ancient site known as Adam's Calendar, the oldest man-made structure in the world, predating even the Sphinx and Great Pyramid of Giza by tens of thousands of years.[ccxcvi]. Various astronomical alignments have been identified at the site, and it is possibly the only example of a completely functional, mostly intact megalithic stone calendar in the world.[ccxcvii] Adam's pyramid and calendar are on the same thirty-one degrees east longitudinal line as Great Zimbabwe ruins and the Great Pyramid of Giza.[ccxcviii]

There are thousands of stone circle ruins scattered throughout the mountains of Southern Africa. The first estimates of the number of these ruins were made in 1891 by English explorer Theodore Bent. He estimated there were about 4,000; by 1974, the estimate had risen to 20,000. Today, a researcher and authority on the subject, Michael Tellinger, has estimated the number of stone ruins to be 100,000 or possibly much higher. Some of these "stone circles" have no doors or entrances, while most are connected by an expansive network of channels that are often misinterpreted as "roads" by some historians. This connected grid of circular ruins is immersed in a seemingly never-ending expanse of ancient agricultural terraces surrounding the structures. Adam's Calendar is considered to be the most famous among these ruins.

By establishing mitogenomic timelines, frequencies, and dispersals, it has been shown that the Khoisan lineage originally first emerged within the residual Makgadikgadi-Okavango paleo-wetland of southern Africa over 200,000 years ago. Genetic divergence points to a sustained 70,000-year-long existence of the Khoisan lineage before their "out-of-homeland" migrations and expansions eastward, southeastward, and finally northward between 120,000 and 12,000 years ago. The Okavango Delta and Makgadikgadi wetlands were each a feature of the Pre-Ice Age pluvial, formed simultaneously in northeastern Botswana, where the river is dammed by the southern fault lines of the Great Rift Valley, causing its waters to form and give shape to the huge Wetlands.

The ancestral Proto-Khoisan and the descendent *Khoisan* of the *Naga* ethos each used their early maritime skills and abilities to spread southeastward, beyond the near southern islands, to eventually reach what was then the contiguous continent size landmass of Australia and Tasmania, known as the Ice Age continent of "Sahul*,*" and, ultimately, to the huge Sunda sub-continent, a massive sub-continent size peninsula that existed where the present day Indonesian Archipelago (with over 17,000 **islands**) emerged when ocean levels rose and submerged the great landmass after the end of the Last Great Ice Age.

When sea levels were still near their lowest, the southern islands of the *Crozet Archipelago, Amsterdam,* and *St Paul*, and those along the *Ninetyeast Ridge* were far more substantial land masses, facilitating migration along what then seemed to be an *ancient land bridge* between *Africa* and the massive Sunda Sub-Continent. South of Madagascar, the *Kerguelen Archipelago* was then joined into a single-island landmass, as was the *Crozet Archipelago*. The present-day islands of *St. Paul* and *Amsterdam* became a single land mass, situated approximately halfway between *Southern Africa* and ancient *Sahul*. They were the southernmost island land mass in the *ancient land bridge*.

The island chain marked by the mountain peaks along the *Ninetyeast Ridge* also became more prominent during the Glacial Maximum, extending the eastward leg of the *ancient land bridge* fully to the coast of Asia. The *Ninetyeast Ridge* is actually a narrow submarine mountain range extending from Asia towards Antarctica; the ridge rises to an average height of 10,000 ft, with a number of its peaks emerging as islands during periods of low sea levels. [ccxcix] To the west of the *Ninetyeast* are *Cocos Islands*, then a large single island land mass; situated just north-west of present-day Perth, *Cocos Island* was among the gateways to ancient *Sahul*. The narrower sea crossings intersecting the more significant island land masses greatly facilitated the waves of outbound migrations prompted by the long and severe drought-like conditions in Southern Africa during the *Glacial Maximum*.

As the Kalahari began drying up, small groups of *Khoisan* began to migrate beyond the southern shores towards the promise of a more hospitable climate and terrain in the low-lying islands of the southern seas.[ccc] There were at least three separate migrations of the Khoisan from Southern Africa; the first around 95,000 B.C. Using the early maritime abilities developed by navigating the network of inland waterways and huge inland lakes to venture beyond the ancient riverine corridors and confines of Southern Africa, the *Khoisan* reached Madagascar around 95,000 B.C; these migrations were among the second series of major outbound migrations from Africa. This was followed by waves of *Khoisan* migrations across the narrow sea crossings and *ancient land bridges* of the southern seas, destined for the lands of *Sahu*l and *Sunda*.

The second migration of the *Khoisan* occurred after tropical Africa's climate became wetter (around 70,000 B.C.), dramatically increasing the flow of inland rivers emptying into and expanding the wetlands and estuaries of the Kalahari. The inundation of large areas of fertile land and the dramatic expansion of the wetlands ultimately gave impetus to second waves of migrations by the *Khoisan*, who spread southeastward, ultimately to Sunda. An effect repeated during the pluvial period between 30,000 and 19,000 years ago, when there were again high lake-levels in Paleo-Lake Makgadikgadi as the lake filled to capacity, it overflowed into the valleys below. The waters of huge Paleo-Lake Makgadikgadi drained northwards and then eastwards, forcing the middle and lower Zambezi Rivers to connect, forging the mighty Victoria Falls into existence.[39]

---

[39] Street & Grove (1976). Heine1979

However, the ancient southern Kalahari was characterized by arid conditions during this period. Population levels remained stable in the lake-dependent homeland…until rising temperatures began to result in an intense drying out of the region.[ccci] Warming began abruptly about 15 000 years ago, with a short-lived return to cold conditions between 12 000 and 11 000 years ago. Temperatures then rose again. A second pluvial with less high lake levels occurred around. 12,000 years ago, and by mid-Holocene, the reconstituted lake was somewhat recharged, yet only a frail remnant of its former grandeur. Nonetheless, a patchwork of green islands still filled the massive paleo-lake, and its water still fed an intricate network of rivers connecting Nagu-Naro. When the massive waters of the pluvial preceding the Holocene poured into the Kalahari, it created a huge inland lake, the Holocene-era iteration of Paleo-Lake Makgadikgadi.

Paleolake Makgadikgadi was still situated at the distal end of the Okavango River, which flowed all the way from the Angolan highlands into northern Botswana, forming the alluvial fan defining the Okavango delta.[cccii] It was thus, after all, that an awkward geological twist of fate created the greatest natural oasis on earth, the Okavango Delta northeast of Paleo-Lake Makgadikgadi. At its height Holocene era Paleo-Lake Makgadikgadi covered as much as 80,000 km and was as much as 30 m deep.[ccciii] The Okavango, Zambezi, and Cuando rivers once all emptied into the huge basin of the giant ancient lake.[瀑cciv]

The Kalahari was then again a vast wetland, where huge inland lakes, lagoons, rivers, and waterways provided both sustenance and a means of transport.[cccv] The success of their advanced civilization led to the manmade crisis of 'overpopulation at Nagu-Naro,' a crisis prompting renewed waves of migrations. Migrations of the Khoisan to the southern lands soon transformed into waves, with boatload caravans departing in family and extended family groups, often establishing temporary and permanent settlements on suitable islands along the migratory route to Sunda.[cccvi]

Dawn of the Eon

The Sunda shelf is the name present-day geologists call the largest single section of Asian real estate submerged by rising sea levels after the Great Last Ice Age; a vast sub-continent-sized expanse of land in Southeast Asia where the southern reaches of the South China Sea, the Gulf of Thailand, and the Java Sea are today. During the Glacial Maximum, when sea levels were much lower, this area was twice the size of the Indian Sub-Continent. It included what we now call Indo-China, Malaysia, and Indonesia. The South China Sea, the Gulf of Thailand, and the Java Sea formed the connecting parts. Apparently, the present location of Hong Kong and other present-day Chinese ports were "hundreds of miles inland during the last Ice Age." During the Last Glacial Maximum, Sunda extended northward from Indonesia to Borneo.

During the Ice Age, the Sunda Sub-Continent was characterized by an abundance of mountains, valleys, and rivers; the mountains are still with us today due to their loftiness in Sumatra, Java, and Borneo in particular. The Sunda Shelf connects the major islands of the Indonesian archipelago with the most extensive lowland areas in Sumatra, Java, and Kalimantan. Sunda was comprised of the Indonesian archipelago, Malaysia and Indochina, contiguously linked, forming a single peninsula-shaped landmass twice the size of the present-day Indian sub-continent. In the interior was a gigantic fertile plain that benefitted from heavy rains, rich soils, and the warm winds of the equator, which blew across the Sunda during the Last Ice Age; in consequence, the sub-continent was then home to some of the richest forestry, fauna and agricultural lands on Earth.

Sunrise at Sunda

Amidst and after the Last Glacial Maximum, the Sunda was an ideal location for early agricultural development and expansion. It must have seemed like the Garden of Eden to the migrants who sought to take advantage of this Ice Age refugium. They would settle long-term and develop a uniquely high civilization and cultural variant here. Sunda was blessed with vast fertile plains, abundant rivers and lakes, and rich mineral resources. While the maximum glacial, Sundaland featured high mountains along the south coast, in the region of the present-day isles of Sumatra and Java, and east in the region of present-day Borneo. All three regions were immediately bounded by the main ocean, but the central portion, now forming the submerged Sunda Shelf, was vast, a flat plain.

Underwater mapping of the Sunda Shelf reveals that modern rivers in Indonesia, Malaysia, and Indo-China would have been extended and often combine to form much bigger rivers in the area now inundated. The mountains stretching along the South China and Celebes seas of the Sunda shelf mark the outer (southern) edge of Asia's once-extended continental land mass. The outer edge of the chain of present-day islands marks the mountain ranges extending from Sumatra through Java and the Lesser Sunda islands, forming the then Southeastern edge of the Sunda sub-continent. On the inner (northern) side of the islands, the mountains are graded into swamps, lowlands, and the broad lowland plains that would become the shallow Java Sea.

East of the low land plains were the heights of present-day Borneo, dominated by Mount Kinabalu, the highest peak in the Southeast Asian archipelago. The broad mountain system, which includes Mount Kinabalu, runs roughly from northeast to southwest, dividing the highlands. Kalimantan, which constitutes about three-fourths of the island, consists mostly of forest-covered mountains in the deep interior and lowlands and alluvial swamps near the coast. The present-day island of Celebes then comprised the southern heights of Sunda, situated just north of the Sahul shelf. The heights of Celebes were extremely long, running northeast from the highland's north-south backbone. The Celebes region of had ranges of mountains cut by deep rift valleys; the region was bordered by oceanic troughs in the south, separating the Sunda and Sahul Shelfs.

In the period before the Last Glacial Maximum, many areas that later became completely barren deserts, were far wetter than they are today, notably so in the southern region of present-day Australia, where migrations and occupation by "Early-Sudra" (those called "Aborigines"), which is believed to have coincided with the wet period between 40,000 and 60,000 years ago.[cccvii] An ancient advent later foreclosing extensive settlement by the Nagas, who migrated after that period. From the northern coasts of Sahul, the Nagas made the shortened sea-crossing to Sunda, progressing along the ancient migratory path and settlement areas of the ancestral Proto-Khoisan, who migrated over 40,000 years prior.[cccviii] The Naga first settled in village clusters along the southern coastal region of Sunda, from where they then spread northward and through the coastal valleys and into the vast inner plains.[cccix]

Nascent Naga Sunda

Sunda dwarfed the neighboring Indian subcontinent. Sunda was a massive sub-continent of Southeastern Asia, encompassing the Sunda Shelf, the part of the Asian continental shelf that was exposed during the Last Ice Age. During the Ice Age, lower sea levels connected the Asian continent with the western Indonesian archipelago, defining the massive ancient subcontinent. The huge Sunda Sub-Continent included the Malay Peninsula on the Asian mainland, as well as the large islands of Kalimantan, Java, and Sumatera and their surrounding islands. Sunda, as it was, had high mountains along the south coast, in the region of present-day Sumatra and Java, and also in the east, in Borneo; all three regions were bounded by oceans, and the central interior (now forming the submerged Sunda Shelf), was a vast flat plain.

During the Last Glacial Maximum, the terrain of ancient Sunda consisted of tropical rain forests, woodlands, grasslands, and montane tropical forests. Initial Naga settlements were concentrated in the coastal south, from where they then spread northward, along the coastal foothills, and eventually eastward, through the coastal valleys and gaps between the foothills, into the vast interior plains. Large rivers with fertile lands defined the interior plains and lowlands of ancient Sunda during the Ice Age. Many, if not most, settled along the major river systems linking the vast, well-irrigated interior plains, where soon ancient fishing and agricultural settlements and communities arose, expanded, and thrived. Rivers were the best means of transportation at that time. Like in Southern Africa, the Naga expanded along these rivers' corridors for untold generations.[cccx]

The ancient riverine cultures are evidenced by rock paintings spread all over the archipelago. Most of the paintings are estimated to be more than 10,000 years old. Some of the paintings depict boats. These suggest that they already had the technology from the very ancient time. The ones in Maros were carbon-dated to about 40,000 years old. Sunda was in the ancient tropics, surrounded by major oceans, those now called the Indian and Pacific Oceans, benefitting from the heavy precipitation, with rich volcanic soils which developed into some of the richest agricultural and forestry lands, creating some of the richest fauna on Earth creating ideal climatic conditions for the development and advancement of early agriculture and agricultural technology. The Naga of Sunda was a world leader in agricultural technology, using stones for grinding wild grains as early as 24,000 years ago.

Naga's technological development seems to have been focused on both agriculture and mining and the manufacture of metal alloys. ...Kalimantan Island was rich in gold, while the region of the present-day Malay Peninsula and the regions of the present-day Bangka and Belitung Islands were rich in Tin, with rich veins of Copper, Lead, and Zinc scattered around the southern confines of the massive sub-continent. Pre-historic remains of the era consist of pottery, metal works, cave paintings, burial sites, stone tools, megalithic stones, and step pyramids. Khoisan megalithic culture featured in earth-and-stone step pyramids used in similar purpose as the pyramids of Southern Africa, similarities which demonstrate that they sprang from a common origin. The earth-and-stone step pyramids were normally built on natural or manmade mounds or hillsides.

Like throughout much of Southern Africa, pyramids have been found throughout the vast Sunda Sub-Continent, with most of them found in the region of the present-day island of Java, the largest of which is at the megalithic site of Gunung Padang, discovered in 1914, the largest site of its kind in present-day Indonesia. No one knew the Pyramid was a pyramid until geological surveys were done in 2011. [40]Rather than a pyramid, like the ones in South Africa, Gunung Padang is a terrace-like structure built atop an existing volcanic hill. Gunungpadang is the biggest and the oldest of the earth-and-stone step pyramids, dated about 25,000 years ago.[cccxi] The various layers dating to different periods in time indicate different eras of construction at Gunung Padang; it is believed that 25,000 years ago is when constructions at the site first began.

The whole of present-day Indonesia is covered with mysterious ancient ruins and megaliths, which are largely unknown and uninvestigated. The Nagas were a highly civilized and megalithic culture, the ancient ruins of which include temples that are still in use because very often they were built on ancient sites and retain influences from the ancient past. The ancient Naga of the Sunda were a farming and spice-trading civilization; they developed a guild-based industry and maritime trade system. The Naga were great seamen and were the first to develop early ancient maritime trade in the region. Approaching the end of the Last Great Ice Age, winds were up to 70 percent stronger than prevailing present-day winds, which, together with accommodating equatorial sea currents, made ocean sailing more comfortable.

The prevailing wind and sea currents of the era were ideal for long-distance maritime trading, and the Naga linked with ports supplying expanding markets along the coasts of the Kumari Peninsula and East Africa. Serendipitously, the Nagas discovered the westerly route to the eastern coast of the ancient Kumari Peninsula while following the southern equatorial current flowing from Sunda to Africa past Madagascar. The current churns both north and south after hitting the African coast. The northern section splits again, offering the Naga spice traders the alternative of cruising straight home on the easterly counter-current or striking out northwards along the west coast of the Kumari Peninsula.

The Kumari Peninsula

At the height of the Glacial Maximum peninsular *Kumari* fully encompassed the present-day Maldives islands, then the peninsula's northern mountain range, stretching southward from its central west coast in a slight westerly direction to descend into a series of valleys and vast central highland plains. A broad low land plain extended between the southern foothills of the central highlands and the northern foothills of the southern highlands just north of the cape. The Chagos Arch islands were then the southernmost mountain range and highlands of *Kumari*. A broad southern highland plain stretched from the foothills of the present-day main island group of the Chargos Arch, then situated along the southwestern coast of Kumari Nadu, and extended to the foothill of the southern most of the island of the Chargos, then situated on the southeastern coast Kumari Nadu. From the foot of the southeastern mountains, the highlands stretched slightly to the southwest, descending abruptly into lowland foothills and broad coastal plains just above the southern cape.

---

[40] . Natawidjaja 2013

Migrations of the Sudra

It was conceivably in the highlands of *Mount Meru* and *Kilimanjaro* that the prominent feature differences between the two major branches of the descendant Africoid family became most pronounced. The *Dasas* were, by lineage, direct descendants and a subset of the *Sudra* that settled in and around the highland regions of *Kilimanjaro* and *Meru* during the late Ice Age, around 45,000 B.C., and over the course of time had become far more differentiated than their ancient ancestors. Over the millennium, they gradually adapted to cold, hot, or dry semi-self-contained environments, resulting in differing skin tonality and hair texture, leaving their ancestors far more diverse people.[cccxii]

The *Kolarians* (the '*Kols*") are among the oldest of the *Proto-Sudra*, emerging in the foothills of Kilimanjaro and Meru, with their terrain eventually extending to the adjacent eastern coastal planes during the ice age. The *Kols* exhibited clear affinities with the *Veddha* and were among the first to cross the seas to traverse the *Kumari* peninsula to ancient *Ceylon* (present-day Sri Lanka) and from there into the confines of the ancient *Indian Sub-Continent*. Along with other evident physiological similarities between the *Kols* and other emergent ethno-groups of the *Sudra* over the long millennium, common adaptations to the alpine climate of the highlands culminated in clearly shared characteristics, such as the wavy and often curly hair of the otherwise darkly hued *Adi-Dasas* (pure Dravidians).

The Legends

The *Sudra* emerged in the alpine highlands of *Kilimanjaro* and *Meru*, centered around the vast and fertile Arusha region between the peaks of *Mount Kilimanjaro* and *Meru*. In the alpine highlands, over the long millennium of the Last Great Ice Ag, the Sudra would become further differentiated, with the most apparent difference between Negroids and Sudroids being that of hair texture. The dramatic and sustained decline in temperature levels in the highlands during the Last Great Ice Age, in combination with long periods of near geographic and reproductive isolation, gave rise to the varying physical distinctions; the hair texture of *Sudroids* is generally, though not exclusively wavy or curly, in contrast to the hair texture of *Negroids,* which is generally, though not exclusively, curly to frizzy.

Anchored by the fertility and rich abundance of the greater Arusha region, ideally situated along the southern base of Mount Meru amid rolling green foothills, with Meru towering over the whole region. The *Dasas* spread into Arusha from their home terrain in the ancient highlands. The landscape gets noticeably lusher as you gain altitude at Mount Meru; at about 6,000 feet, the fields are lush and green, providing ample settlement area where early Dasa's villages arose and expanded into early village clusters.

Mount Meru's highlands descend through various landscapes, plains, forest moorlands, and a lava desert, finally into the lush and fertile Arusha region, marked by large leafy banana trees. The western slopes of Meru drain into the Eastern Rift Valley, east of Arusha, where the Ngorongoro highlands rise from the floor of the valley, while the eastern slopes of Meru, and Kilimanjaro, each drain to the Indian Ocean. By these routes, the early *Sudra* of each ethno-group extended their settlement ranges to the adjacent east African coastal planes, from where many would later migrate to and through the fabled *Kumari* peninsula and the later surviving *Isles of Kumari* to the *Indian Sub-Continent* of the era.

Rise of Nagu-Noro

In the heart of southern Africa lies the scattered evidence of a lost civilization whose people built some 20,000 stone structures. These breathtaking ruins constitute the largest continuous stone settlement ever built on Earth, as it stretches over thousands of kilometers from South Africa all the way to Kenya and beyond. South Africa show that these early humans had already developed a feel for the arts and crafts around 80,000 years ago. Until recently, this was the only real link we had to the cradle of humankind in southern Africa and its earliest inhabitants. Southern Africa holds some of the deepest mysteries in all of human history. The re-evaluation of some of these ancient stone ruins of southern Africa has led further back in time than ever before.

These mysterious ancient ruins consist of dwellings, forts, temples, roads, irrigation systems, and agricultural terraces that cover thousands of square kilometers. It is estimated that more stone went into building these features than went into building all of the Egyptian pyramids. It is an archaeologist's dream that will unveil even greater and more mysterious secrets in years to come. Research over the past twenty years has revealed that these stone structures are, in fact, the remains of ancient temples and astronomical observatories of lost ancient civilizations that stretch back for thousands of years.[41] These circular ruins are spread over thousands of square kilometers; there is no real count or audit of the ruins, but it is estimated by those who have flown over them for years that there must be around 20,000 structures scattered all over southern and east Africa.[cccxiii]

It seems the vast lands of ancient Nagu-Naro were brought together, if not formerly united, under a renowned personage whose actual name has long been lost in the dust of early antiquity; thus, in this writing, he shall simply be called "Noura" (a name meaning "the light"); perhaps the first of the "Grand Regents" of the early ancient Nagas, a station arising from prominence among the regional powers (the "Regents") under his greater Grand Regency. A feat achieved not merely by prescience and leadership but more significantly by the influence of esoteric spiritual ethos. An ethos that first attracted the abidance of the Regents and laity of the northern provinces around the ancient City of Nagu-Noro, west of the Khoti Pan in the ancient Okavango Delta, near the then mouth of gigantic Palaeolake Makgadikgadi.

It was an ethos and inculcation that spread first across the northern uplands of Noroland and then southward across the wet Kalahari of the era, through which it spread eastward to the Southern Megalithic City, just west of Maputo harbor, on the coast of present-day Mozambique. Noura himself, though a native of the City of Nagu Noro, would have been deeply influenced by the spiritual tenets of his lineage, which arrived at the delta generations prior by way of the uplands northeast of the Zimbabwe plateau.[cccxiv] Because the "Rainbow Serpent" (the cosmic "Naga") was the universal totem of the clans of the early ancient Khoisan, the clans were distinctive and known by their ancestral terrain.

The ancestors of Noura originally arrived from the ancient Zambezi River Valley, where their ancestral terrain was in and along the corridors of the enchanting and mystical middle river valley. The mighty Zambezi is the fourth-longest river in Africa. The long winding river valley it carved over the early millennium came to be anciently inhabited by both the Khoisan and the Ba-Twa, who, for untold centuries, peacefully coexisted, interacted, and often prospered, even during the most turbulent and difficult times.[cccxv]

---

[41] Research by Cyril Hromnik, Richard Wade, Johan Heine and a handful of others

During earliest antiquity, the meandering Zambezi was described as having the body of a snake and the head of a dragon, with the anatomy of the long winding body of what was then called the "Serpent River" trifurcated by the geographical boundaries along the course of the river, defining the Upper, Middle, and Lower Zambezi River Valleys. The headwaters of the river emerge just east of the divide between the Zambezi watershed and the Congo watershed. From its headwaters, the Upper Zambezi flows southwest about 150 miles, into and through present-day Angola, where the river turns true south and flows through present-day Zambia and Botswana and along the border of Zambia and Zimbabwe.

The Zambezi then bends almost due east, below its junction with the Kwando River. It then slowly flows eastward towards the chasm the Great Victoria Falls plunge into. Victoria Falls is the boundary between the Upper and Middle Zambezi.[cccxvi] Below the falls is a gorge some 60 miles long, where the river descends in a series of rapids. The Middle Zambezi extends about 600 miles from Victoria Falls into present-day western Mozambique. About fifty miles downstream from the Falls, the river flows through an extensive plain, occupying the broad Middle Zambezi River valley. This valley spreads out to a width of three to five miles in places.

Over the long millennia, the mighty Zambezi River has rushed through the plain of the middle valley, creating islands, channels, and sandbanks, turning this section of the river into a fertile valley unique unto itself. The middle valley is a spectacular section of the river with many islands, channels, and crystal clear waters with many species of fish; the river here was broad and shallow, with scattered outcrops that captured fertile alluvial soils. Here were also numerous islands and sandbanks fringed by dense forests of baobab-mingled indigenous trees. The ancient middle valley had a wide variety of trees and open grasslands where early subsistence farming communities arose, perhaps, to some extent, influenced by the early ancient agricultural ethos of nearby Nagu-Naro.

The middle Zambezi anciently ended at the "Kebrabasa," a huge gorge where the river flowed through the western panhandle of Mozambique and into the broad Lower Zambezi Valley. The section of the Zambezi beyond the Kebrabasa is about 400 miles in length. It is where the river becomes shallow in places as it spreads out over the area of Lower Zambezi. The river then splits into a number of branches, forming the Zambezi Delta as it approaches and empties into the Indian Ocean.[cccxvii] Khoisan and BaTwa lived along the river for thousands of years, with the Khoisan occupying the Lower River Valley and the BaTwa inhabiting the Upper Valley. However, it was in the enchanted Middle River Valley they co-existed in semi-isolation and cultivated a unique ethos under which they lived and prospered for thousands of years.

The Parables

The northern Zimbabwe plateau is part of the central Zimbabwean plateau, covering most of the present-day country of Zimbabwe; the relief of the plateau is characterized by three distinct geographic sections. The "highveld" comprises areas of land generally above 1200 m above sea level, and the "middle veld" comprises those parts of the plateau with land between 600 and 1200 m above sea level. The Middle Zambezi River Valley is part of the Zimbabwean plateau known as the "Lowveld," comprising areas of land below 600 m above sea level, a fertile rift valley caused by faulting, through which the waters of the Zambezi River slowly flow, depositing rich alluvial sediments and soil.

The river in the middle valley is broad and shallow, with numerous islands, and abounds in rich vegetation, wild animals, and birds. The waters harbor a variety of fish species, as well as numerous hippos and crocodiles. The variety of trees in the middle valley is also noteworthy, including fascinating baobabs and ilala palms. The vegetation gradually shifts from the tree stands that dominate the valley floor to the woodlands that stretch up the escarpments onto the plateaus to the north and south. Forests line the river with canopies of whipping riverine trees, while vegetation on the alluvial soils dominates the open savannas.[42]

The settlements and terrain of the BaTwa and Khoisan were interspersed throughout and along the forested fertile floor of the middle river valley. Their initial interactions were barter and trade, expanding from there to assistance and aid, and eventually inter-dependence. An advent fomented by the harsh heat and aridity of the glacial maximum, followed by the deadly discontinuous floods of the early Holocene. Clans of the BaTwa brought with them an ethos of connectedness and the notion of their "guardianship of the forests." While clans of the Khoisan brought with them the belief that the "creator" is "power," and given that it is this "power" that imbues and sustains life, to live in harmony with it is to live in harmony with the flow of nature. Concordant ancient beliefs that, when synthesized, derived philosophies of an ancient belief system that, in many ways, were synergistic in effect.

The fetish priests of the BaTwa espoused the belief that all living things possess a spiritual essence, alluding to the "Divine Netjeru" and the omnipresence of the unknowable "Netjer," while the shamen of the Khoisan espoused belief in the notion of an "immanent spirit" (within each life form) that is invigorated by the "power" flowing from the "creator." Though the BaTwa called the Celestial Serpent (the "Southern Borealis") the "Hydra," and the Khoisan called the fabled Rainbow Serpent the "Naga," they each believed it to be an aspect of a mysterious "Creator,"; bestowing the vital energies (the "Mãna") that imbue and sustain life, on its journey across the vast cosmos.[cccxviii]

The Shamanistic Priest, verily called the "Enlightened Ones," observed that just as there were plants and trees in the forests that clearly proved more worthy than others, by the measure of their strength and greater growth, visibly exceeding their peers, some men, and women are more worthy than other, and are endowed greater proportions of the subtle energies that nourish life. The *Enlightened Ones* proselytized that integrity, honesty, and other such ethical virtues were observably things that strengthen one's character, which, they propounded, must surely be reflective of a strengthened soul. The belief system resolved that each person is strengthened by the magnetism of their "Virtues,"; an early ancient philosophy that would come to stress the importance of discipline and empathy.

---

[42] Wild & Barboza 1967; Jachmann 2000

The early proponents and practitioners of the emergent philosophy were not then organized into a hierarchical or proselytizing priesthood. Yet, the allure of their belief system fomented its eventual spread throughout the middle valley, the virtual "Heart of the Serpent River." The early ancient Shamanistic Priests taught of a spiritual path for raising consciousness and emotional and physical healing; they espoused a semi-holistic philosophy rooted in self-mastery via cultivation of the mind and mental discipline. It holds no dogmas, yet instead offers a path to personal awakening. Rationality was the key to virtue and happiness, and discord and depravity were the only things truly bad. Wisdom, justice, courage, and temperance were the four cardinal virtues of the emergent belief system.

Yet, there were two more powerful virtues, the silent virtues of "grace and gratitude"; silent in that they were (and are) discreetly if not tacitly bestowed and received, and as such, were deemed "mutually enhancing." This unique power of the silent virtues was believed to greatly enhance the "magnetism" of one's personal virtues in attracting the flow of Mãna, better endowing one with health and the vital energies of life. It can irrefutably be said that after a period of dissemination and pondering, the individual and collective pursuit of what became known as the "Power of the Virtues" virtually transformed socialization and cultural interaction in the early ancient middle river valley.

It was a transformation that facilitated the emergence of the early pre-historic farming communities whose remnants have recently been discovered in the middle river valley by present-day archeologists.[cccxix] The Enlightened Ones (the Shamanistic Priests) espoused simple tenets for guidance, such as "Treat each as you seek to be treated," "If you seek to be treated with honor and respect, treat others with honor and respect," and "If you seek to be treated with integrity, act with integrity, and honor the integrity of others'. Such tenets were viewed to be in pursuit of the "Power of the Virtues," a broadly adopted and pervasive pursuit that led to ease and facilitation of individual and intercultural interaction and exchange.[cccxx]

To aid, assist or otherwise cooperate for the benefit of others, as well as the self, was seen as act of "Grace," usually followed by acts of "Gratitude," evoking the greater "Power of the Virtues," availing oneself of a greater flow Mãna; a reflexively reciprocal belief system that simultaneously spread and bonded its adherents. This was the earliest iteration of Pre-Buddhist philosophy, an ethos the ancient name of which has long been lost in the dust of antiquity; thus, in this treatise, it shall simply be referred to as the "Path." From the beginning, meditation and observing moral precepts were foundational in adherence and pursuit of the "Path."[cccxxi]

Through discipline and resolutions to the "Path," early practitioners discovered that creating high vibrational levels led to spiritual phenomenology and higher levels of consciousness. The "Enlighten Ones" instructed aspiring practitioners in inducing a physical relaxation so deep that it almost approximated falling asleep. Then, while keeping their eyes closed, with a fixed stare (preferably directed inward toward the forehead), aspirants were instructed to focus attention intently on the center of a visual field kept dark and "emptied" of importuning thoughts or mental images, opening the third eye, a portal to spiritual enlightenment —achieved and sustained through dedicated meditation.

An ideal ethos for the evolution and advancement of early ancient multicultural civilization, an idyllic setting abruptly interrupted by the deadly discontinuous paleo-floods of the early Holocene. It was a period in which the Zambezi River often burst its banks, forcing thousands to flee their villages to escape its floodwaters. Heavy rains and flooding throughout the basin of the middle valley during the early Holocene led to the dislocation and eventual relocation of thousands of people, with many, if not most, resettling on the Zimbabwean plateau above the north-eastern shore of ancient Lake Makgadikgadi. In contrast, others traversed the uplands extending northeastward from the plateau to resettle in the outer precincts of the early ancient City of Nagu-Naro.[cccxxii]

Ruins are spread over the ancient overlapping and amalgamating territories extending from the original home range of the Khoisan in southern Africa through Zambia into the northern reaches of the East African Plateau. An ancient road structure that once connected most, if not all, of the ancient ruins, is still visible from the air for hundreds of kilometers. It is evident that this was no accidental settlement patter but a well-planned and evolved civilization that was mining and had some means of transport. Extended agricultural terraces are spread over large areas, which suggests that these people had a good knowledge of agriculture and planted produce extensively. The ancestors of Noura were among the dislocated clans from the Middle Zambezi Valley who then re-settled in the outer precincts of the early ancient City of Nagu-Naro.

The outer precincts surrounding the core of the early ancient city were adjoining suburbs inhabited by distinctive clans, whose greater clanic families more broadly inhabited the greater regions extending outward from the suburbs. Because the early ancient Naga viewed their culture as an organic collective, rather than the provincial sovereignties of petty kings, leaders of the prominent and defacto governing clans within the given regions were more akin to "regents" than "king," with the true monarch, the "Grand Regent," elevated to such status by the pervasive power of influence and the successes and strength of their example. The clans from the Middle Valley brought the ethos of the "Path" with them, the tenets of which were quickly grasped by those from the middle valley, ushering in an era of prosperity and prominence for their precinct.

Thus, the Regent of the precinct inhabited by the clans from the middle valley rose to become "Grand Regent" of the northern provinces, anchored at the ancient City of Nagu-Naro. The first of his lineage to assume the "Grand Regency," while a product of his heritage from the middle river valley and an adherent to the "Path," Noura was born, raised, and greatly influenced by the precepts of Noroland, and as such, was the first to bring together the ethos of "Path," and Noro spirituality rooted in esoteric Ophiolatry ("Serpent Cult"), which symbolized and masked ancient allegories and myths of the (Aurora Borealis inspired) "Rainbow Serpent," the fabled "Cosmic Naga," and the constellation of Draco (the "Dragon"), which then showed the Great Serpent as ruler of the night sky, with its long body composed of stars revolving timelessly around the universal axis.[cccxxiii]

The powerful combination and influence of the "Path" and esoteric "Ophiolatry" spread southward from Noroland, across the wet Kalahari, and eastward to the regency and provinces of the southern "Grand Regent," anchored at the ancient Megalithic City west of Maputo harbor, on the coast of present-day Mozambique; a grand regency which, in time, yielded to the preeminence of Noura and Nagu-Noro, which then became the Impetus of Naga expansion. Myths and stories speak of legends of the ancient serpent symbolism and reference of the Naga, with evidence uncovered (in the present day) citrusdal district of South Africa, a powerful energy center for the *Khoisan*, in the stadsaal caves, where there is an ancient picture of a human-headed serpent. The Drakensberg, which means dragon mountain in *Afrikaans*, appears to have been another center of reverence; deep in the heart of the Drakensberg, two concentric rings of power are said to surround the specific points of worship, an ancient reverence priests still observe in the region today.[cccxxiv]

The ancient riverine and maritime acuity of the *Khoisan* aided the early expansion of trade throughout the southern sphere, particularly along the courses of the major rivers connecting key seaport towns like *Sofala*. Goods and wares from Zimbabwe were transported along the waterways and exported through the ports of *Sofala*, where they joined the trade flows from *Nagu-Naro*. An ancient port that served the *Nagas* well in their critical role in intermediating trade between *Nagu-Naro*, *Sahul*, and *Naga-Sunda*. The Nagas had become expert navigators and great seamen with considerable maritime resources. Their ships were built with sails and ores, manned and stocked to embark on long expeditions. Such ships were among the earliest plying the southern seas. The *Khoisan* were among the first shipbuilders on earth and used their ships to traverse the *Ninety East Land Bridge* and cross the open seas.

Sealanes of Sahul and Sunda

When sea levels were near their lowest, the southern islands of the *Crozet Archipelago*, *Amsterdam*, and *St Paul*, and those along the *Ninetyeast Ridge* became even more substantial land masses, facilitating passage between the islands of the *ancient land bridge* and the southern coasts of *Africa*, and the western coasts of *Sahul*. What remained of the ancient land bridge extended south of Madagascar to the *Kerguelen Archipelago*, the *Crozet Archipelago*, the isles of *St. Paul* and *Amsterdam*, the remnants of the island chain of the *Ninetyeast Ridge*, to *Cocos Islands* just north-west of present-day Perth, the gateway to *Sahul*. The gradually rising seas of the Holocene slowly inundated the low-lying island that made up much of the land bridge, altering the currents flowing between Southern Africa and *Sahul*.

It has long been speculated that navigation was accomplished not in the open ocean but primarily by short hops between the intersecting islands comprising the land bridge, proceeding along and within view of the coastlines. However, during the course of their trade and discourse with the seaport towns and trading villages of *Sahul* and *Sunda*, the *Naga* gradually adapted to the changes brought on by the rising sea levels of the Holocene and the challenges of open seas. To trade with Sahul and Sunda, they had to cross the strait gap in boats, either on a northerly or southerly route, from island to island, and later, after the submergence of most of the isles of the land bridge, they had to be capable of open-sea navigation, with no land visible on the horizon.

Early on, they had crossed in numerous boatloads, in caravans that launched at about the same time, landing very close to each other in order to establish viable populations for numerous settlements, villages, and civilizations that arose over the millennium. The trade winds and currents allowed regular and direct maritime contact and trade between Nagu-Naro, Sahul, and Naga-Sunda. When sea levels were at their lowest, the fullness of Sahul joined present-day Australia with the whole of nearby New Guinea in the north and the whole of Tasmania in the south, forming ancient 'Sahul.' The seas around the Sahul Shelf are shallow, and the islands closer to Sahul were more closely linked to Sahul than neighboring Sunda, affording the Naga interim ports between Sahul and the harbors of *Naga Sunda*.

Little Freeze: The Younger Dryas

Climatic conditions continued to gradually warm over the following millennium, with sea levels rising to inundate low-lying islands and reshape coastal boundaries. With the rising seas came extenuated and longer voyages, as island land areas shrank in size and proportion or disappeared altogether. Average temperatures gradually rose until around 12,000 BCE, when temperatures suddenly plunged into a new ice age known as the *Younger Dryas*. [cccxxv] At the peak of the Younger Dryas, the north pole snow cap spread southward, covering all of Europe, down to the Baltic shores, extending in Britain down to the Thames, and in North America down to New England, and more centrally as far south as Ohio. Even the mountain ranges of Central Africa were again covered by expanding glacial ice caps.

The *Younger Dryas* climatic event was abrupt in its rapid onset, fully halting the *Holocene* warming trend at the end of the *Glacial Maximum*. After the Glacial Maximum, the world began to slowly warm in a period known as the *Bølling-Allerød*, which began at approximately 13,900 BP. The *Younger Dryas* began with a rapid reversal of the warm conditions of the Holocene and a return to glacial conditions. With the resurgence of glaciation, once again, enormous volumes of water were withdrawn from the world's oceans and locked up in the expanding ice-caps. As the great glacial ice sheets expanded, global sea levels gradually fell, once again exposing vast tracts of low-lying island mass extending southeast from southern Africa toward Southeast Asia. Lowered sea levels re-exposed most of the island chain comprising the ancient southern land bridges.

With the *Younger Dryas* had also come a resurgence in cold arid conditions, which, over time, reduced the fertility and abundance, prompting a renewed series of outbound migrations. Among the first impact areas were the most remote of the highland valleys populated by the *Dasas*. Because of the greats droughts brought on by the Younger Dryas, people living in the affected areas could no longer obtain sufficient food by hunting and gathering and, as a result, had to turn to farm and then to the establishment of settled, larger communities in order to ensure a more stable and abundant food supply. The *Younger Dryas* triggered a revolution in human life by driving people to concentrate in oases-like areas where they could exploit agricultural techniques while still driving others to migrate to open and fertile lands.

With the low sea levels of the early Younger Dryas also came shorter and narrow sea voyages to the east, to Kumari. Long cold drought-like conditions in the highland valleys would prompt a gradual but mass dislocation of the Dasas, populating these areas over time. Migrants mobilized by the dislocations no doubt first impacted regions like Arusha, but over-population pressures would ultimately force many to re-settle in the foothills and lowlands and, ultimately, voyage across the east island chain to reach the promise of an abundant and fertile *Kumari*.

As the Younger Dryas progressed, the glacial ice caps and cold temperatures in the northern hemisphere began to function as a sort of global 'cap' under which the drought-like conditions in the highlands of Kilimanjaro and Meru prompted a steady flow of outbound migration destined for *Kumari*. The seas have typically fallen about one hundred meters during each of the last four glacial episodes. With the fall in global sea levels, many near-shore islands were again exposed as hills along the coastal plains. In contrast, offshore islands within a fifty-fathom contour were again transformed into contiguous land masses during the height of glaciation.

The *Dasas* migrated and colonized many of the isles of the Indian Ocean and the South Seas, with the larger preponderance settling in *Kumari*, preceded by the *Kols* and the *Veddas*, who in turn pushed further into the Indian sub-continent and Asian mainland. Perhaps the dislocations, migrations, and colonization of the Dasas prompted the waves of eastern migrations of the *Asuras*, who established settlement areas as far north as the central (Indian) sub-continent, and as far east as western Sunda. The *Dasas,* in turn, extended their range from the highlands of Kilimanjaro and *Meru* to the Kumari Peninsula. While to the south, the Kalahari ended its wet phase with the onset of the Holocene, after which the rivers, lagoons, and lakes gradually gave way to the region's new drier conditions.

The added aridity brought on by the Younger Dryas only served to further exacerbate the situation, prompting vast dislocations and outbound migrations of the *Khoisan*. Aided by the eastern currents of the southern seas, south of the Mozambique Channel, and the re-emergence of the low-lying lands surrounding the southern islands comprising the ancient 'land-bridge' extending eastward towards *Sahul*, the migrations of the *San*, in large part, were pre-disposed towards colonization and settlement in the lands of the southern seas, with the greater preponderance ultimately destined for *Sahul* and distant *Sunda*.

The Allerød Warming

For centuries outbound migrations of the *San* had both colonized and swept across the southern islands of the ancient land bridge. In contrast, to the north, the northernmost islands of the land bridge had been settled and traversed by the *Sudra*. The cold arid conditions of the *Younger Dryas* ensued for several centuries until the cold glacial conditions were interrupted by the *Bølling* warming event, a period in which the great ice flows again began to recede, and the rains returned to replenish rivers, lakes, and valleys; slowing the outbound migrations of the *Dasas*, as habitable conditions improved in the highlands of *Kilimanjaro* and *Meru*.

To the south, outbound migrations of the *San* would continue nearly unabated as the *Kalahari*. Much of the whole of the southern sphere endured an even greater intensity in the seemingly endless dry and drought-like conditions. The land bridges exposed during the *Younger Dryas* remained largely available during much of the *Bølling* warming event, facilitating outbound migrations to and across the islands southeast and east of the Cape. Upon clearing the coast south of Madagascar and southeast of the Cape, the ancient migrants would rely upon the southward flowing currents of the *Mozambique Channel*, which pushed southward into the southern seas to where the poleward branch of the current turned eastward, creating a broad ancient sea lane extending from the juncture with the Mozambique Channel currents, towards the western coast of *Sahu*l.

The southern island land mass of the present-day *Crozet Archipelago* was situated near the juncture of the currents, where southward currents of Channel met and were turned eastward by the poleward current; from where the currents of the sea lane flowed eastward, toward *Kerguelen, St. Paul, and Amsterdam,* and *Cocos Islands,* off the western coast of *Sahul*. Reduced precipitation during the onset of the *Younger Dryas* glacial event left much of western *Sahul* covered by extensive grasslands, rather than the riverine or rainforest environ to which San was then most adapted, and with drier grasslands extending to the well-watered surviving rainforest to the northeast region of present-day *Papua*.

In consequence, the northeastern regions and highlands functioned as a magnet in attracting large settlements and colonies of the migrating *San;* from here, many would eventually migrate into the eastern *Sunda* region to the north, where they would add to the population and settlement areas of the earlier waves of migration. With this, the then-latest migration of the *San* came a reinforcement and strengthening of the emerging influence of the cult of the *Naga*. An advent that would enhance inter-regional transport and trade, facilitated by the currents of the eastward flowing sea lanes, was countermanded by the westerly trade winds, which allowed reliable voyages between *Southern Africa* and *Sahul*.

Excursions of the Khiosan: Naga-Sunda

Increased rains at the end of the *Younger Dryas* caused years around the flooding of rivers and lakes and increasingly inhospitable conditions along the coastal and lowland settlement areas of the *Southern African Sphere*. Relocation from the lowlands served to further add to population concentrations in the highland foothills, with later arrivals forced to move on to other environs, gradually beginning a new wave of migrations into the Indian Ocean and south sea regions; migrations which had theretofore occurred in only a piecemeal fashion during the immediately preceding century; but now the stream of migrants increased dramatically and became steady. Century after century, as the glaciers receded, more temperate conditions prevailed in Africa and over the globe, allowing an increase in vegetation, as well as more abundance of game and fertile environs throughout the Indian and south Pacific island regions.

When the ice age finally ended, it did so relatively rapidly, in a hundred years or so. Sea levels rose three hundred feet in just one hundred years, flooding and swamping the coastal and low-lying communities, causing mass relocations and forced migrations of whole village communities. As temperatures rose, susceptible regions suffered long periods of drought, with the Kalahari being among the first to begin to dry up, prompting a large and sustained outbound migration of the (Khoisan) Nagas. While sea levels remained sufficiently low, migrants quickened the rate of their still fairly unencumbered movement from and between eastern and southern Africa and the low-lying islands bridging the Southern Seas from Southern Africa to *Sahul* and *Sunda*. From south of Madagascar, the *Kerguelen Archipelago*, the *Crozet Archipelago*, and the isles of *St. Paul* and *Amsterdam,* situated about halfway between *Southern Africa* and *Sahul*, continued to form the backbone of the *ancient land bridge*.

The narrow island chain stretching eastward along the mountain tops of the *Ninetyeast Ridge* remained the backbone of the eastward leg of the *ancient land bridge*, reaching *Western Sunda* and ultimately *Southern Asia*. To the west of the Ninetyeast Island Chain, Cocos Islands, situated just northwest of present-day Perth, continued to be the gateway to Sahul. While the land bridges lasted, final waves of migration spread from Southern Africa to the lands of the southern seas. Sea levels ultimately began to rise as thick sheets of ice, which, until then, covered large parts of Earth, melted in the warmer temperatures. Entire land masses 'detached,' one from the other, as waters rose; from a geological perspective, this happened overnight. However, in human cultural terms, it was an extremely protracted process. Drought-like conditions in Southern Africa prompted increased outbound migrations, using what remained of the dwindling land bridges and taking advantage of still relatively short sea voyages between the islands bridging Southern Africa, Sahul, and Sunda.

The warm climate of the *Bølling* warming event ultimately gave way to yet another reassertion of cold, dry, glacial-like conditions, referred to as the *Older Dryas*. Massive glaciation again ensued, and again dry drought-like conditions in the highlands prompted new waves of outbound migrations among the *Sudra* of *Kilimanjaro* and *Meru*. Renewed waves of migration again destined for *Kumari* flowed from the highland valleys. While to the south, even more intense drought-like conditions portended the beginnings of gradual desertization of the Kalahari, prompting waves of outbound migrations by the Nagas. The *Older Dryas* ended after only a few decades with the onset of the *Allerød Warming*. Once again, the great glaciers began to recede, and wetter weather ensued, bringing the Younger Dryas a close.

Exodus of the Adi-Dasas: Kumari Kandam

Mount Meru's highlands descend through various landscapes, plains, forests, and a lava desert, finally descending into the Arusha region, leafy with banana trees. Arusha is about 160 miles east of Ngorongoro, at the southern base of Mount Meru, and is divided into two sections by the small Naura River Valley, with the landscape noticeably lusher at the altitude near Mount Meru. At about 6,000 feet, the fields are lush and green, providing a rich and abundant settlement area where early settlement clusters and townships arose and expanded, with the fertile highlands destined to become the center of the emerging regional corridor.

Arusha was centrally connected to other settlements by well-established trails and routes interlinking population clusters, with Mount Meru as the topographic centerpiece of the eastern highlands. To the immediate east was Mount Kilimanjaro, towering above Meru and the Rift Valley highlands. Kilimanjaro was populated on both the southern and eastern slopes, which were exposed to the prevailing winds and rain from the Indian Ocean. It was thus well watered and fertile from the mixture of volcanic soil. Archaeological discoveries have found rings and bowls made from obsidian flakes found on the western slopes. Arusha, at the southern base of Meru, was easily accessible from these particular settlement areas of Kilimanjaro.

Kilimanjaro and Meru are each ancient volcanoes, with Kilimanjaro rising to 5,895m and Meru rising to 4,500m. The highlands of Kilimanjaro were characterized by Equatorial to Arctic vegetation, passing through near tropical rainforest, savannah grassland, semi-arid to arid, semi-desert, temperate, moorland, alpine desert, and finally to the permanent snowlines. Among the Sudra in the region, the *Adi-Dasas* (Pure Dravidians) came to dominate and control the trade routes extending between the interior highlands and the adjacent east African coast, interposing the raw materials and commodities traded by the *Sudra* of the lowlands, and perhaps Kumari itself.

The terrain and range of the *Sudra* then extended from the foothills of Kilimanjaro and Meru eastward to and across the Kumari peninsula; into what was then a larger Indian Sub-Continent, with more extensive coastal planes. This while the early *Dasas* remained largely centered and concentrated in and around the highlands of Meru. The western slopes of Meru descended into the Eastern Rift Valley, where the Ngorongoro highlands rise from the valley floor. The *Dasas'* neighboring settlement area in Arusha was a relatively short distance away;. However, in the latter part of the era *Adi-Dasas* attention was turned more toward the foothills of Meru, which had become provinces of the *Nagas*, which were spread northward from the south.

The Adi-Dasas ("Pure Dravidians") legends mention an ancient landmass that disappeared into the Ocean. Present-day Tamils say it was highly populated and included large cities, now buried beneath the sea.[cccxxvi] Until 9,000 years ago, Southern India extended southward below Cape Comorin, Kanya Kumari, incorporating present-day Sri Lanka (ancient Ceylon), with an elongated peninsula extending southward beyond the Equator. The Indian sub-continent was then a far long land mass than exists today; the southern peninsula engulfed the whole of the present-day island of Sri Lanka which was then a mere mountain range, and the highland region at the northeast of the peninsula, anciently known as *Kumari* Kandam.

From Sri Lanka, Kumari stretched southward into the Indian Ocean beyond the equator, with broad coastal plains along the western coast of the peninsula. The coastal plains extended first in a westerly direction, along the southern shoreline of Sri Lanka, abruptly turning southwestward for several hundred miles beyond the shores of Sri Lanka before assuming a true south direction along the Lakshadweep-Chagos Ridge to the peninsula's southern extent, just beyond the present day Chagos Archipelago. The heart of *Kumari* was situated south of Cape Comorin, from where the heartland stretched southward across the northern plains to the foothills of the Maldives' central highlands. The Kumari peninsula extended southward across the central highlands and southern foothills to where it spanned southern plains to the interior foothills of the present-day Chagos Archipelago. [cccxxvii]

The *Dasas* had long prior established well-worn trade and migration routes between the regions of Kilimanjaro and Meru and those of the Kumari peninsula. The highlands of Mount Kilimanjaro and Mount Meru descended through plains, forests, desert, and valleys, with the eastern slopes ultimately descending through the lowland foothills to the adjacent seaside settlement on the coast. There were a series of islands between the seaside launching points on the East African coast and the southern coasts of Kumari; there were the greater Seychelles, followed by the Mauritius and Reunion Isles, each a steppingstone in the direct trade and migrations routes to *Kumari*. With the retreating glaciers came melting ice. As the ice melted and the rains increased, the rivers overflowed, the lakes expanded, and all of the world's Oceans rose, causing floods of unimaginable disastrous enormity.

This ancient tropical warming caused rapid atmospheric changes in the broader region surrounding the equator. The flooding and incessant dislocations in the highlands valleys and plains, as well as the lowland foothills of Mount Kilimanjaro and Mount Meru, led to a gradual but constant flow of outbound migrations of the *Sudras*, with large groups of the *Dasas* ultimately destined for the shores of *Kumari*, following the earlier migratory paths of the *Veddas* and *Asuras* who were among the first to migrate across peninsular *Kumari* into the *Indian Sub-Continent*, and ultimate destinations in the north, east, and west.

Rise of Kumari: The Adi-Dasas

Dasas (Dravidian) civilization commences with the records that have come down to us from the Tamil literary writings during the past 12,000 years, which have been divided by historians into three periods, called the First Sangam period from 9600 BC to 5200 BC, the Second Sangam period from 5,200 BC to 1,500 BC, and the Third Sangam period from 1500 BC to 600 AD. According to legend, the formation of the First Sangam of the Dasas was held in *Kumari*, first convened on Mount Mahendra at southern Maturai by the rishi Agastya. . The first Sangam had been headquartered in the city of *Then-Madurai* (Southern Madurai) and was patronized by a succession of eighty-nine kings, surviving unbroken for over four millennia. During that time, it approved an immense collection of poems and literature. [cccxxviii]

Very little more is known of the First Sangam other than that it was destroyed by the deluge at the end of that golden age, when the city of *Then-Madurai* was swallowed by the sea, along with large parts of the land mass of peninsular *Kumari*. According to legend, over about 11,000 years, a historical dynasty of Dasas kings formed three Sangams to foster the love of knowledge, literature, and poetry among their subjects. These Sangams were the fountainhead of *Dasas* culture, and their principal concern was the perfection of their culture and traditions. The first two Sangams were located in the antediluvian land of peninsular Kumari, which in ancient times bore the name of Kumari Kandam, literally the Land of the Virgin or Virgin Continent.

The first Sangam, head-quartered in the early city of Then-Madurai (Southern Madurai), was patronized by a succession of eighty-nine kings, and survived for an unbroken period of 4,400 years, during which time it approved an immense collection of literature in the advancement of Dasas culture and traditions; attributes which acted as a magnet in attracting the attention and aspirations of large communities of disaffected Dasas adversely impacted by the increasing migrations of Nilotics into the highlands of Arusha and Mount Meru. Then, the steep upper slopes of a youthful cone of Mount Meru, which ascended well over 10000 ft to tower above the southern edge of Arusha, were utterly shattered by a massive volcanic eruption that formed the oblong 5-mile-wide caldera that remains open to the east to the present day.

The main summit of *Mount Meru* lies on the western edge of the caldera, perched above the 12,000 ft high crater known as the Ash Cone. *Dasas* legends say that Mythical Mount Meru rested on the hood of the coiled primeval cobra Vasuki, who, it was said, caused earthquakes when he yawned. It was believed that the existing world would be devoured by this ancient serpent at the end of the age and world cycle. The legend also tells a story of the remaining *Dasas* and *Asuras* of the region assembling on ancestral *Mount Meru*, presumably to plan, organize and begin what would be the final exodus of *Sudra*. An increasing flow of outbound migrations of the Dasas ensued following the catastrophic eruptions of *Mount Meru*, migrations spanning many generations, with most destined for *Kumari*.

Northward Push of the Nagas

The influence of the Naga spread throughout the interior highlands and coasts of Kenya as well as Somalia, on the Horn of Africa. The Anu had aided in spreading and assimilating the familiar tenets of the serpent cult in the north. Precepts of the ancient Hydra cult which had long functioned as both organizing principles and channels of spiritual and personal development among the Anu of the region; tenets which spread throughout the far reaches of the settled north, well before the *Allerød Warming*. Nonetheless, before and after the final cataclysms at Mt. Meru, the Khoisan had gradually extended their range northward, through the intermediate highlands and coastal lowlands of Tanzania, through the highlands and lowlands of Kenya, to the highlands and coastal lowlands of Somalia, the land of Punt itself.[cccxxix]

The ancient terrain and traditional provinces of the Anu stretched from the highlands and coastal lowlands of Punt on the Horn of Africa through present-day Kenya and Tanzania and well into northern Mozambique. It was here, in northern Mozambique, where, as the Khoisan grew to prominence, the Naga soon supplanted the early influence of the Anu. Naga trading patterns cast a wide net, exceeded only by the weight and reputation of their ideas. This attracted a broad range of northward trade opportunities, extending through Tanzania into southern Kenya. Once such trading networks were established, they became more or less routine, a fundamental factor in maintaining and expanding ancient trade and relations.

Trading networks were viewed as solutions to the problem of acquiring commodities not locally available. Cross-cultural interaction catalyzed by the exchange of commodities served as a means for people to acquire new technology and assimilate cultural ideas. The Naga fomented a tradition as cultural brokers and middlemen and, over the ensuing centuries, played a vital role in forging the early trade relations throughout the ancient world. The Naga employed a cooperative strategy in acquiring and trading desired commodities, an early bulk approach to trade that rendered them the early masters of the art. While it is not clear that anything resembling formal trading relationships was established between the Naga and other peoples, it is clear that the Nagas learned early that commodities that lead to mass consumption have the potential to shape socio-political and economic relationships.

As the Naga spread ever northward into the region of present-day Kenya, Ta Netjeru, the "Land of the Gods," they met their first true resistance. Intrusion into the "Land of the God" was surely viewed by the Anu as something akin to heresy. Though habitation had not been exclusively theirs in the region, trade across Ta Netjeru (the "Land of the Gods") had been their exclusive province for thousands of years. As the radiating influence of Nagu-Naro, and the emulative Regencies it spawned, spread fully into and across the region of present-day Kenya, it alas met s determined resistance in the form of the Anu, who traditionally controlled trade routes through the region.

Compounding what the Anu sure viewed as heresy and intrusion, the Naga traded not only in their own commodities and wares, but they also brought the direct spice trade to the region, trading in exotic spices from Naga Sunda, a trade which gained their deeper penetration into the region, raising the ire of the Anu, and ushering a period of back-and-forth skirmishing. The first real provocations for war came from the Anu, when, alas, they responded violently to what they viewed as a heretical intrusion into Ta Netjeru, the "Land of the Gods"; from present-day archeological assessment, interpretation, and depictions, it appears to have been a planned attack at a Khoisan settlement site called Nataruk, a few miles from the present-day shores of Lake Turkana, in Kenya.

Nataruk was along the shore of a lagoon, a marshy area surrounded by woodland, offering the perfect setting for hunting and fishing and an abundance of clean drinking water. The area on the edge of the lake, at that time, must have seemed the perfect place, with all the amenities to live, prosper, and expand. Though the attack upon the village at Nataruk was most certainly one of surprise, the twenty-seven people whose remains were excavated there died wielding clubs, knives, and projectiles. The projectile points are the clearest evidence that this was an organized attack; projectile points are a "fingerprint" of inter-group conflict and can often be used to determine assailants. Two of the points were made from a hard black stone called obsidian, which wasn't common in the area around Nataruk but in the highlands of Punt, a sign that the mighty Punt had seen enough.[cccxxx]

Another provocation occurred further north, in present-day Southern Sudan, at a former ancient Khoisan settlement site presently called Jebel Sahaba. An attack similar to the attack at Nataruk left over sixty people dead or dying. Present-day archaeologists have discovered and excavated the skeletons of sixty-one people found in a mass grave, forty-five percent of which show injuries consistent with acts of war. People died from wounds inflicted by arrows and spears, with direct wounds to the victims' chests, necks, jaws, and heads. Work on the skeletal material suggests there are even more taphonomy indicators of violent death in the form of arrow impact marks, suggesting that some of the individuals succumbed to attacks from archers, with a few projectile points embedded in the bone fragments themselves.

The archaeological record indicates that it was an era (between 12,000 and 10,000 BC) when there was a revolution in weapons technology. During this period, four new weapons first make their appearance-the bow, the sling, the dagger (short sword), and the mace. The bow and the sling were important for hunting, but the dagger and mace were most useful for fighting other humans.[cccxxxi] Among longer-range weapons, arrows can kill at maximum distances of 50 to 200 meters depending on their weight, their point type, and the bow's power; the fire rate of bows is potentially high, with approximately five to ten aimed shots per minute. Very short-range weapons and battles create severe psychological and social difficulties that render long-range shock weapons the weapon of choice among the more disciplined forces of early antiquity. [cccxxxii]

First Neolithic War

While the "Neolithic," or the Agricultural stage of development, began in Africa well before 15,000 B.C., the "First Neolithic War" began thousands of years later, during the onset of the Younger Dryas. The Younger Dryas was a cold, arid era, which began around 12,000 BC, disrupting the Holocene with a rapid return to glacial conditions in the Northern Hemisphere and drought-like conditions in the Southern Hemisphere, an advent that prompted the northward migrations and expansions of the Khoisan. The Khoisan, that is, the Naga, expanded northward through the regions of present-day Zambia and Tanzania just after the onset of the Younger Dryas; the Dasas report Naga settlements at the base of Mt Meru in Tanzania at a very early age. The Naga expansion into and through Kenya had been uneventful until the attack and massacre at Nataruk. [cccxxxiii]

The second provocation for war came with an Anu attack at Jebel Sahaba, which was then met with swift reprisal, as the Naga massed forces of the northernmost regencies, and mounted an exacting retaliatory attack north of Jebel Sahaba, at an Anu village near Wadi Halfa, in present-day Sudan, where they slay nearly sixty people. Archaeological evidence at the site was discovered in the 1960s when archaeologists uncovered and excavated a large burial plot dating about 12,000 BC. Archaeologists found fifty-nine ancient skeletons with a variety of stone projectile points in their skulls, spines, pelvises, and limbs: reflecting their violent deaths. Whether their deaths were the result of an organized military campaign or a brutal skirmish is unknown; however, what is known, is that the attacks and reprisal launched what can appropriately be termed the "First Neolithic War."

There is a difference between fighting and organized warfare; when small groups of warriors fight, they often engage each other in individual combat and fight as an undisciplined hoard, swarming over and destroying whatever is in their way, with minimal regard for strategy and tactics. However, when larger groups of warriors band together, they require greater elements of forethought and planning; campaigns may last a day or a few days once some goal or vengeance has been met. True war requires a disciplined army of warriors that can take orders and fight in line. A truism of military science says that a disciplined army always has the advantage over one that lacks training and discipline. Warfare has always involved discipline, logistics, and transport, as well as weapons; an early advantage granted the Nagas.

The Parables

By the act of nominating a regional warlord to lead their lot, the northern Regencies of the Naga, in effect, selected their first true "Grand Regent,"; a personage the actual name of whom has long been lost in the dust of antiquity, whom, in this work, shall simply be referred to as "Akor," a name meaning "War Leader," who, after the reprisal near Wadi Halfa, set about alerting, preparing and amassing his forces, in anticipation of a retaliatory attack, and more sustained campaign by the Anu.

The Naga early surmised the predominant perennial power, the mighty ancient Kingdom of Punt, to have been the source of the organized aggressions against them. The Regencies sought, at first, only to strike a blow that would command its mutual respect. But it seems that from the beginning, Akor's objective was possession of the highly valuable frankincense forest; indeed, he deemed the provocation for war to have been fortuitous, if for no reason other than that, a reason for which he rose to the challenge. The first major battles took place as the Nagas sought to push into the southern highlands of southern Punt, only to be met by the disciplined warriors of the Crocodile Clans, who slowed, if not thwarted, the Nagas advance into the highlands.

An advent prompted Akor to add another dimension to the Naga assault, to gain a foothold and a base of operation within the confines of Punt itself. Leveraging their maritime capabilities and prowess, the Nagas played to their strength by attacking and subduing the totem Anu clans of the Dugong, on the four largest islands of the Bajuni archipelago, off the southern shores of southern Punt. Four of the six clans of the Dugong inhabited the four largest islands of the archipelago, with the largest and main clans of the Dugong at the villages around (present-day) Kismayo, near the mouth of the Jubba River on the southern coast of southern Punt.

As the Naga again sought to push their way into the southern highlands of Punt, again encountering strong resistance and, indeed, counter-attacks from the warriors of the Crocodile Clans, this time buttressed by Anu warriors from the totem clans of the Cobra, Viper, Hippopotamus, and Grey Owl. A battle and diversionary tactic planned by the ever-clever Akor, who launched an attack from the offshore Bajuni Isles, subduing the ancient villages of Kismayo, near the mouth of the Jubba River, on the southern coast of Punt. All the while, though badly outmanned in their effort to push into the southern highlands, because of their centralized ethos, their Naga fought as a cohesive army. In contrast, warriors of the Anu clans fought as separate legions, allowing the Naga to hold their ground.

Understanding now that the Naga were not to be taken lightly, upon receiving word of their subduing ancient Kismayo and gaining a foothold in the southern highlands, Lord Ba-tau sent word to alert and instruct that clans east of the Ogaden prepare and send warriors to defend the land. A wise man once said that "the sons of giants are dwarfs," an observation with resonance in this instance, given that Bes (Bisu, Aha (the "Fighter")) would surely have organized and led his counter-offensive rather than commanding from the distance and safety of the capital City of Barbara, on the northern coast of Punt. Alas, Ba-tau dispatched legions of warriors from the large totem clans of the Ibis, summoning and retaining warriors of his native clans of the black leopard to protect the city. The edict to protect and defend Barbara by Lord Ba-tau, albeit a bit too little, too late, was a stroke of prescience, nonetheless.

With their success in using the Isles of the Bajuni archipelago in the south to subdue Kismayo as a stronghold on the coast of southern Punt, the Naga amassed an armada. It attacked and subdued the largest Isles of the Socotra Archipelago, off the coast of northern Punt, from where they launched a direct assault upon Barbara itself.[cccxxxiv]. Serendipitous was the arrival of the adept warriors of the Black Leopard, whose archers exacted a grim toll on the attackers, thwarting an over-run of the City. Ancient Barbara nonetheless fell under siege, with the Anu warriors of the clans of the eastern plateau otherwise preoccupied with their efforts to dislodge and drive the Naga from their foothold in the southern highlands, as well as from ancient Kismayo, where the Naga were pushing into the Jubba River Valley, toward the strongholds of the Crocodile Clans in southern Punt.

This was another altogether adept strategy by Akor to prompt factions of the Crocodile Clans to withdraw from their efforts in the southern highlands to defend their own strongholds, lessening the stress and granting time for reinforcement of the increasingly out-manned Naga fighting to retain, if not gain ground, in the southern highlands. To further seize the momentum, Akor called upon those at the southern extent of his new northern "Grand Regency," those in the regions of present-day central and southern Tanzania, to commit warriors to aid and assure victory against the Anu of Punt. This call was heeded by southern Regencies as far south as Nagu-Naro itself, who each responded with small legions of warriors that independently headed northeastward to join the endeavor under the battle-wise leadership of Akor.

Yet, as faith would append, it was then that Lord An of Ta-Nebiru beseeched that the powerful Elephant Clans of Mount Elgon assume leadership in protecting Ta-Netjeru (Mt Kenya), the "Land of the Gods," and aid in defense of Punt. It was thus that the Elephant Clans of the cavern cities, joined by the clans from the slopes of Elgon and the reverent Hippopotamus clans from the caves and forest at the foothills of Mt. Kenya, intervened to intercept the Naga legions from the south, forestalling the reinforcement of the Naga in the southern highlands of Punt. An advent caused Akor to tighten the siege of Barbara until the city was forced to surrender. Those who survived the attack and siege on the city, including Lord Ba-tau, escaped to the northern plateau, where they regrouped and strengthened their defenses. Frustrated in his efforts to reinforce his warriors in the southern highlands, Akor again enlisted the aid of the Naga fleet.

Ships from a Naga armada soon descended with reinforcements, one after another, on the coasts near Barbara in the north and Kismayo in the south. Advents prompting the aging Lord An to again intervene, this time by direct message to the House of Noura in Nagu-Naro; a message advising that continued aggressions risk broader hostilities and disruptions in what had for untold generations been a peaceful relationship. Lord An informed that such aggressions risk broader mutual hostilities between Anu and Naga, extending even to the Anu of the fabled Mountains of the Moon and Hapi Valley, as well as those in the Zambezi River Valley …in reach of Nagu-Naro itself.

A message interpreted as a subtle threat, to which the House of Noura reminded that the hostilities were first exhibited by Punt, not the Naga, who responded only after a second massacre of innocent villagers. Howsoever, the House of Noura agreed that broader warfare and lasting mutual hostilities must be avoided at all costs, a sentiment to which Akor appended that hostilities shall cease "where the combatants stand." An appendage meaning that the Naga would retain Barbara, Kismayo, and much of the Jubba River Valley. Though his forces on the eastern plateau and the valley separating the plateaus, as well as those in the eastern regions of the western plateau, were considerable, Lord Ba-tau surmised that re-taking Barbara would cost many lives.

Nonetheless, Lord Ba-tau held fast to the relinquishment of Kismayo …and all lands south of the acceded province of Barbara. It was an accord requiring Akor to abandon any and all land acquired in the southern highlands, as well as abandon and relinquish control of the southern islands. An accord strongly supported by the House of Noura and the regency of Nagu-Naro, and though Akor deemed it less than victory, it was far from a total loss in that the Naga retained control of Barbara and a large swath of the rich Frankincense Forest. This was the beginning of Nagu-Punt (the "Naga in the Land of Punt"), the northernmost regency of the early ancient Naga in Africa.

A lasting but uneasy peace ensued from the highlands of Nagu-Punt, through old Punt and into ancient Sudan. Continued expansions of the Khoisan and the Ethos of the Naga beyond the confines of Nagu-Punt and into the retained lands of old Punt prompted renewed waves of Anu migrations into the Nile River Valley. The discontent was such that the Crocodile clans at Dolo, in the border area between present-day Somalia and Kenya, and at nearby Doolow on the Jubba River, together with the clans at the townships of Mandera, Bandera, Belad Hawo, and Bu'ale in the southern Jubba River valley, migrated from southern Punt into Lower Nile River Valley en masse, where they settled and eventually founded the City of Crocodilopolis (the "Crocodile City") on the shores of Paleo-Lake Morris in the huge Fayyam depression. [cccxxxv]

The pervasive spread of the Naga throughout the lands south of old Punt caused descent and disruption even the sacred lands of Ta-Netjeru (Mount Kenya (the true "Mount Zion")), the "Land of the Gods, where the Naga enshrined the notion and tradition of the "*Ng ai*" as an aspect or instrument of the creator that inhabits the peak of Mount Kenya. Such incursions of the ethos of the Naga prompted the migrations of the clans of the Dogon (and the "Nomo Legends") from the highlands of Ta-Netjeru to the fertile lands of the Nile Valley.[cccxxxvi] By 9,600 B.C., the *Naga* had all but fully subsumed a region extending from the Horn of Africa in the north to Tanzania and northern Mozambique in the south, the defining boundaries of emergent *Nagu-Punt*.

The preeminence of the Naga on the Horn of Africa in many ways severed the incidental empire of the Anu, disrupting the flow of trade between early Sumer, Punt, Ta-Nebiru, and the Nile Valley, weakening the erstwhile empire of the Anu. The growing preeminence of the Naga in the frankincense trade, along with the re-charging of Great Lake Victoria after the Holocene rains returned (lessening the need for the existence of the "Great Pass" ("Ta-Nebiru"), together with the death of Lord An, combined to mark the decline of the fabled City of An, which eventually succumb through ages, and was lost to the ancient forests. With the decline and eventual demise of the "Great Pass" ("Ta-Nebiru"), the kingdoms of the Mountains of the Moon once again became the foremost stronghold of the Anu in Central Africa.

Rise of Nagu-Punt

The coastline of *Nagu-Punt* stretched over 3,000km, from Mogadishu (in Somalia) on the north to Mozambique in the south. The coastal terrain was diverse but was dominated in the interior by a low-level coastal plateau with low-lying estuaries, lagoons, and natural harbors. Early trading networks along the coasts were guided by supplying the need for raw materials rather than for meeting the demand for commodities or finding markets to export products. South of the Zambezi River is a natural corridor route from Zimbabwe to the port towns along the Mozambique coast. Mozambique consists of a series of ancient sea and river ports connected to trade emanating from the interior hinterlands. Ancient seaports and coastal trading posts arose and expanded along the coast, from northern Somalia in the north to northern Mozambique in the south.

The port town of *Sofala* on the northern coast of present-day Mozambique was the southernmost of the seaport towns of Nagu-Punt. *Sofala*, however, was only nominally within the province of *Nagu-Punt*. The *Khoisan* of Nagu-Naro were the first inhabitants of Mozambique, which is mostly a low plateau with a bunch of rivers flowing through to the Indian Ocean, the largest of these rivers is the Zambezi, which flows through Central Africa. The other rivers, except for the Ruvuma, which is the border river between Mozambique and Tanzania, originate from the plateau and mountains within the region. The ancient riverine acuity of the *Khoisan* had aided their early expansions and settlement throughout the region, particularly along the course of the major rivers emptying into the Indian Ocean, where early port villages arose at natural harbors like *Sofala*.

The maritime aspect of the trade was dominated by the Naga of Nagu-Punt and Nagu-Naro, the Dasas of Kumari, and the Naga of Naga Sunda, who established the early post-ice age maritime trade route eastward from Nagu-Naro to and along the western coast of Sunda, and from there, westward, to and along the eastern coast of the Kumari peninsula, an ice age extension of the Indian Sub-Continent which then extended southward to the present day Chagos Archipelago; then the southern mountain range at the Cape of Kumari. The ancient maritime trade route of the Naga proceed southward along the eastern coast of Kumari, rounding the Cape to then sail westward toward Seychelles, then a far larger contiguous landmass, and from there to the ports of Nagu-Punt along the ancient East African seaboard.

This early ancient maritime trade route served as a channel for trading frankincense and myrrh, as well as spices such as cinnamon, ginger, pepper, nutmeg, clove, and turmeric, and precious stones, pearls, ebony, silk, and fine textiles. Added to this, specifically from Nagu-Punt, in addition to frankincense, from the interior came rare woods, feathers, animal skins, and gold. All were traded from the seaports of Nagu-Punt, including the ports of *Berbera*, *Marka*, *Baraawe*, and *Mogadishu*, and the ancient seaports at *Mombasa* and *Zanzibar islands*, along with the coastal seaports at *Dar es Salaam*, *Kisiju* and *Kilwa* along the central East African coast.[cccxxxvii] Despite the intent of the accord between Nagas and Anu, the rise and prominence of Nagu-Punt, in many ways, forever weakened and severed the ancient empire of the Anu.

The Legends

With the early ancient City of Barbara, the Naga also acquired the rich Frankincense Forest, along with lands surrounding and including the ancient sanctuary at Lass Geel, which had long been an ancient Monastery of the Hydra Cult, with a cadre of older monks still in residence when the Naga arrived. Contextualizing the Ophiolatry of what can best be described as the Pre-Buddhist ethos of the Naga cult, with the Ophiolatry of the evolved Animist orthodoxy of the Hydra cult, who ascribe creation to the divine forces of Netjer. Though each, at onset, believed the "Southern Borealis" to be an aspect of the creator, in the evolution of their respective beliefs, each derived different perspectives on the mystical existence and interactions of mythical deity.

The Pre-Buddhists orthodoxy of the Naga did not ascribe creation to any kind of deity, although they believed in supernatural beings who could help or hinder on the path towards enlightenment; divine beings called "devas" (often called "gods"), a type of celestial being who shares the god-like characteristics of somehow being more powerful and longer-lived than humankind. Pre-Buddhist priests pontificated that none of these" gods" is a "creator" or an "eternal being," though they live very long lives; the Pre-Buddhist nonetheless believed in heavens and rebirths (or cyclical rebirth).[cccxxxviii] The orthodoxy of the early Pre-Buddhist presumed that the cosmos had no ultimate beginning. Thus they saw no need for a creator god or deity.

In contrast, the Animist orthodoxy of the Hydra cult held that creation was caused and maintained by the divinity and plurality of Netjer; divine forces or energies called the Netjeru (or "Netjeru"). The Netjeru were believed to be the forces of Nature, which maintain the world and cosmos, yet to simply call or equate them as gods and goddesses gives a false impression.[cccxxxix] The orthodoxy of the ancient Hydra Priesthood held that creation was and is the sorting out and bringing order to the primeval chaos of undifferentiated energy and consciousness, the waters of the fabled numinous seas in the time before time. The duality of chaos and cosmos was central to the precept of creation held by the Hydra cult, a precept presuming an eternal struggle between chaos and cosmos.

While the Pre-Buddhist orthodoxy of the Naga viewed the unfolding of creation as an endless chain of causality, a precept viewed only within the context of Kundalini. Pre-Buddhist Priests of the Naga called Kundalini "the face of the Creator" proselytizing that 'just as we recognize someone by his or her face, the Divine is recognized by its power of Consciousness, Kundalini.[cccxl] The Pre-Buddhist of the Naga proselytized that Kundalini clothes the formless in form, giving the Absolute a face to adore, a presence to inspire, traditions to revere, and a body of wisdom to serve and guide. She is the esoteric goal of the awakened mind and the transcendent vision of sages and saints. By knowing Her, all is known, and life becomes suffused with sublime joy.

The Pre-Buddhist proselytized that believing in gods was not useful for those seeking enlightenment, instructing instead that aspirants "drown the ordinary ego-mind in Stillness, if one truly seeks to know the Knower."[cccxli] A system of belief in which there appeared a repugnant hint of heresy to the reverent priests of the Hydra orthodoxy, who viewed themselves as preservers, guardians, and protectors of the "Sacred Mysteries." In the orthodoxy of the Hydra Priesthood, "Netjer" was deemed the One Self-Created Deity, a deity that manifests in myriads of forms. These forms and forces were believed to be interrelated and immanent in the phenomena of nature, with each recognizable force corresponding to a deity (a "Netjeru") in nature[cccxlii] Nonetheless, the gods and goddesses embodying the "Netjeru," though invoked in the plural, were viewed as aspects of the singular form of Netjer. The priest of the Hydra orthodoxy conceived the deity as singular, with only one true god, "Netjer," responsible for the emergence and maintenance of the Cosmos.

Age-old adages and legends of Ptah and Bes (Bisu) affirmed and informed of the interactive plurality of Netjer (a word meaning "divine power") and the contention that persists between Cosmos and Chaos, the eternal dissonance defining the divine duality of existence. In the evolved Animism of the Hydra priesthood, it is the vital energies (or "Quintessence") flowing from Netjer that imbues and sustains the cosmos, a cosmos that is basically a hierarchy or matrix of different planes of existence. Each plane of the hierarchy was believed to be a theophany, a creation by the consciousness of the plane of existence or level of being above it, with each plane sustained by the plane below it. [cccxliii] An architecture emphasizing the critical importance of this, the physical realm, is deemed to be the lowest plane of existence or level of being.

The will of Netjer was believed to be made manifest through the reverent and in the Netjeru, the divine energies and forces that, through their actions and interactions, maintain and defend the cosmos. In this context, it was the self-ascribed purview of the warrior priest of the Hydra cult to preserve and defend the orthodoxy, as its precepts were deemed vital in the spiritual defense of the physical realm. This disposition left them with an uninformed growing disdain for the precepts and ethos of the Naga. In the mysticism of the early Pre-Buddhists, it was said that when *kundalini* touches the spleen center, it gives man the power to travel at will on the vast plane of the Astral Sea whilst away from the physical body.[cccxliv] Astral Plane is what the Aethereal Plane sits in, surrounded at a great distance by the Outer Planes.

The 'astral substance' of the Astral Plane is far more sensitive and responsive to psychic energies flowing through the 'cosmic medium' than the 'ethereal substance' of the Ethereal Plane. The Astral is essentially a transitive plane with thoughts flowing through to other sub-planes and planes; the collective flow of these psychic energies gives form to the endless Astral Sea. The Astral Sea is, for the most part, a dreary and empty expanse of nothingness, broken up upon by sporadic numinous island-like floating landmasses, the fabled floating Isles of the Astral Sea. There are innumerable floating islands and island archipelagos in the immensity of the Astral Sea, most of which are uninhabited. However, there are four prominent, continent-size islands that are indeed inhabited.

Each of the four prominent islands is said to offer different gifts, with each a unique expression and manifestation of the consciousnesses constituting its being: each functioning as separate "sub-planes," a lot bigger inside than out. The largest of the prominent islands is, without question, an island called "Pler-oma," known as the "Island of the Blessed,"; an island equally influenced by psychic winds of the Spiritual, Causal, and Ethereal Planes. The word "Pleroma" literally means 'fullness.' It is said that the "Island of the Blessed "avails of all things; it is said 'that "there is nothing outside of Pler-oma that cannot be availed from within.' Then there is the island of Psi-om, known as the "Island of Wisdom," and the island of "En-sisi, known as the "Island of Peace." En-sisi is similar in vibration and nature to the "Island of Wisdom," like En-sisi, Psi-om is equally influenced by the Physical and Ethereal Planes, and to a lesser yet significant extent, by the Causal Plane; with the two Isle thus somewhat similar in nature.

Nonetheless, the island of En-sisi is perhaps the most distinctive of the four prominent isles, with a distinctive half-moon shape island amidst a huge blue lake at its heart, an island seemingly engulfed in a white-hot astral fire that covered and obscured the view of its mountainous terrain: an isle known as the "Island of Fire" (also known as the "Island of Flame"), a portal for the powerful psychic winds of the Causal Plane. Because the locus of one destination in the Astral plane is determined by subliminal or subconscious intent, for the "Enlightened Ones" among the Naga of Pre-Buddhist orthodoxy, the destination was the second largest of the floating islands of the Astral Sea, an island called "Nur-vna," known as the "Island of Bliss." The vast island of "Nur-vna" was formed and influenced by the winds of the Physical, Ethereal, and Causal Planes, and it is here, basking in the psychic winds of the Causal Planes, in the highlands of the "Island of Bliss," that early "Enlightened Ones" first discerned the endless chain of causality that underlies creation.

For thousands of years, the wisdom and sacred science of *kundalini* was veiled in secrecy, passed along in oral tradition from enlightened master to chosen disciple; a core belief system informing the ethos of the Naga. Nonetheless, contrary to the claim of doctrinal stability, Pre-Buddhism was dynamic, with a number of different sects. Early Pre-Buddhists adopted many traditions from the local culture. Pre-Buddhist sects adopted animistic beliefs, propounding that the forces of nature are anthropomorphized and personified in the form of guardian spirits or angelic beings. They also venerate ancestors in the spiritual realm. Beyond this, there was not much variation in practices among the Pre-Buddhist sects. Karma was universally accepted as the moral law of cause and effect. One was expected to move toward enlightenment alone. Alien concepts to those of the Hydra orthodoxy, who, despite the adoption of certain tenets of animism by some Naga sects, found offensive the lack of reverence for Netjer and the Divine Netjeru.

A festering disposition culminating in abandonment of the lands of the eastern plateau by the totem clans of the Ibis and Grey Owl, along with others, though not most of the clans of the eastern plateau. The Anu of the orthodoxy migrated northeastward from the old eastern plateau of Punt, and then westward through the lands of the present-day southern Sudan, to avoid the northward growing influence and expansions of the Naga. From southern Sudan, *Anu* migrated westward into present-day Chad, where they initially settled around the southern shores of Paleo-Lake Chad of the era. However, many eventually migrated northeastward to settle in the forested foothills along the western coast of the ancient inland Sahara Sea of the era.

Through their early trading networks, the Naga facilitated the flow of goods and commodities throughout their central terrain in East Africa, southward, extending fully from the highlands of Punt in the north to KwaZulu-Cape in the south. Livestock, hides and skin, aromatic woods, and raisins were exported, while rice, other foodstuffs, and hides were imported. The *Naga* were maritime culture, among the earliest to become well adapted to the open seas for both transit and trade. There were always movements of traders and settlers up and down the coast and between coastal and island port towns and settlements. Oral traditions recall that the coastal port town of *Berbera* served as the early northernmost departure port for both goods and pilgrims destined for points south and east.

The *Naga* were the first to use the monsoons to travel from Berbera to Mogadishu and along the East African seaboard to the ports of *Mombasa* and *Zanzibar*. They Used the northeasterly monsoons to travel back to Mogadishu and Berbera and the islands off the coast or further on to the Kumari Peninsula. Ancient overland trade routes joined northern *Nagu-Punt* with the flow of goods and trade from the regions of their interior as well as *Sudan* and *Upper Nile valleys*. The *Nagu-Punt* port at *Berbera* was linked with the ancient ports at *Marka, Mogadishu* and the central coasts ports at *Mombasa, Zanzibar,* and *Dar es Salaam*. From there, the early ancient maritime route continued southward to the southern-most ports of Nagu-Punt in northern Mozambique, and from there, southward to the coastal ports of Nagu-Naro on the central coast of Mozambique and the southeastern coasts to the Cape of South Africa.

The southwest monsoon allowed the flow of goods and commodities from Nagu-Punt, such as spice, grain, ivory, hides, and obsidian, to the port towns and trading settlements along the coasts and on the islands to the south. From *Dar es Salaam* to the *Seychelles* Isles and onward to southern *Kumari*. Or, proceeding further southward, from the port town at *Sofala* on the northern Mozambique coast to the *Chamorros* Isles and onward to northern Madagascar and the western coast of Kumari. The northeast monsoons allowed the flow of goods, commodities, and trade from the port towns of the south, as well as the off-shore islands and *Kumari*, into the heart of *Nagu-Punt*. If the winds were seized at the right times, then overseas sailing was quick and easy, allowing ancient trading vessels of the Naga to ply the open seas.

Foreshadows of Empire

The suzerainty of the Grand Regency at *Nagu-Punt* ultimately expanded to encompass the whole of the Ethiopian and Eritrean highlands, from where the influence of the Naga spread northward through present-day southern Sudan into the Upper Nile Valley. The highlands of Punt were cool enough and well-watered enough to facilitate the growth of agriculture in suitable areas. To the east, the plateau was a grassy savanna stretching to the marshlands of the Kagera River. Across the hills, to the southeast, was the Nyungwe Forest, the largest and one of the most ancient surviving forests in East Africa. To the south, the Nagu-Punt regency claimed the pastoral domain from the Horn through present-day Kenya to the well-watered plains of northern Tanzania.

Highlands of Nagu-Punt: The Naga

Nagu-Punt was the northernmost regency of the emergent empire of the Nagas. It came to embrace a broad amalgamation of clinic domains, provinces, townships, and early ancient cities scattered across its territory, underpinning the emergence of a diverse, high culture. The ethnic makeup of the early populous of Nagu-Punt was a mixture of Khoisan, Anu, and Nilotics, ranging southward from the highlands of Nagu-Punt to northern Zambia. Nagu-Punt became an important source of manufactured and raw goods and a source of incense and other exports, such as myrrh, ivory, black ebony wood, cinnamon, spices, obsidian, seeds, and grains from the interior. Commodities and goods were imported and exported through the Nagu-Punt ports of *Berbera* and *Marka* in the north, with *Mogadishu* and the central ports at *Mombasa*, *Zanzibar,* and *Dar es Salaam* in the midlands, and the ports of northern Mozambique in the south.

The ancient mariners of Nagu-Punt used the then-seasonal monsoon winds to sail eastward from the ports of Nagu-Punt to the Cape of Kumari and then northward to trade along the eastern coast of the post-ice age peninsula. Naga mariners sailed northward to the fertile terrain and highland valleys of the ancient peninsula's northernmost mountain range in the region of the isle of ancient Ceylon (and present-day Sri Lanka) before the great inundation. By word of the ancient Dasas (Dravidians), it was here, in the region of (ancient Ceylon) the northern-most mountain range of Kumari, where the Naga eventually established the third of their Great Regencies, Naga Nadu, which was centered in the area of the present day the Jaffna Peninsula.[cccxlv]

No doubt attracted to the highlands of northern Kumari as a key source of true cinnamon, the Naga found vestiges of the early ancient Veddha vanguard in long residence when they arrived, but unlike the Anu, the Vedda felt no intrusion as the was very little if any overlap in their territorial domains. Ancient Naga mariners continued northward, along the far more expansive western coastal plains of the Indian Sub-Continent of the era, sailing as far north as the mouth of the ancient Saraswati River Valley, from whence they sailed southward, returning along the western coasts of the Indian Sub-Continent and Kumari Peninsula, avoiding trade with early Sumer and Incense Coast, in abidance of their accord with the Anu, the ladened ships of the ancient mariners returned to the ports of Nagu-Punt.

Mountains of the Moon: The Anu

The accord with the Nagas left the *Incidental Empire* of the Anu forever severed, with direct trade along the ancient eastern coasts of the Arabian Peninsula (the "Incense Coast") and direct trade with the Anu of earliest Sumer. Traded for frankincense from the Incense Coast was still possible through the old northern ports of Punt. Still, alas, trade through Nagu-Punt soon became predominant throughout the greater region. The rise and expansions of Nagu-Punt, together with the return of the re-charge of Great Lake Nyanza (Lake Victoria), culminated in Ta-Nebiru ("the Great Pass") being little used and falling into decline, leading to the eventual demise of the ancient "City of An," returning the nucleus of the *Incidental Empire* to the fabled Mountains of the Moon.

The fragmented *Incidental Empire* of the Anu then extended northward through the suzerainty of the Nagas in Upper Nubia, into and through Lower Nubia northward into the Anu bastion in the Lower Nile River Valley and Delta. The vast lands descending from the southern highlands along the course of the *White Nile* through the plains of the *Sudan* south of the *Sudd* had previously long been the unquestioned terrain of the Anu. However, the northern expansion of Khoisan and ethos of the *Nagas* beyond the highlands of Old *Punt* and into vast Sudan and the land that would become Upper Nubia now was cause for growing resentment and discontent among the ancient *Hydra Priesthood,* guardians of the "Sacred Mysteries. Discontent culminated in the outbound migration of the faithful from the highlands of Old Punt, migrations westward towards the Anu settlements north of the massive Central Saharan lake, *Paleo-Lake Chad.*

Nonetheless, the strength, resilience, resolve, and resistance of the Anu were most reflected along the corridors of their stronghold in the Lower Nile River Valley, where all those ancient cities [Ant, Annu Menti, Aunti, Aunyt-Seni today called Esneh, Erment, Quoch, and Heliopolis] have the characteristic symbol which serves to denote the name, Anu. As it has been said of the Anu migrating into the Nile Valley from the highlands of Old Punt, "these Anu [Puntites] were agricultural people, raising cattle on a large scale along the Nile, shutting themselves up in walled cities for defensive purposes." The *Anu* of the *Lower Nile Valley* and *Delta*, including those around *Paleo-Lake Morris*, organized into a loose federation of kingdoms around the shores of the ancient lake, coalescing to protect their province.

Paleo-Lake Morris was west of the *Lower Nile River Valley* proper; it began as a natural lake in the huge *Fayum Depression* in the Western Desert. The *Anu* kingdoms around the ancient lake-built canals, dams, and channels, diverting part of the flow of the *Nile* into the d*epression*, preserving and maintaining the massive freshwater lake. The huge Faiyum *Depression* was anciently transformed into a fertile garden by the natural flow and silt of the Nile, which once diverted significant freshwater into the d*epression*. The flow of the water carried with it the rich soil which settled around the shores of the newly-created lake, sprouting vegetation along its banks. According to legend, the federation of kingdoms around the lake, led by the early Crocodilopolis, produced formidable weapons, aiding powerful armies prepared to protect the whole of the Lower Nile Valley.

The Vela X Supernova

The *Vela* supernova exploded approximately 13,500 B.C. (and was about 800 light-years away). Ancient humans on earth at that time would have noticed a very bright new star in the sky, which would have been the supernova explosion itself. Light from the supernova explosion that created the Vela remnant reached Earth about 11,300 BC.[cccxlvi] There are core samples that support that light or energy from the Vela Supernova impacted Earth approximately 11,300 years ago, possibly contributing to the significant climatic and ecological changes that date to that time period, specifically, the end of the Younger Dryas, roughly 11,200 BC, ushering in the Age of Leo, at 11.000 BC.[cccxlvii]

In the wake of the *Vela X supernova,* the *Holocene* warming perioding resumed, resuming the great glacial melt, causing global sea levels to rise. During the Holocene's warmer, rainier climate period, central Africa became increasingly wetter, with expanding rivers and lakes routinely overflowing their banks, flooding low-lying areas. The melting glaciers and increased rainfall gradually transformed the former lakes and rivers of the interior into massive inland lakes and huge rapidly flowing rivers and tributaries, transforming the Nile into the "Wild Nile" of the era. In adjustment to the times, the Anu of the Nile River Valley built their settlements and homes atop mounds along the river, with those along the former lower shoreline and on the low-lying island forced to move to higher ground.

The Great Floods

The Holocene Epoch resumed in earnest around 12,000 BC, with the return of the rains, rapid warming, and glacial retreat in the period up to around 11,500 B.C. With the retreating glaciers came melting ice, and as the ice melted, the rivers overflowed, and the lakes expanded. Lake Victoria reappeared and overflowed; Lake Albert also overflowed into the White Nile around 12,000 BC, and so did Lake Tana into the Blue Nile. The increase in monsoonal rains and rising sea levels caused unprecedented flooding and disaster. Entire land masses 'detached,' one from the other, as waters rose. This marked the true end of the Ice Age, when it literally collapsed, as compared to the long build-up phase of the great glaciers. The meltdown, in contrast, occurred more swiftly as temperatures gradually rose to 14 degrees below present-day levels. As the great glaciers and thick layers melted, sea levels gradually rose.

In some parts of the world, it was an ecological disaster, reconstructing whole coastlines and ecological systems as seas rose about 35 meters to present levels, a process that took over four thousand years. While, from a geological perspective, this happened overnight, in human cultural terms, it was an extremely protracted process. Maximum sea levels were not reached until around 8000 years ago when the neck of land near Cape York, Australia, connecting Sahul to its northern appendage (New Guinea), finally disappeared under what would become known as the Torres Strait. New Guinea had become a separate island. At 13,500 B.C., ocean levels were still as much as three hundred feet lower than today, and many of the existing and growing settlements of the time were experiencing increases in population and expanding beyond the river valley and highland vegetation belts to the coastal zones, where they established fishing and ultimately early trading communities at the ocean's edge, at early ancient ports established in natural harbors.

Deluge at Sunda

The Sunda Sub-Continent remained dry and in full prominence between 23,750 BC to at least 15,250 BC, after which climatic temperatures began to rise, causing the gradual melting of the great global ice sheets, causing the gradual rise in world sea levels, which gradually began to encroach and submerge the low-lying regions of Sunda. The sea levels continued to rise, causing land loss on tropical coasts with flat continental shelves. Cracks in the earth's crust as the weight of the water shifted set off catastrophic earthquakes, volcanic eruptions, super waves, and floods which drowned the coastal villages along the coasts of the Sub-Continent. The gradual rise in sea level submerged significant parts of Sunda, submerging the lowest-lying areas of ancient Sunda beneath the South China Seas; this occurred between 14,000 and 12,500 years ago.

Archaeological evidence exists of ancient villages under a "silt curtain" left by the sea floods in the drowned coastal regions. A period of rapid flooding ensued between 14,000 to 12,000 years ago. By its end, the *Sunda* sub-continent had lost over half of its surface area. Sunda had been well populated when sea levels began to rise. After the long period of flooding, surviving and emergent societies reconstituted along southern and eastern coasts and what remained of the great plain. Sundaland was the widest area to be drowned after the Last Glacial period as the glaciers started to retreat in earnest. When sea levels rose to the extent that encroaching waters flooded vital low-lying terrain, whole villages migrated into vacant areas at higher elevations of the receding central plains. Many migrated along major inland rivers and waterways to re-settle further north in the central plains.

The receding Great Sunda Plain had by then been the home terrain of the Naga for several millennia; from there, they had revived their de facto empire, prospered, and expanded their trade and influence from the mainland of southern Asia in the north to the far reaches of Sahul and Tasmania in the south. This had been an era in which the advanced agricultural traditions and the spice trade brought prosperity and renown to both *Sunda* and the *Naga*. Still, by 11,000 BC, the rising seas and encroaching inland waters had reclaimed much of the vital lowlands of the great central plains and eroded the reach and overriding influence of the Naga in what had traditionally been their southern terrain. The great central plains had been reduced in the south to the expanse extending between Sumatra in the west and Borneo in the east.

The lowland in the great central plains of Sundaland was, for the most part, some 327 feet below 1999 AD sea level, so they would have been 98 to 65 feet above sea level at the time of the maximum itself. The great ice sheets melted as temperatures rose, and sea levels rose about 400 feet, gradually submerging much of Sunda. When the bulk of the central plains became submerged in the rising seas, there were agriculturalists and urban dwellers who lived along the coasts and inland rivers and lakes. The first and second floods impacted these communities more than those settled in the interior of the great central plains. In the north, the central plain receded into an area bordered by the Malay peninsula on the west, and the southern coasts of Thailand, Cambodia, and Viet Nam, in the region the present-day Gulf of Thailand, on the east.

Before and especially during the gradual flooding of the lowlands, many people migrated northward along the river valleys of the receding Sunda into surviving southeastern Asia. The North Sunda River provided a vital connection to the Mekong River in Vietnam, the Chao Phraya River in Thailand to the north, the Baram and Rajang rivers to the east, and the Pahang and Rompin Rivers to the west of the receding Sunda landmass. The submergence of the great Sunda plain occurred over thousands of years, with most of Southeast Asia's present-day southern coastal region remaining an integral part of the central plains of Sunda (until roughly 9,000 BC). Nonetheless, the increasingly fragmented influence of the Naga in the south, from New Guinea to Tasmania, over time, culminating in the northward shift in the sphere of their influence, as most gradually migrated northward into mainland southeastern Asia, while others inhabited the surviving island archipelago.

Inundation at Kumari

To the west of the Sunda peninsula, beyond the expanse of the Indian Ocean, was the eastern coast of peninsular *Kumari*. The Kumari Peninsula of the era extended southward from the southern extent of the Indian Sub-Continent to the present-day Chagos Archipelago at the southern cape of the Ice Age Peninsula. The eastern coast of the Kumari peninsula bordered the then far more encompassing Bay of Bengal, bounded by the coasts of *Kumari* on the west and the ancient coast of *Sunda* on the east. Submergence of the land south of the Malay peninsula opened southern channels connecting the South China Sea to the East Indian Ocean, opening direct trading routes between the *Dasas* of Kumari and the *Naga* of Sunda. The *Dasas* were excellent mariners, with well-established seaports supported by interior trade routes into the heart of central Kumari.

From the Ceylon highlands, Kumari stretched southward into the Indian Ocean beyond the equator; broad coastal plains extended southward along the western coast of the peninsula, with much broader coastal plains extending first in a westerly direction, along the southern shoreline of Ceylon, abruptly turning southwestward for several hundred miles beyond shores of Ceylon, before assuming a true south direction along the Lakshadweep-Chagos Ridge, to the peninsula's southern extent, south of the equator just beyond the present day Chagos Archipelago. Broad southern highland plains stretched from the foothills of the main island of the present-day Chargos Arch, then situated along the southwestern coast of Kumari, to the foothill of the southernmost island of the Chargos.

Peninsular *Kumari* was about a couple thousand miles long and several hundred miles wide in places along that length. Harbor towns and port cities were reconstituted along the redefined eastern, southern, and western coastal belts, again serving as trading ports for interior trade routes. The heart of Kumari still stretched from the Pahruli River in the north to the Kumari River in the south. The peninsula was interspersed with mountains, marked by the present-day *Lakshadweep Isles* in the north and the *Chargos Archipelago* at the southern cape. The western coastline of *Kumari* stretched northward from the southern cape, along the Lakshadweep-Chagos Ridge, to the present-day Laccadive Islands, which were then the northern coastal mountains of the antediluvian peninsula. The submergence of the Kumari, like Sunda, while often abrupt, was generally a slow, gradual process, and just like Sunda. Still, perhaps more decidedly so, the submergence of the Kumari was due to the rise in sea levels and the resulting great floods.

The first extended period of flooding between 12,000 BC to 11,000 BC claimed a large portion of the broad coastal seaboard surrounding peninsular *Kumari. As sea levels rose, flooding ultimately submerged the early seaboard village*s well as much of the coastal plains. Freshwater coastal waterways and wetlands were subsumed by the rising seas, creating estuaries extending far inland. Coastal spots that had formerly been above the water line were then submerged, and plates that supported dry land were undermined, with vast regions succumbing to the seas. How much land remained above the waves depended on how deep and wide the ocean rifts were; tectonic plates supporting land masses may rise and fall, depending on the interaction and pressure placed upon the plates; these tectonic interactions often give rise to extended periods of violent volcanic eruptions, earthquakes, and upheavals, as the land mass settles into its new disposition.

The climate shift around 10,000 BC and an ensuing 500 years of heavy rains and rising seas brought the second period of flooding and inundation of the coastal plains; what remained was essentially the highlands and interior plains, surrounded by narrower coastal plains. A long series of mountains was situated at the southern cape of the peninsula, in the region where the first Sangam was situated, at the early city of ancient *Then-Madurai* (Southern Madurai). The major southern interior trade routes still converged south of the southern mountains, at the cape of the peninsula, with all roads still leading to the early ancient southern city of *Then-Madurai*. Before the beginning of the deluge, *Then-Madurai* remained a key destination point for commodities, goods, and wares flowing from the southern interior of Kumari and, accordingly, remained a key destination for Naga maritime traders. From *Then-Madurai*, the maritime route proceeded to the harbor town of *Kumar*, at the southern end of the *Kumari*. From there onward to *Seychelles*, *Zanzibar*, and finally, the coast of *Nagu-Punt*.

Prosperity at Nagu-Punt

The *Naga* traded at the ancient seaports of *Berbera*, *Marka*, *Baraawe*, and *Mogadishu* in northern *Punt*, where early trade patterns formed around valued commodities and resources located in one place and desired in another. Agriculture had developed in the great lakes region and on the whole of the east African plateau out of the pastoral culture; with organized agriculture beginning sometime before 10,000 B.C. Archeologists and Scientists have discovered grains of sorghum that were planted and harvested in the region of present-day Sudan, which were dated to be more than 10,000 years old. These grains and many others were used for food as well as trade during the era of the Naga.

A wide network of trade and commerce emerged from the practice of storing surplus grains, other commodities, and crops. Prosperous interior trade routes on the plateau connected to the maritime trading network at seaports and harbor towns along the East African coast. Goods from *Kwale* and *Koma* islands and a large amount of the trade from *Mafia* passed through the seaports on the *Kisiju* coast, a key trading seaport in the region. These seaports became calling and stopping ports for boats plying between *Dar es Salaam* and *Kilwa*; *Kisiju* eventually became the largest port between *Dar es Salaam* to the north and *Kilwa* to the south. This period was one of flourishing and rapid expansion of trade and trading entrepots, with extending trade networks connecting and harmonizing the culture and evolving civilization of *Nagu-Punt*.

Agriculturalists traded food crops in exchange for meats and dairy products from the pastoralists, meat, hides, ivory, plants, food crops, and forest products from the hunter-gatherers, and forest products from the forest dwellers. Key central seaports arose to service the regional trade on the islands off the coast of present-day Tanzania, marked by the present-day ruins of *Kilwa*, *Kisiwani*, and *Songo Mnara*. As trade and trade patterns evolved, demand increased for the specialized craft of artisans who manufactured tools and pottery and transformed raw materials and minerals into products and commodities. The seaport on *Mombasa* Island, in present-day *Kenya*, became home to a microlithic stone-tool technology, using a wide variety of raw materials, contributing to an increasing diversity of trade and expansion in the region; the island seaport became an entrecote for broader regional maritime trade.

Archaeological investigations around *Mombasa* and south of *Dar es Salaam* point to high levels of early density at the sites and the settlements annexing the urban area. The seaport town expanded to urban proportions at an early stage; terrestrial surveys and excavations on the island have uncovered two of the earliest urban-like settlements of the era. Several of the other early seaports of *Nagu-Punt* experienced similar growth and prosperity; eventually, they extended their influence over the whole of the Indian Ocean and South Sea regions. A wider variety and diversity of goods and products were eventually traded along the rapidly expanding and ever-emerging links in trading networks during the era, including greater varieties of plants, food crops, exotic woods such as black ebony, flint, stone tools, copper, red ochre, animal skins, minerals, herbs, incense, salts, spices, textiles, and a variety of other manufactured products.[43]

---

[43] Susu Economics: History of Pan-African Trade, Commerce, Money and Wealth (Part 1), by Paul Alfred Barton

For centuries before Mount Meru's eruption and Sudra's exodus, the Puntites of Nagu-Punt had grown prosperous and powerful from their vast dominance of early maritime trade in the region. The seaport of *Sofala,* southernmost of the seaports of *Nagu-Punt*, was a trading entrepot for raw materials and commodities from the southern interior, with the network of rivers flowing through the *Mozambique* plateau to the Indian Ocean used to transport goods to the coast. Riverports connected to trade centers in the interior aided the flow of goods and raw materials along the network. The region's largest rivers is the *Zambezi*, which winds through most of Central Africa; south of the *Zambez*i is the ancient corridor extending from *Zimbabwe*. Ancient riverports were situated at natural harbors along the course of the major rivers flowing to the coast, where the 'riverine trade' linked with 'seaports like *Sofala.*

The Finanal Inundations

Inundation of the low-lying coastal areas and islands occurred over thousands of years; during some periods, the sea levels rose rather drastically, forever claiming the once prized coastal zones and seaside communities. From a geological perspective, this happened overnight. However, in human terms, it was an extremely protracted process. Sea levels rose, reclaiming large tracts of the coastal area, causing flooding and dislocation in communities at the ocean's edge and on low-lying islands. Entire sections of land mass literally 'detached,' one from the other, as the waters rose. There were three major ancient floods, the first occurred about 14,000 years ago, the second about 11,500 years ago; a shift in climate then occurred after 10,500 BC that brought 500 years of persistent, heavy rains and an increase in the rise in sea levels that caused the first in the long series of land mass brake-ups, fragmentation, and ultimate disappearance into the seas.

The *East African* coast has a relatively uniform topography, with a fairly narrow strip of coastal land that parallels the shoreline and a seaboard stretching from Somalia in the north to Madagascar, Mozambique, and finally, the Cape in the south. The coast of East Africa and *Nagu-Punt* thus did not undergo the type of utterly transformational change that impacted the other lands and major centers of an ancient civilization. However, coastal harbor towns and island seaports were adversely impacted by the rising sea levels; Seychelles was greatly reduced in land mass, size, and prominence, as were most of the other surviving offshore islands. The rising seas of the *Holocene* ultimately submerged the last of the low-lying islands comprising the ancient land bridge and separated *Tasmania* from mainland *Sahul*; Tasmania emerged as a separate island, slightly larger in size than West Virginia, roughly two-hundred miles off the southeastern coast of mainland Sahul.

The gradual inundation and brake-up of Sahul into the present-day configurations of Tasmania, Australia, and New Guinea disrupted and altered ancient trade patterns and routes, as well as the frequency of communication and the cultural discourse and exchange that had for millenniums served to connect and link the divergent groups of the regions. The separation of Tasmania prompted outward migrations of the able and increased isolation for those who remained. The brake-up of Sahul greatly diminished the influence and reached of the *Eastern Naga* in what had been a southern extension of their home range. For centuries, they and their confederates had been concentrated along the eastern coastal belt of Sahul, from Tasmania in the south to New Guinea, the Isles of Sunda, and what remained of the Sunda Peninsula. And now, as sea levels once again rose and claimed large coastal and low land regions, the inhabitants of the old eastern Naga terrain and spheres of influence were adversely impacted.

Isles of Sunda: Sunda Archipelago

Rising sea levels in three massive pulses caused flooding and the submerging of the Sunda Sub-Continent, creating the Java and South China Seas and the thousands of islands that make up Indonesia and the Philippines today. The actual disintegration of Sunda was the outcome of a series of volcanic disturbances and eruptions that gradually undermined the substrate comprising the foundations of the sub-continent. The Sunda Strait between the islands of Sumatera and Java and the Bali Strait between the islands of Java and Bali opened about 10,000 BC, connecting the Java Sea to the Indian Ocean and separating the island of Java from the Asian Mainland. Thus, the Southwestern part of the South China Sea and the Java Sea was then created.

After 10,000 BC, a new climatic shift brought on 500 years of heavy rains, aiding rising sea levels and the inundation of much of the central plains. What remained of the sub-continent formed a narrower 'boot-shaped' peninsula, with southern Burma and Sumatra forming a north-south highland mountain range along the peninsula's western coast. The highlands of Java formed the heel of the boot' at the southwestern extent of the peninsula, while Borneo formed the upward-pointing 'foot of the boot,' with the 'toe of the boot' extending fully to Palawan in the Philippines at the eastern extent of the *Isles of Sunda*. More than 13,000 islands emerged south of the *Sunda*, beginning what would ultimately be the world's largest island archipelago. The main islands are Java (Jawa), Sumatra (Sumatera), Sulawesi (Celebes), and Borneo, with New Guinea at the southern reaches of the archipelago.[cccxlviii]

By 8,500 BC, much of what remained of the great central plain had been inundated by rising seas, giving form to much of the present-day Indonesian Archipelago. The Malay Peninsula, Sumatra, and Java were still nominally connected, while Borneo was fully severed and bounded on all sides by the seas. Whilst much of the territory was lost in the first and second 'global superfoods, almost all the antediluvian continental shelf was inundated during the third flood, roughly 8,500 BC.[44] By 8,000 B.C., the central plains had been totally inundated, forming the present-day islands of the Philippines and Eastern Indonesia as we now know them. The islands that makeup Nusa Tenggara, along with Maluku and Sulawesi, emerged between Sunda and Sahul at this time; this was also the period that the land bridge that joined Sahul (Australia) and New Guinea was submerged (by 8,000 BC).

There are ancient tales and legends throughout the coastal regions of Southeast Asia, Africa, and the South Seas Isles, eluding to the destruction of the Sunda sub-continent. Geophysicists have discovered "currently submerged plateaus" in the oceans near Australia and Java, in the region of present Indonesia, that are clearly associated with the emergent Isles of Sunda, marking the remnants of the lost sub-continental land mass. The Naga were concentrated in the river valleys of the great central plain as well as the central plain itself, from where they led and augmented earlier the migrations into Southeastern Asia, where their sphere of influence spread northward up the Chaopraya River Valley into the central plains of Thailand, westward to the Bay of Bengal, and eastward to Cambodia and Vietnam, giving form to earliest ancient Kampuchea-Krom.[cccxlix]

---

[44] Stanford Geophysicist, Amos Nur (1977)

The mythology of the Naga in southeastern Asia is centered upon ancient Kampuchean (and present-day Cambodian) legend, which depicts them as a 'serpentine race' of beings who possessed a vast empire or kingdom; they were depicted as an ancient Africoid people, physically short in stature, dark skin, curly or even frizzly hair, broad nose, and thick negroid lips.[cccl] The Naga, known as the "Khmer: in Southeast Asia, were among the first inhabitants in the region. In ancient Kampuchean culture, the fundamental identification with the Nāga stems from two ancient beliefs, the ancient belief that the Khmers are the descendants of Phra Thong and Nang Nāga, the belief in Buddhism which depicts the Nāga as the protector of the religion. These two beliefs blend to form the fundamental belief system of the Nāga Khmer.

Historically, the identity and name of the Khmer-Krom people and their ancestral lands have been changed and/or referred to differently by various civilizations as well as the colonizing governments. Under the colonization of France, Kampuchea-Krom was called Cochin China. Ancestors of the early Khmer are believed to have arrived in the Angkor area of ancient Kampuchea (and present-day Cambodia) as early as 10,000 years ago. Thanks to archaeological work carried out since 2009. This can now be traced back to the Neolithic period. As excavation sites have become more numerous and modern dating methods are applied, settlement traces of all stages of development, from neolithic groups to organized preliterate societies, are being documented in the region.[cccli]

Ancient legends memorialize the Naga throughout the region as Asiatic black men who were the earliest ancestors of the descendent Afro-Asiatics, who would become the earliest and predominant inhabitants and culture through present-day southeastern Asia[45] These Afro-Asiatics cleared the forest for settlements, where they practiced forms of early agriculture in irrigated paddies, used buffaloes in farming, and hunted with axes, spears, arrows, slingshots, and fishing hooks. Because of the widespread correlations between early centers of agriculture and major language family homelands, demographically expanding agricultural populations moved outwards from primary agricultural homeland regions, expanding slowly into and occupying lands previously occupied by the earlier foraging cultures, creating for themselves a new homeland in southern Asia.

To the Southwest vestiges and admixtures of the Nagas and Väddas, in what had become the predominant land of Väddas, whose range extended southward along the western coast of the Malay peninsula, across Sumatra, Java, the Lesser Sunda Isles, into the region of present-day Papua New Guinea. The admixtures of the Nagas and Väddas were full statured, dark complexion, and somewhat lanky, with curly hair. The purer descendent Väddas remained a dark-skinned, short-statured people, adding a degree of continuity to the full extent of the Väddas settlement and trade range, which included areas they share with the Naga in Southeast Asia, including Thailand and Malaysia, and into the Indian subcontinent and Ceylon (Sri Lanka), which still annexed the ancient Kumari peninsula.

---

[45] Introduction to African Civilizations, John G. Jackson

Isles of Kamari: Kumari Nadu

The mountain ranges of Kumari had forty-eight high peaks, with the Indian continental shelf extending all the way from the Lakshadweep Isles at the Northern end of peninsular Kumari to the Maldives and the Chagos Archipelago at the Southern cape of the peninsula. The submergence of the *Kumari* peninsula, like *Sunda*, while often abrupt, was generally a slow, gradual process, and just like Sunda, but perhaps more decidedly so, the submergence of the Kumari was partly due to the last of the great floods, and partly due to the cyclical shift in the "tilt" of the Earth[ccclii]. The weakening of the substrata supporting the Kumari peninsula occurred over many thousands of years as rising sea levels and the eventual culmination of a long series of volcanic eruptions, earthquakes, and upheavals gradually undermined the foundation of the landmass.

Natural cataclysmic landslips occurred as a result of earthquakes and volcanic eruptions, which fragmented and weakened the surface of the peninsula and the surrounding ocean beds. Finally, a vast part of the landmass was swallowed by a cataclysmic landslip, followed by an on-rush of the sea and the massive flooding and inundation of vast areas of the landmass. The submergence of the peninsula was thus, in part, a result of the shift in tectonic plate, causing devastating tremors as large as 8.6 on a Richter scale basis, and in part a result of the rise in global sea levels. Half of Kumari sank in the first great flood, fully inundating and destroying the provinces of Ezh Thenga Naadu, Ezh Munpaalai Naadu, etc., the vast Pahruli river and, of course, the city of *Old Madurai*, seat of the first Sangam (Literary Academy) of the Dasas.

Dasas legends speak at length about the culture and civilization that prospered in *Kumari* during the ice age; the legends describe ancient Kumari as the large land mass beyond the southernmost tip of the present-day sub-continent, extending halfway between Africa and India, which disappeared into the Ocean. The legends also bear witness to the dramatic rise in sea levels and the massive floods and upheavals, which ultimately brought about the final destruction of the ancient southern land mass appending the sub-continent. The final convulsions and rising seas levels engulfed all but the remaining islands, including the Lakshadweep (Laccadive) and Maldives, Chagos, and ancient Ceylon, and Legends common to many Dasas groups give reference to the vast, now-sunken land mass and their migrations in the wake of the destruction of their homeland.

The Legends

Kumari was highly populated and included large cities before a series of major eruptions shattered the very foundations of the extensive landmass. In the first upheavals and inundations, fully one-half of the land mass was lost, leaving the then surviving land mass broken asunder in many places, as a long series of earthquakes and volcanic disturbances continued to gradually undermine the substrata comprising Kumari's foundation. Ultimately a new separate and distinct lesser, but nonetheless huge, island land survived as southern Kumari was separated from the receding peninsula. As the northern portions of the great landmass gave way, it broke up and gradually sank; survivors migrated to the two major surviving land masses.

At the final end of the first series of upheavals, half of the land mass was again lost, leaving the remaining land broken asunder in many places; the continuing series of earthquakes and volcanic disturbances gradually undermined the substrata underlying the very foundation of Kumari. Finally, two separate smaller, but nonetheless large, island land masses survived, as the original land mass succumbed to fragmentation and flooding. The second series of upheavals resulted in the fragmenting and ultimate destruction of the two surviving land masses, each giving way to further fragmentation, divisions, and inundations.

The final series of upheavals gave left a vast, sprawling island archipelago in its wake, marked by the mountain peaks and highlands of the now largely submerged continental peninsula of *Kumari*. As sea levels rose, the inhabitants of the coastal grasslands and plains and the interior lowlands migrated at first to the highlands of what would eventually become the first two major surviving divisions of the former peninsular land mass. Following this third series of upheavals and flooding, the survivors sought were forced to seek refuge and migrate to those islands surviving peak sea levels and, more significantly, into the heart of the mainland sub-continent itself.

The final rapid rise in sea levels occurred about 8,000 years ago, approximately 6,000 B.C., launching the last of the three global super-floods when the Indian Ocean swelled and submerged the core surviving remnants of *Kumari*. By the time the Holocene neared its close, Southern Asia had lost over half its surface area; sea levels had continued to rise until reaching peak levels about 5,500 years ago, stranding many of the most primitive inhabitants of the surviving islands as they became increasingly isolated. Peak sea levels finally engulfed all but the present-day surviving islands, from *Ceylon* off the coast of the Indian sub-continent, to the *Maldives* Isles and the *Chagos* Archipelago, approaching the coast of east Africa. [cccliii]

The rising seas submerged forty-nine Nadus (districts) south of the Kumari River. Before the floods, the forested and populated lands between the Prahuli and Kumari rivers stretched for about 1,000 miles; the abrupt submersion of the land area encompassing the two rivers resulted in the vast destruction of whole villages and many lives.[cccliv] As told by the Tamils in southern India and Sri Lanka, the people of the kingdom of Kumari migrated from a drowned large landmass in the Indian Ocean into Southern India. Dasas (Dravidian) civilization commences with the records that have come down to us of the Tamil literary writings during the past 12,000 years, which have been divided by historians into three periods, called the First Sangam, from 9600 BC to 5200 BC, the Second Sangam, from 5200 BC to 1500 BC, and the Third Sangam from 1500 BC to 600 AD.

The first Sangam had been headquartered in the city of *Then-Madurai* (Southern Madurai) and was patronized by a succession of eighty-nine kings, surviving unbroken for over four millennia, during which time it approved an immense collection of poems and literature. Very little more is known of the First Sangam other than that it was destroyed by the deluge at the end of the golden age, when the city of *Then-Madurai* was swallowed by the sea, along with large parts of peninsular *Kumari*. Kumari Nadu was the largest island remnant of the surviving archipelago. After the first academy at southern Maturai was terminated, *Dasas* were concentrated at Kumari Nadu, where they gradually constructed a new city and established the second Sangam at a place called *Kapatapuram*. The Second Sangam is said to have lasted over 3,000 years, when the same fate befell this city; it too was swallowed by the sea around 5,300 BC and lost forever. Following the inundation of Kavatapuram, the survivors once again relocated northward to a city in present-day Tamilnadu, then known as *Vada-Madurai* (Northern Madurai), located on the shores of the Bay-of-Bengal.

The Northern Sphere

The long and varied migrations and cultural flows from Sub-Saharan *Alkebu*-lan ("Africa") northward towards the fertile grasslands and wetlands of the *Sahel* and the *Sahara* underly the earliest diffusion of emergent cultures and microlithic industries in the northern sphere. The demographics of the north were largely shaped by drought-like conditions in *Central Africa*; the heightening aridity, expanding drought, and increasing severity of life prompted successive waves of migrations towards the fertile wetlands of the *Sahel* and *Sahara*. Though palaeoecological and paleo-anthropological data are sparse, there is significant evidence of synchronous humid periods in the *Sahel* and *Sahara* around the times of the northern migrations. The valleys, highlands, and forest lands of *Central Africa* had, on each occurrence, become extraordinarily dry and unyielding, mobilizing long migrations towards the wetlands of the north.

Among the first mobilized were those first impacted, such as the *Anu,* whose range then still extended from the lowlands of the Rift Valleys to the highlands surrounding *Great Lake Nanza* (colonial and post-colonial "Lake Victoria"), crossing the northern Serengeti highlands, intersecting the range of the *Sudra,* which stretched from the northern *Serengeti* through the *Kenyan* highlands. During the early (*primal*) migrations, the *Anu* range extended across the eastern highlands to the adjacent coastal plains and nearshore islands, in effect, intervening with the range of the *Proto-Sudra*.

During the *Primal Migrations*, diminutive *Väddas* inhabiting the coastal plains migrated northward along the eastern coastal belt, around the *Horn of Africa*, where some settled while others pressed eastward beyond the *Gulf of Arden* to the *Mandab Strait*, where many crossed and first settled along the fertile western coast of the land presently known as the "Arabian Peninsula."[ccclv] *Proto-Anu*, in turn, migrated northward along the ancient *White Nile* into *Sudan,* the *Sahel,* and the ancient *Sahara*.

The Saharan Pump

The 'Saharan Pump' hypothesis postulates that long periods of heavy rainfall for thousands of years have alternated with long periods of drought in the Sahara. The so-called "wet Sahara" phase, during which rivers, large lakes such as mega-lake Chad, and the Saharan Inland Seas existed alternately with an immense "Sahara desert." Extended periods of rainfall, lasting thousands of years (the "pluvial" periods) precede the "Wet Sahara" phase, during which the Saharan terrain becomes green and fertile, with an abundance of plants, trees, and forests, as well as large lakes, vast river networks, and huge inland seas. People have anciently migrated into the Sahara from Sub-Saharan Africa during the "green" or "wet Sahara" phases and migrated out of the Sahara during the transition to the "Sahara desert" phase.

During the transition, which is essentially the closing period of the "green" phase, the Sahara becomes a vast savanna-like grassland, and during the subsequent inter-pluvial (or arid) periods, the Sahara gradually reverts to desolate desert-like conditions. This back-and-forth climate shift and the resulting migration(s) are together called the *"Saharan Pump,"*; describing the ancient movement of people, primarily between Sub-Saharan Africa, the Sahara, and Eurasia, during cyclical climate shifts.[ccclvi] Pulsing like an explosion of plants after a rare rain and the desert's terrain almost completely covered with vegetation, when moist eras visited, they thrived.

The Sahara passed through several wet and dry phases over the past 120,000 years; pollen counts and other climatological data indicate that the earliest two of the last three phases were marked by an extensive wet period between 28,000 BC and 18,000 BC. However, the great Saharan mega lakes and paleo-rivers were formed during the much earlier Middle Pleistocene era. [ccclvii] Nonetheless, by 30,000 years ago, before the onset of the second of the great northern migrations, long, extended periods of persistent rainfall produced and expanded huge lakes throughout the Sahara. Southeast of *Lake Moeris,* a giant lake roughly the size of England, *Paleo-Lake Fezzan,* formed in the Fezzan depression when the great rains fell.

Central Saharan Seas

The present-day *Fezzan* basin is east of the Nile Valley, an area in which a gigantic ancient lake existed throughout much of antiquity, around which a distinct culture emerged and rose to great prominence. The present-day Fezzan depression is a large, closed basin that contains numerous ancient palaeolake sediment outcrops, shorelines, and a wealth of ancient lake deposits that have been dated, using up-to-date techniques, to produce a chronology of climate change in the *Central Sahara*. The chronology demonstrates evidence of warm, humid conditions prevailing in the Sahara during the interglacial periods, generating high enough rainfall to produce a giant lake roughly the size of England in the Fezzan. This was "*Paleo-Lake Fezzan.*" [46];[47]

Paleo-Lake Fezzan was one of several great lakes that once existed in the Sahara; these were part of a larger network of greater and lesser lakes and inland seas which included immense *Mega-Lake Chad* in the south, the mysterious *Mauritanian Sea* in the west, and legendary *Lake Tritonis* and the fabled *Triton Sea* in the central north, paralleling the southern foothills of present-day Tunisia and Algeria. *Lake Moeris* to the east was among a number of other smaller lakes linked through interconnecting rivers and basins, forming waterways and corridors across the ancient *Sahara*. There were other lakes bridging the central Sahara, including the *Ahnot-Moyer Lake* in central Algeria; their catchments broadened the network of rivers, lesser lakes, and tributaries forming the corridors across the Central Saharan lowlands.

The *Sahel* is a transition zone between *Sub-Saharan Africa* and the *Sahara*, bordering the *Sahara* in the south. The *Sahel* is predominantly flat, with a few isolated plateaus and mountains; it extends from the *Indian Ocean* in the east to the *Atlantic Ocean* in the west. Between 70,000 BC and 30,000 BC, the *Sahel* was very wet, rainy, and humid and, in consequence, contained a series of large and small lakes. Ancient lithic art in the region portrays crocodiles and elephants, depicting remnants of the vast wetlands that once existed. *Mega-Lake Chad* was then a huge lake straddling the *Sahel* and *Sahara* along the borders of present-day Chad and Niger. At its peak, the lake was bigger than the present-day Caspian Sea and fed a broad band of tropical vegetation extending northwards into the Sahara, attracting those who migrated northward from central Africa.

---

[46] Brooks *et al.*, 2003
[47] Thiedig *et al.*, 2000

Other paleo-lakes and large wetlands existed at the southern reaches of the Sahara and Sahel, the southernmost being *Lake Turkana* and the *Lotagipi Swamp* west of *Lake Turkana, Lake Sudd*. During interglacials, Lakes Chad and Sudd expanded to fill about half the gap between them, resulting in vast areas between Chad and Ethiopia-Kenya alternating between deserts and wetlands. *Paleo-Lake Sudd* was an immense shallow wetland fed by the *White Nile* descending from *Lakes Mwitanzige* (Albert*)*, *Rutanzige* (Edward), and *Nanza* (Victoria*)*. The *Sudd* wetlands expanded into Sudan, forming a formidable obstacle to migration; it was considered nearly impassable either overland or by watercraft. A swamp that no one could pass through for most of antiquity, altering the paths of early migration in the central Sahel and southern Sahara.

The Northward Migrations

In the first of the great northward migrations, the *Proto-Anu* and *Kwa* inhabiting the *Albertine Rift* migrated along the foothills of the *Western Rift Valley* to the *Lu-ku-ga River,* where they progressed along the river's westerly course, exiting the *Western Rift* through the *Mitumba Mountains,* to where the *Lu-ku-ga* River merges into the *Lu-al-a-ba River*. *Proto-Anu* (Ba-Twa), accompanied by the *Kwa*, whom evidence supports migrated from around the *Virunga Mountains*, and the related *Nwa Nshi* from the lowlands of the *Western Rift,* each separately yet together migrated along the course of the *Lu-al-a-ba River* to the mighty *Congo River*, which directed the long migrations northward, toward the *Ubangi River*.

Thus began the northward migrations along the river corridors of *Western Africa* towards the fertile wetlands of the ancient *Sahel* and inland seas of the Sahara. Proto-Anu migrations pushed northward along the *Ubangi* to the *N'Dja-mena* region, in present-day *Chad*, just beyond the northern fringes of the *Great Rift Valley*. From *N'Dja-mena*, the *Proto-Anu* migrated northward to settlement areas around the southern shores of *Paleo-Lake Chad*. This while migrations of the *Nwa Nshi, Igbo,* and other subsets of the *Kwa* progressed northward along the *Congo, Ubangi, and Chari Rivers,* with many arriving at the southern shores of *Mega-Lake-Chad,* where all encountered the *Sao,* fully statured aboriginals, which first emerged around 45,000 years ago.

Northern Migrations of the Dasas

The *Dasas* inhabiting the east African foothills around *Mount Meru* are thought to have begun northward migrations about 20,000 years ago, after the end of the second *Mousterian Pluvial*, prompted by the expanding droughts and heightening aridity blanketing Central Africa during the Glacial Maximum. The actual migration path of the Dasas is a matter of study and debate. However, the field of genetics has shed some light on the matter. Conceivable maps of human migrations can be made based on current genetic and climatological evidence. For instance, an analysis of the distribution of the R-V88 haplogroup in African populations revealed a striking genetic contiguity between the Chadic-speaking peoples from the *Paleo-Lake Chad* region and several Afro-Asiatic-speaking groups, such as the *Dasas*.[ccclviii][ccclix]

The route of the *Dasas* has been traced through *Kenya*, suggesting the path of their northern migrations progressed through the Kenyan highlands descending into Sudan, west of Lake Turkana. Expansion of the *Nilotic* settlement range west of *Lake Turkana*, together with the expansion of the *Lotagipi Swamp*, as *Lake Turkana*, drained westward, combined to push the *Dasas* migrations towards the *White Nile*, where they moved northward along the river's course, toward the *Great Plains of Sudan*. The *White Nile* enters *Southern Sudan* at the current *Sudan-Uganda* border, flowing across forested hillsides and cataracts before slowing as it approaches the present-day *City of Juba*. Southern Sudan is trough-like, shaped by the highlands, mountains, and hills at its eastern, southern, and western borders. Numerous rivers flow from the surrounding mountains into the central Sudan valley, where the *Dasas* took respite before migrating westward toward *Mega-Lake Chad*.

The largest waves of migrations occurred during the *Wurm* glaciations (approximately 16,000 BC), a period characterized by a climate fluctuating between extreme aridity and sustained rains. During wetter periods, rainfall reached the Saharan highlands as far north as the *Tropic of Cancer*, engorging rivers, lakes, and tributaries draining southward, filling and often overflowing the central southern Saharan drainage basins in the *Sudd* and *Mega-Lake Chad*. *Paleo-Lake Sudd* expanded the wetlands, filling about half the gap between it and *Mega-Lake Chad*, which, in turn, also expanded into the wetlands, connecting the two immense bodies of water. In drier times *Paleo-Lake Sudd* and *Mega-Lake Chad* dwindled and contracted their shorelines, while in wetter times, the lakes expanded into the lowlands transforming the *Sudd* into an impassable swampland.

It appears the Adi-Dasas migrated along the course of the White Nile through the plains of the Sudan, where some temporarily settled along the banks of the river south of its ostensible terminus point at the *Sudd Wetlands*. The White Nile then all but disappeared under the floating canopy of the Sudd swamplands, with the migrating *Dasas* temporarily settling along the upper part of the river before pressing onward towards fertile lands in which to settle. Expansion of the *Paleo-Sudd Wetlands* along with the villages of *Nilotics* in the natural harbors and best settlement areas around the *Sudd* combined to push the *Dasas* migrations westward toward the fertile and well-watered lands along the eastern shores of *Mega-Lake Chad*. [ccclx]

The Adi-Dasas settled and expanded northward along the eastern coast of *Mega-Lake Chad*, the northern basin of which was the Bodélé Depression, the lowest point in *Mega-Lake Chad*. The fertile lands around *Mega-Lake Chad* acted as a center of gravity for the *Adi-Dasas* and neighboring populations of the autochthonous *Si* (Xi, Shi), whose ancestors had been the northern-most and first of the sacred tribes of Yam to migrate into the Sahara (during earliest antiquity). Though the *Si* (Xi, Shi) anciently inhabited the coastal lands along the northeastern and northern shores of *Mega-Lake Chad*, their core stronghold was in the highlands of the great mountains to the northeast of the Mega-Lake.

The entire *Ounianga Basin* between the *Tibesti* and *Ennedi* mountains in present-day Northern Chad was anciently occupied by *Paleo-Lake Yoa*, a large highland lake replete with several islands, transforming the basin into a rich green valley, filled with trees, grasslands, and a variety of wildlife; an ideal environment for the early habitations of the ancestral *Si* (Xi, Shi).[ccclxi] The interactions between the *Adi-Dasas* and *Si* (Xi, Shi) around Mega-Lake Chad's eastern, northeastern, and northern shores led to resemblances and affinities in certain beliefs; this is particularly evident in the affinity for spiritual beliefs.[ccclxii] Like the Si, the Adi-Dasas worshipped Amun/ Amon/ Amma, a Deity representing the flowering life force hidden in the primordial waters of consciousness.

The *Mega-Lake Chad* basin was situated within the bidirectional corridors of both the *Sahara* and the *Sahel* of distant antiquity and thus became one of the most populated places in the Northern *Sphere*. The impetus for settlement in the lands along and around its shores appears to have been connected if not driven by a series of heavy and extended pluvial (rainy periods) during distant antiquity, climatic ameliorations that started over 60,000 years before the present (YBP).

Mega-Lake Chad

The *Sao*, whose origins were southeast of *Mega-Lake Chad*, were amongst the earliest of the "full-statured' *Negroid* types to emerge in the tropical interior river valleys, with characteristics and affinities identifiable as early as 45,000 BC. According to legend and oral traditions, 'the *Sao* were as tall as giants'; the legends described them not only as giants but as keen hunters who planned and constructed towns and walled villages. They were among the earliest people to migrate along the course of the *Chari River and* settle in the delta and along the southern shores of *Paleo Lake Chad*.[ccclxiii]

The *Sao* was comprised of several clans united into a single polity by language; they were the earliest people to have left clear traces of their presence in *Cameroon* and the southern *Lake Chad* basin. The *Lake Chad Basin* is situated at the intersection of *Cameroon*, *Chad,* and *Nigeria;* the Sao spread from northeastern *Cameroon* to areas around the *Mega-Lake Chad* basin. The largest archaeological finds of the *Sao* have been uncovered in their original homeland, by the *Chari River*, south of the *Lake Chad Basin*, in northern, eastern *Cameroon*. Archaeological evidence suggests that while societies of distant antiquity in the southern basin were not yet farming, they were harvesting wild grains. They did not have to cultivate in order to support themselves in one place; this is probably the way domestication of cereal crops first emerged around the basin.

By the time of the *Proto-Anu* and *Adi-Dasas* migrations, the Sao inhabited much of the coastal belt along the southern basin east of the *Chari-Logone Delta,* at the southeastern extent of *Lake Chad*.[ccclxiv] Upon arrival, the *Adi-Dasas* found the jealously guarded territories of the *Sao*, whose terrain stretched along the southeastern coast of the lake and throughout much of the eastern *Chari-Logone Delta*. *Adi-Dasas* migrations were thus pressed further westward, through and past the long-established settlement ranges of the *Nwa-Nshi, Ndi-Igbo,* and other descendants of the *Kwa"* who anciently settled on the southwestern coast of *Lake Chad*.

The *Ndi-Igbo* and most of their neighbors were descendants of the *Proto-Kwa* who migrated from the Western Rift Valley.[48] "*Ndi-Igbo*" simply means "the Ancients, the First People, the Aboriginals (*Ndi Gbo*)." *Ndi-Igbo* synthesized over thousands of years from their ancestral Proto-Kwa. *Proto-Kwa* clans migrated northward along major West African river corridors until finally reaching and progressing northward along the *Logone River*, which forms a broad delta with the Chari River, the "*Chari-Logone Delta*," at the southeastern extent of *Lake Chad*. The *Chari* and *Logone* were key corridors leading ancient migrants to the delta and lands surrounding the southern basin. The Logone is situated west of the *Chari River*, leading the *Nwa-Nshi* and *Ndi-Igbo* to settlement areas west of the territories of the *Sao*.

---

[48] Acholonu-Olumba, Prehistoric Origins of the Igbo

Satellite imagery has enabled a detailed mapping of the paleo-shoreline of *Lake Chad*, which has been identified to the north-west of the present-day lake, where the north-central basin of the lake was then still filled with water, and people settled and farmed around its shores.[49] The westernmost shoreline of *Paleo-Lake Chad* consisted of an extensive beach ridge, known as the "Bama Ridge," extending around the western shores of the palaeolake in a relatively straight shoreline. The *Bama Ridge* terminates in the north at the *Komadugu-Yobe Rivers*, which enter the lake in the northwest. The main rivers flowing into *Paleo-Lake Chad* are the *Chari-Logone, which* enters the lake in the southeast, and the *Komadugu-Yobe*, which enters in the northwest. The flow patterns of the two rivers gave rise to a massive swampland across the middle of the lake: dividing its southern and northern basins.

The greater *Chad Basin* is actually comprised of two separate basins, a northern and a southern basin. The northern basin is primarily fed by the *Komadugu-Yobe Rivers,* which flow eastward through *Nigeria* and *Niger* to enter Lake Chad in the northeast; while the southern basin is primarily fed by the *Chari-Logone Rivers,* which flow northward from the southeast to enter the lake in the southeast. The *Adi-Dasas* settled in the region straddling *Lake Chad's* southern and northern basins along the western coast of the lake, well north of the settlement range of the *Ndi-Igbo*. The final *Adi-Dasas* settlement range straddled the great central swamplands separating the southern and northern basins, affording them access to the resources of the wetlands, as well as those of the southern and northern hemispheres of the greater *Chad* basin.

To the north of the *Adi-Dasas* settlement range was the *Komadougou-Yobe Delta*, where the *Komadugu-Yobe River* then emptied into the western end of *Paleo-Lake Chad,* the then settlement province of those referred to as the "*Oru."* The Oru was a descendent *Proto-Anu* and *Anu* who migrated from the southern shores of *Paleo-Lake Chad* prompted by expansions of the *Sao* and migrations of the *Nwa* and *Ndi-Igbo* into the region. The term "*Oru*" was a survival of the ancient term "*Heru*" (for the "Followers of Heru").[ccclxv] The *Oru* was Anu of the *Hydra Cult,* who, having rejected the overlordship of the *Nagas*, immigrated seeking new lands beyond the reach of the *Nagas,* prompting their settlements around the southern shores of *Paleo-Lake Chad*.

By the time the *Adi-Dasas* settled along the central western coast of Lake Chad, the *Oru* had migrated westward through the delta along the courses of the *Komadugu-Yobe* river. The *Komadugu-Yobe* is actually a network of rivers flowing eastward over hundreds of miles, ultimately converging to form the Yobe and Komadugu Rivers, which, in turn, converge to form the *Komadugu-Yobe River*. The rivers flow through a sub-basin of the *Lake Chad* basin, forming extensive ancient floodplains and a rich fertile terrain in which early *Oru* settlements grew quickly, prompting further settlements and further westward expansions of the *Oru* along the courses and tributaries of the river.

---

[49] Leblanc, 2002; Leblanc et al., 2006

The *Oru* had become a primarily aquatic-based culture, settling on the banks and tributaries of the *Komadugu-Yobe*. The "*Oru*" were a subset of the *Anu* who, in the west, had become known as the '*Water People.*' According to oral tradition, their migrations and settlements would eventually make their way to the *Niger Delta*, where they are said to have first settled along the coasts. The northern migrations of the *Oru* along the east-west corridors of the river intersected the far more ancient northern migrations of the *Kwa,* who traversed the course of the *Lower Niger* in present-day *Southern Nigeria*, thousands of years before the *Oru* migrations into the region. Nonetheless, the infusion of the orthodoxy of the *Oru* would prove influential and instrumental in adapting similarly constructed belief systems and organizing principles by other [existent and emergent] cultures in the region.

Kwa of the Niger

The *Kwa* was essentially a land-based culture whose descendent subsets settled in and along the fertile interior valleys and river corridors of *West Africa* on their northward migrations towards the wetlands of the *Northern Sphere*. The *Niger River* became a key corridor in their northern migrations through present-day *Nigeria*, *Benin*, *Niger,* and *Mali* and across *Western Sudan* into the wetlands of Western Sahara. The *Niger River* is to *Western Sudan* what the *Nile River* is to *Egypt*, but rather than one delta, as in Egypt, the Niger River has three, forming a broad irrigation system that spreads over thousands of miles. The *Niger River Valley* follows the course of the river, from *Kanji Lake,* in present-day *Nigeria* in the south, to *Niamey* in present-day *Niger* to the north, and from there through *Ago* and *Bourse,* in present-day *Mali*, where the ancient river channel is well defined, but shallow, and interrupted by several rapids.

Early northward migrations of the *Kwa* progressed beyond the *Niger-Benue* confluence thousands of years before the *Oru* entered the region. *Proto-Kwa* migrated northward against the course of the *Niger River*, which flows southeastward from *Bourse*, in the region of present-day *Mali* in the north, where it is received from the east, flowing from *Timbuktu* to *Bourse*. The course of the *Niger* of distant antiquity ran through an enormous marshland to the north of *Timbuktu* that covered a surface area exceeding several hundreds of square miles. Early clans and village clusters of the *Kwa* settled, survived, prospered, and expanded, largely on fish diets and the lush abundance of vegetation and wild game in the surrounding ancient terrain.

During this period, what we today call the "*Niger River"* was then actually two rivers, the *Upper Niger* and the distinctly separate *Lower Niger*. The *Upper Niger* rose in the highlands of southeastern Guinea and flowed northeasterly into a closed basin and ancient salt lake known as the "*Juf,"*) a remnant of a more ancient inland sea to the north, which once occupied a large portion of Western Sahara. The *Upper Niger* flowed north and northwest to empty into the *Juf*, which in the quaternary age was a salt-water lake remnant of the earlier ancient inland sea which, in the tertiary age, once extended as far east as *Bilma*. Lake Fagubini is regarded as a remnant of the ancient course of the upper river.

The *Lower Niger* traversed the central Sahara flowing southward, aided by tributaries descending the *Adrar Massif*, with the Lower Niger then emptying into the *Gulf of Guinea*. The *Upper Niger*, in Trun, was once aided by tributaries from the Ahaggar mountains that flowed along the course of *Wadi Taffassassent*, now a dried-up ancient riverbed in the central Sahara. Although the upper and lower parts of the *Niger River* have all the appearance of ancient rivers, the *Middle Niger* is the result of a "recent" capture; "it has no past, it scarcely has a present."[50] Though the geological changes that have taken place are imperfectly known, it is theorized that climatic conditions and shifts in the topography over the millennium caused the river to assume its present course.

When the *Middle Niger* arose in the hills near the *Juf* ... from where it flowed southward, connecting with the *Lower Niger* on its course to the *Gulf of Guinea*, creating the boomerang-shaped geography that ultimately joined the courses of the rivers together. At the height of the *Last Great Ice Age* (the "Glacial Maximum"), sea levels were at their lowest, and a distinctly separate *Upper Niger* cut deep gulfs into the developing *Inland Niger Delta*, forming the valley of the Upper Niger and the floodplain downstream where the river's floodwaters spread through a maze of channels, replenishing the vast wetlands.

Emergence of the Manding

Early settlers of the *Inland Niger Delta* formed riverine communities where vegetation, fish, and other small aquatic animals were eaten.[ccclxvi] The *Manding* emerged as full-statured *Negroids* from the ancestral *Kwa* in the fertile wetlands of the *Inland Delta*.[51][52] Like that of the *Nilotics* from the *Anu* in the wetlands of *East Africa* and the *Sao* in the *Chari River* wetlands south of *Paleo-Lake Chad*, the *Manding* emerged in the abundance of the wetlands of the *Niger Basin*, with characteristics identifiable as early as 40,000 BC.[53] The early *Manding* lived in mounds along the corridors and tributaries of the *Niger* and, like the *Sao* of the *Chari River* wetlands, were formed essentially by clans, united into a single polity by one language.

Over the centuries, they spread throughout and beyond the *Middle Niger*, extending their settlement range northward into and beyond the *Inland Niger Delta*.[54] Hunter-gatherer groups, who had specialized in hunting used their knowledge of the habits of game to shift to animal husbandry. Growth, specialization, and rising demand stimulated trade throughout the region. During the *First Mousterian Pluvial,* the *Sahara* bloomed like never before, not only in vegetation and wildlife but also in new settlements.[ccclxvii]

Saharan terrain then consisted of rolling grasslands with thick and abundant vegetation, nourished by ample seasonal rainfall, which fed a vast network of rivers, tributaries, and greater and lesser lakes scattered across the ancient landscape. A period that lasted over twenty thousand years, until about 30,000 BC, when pluvial conditions began to gradually end, and desertification gradually began to overtake the interior Sahara. It was prior to this that the *Manding* pressed northward beyond the *Inland Niger Delta* into the wetlands south of a huge inland sea that then occupied much of *Western Sahara*.

---

[50] R. Chudeau, *Sahara soudanais,* Paris, 1909
[51] Ehret and Posnansky 1982
[52] Proto-Mande (Niger-Congo subset)
[53] Ehret and Posnansky 1982:242
[54] Bimson 1980

The Legends

The *Manding* call themselves *Ma-nde*: children of *Ma*, in acknowledgment of their ancient concept and reverence for truth, balance, order, morality, and justice, ideals they propounded as the essential order of the Cosmos. [ccclxviii] *Maat* was the personified Goddess of the Virtues of Truth, Balance, Justice, and Order and was said to regulate the actions of both mortals and the deities. It was said to be *Maat* who set the order of the Cosmos from Chaos at the moment of Creation.[55] [ccclxix]

Maat is the eternal antagonist of *Chaos*. It is said that Maat's battle with Chaos commences on several levels; Maat is said to battle all forms of destructive chaos and uncreation, the essence of imbalance or imbalance impurity. How *Chaos* manifests in each person's life is different, but many souls can identify the sort of turmoil that leaves them feeling undone, as if their selfness is being stripped away and destroyed, their very sense of identity: that is Chaos. *Chaos* acts counter to *Ma'at*. Chaos is the opposite of Ma'at. It is an imbalance, impurity, destructive power, and worse – it is "uncreation." The opposite of "Ma`at, "chaos" is untruth, falsehood, disorder, unrighteousness, and injustice.

Ancient Scriptures teach that chaos is an abomination to the Deity. It may gain ground for a while; it may bring pleasure for a while; it may bring gratification for the moment, but in the end, it leads to destruction. Ma'at was the solid reason the sun rises and the earth maintains its movement. Without Ma'at, there would be no balance. The low-lying basins of *Western* Sahara were then still occupied by remnants of the once massive ancient Saharan Inland Sea that fully occupied the low-lying basins and thus covered much of the *Western* and *Central Sahara*. Though greatly diminished before the onset of the *First Mousterian Pluvial*, surviving remnants of the ancient perennial sea, the most significant of which was a huge *Western Inland Sea,* occupying the basins and depressions of the present-day *'Spanish Sahara'*.

An inland sea that expanded and was annexed after the opening phases of the first pluvial, bringing the gigantic, perennial ancient *Saharan Inland Sea* of faint fable back to life and near full form and dimension, occupying the huge northern, central, and western basins of the *Sahara*. After the closing phases of the *First Pluvial*, over five thousand years after the end of the prolonged rains, the perennial inland sea again dwindled and fragmented into the huge remnant inland seas and salt-water lakes of distant and early antiquity.

The surviving inland sea in the west was the largest of the fragmented remnants of the ancient Saharan inland sea; this was the fabled *Mauritanian Sea,* around whose shores the *Manding* settled before the end of the *First Mousterian Pluvial.* As pluvial conditions waned and arid conditions ensued, desertification spread throughout the Sahara, claiming large portions of the wetlands, and mobilizing migrations north of the *Inland Delta* towards the southeastern shores of the fabled inland sea.

---

[55] Later called Sophia by the Greeks

The *Upper Niger River* arose and flowed from its source in the highlands of *Guinea* and flowed north-west, emptying into a now-gone lake (the *"Jug"*), a salt-water remnant of the massive ancient Saharan inland sea, whose own Outlet Rivers still drained northward into the basins of the Mauritanian *Sea* as late as 28,000 BC. The *Middle Niger* arose in the hills near *Lake Jug* and flowed southward, connecting with the *Lower Niger* on its course to the gulf. It was the upper course of the *Middle Niger* that led the Manding to the wetlands of the *Jug* and from there to the southwestern coastal plains of the *Mauritanian Sea*.[ccclxx] The *Upper Niger* and *Lower Niger* were then two distinctly separate rivers.

Western Inland Sea: The Mauritanian Sea

It is difficult to imagine now, but the interior region of present-day *Mauritania*, today an almost entirely arid desert, once retained a great Inland Sea. Estuaries and a network of paleo-rivers and lagoons nurtured by the ancient sea yielded a variety of vegetation sufficient to support an abundance of elephants, rhinos, and hippopotami around the former coastal belt, as well evidenced by the numerous rock art portrayals of the era scattered across the region. Long after the end of the *First Mousterian Pluvial*, this western inland sea became the largest surviving remnants of the more ancient inland sea that once covered much of the northern, central, and Western Sahara. The second largest of its remnants was the northern inland sea of the era, on the chotts plateau to the northeast.

The western inland sea was fed by paleo-rivers that flowed from the highlands of the *Anti-Atlas* to the west and the heights of the *High Atlas* to the north. The ancient *Mauritanian Sea* occupied the immense low-lying depressions formed by the *Mauritanian-Sénégal Basin*, which lies in silent witness and testimony to the size and dimensions of the once huge ancient western inland sea. The *Mauritanian Sea* covered an area extending from present-day *Morocco* in the northwest to present-day *Guinea-Bissau* in the south. Geologically the '*Mauritanian-Sénégal Basin*' was a consequence of the structural detachment and separation of the South American and African continents. A structural detachment resulted in the basin's slightly seaward tilting disposition, with a definitive uplift along the marginal areas accentuating the interior coastline. According to relevant gravimetric data, the *Mauritanian -Sénégal Basin* occupied by the ancient inland sea is essentially a giant 'Rift'.

Faint legend would add a 'Rift' first filled by the waters of an even larger and more ancient inland sea that once covered most of the north-central and southwestern Sahara. A sea that once connected with the Mediterranean Sea at the *Gulf of Gabes*, on the central coast of North Africa, and connected with the Atlantic Ocean at the coast of *Mauritania*, on the coast of West Africa, where the low-lying coastal barrier tilts seaward.[56] Over time, tidal cycles and falling sea levels re-established the integrity of the western coast, sealing and rendering the inland sea self-contained. Warming climatic conditions and prolonged periods of heightened aridity combined to facilitate the drying out of the northern Sahara and the further contraction of the ancient inland sea, as the huge body of water gradually yielded the higher land formations surrounding the basins.

---

[56] Western Senegal, West Africa; Abdoulaye DIOP - Départment de Géologie, Faculté des Sciences et Techniques Université Cheikh Anta Diop, Dakar, Senegal.

The ancient western and northern inland seas of the inter-pluvial periods were actually remnant fragments of a far more ancient and perennial inland sea formed and reconstituted during the first and second pluvial. Desertification in the Sahara has come and gone in varying degrees of severity with the ice ages; during the last three hundred thousand years, the Sahara has undergone a succession of glaciation-induced dry, arid periods, each separated by about one hundred thousand years from its predecessor. The massive *Saharan Inland Sea* of the pluvial shrank in size and dimension over thousands of years during the following inter-pluvial periods, fragmenting into the two inland seas of the earliest antiquity, interconnected by a remnant network of paleo-rivers and tributaries linking the basins.

When the *First Mousterian Pluvial* finally ended, the *Mauritanian Sea* covered an area extending from present-day *Morocco* in the northwest to southern Mauritania in the south, covering roughly half the Western Sahara. Rock art engravings and depictions of animals dependent on large bodies of water have been found at numerous sites around the former coastal belt, most notably, the ancient buffalo of the era. As the desert again began to gradually reclaim the *Sahara, Manding* migrations coalesced around the fertile southern coastal belt and the network of rivers, lagoons, and tributaries to the south and southwest of the *Mauritanian Sea*.

Ensuing migrations and settlements advanced northward along and around the huge inland sea's southeastern, southern, southwestern, and western coastal belts. Migrations along the eastern coastal belt progressed northward from the *Juff* wetlands, above the *Inland Niger Delta*, from where they spread along the large paleo-major rivers flowing towards and into the *Mauritanian Sea* from the highlands of the far northeast. The progression of new settlements along the western coastal belt was channeled through the broad-peninsula-like landmass of the era bordering the western coast, geographically defined by the southern highlands, foothills, and savannas of the *Anti-Atlas* mountain range, situated between the immense *Mauritanian Sea* on the east, and the vast *Atlantic Ocean* on the west.

Rise of the Manding-Si (Xi)

The earliest arriving clans of the ancestral *Si* (Xi, Shi) made temporary settlements along the northern coastal belt of the *Western Inland Sea*, where they found an abundance of fish, local game, and plant life, and the adjacent highlands were surveyed for permanent settlement areas. The temporary settlements were converted to seasonal villages for fishing, hunting, gathering and livestock once permanent residences were secured in the highlands. First had come the fishing and hunting clans, attracted to permanent settlement by the shift from hunter-gatherers to herders; some clans practiced a combination of herding, hunting, and fishing. Then came the artisan, artisans, seers, and boat builders.

The broad coastal grasslands north of the huge western inland sea became home to the pastoral clans and large herds of cattle, with grazing, ranges extending beyond the foothills, well into the highlands. Fishing clan villages formed and expanded around the immediate northeastern and northern shorelines and on several small islands in the northern and central confines of the huge *Western Inland Sea*. As pastoral clans grew, the seasonal villages along the northern and northeastern coastal belt gradually obtained a semi-permanent aspect, but in keeping with custom and tradition, more permanent villages were established in the adjacent highlands of the *Atlas*.

The need to exchange useful goods, such as ceramics and textiles, encouraged early trade between the clans and villages and gave rise to trade and transit corridors along the coastal waterways linking major settlement areas around the huge inland ` 1111i`1jkisea, eventually bringing the *Si* (Xi, Shi) into contact and commerce with the agricultural settlements of the *Manding,* beyond and along the southern coastal belt of the *Western Inland Sea*. Early *Manding* settlements were established along the southern coastal belt, with later expansions northward channeled along the western coastal belt and the mountainous, peninsula-like landmass formed by the southern *Anti-Atlas*, bordered on the east by the *Mauritanian Sea,* and on the west by the *Atlantic Ocean*.

The oldest farming and cultivation of sorghum, rice, millet, yams, and other grains were cultivated by the *Manding* of the era, albeit closer to their initial home range, south of the *Western Inland Sea*. Here the inimitable and resourceful *Manding* cultivated and farmed vast areas, eventually expanding to the fertile lands of the southern coastal belt itself. While the northern highlands were bastions of the *Si* and the center of the highest state of development of flake tooling of the era, referred to as the *Alterian* tradition, characterized by high standards of workmanship, variety, and specialization.[ccclxxi] It is theorized that the bow and arrow were first invented in the *Aterian* tradition.[ccclxxii]

Eventual amalgamations of the *Si* and *Manding* marked the beginnings of the great Saharan civilization that emerged during the ice age. Prosperity from the amalgamations and expansions of them and the descendent *Manding-Si* reverberated across time and distance in the Sahara of the era. *Si* (Xi, Shi) and descendant *Manding-Si* clans-built irrigation canals and boats and used both natural and constructed waterways as transit routes. The rise of pastoral farming and the raising of livestock may have been a direct result of the invention of irrigation and sustained farming. Once crops could be grown in one place and there was no need to forage, people began to find ways to keep animals near them as well.

The emergent economy became increasingly diversified, encompassing fishing, herding, and farming methods of food production. Farmers grew wheat, barley, fruits, nuts, vegetables, and olives for oil in the lowlands in the winter and grazed herds of cattle and goats in the mountains during the summer. Semi-nomadic pastoral clans lived in permanent villages in the highlands for part of the year and moved between their summer pastures in the highlands and the lower-lying winter grazing lands. The Sahara got greener as temperatures rose near the end of the *First Pluvial;* as the warmer air absorbed more moisture from the glacial melt and oceans, the rains returned for a short but protracted period.

Early trade routes of the era linked the western coastal belt of the *Mauritanian Sea* with the *Western Sahel* (anciently viewed as the "*Western Sudan*"), extending the emerging influence of the *Manding-Si* to the Southwestern Sahara. This was during the earliest antiquity in the Sahara, the latter part of the Stone Age, to some extent over-lapping the Bronze Age in certain areas. It began when man ceased the semi-nomadic way of life and started settling in permanent agricultural communities. The early formation of informal state-like provinces was linked not only to agricultural improvements and the population growth and expansion that followed but also to the growth of inter-regional trade. The fusion of the new with the older communities along familial lines of affinity served to bond and seed populations into early urban-like communities across the terrains of the *Manding-Si, Manding,* and by osmosis, to the peoples of the adjoining and surrounding territories.[ccclxxiii]

This was the long closing period of the *First Mousterian Pluvial* when the rains had diminished, but the Sahara was still crossed by vast but waning networks of rivers interconnecting the huge inland seas and large lakes of the era. Desiccation occurred gradually at first, over hundred years, but then accelerated as the vegetation which helped generate rain was lost, causing the soil to lose its ability to hold moisture when it did rain. Light-colored land without plants reflects rather than absorbs sunlight, producing less warm, moist cloud-forming updrafts, causing even less rain.

Clans and villages along the receding shorelines of the *Western Inland Sea* intensified their collection of wild grains, some of which they cultivated. In the south, along the western coastal belt, *Manding-Si* clans lived in upland villages in the *Anti-Atlas* in the summer, while in winter, like the *Ancestral Si*, they migrated with their herds to the lowlands, returning to the uplands in summer to irrigate and grow sorghum, vegetables, apricots, and apples. Over two hundred fifty settlement sites of the era have been identified (so far) in the highlands along what was once the western coastal belt of the *Mauritanian Sea* in present-day southern *Morocco*.

Some sites and artifacts date back thousands of years; fractured rock strata can be seen scattered throughout the foothills covered with incised animals and enigmatic symbols, the meanings of which remain obscure. The *Manding-Si* were a mix of *Manding* in Western Sahara and the far more ancient *Si* of the Central Sahara. It was the ancient westward migrations of the *Si* that brought them into early contact, commerce, integration, and eventual miscegenation with the *Manding*. The *Si* (Shi, Xi) were ancient master boat builders, seafarers, and fishermen who had traded across the Sahara when the region was still partially inundated by the massive ancient inland sea that once occupied parts of the northern and much of the central and Western Sahara. By the time of the emergence and expansions of the *Manding*, the ancient inland sea had long dwindled and fragmented into the massive inland seas that came to define the region during the waning years of the last Ice Age.

Translated in *Manding*, the word *"Si"* (or *"Shi"*) referred to *"the race"*, probably relating to the *Manding* term *"Si,"* which was used as an ethnonym.[ccclxxiv] [57] *Manding* settling around the shores of the *Mauritanian Sea* intermixed with the ubiquitous *Si*, who spread westward from the central highlands. Early provinces of the *Si* were concentrated along the northern coasts and isles of the huge western inland sea and the interconnecting waterways emptying into the northern basin from the north, northeast, and central Sahara. The *Manding-Si* was the culmination of several centuries of intermixing and miscegenation between the *Manding* and *Si*. The *Manding-Si* arose to prominence over the ensuing millennium, subsuming the preeminence and hegemony of the ancestral *Si* in the inland seas.

As desert-like conditions transformed and slowly reclaimed the lowlands, *Manding-Si* clans spread into the highlands, forming loose networks of villages, with trade between the highland and coastal communities forming the foundation of the earliest kingdoms. The *Manding-Si* built several types of homes and villages; in the highlands, they built cliff dwellings and early masonry houses, while in the lowlands, near the coasts and waterways, they constructed large mounds, where they built circular huts made of stone and wood. The earliest Saharan kingdoms arose among the *Manding-Si* around the southern and western coasts of the *Mauritanian Sea*.

---

[57] Clyde Winters

Archaeological testimony supports that the *Manding-Si* were among the first peoples on the continent, outside the greater regions of the *Nile Valley* and *Punt*, to produce stone settlement civilizations. These were built on the rocky promontories of the Tichitt-Walata and Tagant cliffs of Southern Mauritania. The oldest farming and cultivations of sorghum, rice, millet, yams, and other grains were cultivated by the *Manding-Si* in the southern extent of their settlement range during this period. They employed forms of ancient agriculture and horticultural in long development, practice even at that early-stage antiquity. The archaeological findings and data suggest the *Manding-Si* migrated first north ...and then eastward.[58]

The northern highlands of the Atlas had been an early ancient province of the ancestral Si, whose clans and villages inhabited the highlands long before the emergence and expansions of the descendent *Manding-Si*. The *High Atlas* is the most northerly of Africa's mountains, with the whole of the Atlas range extending over one thousand miles across present-day *Morocco, Algeria,* and *Tunisia*. Three large mountain ranges make up the Atlas chain in the west; the *Anti-Atlas,* the *High Atlas,* and the *Middle Atlas*. The *Manding-Shi* initially came to inhabit the western foothills and highlands-western coast of the ancient *Mauritanian Sea.*

Eastern migrations of the *Manding-Si* seem to retrace the earlier western migrations of the *Ancestral Si*, the migratory paths which brought the *Si (Xi, Shi)* to the *Western Inland Sea*. Following the ancient path of their ancestors led the *Manding-Shi* to the *Northern Inland Sea*. Prompted by word of well-watered and fertile lands on the northern plateau and the broad fertile valleys of the *Fezzan*, the *Manding-Shi* migrated along the waterways linking with the large inland sea of the north, on the high plateau. During the long-wet periods of the pluvial, the Sahara became home to numerous rivers and shallow lakes, supporting rich flora and fauna along the river corridors connecting the inland seas. *Manding-Shi* clans pressed eastward along these waterways on boats made of papyrus and sewn-plank, with sails, settling intermittently around large lagoons and lakes.[59]

Northern Inland Sea: The Fabled Triton Sea

To the northeast was the large *Northern Inland Sea*, the present-day remains of which is a chain of large salt lakes that lay below sea level on the *High Plateau*. The High Plateau is really a great basin, stretching over six hundred miles eastward from *Morocco* to *Tunisia*, situated between the parallel ranges of the *Tell Atlas* to the north and the *Saharan Atlas* to the south. The floor of the *Plateau* descends into a series of depressions along its central axis, forming a chain of present-day salt-lake basins, which get progressively deeper from west to east, remnants of the ancient northern inland sea. The chain stretches eastward across the *High Plateau* through present-day northern Algeria at the western extent of the belt basins, leading to the *Mediterranean Sea* at the *Gulf of Gabes*, on the coast of present-day Tunisia, at the belt's eastern extent.[60]

---

[58] Winters 1981b:81

[59] Natiional Geographic published pictures of these prehistoric boats painted on cave walls in the Western Sahara.

[60] Swezey, 1996

The basins of the present-day chain of salt lakes (known as the "*Chotts belt*") consist of northern and southern chains of '*Chotts Lakes*', presently separated by the depocenter of *Chott Rharsa* in southern Tunisia.[61][62][ccclxxv] The southern chain is comprised of *Chott Fedja, Chott Djerd,* and *Chott Rharsa* in southern Tunisia, together with *Chott Melghir* and *Chott Merouane* in northern Algeria.[ccclxxvi] The northern chain of Chott Lakes includes *Chott Hodna,* the lowest in elevation of the northern Chotts, and *Chott Chergui, the* westernmost of the Chotts, in southern Algeria. From earliest through late antiquity, the entirety of the *Chotts Basins* was geologically aligned, forming the contour of the huge *Northern Inland Sea* that once occupied and conjoined the combined basins. An ancient *Northern Inland Sea* that covered a surface area of approximately two thousand six hundred square miles during most of antiquity.

Recent geological and tectonic studies in the area appear to support the findings that seismic activity in the region was ultimately responsible for shifting and delimiting the northern and southern basins of the *Chotts*. A deformation, mostly in northern *Algeria*, characterized by northwest-to-southeast seismic steeping in the northern range, associated with horizontal thrusting along the fault zones. High subsidence in the faults of the southern range, in turn, caused the southern and northern chains to move differently during the geological history, concomitantly falling out of alignment. The historical seismic activity in the region has been characterized by moderate to destructive magnitude events, over time accentuating the divergence between the northern and southern Chotts basins.[ccclxxvii][ccclxxviii]

At the end of the first *Mousterian Pluvial,* the combined basins of the aligned Chotts belt were inundated and flooded by intrusions of the *Mediterranean Sea* and conjoined into a large single inland sea, forming the deepest and second largest of the perennial Saharan Inland Seas of the era (ancient Seas that once occupied the basins of the northern, central, and western Sahara). Buttressed by the massive rains and drainage of the *Pluvial,* the *Northern Inland Sea,* which would later become known as the fabled *Triton Sea* of the classical era, attained broader scope, depth, and dimension.[ccclxxix] The confines and isles of the *Triton Sea* were, even at that early age, inhabited by numerous closely knit clans of the *Ancestral Si* (Xi, Shi), an ancient people who had long been prominent throughout the highlands and valleys of the Sahara.[ccclxxx]

The *Ancestral Si* (Xi, Shi) were the eldest and most pervasive of all the peoples in the Sahara, having migrated and settled throughout the habitable regions thousands of years before the onset of the *primal migrations*. Their early migrations from the *Central Sahara* brought with them a multifaceted yet ostensibly homogeneous culture and a diffusion of the early microlithic industries of the northern rift valley and eastern highlands into the *Northern Sahara*. A technology transference put to effective use in the adaptations required of habitation in the Sahara of the era. A protracted cold and arid climate blanketed the Sahara around 70,000 years ago, after the onset of their migrations, culminating in an arid maximum and intense cold phase that subsumed the region for thousands of years.[ccclxxxi]

---

[61] Also known as Chott Gharsa
[62] Rabia, 1985; Zargouni, 1985; Abdeljaoued and Zargouni, 1985; Fakraoui, 1990; Ben Ayed, 1993; Bouaziz, 1995; Hlaiem, 1999

Several dryers and wetter (*pluvial*) cycles were obtained for extended periods during the middle and upper paleolithic, with wet peaks during Mousterian (70,000-50,000 b.p.) and Aterian (35,000-25,000 bp) pluvial times. These were followed by fairly long hyper-arid phases (*Inter-Pluvial*) when conditions were very similar to those at present. During the height of the *Pluvial* and *Inter-Pluvial* periods, the highlands became virtual refuges for both animals and humans, providing greater safety from floods during the *Pluvial*, capturing more precipitation than the plains, and providing reservoirs of water and fertile habitat during the *Inter-Pluvial*. The heightening aridity and expanding desert-like conditions in the lowlands prompted mass migrations, setting in motion the eventual diaspora of the *Si* (or *Xi* (Shi)) across the *Northern Sahara* of earliest antiquity.

Shrouds of the Si (Xi, Shi)

They called themselves *Si* (or *Xi* (Shi)) people, though much of their origin is shrouded in mystery, with even the most ancient of legends and myths somehow intentionally misleading. Archeological findings suggest they are among the most ancient of peoples to have arisen in the Sahara and were, by all evidence, autochthonous to the *Central Saharan Highlands* of the *Ennedi, Tibesti, Tassili, Ahaggar, and Tadrart Acacus* Mountains, where hundreds of sites and thousands of ancient inscriptions, engravings and rock art have been discovered.

Their migrations into and permanent habitations in the sheltered confines of the highlands actually began thousands of years before the onset of the cold, bitter climate that enveloped the Sahara 70,000 years ago. Waves of migration were prompted into mobility by the heightening aridity and expanding desert-like conditions transforming the fertile savanna-like grasslands into all but barren terrain, barely able to sustain life.[ccclxxxii] Conditions in the Saharan lowlands became much as they were at the height of the later *Glacial Maximum,* with greater-than-present-day desert-like conditions expanding across much of lowland Sahara, waves of *Si* (Xi, Shi) pressed into the sheltered and still well-watered and fertile valleys of the highlands.

The early ancient *Si* (Xi, Shi) eventually established a network of villages, bridging and linking major settlement areas across the core highlands of the *Central Sahara*, a construct affording easy trade and technology transference. More efficient stone tooling techniques and industries emerged to greater use, enhancing capabilities, and aiding a measure of abundance, allowing early village settlements to flourish and clans to expand and settle throughout much of the central highlands. Tools have been unearthed throughout an area covering hundreds of miles within the highlands; ancient inscriptions, cave paintings, and carvings of the *Si* are scattered across almost all of the inhabited central Saharan highlands of the era.

Adaptation to the harsh, colder climate of the highlands culminated not only in tool innovation but also the evolution of physical features distinct to the highlanders, most notably the semi-straight hair textures of the ancestral *Si* (Xi, Shi), a purely (autochthonous Alkebu ("African") Negroid people. [ccclxxxiii] [ccclxxxiv] [ccclxxxv] Straight hair was an evolutionary attribute of the highlands, aiding in insolating from the cold climate blanketing the Sahara, particularly in the highlands during an era in which the ancestral *Si* (Xi, Shi) arose. Variants of their emblematic "Round Head" style rock art mark the settlement areas of the ancestral and descendant *Si* (Xi, Shi) as they expanded throughout the Sahara.

Ancient rock art in the *Ennedi* is said to represent the oldest depictions of the primordial culture of the highlands. Historian, Dr. Clyde Winters, has been able to decipher and identify inscriptions of the *Shi* ("*Si*") using analogous inscriptions of the *Manding-Shi* recorded by anthropologist Maurice Delafosse at the end of the nineteenth century, suggesting they first arose in the highlands where their inscriptions of the greatest antiquity are found.[63] [64] Rock art found in the *Ennedi* mountains is said to be the oldest evidence of Neolithic culture and industry in the *Sahara*. The *Ennedi* is mostly forgotten in the heart of the Sahara, extending between northwestern Sudan and northeastern Chad. The mysterious mountains and gorges of the *Ennedi* shelter secret river canyons and deep highland valleys of breathtaking beauty; the second largest natural arch in the world can be found in the *Ennedi*.

Situated in the *Sahelian* transition zone where high mountains abruptly rise from the great basins and plains of the Sahel and Sahara, the very height of the *Ennedi Massifs* creates an environment unlike that of the immediately surrounding region; in the highlands, water was not scarce, and desert sand does not dominate the soil structure. Remnants of ancient acacia forests can still be found in the *wadis* and *enneris* of the southern *Ennedi,* and crocodiles are still found in a few of the ancient pools in the river canyons; each relic of distant antiquity. The *Ennedi* are home to one of the last groups of Saharan crocodiles, as well as the last lions in the Sahara, who survived there until they became extinct, with the last seen in 1940.

The *Ennedi* contains many sandstone formations and natural arches, like the great *Aloba Arch*, which at a height of nearly 120 meters, is one of the most awesome natural arches in the world. The Rock Art in the central (and broader) Sahara goes through several phases, with the earliest depicting 'people' in the so-called '*Roundhead*' style. The older Roundheads look very much like black Africans, many with white paint showing sharply on the dark skin and clear Negroid profiles and hair.[ccclxxxvi] Ancient rock art tells us many things about the customs in an area at any given period; in this sense, it is a living representation of cultural transitions in a geographical context. Notwithstanding, the Rock Art in the Ennedi is among the least studied in the Sahara.

Highland Sanctuaries

The *Ennedi* consists of a succession of plateaus, rising in tiers from a base level of about 1,600 feet to elevations of 5,000 feet, forming a huge geographic triangle covering roughly 12,000 square miles of northwestern *Sudan* and northeastern *Chad*. The plateaus are ravined by many valleys, most of them deep ancient river valleys, with what were clearly once fertile grasslands found in virtually all the valleys of the plateaus. Ancient rock art has been found on the eastern side of the massif, with petroglyphs and rock paintings abundant throughout the whole area. Stone-age gravesites are plentiful in the highlands; indeed, artifacts uncovered in the highlands suggest the *Ennedi* as the starting point in their early ancient migrations of the ancestral *Si* (Xi, Shi).[65] Archaeological findings in the *Ennedi*, from the *Acheulian* through the *Aterian* periods, appear to depict the earliest continuity of *Si,* Xi, and Shi cultures.[ccclxxxvii]

---

[63] Delafosse, "Les Vai Leur Langue et Leur Systeme d"Ecriture," 1899
[64] Winters, 1983, 1986
[65] Winters 1979, 1997

Research conducted in the 1950s around the northwestern tip of the *Ennedi* discovered larger-than-life engravings of women at early ancient settlement sites such as *Niola Doa* in the northern highlands.[66] Other sites have since been discovered, explored, and studied along the outer rim, though no exhaustive inventory has been established. Nonetheless, what has been uncovered is a literal "gallery" of paintings, engraving, and inscriptions, by the hundreds, in the *Ennedi*, with new findings discovered each year.[ccclxxxviii] Recent research has provided radiometric dates, geo-archaeological strati-graphic sequences, and lithic assemblages, revising the chronological interpretation of the engravings, artifacts, and tool traditions in the highlands, finding them to be far older than conventionally held.[ccclxxxix]

The wet phase of the *First Mousterian Pluvial* was followed by a long hyperactive arid, sub-humid phase that enveloped much of the *Sahara*. The growing barrenness in the lowlands during the initial phases of aridity and drought prompted settlements to dwindle, and survival to once again depend on re-location into the sheltered confines of the highlands. From this period onward, tool advancement in the highlands, particularly the Aterian, show characteristics of the first industries of the upper Paleolithic.[67][68][69][70] Aterian tool traditions in the central highlands arose around the time of the migrations of the *Si* (Xi, Shi) into the highlands, while the Mousterian tool traditions appeared later, with descendent the *Si*, who would improve upon tools in the Aterian traditions.

During the long rainy periods punctuating the aridity, ancient lakes would recharge in the basins of the highlands and depressions of the lowlands. However, in the lowlands, even during the wetter periods, desert-like conditions prevailed, causing the lakes in the lowlands to quickly dwindle and vanish. Isolated lakes persisted in the cooler valleys of the highlands. One such ancient lake existed (and exists) in a huge crater-like valley (the "Ounianga Basin") between the *Ennedi Massifs* in the southeast and the *Tibesti Massifs* in the northwest; a lake known as *Lake Yoa*, the second largest of a handful of lakes in the ancient *Ounianga Basin*. The entire series of present-day lakes in the *Ounianga Basin* are remnants of a larger ancient lake, *Paleo-Lake Yoa*, which occupied the entire basin during the wet phase; a paleo lake recharged to near full prominence during the *Mousterian Pluvial* (50,000 BC and 25,000 BC).

Paleo-Lake Yoa

The *Ounianga Basin* is a large basin of over nineteen hundred square miles; archeologists and researchers have found numerous fossils in the basin. Flint tools dating back over 100,000 years have been discovered around the shorelines outlined by the huge lake once occupying the basin.[71][cccxc] During the last millennia, steadily blowing northeast trade winds have blown extended sand dunes into the large ancient basin, subdividing the once continuous freshwater lake into separate compartments, which presently host some fifteen lakes, covering a total surface area of thirty-two miles. At its height, *Paleo-Lake Yoa* filled and merged the lowest-lying depressions of the basin to form a huge lake replete with several islands, transforming the basin into a rich green valley filled with trees, grasslands, and a variety of wildlife.[cccxci] Settlements around the shores of the lake and on the islands occurred early and lasted for several millenniums.

---

[66] Bailloud1997
[67] Camps, 1973; Clark e t a l , 1973
[68] Maley e t al, 1971
[69] Mc Burney, 1967
[70] Werdorf, 1968
[71] Disoveries by French Paleontologist Yves Coppens in Ounianga-Kebir

Stone structures found on one of the islands of *Paleo-Lake Yoa* date back thousands of years, foreshadowing the culture of the emergent *Si* (Xi, Shi). A study of ancient pollen and aquatic organisms in sediments in the basin indicates that the sheltered valley and ancient lake yielded slowly and begrudgingly to the aridity subsuming the lowlands; a process taking over two thousand years after its onset; an ideal environment for the early habitations, development, and expansions of the *Proto-Si* (Xi, Shi). The *Tibesti Mastiff* to the west of *Paleo-Lake Yoa* and the *Ennedi Mastiff* are in precise geographical alignment to funnel and compress rising winds through the north-south corridor of the valley spanning the length between the two ranges. The corridor gradually narrows to a cone-shaped pass at its southern extent, creating a natural wind tunnel, intensifying the winds as they blow towards the *Bodélé* depression at the southern edge of the *Sahara*.

The winds become more intense as the distance between the mastiffs narrows, with wind tunnels forming over six hundred miles north of the pass. Similar winds swept through the corridors and across *Paleo-Lake Yoa*, with rising northeast wind currents contravening the southward flowing currents of the paleo-lake, which discharged at its southern extent. The winds and currents of the lake created an ideal environment to adopt the early sailing skills so aptly exhibited by the *Si* and for which would become so renowned in later periods. The shores of *Paleo-Lake Yoa* were fertile habitats for wildlife from the lowlands, making them also ideal hunting grounds for the *Proto-Si*, while the lake itself provided a wide variety of fish. The early ancient *Proto-Si* (Xi, Shi) appeared to maintain specific sites for specific purposes; base camps (residential) in the mountains, food procurement sites around the shores and on the isles of the lake, and workshops maintained elsewhere where needed. [cccxcii]

Researchers also uncovered and identified sites with seasonal occupation characteristics, some devoted to hunting, others to a gathering, and still others to the exploitation of mineral resources and tool workshops. Survival and technological skills during this period were high; the stone tools discovered in the highlands were versatile, generally used for processing, and exhibited homogeneity throughout the sites that have been studied. Pollen data from lake sediments indicate a mild tropical climate existed in the valley during the era, with wooded grasslands, ferns growing in the floodplains, and shrubs that now occur only on the high cool summits of the Tibesti Mountains growing in throughout the basin.

Erica pollen and the array of humid plant growth in the valley suggests a significant paleo-river discharging the highlands of the Tibesti to the northwest, flowing into *Paleo-Lake Yoa* until perhaps as late (or as recently) as 4,300 BC. The present-day *Tibesti* are rugged mountains where the poor grasslands, marshes, and mountainous terrain are remnants of the rich grasslands and rainforests that once covered these highlands. The *Tibesti Mastiff* is nonetheless all at once both alluring and visually impressive, its most prominent feature being the highest mountain in the *Central Sahara*, which rises abruptly from the floor of the *Chad* basin, beckoning early migrants from the valley between the *Ennedi* and *Tibesti*.

Central Saharan Highlands

The summit of the *Tibesti Mastiff* is the highest point in the Sahara, rising from the floor of the *Chad* basin to over 11,100 feet above sea level. The *Tibesti* is a giant triangular Massif covering over 38,000 square miles, with ancient rock art scattered across the whole of the habitable regions of its highlands. When the French (colonial troops) first explored the interior of the range (in 1914), they made absolutely no mention of the vast array of ancient artifacts and rock art spread throughout the highlands; it is inconceivable that it could have gone unnoticed.[72]

The Tibesti was clearly once a far more biologically productive range, with rain forests and large wild game, evidenced by the animals depicted in ancient rock paintings in the highlands. Inside the massif, rainfall is and was generally higher than outside or in the Saharan lowlands. The ancient interior had a far wetter climate, with many rivers and several large lakes. The aquatic character of the predominant fauna suggests surroundings that were once far damper, with a number of streams and rivers often in full flood. Huge volumes of water flowed from the highlands of the *Tibesti* during the *Last Great Ice Age*, carving and shaping an array of deep diverging canyons and river valleys, spreading and descending in all directions.

The grasslands surrounding the base of the *Tibesti* thus provided rich grazing and hunting grounds for wild game, with enlarged shallow lakes occupying the river pans, providing plentiful food sources from fish, large game, and aquatic plants. The *Tibesti* are actually a group of extinct volcanoes, with the backbone of the range in northern *Chad* and its northern slopes extending into southern *Libya*. While the range is crossed by many dried paleo-rivers descending the highlands, orbital radar satellite imagery mapping the major paleo-drainage systems, show a large, significant paleo-river, over five hundred miles long, with three large tributaries, flowing from the northeastern highlands of the *Tibesti* northward, through the lowlands intervening the *Tassili n'Ajjer,* meaning "Plateau of the Rivers."

Situated northwest of the *Tibesti*, the *Tassili Plateau* is part of the central Saharan divide between northward and southward flowing watersheds. It was this permanent availability of water that incented *Si* (Xi, Shi) migrations into the highlands. The *Tassili Plateau* is scared by ancient valleys, ravines, and wadis (or dry riverbeds), the skeletal remains of the well-watered, fertile highlands of the bygone era. The Si expanded throughout the habitable highlands, where rock art and archaeological sites aid in reconstructing key aspects of their migrations and expansions during the era. An impressive array of archaeological sites and prehistoric artifacts scattered between the *Tibesti* and *Tassili* clearly trace the migrations of the Si across the intervening lowlands into the highlands of the Tassili plateau.[cccxciii]

The *Tassili* is famous for rock art documenting the vivid scenes of everyday life during early antiquity in the highlands and depicting lowlands teeming with animals and rich in vegetation.[cccxciv] The plateau is renowned for bizarrely shaped rock formations, covered by a layer of iron-manganese-hydroxide, providing them both a protective shield and a renowned reddish-black tint, best known for the extensive rock art and paintings from the emblematic 'Round Head Era' of the *Si* (Xi, Shi). Early spiritual use of hallucinogenic plants to open gateways to other dimensions also arose in the *Tassili*. The use of hallucinogens as a source of spiritual inspiration is an ancient practice confirmed by archeological findings in the highlands.

---

[72] Tilho 1920

The oldest representations of hallucinogenics were of sacred mushrooms in the Tassili, where ancient rock art depicts polychromic scenes of harvest, adoration, the offering of mushrooms, and large godlike figures. The center of this style is in the *Tassili,* but examples are also found in the *Tadrart Acacus* and the *Ennedi.*[73] This Saharan testimony shows that the use of hallucinogens for spiritual enlightenment extends back in antiquity well beyond the Paleolithic and, further, that their use always took place and was primarily confined within rituals of mystic religious contexts. According to the infamous Henri Lhote, European "discoverer" of the *Tassili* frescoes, "it seems evident that these painted cavities were secret sanctuaries."

At least two species of entheogenic mushrooms frequently occur in the images at *Tassili* and *Acacus* mountains, with interest in hallucinogens typically represented within the context of medicinal mushrooms and herbs. Pollen examinations carried out at *Tassili* reveal that, during the *Round Heads* period, the area was vegetated by highland flora with the presence of coniferous trees and oaks.[74] The large mushrooms represented were indigenous to this wooded area in that they are associated with these species of tree. However, in addition to Psilocybin cubensis (mushrooms), rock images depict other psychoactive fungi, including Psilocybe cyanescens and Panaeolus spp.[75], though it is not easy to identify them in the rock art of the era. The biochemical characteristics of each determine the action of the human mind, and it either belongs to a flora that has disappeared or retreated to the Saharan basin, which later became a desert.

From the paintings, it would seem there are at least two species, one of which is small, topped with "papilla" images found in the Tassili and Acacus highlands, and the other symbolized in abstract by what the French called the *forme symbolique*g. A symbol that looks like a large tulip—a long stem topped by circles within circles. The use of hallucinogens is always depicted within a context of mystico-religious ritual and initiation, suggesting the presence of an ancient mushroom cult, with a complex differentiation between botanical species and related mythological representations. Since fungi are not able to be preserved as organic material over long periods of time, they and their fruiting bodies are almost never found during archaeological excavations. Petroglyphs are the only evidence of the lost culture; it was through ancient rock carvings that the "*Mushroom Cult*' was re-discovered. One group of rock drawings appears to be of pre-Neolithic early gatherers, in which mushroom effigies are repeatedly represented.

However, the most impressive is a scene of several different animals chased by hunters; in the lead, there is an antelope, a small, baby-like ghost figure floating over his back. Out of the scene rises a huge figure with outstretched arms and a white mask. His muscles are flexed, and on his stomach, an abstract symbol — a circle within a circle. These were the first vestiges of religious belief inscribed on the cliffs. Other rock engravings traced the migration northward from the highlands of the *Tassili.* Easy access into the *Wadi al-Hayat* on the northern edge of the massif made that wadi an important corridor for the groups of migrants pressing further north to the well-watered, fertile, and abundant lands surrounding the gigantic *Paleo-Lake Fezzan*...in the huge Fezzan basin. There the *Wadi al-Hayat*, known as the "*Valley of Life*," contains one of the richest concentrations of rock art along the ancient migratory corridors of the region, where an array of ancient engravings and pictorials depict migrations along the wadi well before, during, and for thousands of years after the *Last Ice Age*.

---

[73] Muzzolini, 1986:173-175
[74] AAW., 1986:97
[75] Gartz 1992

The *Tadrart Acacus* Mountains are the northernmost arm of the *Tassili-n-Ajjer* maintain range, anchored in the *Central Sahara*. Nonetheless, the *Tadrart Acacus* are unique and quite independent. The natural forces that shaped the *Tadrart Acacus* are visible in the mountains, and the societal forces that shaped the evolutions of the *Si* (Xi, Shi) are visible in the rock art of the highlands. Ancient rock art in the *Tadrart Acacus* creates a sort of mystical environment where the stories of antiquity can be read like a book. Millennia of winds and flashfloods have carved the mountains into bizarre shapes, with astonishing and innumerable natural arches spanning the base of the mountains. A prolonged wet period at the end of the Pleistocene, evidenced by the sedimentation in the highlands, aided in reshaping the hydrographic network of lakes and rivers discharging the highlands.[76]

Aided by extended periods of reproductive isolation, the *Ancestral Shi* emerged in the Central highlands as full-statured *Negroids*, with distinctive wavy, often straight hair, providing better layering, forming a more compact coat against the cold of the ancient highlands.[cccxcv] Archaeological finds in the earliest settlement areas reflect multi-functional, tool producing and using cultures extending throughout the highlands for over 20,000 years before the onset of the *First Mousterian Pluvial* brought an end to the long cold phase that blanketed the Sahara. Cold conditions along the Mediterranean coast from Cyrenaica continued to prevail from 50,000 BP to 43,000 BP when the *Würm Glaciation* advanced over much of *Northern Eurasia*, displacing the climatic zones of the northern hemisphere southward. As the temperate zones of the northern hemisphere acquired an 'arctic' climate, the rain bands typical of the northern temperate zones dropped to the Saharan latitudes; thus began the rains of the *First Mousterian Pluvial*.

The first *Mousterian Pluvial* was an extended Rainey period that brought a final end to the arid cold blanketing the Sahara. The *Pluvial* began around 50,000 years before the present ("BP") and lasted about 20,000 years to around 30,000 BP. The arrival of the Pluvial was the beginning of an extensive rainy and wet phase lasting for thousands of years; massive rains with the persistence and shaping force of water transformed much of the geographic features of the central highlands. During the earliest phases, the highlands became inundated, with highland basins and depressions (or "Wadis") transformed into lesser and greater paleo-rivers which once descended the highlands to re-charge the massive paleo-lakes and ancient inland seas of the lowlands. During the opening phases of the first *Mousterian Pluvial*, the watercourses of the central highlands quickly became filled beyond capacity, with the massive waters overflowing through the channels and river networks of the highlands to recharge and often re-shape the great paleo-lakes and huge inland seas of the Sahara.

The network of ancient lesser and greater paleo-rivers and lakes facilitated the spread and homogeneity of the *Si* throughout the settlement areas of the central highlands. The lowlands were again gradually transformed into vast savanna-like grasslands punctuated by woodlands, teaming with the wildlife of the era.[cccxcvi] The *Tadrart Acacus* approach heights of 5,000 feet above sea level and are bordered on the west by *Wadi Tanezzuft*, a deep valley-like ravine transformed into a large paleo-lake during the *Pluvial*, feeding an intricate network of rivers flowing from the central highlands to the lowlands. The *Tadrart Acacus* range is tilted slightly to the east, dissected by the ancient rivers descending the highlands.[77] The paleo-rivers of *Wadi Tanezzuft* cross the highlands and interconnect with *Wadi Teshuinat*, one of the main wadis where a number of ancient sites have been uncovered, several around the ancient shoreline of *Wadi Teshuinat* and the side wadis that branched off the main wadi.

---

[76] Carrara et al. 1998
[77] Cremaschi, 1998

There are over one hundred wadis within *Wadi Tashwinat*; its intricate network of caves provided shelter for thousands of years and are home to thousands of drawings and engravings depicting life in the highlands. *Wadi Tashwinat* is the largest wadi of the central *Tadrart Acacus and* is situated in the largest valley in the area. Over three hundred ancient settlement sites have been discovered in the valley, with tools of the 'Aterian Tool Tradition' uncovered at several sites and tools of the 'Mousterian Tool Tradition' discovered at other sites. A significant Aterian tool innovation of the era was the 'spear-thrower', a small length of wood with a notch at the back of the spear shaft, allowing greater power and accuracy in hunting; discoveries of large stores of animal remains attest to the success of the new technique.[cccxcvii][cccxcviii]

Paleo-Lake Fezzan

As the rains returned, clans of the *Si (Xi. Shi)* descended the *Tadrart Acacus* via the rivers formed by *Wadi Tanezzuft* as it discharged the massive waters of the first *Mousterian Pluvial* to the lowlands, an advent subsuming the *Fezzan* basin, bringing *Paleo-Lake Fezzan in*to renewed life and vigor. This was another aspect of the Saharan pump effect, prompting major inbound and outbound migrations of people and animals into and out of the most vulnerable regions of the Sahara as the climate shifted. Ancient rock art and engravings found in the Fezzan basin are said to be about 20,000 years old, although, according to informed sources, the dating processes need to be credibly and duly revised, extending the dating further back into prehistory. The Fezzan basin forms a large, closed depression, where one of the largest ancient lakes of far distant antiquity once occupied much of present-day southwestern Libya, along its borders with Niger and Algeria.

The Fezzan basin contains outcrops and shorelines recognized to have once formed the gigantic lake that anciently occupied and contributed to forming the basin, a lake known as *'Lake Megafezzan'*, a huge body of water the size of England that occupied the basin as late as 200,000 B.C.E.[cccxcix] The plateaus of the *Tassili* and *Ahaggar* mastiffs form the southern border of the huge basin. The massive basin is punctuated by interior mountains, uplands, and valleys, with the outline of the gigantic ancient lake marked by two huge rolling sand seas, dissected by the "Black Messaka" mountains northeast of the *Tadrart Acacus*. Archaeological research in the basin has uncovered the existence of several smaller paleo-lakes sharing the huge basin with an expanding Paleo-Lake Fezzan during the earliest phases of the first *Pluvial*. Archeologists confirm the small lakes emerged during the initial heavy rains in the basin and surrounding highlands during the opening of the first pluvial.

Prehistoric settlement sites containing an array of Aterian tool artifacts have been uncovered around the shores of many of these small paleo-lakes, many of which were in existence for thousands of years. *Paleo-Lake Fezzan* was but the last of several large palaeo-lakes that once existed in the Fezzan basin; its catchment basins linked navigable corridors across the expanse of the Sahara. Drainage of the massive waters led to an intricate network of interconnecting rivers and lakes, enabling Si (Xi) migrations across the central and northern Sahara. Where alluvial fans were situated on the boundary between two river catchments, their channels linked the adjacent rivers, allowing waters to flow from one basin to the next, aiding migrations of the Si (Xi) throughout the region.[78][79]

---

[78] Migrations Project team Kevin White and Nick Drake
[79] Paleoanthropologists Robert Foley and Marta Mirazón

The *First Mousterian Pluvial* reshaped the waterways descending the *Tadrart Acacus*, with *Wadi Tanezzuft* forming the most significant of the palaeo-rivers descending the watershed. Its ancient waters flowed northeast, emptying into the depression that formed huge *Paleo-Lake Fezzan,* around whose ancient shores rock art of the era still depicts memories of a time when large water-dependent animals such as hippopotamus and elephants thrived in abundant numbers throughout wetlands of the basin.[80 cd] Archaeological artifacts of the most recent discovery around the shores of Paleo-Lake Fezzan have been dated to the late Acheulean and Aterian periods (circa 100,000 - 30,000 BC.). Conclusively vivid scars tracing the ancient shoreline of *Paleo-Lake Fezzan* are still visible through satellite imagery, providing testimony to the size and dimension of the huge lake. [cdi]

Archeological investigations have uncovered settlement sites and artifacts around the shorelines of *Paleo-Lake Fezzan* dating back more than 75,000 years. Frequent overspills of the lake were a key mechanism linking catchment basins across the Sahara. Overflows fed a network of paleo-rivers linking smaller and larger lakes to the inland seas of the era. When *Paleo-Lake Fezzan* overflowed, its waters drained into the *Serir Tibesti River* that then linked the *Kufra River* via a giant fan connecting most of the fluvial systems of the lowland Sahara. Normal discharge of *Paleo-Lake Fezzan* was through a series of narrow river valleys, where its waters poured into a large Bay at the terminus of a huge river flowing northward …from the Tropic of Cancer

Tropic of Cancer

The *Ahaggar Mastiff* lies on the *Tropic of Cancer*, in the central Saharan uplands, northwest of the *Tassili,* where it forms a virtual shield, anchoring an alignment of great mastiffs that stretch across the heart of the Central Sahara. The *Ahaggar* alone is over thousand three hundred miles long from east to west and nine hundred miles wide from north to south. Prehistoric settlement is evident from extant rock paintings, and the *Ahaggar* still bares the distinctive scars of the once intricate network of ancient rivers and tributaries that arose and descended from its highlands. The present-day *Ahaggar* is deeply incised by the network of ancient wadis that once drained the waters of the pluvial from the highlands. The courses of two great paleo-rivers, now dry wadis, played prominent roles in the river networks and channels emanating from the *Ahaggar* and served as key arteries in the migrations and expansions of the *Si* across the Sahara of distant antiquity.

The *River Tafanasset* draining the southern highlands, flowed westward fully to the river *Niger*, while the *Igharghar River* draining the northern highlands, flowed northward to the *Chott el-Jerid*, bridging western and northern extents of the Sahara. The density of rock art pictograms and engravings and a large number of ancient settlement sites along the corridors of the ancient rivers reflect the significance of the Ahaggar as an early central locus of the ancestral *Si* (Xi). The *Tafanasset* and *Igharghar* rivers became early key corridors of settlement, migration, mobility, and trade across the central highlands and the western and northern Sahara. Although now mainly waterless, the Sahara still possesses the skeleton of ancient river networks of distant antiquity; much of it centered on the rivers and channels spreading out from the *Ahaggar*. Ancient rock art along the courses of the ancient waterways bear testimony to those who once inhabited and traversed these ancient corridors. The massive rains of the first pluvial reached beyond the *Tropic of Cancer*, enlarging and overflowing the highland rivers and lakes of the *Ahaggar*, opening connections between drainage basins that had theretofore been separated. [l]

---

[80] Cremaschi 2004

The *Ahaggar* mastiff is situated in a position that allows heavy rains to invade the interior highland valleys of the mountain range, where the unrelenting rains of the first pluvial caused massive flooding and a huge rise in rivers discharging the highlands. The *Tafanasset* and *Igharghar* were fed a web of highland (tributary) river valleys through which the waters of the pluvial descended, giving shape, form, and impetus to the two great rivers. Surrounding the *Ahaggar* are ancient sandstone plateaus cut into deep gorges by the rivers of the pluvial, as the massive waters flowing from highlands mobilized the hydrological network spread across the western and northern Sahara. When the *River Tafanasset* drained the southern highlands of the *Ahaggar,* its massive waters descended southward, flowing westward across what is now a *sand sea* to meet the *Lower Niger* at its western terminus.

The *River Tafanasset*, now a dried-up wadi, formed the ancient upper course of the *Lower Niger* during the pluvial. Ancient rock art along the route attests to migrations along the course of the river. The *Igharghar River* drained the peaks of the northern highlands of the *Ahaggar*, flowing through a deeply incised canyon to its headwaters between the *Tasili Plateau* and the *Irawen Mountains*. The ancient *Igharghar River* was the fabled *"Triton River"*, alluded to by *Herodotus* as flowing from the *Ahaggar* into *Lake Tritonis*. A historical representation of this paleo-hydrological system survives in the form of the *Piri Re'is* map of 1513. At the eastern end of the African portion of the map is an apparent mastiff, surrounded by rivers that flow in the four cardinal directions, a distinct reference to the central highlands where the *Ahaggar* anchors an alignment of mastiffs forming a *"fertile crescent"* across the central Sahara. A major *Nile* tributary of the era, known as the *Yellow Nile*, flowed eastward from the southern *Ennedi* to meet the *Nile* at the *Great Bend*, while the ancient *River Tafanasset* flowed westward from the *Tibesti* to connect with the *Lower Niger*.

In a much later reconstruction of the *Piri Re'is* map, Hapgood appropriately places the 'apparent' mastiff on the Tropic of Cancer, making it clear that this is the "Ahaggar" of the central Sahara; its existence must clearly have been known from ancient legend, rather from the European Age of Exploration. The *Ahaggar* is geographically close to the *Tassili,* with only a few hundred miles separating the two mastiffs. Some of the rock paintings of distant antiquity in the *Tassilli* actually depict and show the use of ancient boats, such as at the ancient sites at *Sefar* and *Aouanrhet*, clearly affirming the use of the crafts on the waters of the *Central Sahara* during earliest antiquity. A mere six hundred miles separate the *Ahaggar* highlands from where the *Igharghar River* flows northward through the huge Triton River Valley towards *Lake Tritonis*. The *Igharghar River* was indeed the fabled *"River Triton"* hypothesized by the ancient historian *Herodotus*. At its height, the *Igharghar* was the most prominent river in the ancient *Sahara*, more so than even the mighty *Nile* of the era.

Nonetheless, there remains a dearth of knowledge regarding the course of the *Igharghar* and the huge wadi hosting the ancient river, despite numerous explorations. Topographic depressions of *Wadi Igharghar* appear too large to have been formed entirely by a river, even a very large river, confounding the discovery of its ancient course. Nonetheless, the terminus of that ancient river today is a huge sand sediment, the *Great Eastern Erg*, one of biggest sand deserts in the world, a testament to thousands of years of alluvial deposits and the past prominence of the mighty northward flowing *Igharghar River*. Its ancient corpse, the now completely dry "*Wadi Igharghar"*, still extends over seven hundred miles from the *Ahaggar* highlands in the south to Chott el-Jerid, *Lake Triton* in the north. The *Igharghar* was over seven hundred eighty miles long and, in some places, nearly six miles wide; its perennial waters nourished the fertility of the lands surrounding its course, transforming the *Igharghar River Valley* into a vast paradise of fertility and abundance.[cdii]

The Triton River Valley

The *Si* (or *Xi* (Shi)) who settled in the valley made adequate use of local game and plant life and established seasonal settlements along the river corridors of the valley. Abandoning the safety and shelter of the highlands in phases, seasonal hunting campaigns and temporary settlement areas gradually gave way to permanent settlements along the floor of the valley and the course of the river. When the rains subsided around 70,000 years ago, the climate became more humid; this was during the ice age when snow still lay atop the peaks of the central massifs. Highland river tributaries still flowed down to recharge lowland rivers tributaries and minor lakes.

At the foot of the mountains grew cedars and hackberries, cypresses, junipers, oaks and olives, and occasionally birches, beeches, or lime trees. Countless archaeological remains, rock paintings, and engravings give witness to the former rich human life under such favorable ecological conditions. There were woods, shrubs, extensive areas of savanna, rich grasslands, vegetation, and thick fauna and foliage. Until finally, the snowcaps atop the massifs were depleted, and more and more often, the rains failed to appear. Rainfall anomalies occurred over a relatively short period. However, the weakening in the snowcap retention rates occurred over a long period and contributed disproportionately to the decline of the sizable river tributaries flowing from the highlands to the rivers flowing across the valley floor.

Minor rivers and tributaries dwindled and evaporated before reaching the *Igharghar River,* and the ever-mounting aridity and dry winds caused the grasslands and foliage to ultimately wither and die. Advents prompted the *Shi* to retreat to the plateaus where in the initial phases, the rains were still plentiful. From there, they retreated further into the mountains, their islands of sanctuaries in the midst of the mounting aridity in the lowlands. One of these islands was the *Tassili Plateau*, where the persistence of the wind-blown sand has worn surreal cities of rock out of the sandstone of the plateau, forming cave systems with narrow alleys, broad streets, bridges, pillars, rock cathedrals, and wide squares. An almost endless labyrinth about 5,000 feet up. Generations of *Shi* lived in these *'Cities of the Wind'* for thousands of years, leaving their marks on the sandstone walls.

Present-day nomads have ascribed names to each of the "Cities of the Wind": *Tin Tazarift, In Itinen, Tin Aboteka,* J*abbaren,* and *Auanrhet.* In the rock labyrinth of *Tinterhert*, adjacent to the middle of the *Igharghar River Valley,* there is a fifteen-foot-long engraving of a herd of cattle, connoting the highlander's adaption of pastoralism during the era, in addition to their traditional hunting, fishing, and gathering techniques. In a painting at *Jabbaren* - one of the most richly endowed *Tassili* sites - there are at least five people portrayed in a row kneeling with their arms held up before them in front of three figures, two of which are clearly anthropomorphous. A scene of adoration in which the three figures represent mythological divinities; the two anthropomorphous figures have large horns while the upper portion of the third figure, behind them, is shaped like a large mushroom, a testimonial to mystico-religious rituals and beliefs of the Seers and Priest of the mushroom cults.[cdiii]

Images of mythological beings of human or animal form cover the rock shelters of the high plateaus, which in some areas are so interconnected as to form true citadels with streets, squares, and terraces. Almost 100 miles from the cattle herds of *Tinterhert*, the persistence of the wind-blown sand has worn surreal cities of rock out of the sandstone of the plateau, cave systems with narrow alleys, broad streets, bridges, pillars, rock cathedrals, and wide squares; an almost endless labyrinth about 4,500 to 6,000 feet up. One of the most important scenes to be found at *Tassili* is in the labyrinth of *Tin-Tazarift*, in which a series of masked figures dressed as dancers are surrounded by long and lively festoons of geometrical designs of different kinds. This could be the most ancient ethno-mycological finding to the present-day depicting early religious ritual.

Each dancer holds a mushroom-like object in the right hand; two parallel lines come out of this object to reach the central part of the head of the dancer. It would seem that these lines - in themselves an ideogram that represents something non-material in ancient art - represent the effect that the sacred mushroom has on the human mind.[cdiv] Perhaps the most fundamental of all mushroom uses is the use of them as mediators to the Gods. It is this very aspect that trumps all other mushroom potentials in human culture. It is the essence of the spiritual link of man to nature and to the Gods. Many seers believe the visionary dream state induced by mushrooms allows them to contact spirits in the spirit world to gain knowledge about medicinal plants and how to treat illness and disease.

There seems to have been no clear dividing line between the Sages' prescription of spiritual or medicinal plants. These mushrooms can be distinguished by means of a complex system, every type having its own mythological representation.[81] According to the depictions of the many works of art left us, the *Shi* were gatherers of wild vegetal foods, "people who lived in a sort of Garden of Eden and who used mind-altering substances." In the valleys, there were perennially flowing rivers bordered by seed-bearing grasslands. Sacramental use of psychotropic mushrooms amidst the ever-growing abundance led to the creation of religious rituals and initiation under the careful oversight and tutelage of the emergent cult of spiritual Seers. The deepening of this eschatological dynamic goes back to the Palcolithic (the long period of the hunting of large game); there are several therianthropic images portraying the painter and the animals around him as one.

It is most likely that it is within these contexts, related to religious initiation, that the origins of individual specializations concerning the medicinal, therapeutic, and culinary aspects of herbs and vegetals first arose. Enlightened hunter-gatherers who had theretofore specialized in the hunting of animals, evidenced by the large number of prehistoric arrowheads discovered throughout the highlands, gradually became animal herders. Capitalizing on their familiarity and awareness of the habits of the local game, enabling a natural shift from hunter-fisher-gatherers to animal husbandry. They rapidly increased, keeping livestock once climatic conditions made it impossible to collect grains.[82] The ancient rock art in the region depicts herds of cattle and large wild animals in highland valleys where herds once roamed free and highland rivers still flowed freely.

---

[81] Samorini 1992, 69
[82] Proto-Saharan Civilization, by Dr. Clyde Winters

Geologically speaking, this was a major turning point in human history, marking the transition from hunter-gatherers to herdsmen. From this point forward, the *Si* (or *Xi* (Shi)) engaged not only in hunting, gathering, and fishing but also in livestock raising, as shown by cliff drawings in various parts of the highlands. The nourishing rains returned to the Sahara with the *First Mousterian Pluvial* around 50,000 years ago, and, like the rest of the Sahara, the extensive rains brought the *Igharghar River Valley* renewed life. The massive rains of the pluvial collected in the huge watersheds of the *Ahaggar* central highlands, from where the waters descended through a network of tributaries, ultimately conjoining to recharge the mighty *Igharghar River*. The *Ahaggar Plateau* is not inferior to the *European Alps* in the area; the Ahaggar range is part of the mid-Saharan Massifs that forms a huge shield across the central Sahara, where the massifs collected and channeled the huge waters of the pluvial into reinvigorating the mighty *Igharghar*.

The early ancient *Igharghar River* was once again joined along its long course by large tributaries descending the southwestern plateau through the drainage of the numerous river valleys of the *Tassili*, augmenting the waters of the *Igharghar* on its journey to the northern sea. The *Igharghar River Valley* was again transformed, becoming very well-watered and extremely fertile, with an abundance of grasses, grains, wild flora and fauna, and a variety of wildlife re-inhabiting the floor of the valley. The semi-sedentary fishing clans of the highland rivers and the hunter-gatherer clans of the highland periphery were the first to re-assume permanent rather than seasonal settlement along the floor of the valley. Early *Si* (Xi, Shi) settlement sites in the valley depict their exploitation of the surrounding habitat. Prehistoric pottery and baskets of the era uncovered in the valley were anciently used by women, the Si (Xi, Shi), to collect wild grains, as evidenced by the abundance of such discoveries at early settlement sites all along the floor of the valley.

After the fisher-hunter-gatherer clans came the artisan and craft clans from the 'cities of the wind' and the pastoral clans from the plateaus with their herds of livestock. What is now the *Wadi Igharghar*, an arid, desolate part of the Sahara, was then vast open grasslands broken by green hills, blue lakes, lagoons, and river tributaries. During the pluvial, the *Igharghar River Valley* bloomed like never before, not only in vegetation but also in expanded human habitation. Pastoralism and fishing preceded food production in the valley, attested to by ancient rock art in the region, affirming that the transition from hunting to raising livestock occurred before permanent human habitation resumed in the valley. Rock art depicting herds of cattle was first discovered in 1850.[cdv] Since then, many more drawings have been found; many of the animals depicted in the rock art no longer inhabit the region, having gone extinct. More recently discovered scenes show people in their daily activities, all in a very artistic and refined manner.

At first, they lived in small clans with between 30 and 100 family and extended family members. However, over the centuries, these clan and extended clan settlements expanded and merged into densely populated and defined community clusters along the course of the river. Adjacent grasslands were home to the nomadic pastoral clans and large herds of cattle, where today, enormous arid expanses of sand stretch for hundreds of miles. Ancient rock art along this sector of the valley shows hippos, crocodiles, elephants, and fishing, evidencing the once aquatic environment prevalent throughout the greater *Sahara*. With its massive waters and numerous tributaries, the *Shi* residing along the river transported and communicated mainly by boat. Rivers discharging the highlands formed a number of sizable tributaries snaking across the floor of the valley to join the *Igharghar*, creating a mosaic of semi-autonomous fertile habitats in the valley, where extended clans gradually settled.

Ancient tributaries crossing the valley floor to the *Igharghar* depict widely meandering courses, with signs of frequent flooding, where the tributaries often over-flowed their banks, transforming broad areas of the valley into well-watered hill and grasslands, inter-connected by streams and lagoons. These places served as ideal settlement areas; fishing clans settled along the banks of the river and its tributaries, building boats and habitation mounds safe from the numerous floods. Water resources were essential for the cattle herds of the semi-nomadic pastoral clans who settled in the grasslands. Scientists have found microscopic stains of dairy products on cooking pots from these areas dating back thousands of years.[cdvi] [83] The sedentary artisan and craft clans settled away from the marshlands, constructing clay, stone, or mud dwellings, forming the early villages of the valley. Investigation of several of the sites revealed a complex pattern of specialized settlement types, including living sites, primary and secondary workshops, and primary and secondary butchery sites. Specific types of sites were closely related to the local landscape.[cdvii]

The ancient *Igharghar River* (the fabled *"Triton River"*) was nearly six miles wide in places, with strong current and several islands scattered along its northwestern course. In the tradition of the *Si* (Xi, Shi), each community cultivated groups of astute boat architects and builders and a cadre of expert sailors to ply and fish these waters. Those early *Si (Xi, Shi)* sailors were the ancestors that would be later renowned as the ancient *"Fish and Reed-Boat Navigators"* of earliest antiquity. It was they who plied and fished the immense open waters of the mighty *Igharghar River,* establishing fishing villages and later permanent settlements on the islands along the northwest course of the river. These settlements played a significant role in the migrations and settlements of the *Si (Xi, Shi)* beyond the confines of the *Igharghar River Valley* (the fabled *"Triton River Valley"* of later Greek mythology). At its northern terminus, the ancient *Igharghar River* emptied into a gigantic estuary, a huge body of water known in Greek mythology as *"Lake Tritonis."*

Legendary Lake Tritonis

Lake Tritonis was a huge estuary, fed in part by the discharge of the *Igharghar River*, which emptied into the estuary at its southern extent. By definition, an Estuary is where a freshwater river meets the sea, and the saltwater of the sea mixes with the freshwater of the river, resulting in somewhat salty water, not as salty as that of the sea. Estuaries form transition zones between riverine and maritime environments and are subject to the influences of each, such as tides and the influx of salt water, and riverine inflows of fresh water. Many downriver valley estuaries were formed during the pluvial as rises in sea levels flooded low-lying interior basins, in some instances creating habitable islands of submerged mountains within the flooded basins.

The confluence of both sea and fresh water in these environments provides high levels of nutrients and sediment, making downriver estuaries among the most productive natural habitats in the world, beckoning the expeditions and expansions of the *Shi*. While the precise location of *Lake Tritonis* is a matter of debate, it is increasingly acknowledged that the huge shallow lake in every way resembles and is fittingly identified, in both characteristics and location, with the combined basins of *Chott El-Fedja* and *Chott El Jerid*. The vast present-day salt lakes lying below the sea level, appropriately situated and postured in the northern Sahara, *Chott El-Fedja* and *Chott El Jerid* are the first in a chain of present-day salt lakes extending to the Gulf of Gabes, on the coast of present-day Tunisia.

---

[83] African Archaeological Review, Volume 5, Number 1 (1987),[49-63, DOI: 10.1007/BF01117082]: Recent work on the Middle Palaeolithic of the Eastern Sahara; Fred Wendorf, Angela E. Close and Romuald Schild

The huge depression formed by the combined basins of *Chott El-Fedja* and *Chott El Jerid* is continuous, stretching over one hundred twenty miles from west to east; *Chott El Jerid* has an elongated arm in the form of *Chott El-Fedja,* extending eastward to the *Gulf of Gabes*. Several large paleo-rivers discharging the *Tadrart Acacus* and *Paleo-Lake Fezzan* emptied into the huge estuary along its eastern coasts. As did several smaller but less significant paleo-rivers discharging the *Aurès* at the eastern extent of the Atlas. Paleo-Lake Fezzan also emptied into the huge estuary through several large paleo-rivers flowing westward through a series of long ancient fluvial valleys along the western rim of the Fezzan plateau.

Present-day *Wadi* banks mark the ancient courses of the rivers through the long fluvial valleys, then connect *Paleo-Lake Fezzan* and *Lake Tritonis*. The *Wadi* banks are deeply incised into the bedrock, allowing narrow canyons upstream, then widening along the lower part of their courses, where *Wadi* bottoms become flat, containing ancient fluvial sediments that geo-archaeological data confirm relates to the hydrographic activity of the pluvial when the discharging rivers of *Paleo-Lake Fezzan* fed the huge estuary along its eastern coast. [84] Triton River clans settled along the southern and western coasts of *Lake Tritonis*, while clans from the *Fezzan* basin and the *Aurès* and *Tadrart Acacus* highlands settled along the northern and eastern coasts of the ancient estuary.

The settlers and settlements from the highlands to the north and west, and those from the western river valleys of the *Fezzan*, together with those of the *Triton River Valley*, placed *Lake Tritonis* at the center of one of the earliest nautical crossroads of distant antiquity. Rising cultural influences within the huge lake were centered on its two islands and coastline characterized by a large peninsula in the west, lagoons of varying sizes, and expanding village clusters in the Deltas at the mouths of the larger and lesser rivers flowing into the huge lake. Ancient *Lake Tritonis* was home to two islands that would play significant roles during the classical era, the isles of *Phla* and *Mene*.[cdviii]

According to Greek mythology, Athena, the "Goddess of Wisdom," was born beside *Lake Tritonis*. The *Periplus of Skylax* says: The Islands in this Lake were also associated with the *Holy Spirit of Amun*, the deity representing the flowering life force, which is hidden and established in the primordial ocean (waters) of consciousness. [85] One can still see erosion patterns on the valleys and lake beds of the Chotts, patterns left by early ancient *Lake Tritonis,* together with relics of distant antiquity from the lush lands that once thrived around the shores of the ancient lake. Two intervening factors aided the seas in flowing freely through the Gulf of Gabes during and after the *Last Great Ice Age*; these being the closing of the *Black Sea* as global sea levels declined and isostatic subsidence along the North African sea coast caused by glacial loading.[cdix cdx]

As global sea levels fell during the initial phases of glacial loading, the Black Sea became increasingly isolated and ultimately land-locked. As Mediterranean sea levels fell below the elevations of the Dardanelles and the Bosporus, the Black Sea gradually but ultimately became completely cut off from the Mediterranean, depriving the Mediterranean Sea of a key and significant outlet in the Black Sea basin.[cdxi cdxii] To the south, as sea levels fell, proximal glacial loading in the Atlas mountains resulted in isostatic subsidence along the North African coastal sea bed, lowering the *Gulf of Gabes*, allowing the diverting tidal flows of the Mediterranean to first gradually and then freely flow through its narrow corridors into *Lake Tritonis*, and ultimately into the great northern inland sea, the fabled Triton Sea.[cdxiii]

---

[84] Zerboni et al.,2011
[85] Nordenskiöld, 1897

By the middle of the First Mousterian Pluvial, *Lake, Tritonis* was near full size and dimension, with clans of the *Si* settling around its shores and inhabiting its islands. During the rise of the Mediterranean Sea through the Gulf of Gabes, tidal surges flooded Lake Tritonis, with natural geographical features such as the large islands at the entrance of the Gulf protecting the huge estuary from the full forces of the sea.

Watergate at Gabes

The Gabes drainage system was far larger during the earliest antiquity than at present; the ancient architecture of the channelized bodies and depositional facies indicate high-magnitude flood events, such as major sea tides, passed into the basins of the Chotts during the earliest antiquity. The confluence of the massive rains of the *Mousterian Pluvial,* and the increased glacial melt released by the rains, together with the foreclosure of the *Black Sea* basin as an outlet for the rising waters of the *Mediterranean Sea*, and finally, the delayed isostatic rebound from reduced glacial loading in the *Atlas*, combined to open a *Water Gate at Gabes*; through which the massive discharging waters of the Mediterranean Sea flowed freely into the then aligned basins of the Chotts.[cdxiv][cdxv]

The *Mediterranean Sea* connected with *Lake Tritonis* through two canal-like channels at the mouth of a huge estuarial harbor. Northern and southern channels, straddling an island at the mouth of the *Gulf*, stretched eastward for several miles before discharging the waters of the *Mediterranean* into the Estuary at the eastern extent of *Chott Fedjadj*. Chott Fedjadj is actually a narrow extension of the much larger *Chott Djérid*, forming the eastern extremity of the Chotts basins.[cdxvi] Inundation of the *Chotts* required only the flooding of an isthmus about thirteen miles wide and 150 feet. High, between the *Gulf of Gabes* and *Chott Fedjadj*.

The basin of *Chott Fedjadj* extends southwestward into *Chott Djérid,* which, in turn, is separated from the basin of *Chott Rharsa* by only a narrow ridge. *Chott Rharsa* is succeeded westwards by a series of depressions extending to the basin of *Chott Melrhir*, which is then separated from *Chott Meorouane* to the southwest by a stripe of dry land as narrow as two and one-half miles in places. The dramatic rise in sea level submerged the intervening surface areas, transforming hills and higher areas into islands and peninsulas in the newly forming northern inland sea. Nearly twelve cubic miles of water gushed through the channel, inundating over a mile of newly formed shoreline a day.

The waters of the *Mediterranean Sea* poured through the channel, raising the ancient inland seas about a foot a day, inundating, and spreading surface waters over the lowlands and around the intervening higher ground of the then-aligned basins of *Chott Hodna* and *Chott Chergui,* westernmost of the Chotts basins, in southern Algeria. The rising waters inundated the chain of lake basin on the *Chotts Plateau*, bringing to life the ancient *Northern Inland Sea*, the fabled Triton Sea of later Greek mythology. The chain of lake basins on the *Chotts Plateau* was rather quickly overwhelmed, on a geologic time-scale, with the waters of the *Mediterranean* eventually breaching the southern banks of *Chotts Melghir* and *Meorouane* in the east and *Chott Hodna* in the west, sending cascades of seawater southward into the huge basins of the central and western Sahara.[cdxvii]

Much of the Saharan central lowlands are below sea level, with its major aquifers comprised of three great basins; the *central basin*, the most extensive of the three, encloses the *Great Eastern Erg* and is limited on the east only by the *Hamadah Hamra*. Beyond which is the *eastern basin,* which was largely unaffected by the rising waters at *Gabes*. To the west is the *central basin,* bounded by the *Mzab Dorsal,* which was transformed into a peninsula within the *Saharan Inland Sea* of the era; beyond which are the *western basins* and low-lying depressions, dominated by the basin of the *Great Western Erg,* the *Foggaras,* the *Juf* depressions, and the huge *Mauritanian-Sénégal Basin,* near the western edge of the Sahara.[cdxviii][cdxix]

As the basins of the central lowlands were overwhelmed, the rising waters drained westward, joining the waters descending from *Chott Hodna,* flooding and eventually submerging the western basins and depressions. The central and western basins were eventually all but completely flooded and fully inundated, forming the greater proportion of the ancient Saharan Inland Sea (the fabled "*Atlantean Sea*" of later legend), bounded on the south and east by the *Ahaggar* and *Tasili* mastifs, and on the north and west by the *Atlas* mountains. The huge *inland sea* covered much of the northern, central, and western Sahara for thousands of years. Its cresting waters eventually found an outlet to the *Atlantic Ocean* and formed a Delta at the lowest point on the West African Seaboard, on the southern coast of present-day *Mauritania*.[86] For thousands of years, the huge *inland sea* connected the waters of the great eastern ocean (the "Atlantic") with those of the external northern sea (the "Meditterean"), rendering the *Atlas Mountains* perennially surrounded on all sides by water.

The Parables

The most ancient of myths attest to accounts in which the oldest of all deities, *Neith*, brought forth the first land from a 'primeval ocean' called *Nun* (the primeval waters of chaos).[cdxx] *Nun* is deemed the source of all that appears in the differentiated world, encompassing all aspects of divine and earthly existence. Legends hold that in the beginning, there was nothing more than the watery mass "*Nun,*" from which the *Divine Spirit, "Neith",* arose; described as the "*Virgin Mother Goddess"* who came to be in the beginning and caused everything to come to be... [cdxxi][cdxxii]

Neith is described as the feminine aspects and personification of the primeval waters of *Nun*, which, in an undifferentiated fashion, personifies and encompasses the masculine aspects that enable her creative aspects to function. Ancient texts describe *Neith* as the active element that causes creation, utilizing her powers to permeate the inert and void qualities of *Nun,* giving rise to living, formed matter. *Neith* is the personification of the first conscious *Act of Creation* from the *Void;* it was she who took the engendering potentials of a *Nun* and caused creation to begin.

Everything in creation emanates from *Nun* and expresses in the form of elements in succeeding levels of denseness. These elements also manifest in the form of the opposites of Creation, man-woman, up-down, and white-black, which appear to be exclusive and separate from each other but are, in reality, complements of each other. Causing matter to exist and to live is the fundamental nature of *Neith's* role in creation; ancient legends report accounts of Creation in which *she* brought forth the first land from the primeval waters of chaos.[cdxxiii]

---

[86] Western Senegal, West Africa; Abdoulaye DIOP - Départment de Géologie, Faculté des Sciences et Techniques Université Cheikh Anta Diop, Dakar, Senegal.

The primordial waters of chaos covered the earth during the reign of *Neith* (Nunet), the *Virgin Mother*, who is said to have been "born the first, in the time when as yet there had been no birth.[87] Ancient legends record that *Neith* (Nunet), whose very name may be interpreted as symbolizing the existence of *God* before creation, was the first to emerge from the primeval waters of *Nun* to give expression and bring creation to the world.[cdxxiv]

As recently as 30,000 years ago, at the end of the first pluvial, the Sahara was partly covered, once again, by remnants of the huge perennial Saharan Inland Sea of earliest antiquity (the fabled "*Atlantean Sea*") that once emptied into the great eastern ocean (the present-day "Atlantic Ocean"), on the coast of West Africa'. Outcrops of the northern, central, and western Saharan basins outline the immense size and structure of the ancient inland seabed once occupied by the *Atlantean Sea*. To the north, the land rises in a series of escarpments, and as the waters of the *Atlantean* gradually drained into the deeper basins of the eastern ocean, vast swaths of land began to re-emerge, first in the north and then increasingly across the Saharan lowlands.

Howsoever, the great perennial inland sea did not go peacefully into the passages and fables of earliest antiquity; it was revived and reinvigorated on several occasions for comparatively shorter and shorter periods by the fading rains of the pluvial and the still massive waters flowing from of the watersheds of the *Tassili* and *Ahaggar* highlands. As the waters of inland sea fluctuated, some areas emerged and were then re-submerged again, only to re-emerge over the long passage of time. Over time, the immense waters of the *Atlantean Sea* finally gradually receded, eventually fragmenting into the huge Northern and Western Inland Seas and the lesser residual salt lakes and marshlands occupying the low-lying depressions of the northern, central, and Western Sahara.

From an archaeological perspective, early arrivals "into" and "out of" *West Africa* during the era are of particular importance in understanding key aspects of 'east-to-west' and later 'west-to-east' cultural transmissions in terms of both the geographical extent and sociological impact during early antiquity. The topography of the migration routes to the fertile coastal lands surrounding the western inland sea is marked by a high density of ancient drainage networks, supporting the headwaters of large ancient river systems. Several archaeological sites, including rock shelter areas with a rich diversity of paintings, burial sites, and other evidence of human habitation in the era, have been uncovered near the ancient river system.

With the reinvigoration of the vast but intricate network of remnant and interconnected rivers and waterways crossing the Sahara of the era, those who could harness the powers of the water currents and were knowledgeable about navigation became the great explorers and masters of the era. In many places, large paleo-rivers flowed into depressions where they formed delta systems that fed lakes and playas with both inflow and outflow channels, providing navigable ingress and egress waterways linking the greater and lesser lakes with the huge northern and western inland seas. Having early-refined skills in celestial navigation, mariners of the Si (Xi, Shi) were the first of the ancient explorers and traders to ply the waterways of the Sahara and the first to bridge the northern and western inland seas.

---

[87] Creation Records, p. 176;. George St. Clair, (London, 1898)

Rise of the Atlas

The *Atlas Mountain* range is actually a series of sub-ranges, trending southwest to northeast, stretching from the highlands of the *Anti-Atlas* in southern Morocco to the heights of the *Grand Atlas* in northern Morocco. The range turns eastward for over twelve hundred miles, from its northwestern extent in northern *Morocco* to its northeastern extent in eastern *Tunisia,* forming the geologic backbone of North Africa. Morocco is dominated by four of the six sub-ranges that comprise the ancient *Atlas Mountains,* the *Anti-Atlas* in the south, the *High Atlas* and the *Middle Atlas* in the north, and the *Rif* mountains in the north. As the impact of the waning rains and mounting aridity became increasingly encroaching, towards the end of the *First Pluvial*, migrations into the sheltered and still well-watered valleys of the *Atlas* ensued en masse from the lowlands. The paleo-river valleys of the ancient *Atlas* were important factors in the migrations and settlements in the highlands. Several large paleo-rivers discharging the *Anti-Atlas* and *High Atlas* provided fertile areas for permanent re-settlement and expansion; the *Souss River Valley* was one such area.

The *Souss* is an ancient river rising from the *High Atlas* from where it flows westward into the *Souss Plain* of southern *Morocco*, an area sheltered from the encroaching aridity of the lowlands by the shielding heights of the *Anti-Atlas*. The hot, arid winds of the lowlands at the end of the *First Pluvial* were foreclosed from ascent into the highlands by the *Sahara*-facing slopes of the *Anti-Atlas;* as the hot air climbed the windward slopes, it expanded and cooled until it became saturated with vapor, creating a blanket of moist air up the windward slopes; moisture condensing as rain or snow in the highlands, releasing the latent heat. The *Souss* plain of the era was characterized by a semi-tropical climate, where rainfall was plentiful, especially in its coastal area, which is bounded by the *Atlantic Ocean* at the west, the *High Atlas* in the north, and the *Anti-Atlas* in the southwest. The *Souss River Valley* is situated where the *Anti-Atlas* and *High Atlas* parallel each other from southwest to northwest, with the fertile *Souss-Massa Plain* nestled between the two mountain ranges in the southwestern *Moroccan* highlands. The *Souss-Massa Plain* of the era was an ideal environment for clan re-settlements and growth in the highlands of the era.

Geologically the *Souss-Massa Plain* is an alluvial basin and, as such, remained well-watered and irrigated after the end of the first pluvial. There are still remnants of the large forests of the ancient *Argan* trees endemic to the highlands scattered along the valley. Moroccan *Argan* trees are still valued for their exotic and medicinal oils; the ancient forests of the *Souss* were home to a wide variety of species.[cdxxv] The oil extracted from the fruit of the tree has several medicinal properties and is known to enhance immunity against infections and diseases and provide relief from joint pain.[cdxxvi] There is a nut inside the fruit, with an extremely hard shell, usually containing one to three almond-shaped kernels. The nuts were collected to extract the oil; what remained was fed to the cattle, and the leftover shells were used for heating. Nothing was wasted. Argan trees live much longer than olive trees and require no cultivation; forests of the ancient trees were a valuable resource during and after the close of the first pluvial.

The *Souss Valley* remained green and fertile after the end first pluvial and the heightening and encroaching aridity from the lowlands, particularly around the sediment-laden banks of the river, whose waters flowed unabated from the rain, snow, and glacial melt in the *High Atlas*. The summit of the *High Atlas* forms a broad barrier to moisture and air masses from the Atlantic, capturing and releasing their humidity on the northern slopes in the form of snow and rain to the benefit of the highland valleys. The *Anti-Atlas* is a lower mountain range than the *High Atlas*, forming the upper catchment of *Morocco's* longest river, the *Drâa.*

The *Drâa River* rises in the *High Atlas,* at the confluence of the *Dadès* and *Imini* rivers, from where it first flows southeastward and then turns westwards into southern Morocco, from where it once flowed into the *Atlantic,* at the ancient mouth of the river, opposite the *Canary Islands*. During the waning era of the first pluvial, several large but less significant paleo-rivers zigzagged down the eastern slopes of the *Anti-Atlas,* in northern *Mauritania* and southern *Morocco*, providing migratory and settlement corridors into the highlands for clans from the southwestern coastal belt of the *Mauritanian Sea*. Migrations and re-settlements in the highlands during the era are evidenced by the vast array of rock art and petrographs scattered across the foothills and highlands between northern *Mauritania* and southern and northern *Morocco*. The oldest is dated to about 35,000 years ago, coinciding with the closing era of the first pluvial. The *Drâa River Valley* was a major resettlement area in the southern *Moroccan* highlands during this era, again evidenced by the array of rock art, artifacts, and petroglyphs.[cdxxvii]

The greater *Drâa* basin is actually an immense catchment system stretching across Morocco into Algeria. The upper and middle catchments are located between the southern margin of the central *High Atlas* and the *Anti-Atlas.* The valley in between drains the surrounding plateaus, and, after merging with the *Dades River,* at the junction of the three rivers in the *Ouarzazate River Valley,* the *Drâa River* flows nearest the Sahara and the ancient coastal belt of the *Mauritanian Sea.* The *Drâa* River then turned southwestward, flowing from southeastern Morocco to the *Atlantic*.[cdxxviii] The benefits of the amalgamating clans were first and most pronounced in the *Drâa Valley,* where almost 300 sites have been discovered and are now known, although few have been fully studied.

In the absence of radiocarbon or another dating, the only clues to the chronology of the rock art and engravings come from datable material objects; nonetheless, the findings point to a definite cultural homogeneity over the broader Saharan complex. None of the art is thought to be no older than the era of *North-African* antiquity starting about 30,000 BCE. The distribution of sites in the western highlands can be roughly divided into two areas, those in and adjoining the *Anti-Atlas* to the south and those in and adjoining the *High Atlas* to the north. The rock art and burials in both the south and north portray a direct continuity with the wider central Saharan cultural complex of the era, analogous to the marking of the early migrations of the ancestral *Si*.

Early village sites in the *Atlas* appear increasingly more numerous and larger, with increased density in the innermost valleys nearing and approaching the end of the first pluvial. Ancient shaping tools of the era discovered in the region demonstrate a considerable degree of ability. Flint, cut into pieces that can be thin, sharp, and strong, replaced the hard rock of the previous period, the lava and quartzite, which were difficult to carve. One theory suggests that the population growth of the era in the highlands was aided in large part by the improved tools and weaponry of the hunters: making them more efficient and far more productive. Examples of tools produced using the new materials and techniques were fine blades, scrapers, and improved hunting weapons.

Early industry included ensembles with and without hand axes, cleavers, chopping tools, and small finely crafted instruments and cutting tools. Agriculturalism in the highlands spread eastward with the influences of the *Manding-Si*, while refined tooling and pastoralism were the inheritance of *Ancestral-Si*, spreading westward with their earlier migrations. The Discovery of the necropolis of *Rouazi* in the present-day region of *Skhirat*, on the *Atlantic* coast of *Morocco*, has proved of particular importance in demonstrating the features and prosperity of the mixed economy of agriculturalism, pastoralism, hunting, and fishing and its expansion throughout the *Atlas* during the period.

The *High Atlas* is where the highest mountain peaks are situated and form the intricate drainage basins that feed the vast network of rivers descending to the lowlands. North of the *Middle Atlas,* the *High Atlas* is separated by the *Moulouya* and *Oum Er-Rbia Rivers*. The *Middle Atlas* is the westernmost of the three northern chains, which together surround a large, plateaued basin that trends east-west into the Algerian highlands, where the eastern extension of the *High Atlas* forms the backbone of present-day *Algeria* and *Tunisia*. Most rivers in the *High Atlas* flow westward toward the *Atlantic*, creating rich, fertile east-west trending valleys in the temperate northern highlands. Two major paleo-rivers of the era, the *Ziz,* and the *Rheris,* flowed eastward into the Sahara, providing convenient entrance into the highlands for clans clustered along the northern coastal belt of the *Western Inland Sea.* The *Ziz* rises in the *Middle Atlas* in *Morocco*, from where it flows over one hundred sixty miles through southern *Morocco* and *Algeria* and ultimately into the *Sahara,* where it once emptied into the northern basins of the ancient *Mauritanian Sea.*

The river valley corridor of the *Ziz* was an active route into the highlands, while the *Valley of the Rheris* became more broadly settled, with numerous settlements, even as others pushed through the valley into the highlands. Remnants of the ancient cedar forests that filled the highlands during the migrations of the era still cover much of the *Middle Atlas;* the geography of the highlands is still defined by large mountains dissected into the valleys and plains into which the clans settled and found sanctuary. The steep cliffs and long ridges of the *Aurès Mountains* to the south create an almost impenetrable refuge. The *Rif* Mountains to the north, a sub-range of the *Tell Atlas,* stretch eastward, paralleling the *Mediterranean* coast, where the mountains enclose the *Atlantic plains*, catching the rainfall blown in on the winds of the *Atlantic Ocean.* The eastern ranges of the *High* and *Middle Atlas* take the shape of an extended oblong, stretching eastward over one thousand miles from present-day *Morocco* through *Algeria* to *Tunisia,* enclosing a vast complex of plains, grasslands, and plateaus.

Once in the highlands, the pastoral clans spread into the rich, well-watered grasslands, from where they then expanded onto the *Atlantic plains*. Some of the first rock engravings of *North Africa* were actually discovered in this area, on the northeastern *Algerian-Moroccan* border, particularly on the mountainous ridges of the *Figuig* and *Ksours Mountains*.[cdxxix] The *Figuig Mountains* are part of the continuation of the *High Atlas;* it is through the *Ksours Mountains* that the *High Atlas* joins the *Saharan Atlas* to the east. To the west, in north-central Morocco, a narrow ancient mountain pass known as the "*Taza Gap"* runs east-west between the *Middle Atlas* ranges, linking present-day *Algeria* and *Morocco*. Pastoral clans moving into the highlands spread westward through the *Taza Gap* onto the Atlantic coastal plains. Others moved eastward into the foothills and valleys of the *Tell* (or "*Maritime"*) *Atlas*.

The northern coast of the *Tell Atlas* parallel the *Mediterranean* with a narrow belt of foothills and plains, once heavily forested with cedar, pine, and cork oak trees. In the south, the *Tell* parallel the *Saharan Atlas*, with the two ranges trending east-west, separated by the *Plateau of the Chotts,* anciently known as the "*High Plateau."* The *Saharan Atlas* forms the sixth chain of the *Atlas Mountains* complex, arising to the south and leeward of the *Tell Atlas*. The *High Plateau* extends westward from the *Gulf of Gabes* (on the present-day Tunesian coast) at its eastern extent, stretching westward across present-day *Algeria,* bordered by the *Tell Atlas* on the north and the *Saharan Atlas* on the south, reaching just beyond the present-day border of Morocco, at the plateau's western extent. The floor of the plateau descends into a series of east-west trending lakebeds (or *'Chotts'),* forming a huge depression along the central axis.

The present-day *Chotts* basins still descend nearly seventy feet below sea level at their lowest point, reminders of the large navigable inland sea that once occupied the combined basins on the *High Plateau*. Following the end of the *First Pluvial*, the *Northern Inland Sea* (the fabled *"Trident Sea"* of later Greek Mythology) stretched over two hundred fifty miles westward from the *Gulf of Gabes* to its western extent just east of present-day *Biskra*. Along the southern border of the *High Plateau* are the *Saharan Atlas*, a far higher range than the *Tell Atlas*, which borders the plateau on the north. The *Tell Atlas* create a broad mountain shield capturing the moist winds and rains blown southward from the Mediterranean Sea while simultaneously acting as a natural barrier to the aridity rising from the deserts to the south. By virtue of this arrangement, the three sub-ranges of the *Saharan Atlas* receive far more rainfall than the *Plateau*, with the continual drainage of the mountains flowing mostly northwards to the *Plateau* and the basins once occupied by the *Northern Inland Sea*. Large river valleys descending the *Saharan Atlas* during the era provided routes to the well-watered highlands for clans along the southern coastal belt of the inland sea.

As the *Interpluvial* ensued, many areas in the lowlands would no longer support fruiting plants or grow sufficient grasses. Clans depend on rainfall to collect, and harvests could only do so in shrinking areas, yet in the highlands. There were still fruit-bearing plants and good grazing areas. A palisade is formed in the center of the *Saharan Atlas* by its shorter sub-ranges (the *"Ksour"* and *"Ouled-Naïl,"* joined by the most eastern massifs of the *Aurès*.[cdxxx] Even at the height of the interpluvial, the palisades collected rains captured by the mountains, channeling it to the highland plains and river valleys, a natural ancient irrigation system that provided fruitful harvests in the valleys, and rich grasslands on the plains. In the eastern highlands, the rivers discharged into the eastern end of the *Northern Inland Sea* (the *"Triton Sea"*), connecting the clans of the *Saharan Atlas* highlands with those of *Lake Tritonis* and the *Triton River Valley*.

Coalescence of Fire: The Inter-Pluvial

Where the rains of the *Mousterian Pluvial* had once transformed the whole of the *Sahara*, and indeed all of *Northern Africa*, into a well-watered, rich, fertile, and bountiful terrain, the mounting aridity of the *Inter-Pluvial* now slowly began to transform the *Sahara*, and much of the *North African lowlands* into an increasingly hot, dry, desolate and inhospitable area; prompting mass dislocations and migrations across the whole of the Saharan lowlands. The end of the *Pluvial* was accentuated by a widespread arid event blanketing the Saharan *lowlands*, announcing an *Interpluvial* that would span six thousand years, from 30,000 BCE to 24,000 BCE. As the Saharan lowlands gradually reverted to desert terrain, flora and fauna of the pluvial era slowly retreated northward and westward toward the *Atlas* or southward toward the surviving forest zones.

Vast patches of savanna emerged and broadened across the Sahara, characterized by large stretches of grasslands mixed with sparse groupings of trees, serving as intermediate zones between the highland forests and desert lowlands.[cdxxxi] Trees of the savannas were widely spaced, with the canopies of the tropical era no longer closing. The open canopies allowed sunlight to reach the ground and transform the topography into a terrain of grasslands. The growing barrenness caused many of the sedentary clans, those most dependent upon hunting and gathering in the lowlands, to virtually perish. The increasing lack of vegetation across the lowlands forced the migrating clans to travel between pastoral valleys, remaining acutely aware of subtle changes in climate and the shrinking habitable zones. Once again, survival came to depend on resilience, mobility, and adept and keen adaptation.[cdxxxii] Movements became tied to the rains or seasonal runoff from the snow-capped mountains.

Surviving clans fleeing the expanding deserts gravitated towards the large paleo-river valleys of the era; river valleys were a remnant of the highland drainage systems active throughout the waning years of the *Pluvial,* yet they still provided ample water and refuge for those fleeing the encroaching deserts.[cdxxxiii] Desert-like conditions gradually claimed the remaining fertile areas as populations concentrated in and around the large, habitable paleo-river valleys descending the highlands. Settlements and migrations proceeded along the lower ascending corridors of the river valleys into the temperate and vastly more fertile river valleys of the highlands. Inter-connected settlement clusters or provinces were forged in the process, chaining from the lowland corridors of the river valleys to the larger, more fertile valleys in the highlands. In the highlands, the ability to secure permanent and abundant sources of food became inextricably related to the emergence of larger, more organized, and diversified communities. This was the time in which the clans began to trade along provincial networks, leading to informal and later formalized trading corridors.

The passes through the *Moroccan High Atlas* played key roles in the mobility and transit of people and wares between the northern highlands of the *Middle Atlas* and *High Atlas*, and the southern highlands of the *Anti-Atlas,* as well as along the seaboards of the *Western Inland Sea* (the "Mauritanian Sea") and the *Atlantic Ocean*. Key transit and trade routes of the era linked the southern provinces with those of the *Drâa* and *Sous* valleys in the southern Moroccan highlands in the north. Settlements quickly took root and expanded throughout the broad *Souss* plains, transforming the highland valley into a key population center. Similarly, settlements also quickly expanded around the catchment areas of the *Drâa* and along the ascending and descending corridors of its river valley. The *Drâa River* drained the southern slopes of the *High Atlas* and the northern slopes of the *Anti-Atlas and* collected migrants from each on its journey to the Atlantic Ocean.

The *Drâa River* flows southwestward to the West African Atlantic seaboard, where the mighty river once emptied into the ocean at the river's ancient mouth, just opposite the *Canary Islands*, facilitating what was, at first, seasonal excursions to the bountiful islands.[cdxxxiv] Coastal and fishing clans descending corridors of the *Drâa* settled around the delta at the ancient mouth of the river, from where settlements expanded along the Atlantic seaboard. Over twenty sites of the era are found overlooking the *River Chebeika* along the Atlantic seaboard of southern Morocco.[cdxxxv] The majority of the sites are marked by open-air rock art engravings, in proximity to nearby rock shelters, with walls and ceilings full of painted images. Over one-hundred red-ochre paintings have been discovered in several rock shelters along the coastal settlement zone. One of the most striking scenes – visible on one the roof of one of the cave sites – is of a line of ostriches and a giraffe following two archers.

The two archers faced two other similar figures, one carrying a bow. The human figures, with their oval heads, prominent buttocks, and powerful thighs, are clearly identifiable with the indigenous *Negroid* types of the era. The pictorials themselves seem to portray a period of tension between the clans as the once seemingly endless abundance increasingly gave way to scarcity. As the grasslands gradually dried and transformed into desert terrain, extended clans and villages impacted by the encroaching wastelands were mobilized into waves of migration. Some, those so acclimated or inclined, continued northward along the Atlantic seaboard, while others, many, not most, migrated by boat on the currents of the *Drâa* to the virgin coastal fishing grounds and bountiful forests of the *Canary Islands* just off-coast.[cdxxxvi]

The microclimate and forests of the *Canaries* provided a rich and diverse plant and wildlife environment, which, in turn, played a vital role in preserving the watersheds that enabled the abundance on the islands. The *Canaries* were welcomed respite and refuge for those fleeing the mounting barrenness of the Sahara. Ancient sites and rock art have been discovered on the islands, which are of particular interest due both to their characteristics and the chronological and cultural implications they portend for the study of prehistory on the islands.[cdxxxvii] One noteworthy archaeological site consists of six panels containing representations of geometric and figurative motifs; within the group of figurative motifs are schematic anthropomorphic engraved on the panels. From a chronological and cultural perspective, the portrayal presented in rock art emphasizes the direct archaeological relationship between inhabitants of the southwestern Sahara and the early cultures introduced in the *Canary Islands*. Uncovered sites portray clear resemblances to rock art and sites of the era in the southwestern Sahara.[cdxxxviii] The characteristics are generally the same as those observed in the Sahara, although minor differences are discernable.[cdxxxix]

Nonetheless, *Canarian Rock Art* depictions, such as those at *Risco Blanco*, portray a clear relationship to that of the era in southern *Morocco* and the southwestern Sahara.[cdxl cdxli cdxlii cdxliii] Along the coast of Morocco, in the present-day region of Témara, numerous sites predating those of the Canaries have been discovered in caves paralleling the seaboard, with distinct similarities to sites on the *Canaries*.[cdxliv cdxlv cdxlvi] Many of the caves were occupied by the first farmers, suggesting a close relationship between early farmers and the more mobile fishing clans. In the north, as the interpluvial progressed and arid conditions became pronounced, the *Drâa*, which was the largest river during the pluvial, became the southern boundary-line of cultivable land in the western highlands. During the heavy rains of the pluvial, the *Drâa* had been a natural source of irrigation; however, at the height of the interpluvial south of the valley, the mighty *Drâa* had been reduced to little more than a perennial river.

From the *High Atlas,* which rises at the Atlantic coast of *Morocco*, the newly green *Iberian Sub-Peninsula* was (and is) fully visible and was surely beckoning to those weary of the heightening desolation rising from the lowlands. The *Rif Mountains,* the most northern of the *Atlas* ranges, enclose the *Atlantic Plains* on the northwestern tip of the continent, at the Straits of Gibraltar. From here, again, the *Iberian Sub-Peninsula* was (and is) all but fully visible, just beyond the horizon across the straits.[cdxlvii] Situated at the southwestern tip of *Europe*, the *Iberian Peninsula* is a mere five miles away at its nearest point.[cdxlviii] Clans along the coast pressed the first forays of the era into the thawing land of the north. Fishing clans, followed by hunting and gathering clans, established first seasonal and later permanent settlements, later attracting sedentary clans who annexed and transformed settlements into villages emulative of the mixed economies and culture of the Atlas.[88]

While it is generally refuted that *North Africans* crossed the *Strait of Gibraltar* around the *Last Ice Age,* archeological evidence suggests their maritime adaptations and seafaring played significant roles in the early settlement and geographic expansion throughout the *Southern European Peninsula*, with the development of more sophisticated seafaring and marine abilities employed during the *Last Glacial Maximum*.[cdxlix] The areas of *Iberia* first colonized appear to have been devoid of human occupation until the new immigrants brought their sedentary mixed-economic style and culture to the *Peninsula*.[cdl] Recent DNA evidence now firmly affirms that there was, indeed, definitive gene flow from *North Africa* to the *Iberian Peninsula* during the *Glacial Maximum*.[cdli] The *Iberian Peninsula* has a rich heritage of rock art, with numerous sites along its main river, the *Douro*, and its tributaries, the *Côa* and *Aguiar*.

---

[88] The 'Aterians', starting about 30,000 B.C'

Early settlements were established in the lush southern river valleys, where analysis of surviving archaeological evidence suggests the sites were recurrently occupied on a seasonal basis.[cdlii] The magnificent array of rock art of the era in the Atlas depicting wild game, such as gazelles and bovines, portrays the importance the hunt continued to play, even in the increasingly mixed economies of the Atlas. So, it should come as a little surprise that when an abundance of wild game animals, gazelles, antelopes, long-horned Oxen, large red deer, ibex, and other now-extinct species native to the sub-peninsula, were reported by the seasonal migrants, large groups were soon attracted across the Straits. It was not until the establishment of permanent sedentary agricultural communities that it appears the rock art along the eastern region of the sub-peninsula began to flower.[cdliii]

The iconic prehistoric rock art of the North African immigrants of the era along the southern and coastal regions of the sub-peninsula stands in stark and distinct contrast to the cave art of the somewhat more primitive inhabitants of the norths, those whom the North African clans must have considered the native peoples of the sub-peninsula.[cdliv] During the era just prior to the arrival of the clans from *North Africa*, native *Eurasian Neanderthals,* emanating from *Southern France,* had themselves just immigrated into the northern confines of the *Iberian Sub-Peninsula*; this around 35 000 BC.[cdlv] Most of northern *Europe* remained covered by thick sheets of ice during the *Glacial Maximum*, while the southern regions of the peninsula were blanketed by permafrost, rendering even the more temperate south unsuitable for habitation, an advent prompting southward migrations of native *Eurasians*.

Neanderthals migrated into the more temperate *Iberian Peninsula*, slowly expanding southward. They were in residence in the central peninsula well before and after 28,000 BC,[cdlvi] when they are purported to have succumbed to extinction.[cdlvii] *Mousterian* tools associated with their culture were discovered in 1995 that has been dated as late as 25,000 BC, three thousand years beyond their presumed extinction, confirming, by dent of archeological evidence, that they survived far beyond the conventionally accepted notions of their demise.[cdlviii] There is little question that the *North African Clans* who colonized the peninsula at the same time as the *Neanderthals* were anatomically modern humans. However, it is an error of conventional academics to classify *Neanderthals* as sub-human.[cdlix] While the two groups varied significantly in physical appearance, *Neanderthals* were early humans native to *Eurasia*, those who migrated into the northern Iberian sub-peninsula shortly before the arrival of the *North Africans* to the south.[cdlx]

The rock art found in southeastern Spain portrays early North African colonization, depicting lively scenes of everyday life with warriors, hunters, dancers, and animals. While dating has been the subject of long debate, its style is nonetheless distinctly unlike the cave art found in the north, where the figures are small and painted in solid colors, with no attempt at light and shade. [cdlxi cdlxii cdlxiii] Rock Art sites in the *Côa Valley* of present-day *Portugal,* and *Siega Verde* of present-day *Spain,* on the banks of the *Côa* and *Agueda* rivers, document the continuous occupation from the end of the Paleolithic Age (with hundreds of panels carved over several millennia) provide a most remarkable open-air ensemble of Paleolithic art on the peninsula. They uniquely represent the prehistoric evidence of the ancient settlements on the peninsula. [cdlxiv] The first colonization of the central interior of the peninsula began during the Middle-Upper Paleolithic.[cdlxv cdlxvi] This was perhaps the first time during the *Paleolithic Age* that a disjunction emerged between the paces of biological and cultural evolution.

It was anatomically non-modern European Neanderthals and coeval modern African Middle Paleolithic people who now shared the peninsula. A 24,500-year-old skeleton found in Portugal shows Neandertals and early modern humans intermixed and produced children. Radiocarbon dating recently confirmed the age of the skeleton, indicating the child lived 4,000 years after the time that Neandertals and early modern humans coexisted on the *Iberian Peninsula*.[cdlxvii] The discovery challenges the commonly held theory that *Neandertals* played no role in the direct ancestry of modern humans.[cdlxviii] The sustained heightened temperatures of the *Interpluvial* pushed the habitable zones on the *Peninsula* further northward during the closing millennium, while, to the south, relentless heat and aridity in the Sahara prompted increased population concentrations in the interior and northern highlands. Evidence suggests moist habitats in the *Ahaggar, Tassili, Tibesti,* and *Aïr* mastiffs, at mid-altitudes between 5,000 to 8,000 feet, became prime climate refugia for the clans and village groups coalescing in the interior highlands. These were elevations where humidity levels were significantly and sufficiently higher than that of the lowlands, and the cooler temperatures created conditions favorable to the survival of people and animals.

In the *Atlas*, despite the arid conditions in the Saharan lowlands, with the climate divide, snowcap melt and rainwaters continuously recharged the aquifers, feeding the network of tributaries irrigating the river valleys and plains. Population concentrations inevitably coalesced around the river valleys and the seaboards of the *Atlas*. The *High Plateau* nurtured its own populations, combining the clans along the northern coast and those along the southern coast of the *Northern Inland Sea*, with those along the eastern corridors of the estuarial harbor at the *Gulf of Gabes,* where the waters of the *Mediterranean* flowed into the inland seas. The clans and provinces of the *Atlas* developed internal systems of communication, with village clusters linked trails and paths that avoided the valley floors, allowing the free flow of people, trade, information, and technology transference, an advent facilitating the homogenization and eventual amalgamation of the clans and provinces in the Atlas.

Return of the Rains: The Second Pluvial

The prolonged arid phase in the *Sahara* was followed by a sub-humid phase, lasting from about 24,000 BCE to 22,000 BCE, followed by a cold, arid event, followed by torrential rains of greater and lesser proportions, causing broadscale flooding across the Sahara.[89] [90] The latter phases of the *Second Mousterian Pluvial* caused flooding of the type that occurs when extensive rainfall is unable to be fully absorbed by the ground or drained away. Pluvial flooding gradually inundated the depressions and basins of the *Saharan* lowlands in some areas due to the rains, and in others due to the volume of water discharged by the highland rivers. In all instances, the lowlands became saturated, causing flooding across the central and Western Sahara basins. The onset of the *Second Pluvial* resulted from climatic patterns caused by the *Wisconsin Glaciations* in the *Northern Hemisphere*.[cdlxix]

Bitterly cold temperatures rising from the huge glacial expanse ultimately displaced and compressed the climatic zones southward, where the steep temperature gradient between the *Arctic* and *Equatorial* fronts accelerated winds meridionally, further compressing northern climate zones southward toward the *Equator*.[91] *Europe*, in consequence, experienced a dramatic drop in temperature, marking the onset of the *Glacial Maximum,* the coldest phase of the *Last Great Ice Age*. [cdlxx] [92]

---

[89] Conrad, 1969; Servant, 1973; Maley, 1976
[90] Maley, 1976, 1977a
[91] Rognon, 1976
[92] Maley, 1977b

The *Glacial Maximum* was *the* period of maximum glacial extent during the *Ice Age,* an era that lasted over six thousand years in the *Northern Hemisphere* and notably less in the *Southern Hemisphere*. Cold arid conditions ensued at its onset in both the northern and southern hemispheres; this was a time when desert-like conditions in the *Sahara* became far more extensive than at present, and tropical forests were significantly reduced.[cdlxxi] When the northern ice sheets began to expand in earnest, the intense cold rising from the glacial expanse altered existing weather patterns, creating their own air masses. These new weather patterns reinforced themselves, plunging the north and parts of the southern hemispheres into the cold, arid era of the Glacial Maximum.[cdlxxii]

To the south, somewhat smaller but still large and nonetheless significant glaciers formed and expanded in the heights of the *Atlas*, especially the *High Atlas* in northern *Morocco* and the huge massifs in southern *Algeria*. Tell-tale geological signs are evident of large glaciers of the era also forming and expanding in the heights of the *Tell* and *Saharan Atlas;* huge glaciers, although smaller than those of the *High Atlas*, may nonetheless have been clearly visible from the seas and coastal belt of the *Northern Inland Sea* on the *High Plateau*.[93] [94] During the most extensive phases of the glacial maximum, snowlines fell across the *Atlas,* from the *Anti-Atlas* in the southwest to the *High* and *Middle Atlas* in the north, the *Tell Atlas* in the northeast, and the *High Plateau* and *Saharan Atlas* south of the *Tell*. During this time, the habitable zones in the *Atlas* were compressed between the mounting aridity arising from the *Saharan* lowlands and the descending frigid temperatures from the expanding glaciers in the highlands.

Conditions prompted increased settlement along the mid-corridors of the major river valleys descending the highlands; this, over time, resulted in near urban-like densities across the favorable provinces of the *Atlas*. Those fleeing the spreading desolation of the lowlands, and those fleeing the expanding glaciers of the highlands, each added to those who had long settled in the highland river valleys, an advent that simultaneously disrupted and enriched the cultural ethos and diversity of the village settlements in the Atlas, with reverberations that would affect and aid much of what was to follow. To the north, the dramatic drop in temperatures across *Europe* at the onset of the *Glacial Maximum,* particularly on the *Iberian Peninsula,* prompted a reversal of the northern migrations and expansions of *North African Clans* on the *Iberian Sub-Peninsula*.

As the intensity of the *Glacial Maximum* ensued, many, if not most, of the clans and village groups who had by then resided on the *Peninsula* for several thousand years opted to retrace the ancient migrations of their ancestors and return to re-settle, at first, along the Atlantic and Mediterrean seaboards of the North African coasts. Eventually, upon incursion of the frigid temperatures of the north, again many, if not most, settling along the coasts re-settled along the corridors of the river valleys ascending to the highlands. Many of those settling along the *Atlantic* coast joined the precessions moving through the *Drâa* delta to settle along the ascending corridors of the *Drâa River Valley,* while others in proximity to the delta of the *Souss* joined those moving through the *Souss* delta of the era to settle along the corridors the *Souss River Valley*. Many who initially re-settled along the *Mediterranean* seaboard would later opt for permanent re-settlement along the corridors of the lower *Moulouya River Valley*.

---

[93] Barbier & Cailleux, 1950; Büdel, 1952; Tihay, 1972, 1973
[94] Ballais, 1983

Each group and community added to the increasing population density occurring throughout the *Atlas*. At its apex, the aridity spreading across the lowlands prompted even the fishing clans along the interior coast of the *Western Inland Sea* to seek permanent abode in the *Anti-Atlas*, opting for the use of temporary fishing villages along the inland seaboard. The long period of cold, desolate aridity across the lowlands was eventually broken by a steep thermal gradient that formed over the central Sahara; this as the southward progressing *Polar Front* was ultimately subsumed by the northward progression of the *Equatorial Monsoons,* marking the retreat of the Glacial Maximum, and beginning of the *Humid* phase in *North Africa.* Palaeo-hydrological strata in tropical and subtropical Africa depict the first indications of de-glaciations, with wetter and vastly more humid climates than obtaining across most of Northern Africa. The region falls mostly within the domain of the *African Monsoons;* changes in palaeo-hydrological records of the era reflect the strength of the *Monsoons* as they pushed northward, ultimately invading and finally overwhelming the *Polar Front*.

The wet conditions and floods that followed the progression of the *Second Pluvial* are recorded within the mountain ranges of the interior Sahara and across the basins of the Saharan lowlands. At the heights of the *Atlas*, the ensuing rains and warmer climate facilitated the glacial melt of the ice-capped mountain peaks. It was this progressive glacial melt that ultimately caused the final collapse of huge parts of the gigantic ice sheets, releasing large volumes of meltwater descending to the lowlands through the network of tributaries feeding the major rivers flowing from the highlands. The increased rains and glacial melt added to the ongoing rise in sea levels, and, with the adjustment to global sea levels in the *Mediterranean* frustrated by restricted flow through the narrow Strait of Gibraltar and outlet to the *Black Sea Basin* still foreclosed, delayed isostatic rebound (from reduced glacial loading) in the *Atlas*, once again, aligned with the other key variables to render open the *Water Gate at Gabes*.

Pent-up and rising waters of the Mediterranean *Sea* burst through the narrow canals at the Gulf of Gabes, fully subsuming the huge estuarial harbor at the mouth of the *Northern Inland Sea* (the fabled "Triton Sea"). The sheer force of the intrusion caused the salt waters of the Mediterranean to virtually overwhelm the vast volumes of freshwater flowing northward into the estuary from the *Triton River*; evidence suggests *salt water* penetrated far into and up the *Trident River Valley*. To the west, the rising waters pushed through the *Channels of the Chotts* with equal if not greater force, as the still rising waters of the Mediterranean Sea once again ultimately subsumed and eventually breached the southern banks of the basins of the *Northern Inland Sea*.

The breaching waters once again created huge north-to-south flowing wadis across the *Sahara* as the massive discharge poured southward into the enormous *Central* and *Western* basins of the *Sahara*. The force of the initial breach caused large sections of the terrain to deteriorate and be carried away in the waters unleashed by the breach. The massive waters ultimately filled the *central* and *western basins* and the adjacent *depressions of the Juff,* finally inundating each, bringing the perennial *Saharan Inland Sea* to renewed life. The immense inland sea once again fully occupied the combined *central* and *western basins* of the Sahara, conjoining the *Inland Seas* to eventually reach the *Atlantic* off the *West African* seaboard, once again rendering the *Atlas* surrounded by water.[cdlxxiii]

The Parables

It was *Amun* who came to the aid of the people at the time of their greatest distress and ignominy, guiding them into the sheltered confines of the highlands and teaching the early Seers to use the Cycles of the Moon as their Calendar. *Amun* arose from the primordial waters of consciousness (the *'Nun'*) during the time the *Pole Star* in the northern sky was in the *Constellation Draco*. *Amun* suddenly appeared out of the primordial waters to awaken humankind as the supreme deity, representing the flowering life force hidden and established in the primordial waters of consciousness. [cdlxxiv]

The state of Man's consciousness before the arising of *Amun* was that of an undifferentiated potential within a vast primordial mist. There were two dual precepts inured by the Priest of Amun, awakening consciousness of Man, those of *Mind* and *Matter*. *Mind* itself is "dualized" into *'Consciousness'* and *'Will'*, with *Consciousness* representing the passive polarity and *Will* the active polarity of the essential aspects of the *Mind*. While *Matter* is said to represent a state of being (or energy) along a continuum of change.

Amun's unknown form originated from the conception that he was "first formed" by the *Gods*. His name is generally translated as "the hidden one" or "the secret one," and it is thought that he created himself and then created everything else while remaining distanced and separate from the world. *Amun* was unknown because he represents absolute holiness and, in this regard, is different from any other deity. Both his name and physical appearance were unknown, thus indicating his unknowable essence.

Amun was not considered immanent within creation, nor was creation seen as an extension of himself. So holy is he that he remains independent of the created universe. Legend holds that he was self-created, and "everything happens within him, and nothing exists outside him." He is "the one maker of all things, and beings; from whose eyes mankind proceeded, from whose mouth the Gods were created." The one who is said to abide in the hearts of all creatures as the indestructible "Self"; whose "unknowable form" is said to pervade the entire cosmos.[cdlxxv]

Pollen cores off the coast of *West Africa* indicate that shortly after the onset of the *Second Pluvial*, as early as around 23,000 BCE, rainforests were re-emerging along the Mediterranean and Atlantic seaboards of Northern Africa. Conditions were such at the height of the *Second Pluvial* that the highlands again became well-watered, with networks of rivers flowing to the lowlands. Freshwater springs and grasslands covered much of the highland valleys, in some regions even surpassing conditions that had prevailed in the heyday of the *First Pluvial*. Settlement areas arose and expanded along the *Kert* and *Moulouya River Valleys* in the mid-northeastern highlands of *Morocco* and the *Medjerda River Valley* in the mid-northern highlands of *Tunisia*.

The consistent seasonal rains and floods contributed to the re-emergence of mixed economies in the highlands. With the revival, restoration, and expansions of many of the older settlements and provinces experienced inbound migrations, renewed economic intensification, and an element of territoriality among some of the most favorable environments of the middle highlands. Archeological sites of the era suggest settlements expanded across the *Atlas* highlands, eastward from *Morocco* through *Algeria* to *Tunisia*, and southward to the *High Plateau* and central palisades of the *Saharan Atlas*.

The basins in the northern, central, and western Sahara remained fully occupied and gave shape to the huge *Inland Saharan Sea* until, around 20,000 B.C., the perennial inland sea once again began to recede and fragment. During the waning centuries of the pluvial rains, highland river valleys across the whole of the Sahara blossomed with renewed vitality. The basins of *Paleo-Lake Yoa,* in the southeast, were again submerged and gave shape to the large perennial lake that again transformed its surrounding terrain into a rich, green highland paradise filled with trees, grasslands, and a variety of wildlife.

To the northwest, the mountainous highlands and valleys of the *Tibesti Mastiff* were reinvigorated by the pluvial. The *Tibesti* is crossed by a number of descending paleo-rivers flowing through the highlands to the lowlands intervening the *Tibesti* and the *Tassili* mountains. The *Tassili plateau* is part of the divide between northward and southward flowing watersheds in the *Central Sahara*, where renewed forests and wild plants and the return of large and small game anchored settlement patterns and expansions along the adjacent highlands. Huge volumes of water again flowed from the highlands, reinvigorating the grasslands surrounding the base of the mountains, which again offered rich grazing, large lakes, and varied types of fish and aquatic life.

In the *Tadrart Acacus, the* northern arm of the *Tassili* range, a network of ancient river tributaries again descended the highlands where *Wadi Teshuinat*, the largest wadi in the central *Tadrart Acacus,* was revived in the largest valley in the region. Paleo-river tributaries of *Wadi Teshuinat* dissected the highlands and interconnected with *Wadi Tanezzuft,* again encouraging settlements and villages to expand along the shores of *Wadi Teshuinat* and its tributaries. With the massive pluvial rains, highland rivers and lakes once again were soon overwhelmed and discharging huge volumes of water through the network of tributaries, recharging and adding size and dimensions to *Paleo-Lake-Fezzan*, and *Lake Tritonis* at the mouth of the fabled *Trident* Sea.

The massive *Ahaggar Mastiff* in the mid-Saharan uplands formed a virtual shield anchoring the alignment of mastiffs stretching across the *Central Sahara* and once again channeled the massive waters of the pluvial from the highlands. The headwaters of two great *Central Saharan* paleo-rivers of earliest antiquity again arose in the heights of the *Ahaggar;* the *River Tafanasset* draining its southern highlands, flowing westward to the *Niger River*, and the mighty *Igharghar River,* draining its northern highlands and flowing northward through the fables *Triton River Valley*, to empty into the huge estuarial-harbor that was the *Lake Tritonis*, at the mouth of the *Trident Sea.*

The *Triton River Valley* was once again transformed, becoming well-watered and fertile, with an abundance of grasses, grains, wild flora and fauna, and a variety wild life re-inhabiting the floor of the valley. Renewed and expanded settlement and revival of cattle herding along the valley and in the adjacent highlands soon ensued. The Sahara once again bloomed and regained its lost abundance, not only in vegetation and wildlife but also in the return of human habitation. With the rainfall, and ample rivers, lakes, and marshland, settlements revived and improved methods to tame the waters by irrigation channels and constructing dams.

Yet none rose to prominence like the clans of the *Atlas-Si,* whom later legend would call "*Atlatians*," and their perennial homeland "*Atlatia."* The Atlas reverts to perennial 'Atlatia' when the ancient massifs become surrounded, usually for thousands of years, on all sides by water. The seaboard of the ancient *Saharan Inland Sea* (the fabled "*Atlantean Sea"*) then borders *Atlatia* to the east and south, while the *Atlantic* seaboard *Atlatia* borders on the west. The *Mediterrean* seaboard then borders *Atlatia* to the northwest and north. The *Northern Inland Sea* (the fabled Triton Sea) borders *Atlatia* to the south, and the *Gulf of Gabes* borders *Atlatia* at its extreme east.

Ascendance at the Atlas: Rise of Atlatia

Early vestiges of the first kingdoms arose in the highlands and coastal plains of southern *Atlatia*, with the earliest of the emergent kingdoms forming well before 20,000 BCE in the highlands of *Southern Atlatia* (in present-day *Mauritania*).[95] Small coastal and interior fiefdoms were formed and asserted from the Atlantic coast through and across the highland valleys of (the *Anti-Atlas* in) *Southern Atlatia*, encompassing the western and southwestern coastal plains and shores of the *Saharan Inland Sea* of the era. Horticulture, arts, crafts, building, and a rich, green environment of seemingly endless abundance were obtained at that time. Large highlands lakes and descending rivers irrigated the highland valleys and the coastal foothills and plains along the two seaboard. The return of rains brought renewed interest in plant collection and a later return to cultivation.

The southern *Atlatians* (the *Manding-Si* of the *Anti-Atlas* and surrounding coastal plains) practiced a form of agriculture characterized by the use of the hoe and water storage and irrigation techniques, together with the use of available soil fertilizers. Early agricultural techniques were being refined long before iron tools came into use, and productivity improved in this region. The ability to produce surplus food led to an increase in population; as people spread into more marginal areas, they were forced to domesticate plants and animals to preserve accustomed levels of food production. This led to further population growth and, with it, larger, more complex social and political organizations and occupational specialization. As before, revived agricultural centers did not grow automatically into more complex village clusters and townships, but a result of their formation was an increased demand for materials necessary to make cultivating-tools and other equipment.

Moderate climatic conditions have made it possible to engage in intensive plant domestication. Food surpluses led to the renewed rise of townships, towns, and complex political organizations. Social ranking of individuals in society, and craft specialization, as the prosperous clans and provincial townships and village clusters, became more sedentary. The advent of revived prosperity made the inhabitants much less mobile and able to obtain materials for themselves, encouraging renewed trade. Early goods traded included tools, precious stones, wood, ostrich eggs and shells, animals, ivory, alabaster, vessels, pottery, herbs, and oils.Trade routes intersected at key junctures between the expanding population centers of the highlands and natural harbors along the inland seaboard, where makeshift ports arose and nurtured fledgling coastal villages.

Maritime trade across the *Atlantean Sea* began at least as early as the final phases of the second pluvial, with boats and fishermen, craftsmen, and coastal villages active along the inland coastal zone of the era. The inhabitants of Southern Atlatia were masters of the highlands lands as well as the inland seas of the era; they were among the first shipbuilders in the ancient Sahara and used watercraft for both fishing and trading expeditions across the expanse of the huge inland sea. Though smaller in size and dimension than the *Saharan Inland Sea* of the *First Pluvial*, the *Saharan Inland Sea* of the *Second Pluvial* was nonetheless of considerable size and magnitude. Each time the pattern of inundation from the *Mediterranean Sea* had been a little different.[cdlxxvi] Each cycle had its own idiosyncrasies in terms of timing and magnitude, yet each was precipitated by an alignment variable opening the *Watergate at Gabes*.[cdlxxvii]

---

[95] Blisshords Communications

Once the sea levels of the Mediterranean gained unfettered discharge through Gabes, the pent-up waters of the *Mediterranean Sea*, once again, first inundated and overwhelmed the estuarial *Lake Tritinus*, and the combined basins of the Chotts, giving form to the perennial the *Trident Sea* of the era. The overflowing waters again found an outlet by breach of the southern basins of *Chott Melghir* and *Chott Merouane*, at the eastern end of the *Triton Sea,* with the cascading waters pouring into the *Great Eastern Erg* in the central Sahara. The force of the cascade excavated flow channels through the western banks of the *Eastern Erg*, releasing the rising waters into the *Western Erg* of the Sahara and joining the waters descending from *Chott Hodna* at the western end of the *Triton Sea*. The *overflow from the northern basins eventually filled the Erg*s. The rising waters eventually transformed the mountainous areas within the central and western basins into islands, giving full shape to the perennial *Saharan Inland Seas* covering much of the northern, central, and Western Sahara.

The great inland sea was defined by its three major basins, the contiguous northern basins of the *Chotts*, the huge central basin, limited westward by the *Mzab Plateaus*, and the huge western basin dominated by the *Western Erg*.[cdlxxviii] [cdlxxix] Thus were the Saharan basins transformed, once again, into the perennial *Saharan Inland Seas*, whose waters washed against the foothills of the *Tassili* and *Ahaggar* mastiffs in the *Central Sahara*.[96] Waters of the inland seas again eventually found an outlet on the western coast of present-day *Mauritania*, where the coastal barrier then tilted seaward toward the *Atlantic,* again, rendering the *Atlas* surrounded on all sides by water, again giving full form to perennial *Atlatia*. Though shallower than the present-day *Black Sea,* which reaches depths of 7,200 feet, and covers a surface area of 168,495 square miles, the *Saharan Inland Sea* of the *Second Pluvial* reached depths of 2,500 feet, covering a surface area nearly half the size of the *Mediterranean Sea*.

The tropical blue waters of the inland sea were reminiscent of the blue waters of the present-day Caribbean Sea. Its surface waters were generally warm, although colder waters were found in the northern basins, closer to the discharge of the *Mediterranean Sea*. The current of the sea was generally clockwise, influenced by inflow in the northeast from the *Mediterranean* and discharge in the southwest into the *Atlantic*. *Atlatians* were adept seafarers and masters of the inland seas. As the early kingdoms took shape, trade became increasingly important; those communities that happened to have vital materials within their territory were in positions they could exploit. Over time, such communities increased in wealth, size, and prominence. Highly valued obsidian was exported from the *Atlas* to the inland seacoast of the *Ahaggar*, from which it was bartered and traded in the *Central Highlands*. Surviving obsidian and ceramics artifacts of the era, most of which are likely to have come from the ancient maritime trade, number in the hundreds.[cdlxxx]

The *Atlatians* had an early monopoly on obsidian, a product of vital importance for the production of blades and other objects. Obsidian is a natural form of volcanic glass that is created when lava cools too quickly to form a crystal. It was valued and widely used during the earliest antiquity because it could be fractured to create arrowheads and sharp blades.[cdlxxxi] Obsidian's sharp nature made it a stone of choice in making blades and arrowheads; polished Obsidian was even used to create the earliest mirrors.[cdlxxxii] Obsidian is generally pure black in color, and while it is extremely rare to it in other colors, natural blue Obsidian, one of the rarest of colors, could be found (and has been re-discovered) in the Atlas of Morocco; from where it was once traded, during earliest antiquity.[cdlxxxiii]

---

[96] Herodotus

After the long favorable wet period in the Sahara, a pronounced aridity ensued, blanketing the Saharan lowlands around 20,000 BC. Starting at about 20,000 BP, the period was relatively dry throughout North Africa, with a maximum peak of aridity and extreme dryness occurring around 19,000 BP. As the climate dried, the rolling grasslands in the southern Sahara were the first to recede. Once global ice sheets began to expand, the northern Sahara began to dry as well. However, the monsoons, which had previously brought rains to the *Sahel*, shifted northward, counteracting the drying, as lakes in the *Central Sahara* drained southwestward through tributaries and rivers. As arid conditions subsumed in the lowlands, the *Manding-Si* gradually spread into the fertile river valleys of present-day Mauritania, Morocco, and Algeria. By 17,000 BC, the climate of the Sahara was desert-like terrain, with arid plains reducing the forests and lush coastal lands surrounding the inland sea.

The Parables

It was during *Ra's* reign that the *Great Ice Age* began its gradual but eventual end. To the people inhabiting the Sahara at the end of the Ice Age, this time, the welcomed warmth and abundance were a reflection of the power of *Ra,* a celestial *Deity*, nearly always portrayed with a *solar disc* above his head; he was the *god* of the sun, the bringer of light, *ruler* of the heavens. *Ra* was the deification of the visible sun, the highest of the cosmic powers, and deemed the creator of the Cosmos. He was believed to have separated the primeval elements and created the other deities; from this belief came the conception of the "*Ennead,"* a group of nine divinities, and the triad consisting of a divine *father, mother*, and *son*.

Known as *Amun* when representing the flowering life force hidden in the primordial waters of consciousness, *Ra* was the emanating essence of *Deity*. *Ra* embodied the divine features of power, energy, light, and warmth. *Ra* is what made the crops grow each season, so it is no surprise that the cult of *Ra* grew to immense power and was widespread. In his most divine form, *Ra* was known as "*Amun-Ra,"* the hidden, emanating essence, the secret *god*. The very name '*Amun*' meant "hidden," and the contraction, *Amun-Ra*, meant "the hidden one" or "the secret one." When merged with *Ra*, *Amun* became both a visible and invisible *deity*.

Amun represented the essential and hidden, whilst *Ra* represented revealed divinity; the addition of the name "*Ra*" to the hidden divinity of *Amun* revealed the god to humanity. Hence, *Amun-Re* combined within himself the two opposites of divinity, the *hidden* and the *revealed*. Amun-Ra was said to have emerged from the primordial waters of consciousness; as *Amun,* he was secret, hidden, and mysterious, but as *Ra,* he was visible and revealed. This duality was an aspect of the essential balance inherent in creation, further exemplified by the relationship between *Amun-Ra* and *Ma'at*.

After this period, the climatic evolution became different, region by region, and drier, more humid conditions were seldom experienced simultaneously over the entire *Sahara*. The severe aridity that blanketed much of the Sahara gradually extended southward, beyond the *Chad Basin*, causing a gradual regression of *Paleo-Lake Chad* (until about 12,500 BCE).[97] The *Central Saharan highlands* avoided the hyper-arid conditions and instead experienced extended wet climatic conditions, lasting until about *Mid Holocene*, although interrupted by several short dry events.

---

[97] Maley 2004

The Saharan lowlands suffered a prolonged arid phase, during which climatic data suggest human occupation again became concentrated in the well-watered highlands. Environmental conditions across the Saharan floor included increased desiccation, with constraints on food sources, prompting the expansion of urban-like communities in the highlands. This was the period during which the petty kingdoms in *Southern Atlatia* coalesced across the highlands and adjacent seaboards. Early kingdoms in *Southern Atlatia* were nurtured in the fertile river valleys of the *Anti-Atlas*, from where they traversed the highlands to the eastern and western seaboards of *Southern Atlatia.*

Increased demand for raw materials by expanding provincial kingdoms led to increased trade between southern and northern *Atlatian* provinces. However, this was also an era in which rivalries for access to strategic minerals, valued commodities, and trade routes prompted internal animosities as early *Southern Atlatian* kingdoms competed for dominance over trade routes, trade routes linking the southern, northern, and inland *Atlatian* highlands. The growing rivalry, competition, and quest for prominence and influence through exhibition and force of prosperity led to faster innovation and technology transference, accelerating cultural development across the Atlatian complex.

The Legends

It was before the dawn of the megalithic era, in the age of the reign of the first of the *prescient leaders* in the highlands of northern *Atlatia*, a legendary leader whose name has long been lost in the dust of earliest antiquity, a leader legend simply knows as *"Ouranos,"* the king who first gathered the northern clans and instructed in the construction of refined sheltered habitation within secure walled cities. *Ouranos* caused the nascent kingdoms to cease their trivial rivalries and opt instead for a mutually productive, secure, and beneficial mode of living. It was he who guided them in the uses of cultivated fruits and how to store them. *Ouranos* (revered as *"King of the Sky"*) reigned over northern Atlatia, where his ingenuity and wit brought widespread prosperity to the highlands of the north.

To the south, among the provinces of *Southern Atlatia* reigned an equally prominent leader whose name again has been long lost in the dust of earliest antiquity, a renowned Queen legend simply known as *"Gaia,"* whose rule extended from the highlands of the *Anti-Atlas* of *Southern Atlatia,* to the broad coastal plains along its then southeastern seaboard. The agricultural prowess of the *Manding* and *Manding-Si* of *Southern Atlatia*, and the seemingly endless abundance in the region, led *Gaia* to be revered as the *"Great Mother,"* a name (then) synonymous with the fertility of the Earth. The eventual union between *Ouranos* and *Gaia* served as a catalyst, fusing the provinces of the northern and southern highlands, launching the beginning of the *Golden Age.*

During the early phases of the *Golden Age*, the use of gold was necessarily infrequent; while there were the occasional finds of alluvial gold, such finds occurred only rarely. Eventual mining and extracting the newly discovered metal required extensive procedures, particularly given that the tools used were barely harder than the rock they were supposed to crush. Thus, the increasing prevalence and use of the new metal did not presage or signify the abandonment of longer-known and used materials. Gold nonetheless came to be considered the flesh of *Ra*, and association with it inferred immortality. Gold was discovered and mined from the highlands of the *Atlas of Algeria* to the highlands of the *Tell Atlas*.[cdlxxxiv]

However, by the middle of the *Golden Age*, there was a game changer, a natural alloy of gold and silver known as *"Electrum"* was discovered in the highlands of *Southern Atlatia*. Electrum is a naturally occurring alloy of gold and silver, with trace amounts of copper and other metals. After the onset of the Golden Age, gold was mined broadly throughout *Southern Atlatia*, both as hard rock deposits and as alluvial gold washing down from the highlands. But silver had been a fairly recent discovery during the middle of the *Golden Age*, and the discovery of *Electrum* as a natural alloy launched a new phase of the age. This era would open the way to new technologies in metallurgy.

The reign of *Ouranos* and *Gaia* eventually passed to their progeny, the legendary and fabled *Khem* (also known as *Kham, Ham, Khronos,* and *Chronus*) first of the early Kings to add parts of the *Tell* …lands beyond the confines of *Northern Atlatia,* to his reign. Yet he was precluded from incorporating *Southern Atlatia* by the coalescence of its provinces into a loose federation by the legendary *Tyru, the* first of the imperial kings. Nonetheless, *Khem* (*Kham, Ham, Khronos, Chronus*) was the most acclaimed of the '*prescient leaders'*. [cdlxxxv] As a careful observer of the stars, he foretold many things that would take place throughout and beyond the realm. It was he who introduced the year based on the movement of the sun and the months on that of the moon.

The reign of *Khem* (*Kham, Ham, Khronos, Chronos*) spanned the middle of the *Golden Age,* when the fabled emperor is reputed to have overseen the building of the ancient megaliths and megalithic sites of *North Africa*. [cdlxxxvi] *Khem* presided during the era in which *Northern Africa* became the center of the megalithic building. Indeed, megalithic building originated with his rule in *Northern Africa*, when *Atlatia* was the stronghold of early megalithic civilization.[cdlxxxvii] Megalithic sites arose and flourished during the closing era of the *Last Great Ice Age,* first along the coasts of the Atlantic and then along the ancient seaboards of the *Mediterranean, Aegean,* and *Euxine* (the 'Proto-Black') *Seas*.

Along the inland coasts of *Southern Atlatia,* the relatively calm waters of the *"Atlantean Sea"* prompted maritime excursions to well-known seaside towns for barter and trade. The currents of the inland sea moved clockwise, influenced by the (then) inflow of the *Mediterranean* in the northeast and discharge into the *Atlantic* in the southwest. Prevailing northeasterly winds, while seasonally stronger, blew year around, compressed between a high-pressure cell in the *Sahara* and a low-pressure cell in the equatorial zone farther south. Advents that provided reliable northeasterly trade winds counter to the southwesterly currents, ideal for full cycle maritime excursions.

Coastal and interior kingdoms of the era occupied areas of the sub-tropics now partially covered by dense vegetation, just south of the former shorelines of the ancient inland sea. Trading activity during the era became particularly intense between southern and northern *Atlatia*, as the southern Atlatians became intermediaries linking the interior kingdom of the sub-tropics to northern *Atlatian* trade networks, which, in turn, were connected to eastern *Atlatia*. Compounding this, ensuing ecological changes across Sahara caused periods of sustained economic crisis and turbulence that were highly disruptive to the further development of the trading networks. Among the most significant advent was the onset of the not-so-gradual regression of the great inland sea.

Following the peak of the *Glacial Maximum* climatic conditions became extremely arid, and deserts encroached into the *lowlands* as forests shrunk into refugia. The aridity reached its optimum around 19,000 BCE, the point at which global ice extent was at its greatest. There is extensive evidence of the exploitation of marine resources along the former shorelines of the inland sea as it hastened the pace of its regression. Savannahs and grasslands gradually replaced the retreating forests, with desert-like terrain expanding into the retracting contours of the *Atlantean Sea*.

When the *Mediterranean Sea* finally adjusted to global sea levels, its waters slowly receded from the Sahara, and the *Atlantean Sea* eventually regressed into its three major basins until (around 16,000 BCE). Nonetheless, the presumption that the whole *Sahara* became entirely empty and devoid of life during this period of hyper-aridity is simply not supported by the research.[98] The climatic record from the different geographical regions of the Sahara indicates that the highlands experienced significantly wetter conditions than the lowlands during the period, resulting in vastly differing environments. The highlands had significant rainfall, sufficient to sustain highland rivers and lakes, even though surrounded by the hyper-aridity of the lowlands.

Archaeologists have studied many ancient habitation sites in the Sahara of the era, the relics of which show how climate affected but did not eliminate human habitation in the tablelands. Remains of a prehistoric town dating back to the era (about 15,000 BCE) were uncovered in *Western Sahara*. The remains of a place of worship, houses, and a necropolis, as well as columns and rock engravings depicting animals, have been found at the ancient site.[cdlxxxviii] The ancient town thrived as refinements of the early blade industries spread throughout the (then) coastal plains of the eastern seaboard during the era. This undaunted progress was nonetheless interrupted around 13,000 BCE by an abrupt global warming and moistening of the Saharan climate, an advent occurring within the space of only a few decades. Once the glaciers began to withdraw, a rise in *Mediterranean Sea* levels followed, ushering in a new wet and rainy era around 12,500 BC.

The Holocene: Neolithic Sub-Pluvial

The *Holocene* was a prolonged and relentless rainy period, causing widespread floods across the floor of the Sahara.[cdlxxxix] It began about 12,500 BC and was strong for about 3,000 years. The *Sub-Pluvial* was the most recent of the extended rains and floods in the Sahara and marked the beginning of the era of the "*Green Sahara*," when the rains of the *Sub-Pluvial* transformed the *Sahara* from varied grasslands into watery wetlands and rain forest. In some areas, the wetlands were widespread and became part of a complex web of rivers, tributaries, and waterways snaking across the lowlands. In contrast, in other areas, the landscape supported rich soils and thick forests.[cdxc]

The intense rainfall levels eventually expanded and overflowed the banks of rivers and shallow lakes across the lowlands. As the torrential rains persisted, the floods transformed the Saharan tablelands into a riverine ecosystem, expanding the remnant *Western Inland Sea* (the "*Mauritanian Sea*") to the foothills of present-day northern *Mauritania*, at sea's then northwestern extent. Finally, the smaller lakes across the central tablelands merged into larger lakes. As the inundation progressed, large lakes merged into even larger lakes, with the relentless rains lasting until about 10,000 BC, when much of the central lowlands were partially submerged beneath the waters and swamps of a massive shallow freshwater lake.

---

[98] The 'Late Pleistocene

Interstadial deglaciation called the *Allerød Oscillation* occurred around this period, weakening the conditions underlying the *Last Ice Age*. The *Allerød Oscillation* was, in effect, a moist global warm period that occurred at the end of the last glacial period. It significantly raised temperatures in the northern Atlantic, causing sea levels to eventually rise across the globe, not just in the northern Atlantic.[cdxci] The climate warmed dramatically and abruptly ...in no more than a decade or two. This was all the more remarkable because it occurred in the presence of massive ice sheets and the continuation of the *Albedo Forcing* that presumably helped maintain glacial conditions up to that point. We now know there was at least a three-hundred-foot rise in sea levels at the end of the *Last Ice Great Age*.[cdxcii] As before, the confluence of delayed isostatic subsidence from reduced glacial loading in the *Atlas* and the continued inaccessibility of the *Black Sea* basin as an outlet for the rising waters of the *Mediterranean Sea*, together with the relentless rains of the *Sub-Pluvial*, again aligned and rendered open the *Watergate at Gabe's*.

Once again, the waters of the *Mediterranean Sea* poured through the *Gulf of Gabes* into the northern basins, flooding and eventually breaching the southern banks of the basins, with the massive waters cascading southward into the central depression with a direct impact on the shallow lake and then partially occupying the basin. The waters in the central basin rose and eventually drained into the lower western basins as the revived perennial inland seas once again covered much of the northern, central, and western Saharan lowlands, leaving only highlands such as the *Tassili, Ahaggar,* and *Atlas* exposed. As the floods waters fluctuated, some areas were exposed as plains and then re-submerged until finally, the inundated basins were conjoined to reincarnate the last iteration of the perennial *Saharan Inland Sea,* the fabled "*Atlantean Sea*" of later Greek legend. Once again, the ancient inland sea covered the Saharan lowlands and came out where the landscape was at sea level, on the coast of present-day *Mauritania*, rendering the *Atlas* once again surrounded on all sides by water, reincarnating perennial *Atlatia*.

The *Atlantean Sea* also received waters discharged from the southern slopes of the *Tassili* and *Ahaggar* drainage basin and grew and receded with the seasonal run-off related to the *African Monsoons* of the era, which then reached directly into and beyond the central Sahara. The monsoons penetrated northward, with seasonal runoff from the slopes of the central highlands and interior slopes of the Atlas, enhancing the size of the inland sea.[cdxciii] Because some parts of the Saharan floor were (and are) below sea level, while other parts rise well above sea level, the huge inland sea obtained a rather irregular shape, with coves, peninsulas, natural harbors, and islands, on which coastal trading villages settled and expanded during the era. The largest of the islands in the *Atlantean Sea* was structurally part of the Saharan floor that rises above sea level in the northern, central, and western basins. The heights of the (then marine) ridgelines separating the huge central and western basins formed a small island archipelago where the two huge basins were conjoined into the main body of the revived *Atlantean Sea*.

Fishermen and traders once again took to the open sea, eventually colonizing the isles and re-establishing ancient trade relationships and networks along and around the coastline of the huge ancient inland sea. *Atlatian*-borne culture prospered from this period onward, with the perennial inland sea once again providing a readily available and viable means of trade and transport. The currents of the ancient *Atlantean Sea* (once again) generally moved clockwise to the south-southwest, influenced by the inflow of the *Mediterranean in* the northeast and the discharge of the *Atlantean into* the *Atlantic* in the southwest. When the *Tafanasset River* of the era drained the southern slopes of the *Ahaggar*, its massive waters flowed westward into the *Atlantean Sea,* reinforcing the westward flowing currents along the southern margins of the inland sea to its terminus at the southern extent of the *Anti-Atlas* ...and *Southern Atlatia*.

Northeasterly winds in the *Sahara*, again, while seasonally stronger, blew year around, providing trade winds counter to the southwesterly currents of the inland sea, enabling renewed maritime trade and excursions. On this sea, latter-day ships of the era sailed and moved from place to place, bartering, trading, and exchanging goods, commodities, and wares. Maritime trade, transit, and commerce of the era contributed to the mobility of people around the coasts of the *Atlantean Sea* and, thereby, to a degree of cultural homogeneity across the ancient Sahara. There is evidence of a port city at the base of the *Ahaggar* Mountains that was active during the era, a distance of nearly a thousand nautical miles from the seaboard of *Southern Atlatia*.[cdxciv] Once again, for thousands of years, the submerged *Chotts Basins* became a navigable inland waterway accessible from the *Mediterranean Sea* through the Gulf of Gabes.

Inundation of the Chotts Basins gave shape to the ancient *Triton Sea*, with its mouth at estuarial *Lake Tritonis,* which received its waters through the *Tritent River Valley* from the northward flowing *Tritent River*, and the *Mediterranean Sea* through the "*Channels of the Chotts*". The relentless rise in sea level allowed progressive marine incursions into the huge northern, central, and western Saharan basins, which were ultimately inundated and re-occupied by iterations of the perennial inland seas of bygone eras. It is again difficult to imagine now, but almost all of the central and western Saharan lowlands were all but completely submerged and covered by the waters of the huge perennial inland seas. Estuaries and networks of paleo-rivers and lagoons nurtured by the relentless rains yielded a variety of vegetation sufficient to support an abundance of elephants, rhinos, and hippopotami around the former coastal belt.

At the height of the *Sub-Pluvial* ecological conditions became vastly different from those prevailing earlier; by this time, the expansive waters of the inland sea fully covered the northern basins of the high plateau, draining into and ultimately inundating the massive central basins of the tablelands, and the huge lower basins of the western lowlands. Following the height of the *Sub-Pluvial,* the lowlands and much of the midlands intervening the central and western basins were all but completely submerged and conjoined, forming the core lower body of the ancient *Atlantean Sea*. The *Triton Sea,* the northern upper arm of the huge inland seas, remained attached to the *Atlantean Sea* for hundreds of years by excavated channels flowing into the *Great Eastern Erg,* and the channels excavated through its western banks flowing into the basins of *Great Erg*. Only the major highlands such as the *Atlas, Ahaggar,* and *Tassili* appeared to rise above the surface of the huge Inland Sea from a distance, appearing as vast islands in the *Sahara*.

Islands in the Sahara

This was the era during which *African Aquatic Civilization* blossomed from the *Atlas* in the northern, western, and central Sahara and regions further east. Its greatest extent was achieved during the wettest times, reaching its fullest flower at the western and northern margins of the Sahara. Dispersions into areas populated by the aquatic civilization were characterized by inter-regional migrations, with the polarity of aquatic civilization centered in the *Atlas*, where the preeminent culture of the era was seated. There were again islands in the *Atlantean Sea* of the era where fishing and trading communities arose. Traditional papyrus and plank-lashed boats, together with larger ships with elevated bows and sterns with bowstrings astern for rudder oars, again plied the open seas for fishing and transit of goods. [cdxcv]

As maritime trade again facilitated communications and cultural transmission across the Sahara, contention with heavy rains and flooding during the *Sub-Pluvial* again prompted permanent relocations and concentrations in the upper river valleys, where life was more predictable. Here villages and hamlets gradually merged into larger urban-like communities, each developing somewhat autonomously in the semi-isolated island-like highlands of the 'aquatic' era. Separated by the vast expanse of the inland seas, village communities were pressed into petty kingdoms centered in the highlands of the *Ahaggar, Tassili, Tibesti,* and *Ennedi* across central Sahara, central highlands which formed the "*Saharan Fertile Crescent*" of the era. Together with the *Saharan Atlas* in the northwest and the *Atlas* spanning the western and northern margins of the *Sahara*, the *Ennedi, Tibesti, Tassili,* and *Ahaggar* were figurative islands rising above the mist of the ancient inland sea.

The Ennedi

The *Ennedi* served as a crossroads for inter-regional trade, connecting the southern trade routes to those of Sudan and the highlands of Ethiopia. Ceramics spread from Sudan through the *Ennedi* into the Sahara's central, western, and northern highlands. Ceramics and pottery of Sudan were traded and used from the *Ennedi* to the *Ahaggar* and points beyond.[99] *Paleo-Lake Yoa,* situated in the *Ounianga Basin* in the crater-like valley between the *Ennedi* and *Tibesti,* was once again filled during the Sub-Pluvial, transforming the surrounding basin into a rich green valley with trees and bounding grasslands. The *Ounianga Basin* of the era was teaming with vibrant village clusters around the shores and islands of the lake, populated by lineal descendants of the *Ancestral Si*.[cdxcvi] The neighboring *Tibesti,* with its series of massifs in the south, allowed transit and trade from *Paleo-Lake Yoa* to the *Tibesti*.

The Tibesti

The *Tibesti* is a giant triangular volcanic *massif* covering over thirty-eight thousand square miles in northwestern *Chad*. The mountain range had thick rain forests and rich, fertile valleys during the *Sub-Pluvial,* evidenced by the rock art of the era in its highlands. Rainfall inside the massif was higher than outside, with the interior once again obtaining an aquatic character, with rivers and large lakes often in full flood. Grasslands surrounding the base of the mountains provided rich grazing and hunting grounds for wild game, while enlarged lakes in the lower river pans provided ample sources of fish and aquatic plants. The *Tibesti* is actually a group of extinct volcanoes, with the backbone of the range in northern *Chad* and its northern slopes extending into southern *Libya*. The towns along its trade routes were well known by ancient traders as marketplaces for goods in route to and from the southeastern, central, northern, and western Sahara.

To the northwest of the *Tibesti,* the *Igharghar River* (the "*Triton River*" of classical Greek Mythology) discharged the northern slopes of the massive *Ahaggar* mountains, flowing into and through the "*Triton River Valley*" to the estuarial harbor that was fabled "*Lake Tritonis*" in the north. The *Tefassasset River* discharged the waters of *Ahaggar's* southern slopes, flowing into *Paleo-Lake Chad* to the south. The *Tamanrasset River* (precursor to the "*Lower Niger*") ran south southwestward, descending the highlands of the *Tibesti* into the *Tilemsi Basin* in the southeast. While most models of human cultural evolution conveniently ignore the role of maritime adaptations during this period of early antiquity in the Sahara, rock art along the ancient courses of these key waterways bears clear testimony to those who once traversed these corridors, bridging key areas of the ancient *Sahara*.[cdxcvii]

---

[99] Andah 1981

The Tassili

The *Tassili* and nearby *Ahaggar Massifs* were central to the ancient trade, communications, and cultural transmission spreading across the *Sahara*. During the earlier phases of the era, economic strategies across the region were mainly based on hunting and fishing. However, a dramatic shift occurred in plant exploitation, with intensive and specialized use of wild cereals. as the era progressed.[100] The processing of cereal seeds led to an increase in grinding equipment and the development of a dedicated microlithic industry struck from silicified sandstone. Sites evidencing this phase are rare in the lowlands, underscoring the concentrations of permanent communities in the highlands.

The Tadrart Acacus

The *Tadrart Acacus,* the northernmost extent of the *Tassili*, is a relatively small range, slightly more than ninety (90) miles long, covering an area of roughly eighteen hundred square miles, with a maximum elevation of thirty-six hundred feet. There is sound chronological evidence of active pastoral communities in the Acacus highlands during the *Sub-Pluvial*. Archaeological sites in the *Acacus* make it possible to hypothesize the existence of multi-faceted communities that once built stone structures and lithic artifacts struck from different raw materials.[cdxcviii] The pastoral-sedentary tradition in these ancient highland communities required an evolution of highly developed specializations for exploiting the food resources of the lowlands and herding and managing cattle and other livestock in the lowlands and highlands.

Clans routinely dispersed into the lowlands during summer and returned to the highlands during the winter. It was in the highlands where settlements appear to have been larger, where water sources were permanent and more manageable.[101] It was also in the highlands that the *Harp* was first depicted in rock art dating back to the *Sub-Pluvial*. Highland clan communities grew to be larger, and many indicators suggest highland villages were inhabited for longer periods during the year; organization of lithic technology, grinding equipment, and pottery underscored an increase of sedentism. Moreover, the sites were more complex, with separated specialized areas, such as fodder stocking and animal corralling. Early petty kingdoms eventually coalesced and emerged from the highland communities of the *Sub-Pluvial,* where they harvested and gathered fruits and grains in the lowlands, fished in the wetlands, and participated in riverine and maritime trade.

While the kingdoms in the *Acacus* were dynamic in their own right, it was in the *Tassili*, about five thousand feet up, where highland clans had for thousands of years found refuge and occupied the labyrinths of the *Tassili Plateaus*, the ancient *"Cities of the Wind"* where a unique form of spiritual vision first arose. The *Cities of the Wind,* the ancient cities of *Tin Tazarift*, *In Itinen*, *Tin Aboteka*, *Jabbaren*, and *Auanrhet,* with their famed narrow alleys, broad streets, bridges, pillars, cathedrals, and squares, were formed from sandstone rock. It was here that the ancient Seers believed the visionary dream-state induced by mushrooms allowed them to contact Beings in the spiritual realm, gaining knowledge of medicinal plants and how to treat illness and disease.

---

[100] Wasylikowa 1992; Castelletti et al. 1999; Mercuri 1999
[101] Cremaschi and Di Lernia 1999

Here the descendents of the *Ancestral Si* remained a devoted and spiritual people; faithful followers migrated to this labyrinthine realm seasonally, congregating in great numbers, meeting for trade, fellowship, and enlightenment. Ancient rock art at *Jabbaren* portray scenes of adoration for representations of the divinities as testimonial to the mystico-religious beliefs of the Seers and Priest of the sacred cults.[cdxcix] Simultaneously, at the labyrinth of *Tinterhert*, adjacent to the middle of the *Igharghar River Valley,* ancient rock art of the era depicts the adaption of pastoralism, with engravings of herds of cattle by the descendants of *Ancestral Si* of the era.

The Ahaggar

The *Ahaggar Massif,* situated on the *Tropic of Cancer* in the central Sahara, is geographically close to the *Tassili,* with only a few hundred miles separating the two mastiffs. The *Ahaggar* tower was prominently above the central highlands to its east and anciently towered prominently over the expansive surface of the *Atlantean Sea* to its west. The port city at the western base of the *Ahaggar* during the era imported and exported goods, commodities, and wares aboard ships of papyrus and plank, sailing to and from ports along the inland seaboards of *Southern Atlatia* in the south and *Central, Northern,* and *Eastern Atlatia* in the north. The plateaus in the south of the *Ahaggar* are filled with petroglyphs of giraffe, ostrich, gazelle, and other game animals inhabiting the highlands during the *Sub-Pluvial*, together with the many frescoed shelters and burial mounds of the clans who inhabited the highlands during the era.

To the east, the *Ighassan* plateau has numerous paintings and archaeological sites, and the *Fadnoun* plateau has hundreds of stone monuments of the era. In the northeastern area are Neolithic sculptures, pottery, grinding implements, enclosures, and other materials used by highland clans during the era. The plateaus have over fifteen thousand well-preserved Neolithic rock engravings and paintings of great variety and vitality. Yet, it has been estimated that at least two million artifacts of the era have been removed from the more accessible areas of the *Ahaggar*. The *Ahaggar* is renowned and reputedly full of ancient treasures and metals intentionally left behind by *Ancestral* and *Descendent Si* inhabiting sacred refugees before, during, and after the *Last Great Ice Age*. These places, the legends say, have been deserted for many thousands of years. It is said that one can enter caverns in the mountains and there find ancient treasures, cities, and lakes.

According to legendary tales, the oldest libraries on Earth are hidden away in these mountains and will someday be rediscovered. They contain knowledge of times before and after the deluge of the *Sub-Pluvial*. A time when ancient ships of the era plied the perennial inland seas, busily serving as transport and transit, carrying trade, commerce, and communications across and throughout the isles, coastal ports, and confines of the massive *Atlantean Inland Sea*. The *Ahaggar* is between fifty and one-hundred eighty miles in width, with extremely broken terrain towards the north, characterized by north-facing cliffs marked by deep gorges and steep-sided well-watered valleys, with semi-permanent rivers still running northward. The Massif's present-day characteristic red to black-weathered sandstone has been deeply eroded over the ages into forests of sixty to one-hundred feet high pillars, standing like ancient ruins. Ancient drawings and engravings in the highlands record the climatic changes, with animal migrations, and the evolution of cultural life in the highlands during the *Sub-Pluvial*.[d]

Permanent settlements were concentrated in the highlands, with specialized sites to exploit local raw materials like silicified sandstone, quartz, and quartzite. Seasonal hunting villages were in the lowlands, with fishing villages and ports along the course of the river. Silicified sandstone was fairly common in the highlands, while other useful materials and metals required trade. In the lowlands, along the corridors of the *Triton River Valley,* economic strategies were centered on hunting, fishing, barter and trade intermediation between the *Ahaggar* highlands to the south and *Lake Tritonis* to the north.[di] In the north, the *Igharghar River* (the fabled "Triton River") drained the massive watershed of the *Ahaggar*, flowing through the deeply incised canyon marking the course of its headwaters along the escarpment on the northern edges of the mastiff, between the *Tasili* and *Irawen Mountains*. The *Igharghar* ran north for over seven hundred eighty miles and, in places, was nearly six miles wide, with its waters nourishing the fertility of the *Igharghar River Valley* (the fabled *"Triton River Valley")* as it flowed into the estuarial harbor that was fabled *"Lake Tritonis."*

Atlatian Archipelago

Because the Atlas Mountains, for the most part, were (and are) a nearly contiguous land mass, perennial *Atlatia* had features of an archipelago, with the largest island-landmass comprised of the Anti-Atlas in the southwest, the High and Middle Atlas in the north, and the Tell Atlas in the east.[dii] A smaller island landmass consisted of the Saharan Atlas, leeward of the Tell Atlas; the entire Atlatian complex stretched across and just off the then nominal northwestern seaboard of Africa. From present-day *Morocco* in the west to *Tunisia* in the east, the two main isles were nominally surrounded by water, with several sizeable islands and smaller isles off the western seaboard: all of which comprised the *Atlatian Archipelago.* Along the southwestern seaboard, off the coast of present-day Mauritania (and Senegal), are the Cape Verde Islands of Boa Vista, Sal, São Nicolau, Santa Luzia, São Vicente, and Santo Antão.[102] With the smaller islets of Branco and Raso between Santa Luzia and São Nicolau, and Pássaros near São Vicente, the islets of Rabo de Junco off the coast of Sal, and the islets of Sal Rei and Baluarte off the coast of Boa Vista.

To the south were (and are) the islands of Maio, Santiago, Fogo, and Brava, with the smaller islet of Santa Maria near Santiago, and the islets of Grande, Rombo, Baixo, de Cima, do Rei, Luiz Carneiro, and Sapado near Brava, and the islet of Areia also close to the coast of Brava; all part of the *Atlatian Archipelago*.[103] To the north, off the southwestern coast of present-day Morocco, are the Canary Islands of Lanzarote, Fuerteventura, Gran Canaria, Tenerife, La Gomera, La Palma, and El Hierro, and the smaller islands of Isla de Alegranza, Isla Montaña Clara, and Isla Graciosa, Isla de los Lobos, Roque del Este, and Roque del Oeste.diii Further north, off the coast of central Morocco, were (and are) the islands of Madeira, Sao Tome, and Principe, and still further north, off the coast of northern Morocco, are the Azorean islands of Sao Miguel and Santa Maria, Terceira, Graciosa, Sao Jorge, Pico and Faial, and Flores and Corvo. While Cape Verde and the Canary Islands share affinities with the southwest, Madeira, Sao Tome, Principe, and the Azores share closer affinities with northwestern Africa; again, all are part of the *Atlatian Archipelago.*

---

[102] The Windward Islands
[103] The Leeward Islands

To the east, leeward of the *Tell,* was the *Saharan Atlas* island landmass, nominally surrounded by water. The *Northern Inland Sea* was bordered by the *Saharan Atlas* on the north, stretching from the basin of *Chott Ech Chergui* in present-day northern Algeria in the west to the *Gulf of Gabes* on the coast of present-day Tunisia in the east. Waters flowed southward from the *Northern Inland Sea* basins of *Chott Melrhir* and *Chott Hodna* into the central and western basins of the *Atlantean Sea,* bordering the island landmass on the east and west. The *Saharan Atlas* island landmass stretched over 1,500 miles, rendering it the second largest isle in the *Atlatian Archipelago*.

The *Saharan Atlas* still rises to heights of 7,600 feet. However, little survives of the once extensive cedar forests that populated the highlands during antiquity.[div] The highlands of the *Saharan Atlas* included a central palisade formed by its shorter ranges (the *Ksour* and *Ouled-Naïl* mountains) grouped between massifs to the west and east. To the north, windward of the *Saharan Atlas* and *Northern Inland Sea*, the *Tell Atlas* had an entirely different climate than the *Saharan Atlas*. The *Tell* is over 900 miles in length, paralleling the Mediterranean seaboard, stretching westward from present-day Tunisia through Algeria to Morocco. Due in large part to the compression of the typography between the Mediterranean towards the Equator, the rain was far more common in the highlands and to the immediate south of the *Tell* during the Sub-Pluvial.

In consequence, the east-west trending ranges and intervening plains of the *Tell Atlas* and the grasslands surrounding the *Northern Inland Sea* were then among the most agriculturally productive of the eastern *Atlatian* complex. Several prehistoric sites and megalithic monuments have been discovered in the highlands of the *Tell,* depicting an evident history of extensive ancient habitation and cultural evolution by the autochthonous clans and communities of the highlands. While autochthonously and culturally related to the *Ancestral Shi* of the *High Plateau* and the *Saharan Atlas*, the communities of the *Tell Atlas* were nonetheless autonomous. Numerous paleolithic flints have been discovered in the *Mina River Valley*, where a number of megalithic monuments have been discovered.

As with megalithic found in other parts of the Tell, little is known about this large group of monumental structures, and further study and (unbiased) analysis are needed. In the lofty altitudes of the north, where *Ouranos* reigned over *Northern Atlatia* in the past and led the northern clans to prosperity, the high divination and inter-regional relationships imbued with the northern provinces of *Southern Atlatia* remained intact and indeed had evolved. An advent lustrated by the rock art of the *Sub-Pluvial* in the northern highlands. Rock art sites in the lofty altitudes of the *High Atlas* began to be discovered in the early 1950s, at first by chance, where ancient sites could only be visited in the summer or early autumn since the rest of the year they risked being under snow

Prehistoric petroglyphs in the *High Atlas*, like other prehistoric art in the Saharan highlands, clash against the problem of meaning. Researchers who have undertaken such interpretation generally consider techno-typological similarities and affinities as suitable tools for classifying and implying inter-regional relationships and probable meaning. The petroglyphs in the heights of *Northern Atlatia* depict clear, distinct, and evident affinities with the rock art of the era in *Southern Atlatia*, supporting the inter-regional and cultural relationship between the two regions at the onset and throughout the *Sub-Pluvial*. The *Souss River Valley,* nestled between the *Anti-Atlas* and *High Atlas*, facilitated continued and close trading relationships between Northern Atlatia and the northern provinces of Southern Atlatia.

The *Souss* River rises in the *High Atlas,* from where it descends westward into the broad alluvial basin of the *Souss River Valley,* nurturing the ancient forests of *Argan* trees still valued for their medicinal oils. Oil extracted from the fruit of the tree was renowned for enhancing immunity against infections and diseases and providing relief from joint pain and continued to be traded throughout and beyond the Northern provinces of *Southern Atlatia*. Also rising in the *High Atlas* is the *River Draa*, which cut a deep channel between the *High Atlas* and *Anti Atlas,* descending through and carving a series of canyons famous for their cliffs of green and black rock. The *Drâa River Valley* was a major early ancient settlement area for disparate and diverse groups of *Si* and *Manding-Si* in southern Morocco, where the early benefits of such amalgamations were most pronounced. It was from here that the prosperity of an early mixed economy of agriculturalists, pastoralists, hunting, and fishing expanded into the northern highlands. From those highlands, the *Drâa* flows southeastward and then turns westwards toward the *Atlantic,* where it once emptied into the ocean at its ancient delta, opposite the *Canary Islands*.

Height of Atlatia: Plato's Atantis

A number of researchers conclude the core of early Atlatia was in the northern precincts of *Southern Atlatia,* in present-day *Southwestern Morocco*, presumably in the *Souss-Massa Plain,* a large caldera-like formation surrounded by the *High Atlas,* the *Anti-Atlas* and the *Atlantic Ocean*.[dv] This was northern *Southern Atlatia,* where *Queen Gaia* reigned and later formed a union with *Northern Atlatia* through her marriage to *King Ouranos,* beginning the great *Golden Age*. However, competing theories also exist, the most common being that the core of the earliest *Atlatia* was in the heart of *Southern Atlatia*, in present-day *Mauritania*, the first area to build large towns, sophisticated irrigation systems, water wells, roads, canals, and many other foundational aspects of early *Atlatian* civilization.

On the promontories of the Tichitt-Walata and Tagant Plateaus in present-day *Mauritania*, the *Southern Atlatians* built what are among the earliest known features of the Saharan civilization of earliest antiquity, evidenced by more than 400 ancient stone masonry settlements, with clear street layouts, where some had massive surrounding walls, while others were less fortified. Archaeology has shown they had agriculture, cities, and an advanced society; a society well organized with advanced social relations and an egalitarian societal structure. The bio-archaeological remains from the area suggest an early mixed economy based on the herding of livestock and the collection of sorghum, millet, yam, and rice along the lowland marshes and inland seaboard of the era.[104] In an environment where arable land and pasturage were at a premium, the population grew, and large-scale political organizations emerged, factors underscored by the homogeneity of architecture, settlement patterns, culture, and traditions.

This agro-pastoral society traded in jewelry and semi-precious stones from distant parts of the Sahara and Sahel, while early agriculture, pastoralism, hunting, fishing, and crafts continued to be expanding aspects of their mixed economy. The emergent empire in *Southern Atlatia* had several ethnicities and embraced a number of advanced cultures in the tropics, where a number of large ancient kingdoms existed. Atlatian maritime exploration and trade along the inland seaboard led to improvements in boat building, leading to the construction of larger and more capable boats and ships.[dvi] The influence of *Southern Atlatia* extended northward along the inland seaboard, traversing the ancient coasts along present-day central *Mauritania* into southwestern Algeria.

---

[104] The Fertile African Crescent, by Dr. Clyde A. Winters

The earliest iteration of the empire, incepted by the *Manding-Si*, brought together related groups such as the *Manding* and *Kwa,* extending their influence along the southern coastal zone of the *Atlantean Sea* to trade with the kingdoms in the ancient *Sahel*. Along the coasts of the huge inland sea were forests, savannas, seaside villages and ports, early cities, towns, meadows, and corridors of trade. Several early maritime kingdoms arose around these shores, with faint memories of their maritime prowess still surviving along the old trading routes adjacent to the former seaboard. Hints of the old maritime culture can be found in the languages of the descendent peoples inhabiting the *bordering tropics*, where names such as "Barakunda" and "Barokunda," both meaning "Boat-Towns," are still in common use in Gambia and Senegal.[105]

The *Manding-Si* of *Southern Atlatia* were among the earliest ship-builders in the *Sahara* and had long conducted maritime trade throughout the inland sea. The presence of elevated bows and sterns on their boats depicted in the era, with the renowned "bowstring" astern (used for rudder oars), affirms the use of these ancient ships for navigation across the open seas. On the Atlantic seaboard, the islands off the western coast of Southern Atlatia had been part of their maritime navigational realm for several millennia. Fishing and trade expeditions took place on several offshore isles considerable distances from shore. Such was the case with *Cape Verde Islands,* off the coast of Mauritania, where currents flowing past the islands bring large quantities of plankton, making the area extremely fertile fishing ground.

Vessels that sailed the *Sahara Inland Sea* sailed across the open waters of the Atlantic to avail *Southern Atlatians* of these rich fishing grounds. Merchants and traders also ventured the voyage, nearly three-hundred miles from the shores of *Southern Atlatia,* to avail themselves of resources and trade opportunities with communities on several islands. Ancestors of the earliest settlers of the islands originally came from the region of the present-day Spanish Sahara in *Southern Atlatia* and welcomed trade from the mainland. Though archaeological research on the *Cape Verde Islands* has been limited, 142 artifacts of the era have been discovered on the aisles. However, examination of the archeological dating procedures used reveals them sadly lacking and often misleading.[dvii]

The island of *Sal* is the closest to the shores of *Southern Atlatia;* here, there was (and is) an abundance of tuna and large numbers of turtles nesting on the beaches, which attracted the ancient fishing fleets. These, together with trade for wild asparagus harvested around the island, brought merchants to the isles. During the earliest phases of the Holocene, the *Cape Verde Islands* were larger than at present, with more extensive coastal landmasses and harbors, enabling the construction of seaside villages, townships, cities, and ports. These were uncovered by the so-called "Buache Map," proffered in 1737 by the French geographer Phillip Bauche, copied from sources whose origins are based in antiquity.[dviii] This map correctly portrays the location of the islands and the outline of an underwater plateau, which once formed an extended shape before inundation. A submerged city has been discovered off the coast of the islands.

---

[105] Cheikh Anta Diop (The African Origins of Civilisations 1974)

Imperial *Atlatia* took shape from the highlands of the *Anti-Atlas*, with its earliest center just north of *Arghilas,* in present-day Western Sahara, extending first to the highlands of *Morocco*, then to the *Grand Atlas* and then eastward to the *Tell* and the *Saharan Atlas*, extending fully to the original *Pillars of Hercules,* at the *Gulf of Gabes*. The expansion of provinces in the *Tell* and *Saharan Atlas* led to increased trade and technology transference throughout *Atlatia*. Archaeology has shown they had cities, agriculture, and a phenomenally advanced system of water irrigation, where they cultivated a variety of high-grade cereals, wheat, barley, and other crops, including date palms, vines, and olives. They cultivated cultured meats, both dry and edible kinds of fruit and species of vegetables, and maintained storages of nuts of various varieties. There was an abundance of wood for carpentry and specific areas allotted for tame and wild animals; all these the archipelago provided in seemingly endless abundance.

*Atlatian*s mined minerals as well as metals, including *"orichalcum,"* which was mined in parts of the main islands and, with the exception of *gold*, was the most valued precious metal of the era. The *Atlatians* employed themselves in building temples, palaces, harbors, and docks and continued to ornament these in successive generations, every king surpassing the one who came before, until they made the whole countryside a marvel to behold. The plain on the main island, which had been cultivated over many ages, was rectangular for the most part and received streams that came down from the mountains, winding around the plain and touching the *Capital City* at various points, from where the streams then discharged into the sea. Straight canals, a hundred feet in width, were cut into the plain at intervals of sixty thousand feet, used to float wood down from the mountains to the city and convey harvested fruits and vegetables to ships in the harbors. Twice a year, they harvested fruits and vegetables, once in winter, with the benefit of the rains, and once in summer, with the benefit of the water in the canals.

The Legends

Khem (known anciently as "*Khronos"* or "Chronos" by the later Greeks and as "Ham by the even later Semites) presided during the building of the Megaliths and Megalithic sites that flourished along the ancient coasts of the "Western Ocean" (the present day "Atlantic Ocean") and the Mediterranean Sea.[dix] *Khem* (Kham, Cham, Ham, Khronos) was known as the "Lord of Justice," punishing anyone who lied or broke an oath, yet was said to be always fair, striving to achieve balance among all things; he was closely associated with what was then known as the "Western Ocean," anciently known by the later Greeks as the "*Sea of Khronos.*" According to the early Greeks of the *Atlatian* era, *Khem* was the builder of the ancient Megaliths around the Mediterranean. Megaliths were used as early ancient celestial observatories, shelters, and territorial landmarks.

In inculcating the early suzerainty of *Atlatia* over lands around the Mediterranean, *Khem* commissioned construction of impressive Megaliths honoring local kings and the Megalithic Coastal Cities around the Mediterranean of the age and spent long periods abroad on such campaigns. It was during this, the *Megalithic Age*, that *Khem* (Kham, Cham, Ham, Khronos) directed the building of the ramparts of earliest *Troy* …at the western extent of *Asia Minor*, gateway to the ancient *Euxine Sea* (the "Proto-Black Sea"). During the construction of the earliest Troy, *Khem* had an illicit affair with the daughter of a renowned but dethroned *Atlatian* king, a beautiful woman named *Philyra* by whom he sired a son with the given name of *Kheiron* (Chiron), a son who would later honor him by being instrumental in the rise of *Phrygia,* an important early ancient province of *Asia Minor*. Mischievous *Khem* sired a second son on a mission in the distant land that would become *Canaan*.

While constructing a megalith east of present-day Lebanon, *Khem* had an illicit affair with a beautiful woman known as *Nuit* (Nwt), the wife of a nobleman from Nagu-Punt.[dx] [dxi] The woman was of royal lineage and the wife of a respected herb and incense trader, a woman by whom *Khem* sired a son with the given name of *Seteth* (Set), an advent so dishonoring it left the nobleman's family in disgrace. Khem (Khronos, Chronos, Kham, Cham, Ham) sired six children by his wife Rhea, three sons, Hāidēs (Ἅιδης), Poseidon (Sidon), and Ausar (Osiris), and three daughters, Hestia, Demeter, and Hera. Hestia, the eldest, was the oldest daughter, and Hāidēs, the second eldest, was the oldest son. Demeter, the third eldest, was the second and middle daughter, and Poseidon, the fourth eldest, was the second and middle son. Hera was the youngest daughter, and her younger brother *Ausar* (known as Osiris by the early Greeks and Zeus by the later Greeks) was the youngest and last of his progeny. [dxii]

There was a federation in *Atlatia* that had ruled over the whole archipelago and several other islands, as well as the lands extending and beyond the original *Pillars of Heracles,* in addition to parts of southern *Eurasia* as far as *Tyrrhenia*. Poseidon, receiving for his lot the main island of *Atlatia*, settled on the side toward the sea. In the center of the main island of *Atlatia*, there was a plain, said to have been the fairest of all plains and very fertile. Near the plain, there was a mountain, where there dwelt a man of that countryside whose name was *Evenor;* he and his wife, *Leucippe*, had an only daughter, whose name was *Cleito*. *Cleito* was growing up to womanhood when her father and mother died; *Poseidon* fell in love with her, had intercourse with her, and built her home on a high hill at the very center of the island. The home overlooked a fertile plain bordered by the sea, where *Poseidon* and *Cleito* eventually begat and raised five pairs of male children.

Dividing the island of *Atlatia* into ten portions, *Poseidon* gave to the firstborn of the eldest pair, his mother's dwelling, and the surrounding allotment, which was the largest and best and made him king over the rest. For the others, he made princes and gave them rule over other territories. It was *Poseidon* who named each of the twins; the eldest he named *Atlas*, who was given the largest province and named the entire archipelago as well as the *"Western Ocean"* after himself. [dxiii] [dxiv] To his younger twin-brother, who obtained the eastern extremity of the main island, toward the original Pillars of Heracles, *Poseidon* gave the country, which is named after him, *Gadeirus,* a region still known as the of *Gades*. To the second pair of twins, *Poseidon* gave the elder the name *Ampheres* and the younger the name *Evæmon;* the third pair were named *Mneseus* (the elder) and *Autochthon* (the younger). To the fourth pair of twins, he named the elder *Elasippus* and the younger *Mestor;* and to the fifth pair, he named the elder *Azaes* and the younger *Diaprepes*. Each of these and their descendants were the rulers and inhabitants of the adjacent islands in the open sea and also held sway over the country within (that is, "west of") the original *Pillars of Heracles*.

Thus did the ruling coalition of *Atlatia* come to descend from *Poseidon*. These powerful rulers formed a federation by which they controlled all of *Atlatia,* but their authority over one another and their mutual relations remained governed by the *Laws of Poseidon*. *Atlas* ruled the largest province, in which he built the new capital *city of Atlatia*. It is said the tops of the city walls were clad with brilliant metals, including an iridescent golden-red alloy known as orichalcum, and shiny metallic silver, each metal glowing together in the dawn. The finest structure on the island was the *Temple of Poseidon,* and it served as the home of the primary ruler. The outside of the temple was covered with silver, with its pinnacles covered with gold. The interior roof was ivory, adorned with gold, silver, and orichalcum.

They placed statues of gold inside the temple, with one of *Poseidon* himself standing in a chariot led by six winged horses of such size that his head touched the roof of the building. There were also other images in the interior of the temple that had been dedicated by private individuals. Some of the other buildings were simple, while in others, they put together different stones, which they intermingled to be a natural source of ornament. They used fountains of cold and hot springs and built cisterns, some open to the heavens and others with roofs for use in winter as warm baths. There were many temples built and gardens and places of exercise, some for men, some for women, and some set apart for horses, on both the two main islands. In the center of the larger of the two islands, there was a racecourse for horse races that extended all around the island.

The surrounding mountains were celebrated for their size and beauty, in which they exceeded all that are now to be seen anywhere; they inhabited by many wealthy villages and blessed with many natural rivers, lakes, and meadows, supplying food enough for every animal, wild or tame, and wood of various sorts, abundant for every kind of work. For generations, *Atlatia* remained peaceful and prosperous. Almost all of the population's needs were met by the fields, forests, and mines of the islands. Anything the kingdom did not produce was imported. This was possible because the ruling body met regularly; it came to consist of ten rulers who were, in essence, *Atlas* and his nine brothers. These meetings occurred in the *Temple of Poseidon,* where the rulers inscribed the laws on a pillar of orichalcum.

Thus, the island came to be divided among *Atlas*, the first King of a unified *Atlatia*, and his nine brothers, with *Atlas* assuming control over the central hill and surrounding areas.[dxv] *Atlas* had a large and honorable family, and his eldest branch always retained leadership of the kingdom; they had wealth in an amount as was never before possessed by kings; they were furnished with everything they could have wanted. Because of the greatness of their empire, many things were brought to them from foreign lands, and the archipelago itself provided much of what was required for their uses of life.

Nonetheless, each succeeding king tried to outdo his predecessor in building a greater kingdom, an endeavor that led to their corruption. *Atlatia* assembled and developed a powerful army of soldiers, as did each of its nine provinces, and with the passage of time, their military and economic influence grew. Their powerful armies assailed parts of present-day *Libya* and the prosperous early ancient lands in the *Lower Nile Valley*. They also launched unprovoked expeditions against southern *Eurasia* as far as *Tyrrhenia* (present-day Italy) and the *Anatolian Peninsula* (present-day Turkey), as well as other parts of *Western Asia,* acts in clear contravention of the *Laws of Poseidon*.

Ausar, known as *Osiris* (a corruption of the name *Ausar*) by the pagan Greeks and *Zeus* by the classical Greeks, called together the older rulers and asked for their advice in putting down the rebellion against the *Laws of Poseidon*. However, dissension between him and his nephews led to his frustration and no resolution to the matter. The ensuing rivalry caused *Ausar* to first relocate to far Southern Atlatia, where he followed a manner of life opposite to that led by his siblings. Some say his rise to kingly stature over the region was due to his own accord, while others say he was chosen by the masses because he showed himself honorable …as well as the distrust they bore towards his corrupt kindred.

Ausar was pre-eminent in strength and qualities of virtue; he demonstrated zeal in punishing impious and wicked men and displayed kindness toward the masses; for this reason, the name "*Kush*" was conferred upon him, a title meaning the "Perfect Black Sovereign."[dxvi] *Ausar* departed *Atlatia* before the fall, relocating to land south of the Atlantean seaboard; there, he built a city among the *Igbo* (one the peoples from the sacred "Land of Yam"), where he settled in anonymity and peace. *Atlatia* eventually fell, but *Ausar* (whom the *Igbo* called "*Eshi*") was said to have recorded the knowledge of *Atlatia* on stone and hid them (365 of them) in the northern forests of ancient *Nigeria*.[dxvii]

Atlatia was governed according to the *Laws of Poseidon*, as they had been handed down; besides the laws, there was an oath invoking renunciation of the disobedient, inscribed by the first rulers on the column of orichalcum at the *Temple of Poseidon,* where the people assembled every sixth year. At each assemblage, they gave pledges to one another, consulted about public affairs, inquired into transgressions, and passed judgment on those who transgressed. They drank from golden vessels, and, at night, sitting around the fire at the temple, they received and gave judgment. If any had accusations to bring against another, they did so in an open forum; when conferring judgment, each swore they would judge and punish those deemed to have transgressed according to the laws on the column.

Each swore that for the future, they would not transgress any of the inscriptions and would not obey any ruler who commanded them to act other than in accordance with the injunctions of *Poseidon*. There were many special laws, which several kings had inscribed about the temples, but the most important was that they were not to take up arms against one another. They were all to come to the rescue if anyone in any city attempted to overthrow the royal house. Like their ancestors, they were to deliberate in common about war and other matters, giving supremacy to the family of *Atlas*; the king was not to have the power of life and death over any of his kinsmen unless he had the assent of the majority of the ten kings.

As to the population, each lot in the plain of the main island had an appointed leader. In the rest of the archipelago, there was a vast multitude, with leaders to whom they were assigned according to their villages. As regards manpower, it was ordained that each leader furnish war chariots so as to make up a total of ten thousand chariots; also, two horses and riders upon them, a light chariot, accompanied by a fighting man on foot carrying a small shield, having a charioteer mounted to guide the horses. In addition, he was bound to furnish two heavy-armed men, two archers, two slingers, three stone-shooters, and three javelin men, together with all the men who were fit to bear arms or serve as sailors to make up a complement of twelve hundred ships. Because of their shipping fleet, the *Atlatians* had a large supply of imports from abroad. However, early on, the archipelago itself furnished most of the requirements of daily life.

In addition, the *Atlatians* produced and brought to perfection various metals, both the hard kind and the fusible kind, including mountain copper, which was among the most precious of metals then known, except orichalcum and gold; each extracted by ancient mining, with a large number of mines in many places within the archipelago. Yet, over time, economic strategies became increasingly directed toward foreign expeditions, with long-distance voyages made in search of precious metals and other resources. Rock art depicting ships of the era is found in the Atlas, associated with the large rivers, then discharging into the open seas. All of these ships are depicted with much the same design and include sails and many oars. A prehistoric city of the era, probably used in preparation for river-based launchings of maritime endeavors, was discovered in southwest *Morocco*, in the *Souss-Massa-Draa River Valley*.[106]

---

[106] Discovered in 2008

The ancient city has a great manifold of ruins with clearly prehistoric features, with large numbers of ruined buildings, caverns, cisterns, paths, stone heaps, and traces of agricultural landscaping.[dxviii] A multitude of stone tools was found next to the ruined buildings. Some rather unusual constructions were also discovered, including a large stone circle complex, and a large triangular complex, nearly thirty-thousand feet in length. The unusual size and presence of several unique stone monuments make it distinct from neighboring archaeological sites. A remarkable oval building is situated in the northeast of the central area, and a freestanding house (measuring 30m x 18m.) was the best preserved of the ruins found.[dxix] Neolithic ceramics and stone tools were found inside the ruins.[dxx] There were also megaliths situated in the vicinity and other buildings with prehistoric features.[dxxi]

A central hill surrounded by a long broadway (while its purpose remains unclear) appears to have been a circular rampart or an aqueduct. The whole area is traversed by paths, and in the central area, a path paved with stones was discovered. Some of the paths form straight lines that seem to run parallel to one another and may have been avenues. Caverns were found all over the area, especially near the ruined buildings. It is estimated that there were over five-hundred caverns, with many, but not all, sunken; most appear to be old cisterns cut into the limestone, while others appear to be cellars of ruined buildings. Unfortunately, most of the monuments have already been destroyed or are currently being demolished by stone grinding mills.[dxxii] [dxxiii] The megalithic site of *Mzora* is located in a rarely visited part of *Morocco*, not far from the Atlantic coast and the prehistoric ruins of *Lixus*. Lixus was once a prehistoric seaport perched on a hilltop overlooking the Atlantic Ocean near the *Loukkos River*, constructed on the bank of the river. [107]

Archaeologists have uncovered an amphitheater with hundreds of seats for spectators at this unique site; behind it are the city baths, which seem to be in excellent condition. In the center of the ancient seaport is a Basilica, which is also reported to be in very good condition.[dxxiv] *Mzora* is also home to a *Neolithic Ellipse* of 168 surviving stones, with the tallest over sixteen feet in height.[dxxv] [dxxvi] [108] Off the southwestern coast of Morocco are the *Canary Islands* of *Lanzarote, Fuerteventura, Gran Canaria, Tenerife, La Gomera, La Palma,* and *El Hierro.* Sailing southwest from the harbor at the ancient *Draa River Delta* on the Atlantic coast, *Atlatian* sailors easily sailed to the *Canaries*. Obviously, before they accomplished this feat, the art of navigation on the open seas had been considerably advanced.

Atlatian colonization of *Tenerife* can be seen from the study of the rock art sites of Aripe I and Aripe II, as well as from the Zanata Stone. [dxxvii] [dxxviii] [dxxix] Rock art engravings of the era in the Canaries bear a clear likeness to those in the Southwestern Sahara.[dxxx] There are tens of thousands of examples of the Western Sahara of rock art that appear at sites in *Tenerife* and on many of the *Canary Islands;* indeed, many elements can be traced directly back to the Atlas and the highlands of the Central Sahara. What is apparent is that there was a direct relationship between the *Atlatians* of ancient *Southwestern Morocco* and *Mauritania* and the colonization of the *Island of Tenerife*.[dxxxi] The rock art at *Risco Blanco* should also be added to the archaeological evidence catalog explaining Tenerife's colonization.

---

[107] Also spelled variously Msoura/Mezorah
[108] Temple, Robert (2010). Egyptian Dawn. London: Century. p378.

The rock art at *Tenerife* is on the western side of the island, on the south face of the *Risco Blanco* site, on a small volcanic point standing over two-thousand feet above sea level. It consists of six panels in which all the geometric and figurative engraved motifs have been executed using the incision technique. The site is inside a small hollow on a horizontal surface, three feet wide and nearly four feet long, with the engravings occupying the northeast area of the panel; the incision technique varies in depth and width, depending on the motifs. [dxxxii] There are also *ancient-stepped pyramids* of the era in the *Canaries*, on the islands of *Tenerife* and *La Palma,* complex structures with thousands of stones, all structured in layers. Although of different sizes, they share a similar rectangular ground plan. Astronomical connotations are also associated with the ancient construction and use of the pyramids. If you were able to climb to the top of the largest pyramid during the summer solstice, you would witness a double sunset as the sun sets behind a tall mountain peak, passes it, and then reappears and sets behind the next mountain.

The *pyramids* all have stairs on the western side, which were climbed exactly as the sun rose on the morning(s) of the winter solstice. While the *Canary Islands* may hardly seem a place for pyramids, those that have been discovered on Tenerife alone, near Güímar, have long been known to exist on the island.[dxxxiii] The pyramids on both the islands of *Tenerife* and *La Palma* have yet to be recognized as historical monuments and are thus not protected. Only those in *Güímar* are safe because they are on land, which now forms an Ethnographic Park. Nonetheless, it seems evident that what is really needed is a properly funded investigation into these pyramids by a non-biased team of archaeologists. In addition to the pyramids of the present-day coast of the *Canary Islands*, a central pavement and wide engraved stone steps have been discovered on the fifty-foot-deep sea bottom, items that are clearly of prehistoric archaeological origin.

The *Canary Island* of *Madeira,* off the central coast of present-day *Morocco,* is an island rich in prehistoric archaeology, with a large number of unexplained ruins and walls hidden under geological sliding and conditions that have lasted for thousands of years. In this writing, these prehistoric archaeological sites have yet to receive the serious study they deserve and are in danger of being eradicated by "modern development." Of equal significance, further north off the coast of central Morocco is the *Azorean islands* (the "*Azores*") of *Sao Miguel* and *Santa Maria, Terceira, Graciosa, Sao Jorge, Pico, Faial, Flores* and *Corvo,* where rock art and other artifacts have been discovered which archeologists believe can be dated back to the Bronze Age." [dxxxiv]

A large number of prehistoric pyramidal structures have also been discovered on the island of *Pico,* some exceeding forty feet in height. One hundred and forty pyramids have been observed by researchers, and according to archaeologists studying the pyramids, they seem to be oriented to the stars. Some of the pyramids have inside chambers that have yet to be explored and studied. Archeologists indicate the structures may have been built according to an oriented plan aligned with the summer solstices, which affirms they were built with intent and purpose.[109] Researchers working on sites say artifacts were also found and believe the structures were places of worship. They also believe the pyramids are analogous to similar prehistoric structures found in *North Africa* and the *Canary islands*. [dxxxv] As with certain of the *Canaries*, there have been reports of underwater ruins off the coasts of the *Azores*.

---

[109] APIA archeologists Nuno Ribeiro and Anabela Joaquinito

An underwater pyramid has been reported off the coast between *São Miguel* and *Terceira*; the structure is said to be perfectly squared and oriented by the cardinal points. It is thought to be approximately one-hundred ninety-six feet tall with a base of roughly eighty-six thousand square feet.[dxxxvi] Additionally, in 1985, several hundred miles east of the *Azores*, a Russian vessel was filming the ocean floor with a special deep-diving camera when, at a depth of 120 feet, they noticed a string of stone columns and a massive dome-topped building.[dxxxvii] "We couldn't believe our eyes," they said. "We were viewing an entire city with magnificent boulevards and avenues, and they were lined with what looked like temples, halls, government buildings, and homes."[110] To the east, an undersea wall has been discovered on the Mediterranean side of Gibraltar, just off the Moroccan coast of the once the main island of the *Atlatian Archipelago*.[dxxxviii] The wall extends for nine miles atop a submerged mountain 120 feet below the surface. Some of its stones are each larger than two-story houses, and the researcher observed roads going down the mountain further into unknown depths.[dxxxix]

On the mainland, in present-day Morocco, another megalithic monument was discovered to south of Casablanca (in 1926). Just off the coast, to the west, is the *Island of Essaouira*, opposite the ancient *Port of Lixus*; the island was anciently known as the "*Island of Amogdul*" by descendants of its original *Atlatian* inhabitants and became known as *Mogador* during the French protectorate of 1912 - 1956. With the independence of Morocco, the island was renamed '*Essaouira*'.[dxl] Archaeological research shows that Essaouira has been occupied since prehistoric times, primarily because the island has long been considered one of the best anchorages on the Moroccan coast. The bay at Essaouira is partially sheltered, making it a peaceful harbor protected against strong marine winds, with the added benefit of sheltered passage between the island-mainland. The archeological value of the island is said to be of unmeasurable importance for learning about prehistoric methods of construction adapted to the supply of local building materials. The ancient supply of woodland stones facilitated the building of fortifications on the island.

The *Atlatians* first became interested in the island because of its proximity to the coast, the island's rich fishing waters, and its famous seashell "Murex" from which a valuable purple dye was produced; this, as well as the access it afforded for freshwater replenishment during long maritime undertakings. Ideally situated with regard to the trade winds of the North Atlantic, the island prospered during the earliest maritime expeditions and incursions into Europe. The coasts of *Europe*, from the *Iberian Peninsula* in the south through *France*, the *British Isles,* and *Scandinavia*, are dotted with megaliths of the era.[dxli] According to archaeologists, most of these were erected during the Neolithic Age (the era of Atlatia).[dxlii] The oldest of the megaliths were constructed in *Portugal*, followed by western *France* and *Ireland*, before spreading eastward to *Sicily* and *Tyrrhenia* (present-day Italy) in the south.[dxliii]

Most *Atlatian* long-distance expeditions were in pursuit of metal and mineral deposits, such as Tin, mined and exported from the *Iberian Peninsula* and the *British Isles* at the onset and height of the *Bronze Age*. The capital of *Atlatia* had been long situated south of Gibraltar, at *Arghilas*, where some of her ports are now submerged off the Moroccan coast. However, after unification under *Atlas*, a new capital city was constructed, where it is said: "the tops of the city walls were clad with brilliant metals, including an iridescent golden-red alloy known as orichalcum, and metallic silver; each metal glowing together in the dawn." While reports from antiquity are silent on the location of the city, archeologists believe it was located northwest of the *Souss-Massa* plain, where a large circular caldera-like structure was discovered. A structure covered with hundreds of ruins that appear to fit the dimensions of the city.[dxliv]

---

[110] Australasian post, January 30, 1986

Archaeological evidence along the coastal belts of the *Northern Inland Sea* basins suggests herding became common practice, with villages and towns practicing a combination of herding, hunting, and fishing, while others practiced and refined farming, irrigation, and agricultural techniques. Archaeology has shown they had agriculture and a phenomenally advanced system of irrigation, where they cultivated a variety of high-grade cereals (wheat and barley) and other crops (date palms, vines, olives, cotton, vegetables, and pulses). On the High Plateau, a mixed farming and pastoral economy emerged around the *Northern Inland Seaboard* and throughout *Tell*. From this time onward, the presence of large, stonewalled corral areas and numerous granary foundations indicate the importance of the mixed farming and pastoral economy, which spread from the *Tell* to the *Saharan Atlas*.[dxlv]

The area of the *Saharan Atlas,* currently known as *South Oran,* is where prehistoric engravings have been studied since 1863; the oldest show affinities with those in the *Tassili* (in the central Sahara). There is evidence that by 10,000 B.C., there were fertile grasslands, forests, meadows, rivers, streams, and large towns and cities in the *Saharan Atlas*. On the main island, the *Moulouya River* (in northeast *Morocco)* was a key water course emptying into the *Mediterranean Sea;* Neolithic open-air sites have been found around its lower basin, with remnants of habitation in the floodplain, including ceramics and geometric triangles; artifacts of river valley villages in proximity to ports along the Mediterranean seaboard.[111][dxlvi] The northern province of *Oran*, with its many vineyards, citrus groves, orchards, and gardens, was situated between the *Moroccan border* on the west and the *Soummam River* on the east, on the main island of the *Tell Atlas* ().

Northern Oran was home to an ancient port city on the *Gulf of Oran*, an inlet of the Mediterranean Sea that had been occupied since prehistoric times; it was one of the early maritime hubs of eastern *Atlatia*. The river valleys ascending from the Mediterranean seaside ports of the era connected with the passes through the *Moroccan High Atlas* and played key roles in trade between the eastern seaboards, the river valleys, the highlands of the *Tell At*las, and the northern highlands and river valleys of the *Middle* and *High Atla*s. Trade flows continued through the highlands, river valleys and inland seaboards of the *Anti-Atlas*. In the second half of this era *Atlatia* extracted large amounts of copper from mines in the *Akjoujt Mountains* in the *Anti-Atlas,* and transformed a significant portion into tools, weapons, and jewelry. At least three thousand (3000) artifacts of the era have been uncovered in the region; it is thus safe to assume that production in the region was far higher.

Though hardly anything is known about the miners and metal workers of the Akjoujt Mountains, their production was broadly exported, notably, from the Atlantic coast, particularly around Nouakchott in eastern Mauritania, down to the *Senegal* and *Niger Rivers* of the era. The geological formations of the Atlas had remained rich in minerals, with the *Moroccan High Atlas* containing deposits of lead and zinc and the *Middle Atlas* containing deposits of copper, silver, and manganese. The use of copper in antiquity was of more significance than gold; the first tools, implements, and weapons were made of copper; nonetheless, as the era progressed and the "Copper Age" neared maturity, the *Atlatians* launched returning expeditions to the Iberian Peninsula, where they first established mines in the southern regions of present-day Spain.

Copper from the Peninsula had become increasingly important by the mid-millennium when the valued metal was mined and imported from the north and northeast regions of the Iberian Peninsula. Mines of native copper were also still productive in the mountains of Atlatia, but a great technological innovation, "bronze," an alloy of copper and tin with better hardness and resistance than pure copper, had changed the entire dynamic. The mountains of *Atlatia* lacked sources of Tin, and the mountains of the Iberian Peninsula had large sources of highly prized metal. The strategic objective of Atlatia was then, in order to obtain a monopoly of bronze, to control the mines of tin, which Atlatia was lacking. The tin of the era was imported by the southern and northern kingdoms from the southwest Iberian Peninsula and as far away as Cornwall in the present-day British Isles.

Bronze was the first alloy or combination of metals to affect the order of kingdoms and nations during antiquity; harder and more chemically resistant than copper, societies that utilized bronze tools and weapons easily ruled their neighbors. According to Plato, the *Atlatians* fused metals and practiced expansionism. In this pursuit, they used their naval power to explore parts of Europe as early as 9,600 BC. According to Critias, they first conquered parts of Libya, where megalithic remnants can be seen in the Terrgurt Valley, "there had been originally no less than eighteen or twenty megalithic trilithons, in a line, each with its massive altar placed" according to 19th-century explorer H.S. Cowper.[dxlvii][dxlviii] Critias advises that they sought conquest as far as the Nile and in Southern Europe as far as Tyrrhenia.

The first incursions into southern Europe were launched from the *Port of Lixus,* on the Atlantic seaboard, in concert with expeditions from the *Isle of Essaouira,* opposite *Lixus,* an ancient port ideally aligned with the *North Atlantic* trade winds for voyages to Europe from the *Moulouya River Delta* in northeast *Morocco,* and further east from the *Port City of Oran.* Expeditions from eastern Atlatia were launched from the *Gulf of Gabes* and the *Port City of Cyrene* on the Cyrenaican (Libyan) coastal plateau. *Cyrene* is a city steeped in legends, and one of the most complex archaeological sites along the Mediterranean seaboard, a site whose antiquity is affirmed by a single surviving megalithic discovered over a century ago. [112][dxlix]

Though unquestioned loyalty and unity were inherent in the ethos of *Atlatia*, the constituent kingdoms competed mightily to excel in progress, prestige, and honor. Ships could then be constructed more stoutly and with greater speed and were constructed in increased numbers as experienced seafarers made voyages of exploration and opened up new routes in all directions. In competition with the kingdoms of the north and south, the eastern kingdoms sailed over the open seas from the coast of eastern *Atlatia* (Libya) to the *Isle of Crete* as skilled mariners aboard well-equipped vessels, capable of conducting long-distance voyages over the inland seas, sailed the open water of the *Mediterranean Sea* and returned to their home ports. The *Island of Crete*, off the coast of the *Port City of Cyrene* in the *Mediterranean*, was the entryway to the *Aegean Sea* and the first island colonized by eastern *Atlatia*.

---

[112] Giuseppe Haimann, Cirenaica (1882)

The founding of the ancient settlement on the *Island of Crete* that later became the *City at Knossos* has been dated to about 10,000 B.C. (an approximate dating based on the archaeological strata).[dl] The earliest settlers on *Crete* brought a high degree of culture with them during the Neolithic Age, as their artifacts demonstrate. Houses were built of stone as well as of wattles daubed with clay, and they had an active sea trade, with obsidian imported from the *Isle of Melos*, as well as an early agricultural economic base.[113][dli] Descendent *Atlatians* on *Crete*, later called *"Minoans"* (a term coined by a 19th-century British archaeologist after 'King Minos' of Knossos), in keeping with their heritage, were master builders, as attested to by one of their greatest achievements, an aqueduct that brought fresh water from the mountains to their capital city at Knossos, supplying water for the first known "flush" toilets, as well as other uses.[dlii] Paved roads and multi-storied townhouses were also prominent on *Crete*, with archaeological evidence suggesting that theirs' was a peaceful society with no need for fortifications.[114]

Eventual trading expeditions and incursions into continental *Southeastern Europe* from *Crete* enabled them to mine and procured valued mineral deposits, such as cassiterite, which, when mixed with copper, rendered it harder. However, *Crete* had long imported obsidian from *Melos* before the introduction of metalworking and alloys and was well developed during the earlier phases of the Neolithic, as evidenced by the refined obsidian knives discovered at Knossos. Nonetheless, regular shipping traffic on the Mediterranean and Ægean Seas increased greatly after knowledge of metals and metal alloys became widespread. While copper could be found on *Crete*, tin had to be imported, and trade-oriented traffic by sea was greatly increased.

After establishing trading settlements on several of the Ægean Islands, the earliest incursion into the Southeastern European mainland was into the ancient lands of Arcadia, Thessaly, and Thrace, with the Atlatians expanding throughout *Thrace*. It is generally accepted that a miscegenated people, called *"Proto-Thracians,"* arose from admixtures of Atlatians and indigenous peoples then inhabiting the land (with the *Atlatians* later called *"Pelasgians"* by pagan Greeks as a term for Africans inhabiting Southern Europe when they arrived in the area). The *Proto-Thracians* became a fusion of several different tribes and cultures throughout the region. However, the history of these times is shrouded in veiled legends and myths.[dliii][dliv] Early *Thrace* was a rich and fertile region, prime for agricultural development, providing an ideal base for Atlatian colonization and expansion.

The term "*Proto-Thracian*" was originally coined for descendants of the first *Atlatian* settlers and colonists, those who would so eventually inhabit much of the area from Greece up to the Danube.[dlv] *Proto-Thracians* shared and preserved age-old *Atlatian* abilities for discovering and extracting natural metal and mineral resources and deposits without harming nature. Present-day archaeologists and anthropologists continue to be surprised by the kinds of advanced technological practices they employed during the era and have further affirmed that through ancient Thrace, the *Atlatian* colonists and their *Proto-Thracian* descendants came in direct contact with *Western Europe* during the Neolithic Age. Evidence has been forthcoming that two main trade routes crossed Germany, one from the head of the Adriatic and the other from the lower Danube River Valley.[dlvi][dlvii] France was similarly crossed by the Rhone River Valley, a trade route used to bring tin down from Cornwall in the British Isles.

---

[113] Myths of Crete & Pre-Hellenic Europe; By Donald A. Mackenzie (1917)
[114] Myths of Crete & Pre-Hellenic Europe; By Donald A. Mackenzie (1917)

The *Atlatians* of *Crete* were the earliest seafarers to trade along these routes, as is supported by various pieces of evidence.[dlviii] According to researchers in the late 19th century, by the beginning of the "Atlatian Bronze Age," the Rhone River Valley played a key role in transit between the north and the Mediterranean, suggesting that the Rhone Valley was already a continental trade route to the tin mines of Britain.[dlix] It is only within recent years that necessary archaeological data has been available to enable researchers of antiquity to conclude, with some degree of confidence, that *Crete* was the birthplace of the *Aegean Civilization*, which, in turn, radiated throughout Europe. The influence of *Aegean* culture (which assumed its character in early *Crete*) extended east as far as western Anatolia, where *Crete* was in contact with early *Troy*.

Troy's connection with Crete extends back to the Neolithic Age, evidenced by discoveries of small obsidian artifacts uncovered in the stratum of the 'first city of Troy' (or Troy I). Howsoever, at home in *Atlatia* proper, according to Plato's account, *Atlatian Kings* had become corrupt and greedy in their colonization and expansions. Putting "selfish pursuits above the greater good, they soon began invading foreign lands" and subjecting their peoples to slavery. In Plato's account, the rulers of *Atlatia* had become corrupt to such an extent that they wanted to conquer everyone and embraced the idea of world domination. They began wars and dispatched fighting troops to Europe and Asia Minor. Yet shortly after failing in their aggressions, earthquakes, and floods ravaged their homeland; until, presumably, the entire *Archipelago* suffered catastrophic convulsions, and all of *Atlatia* finally disappeared beneath the sea; within the course of a single day and night.

An ending that does not exactly comport with interpretations of the legends recorded in the prehistoric text of *Khemet*, those transmitted through oral traditions until about 5,200 years ago, when preserved forms of ancient record-keeping first began.[dlx] Although, in deference to those who ascribe to the myth, there are several consistencies between legend and myth; for instance, both are centered on large islands, between *Gibraltar* and the *Pillars of Heracles*. Both were on an island larger than Libya, and Asia Minor (the latter referring to the *Anatolian Peninsula*) combined. From where travelers could reach the other islands, and from there, the opposite continent (referring to Africa), "which surrounds what could truly be called the ocean" (the 'Atlantean Sea'). The crux of the departure is in the story of the actual demise of *Atlatia*.

Traces of the Fall

Plato describes a nearly unfathomable destruction marked by violent earthquakes and floods lasting "a single day and night," in which Atlatia (Atlantis) was utterly destroyed and sunk beneath the sea, completely disappearing. A powerful and improbable event and a catastrophic ending that surely would have dramatically and adversely impacted the surrounding geography for thousands of miles, leaving clear and definitive evidence that a major landmass had, in fact, disappeared beneath the seas. However, no such evidence, to date, has been found to exist. Alternatively, recent tectonic models appear to challenge the myth of the demised and instead demonstrate a chain of events that depict an abrupt continental upheaval, a seismic eruption of catastrophic proportions, culminating in a sub-continental uplift along the Atlas Mountains.[dlxi]

Here, at long last, is perhaps the answer to the riddle of historically delayed subsidence along the coastline of the Atlas, that which repeatedly rendered open the "Water Gate at Gabe's." According to a recent hypothesis developed from Plato's geographic and dimensional descriptions, the Atlas was physically deeper in the Earth's mantle prior to the catastrophic convulsions. Fortuitously, a more recent scientific study of the tectonics underlying the Atlas appears to support this hypothesis. In a study released in 2014 by a team of University Researchers in the field of Earth Sciences, it has been found that the Atlas is floating on a layer of hot molten rock flowing beneath the lithosphere, the Earth's most rigid outer layer, an underlying condition extending perhaps all the way to the volcanic Canary Islands, off the northwestern coast. [dlxii]

A seismic event was precipitated by a combination of extended unrelieved down-thrust subsidence caused by glacial loading in the Atlas, followed by a delayed isostatic rebound from glacial unloading (due to the "floating" nature of the Atlas), exacerbated by the increasing weight of the *Atlantean Sea*.[dlxiii] Eventually, the unleashing of the constrained forces came with volcanic eruptions and earthquakes of unprecedented proportion. When the greater force of the African Plate suddenly slipped past the critical gravitational tipping point, the result was a powerful series of upward thrusts and convulsions. Convulsions caused a dramatic uplift that, in turn, caused powerful tsunamis to race westward and northward, colliding with offshore islands and overwhelming and destroying all within their path.[dlxiv] The dramatic uplift caused harmonic waves of earthquakes rolling across the mantle of the Atlas; these, in turn, resulted in a series of tsunamic waves rushing across the Atlantic and Mediterranean.

In the Atlantic, the tsunamis swept over many of the offshore islands in their path. The plateau that once formed the extended shape of the *Cape Verde Islands* was submerged by the tidal waves, as was the drowned city discovered off the coast of the islands. The massive waves also submerged the central pavement, engraved stone steps, and a large number of ruins off the coast of the *Canary Islands*. Submerged ruins from the tsunamis can also be found off the coasts of the *Azores,* including the submerged pyramid found between *São Miguel* and *Terceira*. The long series of tsunamis overwhelmed the smaller islands, which eventually sunk beneath the ocean. In a similar fashion, the coasts of several larger islands were impacted and nearly obliterated, exiling to mystery the "people of the megaliths" who laid the foundations following generations (traces of their works are the present-day "mysteries" of those islands). Tsunamis also swept across the Mediterranean, from the coasts of Morocco and Algeria to the coasts of southern Europe, destroying cities and villages, including the original city of ancient Athens.[dlxv]

Across the Mediterranean, the tsunamic flooding receded with such force as it swept back into the Mediterranean basin that it denuded much of the fertile topsoils along broad swaths of the coast of Southern Europe. Soils that were eventually commingled at the strait flowed into the Atlantic basin, contributing to the formation of the Spartel mud bank that is similarly dated.[dlxvi] It was Plato, or perhaps Solon, who first noted that ancient Athens had been destroyed by the same catastrophe that had destroyed Atlatia, saying of it that "all the richer and softer parts of the soil, having fallen away, and mere skeletons of the land being left," and of the ancient coastline that "the Earth has fallen away all round and sunk out of sight." Tsunamic destruction, accordingly, also caused the submergence and, in some instances, total obliteration and disappearance of the megalithic monuments and cities along all the coastal areas of the Western Mediterranean. And this, since the fall of Atlatia, had very wide ramifications; its destruction precipitated the "mysterious" interruption of megalithic civilization and culture in the Western Mediterranean.

Megalithic civilization was similarly interrupted on the Atlantic coast of western Europe; from the Iberian peninsula in the south, where there are ruins off the coasts of Ceuta, Tarifa, Zahara de Los Atunes, and Chipiona (in the present-day Cadiz) on the Peninsula, northward, beyond the British Isles. With the fall of *Atlatia,* an important center of civilization all but disappeared; ended was the transmission of ideas, along with the traditions in culture and commerce that emanated from this early fount of civilization.[dlxvii] An empire of great navigators who colonized regions of western and southern Europe to mine tin, silver, and gold and regions in Asia-Minor to mine other valued metals, minerals, and precious stones. In exchange, they exported technology and refined products and wares, together with their very culture. Not long after the fall, many of the coastal regions of Europe and Asia Minor fell back into subsistence, no longer capable of great works.

At *Atlatia*, the recoil of the tsunamis caused widespread destruction along the coast of Morocco, where ruins have been discovered at several sites off the coasts on both sides of Gibraltar. Similarly, evidence of widespread tsunamic destruction can be found along the coasts of Algeria, Tunisia, and Libya, where several submerged ruins of the era are located, including massive temple ruins like those discovered onshore.[dlxviii] Along the northern interior coasts of Atlatia, the continental uplift decimated the farming and seafaring economies around the seaboard of the *Atlantean Sea*. A disastrous draining of the *Northern Inland Sea* (the "Triton Sea" of later Greek mythology) began because of the uplift in the Atlas highlands. The catastrophic convulsions and upheavals in the *High Atlas* literally lifted and disjunct the chain of *Chotts* basins on the *High Plateau*, forever severing the alignment that gave full scope and dimension to the fabled *Triton Sea.*

The basins of *Chotts Chergui* and *Hodna,* westernmost of the Chotts, were elevated and disjoined from one another, thrown out of alignment with the then lower chain of basins comprised of *Chott Merouane* and *Chott Melghir* in northern Algeria, and *Chott Rharsa, Chott Djerd* and *Chott Fedja* in southern Tunisia. The uplifting and tilting of *Chott Hodna* facilitated the discharge of its waters into the Western Inland Sea, while reverberations of the uplifting caused tsunamic waves to rush eastward across the basins and intervene in the lowlands of *Chotts Merouane, Melghir, Rharsa, Djerd,* and *Fedja*; disrupting and reversing the historical inbound flow from the Mediterranean Sea. These advents caused confusion in those *Atlatians* who fled the upheavals centered in the northern highlands of the *Moroccan Atlas* and reverberated in the *ell Atlas* highlands; those seeking refuge around the coast of estuarial *Lake Tritonis*, at the Pillars of Hercules - the eastern extent of ancient Atlatia, proper.[dlxix]

Similar catastrophes befell the western extent of *Atlatia* when the *Adrar Mountains* beyond the southern reaches of the *Anti-Atlas* suddenly erupted in a gigantic volcanic explosion of immeasurable proportion, an event obliterating and imploding the volcanic mountain at the heart of the eruption.[dlxx] As a consequence of the massive eruption, the volcanic mountain, voided of its magma, collapsed, and its enormous peak sunk, turning into a giant caldera over thirty miles in diameter, forming a circular geological configuration known as the *"Richat Structure."* At the heart of the huge *Richat Structure* (also known as the *Eye of the Sahara*) is a deeply eroded, slightly elliptical, over twenty miles in diameter, circular dome. Present-day geologists concur that the *Richat Structure* was indeed the result of geological uplifting, followed by centuries of erosion. The present-day form of the structure is characterized by concentric bands of resistant quartzite rock ridges, with intervening valleys of less-resistant rock in between.[dlxxi]

The scope and pervasiveness of the dramatic eruption in the *Adrar Mountains,* which had been heavily settled throughout the Neolithic era, reached far beyond the ancient mountain range, impacting and disrupting the surrounding terrain for hundreds of miles. Like in the eastern extent of *Atlatia,* many people had fled to Southern Atlatia... seeking refuge and respite from the convulsions and upheavals in northern highlands; like those at the eastern extent of Atlatia, the advents at the southern extent caused deep confusion, resulting in the ultimate abandonment of Southern Atlatia. Before the upheaval and uplift, the formation of the *Atlantean Sea* was made possible by inbound water flowing from the Mediterranean Sea and discharged from the watershed of the Central Saharan Highlands into the central and western basins. After the upheaval, the Northern Inland Sea (the fabled "Triton Sea") gradually drained from the uplifted continent in the north, reversing the flow into the Mediterranean basin, through, among other places, the *Gulf of Gabes*. To the south, the core body of the massive (Atlantean) inland sea gradually, if haltingly, drained from the uplifted African Plate, down into lower basins of the Sahara, finally, in large measure, discharging into the even lower basins of the *Atlantic Ocean* on the West African coast.[dlxxii]

Contrary to the myth, the destruction and final fall of *Atlatia* was an occurrence that took place over a number of years and, in some areas, decades. Many of those who survived the first series of convulsions and earthquakes either migrated earlier, ahead of the imminent disaster or survived and migrated after the upheavals. Alarmed *Atlatians* hurriedly migrated to surrounding areas and colonies deemed far enough to be safe. There were some who fled to *Crete* and assimilated into the *Atlatian-Minoan* populace, while others opted for what would later be known as the '*Greek Mainland'*, the '*Cyclades Islands',* and '*Hissarlik'* (Troy). Still, others immigrated to *Arcadia* and *Thessaly*, while others settled in *Thrace* and assimilated into the *Proto-Thracian*. From the northwestern coast of the Atlas, groups migrated to colonies on the east and west coast of the *Iberian Peninsula*, with a few opting for the *Island of Essaouira*, opposite Lixus. Along the northwest coast of Atlatia, some migrated to the *Azorean Islands*, while those further south migrated to the *Canary* or *Cape Verde Islands*. Along the inland seaboard, the draining of the *Atlantean Sea* was a process that occurred over hundreds of years, in some areas, thousands of years.

During the upheavals in the Atlas, a series of tsunamis were launched across the *Atlantean Sea*, destroying cities and ports around the inland seaboard. The tsunamis scored a direct hit on the eastern seaboard, with many traumatized coastal dwellers fleeing into the *Ahaggar* highlands, while others continued on to the *Tassili,* and still, others opted for the *Tibesti*. The people most fortunate and first to recover were those who had previously departed Atlatia before the brunt of the catastrophes. Those such as *Ausar* (Osiris, Zeus, Kush), who was in self-exile from the corruption and chaos of the filial rivalries in *Atlatia,* ultimately relocated south of the inland seaboard, where he settled in anonymity and built a royal city among the *Igbo*[dlxxiii]. This was the city in which faint legend reports he recorded the knowledge of *Atlatia* on stone tablets and hid them in the forests. This is also where he cultivated the seeds of what would eventually become an alliance of kings and kingdoms across the *Sahel* (the "Ancient Sudan"), from the Atlantic coast in the west to the coast of the Red Sea in the east.

The effects and consequences of the upheavals and convulsions along the Atlas Mountains were felt as far away as the Eastern Sahara, where geological findings indicate that reverberations from the uplifting of the continental table in the central Sahara seem to have caused an uplift in the Nubian Swell, in eastern Sudan. An uplift contributed to a re-direction of the Nile, which forced it to flow along the geotectonic faults around the Nubian Swell, resulting in the part of the course Nile River known as the *"Great Bend,"* where the river makes a sweeping loop south-west and then gradually curves back its northward course toward the Mediterranean Sea, rejoining the original course along valley about 250 miles further north.

Revenge of Ra: Return of the Sun

In the middle years of the *Sub-Pluvial* (around 9,500 BCE), the Sahara experienced an extended, though relatively brief arid phase, punctuated by the generally moister conditions of the *Sub-Pluvial*. The mid-*Sub-Pluvial* began with a general increase in temperature, with conditions becoming arider each year. Scientists surmise that the Sahara began its final transformation into (present-day) desert-like terrain after the Earth began its periodic change in orientation. This long process may have begun as early as the mid-*Sub-Pluvial*.[dlxxiv] Nonetheless, the catastrophes that befell *Atlatia* occurred, in part, during the opening phases of a long, arid climatic episode embracing all of North Africa, particularly the Sahara.[dlxxv] During the latter phases of what became an intense hyperacid episode, grasslands, and fauna retreated to the river valleys and mountains across the Sahara.

During this period, *Ancient Sudan* (the "Sahel") was transformed into a far more habitable and fertile region, attracting migrants fleeing *Atlatia* and the Sahara. In eastern *Sudan,* sheep and goat husbandry preceded cattle domestication because cattle were less adaptive to the landscape, in sharp contrast to western Sahara, where cattle was the mainstay domesticate for sedentary pastoral economies. Manding-Si and ancestral *Manding* from southern *Atlatia* were all familiar with the cultivation of rice, yams, and millet. Migrants from these groups were early re-adopters of agriculture and made animal domestication secondary to the cultivation of millet, rice, and yams. Farmers from all groups throughout the region practiced a form of intensive agriculture characterized by the use of hoe, irrigation, and use of manure fertilizers to maintain soil fertility.

Archaeological evidence from the region suggests changes in the previous subsistence economy resulted from a combination of ecological and demographic changes. Agriculture expanded in the context of gradual changes in climatic conditions. Pastoral clans, in response, settled near grassland habitats essential for their herds, adding the benefits of domesticated cattle resources to the economies of the agricultural communities. The combined groups established centralized, permanent villages and complimentary economic patterns, with the agriculturalists cultivating sorghum, a grain is grown for both human and animal consumption, and the pastoralists providing sustainable supplies of meat, milk, and hide.

As semi-desert like-terrain advanced into the Sudan, arid conditions obtained as far south as the northern Sahel, intruding into the newly cultivated refuge. Some shallower lakes and rivers that existed during the early part of the sub pluvial gradually disappeared, the remains of which are detectable today only by radar and satellite imagery. The economic and social disruptions caused by the encroaching aridity and desert-like terrain resulted in expanding distances between village clusters and a sense of semi-isolation of population centers across Sudan. In consequence, existent and emergent kingdoms expanded autonomously, leading to rivalries that threatened the unity and security of a fledgling and still embryonic early ancient Sudanic Civilization

The Parables

Faint ancient legends say that after the fall of *Atlatia,* it was the revenge of *Ra* (the "Sun-God") that then befell the survivors of once noble Atlatia and the ancient Sahara as inescapable punishment for their wayward misdeeds, corruption, and transgressions. *Ra* was considered the ancient aspect of the God personified by the Sun (was thus called the "Sun God"), ruler of the Sky and Earth. One myth says that Ra emerged from the waters of the Nun, and the first rays of the Sun fell on him, announcing the way to Heaven. Ra was thought to have his throne inside the Sun as its sole ruler, a benevolent entity, the original creative force of the Earth, the stars, and the Cosmos.

The Sun was believed to be ensouled by the Sun God Ra and was seen as a symbol of light, enlightenment, resurrection, and rebirth. Ra was thought of as the spirit and substance of the Sun and as the cosmic light, the "Spiritual Sun" where all is resolved and to which all returns. As ancient deification of the Sun, *Ra* was considered among the most important aspects of an unknowable *God*. In that aspect, he was considered the light which shone through the very spirit of Man and was thus called "the Divine Will-Power." The solar power from Ra was believed to be transferred daily to the people, and thus it was Ra who ultimately evoked the direction of the country and civilization.

In ancient cosmology, the "First Time" began, and then *Ra* was thought to have created the *Cosmos*, including his children – the other aspects of the unknowable *God*. He aided *Ma'at* in bringing order to *Chaos*. Nun was thought to be the father of Ra, who, in turn, was known as the father of the Gods. It was believed that all forms of life were created by Ra, calling them into existence by speaking their secret names, while humans were created from his tears and sweat. It was believed that all things needed to exist physically on Earth could not come about without the light, warmth, and energy of the Sun, just as Man needs God (the Source and Creator) in order to live and grow spiritually.

The most common symbol of Ra was a solar disk, and more than a dozen (undamaged) carvings of such disk, depicting his divinity, are still visible on rocks in the middle of the valley south of Marrakesh, near Mount Toubkal, the highest peak in the Moroccan Atlas. Since Ra was of great antiquity, there are far too many stories connected with him to relate them all in concise legend. One of the most broadly known myths about Ra is the one about *His Divine Eye*. During the *Golden Age,* everything Ra saw was perfect and so beautiful that it brought tears to his eyes, which became human beings. After some time, *Ra* noticed humankind was plotting against him, so he decided to punish them. In his vengeance, *Ra* sent the harsh rays of the *Sun* to destroy the insubordinate.

The changes in the Saharan weather patterns have been identified by scientists using geochronology, *archaeological traces of climate change, and, most recently, high-resolution sediment cores*. Research suggests that it started and ended abruptly, on a geologic timeframe, lasting perhaps as briefly as a few decades, triggered by an insolation tipping point whereby the subtropical African climate abruptly flipped between humid and arid conditions.[dlxxvi] Desert-like conditions and terrain advanced well into Sudan around this time, with many impacted communities relocating to still well-watered areas surrounding the rivers and lakes, where conditions provided the necessities of life, and they again established new village communities

Sudanic culture evolved in the context of these gradual but momentous changes in climatic conditions. The sedentary craft, artisan, and merchants led the way in constructing dwellings and relocating whole villages near viable rivers and lakes deemed suitable by the agricultural, pastoral, and fishing clans, with merchants attracting, conducting trade, and establishing trade routes between villages throughout local regions. The capacity to collectively adapt to the environment was one of the most powerful and enduring characteristics of each of the divergent and disparate "Proto-Saharan" groups from the time of their respective origins, a characteristic on full display during the evolution of (early) Sudanic Civilization.

As *Sudan* became dryer, with increasingly barren pastures, the central *Sahel* still held lush grasslands, green plants, fertile soil, trees, and wetter conditions. The humid savannah and forests of the *Sahel* enabled man-made landscapes, bigger settlements, and the growth of early Sudanic Civilization, notwithstanding the intermittent variations in climatic conditions. The situation of inter-regional isolation and semi-stateless existence among the newly enshrined communities in *Ancient Sudan* was changed with the arrival of immigrants from varying parts of the Atlatia. Many of the newly infused immigrants knew important crafts and arts and were familiar with the tenets of good governance; this, together with the existing agriculture, pastoralism, fishing, and inter-regional trade, enabled the peoples of Ancient Sudan to organize small-scale city-states.

Rise of the Sahel: Ancient Land of Kush

Perhaps it was the word of his reputation and abilities spread by the *Atlatian* diaspora in the Sahel, or perhaps the selfish desire of the emergent Sudanic Kings in the Western Sahel to define themselves as constituents of a new "Quasi-Atlatian" dynasty, with *Ausar* (Osiris, Zeus), ascended to leadership, uniting the diverse kingdoms of *Ancient Sudan*. Under his rule, a new form of centralized government based on a theocratic monarchy focused on receiving spiritual inspiration from *Amun* was implemented, with tribute, honor, and reverence rendered to sustain his *Divine Law*. Under the sovereignty of Ausar, their authority over one another and their mutual relations were governed by *Divine Law* reminiscent of the *Laws of Poseidon*.

There was an oath invoking renunciation of the disobedient and regular assemblages of the Rulers; at each assemblage, they gave pledges to one another, consulted about public affairs, inquired into transgressions, and passed judgment on those who transgressed. If any had accusations to bring against another, they did so in an open forum, and when conferring judgment, each poured a libation on the fire and swore they would judge and punish those deemed to have transgressed according to the law. There were many special laws promulgated by the several kings, but, again, in emulation of Atlatia, the most important was that they not take up arms against one another and that they all come to the rescue if anyone attempted to overthrow the royal house. Like the *Atlatians*, they deliberated in common, giving supremacy to the house of *Ausar*. *Ausar* (Osiris, Zeus) encouraged inter-regional trade, inter-mixing, and the spread of social traditions across Western Sudan.

As was common during antiquity, many men, particularly those of prominence or royal lineage, had many wives, as did *Ausar* over time. *Thoth* (whom the classical Greeks called Hermes) was born of a union between *Ausar* and *Maia,* a woman of high standing in the *Holly City*. *Maia* was of prominent lineage among both the *Oru* and *IGBO;* her mother was from a royal house among the *Oru* (Western Anu), and her father, part *Oru,* and part *Igbo,* was a prominent merchant and trade intermediary. *Thoth* was the fourth son of *Ausar* (Osiris, Zeus), and *Maia* was his third wife. *Ausar* had married his first wife, *Hera,* at the height of *Atlatia* when each was a young adult, and through this union, *Ausar* had his first son, *Ares*. When *Hera,* herself a woman of royal lineage and high standing in *Atlatia*, became aware that *Ausar* had fallen in love with *Leto*, a woman of equally high standing, she became extremely jealous. *Leto* was gifted with wonderful beauty and was loved deeply by *Ausar*, and from their union, Leto bore twins, a beautiful daughter, *Artemis*, and a second son, *Apollo*.

When Hera found out about the approaching birth of *Ausar's* third son, she was outraged with jealousy. His third son, *Herakles* ("Hercules"), was by *Alkmene*, his third wife, a woman considered a "commoner," far beneath Hera's stature and standing among the most influential of the royal houses of Atlatia. To be certain, men of prominence or royal lineage during the era had many, many wives, but typically wives of roughly equal standing and station. That Ausar (Osiris, Zeus) should prefer the favors of a mere commoner was perhaps hurtful enough, but that he would now permit her to bare him a son was unforgivable. Hera became enraged and full of vengeance and hostility, an advent leading to the estrangement of her and Ausar upon his self-exile to far Southern Atlatia. Before his final departure from Atlatia, Ausar (Osiris, Zeus) sought to amend the discord between him and Hera, imploring that she and Ares join him on his journey.

However, Hera was adamant, and Ares had reached majority, and just like his mother, became very difficult to deal with. Ares was an enthusiastic warrior who, in contravention to his father, embraced the corrupt wars of Atlatian expansionism. In consequence, *Ausar* (Osiris, Zeus) was left with little alternative but to leave without them, departing with his second son *Apollo*, second wife *Alkmene*, and third son *Herakles*. Soon after his third wife *Maia* gave birth to his fourth son *Thoth* (Hermes) in the *Holly City* - legends say she could sense her son's genius – and set out to cultivate his capabilities in every way. Under the tutelage of his mother and priests of the *Oru Thoth* learned of the history of the *Anu* from the dawn of time; under his father and the priests of Amun, he studied Atlatian script and learned of its sciences and its history and legends together with those of his royal lineage. [dlxxvii]

Under the aegis of his grandfather and the priests of the *Igbo, Thoth* studied and learned *Ogam,* among the most ancient of the arts of writing. In the *Holly City,* he was availed of the wisest philosophers, healers, and seers, the most reverent of high priests of the various sects, the most capable of generals, builders, and craftsmen, and the most honorable of noblemen, merchants, and traders of every rank and from every corner of the vast region. [dlxxviii] *Thoth* studied philosophy, religion, astrology, alchemy, medicine, and the sciences while growing to the majority, becoming his father's first scribe at a rather early age. Similarly, Herakles was also driven to develop his natural abilities; gifted in physical attributes, he cultivated and refined his skills as a warrior and military officer, assuming a position as a senior officer in Ausar's command regiment.

Their older brother *Apollo*, whose most famous attribute was the art of prophecy, aspired to be like his father; an excellent archer and better politician; he cultivated his skills as a liaison to the royal houses. *Ausar* (Osiris, Zeus) is said to have gathered a great army with which to subdue the width and breadth of ancient Sudan. He supposed that if he made men give up their savagery and adopt a gentle manner of life, he would receive the immortal honors of *Ra* in recompense for his deeds. Beyond the expanse of *Ancient Sudan,* he planned to visit all the inhabited regions of the earth, from Alkebu-lan to Arabia, India, and Eurasia, and teach men how to cultivate and live in harmony. As regards manpower, it was ordained that each ruler furnish men who were fit to bear arms, along with archers, slingers, stone-shooters, javelin throwers, horses with mounted riders, and war chariots with mounted charioteers, in numbers to advance the pursuits of the alliance under the leadership of *Ausar* (Osiris, Zeus).

A peak period of aridity occurred during this time, followed by a marked regression, with intermittent rains and a return of humidity as the *Sub-Pluvial* reasserted itself. This was then followed by a second gradually heightening, but less extreme peak in aridity, of shorter duration. At the time of the migrations toward the east, the entire ancient Sudan was still a thriving region; the stresses and depletion of resources in the west prompted the expansions and later migrations toward the east. *Ausar* (Osiris, Zeus) beckoned contingents to gather outside the *Holly City* ("Igbo Ukwu") he founded among the Igbo (a subset of the Kwa), who influenced spread over a number of other cultures. A British Archaeologist, Thurstan Shaw, excavated remnants of the ancient *Holly City* of "Igbo Ukwu" in 1950, unearthing what could fill an entire museum from only three pits.

The artifacts uncovered at *Igbo Ukwu* proved to be an enigma because they had no relationship with any other artifacts excavated in other parts of the forest of eastern Nigeria, where the city was located. Shaw had uncovered a lost city and link to early civilization in the rain forest; he later noted in his book that one of the excavated ruins was a temple with over three thousand pots for offerings and a dried cistern that supplied the temple with spring water; suggesting a city with a vast spiritual influence, comparable with that of Delphi.[115] In 1990, Professor Catherine Acholonu began conducting field and library research on African Pre-history. In the process, Professor Acholonu discovered most of the items found in *Igbo Ukwu* carry symbols also found in ancient *Khemet*, India, and the Middle East. Based on these findings, she took her research team to *Igbo Ukwu* to conduct further research and discovered that random excavation had been going on for as long as the present town (constructed over the ruins) had been in existence. Yet, no one within living memory knows who left the artifacts.[116]

Also uncovered were bronze artifacts that stood alone in their method of manufacture, technique, and style.[dlxxix] Equally astounding, well before the excavations and discovery by the archaeological expedition led by Thurstan Shaw, British colonialists, missionaries, and anthropologists, decades and perhaps as much as a century earlier found ten-step pyramids in the area of Nsukka in Nigeria, each the size of a single story building, when they first arrived in Igboland. It was certainly not an accident of history, but a well-orchestrated plot aimed at extinguishing Igbo links with Khemet, that the pyramids, which were located in the village of Abaja in Nsude (town), near Nsukka in northern Nigeria, disappeared without a trace and without any official entry being made of them in any archive or historical record by the otherwise very meticulous British anthropologists, colonialists and missionaries.[dlxxx]

All the ancient African mythologies under reference say that the *Holly City* was constructed by a god called *Eri* (in Igbo). The mythologies of the Yoruba (as recorded in *Ifa*) and of ancient Benin as well as those of the Igbo, all confirmed that the *Holly City* was constructed in eastern Nigeria.[117] Igbo *Nri mythology* says the project was connected with the Omambala River (now called Anambra River, a tributary of the River Niger), which then used to flood the whole area. The mythology says that the *god* who undertook this land reclamation project did so by raising a plateau, hilly terrain with a flat surface, and then building on it a *Holy City*, a forbidden city that only priests could enter. The mythologies make it apparent that the founder of the *Holy City* was *Ausar* (known as "*Kush*" in Ancient Sudan).[dlxxxi]

---

[115] Unearthing Igbo Ukwu, 1977 and Ekpo Eyo, Two Thousand Years of Nigerian Art, 1990; by Thurstan Shaw
[116] Unearthing the Lost City of Heliopolis (Igbo Okwu); By: Professor Catherine Obianuju Acholonu; Institutional Affiliation: Director, Catherine Acholonu Research Center, Abuja, Nigeria.
[117] Illustrated in Titi Euba, "Ifa Literary Corpus as Sourcebook of Yoruba History," in Alagoa, see index 3, above.

Tribes of Kush

First, Ausar (Osiris, Zeus, Kush) brought together the representatives of the royal houses and the priests of the *Igbo*; secondly, he summoned emissaries from the royal houses and priests of the *Oru* (followers of Horus, the Elder). The *Oru* (a subset of the Anu) were spiritual adherents to the orthodoxy of the old *Hydra* priesthood emanating from the fabled Mountains of the Moon, direct descendants of those who first studied the celestial heavens and plotted courses between the great lakes and rivers purely by the stars. The very term "*Oru*" was a survival of the epithet "Heru," referencing them as "Followers of Heru," who, having rejected the overlordship of *Nagu-Punt* in the east, sought new territories in the west, beyond the reach and influence of the *Naga*. The *Oru* was an aquatic-based culture that came to be known in the west as the '*Water People*'; many initially settled along the corridors of the *Komadugu-Yobe River*, while others settled further north along the corridors of the ancient *Niger River*.

According to oral tradition, the *Oru* migrations and settlements eventually made their way through the *Niger Delta*, where some settled along the banks of the river, while others settled further west along Niger, south of the *Adrar Mountains* and the southern extent of Atlatia.[dlxxxii] Following the massive eruption and implosion of the volcanic peak in the *Adrar*, those at the northern and northwestern extent of the settlement range of the *Oru*, like others, sought safety back in Western Sudan.[dlxxxiii] The gradual transformation of the Sahara drove many of the *Kwa* to migrate south of the Niger Benue confluence, where they interacted with the Igbo and became an integral component of early Sudanic civilization. The *Niger River* is to western *Sudan*, and the *Nile River* is to *Khemet*, flowing through Mali, Niger, Benin, and Nigeria. They traded copper from mines in the Air Mountains, where there are rock drawings of chariots and evidence of early copper smelting.

During the migrations of the Kwa, the *Niger River* was still two separate rivers. What is presently the "*Upper Niger*" rose in the highlands of southeastern Guinea and flowed northeasterly across Western Sudan into the closed basin of an ancient lake. The "*Lower Niger*" was a separate river east of the "*Upper Niger*," where, aided by tributaries from the *Adrar Mountains*, it gained full form as it received over a dozen tributaries along its southwesterly course through Western Sudan. The ancient *Taffassassent River* then rose in the *Ahaggar Mountains*, from where it flowed westward across the southern Sahara to join the then upper course of the *Lower Niger River*, which then flowed through southern *Niger* and northern *Benin* into *Nigeria* to empty into the *Gulf of Guinea*.[dlxxxiv] As the Kwa migrated along the banks of the river, some settled or joined existing village clusters along the upper course of the 'Lower Niger', while others opted for settlement further south, where they established a nascent kingdom in proximity to the *Igbo*. The *Manding*, whose settlement range stretched along the corridors of the *Atlantean Sea*, were also in flux after the upheavals and eruptions in the *Atlas*.

The Legends

The legends say *Ra recognized Ausar (Osiris, Zeus, Kush)* as heir to his throne, which he then assumed. Ausar grew and became a mighty king, and he went about the job of bringing civilization to his people. He taught them agriculture and animal husbandry. He gave them a code of laws to live by and showed them the proper ways in which to worship. The legends report his armies moved eastward, departing the area north of *Lake Chad*. As he progressed eastward, his army gathered even greater strength, absorbing contingents summoned from the lands falling under his sway. *Ausar* brought many lands under his rule, not by violence or force, but by rectitude and persuasion; he supposed that if he aided men in giving up savagery and adopting a gentle manner of life, he would receive immortal honors.

It was, perhaps, the evolution of his noble vision that *Ausar* came upon his desire to visit all the inhabited lands and teach the race of men how to cultivate the vine and sow wheat and barley. A noble deed that would benefit not only the men of his time but all succeeding generations, who, in turn, would be delighted at the abundance of foods they are able to produce. The empire became a mighty land under the rule of *Ausar*, and his subjects gladly worshiped the ground upon which he walked, yet the priesthood would also be of great service in molding early *Kushites* ethos. A commonality of certain beliefs and practices among the Manding and Mande (the "children of Ma"), as well as the Dasas of the central Sahara (who also honored 'Ma'at'), gave rise to the core beliefs of the newly forming Kushites. [dlxxxv]

Ma'at represents the Virtues of Truth, Balance, Justice, and Order and is the antagonist of *Chaos*. The opposite of "Ma`at" is "Chaos," untruth, falsehood, disorder, and injustice. It was believed Maat's battle with Chaos is on several levels: personal, world, and cosmic. Maat battles a destructive form of chaos, uncreation, and un-naming. It is the essence of imbalance or impurity. Beyond their esteem for *Ma'at*, the Kushites held great reverence for *Amun,* the "hidden" one; unknown because he represents absolute holiness. It was he who would come to the aid of the people at the time of their greatest distress, guiding Seers to use the cycles of the Stars as their Calendar.

The *Priests of Ra*, as astute theologians, succeeded in persuading the priesthood and royal houses in the belief that all the (indigenous) Gods were forms and manifestations of *Ra* and so secured his supremacy and rule of Devine Law. In addition, they incorporated and gave reverence to Amun. *Amun* was said to represent the life force hidden in the primordial waters of consciousness, while *Ra* was the emanating essence of *Deity*. Ra was power and energy, light and warmth; Ra was what made crops grow each season. *Amun* represented the essential and hidden, whilst *Ra* represented revealed divinity. In his most mature form, *Ra* became known as *Amun-Ra*, the hidden, emanating essence, the secret god. When merged with *Ra, Amun* became both a visible and invisible deity; hence, *Amun-Ra* combined within himself the duality of the two opposites of divinity; the hidden and the revealed.

As *Amun,* he was secret, hidden, and mysterious, but as *Ra*, he was visible and revealed. This duality appealed to the precept of balance and duality, leading to the association between *Amun-Ra* and *Ma´at; Ma´at* imbued the necessary self-regulating tenets of integrity, ethics, morality, and justice. Under Ausar (Kush), a great Kushites civilization first emerged in Western Sudan, expanding to the lands of Central Sudan and from there to Eastern ancient Sudan, where the Kushites established themselves in the land that would later become known as ancient Nubia. Moving northward along the corridors of the Nile Valley, Ausar established colonies and cities as he moved into what would later become known as "Lower Khemet."

The legends say *Ausar* (Osiris, Kush) founded the city of *"Thebaid,"* a city of a hundred gates, which he named after his mother, a city later generations called *"Thebes."* There appears to be no existent record or agreement however as to exactly when this city was founded, the legends report that *Ausar* built a temple to his parents, famous for its size and two golden chapels in *Thebaid*. Ausar(Osiris, Zeus, Kush) bestowed the name of *"Khem"* upon the lands of the Upper and Lower *Nile River Valley* in honor of his father, anointing the lands of the *Nile River Valley* - the *"Land of Khem"* (*"Khemet"*).

Manding-Si migrations toward ancient *Western Sudan* began sometime after the third prolonged sequence of earthquakes and upheavals in the *Atlas*, with each sequence of earthquakes and upheavals reverberating further and further southward, well beyond the *Anti-Atlas* into the *Adrar Mountain Range* to the south. The earliest of the *Saharan* kingdoms of the *Manding-Si* ancient arose in southwestern *Mauritania;* it was from there they migrated into Western *Sudan,* many seeking to join *Ausar* (Osiris, Zeus, Kush), the last lineal king of the *House of* Khem. Elders of each group sent emissaries to the *Holly City*, only to be rebuffed and told that the *City of Igbo Ukwu* was a "Forbidden City" into which only priests were permitted to enter.

The priests among the emissaries of the *Manding-Si* were then allowed entrance and opportunity to confer among the assembly, headed by *Ausar,* where the knowledge and merits of the Devine Laws by each priest were discussed, examined, and weighed at length, together with their disposition concerning the transgressions that befell Atlatia. Only those deemed faithful and those seeking penance by oaths of rectitude, commitment, loyalty, and tribute were brought into the heart of the growing alliance. The *Manding-Si* brought with them all the knowledge, technologies, and tenets of southern *Atlatia;* they fomented networks of trade between themselves, the Manding, Kwa, and Igbo, forming the foundations of their early kingdoms.

The *Manding-Si* were master boat builders and seafarers, well acquainted with trade along rivers, tributaries, and waterways, and facilitated inter-regional trade over a broad area of Western Sudan. *Manding-Si* were among the first peoples in Western Sahara to build stone settlements, such as those built on the rocky promontories of the Tichitt-Walata and Tagant cliffs of southern Mauritania. In ancient Western Sudan, the *Manding-Si* constructed large mounds, where they built dwellings and buildings made of stone and wood; they also conducted farming and cultivation of sorghum, rice, millet, yams, and other grains and were thus a positive addition and a contributing factor to the growth and growing prosperity of early ancient *Kush*.

Another important group was the Dasas (Dravidians), whose expansions were pushed northward, above Paleo-Lake Chad by the warlike *Sao,* whose settlement range expanded along the lake's western coast, dislodging the *Dasas* whose settlements had straddled the central swamplands separating the southern and northern basins of Paleo-Lake Chad.[dlxxxvi] The area around *Paleo-Lake Chad* was controlled by an array of walled city-states belonging to the *Sao*. According to oral histories, the *Sao* once dominated much of the region around the lake and saw their leaders as divine rulers. The Sao were skilled builders, potters, and metalworkers and built large clay buildings with thick walls to protect their towns. They were well-known for their urban culture, walled towns, and political organization. Yet even the contentious and decidedly autonomous *Sao* were induced by *Ausar* to cease their aggressions and aid in prosperity by inter-regional trade. At his bequest, the Sao sent contingents to support the armies and noble pursuits of *Ausar* (Osiris, Zeus, Kush).

The Kushite Migrations

The *Kushites* were highly organized, with the armies and migrants from each of the numerous kingdoms advancing in order, with contingents of cavalry, mounted war-charioteers, archers, javelin throwers, stone-shooters, and slingers represented from each kingdom; these were followed the legions of men who were fit to bear arms. The huge entourage of the Kushites armies included mothers, wives, sisters, and cousins, which gave the Kushites advance across Ancient Sudan the characteristics of migration. The Kushites were agro-pastoralists who cultivated millet and sorghum and maintained large herds of cattle, including the migratory herds of the northern Nilotics, which depended on a sequence of wetlands for their dry-season grazing. Wild donkeys were domesticated by the *Kushites* and used as beasts of burden, enabling the transport of cargo across Sudan.

As they progressed eastward use of the epithet "Kushite" came to be used as a general term to describe the constituent masses of *Manding-Si, Igbo, Kwa, Oru, Manding, Dasas, Nilotics, Manding-Kush, Kush-Si, Anu, Sao* and others amassed in advance through *Sudan* into the *Upper Nile River Valley*. However, migration and commerce do not sufficiently explain how the people living across such a vast expanse developed a common worldview and linguistic heritage. Evidence suggests a more complex picture of migration, commerce, and alliances among the peoples of Ancient Sudan. Perhaps it was reverence for *Atlatia* and the reputation of *Ausar*, or perhaps it was the natural affinities and desire of the traumatized peoples of the era to seek alliances, prompting the allegiance that later gave rise to the epithet "*Kushite*."

During this period of the Sub-Pluvial, the southern edge of the Sahara was some 300 miles further north than at present, with a larger land area in Sudan. By the end of mid-Sub-Pluvial, during what must have seemed like the height of the heat and aridity, groundwater along the northern periphery of Sudan was recharging for the last time. With the increasing aridification, desert-like terrain encroached southward, even during the moister periods. The Kushites were a highly organized people with numerous clans; they were great builders who went to great lengths to construct irrigation systems as they moved eastward, to the benefit of both they and the other peoples of the area, at a time when rising aridity began to spread into Sudan. The *Kushites* maintained control over the irrigation and water systems they developed along their migration, leaving emissaries at hubs along the trade routes as they progressed eastward.

When the *Ennedi Erg* and *Lower Wadi Howa*r (the *Yellow Nile*) would no longer support permanent settlement, the Kushites used the remaining drainage and water table as a source of irrigation and water supply along the largely dried riverbeds, allowing their migrating herds of cattle and livestock to use the wadi as a thoroughfare as they pressed on eastward. *Lower Wadi Howar* drained an area over two-hundred miles wide, and as the *Yellow Nile* entered the main *Nile River* between the third and fourth cataracts. With heightening aridity blanketing the *Sahel*, the *Kushites* pressed eastward through Sudan towards the fertile lands of the *Upper Nile River Valley*. It was the *Nilotics* north of the *Sudd* who first encountered and interacted with the *Kushites* migrating into the region.

The socio-economic activities of the northern Nilotics depended heavily on regular rains and annual floods to regenerate floodplain grasses to feed their cattle. Because climatic changes had begun to impact even the Sudd Wetlands, seduced by the water resource aptitude of the *Kushites*, the Nilotics made a mutually beneficial alliance with them. It was by the accord of this alliance that, as the *Kushites* pushed into the *Upper Nile River Valley,* Nilotic elders informed Ausar of the preeminence of the Naga. The elders of the *Oru* further told of legends of the *Naga,* informing that *Nagu-Punt* was very much an empire, in many ways equal to and perhaps even exceeding Atlatia in the scope of its influence. *Oru* and *Nilotic* elders advised that, in all likelihood, having by now surely been observed, the *Naga* would send a force of sufficient size to protect their presumed sovereignty over what they deem the northern frontier.

Encountering the Nagas

The Kushite horde migrated along the riverbed of the *Yellow Nile,* entering the *Nile River Valley* between the fourth and third cataracts opposite *Old Dongola*. [dlxxxvii] Here is where they were finally able to water their large herds of cattle and livestock and set up encampments adjacent to the banks of the river. *Ausar* directed a third of his force to establish formations north of the third cataract to defend against any possible aggressions from the *Anu* allies of Nagu-Punt in the Lower Nile Valley. The remaining two-thirds of the *Kushite* armies were directed to station themselves in the plains between the fourth and the sixth cataract. "Cataracts" are shallow stretches of the Nile River where the water's surface is broken by small boulders on the riverbed, creating rapids along the river's course. Measured upstream (from north to south), the first Cataract is near present-day Aswan, at a length of approximately 6.5 miles. The other Cataracts are in Sudan, with some consisting of three or four separate groups of rapids.

At the "*Great Bend*" of the *Nile River*, the river changes direction from south-north to east-west and then turns to flow westward for a good portion of its course before it again turns to flow northwards to the sea.[dlxxxviii] The *Kushites* increased the size of their domesticated cattle. They settled into a sedentary way of life, constructing fortified mud-brick villages, cultivating wild grains, and supplementing pastoralism with hunting and fishing in the *Upper Nile Valley.*[118] The *Kushites* were the first to domesticate wild sorghum and millet, and these became staple grains in the early Kingdom. The center of the *Kushite Kingdom* was at the confluences of the Blue Nile, White Nile, and Atbara Rivers. The region at the confluence of White and Blue Niles was conducive for large-scale farming; the river's wide-open banks were enriched with sediment from the volcanic highlands of Central Africa, carried down by the annual floods.

Despite the lack of significant rainfall, at the confluence of the White and Blue Niles, the annual inundation of the riverbanks provided fertile grounds to foster widespread cultivation. Controlling water was greatly simplified by the valley's reliable three 4-month seasons: the annual flooding during June-September, the growing period of October-January, and the harvesting during February-May. As a result, the *Kushites* were able to accurately time both sowing and reaping. The earliest settlements were at *Nabta Playa,* an internally drained basin spread over 1.8 miles in the southernmost Upper Nile Valley.[dlxxxix] During the early Sub-Pluvial, Nabta was seasonally filled with water, which encouraged migration into the area. [dxc] The region became increasingly habitable because of a climatic change caused by a northward shift of the summer monsoons.[dxci] This shift brought enough rain to the Nabta to enable it to sustain broad diversities of life for humans and animals.

---

[118] Hoffman 1979:102

Although it was a small amount of rain, usually around four to eight inches a year, it was enough to fill the playas with water for months at a time; in the earliest settlements, people made ceramic vessels and set up seasonal cattle herding camps around the rim of the playas.[dxcii] The Kushites were able to dig large, deep wells to supply enough water year-round and live in organized villages arranged in straight well-planned rows. The people at Nabta herded and regarded cattle in much the same way as present-day peoples of West Africa regard them. Though they were able to dig wells that supplied them with enough water to live at Nabta, once fall came, and the playa dried up, many people migrated to the Nile River, where water was readily available. Artifacts indicate that those at Nabta built houses, dug wells, and manufactured items, including stone tools, weapons, and pottery.

Evidence suggests that the community at Nabta adopted a complex and centralized form of organization. Ceramics uncovered at Nabta from this period are few but are considered some of the oldest identified in Africa. Settlements became larger and more sophisticated; one settlement from this period contains 18 houses arranged in two, possibly three straight lines. It also contains numerous fire hearths and amazing walk-in wells. This settlement also shows the establishment of an organized labor force. The region hosts the world's oldest known example of sorghum farming and storing along the Blue Nile in Central Sudan, near Nabta Playa. Archaeological findings reveal Kushite culture involved a higher level of organization than their contemporaries closer to the Nile Valley. Kushite villages were designed in pre-planned arrangements, with above and below-ground stone construction and deep wells that held water year-round. During the second season after fall, after the playa dried, approaching legions from Nagu-Punt aroused the suspicions of the Kushite lookouts.

The Nagas had powerful armies whose warriors were divided like regiments, armed with swords, spears, javelins, slings, longbows, shields, and other weapons reflecting their warrior prowess. *Nagu-Punt* was known for its warriors, who were known and feared by those who saw them in battle. The Naga had at first tolerated Kushite incursions, that is, while the largest proportion of the Kushite settlements remained in Sudan rather than the Upper Nile Valley. However, the Kushites were now encroaching into the Upper Nile Valley, exhausting the limits of *Naga* tolerance. Each season, once fall arrived and the playa dried up, scores of Kushites would relocate into the Upper Nile River Valley, angering and eliciting hostilities from the Naga. The ethnic makeup of Nagu-Punt was largely a mixture of peoples from the greater region, including *Nilotics* from the southern highlands and, of course, *Anu* from the highlands of *Punt* who found common cause with the Khoisan, progenitors, and principal ethnic group of the Nagas.

In time the Nagas had attracted and were comprised of a diverse mixture of peoples, suggesting their annoyance with the *Kushites* was over *beliefs* rather than ethnicity. Anthropologists have identified several common strategies in Neolithic warfare; one of them was to interdict the use of unoccupied territory to prevent exploitation of its resources by others. And, most importantly, control of the 'no man's lands' between the centers (or capitals) of the disputing Neolithic states. Kushite encampments were centered near the confluences of the Blue Nile, White Nile, and Atbara Rivers, the stronghold and heart of the emergent Kushite Kingdom. The Blue Nile, White Nile, Wadi Howar (the "Yellow Nile"'), and the Atbra of the era provided year-round supplies of water, and an abundance of food, with ample lands for a new settlement, characteristics facilitating the expansion of the *Kingdom of Kush*.

Until most recently, anthropologists and prehistorians have, for the most part, ignored the role of warfare and political influence, and conflict resolution between cultures and civilizations of antiquity. Within the last generation, there has been a dramatic change, with at least some anthropologists realizing that patterns of a military assertion within prehistoric societies are as important as the political, economic, and religious systems they developed.[dxciii] The incentive for armed conflict between groups grew once the agricultural revolution began. The food disparity widened between newly rising agricultural towns and less proficient older communities. Stockpiles of grain and animal herds owned by the new towns were a powerful attraction to the more dominant power in the region. As the towns grew richer in goods through the specialization of labor, their attraction as targets only increased. The increased *Kushite* incursions into the *Nile River Valley* served as both a catalyst and apt subterfuge for aggressions from *Nagu-Punt*.

The main difference between prehistoric and historical *war* is that, in many cases, prehistoric states did not share a common frontier, there was usually a "no man's land" separating them, and most military confrontations, at least, began there. Eastern *Sudan* was characterized by a flat surface plain that rises gradually in the Upper Nile Valley in the far south of Sudan. In the southeast, the interior plains give way to the high plateau of *Ethiopia,* where among the main rivers flowing off the plateau are the *Blue Nile* and *Atbara*. The discharge of the Blue Nile and Atbara caused the annual floods in the Nile Valley, which formed cultivable land along the banks of the river. The Nile rises in June from the annual floods, reaching a peak in August, and begins to decline in September. For most of its course, the *Nile* flows south to north, but in the heart of Sudan, it suddenly turns eastward towards the Red Sea, then mostly northward, before turning rather abruptly westward again. With a final turn, the *Nile* resumes its original northward course to the Mediterranean, creating a huge 'Great Bend' in the course of the river.

The Nagas understood that occupation of the *Bayuda*, in the heart of the *'Great Bend'*, would enable control of a large sweeping area of the *Upper Nile River Valley* in *Sudan;* this north of the confluences of the Blue Nile, White Nile, and Atbara at the center of the early Kushite Kingdom …and that this would certainly provoke a response. The *Naga* were a maritime rather than land power and possessed considerable naval resources, resources used to transport warriors from the ports of Berbera, Seylac, Marka, Baraawe, and Mogadishu, to the *Port of Suakin*, on the Red Sea coast of *Sudan*. The *Port of Suakin* was on *Suakin Island*, an island amid a large natural harbor; the strategic importance of Suakin was that it had unique defensibility attributes, making the island difficult to attack from land or sea. An additional important strategic attribute was the proximity of *Suakin* to the *Bayuda*.

The *Bayuda* is an area of roughly 186 square miles, with its southeastern border marked by Meroe and Kamil in the southwest. The *Bayuda* was contiguous with the ancient expanses of the *Northern* and *Nubian Deserts*, between which the *Bayuda* is sandwiched. The *Bayuda Desert* marked the southern half of *Nubia* and was of vital strategic importance in the formation of early *Kush*. Though faster and shallower along the Great Bend, the Nile River was the source of everything in the region …the source of water, invention, irrigated lands, and the crops of the Kushite villages and towns. Yet, by the time the *Kushites* became aware of warriors of *Nagu-Punt* from the southern highlands, the Nagas had taken firm control of most of the *Bayuda*.

Second Neolithic War

Because there are no written documents from prehistoric times, we do not know about the great wars that must occasionally have broken out, and obviously, we cannot know about the tactics of individual battles. However, there is every reason to believe that even in Neolithic times, man learned to fight in an organized fashion, with leadership, discipline, teamwork, and order. General tactics, in terms of maneuvering large bodies of men, were basic and had not changed much for thousands of years; archers generally opened the battle, followed by masses of infantry in general hand-to-hand combat mode. In the conflict between the Naga and the Kushites, strategy and tactics would become more finely ingrained in the art of warfare. Reconnaissance along the navigable tributaries of the Nile, and key overland routes, kept the Kushites informed regarding security on the periphery, as well as the unfolding strategy of the Nagas.

Ausar convened his Generals to develop a counter-occupation of the *Bayuda* by the *Nagas*. Compounding the situation were the indigenous people of Sudan, the ubiquitous Nubians. Nubians (or more aptly the *"Anu-bians"*) descended from ancestral *Anu* as full-statured Negroids in the northern lowlands of Eastern *Sudan* and the *Upper Nile River Valley*, near the end of the *Second Pluvial*, sometime around 18,000 BC. *Nubians* did not coalesce as a separate and distinct people until around the beginning of the *Sub-Pluvial*, remaining fairly disbursed among the *Anu* until about 12,500 BC. Following the onset of the Sub-Pluvial and revitalization and return of abundance throughout much of the region, the *Nubian* population grew to become second in size only to that of the ancestral *Anu* in the *Lower Nile River Valley*.

The heart of the ancient *Nubia* stretched from the Middle and Upper Nile River Valley, from the first cataract down to the confluence of the White and Blue Nile Rivers, where the Nuba (Anu-Ba) had inherited and were in residence in many of the ancient cities of the old empire (of the ancestral Anu). Greater ancient Nubia consisted of four regions with varied agriculture and landscapes; the Nile River Valley in the north and central parts of Nubia, allowing farming using irrigation; western Sudan with mixtures of agriculture. And eastern Sudan with a few areas of irrigation and agriculture. Ancient Nubia was dominated by kings from clans that controlled the region's gold mines and trade in exotic goods from other parts of Africa (such as ivory, furs, and skins) and kings from clans that controlled the rich agricultural lands.

At the heart of early ancient *Nubia* was the vast settlement area where the *Blue* and *White Niles* meet, which, in the *Nubian* context, is referred to as *"Early Khartoum"*. Evidence of an early culture from this time has been uncovered near the modern *City of Khartoum*. Fledgling *Early Khartoum* evolved at a time when the Sahara was enjoying favorable climatic conditions.[119] The *Nuba* developed a common since of identity, yet they lacked political coherence as a single polity. The *Nuba* were largely influenced by the geography of the vast terrain they inhabited, a terrain often divided against itself. Nubians were broadly disbursed throughout their terrain; this dispersion, together with their still parental-like association with the *Anu,* were contributing factors to their lack of political polity.

---

[119] Midant-Reynes 1992/2000 p.98

Nubians of the *Horn*, like the *Anu* of the highlands, were "*Puntites*", subjects of *Nagu-Punt*. *Nubians* in the *Lower Nile Valley*, like the *Anu* around ancient *Lake Moeris* and the *Nile Delta*, proclaimed only "a vague alliance" with the *Naga*. *Nubians* in *Sudan* were treated as "vassals" and felt little, if any, allegiance to the *Nagas*. The *Kushites* were vying with the *Naga* for control of trade routes from the interior of Africa and those leading north toward the coast of the Mediterranean, further reinforcing the impetus for war. In somewhat of a counter-initiative, by taking control of *Bayuda*, the *Nagas* had hoped to not only outflank the *Kushites* but also resume control of vital trade routes along the *Nile* as it proceeded through *Sudan*.

The *Kingdom of Kush* was situated in the heart of ancient *Nubia*. Thus, the Nubians found themselves lodged between two powerful forces, the *Nagas* and *Kushites*. Though the Nagu-Punt were presumed to have unchallenged control over the region, they were unaware of the Kushite read guard near Old Dongola, a contingent comprised of nearly one-third of the huge *Kushite Army*, outnumbering the *Nagas* in the *Bayuda* by a factor of three-to-one. Nonetheless, for *Ausar,* the risk of dispatching his rear guard against the *Nagas* in *Bayuda* was the possibility of attack by the *Anu* of the *Lower Nile Valley*, a prospect that would require a force near the size of the rear guard to repel. To reduce the risk, *Ausar* dispatched *Oru* priests and emissaries to provide assurances to the *Anu* that the intentions of *Kush* were only to defend its territories, a delegation requesting, at minimum, the *Anu* remain neutral in any conflict.

The delegation returned having been well received and indeed exalted by the *Anu* priest, but the powerful Anu kingdoms around *Lake Morris* were non-committal regarding their disposition should conflict erupt between the *Kushites* and *Nagas*. However, even without the assurances of the *Anu* in the *Lower Valley*, the alternative of not eliminating the threat at *Bayuda* would have been to leave the heart of *Kush* vulnerable from both north and south. *Ausar* (Osiris, Zeus, Kush) thus directed that half the contingent of the *Rear Guard*, a force larger than the sum of the warriors of *Nagu-Punt* at the *Bayuda*, assail the *Naga* from three coordinated points of attack; with the objective of corralling them inside the "Great Bend", with their backs against the *Nile River*, reassuming *Kushite* control of the *Bend*.

From the confluences of the three main tributaries of the *Nile*, Ausar dispatched half the Kushite army to engage forces of *Nagu-Punt* approaching from the south. Even in such remote times, an elementary and basic requirement of organized warfare was the ability to form troops in column and line; if a body of warriors cannot march in column and fight in line, it is not an effective army. Forming a column and holding a line requires teamwork, training, and discipline. The natural instinct in a clash of arms is to run, an act that jeopardizes everyone, but there is safety in the line. You win if the enemy cannot break through your line or come around behind it. If your line is penetrated, you are finished, and your life is in grave danger.[dxciv] True to their heritage, the Kushites fought from chariots, and the plains of the *Bayuda* were an ideal battlefield for the Kushites.

The plains between the Blue Nile and Atbara, south of *Khartoum* and the *Bayuda,* presented the best opportunity for the Kushites to engage the enemy on the advantageous ground; strategically, the site also availed the Kushites of the latitude to intercede Nagas approaching via the Blue Nile before they could disembark and join the battle, or proceed onward to attack *Khartoum* itself. Eastern Sudan is characterized by a flat surface that dominates the area, a plain that rises gradually from under 1,000 feet above sea level in the Upper Nile Valley to over 2,500 feet above sea level in the far south of Sudan. The plains were an area of strategic significance to the *Naga* in *the* occupation of the *Bayuda*. Thus, the stage was set, and in preparation for their confrontation with the Nagas, the Kushites assembled formations of archers, infantry, and long spearmen. Formations followed by columns of mounted war chariots with drivers and archers.[dxcv]

At this stage of the Neolithic, the short bow had advanced to the point where archers mounted on war chariots were a devastating mobile military force. The *Kushites* used the *Atlatian* short bow, with which archers mounted on war chariots could hit a target at a distance of 200 yards. Much of the early success of the *Kushites* was due in large measure to the mobility of their archers; *Kushite* archers mounted on war chariots quickly became among the most feared of all mounted archers. While the warriors of the *Naga* also used the bow as a primary weapon and were equally revered for their skills, the speed and mobility of the Kushite mounted war chariots put the Nagas at a distinct disadvantage, culminating in a series of early defeats in the plains.

Next, it is said the *Kushites* marched on the early ancient outpost of *"Naqa"*, a little over a hundred miles northeast of *Khartoum*. Present-day *Naqa* is a ruined city generally associated with the ancient *Kushite Kingdom* of *Meroë*. Still, at its earliest founding, it was an outpost of *Nagu-Punt*, set along the Nagas' northern trade routes. It is significant to note that the *Naga* icon, with a serpent body coming out of a lotus with Lion's head, is prominently depicted on a pylon relief at the *Lion Temple* in *Naqa*. The *Kushites* advanced upon, quickly subdued, and captured ancient *Naqa*. After leaving a detachment to secure the outpost, *Ausar* (Osiris, Zeus, Kush) had his generals reassemble their troops and marched southward to engage the advancing armies of the *Naga*.

The *Nagas* had powerful armies whose warriors were divided like regiments, armed with double-edged swords, sharp-edged spears, and long and short bows and shields. These regiments were followed by the most elite of *Naga* warriors, renowned and feared warriors whom the Kushites first encountered on a broad plain southeast of *Naqa*, where the Kushites had the advantage of mobility and, for the moment, had accomplished their objective of seizing the initiative. Kushite generals assembled columns of their war chariots, with mounted riders and archers at the ready. The chariots formed the frontal lines, followed by columns of long spearmen, interspersed with javelin throwers who, in turn, were followed by warriors comprising the Kushite infantry. As the *Kushites* readied their charioteers for a frontal assault, the *Nagas* unleashed their longbow archers, who, in tandem, launched a coordinated salvo of arrows over distances of nearly 500 yards onto the *Kushite* ranks.

Many of those exposed on the front lines of the Kushites raised their shields to protect against the arrows, but many did not, and of those who did not, many were severely or mortally wounded. The ranks of Kushites were visibly shaken by the barrage when the *Nagas* unleashed a second and third round of longbow salvos raining down on *Kushite* ranks. As the second and third salvos took flight, the Kushites unleashed a full-frontal charge – with charioteers and mounted archers racing beneath the arc of arrows, quickly closing over the half distance between them and the Nagas near the opposite end of the battlefield. As the charging Kushites came into the range of their short bows, the archers mounted on the chariots unlashed their own barrage of arrows into the ranks of the Nagas.

The *Nagas,* in turn, responded to the charge of the *Kushites* by unleashing their own vaunted infantry, who raced toward the charging *Kushites* with a shield and long sword in hand. The two forces clashed in pitched close combat as the distance closed between the charging Kushites charioteers and Nagas. Here the elite swordsmen of the Kushites were in their element, bringing out the swords of the charioteers who then fought the Nagas at close quarters. The foray was mercifully interrupted when Kushite mounted archers seized the momentum by encircling the clashing warriors, picking-off Naga warriors in the midst of battle. Witnessing the shifting momentum, *Naga* archers launched barrages of arrows into the hordes entwined in desperate combat on the battlefield.

The response from the *Kushite* charioteers on the battlefield was to launch a barrage of arrows of their own to meet the challenge; this while the *Nagas* in close combat were suffering casualties by errant arrows from their own archers. It was a contest in which the Kushites won the day, with the two sides each retiring their forces from the battlefield, making encampments at safe distances, and leaving small contingents to guard against surprise attacks. Kushite generals sent word of the outcome of the campaign to *Ausar* at *Khartoum,* advising they had halted, but not turned back, the advance of the Naga – more warriors would be needed to ensure victory. However, *Khartoum* itself had just repelled a near-surprise attack by Naga forces that advanced on the Kushite stronghold from along the *Blue Nile*. *Kushite* lookouts observed the Naga warriors disembarking upriver from *Khartoum and* warned of the impending attack on the early ancient city.

Ausar directed his generals to dispatch the standing infantry to meet the Nagas head-on, outside the city's perimeters, with several contingents of infantry remaining in the city for its defense. Two contingents of infantry were assembled along the southern entrances of the city, and Ausar directed that every able-bodied man be alerted to arms to defend the city. Ausar then dispatched messengers to alert the encampments of Kushite armies surrounding the city; then came the first of several barrages of long arrows raining down from the sky, announcing the arrival of the Nagas. The salvos by the longbow archers of the Nagas both stunned and caught the Kushites off-guard… they had wrongly assumed that they had more *lead* time. The Nagas besieged and nearly over-ran the city early on, with their early success halted as the standing *Kushite* infantry finally entered the fray. As warriors from the surrounding Kushite armies poured into the city, the Naga forces were soon outnumbered.

Though their warriors fought on in a famed fanatical fashion, they eventually gave ground to the superior numbers of the Kushites. It was shortly after this victory the Kushites generals leading the *Bayuda* offensive reported that while they had disrupted Naga control over the Ohio-sized *Bayuda* and Great Bend of the Nile River, the 0 Nagas who had control over the region proved more cunning than first imagined or presupposed. The Kushite strategic objective had been to corral the Nagas inside the 'Great Bend' with their backs against the Nile River. This strategy underestimated the vastness and diversity of the terrain within the *Bayuda*. However, the Kushites generals informed that, by several measures of tactical success, they had been able to confine the *Nagas* to the northeast of the *Bayuda,* above the fourth cataract: with much of the fighting devolving into guerrilla warfare along skirmish and containment lines. A scenario the generals informed could last for months, if not years – advising that they needed more forces to ensure an immediate victory.

Nubian clan leaders had theretofore been dubious of the ability and resolved of the *Kushites* to contend with the power and authority of the *Nagas. H*owever, they were both surprised and impressed at the adeptness displayed by the *Kushites*. Most significantly, the *Nubian* leaders then believed the *Kushites* could prevail; where they had been reticent before, they were now eagerly receptive to aligning themselves with the cause of the *Kushites*. Nuba clan leaders near *Khartoum* advised the *Kushite*s that the *Nuba* in the highlands of *Old Punt* forewarned that the *Nagas* were amassing a huge army of warriors, larger than the one now dispatched in what they viewed as the *northern backlands*. A massive force that would be added to the forces now engaged in battle with the Kushites… and this soon as at the beginning of the next dry season.

Upon conferring with his generals, *Ausar* (Osiris, Zeus, Kush) dispatched his son *Apollo* to the kingdoms of the *Saharan Highlands*, the *Trident River Valley*, and those along the waning shores of the old *Atlantean Sea* …in the solicitation of their alliance and military assistance – to open access to *eastern lands* far larger and with far greater resources than the frozen lands of the north. Though amalgamation of the *Nuba* into the *Kushite* fold alone might have added sufficient warriors to counter-balance the pending doubling of the *Naga* forces joining the battle, *Ausar* (Osiris, Zeus, Kush) reasoned that a formidable force of tested former soldiers from the *Atlatian Diaspora* would add the depth and proficiency needed to defeat a significant power like *Nagu-Punt*. [dxcvi]

At the height of its glory, *Nagu-Punt* was an economic and maritime power with a profound effect on eastern Sudan and Upper Nile Valley. The economic influence of *Nagu-Punt* anciently extended northward through the highlands of *Old Punt* into eastern Sudan, a region hitherto deemed little more than a 'backwater'. Still, the intrusion of the Kushites had now challenged the primacy of the *Nagas*. During the weeks and months between dry seasons, the conflict de-evolved into a form of guerrilla warfare. The *Kushites* in the plains took the lead, using their maneuverability to frustrate, their stealth to surprise, and their rapid movement to harass, ambush, and terrorize, while minimizing their own casualties through rapid retreat when confronted by equal or stronger forces.

Determined to tighten the noose around the *Naga*s corralled at the northeastern extent of the *Bayuda,* the Kushites formed small guerrilla bands to conduct "hit and run" raids behind the skirmish and containment lines; to weaken and distract the Nagas as they pushed them to the northeast, to further tighten the noose of their containment. The nature of the conflict continued in this trend over the next few weeks and months, with the *Kushites* somehow seeming to gradually gain momentum and a modicum of advantage. Perhaps as little as four months had elapsed since *Appllo* had been dispatched to solicit assistance from the Old Saharan Kingdoms, and yet, after such a short period, he had returned to *Khartoum. Apollo* returned with emissaries from the Saharan kingdoms, emissaries from the central highlands, the *Triton River Valley,* the kingdoms around the waning shore of the Atlantean Sea, as well as those around the ancient shores of *Paleo-Lake Fezzan,* where many settled after the fall of *Atlatia.*

Several large kingdoms had arisen in the Fezzan and were keen on the idea of access to the eastern lands. However, like the emissaries of the central highlands, they sought a formal Confederation under the leadership of Ausar (Osiris, Zeus, Kush). They sought assurances that such a confederation would be ruled under the *Laws of Poseidon;* thus was the *Maa Confederation* bound, and the emissaries sent word to their sovereigns, summoning allotted contingents of their armies. It was thus, by the oldest of legends, that Ausar unified the *Ma Confederation*, whom he enlisted in his struggles against the Nagas, who, as legend and fate would have it, were led by a half-brother of *Ausar* (Osiris, Zeus, Kush) of whom had no knowledge, *Setekh* (Set, Seth, Typhon).

The conflict between the *Kushites* ("followers of Ausar" (Osiris, Kush, Zeus)) and the *Nagas* ("followers of Setekh (Set, Seth, Typhon)) continued at varying degrees of intensity over the following months before the next dry season - punctuated by four major campaigns. Three were offensive campaigns on the plains, one Kushite effort failing to push the Naga off the plains, and two failed efforts by the *Naga* to break through the lines of defense of the Kushites to aid the Naga regiment cornered in *Bayuda*. The fourth was a successful campaign by those Naga cornered in the *Bayuda.* While holding the *Kushites* at bay, the ever-resourceful *Naga* constructed a flotilla of rafts and boats and eluded the grasp of the *Kushite*s by night on the currents of the Nile. In abandoning the *Bayuda,* the *Naga*s had opted to flee northward into the Lower Nile Valley, the land of the *Anu*, where they implored the Anu to honor their alliance with *Nagu-Punt* in their war against the Kushites.

To demonstrate Kushite vulnerability, the Nagas left a trail of destruction through the heartland between the fourth and first cataracts of the Kingdom of Kush, besieging Kushite and Nubian villages along the course of the river through Sudan and Upper Nile Valley.[dxcvii] For the most part, Kushite villages in the Lower Nile Valley became indistinguishable from those of the Nuba; in consequence, more than a few Nubian villages were besieged or altogether destroyed by the *Nagas* in route to refuge with the *Anu* in the Lower Valley. The *Anu* of the *Lower Nile Valley* and *Delta* were organized into an informal alliance of petty kingdoms and fiefdoms along the course of the river. Howsoever, the most powerful kingdoms in the *Lower River Valley* were those around the shores of *Paleo-Lake Morris* in the Fayum.

Paleo-Lake Morris was west of the *Lower Nile River Valley* proper, where it began as a natural lake in the huge Fayum depression in the Western Desert. The *Anu* of *Palaeo-Lake Morris* were organized into a loose federation of kingdoms around the shores of the ancient lake, coalescing to build and protect their provinces; they built canals, dams, and channels, diverting part of the flow of the *Nile* into the *Fayum*, creating a massive freshwater lake. According to legend, the Anu around *Palaeo-Lake Morris* were able blacksmiths that produced formidable weapons, aiding the powerful armies maintained by each of the kingdoms. The most prominent of the kingdoms was that of early Crocodilopolis and the formidable Crocodile Clans, devout opponents of the northward spread of the influence of Nagu-Punt.

The Anu kingdoms around *Palaeo-Lake Morris* were largely adherents of the old *Hydra Priesthood*, "*Followers of Heru,*" whom they revered as "*Horus of the Two Horizons*". It was in this spirit that the *Anu* kingdoms around *Palaeo-Lake Morris* and in the *Nile Delta* marshaled their forces to meet the marauding *Naga* armies as they crossed the borderlands into the Lower River Valley. Face-to-face, the *Naga* and *Anu* armies appeared equally disciplined, granting Anu commanders comfort that they were not facing an 'out of control' ban of pure marauders. In conferring with the *Anu*, the *Naga* commander requested both refugees, and the *Anu* honored their centuries-old alliance by joining the Naga effort to expel the intruding *Kushites*. As the *Kushites* pressed northward in pursuit of the marauding *Nagas* fleeing the *Bayuda, Kushites* commanders surmised that should the *Anu* enter the battle or form an alliance with the *Naga. T*hey should be made to understand that the war will then be at their doorstep and perhaps even within their very territories.

To the south, the armies of the *Maa Confederation* were arriving and forming encampments around *Khartoum* and, within a matter of weeks, had increased the ranks of the Kushites by more than half. Armies of the *Confederation* were promptly deployed to the plains, joining the *Kushites* locked in a standstill battle with the *Nagas*, a standstill in which neither side had been capable of holding new ground. However, the combined forces of the *Kushites* and *Maa Confederation* were able to penetrate the defenses of the *Nagas* in several places at once, overwhelming the Nagas by sheer force of numbers. The Naga battle lines then broke as they retreated southward, with the seasoned warriors of the *Confederation* and *Kushites* in pursuit. *Kushite* and *Maa Confederation* warriors moved swiftly to maintain 'battle contact' with the fleeing Nagas, granting them neither time nor opportunity to reform their ranks. *Kushites* and *Confederation* warriors pursued the *Nagas* into the highlands of *Old Punt,* from where they eventually fled to the very heart of *Nagu-Punt* itself.

The collapse of the *Nagas* on the plains had happened both abruptly and by complete surprise, followed by an equally unexpected fast-paced retreat into the highlands of Punt, bringing the whole ugly affair of the war directly into the *Naga* homeland. It was still a month or so before the dry season, and several armies from the *Southern Regencies* of *Nagu-Punt* had gathered and made encampments just south of Nagu-Punt, where they were largely unaware of the *Maa Confederation* or its entrance into the war. Once advised of the impending fall of the ancient *City of Berbera*, the Regents at the southern encampments rallied their forces to join in defense of the city, where the armies of the *Naga*s had finally slowed *Kushite* incursions.However, the momentum of sheer numerical superiority remained with the *Kushites* and *Maa Conferation*. It was about this time, perhaps because of cunning or simply a twist of fate, that the *Anu* of the *Lower River Valley* opted to honor their alliance with the *Nagas,* assailing the "Rear Guard" of the *Kushites*.

Ausar and his generals were undoubtedly aware that with a strong contingent to augment their forces in the southern highlands, *Nagu-Punt* would be forced to surrender the *Horn*. However, those forces would now have to be diverted to contend with the *Anu* in the north. The assault unleashed by the *Anu* quickly overwhelmed the *Kushite Rear Guard*, forcing their retreat back into the Upper Nile Valley before finally bringing the 'blitzkrieg-like' offensive of the Anu to a halt by mounting a counter-offensive of their own. The counter-offensive took the then recklessly overconfident advancing warriors of the *Anu* by complete surprise; in the midst of what appeared a full retreat, the *Kushites* had suddenly dug in and turned to fight. The *Kushites* had retreated to the open plains, a battlefield suitable to their style of warfare; when the advancing *Anu* became visible, and within range of their lines of defense, the *Kushites* unleashed a barrage of arrows, followed by a full-throated charge of Kushite warriors; a tactic that turns the tide of the battle.

As the Kushites brought war chariots to their aid, the *Anu* astutely retreated rather than render themselves vulnerable on a battlefield advantageous to their adversaries. With a pending stand-off developing in the north, after due consideration *Ausar* dispatched a small group of emissaries, including an esteemed delegation of priests from the *Oru,* to meet with the *Anu* and, if possible, dissuade them from their alliance with Nagas and instead, persuade them to make common cause with the *Maa Confederation*. The *Oru* delegation, together with a military envoy and security detachment, were directed to and allowed entrance into a small borderland town, where the priests and military envoy were shown entrance into a temple and, in keeping with ancient *Anu* tradition, offered libation, before introduction to an Anu High Priest whose name has been lost to antiquity, and shall simply be known as *Tera-Neter* (a name meaning "God's Devotee"). [dxcviii]

Tera-Neter advised that in respect for their *Naga* guests, who were also present, they shall be permitted as observers, with a small delegation led by one known as "Yorith", commander of Nagas seeking refuge, if not alliance, with the Anu in the Lower River Valley. [dxcix] As a show of respect and good faith, the delegation of the *Oru* from the *Kushites* was led by the renowned scribe and third son of *Ausar*, the *Oru High-Priest Thoth* (Hermes). There was no priesthood or priests to divine the faith and expound the wisdom of the *Nagas*. They were instead spiritually guided by clerics of a different nature, and politically guided by the *Provincial Regents* of *Nagu-Punt*, united under the *Grand Regency* of *Setekh* (Set, Seth, Typhon), who asserted dominion over the entire *Nile Valley*. The *Kushites*, in turn, were united under *Ausar* (Osiris, Zeus, Kush) and offered nothing less than liberation for the *Anu* and the entire *Nile Valley*.

The *Anu* of the Lower Nile Valley of the era were largely adherents of the ancient tenets of the old *Hydra Priesthood* and thus shared many of the beliefs of the *Oru*; accordingly, the *Anu High Priest Tera-Neter* held the *Oru High-Priest Thoth* in high esteem. In first seeking peace for the Anu of the Lower Valley, *Tera-Neter* informed that they "will accede to the secession of hostilities, provided the *Kushites* withdraw from our borders," To which *Thoth* advised that "the *Kushites* are not your enemy …we will, of course, withdraw from the borderlands of the Lower Valley. However, honorable *Tera-Neter"*, the *High Priest Thoth* continued, "be advised that the kingdoms of the Sahara (the "*Maa Confederation*") have aligned to seek access to the eastern lands, access forestalled by the Nagas; lands that remain within the ancient memory of the *Anu* – and in your deliberations, we hope you will give favorable consideration to joining the alliance – for which we shall patiently await your determinations; but I can make no promise regarding the prosecution of the war in the highlands of *Nagu-Punt*. Again, we shall patiently await your determinations, *Thoth* repeated – "yet let us each be mindful that time is of the essence. The armies of the *Kushites* and the *Maa Confederation* have already pushed their way into the heart of *Nagu-Punt*.

With the arrival of the dry season, the full complement of armies from the southern regencies of Nagu-Punt joined the battle against the *Kushites* and *Maa Confederation*. The combined forces of the *Kushites* and *Maa Confederation* nonetheless held the regions of present-day *Eritrea* and *Ethiopia*, while the forces of *Nagu-Punt* held the regions of present-day Somalia and the Horn. After months of campaigning, with neither side able to gain ground, it had become apparent to the Nagas, particularly the Regents of the southern provinces, that the northern highlands would eventually be lost. In the ongoing diplomatic efforts to find a resolution, *Tera-Neter* inquired, "Will the *Kushites* stay their hand ?" to which *Thoth* then inquired, "to what end?", With *Yorit*h then advised that the *Nagas* have long memories and would never truly resign to loss of the highlands. To which *Thoth* retorted that 'though a nascent power, the ancestral lineages of the *Kushites* are long, and they will never relinquish lands they have spilled their blood to win and hold.

The *Kushites* were a mounting power, and for their leader, *Ausar,* it had become important to retain strategic and maritime control of the *Horn* and the coastlines and natural harbors of *Sudan, Eritrea, Ethiopia,* and *Somalia*. The *Kushites* thus sought an uneasy peace with the *Nagas*, with the provision that "the *Kushites* shall not withdraw from lands that they have spilled their blood to win. It was a peace later ratified under the duress of their distress, by none other than Setekh (Set) himself, as the Kushites, demonstrating their maritime prowess, landed a coastal assault, claiming the Port, if not the City of Berbera, the capitol of *Nagu-Punt*. With the Naga retaining Berbera and coastal Somalia, from that point forward, the '*Land of Kush*' encompassed the northern coast of the *Horn of Africa*, the coast and highlands of present-day *Ethiopia, Sudan,* as well as the entire *Nile River Valley* and huge *Nile Delta"*. The victory clearly belonged to the *Kushites* and the *Maa Confederation*. A jubilated *Ausar* extended an immediate invitation for *Tera-Neter* and delegates of the royal houses of the lower valley to join the *Confederation*.

To celebrate the Anu entry into the Confederation, *Ausar* (Osiris, Zeus, Kush) expanded the 'City of a Hundred Gates, which the men of later generations called Thebes.[dc] Legends say *Ausar* directed the building of a grand temple (famous for its size and two golden chapels) dedicated to his parents at the heart of *Thebes* and appointed priests to have charge over these. Here, the Assembly of the Maa Confederation gathered to welcome the Anu of the Lower Valley, assess opportunities presented by their victory over Nagu-Punt, and, most significantly, hear the inspired vision of *Ausar* - regarding the mysterious lands of the east. It was at the convening of this assembly that *Ausar* (Osiris, Kush, Zeus) named the Nile River Valley and Delta in honor of his father, *Khem,* proclaiming that from that day forward, the Upper and Lower Nile River Valley and Delta would be known a the '*Land of Khem*' ("Khemet").

When *Ausar* (Osiris, Kush) arrived in the borderlands of *Old Punt*, he built dikes to curb the river (on both banks) so that floods would no longer form stagnant pools over the land, instead directing the floodwaters instead through floodgates he had constructed. After completing the affairs of greater *Kush* and *Khemet*, *Ausar* (Osiris, Kush) turned the supreme power over to his wife *Isis* and placed his son *Thoth* (whom the classical Greeks would later call Hermes) at her side as a counselor because of his prudence. He left *Heracles* renowned for his valor and physical strength as supreme commander over all armies throughout the land.[dci] Homer described Hercules as "black he stood as night his bow uncased, his arrow string for flight". As military general of the combined forces, his charge was the entirety of the lands of *Khemet* and *Kush*, from the delta to the highlands. *Ausar* (Osiris, Kush) appointed two of his most trusted Generals to serve under the joint command of Heracles, *General Hu* as commander of Upper Egypt and *General Sia* as commander of Lower Khemet.

To support the rule of *Isis* in *Khemet*, *Ausar* (Osiris, Kush, Zeus) appointed his most trusted confidants, *Bousiris* as Governor of the Delta and the East, and *Antee* as Governor of Upper Khemet (Egypt) and the West.[dcii] Ausar (Osiris, Kush, Zeus) then gathered his remaining Commanders and those accompanying his expedition and departed with his army, taking his son (whom the Greeks called) *Apollo* with him. Legends hold that *Ausar* and his expedition crossed into ancient Yemen (in the south of the present-day Arabian peninsula) from the coast of *Old Punt*, just north of the *Horn of Africa*. From there, the Kushites marched through Southern Arabia along the shore of the Red Sea to ancient Oman, Sumer (Southern Mesopotamia), Elam (early ancient Persia), Indus (early ancient India), and the limits of what he knew to be the known inhabited world.

Allies at Kumari Nadu

Kumari Nadu was ruled by the *Pandyans* at Madurai before it sunk beneath the sea. According to Dravidian scholars, the Pandyans worshipped Amman (corresponding to Amun of the Kushites). According to legend, over a period of about 11,000 years, the *Pandyans*, a dynasty of *Dasa's* kings, formed three Sangams in order to foster among their subjects the love of knowledge, literature, and poetry. These Sangams were the fountainhead of *Dasa's* culture, and their principal concern was the perfection of their culture and traditions. The first two Sangams were located in the antediluvian land of peninsular *Kumari*, which in ancient times bore the name of *Kumari Kandam*, literally meaning the "Land of the Virgin or Virgin Continent".The *Dasas* fleeing the flooding and final inundations, migrated northward, settling over broad regions of southern, central, and northern India, where they diverged into the *Adi-Dravida*, Tamiloid, Kannadigoid, Telugoid, Malabaroid, Malayaloid, and Tuluvoid.

The Kalittokai (104) historical writings makes it clear that after the *Pandyans* were forced to migrate off their Island into South India, "to compensate for the area lost to the sea, King Pandia moved to the other countries and won them; removing the emblems of tiger (Cholas) and bow (Cheras) he, in their place, inscribed his reputed emblem fish (Pandias) and valiantly made his enemies bow to him". The *Nagas*, described as fierce warriors with long and curled locks of hair", heavily resisted the invasion of the *Cholas*. The Kalittokai (IV,1-5) reports that the Nagas of *Naga-Nadu* were eventually defeated by the *Dasas* (Dravidians) from *Kumari-Nadu*. This landmass is mentioned in the *Silappadikaram*, in which it is said that *Kamari-Nadu* was made up of seven nadus or regions; the Dravidian scholars Adiyarkunallar and Nachinaar wrote about the ancient principalities of *Tamilaham*, which existed on *Kamari-Nadu*.

The Asian Excursion: Crossing the Straits

To the east of the Horn of Africa, on the opposite side of the Gulf of Aden, beckoned Southern Arabia and the green and fertile lands that would become *Ancient Yemen*. The Strait, which separates Africa and Arabia, is quite narrow at some points, averaging a couple of day's journey by small boat. The land of *Ancient Yemen* is a mountainous region where the highest mountain (Nabi Shu'ayb) rises to a height of 12,336 feet. The highlands of ancient *Ethiopia* and *Yemen* were (and are) physically and environmentally related and similarly configured, forming part of a greater region that has close geographical, climatic, zoological and botanical connections. [dciii] [dciv]

Ancient Yemen then occupied all of the southern *Arabian Peninsula*, including the regions of present-day Saudi Arabia in the north and *Oman* in the east. The valleys, which open into the eastern deserts, did not then form the arid landscape they do in the present era. Rainfall was more frequent and created floodwaters that channeled into the broad fields through numerous tributaries, irrigating and giving rise to vast grasslands. Southern Arabia, especially the regions of Ancient Yemen, was anciently known as *Arabia Felix* (or Happy Arabia or "Flourishing, Arabia").[dcv] Geographically, Arabia Felix was the fertile region of southwestern and southern Arabia. This region contrasted with *Arabia Deserta* in barren central and northern Arabia and with *Arabia Petraea* ("Stony Arabia") in the northwestern region of the Arabian Peninsula. *Arabia Felix* was bounded by the Shiraz region of the Persian Gulf, the Eritrean or Red Sea, as well as the Indian Ocean.[dcvi]

The Kushites who chose to settle in the region first settled in the extreme south west of the Peninsula, from where they then spread northward and eastward over Yemen, Hadramaut, and Oman.[dcvii] The land within Arabia Felix was a very fertile sub-region that would prove to be rich and productive for the transplanted spice trade. *Ancient Punt* was the original homeland of incense, such as frankincense and myrrh, and spices like cinnamon, as well as coffee. With the *Kushite* migrations and expansion, the traditional *East African* planters of these crops and the merchants of this most lucrative of ancient trades extended their operations from *Kushites-Punt* across the straits of Bab-el-Mandel, to take advantage of the fertile land and natural harbors of *Arabia Felix*, which subsequently (and for thousands of years) became export hubs of the ancient trade.[120] [dcviii]

The central role of *Arabia Felix* in the ancient incense trade has long been known from historical accounts. However, until now, archeologists have had few opportunities to investigate the incense-growing regions of this ancient land, which included Ancient *Yemen* and part of *Oman*. Seven years ago, a team of American and British explorers found in southern Oman the ruins of two frankincense trading centers that appeared on the maps of Claudius Ptolemy (the Alexandrian geographer of the second century A.D); the team's more recent excavations uncovered a previously unknown pattern of sites associated with frankincense from 5000 B.C.

---

[120] See Strabo, Geography (Book XVI.iv.19)

The early *Veddas* constituted a significant factor in the initial peopling of *Southern Arabia*, with their skeletal remains having been exhumed from sites as far as early Sumer. The *Veddas* were the first native peoples of Arabia. However, in this writing, they have essentially disappeared from the present-day "Middle East" with the exception of a very small number of partial *Veddas* in Somalia, Yemen, Oman and some regions of present-day Iraq, Saudi Arabia, and the Persian Gulf.[dcix] The *Veddas* were still a viable and significant factor in the population of Southern Arabia when the Kushites arrived; surveying the conditions of their existence, Ausar deemed them the first trial of his vision and mission.

Ausar supported agricultural development and expansion in Arabia Felix, particularly due to the soil fertility and prospects for the growth of frankincense and myrrh. Another factor was surely the region's close proximity to the sea and strategic position on emergent maritime and overland trade routes. Annual floods deposited sediments in irrigated areas, creating fertile fields where grain was planted and even some small groves.[dcx] Faint legend reports that it was in *Arabia Felix* that *Ausar* discovered the grapevine and that having devised the proper treatment of its fruit, it was here that he was the first to drink wine and taught mankind at large the culture of the vine, as well as the way to harvest the grape, and to age and store the wine, together with the prudent use of wine,[dcxi]

Yves of Yemen

Yemen lies on the edge of one of the world's great sand seas, the *Rubh-al-Khali*, but even this dry desert bears the unmistakable imprint of flowing streams and rivers. When the Earth emerged from the last Ice Age, the Sahara and the *Rubh-al-Khali* were savanna grasslands with a more temperate climate and much higher rainfall than they experience today. Runoff from the coastal mountains carved the dendritic drainage pattern, which was then "fossilized" when the climate became more arid. The earliest settlements arose when climatic conditions were still moist and wet, with inhabitants settling in the highlands. Geography is often destiny, and Yemen's destiny was that it is walled off from the rest of the Peninsula by mountains and deserts.[dcxii]

While most settlements were on hilltops, above the lowlands floods, the largest settlement (at *Hawagi*) was the exception, situated on the cultivable plains of eastern *Qa Jahran*, availing the settlement of its position on a major trade route skirting the eastern edge of the plain. According to legend, Ausar's fifth son, *Raama(h)*, who began the ancient lineage of S(h)eba, was fathered in what would later become the eponymous village of Raamah, just beyond the northern borderlands of present-day Yemen, in southern Oman.[dcxiii] *Raamah* is anciently described as a kingdom of the Arabian Peninsula, and following the later birth and rein of *S(h)eba*, his kingdom and its countrymen would be commonly referred to as "*Sabeans*". Accordingly, it is clear that *Yemenites* and *Sabeans* are the purely *Africoid* progenitors of the later *Ancient Kingdom of Saba* (historically cited as distinctly Kushite), which rose on the southwestern side of the Arabian Peninsula.

Aromatics such as myrrh and frankincense were greatly prized in the ancient, civilized world and were used as part of rituals in many cultures. With the rise of the great ancient civilizations in *Khemet, Mesopotamia, Elam, Indus*, and the ancient *Sahara*, ancient *Yemen* would become an important overland trade link between these countries and the highly prized luxury goods of *Southern Arabia*. As a result, several trading kingdoms grew up astride an incense trading route that ran northwest between the foothills and edge of the desert. Because of their prosperity, the states of ancient Yemen were collectively called *Arabia Felix* in Latin, meaning "*Happy Arabia*." Thus, Ancient Yemen become the oldest civilization in the Arabian Peninsula.

On to Oman

Frankincense attracted early settlements to the area of *Southern Oman*, bringing the region of Dhofar to prominence. *Dhofar* became a prime source of this exotic commodity from the earliest of times; *Dhofar* was a habitat uniquely suited to the cultivation of frankincense. Frankincense from Dhofar was transported by land and sea. The crop was collected for outward transport through Yemen; the land route started to the west of Dhofar and passed through Nejd to the southern Arabian peninsula; another significant route linked Dhofar with the eastern Arabian peninsula and continued to settlements in early ancient *Sumer*. The Arabian Peninsula received much more rainfall at that time, sufficient rain to support a flourishing civilization in what is now desert to the west of the mountains along the Gulf of Oman.

The earliest known city in Oman, which dates back at least 9,000 years, is *Dereaze*; archaeological finds at the site include flint tools, hearths, and hand-formed pottery. Until very recently, almost nothing was known of the past of Oman. However, archeologists have recently discovered that ancient Oman had a flourishing copper mining and processing industry from where ancient copper was actively exported. At the height of the incense trade, frankincense was more precious than gold, yet the ancient *Frankincense Road* would safely carry caravans of the sap from *Dhofar* in *Oman*, through *Yemen*, and then north along the *Red Sea* to *Khemet*. Sumerian tablets call *Oman* "Magan," a reference to Oman's history of shipbuilding (Magan is a type of ship's chassis). Due to its strategic position lying on some of the world's most important trade routes, the ports of Oman have held great prominence among spice and trading merchants.

Isles of Dilmun

Dilmun was also the name given to the region of the islands and adjacent coastal lands extending northward along the central-eastern seaboard of the Arabian Peninsula to the Persian Gulf. The Kushites largely pushed past the *Isles of Dilmun* into Lower Mesopotamia, initially settling along now-vanished rivers and tributaries until moving northward into the *Sumerian* Plains and the Delta. Those who first migrated into the area found it to be a land of marshes and swamps, rich in fish, wildlife, and date palms; it was the most fertile of the three areas into which the river valleys were divided. River channels, teeming with fish and fertilized by alluvial silt laid down by uncontrolled floods, gave the delta excellent agricultural potential, once made habitable by the use of traditional irrigation and flood control techniques.[dcxiv]

Sunrise at Sumer

The prodigious rains of the Holocene resulted in near complete inundation of the alluvial plains characterizing much of lower Sumer. When the *Kushites* entered the area, the *Eastern Anu* and *Proto-Elamites* (*Dasas*) constituted a significant factor in the peopling of the greater region. The intermixing of these groups, *Eastern Anu, Proto-Elamites,* and *Kushites,* came to constitute the roots and collective beginnings of the people's ancient history that would later refer to as "Sumerians". Notwithstanding, at this writing, scholarly controversy still purportedly surrounds the "origins" of the "Sumerians". The term "Sumerian" is actually an exonym (a name given by another group of people), first applied by the Akkadians. It is significant to note that the "Sumerians" described themselves as "*the black-headed people*" (sag-gi-ga) and called their land - ki-en-gir, the "place of the civilized lords".[dcxv]

In view of the important role played by this race in the development of civilization in Western Asia, it is pertinent to recall the fact that not many years ago, the very existence of the *Sumerians* was disputed by a large body of those who occupied themselves with the study of the history and languages of 'Babylonia'.[dcxvi] What was known as "the Sumerian controversy" engaged the attention of writers on these subjects and divided them into two opposing schools. At that time, not many actual remains of the Sumerians themselves had been recovered, and the arguments in favor of the existence of an early non-Semitic race in Babylonia were, in the main, drawn from a number of Sumerian texts which had been found in the palace of the Assyrian king, Ashurbanipal, at Nineveh. A considerable number of the tablets recovered from the royal library were inscribed with a series of compositions written in the cuneiform script (but not in the Semitic language of the Assyrians and Babylonians).

Assyrian translations had been added to many of these compositions by the scribes who drew them up. On other tablets were found lists of the words employed in the compositions, together with their Assyrian equivalents. The late Sir Henry Rawlinson (rightly) concluded that these strange texts were written in the language of a race who had inhabited *Babylonia* before the *Semites*; he explained the lists of words as early 'dictionaries' compiled by the Assyrian scribes to help them in their studies of this 'ancient tongue'. Henry Rawlinson correctly assigned the non-Semitic compositions that had been recovered to the early non-Semitic population, who are now referred to as "*Sumerians*". It was not until the renewal of excavations in Babylon that evidence was obtained which put an end to the so-called '*Sumerian controversy* 'and settled the problem once and for all - in accordance with the views of Rawlinson.

But not without a measure of subterfuge, in 1928, the Field Museum and Oxford University conducted joint excavations in northern *Sumer*, in which they found that eight of the earliest crania from the region were "hyper dolichocephalic" or "long-headed," a trait typically (but not exclusively) identified with *Africoid* types, as well as broad-nosed. A second study and physical examination of *Sumerian* skulls was conducted [presumably from an earlier site] in upper *Sumer* and found that of twenty-six of the crania examined, twenty-two were *Afro-Sudroid*. The African connection should not be surprising. Like the *Arabian* peninsula, for thousands of years, Mesopotamia (Sumer in particular) became populated by *Vedoid Veddhas* (from the *Veddha Vanguard*), *Negroid Anu* (from *Ta-Nebiru*), miscegenated *Eastern Anu* (from the aforementioned parentage), and *Proto-Elamite Dasas* (from neighboring embryonic *Elam*), and the later arriving *Kushites*.[dcxvii]

The spiritual ethos of early Sumer was informed by the ancient beliefs of the *Anu*, which were based on *Animism*, the worship of nature, such as the wind and water and elements. However, the ancient sages of *Sumer* found it necessary to bring order to that which they did not fully understand, and to this end, they surmised that a force more indicative of humankind was at work. Over time, the human form became associated with this force; "*Gods,*" in human form, were then seen as having control over nature. By the time *Ausar* and the *Kushites* arrived at *Sumer*, just as *Ptah* had been deified in ancient *Khemet*, so too had *An* been deified in ancient *Sumer*.

The Parables

In Sumerian mythology, *An* became a deity whose name was synonymous with the sun's zenith, or heaven. He was considered the oldest god in the Sumerian pantheon and was originally deemed the supreme deity. His major roles were as an authority figure, decision-maker, and progenitor. He was said to allot functions to other gods and could increase their status at will. An's power was so deeply respected that, in many ways, An *was* power.[dcxviii]

According to ancient Sumerian texts, *An* (known in later Assyrian and Babylonian times as "Anu") was said to be the reigning titular head of the Sumerian Ontological Family Tree along with his two sons.[dcxix] *Enki* was deemed *Lord of the Earth and Waters*, and *Enlil* was deemed *Lord of the Air and Command*.[dcxx] In Sumerian mythology, it is *An* who took over heaven when it was separated from the earth, creating the *Cosmos*. An was said to be the personification of the sky, the utmost power, the *supreme god* "who contains the entire Cosmos". Indeed, the very name "*An*" is the *Sumerian* word for heaven.

An was deemed the father of all the gods and was identified with the north ecliptic pole centered in the constellation "Draco" (the "Serpent"). It was a mythology and belief system that formed a triune conception of the divine, in which *An* represented "transcendental" obscurity, Enlil the "transcendent", and Enki the "*immanent*" aspect of the *divine*.[dcxxi] An's primary role in the pantheon was as an ancestor figure, with the deities in the Sumerian pantheon believed to be his offspring (known as the *Anunnaki*, a word derived from the name "Anu", and translates properly as the "offspring of Anu").[dcxxii] [dcxxiii]

Although one of the most important deities, by the time of the earliest written records of Sumer, *An* was rarely worshipped, and veneration was instead devoted to his son *Enlil*. In later mythology, the only deity who had access to *An* was his son Enlil who gradually took on his father's characteristics, yet *An* continued to be venerated.

Mesopotamia was a large area, and there were differences between the northern and southern regions. The Tigris and Euphrates had been depositing alluvial sediments in *Southern (Lower) Mesopotamia* for thousands of years, building-up an immense flat plain that, when irrigated in ancient times, became highly fertile. This was a time of early development of agriculture and animal domestication, the emergence of small villages, some of which were fortified, and pottery manufacturing in various locations. [121] [122] The geography of each region and the natural resources found there affected, and, in many ways defined, the way people lived. [dcxxiv]

By the time of the arrival of the *Kushites*, small villages and towns were common across early *Sumer*. The rivers played a formative role in Sumer, with the larger portion of the countryside formed by deposits carried down by the waters of the two rivers, creating the alluvial plains at the head of the *Persian Gulf*. The *Kushites* were among the earliest settlers of the newly formed alluvium of the era, where they plowed and used swampland and rich alluvial soil for agriculture. Under the threat of unpredictable floods, they began the practice of building settlements upon artificial mounds to preserve the structure of buildings against the flood. Summer had great agricultural potential once the environmental problems were solved.

---

[121] Smith, 1998
[122] Redman, 1978

"Arable land had literally to be created out of the chaos of swamps and sandbanks through a separation of land from water, with the swamps drained, floods controlled, and irrigation canals constructed. In the course of several successive cultural phases after arrival of the *Kushites*, these and other problems were solved by cooperative effort. The Tigris and Euphrates each take winding courses through the alluvial plains, constantly changing directions as the silt builds up along their riverbeds during the annual floods. The Tigris has undergone less change in its course than the Euphrates, with the latter having actually undergone far more changes in its course over time. When the courses of the rivers shifted sufficiently, mound communities had to relocate to the new riverbed; all the mounds marking the sites of the former settlements lie east of the present-day riverbed. Historically, the course of the *Euphrates* has shifted westward. The first true appearance of the *Sumerian* admixture was in the *Delta* flats of the *Tigris* and *Euphrates* riverbeds, where, in their own writings, they called themselves the "black-headed people" and their land, in cuneiform script, was referred to as "the land of the black-headed people".

Although the earliest settlements were established in a remote period, it is apparent that they inherited an already high level of civilization; from the onset, history finds them building houses and temples. They were also rich in cattle and sheep and increased their country's natural fertility through a regular system of canals and irrigation channels. High water tables prompted experimentation, innovation, and expansion of agricultural irrigation systems, enabling the population to grow. At first, the *Kushites* formed small agricultural villages. As farming advanced from the cultivation of small plots to the tilling of extensive fields, the people found not only that the richness of the delta permitted larger settlement but that the vast engineering and irrigation works in the dikes and canals necessary to harness the annual floods were an absolute necessity. This required a workforce of hundreds of men; the layout and clearing of the canals required experienced and expert planning, while the division of the irrigated land, the water, the grasslands, and the crops required political development.

The fertility of the rich silt is what made it possible for the *Sumerians* to gather and make farms and cities. The silt left from the rivers moving out of place and flooding is what caused the area to become so fertile; flooding provided the necessary minerals to the soil so that staple foods, such as wheat and barley, could take root and flourish. The *Kushites* were the first to domesticate wild sorghum and millet, which became staple grains and were exported to Pakistan and India. Mud, clay, and reeds were the only building materials the *Sumerians* had in abundance; trade was thus necessary to supply workers with materials. Merchants went out in overland caravans or in ships to exchange the products of the *Sumerian* industry for wood, stone, and metals. The largest of the ancient cities was at *Eridu,* in the southernmost part of the land, where the layout and clearing of the canals required expert planning, while the division of the irrigated land, the water, and the crops demanded political organization and dispatch.

Summer was already in the first stages of civilization when the settlements first appeared at *Eridu*; early settlements had long prior waxed, waned, relocated, and combined to form the foundation of the City of Eridu. The *Kushites* found the richness of the alluvial soil, easily accommodating to a larger settlement, at *Eridu,* a major benefit in a location where they realized that vast engineering and construction work in building canals and dikes would be necessary to harness the annual floods. Sumerian civilization was shaped by the forces of the Tigris and Euphrates rivers, which at any time could unleash devastating floods and wipe out entire populations. Summer was subject to constant inundation, and the remains and settlements were, in many places, swept away, with all traces of them destroyed. A series of such large inundations, over thousands of years, had previously overflowed the banks of the *Persian Gulf*, wiping out much of the arable lands further south, which may, in fact, have led to the original site and founding of *Eridu*.

In general, the lands of Sumer consisted of a flat alluvial plain and formed a contrast to the northern half of the Tigris and Euphrates valley, known as Upper Mesopotamia. Northern, or "Upper Mesopotamia," is made up of hills and plains; the land was quite fertile due to seasonal rains and rivers flowing from the mountains. The dual nature of the Tigris and the Euphrates [their potential to be destructive or productive] resulted in two distinct legacies; on the one hand, plentiful water resources and lush river valleys for the production of surplus food -- on the other hand, it could also be an extremely threatening environment, driving its peoples to seek safety.

The civilization at Sumer was also shaped by conflicting factors, such as the unpredictability of the Tigris and Euphrates and surplus food production in the alluvium facilitated by irrigation and flood control projects. As the repute of the fertile river valleys of Sumer attracted further migrations, the volatility of the rivers necessitated a form of collective management to protect the marshy, low-lying land from flooding. The Sumerians were highly innovative people who responded creatively to the challenges of the Tigris and Euphrates rivers. As surplus production increased, management became more advanced, and a process of early urbanization evolved, culminating in a new social order that spread eastward from *Sumer* to the earliest *Elam*.

Enter Elam

The *Susiana Plain* to the east of *Sumer* was a continuation of the lower alluvial topography, albeit in gradually higher land as it slopes upward toward the *Iranian Plateau*, between the *Tigris* and *Euphrates* river mouths, and the *Zagros Mountains*. Early Dasa's settlers on the *Susiana* Plain chose to settle atop low-lying natural hills, surrounded by shallow marshes, at heights and elevations sufficient for dry farming. *Kushites* settled on the plain with clusters of small dry-farming villages, which later developed into a network of villages centered on the largest; the *Dasas* of *Susa* emulated this strategy in establishing their own early villages on the plan. *Elam* was the earliest civilization in *Persia* (present-day Iran) and anciently bordered *Sumer* to the east. The first *Kushite* settlements in *Elam* were part of their settlement range extending eastward from ancient *Sumer*.[dcxxv] Several ancient scholars have noted that the first rulers of *Elam* were *Kushites*; indeed, according to the Greek Geographer and Historian *Strabo*, the first *Elamite* colony at *Susa* was "founded by *Tithnus*, a *King of Kush*".[dcxxvi]

Notwithstanding, the *Elamites* themselves appear to have been an admixture of *Dasas* and *Kushites;* archeologists have compared pottery uncovered in prehistoric *Elam* with similar ware found in ancient *Kush* and found the fragments at earliest *Susa* to be similar in dating and other aspects.[dcxxvii] Perhaps the best way to think of *Elam* is as an extension of the earliest *Sumer*; the two were culturally pretty much the same, and the people were ethnically similar.[dcxxviii] They had the same high level of civilization, with the same agriculture, the same architecture and technology in mathematics and the sciences. The earliest *Elam* was essentially an extension of the spread of *Neolithic* settlements and *colonies* along the alluvial valleys of the *Euphrates, Tigris,* and Karun *Rivers*.[dcxxix] There was but one navigable river to the east of Sumer, across the vastness of what would later become ancient Persia, the *Karun River*, on the left bank of which was ancient Shoosh (Susa).

It was along the *Karun River Valley* that the earliest *Elam* arose, nurtured from the cluster of settlements that formed early Shoosh (Susa). The ninth millennium (BC) marked the beginning of the Neolithic age throughout the region, when agriculture spread throughout and beyond southern Mesopotamia, and the use of pottery became widespread.[dcxxx] Early ceramic assemblages in *Elam* and *Sumer* at this time were similar in composition and the types of symbols displayed. Elam was centered southeast of the Tigris, at the site of Susa, their largest village, the mounds of which are about thirty miles from the hills and are, to judge from their position, of great antiquity.[dcxxxi] The coast of the Persian Gulf has advanced considerably since early antiquity; during the Neolithic era the coast was about one hundred twenty miles farther north than at present. The *Persian Gulf* was dry throughout and just after the Ice Age; rivers of the era flowing into the Gulf can be traced to the ancient coastline, with the *Euphrates*, *Tigris*, and *Karun* each reaching the Gulf and forming a separate delta.

The earliest Kushite migrants settled along the major tributaries and rivers in what amounted to a long dry plain along the coastal expanse of the Gulf. At the earliest stages of the Kushite push eastward, the vast dry plain of the Persian Gulf was linked by riverine travel, much of it through *Elam*. As the Kushites pushed eastward into the alluvial plain and foothills of the *Zagros Mountains*, they christened the area '*Khuzestan*' (or more aptly, '*Khoozestan*'), meaning "Land of Kush in Elam". *Khuzestan* eventually became the center of a loosely organized federation at the heart of *Elam*. Infilling of marine waters into the *Persian Gulf* gradually drowned the major river tributaries along which the Kushites settled, pressing the growth of Elam to the north and east. It was then that Elam first came to include the lowlands in the south and west and the highlands to the north and east. The highlands gave them wood, marble, alabaster, lapis lazuli and metal ores, all of which were sought during the rise of Mesopotamia, which was short on raw materials.

As the marine waters gradually rose in the Gulf, *Elam* slowly rose to prominence by expanding its vast overland trade routes. The Kushites and Elamites expanded into the highlands, where the *Zagros Mountains* came to constitute a major physiographic region of *Khuzestan*. The Zagros form an arc that stretches over one thousand miles long and one hundred to two hundred miles wide from the plains of *Khuzestan* in the south to present-day *Turkey* in the north.[123][dcxxxii] Archaeological findings indicate that when the *Kushites* migrated into the *Zagros*, *Dasas* lived in the highlands and on the plateau and assimilated and adopted ancient Kushite culture.[dcxxxiii] Early Elamites retained vestiges of their Kushite identity as they spread throughout the region, as evident in the annals of history. Underscoring the point, George Rawlinson noted that "in Susiana (Susa), where Kushite blood was maintained in tolerable purity ...there was, if we may trust the Assyrians, a very decided prevalence of a Negro type of countenance... The head was covered with short, crisp curls and thick lips.[dcxxxiv][dcxxxv]

In time, *Ausar* gathered his trusted advisors to plan the next leg of their expedition and route to the lands and riches of the east. *Anu* priests and guides who accompanied the *Kushites* into Asia spoke at great length of the riches and futility of the lands along the coastal route eastward, through what would later become the ancient land of *Baluchistan* ...leading to the settlements in the *Sarasvati* and *Indus* river valleys. Yet they spoke in equal praise about the mineral riches in the mountains of the north, those that would later become known as the *Hindu Kush Mountains*. The allure of each route should be tempered, cautioned the *Anu*, for each route is interspersed with provinces of the *Nagas*, who are quite powerful in these lands.

---

[123] Oberlander (1965:12)

Ausar conferred well into the evening with his *Commanders* (or "Generals"), who strongly advocated the northern route toward the mineral-rich mountains, expressing confidence in the ability of their forces to insure Kushite security and arguing that experience has shown that territory cannot be settled peacefully or passively with the *Naga*. While the *Clan Leaders* opted for the less rigorous and seemingly more inviting coastal route, reminding all of the several ship armadas accompanying their migrations along the coast, where the majority of the merchants' goods for trade were stored. Prompting the *Merchant Leaders* to inquire about what utility the ships would be, asking, "Should we abandon them for the inland route to the highlands?" After several moments of reflection, a sanguine *Ausar* decided upon both routes.

"Our forces would be divided", objected the Generals, to which *Ausar* responded, "Yes, and we shall appear less like an invasion and more like a large migration, deserving of attention perhaps, but certainly less threatening". "Two-thirds of our forces and entourage shall take the northern route into the highlands", Ausar commanded, adding, "The remaining third shall take the coastal route, accompanied by the Armada, to the mouth of the great river valley. This will allow sufficient size and strength of force, should the need arise, to defend the migrations in the northern highlands, and adequate strength to defend the migrations along the coast, with the added dimension of the *Armada* should the need arise. Apollo shall lead the coastal migrations, Ausar advised and instructed.

The Generals were in unanimous support of *Apollo's* leadership, as were the Merchant and Clan leaders, with only the apportionment left to decide. A determination *Ausar* assigned to his most senior Commanders and most experienced Captain of the Armada. After several days of planning, dissemination, and realignment of the Kushites into coastal and highland factions, the physical apportionment took place on the *Khuzestan* Plain. The morning following the apportionment, *Ausar* and *Apollo* and their most trusted advisers, most particularly the priest of the *Anu*, met well into the afternoon, planning and coordinating their eventual rondevu at the delta of the *Saraswati River* in the *Gulf of Cambay* along the ancient northwestern coast of the Indian Sub-Continent.

The Anu informed Ausar of a natural harbor in the *Gulf of Cambay* that was uninhabited or controlled by the Naga, making an ideal locale for the rondevu along the coast. This would require Ausar and the northern faction to make the long trek southward from the highlands to the coast; a trek that would not be without benefit, the *Anu* informed, it would open a trade route between the highlands and coast. "When we arrive at the harbor", Ausar added, "we will build a 'three fire' signal to guide the *Armada* to our location, which should then be relayed to *Apollo* along the coast before the ships make anchorage that evening". That being said, the following morning, Ausar led the highland faction toward the foothills of the *Zagros Mountains*.

Hindu Kush: Base at Bactria

The *Kushites* and *Elamites* each sent colonies across the Iranian Plateau, as far as *Tepe Yayha*, in present-day southeastern Iran.[dcxxxvi] The *Kushites* progressed northeastward through the mountainous high country later known as *Northern Elam,* establishing settlements as they traversed the highlands.[dcxxxvii] [dcxxxviii] The allure of rich deposits of *lazuli* attracted the *Kushites* toward what would later come to be known as the '*Hindu Kush Mountains'* in northern Afghanistan.[dcxxxix] The *Kushites* discovered that every piece of *lapis lazuli* in Sumer came from the area of early ancient *Bactra* ...in the *Hindu Kush Mountains*.

The ancient path taken by the *Kushites* is traced by the *oldest* settlement mounds built [by soil compressed into artificial hills] across the *Iranian plateau*.[dcxl] The still-existent prehistoric mounds are replete with mud-brick structures from later habitations, built atop those of earlier occupations, with the latter compressed into the base of the artificial hills to add further height to the mounds. [dcxli] This technique was repeated during the eastward migrations, with treeless areas of the present-day central highlands signifying the presence of the ancient artificial mounds (or 'Tepes') of the era, which rise suddenly from the otherwise flat plateau. Among the earliest of which was *Čoḡā Bonut*, in the *Khuzestan* (Susiana) plain.[124]

Čoḡā Bonut is situated in the central part of the *Khuzestan* plain and is one of the few ancient sites excavated since the Iranian Revolution, containing pre-ceramic and early pottery from the Neolithic occupations.[125] [dcxlii] [dcxliii] Evidence excavated from the archaeological sites at *Čoḡā Bonut* includes Aceramic, the oldest known on the Khuzestan plain. Čoḡā Bonut has also provided the best evidence (to date) of the earliest stages of settled agricultural life in *Khuzestān*.[dcxliv] The *Chogha Bonut* settlements were among the earliest villages on the ancient Susiana plain; they, along with even earlier agricultural communities such as *Chogha Golan*, which arose in 10,000 BC in the Zagros Mountains (in western Iran), formed much of the earliest *Elam*.[dcxlv]

Agricultural communities such as *Chogha Golan* in the Zagros foothills flourished along with *Čoḡā Bonut* and other settlements in and around the Zagros. *Chogha Golan* was continuously occupied from 10,000 BC until around 7,000 BC. The subtle influence of the *Kushites* during the latter part of the era has been detected by archaeologists and experts who have noted the gradual change in grains: wild at first, but over time showing evolution towards crops still in cultivation today.[dcxlvi] [dcxlvii] *Chogha Golan* preserves the rich archaeological sequence in the foothills of the Zagros Mountains, with artifacts suggesting substantial inhabitation at the site for thousands of years.[dcxlviii] [dcxlix]

Tepe Gurân [excavated by a Danish archeological team in 1963] is in the highland valleys of the central Zagros. The Tepe was home to a settlement in the Hulailan valley of the Zagros, where archeologists have uncovered a sequence from pre-pottery through the early stages of pottery manufacture. The single radiocarbon date from the preceramic component suggests an age of about 9,000 B.P., concordant with the era of Kushite migrations through the region. [126][127] Tepe Gurân was a temporary settlement at its earliest stages, accommodating herders who lived in wooden huts during the winter to take advantage of the natural pasture. Not until later did the settlements become permanent villages.

---

[124] Alizadeh 2003
[125] Alizadeh, 2003
[126] Mortensen, 1963; 1972
[127] Voigt, p. 637

The *Iranian Plateau* covers much of present-day Iran and Afghanistan, with the western edge bordered by the Zagros Mountains and the eastern edge ending with the Hindu Kush range. The Zagros stretches from the northwest to the south, diverting to the east just north of the Persian Gulf. Early Dasas and Kushite farmers expanded throughout the lower and mid-level valleys of the Zagros, where they found conditions most favorable. In contrast, rivers on the Iranian plateau were few and mostly seasonal, and the lack of water and fertile soil rendered much of the plateau unfit and undesirable for settlement. [128]

Two huge deserts, the *Dasht-i Kavir* in the north and the adjoining *Dasht-i Lut* in the south dominate the center of the *Iranian Plateau*; these wastelands constituted a formidable barrier, forcing the Kushites to the south or north of these empty expanses. From the west, the northern route led past present-day *Tehran* to where a pass between the mountains allowed passage (through northeast Iran) to the ancient staging post at Herat (in present-day Western Afghanistan). The Hindu Kush Mountain range has two highland passes connecting Western Afghanistan and the region that would become known as ancient *Bactra*.[dcl]

Bactra was situated between the *Hindu Kush* and the *Amu Darya* River, where its earliest territories were confined to the area south of the Āmū Daryā. During early antiquity, there was a semi-arid zone between the fertile areas and the river, with large mountain streams reaching the *Āmū Daryā* (or 'Oxus') river, forming lush, fertile corridors through the steppe. The province of ancient *Bactra* expanded throughout what is now northern Afghanistan, southern Uzbekistan and Tajikistan; the presence of these varied types of landscape throughout this vast terrain aids in explaining the beginning of agriculture and urbanism in early *Bactra*. While its pre-history is not very well known, Bactra's unique role in history cannot be over-emphasized. [dcli]

The Hindu Kush is actually a sub-range of the *Hindu-Kush Himalayan* range that stretches between central Afghanistan and northern Pakistan and divides the *Amu Darya* (or Oxus) river valley to the north from the *Indus* river valley to the south. [dclii] Consequently, this is a very fertile area where *Kushite*, *Dasas* and *Asuras* farmers produced wheat and barley in very ancient times. The *Amu Darya* (or Oxus) river basin in present-day northern Afghanistan and southeastern Uzbekistan, consequently, became the heartland of the *Kushites* and the foundation for early *Bactra*.

When *Ausar* departed *Bactria* for the *Indus Valley,* he left a large garrison to administer the settled lands of Bactria as a key trade corridor. [dcliii] The *Kushites* organized the first major trade that moved through the territory, bringing early prosperity to Bactra. Archaeological evidence points to a rich ancient civilization existing in the area for thousands of years (evident by massive irrigation systems); *Bactria* traded with *Elam, Sumer, Kush* and *Khemet*. For untold centuries, eastern storytellers in the ancient highlands lamented and preserved the departed glories of the *Kushites* in the *Hindu Kush Mountains*.[dcliv]

---

[128] Bernbeck, 2001; Hole, 1987a; 1987b

The Sea of Knowledge: Island City of Shambhala

Kushite settlements in the central Asian highlands along the *Amu Darya River Valley* were situated just beyond the confines of northern *Naga Mandla*, the empire of the *Nagas* in western and southern Asia, near the intersection of two key *Naga* trade routes; the northwest-northeast trade route from the *Khyber Pass* along the upper *Indus River* to the *Kashmir Valley,* and the main north-south trade route along the *Ganges River*, across its watershed, and through *Punjab* and the edge of *Bactria* to *Kashmir*. The southern *Kushite* expedition, led by *Apollo*, skirted along the western borderlands of *Naga Mandla* on an excursion to the *Malabar Coast,* an advent that surely hadn't escaped the watchful eye of *Shiva*. Like *Ausar* (Osiris, Kush), *Shiva* was a highly capable leader and military commander who oversaw the well-equipped and strong armies in *Naga-Mandla*.

Shiva himself was comparable by some to *Apollo* in his ability to dispatch enemies with his bow. He always wore an ornamental cobra as a symbol of his power and the royal authority of the *Naga*. The *Anu* guides advised Ausar that there was a highland route through the *Karakoram Pass* that was not one preferred by the Nagas in the region, a highland route that might be available should the Kushites desire to continue further eastward. [dclv] The Anu guides instructed that " the route begins near *Leh*, on the *Ladakh plateau* in the hills of the *Karakoram Mountains,* near the banks of the *Indus River*, and ends at a trading village on the other side of the mountains (in the vicinity of present-day *Kashgar*), on the north-western coastal belt of a large inland sea occupying the *Tarim Basin,* in the *Takla Makan* depression, at the northwestern extent of present-day China.[dclvi]

The Legends

The *Tarim Basin* in the *Takla Makan* depression was once occupied by an immense inland sea, with waves that once washed against shores along the southern foothills of the *Tian Shan Mountains* to the north and against the coasts of the northern *Tibetan Plateau* to the south. The eastern prolongations of the inland sea once washed against shores at the western reaches of present-day *Mongolia*. The huge inland sea was formed following the *Last Great Ice Age*, during the Holocene Optimum, when it expanded to immense proportion from the increasing ice melt of the northern glaciers; until a series of earthquakes caused its waters to slowly drain southeastward.[dclvii] Near the end of the *Holocene,* a significant remnant of the ancient inland sea still occupied much of the *Tarim Basin*. [dclviii]

At the time of the *Kushite* settlements in the highland river valley at *Baktra*, a large, sapphire blue inland sea known as the *"Sea of Knowledge"* was said to still exist in the *Tarim Basin* to the east. Thriving towns, villages and seaports were said to be around its shores, including the ancient trading village at the end of the eastern trade route from northern *Naga Mandla.* There was a small trading post at the intersection of the overland trade routes on the northwestern coast of the inland sea. The *Sea of Knowledge* extended nearly five hundred miles from west to east and over two hundred fifty miles from north to south, covering a surface area of over one-hundred thousand square miles. A small mountain range rose from the western interior floor of the basin, where several of the highest mountains breached the surface of the water to form a cluster of small islands across the center of the *Sea of Knowledge*. [dclix]

Among the small archipelago was an island upon which a city of sacred repute was said to exist, a mystical ancient island city-state known throughout the region as *Shambhala* (the "Hidden Kingdom"), of which the *Kushite* merchants had been told.[dclx] Ancient Tibetan texts describe the physical make-up of the fabled kingdom as a beautiful place, formed of eight regions, each surrounded by a ring of snow-capped mountains; the greater kingdom was thus said to resemble an eight-petaled lotus blossom.[dclxi] The *Sea of Knowledge* was ringed by the *Kunlun Shan* and *Tien Shan Mountains*, forming an outer ring of mountains, with the circular shape of the *Tarim Basin* and surrounding landforms of the *Takla Makan Depression* forming a lotus-like geographic depiction of the ancient realm. Enormous and formidable outer walls, running several miles, were said to encircle the *Island City of Shambhala*, enclosing hundreds of buildings, within a labyrinth of internal pathways, temples, inner sanctums, and towering gates of entry at each of the four cardinal directions dissecting the city.

Legends say adepts from every race gathered within the island sanctum and that from among them, great Sages are said to be in perpetual residence, forming a continuous inner circle of human wisdom. From the north came southern Siberian tribes autochthonous to the *Tien Shan Mountains*, who were among the first to settle along the northern coastal belt of the ancient *Sea of Knowledge*.[dclxii][dclxiii] At heart, their settlements were the *shamans*, who brought with them their belief in animated nature and the existence of 'entities' in all natural objects, with their own spirits (or souls), and the existence of a supreme god, whom the Shaman was in contact with by sending their souls into the spiritual world, an advent aided by intoxicating herbs such as juniper and toadstool.

Within their villages, the *Siberian shamans* were worshipped like "saints"; a reverence emanating from their knowledge as healers of illnesses and diseases and their acuity and adeptness in the use of medicinal herbs as cures. In the midst of the high mountains of the *Tien Shan* are enclosed valleys where numerous hot springs nourish a variety of rare plants and medicinal herbs able to flourish in the unusual volcanic soil; renown was based on their success in inuring good health, longevity, and spiritual growth within their villages.[dclxiv] The *shamans* were also the repositories and guardians of their cultural traditions, belief systems, and cosmology. *Siberian shamans* are said to gain their knowledge and power to heal by entering the spiritual world through dreams and visions, which left them enlightened, the wisdom that the *Siberian shamans* would eventually bring to *Shambala*.

From the east came the clans and tribes of southern Mongolia and the lands forming the eastern coastal belt of the ancient *Sea of Knowledge*.[dclxv] The peoples of greater southern Mongolia were predominantly nomadic pastoralists until the dawn of the new age brought with it a rise in agriculturalism and sedentary, permanent settlements. A source of mounting friction during the earliest part of the era, prompting migrations by the sedentary clans in search of fertile and uncontested lands in which to settle. Ancient, marked rocks ("petroglyphs") have been found at strategic locations as territorial markers identifying the traditional grasslands, rivers, and valleys of the nomadic herders against the encroachment by permanent settlers, making clear the lines of demarcation. Sedentary clans from southern Mongolia and adjacent lands were the first to settle along the eastern coastal belt of the *Sea of Knowledge*.

The coalescing and guiding principles were embodied in the *Shaman; the* Mongolian Shaman values the importance of keeping the world in balance, which implies doing things in moderation and with consideration of the effects of one's actions on others. From their perspective, all animals and plants have sentient souls, and for that reason, respect for the spirits of nature in all living things shapes their worldview.[dclxvi] *Mongolian Shamanism* espouses that one's personal power is directly related to one's positive and negative actions, and though no one is capable of only positive actions, as long as the positive and negative are in balance, one can live in health, peace, and safety. However, when one's actions are too negative, one's personal spiritual power shall be depleted, and one will be susceptible to disease and other dangers. The essential ethos embodied living temperately and conscientiously, keeping negative and positive actions in balance.

Ancient *Mongolian Shaman* revered the unifying spiritual force flowing through and inhabiting all living things, the wisdom they would bring to *Shambala*.[dclxvii] From the west and south came the *Nagas*; in the west, they came from *Kashmir,* across the Ladakh highlands through the *Karakoram Pass*, and established a cluster of settlements and an early trading village(in the vicinity of present-day *Kashgar*) close to the northwestern coast of the ancient inland *Sea of Knowledge*.[dclxviii] Early ancient settlements grew into villages that expanded along the northwestern coast, as others migrated from *Kashmir* and through the *Pamir* and the *Fergana* valleys. These were the ancient farmers responsible for the introduction of early agrarianism along the former northwestern and western coastal belts of the ancient inland sea. Wheat, barley, domestic sheep and horses were each import of the era from *Naga Mandla*.

Ancient settlements along the northwestern coast were situated between the *Kashgar* and *Yarkand* rivers, with the Kashgar flowing north and the Yarkand flowing south, creating a corridor of fertile, well-irrigated land between the two rivers, with each flowing into the *Sea of Knowledge* along its west coast. To the south, the *Nagas* descended from the Himalayan highlands to the Tibetan Plateau through the valleys of the *Kunlun Shan Mountains*, which then formed the southern coastal belt of the ancient inland sea. The *Tibetan Plateau* stretches northward to the *Kunlun Shan Mountains* in a south-to-north slope, causing the ancient rivers running off the mountains to flow towards and into the ancient inland sea. Prominent rivers such as the *Khotan* and the *Keriya* flowed from the highlands of the *Plateau* through the *Kunlun Shan Mountains,* guiding the *Nagas* of the highlands to the fertile southern coastal lands of the *Sea of Knowledge*.[dclxix]

The *Nagas* of the Himalayas and Tibetan Plateau were renowned for their ingenuity. They not only cultivated and harvested vast fields of barley grown in Himalayan valleys at elevations up to 14,000 feet, but to escape the bitterness of the semi-arctic cold that blankets the *Himalayas* each winter, the *Nagas* took refuge in a large network of caves stretching hundreds of miles inside the mountains. Ancient legends tell of vast caverns illuminated by precious stones, inhabited by the *Nagas* beneath the *Himalayas*; the legends say the *Nagas* lived in palatial cave-side residences in an underground city called *Bhogavati*, a subterranean city said to be inhabited throughout the year by monks in the tutelage of yogis'. Tibet was the easternmost province of *Naga Mandla,* under the direct Regency of *Lord Shiva* (Siva); to the west of the plateau is *Mt. Kailash,* the highland abode of Shiva in southwestern Tibet.

Mount Kailash dominates the region with its prominent four-sided summit, each side facing one of the four cardinal directions (of the compass). Though hardly attaining the heights of grand Himalayan peaks such as *Everest*, the mystique of *Mount Kailash* is in its majesty; it resembles a vast cathedral in shape, with sheer perpendicular sides that drop for hundreds of feet from its peak, exposing horizontal layers of stone with slight variations in color, giving the mountain the appearance of having been built by giant hands.[129] It was from here that *Shiva* sparked a spiritual revolution that transformed *Naga Mandla*, awakening its people to a new enlightenment. [dclxx] The image of *Shiva* in meditative repose at *Mt. Kailash* was etched in the psyches of *Rishis*, *Yogis*, *Gurus*, *Monks* and *Adepts* throughout *Naga Mandla*.

It was from his repose at *Mt Kailash*, in southwestern Tibet, that *Shiva* (Siva) systematized the spiritual traditions of *Tantra*. It was then that he came to be addressed as '*Shambo*' (the "Auspicious One") and referred to as the '*Adi Yogi*'; the first teacher of the sacred science of Yoga and the first master to practice spiritual feats to attain salvation.[dclxxi] All *Yogic* and *Tantric* systems consider *Shiva* the *"Adi Guru"*, the first *Guru* and *Divine Master* of *Tantra*; his teachings did not give philosophical explanations but instead gave distinct instructions on the methods of liberation.[dclxxii] According to them, the cosmic consciousness descends towards manifestation as individual consciousness enveloping all of existence. The word *Tantra* is *Sanskrit*, an ancient language given the *Vedic Rishis* by *Shiva*; it derives from the root word 'tan', which translates as "to weave, to put forth, or manifest's."[dclxxiii dclxxiv]

Like the universe we inhabit, *Tantra* continually expands, spreads, and manifests itself like a "cosmic weave" made up of different energies. We are part of this weave, as all life and every type of energy, including thoughts, actions, and all physical matter.[dclxxv] Tantra allows for ways of knowing, feeling, and processing that goes beyond intellectuality or limited rationality; it is a spiritual and metaphysical science, which means it is also mystical in its explorations and uses of the interconnectedness between ourselves and the Cosmos. [dclxxvi] There are legends of the African origin of "Tantrism" among the early Nagas in scattered, unorganized forms for thousands of years. [dclxxvii] *Shiva* himself was born and raised in a culture founded upon such beliefs, notwithstanding that it was he who was the first to propound and proselytize these beliefs, collecting and systematizing all its branches.[dclxxviii]

The Tantric path, as espoused by *Shiva,* is predicated on the idea that an enlightened nature already resides within each of us, though temporarily obscured.[dclxxix] Focus is thus given to spiritual development because Tantra's essence is to awaken latent spiritual force and unify oneself with Cosmic Consciousness. [dclxxx] *Tantra* was used to explain, teach and initiate people into a radically different way of looking at and acting in the world. Tantra is an oral practice and tradition with direct links from teacher to student. In the tantric tradition, it is not the student who finds the teacher but the teacher who finds the student. Tantrism is an esoteric system of practices handed down from teacher to student by word of mouth. Thus, a tantric connection is more than a lineage association or affiliation to a tradition; belonging to a certain tantric lineage means the skills are learned, mastered, and handed on with a special kind of permission.

---

[129] G.C. Rawling, The Great Plateau, London, 1905

Tantra's learned teachers see the mind's nature as "trapped", striving to escape its confinement; through initiation and practice, they guide the aspirant to enlightenment. Yet the Tantric path is said to be not for the faint at heart and those of dubious internal fortitude; it is best approached by the brave and resolute in that it requires that each practitioner adheres to strict disciplines in their spiritual practices. Meditation is the main practice of the tantric tradition, and through it, the practitioner struggles to overcome weaknesses and imperfections; to proceed, one must overcome whatever obstacles one faces in the path of self-emancipation.[dclxxxi][dclxxxii] Practitioners of higher Tantra, the *Gurus* (Masters), look upon things from a broader perspective, renouncing all narrow thinking through self-realization and selfless service; they would strive to advance the welfare of the masses. In ancient *Naga* villages, the advice and guidance of *Gurus* and *Yogis* were routinely sought to help villagers to cure their illnesses and solve their problems (like Shaman).

In the Tantric tradition, the Guru plays a special role, guiding aspirants on a spiritual path to enlightenment, a path likened by *Tantric Yogis* to overcoming one's internal struggles to awaken the unfathomable power (the "*Kundalini*") within. The iconic *Naga 'Serpent* is the symbol of the *Kundalini,* is said to lie dormant, coiled at the base of the Spine (beneath the Muladhara Chakra), until awakened.[dclxxxiii] *Kundalini* is sometimes described as the individual bodily representation of the great cosmic power which creates and sustains the universe because each of us is a microcosm of that macrocosm. It was through *Tantric* enlightenment that the location of the centers of psychic energy (the 'chakras') in the subtle (or astral) body was discovered.[dclxxxiv] The passage of the awakened *Kundalini* (coiled snake-like energy) is a unique branch of esoteric tantric knowledge, ultimately unfolding the mysteries of the Cosmos. [dclxxxv]

Yogis of the tantric path facilitated the liberation of energy and expansion of consciousness through practices of internal alchemy, by which they attained enlightenment. These were the *Yogis* of the *Kunlun Shan Mountains,* forming the southern coastal belt of the *Sea of Knowledge*. The holds a distinctive place in ancient Chinese mythology, which alludes to the lush, fertile. Naga cave communities in the highlands of the *Kunlun Shan* were the source of the ancient mythologies about the subterranean realms of the Nagas.[dclxxxvi] The ancients' believed the great *Yogis* inhabiting these coastal highlands could, through meditation, leave their bodies (astral projection) and confer in the higher realms; the wisdom they surely brought to *Shambala.* In keeping with their maritime tradition, the ships of the *Nagas* plied the open waters of the ancient *Sea of Knowledge,* cultivating and facilitating trade, which is how they, like others around the shores of the great inland sea, first encountered the archipelago and the *Island City of Shambala.*

The sea lanes of the inland sea were the earliest means of transit across the vast expanse of the *Takla Makan* during much of antiquity.[dclxxxvii] Early trade began between neighboring villages along the coastal belt of the *Sea of Knowledge* and spread across the sea as each sought to obtain needed and valued things for survival and advancement.[dclxxxviii] The island city was at the nexus of trade and culture throughout and well beyond the coastal confines of the ancient *Sea of Knowledge*. If not the direct source, the island city was surely an ideal locale to trade and acquire exotic goods such as those the *Kushite* merchants witnessed trade among the *Nagas* at their northern provincial capital and trading hub at the ancient *City of Oudh*. Though the *Kushite Merchants* who were told the tale of *Shambala* were most emphatic in their lobby for the expedition farther east, as were *Priests* of the various *Kushite* sects, *Ausar* (Osiris, Kush) resolved that any such venture need to await his return.

Naga-Mandla: Realm of Shiva (Shambo)

Lord Shiva, Grand Regent of *Naga-Mandla* (Ancient Eastern India, Kashmir, and Tibet), was the presiding authority over the region; the Naga of the northern highlands were deeply committed to the precepts of *Shiva*. The main principles of Shiva's existence, like minimalism, living on the hills, and leading a life cut off from others, were an ethos that spread from the northern highlands throughout the Greater region. Shiva was not a *sacred god* but a real personage, as suspected by those Indian scholars who have sought to interpret him historically. Indeed, *Shiva* was among the *Nagas* that migrated into *Asia* and the (Indian) *Subcontinent* during the centuries of upheavals, inundation, fragmenting, and the eventual submersion of much of the ancient *Sunda Sub-Continent*. [dclxxxix]

The Legends

There are legends about Nagas in the folklore of the present-day tribal's of Southern India (Adivasis) and the aboriginals of Australia, about the ancient Nagas who once inhabited a big continent that existed between the Indian Ocean and the Pacific Ocean and gradually sank, over thousands of years, with its remnants forming the present-day Indonesian archipelago. In those days, very few primitive tribes (Kols, Asuras, Munda, Veddas, etc.) inhabited Asia and the Subcontinent. The Nagas did not entrust their highly developed technologies to such aborigines. However, they did teach them how to build simple thatch and adobe homes and to raise vegetable and animal foods. They also taught them about the Creator of All Life,

There once dwelt in a dense forest a group of hermits engaged in the most difficult of austerities. The hermitage had a large number of knowledgeable and mighty sages. Still, they were, for the most part, ritualists, more involved in the actual process rather than appreciating the symbolic significance behind the liturgies they performed. Lord Shiva, in his role as an ascetic mendicant, approached this group of recluses. Shiva taught the use of tools and the production and use of fire and other essential aspects of early civilization. From the very beginning, He was an omnipresent entity. Whenever, in the undeveloped and simple human society of those days, any need arose, Shiva was there to help; whenever any knotty problem developed, Shiva was there to solve it.

"He [was] both severe and tender. He [was] tender, so naturally, people love Him. Although He [was] severe, people still adore[d] Him because underlying His apparent severity, there [was] tenderness. Thus, the role of Shiva [was] predominantly the role of a promoter of welfare. So, the first meaning of the term Shiva is 'welfare'... [One] who looks upon everything with His special expression of sweet benevolence, who views everything with compassion. Shiva's uncommon erudition, unmatched dynamism, his dexterity in action... his sweet touch... his glow of positivity... his extraordinary personality and genius... his radiant splendor... the dazzling brilliance of his effulgence... his pervasive influence in all spheres of human life... and, at the same time, his own philosophy – all these things together elevated Shiva to the status of a [god].

Shiva was a great personality whose entire life and his very way of life became a philosophy. And when one's personality becomes fully identified with one's philosophy of life, one becomes a *god*. Shiva's ideology was in all ways identified with his life and way of life. Though he had occult powers, there was no pomp and show in any aspect of Shiva, before whom everyone bowed; Shiva was completely indifferent to his powers. Given his unprecedented wisdom and unique leadership qualities, spiritual aspirants and the laity alike saw divine qualities in him. In his simple personality, they found many admirable virtues. Wedded to Parvati, father of Ganapati and Subrahmanya, Shiva is said to sit in deep meditation on the *Mount Kailas* of the Himalayas, the patron of all ascetics, and the one who represents everything that is pure and auspicious. [dcxc][dcxci]

In the earliest ages, India was inhabited by several tribes belonging to three races, *Nagas*, *Dasas*, and Munda (also called "*Kolarans*" (or "*Kols*")).[dcxcii] Mundas lived in the north, while the *Dasas*, who became more numerous, inhabited every part of the sub-continent. The *Dasas* were pastoralists with large herds of cattle, requiring vast grasslands; it was they who cut down and cleared the forests, made pastures, and cultivated the land with grains, like wheat and barley in the north and rice in the wetter parts of the east and south. The Mundas (*Kols*) lived largely by hunting and were divided into distinct clans. [dcxciii] The *Nagas* were most prominent in the east and north, from *Old Lanka* in the south to *Kashmir* in the north and *Tibet* in the east, as chronicled in the ancient literature of those lands.

Shiva founded and made his capital at the ancient cosmopolitan *City of Kashi,* at the heart of the main northern trade route of the *Nagas*. The ancient northern route ran along the course of the Ganges River, across its huge watershed, and northward through the Punjab and Taxila (Gandhara), along the edges of *Bactria,* en route to *Kashmir*, in the central highlands. Since the city was located on the banks of two tributaries of the *Ganges*, the *'Varuna'* and *'Asi'*, the new 'contracted name' of '*Varanasi*' has been given to the old city.[dcxciv] The ancient name of 'Kashi' meant 'luminous one' because the city was the capital of *Shiva* and his wife *Parvati,* and it was from ancient *Kashi* that Lord Shiva governed all of *Naga Mandla*. During the era of *Shiva's* regency, a new ethnic group migrated into and intermingled with those then inhabiting the northeast, resulting in four major groups in the north. There were, of course, the *Nagas* who had come from Sunda and Africa and *Dasas* who had arrived from Kumari and Africa.

Expansions of the *Nagas* and *Dasas* aided in prompting the migrations of the Mundas ("*Kols*") from the north into central India. The latest arrivals from the north were purely *Mongolian* people who migrated to Tibet from Mongolia. *Shiva* was the first and last person able to unite all of these tribes and races into a unified people; he was able to foster genuine peace by marrying his three wives, Naga *Parvati*, Dasas *Kali* and Mongolian *Ganga*. [dcxcv] The Indian subcontinent is shaped like a four-sided parallelogram, with its two northern sides bounded by the *Hindu Kush Mountains* across the northwest and the *Himalayas* across the northeast. The *Nagas* inhabited the *Himalayas* extending as far as *Mount Kailash*, the highland abode of *Shiva,* depicted there as an *Omniscient Yogi* and devoted husband to his wifes Ganga, Kali and Parvati, and father to his children, Ganesha and Kartikeya. [dcxcvi][dcxcvii][dcxcviii]

The *Nagas* of the *Himalayas* were followers of Shiva and cultivated and harvested fields of barley grown in Himalayan valleys at elevations up to 14,000 feet. Trade along the highland routes through northern *Naga-Mandla* was assessed by the Nagas at the northwestern border (or boundary), under the Vice Regency of *Kuvera,* from the northwestern capital *City of Oudh,* where he administered trade flows through the *Khyber Pass* …and monitored trade along the northwest-northeast highland route. Trade was assessed again at the boundary of the northeast / northwest highland route, north of the *Himalayas* in *Kashmir,* at the mouth of the *Karakoram Pass'*. Immediately north of the *Himalayas* are the *Zanskar* mountains, beyond which are the *Kailash* mountains, beginning at *Mount Kailash* and ending northwest of the ancient village of *Leh* on the Ladakh plateau in eastern *Kashmir*.[dcxcix] *Kashmir* is the northernmost province of the sub-continent, yet is cut off from its northern plains by three ranges of the *Himalayas*, the *Pir Panjal, Karakoram*, and *Zanskar*.

The *Himalayas* divide the *Kashmir Valley* from the *Ladakh* plateau, while the *Pir Panjal* range encloses the valley from the south and west, separating it from the plains of the northern sub-continent.[dcc] The *Karakorum Mountains* are situated northeast of the *Kailash* range, stretching across the northern sub-continent in a mostly east-west direction. The *Karakoram Pass* is a long narrow valley traversing the *Karakorum Mountains* from *Ladakh* (on the Tibetan Plateau) in eastern *Kashmir* to present-day western *China* at the opposite side of the range.[dcci] It is impossible to state with certainty exactly when trade through the *Karakoram Pass* first commenced; however, what is clear is that it occurred earlier than had long been thought.[dccii] With one part of the northern *Himalayan* pass located in (Indian) *Kashmir* and the other part situated in western *China*, just north of *Tibet*, the impetus to traverse the pass during the earliest of times (in both directions) was certainly not lacking.

At the dawn of antiquity, the *Nagas* were the earliest of civilized peoples and the primary inhabitants of *Kashmir*; there, they are described as the *"civilized humans"* of Kashmir in Kalhana's Rajatarangini, and far more ancient accounts make reference to the earliest protector ("Regent") of *Kashmir* as a King of *Nagas*. Though it has been soundly promoted and, in consequence, generally accepted that *Kashmir* was originally settled by the late-arriving Aryan tribes, *Kashmiri* ancient accounts make prominent note of the far earlier arrival and civilizing ethos of the *Nagas* throughout the region.[dcciii] Ancient *Kashmir* was once a principal center of northern *Naga Mandla*, with proof of the ancient prevalence and prominence of the *Nagas* evident in the ancient historical accounts of the *Kashmiris* themselves. There are literally hundreds of shrines and places in *Kashmir* adorned with artifacts and carved symbolic images of the *Nagas*. In its prehistoric mythology, *Kashmir*, like other provinces under his regency, is said to have been an abode of *Shiva* himself.[dcciv]

Into India

Sub-Continental India is marked by the massive Himalayas to the north and the Indian Ocean to the south, with mountains and deserts to the West and mountains, jungles, and rain forest to the East, making for clearly defined natural boundaries. *Bactria* was bounded on the east by the region of *Gandāra* in present-day northeastern *Afghanistan* and northern *Pakistan*, on the Indian subcontinent. The *Kushites* (or '*Saka*' as they were called on the sub-continent) entered India through several paths: some entered northwest India through the Khyber Pass, while others entered through the more southerly Bolan Pass, which opens into Dera Ismail Khan in Sindh, an entry point into Gujarat.[dccv] Once through the passes and across the *Indus River*, they had a choice between the desert to the south and the fertile plain called the *"Punjab"* to the east.

The *Kushites* chose the *Punjab*, which literally means 'five rivers', on the *Baluchistan* rim of the *Indus Valley*. Here is where the earliest agricultural communities of the *Indian Subcontinent* came into being ---where the *Baluchistan Mountains* were good for both pasturing herds and contained valuable minerals and metals.[130] Agriculture was first spread into the *Indus Valley* by *Proto-Elamite* agriculturalists, who brought farming from *Elam* into the *Indus*, an advent occurring simultaneously to that of *Kushite Bactria*.[dccvi] There were four major subsets of Sudra that came to inhabit the *Indian Sub-Continent:* Proto-Elamites taking the sea route via the Persian Gulf and settling on the west coast of the sub-continent; a separate Proto-Elamite group taking the land route through the *Bolan Pass,* and finally, a third group who spread eastward from *Elam* through *Baluchistan,* where survival of the *Dravidian* language is a remnant of their migrations as they pushed into India. The pastoral villages that spread eastward through Baluchistan prepared the way for the *Kushites,* who later followed.

As the *Kushites* who took the northern route crossed the *Hindu Kush Mountains* into what is now northern Pakistan, the *Kushites* who crossed the *Bolan Pass* came into Indus, leaving the *Brahui* language in Baluchistan as a remnant of their passage. *Kushite* settlement groups who first migrated into the *Indus Valley* slowly developed trade, starting with small trade settlements in the major agricultural areas or along established trade routes. The availability of large waterways made trade convenient, and trade networks used boats along emerging maritime routes, such as the routes through the *Persian Gulf* and the *Gulf of Oman*. Overland trade was accomplished by wheeled carts drawn along regular caravan routes. Farmers in the alluvial plain of the *Indus River Valley* had established full-sized villages using copper and bronze pins, knives, and axes.[dccvii] The *Kushites* established trade relations with the *Adi Dasas* (pure Dravidians) inhabiting the Indus-Saraswati River Valleys and much of the Southwestern Sub-Continent.

Those who migrated northward along the western coast of peninsular *Kumari* (to the south), from whence they spread to the *Bay of Cambay* and into interior *India,* were a diverse population of predominantly *Adi-Dasas*; however, it was the *Nagas* who were most influential throughout the ancient *Sub-Continent* and other parts of *Asia* from the earliest of ages. *Nagas* had unchallenged control of trade in large parts of Asia long before the arrival of the *Kushites*.[dccviii] As far back as can be traced, the *Nagas* lived in prosperous villages with economies based on agriculture and pastoralism and were considered an *advanced civilization*.[dccix] The *Nagas* migrated to *Sindh* at a very early age. It was they who ruled much of *Indus* during the earliest antiquity; indeed, it was they who created *Sanskrit*.[dccx] The Nagas from *Nagu-Punt*, and great seamen who ruled the ancient *Indian Ocean* and *Southern Seas* for untold centuries before the ascendance of the *Kushites*.

The *Kushites* and *Puntites* were each from east *Africa,* each similarly characterized by dark skin, full lips, broad nose, and usually black hair, with generally woolly and often curly hair texture in subtle contrast to the *Adi Dravidas*, also of *African* descent, who were also distinctive by their dark skin, dark brown or black eyes, and generally black hair, yet with a generally wavy, often curly texture, with full lips and broad nose.[dccxi] The *Väddas, Anu, Adi Dasas, Kolarians* ("Kols") and *Nagas* were the earliest and original inhabitants of the *Indian Sub-Continent* and the *Indus Valley*.[dccxii] They were each well-established in India for thousands of years before the arrival of the *Kushites*. The *Adi Dravidas* and *Kolarians* lived side by side for centuries before the arrival of the *Kushites*; the *Adi Dravidas*, being more numerous and stronger, took the more fertile lands.

---

[130] Iyengar 1925, p.57

The *Adi-Dasas* were great maritime traders, trading commodities and goods with other countries by sea. This proclivity comported well with the maritime heritage of the *Kushites*, who had become well-known for their boldness in trade and seafaring expeditions. Again, the availability of large waterways throughout the region made trade convenient, with trade using boats and ships along the maritime routes linking major rivers with the Arabian Sea, the Persian Gulf, the Gulf of Oman, and the Indian Ocean. *Punjab* formed the heartland of the *Kushites,* who traversed the *Hindu Kush Mountains* to enter the Indus. Though "*Punjab*" literally means 'five rivers', Vedic literature informs that the area of northwestern India in which *Punjab* is located was more anciently known as the "*Land of the Seven Rivers*", the mightiest of which was the *Sarasvati River* (the present-day Ghaggar-Hakra River) that once traversed the vast *Thar Desert*, which was then fertile and hospitable. [dccxiii]

Early Indian Civilization emerged in the 8th millennium BC along the banks of the legendary *Sarasvati River* in ancient *Baluchistan*. The earliest settlements have been uncovered where the Indus Valley plains of northwestern India meet the hills at Mehrgarh. *Mehrgarh* was an early ancient *Dasas* village on what is now the northwestern "Kaachi plain" near the *Bolan Pass* in Baluchistan (in present-day Pakistan). The *Kaachi Plain* is located where the Iranian Plateau meets the Indus floodplain, a great alluvial expanse that merges with the Indus Valley. The *Mehrgarh* archeological site covers an area of about 200 hectares, situated along the banks of the ancient *Bolān River* in the *Baluchistan. Mehrgarh* is one of the earliest sites with evidence of farming (wheat and barley) and herding (cattle, sheep and goats) in South Asia. Lowest level settlement sites uncovered (thus far) at Mehrgarh date back to 8,500 BC. From here, Adi-Dasas (Proto-Elamites), migrating eastward from Elam through Baluchistan, first spread to the eastern side of the Indus *River Valley*.. [dccxiv]

The Saraswati River was not a mere legend but a vibrant and mighty river during early antiquity, an era when the *Saraswati River Valley* was the cradle of early civilization in Northwestern India. The *Sarasvati* in the Vedas, flowed from the Himalayas through Ghaggar Hakra in Punjab, Haryana, Rajasthan and Bahawalpur and then through the Sind, making a delta at the *Rann of Kutch,* flowing from there into the Arabian Sea.[dccxv] The Saraswati originated from the *Har-ki-Dun Glacier* in West Garhwal, the Bandarpunch Massif in the Himalayas, and the Yamuna River. The ancient two rivers flowed parallel for some distance and later merged southward as the Vedic Saraswati. The seasonal rivers joined the Saraswati as it followed its course through Punjab, bringing prosperity to northwestern India and early "*Vedic Civilization*".

The *Saraswati-Indus River Valley* civilization included over 1600 sites, with most of the ancient villages and later cities laid out on an exact north-south grid on sites west of the river, which were built with kiln-fired brick (of uniform size).[dccxvi] A striking cultural continuity exists between the *Indus-Sarasvati Valley Civilization* and early *Vedic Society*. At *Mehrgarh,* there is evidence of the use of copper, barley and cattle at a very early time – all characteristics of the *Vedic* culture; there is also a striking racial continuity.[dccxvii] Vedic texts show that cities were an integral part of their ethos; their cities were cosmopolitan centers in which different ethnic groups came together for commerce and interaction and lived together relatively peacefully for thousands of years.[dccxviii]

The *Sarasvati* was the largest and most vibrant of the waterways, a broad and navigable river upon which *Kushites* in *Punjab* sailed southward, ultimately re-connecting with the Proto-*Elamites* and *Kushites* who traversed *Baluchistan* and the *Bolān Pass* to enter into the lower corridors of the *Indus* and *Saraswati Rivers*. The headwaters of the ancient *Saraswati*, then by far the largest and more substantial of the two largest ancient rivers, arose and flowed from the *Har-ki-Dun* ("Valley of Gods") glacier in *Garhwal*. The ancient highland course of the huge river is said to have descended through Adibadri, Bhavanipur and Balchapur before finally assuming a long southwesterly course through the plains of *Punjab*, *Haryana*, *Rajasthan,* and *Gujarat*, enroot to discharge into what was then the *Bay of Kutch (Kush)*, on the coast of the ancient *Arabian Sea*.'[131] [dccxix] [dccxx]

The Legends

The mighty *Saraswati River* is glorified in the ancient texts of the *Rig Veda,* where it is described as 'flowing rapidly' and 'possessing unlimited strength' and extolled as 'the purest of all rivers'; called the 'best of the seven major rivers' of *Vedic* times. [132] [dccxxi] At its height, the *Saraswati* was far larger and more prominent than the more historically famed *Indus River;* it is significant to note that the *Indus River* is completely absent from the text of the *Rig Veda* (most ancient of the four *Vedas)*.

'*Old Rig Vedic*' literature praises and glorifies the fullness of the ancient course of the *Saraswati,* describing it as extending from the "mountains to the sea". The ancient text of the *Rig-Veda* account in detail the social, religious, and economic background of *Saraswati-Indus River Valley Civilization* during early antiquity, a time referred to as the '*Vedic era*'. The *Vedas* are the records of the 'Maharishis' ("Great Sages"), who meditated upon and comprehended the truths through their divine power. According to Vedic traditions, the Rishis ("Sages") to whom the Gods revealed the Vedas are the hierarchy working under the guidance of the Highest Creative Intelligence, the Devine Deity.[dccxxii]

Knowledgeable scholars date the *Rig Veda* as early as 12,000 BC to 4,000 B.C; it was transmitted orally, from teacher to student, by learning its vast amounts of verses by heart, from 9,000 BC to 7,000 BC. [dccxxiii] [dccxxiv] The earliest center of *Vedic* civilization was the *Punjab*, which literally means 'five rivers'; two of the main rivers that flowed during the Vedic era disappeared over 5,000 years ago. It for this reason, in Vedic literature, *Rig-Veda* authors describe their land as the '*Land of the Seven Rivers*', when all seven rivers were active, the mightiest of which was the Sarasvati. [dccxxv]

The *Veddas*, *Anu*, *Nagas*, *Adi Dasas,* and *Kushites* (Negroids and Sudroids of Africoid derivation), were unquestionable originators of India's earliest civilizations, most notably the ancient *Saraswati-Indus River Valley Civilization* and later *Vedic Civilization*.[dccxxvi] The *Kushites* were one of the early migrating branches of the *Vedic family* when they crossed the *Hindu Kush Mountains* into the *Punjab plain*, where they eventually migrated across *the Punjab Rivers* to reach upper Ghaggar, where they merged with the *Adi Dravidas*, producing the earliest vestiges of ancient northern *Vedic* culture in Indus (sometime before 7,000 BC).

---

[131] A. V. Sankaran
[132] A. V. Sankaran

The *Kushites* took Adi *Dravidas* wives on the fertile plains of *Punjab,* where they settled down and introduced the use of the plough drawn by oxen and bulls to till the fields. *The early Vedic* economy in the north was, at first, primarily agriculturally based. The upper course of the ancient *Sarasvati* flowed through the plains of *Punjab*, where, according to sacred Vedic texts, the mighty *Saraswati River* of the era was so powerful and majestic that it inspired the *Rig Veda* to be composed on its banks.[dccxxxvii] The *Vedas* are considered the world's oldest intellectual legacies and were composed on the banks of the ancient Saraswati River. The *Rig-Veda* is the work of many authors or seers (called "*Rishis*").[dccxxxviii] The *Rishis* are said to have heard the *Vedas* (meaning "Wisdoms") during their deep meditations.

The *Vedas* are not considered the works of the human mind but an expression of what has been realized through intuitive perception by *Vedic Rishis*, who had powers to see beyond the physical phenomena. They are called *apauruseya grantha* (authorless works). After 4,000 years of oral transmission from master to pupil, in 5000 BC, the *Vedas* were compiled for the benefit of future generations. The *Rig-Veda* is said to have been written in *Punjab* and embodies a literary record of the cultural development of ancient *Punjab*.[dccxxxix] In *Vedic* tradition, there were seven great seers: *'Gautama, Vishwamithra, Jamahagni, Bharadwaaja, Kashyapa, Vasishtha* and *Athri'*. These are considered ancestors of humankind; in *Vedic mythology,* it is held that humankind originated from the *Seven Sages*, the "*Sapta Rishis,*" who are said to come from the *Creator*.[dccxxx dccxxxi dccxxxii dccxxxiii]

Rig Vedic seers taught that the Cosmos was created through harmonious efforts of the gods, who were essential aspects of a *Creator* unveiled as *One* who is unborn and, above all gods, the creator and architect of the *Cosmos*. Vedic seers used symbolic language and had many ways of referring to that which is *One*. He is called the nonexistent because he is eternal, beyond existence. *Deity* manifest is the fabric of creation itself; they are *One*.[dccxxxiv] The *Vedas* teach that creation is without beginning or end.[dccxxxv] Many archaeological, anthropological, geological, and remote sensing evidence corroborate astronomically calculated dates giving evidence that Vedic civilization is far older than concluded by conventional historians.[dccxxxvi] The *Sarasvati* is actually the only river described in some detail in the *Rig-Veda*. It is said to have been a long river because many kings lived on its banks; five kings each are said to have derived their prosperity from the mighty Sarasvati.[133][134][dccxxxvii] At its peak, mature Sarasvati-Indus River Valley Civilization extended across the alluvial plains of *Punjab, Sindh, Baluchistan*, and the *Gujarat* coast and surrounding valleys.

There were two main *Vedic cultures* of the era. The first were in the north, in the *Sarasvati-Drishadvati* river region, where the *Kushites, Adi- Dravidas,* and the *Nagas* of the *Iravati River Valley* in northwestern *Indus* formed the early foundation of *Northern Vedic Civilization*.[dccxxxviii] The second main *Vedic culture* was a southern culture along the coast of the *Arabian Sea*, dating back to the *Kushite* migrations through the foothills and valleys of *Baluchistan*. In the earliest *Elam*, the *Kushites* had been joined, if not led, by indigenous and regional clans of *Adi Dravidas* (Proto-Elamites), guiding their eastward migrations across *Southern Elam* through *Baluchistan* and the *Bolan Pass* into *Southern Indus*. This explains the close relationship between the *Elamite* and *Manding* languages.[dccxxxix] *Adi-Dravidas* of southwestern Indus, together with the *Kushites* who traversed the Bolan Pass, formed the foundation of *Southern Vedic Civilization*.[dccxl]

---

[133] Rig-Veda 8.21.18
[134] Rig-Veda 6.61.12

Based on evidence gathered through excavations, Archaeologists have concluded that an advanced civilization, *Vedic* in nature, arose and flourished along the long corridors of the *Sarasvati Rivers* during the earliest antiquity. The (heavily revised) *Rig-Veda* of later ages notes five Vedic tribes that dwelled near the banks of the ancient Sarasvati, tribes identified with the nomadic *Arya* from Central Asia, who would later invade and supplant much of authentic Vedic history and culture. [dccxli] The *Vedas* were originally Black Kushite literary works; according to Drucilla Dunjee Houston, the sacred text was stolen, appropriated, and corrupted by invaders, who then added self-serving, racist ideas. The Author explains in the book "Wonderful Ethiopians of the Ancient Kushite Empire" that it has been shown that (over) 5,000 years ago, there was no branch of the Aryan race that could have produced the Rig Veda. In 5000 BC, no *Aryan* (or *Japhetic*) peoples had blacksmiths, carpenters, practiced agriculture, or possessed the civilization the *Rig Veda* reveals." [dccxlii] Houston notes that according to the Rig-Vedas, the Kushites of India were blacksmiths, goldsmiths, coppersmiths, carpenters, and husbandmen who practiced agriculture; "they fought from chariots as did all the Kushite nations".

The Kushite pantheon of deities included Suriash (from Sanskrit Surya, meaning the Sun), Maruttash (from Sanskrit Marut, a storm god) and Indas (from Sanskrit Indra, the king of the gods). Names of gods also appear in the names of Kushite kings, as is very typical among the *Vedic* people. These northern and southern groups influenced each other in various ways, as the *Vedas* indicate. The northern culture ultimately prevailed, making its main ancient literary record the early Vedas. Kushite kings, in turn, established trade and diplomacy with *Elam, Sumer, Kush* and *Khemet,* and established royal alliances with them. They also governed with the order, introduced advanced technologies, and followed the Vedic policy of honoring the customs and religious beliefs of the peoples whose land they occupied. Over twelve hundred ancient settlement sites have been uncovered along the Sarasvati basin, evidencing that a mighty river once nurtured and sustained the ancient maritime civilization that arose along its banks.

It was possible to travel on the currents of the *Sarasvati* from the *Gulf of Chambay* to Mathura via Lothal, Dholavira, Granweriwala, Kalibangan, Banawali, Paonta-Doon, and Indraprastha. *Kushites* living near the mouth of the river traded by sea with Sumer, Kush and Khemet. There is a surprising lack of scholarly resources regarding the expansion of the Kushites, although ancient sources extol their numerous achievements. The *Kushites* sent out many colonies; in some places, they mixed with the people of the land and were nearly absorbed. In others, they excluded the natives and maintained themselves solely and separately. However, in spite of their formidable achievements, the contributions of the *Kushites* have been largely ignored by 'conventional' historians. As noted by Drucilla Dunjee Houston, "to those who read the *Rig-Veda* intelligently and without the confusing glasses of prejudice, these mutilated and interpolated writings are but a description of the familiar traits and customs of Kushite Ethiopians. Drucilla Dunjee Houston concludes that the Brahmins were probably a much later and intermixed branch of the inhabitants of *Hindu-Kush*."

Drucilla Dunjee Houston states further that "the fact that the *Brahmins* altered *Sanskrit* writings to such great extent is proof itself that they were not the original authors of these works. They took over and appropriated much from Buddhism that would appeal to the masses when they found it otherwise impossible for them to sit in the saddle of the priesthood." [dccxliii] Vedic knowledge in India clearly preexisted the arrival of the *Aryans* [around 1,200 BC]; the proof is that the *Saraswati River* dried up about 5,000 years ago, over 2,000 years before the arrival of the *Aryans*. The *Rig Veda* was composed while the *Saraswati* was still in full flow, well before 3,000 BC; the Vedic and early Harrapans belonged to the same civilization.[dccxliv] When the *Saraswati River* flowed, the current desert of Rajasthan was a green land full of vegetation. The existing rivers, Sutlej, and Yamuna, are believed to have been major sources of the Saraswati River during the Vedic era. [dccxlv]

It is believed that about 12,000 BC, during the liquefaction of the glaciers in the Himalayas, the Ghaggar River was flowing in full strength, which is underscored by the broad palaeo-channel of this river. It is also seen that it gradually joined the currently waterless canal of the Hakra River, which led to the river discharging into the *Rann of Kutch*. Recent photographs taken by satellite have demonstrated the existence of the dried upriver, which is, in fact, the Saraswati. The ancient *Rig Veda* says 'that the Saraswati ran unbroken from the mountains to the Sea, allowing maritime trade from the northern Vedic realm to the foreign ports abroad. During the last decades, a great number of Northern India archaeological sites have revealed remnants of Vedic cities, which formerly stretched out on the banks of the Saraswati. The *Saraswati* descended from the height of the *Himalayas* through Adibadri, Bhavanipur and Balchapur in the foothills to the plains, the river took roughly a southwesterly course, passing through the plains of Punjab, Haryana, Rajasthan, Gujarat and finally, it is believed to have flowed into the *Arabian Sea* at the *Rann of Kutch* near Prabhas Pattan.

The Rig-Veda mentions petty kings dwelling along the course of Sarasvati during the Vedic era and makes almost one-hundred references to the ocean (Samudra) and dozens of references to rivers and ships flowing to the sea for maritime trade.[135][dccxlvi] The *Kushites* traversed the mouth of the Persian Gulf, adhering to the coasts of Oman, *Yemen,* and eastern Arabia, and sailed the *Red Sea* to the coasts of *Punt, Kush and Khemet*. Archaeologists have uncovered several of the ancient maritime routes of the Kushites, most notably the spice routes between the ports of *Indus, Elam, Sumer, Yemen, Kush* and *Khemet*.[dccxlvii] Many such voyages were launched from the port city of *Kususthali*, built by *Ausar* in the *Bay of Kutch (Kush),* in the *Gulf of Cambay,* along the ancient northwestern coast of the sub-continent. Though legends mistakenly attribute the construction of *Kususthali* to *Krishna, Kush* (Ausar, Osiris) was the original builder of the ancient port city and the original *City of Old Dwarka*, now submerged in the ancient *Bay of Kutch (Kush)*.[dccxlviii]

The name of the ancient port city actually became a key to deciphering *Indus Valley Script* because the ligature in the Indus Script for thalassocracy is a triton-looking sign, a *Semitic* alphabetic symbol written as *Vedic Sanskrit*.[dccxlix] The name "Kususthali," as described in the *Vedas,* essentially means "ocean port". Thus, the 'Thalassocracy of Kush" is translated as *"Ocean Port City of Kush"*.[dccl] Thus, it was clearly *Kush* (Ausar, Osiris) who built the *Port City of Kususthali*, the ancient maritime City of Kush now submerged by rising seas in the *Gulf of Kutch*, in the distant shadows of the *Hindu Kush Mountains*.[dccli] Underwater ruins in the *Gulf of Cambay* extend out fifty miles from the shore on the submerged channel of the extinct *Sarasvati River* across the then far broader coastal plains of the early ancient era. There are legendary bronze age ruins of the early *Sarasvati-Indus Valley Civilization*, far out at sea, including at the *Port City of Kush* ('Kususthali') in the *Gulf of Kutch* (Kush).

Guided by the accorded 'three fire' signal, the *Kushite Armada* found anchorage in the then-natural harbor at the *Bay of Kutch (Kush),* joining merchants, traders, craftsmen, and mariners from the *Upper* and *Lower Saraswati River Valley*. The *Port City of Kush* was then under construction in the now submerged *Bay of Kutch* (Kush), under the direction *Ausar* (Osiris, Kush), to both accommodate the ships of the *Armada* and serve as a trading port city, with proximity to the mouth of the *Saraswati*, on the sub-continent. *Adi Dasas* from areas of the delta and mouth of the *Saraswati River* aided in the design and construction of the ancient port, many of whom spoke of a grand port and center of (ancient maritime) trade along the coast to the south.

---

[135] Rig-Veda 8.21.18ab

Merchant ships of the *Kushite Armada* were directed due south, along the coast, to the ancient *Port City of Lothal*, just south of *Kususthali* in the *Gulf of Cambay*, on the coast of the Arabian Sea. *Adi Dravidas* built the first major port in history at the *Gulf of Cambay*, in *Gujarat*, when they constructed ancient *Lothal*. Here archaeologists have found large warehouses ready to hold goods for export and import. In addition to warehouses, there were also many granaries and factories at *Lothal*. The city was destroyed by floods over and over but was rebuilt over and over also on higher platforms; a huge wall was built to encircle the city to protect it from floods. *Lothal* was both an important port city of the *Sarasvati-Indus Valley Civilization* and the center of the all-important bead industry of the era. There were warehouses for storing the commodities uncovered during the excavations at ancient Lothal; recently, a warehouse having 64 rooms with passages for each room was discovered.

The dockyard and warehouse at Lothal were connected by a long wharf; dockyards of those times could handle thirty ships of sixty tonnes each, making Lothal a key port city of the era. From the ancient *Port City of Lothal,* the Kushite armada was directed and preceded southward along the coastline, to the ancient early coastal cities of *Goa* and *Kerala,* on the *Konkan Coast*. The plains along the western coast of the Sub-Continent were far more extensive than at present. Now submerged hills and valleys of the broader coastal plains were well above sea level during much of the early Neolithic era. As sea levels rose, the ensuing flooding ultimately submerged and forever claimed many of the coastal fishing villages, towns, and cities, as well as much of the coastal plains and grasslands. From the ancient *Konkan Coast* southward to *Cape Comoran* are submerged ruins of the northern coastal villages and cities of *Kumari Kandam*, flooded according to the Vedic literature, such as the flooding of *Kususthali* by the post-glacial rise in sea level.

The oldest *Dravidian* traditions speak of prehistoric cities and kingdoms in the Southern on the now largely submerged *Kumari Peninsula*. The western coast of *Peninsular Kumari* once stretched northward from its southern cape, where a series of mountains punctuated the end of the peninsula. This was the region where the first *Sangam* was situated, in the *City of Then-Madurai* (Southern Madurai), along the Lakshadweep-Chagos Ridge. Peninsular Kumari was then about a couple of thousand miles in length and several hundred miles wide in places.[dcclii] The ancient history of *Goa* dates back to the time of the *Kumari Peninsula*; rock engravings found at various places in Goa indicate that people settled in this region between 10,000 BC – 8,000 BC. Goa possessed rich flora and fauna, owing to its location on the Western Ghats range (a biodiversity hotspot).[dccliii] Throughout much of antiquity, Goa was renowned for different kinds of spices and fruit, as well as cloves, nutmeg, cumin, curry, cinnamon, pepper, vanilla, coriander, turmeric, banana, coconut, pineapple, mango, pomelo, jackfruit, bimbli, guava, papaya, and cashew, citrus. And it was at ancient *Goa* that the *Kushites* would again encounter the *Naga*.

Goa was a land that had fallen under the influence and province of the *Naga*, a land in which the *Naga* had been prominent for untold centuries of antiquity.[dccliv] The ethos of the *Naga* was an ancient cult in *Goa* long before the arrival of the *Kushites*. More than one-hundred twenty-five prehistoric petroglyphs are displayed on the banks of the *Kushavati River* in southeastern *Goa*, evidencing the spiritualism and prowess of the ancient cult. For hundreds of years, the *Kushavati* rock art gallery of *Goa* was known locally, but the people did not know the antiquity of the work, nor could they interpret it. After a thorough study, it was concluded that these petroglyphs are different from those found elsewhere in *Goa*.[dcclv] Deeper studies and analysis over a period of years showed that it was an exquisitely carved ocular labyrinth, one of the best in India. Its ocular nature also clinched the evidence of prehistoric shamanism.

They were experimenting with fungi and wild mushrooms, psilocybin mushrooms gathered from local termite hills.[dcclvi] Psychedelic mushrooms have mind-altering substances called "entheogens' that can produce profound, indescribable spiritual experiences. The discovery of rock art engravings on lateritic platforms and granite boulders from *Usgalimal* on the banks of the (west-flowing) Kushavati River has shed light on the prehistory of *Goa*. An anthropomorphic figure of a *Mother Goddess* and tectiforms resembling tree-like motifs have been found, which a detailed study has dated to 8,000 BC.[dcclvii] The earliest ancient *mystic cults* of *Goa* appear to have clearly been *Nagas*, as evident by both the age and their inherent pursuit of enlightenment.[dcclviii]

The Parables

Only those spiritually advanced seekers whose *Kundalini* was said to be 'awakened' were bestowed the privilege of being called "*Naga*". The Naga was worshiped as a symbol of the serpentine-like spiritual energy (fire) that flows through all living things. *Kundalini* is a Sanskrit word meaning "coiled up like a snake" (there are a number of other translations emphasizing a more serpentine nature to the word— 'serpent power'), so-called because it is believed to lie like a serpent in the root chakra, at the base of the spine. *Kundalini* was (and is) the *Serpentine Fire* as used by yogis, the sub-atomic force located in the Sacral Bone area at the base of the spine. The *Kundalini* has seven layers; each layer has seven sub-layers. Therefore, there are forty-nine degrees of awakening it. In ancient *Khemet* (Egypt), the awakening of the Kundalini energy, which has risen up to the brow chakra or the forehead center, is symbolized by a serpent on the crown of the Ngu (Pharaoh).[dcclix]

Kundalini is a psycho-spiritual energy of the consciousness, thought to reside within the sleeping body; a form of serpentine energy residing in the body has potent force, coiled like a serpent at the base of the vertical axis, and aroused either through spiritual discipline or spontaneously to bring new states of consciousness (including mystical illumination). The power of Kundalini is said to be enormous, and those are having experienced it claim it to be indescribable. Kundalini has been described as liquid fire and liquid light; the concept comes from ancient yogic philosophy and refers to the "mothering intelligence" behind yogic awakening and spiritual maturation (known as Kundalini Shakti). According to yogic tradition, *Kundalini* is curled in the *root chakra* in three and one-half turns around the sacrum.[dcclx]

Yogic phenomenology states that *Kundalini* awakening is associated with the appearance of bio-energetic phenomena that are said to be experienced somatically by the yogi, an advent referred to as "*pranic awakening*".[dcclxi] "Prana" is interpreted as the vital, life-sustaining force in the body. Uplifted or intensified life energy is called pranotthana and originates from the reservoir of subtle psycho-spiritual and bio-energy at the base of the spine. This energy is also interpreted as a vibrational phenomenon that initiates a process of vibrational spiritual development. The phenomena associated with it vary from bizarre physical sensations and movements, pain, clairaudience, visions, brilliant lights, super lucidity, psychical powers, ecstasy, bliss, and transcendence of self.

The serpent is the symbol of the energy flowing through both the cosmos (on a macro basis) and the individual (on a micro level). As the cosmic energy circuits have an inherent serpentine form, the *Kundalini Shakti*, the coiled and dormant cosmic power, the supreme force in the human body, the coiled-up energy, also has the shape and character of the serpent. Under *Tantra*, this *Kundalini* is the supreme instrument of all achievements, absolute light, knowledge, and bliss. By arousing the Kundalini, it is dormant, is reoriented and undergoes a transformation. When the Kundalini keeps sleeping, man's awareness of the world restricts to his immediate earthly circumstances; however, when the Kundalini awakens, the individual does not remain restricted to his own perception but participates in the divine source of light and attains cosmic transformation.[dcclxii] Descriptions of Kundalini-type experiences are found in the ancient esoteric teachings of *Khemet*, *Tibet, China,* and *East Africa*. The epithet "Naga" was bestowed upon those who had attained access to *Kundalini energy*, the serpentine force within.

To be referred to as a "*Naga*" was to be referred to as *enlightened* and as *wise* as the mythical serpent. With the passage of time, the term "*Naga*" thus became used to refer to those who were spiritually awakened.[dcclxiii] The *Nagas* treated medicinal and psychoactive plants and herbs with the greatest of respect; they were considered doorways to the higher realms. It was taught and understood that the use of psychoactive mushrooms without using yoga limited the vast potential and strayed from the ancient use of wild mushrooms. Over forty-five locally known wild edible ancient mushroom species are found and harvested in Goa, one of which the Goan Nagas considered sacred. The *Termitophilic* species are found in tropical and sub-tropical parts of Asia and Africa. About thirty different types of wild Termitomyces mushroom species are grown and harvested in ancient *Goa*.

The mushrooms in *Goa*, which sprout from the termite mounds, are known by various names in different areas; a species with a beaklike protrusion (umbo) is known in Canacona as "chochyale or Toshale".[dcclxiv] One, which grows solitary, is known as 'Khutyale'. Edible Russulas are known in the Cotigao sanctuary as "Pava alami or Shendari alami'. Those who collect mushrooms from the wild and sell these by the roadside or in markets are expert mushroom collectors. They have traditional knowledge of mushroom habitats, morphology, and seasons and can distinguish between edible and toxic species. Being at the epicenter of the ancient mushroom and spice trade, the *Naga* kingdom of the era in ancient *Goa* was both significant and prosperous. Though not under the suzerainty of *Nagu-Punt*, the *Naga* of *Goa* had long been ancient trading partners with *Nagu-Punt*, and their sentiments were muted in what they deemed to be essentially a territorial dispute in *East Africa*.

Accordingly, the trade relationship with *Nagu-Punt* did not prevent the *Naga* of *Goa* from establishing a fruitful trade relationship with the *Kushites*. Spices had actually been both cause and stimulus of economic development during the earliest phases of antiquity; it was the importance of the early spice trade that originally attracted the *Nagas* to *Konkan*, leading to later incursions into the southern interior where they uncovered new herbs, prompting their further entrenchment in the south. The *Nagas* had a capital city in the southern part of the sub-continent, which is said to have been situated in the heart of the Dekkan, evidencing the pervasiveness of their influence.[dcclxv] Though their sentiments regarding the dispute between *Kush* and *Nagu-Punt* remained muted, the *Nagas of Goa* astutely advised the *Kushites* that the further south, and the closer to *Nagu-Punt* that they venture, the more acute sentiments might become between them and the Nagas they may encounter.

The captains of the *Kushite* merchant fleet were given a second pause for consideration by the answer to their inquiry about the need for such a large sea wall, recently constructed [at a length of roughly fifteen miles] along the ancient *Konkan* coast. Towards the end of the Ice Age, some say 11,000 – 8,000 BC, sea levels began to rise with the run-off from the melting of glaciers. In 8,000 BC, it had increased by 400 feet and submerged most of the submerged part of the peninsula between the oceans off the coast of India. [dcclxvi] By 8,500 BC, much of what remained of the great central plain of the *Kumari Peninsula* had been inundated by rising seas. Right before 8,000 BC, thousands upon thousands of miles of coastline disappeared, wiping out entire coastal communities. Rising sea levels caused flooding and dislocation at the ocean's edge, forever claiming once prized coastal zones.

For the Nagas, the indelible experience of the earlier *Sunda* floods had been passed down over the generations; prospective and actual dislocations thus prompted the *Nagas* to migrate to the *Konkan* coast, beginning around 8,400 BC. Then as the coastal dwellers of *Goa,* they closely observed the rising seas and tides advancing toward the fragile shoreline, prompting them to build a sea wall to shield and protect the coastal villages, harbors and coastline. [dcclxvii] The continuous efforts of the sea to scale as much land as possible before receding provided the inspiration and fortitude to develop the engineering skills and abilities to build and add to the large sea wall. In this battle between land and sea, there were times when, for brief and prolonged periods, the sea or land had an advantage over the other, resulting in either sea conquering and occupying otherwise exposed land or land, forcing the sea to recede thus extending its rule to a greater area.

The structure of the ancient "Konkan Sea Wall" was not continuous, but it was (and is) uniform and less than ten feet below present-day sea levels.[dcclxviii] Forewarned, the captains of the cargo-laden *Kushite* fleet raised anchor in the *Harbor of Goa*, and set course due south, bound for *Kerala*. The earliest *Sanskrit* text to mention *Kerala* by name is the *Rig-Veda*. [dcclxix] Geographically, ancient *Kerala* was situated between the *Western Ghats Mountains* and the *Arabian Sea*, at the southern reaches of the *Malabar Coast*. The "Malabar Coast" was a name given to the stretch of coast extending southward from *Goa* to *Kerala*. The *Malabar Coast* consists of a continuous belt of sand dunes, behind which are lagoons paralleling the coast, linked by canals, forming inland waterways. The inland is level alluvial land, well-watered by rivers descending the *Western Ghats*. *Kerala* is one of the most beautiful places on earth, blessed with endless beaches, lush green forests, waterfalls, fertile land and palm-fringed lakes. Ancient Kerala became known as the land of spices sometime in the distant fog of early antiquity.

Notwithstanding, there is little unanimity among historians about the region due to few written historical accounts. Kerala's ancient history has thus been shrouded in the mists of tradition, interwoven with legends and myths. The history goes back thousands of years, though there is limited information available regarding the ancient period. The *Veddas* were amongst the earliest inhabitants of the southern sub-continent and Kerala. The *Kadar*, who live in the present-day forests of Kerala, is a Vedda group who are probably descendants of the original people of India. The first of the Nagas and Dasas to reach the southern sub-continent appear to have done so by way of the ancient Kumari peninsula. The *Adi-Dasas* was perhaps the last of the earliest arrivers on the southern sub-continent, having migrated and settled throughout central and northern India thousands of years before the arrival of the *Kushites*.

The *Nagas, Veddas, Kols* and *Adi-Dasas* were amongst the early diverse inhabitants of *Kerala* when the *Kushites* arrived. Kerala was famous for spices like cinnamon, cardamom, nutmeg, ginger, turmeric, and black pepper; unlike salt, which can be found practically anywhere in the world, black pepper, like certain other spices, is indigenous only to *Kerala*. Kerala rose to fame solely based on its early *monopoly* over *spices* and certain *medicinal herbs*. Over seven hundred species of medicinal herbs are found in *Kerala*, and like the wild mushrooms harvested in Goa, those who harvested spices and herbs in Kerala had a keen knowledge of plant habitats and seasons.[dcclxx] Ancient *Kochi* (Cochin) was the main port of *Keralla* well into the historic era; ancient Kochi dates back to 8,000 BC when it is believed to have been submerged in the Arabian Sea. Kochi is reputed to have been the ancient world's greatest trading center in spices.[dcclxxi]

The ships of the Kushite Armada dropped anchor in the natural harbor of ancient Kochi, where, as forewarned, they found the *Nagas of Kerala* less than forthcoming, accommodating or willing to trade. However, they found and connected with willing and experienced harvesters and traders among the *Adi-Dasas, Kols* and *Veddas*. With their aid, traders of the Kushite fleet were able to add hundreds of pounds of dried spices and medicinal herbs to their cargos. In their barter, exchange, and discourse with the *Adi-Dasas*, the commander of the Kushite armada inquired about the rising seas and coastal floods and how they might affect the currents and tides on the voyage north to the *Port City of Kush (*'Kususthali'*)*. The Dasas advised of the history of great floods devastating the Kumari peninsula; the first period of flooding (between 12,000 to 11,000 years ago) claimed a large portion of the coastal seaboard surrounding the peninsula.

As sea levels rose, coastal flooding ultimately submerged and forever claimed many of the seaboard townships and fishing villages, as well as much of the coastal plains. The coastal flooding forced al dislocation of those who had settled along the ancient seaboard for thousands of years. Peninsular *Kumari* then still extended to the present-day Chagos Archipelago, at its southern extent, with the eastern shores of the peninsula bordering the then far more encompassing Bay of Bengal. The global climate shifted around 10,000 BC, and the following five hundred years of torrential rains and rising seas brought on second-period flooding, causing further diminishment of the coastal plains. What remained was essentially the intact highlands and interior of the peninsula, surrounded by narrower coastal plains. Peninsular *Kumari* was then about a couple of thousand miles in length, still stretching from the *Pahruli River* in the north to the *Kumari River* in the south, interspersed with mountains, valleys, and interior plains; extending from the present-day *Lakshdweep Isles* in the north to those of the *Chagos Archipelago* in the south.

Inundation and weakening of the low-lying coastal areas progressed over thousands of years; during some periods, the sea levels rose rather drastically, forever claiming the once prized coastal zones and seaside communities. Sea levels rose to reclaim large tracts of the coastal area, causing flooding and dislocation of whole communities along the seaboard. The rapid rise in sea levels began around 8,000 BC, launching the last of the three global super-floods, with the Indian Ocean swelling and submerging core parts of *Kumari*. Peak sea levels are reaching all but the highlands of *Ceylon* at the (then) southern extent of the (Indian) Sub-Continent, and the *Maldives* and *Chagos* highlands on the southern peninsula, approaching the coast of east Africa. The rise in the seas had already begun to impact and affect the fragile *Malabar Coast*; however, the *Adi-Dasas* advised the currents, and rising tides should not hinder the *Kushite* return voyage.

With the ships of the merchant fleet heavily laddened with cargoes of spices and commodities like Sandalwood, Ivory, and Teakwood, *Kushite* captains raised anchor in the harbors of Kerala and set an urgent course due north, bound for the *Port City of Kush'* (*'Kusustuali'*) to apprise Ausar (Osiris, Kush, Zeus) of the calamity approaching from the rising seas. A voyage that would initiate relations with the *Saraswati-Indus River Valley, Elam, Sumer, Dilmun, Yemen* and eventually *Kush, Khemet* and destination ports in the Mediterranean. Upon return to the *Port City* of *Kush* (*Kusustuali*), the merchant fleet found the early ancient port still under construction but substantially complete. Nonetheless, the fleet was met with great fanfare and expectation, with Kushites at port having heard lavished tales from the local *Adi-Dasas* about the rich southern lands from which the fleet was now returning, the exotic spices of *Kerala*, and the mystical mushrooms of *Goa*.

The fleet's commanders, captains and merchants were brought together to update *Ausar* (Osiris, Kush) on the expedition later that evening. Small quantities of all they had procured were on display, with the prospects of new trade opportunities discussed; yet perhaps most concerning issue discussed was the rising seas. To *Kushites* of *Atlatian* derivation, whose native lands once adorned the ancient shores of the old *Atlantean Sea*, such as *Ausar*, the destructiveness of the rising seas were signs of approaching floods, and perhaps tsunamis, of potentially catastrophic proportion. A threat to all coastal communities, as well as those along the major rivers, deltas and corridors susceptible to vast inland flooding and destruction from the seas. Many of the *Kushite* merchants expressed concern for what dangers the rising seas might portend for *Kush, Khemet*, the *Nile Delta* and the safety of their families. *Ausar* and the fleet commanders surmised that any threat to *Nile Delta* would, by necessity, arise in the northern seas; seas quite familiar to *Ausar* (Osiris, Zeus, Kush).

It was thus resolved that the *Kushite* merchant fleet, laden with cargo, should depart for home and the ports along the Red Sea coasts of *Kush* and *Khemet*. Fleet commanders would again proceed along the coastline in order that they might avail themselves to alert the colonies of the impending danger as they progressed back to the coast of *East Africa*. Roughly a third of the *Kushite* merchant entourage opted to settle at *Kusustuali* and complete the *Port City* of *Kush. Ausar*, in turn, advised that he, his security detachment, and those of the overland entourage opting to continue onward would return across the *Hindu Kush* to collect and reunite with the main *Kushite* armies and entourage at their encampments in the highland river valleys of *Bactria*.[136]

Kusha-Dwipa: Nascent Kushite Empire

According to the *Matsya*, an ancient historical text from India, the world belonged to the Kushites for 7,000 years. According to a separate ancient Indian historical text, the Puranas, the world was divided into seven Dwipas (or divisions); the *Kusha-Dwipa* was said to extend from Africa to Asia, encompassing Old Punt, Sudan, Nubia, Arabia, Mesopotamia, Elam, India, and Asia Minor. According to the ancient Sanskrit writings, under the reign of the Kushites, these areas arose to become the most powerful and enlightened parts of the world.[137] Yet, in many ways, the nascent Kushite empire had been aided and propelled to prominence as part of the Maa confederation. At its nascency, the *Kushite Empire* extended from ancient Bactra and the Indian Sub-Continent in the east through Elam, Sumer, Mesopotamia, Arabia, Ethiopia, Sudan, and Khemet. From where nascent *Kusha-Dwipa* then stretched westward, fully across the *Sahel* ('*Ancient Sudan*') into *West Africa*, at its western extent.

---

[136] In Greek: Βακτριανή; Old Persian: Bāxtrish; Avestan: Bāxδī)
[137] The Wonderful Ethiopians

The *Puranas* say the *Kushites* ruled the parts of India in which they became prominent before returning west. Though ancient history, legend, and mythology are each silent on the story of their return to Africa, we can construct a picture of what happened from various available sources. From their base at Bactra, *Ausar* clearly led the Kushites westward, retracing the route they migrated across Elam's mountainous high country. Ancient *India* and *Bactra* were the most eastern provinces of nascent Kusha-Dwipa; the mound colonies to the west were established during the eastward migrations across the Iranian Plateau and Elamite highlands, were now self-sustainable and contributive to commerce along the highland trade route. Cultural and ethnic affinities between the *Kushites* and *Dasas* of earliest *Elam* facilitated coalescence and encouraged the development of well-organized trade networks across the highlands. Settlements in the mountainous high country became the sources of wood, marble, alabaster, metal ores and precious stones traded along the highland trade route.

The southern trade route traversed the southern Iranian plateau through Baluchistan (the westernmost province of present-day Pakistan), where trade along the corridor increased as Kushite and Proto-Elamite settlements and colonies expanded eastward.[dcclxxii] Anciently, the whole of present-day 'Baluchistan' was then called 'Kush', or 'Kuj' as the Persians pronounced it; also known as 'Kach' or 'Kaj'(each corruption of 'Kush'), a name appearing in eastern and western Baluchistan as 'Kach Gandava' and 'Kach' or 'Kaj Makran', respectively. The whole region was predominantly inhabited by Kushites and Proto-Elamites, the 'Asiatic Ethiopians' of Herodotus.[dcclxxiii] Retracing the route across the northern highlands, Ausar (Osiris, Zeus, Kush) and the Kushites revisited the settlements and colonies established across the northern Iranian Plateau during the eastern migrations. The ancient highland route traversed and linked colonies in the central Zagros highlands with villages and colonies on the central *Khuzestan* (Susiana) plain in southwestern Iran (where Rawlinson affirms the finding of ancient Kushite inscriptions in Susiana).

Back to Bactra: The Northern Highlands

The return of *Ausar* and his entourage and remaining detachment to the highlands of Bactria was met with both festivity and formality. Festivities lasted well into the evening, beginning the very morning of their arrival, with *Ausar* providing tours and celebrating at each of the settlements raised since his departure. *Bactra* was comfortably nestled between the *Hindu Kush Mountains* and the *Āmū Daryā River*. The earliest *Kushite* settlements spread along the area south of the river in what is now *Northern Afghanistan*, *Southern Uzbekistan* and *Tajikistan*. This was the early 'heartland' of early ancient *Bactra*, once a very fertile region, where the seeds of early agriculture took firm root and thrived; leaders of the early *Kushite* settlements sought to promote *Bactra* as an ideal locale for the 'provincial capital' of '*Kush*' in Asia.

Foundations of the region's earliest ancient city, *Bactra (Bactra)*, were formed by the constellation of early *Kushites* settlements situated along the southern bank and to the south of the *Amu Darya* (Oxus) River. The original settlement sites are still found approximately forty-five miles south of the present-day course of the *Amu Darya*, which ran closer to the early ancient city of *Bactra* throughout most of antiquity.[dcclxxiv] Early Kushite settlers along the banks of the *Amu Darya* lived on river terraces and devised methods of irrigation that allowed them to grow crops on the northern plains. From there, according to pre-historical accounts, farmers and herders expanded throughout much of the highland plains surrounding the *Hindu Kush*. In discussing the prospect of making *Bactra* the provincial capital of '*Kush*' in Asia, *Ausar* (Osiris, Zeus, Kush) and leaders of the settlements forming early *Bactra* gathered, ate and drank in lively discourse well into the evening.

Priests from *Ausar's* entourage told stories of the expedition to the south and their discoveries in the mystical land of *Goa,* while merchants from the expedition told of *Kerala,* the land of exotic spices, a few of which they were enjoying that evening. And yet, as captivating as the adventures of the expedition were, the *Kushite* settlement leaders, particularly the priests, believed they had made a discovery equally as enthralling. In trade and discourse with the *Nagas* of the north, *Kushite* merchants were granted a tale of a rich, rich mystical city, perhaps the source of much of the exotic highland trade of the *Nagas*, some distance to the east. The *Nagas* had their provincial *Capital City of Oudh* in the northwest, near what is now *Herat* in present-day Afghanistan, where the city served as a trade center for a string of villages along their highland trade routes to the east. [dcclxxv] [dcclxxvi] The ancient trade route began at the *Khyber Pass* (in present-day southeastern Afghanistan and southwestern Pakistan) and ran through *Northwestern India* to the tablelands of *Tibet.*

The omnipresent symbol of the *Naga* (the "Self-Consuming Serpent") marked each village along the ancient route, connoting their unison, affinity and identity with the *Nagas*.[dcclxxvii] The serpent symbol is often found at the sites of the ancient cities and villages along the old trade route, as are the earliest symbols of *Shiva*.[dcclxxviii] Legends hold that a brilliant, deified *Naga* king by the name of *Kuvera* (also called 'Kubera') brought the ability to smelt copper, gold, and other metals to the highlands; activities which occurred in the kingdom subsequently named after him, '*Khyber*', in what are now Southeastern Afghanistan and Northeastern Pakistan. This was an early *Kingdom* that the *Nagas* inhabited in the *Khyber Pass.* According to *Hindu* mythology, *Kuvera* and *Shiva* once each lived as *ascetic yogis* at the frigid heights of the pyramidical peak of *Mount Kailasa* in the *Himalayas.* For the *Kushites* of the era, the *Tibetan Tablelands* beyond the *Himalayas* were the known extent of the *Naga* highland trade route to the distant east.

Though the prospect of *Bactra* as a 'provincial capital' of '*Kush*' in Asia had a certain appeal to Ausar (Osiris, Kush), he felt it incumbent to then apprise of the calamity approaching from the rising seas. *Ausar* informed of the calamitous destruction along the *Konkan* and *Malabar Coasts* from the rise in sea levels in the great eastern ocean. Mariners and Merchants who took part in the southern expedition gave eyewitness accounts of coastal flooding that had already begun to impact the fragile *Konkan* and *Malabar Coasts.* The plains along the western coast of the Indian Sub-Continent were far more extensive than at present, and now submerged hills and valleys of the ancient broader coastal plains were at risk all along the western seaboard. The sea level rise had prompted the Nagas of the *Konkan Coast* to construct a large sea wall to protect their coastal villages and natural harbors from the unrelenting force of the rising tides. Beyond the *Malabar Coasts* and Ceylon, then still part of peninsular *Kumari* that extended to the present-day Chagos Archipelago. *Peninsular Kumari* was then about a couple thousand miles long and several hundred miles wide in places along that length.

As sea levels rose, coastal flooding submerged much of the seaboard, forcing the dislocation of those who had been on the seaboard for thousands of years. The Dasas of the southern coasts say that from the *Konkan Coast* southward are submerged ruins of the northern coastal villages and cities of *Kumari*. The *Dasas* of the *Malamar Coast* told of great floods that devastated *Kumari*, inundating and weakening the substrata underlying the coastal belt, eventually submerging and fragmenting large parts of the peninsula. The destruction was of a magnitude and proportion unheard of or seen since the dramatic destruction of ancient *Atlatia*, an advent and nightmare still resonant in the memories of all *Kushites* of *Atlatian* derivation. As the *Kumari* peninsula became weakened by the inundations and upheavals, core parts of the peninsular landmass gradually fragmented, forming several islands. Many of the smaller, low-lying islands eventually also succumbed to the rising tides. *Ausar* advised that ships of the armada had already been dispatched back to *Kush* to survey and prepare the eastern coast.

Ausar (Osiris, Zeus, Kush) surmised that any such danger or threat to *Khemet* would come from the *Great Northern Sea* (the 'Mediterranean Sea'), with which he was familiar and vowed to personally survey before his return to Kush. He further surmised that the highland villages (of early *Bactra*) in the *Hindu Kush,* along the *Āmū Daryā River Valley,* were ideally situated to be *the* key trading hub and provincial *Kushite* capital in Asia; however, he mused, "only if a great city could be raised, a great trading city that would attract and serve as a center for merchants near and far. A great port city is being built in the south, the ancient '*Port City of Kush'* ('Kususthali'), in the Gulf of Kutch Ausar extolled and urged the merchants, traders and settlers of early Bactra to raise a great city worthy of being capital.[dcclxxix]

To aid in the endeavor, *Ausar* would leave most of the Kushite army, advising that those who needed a return to Kush would depart and soon as rest, replenishment of supplies, and preparation by returning merchants, and the loading of their goods would allow. The returning Kushites would depart along the highland route (to the west) by which they arrived and, in so doing, inaugurate the ancient east-west highland trade routes between the *Kushite* settlements and villages across the high plains. Ancient history reports that the *Kushites* organized and controlled the first major trade through the territory, bringing early prosperity to *Bactra*. Archaeological evidence points to the ancient city-state as a hub of eastern trade with *Elam, Sumer, Dilmun, Yemen, Kush and Khemet* for thousands of years.[dcclxxx]

Return to Sumer

The name *Kush* (or "*Khuzistan*") was applied to the whole of the eastern side of the lower Tigris river in Mesopotamia. The northern and southern trade routes came together along the *Karun River,* the only navigable river east of *Sumer*, in the vicinity of *Ancient Shoosh* (Susa). To the east, in the region of the earliest Sumer, were the Kushite and Dasas villages along the alluvial valleys of the Euphrates and Tigris Rivers. The largest Kushite villages had been established in the southern-most part of the land that would later come to be called *Sumer*. Arable land was literally created out of the marshes and swamps by a 'separation' of land from water; the swamps were drained, and floodwaters were controlled and diverted to the rainless desert by canals. Sumer was already in the first stages of civilization when the southern settlements formed the early City of Eridu; Dasas settlements had long prior waxed, waned, relocated, and combined to form the foundation of the largest cluster of villages the came together to form early Eridu.

Eridu was the southernmost of the early Sumerian settlements. Built on the shoreline of an ancient northern Arabian lake, the city acted as a prime entrepot. During its heyday, Eridu had access to both the Gulf and Arabian markets. The incense trade to southern Mesopotamia either followed overland routes across Eastern Arabia or maritime routes in the (Persian) Gulf. In both cases, they converged on the lower Mesopotamia delta. Sumer would ultimately expand to encompass the whole plain between and on both sides of the Tigris and Euphrates rivers. The Kushites found the richness of the alluvial soil at *Eridu* would accommodate a larger settlement, a major benefit in a location where they realized engineering and construction work in building canals and dikes would be required to harness the annual floods and that this would require a work force of hundreds of men. Countless books have been written about the "mysterious origins" of the (allegedly) racially ambiguous *Sumerians*.[dcclxxxi]

Usually, when Eurocentric authors write about the "*mysterious origins*" of influential people in the ancient world, it's a veiled allusion to the fact that those *mysterious people* were of *African* derivation.[dcclxxxii] Nonetheless, the *Kushites* were at the heart of archaic civilization, becoming widespread in Africa and Asia for thousands of years; the annals of the great nations of these lands are full of them. When *Ausar* (Osiris, Zeus, Kush) and the *Kushites* settled again in the land that became Sumer, he took his third wife, with whom he had his fifth son, whom they together named "*Nimrod."* Nimrod is said to have been the son of a virgin queen who was overtaken by the prominence and majesty of Ausar (Osiris, Zeus, Kush).[dcclxxxiii] *Nimrod* was raised in an *African* tradition that goes back thousands of years, with high priests of the faith and hunters so at one with *Deity,* they could commune with nature, tame wild animals, and combat the unseen forces that corrupt man and beast.[dcclxxxiv]

The scriptures imply that *Nimrod* was a *Priest-King* who worked to achieve *God's* will, which was always to build a spiritually uplifted civilization, traditions for which the *Kushites* were renowned. Wherever the *Kushites* went, they took their royal priests and scribes. Kushite religious life was diffused through the agency of these priests, who helped lay the foundation for civilization by policing the natural order of creation and were thus deemed "*Mighty Hunters before the Lord."* They built shrines and temples along the major waterways and were instrumental in collecting taxes for commerce along the waterways they controlled. Most people do not know there was another iconic tradition of the ancient *Kushites,* a cultural tradition that not only points to spiritual abilities and mastery but says explicitly that *Nimrod* was such a *master*, a form of spiritual mastery that led to the rise of Sumerian civilization.

African priests and shamans of all types worldwide share in this tradition; Saint Francis of Assisi and Saint Anthony (in the Catholic tradition) are great examples. It was said that once you achieve "God Consciousness", you will share in some of the Creator's abilities, including the ability to communicate with animals. Nimrod became a masterful leader because he was one with the Creator and living in a sort of "God Consciousness." For reasons that become quite apparent later, there has been an ongoing chorus of deceit about Nimrod; lies and distortions that largely emanated from 'extra-biblical sources' and legends authored thousands of years after his reign. For centuries the perpetrators have sought to usurp the lineage and personage of the Sumerians and later Babylonians; it is time, at last, to dispel these lies.

Rescuing Nimrod

The *Kushite* prince *Nimrod* is said in ancient literature to have been a very charismatic young man who slew a "Serpent" [a Naga], a deed which made him popular among the people of Sumer. He is described as a big and strong and very handsome, athletic "black man" whose looks dazzled the eyes of his female admirers and whose charisma spellbound his male followers. *Nimrod* became very skilled in archery and warfare and, according to Genesis 10:8-12, became "a mighty hunter before the Lord."[138] At this time in history, the beasts of the land were still aggressive toward people, causing them to become fearful for their lives. Nimrod emerged as their protector by hunting the animals on horseback with a bow and arrow.

---

[138] Ridpath 114 -15

All ancient traditions agree Nimrod was of the black race that passed from east Africa through Arabia to the valley of the Euphrates, where Sumerians such as he would call themselves the 'black-headed people' and speak a derivate language initially from Ethiopia (the 'Land of Punt and Kush').[dcclxxxv] Semite myths recount the heroics of *Nimrod* in their book of Genesis, which states that he was a mighty hunter of renown who was said to have built *Erech*, *Sumer*, and parts of *Elam*.[dcclxxxvi] [dcclxxxvii] Nimrod developed a concept of state, which was a monarchy modeled after his understanding of Heaven's governmental system, to mirror it on earth; hence, it was considered a divine monarchy, representing the Kingdom of God on Earth.[dcclxxxviii]

The Legends

The Scriptures say Kush begat Nimrod who began to be mighty upon the earth. Nimrod is said to have been the son of a virgin queen who was overshadowed by the prominence and majesty of his father, Kush.[dcclxxxix] *Ausar* (Osiris, Kush) begat *Nimrod* (his fourth son) with *Semiramis*, whom he took as a wife. The sons of Ausar thus far were six of his eight sons and, in order of their birth, his sixth and third youngest, *Nimrod,* was he who first rose to greatness as a Monarch, which until this day has made his name famous among the greatest princes.[dccxc]

By all accounts, the Kushites adhered to a spiritual tradition focused upon becoming *one* with the *Creator*, to be "in the face" of God, just as the scriptures say of Nimrod. These Kushites systematically built civilizations using this spiritual reverence, making their art and architecture ultimate proof that *Nimrod* lived, as the original scriptures said, "in the face" of God." Nimrod was renowned for having established an early ancient territory that extended the length of the *Tigris-Euphrates Valley*, where he was seen as a benefactor to the people.

Nimrod was a warrior king who expanded his empire to include much of the northern and eastern territories, where he met and married his first wife *Eneth*, who bore him twin sons called *Hunor* and *Mugor*.[dccxci] In the book "Legend: The Genesis of Civilization", the British Egyptologist David Rohl equates the Sumerian king *Enmerkar* with the biblical *Nimrod*. Nimrod was closely associated with Erech (the biblical name for *Uruk*), where *Enmerkar* ruled [cf. Gen. 10:8-10]. Erech was a city of ancient Sumer founded by Nimrod.[dccxcii]

In most Sumerian literature, Enmerkar's name is written En-me-kar; in slightly later texts, we find En-me-er-kar.[dccxciii] The Sumerian King List adds that Enmerkar was "the one who built Uruk." Enmerkar built a great sacred precinct at Uruk and constructed a temple at Eridu; that much we know from the epic poem 'Enmerkar and the Lord of Aratta'.[dccxciv] By all accounts, Nimrod was the founder of ancient Babylonia and the City of Babylon, though the date of the latter's foundation is still disputed.

The City of Babylon was the capital of the ancient land of Babylonia in southern Mesopotamia, where it became an important marketplace along the ancient trading corridor. Babylon was the ancient "*Land of Shinar*" alluded to in the Bible (Gen 10:10), and its general location has never been disputed. The earliest Sumerian settlements in Southern Babylonia arose in remote times, settled by people who had clearly already attained a high level of culture and spiritual development, building houses and temples of burnt and unburnt brick. Babylon means "Gate of the God."

The founding of the earliest cities of Babylonia and their federation into one great kingdom is ascribed to Nimrod. Attributed to Nimrod is the building of Erech, Accad, and Calneh in the *Land of Shinar*.[dccxcv] Many legends have been spun around his name, some claiming Nimrod was "Ninus", the earliest Babylonian king. This individual ruled at the beginning of Babylonia and was the founder of Nineveh and other cities in Assyria. Genesis 10:11 indicates that Nimrod was the builder of Nineveh, and the very word Nineveh (Nin-neveh) means "the habitation of Ninus."

By all truly credible accounts, Nimrod was the founder of Babylonia, Akkad, and Assyria. Gen. 10:11 reports that Nimrod built the city of Nineveh, which identifies him with king Ninus. The historian Apollodorus clarified that "Ninus is Nimrod."[139] In the ancient records of Justin and Diodorus Siculus, Ninus is credited with those kingly powers attributed to Nimrod in the Scriptures.[dccxcvi] Many authorities translate Genesis X to read, "Out of that land, he (Nimrod) went forth into Assur ("Assyria") and builded Nineveh." This is the proper translation of the passage (and not that "Asher went forth and built Nineveh"). [dccxcvii]

Ashur was an old Sumerian settlement in the north that grew into the capital of early ancient Assyria. The name is taken from the god "Ashir," about whom Sumerian texts of all periods are silent. His name is sometimes written "Aššur", meaning means "a deity of light." Ashur (or Aššur) was north of the Fertile Crescent in a well-irrigated region that stretched north across Mesopotamia to the Mediterranean coast. A land that included present-day Syria and the southeastern Anatolian Peninsula. Mountains were in the north and northeast of early Assyria along the borders of present-day Turkey, Syria, and ancient Elam.[dccxcviii]

As all Bible students have been taught, the Assyrians are said to have descended from Ashur, who is asserted to have been the second son of Shem, who was said to be the first son of the fabled "Noah of the Great Flood" (Genesis10:22), adapted from the story of the "Great Flood" in the "Sumerian Epic of Gilgamesh."[dccxcix] Flavius Josephus, a first-century Romano-Jewish historian, purported thousands afterward that "Ashur (or Aššur) lived at the city Nineveh, and named his subjects Assyrians. Ashur (or Aššur) remained the chief Deity under the later arriving Semites, even when the Assyrian capital was moved to Nineveh (about 800BC).

In truth, Ashur (or Aššur) was a deified form of the early ancient Sumerian *City of Assur*.[dccc] Archaeologists have discovered that the further back in time the digs in this region go, the more advanced, the earlier founding culture is found to have been. The first Sumerian remains were unearthed in the middle of the nineteenth century by Hincks, Oppert, and Rawlinson; Rawlinson called these people Cushites ("Kushites").[dccci] Repeated references from Akkadian and Old Babylonian writings clearly refer to the Sumerians as "black-headed peoples," differentiating them from the later Akkado-Babylonian Semites and other surrounding peoples.[dcccii]

It has been recognized from the earliest days of archaeological discovery that Sumerians depicted themselves in ways that are recognizably different from their depictions of Semites in their own pictographic tradition. Though it would arise thousands of years later, the fatherland of the Semites was along southeastern Anatolia; a region portioned off from the remaining portion of the peninsula by the imposing Taurus mountain range from the north to the east and by the Nur mountain range from the west.

---

[139] Apollodori, Fragm. 68 in Willer, Vol. i, p. 440

This three-sided natural shelter significantly affected the lives of the people during this troubled period. This area is only exposed on the south, the side of the Syrian lowlands. The upper courses of the Tigris and Euphrates rivers and their tributaries supply this area with water. It was precisely from this area that the Semites began to descend south along the Tigris and Euphrates river valleys in the 3rd millennia BC.

Thus did the emergent Semites migrate into ancient Assyria and Akkad rather than "found or build" those early provinces as they purport. There can be no doubt that the peoples originally inhabiting southern Mesopotamia (Shinar) and Northern Mesopotamia (Assyria and Akkad) were black. Nimrod and his people were undoubtedly Kushites of the same elk that ruled Khemet well before the founding of Babylonia and Babylon. There is no doubt that Nimrod was of African ancestry, so let us settle that once and for all time.

The Bible is, in essence, a retranslated and condensed copy of all African spiritual, religious, cultural, and iconographical events; a retranslation in which (Biblically and extra-Biblically) Nimrod is shone to be a powerful black King, a Kushite King.[dccciii] Every Christian scholar, theologian, and minister to the laity has pontificated on the blackness and evilness of the purported versions of the Biblical Nimrod.[dccciv]

There have been a lot of terrible things said about Nimrod over the centuries, and it all comes from extra-biblical sources and legends. The perpetrators took the original history, legends, and biblical tradition, turned it on its head, and pretended that what they were teaching was biblical and from *God*. This, of course, means they are pure and simple liars, and it is time these lies be laid to rest.[dcccv]

The Mosaic records frequently allude to the prominence of the *Kushites*. They are described as the most powerful, the most just, and the most beautiful of the human race and are constantly spoken of and described as "black." There seems to be no other conclusion to be drawn than that during remote ancient history, the Kushites and their civilization were among the most prominent in the world.[dcccvi] The defamation and slander against *Nimrod* (and, by inference, the *Kushites* and the entire lineage of Khem (Kam, Ham, Khronos)) began with a people who migrated into the area of ancient Sumer thousands of years after his reign. These were the infamous Chaldeans, tribes who first appeared in the annals of history living in the marshlands of southern Mesopotamia.

The Chaldeans were a Semitic people who settled in the then relatively poor area around the head of the Persian Gulf.[dcccvii] When they migrated into the region, they were no more than a few nomadic tribes with little civilization to their credit compared to the more mature civilization of Sumer, and they were no doubt perceived to be of little or no threat. They lived among the swamps along the lower courses of the Tigris and Euphrates, where each tribe was under the leadership of a Shaikh, who at times called himself a king.[dcccviii] The Chaldeans integrated themselves by marrying into local Sumerian families, a theory supported by the apparently mixed traits of their descendants. The Chaldeans coveted the rich cities and richly cultivated lands of Sumer and eventually began a host of efforts to possess themselves of the country. They immigrated in great numbers to the borderlands of Elam, where they settled and perpetually harassed Sumer.[dcccix]

The Chaldeans then began to expand around the head of the Persian Gulf, settling at the foot of the eastern mountains.[dcccx] When the opportunity presented itself, during a civil war weakening the Babylonian political structure, the Chaldeans took advantage of the internal strife and attacked Babylon in 626 BC.[dcccxi] Once in full possession of the country, later scribes of Chaldeans, seeking to usurp the heritage of Sumer and descendent Babylon, began their campaign of slander and defamation against Nimrod, the founder of Sumer. Purportedly using ancient Babylonian records and texts that are lost to us, the Chaldean scribe Berossus published his "Babyloniaca" ('History of Babylonia') in three books around 290–278 BC.[dcccxii] Berossus referred to Sumerians as "black-faced foreigners" in his *History of Babylonia*, which has itself been lost (except for fragments written by the later Semite scribe, Flavius Josephus).[dcccxiii] The corrupted Biblical word for Babylon was *Babel*.[dcccxiv]

The earliest reference to the "Tower of Babel" is also found in the "*History*" Berossus handed down.[dcccxv] This is the "Biblical" account of the *Tower of Babel*, and thus far, no Babylonian record or document has been discovered that corroborates or refers to the subject.[dcccxvi] Not so ironically, there is an ancient *Sumerian* myth that far predates, and is strikingly similar to the tale of the *Tower of Babel*, called "*Enmerkar and the Lord of Aratta*." A tale wherein Enmerkar of Uruk is building a massive ziggurat in Eridu and demands a tribute of precious materials from Aratta for its construction; at one point, reciting an incantation imploring the god *Enki* to disrupt and restore the linguistic unity of the inhabited regions — named as Shubur, Hamazi, Sumer, Uri-ki (Akkad), and the Martuland, "the whole universe, the well-guarded people — may they all address *Enlil* together in a single language." A recent theory advanced by David Rohl associates Nimrod, the hunter, and builder of Erech and Babel, with Enmerkar, the king of Uruk, also said to have been the first builder of the Eridu ziggurat. This theory proposes that the remains of the building that (via Mesopotamian legend) inspired the story of the Tower of Babel are the ruins of the ziggurat of Eridu (just south of Ur).[dcccxvii]

Semite scribes who later took up the mantle of slander against *Nimrod* knew that he remained well-known and respected in ancient civilizations, such as the Greeks, whose poet Homer called the Kushites "most favored of the gods" and said that the gods would come down off mount Olympus to dine "face to face" with them. At the same time, everyone else had to go to the temple to commune with divinity. And the writer Herodotus said they were the "most long-lived and the most just of men." The Semites knew that Nimrod was the subject of many ancient Kushite stories and parables, even in their time, and remained so renowned they dared not exclude or minimize him or his role in the rise of civilization. Later Semite scribes, far removed from the original authors, who apparently hated the Nimrod tradition for its implications, began their long and insidious campaign of slander and defamation against his reputation and personage.[dcccxviii][dcccxix]

It was *Flavius Josephus*, the Roman-Semite scribe, who said that "Nimrod caused the people to revolt against God", and in his "*Antiquities of the Jews*" (c. AD 94), he recounted the story as found in the Bible, writing that seeing no other way of turning men from the fear of God, Nimrod turns to tyranny to bring them into dependence on his power. According to Flavius Josephus, Nimrod inspired the people to build the Tower of Babel.[dcccxx] The *Tower of Babel* is a story told in the *Book of Genesis* of the Tanakh (the "Torah"), the phrase "Tower of Babel" never actually appears in the *Hebrew Bible*.[dcccxxi] Some suggest the story came from the "Yahwist" of the era; its etiological nature appears typical of the early Yahwist. The wording regarding the *City of Babel*, referring to the noise of the people's "babbling," was a term in common use among Semites and typical of the early *Yahweh Cult*, which began in 1AD.[dcccxxii] The gist of the story is that Nimrod encouraged the people to build a tower to reach heaven to make them equal to God.

The Talmud goes so far as to infer that Nimrod incited them to war against heaven, yet the biggest lie was that he declared himself God. The *Tower of Babel* story implies that God took offense at the efforts of the people to build a tower to heaven and confounded their tongues so that they did not understand one another's speech, and they thus ceased to build the tower.[dcccxxiii] Until that time, according to the story, everyone evidently spoke a single language, and "God's action" caused the development of different languages.[dcccxxiv] Of course, the development of languages is a subject that has been intensively studied, and virtually no evidence has been found to suggest that all languages originated from a single point or time. In fact, languages are known to have developed worldwide over great time spans; in essence, linguistics history alone has found the story to be a myth.

Given that the "Tower of Babel story" was almost certainly derived from the more ancient Sumerian myth about "Enmerkar and the Lord of Aratta", in proper context, it (and the slander against Nimrod) should be viewed as the earliest in a continuing series of nefarious efforts to usurp the heritage of the civilization he built in Sumer (and descendent Babylon). Fortunately, this insidious usurpation of Sumer and Babylon is refuted by the uncorrupted annals of antiquity; when a late 18th-century English traveler visited the Kushite temples at Abu Simbel (in Nubia), he saw sculptured on its walls the story of the Fall of Man, as told in Genesis. Commenting on this, British Historian Godfrey Higgins inquired as to how it was that the myths of the "Book of Genesis" were found in Nubia, a thousand miles above Heliopolis.[dcccxxv]

A more salient query would have been to question how it was that the myths inscribed at Abu Simbel so clearly predate the original authorship asserted by the Semite scribes (by well over a thousand years). As the son of *Kush* (Ausar, Osiris, Zeus), the era in which *Nimrod* lived and ruled was thousands of years before the arrival of the Chaldeans in Sumer (and the Semites later in Babylon). The most ancient legends describe Nimrod as a masterful hunter "before the face of God", inferring that he was closer than just being 'before' the Lord, he was literally 'face to face' with the Lord; interpreted anciently to mean that he was not merely doing something "before the Lord", but also with the "blessings of the Lord." Irrespective of interpretation, it is clear that *Nimrod* was a person of high moral character and an esteemed repute "before the face of God."[dcccxxvi dcccxxvii dcccxxviii]

Nimrod carved a territory in the primitive days of Mesopotamia that extended beyond the length of the Tigris-Euphrates Valley into the land that would become known as Kanaan. The oldest legends extol him as a great hunter but are somewhat ambiguous about all he hunted. According to comparative religion and other sources, it was not merely animals that were problematic for those gathered to build their civilization. It was the tendencies of men, represented as spiritual metaphors and symbolic appellations, called "leviathans"; forces devoted to the disruption of their civilization and the desecration of their belief in "God Consciousness."

A familiar "leviathan" from ancient *Khemetic* tradition was 'Apep', a serpent who purportedly opposed those on the road to spiritual enlightenment.[dcccxxix] Set and Apep were each representations of the ancient Nagas in Mesopotamia; in Mesopotamian mythology, a Naga leader, who first arrived by ship, is symbolized by an amphibious wisdom-disseminating god called 'Oannes'. The traditions of ancient Mesopotamia recount the story of this "amphibious ancestor" who taught the inhabitants the arts and crafts of civilization. About which the archaeologist Benno Landsberger writes, "the legend of the Seven Sages who emerged from the sea and imparted technical skills and knowledge to the Babylonians, may quite possibly have some (pre)historical basis." [dcccxxx]

The *Rig Veda* refers to a *Naga* leader named *Ahi* who fought against Indra (the God of the Aryans who invaded the south). According to its accounts, this ruler belonged to a lineage of Naga ruler-priests from the area of Sumer. The ancient Sumerian King List bequeathed two principal lineages of ruler-priests and spiritual teachings, the earliest being that of the Nagas, whose influence was widespread and was the source of the Tantric tradition that spread westward from the Kashmir valley. Gurus and Yogis of the Nagas were almost universally symbolized as "serpents" that sought to impart greater knowledge and intelligence to the earliest inhabitants of the region. The contest with the Nagas for preeminence in the area of early Sumer and dominance in the Tigris-Euphrates Valley defined the issues confronting Nimrod as he sought to develop a state modeled upon his understanding of the governmental system of Heaven, a divine monarchy, representing the Kingdom of God on earth.

When the *Kushites* entered Western Asia, they were noticed but undisturbed and, more importantly, unchallenged by the Nagas. However, by the time of the territorial expansions of *Nimrod*, the Nagas had apparently moved forcefully to preserve a measure of their hegemony and influence and counter his further expansions eastward. Nascent *Kusha-Dwipa* met no such challenge or resistance in Western Asia during the time of *Ausar* (Osiris, Zeus, Kush) and the Kushite migrations. Early Kushites settlements and colonies of Sumer united the southern part of Mesopotamia with southern Arabia (Yemen), where they had founded many kingdoms, including Saba (present-day Yemen). The overland trade route of Kusha-Dwipa ran through the regions of early Sumer, Oman, and Yemen, from where, after crossing the Red Sea, it extended into Northeast Africa, where the overland route linked with the ancient north-south trade route, leading to the heart of early ancient Kush in Sudan.[dcccxxxi]

This was the route taken by the remaining merchants, traders, and their entourages, who, together with a detachment of the Kushite army, were now tasked with inaugurating the trade route from Sumer across Arabia and the Red Sed to the heart of Kush. But this was not the route taken by *Ausar* (Osiris, Zeus, Kush) and the remainder of the Kushites who stayed for a time in Sumer before departing northward through the Tigris-Euphrates Valley to the coastal land that would become known as '*Kanaan*' (or "Canaan"). Ausar and the Kushites proceeded to Kanaan and the *Great Northern Sea*. He reunited with his nephew *Agenor*, who planned to give homage to his late father *Poseidon* at an early ancient island city that would become known as *Sidon*.

On to Kánaán: Eastern Mediterranean

Mesopotamia is geographically situated between the Tigris and Euphrates Rivers, which each flow much slower in Southern Mesopotamia, the region of Sumer, where the topography is mostly flat with wider basins than in the north.[dcccxxxii] Northern Mesopotamia is mountainous, in contrast, where the topography restricts areas of cultivatable land for planting; the mountains compensate for this by being rich in timber and mineral resources. Attributes noticed by *Ausar* (Osiris, Kush) and the remainder of *Kushites* on their expedition through Northern Mesopotamia to the coast of the *Great Northern Sea* in the land that would become known as *Kanaan*. Mesopotamia was at the heart of an area anciently known as the "*Fertile Crescent*", a region encompassing a wide swath of land stretching northward from the mouths of the Tigris and Euphrates Rivers in Southern Mesopotamia through the fertile plains and plateaus of Northern Mesopotamia, to the forested coasts in the north. It was the forest belt of the north which became known as the "*Levant*", where the Fertile Crescent turns west along the coast of *Kánaán*, at the eastern extent of the Mediterranean Sea.[dcccxxxiii]

It was the Levant that defined what came to be known as *Kánaán*. *This land* encompassed the geographical area extending from present-day Syria in the north, through present-day Lebanon, Gaza, and Israel, to the southern extent of the present-day Palestinian Territories in the south. The width of *Kanaan* spanned eastward from the Jordan Valley, fully encompassing present-day Jordan and all that was anciently between the Jordan River and the eastern coast of the Mediterranean Sea.[dcccxxxiv] The earliest known inhabitants of *Kanaan* were those whom archaeologists euphemistically refer to as "Natufians", an Epipaleolithic culture of *East Africans* who migrated into the region between 15,000 and 9,000 years ago.[dcccxxxv] The term "*Natufian*" is taken from the archeological site in the Southern Levant, where their remains were first discovered and had no historical significance. Evidence supports that they migrated along the Nile Valley into the Delta, from where they entered the Levant.[dcccxxxvi]

They are said to have been small-statured Negroids who spread agriculture from the *Lower Nile Valley*.[dcccxxxvii] These were migrations of *Anu* from beyond the confines of the then swamp-like Nile Delta to the open fertile lands of the Southern Levant. Though archaeologists call them "*Natufians*", it was the *Anu* who was, by 13,000 BC, collecting the grasses, which later became the domesticated crops of the Levant.[dcccxxxviii] It was the Anu who entered the *Levant* with implements of the Maurusian tool industry and established the ethos of grass collection in the land.[dcccxxxix] The Anu (or "Natufian") culture in the Levant is said to have been unusual in that it was sedentary before the introduction of agriculture while still populating an area that extended from its stronghold around Lake Moeris in the Lower Nile Valley. All authorities generally concede on the matter that the earliest evidence of agriculture was found among the Black Africans of Jericho.

During the Holocene, the region from the Nile Delta to the Jordan River was wet, and this was the era in which the Anu first cultivated modern wheat. Modern wheat was a fertile mutation of wild wheat, it made much better food, but its seeds are bound more firmly to the stalk and cannot ride the wind. Without farmers to collect and sow this wheat, it dies; modern wheat created farming by wedding its own survival to that of the farmer. The Anu was the first to cultivate this new mutation (around 8,000 B.C.), the wheat which the world still prizes. The Anu were the ancestors of the builders of the first Neolithic settlements in the Levant, where there is evidence of deliberate cultivation of cereals. However, they generally made use of wild cereals. They called themselves "Kena Anu" and were consequently known as "*Kánaánites.*"

The *Kena Anu* established an ancient fishing village and seaside port at the natural harbor that would later become known as the "Port City of Byblos" on the *Mediterranean* coast. Byblos was actually the *Port City of Gebal* (called Byblos by the Greeks) in northern Kanaan. Ancient Byblos is one of the most archaeologically rich places on the earth because it has been around for such a long period of time; it is believed to have been first occupied between 8,800 BC and 7,000 BC. According to fragments attributed to the pre-Homeric Phoenician priest *Sanchuniathon*, it was built by *Khronos* as the first city in *Kánaán*; Neolithic remains of the city can still be seen at the site.[dcccxl]

Port City of Gubal: Old Byblos

The *Kánaánites* were a people who assimilated many of the other cultures of earliest antiquity. According to *Philo of Byblos* (quoting Sanchuniathon (quoted in Eusebius)), *Byblos* had the reputation of being among the oldest cities in the world, founded by Khronos (known as *Khem* to the Kushites, *Chronos* to the Greeks, and *Ham* to the later Semites). Byblos was considered a city of great antiquity, even by Kánaánite standards.[dcccxli] Before the intervention of Khronos, it was said to have been a small fishing village and a cluster of settlements on the coast; tools of this period have been found at the site. Several monocellular huts with crushed limestone floors can still be seen at the site. It is said that one of the earliest attempts at city planning was conceived in *Byblos;* a massive wall surrounded the city, and a narrow winding street led from the center, with secondary lanes that branched off, taking irregular paths among the houses. Legends say that settlers from Byblos formed Tyre, led by a man of *Royal Atlatian* lineage known as *Agenor*.[dcccxlii]

Agenor was the son of *Poseidon* and *Eurynome*, daughter of *Ōkeanós*, king of the old northern *Atlatian* colonies spanning the southern Euxine Se*a* (the Proto-Black Sea). *Eurynome* bore twin sons to *Poseidon, Agenor,* and *Belus,* who, after the fall of *Atlatia,* each migrated eastward into the lands that would become *Lower Khemet*). According to legend, after a time, Agenor departed Khemet for the land that would become *Kanaan*, where he became a king and founder of a great line (as evidenced by the Armana letters found in *Khemet*). During the final cataclysms (and fall of Atlatia) in the *Atla*s, a series of powerful tidal waves swept across the *Mediterranean Sea*, from the coast of Morocco and Algeria to the coasts of southern Europe, destroying the ancient cities along the coasts of the Western Mediterranean.

Tsunamic destruction spanned the breadth and length of the Mediterranean, with the least impacted area being the eastern Mediterranean, the coast of Kánaán. The Atlatian Diaspora in the Mediterranean spread to the colonies least affected by the destruction. Some opted for the Isle of Crete, others spread to colonies protected by the Ægean, such as Thrace. Still, others chose Hissarlik (*Troy*) high over the western promontory of Asia Minor, while many others opted for the old Kena Anu Port City of Gubal (Gebal) in ancient Kanaan. The old Kena Anu city had been called "*Guba*l" and later "*Gebal*" for thousands of years before the arrival and intervention of *Khronos* (*Khem, Kham, Ham*); that early *Gebal* became ancient *Byblos* was made clear in the *Septuagint,* which routinely translates and refers to *Gebal* as *Byblos*. The old *City of Gubal* (Gebal) came to be known as "*Byblos*" by the later Greeks, which is where the word "Bible" came from, which literally means "Papyrus Book." Migrants and refugees from Atlatia numbered increasingly among the inhabitants of Byblos during the final years of upheaval and calamity in the Atlas; this was a period of prosperity at Byblos, perhaps this that had attracted Ageno*r*.

Island City of Tyre

Agenor's arrival and sojourn in *Byblos* were serendipitous in that expansion of the ancient city had brought it to the brink of early city-state status. With the increasing influx from the Atlatian Diaspora, circumstances for establishing a nearby sister city presented a unique opportunity for an ambitious leader of royal *Atlatian* lineage like *Agenor*. Pliny and Justin hint at the *Atlatian* connection when they note that *Tyre* "was founded by (those whom Pliny and Justin each referred to as) "Phoenicians" who, being disturbed by an earthquake and leaving their native land, settled first on the Assyrian Lake, and subsequently on the shore near the sea, (and) founded there a (second) city which they call *Sidon*. The location of the first city, "*Tyre*," was on an island with a superb natural harbor and great wealth and has been seen as a mirror of *Atlatia.*"

Beyond its founding by *Agenor,* nothing is known of the circumstances, and there is much uncertainty even as to the date of the founding of ancient Tyre.[dcccxliii] The City of Tyre had a rather interesting and beneficial geographical layout. The original city was founded on a small rocky island about half a mile off the central coast of Kánaán. Sometime after the founding of the Island City, a Mainland City of Tyre (called "Old Tyre" by the Greeks) was founded.[dcccxliv] It was shortly after the founding of the city that Ausar (Osiris, Zeus, Kush) dispatched Apollo to Byblos to arrange their reunion with Agenor. Upon learning of his arrival at Byblos, Agenor took leave of Tyre and met his cousin in the city built by their grandfather, Khronos (Khem, Kham, Ham). In the days and weeks required for Ausar and the remainder of the Kushites to make their way southward, Apollo and Agenor reacquainted at the old city of Byblos. Apollo enthralled Agenor and select members of his court with tales of the Kushite expedition across the Western Asian highlands and into the Indian Sub-Continent.

Apollo described the magnificence and prospects of the Āmū Daryā and Saraswati River Valleys, and Ausar's founding of Kususthali (the 'Port City of Kush') on the northwestern coast of the sub-continent, availing the Kushites of prosperous maritime trade across the Southern Sea. Agenor, in turn, invited Apollo to tour the grand new city he himself had founded, the island City of Tyre, prosperous in its own right. Early settlements were made on the island. Due to its advantageous geographical position and good ports, Tyre became among the wealthiest trading cities on the coast of Kánaán, soon rivaling its parent Byblos. Tyre was the most southern of the commercial and trading cities on the coast of Kánaán, soon producing and transiting commodities to trading partners in the *Aegean,* at first in cooperation and later in rivalry with Byblos. As the island city became a major commercial seaport in its own standing, it soon cultivated the closest relationship with *Khemet* of all the port cities of Kanaan. Agenor boasted of the island city's great wealth and his efforts to develop other colonies along the central coast, the first of which, he informed, was already established on a small island just north of Tyre.

Island City of Sidon

Remnants of the since sunken small island city have been discovered offshore between the Island of Tyre, the Mainland City, and the Island of Sidon. The small island colony and the city were the second but most significant of the early colonies established by Tyre under Agenor. Neighboring Sidon and its companion island to the north of Tyre were originally colonies founded by settlers from Tyre, led by Agenor, who then became king of the central coast of Kánaán. The smaller island between Tyre and Sidon was actually the first colony established by Tyre under Agenor. Though lacking the attributes of Tyre and Sidon, this bygone island colony encouraged Agenor's later building of the far larger and more complex colony at Sidon.

Agenor modestly relished and took pride in pointing out the grandeur of the bygone Island colony and early city to *Apollo*; all, he noted, afforded from the growing prosperity the colony shared with its parent, burgeoning *Tyre*. In a less modest moment, he (*Agenor*) boasted that Tyre and its colonies would one day overtake ancient *Byblos* as the preeminent maritime trading power on the coast of *Kánaán*. After two weeks as an honored guest of Agenor, *Apollo* returned to *Byblos*, both inspired and concerned for the challenges *Tyre* posed to the ancient trading prowess and influence of the old city. Upon his return to Byblos, *Apollo* sought an audience and conferred with the royal court on means at their disposal to strengthen trade with *Khemet*.

Byblos was the earliest ancient seaport on the coast of *Kanaan*, the main archaeological site of which is comprised of an extensive complex to the immediate south of its ancient harbor, a site containing Neolithic and prehistoric-era houses. Within *Old Byblos* proper, along the fringe of the harbor, are a number of ancient circular pits that have been cut into the rock at the base of the cliffs and lined with lime mortar, no doubt to provide guidance to ships seeking safe harbor and anchorage after sunset. Despite its ancient significance, the archaeological site of *Byblos* is under threat. Its ancient walls have long been adversely impacted by a light railway used to move soil in the early 20th century, and while an ancient "sea door" at the base of one of the cliffs is still evident, a collapse from the slope above threatens to engulf it. *Byblos* was in its rise to early prominence in the era during which Apollo returned to the city and informed the royal court of the imminent arrival of *Ausar* (Osiris, Kush) and beseeched that they seek to gain favor with him and the *Maa Federation*. It was also *Apollo* who advised that they improve access and safety of the harbor for ships at anchorage.

The seaport at *Byblos* was exposed to strong waves and prevailing winds from the southwest, often-threatening ships at anchor in the open harbor; Apollo advised that a well-placed seawall would better shield the harbor from the swells and waves. A late Holocene rise in sea level along the coast of ancient *Kanaan* during the era can be seen in the form of stratified marine platforms commensurate with changes in the ancient sea levels of the era.[dcccxlv] While the southwest winds, which were strongest in winter, facilitated maritime trade and excursions northward along the coast of *Kánaán*, the narrow-embayed beach at *Byblos* provided little protection from storm waves raised by those winds. It was again *Apollo* who advised on the configuration and construction of the seawall they ultimately designed and built in the harbor at *Byblos*.[dcccxlvi] Construction of the seawall modified the local currents. It changed the focus of the energy of the waves, protecting and enhancing the appeal of the harbor and anchorage at Byblos. *Apollo* later became celebrated and worshipped at *Old Byblos;* they built an ancient temple (the 'Temple of Apollo') at the city in his honor.

Early Ancient Ugarit: The Kena-Anu

When *Ausar* and the *Kushites* reached *Kanaan*, they first replenished and stayed in northern Kanaan for a time in the early ancient town of Ugarit. The early ancient village of *Ugarit* was a small, fortified town (established before 8,000 BC) on the northern frontier of what had been the homeland of the *Kena'Anu*. That these descendent *Anu* were prominent in the founding of *Ugarit* is evidenced by the reverence held for the *Ugaritic Goddess of the Duat* in the city. Nonetheless, *Kena'Anu* preeminence at *Ugarit* would later be supplanted by the *Nagas*. Northward maritime expeditions from *Nagu-Punt* brought *Nagas* down the *Nile* to the eastern *Mediterranean* and *Kanaan,* while others sailed north on the *Red Sea* to the Sinai Peninsula to reach *Kanaan*.[dcccxlvii]

There is also ample evidence of (*Shaivite*) *Nagas,* from *Naga Mandla,* entering northern *Kanaan* and *Ugarit* via the *Mesopotamia Valley*. Ugarit was perhaps the only region where the *Nagas* of *Nagu-Punt* and *Naga Mandla* would come together to form (what would become) the northern Kanaanite Kingdom of Ugarit. During this period, the ethos and iconology of the *Nagas* became prevalent throughout and eventually beyond the confines of northern *Kánaán*. Regarding the exact date when the serpent cult and totem became prevalent beyond Ugarit, no direct testimony is available. However, a later-era adaptation of the iconography of the Nagas (which came to be known as the "*Cult of Bronze Serpents*") by the Semitic invaders of Ugarit is firmly attested to in the archaeological record.[dcccxlviii]

The biblical myths surrounding ancient *Ugarit* infer the religion of its inhabitants was a crude and debased form of ritual polytheism associated with sensuous fertility-cult worship.[dcccxlix] Myths that allude to corruptions of the spiritual practices of *Tantra* brought to Ugarit by the (Shaivite) *Nagas* of *Naga Mandla*. Latter-day usurpers severely misinterpreted the esoteric part of this belief system and its rituals in their efforts to emulate the civilization they found at Ugarit. For the Nagas, *Tantra* was used to teach and initiate people into a radically different way of looking at and acting in the world. At the heart of *Tantra* is the expansion of the mind and the liberation of energy from the clutches of matter to spirit. The union of Male and Female (Female primordial energy and Male primordial consciousness) is its ultimate symbol, along with the sacred weaving of polarities that melt into one unified whole. In *Tantra*, the Kundalini, a force of enlightenment said to lie dormant, coiled at the base of the Spine, is awakened.

Kundalini is a creative power and, thus, very sexual in nature, rendering it amenable to meditative, yogic, and sexual stimulation. It is this spiritual aspect of *Tantra* (the quest for the liberation of *Kundlini*) that so escaped the understanding of the latter-day usurpers at *Ugarit*. The latter part of the Early Bronze Age (3,000–2,000 B.C.) is when the first wave of invaders, the *Amorites*, a nomadic *Semitic*-speaking people from the *Southern Anatolian Peninsula*, gradually spread into *Kanaan*. They migrated (over several centuries) into northern *Kánaán*, inhabiting the hills around the cities, from where they then eventually rose up against their host and launched hostile raids and attacks on *Ugarit*.[dcccl] First came the *Amorites*, an illiterate people from *Southern Anatolia*, and then came their more sedentary brethren, who previously resided in *Babylon* until their expulsion after the fall of *Hammurabi*.

Migrants from Babylon joined the Amorites and became the dominant population in northern *Kánaán*; and once they found their numbers sufficient, they invaded *Ugarit* overthrowing the Kanaanites.[dcccli][dccclii] Amorites ruled Ugarit from about 2,100 BC until 1,720 BC when the *Hyksos*, also a Semitic people, invaded northern *Kanaan* and overthrew the Amorites. The Hyksos eventually pushed through Kánaán and invaded and ruled parts of Lower Khemet until the *Pharaoh Ahmose* drove them back into Kánaán in 1,538 BC.[dcccliii] Historical knowledge of the Kánaánites before 1928 was limited to three sources; archaeological excavations at sites within the ancient cities of *Kánaán*, literature of contemporaries who lived outside Kánaán, and the Hebrew Bible and Old Testament.[dcccliv][dccclv]

Archaeologists, linguists, and biblical historians have pored over the Ugaritic texts for nearly a century, trying to understand the world they chronicle; the documents uncovered contain literary texts that open a new door to the religious concepts and practices of the time. They provide not only direct insight into the culture and religious practices of the era but also have an important bearing on the Old Testament. The Ugaritic Texts reveal that the patriarchal stories in the Old Testament were not transmitted orally but were actually of ancient *Kanaanite* origin, which has led to a new appraisal of the Old Testament.[dccclvi] Ancient *Ugarit* of the era in which the 'Ugaritic Texts' were created was a city ruled and largely inhabited by the *Hyksos* and remnants of their *Amorite* predecessors.[dccclvii]

Historical conflation (and seemingly deliberate obfuscation) of the Amorites as a "Hamitic" people has only served to add to the confusion regarding these ancient 'Semitic' people as *"Kanaanite"*. The *'Amorites*' were clearly not descendants of *Ham* (Cham, Kham, Khem, Khronos), irrespective of much written to the contrary.[dccclviii] The Amorites were a Semitic people from the Anatolian peninsula, anciently described as troublesome nomads who are said to have been one of the causes of the downfall of the 3rd Dynasty at Ur in Sumer. Yet in the Bible, they are named instead of the Kanaanites as the inhabitants of Southern Kanaan (Palestine), whom the Israelites were ordained by their god *Yahweh* to exterminate.[dccclix] They condemned these so-called *Kanaanites* as immersed in idolatry, moral depravity, and sexual immorality, a curse that, after due investigation, appears to say more about their duplicity and internal struggles with (the Amorite) aspects of their own ancestry than it does about the authentic ethos of the Kánaánites.

Kushites at Kánaán

The Kanaanite*s* were an amalgamation of African and Afro-Asian peoples, the earliest of whom, the *Kena-Anu*, were followed by immigrants from the Atlatian diaspora during and after the fall of Atlatia. Then came the Nagas, *Sethians* from *Nagu-Punt,* and *Shaivites* from *Naga Mandla,* followed by the *Kushites*, who entered Kánaán near the end of their great migrations. Each group brought with them deep, rich, societal, and spiritual traditions dating back thousands of years before the earliest Semite tribes departed Anatolia. Cultures that built great civilizations, such as the one the Semites discovered and coveted at *Ugarit* in Northern Kanaan.[dccclx] When the *Kushites* reached *Ugarit* on the coast of northern *Kanaan,* it was but a small-fortified port city on the *Kena Anu* frontier. These founders were still in residence, and prominent within the city. As was done in the Lower Nile Valley, *Kushite-Oru* priests were sent as emissaries and quickly established affinities and close relations between the *Kena-Anu* and Kushites.

Ausar and the *Kushites* settled, for a time, in the hills surrounding and in proximity to the ancient port city, availing themselves of the resources of the city to replenish their stores in preparation for the journey ahead, which for many would be the final leg home. During the sojourns of the *Kushites,* their spiritual beliefs were spread by priests, who brought their religious practices from the heart of Kush to Arabia, Sumer, Elam, India, Bactria, Mesopotamia, and *Kanaan*. For example, the *23rd Psalm,* "The Lord is my Shepherd, I shall not Want," was taken from the Cult of *Osiris* (Ausar, Kush)*,* known as *Mizraim* by the later *Hebrews. Kushite* priests greeted the rising sun with prayers, watched as it expanded across the horizon, and acted as intercessors and prophets to the laity. It was this Kushite conception of "priesthood" that was the antecedent and paradigm for the Hebrew (and Christian) conception of the priesthood; they even adopted the principal God of the *Kushites, "Amun'*, by ending their prayers in his name.[dccclxi]

After a period of rest, recuperation, and replenishment in the hills around Ugarit, *Ausar* and the *Kushites* broke their encampments and began their journey southward, through northern Kanaan, en route to *Byblos* in central Kanaan. Kanaan was a rich land of varied terrain characterized by mountains, hills, and coastal plains. Its topography was notoriously unfavorable to formal political unity; its headlands project to the sea cutting the coastal lands into a number of small plains named after their main cities, like the Plain of Tyre and the Plain Sidon, fostering a sense of regional autonomy. Kushite diffusion across the Levant (documented by research in fields such as genetics, linguistics, archaeology, and anthropology) revived a sense of affinity in Kanaan.

Kanaan was not considered a united land in the traditional sense. Distance and mountains separated its major population areas, with the most prominent of its early cities eventually devolving into a collection of independent city-states. Though the *Kena-Anu* had a cultural tradition of agricultural cultivation centered on barley, wheat, olives, grapes, dates, figs, and pomegranates (as early as 9,000 BC), over time, their mythologies came to vary from city to city, inuring an increasing sense of divergence between the *Kanaanite* cities. The mindset of the *Kushites* migrating through *Kanaan* was driven by *Amun* and the precept of raising order from chaos through coalescence, which gave impetus to their reverence for *Ma'at*. Throughout their endeavors, the Kushites strove to maintain Ma'at, the principle of balance, harmony, justice, and order. The Kushites migrating through Kanaan were highly organized people, skilled in agriculture, irrigation, engineering, mining, and metalworking. From among their ranks, many opted to settle and were absorbed into communities in the hills and plains of Kanaan as they continued southward.

The countryside of the Levant was rich and fertile. However, because most river valleys in Kanaan were unsuited for large-scale irrigation, early farmers were entirely dependent on rain, restricting their yield and harvests. *Kushite* settlers were welcomed because they brought new skillsets and approaches to this age-old problem. *Kanaan* was surrounded by *Kushite* countries with successful farming methods. The *Sumerians* in Southern Mesopotamia and *Khemetans* in the Nile Valley had done so largely by mastering Kushite irrigation techniques. Kushite settlers built stone terrace walls to retain water on the steep slopes of the highlands and tapped springs and underground waters welling up in the valleys and hills. They used systems of conduits and check-dams to redirect rainwater into fields and thus were able to irrigate crops over broader areas. Though they would eventually be assimilated into the cultures among whom they settled, their addition to the "Kanaanite stock" of the era revived a sense of consecutiveness between the emergent city-states.

Each prominent city, Ugarit, Byblos, and Tyre had its own king. However, as legend holds, the histories and monarchies of Tyre and Sidon were interwoven from the earliest of times. When *Ausar* reached *Byblos*, after exchanging messengers with *Apollo* and *Agenor* advising of his approach, he and the *Kushites* were met with great fanfare by the king and the royal house of that ancient city. An extended welcoming ceremony was followed by a grand feast that evening with *Ausar,* the personal guest of the royal court, as they sought to gain favor with the ruler of *Kush*. Khemet was the northern province of Kush during the era, and upon the advice of Apollo, the royal house of *Byblos* sought to increase trade and stand with the nascent empire. The feast and spirited dialogue lasted well into the evening. Nonetheless, *Ausar* still rose before dawn (with the priest of *Amun*) the following morning to greet the rising sun with prayers in homage to his father, *Khem (Kham, Ham, Khronos)*, who built *Old Byblos* during the old Atlatian megalithic age.

For his part, *Agenor* departed *Byblos* that evening for *Tyre* to prepare his own court and city for Ausar's impending arrival, while *Ausar* and *Apollo* cordially remained as guests of the royal court of *Byblos* for a brief time before they and the *Kushites* continued onward to *Tyre*. Upon arrival, the Kushites made encampment on the *Plain of Tyre*, located at the foot of the southwestern ridges of the Lebanese mountains, near the gorge of the ancient Leontes River.[dccclxii] The rich, well-watered plain was the island city's major source of food, water, wood, and other living essentials.[dccclxiii] As the Kushites raised their encampments, *Ausar, Apollo,* and a small delegation arrived at the adjacent island city of *Tyre* and were again met with festivities, followed by a grand feast, as *Agenor* sought to ensure *Tyre* did not lose trade to *Byblos*.

The following morning *Agenor* invited and provided *Ausar* with a personal tour of his city, emphasizing the island's great prospects and his efforts to develop it to its fullest potential. The island city was the most southern of the ancient trading cities on the coast of *Kánaán*. It was graced with favorable geographical positioning, about a half mile off the coast of *Kánaán*, and two excellent ports, with harbors hewn out of the natural rock, protected by a wide breakwater.[dccclxiv] The basin of *Tyre's* northern port was a natural semi-protected bay enhanced by the ancient harbor infrastructure (moles and sea walls) of the era.[dccclxv] An urban quarter of the early ancient city arose in a basin protected from the sea to the south; remnants of a number of prehistoric structures, such as walls, foundations, and, most importantly, large quarries of the era, suggest the quarter was home and workplace to the city's masons, artisans and laborers and their families.

At the time of *Ausar's* visit and tour, a modest stone mole (now submerged) was being constructed across the mouth of the basin to protect the quarries and urban quarter from the encroaching tides of the rising sea, a point well noted by *Ausar*.[dccclxvi] *Agenor* boasted of the island city's growing fleet of ships and *Tyre's* mounting wealth and regional influence and told *Ausar* of his plan to establish a chain of such colonies along the central coast of *Kanaan*, the first of which, he informed, was on a nearby small island, he wished to tour with *Ausar,* granted his permission, the following day. In their repose that evening, after another festive meal, *Ausar* turned the discussion to the encroachment of the rising seas, which was clearly to be threatening the coast, requiring the moles and seawalls witnessed in the harbors of *Byblos* and *Tyre*.[dccclxvii]

Agenor concurred that the sea had indeed risen, though the turmoil witnessed in the wake of the cataclysms at Atlatia, those that swept across the western end of the great sea, had not yet reached the coasts of *Kánaán.* However, he, too, feared its arrival. He (Agenor) had been told by captains of several ships of the merchant fleet that most of the cities of the old (Atlatian) colonies had been relocated to higher ground, including those on isles in the midst of the great lower northern sea (the 'Mediterranean Sea'), such as *Crete* and those along the coast of the frigid lands of the north. *Apollo* added that mariners at *Old Byblos* said that the colonies of the (Atlatian) diaspora fare well in the northern lands, but they progress little, for they no longer have the light of *Poseidon*. Not so much in the hearts of the populace but in the minds of those who rule who no longer feel bound by its ethical ethos, not because they no longer *believe*, but because they are no longer *guided* by the *House of Khem* (Kham, Ham, Khronos), the "Lord of Justice."

Ausar, *Agenor* noted, was the *last* of the royal lineage of *Poseidon* and the *last* of the strident adherents to his laws. The stories say, 'a reverent posture caused him (Ausar) to depart *Atlatia* before the upheavals and its final fall'; these stories are told all over the colonies and amongst many in the Diaspora, 'wherever they live, even here in *Kánaán'*. Agenor continued, 'we are told that the great northern sea remains more unsettled in the east, that much of the turbulence since the fall (of *Atlaţia*) has been captured in the (*Aegean Sea*) enclave above the *Crete*, where it reverberates between the northern mainland and isles to the east; gradually releasing its higher seas to the west.' *Ausar* (Osiris, Kush) advised that priests of the *Kena Anu* had informed priests of the *Kushite Oru* that the rise in the northern sea had submerged the *Lower Delta*. They are told that waves wash against the northern edge of the *Giza* plateau, yet the priest advised, "flooding from the great sea reaches little further."

Many of those (Anu) who settled in the delta were said to have once again settled around the shores of *Paleo-Lake Moeris* (in the *Fayoum*), while others remained around the shores of the delta. The Nile was then far broader during seasonal floods, inundating lands as far south as *Bayuda* when the flood level is said to be as much as five meters above the alluvial plain surrounding *Bayuda*, which then became partly inundated.[dccclxviii] Priest of the *Kena Anu* extolled *Thoth* (Hermes), and *Heracles* (Hercules), who they said had well prepared and protected the lands of *Khemet* and *Kush*. Legend holds that *Thoth* preserved his canon of writings inside two great pillars just before the great flood fully subsumed the delta. It was then *Heracles* made ancient *Waset* (Thebes) in *Upper Khemet* the capital from where he and *Thoth* exercised their authority as patron protectors of the land under the auspice of *Queen Isis,* who awaits the return of *Ausar*.[dccclxix] The ancient city of *Waset* developed at a very early date from a number of small villages, particularly one around present-day Luxor, then called Epet; legend holds the city was built by Ausar and Isis when Ausar became Pharaoh of Khemet (Egypt)." [dccclxx]

The priests of *Amun* claim that as the first city in the world, *Waset* (Thebes) became a model for all others. This was the original ancient *Thebes* (Waset) of which the later Greek legends speak when they recount the early feats of Heracles (Hercules), the capital city of early ancient Kush. Heracles was an extremely passionate and emotional individual, capable of performing great deeds. Extraordinary strength, courage, ingenuity, military prowess, and astuteness in battle were among the characteristics commonly attributed to him. He (Heracles) protected and defended the realm against incursions by the Sethian (Nagas) to the south of the greater Kush, while *Thoth (*Hermes) attended to its sustenance, prosperity, and spiritual enlightenment.

South of Waset, in Kush, where two key tributaries of the Nile converge (at present-day Khartoum), forming the main body of the mighty Nile River, the floods carry layers of mud and silt down from the eastern highlands blanketing the floodplains along the riverbed, particularly the huge alluvial plain surrounding *Bayuda,* where the Nile winds through the heart of Kush. This flood-born layering of rich soil and silt over the plains has created broad, fertile corridors along the *Upper Nile*, particularly *Bayuda*, making *Kush* and *Upper Khemet* among the most productive farming regions of the land. In the north *Thoth (*Hermes) is held in high esteem as a renowned priest of the *Oru* (Kushite-Anu) by the petty kingdoms around the shores of *Lake Moeris*, holding fast the unity hard won by *Ausar* with the founding of *Kush*.

As the evening wore on, *Ausar* informed *Agenor* of his decision to forego the trip to the *Bygone Island* and instead move on to the city and isle he (Agenor) planned to dedicate to *Poseidon.* Having given the matter due consideration, he (Ausar) said to wish to consign three ships from Tyre's fleet to both take the measure of the turmoil in the eastern (Aegean) enclave of the Northern Sea, to see what might portend for Khemet, and to reconnect with the old northern colonies. Ausar concurred that the northern colonies needed to be informed of the rise of the *Maa Confederation* from the ashes of *Atlatia*, as well as the rise of *Kush,* particularly that of *Khemet* (the 'Land of Khem' ('*Ham*')). Ausar then advised that he would spend the rest of the evening amongst the *Kushites* in their encampment, where he would inform his priests, generals, and clan leaders of his decision.

Plying the Northern Seas

Before departing for the Plain of Tyre, *Ausar* advised *Agenor* that, although many Kushites might elect to settle in *Kánaán*, most would return to *Kush* and would appreciate any assistance he might avail. *Agenor,* in turn, advised that he would have the vessels requested by Ausar prepared for their departure in the morning and that he would personally ensure the *Kushites* who elect to return are sufficiently provisioned. That next morning *Ausar* and *Apollo,* accompanied by a security detachment and select members of their entourage, boarded the ships made available for the voyage, with Ausar, Apollo, and Agenor aboard the flagship. They then set course for the isle *Ausar* would consecrate in reverence to *Poseidon,* and *Agenor* would dedicate as the *Isle of Sidon.* Sidon's coastal geography made it an ideal location for setting up three natural anchorage havens; *Agenor* took pride and relished pointing out the grandeur of the mainland and its natural ports. A sandstone ridge south of the site of the early city is breached by the sea, forming a large semi-circular embayment, with the early city situated on a promontory overlooking the ridge and embayment.

During its earliest prehistory, Sidon's geomorphology was pretty much defined by the now submerged ridge, which then sheltered the city's two harbors, the Northern Harbor and the so-called "Khemetans (or Egyptian) Harbor." A third insular harbor of the offshore *Island of Zire* formed an outer harbor facility, which operated in tandem with the continental port (a unique feature of the Sidonian harbor complex).[dccclxxi][dccclxxii] The lee side of the offshore island of *Zire* was used as a deep-water anchorage, where large vessels were able to load and unload, and their cargos ferried to and from shore by boats. The promontory of Sidon separated the Northern and Khemetan Harbors; it is generally accepted that both harbors were significantly larger during antiquity. The early city of *Sidon* is of immense antiquity, but few remains of the ancient city have survived the ravages of time; according to legend, the city was inhabited as early as 7,000 BC. and perhaps even earlier.[dccclxxiii]

The inherent relationship between the *Isle of Sidon* and the mainland *City of Sidon* was that the mainland city was built on a peninsula across from the island, a peninsula that sheltered and protected ships at anchor from storms at sea. The northern harbor, anchored by the mainland port city, was the center of activity in Sidon during early antiquity. The early port city and the island had sizeable fishing village communities, with fishing fleets moored in both the outer and mainland harbors, exploiting the abundance of fish along the coast of the mainland and around the shores of the island. The flagship with *Ausar, Agenor, and Apollo* aboard, and their accompanying vessels, anchored in Northern Harbor, where they, and their entourages, disembarked aboard several boats, headed for the mainland to planned festivities and formalities hosted by Agenor's royal court at *Sidon,* awaited their arrival their arrival in the heart of the city.

The old mainland city resembled a maze of narrow alleyways, winding streets, and arched pathways connecting the different neighborhoods, communities, and villages.The festivities lasted well into the evening, with *Ausar, Agenor,* and *Apollo* each retiring early to be rested for the ceremonial dedication to take place after prayers the next morning. Before dawn, Ausar, Agenor, Apollo, and select royal court members joined the *Priests of Amun* atop the highest point on the promontory, which overlooked the city and embayment, as they greeted the rising sun with prayers. Watching as the glow from the rays of the sun slowly expanded across the horizon, *Ausar* stepped forwarded and asked in the name of *Amun* that consecration be conferred upon the city and island in reverence to the piety of *Poseidon.* Agenor, in turn, confessed his direct lineage and gave homage to *Poseidon,* professing eternal adherence to his laws and decreeing the city and island 'to be forever known as *Sidon'*.

The balance of the ship's crews re-boarded their vessels before dawn that morning, joining the skeleton crews already aboard, completing the ship's compliment as all hands then prepared for the voyage ahead. Those of the *Kushite* entourage and security detail not in attendance at the dedication ceremony followed shortly after the ships' crews, re-boarding their ships just after dawn. Later that morning, *Ausar* and *Apollo* took leave of *Agenor* at the dock of the mainland *Sidon*. They, along with the priests and the members of their entourage and security who attended the ceremony, boarded the boats that ferried them to their ships in the harbor. Anchors were raised not long after their re-boarding, and the ships, led by the flagship, were underway.

Voyage to the Isle of Crete

When they departed the harbor at *Sidon*, the captain wanted to sail straight due west to the *Isle of Crete* and from there to the old northern colonies in the enclaves of the *Ægean Sea*. The alternative was the coastal route, northward to the port of *Byblos*, and from there westward along the coast of the *Anatolian Peninsula*, with overnight port stops along the way. Although the course due west wouldn't be as smooth as the coastal route, without the overnight stops, the voyage would be less than half as long, even against unfavorable winds. The course was due west, but the prevailing winds, although not very strong, blew easterly, and the ancient mariners knew the first leg of the voyage would be a continuous tact into the winds, which could extend the length of the voyage. However, the planned course would permit the ships to sail under partial shelter of the *Isle of Crete*; the winds and waves were calmer to the lee of the island, allowing the ships to make better time.

Though the *Kushites* would later become renowned as ancient mariners, at this stage in antiquity, it was the ancient mariners of the *Atlatian Diaspora* (*Kanaanite* and *Kushite* alike) who possessed superior navigational and maritime acuity, particularly on the open waters of the *Mediterranean*. The voyage to *Crete* took all of nine days, with the armada putting into and dropping anchor in a natural harbor on the eastern shore of the island; the harbor and adjacent village served as a port to ancient *Knossos*, the oldest city on the island, located roughly five miles inland from the harbor. The royal house of *Crete* had not yet emerged, and though *Knossos* would later become its seat in early antiquity, it was merely the largest and most prosperous town on the isle. Knossos was built around a raised central court, a top of Kephala Hill, where the oldest structures are razed with their tops made level.[dccclxxiv] *Ausar's* armada planned to stay in port for three days as the ships replenished. As the crews prepared for the next leg of the voyage, the stay-over allowed the merchants aboard to journey to *Knossos* with samples of exotic herbs, spices, and incense from across *Kusha Dwipa*... to exchange and cultivate trading relationships.

They also brought news of the rise of the *Maa Confederation* from the ashes of *Atlatia* and the ascendance of *Kush, Khemet,* and *Ausar*. The sojourn at the *Isle of Crete* was somewhat of a homecoming for *Ausar* (Osiris, Kush, Zeus) and many of the other *Kushites* of *Atlatian* derivation; the island had been among the earliest colonized by *Atlatia* in the Mediterranean and, as such, became a gateway to the later northern colonies. *Crete* was settled during the reign of *Khronos* (Khem, Ham), who ruled during the so-called *Golden Age*, a time of prosperity, peace, and general ease, a time when the people had no need for laws or rules; everyone aspired for the good and betterment of both themselves, and the 'all', so there was no need.[dccclxxv] An ethos *Ausar* and the *Kushites* of his armada found still prevalent among both the *Atlatians* descendants of the original settlers of *Crete* and those of the *Atlatian Diaspora* who later migrated to the island during and after the fall of *Atlatia*.[dccclxxvi]

In that earlier era, the reign of *Khronos* came to be synonymous with the '*Megalithic Age*', as it was he who presided over the building of the megaliths and megalithic cites that once adorned the ancient coasts of the *Aegean* and *Mediterranean*. Crete was situated off the eastern coast of *Atlatia*, adjacent to the port *city of Cyrene*, and served as the *colonial seat* of Khem (Khronos), who resided on the island for months at a time during the building of the megalithic. The island also served as the entryway to the northern colonies. Legends say that though he and *Rhea* held court at *Knossos*, much of the time, *Khronos* resided in *Kronion Cave* while at the *Crete*. Of the six children they reared, only *Hera*, their youngest daughter, and *Ausar* (Zeus), the youngest son, were raised during the height of the megalithic era, and each spent large parts of their youth on the island. *Kronion Cave* is on the *Lassithi Plateau*, at an altitude of 2,800 feet, atop an ascending entry path, with steps hidden in trees leading to the entrance of the cave, making its entrance slightly indiscernible.

The entrance opens to a narrow corridor with moist-green walls, leading to a small hall in which there are broken stalactites and stalagmites, with a large stalagmite in the middle of the cave creating two passageways along its sides. The wrinkled walls of the cave give way to niches and columns hosted in beautiful effect within the walls. The first cavern leads to another at a lower level, where a large stalagmite resembles a comfortable armchair.[dccclxxvii] *Khronos* sought solitude with Rhea in *Kronion Cave*, where he is said to have spent uninterrupted days in recluse and prolonged meditation. *Lassithi* is far cooler than the coast of *Crete* in autumn, winter, and spring. When the snow melts in late spring, water covers the base of the plateau, with no canyon outlet, forcing the water to seep gradually into the ground. The sustained moisture gave rise to morning and evening fog on the plateau and unique strains of fungi thriving in the dampness of the caves and caverns.

During the age of *Khronos,* the narrow corridor forming the entrance of *Kronion Cave* was coated by a fragrant, moist-green fungus, the mycelium of which was said to be luminescent. *Rhea* prepared a sacred potion for Khronos from a rare mushroom that grew only in the depths of *Kronion Cave*; a drink that appeared as a source of enlightenment, inspiration, and an aphrodisiac and stimulant of one's passions, heightening both ecstasy and *prophesy*. Khronos used the potion to better visualize and prophesize the future and aid his path of spiritual evolution. In his meditations, it is said he entered a plane of the spiritual realm where enlightened souls assumed a luminous form with no gross body, unblemished and untainted; imbued by *Amun*, the first light, the unknowable infinite spirit, the "hidden one". It was during such a meditative journey that *Khronos* first envisioned the *Megaliths* which he later constructed across the *Mediterranean and Aegean Seas*.

Rhea did not partake in the potion, repulsed by its pungency and potent effect, opting instead for the milder effect of the vapor released by the mycelium when the cave fungi had been dried, ground into a powder, and used as incense. The fragrant vapor of mycelium in the cave provided the desired effect for *Rhea* and accentuated the effect on *Khronos*, with long periods of deep mediation, followed by long periods of heightened passion, sexual arousal, and intercourse, punctuated by meals and long periods of rest. Legends say that it was thus that *Ausar* (Osiris, Kush) was conceived at *Kronion Cave;* however, in contravention to the most profane of stories, it was the heightened intemperance of *Khronos (*at Kronion*)* that prompted *Rhea* to raise *Ausar* in the comfort of nearby *Dikteon Cave*, a far larger abode, on the slopes of the *Lassithi Mountains* in eastern Crete.[dccclxxviii]

Between its peaks, the Lassithi Mountains and the Lassithi Plateau formed the nucleus of the abode of Khronos and Rhea while on Crete. Dikteon Cave, hidden in the mountains, provided ideal conditions for young *Ausar*. Dikteon lies at an altitude slightly above 3,300 feet on the northern slopes of the *Lassithi Mountains*, which rise above and dominate the Lassithi Plateau. As with *Kronion*, a short path leads to the entrance of the *cave*, and a panoramic view of the whole plateau can be seen just before its entrance. Upon entering the cave, one first enters what is known as the 'ante-chamber', a small room where an immediate difference in temperature can be felt; with the Sun's rays unable to penetrate the cave's depths, the humidity inside often reaches above eighty percent. The interior of the cave has two levels, an upper level of little use other than aiding in ventilation, and a lower habitable level, comprised of five chambers, which archeologists agree were inhabited during the Neolithic.

The ante-chamber at the entrance of *Dikteon Cave* leads to a much larger cavern that is divided into four small chambers; the chamber known as the Great Hall begins on the upper level, but its main room opens on the lower level. Entrance to the Great Hall begins along a downhill staircase leading 100 meters into the mountain to the main room of the Great Hall; a room roughly 38m wide, 84m in maximum length, reaching a height of 5-14m. On the right side of the main room is an insignificant chamber. However, on the left side is the small chamber legend referred to as the '*Cradle of Zeus*', where *Ausar* (Osiris) is said to have been reared under the watchful care of *Amalthea* and *Melissa*, *Rhea's* most trusted handmaidens during his early childhood. At the right of the *Great Hall* is a larger hall, divided into two sections by huge columns; the first section hosts the most impressive sight in the entire complex, a small pristine lake occupying a stone basin at the lowest point in the cave; where *Ausar* once swam and bathed as a young man.

The lake is surrounded by massive stalactites and stalagmites, among which is the so-called "Mantle of Zeus", a stalactite whose shape resembles a cloak which hangs over the lake like a chandelier. At the back of the lake is the small chamber in which young Ausar once sought solitude for his early meditation efforts. Forbade from *Kronion Cave*, he nonetheless revered and sought to emulate the rituals of *Khronos* he witnessed in the caves of the High Atlas, where it was said *Khronos* could actually *see* while *asleep*. [dccclxxix] Elated at having solid ground beneath their feet, *Ausar* and *Apollo* set out and spent much of their first morning on Crete ascending *Mount Ida*, the highest mountain on the island. According to legend *Mount Ida* has the privilege of seeing the Sun before dawn, and *Ausar* and *Apollo* reached the top, overlooking the whole of *Crete* just before dawn, where they greeted the rising sun with prayers and watched as the glow from its rays slowly expanded across the horizon.

They then proceeded to the Lassithi Mountains, where they visited *Kronion Cave*, before continuing on to *Dikteon Cave*, overlooking the majestic *Lassithi Plateau* from the northern slopes of *Mt Lassithi*. The *Lassithi plateau* is one of the most beautiful areas on the isle, defined by a lush, fertile highland valley surrounded by mountains, resembling an enormous natural fortress. *Ausar* and *Apollo* reached the upper slope and descended into *Dikteon Cave* near dusk that evening, using torches to descend and finally rest at the lower level. Along the front bank of the small lake occupying the stone basin at the bottom of the cave, where they then ate as *Ausar* reminisced about his early childhood and adolescence on *Crete*, particularly at *Dikteon Cave*. It was here in the solitude of the small chamber at the back of the lake, during his earliest meditations, that a young *Ausar* experienced his first transcendental epiphany; an epiphany, he confessed to *Apollo*, at first born of resentment.

A resentment arising from a sense of estrangement felt and suffered from the reclusive intemperance of *Khronos* on *Crete*; a simmering resentment assuaged and transmuted into grace and aspiration by the watchful eye and nurturing temperament of *Rhea*. A matter of no trivial consequence, *Ausar* emphasized; indeed, a sacred power had been gifted me by *Rhea*. Imbued in the ability to harness and transmute energies stimulated by one's own emotions is the capability to transform one's moods, qualities, and powers into others; to gain control over one's being. For me, this was the first of the disciplines that informed the path to further enlightenment, the ultimate adventure, where all barriers and demons must be overcome before one's delusions are disclosed and fall away to reveal the Truth. In later adolescence, *Ausar* further confessed, I looked forward to and greatly guarded my solitude and the opportunity for further spiritual enlightenment here, at *Dikteon*. I sought to emulate none other than *Khronos* himself, aspiring to control not only myself but others and the surrounding elements.

Only the most advanced of masters attain the degree of power necessary to affect grosser material conditions, such as the elements. And he, *Ausar* continued, "the *Khronos* whom I had so resented at an earlier age, was such a Master, one who loomed larger than life by my late adolescence. Under his tutelage, I learned that masters affect the elements by *using* the mysteries of Creation rather than being *ushered* along aimlessly by them." A Master, by use of his Will, influences the unfolding of creativity by transmuting mental as well as material conditions. Creation is an unfolding drama *Apollo*, illuminated *Ausar,* participation in which is allotted to those who first master themselves and then the elements. Yet take heed; to attain 'higher enlightenment' and the degree of power necessary to take part, one must also master the mysteries of *Ma'at*. Though often interpreted as "Order", *Ma'at* is far more than that. It is that that holds all that exists together, a force of unity without which all creation would perish, the antithesis of chaos. *Ma'at* is that aspect of *Amun* by which balance, harmony, justice, and reciprocity are created and brings order to all that exists.

But if *Apollo* inquired, by nature, *Ma'at* is a 'sacred mystery', how then can it be mastered? The mysteries of *Ma'at* are unveiled subtly along the course of the life of the Neophyte and less subtly along the path of the Seeker, advised *Ausar*; unveiled, that is, for those who have acquired the wisdom to discern them. Such wisdom is attained both empirically and through inquisition, continued *Ausar,* and you, *Apollo*, are in possession of such wisdom; you need but awaken to them… to gain the enlightenment you have already earned. But how can this be? Objected *Apollo,* all I have done in my life thus far, I have done in honor of thee, *Ausar*; I have yet to heed the call of my own path and destiny. That you have honored me by joining this journey *Apollo*, in no way hinders the rewards of your experiences, assured *Ausar*; much of what you have accomplished, he continued, has been the product of your own making and creativity.

Was it not you, *Apollo,* who gathered and summoned the *Confederation* to the aid of *Kush* when we faced overwhelming forces and was it not you who led the coastal migrations into the *Indus*? Was it not also you, *Apollo,* who spearheaded our migrations through *Kanaan*, making possible this very aspect of the journey? I have dutifully dispatched those tasks you placed before me, *Ausar,* and it is true that I have accomplished much and perhaps learned even more, yet I hardly possess it as enlightenment, uttered *Apollo*. This is because you have not pursued it as enlightenment, *Ausar* illuminated. Pursuit of enlightenment *Apollo* is an endeavor to understand one's relationship with *Amun*, *Ausar* continued*; Amun* is hidden deep within you, and you must 'Know Thyself' in order to find the 'Hidden One', the Invisible Creative Power within. I have given homage to *Amun* all my life and taken strength and resolve from this as I adhere to those tenets of *Ma'at* espoused by the priesthood, divulged *Apollo*; yet, in truth, I know not of the *Amun* within of which you speak.

This much you must ponder within your Contemplations, *Apollo*, advised *Ausar*; the nature of *Amun* is largely unknown, and the fragments that are known are known as sacred "*Mysteries*", enlightenments held tightly secret and revealed only to royalty, high priests, and learned-men *Ausar* elaborated; the degree of revelation nevertheless must be earned through pursuit of such transcendence. These are things availed through practices of meditation *Apollo,* the practice of which one enters a higher contemplative state. Meditation is a form of union with Amun, *Ausar* elucidated, under whose influence the mind receives insights into things of the spirit; its proper practice, *Ausar* explained, requires a measure of solitude, silence, and stillness. The beginning of meditation is brief and frequently interrupted by distractions. Apollo and *Ausar* continued; distractions are readily overcome if one devotes the time, care, study, and practice necessary to master the art.

Meditation is the soul's inward vision *Apollo*, and that subtle energy felt in its deepest repose links the physical body with the immortal spirit of *Amun*. Each of our thoughts and emotions causes our energy to vibrate at particular frequencies *Ausar* illuminated; the lower the frequency, the more corporeal one feels, whilst the higher the frequency, the more spiritual. It is here you will find the *Amun* within… And of those not lacking in reverence or discipline, but perhaps lacking sufficient intuition; those consigned to the lower vibrations, and thus confined to this corporeal reality, *inquired Apollo*; what transcendence avails our lot, *Ausar*? Focusing attention at the highest level of intuition brings to bear that aspect of the Force invigorating one's being, whilst focusing attention at the level of abstract mind brings to bear that aspect of the Force, *Ausar* intoned; these are among the most important things one can do to cultivate one's abilities on the path. Whatever one's vibration, it is possible to raise it and ascend the scale, *Ausar* informed. Yet take heed, *Apollo*, the laws of harmony and discordance are in effect here; discordance, at all frequencies, is associated with unease and chaos, whilst harmony is associated with tranquility and order.

A sublime sensation of harmony and tranquility comes over one as things come into resonance with the vibrations of creation, continued *Ausar*. To take part in its' unfolding, you must first acknowledge your creative abilities and assume responsibility for your reality; acceptance plays a vital role in cultivating one's abilities on the path, *Ausar* advised. Acceptance beyond doubt, *Ausar*? Queried *Apollo*. I have faith in thy word and thy guidance, and this faith undergirds the acceptance you advise in my 'creative abilities' *Ausar*, but in my heart of hearts, I am unable to extinguish doubt in that of which I have little experience, conceded *Apollo*. It is not experienced you lack, responded *Ausar*. It is awareness of your experience; when you gathered the *Confederation* to the aid of *Kush*, did you not influence the consciousness of others, *Apollo*? Inquired *Ausar*. Creation flows from the consciousness which proceeds *Apollo*, and consciousness is shaped by beliefs, beliefs which affect and, in many ways, determine one's reality. Beliefs act as self-fulfilling prophecies, *Ausar* illuminated.

For instance, the belief that reality is purely objective and that your thoughts cannot influence it is nothing but a self-fulfilling prophecy *Apollo*, one in which you abuse power granted to you to make yourself feel powerless. It is only fear that causes you to do this, fear that if you were to fully embrace the creative power of your potentiality, you would be overwhelmed. But that fear is also a belief, one which you are equally free to drop… because it does not serve you. You have the power to let it go whenever you are ready, assured *Ausar*. These fears are the demons and barriers of which I spoke earlier; the rewards of their conquests are endless, *Ausar* illuminated. One's delusions then fall away to reveal the threshold of Higher Contemplation and union with *Amun,* under whose influence one may gain insight into the mysteries of *Ma'at* and the unfolding of Creation.

Granted the powers imbued by this enlightenment, Advanced Masters participate in Creations' unfolding, participation commensurate with their enlightenment. A visualization within Higher Contemplation is the technique underlying this participation; it is a technique of using one's imagination to visualize and create the reality one seeks to shape, a vision focused and made clear in the mind's eye. One must master this fundamental ability if one seeks to affect one's environment, counseled *Ausar*. As you sought to emulate *Khronos*, so shall I seek to emulate you, *Ausar;* I too shall endeavor to become an Advanced Master, asserted *Apollo*. Great Masters ascend through Pureness of Heart and Strength of Will, noted *Ausar*; qualities sufficient in you, *Apollo*, but take heed, though the *path* beckons, its course is arduous. It begins with the quest for enlightenment, and progresses through travails of transcendence, to obscure heights of ascension, to reach the realm of mastery you seek, *Ausar* propounded.[dccclxxx] Enlightened adeptness at complex visualizations and actualization of those visualizations is the method to such ascension, *Ausar* advised.

Know that ascension is not a place, but a state of *Being*; a state gained by participation in the unfolding of *Creation,* and thus the divinity of *Amun*. Such deification, *Ausar* emphasized, is the highest form of enlightenment. But, a last *Apollo*, the evening grows late, and we need awake before dawn in the morrow; the *Kushite* merchants will have returned with replenishments from *Knossos* by midday, and it will surely take the balance of the day and well into the evening for all hands to re-load the vessels for the voyage to the old northern colonies. The most experienced of the ships' captains has advised that we should raise anchor in time for the morning tide, which will ferry the ships to currents favorable to our course. For this we must ensure all efforts are brought to bear, and for my part, I intend to sleep now, *Apollo*, so that we may rise early in the morn, resigned *Ausar*. Should you wish to contemplate on that of which we have just spoken, I recommend the solitude of the chamber at the back of the lake; it has served me well in my Contemplations.

Awakening before dawn the next morning, the two descended from the cave entrance and mountain slope to the upland plain southeast of *Knossos*. The plain is surrounded by pristine cliffs, with a river fed by small creeks and streams flowing from the surrounding hills, traversing the entire length of the plain, from end to end. With no outlet, the upland river flowed northwesterly into a huge cavern, leaving much of the valley floor thick with ancient foliage, irrigated by crystal blues springs flowing across the plain into the river. The Lassithi Mountains and upland plain divide central Crete, providing an ideal locale for *Ausar* and *Apollo* to descend the uplands. They followed the river to the cavern and ascended into the hills to reach an old ancient trail that winds its way down from the uplands. The *Lassithi Plateau* is about nineteen miles from the seaside village near Knossos, where the Kushite Armada was anchored in the harbor, a trek that would take *Ausar* and *Apollo* the better part of the day.

Over half the interior terrain of *Crete* is mountainous, with lower mountains, hills, and valleys in between the higher mountains, so even relatively modest distances take hours to traverse. *Ausar* and *Apollo* arrived back at the seaside village near dusk, shortly behind what appeared to have been a rather large caravan of carts, still trailing into the village square by way of the road from *Knossos*. Smaller boats were busily ferrying cargo to the ships in the harbor, and *Ausar's* senior advisers and several prominent merchants appeared to be coordinating the entire effort from a makeshift dock, at the harbor shore, near the village square. Of all the earliest towns and villages that once adorned the northern and eastern coast of *Crete*, *Knossos* had been the only one to escape the destruction of the tidal waves that swept across the Mediterranean.

Knossos sits inland, separated from the sea by a long range of hills, where the city is situated high on a knoll between the confluences of two rivers. The harbor where the *Kushite* armada was anchored was at the mouth of one of these rivers, the river Kairatos (present-day 'Katsambas'), five miles south of the city.[dccclxxxi] Knossos was the economic heart of the island, connected by roads to other Cretan towns and ports. The *Kushite* merchants of *Atlatian* derivation knew it would be a vital port between *Khemet* and the old colonies, particularly given *Crete's* role as an entryway to the *Ægean*. As *Ausar* and *Apollo* entered the village, *Ausar's* most trusted advisers approached, and each, in an orderly fashion, briefly advised *Ausar* of the status of their efforts in preparing the ships, the crews, and the entourage for the upcoming voyage.

A tired *Ausar* carefully listened to each, then firmly announced, 'all necessary assurances must be made in order that we timely avail ourselves of the morning tide in the morrow; we are advised that morning tide will carry our vessels to currents and winds favorable to our course; thus, we need complete our tasks with lettle haste, listing all hands and passengers aboard tonight'. For now, *Apollo* and I are in need of food and rest *Ausar* continued, our trek has been long and arduous, but we shall join the effort after we eat and rest and retire aboard ship tonight. By dawn, the ancient vessels of the *Armada* had been loaded to the fullest extent possible, prompted largely by the ship's Captains, who anticipated little opportunity for further replenishment until reaching the mainland colonies. Ladened with the combined weight of the replenishments and the exotic goods (spices, herbs, incense, precious stones, and commodities) brought from across *Kusha Dwipa* to trade; the ships each raised anchor just after dawn, availing themselves of the morning tide.

As promised, the tide gradually ferried the vessels further and further out to sea, where the *Armada* met favorable winds and currents just beyond and northwest of the offshore *Isle of Dia*, about nine (nautical) miles north of the ancient harbor of *Knossos*. Although under favorable currents, the ships were buffeted by swells driven by the seasonal northwesterly winds in the *Ægean*. While the designs of the vessels of the era are mostly unknown and highly conjectural, archaeologists believe that maritime activity in the islands of the Mediterranean around 8,000 BC required fairly large, seaworthy vessels that used oars and were also equipped with sails. Such ships were intended as carriers of valuable cargo or perishable goods that needed to be moved as safely and quickly as possible. The ships would have been decked with a row of port holes, coresponding to the number of oars port and starboard.

The use of oarsmen permited the ships to move independently of the winds and currents, but sails would be used as the primary means of propulsion in favorable winds. The vessels of the era had long, slender hulls, with masks and rigging built with large beams, requiring deeper draughts (the measurement of how much of the ship's structure will be submerged), allowing for greater cargo. For maximum efficiency in rowing the vessels, the height of the oarsmen's port holes from the surface of the water was as kept low as possible; to give the oarsmen enough leverage to efficiently move the vessel through the water. Design characteristics that made the ships fast and maneuverable but somewhat vulnerable to rough seas. The oarsman's port holes were usually kept open in good weather but were closed during times of storm unless unfavorable winds required the deployment of the oarsmen to maintain the course.[dccclxxxii]

The Cyclades Archipelago

Though heavily buffeted, the ships were able to abide by the northwesterly winds for a day, followed by a half day of good sailing, reaching the *Cyclades Isles* at the threshold of the *Ægean Sea*. The Cyclades are an archipelago of over two hundred islands, bounded to the south by the *Sea of Crete* and to the north by the *Aegean Sea*. The islands are actually peaks of submerged mountains, with the exception of the volcanic islands of *Milos* and *Santorini*. The *Cyclades* range from the large island of *Naxos* to tiny islands that support only a few thousand people. Before the fall of *Atlatia*, these islands were home to vibrant colonies, the largest of which was *Naxos*. The most ancient descendants on all the islands once attested to their ancestors having derived from the ancient *Sahara* well into the historical period; those were later referred to as the 'Karians'.[dccclxxxiii]

These were the old northern colonists who settled the islands sometime before 10,000 BC, sailing from the coasts of Atlatia to the Islands and the surrounding coasts, where they established prosperous trading colonies and communities. One of which was at the ancient seaside port on the *Isle of Naxos*, the largest of the *Cyclade Islands*. However, the *Isle of Milos*, renowned for the quality of its obsidian, was the first port of destination for the *Kushite* armada. As the ships approached, *Milos,* with its strange horseshoe shape emerged from the blue waters of the *Aegean,* its visible coastline dotted with massive natural caves and almost other-worldly swirled white volcanic rocks. The armada dropped anchor by early afternoon near the seaside village of *Klima*, which, during antiquity, was the first true port of *Milos*. *Milos* had been colonized and inhabited since the early Neolithic and developed much quicker than its neighboring islands due to the quality of the black, volcanic glass-like rock, known as obsidian, on the island. Trade from Milos developed and expanded with exports of obsidian and tools made from the hard glass-like rock, which have been found throughout the Mediterranean.[dccclxxxiv]

The old colonists on Milos also exported minerals from sulfur mines and prospered because of the island's great mineral wealth, as well as its strategic location between mainland *Southern Europe* and *Crete*. The natural harbor at *Milos* allowed for ease of maritime trade, propelling the old *Atlatian* colonies on the island to become the first in the *Aegean* to prosper. The scattered villages that the colonists originally inhabited in the early Neolithic were gradually abandoned as the old settlement communities coalesced into ever larger village clusters. The most prominent of which was *Phylakopi* (Fylakopi), considered the island's first city, where the original settlement and village clusters flourished and expanded into a vibrant trade center and early city by the Mid-Neolithic. Apart from *Phylakopi*, other prehistoric settlements and village clusters of the era have been uncovered in numerous places throughout the island.

For their part, the *Kushite* merchants ferried from the ships anchored in the harbor to the seaside village in small boats, bringing samples of exotic herbs, spices, and commodities from *Kusha Dwipa*, with which to barter. The trade of choice was for obsidian, and after half a day of networking, and an evening of barter and negotiation, the merchants returned to their ships in groups the next morning, each with several boats in tow, manned by locals. The boats were each, in turn, tied to the leeward side of the ships to load the bartered goods; the merchants later returned with several boatloads of obsidian, which were then loaded in a similar fashion into the hulls of the ships. The merchants, crews, and other abled-bodied hands aboard the ships labored into the late afternoon, reorganizing, loading, and best situating the heavier-weighing obsidian and minerals in the ship hulls, after which all but the unlucky skeleton crews were allowed to go ashore, for early the next morning they would raise anchor, and put back out to sea. *Ausar* and *Apollo*, together with the ship's captains, remained aboard their ships, planning the next leg of the voyage, which promised to be somewhat challenging.

The *Isle of Naxos*, the largest and most fertile of the Cyclade islands, was the next port of destination. A voyage requiring that the ships of Armada push southward along the west coast of *Milos*, into and against the northwesterly winds, to circumnavigate the southern tip of the island and set a course due east to *Naxos*. *Milos* is the most westerly of the *Cyclades Islands*, and with a voyage along the coasts of the intervening Islands (Strongyli, Despotiko, Antiparos, and Paros) deemed too time-consuming; it was decided that after rounding the southern tip of the island, the Armada would ply directly eastward to *Naxos*, over open water.

With the added new cargo, the ships were now more heavily laden and sat much lower in the water, an outcome seen as both benefit and impairment. Benefit because the height from the port holes on the sides of the ships to the surface of the water was now much lower, providing greater leverage for the oarsmen to move the vessels through the water. Yet with the ships so heavily ladened and sitting so low in the water, any inability to maintain adequate speed would render the vessels less maneuverable and vulnerable to the rough seas. The ships were buffeted by adverse currents as the Armada plied southward along the west coast and leeward side of *Milos*, turning into unfavorable winds and wind-driven swells as they rounded the southern tip of the island.

Voyage to the Isle of Naxos

The *Armada* raised anchor several hours before dawn the next morning, with all oars in the water, as the ships slowly departed the harbor in caravan formation and plied southward off the east coast of *Milos*. With *Ausar's* flagship leading the Armada, the ships rounded the southern tip of *Milos* just after sunrise and set a course due east toward the *Isle of Naxos*. The *Oarsmen* had set a good strong pace against the currents and attained good speed as the Armada made its way southward along the west coast of *Milos*. But as the vessels turned eastward, the ships heeled heavily, losing speed, as they then plied through swells driven by the northwesterly winds; a loss of speed meant less maneuverability and increased vulnerability to the force of the swells. All able-bodied hands enlisted in the effort as fresh teams of oarsmen rotated every two hours, each battling mightily against the winds and swells until the vessels gradually regained sufficient speed and maneuverability. The Armada plied its way through the opposing winds and swells for the balance of the day until reaching midway between the isles of *Paros* and *Naxos,* where the ships changed course just before sunset.

Following Ausar's flagship, the Armada turned northward into the broad corridor between the islands, availing the vessels of the northwesterly winds as each raised their sails, providing a measure of relief to their exhausted crews. The ships again heeled heavily as they turned, losing momentum, but the winds were strong enough for the vessels to quickly regained speed without loss of maneuverability. Yet, riding low in the water, the heavily laden ships pitched and rolled with their decks incessantly wet with spray, drifting first to port and then to starboard as the rudder men fought to maintain course. The northwesterly winds proved strong enough to scatter the ships of the *Armada*, forcing each vessel to seek shelter nearer to shore at different points along the west coast of *Naxos*. Navigating closer to the shore, under the protection of the leeward side of the island, the ships each redeployed their oarsmen, using both sails and oars, ply their way northward along the west coast of the island. Before the fall of *Atlatian*, there was a trading colony on the cape and others along the coast, but nothing remained of them now, as all had been destroyed by the tsunamic waves which swept across the seas.

Largest of the *Cyclade Islands*, *Naxos* is very different from its neighbors; its steeping cliffs, caves, hidden coves, natural harbors, and large stretches of beach, backed by sand dunes, cedar trees, lush forests and rugged mountains along its coast, give a dramatic effect to its varied landscape. As it was anciently, it remains an island of imposing coastal images from the sea, particularly after sunset. As each of the scattered ships of the *Armada* made their way northward along the coast, the captains of each vessel carefully navigated not to stray too close to the unfamiliar shores, lest they run the risks of hitting large offshore rocks, and similarly, not to stray too far from the shelter the lee side of the island; lest they run the risk of being swept into rough seas by the northwesterly winds. The winds grew calmer as the evening wore on, allowing the ships to venture further from shore, retire their oars, and sail north to their port of destination at the ancient seaside village of Naxos, in the large natural harbor on the island's central west coast.

The last ship of the Armada trailed into the protected waters of the harbor late that evening, dropping anchor in close proximity to the other two vessels. All hands stayed aboard the ships that first night, perhaps recovering, or perhaps simply in need of rest, or maybe both. But early the next morning, *Ausar* (Osiris, Zeus, Kush) and *Apollo*, along with the captains and merchants aboard each vessel, made their way ashore, just north of the seaside village, near the causeway adjoining the Isle of Naxos to the Islet of Palatia. The *Isle of Naxos* is not only the largest of the *Cyclades*; it's situated at the very heart of the archipelago. *Naxos* is to the east of the *Isle of Paros*, to the south of the *Isle of Mykonos*, west of the *Isle of Amorgos*, and to the north of the *Isle of Ios*. *Naxos City*, the islands' present-day capital city and its chief port, is situated on the site of the ancient seaside village and harbor on the bay of Naxos, the largest bay on the island. A mountain range crosses the island from north to south, with the highest point being Mount Zas ("Zas" meaning "Zeus"), known anciently as '*Mount Zeus*'.

In certain versions of Greek Mythology, it was said that *Zeus* (Ausar, Osiris, Kush) was brought up on the island; later, inhabitants on the island of the island even built a temple atop the mountain that bears his name. The first rule of Greek mythology is that there are dozens of different versions of every story and numerous different tales attached to each, with no single version of the 'original' one.[dccclxxxv] However, a truer version of the naming of the tallest mountain on *Naxos* states that *Zeus* (Ausar, Osiris, Kush) visited the island sometime after the fall of *Atlatia*, in celebration of which the inhabitants of the island named its highest mountain in his honor. An occasion upon which they also built a majestic temple in his honor (the 'Temple of Zeus') at the top of the mountain bearing his name.

The Legends

It was under the reign of *Khronos*, during the *Golden Age* and the building of the great *Megaliths* along the coasts of the *Mediterranean* and *Ægean Seas*, that these lands were first brought to civilization. *Khronos* taught men there to change from crude to civilized ways of life and introduced them to the sincerity of soul and justice, ushering in the peace and goodwill that marked the Golden Age. *Khronos* possessed such pureness of spirit and clarity of vision that it is said he precisely prophesized the demise of his earthly body, and when he finally withdrew from this world, that death came peacefully during his sleep. As legend holds, while incarnate here in this world, *Khronos* sired six children by his wife *Rhea*: three sons, *Hāidēs* (Ἅιδης), *Poseidon* (Sidon), and *Ausar* (Osiris), and three daughters, *Hestia*, *Demeter*, and *Hera*.

Following his ascension, it was these descendants who formed the first federation to rule over the whole of the *Atlatia* and its colonies, including those in Southern Europe and those on islands in the *Mediterranean* and *Ægean Seas*. It was *Poseidon* who received the main island of *Atlatia*, where he settled and made his abode on the Mediterranean side of the island. The prescience of *Poseidon's* leadership quickly spread and gained prominence throughout Atlatia, culminating in his ascendance to a mantle previously held only by *Khronos*, that of King of all of *Atlatia* (and its colonies), with the other ruler relenting to lesser sovereignty. *Poseidon* and his wife begat five pairs of male children for whom the main island of *Atlatia* was then divided into ten provinces, giving his first-born, *Atlas*, the largest and best allotment and making him king, with others the made princes and giving rule over the other provinces. Following the ascension of *Poseidon*, his descendants, as provincial rulers of *Atlatia,* formed a second federation that usurped much of the dominion of the first and ruled over all of *Atlatia* and its colonies in the *Mediterranean* and *Ægean*.

Though the descendants of *Atlas* always retained leadership of the most influential kingdom, the other provincial rulers each persistently competed to outdo each other in their attempts to become the second most powerful and influential kingdom of the federation, endeavors which led to their eventual corruption. The corrupt sovereigns raised powerful armies and launched unprovoked aggressions along and beyond the coasts of southern *Europe* in their vain attempts to usurp each other and subdue control of the coastal and island colonies. To the colonist in the *Ægean*, their efforts to control and exploit the colonies were indicative of their decline in reverence and adherence to the *Laws of Poseidon;* a threat portending the destruction of the civilization they respected and swore to uphold. *Poseidon* had been the prime deity of early Cycladic civilization; indeed, in their fables, it is said that he actually created the Cyclades, transforming them into islands and islets.

In truth, it was *Poseidon* who established the earliest colonies at Corinth, Ægina, *Naxos*, and Delphi; it was also he who colonized Attica and founded Athens, naming it after his niece Athena, daughter of Zeus. Most relevantly, it was he who founded the most prosperous of the *Cyclade Island Colonies* in the Aegean*, Naxos. Poseidon's* renown was second to only that of *Khronos,* whom he had aided in building the walls of *Troy*; temples were erected in his honor in nearly all the early colonies and seaport along the coasts of the *Mediterranean* and isles of the *Aegean*; regions where the *Laws of Poseidon* were still held in reverence during the years of corruption, wars, and turmoil; a dark period when word of adherence to the sacred laws of Poseidon, by none other than *Zeus (Ausar, Osiris)*, spread throughout the beleaguered colonies, providing hope and sustaining many through the most troubling of times. *Zeus (Ausar, Osiris)* was a well-known and respected personage throughout the *Cyclades*, particularly on the *Isle of Naxos*, which he first visited under the tutelage of *Khronos* on the occasion of *Poseidon's* christening of the island colony's earliest harbor and port.

The central position of *Naxos*, at the crossroads of the *Mediterranean* and *Aegean Sea* routes, had placed the island colony in the midst of the mounting discord and turmoil until, alas, the unrequited aggressions of the corrupt *Atlatian* sovereigns were driven back, and finally defeated. Only to be followed by the catastrophic upheavals presaging the eventual destruction of *Atlatia*, and the series of tsunamis that swept across the *Mediterranean* and *Ægean Seas,* overwhelming the islands; utterly destroying coastal villages and cities in their path. Tsunamic flooding that receded with such force it denuded the fertile soil on the mainland and island coasts, leaving a wake of destruction, and a vacuum of governance, save only the sacred *Laws of Poseidon*, with *Zeus* (Ausar, Osiris) perceived as its prophet.

Naxos is a diamond-shaped island with mountains in the east that dissect the island from north to south. Rivers flow across the interior in all directions from the mountain range. The western side of the range is gentle, ending in flat and arable land with large green valleys, while the eastern side is particularly steep, with gorges and small cultivated valleys. In the center of *Naxos* is the fertile plain of Tragea, full of trees. Most of those surviving the tsunami floods were in the safety of the highlands, where ample water supply and the rich soil allowed a quick resurgence in agriculture. There was also an eventual resurgence of the island's fishing community and seaside villages, but not as many as on the other islands. In many ways, the recovery at *Naxos* after the fall of *Atlatia* was guided by traditions previously sewn by *Zeus* (Ausar, Osiris, Kush)). As the early colonial settlements had spread and begun to grow across *Naxos*, it was young *Zeus* (Ausar, Osiris), in the service of *Poseidon,* who coordinated coalescing the diverse settlements into a cohesive colony, bridging commerce and trade between the mining settlements in the mountains, and the agricultural settlements in highland plains and valleys, with the fishing and maritime settlements along the coastal lowlands.

At the behest and under the tutelage of *Khronos,* the onus for *Zeus* was to ensure the sustainability of the island colony and enhance its capacity for trade and export. The soil of *Naxos* contained two highly-prized natural resources, marble, and emery, each highly desired commodity and imported at *Atlatia*. In emulation of *Khronos*, young *Zeus* sought spiritual refuge and abode in the mountainous heights of *Naxos;* wisdom inherited from *Queen Gaia,* the first to realize the subtle energies swirling and emanating within certain distinctive mountains. [dccclxxxvi] At the dawn of *Atlatia*, when *Manding-Shi* in the southern highlands took refuge from the bitter winter coldness in the warmth of the deep caves in the *Anti-Atlas* highlands, the *Queen Mother* noted, as she drifted into slumber each night, that she would go into and out of a sleep-like state; seemingly adrift in the moment between being awake and falling asleep. A state of consciousness neither awake nor asleep, but somewhere in between, a state imbued with feelings of overwhelming peace, in which she remained fully aware. [dccclxxxvii]

It was sometime later, after her union with *Ouranos,* on the occasion of her first winter refuge further north, in the immense *Friouato Caves* of *Mt. Toubkal*, that *Queen Gaia* experienced the subtle but pronounced energies of a powerful mountain vortex. Perhaps it was the sheer magnitude and configuration of *Mount Toubkal*, the highest peak in the *Atlas Mountains*, as well as the highest peak in all of North Africa; the subtle energies swirling within the caves at the mountain were decidedly more forceful. As *Gaia* drifted into slumber each night, adrift at that moment between being awake and falling asleep, what followed now was a feeling of subtle vibration accompanied by a sense of overwhelming peace, followed by a feeling like she was floating or having an out-of-body experience. *Mount Toubkal* and the *Friouato Caves* feature prominently in many such legends involving shamanic journey-like experiences and the illumination of one's spiritual nature.

The ancients' believed such mountain vortexes to be portals to higher planes of consciousness and that the subtle energies emanating from within them interact and resonate within the Inner Being of those ('sensitives') amenable and able to detect their influences.[dccclxxxviii] This resonance happens because the energies within the vortex are similar to the subtle energy operating within each person. When one nears a mountain vortex, it stimulates and energizes its etheric energies, making it possible for those who are 'sensitives' to become aware of what mystics have discovered… that our existence is multi-dimensional. Such mountains rise abruptly, shaped like giant pyramids emerging from the earth, and are gathering places for the subtle energies that embrace the planet. The earth experiences the energies emanating from such vortexes as different aspects of consciousness, as do our own bodies.

The ancients' believed these to be places where 'sensitives' could commune with *Amun,* the unknown God, whom they believed was present in the luminous fog that hid the mountain tops. Ancient seers believed this was the answer to the mystery of the atmosphere and warm temperature in the caves of such mountains, caves that appeared to be like transcendental doorways between realms. This is why the spiritual aspects of such mountains were turned into pyramids; pyramids are archetypes of these 'Holy Mountains'. The highest peak on *Naxos* is such a mountain, not merely the tallest on the island but the tallest in all of the *Cyclades*. Tall enough to trap clouds, permitting greater reliable rainfall, making Naxos the most fertile of the Cyclade Islands, with an abundant supply of water in an archipelago where water was usually inadequate. This is the mountain later bestowed the name '*Mt. Zeus,* and within its heights, is the largest cave on the island, known as the '*Cave of Zeus'*.[dccclxxxix] The interior of the cave consists of a chamber extending almost four hundred feet into the mountain, at a width of over two hundred feet in places, adorned with majestic formations of stalactites and stalagmites, giving one the impression of being in a large cathedral.[dcccxc]

It was here that young *Zeus* made his spiritual refuge and abode as Viceroy of *Naxos*.[dcccxci] *Mt. Zeus* is the central focus of the mountainous interior of the island, and it was from these heights, under the governance of *Zeus*, that the discordant collection of early settlements on the island was harmonized into a cohesive, self-sufficient, and unified colony. It began with common paths between village settlements linking coastal and lowland settlements with those in the highlands; paths which became roads linking agricultural settlements in the highland plane and valleys, with mining and quarrying settlements in the highlands and lowlands, and fishing and maritime settlements on the coasts. Roads became trade routes linking and harmonizing the economic vitality of the island; it was only then that a truly cohesive and self-sufficient colony began to emerge and take shape on *Naxos*. Following the tsunami destruction caused by the upheavals and eventual fall of *Atlatia*, all of the coastal towns and villages, and those situated along most of the rivers emptying into the *Aegean*, were totally obliterated.

Much of the destruction was done by the long series of tsunamis and flooding events, each ending with flood waters receding back into the *Aegean* basin with such force that all the villages and early cities along the coast and riverine lowlands virtually disappeared. The resilience of the colony was afforded by its ethos of self-reliance and inter-regional trade, traditions instilled under the governance of *Zeus*. Equally fortuitous, the fertile soils of *Naxos* are in the highland plane and valleys, permitting agriculture and animal husbandry to continue fairly undisturbed as important industries on the island. There was also fine-quality marble in the subsoil of *Naxos*. This was the best quality marble and was exported to *Crete* and other former colonies. Naxos was one of the first islands where marble was worked. It is, therefore, not surprising that here a local school of marble masons and sculptors developed.

The white, brilliant marble quarried today in Naxos is essentially the marble that was used to carve the famous Neolithic Cycladic statuettes. Marble became a key factor in the island's early recovery during this period. Another was 'Emery', a hard rock known from Antiquity as 'Naxian Soil', still mined and has always been used by Cycladic stone carvers, a valued export aiding the early island's recovery. [dcccxcii] A rebuilt capital city on the site of the present-day *Naxos City* remained the capital of the former island colony, and it was from there that a group of the city's prominent citizenry made their way towards *Ausar* (Osiris, Zeus) and his entourage as they approached the city from the seaside village adjacent to where their vessels were anchored. Word had spread through the capital overnight that the small armada anchored in the harbor was led by none other than *Zeus* (Ausar, Osiris) himself, prompting an impromptu gathering of prominent citizens, local craftsmen, merchants, traders, and others, to form the ad hoc welcoming committee that approached as *Ausar* (Osiris, Zeus) and his entourage entered the city.

Diasporic migrations after the fall of *Atlatia* increased island populations throughout the greater region, with *Naxos*, like *Crete*, attracting diverse talent pools of craftsmen, mariners, agriculturalists, merchants, fishermen, pastoralists, traders, and others. Immigrants of the diaspora integrated seamlessly into both new and existing settlements, aiding in the former colony's recovery and prosperity. Yet what they lacked and most sought was reaffiliation with the *House of Khronos* and the moorings of the *Laws and Poseidon*. But perhaps as a testament to the true antiquity of the former island colony, the *Goddess Neith*, mother of all the gods, regarded as the source of all life, had, for all practical purposes, remained the patron deity of *Naxos*, as well as many if not most of the other Isles of the *Cyclades*. Perhaps befittingly so, for in the ontology inherited by the first colonists of the *Cyclades*, it was the Mother Goddess *Neith* (the female counterpart of *Nun*), who brought forth the first land from the primeval waters of chaos, the *void* that existed before creation, and it was she who was most worshipped after the trauma of the floods.

Yet, strangely, in the same proportion that she was worshiped as a caring and protective mother goddess, she was also feared as a bringer of mayhem, violence, and destruction. Present-day archeologists have uncovered numerous artifacts depicting her likeness at the sites of many of the ancient households on *Naxos*, the most distinguishing of which being the so-called 'Cycladic Figurines'; statues symbolizing the worship of the 'Mother Goddess' on the island during the prehistoric the era. In the fullness of *Atlatian* ontology, *Neith* (wisdom), the *Mother Goddess* whose very name has been interpreted as symbolizing the existence of *God* before creation, together with *Nun* (chaos), was the progenitor(s) of *Amun* (mind), the bringer of *Ma'at* (order); who existed before *creation* came into being. Yet it was the worship of the former rather than the latter, *Neith* rather than *Amun*, that prevailed on *Naxos*.

Thus, during the warm greetings and later planning of festivities and accommodation for the weary crews of the Armada with the prominent citizenry of the city, what a far more worldly *Zeus* (Ausar, Osiris, Kush) found most apparent was their lack of reverence for *Amun* and the guiding light of *Ma'at*. A grounding without which he realized renewed allegiance to the *Laws and Poseidon* would be of little lasting avail. *Ausar* (Osiris, Kush, Zeus) and the *Captains of the Armada* resolved that the ships would layover in port for ten days. Sufficient time allowed an expedition of *Kushite* merchants to traverse the interior trade routes, presenting exotic goods from *Kusha Dwipa* and obsidian from *Milos* in trade for the prized marble and emery found by Naxos. *Apollo* was appointed to lead the expedition in the name of the *House of Khronos*, accompanied by the high priest of *Amun*, with the admonition that the merchants be allowed to add no new weight to the ship's cargo, exchanging no more than equal weight for equal weight.

Ausar decreed that the expedition be brought to an end on the seventh day, with the festivities the host had planned at the ancient village of present-day *Filoti* on the slopes of the mountain to be ceremoniously bestowed the name '*Mt. Zeus*'. Traders and merchants of ancient *Naxos City* worked in concert with those of the *Armada* as they off-loaded goods and prepared for the rigorous expedition into the populous interior highlands of the island. The goods were loaded aboard a caravan of pack animals, and after a day of rest, the expedition set off for the interior highlands on the morning of the *Kushites'* third day on the island. *Ausar* (Osiris, Zeus) and the captains and crew of the *Armada* remained behind in the city to plan and prepare for the last leg of their voyage before plotting a course for home. *Ausar* had initially planned to visit the most influential of the former lowland colonies as the final port of destination, presuming it would be best suited to spread the word of the rise of *Kush* and the *Confederation* from the ashes of *Atlatia* and the survival of the *House of Khronos*.

But what had become apparent to *Ausar* was that most, if not all, of the former colonies, had been forever altered, with many never fully recovering. *Naxos* had been among the few to recover its former prowess and influence, and, Ausar surmised, its mariners might be well suited to aid in assessing the Armada's final port of destination. The opportunity presented itself following the departure of the highland expedition, after a group of prominent citizens, including several merchants, informed *Ausar* (Osiris, Zeus) of plans to dedicate '*Mt. Zeus*' in his honor, at the festivities and a trade fare planned for the final day of the expedition, at the highland village (at the site of present-day *Filoti*) on the slopes of the mountain. *Mt Zeus* will then be the tallest in all of the *Cyclades*, they inferred, announcing the survival of the *House of Khronos* to all. In their discourse, several of the merchants and traders of the city made mention of the great void felt after the fall of *Atlatia* and the *House of Khronos*. And that only *Agenor*, son of *Poseidon,* who had built his kingdom in the distant lands of *Kanaan*, and *Haides* (Aides, Hades), eldest son of *Khronos*, who ruthlessly rules the lowlands of the great frozen lands, had been known to them, until the return of *Ausar* (Osiris, Zeus).

The prominent citizens proclaimed that his return, and the dedication of the highest mountain peak in all the islands in his honor, would do much to reclaim the reverence of the *House of Khronos*, a reverence so besmirched by the vile rule of *Haides* in the lowlands. As though anticipating his thoughts, the mariners of the city advised that the Captains of the *Armada* avoid the lowlands ruled by *Haides*. When pressed, all but one of the mariners could offer direct insight, a lone mariner who served aboard a ship venturing as far west as the *Balearic Isles*, where he encountered a trade network of *Atlatians* who settled in the islands, and those who settled on the nearby *Iberian Peninsula*. The islanders traded in metals mined on the peninsula and told of its native peoples being pressed into servitude by the forces of *Haides*. Beyond which, the mariner could offer little else other than a stark warning from the islanders against sailing too close to the coastal lowlands; these coasts, they warned, are plagued by rumors of war, threats of war, or open warfare itself. Only the largest of the former colonies is capable of standing against this tyranny, the merchants opined, but sadly they seem to lack the resolve.

Excursion into Eurasia: Earliest Thrace

The former colony to which the *Naxos* merchants eluded was none other than Neolithic *Thrace*, among the earliest *Atlatian* colonies on the Southeastern European mainland. Somewhat shielded from the full brunt of tsunami destruction that so devastated the isles and coasts of the Southern Ægean, *Thrace* continued to prosper almost unabated; early colonial-settlements evolved into provinces that expanded along trade routes crossing into present-day Germany from the lower *Danube River*, and France from the *Rhone River Valley*, at their western most extent. However, geographically speaking, the heart of *Thrace* of the era encompassed part of present-day northeastern Greece, southeastern Yugoslavia, Bulgaria, and the parts of Turkey that separate the *Black Sea* from the *Sea of Marmara*. [dcccxciii]

Meaning that the voyage from *Naxos* to *Thrace* would require the heavily laden ships of the Armada to sail across the open waters of the *Ægean Sea*. Yet for Ausar, the haunting rumors of *Haides* persistence in that which wrought such destruction upon the *House of Khronos* compelled his counterbalance. Nonetheless, he informed the merchants of *Naxos* that he would confer with the Captains of his Armada before concluding his decision on their final port. *Ausar* knew well that the *Ægean Sea* was far more demanding in terms of sailing skills and experience than the *Mediterranean* and that the hulls of the ships of the *Armada* were laddened to the extent that the vessels had lumbered badly in the seas between *Milos* and *Naxos*; concerns to be duly discussed.

Convening a meeting aboard the vessel serving as his Flagship that evening, *Ausar* (Osiris, Kush, Zeus) inquired into the prudence of a voyage to *Thrace*. The Captains of the *Armada* each had varying degrees of experience, with the most proficient being the Captain of the Ausar's Flagship, a *Kanaanite* of *Atlatian* derivation who had sailed the *Ægean* to *Thrace* on several occasions since the fall. The other two captains were each equally capable, though neither had experience sailing the *Ægean,* for which each insisted they be assigned a celestial navigator 'knowledgeable in these waters.' But what of our heavily laddened vessels? *Ausar* inquired of the three. Were they not scattered along the coast of *Naxos* from the winds and rough seas as we arrived? How might they fare on such a voyage? The ships lumbered in the turbulence of wind and currents between the islands, my lord; sailing between islands under such conditions is far more rigorous than sailing over open water, advised the *Captain of the Flagship*.

Ships often struggle to hold sufficient speed while working through islands under such conditions, concurred the other captains. Under favorable wind conditions, ships travel much faster, with greater maneuverability over open water, the three agreed. The course to *Thrace* would be due north, my lord, the *Captain of the Flagship* added; the prevailing winds are strongly northwesterly this time of year, precisely the most desirable for our destination. Sailing vessels travel best under such favorable winds, that is, winds blowing abaft of beam, he further advised; such winds propel ships to their fastest pace.[dcccxciv] Let us then have the crews prepare the ships for this… the final leg of our voyage, resolved *Ausar* (Osiris, Kush, Zeus), and let us proceed without undue haste, as we have less than a week before the return of the expedition from the interior highlands.

The next morning *Ausar* informed the prominent merchants and traders of the city that he and his *Armada* would indeed proceed to *Thrace* from *Naxos;* to both apprise the former colonies of the rise of *Kush* and the *Confederation* from the ashes of *Atlatia* and, more pointedly, to rekindle the light of the *House of Khronos,* and reverence for the *Laws and Poseidon*. Coalescence among the former colonies shall be sought around this polity, advised *Ausar*, coalescence sufficient in size and strength to countervail and perhaps dissuade the intransigence of *Haides*. As planned, *Apollo* and the merchants and traders of the interior-highland expedition joined *Ausar* and the prominent citizenry of the city for festivities at ancient *Filoti*; on the slopes of the mountain, they then ceremoniously bestowed the name '*Mt. Zeus,*' in honor of *Ausar* (Osiris, Zeus, Kush).

The festivities lasted throughout the day and into the early evening, with piecemeal groups of those who formed the expedition and their pack animals departing and descending the highlands in route to the capital city and its main port in the bay of *Naxos;* this throughout the balance of the second half of the day. Goods from the expedition were boarded the following morning, bringing the ships to full preparation for the next leg of their voyage, permitting the crews and full complement of the *Armada* a half day to relax and a full night of rest. The ships of the *Armada* lifted anchor just before sunrise and the early tide the next morning, then employed both oars and sails until rounding the eastern cape of the *Isle of Mykonos*, where the oars were retired, and the ships sailed freely as the vessels availed themselves of the northwesterly trade winds. The *Armada* picked-up pace, traveling more quickly once the ships entered the open waters of the *Ægean,* riding solely upon the wind. The vessels reached and maintained maximum speed for two days of good sailing, interrupted by a day and a half of storm and rough sailing, followed by four days of good sailing again, arriving along the southern coast of what was then late *Neolithic Thrace* on the morning of the ninth day.

The coast of *Thrace* was then far different than that of the present-day coastal zone. The present-day *Isle of Thassos* was still attached to the coast of *Thrace* and was then called *Odonis*, with *Proto-Thracian* agricultural villages of the era thriving in the now submerged ancient *Plane of Odonis* that connected the present-day island to the coast.[dcccxcv][dcccxcvi] Though shielded from the brunt of the tsunamic waves that reverberated across the *Ægean* during the upheavals in the *Atlas*, coastal *Thrace* was nonetheless impacted by the eventual rise in sea levels following the final fall of *Atlatia*. Most of coastal *Thrace* was slowly inundated and gradually submerged by the rising tides, leaving a large gap in the archeological record (and discoveries) along the seaboard prior to the late Neolithic (6,000 B.C.E.).[dcccxcvii]

Old Kavala City

Long gone are the seaside villages that populated the ancient coastline during the late Atlatian era, such as the colonial city and seaport known as '*Old Kavala City*, at the northern extent of what was then the *Odinis Peninsula,* in the *Gulf of Kavala*, where the ships of the *Armada* found safe harbor and anchorage. *Old Kavala City* was built at the apex of the ancient peninsula on the coast of the *Bay of Kavala,* where, from earliest antiquity, the prosperity of the city was intricately connected to the port.[dcccxcviii] The old colonists and their descendants (the 'Proto-Thracians') exploited the rich gold and silver deposits in *Thrace*, trading precious metals mined in the mountains for goods and wares supplied at first by *Atlatia,* then after the fall by an array of ports throughout the *Ægean,* and ultimately the broader *Mediterranean*.[dcccxcix] The original colonial city and seaport (that later became '*Old Kavala City*') were founded to take advantage of the rich gold and silver deposits discovered on nearby *Mount Pangaion,* the upper slopes of which were found to have been rich in marble rock, with gold and silver deposits found at the lower elevations.[cm]

Due to its proximity to the mines and the strategic location of its port, the colonial city grew increasingly prosperous in maritime trade. It was in part this growing wealth (particularly after the fall of *Atlatia*) that led to the incessant discord and disunity that seemed to plague the land when *Ausar* (Osiris, Kush, Zeus) and his advanced party reached the precincts of the old colonial city. The merchants of the old colonial city were open and eager to trade, but upon each encounter with traders of the *Armada*, they appeared apprehensive and particularly suspicious of what they considered the threatening size of the *Armada* anchored in the harbor. *Neolithic Thrace* had been mired in political turbulence since well before the fall of *Atlatia,* a period marked by inter-regional invasions, wars and oppression for the mere sake of greater power and wealth.

The old colonial provinces had since coalesced into a number of powerful kingdoms, with the royal families of each strategically inter-marrying to solidify allegiances and enhance their power. What was clear to *Ausar* (Osiris, Kush, Zeus) was that the *Thracians* had descended into the insidious materialism and avarice that had so beguiled and weakened the *Atlanteans*. Upon inquiry, and at each encounter, former colonialists and their (*Proto-Thracian*) descendants of the oldest lineage warily imparted similar accounts of the onset of the dissension and treachery that for so long had plagued their land. It began as early as the formative dawn of *Atlatia* itself, with the slighting of *Haides,* eldest son of *Khronos* (Khem, Cham, Ham), when *Khronos* allotted his second eldest *Poseidon* the heart of *Atlatia* while allotting *Haides* the forsaken lowlands.

Usurpation was made complete by the succession of *Poseidon's* eldest son *Atlas* to the throne and his assertion of preeminence over all of *Atlatia* and its colonies by him and his lineage. Acts imbued a mounting resentment within *Haides,* resentment that at first spawned disaffection and then, finally, actual rebellion against the *House of Khronos* and the *Laws and Poseidon*. Incidence, the depths of which *Ausar* (Osiris, Zeus, Kush) had only then begun to fully grasp; there had been rumors of such discord in his youth, trivialities attributed by *Khronos* to immaturity and growth in his eldest son, to whom he had granted sovereignty over his most treasured and earliest of colonies, the rich lowlands of the *Iberia*. Lands from which *Atlatians* had once been forced to withdraw (by the onset of the *Wisconsin Glaciations*) and to which none other than *Khronos* himself had led their triumphant return and entrusted to *Haides,* his eldest son. *Haides,* it seemed, was trapped in a paradox of perspective, believing himself slighted, though he had been honored, and deeming his younger brother the recipient of undue honor, though he instead was held close under the watchful eye of *Khronos*.

It had, in fact, been his faith in the stewardship of *Haides* that allowed *Khronos* latitude for wider exploration, the founding of the later colonies, and the megalithic era that followed. All the while, with *Haides* seething in undue resentment and disaffection, his furor increasingly exacted against the autochthonous (born of the soil or indigenous) peoples of the peninsula. It was not long after the ascension of *Khronos* and the presumptive overreaching of *Poseidon* that *Hāidēs'* unleashed his aggressions against the coveted lands and territories he had long sought adjacent to the peninsula. Aggressions that initially won *Haides* increasing control over the mineral resources of these lands once conquered before his eventual defeat, greatly expanding his wealth, power, and regional kingdom in the interim. *Haides* sought conquest and control of these lands to interpose strategic metals such as *Tin,* a vital alloy in hardening *Atlatian* armaments; his intent was also to gain control of valuable minerals and precious metals such as gold and silver.

The forces of *Haides* swept eastward from the *Iberian Peninsula*, assailing and subduing the islands and coastal lowlands of *Southern Europe* as they advanced. His unprovoked aggressions were simultaneously launched against the adjacent islands and mainland of the *Italian Peninsula* and then inhabited by several barbarian tribes who arose in a vain effort to defend themselves and their lands. The armies of *Haides* made quick dispatch of all resistance, enslaving the captured prisoners, who were placed in chains and pressed into hard labor in the mines within the captured territories. The geography of the Italian peninsula (*Tyrrhenia*) of the era was far different from that of its present-day configuration; the islands of *Elba* and *Sicily* were then still nominally connected to the peninsula. Gold was somewhat scarce in *Tyrrhenia*, with the earliest discoveries found in the central peninsula; silver, on the other hand, was far more prevalent, with several mines of the era developed on the coasts of the *Tyrrhenian Sea* and the *Isle of Sardinia,* where obsidian was also mined (in the central-eastern part of the island).

Proclaiming himself '*King of the Lowlands,* ' the reputation of *Haides* soon spread as the possessor of all wealth that came from the lowlands; indeed, his very name became synonymous with the lowlands.The renown of *Haides* as the *'Patron of Hidden Wealth'* from the lowlands, particularly the mined wealth of gold, silver, and other precious metals, soon spread beyond the islands and colonies of the lowlands to the haughty heights of *Atlatia* itself. There, seduced by envy and corrupted by greed, susceptible sovereigns of *Atlatia* soon raised their own powerful armies to join in common cause with *Haides* in their desire and efforts to gain a measure of the wealth and influence he had attained. An influence that, in many ways, usurped the prestige and authority of *Atlas* himself, a mantle *Haides* both relished and needed to further advance his eastward conquest. The coveted lands ahead, those across the *Ionian Sea* were inhabited by *Atlatian* colonies that would be more formidable than the barbarian tribes of *Tyrrhenia*.

Early Ancient Athens

These were the colonies of prehistoric *Greece*, the allure of which was the precious gold and silver discovered and mined in their lands. It was indeed silver from mines in eastern *Attica*, near fledgling *Athens*, that financed the rise of that early state.[cmi] There were also rumors of gold discovered and mined further east, on the *Isle of Thasos,* an island celebrated for the wealth of its mines. Yet even more alluring were the rich gold and silver discoveries at *Mount Pangaion* of *Thrace,* in the distant northeast of the land. A lust against which *Cecrops*, king of *Attica* and founder of *Athens,* united the colonies of *Athens* and *Thessaly* along with those of *Thrace* to rise in defense against the vile invaders of their lands. According to legend, the colonies of *Attica* were comprised of twelve rural city-states during the reign of *Cecrops*, which he united within a single *Athenian* state. To further buttress his forces, he also sought and entered into alliances with the former colonies of *Thrace,* most inclined to ally with *Athens* against the invaders, those engaged in defending the mines of *Thrace* against the encroachments of interlopers.

The invasion occurred in the same epoch as the rise of early *Athens*, and, fittingly, it was the forces of *Athens* who met the invasion and mounted first resistance, with *Cecrops* then summoning and rallying the ready forces of their allies to the fight.[cmii] It was thus that the *Athenians* were the first to confront the vast forces assembled to subdue their lands and reduce their peoples to slavery. In the beginning, *Cecrops* led only the united *Athenian* forces against the invaders, including the armies of *Erysichthon*, king of *Thessaly,* and *Erichthonius*, king of *Athens.* Upon the arrival of the *Thracians*, he then rallied the combined and allied forces, halting the advance of the invaders and, eventually, the eastward conquests of *Haides*. The duration of war lasted over half a generation, with *Athens* fighting throughout its entirety, even when all her allies had become exhausted and fallen away from her, leaving the *Athenians* to stand alone against the equally spent forces of *Haides* and *Atlatia*. The *Athenians* eventually triumphed over the invaders, repelling and driving them from what would later become *Neolithic Greece,* preserving their lands and peoples from sure subjugation and slavery.[cmiii]

Ancient Greek historians had aptly described *Cecrops* as a hero of the '*Pelasgian*' race, an epithet used by their much later arriving *Indo-European* ancestors to describe the *North African* inhabitants (and their descendants) whom they found throughout the region when they arrived. [cmiv cmv] A description also aptly affirmed by *Plato*, who placed the war between *Atlatia* and *Athens* to the time when *Athens* was inhabited by its original *Pelasgians* founders, again referring to the *North Africans* who inhabited the area throughout most of antiquity.[cmvi] Greek writers of late antiquity concurred that *Cecrops* immigrated to the area with a group of *Pelasgian* colonists, comprised of artisans, agriculturalists, husbandmen, and a warrior class who protected the colony, maintaining as many of the latter as deemed needed. [cmvii]The end of the war ushered in a period of subdued tension and hostility between the spent and weakened forces of *Haides* and *Atlatia* and those of the fledgling informal alliance that would later become *Neolithic Greece*.

The forces of *Haides* continued to launch raids into and across *Europe,* to their immediate north, taking numerous captives into slavery to work the mines in the captured territories they retained in *Tyrrhenia* and what would later become *Western Greece.* It was that *Haides* became worshipped in *Tyrrhenia* and *Western Greece*, depicted as a regal patron and giver of wealth, pouring fertility from a cornucopia of precious metals and mineral resources. Repute that both seduced and gave the *Thracian* kings cause for concern opined the old colonists in their discourse with *Ausar* (Osiris, Kush, and Zeus).The kingdoms of *Thrace* are rich in gold and silver, informed the old colonist, seeking to further explain the discord and treachery that gripped their land.

With the threat to the provinces of *Thrace* abated by the *Athenians*, the old colonists continued, and the *Thracian* kings sought to avoid any further conflict with the rejuvenated forces of *Haides*. They seek to conciliate and contain rather than confront, each benefiting from the fruits of trade with his corrupt kingdom. The *Thracian* kings purport to abhor the vile ethos of slavery at the heart of the *Kingdom of Haides*, the old colonists added, particularly given that *Thracians* have intermixed and interbred with rather than enslaved the autochthones of *Thrace*. Yet, the *Thracian* kings have nonetheless become mired in avarice and the lust for material wealth and power.[cmviii] It is their rivalry and thirst for wealth and power that undergirds the discord and tyranny that plagues *Thrace*, concluded the old colonists, a tyranny that harshly oppresses the people, and is the bane of our very existence. *Ausar* (Osiris, Zeus, Kush), who was called "Dionysus" (in the in *Thrace*), informed the colonists that he would intervene on their behalf if they would aid in the provision of the needed supplies and animals and assist in gathering able men to join common cause with the endeavor.

At hearing this, the old colonists informed that all *Ausar* might require would be provided by those inhabiting the planes between the highlands of *Thasso* to the south and those of the mainland to the north. The old colonists explained that the peoples inhabiting the planes were being slowly dislodged by the encroaching seas, which were gradually submerging the fertile plain, describing the peoples as "agricultural villagers inhabiting the dwindling plane who are nonetheless annually assailed by the powerful kingdoms of Thrace and forced to surrender portions of their harvest." According to ancient sources, the mountains of *Thrace* were then home to an array of covetous and warlike tribes, while the plains were provinces of equally warlike but somewhat more settled tribes. Nearly ninety different *Thracian* tribes are attested to in ancient accords, with those in both mountains and plains aligning themselves into petty fiefdoms, with several forming strong regional kingdoms.

Early Ancient Thrace

Ausar resolved to seek an audience with the most influential kingdoms, whom he would apprise of the rise of the *Maa Confederation* from the ashes of *Atlatia* and the emergence of *Kush* as a part of that Confederation. But most particularly, he would advise *Khemet*, the reconstituted *House of Khronos*. Ancient *Thrace* of the era was situated on the northern periphery of earliest ancient *Greece*, and it is by the name and personage of "Dionysus" that Greek legends best trace the travails of *Ausar* (Osiris, Zeus, Kush, Dionysus) in early *Thrace*.[cmix] Aptly, the first ancient Greek historian, *Herodotus*, used the names of *Osiris* and *Dionysus* interchangeably, declaring, "*Osiris* is named *Dionysus* by the Greeks."[cmx]

In keeping with this tradition, *Dionysus* (Ausar, Osiris, Zeus, Kush) resolved to inaugurate his expedition near the peak of the highest mountain in the land, *Mount Pangaion* (at 6,417 feet), where he and the priests of *Amun (Ammon)* greeted the rising sun with prayers and watched as the glow from its rays slowly expanded across the horizon. And from this vantage point, he also surveyed and gained an intuitive lay of the land. After first conferring and arranging that all but a third of the *Armada's* company, merchants, and security forces would remain and await his return at the old colonial city ('*Old Kavala City*') and seaport, together with the mariners who, in turn, would remain with and secure the vessels in the harbor, each under *Apollo's* command; *Dionysus* (Ausar, Osiris, Zeus, Kush) in turn then set out on the expedition at hand.

The Legends

According to legend, *Dionysus* set out eagerly on his expedition through *Thrace* to *Mount Pangaion* ("Pangaios Mountain," referred to as 'Mt. Nysa' by Homer) to await the sunrise so as to be the first to catch sight of Helios (the 'Sun'[cmxi]). Old Kaválla City was on the ancient road leading from the *Aegean* coast to Pangaios Mountain. Pangaios ('Mt. Pangaion') is situated northwest of *Old Kaválla City* at the mouth of the Struma (or 'Strymónas') River, with the *Aegean Sea* to the south and a vast marshland interspersed with thick woodlands that covered the entirety of what later became the *Plains of Kaválla,* to the north. [cmxii] Mt. Pangaion is situated between the Strymónas and Xiropotamos rivers and towered above the vast marshland to its north and a lesser fertile plain to the south separating it from the Pangaion hills on the coast of the *Aegean*.

The mountain range and its immediate terrain covered the northwestern portion of the ancient province of Kaválla. Where at its lower levels, Pangaios is rich in forest and streams and is surrounded by the fertile alluvial plain of the *Struma River Valley*. There, the mountains' dense vegetation and the seemingly unapproachable slopes at its higher altitude conceal centuries-old secrets in its depths and on its surface. On his passage through *Thrace*, in route to Pangaios, *Dionysus* was ill-received and insulted by an arrogant Thracian King who bitterly opposed his religion, *Lycurgus* (Lykourgos), son of Dryas, and King of the Edonians who lived beside the *Struma River*. When *Dionysus* and his expedition came upon the kingdom of *Lycurgus*, this impious king relished exhibiting his hubris, ordering the immediate and complete expulsion of Dionysus and his expedition from the territory of his kingdom. The irreverent king went so far as to actually attack *Dionysus* and his expedition as they sought to depart his realm.

Thracians were very skilled warriors, and in fleeing the land of the irreverent Thracian king, *Dionysus* and the members of his expedition were forced to fight desperately for their very lives as they retreated back towards the coast of the *Aegean Sea*. When they eventually turned fled the forces of *Lycurgus*. Some were struck down while others were captured; the rest escaped towards the sea, where they were given refuge by Nereus' daughter Thetis; *Dionysus* himself also escaped to the sea, where he, too, was received and given shelter by *Thetis*. The legends hold that later on, the captives were suddenly set free, and *Dionysus* avenged himself by causing *Lycurgus* to go mad, in which crazed state slew his wife and sons and cut off one (some say, both) of his legs, or according to others, actually made away with himself altogether.[140] Thus, according to the legends, *Dionysus* proved his eminence to the *Thracian kings* and reasserted reverence for the *House of Khronos*, an advent marking the beginning of a great change throughout much of *Thrace* thereafter.

That *Lycurgus* may have used 'religion' as a pretext to rally the hearts and minds of his warriors in their attack against *Dionysus* (and his expedition) is both plausible and probable; however, the most compelling motivation for his assault was a furtherance of his control over the valuable gold and silver deposits of Pangaios ('Mt. Pangeon,' the 'Transylvanian Alps').[cmxiii] Pangaios had quickly become one of the most valuable precious metal mining areas in *Neolithic Thrace*; there were gold and silver veins in both highlands and lowlands of the mountain. Early *Proto-Thracian* tribes exploited these riches by panning gold from the rivers, mining silver, and trading these precious metals for goods supplied by more refined colonies on the far southern coasts.

---

[140] Hyg. Fab. 132, 242

When *Lycurgus* and his warriors launched their unprovoked attack on *Dionysus*, he and his troupe fought desperately against the surprise onslaught and sought retreat towards the coast of the *Aegean*. *Dionysus* and most of the troupe eventually eluded the Edonians as they fell back to the coast, but in their haste, several members of the expedition were slain, and others were taken captive, including several of those from *Odinis* who had aided in guiding the expedition through the countryside. *Thetis*, daughter of *Nereus of Odinis*, a renowned benefactor of protection and benevolence in *Old Kavalla City,* met and aided the troupe in finding refuge. Her father, *Nereus,* was a Patron of *Old Kavalla,* from what was then his slowly vanishing dominion, in the *Plain of Odinis,* intersecting the present-day northern coast of *Thasso* and the southern coast of *Thrace*. Tradition says that a larger iteration of the present-day *Isle of Thassos,* then called *Odonis,* was attached to southern *Thrace* throughout much of the Neolithic, connected by the low-elevation coastal *Plain of Odinis,* intersecting the northern hills of the present-day *Isle of Thassos* to the south, and those of southern of *Thrace* to the north.

The *Plain of Odinis* was then far broader than the *Thassos Strait* that now separates the island from the mainland, particularly when sea levels were four hundred feet lower than at present. *Nereus'* dominion encompassed the entire low-elevation plain, from the northern highlands of *Odinis*, to what were then the more extensive southern coastal plains of southern *Thrace*. [cmxiv] His capital city was situated in the very heart of the *Plain of Odinis,* roughly five miles north of the present-day northern coast of *Thassos*.[cmxv] *Nereus'* sunken capital city has recently been re-discovered (at a depth of 328 feet) off the southern coast of the present-day *Island of Thassos*.[cmxvi] A sunken quarry of the era has also recently been re-discovered just off the *Peninsula of Alyki,* on present-day *Thassos.* The word 'Alyki' translates literally as "the salt pans" (or 'salt marshes'); the ancient salt quarry is located at the southeastern most point of the *Cape of Thassos.* The Discovery of the capital city and ancient salt quarry provides a measure of dimensionality to the once prominence of the realm of the *Plain of Odinis* and *Nereus* as its Sovereign. It was with *Nereus*, in the broad fertile *Plain of Odinis,* that *Thetis* sought refuge for *Dionysus* and secreted him and his troupe.

It was *Nereus,* noted for his gift of prophecy and wisdom, who had heightened the alertness of his daughter, *Thetis,* to the prospect of conflict arising between *Dionysus* and *Lycurgus*. Known for his old age, kindliness, and trustworthy knowledge of the future, *Nereus* also advised the village leaders on the *Plain of Odinis,* who had long chaffed under the tyranny of the Edonian King, of prospects of mounting a meaningful campaign against *Lycurgus,* under the renown leadership of no less a figure than *Dionysus* (Ausar, Osiris, Zeus, Kush), of the House of Khronos. *Dionysus* summoned the balance of his security forces to the *Plain of Odinis,* where, with the aid of *Nereus,* he gathered a sizeable band of local warriors, redoubling his forces and forming a well-equipped army. After ample preparation and a survey of the terrain, *Dionysus* returned and launched a vicious counter-offensive against *Lycurgus* at the very heart of his kingdom.

When the two armies clashed, the arrows flew in such mass that they darkened the sky. However this time, it was now *Lycurgus* and the *Edonians* who fought desperately for their lives, as well as their kingdom, but alas, they faltered, fell back, and finally turned in headlong retreat. Thus did *Dionysus* overpower the *Edonians* and slay *Lycurgus*, the barbarian king most opposed to his undertakings. Nor was Lykourgos' fate unique; other *Thracian* tribes, such as the Proitides, Pentheus, Orpheus, and Minyades, also suffered severe punishment …for having allied with the fallen king of the Edonians. *Dionysus* then proceeded through *Thrace* largely unopposed. Though best known in later Greek mythology, long before the arrival of the authors of that mythology, *Dionysus* was known throughout the greater region as the bringer of peace, the rule of law, and the tenets of civilization.

In Thrace, he was revered and known as 'Eleutherios,' "the Liberator," and 'Liber Pater,' "the Free One," because he freed its people from ancient suppression and tyranny. The (misplaced) worship of *Dionysus* (Ausar, Osiris, Kush, Zeus) was first established in *Thrace*, from where it spread southward to Helicon, Parnassus, Thebes and eventually throughout Greece, Sicily, and Italy.[cmxvii] *Neolithic Thrace* was then covered with thick forest, fertile lands and valuable mineral deposits, particularly gold and silver, making it a desired and coveted possession; the spread of the repute of *Dionysus* only heightened the desire for its coveted territories by *Haides*... After proceeding through *Thrace* without meeting with further resistance, *Dionysus* (Ausar, Osiris, Kush, Zeus) returned to *Old Kavalla City,* where he rested and laid with *Thyia*, daughter of *Deucalion*, and, at length, as related by a later Greek poet, she became pregnant and bore *Dionysus* (Ausar, Osiris, Kush, Zeus) seventh son, *Macedon* (Makedon).[cmxviii]

It would be none other than *Macedon* (Makedon), son of *Dionysus* (Ausar, Osiris, Kush, Zeus) and *Thyia*, who would later conquer and appropriate the southern territories of *Thrace* and call this new kingdom 'Macedonia,' after himself. Thus, would ancient Macedonia be carved out from the southern territories of *Neolithic Thrace*. But for the expedition of *Dionysus,* notwithstanding all of his valor and accomplishment, he had nonetheless been unsuccessful in uniting the *Thracians* against *Haides*. When *Dionysus* (Ausar, Osiris, Kush, Zeus) informed the old colonists that time had arrived for his departure and return to *Khemet* (House of Khronos), and the eternal land of *Kush* (Kusha Dwipa), he promised he would send his second eldest son, *Hercules*, to aid in their efforts against *Haides*. But alas, for now, *Dionysus* intoned, his stay had been extended far beyond that envisioned, and the winter months were now upon them.

Northwesterly winds prevail in the *Aegean* for the most part during the winter, yet from the end of September to that of May, the winds alternate with south-westerly. Voyages during these months, when stormy conditions are frequent and daylight hours short, are best avoided; conditions were often bad enough to force vessels to layover in the islands for days, sometimes weeks, or even months. A direct course from the *Gulf of Kavala* would entail sailing mostly east southeasterly, sailing against the prevailing winter winds. *Ausar* (Osiris, Kush, Zeus, Dionysus) and the Captains of the *Armada* thus resolved that the ships would instead take the coastal route due east, between the shore and offshore islands of *Thrace,* to the coast of *Asia Minor,* from there to the northern coast of *Kanaan*. They planned to then proceed southward along the coast to *Sidon* and from there on to *Khemet*.

The coastal route would be more time-consuming than sailing directly over open water; ships traveling along the coast were put into convenient ports at night to avoid off-shore hazards; the length of such voyages often takes several times longer than direct routes during the sailing season, depending on the number and length of layovers. After having rounded the *Cape of Odinis* and departing the *Gulf of Kavala,* the first layover would be at a former colony on the coast of *Asia Minor* (the "Anatolian Peninsula"), in a valley in the northwest of the peninsula, just south of the ancient inland waterway known as the *"Hellespont"*. *Asia Minor* (Anatolia) was surrounded by seas on three sides; the ancient inland *Euxine Sea* in the north, the *Mediterranean Sea* in the south, and the *Aegean Sea* in the west.[cmxix] Peninsular *Asia Minor* juts out westward from the Asian continent, to within half a mile of Europe, with the narrow *Hellespont* strait separating *Europe* from *Asia*, as it connects the *Aegean Sea* to the *Sea of Marmara* (known anciently as the 'Propontis Sea').[cmxx]

Proto-Black Sea: The "Euxine Sea"

The much smaller Proto-Black Sea, the early ancient "Euxine Sea",' was connected to the Aegean by what was essentially an ancient river. With sea levels during much of the Neolithic too low (some 300 to 400 feet lower) for the two seas to interflow, the Hellespont's long, narrow, winding shape resembled more of a river than a strait. The ancient river connected the *Aegean* to the *Sea of Marmora* (known anciently as the '*Propontis Sea*'), which in turn connected to the *Euxine Sea*. During most of antiquity, the *Sea of Marmora* separated *Thrace* and *Asia Minor and* formed (as it does now) an intermediate sea between the *Aegean* in the south and the *Euxine Sea* in the north. The waters of the *Sea of Marmora* through the *Hellespont*, as did the waters of the *Euxine Sea,* flowed through the narrow Strait, thus allowing ancient mariners access to the inland seas.[cmxxi]

The Hellespont, the Sea of Marmora, and the ancient Euxine Sea (the "Proto-Black Sea") are each steeped in ancient mythology. According to the ancient Greek poet Apollonius Rhodius, and the Latin poet Publius Vergilius Maro ('Virgil'), the Isle of Philyra, at the eastern end of what was then the southern coast of the Euxine Sea, was the hideaway where Khronos (Khem, Kham, Cham, Ham), in deceiving his wife Rhea, lay with Philyra, daughter of Okeanos; this in the days when Ausar (Osiris, Zeus, Kush, Dionysus) was still a child tended to in Dikteon cave on the Isle of Crete. Ancient legends and lore hold that Khronos and Philyra were surprised in the very act by Rhea, whereupon Khronos then leaped out of bed and galloped off on a long-maned stallion.[cmxxii]

The Isle of Philyra was also where Rhea is said to have purified Dionysus (Ausar, Osiris, Zeus, Kush) and taught him the mysteries.[cmxxiii] The Euxine Sea (Pontus Euxinus) was an inland sea (the 'Proto-Black Sea') enclosed by the Northern Caucasus Mountains on the north, the Southern Caucasus (or 'Transcaucasus') Mountains on the east; ancient Thrace on the west, and Asia Minor (Anatolia) on the south, with no outlet other than the Bosporus Thracius flowing between the Pontus Euxinus and the Propontis Sea (the "Sea of Marmora"). The main river in Thrace, the Istros River (the present-day Danube), flowed from the interior of Europe into the Pontus Euxinus; the Thracians settled on the coasts of the Euxine Sea, the Propontis Sea, and parts of the Hellespont.

The Hellespont and Sea of Marmora were familiar sea lanes for Atlatian ships plying the Euxine Sea as early as the middle of the Golden Age. These waters were thus not altogether unfamiliar to mariners of Atlatian derivation aboard the Armada. After rounding the Cape of Odinis, the Armada plied eastwardly, some distance from the coast of southern and eastern Thrace. The ships again deployed oars as they sailed near and around the southeastern tip of mainland Thrace, a peninsula extending southwesterly into the Aegean Sea, anciently known as the Gallipoli Peninsula, surrounded by the Bay of Melas on the west and the Propontis Sea and Hellespont on the east.[cmxxiv] Ships of the *Armada* used both sail and oar as they plied past the *Hellespont* toward the northwestern coast of *Asia Minor*.

The mountains beyond the *Hellespont,* extending along the southern coast of the *Sea of Marmora,* stretch eastward as part of a range extending above the southern coast of the *Euxine Sea* inhabited by the *Thracians,* known anciently as *Hieron Oros* (the 'Sacred Mountain'), which aids in compressing the winds through the *Hellespont*. The mountains further east, in *Asia Minor* proper, were rich in metals such as copper, tin, and silver, which, particularly after the discovery of metallurgy in *Atlatia,* led to early *Atlatian* exploration, mining and colonization, with several colonies established along the *Aegean* coast. Ancient mariners accustomed to these seas knew of the force of the winds through the *Hellespont*, which generally forced ships to stopover along the northwestern coast of *Asia Minor*, and the Captains of the ships of the Armada planned accordingly.

Early Ancient Troy

The port of destination for the *Armada* was a former *Atlatian* colony and maritime trading hub on the northwestern coast of *Asia Minor*. The original colony had been established as both a maritime layover and sentinel, guarding *Atlatian* colonial interest on the Anatolian peninsula, a colony known to later antiquity as ancient *Troy*. The founding and very location of *Troy* have long been subjects of much speculation and controversy; latter-day mythology suggests the ancient city was founded as late as 3,000 B.C. by *Ilus,* son of *Tros*, from whom the name *Troy* was purportedly derived. The son and successor of Ilus were *Laomedon*, who is said to have employed *Poseidon* to build the city walls, and then refused to pay him. The most ancient aspects of the latter-day mythology infer that earliest *Troy* was established not merely before the fall of *Atlatia,* which, by *Plato's* accord, occurred around 9,600 BC, but before *Poseidon* himself assumed the throne. This places the establishment and founding of the colony in the Megalithic age and suggests founding by none other than *Khronos* himself.

Alignment of the most ancient aspects of the pertinent myths suggests that it was during the building of *Troy* that *Khronos* (Khem, Kham, Ham) took interlude and lay with *Philyra,* daughter of the de-throned *Atlatian* king, *Ōkeanós,* on what would later become known as the '*Isle of Philyra,*' off the northwestern coast of *Asia Minor,* in the ancient *Euxine Sea*.[cmxxv] According to legend, the abrupt discovery of the illicit affair by *Rhea* prompted *Philyra,* in her shame, to flee the island for the *Pelasgian* ridges on the northwestern *Euxine Sea* coast of *Asia Minor,* where the old colonies prospered from mining in the mountains. There, at length, *Philyra* gave birth to a son, born of her union with Khronos, *Kheiron* (Chiron), half-brother of *Zeus* (Ausar, Osiris, Kush, Dionysus). The place of his birth, earliest *Phrygia,* was one of the most enigmatic provinces of *Asia Minor*, where the early *Phrygians* (the 'Proto-Phrygians') formed one of the most obscure nations in antiquity.

This was when *Pelasgians* were still, if not the dominant population, at least the most important in *Asia Minor*; *Phrygia* was among the earliest of descendent nations to supplant Atlatia on the peninsula. When the *Armada* arrived off the coast of *Troy, Phrygia* was the most prominent kingdom in *Asia Minor,* with its kingdoms under the sovereignty of *Kheiron.* Proto-Phrygians (like *Proto-Thracians*) were a mulatto race, descendent *Atlatians* (referred to as '*Pelasgians'*) intermingled with autochthones inhabiting the areas surrounding the old colonies on the coast and in the mountains, giving rise to several tribal groups and minor kingdoms along the seaboard, and in the *Pontic* highlands above the Euxine Sea (the "Proto-Black Sea").[cmxxvi] Earliest *Phrygia* took shape when *Ōkeanós,* a prominent but de-throned *Atlatian* king, brought together with many of his followers, re-settled on what became the *Phrygian* coast (also known as the "*Pelasgian* ridges"); forming the largest and most influential of the old colonies.

Ōkeanós astutely used his former *Atlatian* repute to unite several of the key tribal groups, forming the nucleus of the early kingdom. *Ōkeanós* was the eldest and had been most renowned of the early eastern *Atlatian* kings; an authority usurped when *Khronos* conjoined the eastern Atlas, bringing all of *Atlatia* under his sovereignty. The advent of Khronos's rise prompted *Ōkeanós* and his loyal subjects to depart *Atlatia,* re-settling first amongst the colonies that became earliest *Thrace,* where *Ōkeanós* prospered, and his wife, *Parthenope,* gave birth to their daughters, '*Europa*' and '*Thrace.*' The latter ('*Thrace*') was the eponymous princess (some say sorceress) whose name the ancient colonial province adopted, thereafter becoming known as the 'Land of Thrace.' [cmxxvii] But alas, the pre-eminence of *Khronos* pervaded even distant *Thrace,* compelling *Ōkeanós* and his compatriots to re-settle on the periphery of the empire, on the northwestern coast of Asia Minor, on the ancient *Euxine Sea*; along the "Pelasgian ridges,"

Khronos had so respected *Ōkeanós* that he was the only one of the 'elder kings' of early *Atlatia* permitted to re-establish his dominion in a new territory under a new dynasty; a task begun when *Ōkeanós* united several key *Proto-Phrygian* tribal groups and early kingdoms, forming the nucleus of earliest *Phrygia*. A task later completed by his grandson, *Kheiron*, who united the remaining kingdoms when the *Phrygians* and *Thracians* allied to defend against the *Atlatian* attempt to subdue their coasts. It was indeed the long-established and enduring affinity between the *Thracians* and *Phrygians*, in all things, but particularly overland and maritime trade, that allowed *Kheiron* to learn of the triumphs and travails of *Ausar* (Osiris, Kush, Zeus, Dionysus) in *Thrace*; an affinity that also allowed him to learn of the *Armada's* intent to layover at *Troy*, on their journey home. *Troy* was a *Phrygian* city in northwestern *Asia Minor*, in the ancient province, called the 'Troad'; the history of Troy is that of a wealthy maritime trade city, with a citadel on the *Aegean* coast, overlooking the *Dardanelles*, at the north-western extremity of *Asia Minor*.

Earliest *Troy* had been an *Atlatian* colony where its inhabitants dwelled in a tiny village built on a mound of 16 meters, enclosed by a nearly 300-foot wall with two towers surrounding several houses overlooking the Aegean. As the colony prospered, it grew into the first iteration of the old city, surrounded with fortified walls for protection against marauding barbarians, with larger houses constructed in rectangular shapes, on stone foundations, with sundried brick walls, built in the interior. Agriculture, animal husbandry, merchandise-manufacture, mining, and trade gave the old city a diverse economic base. After the fall of *Atlatia,* inhabitants of the old city, and indeed the greater region came to be known as "Pelasgians," a race whose history began with the *Atlatian* colonization of Europe and Asia Minor.[cmxxviii] Though the origin of the *Pelasgians* is somewhat shrouded in mystery, reports by ancient historians and the poets before them provide a measure of insight, nonetheless.

According to the poet Asius, Pelasg, the first king of the *Pelasgians,* was born in "Mountains with high ridges," in the territory called 'Gaia Melaina,' meaning the "Black Country,"[cmxxix] This was the land or "blessed country" of the Pelasgians in early Greek Mythology; a land that, according to Diodorus Siculus and the poet Hesiod, was "near the high Atlas Mountains," in the geographical region they knew as 'Gaea' or 'Terra'; ancient *Atlatia.*[cmxxx] Attracted by the gold, silver, and copper discovered in the mountains of Asia Minor, the *Pelasgians* were, for several centuries, the predominant population on the peninsula. However, *Pelasgian* preeminence had been in long decline by the time of the arrival of the *Armada* off the coast. A prominent but fragmenting descendant nation known as *Phrygia* (Frugia) inhabited the northwestern peninsula (to the Hellespont) when *Ausar* and his Armada arrived off the coast. Under the founding sovereignty of an aged *Ōkeanós,* the (Proto) *Phrygians* supplanted the ancestral *Pelasgians* across the entire western half of Asia Minor.

However, weakened by internal political strife, *Phrygia* limited itself to the northwestern half of the peninsula, which it struggled to expand beyond at the time of the arrival of *Ausar* and his Armada.[cmxxxi] The inhabitants of the earliest *Phrygia* (the "Proto-Phrygians") were a 'miscegenated' but still predominantly *Pelasgian* people, who, like most *Pelasgians* of the era in *Asia Minor,* were autochthones of the peninsula.[cmxxxii] Their fragile unity on the peninsula had been one forged by *Kheiron* under threat of *Atlatian* subjugation, a threat that had long passed by the time *Ausar* (Osiris, Kush, Zeus, Dionysus) and his *Armada* dropped anchor off the coast of the old colonial city known to later antiquity as *Troy*. It was precisely the subject of the "fragmentation of the old unity" that *Kheiron* (Chiron) had hoped to broach with *Ausar* (Osiris, Kush, Zeus, Dionysus), his half-brother, during *Ausar*'s sojourn at *Troy*. The unity of ancient *Phrygia* was fragmenting along the borders of new provincial federations, redefining *Phrygia* and placing <u>all</u> at greater risk.[cmxxxiii]

Above the old "*Pelasgian* ridges," on the northwestern *Euxine* coast of *Asia Minor*, was the emergent provincial federation known to later antiquity as '*Paphlagonia*,' where the ancient *City of Gangra* served as the capital and the seat of power. *Paphlagonia* was the oldest and most prominent of the provincial federations into which early *Phrygia* was fragmenting.[cmxxxiv] Its capital, the ancient *City of Gangra*, was the old colonial city originally founded by *Ōkeanós*, from where his grandson, *Kheiron*, half-brother of *Zeus* (Ausar, Osiris, Kush, Dionysus), ruled what had devolved into the most prominent of the provincial federations that had come to comprise ancient *Phrygia* when *Ausar* (Osiris, Kush, Zeus, Dionysus) and those from his Armada arrived at the gates of Troy.[cmxxxv] According to legend, after the fall of *Atlatia*, the royal lineage of the *House of Troy* began with *Teucer*, the eponymous king of the *Teucrians*, the first king of non-colonial *Troy* and the greater province known to later antiquity as '*Troas*.'[cmxxxvi]

Troas (or the 'Troad') was the historical name of the *Biga Peninsula* in northwestern Asia Minor (Anatolia), bounded by the Dardanelles to the northwest and the Aegean Sea to the west; separated from the rest of Asia Minor by the massif forming Mount Ida. *Teucer* was the son of the Patron *Scamandrus* and his wife Queen *Idaea*, an autochthon (local queen) whom later Greek mythology referred to as the 'queen nymph' of *Mount Ida*.[cmxxxvii] *Scamander* was the eldest son of *Ōkeanós* and *Tethys*, and thus the half-brother of *Kheiron*, a familial affinity that aided *Kheiron* in forging the alliance against the *Atlatian invasion*. In the Aeneid, Anchises recalls *Teucer* as being the Trojans' "first forefather," suggesting that he was considered the first figure to bear the bloodline of the Trojans as his father *Scamandrus* did not have such acclamations. Teucer was a first-generation (miscegenated) *Phrygian*, unlike his father *Scamandrus*, who was purely (descendant Atlatian) *Pelasgian*. In most myths mentioning King Teucer, he is described as being a distant ancestor of the Trojans.

Diodorus states that *Teucer* was "the first to rule as king over the land of Troy,'[cmxxxviii] And *Teucer* envisioned his role as a 'native king of *Phrygia*,' and in his opinion, portending a significantly different station than the 'quasi-vassal' relationship his father (*Scamander*) had with his grandfather (*Ōkeanós*). Nonetheless, at the behest of his father, the aging *Scamandrus*, and in respect for the preeminence and influence of *Paphlagonia* among the emergent provincial kingdoms of Phrygia, *Teucer* had hosted his cousin *Kheiron* in grand fashion, as the two awaited arrival of *Ausar* (Osiris, Kush, Zeus, Dionysus) and *Apollo*. The mariners, traders, merchants and others of the *Armada* were met with immediate accommodation as they entered the gates of the citadel, with *Ausar* and *Apollo* immediately invited and ushered to the palace, where they were warmly met and greeted by *Kheiron* and offered accommodation by *Scamandrus*. *Teucer* informed *Ausar* and *Apollo* of a small intimate feast planned that evening in their honor; after, of course, they had availed themselves of the opportunity to rest. He then inquired as to the length of their layover.

Upon unanimous advice of the ship's captains' of the *Armada*, responded *Ausar* (Osiris, Kush, Zeus, Dionysus), our stay will be but a brief one; a day and a night, perhaps two, at most. Then rest well, brother! Interjected *Kheiron*, for tonight we eat and drink; it has been ages since we last conversed, and we have much to share. Agreed, intoned Ausar as he and Apollo retired to separate accommodations within the palace. The feast that evening was festive but small and intimate, with but an intimate few in attendance; after a hearty meal, they drank wine late into the evening and spoke of the changes in their lives since the fall of Atlatia. *Ausar* and *Apollo* spoke of the rise of *Kush* and *Khemet* (House of Khronos) from the ashes of *Atlatia*, and *Scamander* and *Kheiron* told of the rise of *Phrygia*.

As the evening worn on, *Kheiron* finally broached the issue at heart, in his view ...the literal disintegration of (earliest) *Phrygia,* which once occupied the entire western half of Asia Minor; that is, before the emergence of the provincial federations, now re-shaping and weakening the political landscape. Under the wisdom of *Ōkeanós,* the land that became *Phrygia* grew and prospered to its fullest extent; that is, before the rot of disintegration began to eat away at its very core and vitality, intoned *Kheiron*, with a tinge of regret in his voice. Appears we are the victims of our own success, he continued; the alliances forged to fend off the aggressions of those corrupt kings of *Atlatia* also planted the seed of the new provincial federations, an advent now undermining our growth, prosperity and security. How then do the aspirations of the provincial kingdoms undermine, or indeed in any way inhibit growth or prosperity, or in any way endanger greater *Phrygia*? retorted *Teucer*. *Kheiron* refers to the *Phrygia* of old, interjected *Scamander;* the *Phrygia* first ruled by the patriarch, *Ōkeanós,* and then the sons of *Ōkeanós,* just as *Khronos* and then the sons of *Khronos* had ruled *Atlatia.*

It is a time that I, too, a lament for, opined old *Scamander.* Just as *Khronos* had allotted the choice lands of *Atlatia* to his most worthy Sons, 'so too did *Ōkeanós* allot the fertile lands nurtured by the most prominent rivers of the peninsula to those of his Sons he deemed most worthy,' continued *Kheiron*. The prominent rivers flowing through the allotted lands were each named in honor of the sons appointed by *Ōkeanós,* signifying their sovereignty over the allotted lands. *Scamandrus* (Skamandros or Scamander), eldest of the three, was allotted the lands that would later become known as Troas 'the Troad' (the historical name of the Biga peninsula), bounded by the *Dardanelles* to the northwest and the *Aegean Sea* to the west; separated from the rest of *Asia Minor* by the massif forming Mount Ida. The *River Skamandros*, which received its name from its sovereign, was the largest river on the plain of *Troy;* its headwaters rose in the foothills of Mount Ida, from where it flowed across the plain beneath the old port city of Troy to its mouth near the entrance of the Hellespont, north of the old port city.[cmxxxix]

Thus was Skamandrus (Skamandros, Scamander), the original patron of the lands that became known as the 'Troad' and the old colonial city that became known as *Troy*. The second eldest of the three, *Sangas* (Sangarius or Sangarios), was allotted the central-western lands nourished by the circuitous course of the Sakarya (Sangarius) River, the third longest river in *Asia Minor*.[cmxl] Because of the irregular mountain ranges in western Anatolia, the course of the river is unusually curved, flowing northwest, and then northeast, and then southeast, and then turning sharply to the north.[cmxli] The *River Sakarya* (Sangarius) then continues to the west and, after a wide curve, flows the north-northeast until it discharges into the *Euxine Sea*; accordingly, *Sangas* held prime territories in the northwestern heartland. *Meandrus* (Maiandros or Maeander), the youngest of the three, was allotted the fertile Maeander River Valley. The river, again receiving its name from its sovereign, rose in the highlands of southern *Phrygia* and was so celebrated in antiquity for its winding lower course that its very name, "Maeander," became proverbial.

The Roman Poet, Publius Ovidius (Ovid), compared its lower course to that of a labyrinth, a course which prompted the Latin Poet, Sextus Propertius (Propertius), to profess "the stream of the Maeandrus wanders deceptively over the *Phrygian Plain*, and itself conceals the direction of its flow." Nonetheless, the *River Maeander* provides a natural route through mountainous central western Anatolia, linking the interior of *Asia Minor* to the *Aegean* coast; accordingly, *Meandrus* held a prime position in the southwestern heartland.[cmxlii] But, in a twist of fate, interjected *Scamandrus*, it was his daughters, more than the sons to whom he entrusted so much, who were more attuned to the aspirations of *Ōkeanós,* and in many ways, were more like him than any of his sons.

Though in his latter days, he was viewed as a powerful but kindly old man, even then, Ōkeanós remained astute, ambitious, and clairvoyant, with a keen ability to execute the plans he fomented. Traits shared by the shrewd, cunning and calculating *Klymene* (Clymene), the daughter known to many as 'A'sia' (Asia), the eponymous Patron Mother of Asia Minor, whose name literally means 'Famous Might.'[cmxliii] She was seduced at an early age by *Phoebus,* son of *Hyperion* and *Theia,* for whom she bore a son, *Phaethon,* who met an early and untimely death, leaving her distraught, in despair and in the depths of sorrow and pain. [cmxliv] But to her credit, this was a transformative pain, interrupted *Kheiron,* a pain that somehow left her stronger and more resolute in the sense of mission she inherited from *Ōkeanós* (Oceanus).

Ōkeanós was the eldest son of *Ouranos* and *Gaia, Scamandrus* continued, the older brother of *Khronos* (Khem, Kham, Ham), and in many ways, he sought to *prove* to himself, if not to *Ouranos,* that *he*, rather than *Khronos,* had been better suited to guide the destiny of their great empire.[cmxlv] It was perhaps a sense of devotion to this that prompted *Klymene* (A'sia) to marry the *Atlatian King Iapetos* (Iapetus), by whom she bore her second son, the precocious and clever *Prometheus*, over whom she doted and bestowed all of her gifts of cunning, clairvoyance and wisdom. [cmxlvi]

The Prometheus Paradox

Prometheus was clever, always curious, even as a child, and as a young man came to personify intelligence and prudence, becoming increasingly calculative, even cunning; his very name is said to mean "forethought," a trait he inherited and shared with his grandfather, *Ōkeanós* (Oceanus).[cmxlvii] Like him, Prometheus became a great seer, always envisioning the future, preparing things for what might happen in the morrow, next week, next year, or centuries to come. His exceedingly proud parents, *Iapetos* and *Klymene,* were patrons of craftsmanship and early endowed Prometheus with skills of tool making, masonry, metallurgy, building, planning and architecture, leading him to become among the favorites and the very glimmer in the eye of Ōkeanós.[cmxlviii] It is said *Ōkeanós* (Oceanus) once admonished *Prometheus* "know yourself and adapt yourself to new ways," and *Prometheus,* in turn, seemingly channeling the very spirit of his grandfather, sought new ways to push the boundaries of empire to the *Pelasgian* frontier.[cmxlix]

It was actually *Ōkeanós* who removed *Prometheus* from the colonies and sent him to administer mining operations in eastern Asia Minor, beyond the east coast of the *Euxine Sea* ("Proto-Black Sea") and the ancient land of *Aea,* near the *Caucasus Mountains.* The land of *Aea,* known to later antiquity as *Kolchis* (Colchis), was on the then mysterious periphery of the *Pelasgian* world, deemed to be "at the furthest limits of sea and earth,' [cml] Aea (Kolchis, Colchis) was a land bounded by the Pontus Mountains on the southwest, the *Euxine Sea* on the west, as far as the river Corax; the Greater Caucasus Mountains on the north, and what would become the ancient land of Iberia, and the Lesser Caucasus Mountains on the east. Though mining was conducted in the mountains, *Prometheus* did not care to live in the highlands. He was intent on living amongst the autochthones of the region, on living amongst them and helping them, for his heart was saddened when he discovered how wretched an existence they lived. He found them living in caves and holes in the earth, shivering with cold because there was no warmth from fire, dying of starvation, hunted by wild beasts and by one another, the most miserable human existences he had seen.

The Legends

Prometheus gave the autochthones the gift of fire so that they might no longer fear the night eat uncooked food and transform their dark, damp caves into warm, hospitable shelters. According to the ancient Greek playwriter Aeschylus, who wrote (in paraphrase), "Men," said Prometheus, "had, in the beginning, the mind of a child, and I made them wise and gave them the power of thought. In the beginning, the things which they saw, they saw in vain, and what they heard, they did not hear. For a very long time, they confused all things, as the phantoms of some dreams are confused.

These men," continued Prometheus, "did not know how to build brick houses, exposed to sunlight; they did not know how to work the wood, but dwelt in underground places, as ants, hidden inside the dark womb of the caves; they had no sure sign, either for the beginning of winter or of spring, or summer, when the fruit ripens, but lived without any sort of knowledge until I taught them to know the rise and setting of the stars, which is a thing more difficult to remember; I invented the most useful sciences, the system of numbers, I found the way to combine letters, and how things can be memorized, this is the mother of all sciences.

I, Prometheus, first yoked the cattle, to be used for transport… and still, I and not another, discovered the sails so that the ships would be able to navigate on the sea… Moreover, when someone fell sick and had no cure and no way to live, and men died for lack of remedies, I taught them how to make useful medicines with which to protect themselves against all illnesses, and I taught them different ways to prophesy…. Finally, who could affirm to have discovered before me the things useful which are hidden under the earth, the copper, the iron, the silver and the gold… [cmli]

By the most ancient traditions of the autochthones of the region, Prometheus was representative of their enlightenment from their state of culture in the Stone Age to the epoch of metals and the evolution of more civilized forms of existence. Prometheus taught them to build dwellings in the light of the sun and how to use the power of animals. He introduced the sacred knowledge and art of metallurgy and disclosed many of the sacred secrets of nature, including the occult properties of plants to combat sickness and illnesses and open gateways to spiritual development [cmlii]

As the son of *Iapetus,* at the onset of his endeavors, *Prometheus* had requested permission from *Zeus* (Ausar, Osiris, Kush, Dionysus) at the Assembly at the *Temple of Poseidon* in *Atlatia* to give fire and many of the other gifts to the autochthones, so that they might have a little comfort through the long, dreary winter; a request, which, after debate and deliberation, brought near resounding reproach. *Prometheus* was a man of deepest understanding and prophetic or intuitive thinking; though dissatisfied with his reproach, he surely did not misunderstand the underlying prohibitions.

But *Prometheus* had set his heart on helping the autochthones and did not give up, and, little by little, he taught them a thousand things. Among the *autochthones,* he was known as the first *prophet* of his times, and in his hubris, he tried to impart, by the art of divination, the secrets of the future and fate. When discovered, in punishment for his transgressions, by proclamation of *Zeus* (Ausar, Osiris, Kush, Dionysus), the most astute Pelasgian genius of the era, *Prometheus*, was chained to the Caucasus Mountains.[cmliii]

"The pure irony," said old *Scamandrus* drily, "that we should now seek the aid of the *House of Khronos*, and indeed of you, in particular, *Ausar* (Osiris, Kush, Zeus, Dionysus), you who so bitterly bridled our brightest star" To which *Ausar* (Osiris, Kush, Zeus, Dionysus) retorted, "the offenses of *Prometheus* against the oath of the sacred *Mysteries* could not go unrequited. While it is true he sought and lobbied me, among others, to his cause, my argument then was as it is now, give them fire that they might warm their dwellings and learn to cook their food and eat like men. But forbid them the *Mysteries* that they might become strong, and wise like ourselves, and in time, become a threat to our kingdoms'". That *Prometheus* should be forever bound to defend the realm, your realm, against threats arising solely from his insolence and transgressions in the Caucasus,' is only fitting, asserted *Ausar*, rather pointedly. Nonetheless, this was an intrusion upon the autonomy originally granted *Ōkeanós* (Oceanus) by *Khronos* (Khem, Kham, Ham), retorted the aging *Scamandrus*.... An intrusion we could only view as a usurpation of that autonomy… an exhibition of *Poseidon's* sovereignty over *Ōkeanós* scorned old *Scamandrus*.

Let not your resentment distort your memory, father, interjected *Teucer*; the true nature of the transgressions of the not-so-prescient *Prometheus* demanded such intervention. "*Prometheus* had hoped to nurture vassal kingdoms among the autochthones of the Caucasus'," *Teucer* elucidated, "these, he envisioned, when added to the kingdoms of the realm, would render the *House of Ōkeanós*, in its dominion of the *Euxine Sea*, in every way the equal to the *House of Khronos*, in its dominion in the *Mediterranean Sea*. Instead, we now contend with the turmoil so aptly foreseen by *Ausar* in his rebuke of *Prometheus*, emphasized *Teucer;* these days, the accolades most granted the 'gifted' *Prometheus* are those that extol his bravery in defense of the realm or quash tribal uprisings, *Teucer* continued, *Prometheus* has had to undertake many battles …and has emerged victorious. The earliest of *Prometheus'* victories, however, were those aided by *Ōkeanós*, who gathered a significant army specifically to ensure the security of the realm.

Though the usurpation of his autonomy and the rebuke of *Prometheus* were wounds from which *Ōkeanós* would never quite recover, he duly recognized and began to prepare for the dangers portended by the impertinence of *Prometheus*. *Prometheus* had not only shown the autochthones how to build dwellings from stone, tame livestock to make them useful, and protect themselves from the storms of winter and the beasts of the woods; he also showed them how to mine for copper and iron and how to melt the ore and hammer it into shape, and fashion from it the tools …and weapons needed in war.[cmliv] Since the passing of the *Patriarch Ōkeanós* from this world, noted *Scamandrus*, the patriarchy that once held us together has all but dissolved, and with it, the unity of *Phrygia*. Each of the former provinces now vies for autonomy, save only *Paphlagonia,* whose throne has been inherited by the honorable *Kheiron*, who, if I may, seeks to hold the realm together; sentiments which I admittedly share.

The mighty *Red River* (known anciently as the 'Halys River') breaks through the *Pontic Mountains* and flows into the *Euxine Sea* (the 'Proto-Black Sea') on the northern Asia Minor seashore, and the coast of eastern *Paphlagonia*, began *Kheiron* as if to introduce a subject into the discussion; the river forms a large delta where it meets the sea, he continued, around which we now encounter vestiges of perhaps the largest of the autochthon kingdoms we have yet to encounter. It is a kingdom, or more aptly, a collection of kingdoms that have established sovereignty on the high plateau that is the source of the river, interjected old *Scamandrus*. The river has its source on the high plateau, in the *Red Mountains* (the 'Kızıl Mountains'), in north-central Asia Minor, from where it flows southwestward in a wide arc and then turns northward in a great crescent-shaped bend and flows through central Anatolia to where it breaks through the Pontic Mountains and flows into the *Euxine Sea* on the coast of *Paphlagonia*.

Inside the bend of the river are the kingdoms of the *(Hatti)* autochthones. *Scamandrus* then emphasized; the *River Halys* forms the western boundary of their kingdoms, while to the north, it separates the *Pelasgians* of *Cappadocia* from *Phrygia*.[cmlv] Expansions of these primitive kingdoms can also be attributed to the weakness of the kingdom of *Meandrus*, abruptly interjected *Teucer,* sovereignty further weakened by *Kelainos,* the bastard son of *Poseidon,* eponymous king of the *City of Kelainos* (also known as Celænæ), in the central-western highlands.[cmlvi] His city-state is located at the nexus of the *Maeander* and *Catarractes Rivers,* where the *Catarractes* rise in the main square of the city, and issue into the *Meander*. *Kelainos* is both king of the city and what has become the most recent emergent kingdoms into which *Phrygia* is fragmenting. Worst further, continued *Teucer*, in the southwest, opposite the *Isle of Rhodes,* is an emergent kingdom established by a late arriving Pelasgian king, and his followers; the eponymous *King Kar* (Car), from whom the land ("Karia') and its subjects (the 'Karians') now receive their name.[cmlvii cmlviii]

Early Ancient Karia (Caria)

Earliest *Karia* (Caria) arose south of the *Meander River*, bordered by the *Maeander* in the north and the *Dalaman River* in the south; a region intersected by low mountain chains extending out into the sea in long promontories, forming fertile, well-watered coastal valleys inland, and gulfs along the coast. *Karia* is frequently mentioned in ancient literature, though the antiquity of the *Karians* ('Carians') is still said to be largely unknown.[cmlix] Conventional historians purport that it is 'unclear' exactly when the Karians entered into history; however, it is perfectly clear that their earliest capital, the *City of Miletus*, was founded during the 'prehistoric era.' While evidence of the first settlement at *Miletus* has been made and remains inaccessible by the rise in sea level (and deposition of sediments from the Maeander), the first available evidence uncovered at the site is said to be from the Neolithic.[cmlx]

The legendary *Kar* (Car), founder of the capital *City of Miletus* and the kingdom of *Karia,* is also said to have also founded the ancient *City of Alabanda* on the *Marsyas River*, about twenty miles south of its confluence with the *Maeander River*, a city he named after his son *Alabandus*, by his wife *Callirhoe*, the daughter of *Meandrus* (Maeander, Mæander, Maiandros). Like their king, most of the ancient *Karians* (Carians) were themselves *Pelasgi* (descendent Atlatians); most lived in small towns or villages, united in a kind of provincial federation. Their economy was based on the lumber trade and boat building; the region's plentiful cedar and black pine forests contributed significantly to such crafts. The *Maeander River* flowed through *Karia* to enter the *Aegean Sea,* opposite the ancient *Karian* capital *City of Miletus*. *Miletus* was located on the western coast of peninsular Asia Minor, with the *Port of Miletus* situated at the mouth of the *Maeander River*.[cmlxi]

Ancient texts say there were shipyards at early Karian port cities such as Kaunos and Halicarnassus and that the resin and black mastic – the raw materials for tar used in boat building and repair – were among their most important export items. The *Karians* were masters of the sea but were just as comfortable in the mountains of the southwestern peninsula. Indeed their antiquity can be traced back to the Neolithic by drawings they inscribed on rocks in the Latmos Mountains in *Karia*. Because the mountains in Karia met the sea perpendicularly, the coastline, made up of peninsulas, bays and islands, prompted the seafaring Karians to live on both the mainland and on the numerous coast islands. Indeed, the *Karians* have rather quickly become formidable, observed old *Scamandrus,* but be not deluded by the wily machinations of *Meandrus* (Maeander, Mæander, Maiandros)… his seemingly passive form of cunning can leave one as bewildered as the course of the river that shares his name. In *Kelainos,* in the central-western highlands, *Scamandrus* noted, *Meandrus* is building bulwarks against the kingdoms of the *(Hattian)* autochthones on the central high plateau, while his son-in-law *Kar* (Car) build bulwarks in the southwest.

The Phrygian League: Old Phrygia

"For even the noble *Kheiron,"...* continued *Old Scamandrus*, "even he is now seeking to expand *Paphlagonia* eastward into the *Pontus Mountains*, towards *Aea ...* and it has been reported that this is to preserve his mantle and preeminence as the most prominent of the emergent kingdoms of *Old Phrygia",* asserted *Scamandrus*. To which *Kheiron* responded that "it is not the preservation of mantle or preeminence that I seek …however, that I seek preservation of the realm, is true… But of equal import, I seek not to abandon *Prometheus*, who remains true to his bond, and in this *Ausar* (Osiris, Kush, Zeus, Dionysus), you are in no small way involved," he continued, "it is your penance that binds *Prometheus* to the Caucasus,' and 'with the fall of *Atlatia...* and the *Assembly at the Temple of Poseidon,* it is only thee who can free him from his bond,'

It was not I, nor the *Assembly,* that bound *Prometheus* to the *Caucasus,'* retorted *Ausar*, but his own blind ambition; ambition heightened by a misplaced desire to build empire…. at any costs, even the sanctity of the *Mysteries*. The *unanimous* decree that he, by his own hand, had incurred an obligation to defend against that which he himself created was one that required both unanimities… and that *he* himself cast a vote. The epiphany that brought *Prometheus* to cast such a vote came during his brief sojourn in *Atlatia...* with the realization that *Khronos* had never actually sought to build an empire, but only to emulate the edifice of *Maat*, that aspect of *Amun* by which harmony, justice, and reciprocity bring order to that exists, as revealed in his contemplations... and this in the quest for his own divinity.

The enlightenment of *Prometheus* elucidated *Ausar* (Osiris, Kush, Zeus, Dionysus) came at the hands of the priests of *Amun,* from whom he sought advice on a resolution to his dilemma. Under their tutelage, he learned of the revelations of *'Amun'* and *'Maat,'* and of their concordance with the (earlier) revelations of *'Neth';* whom many early colonists conflated with *'Gaia'* (the *"Great Mother"*) and whom you in *Anatolia* have come to know as *'Cybele.'* The priest of *Amun* provided *Prometheus* with rare insight into the arduous path of *Seekers* (of divine wisdom), such as he, and they taught him of the immutable responsibilities that those *Seekers* who become accomplished *("Adepts")* assume as disciples and patricians of the sacred *Mysteries,* as they are revealed.

Prometheus learned that such enlightened *Adepts* acquire a degree of mastery over the creative energies which courses through our very Being, and indeed through all of Nature; a mastery that is the basis of the influence they attain over lesser minds… and that with such mastery, comes great responsibility. Such masters, either voluntarily or involuntarily, come to influence lesser developed minds that orbit about them, influencing their choices, beliefs, and often their very destinies. It is thus, *Prometheus* discovered, that the *burden* of the fate of such *altered* destinies attaches to that of the *Adept* who so altered those destinies... and that for such reasons, the *Mysteries* are concealed from the eyes of the uninitiated (and profane), to protect both *Adept* and *Laity* alike.

With the realization that the *altered* destinies of those he so influenced would, in equal measure, burden the course of his own destiny, *Prometheus* came to see that "true justice" is *redemptive* rather than *punitive* … and, as he further surmised, and later experienced, the *true* purpose of the tribunal (at the *Temple of Poseidon*) was to deduce a path for that redemption. The 'binding' of *Prometheus* to the highest peaks of the *Caucasus'* was symbolic of the arduous dual path of this redemption. He was tasked, on the one hand, to defend against that which he himself created, and on the other, the more daunting task of *mutual liberation* by inuring spiritual growth and reverence in those souls over whom he so influenced; that they might become worthily and better able to use rather than abuse the aspects of the *Mysteries* to which they have been privy.

'And thus, you *should* not… and indeed *must* not, abandon *Prometheus,*' cautioned *Ausar* (Osiris, Kush, Zeus, Dionysus), 'for it is the augmented weight of *his* fate… a fate so deftly pervaded and influenced by the *Patriarch Ōkeanós*… in silent witness and to the benefit of *you,* the *inheritors* of his empire… that now burdens the very providence of *Old Phrygia*… and in many ways *your own* destinies'. 'How then are we to do this,' inquired *Scamandrus*… 'when each of the emergent kingdoms seeks his own autonomy and direction and celebrates none but his own sovereignty?' 'By respecting and honoring that sovereignty,' responded *Apollo*… 'and in so doing you will find a different and new form of unity possible.'

'Is this then the unity you infer when you speak of the rise of your *"Ma Confederation"* rising from the ashes of *Atlatia,*' inquired old *Scamandrus*? 'It is, retorted' *Apollo*, as he further explained…. 'yours' would be a confederation of the emergent provincial kingdoms within the old empire encompassing *Phrygia;* these would be joined with the *City-State of Kelainos* (Kelainai, Celænæ), and the *Kingdom of Karia*, to form what one might call the '*Phrygian League;* with homage to *Old Phrygia,*' connoted *Apollo*. 'A formally constituted body,' he continued, 'governed by a council representing each of the constituent kingdoms; this led by a viceroy bound and dedicated to the individual and collective security and prosperity of the League and its constituent kingdoms,' concluded *Apollo*, emphasizing his final point.

'A unique and novel proposition,' asserted *Kheiron*, 'one most certainly worthy of consideration,' he continued, 'but much has come to pass since the passing of the *Ōkeanós,* and there is now much suspicion, with only guarded cordiality at best, between those who would be the constituents of such a "League," A point on which *Scamandrus* was inclined to concur, noting that… it would require a gifted and adept hand to craft such an alliance… abilities not beyond those of noble *Kheiron* nor *Meandrus,* he continued… but the growing competition and creeping suspicions between these kingdoms surely forebodes, and would most undoubtedly preclude the success of any such undertaking. And yet, inquired *Ausar* (Osiris, Kush, Zeus, Dionysus), can you afford not to at least put forth an effort?

We cannot respond *to Kheiron.* Yet… be that as it may, interjected *Teucer*, emphasizing his point… while it is clear how such an alliance might *allay* the fears and suspicions that weaken us individually and collectively… and further, how such an alliance might aid, and indeed *enhance* (inter-regional) trade and commerce, and indeed prosperity for each and all, he continued… but what I fail to see is how such a 'League' would any way add to our individual or collective security… or that of poor *Prometheus* in the distant *Caucasus Mountains* …that is without usurping our respective sovereignties,' he surmised. This is somewhat beyond a 'zero-sum proposition,' *Teucer* tactfully replied to *Apollo*… each provincial kingdom would allot and commit a fifth of its forces and resources towards all collective military efforts and endeavors.

'This would require the aid and adeptness of one such as <u>thee</u> *Ausar* (Osiris, Kush, Zeus, Dionysus), that is, if we are to hold any possibility of success with such an undertaking,' stated old *Scamandrus*… 'Even if merely on an interim base, quickly added *Kheiron*… 'merely enough time to form and launch such an alliance,' he then further added. 'My sojourn thus far in these, the old provinces of the northern seas, has been far longer planned… as was the expedition that preceded it,' *Ausar* responded rather directly… 'Affairs of equal merit surely awaited my attention in *Khemet* ('House of Khronos') and the vast lands of *Kush* ('Kusha Dwipa'); for these reasons, I must personally decline and aptly express confidence in your abilities and resolve to accomplish that which you must.'

What say you, *Apollo*, inquired *Kheiron?*... the *sons* of *Ōkeanós* mistrust *me* as an *'illegitimate'* heir to the throne... and the *Pelasgians,* while descendent *Pelasgians,* such as the *Karians*, are suspicious, to greater and lesser degree, of both *Meandrus* and *I* ...as mere sons of *Ōkeanós* seeking to reassert the prominence of his old empire. However, your words *Apollo* will have the resonance of objectivity ...and *all* revere and will give homage to a legitimate son of the *House of Khronos,* such as thee.... What say you, *Ausar,* further inquired *Kheiron.* I say the dawn approaches shortly... and we have had a long journey and consumed much wine... and we are in need of rest as a full day approaches. Yes, concurred *Apollo*... we *should* rest... however, I will give your proposition due consideration ...let us discuss it in the morrow.

Yes, of course, responded old *Scamandrus.* Forgive our rudeness ... your accommodations await; someone will show you the way immediately. Let us reconvene at the royal residence in 'the City' for evening meal, suggested *Teucer* ...your ships may re-supply with fresh water up-river 'We have but a few hours before dawn'... noted *Ausar* (Osiris, Zeus, Kush, Dionysus), 'if we are to move our vessels up-river, we should commence at first light...' noting further that 'we shall require stable anchorage and ample room to turn our vessels' Indeed agreed on *Teucer,* advising that 'countervailing winds, compressed by *Hieron Oros* (the 'Sacred Mountain') sweep southward through the *Hellespont*... these winds are channeled through the corridors of the river valley, and shall be at your back... allowing your ships sail up-river.

'Your vessels appear heavily-ladened,' *Teucer* observed, advising that 'they may thus take time to navigate through the winding, narrow course up-river, where you will find stable anchorage at the Cove along the western shore below the City.' 'The Cove is just below where the *River Akçin* joins the *River Scamandrus*... where the converging currents of the two rivers provide a measure of shelter for ships anchored within the Cove'... adding that 'the *River Akçin* flows through a part of the City, allowing entrance and direct trade by small craft.' Adding further 'that the *River Akçin* was a principal tributary of the *River Scamander'*... and that 'the waters of these rivers are apt and pristine'... and 'the ships of your *Armada* may easily re-fill at will'... concluding that 'the Cove allows ample room, and the currents of the river will aid in the turning of your vessels.'

Though most archaeologists agree that the site at 'Hisarlik,' nearest the old Aegean coast, with its many ancient layers, was the original Troy, 'Hisarlik' actually means "Place of Fortresses," and indeed, was a fortress, not a city, but a fortress, a 'citadel.'[cmlxii] Albeit with a surrounding settlement, Hisarlik was a citadel to guard the entrance to the *Scamander River Valley,* where the true inland *City of Troy* was located. The *Citadel at Hisarlik* was actually part of the first line of defenses of a Trojan heartland that stretched much further inland than is generally appreciated; a heartland that encompassed much of the *Scamander River Valley* with its broad, fertile alluvial plains (the legendary 'Trojan Plain'). [cmlxiii] The *Citadel at Hisarlik* was built at the mouth of the river to assert control over both its entrance and trade from the seas. [cmlxiv]

The main *Trojan* territory was behind a defensive line of hills and was far larger and more extensive than generally granted, with the ancient site of the present-day *City of Ezine* as its capital, the true inland *City of Troy*. East of ancient *Ezine* was yet another citadel. This one was posted to guard the overland mountain pass into Trojan territory; it was known as '*Hisaralan,*' which means "Area of the Fortress," Each of the citadels was heavily fortified; however, the local population, who were farmers. Lived in surrounding villages and took refuge in the citadel only in times of danger. The citadels were small, not more than 300 feet in diameter, enclosed by massive walls with gateways and flanking towers, and contained perhaps 20 rectangular houses, a style of narrow, long-room houses in which the residential dwellings shared lateral walls with their neighbors, and surrounded interior courtyards.

Kingdom of Troas: Old Troy

The old inland *City of Troy* was the capital of the *Kingdom of Troas*, the western-most of the provincial kingdoms of the old empire, formed on the large, fertile Troas Sub-Peninsula (the 'Troad') located at the north-western extent of peninsular Asia Minor (Anatolia).[cmlxv] The *Troad* ("Troas") is separated from the rest of *Asia Minor* by the majestic *Mount Ida*, which rises in the northwest of the Sub-Peninsula, roughly twenty miles southeast of *Troy*. The headwaters of the *River Scamander,* anciently far larger than its frail present-day remnant, rose on the northern slopes of *Mount Ida*, from where it descended through the foothills, windings its way westward through the upper river valley, across the plain and mid-river valley, beneath the city, and through the winding, narrow corridor of hills leading to its mouth, near the entrance to the *Hellespont*.

Ancient mariners and ships traveling up the *River Scamander* from the *Aegean* to trade directly with the merchants and traders of the inland port *City of Troy* had to navigate through a narrow pass and winding ridge of hills along the river's course, each providing natural defenses for the inland city. Ships navigating upriver through the narrow, winding course of hills and ridges suddenly found that the river broadened, and the landscape opened into a large, hidden river valley, with the river flowing beneath the ancient inland port city. The *Scamander River Valley* culture of *Troy* was one that included large cities, such as the inland port *City of Troy* itself, and mid-size towns or small cities and small-scale townships and villages along the corridor of the river. The ancient cities, towns and villages along the course of the *Scamander River* and its tributaries were inter-connected by small roads, some paralleling the course of the river, while others inter-connected with overland trade routes.

Noting that 'it will take time for you to collect your crews and prepare your ships for the voyage upriver,' *Old Scamandrus* then advised *Ausar* and *Apollo* that 'we shall depart by small craft just after dawn, allowing ample time to prepare and await your arrival at the castle'; further advising the two that 'there will be a boat awaiting your anchorage in the inland bay; they will ferry you into the city, and guide you to the castle …where we shall have a bountiful feast, with aged libation, prepared for your consumption,' he proudly boasted. The crews, security forces, merchants and ships of the *Armada* were near full preparation the following morning when *Apollo* found *Ausar* alone, awaiting the arrival of the Captains of the two ships accompanying his flagship, whom he had summoned for consultation regarding the next leg of their voyage; an opportunity *Apollo* seized to apprise *Ausar* of his decision to accept the overture presented by *Kheiron* and *Scamandrus'…* to lead the *Phrygian League*; an acceptance he cautioned that should be conditioned upon concurrence by the six royal houses.

'Nearly half of the royal houses are already of the accord,' noted *Apollo* … 'and two of the remaining four, *Kelainos* of the royal house at the *City State of Kelainos* (Kelainai, Celænæ), in the central-western highlands, and *Kar* (Car) of the royal house at the *Karian* capital *City of Miletus*, at the mouth of the *Maeander River* on the Anatolian west coast, are persons of whom we are each familiar… and held in high regard'. "I have known *Kelainos* since youth, continued *Apollo*… when accompanying *Poseidon* to the colonies of *Anatolia* during the reign of *Khronos* (Khem, Kham, Ham),' 'As for *Kar* (Car),' he noted, he 'holds *you* Ausar (Osiris, Kush, Zeus, Dionysus) in highest reverence… which is of particular importance,' *Apollo* emphasized… 'particularly given proximity of the *Isle of Kos,* to what is now the coast of *Karia.'* "

As the two of us are well aware but rarely speak of *Ausar* (Osiris, Kush, Zeus, Dionysus),' *Apollo* mused …we are each tacitly comforted in the thought that my mother *Leto* has been and remains fairly safe and secure nestled in place of her birth, on the *Isle of Kos* …this both during and after the foregone fall of our beloved *Atlatia*. But now,' *Apollo* surmised… 'the rise of *Karia* and the portending political instability between the other emergent kingdoms of western *Anatolia* surely threatens that safety and security. Yet, *Apollo* continued, in my *meditations,* it feels as if destiny itself has ushered me to this juncture. 'None know better than thee how I have *long* been in search of my *own* path *Ausar*, … my *own* destiny, added *Apollo*… and what could be more evident, more compelling than that with which I am now presented,' he queried?

Ausar (Osiris, Kush, Zeus, Dionysus) observed and responded that 'there seems to be a new sense of resolve and prescience about you, *Apollo,'* describing it as a glows about you that I have not witnessed before. 'You speak of your *meditations*, alluding to that that you envision, and though time does not now permit, as the Captains of each vessel are now aboard and I must take leave, I would most be interested in hearing of your vision at a later time, perhaps on the voyage to the port city. Let us then discuss the future you hope to affect here,' decreed *Ausar*. 'As you wish,' *Apollo* responded, with *Ausar* imparting as he left to meet with the *Captains* of the *Armada,* 'there is much we need to discuss, *Apollo*, …yet, as always, know that you have my unwavering support'.

In a meeting with the *Captains* of the Armada*, Ausar* found each in agreement that 'the ships should get underway forthwith, while the coastal winds remained abated … lest the heavily laden vessels run risks of again being scattered along the coasts of off-shore islands or the mainland. 'Once stronger winds re-ensue,' they cautioned, 'the ships would again struggle to maintain maneuverability'… Acknowledging this, *Ausar* advised they await *Apollo* 'for whom they may establish a trading colony in *Troas,'* and that 'in such eventuality a portion of the cargo aboard each vessel would be committed to the venture, lessening freight-loads, and improving maneuverability of the ships, however,' he cautioned… 'Should Apollo be unable to come to terms on the colony… let all hands be prepared to get underway at first dawn, in the morrow'.

With this*, Ausar* instructed the *Captains* of the *Armada* to complete all preparation to 'raise anchor, hoist sail, and get underway… while winds were apt and favorable to sail upriver, where they would find anchorage at (ancient Ezine) the inland port *City of Troy.'* Countervailing winds in the *Aegean* have channeled up the corridor of the river valley, allowing the heavily laden ships of the Armada to hoist their sails and slowly lumber upriver in convoy formation as they made their way through the narrow, winding pass of hills and ridges on the course between the lower and middle river valley. The winds channeled inland from the *Aegean* were compressed in the narrow corridor between the lower and middle valley, providing the ships greater thrust and speed as they sailed upriver, against the current, into the broad, fertile, middle river valley.

Ausar and *Apollo* stood in silence, taking in the view from the bow of the flagship as it led the other two ships of *Armada*, in convoy formation, through and beyond the narrow corridor of hills and ridges into the broad, lush, middle river valley, which opens suddenly and abruptly, with the ancient *Scamander River* widening, and its current slowing, as if to announce a calm, serenity that seemed to blanket the large, green interior alluvial plain that comprised the ancient middle valley. Taking in the full configuration of the lower and middle river valleys, *Ausar* (Osiris, Zeus, Kush, Dionysus) and *Apollo* must surely have found it reminiscent of the other river valleys around which prominent high civilizations were flourishing across much of the expanse of Africa and Asia of the era.

'The *River Scamander* flows westward to the *Aegean* coast, just east of *Cape Sigeum*, the promontory projecting into the southern entrance of the narrow sea corridor (the "Hellespont") bridging the *Aegean Sea* and the *Euxine Sea*,' observed *Apollo*... '*Cape Sigeum* commands the ridge between the *Aegean Sea* and the *River Scamander*,' he continued... 'giving Troy near full control of maritime transport through the corridor.' [cmlxvi] '*The Citadel of Troy* nearest the *Aegean* coast is only a few miles from the Hellespont. *Apollo* noted, 'giving the inland port *City of Troy* a clear maritime advantage in trade passing transiting the corridor between the *Mediterranean* and the *Euxine Sea* (the Greek '*Pontus Euxinus*'; the '*Proto-Black Sea*').'

For ancient mariners, it was common knowledge that the *Hellespont* was one of the most difficult and potentially dangerous waterways in the world; currents produced by the *Aegean Sea*, the *Sea of Marmara* and the *Euxine Sea* were such that ships under sail had to wait at anchorage for the right conditions before entering the strait. The strait is roughly thirty-eight miles long and only three-quarters of a mile to four miles wide, which is a very narrow strait for ships to sail, not to mention ensuing difficulties and danger should a ship need to be turned around at one of the narrowest points along the strait. Additionally, ships entering the strait from the *Aegean Sea* had to wait on the *Isle of Tenedos*, an island controlled by the *City of Troy*, until winds were favorable enough for the ships to enter the strait.

In the age of *Khronos* (Khem, Kham, Ham), the colony that would become *Troy* stood sentinel over the corridor and sea lanes between the *Aegean* and *Euxine Seas*. 'The *Hellespont*, the *Sea of Marmara*, and the *Bosporus* link the *Aegean* and *Euxine Seas*,' noted *Apollo*, 'and it is precisely the strategic position of *Troy* at the entrance of the *Hellespont* that renders it central to fomenting the '*Phrygian League*' of which we aspire, *Apollo* asserted... 'without its maritime centrality '*Kheiron* of *Paphlagonia* and *Sangas* of the *Sakarya River Valley* are each all but confined to the basin of the *Euxine Sea*, whilst *Meandrus* of the *Maeander River Valley*, *Kelainos* of the Central-Western Highlands, and *Kar* of the maritime *Karians* in the southwest are each confined to the basins of the lower seas,' he concluded.

'Troy itself should thus be central to uniting the provincial kingdoms in the '*League*' we seek to foster,' asserted *Apollo*; 'not unlike the constituent kingdoms of *Kush* and the *Maa Confederation*, the incentive to coalesce shall be that of greater security, prosperity, and influence over the broader region. Sovereigns of the provincial kingdoms will surely have interest in such... and the prudent among them will seek not to be excluded,' surmised *Apollo*. "And what of Leto,' inquired *Ausar*. 'Earlier, you spoke of our mutual concern for her unabiding security, particularly amidst the rise of *Kar* and *Karia*... by your words "destiny itself has ushered you to this juncture," recounted *Ausar*... "And though I too sense your destiny is affixed to these lands,' *Ausar* continued, 'share with me your vision of what this destiny portends,'

'What greater *security* for Leto,' *Ausar* further inquired, 'and of what *compensate* for *you*, Apollo'? "It is but *one* destiny," *Apollo* replied, 'a destiny guided by *Ma'at* and formed by the *Reciprocity* to which the *Priest of Amun* so often alludes. So let thy mind be at peace, **Ausar**,' he reassured; 'it has not escaped me that this is an undertaking of significant proportion,' he continued, 'I recognize that it is apt that one be *vested* in the fruits of such an endeavor, a *vesting* I shall duly require in the form of autonomy and sovereignty for the lands adjacent to *Kos* and the (Dodecanese) islands, off the southwestern coast (of Asia Minor), and of this, I envision full accord, *Apollo* predicted... 'an accord shaped by that to be gained by each of the provincial sovereigns, and their kingdoms.'

Early Ancient Lykia

'It is in the land that would become (*Lykia*) the seventh kingdom in the League we seek to foster, that *Leto* will find security... and indeed be held in reverence,' asserted *Apollo*. 'It is thus that binds my destiny,' he explained...' Ausar, you once counseled that *enlightenment* is gained by one's participation in creation, and though its course is arduous, you advised, *enlightenment* so attained is the true path to *deification*, and union with *Amun*. 'You informed me that once my delusions had fallen away, the ensuing clarity would reveal these truths... and my destiny,' *Apollo* recalled. 'Well, my delusions have fallen away, *Ausar*, and what has been revealed is the destiny before me. How can I do less than fully embrace this destiny and, in so doing, seek to participate in the unfolding of creation?' *Apollo* surmised.

'We approach the embayment below the inland port city... where it is said the *Armada* will find safe anchorage,' interjected *Ausar*, 'before we take leave, you should know of our preparation on your behalf,' *Ausar* continued; 'for the autonomy you shall surely require, the captains and merchants of the *Armada* have been instructed that should you reach an accord, we, that is *you*, shall head a trading settlement here... representing the interest of *Kanaan*, *Khemet* (the 'House of Khronos'), and *Kush* (Kusha Dwipa) ... we would invest up to one-fifth of the cargo aboard each vessel toward the venture... which will also better enabling our ships to ply the open seas on our voyage home, *Ausar* opined. 'However, should you not reach accord... all have been instructed that the *Armada* shall set sail at first dawn.'

'Presuming an accord is reached,' *Ausar* continued, 'there will be many merchants in the Armada who will seek to join the venture; there will also be those among the security forces, those who have been at your side since earliest *Kush*,' he further informed. 'It appears Ausar,' *Apollo* interjected, half-jokingly, 'that you have given this as much thought as I'...' but let us not project *too* much into this until we can again take the measure of the hearts of the *Phrygians*,' he cautioned. 'Indeed, you have learned well,' replied *Ausar*. 'The ships have lowered their masts and dropped anchor,' he continued, 'and, as word spreads, those aboard the Armada will await the outcome of our meeting... so let us proceed without haste... 'the craft that will ferry us into the city awaits our departure alongside the flagship so let us gather what we must and disembark,' *Ausar* advised.

The *Scamander River* of the era was broader, deeper, and far more robust than at present, with a strong current, often overflowing its banks; much of the middle river valley was indeed shaped by the overflowing of the river during the early Holocene. The Holocene evolution of the river and the middle valley, in particular, was evident from the alluvium' (interpreted as an indicator of extensive flooding occurring at regular intervals) deposited across the flat basin that defined much of the middle valley and aided in the valley's famed fertility during Neolithic. The ships of the *Armada* were anchored in an inland embayment on the west bank of the river, just below (or north) of where the River Scamander receives the smaller Akçin River, a principal tributary of the Scamander that flowed through (*Ezine Town*) the old inland *Port City of Troy*.[cmlxvii]

The inland bay was just below the nexus of the two rivers, where silting-up of an alluvial fan from deposits drained down from the highlands during the early Holocene created a natural breakwater above the embayment, forming a semi-sheltered inland harbor (that has since been filled with alluvial material), just below where the Scamander receives the Akçin.[cmlxviii] Reaching the interior of the old city from the inland harbor required sailing up the Akçin River against the current, mostly by small craft. Prompted by the waning of the onshore winds, which permit the craft to sail up-river into the interior of the city, *Ausar* and *Apollo* quickly disembarked their ship and were ferried up the Akçin to rendezvous with the guide whom they were advised would direct them to the castle.

To their surprise, they were met and received by none other than *Scamandrus* himself. Old *Ezine Town,* the inland *Port City of Troy*, was most anciently called '*Sigeia*' (Sigia), according to Strabo.[cmlxix] Though the site of the ancient inland port city remains largely unexcavated, at its height, it sprawled over an estimated 990 acres. Successive occupations of the ancient port city during the early historical era have given the city a succession of historical names, depending upon the timeframe of reference; as late as the dawn of the Christian era, during the time of St. Paul, the ancient port city was known as *Alexandria-Troas*.[cmlxx] Ruins surround every aspect of the old port city; *Ezine Town* marks the heart of the old city, with its rough stone circuit walls anchoring the ancient inland port situated on the maritime and overland trade routes between two continents. The Castle was at the village center, the highest point of the ancient site, offering a panoramic view of the inland port city. Like many villages of the era, it was actually the Castle that was surrounded by a circuit of stone walls.

The Castle and its walls were built to provide protection for the inhabitants during times of danger; remains of the old ramparts attest to the importance of the ancient walls. Like the Citadels, old *Ezine Town* contained a style of narrow, long-room, rectangular houses in which dwellings shared lateral walls and surrounded interior courtyards, creating a network of narrow corridors leading to the main avenues to the Castle. The trek through the surrounding townships to the interior village and the Castle availed the wily *Old Scamandrus* of the self-contrived opportunity to confess his enthusiasm for 'the prospect of fomenting a "League" such as that envisioned by *Apollo*... a *Phrygian League* virtually rising from the ashes of the *Old Empire,*' he mused, 'an apt resolution for the increasingly disparate kingdoms that have torn the loyal lands of the Old Empire asunder.' 'These are lands of immense wealth and power,' boasted *Old Scamandrus*, 'wealth that once attracted the attention of *even* the mighty kings of *Atlatia*,' he recounted, but power now sadly diminished by the discord amongst the emergent kingdoms of the realm, a discord that threatens the security and prosperity of all.

'Though, as Ausar eluded, it is certainly within our abilities to foster such a League of our own accord,' *Scamandrus* acknowledged, '*your* leadership in such an endeavor Apollo would far better portend its success, in that it would be emblematic of the re-uniting of two of the greatest houses of *Atlatia,* the *Houses of Khronos* and *Ōkeanós,*' he opined. 'The influence and allure of such a *League* will capture the imagination of the provincial sovereigns,' he surmised. 'You are thus presented with a unique dilemma Apollo,' the wily *Old Scamandrus* deduced, 'surely a grand kingdom awaits you in *Khemet* and the *House of Khronos.*' 'And with due respect to honorable Ausar, he continued, 'in countermeasure, I submit that as *Viceroy* of the *League* you envision, like your *father*, you *too* shall be *above* kings and kingdoms.'

'I seek not to be *above* kings or kingdoms,' replied *Apollo* in retort. 'Yet *here* you shall be at the very nexus of the two great surviving *Houses* of *Atlatia*,' interjected *Scamandus*... "Indeed, you may very well be the *catalyst* for renewed relations between our two great houses," he surmised. 'The words you speak have the resonance of truth, honorable Scamandus,' replied *Apollo,* and though I too can envision a grand destiny here, I seek not to be *above* the kings and kingdoms, but to stand and walk among them... representing a *realm* and *vested* interest of my own, he informed... 'a *seventh* kingdom in the *League* we seek to foster. "Then you have decided to stay and join us," prompted *Old Scamandus*. 'There is much to discuss,' *Apollo* responded, 'I do indeed have a proposition for your consideration, as well as that of *Kheiron* and *Teucer.*'

'Ahead appears to be the entrance of the Castle,' interjected *Ausar*; our journey has been short but trying,' he noted. 'Yes, yes, of course,' responded and concurred *Scamandus*... 'we arrive a bit earlier than anticipated, but I assure you a bountiful feast with libation shall be prepared for our ample consumption shortly in the *grand hall*,' he advised. While we await, two of the loveliest of the *Hand Maddens* of the Castle will receive you at the entrance as we approach... and show you each to accommodations where you may *rest* and *refresh*,' suggested wily *Old Scamandus*, 'before joining us in the *grand hall* ... shall we say in about an hour,' he inquired? 'The *Hand Maddens* will show you the way to the *grand hall*,' he then advised and, by that, took his leave, leaving *Ausar* and *Apollo* in the attentive hands of his seductive *Hand Maddens*.

After rejoining their hosts, *Scamandus* and *Teucer* (of *Troas* and *Troy*), together with *Kheiron* (of *Paphlagonia*) in the *grand hall*, where they partook in the long-awaited feast, and consumed many libations, prompted by *Kheiron*, the discussion returned to the subject of the '*Phrygian League*' envisioned by *Apollo*. 'Scamandus informs us that you have formulated a proposition for our consideration Apollo, *Kheiron* began, 'a proposition under which you might agree to lead our campaign to foster the *League* you so aptly envision,' he queried. 'Any such undertaking should require concurrence by a majority of the six royal houses,' noted Apollo rather abruptly... 'Despite our enthusiasm,' he continued, 'we have here only two of the six royal houses... '*Troas*' and *'Paphlagonia.'*

'A *Phrygian League*, even in *faint* resemblance to the *Old Empire*, will be amenable to *Sangas* (Sangarius, Sangarios),' opined *Old Scamandus*. 'With *Sangas* of the northwestern heartlands, we shall have but *half* of the royal houses,' observed *Apollo*, further noting that 'two of the remaining three royal houses are devotees of the lineage of the *House of Khronos*': these being 'the royal house of *Kelainos* in the central-western highlands, and the house of *Kar* along the southwestern coast. Each will be amenable to a '*League*' at the nexus of the former houses of *Khronos* and *Ōkeanós,*' concluded *Old Scamandus*. '*Kelainos*, son of *Poseidon*, is a cousin whom I have known since youth,' *Apollo* acknowledged... 'while *Kar* is reputed to hold *Ausar* (Osiris, Zeus, Kush, Dionysus) in the highest esteem,' he further affirmed.

'And what of *Meandrus?*' inquired *Teucer*. 'The ever-astute *Meandrus* will seek not to be excluded from a "*Phrygian League*" so reminiscent in scope and dimension to that of the *Old Empire*,' proffered *Scamandus*. 'Through the such alliance, the vested interests and prosperity of each Sovereign and their kingdoms will be better served and protected,' asserted Apollo... 'And for my part, I *too* have vested interest,' he then proclaimed... 'the *Isle of Kos* south of the coast of *Karia* is the birthplace of my mother, *Leto*,' he disclosed; 'the adjacent mainland (that would become the land of ancient Lycia) and off-shore (Dodecanese) islands have long been the province of her people, themselves *Pelasgi*, since before the fall of *Atlatia*,' *Apollo* advised. 'To this, I also can attest,' agreed *Old Scamandus*.[cmlxxi]

The land that would come to be known as ancient *Lycia* occupied a part of the southwestern Anatolian Peninsula; it was a land bounded on the true-north by ancient *Phrygia*, and the northwest by ancient *Karia*, with the *Dmdala Mountains* separating the province of ancient *Karia* from the province that would become ancient *Lycia*. 'This is a land into which the *Karians* have most certainly not encroached, *Apollo*, stated assuredly... 'a land for which I seek recognition of territorial autonomy and sovereignty... as *my* vested interest,' he then declared. 'So your proposition is that you would add to the number of emergent kingdoms into which the *Old Empire* has thus far dissolved,' contested *Teucer*. Would you prefer a more extensive and strident provincial kingdom under Kar instead, solemnly inquired *Old Scamandus*?

'You may be assured *Meandrus* will find appeal in such a kingdom on the southern border of *Karia*,' argued wily *Old Scamandus* ... 'particularly a kingdom under the auspices of one such as *Apollo*... he will seek to leverage such a kingdom as a counterbalance against the ambitions of his surprisingly formidable son-in-law,' *Scamandus* predicted. 'In sum, is this then the crux of your proposition *Apollo*,' inquired *Kheiron*. 'No'... *Apollo* quickly responded, 'there is a *vital* component I deem crucial to formation, cohesion, and governance of the *'League'*... and that is that *Troas* and its capital of *Troy* should be the center of the *"League"* we seek to foster,' he stated rather plainly. Kheiron interjected that '*Paphlagonia* and *its* capital city had always been the *traditional* center and capital of the *Old Empire.*'

Apollo then argued that 'Troy's position at the nexus of the *Aegean* and *Euxine Seas* will be key to attracting the interest of the provincial kingdoms,' noting that 'without its maritime centrality *your* kingdom *Kheiron,* and that of *Sangas,* in the central highlands, are each all but confined to the basins of the *Euxine Sea.* Whilst the kingdoms of *Meandrus, Kelainos,* and *Kar* are themselves confined to the basins of the lower seas'. *Apollo* explained that 'by availing the League's constituents of Troy's strategic maritime advantage, we enhance the facility of each kingdom, and in so doing bind each sovereign to the League's unique and collective strengths.' *Apollo* proposed that 'each sovereign be invited to establish a *trade city* in the middle *Scamander River Valley;* maritime *sister cities* to their *capitals*, connected by overland trade routes to the capitals of their parent kingdoms,' he elucidated.

'A presumptive proposition,' objected *Teucer* 'would this not compromise the sovereignty and maritime prominence that are at present the sole province of Troas,' he protested. 'Conversely,' retorted *Apollo,* 'as host, the establishment of such cities in the middle valley would be at the invitation and pleasure of *Troas*. In the safety of the middle valley, each *trade city* would depend and rely on the protection of the *Citadels of Troy,* for which each would render special dispensation (taxes) to *Troy* as the capital of *Troas*... enhancing both the exercise of sovereignty and the strategic maritime advantages of *Troas*, and *Troy* as its capital,' *Apollo* contended. 'A corridor facilitating both inter-regional and maritime trade,' surmised *Kheiron;* 'a powerful maritime trade corridor... at the very *nexus* of the northern seas,' emphasized *Old Scamandus.*

'The middle valley will become a microcosm of the *League* we envision,' proclaimed *Apollo,* 'a microcosm emblematic of the depth and potentiality of the alliance we seek to foster,' he continued, advising that 'should we reach an accord, then by consent of *Zeus* he,' *Apollo,* 'well established amongst the first of the trade cities in the valley, on behalf of the *House of Khronos.*' Neither legend nor conventional ancient history makes mention of an accord between the early Phrygians and neighboring Pelasgian (and descendent Pelasgian) kingdoms in western Anatolia, though each makes mention of archaic cities of requisite trade scope and dimension which arose in the high places of the valley during the era, rather than in the rich agricultural lands of the alluvial plains that then defined the middle river valley.

Many trade cities arose around (*Old Ezine*) the ancient inland *Port City of Troy;* such were the cities of *Kolonaia* (Colonae) and *Neandreia,* established in the middle valley. Mythology places the founding of the city of *Kolonaia* within the era of the dominion of *Kelainos* (son of Poseidon), King of Kelainai (Celænæ), and though circumstances of the early history of the city of *Neandreia* are said to be unclear, mythological traditions similarly place the founding of the city within the era of the dominion of *Kelainos* of Kelainai (Celænæ). [cmlxxii] Advents which, when taken together, appear to affirm that accord was ultimately reached by *Apollo, Kheiron, Scamandus* and those Sovereigns who would come to form the core of the nascent *Phrygian League.*

Other cities also then arose in the valley, each further enhancing the facility and influence of *Troy* over overland and maritime trade. Yet, the annals of ancient history make no mention, nor do they allude to the existence or prominence of these early *Phrygians* and their ensuing alliance. Part of the problem lies in the various names given to the ancient tribes and peoples who were *Phrygian*, and part is due to efforts by Eurocentric historians to purport an *Indo-European* heritage to a fundamentally more ancient *Pelasgian* people.[cmlxxiii] Classical historians thus deem the *Phrygians* to be among the most obscure peoples in antiquity, at least so far as their origin is concerned. Most ancient travails of the *Phrygians* are generally tied to mythology and the mythical ages, as is the founding of all their cities which were engaged in commercial trade.

The annals of later ancient history finally make mention of what was known as the '*Assuwa League*' (in western Anatolia), a linear and perhaps direct descendent of the *Phrygian League*. Twenty-two member states (or kingdoms) formed the *Assuwa league*, and though the identifications of some are disputed, that of *Troy*, *Troas*, *Lycia* (Lukka), and *Karia* (Karkija, Caria), as core members of the league, is not in dispute.[cmlxxiv] Also not in dispute is the influence of *Apollo* in the kingdoms of the earliest of *Phrygia* and the other states of the alliance. Ruins of ancient statutes and temples dedicated to *Apollo* have been unearthed all over much of western Anatolia, with his influence appearing to have spread from Troas, in keeping with his vision.[cmlxxv]

Kheiron (Cheiron) himself is said to have been personally instructed by *Apollo* and thus became renowned for his skill in medicine and the art of prophecy.[cmlxxvi] Some say that the resolute dedication of *Apollo* to his vision emanated in part from a sense of responsibility he felt for the plight of *Prometheus* since by some accounts, it was from he that *Prometheus* acquired knowledge of the most fundamental of the mysteries he would later so imprudently divulge; others allude to his undying devotion to *Leto*, while still others, particularly the *Priest of Amun*, opine that it was *here* that he found true purpose. As promised, *Ausar* (Osiris, Kush, Zeus, Dionysus) extended the Armada's layover in the middle valley to off-load goods and sort out those who chose to remain with *Apollo* and aid in establishing the new trade settlement.

Isle of Cypress

At long last, with *Ausar* (Osiris, Zeus, Kush, Dionysus) alone at the bow of his flagship, the *Armada* raised anchor and, using the current of the river, slowly navigated downriver through the broad and narrow corridors of the middle and lower river valleys, pass the *Citadel of Troy* at the coast, to ply the open coastal waters of the ancient Aegean Sea once again. With the currents and winds optimal for an expeditious voyage southward, *Ausar* instructed the captain of the flagship to set course and lead the convoy along and around the western and southwestern coast of the *Anatolian Peninsula* to the *Isle of Cypress* and the last leg of their voyage. It was the time of year when the northwesterly winds in the *Aegean* were intermittently interrupted by stronger southwesterly winds, allowing ships to hoist their sails and sail freely along the seaboard.

It was also the time of year when daylight hours were short, and stormy conditions frequent, frequently forcing the three ships of the *Armada* to seek safe harbor at night on one of the off-shore islands along the course. Thus did the *Armada* sail and ply a course along and past the coasts of ancient *Karia* and the land that would become ancient *Lycia*, enroot to the *Isle of Cypress* and the last leg of their voyage. From *Cypress,* the Armada sailed across the open waters of the eastern Mediterranean Sea to the ancient port at *Ugarit*, from whence the three-ship convoy then proceeded southward, paralleling the coast of ancient *Kanaan,* to at last return to the *Isle of Sidon,* from whence their voyage began.

The *Armada* dropped anchor in *Sidon's* northern harbor, near the ancient island city situated on the promontory overlooking the embayment. *Ausar* (Osiris, Kush, Zeus, Dionysus) and key members of his entourage, joined by the captains of the Armada, and a select few merchants, disembarked their (respective) ships and assembled at the center of the island city, from whence *Ausar* dispatched messengers to both the mainland *City of Sidon* and the *Island City of Tyre*, in search of *Agenor,* whom the messengers were instructed to advise of Ausar's return, and request his audience in *Sidon.* Upon learning of Ausar's return, *Agenor* arranged libations for the full complement of the *Armada* (crew and passengers) while secreting *Ausar,* the captains of the Armada, and a few select others, away to his royal residence for a more private setting.

Enjoying his libation in the comfort of the royal residence (at Sidon), *Ausar* (Osiris, Kush, Zeus, Dionysus) shared his observations and assessment of their voyage to the old colonies in the northern seas. The voyage 'first began with the *Isle of Crete,*' he reminded, 'an island that (before the fall of Atlatia) had long served as the entryway to the northern colonies'; Ausar noted that 'those of the *Diaspora* who migrated to *Crete* during and after the great upheavals and final fall of old Atlatia have greatly 'bolstered the island's population and prowess as a key trading hub within the vast island archipelago.' Of the former island colonies '*Milos,*' Ausar advised was again the 'a source of quality of obsidian, and of *Naxos,* he told of the rebuilt capital city and the interest of its merchants in cultivating broader trade for the island's high-quality marble.

The captains of the *Armada* imparted tales of adept celestial navigation in the voyage crossing the open seas between the *Isle of Naxos* and the old colonial seaport at *Kavala City* on the coast of mainland *Thrace.* Ausar (Osiris, Kush, Zeus, and Dionysus), in turn, spoke of the striving autonomy of the emergent kingdoms of *Thrace* and their revival of trade in precious metals to support their efforts. But most significantly, to *Agenor's* delight, *Ausar* told of the new trade settlement established by *Apollo* at the nexus of the upper and lower northern seas on behalf of *Kush, Khemet* and *Kanaan'.* The settlement, *Ausar* (Osiris, Kush, Zeus, Dionysus) elaborated 'lies in the *Scamander River Valley,* within the emergent *Phrygian* kingdom of *Troas;* a kingdom occupying the northwestern (*Aegean*) coast of *Asia Minor.*'

'Ships transiting the corridor between the vast *Mediterranean* and *Euxine Seas* are often forced to seek safe harbor' at the inland ports (of the City of Troy) in the *Scamander River Valley, Ausar* (Osiris, Kush, Zeus, and Dionysus) further advised, 'giving Troas (and its capital City of Troy) near full control of maritime transport through the corridor,' he continued. 'The shores of (the *Sea of Marmora* and the *Euxine Sea*) the upper northern seas are populated by former colonies that have become thriving and emergent kingdoms, such as those that have come to comprise *Thrace, Paphlagonia, Phrygia* and *Aia (Kolchis, Colchis),* among others; theirs is the vast *wealth* of natural minerals and precious metals that first attracted the powerful and acquisitive kings and kingdoms of *Atlatia,*' noted *Ausar* (Osiris, Kush, Zeus, and Dionysus).

To *Agenor's* further delight, *Ausar* (Osiris, Kush, Zeus, and Dionysus) advised that 'as compensate for consignment of the ships, each vessel shall deliver a portion of the most valuable items of their cargoes to his coffers… before departing for *Lower Khemet* at first light in the morrow'. 'At the capital of *Upper Khemet*, after off-loading the balance of their cargoes,' *Ausar* (Osiris, Kush, Zeus, and Dionysus) elaborated, 'each vessel shall be graced with gold from *Kush*, and valuable goods and wares from both *Khemet* and *Kush,* as gratuity for your graciousness *Agenor,* and to compensate the *Kanaanites* among the crews of the *Armada*... who so aided in the success of our voyage'. Thus did the *Armada* raise anchor the following morning and ply southward along the southern coast of *Kanaan* toward the eastern waterways of the ancient *Nile Delta.*

Return to Khemet: House of Khem

The *Nile Delta* is the most dominant geographic feature along the northeastern coast of continental Africa; in its present-day form, it spans over one hundred miles in length and over one hundred sixty miles in width. It was crafted by the *River Nile* of earliest antiquity, which fanned out from its mouth like an enormous tree, branching into different deltaic channels, carving out over ten thousand square miles of *Nile Delta* to reach the *Mediterranean Sea*.[cmlxxvii] The waters of the outer delta were a classic example of a transitional zone between a major river and the sea, while conversely, the inner delta was viewed then as a muddy, swampy barrier to ships and transit. Yet for ancient Anu mariners who knew their way through the intricate waterways of the inner delta, it was seen as both a shield and vital link between the river and sea.[cmlxxviii]

During early antiquity, the inland coast of the *Nile Delta* was over one hundred miles south of where the Armada entered the northeast delta. The experienced *Anu* mariners aboard the flagship of the *Armada* advised that the voyage across the delta 'would take several days, depending upon conditions.' Though, 'under all circumstances,' the mariners counseled, 'the ships of the *Armada* should seek safe anchorage along the course as evening approaches; before the southerly winds subside each night.' During all but the winter months, the southerly winds subsided each evening, prompting ancient ships under sail to seek safe harbor or anchorage rather than push upriver against the currents, by oar, at night. *Anu* mariners piloting ships transiting from *Kanaan* generally sailed into the eastern delta, where temporary and permanent levees and islands, created by alluvium washed down from the southern highlands, provided shelter for overnight anchorage.

Millions of tons of sand, silt and sediments washed down from the highlands along the ancient tributaries of the *Nile* each year, with volumes of alluvium ultimately reaching, settling, accumulating, and adding to the ongoing evolution of the delta.[cmlxxix] Temporary and permanent berms, levees and islands are formed along the main channels of the *Deltaic Nile* by this process, with early settlements in the delta built on permanent high ground along the courses of these deltaic channels. During annual floods, the channels of the *Deltaic Nile* literally inundate the floodplains, transforming the delta into an inland sea, with only the settlements, villages, and early cities visible above the water, appearing as islands in the transitory *Deltaic Nile Sea*.[cmlxxx]

When the floodwaters recede, they left a fertile layer of silt deposited over the huge alluvial plain between the inland *Delta* and outer coast of the *Mediterranean Sea,* reinvigorating the soils of the floodplain, which were then used for agriculture, and facilitating the growth of the early settlements. Though every settlement in the delta, including the smallest, needed some type of port facility, ancient *Kena-Anu* mariners familiar with sailing from the coast of *Kanaan* into the *Delta* preferred anchorage at islands) of sufficient size to provide a safe harbor; such was the port at the early settlement of *Djanet* (a port later Greeks would call 'Tanis'), located in the *Tanitic* channel of the *Deltic Nile*.[cmlxxxi]

Djanet (Tanis) was an early ancient settlement of the era built on a two-mile-wide island, rising just over thirty feet above the floodplain and terrain in the northeastern Delta, with a large adjacent port. The site of the early settlement and later port-city covered about seventy-five acres; its strategic position and harbor on *Lake Manzala*, the largest and northernmost of the *Deltic Lakes*, made it a usually safe and reliable port for anchorage by ancient ships transiting the eastern delta, such as those of the *Armada*. Early ancient *Djanet* (Tanis) was auspiciously situated near the nexus of the *Tanitic* channel of the *Deltic Nile* and the southeastern coast of *Lake Manzala*, a configuration availing the *Armada* of the safe harbor for overnight anchorage… at the port of *Tanis*.

The Armada raised anchor with the recommencement of the southerly winds early the following morning, resuming the voyage across the delta.[cmlxxxii] Sailing before the southerly winds allowed the three ships of the *Armada* to cover the nautical distance from the *Isle of Tanis* (Djanet), in the northeastern outer delta, to the *Giza Plateau*, at the southern inland coast of the delta, in about two days. The mariners of the Armada sailed southward upon the winds as the broad fan and channels of the *Deltic Nile* melded into the main corridor of the *Lower Nile River* of the era. As the ships sailed beyond *Giza*, the river became noticeably calmer and bluer, though it was not always thus.

During the most ancient of times, no part of the *Lower Nile Valley* was above water; in the beginning, the lower valley was an arm of the sea, literally transformed by the flood waters of the *Nile* transporting and infilling enormous quantities of silt and sediment from the southern highlands, gradually in-filling and making the lower valley part of the continent. The massive outpouring of sands, silt and sediments eventually raised and projected the floor of the lower valley into the sea ...beyond the then continental coast. The frequent floods of the Nile routinely overflowed the river's banks, depositing the sediments carried down, creating a fertile lower river valley over twelve miles wide, with an array of channels at the river's mouth, *Nile Delta*.

The early delta was marshy, with a number of large, fertile islands and vast tracks of marshland surrounding several large lakes and small lagoons along the seaward face of the outer delta, with; thick papyrus swamps in the inner delta.[cmlxxxiii] Over the millennia, the river has gradually pushed the inland coast of the bay and delta northward, from its ancient shores at *Waset* (Thebes), to where the river's mouth and delta emptied into the basins of the *Mediterranean* during the periods of earliest antiquity. The inland terrain of the *Lower Nile Valley* was further shaped during the *Holocene* when there was far more rainfall in the middle latitudes, and the mighty *Nile River* of the era flowed with far more volume, and in consequence, the ancient river was four times as wide and twice as deep.

The ancient *Nile* was about sixty feet higher than at present when its swollen waters finally crested and breached the low-lying ridge along its western bank, with the overflow pouring from the main corridor of the Nile into a dry former branch of the river, an ancient riverbed leading into the huge *Fayoum Depression*, a little over twelve miles west of the main corridor of the *Nile Valley*. The overflowing waters of the *Nile* reinvigorated and transformed the ancient riverbed into an active and vibrant channel of the river (anciently known as the "Great Canal"), which flowed into the deepest basins of the massive *Faiyum Depression*, creating a huge paleo-lake of the Ancients' called '*Mr-wr*' (the "Great Sea"); a massive lake latter-day Greeks would call '*Lake Moeris*' ("Paleo-Lake Moeris"). With expansion of *Paleo-Lake Moeris*, much of the *Fayoum* became an inland sea; this was throughout most of the early Neolithic.[cmlxxxiv]

The *Fayoum* (a *Coptic* word meaning "the sea") is a six hundred-ninety square mile depression in the northeastern Sahara, whose surrounding lands were literally transformed into a fertile paradise by the expansion of *Paleo-Lake Moeris*, attracting the first of the *Anu* colonies.[cmlxxxv] *Anu* farmers around the shores of the lake cultivated wheat, barley, and flax, with early Neolithic cities populating the ancient shore of the huge lake. The water levels of '*Mr-wr* (Paleo-Lake Moeris) grew as a result of annual Nile floods, expanding the lake in both size and dimension.[141] *Paleo-Lake Moeris* was situated southwest of present-day *Cairo* and stretched about fifty miles from its eastern shore to its western shore and about thirty-five miles from its northern shore to its southern shore, with an outlet channel returning from the huge lake to the main corridor of the *Nile*, downstream, about fifty miles south of the *Giza Plateau*.[cmlxxxvi]

---

[141] Brewer 1989a; 1989b

As the *Armada* approached and sailed beyond the *Giza Plateau,* the High Priest, prompted by the elders of the *Anu* aboard the flagship, reminded *Ausar* (Osiris, Kush, Zeus, Dionysus) that for many, if not most of the *Anu* traders and mariners among the *Armada's* crew and company, the home was in the region around the *City of Shedet* (a city later ancient Greeks would call 'Krocodilopolis' or 'Crocodilopolis'), on the southeastern coast of *Mr-wr* (Palaeo-Lake Moeris) reached by way of the *Great Canal.*[cmlxxxvii] The mouth of the *Great Canal* was ahead on the west bank of the Nile River, where the magnitude and force of the waters of the ancient *Nile* pouring into and through the canal provided it a northward flowing current parallel and to the west of the main corridor of the Nile, for much of the length of the canal. The northward course of the *Great Canal* paralleled the main corridor of the *Nile* for two hundred miles until the canal turned north-westward, flowing away from the *Nile* and into the northern basins of the *Fayoum* that defined *Paleo-Lake Moeris.*

The Neolithic city of *Shedet* ('Krocodilopolis' or 'Crocodilopolis') was located on the former southern-most coast of *Paleo-Lake Moeris,* with the *Great Canal* (the present-day Bahr Yussef canal) running through the heart of the old ancient city.[cmlxxxviii] Many early ancient *Anu* villages, towns and townships were concentrated in and around the region of ancient *Shedet* (Krocodilopolis), near the entrance into *Paleo-Lake Moeris;* while later villages and towns arose along and throughout the rich, fertile lands surrounding the shores of the huge ancient inland sea. To return home to the shores of *Mr-wr* ("Paleo-Lake Moeris"), the port of destination requested by the priest and elders of the *Anu* aboard the flagship, was the ancient riverport city of "*Saūtī*" (meaning "the Guardian" or "place of the Guardian"), just south of the mouth of the *Great Canal;* providing suitable and ample staging and ease of entry into and through the canal for boats and ships venturing or returning to the great northern inland sea.[cmlxxxix]

The force of the northward flowing current of the canal allowed ships to easily ply northward into *Paleo-Lake Moeris* to the harbors of the ancient *City of Shedet* (Krocodilopolis or Crocodilopolis), and the other *Anu Kingdoms* around the northern inland sea.[cmxc] Ancient *Saūti* was settled on a broad, fertile plain bordering the western bank of the *River Nile* of the era and was both a gateway and center of regional trade.[142] The ancient river port city was situated at the nexus of three great overland trade routes, the first and foremost being a southern route (later called the "road of forty days") connecting Neolithic *Saūti* with the ancient fiefdoms and kingdoms in the huge *Kharga Oasis,* southern-most and largest of the oasis depressions in the Western Desert of Khemet (Egypt). The ancient trade route contused southward from the *Kharga Oasis* to kingdoms in the *Selima* and *Fashir Oasis;* the old trade route continued southward from there to the very heart of ancient Kush.[cmxci]

The second prominent trade route extended westward through what were then the grasslands of the eastern *Sahara,* connecting the ancient city of *Saūti* to the ancient eastern kingdoms of the *Shi* of the era in the large depression defining the *Farafra Oasis.* The third route extended southwesterly, connecting the ancient river-port city and trade center to the provinces of the *Shi* in the *Dakhia Oasis,* on the eastern frontier of the *Maa Confederation.* Ancient *Saūti* quickly became a significant and important regional trade center, with its bustling river port facilitating and inter-connecting trade from and between the kingdoms of *Kush* and *Upper Khemet* and those of *Lower Khemet,* particularly the prosperous cities and kingdoms around the ancient shores of the great northern inland sea, *Paleo-Lake Moeris.*

---

[142] The modern toponym "Asyut" derives from its ancient Egyptian name Z3wt or Z3wty, meaning "the Guard."

The location of the ancient riverport city of *Saūti,* at the mouth of the *Great Canal,* and the nexus of the major trade routes to the eastern provinces of the *Confederation* rendered it an ideal and convenient final port for not only the *Anu* from *Mr-wr* and the *Lower Valley,* but also for the *Shi* among the *Armada's* complement and entourage of priests, merchants, traders, and militia from the eastern provinces of the *Maa Confederation.* The journey upriver from *Giza* to *Saūti* was a voyage of over one hundred sixty (160) nautical miles; a trip of four to five days,' the *Anu* pilot of the flagship advised, 'depending on the conditions on the river,' he concluded.[cmxcii] The *Nile* is blessed with a southerly wind that pushes ships under sail upriver; however, the speed under sail on the river depended then, as it does now, on the time of year, the strength of the wind and the countervailing current of the river.

For the most part, the ancient Nile was fairly predictable, with the winds always blowing from north to south and the current always flowing from south to north, allowing ancient vessels to sail upriver using the wind and row downriver using the current.[cmxciii] Nonetheless, navigation on the ancient river was far from a passive activity, with hazards similar to those of the open sea, such as unexpected gales and storms always present; indeed, ancient accounts are replete with indications of sudden storms causing frequent shipwrecks along the river.[cmxciv] For the pilots and mariners of the Armada, the voyage through the *Lower River Valley* was both tedious and tiring; though calmer than the waters of the delta, they were still tasked with avoiding navigational obstacles such as sandbanks, dangerous shallows and small low-lying islets along the course of the river.

Island City of Henen-nesut: Hēraclĕŏpŏlis

As the winds began to subside, *Ausar* (Osiris, Kush, Zeus, Dionysus) instructed that the pilot of the Flagship 'seek safe harbor of adequate size, so that those aboard the ships of the *Armada* might disembark, for a time, before resuming the voyage with the recommencement of the winds at dawn in the morrow'. The banks of the *Lower River* in the era were lined with thick fruit trees and vegetation, with sandbars and transitory and permanent islets appearing intermittently along the course of the river.[cmxcv] As the *Armada* sailed southward, clusters of riverside villages also intermittently appeared along the banks of the river, prompting a *Priest of Amun* standing near *Ausar* to admonish that the pilot of the flagship 'seek a port of sufficient size to honor a returning King, as this shall mark the return of *Ausar* to *Khemet*... and the land of *Kush*, for which he chose the *Island City of Henen-nesut'*.

The Legends

Fortuitously, or perhaps as fate would have it, not far ahead of the lead ship of the *Armada* was an approaching island city situated on an island that has since become part of the western bank of the present-day *Nile River*. This was the island that Strabo, in his time, would later call the "Great Island'... largely because of the renowned walled city which dominated the island. The island city was called '*Henen-nesut'* (or 'Neni- neswt,' meaning "City of the King's child") in the most ancient of times, a name captured in later Coptic form as 'Hnes' (or "Ahnes"); the present-day Arabic name for the city is 'Ihnasya el-Medina' (or 'el-Medina'). Throughout its long history, the ancient city has had many names, yet the one by which it is most broadly known is its Greek name, 'Hēraclĕŏpŏlis,' the '*City of Hercules'* (Herakles, Heryshaf, Alcides).[cmxcvi]

The date of the founding and settlement on the site of the ancient island city remains unknown; however, what is known is that the earliest *Hēraclĕŏpŏlis* (Henen-nesut), was an ancient fortress city, enclosed by a mud brick wall, situated with its back against the main corridor of the Nile. Earliest *Hēraclĕŏpŏlis* was a fortified citadel with a full garrison and storehouse, the northernmost outpost of early *Kush* in a prosperous but still restive *Lower Khemet*[cmxcvii].

The ancient fortress-city was located on a large natural island, surrounded and formed by two channels of the Nile River of the era; such islands often still take shape when channels of the Nile separate from the main river, forming islands that often do not necessarily last or retain their configurations forever. For example, the ancient *Isle of Thebe*s has changed considerably from what it was throughout much of earliest antiquity. The island of *Hērăclĕŏpŏlis* was formed by a separation of one of the channels of the *Nile,* with the ancient island taking shape between the main corridor of the river to its east and a then western channel which branched–off and defined the west coast of the newly formed island. The early island city was built on the west coast, above and overseeing a natural harbor and river-port on the western channel of the river.[cmxcviii]

The river-port at *Hērăclĕŏpŏlis* (Henen-nesut) was situated in a partially enclosed cove and natural harbor, specially adapted to shifting riverine conditions, on the mid-west coast of the island. The harbor was bordered by a mudbrick casemate structure covered with a limestone veneer to protect its basins from the destructive effects of the rise and fall of the Nile. This created a protected lagoon-like environment that provided a safe abode from dangerous currents, unfavorable winds, and shallow sandbars. [cmxcix] The entrance to the harbor was adjacent and in proximity to the entrance to the city, just above the harbor, on the mid-west coast of the island. The western arm of the Nile, which created the island, was mostly calm and flowed slowly, allowing the ships of the Armada to sail into the harbor and drop anchor. Detachments of the *Armada's* security force then ferried ashore ahead of *Ausar* to secure the area for his arrival.

The security contingent was led by an officer of the flagship who bore specific instruction to 'seek out those in command of the city' and announce the return of *Ausar* (Osiris, Kush, Zeus, Dionysus) so that they may make preparation for the arrival of he and the weary expedition of the *Armada;* last of the *Kushite* expedition to return. It was thus with abrupt but mounting fanfare that *Ausar* and his entourage were warmly welcomed by an impromptu gathering of soldiers and citizenry, jubilantly lining the pathway from the port to the entrance of the city. There they were received by none other than *General Sia*, whom *Ausar* himself had appointed to serve as Commander of *Lower Khemet,* under the combined command of his son *Hercules* (Herakles, Heryshaf, Alcides); this at the onset of the *Kushite* expedition now brought to an end.[143]

The citadel at *Hērăclĕŏpŏlis* was surrounded by an outer fortification and a series of rectangular salients backed by a thick brick wall. The interior of the fortress city was arranged on a grid pattern, with streets lined with long rectangular brick buildings and central garrison quarters built up against the main wall, with a staircase leading to the top of the main wall. Inhabitants of the citadel were largely local recruits, primarily Anubians (Anu-bians) who were autochthonous to the island, commanded by a hierarchy of *Kushite* field officers, who resided at the fortresses along with their families.[144] The island and island *City of Hērăclĕŏpŏlis* (Henen-nesut) were governed by *General Sia,* whose responsibilities centered upon the defense of the citadel, the provisioning of convoy troops, and the protection of the maritime and overland trade routes.

---

[143] Dend. II, 101, 6-7
[144] Hence, Hērăclĕŏpŏlī-tae, the inhabitants of Heracleopolis, Pliny; 36, 13, 19, 86

As reported by the Governor of the island, General Sia, on the evening of the arrival of Ausar (Osiris, Kush, Zeus, Dionysus), the Island City of Henen-nesut (Hērāclĕŏpŏlis) was built upon orders and instruction from Hercules (Herakles, Heryshaf, Alcides) himself, to serve as a northernmost Kushite military outpost in the protectorates of the Lower Nile Valley and Delta. The fortress city was built across from the eastern bank of the Great Canal (the present-day 'Bahr Yusuf 'channel), with the western arm of the Nile that branched–off and formed the Isle of Hērāclĕŏpŏlis separating the island from the western coast of the peninsula-like landmass that then formed the eastern boundary lands of the Great Canal.

As General Sia would further inform, Hercules (Herakles, Heryshaf, Alcides) presided and held court at the palace of the citadel in Hērāclĕŏpŏlis (Henen-nesut) …when in Lowser Khemet. 'Unfortunately,' reported *General Sia*, 'at the behest of *Governor Antee*,' whom *Ausar* (Osiris, Kush, Zeus, Dionysus) himself had appointed *Governor of Upper Khemet* and the *West* at the time of the Armada's arrival at *Hērāclĕŏpŏlis*, marking the long-awaited return of *Ausar* (Osiris, Kush, Zeus, Dionysus), *Hercules* (Herakles, Heryshaf, Alcides) was away on campaign with *General Hu* in the southern highlands, insuring security along the borderlands with the *Nagu-Punt*.

In his absence, the royal court in *Lower Khemet* shifted to the *City of Hermopolis*, where the Vizier, *Thoth* (whom the latter-day Greeks called Hermes), was in residence, *General Sia* advised, noting that 'at present, the *Vizier* is with Governor Busiris, whom *Ausar* appointed as governor of the Delta and the East.[m] *Governor Busiris* had himself recently passed through *Hērāclĕŏpŏlis* in route to *Hermopolis* from the *Delta*, noted *General Sia*. The Governor was enrooted to confer with the Vizier, *Thoth* (Hermes), on the propriety of his newly anointed capital city, the eponymous *City of Bousiris* (Busiris), constructed in the center of the *Delta* (at the site of present-day Abu Sir Bana), the *General* reported.[mi]

The ancient *City of Bousiris* (Busiris) arose in the middle of the ancient *Delta* of the era, near the *Phatnitic* mouth, on the western bank of the *Damietta* channel of the *Deltic Nile,* five miles east of the main corridor of the *Nile River*. The original name of the city in ancient *Khemet* was 'Djedu' (pronounced 'Djedou'); the name 'Busiris' was later attributed to the governor and the city by the Greeks. 'It is the Governor's intention,' *General Sia* reported, "that the *City of Bousiris* (Djedu, Βούσιρις, Bousiris, Busiris) shall be the central customs hub in the delta through which all maritime trade from the *Mediterranean* shall enter *Khemet*; this in pursuant of his charge as Governor of the Northern and Eastern protectorates,' "The controversy,' the General explained, 'was with the preeminent *City of Onu.*' An ancient deltaic city known by several names throughout its long history, it was once known as the "*City of An*" and later the "*City of Anu*" by its *Early Anu* founders.

It was later re-named the *"City of the Sun"* by the *Deltic-Anu* and *Kana-An*u (Kanaanites) inhabitants, but the later *Khemetans* reverted to calling it the "*City of Onu,*' While the *Hebrews* called it the *"City of On,"* and later *Greeks* called it *"Heliopolis"* (the "City of Apollo").[mii] As *General Sia* would go on to explain in greater detail, 'the *City of Onu* (An, Anu, On, Heliopolis) has through the ages, and by long tradition, been the central trading hub between the *Kana-Anu* of *Kanaan,* and the *Anu* of the *Delta* and *Lower Valley.*' 'Most particularly, trade with the *City of Shedet* (which latter-day Greeks called the '*City of Krocodilopolis*') and the prosperous *Anu Kingdoms* around the shores of *Mr-wr* (Paleo-Lake Moeris), the *Great Northern Inland Sea*.' 'The *Vizier* (Thoth, Hermes), as a *Priest of the Oru,* is held in high esteem by the *Priest of the Anu,*' *General Sia* observed; 'this in their mutual reverence for the ethos of the ancient *Hydra Priesthood*, he opined… 'a sentiment more broadly shared in *Onu* (the erstwhile City of the Sun), than in *Shedet* (the latter-day City of Krocodilopolis)'.

After a moment of deliberation, *Ausar* (Osiris, Kush, Zeus, Dionysus) informed *General Sia* that the *Armada* would begin disbanding at the river port *City of Saūti* (Asyūt), further upriver. *Saūti* (Asyūt) was situated above the mouth of the *Great Canal* flowing into *Mr-wr,* Paleo-Lake Moeris, and was also near the juncture of two key trade routes leading to the (eastern) frontier provinces of the *Maa Confederation.*' ' "At *Saūti* (Asyūt)," *Ausar* elaborated, "the *Anu* among our expedition, who are mostly from around the shores of *Mr-wr* (Paleo-Lake Moeris), most notably, the renown *City of Shedet* (Krocodilopolis), shall disembark and make their way home, where they like the *Si* who will disembark and make their way to the frontier-provinces of the *Confederation,* shall bring with them hoards of valuables and exotic goods, and most importantly, accounts of all we that have seen and accomplished together."

'It is true,' conceded *General Sia,* 'that those who previously returned from the (Kushite) expedition have, in many ways, inculcated a new spirit and since of unity and interdependence throughout the realm.' 'Yet you feel it questionable,' observed *Ausar,* 'questionable that this new since of unity will satiate the since of loss felt in *Onu* (the *City of the Sun)…* as a traditional trading hub between the *Anu* of the *Lower Valley* and *Delta,* and the *Kena-Anu* of *Kanaan*." 'Yes, I do find it questionable, Sire,' the *General* confessed. To which *Ausar* (Osiris, Kush, Zeus, Dionysus) surmised that 'that it is *indeed* questionable, requires its utility and perception be strengthen; that *Onu* (An, Anu, On, Heliopolis) and *Shedet* (Krocodilopolis) may come to realize and recognize the benefit of greater prosperity, prominence and security within the unity of *Khemet.*'

'In the context of *unity,* Sire,' observed *General Sia,* 'in my view, it is recalcitrance at *Shedet* (Krocodilopolis) that is at the heart of the discord; a recalcitrance better understood and best explained by the *Vizier* (Thoth) Sire, as he has recently visited the city.' 'He is the city at the heart of the *Island of Khmun*' (a city latter-day Greeks would call *"Hermopolis"* (the "City of Hermes," whom the Greeks identified with *Thoth*); 'a voyage of less than a day, under favorable winds,' the *General* added; 'it is also a convenient lay-over between *Henen-nesut* (Hēraclĕŏpŏlis) and *Saūti* (Asyūt), the port of your destination, Sire.' To which *Ausar,* weighing his words, replied light-heartedly, 'no further encouragement is needed to seek the wise counsel of my son, old friend… we sail with re-commencement of the winds, at dawn in the morrow.'

Isle of Khmunu: Hermolopis "City of the Eight"

As *General Sia* foretold, favorable winds allowed the *Armada* to make the voyage from *Hēraclĕŏpŏlis* (the "City of Hercules") to *Hermopolis* (the "City of Hermes") in less than a day, reaching the *Island* of *Khmun* before sunset. Like the *Isle of Henen-nesut* (Hēraclĕŏpŏlis), the ancient *Isle of Khmun* was formed by a separation of a channel of the *Nile,* with the island taking shape between the main river and a channel that branched off and embraced the island along its west coast. The city (Hermolopis) was on the southern end of a hill or told formed by earlier ancient inundations of the *Nile*; the island city was linked to the river by an artificial canal connecting it to the channel on the island's west coast, and a key trade route (across the channel) leading to the *Bahariya Oasis* in *Western Sahara;* on the frontier of the *Maa Confederation.* [miii]

In *Khemet,* the early ancient island city was known as '*Khmunu,*' the 'City of the Eight,' alluding to the eight ancestors of creation, the "Ogdoad" of the revelation of *Thoth*, whom the classical Greeks called 'Hermes'; his revelation focused on the latent power of *Nun*, or pre-Creation chaos.[miv] *Thoth* (actually a pagan Greek name derived from his true name 'Dḥwty,' pronounced 'Djehuty' ('djih-how-tee')), was the fourth son of *Ausar* (Osiris, Kush, Zeus, Dionysus), born of a union between him and his third wife *Maia*, a woman of prominent *IGBO* and *Oru* lineage, who gave birth to *Thoth* (Djehuty, Hermes) in the Holly City of "*Igbo Ukwu,*" founded by *Ausar* in *Western Sudan*, before the final fall of *Atlatia*.[mv]

In the ancient Holly City of Igbo Ukwu *Thoth* (Djehuty, Hermes) had been availed of the wisest philosophers, healers, and seers, the most reverent of high priests of the various sects, the most capable of builders, craftsmen and generals, and the most honorable of noblemen, merchants and traders of every rank and from every corner of the vast region. He studied philosophy, religion, astrology, alchemy, medicine, and the sciences while growing to the majority. Yet perhaps most significantly, he studied the ontology of the *Hydra* under the guidance of his mother and the auspices of the *Priesthood* of the *Oru*. Later, under the tutelage of his father and the auspices of the *Priest of Amun,* he learned of the cosmology of *Amun* and became his father's first scribe as a young adult.

As an initiate-adept of the ancient *Hydra Priesthood* and a foremost disciple of the *Priest of Amun*, from an early age, *Thoth* (Djehuty, Hermes) sought to reconcile the ontology of the *Hydra* with the cosmology of the *Amun,* the Creator who emerged from *Nun* (the eternal waters of pre-creation) at the dawn of *Creation*. The pre-creation *Nun* was envisaged as a limitless ocean of inert potentialities, induced by its (female) counterpart, *Nunet* (also known as Neith or Nut), whose influence inspired the potentialities of *Nun*, evoking living, formed matter, launching the *Creation* of the temporal Universe. It was said that *Nunet* (Neith, Nut) gave birth to *Amun* while she was still in the waters of *Nun*, and it was thus that *Amun* was conceptualized as the *Creator God* …who existed before creation came into being.[mvi]

Here then, was the ancient precept of *Creation* out of *Chaos,* a cosmology in which *Nun* (Chaos) and its counterpart *Nunet* (Order) are the formative and nurturing forces from which *Creation* springs. *Thoth* envisaged *Nun* as a primordial magnitude of directionless, infinite potentialities, personified by an *Ogdoad* of eight divine beings (literally four, doubled): *Heh* and *Hauhet*, representing its boundless, imperceptible expanses and formlessness (its 'spatial infinity'); *Kek* and *Kauket*, representing its darkness and obscurity, and *Amun* and *Amaunet*, representing its invisible power and the breath of life. The *Ogdoad*, as personified by this pantheon of eight divine beings (four male and four female), is indeed the key to the *Sacred Aunk,* which symbolizes the different aspects of *Pre-Creation* that together form the basis of all existence.[mvii]

The Parables

Nonexistent recreation (the omnipresence, pre-existent, virtual state-of-no-state) was among the first concepts of theology in ancient *Khemet*, evidenced by its founding role in Hermopolitan, Heliopolitan, Theban (and later Memphite) schools of theological thought. There is something before everything, before the order, the architecture and the life of creation, a 'something' manifested as a transformation from a nonexistent state to a state of existing actuality. As alluded to in the later Pyramid Texts, 'to be nonexistent, precludes existence, but does not preclude the possibility of becoming existent'; expressed by the ancient verb "kpr," "kheper," "to become," which also means "to transform,' [145]

Chaos ('Khaos'), the *Nun*, was the nothingness out of which the first objects of existence appeared. Chaos was the first thing to exist and the womb from which everything emerged. Precreation occurred at the conjunction of *Nun* and the sheer possibility of something preexisting as a nonexistent, virtual singularity. Precreation is the dual-union of *Nun* and *Nunet* (Neith, Nut), evoking an infinite energy-field and primordial atom. Hence, although *Nun* is nowhere and everywhere, never and always, it is the primordial, irreversible and everlasting milieu in which the eternal potential of creation unfolds. [mviii]

The ontology of *Nun* is that of a threatening state of affairs into which order could relapse at any moment. It is the opposite of order, light and life; in fact, the cosmos, or temporal Universe, is constantly balancing on the edge of this abyss of Chaos, although periods of extended peace are possible. Precreation is both the source of the first cause of creation and a threatening Chaos; for its darkness and disorder encapsulate *creation* from all sides and all the time. *Thoth* (Djehuty, Hermes) envisaged *Nun* as a primal abyss, a primordial cradle of life, whose female aspect, *Nanuet* (Neith, Nut), is described as the celestial expanse above the abyss, and a dynamic giving rising to the inherent attributes of *Nun*

In the creation myth of *Khmunu* (Hermopolis), *Nun* (Chaos) was made up of four elements, personified as balanced pairs of (male and female) divine beings. *Heh* and *Hauhet,* personifying and representing its spatial infinity and formlessness; *Kek* and *Kauket,* personifying and representing its darkness and obscurity; *Nun* and *Naunet*, personifying and representing its primordial ocean of consciousness, and *Amun* and *Amaune*t, personifying its invisible power ('that which is hidden') and the breath of life. These four pairs of deities form the *Ogdoad*.[mix]

These eight divine beings swirled in and among the primordial oceans of consciousness until they came together in a burst of flame to create and give form to the temporal Universe and its phenomenal dynamics (symbolized in myth as the first mound of earth, called the 'Isle of Fire'). *Amun* arose from *Nun,* the primordial waters of consciousness, living in his own solitude; *Amun*, in this incomplete state, knew not yet his own creation — it would be eons later that the *Divine Mind* (Nous) and the *Creative Intellect* (Logos) would go forth, as emanations of *Amun*, to craft Creation of the temporal Universe.

---

[145] See 'The Pyramid Texts'

Nothing certain is known about *Amun*, although He is given names such as "Atum," "Tatenen," and "Re" ("Ra"). There are those who also say that He is a "Ba" or "soul," but in fact, the papyrus rolls do not unfold or inform of His image. He cannot be perceived, and so He cannot be known. His identity is unknown. Nobody has any power over Him. Not the divine beings (the "Gods" of mythology), not the world, not the people; people may think that *Amun* is this-or-that "neter," but in truth, *only Amun knows Amun. Amun* and *Amaunet* (female aspect and counterpart of Amun) are Alone, a single Singularity; hence the essence (or face) of *Amun* is only known by Him.

His true Name is secret; hence, the word "Amun" (the Hidden) points to the namelessness of the Absolute God who abides as the All in All. Everything happens "in" Him, and He has no second (nothing exists outside Him). Like the ubiquity of *Nun*, the soul-like quality of *Amun* renders him everywhere and nowhere. The *Divine Mind* (Nous) of *Amun*, through his *Creative Intellect*, actualization by the "Word" ('Logos') being spoken, was projected forth as an emanation, giving form and order to the cosmos. It is thus that the Will of the Creative Logos unites and brings together all forms, and it is thus that *Amun* brings *Ma'at* (Order) to Chaos.

Ma'at, an emanation of *Amaunet*, was known as a daughter of *Amun*, without whom it was believed that the waters of *Nun* (Chaos) would reclaim the universe. *Ma'at* was personified as the order established in the universe from chaos at the precise moment of creation. Later called 'Sophia' by the pagan Greeks, *Ma'at* represented the Virtues of Truth, Balance, Justice, and Order. *Ma'at* was said to have not existed exist until *Amun* rose from the waters of *Nun* (Chaos). In empathic emulation of *Nanuet* (Neith, Nut), *Ma'at* (Maat, Maet, Mayet) arose as the goddess of the physical and moral law, goddess of Truth, Justice and Divine Order. *Logos* (the 'Word'), which is the direct emanation from *Amun* that brings into existence all the various states of being in the manifested universe, is *Amun's* instrument both during creation and in the providential administration of the Cosmos.'

In the most general terms, it can be said to represent the face of *Amun* turned towards reality. *Logos* is the all-ensouling Light and Life of the Universe, personified by the *Cosmic Serpent* (the primordial "Light of the Logos"), and sometimes referred to as an independently existing entity (a 'hypostasis'), and sometimes referred to as an aspect of *Amun*. The Pyramid Texts mentions such a Serpent as a manifestation of *Amun* in His emergent form.[146] *Logos* arose as a great spirit (the "*Cosmic Serpent*") that came into being in the midst of the dark waters of (Nun) the Abyss.

A direct emanation of *Amun*, *Logos* was the aspect that assigns to everything its essence and who, as the operative form of the *Creative Word,* laid down the laws of what is to be and what is to be made. *Logos*, the '*Cosmic Serpent*,' came forth yet remained ever with *Amun*, and this 'coming-forth-and-yet-remaining' constitutes its Life. Stated differently, the *Cosmic Serpent* (personified as the primordial 'Hydra' or 'Naga') is no God, but rather an embodiment of the *Word* (Logos) and the creative energy and powers behind it, a living emanation of *Amun*.

---

[146] See Pyramid Texts, paragraph 1146.

It was thus that in the *Revelations of the Ogdoad,* the first creative act envisaged was the setting of the creative energy and force of the *Devine Logos* into motion. The first movement, the primordial impulse and divine emanation induced by the action of the will of *Amun* was envisaged as a spiral in both action and form; metaphorized as the movement of a great *Cosmic Serpent* emerging from the depths of the primordial oceans of conscienceless (the watery Chaos known as 'Nun'), and giving form to the universe. It was said that the great *Serpent* circled the temporal universe for eons, arranging and organizing the *Cosmos.*

Though the great *Serpent* came before the appearance of light, impregnated with the brilliance of *Amun,* which pervades its whole being, in the phenomenal universe, it was perceived by its luminance (its 'light'). The 'light' appearing on earth was metaphorized as the primordial *Hydra* (or Naga): *the* personification of *Logos* (the 'Word') and the manifestation of the spiritual-energy known as *'Kundalini,'* the energy of the DIVINE. It was thus that *Logos,* symbolized by the 'Coiled Serpent,' became the symbol of the school of the "Mysteries" incepted by *Thoth;* and the standard for the reverent *Island City of Khmunu.* [mx]

The island *City of Khmunu'* (Hermopolis) was an important administrative center from inception, auspiciously situated (as it was) on the borders of Upper and Lower *Khemet.* The ancient island was then situated just off the west bank of the *Nile* of the era, where early *Khmunu* (Hermopolis) was surrounded by rich farmlands, made fertile by earlier ancient inundations of the *Nile,* providing the economic foundation for the early settlement on the ancient site.[mxi] The eventual influence of the ancient *City of Khmunu'* (Hermopolis), however, did not lie with the renown city itself; it resided within the hearts and minds of the intellectuals and thinkers within *Khemet* and greater Kush during the era. Most notably, the aspirants, neophytes, scribes and initiates of the early *School of the Mysteries* that arose under the tutelage of *Thoth* (Djehuty, Hermes) in ancient *Khmunu* (Hermopolis). As the first of the ancient *Adepts* ('Masters') of the enlightened theology, *Thoth* (Djehuty, Hermes) incepted, formed and guided aspiring masters of the earliest of the *Mystery Schools,* propagating ideas of self-improvement and enlightenment, furthering his father's philosophy, beliefs and deeds.

Like *Shiva* (Shambo), it is said that he lived a wise and pious life, occupied in intellectual contemplation, giving no heed to the gross things of the material world. He insisted that every man has within him a seed of the infinite indestructible spiritual-energy (the conscious energy) from which his very 'Being' derives, a divine energy that is aroused through spiritual discipline and the aspiration and attainment of enlightenment. *Thoth* taught that there is something special about enlightenment that can illuminate the deep nature of consciousness and, thus, the soul. The individual was trained to pursue his divinity and to be god-like while on earth, and in this, qualify for everlasting happiness. The ancient *Adepts* of the earliest schools called what they put together the *Mystery System*, a secret *Order* with access to the *School of the Mysteries* gained only by initiation and pledge to secrecy.

Priests of the *Ancient Mysteries* were symbolized as the Serpent *"Hydra"* (or "Naga"). The core doctrine was a theory of salvation emphasizing deification as the most important objective, that the soul of a man if liberated from its bodily fetters, could become godlike and more fully participate in the unfolding of *Creation.* Word of the enlightened teachings of the early *Mystery School* at ancient *Khmunu* spread quickly throughout Upper and Lower *Khemet* and greater *Kush,* attracting *aspirants* from across the lands. In addition to reverence and moral order, the *Adepts* disclosed the path to higher spiritual knowledge and enlightenment, leading to renown that transformed the ancient *City of Khmunu* into a major cult center, upping its significance as an early administrative city of *Upper* and *Lower Khemet.*

The ancient *Island of Khmun* was situated just off the west bank of the *Nile* of the era, to the north, but near where the ancient river branched off to the west channel of *Mer-Wer* (the Great Canal). Early ancient *Khmunu* (Hermopolis) was surrounded by a thick quadrilateral wall made of mud brick, and south of the old city was the *Castle of Khmunu*, an ancient citadel overseeing the juncture where vessels from the upper river have levied a toll to continue on to the lower river and beyond.[mxii] Second, only to *Thebes*, the *City of Khmunu* (Hermopolis) was auspiciously situated on the southern side of an ancient hill (the 'Tell of Hermopolis'), which covered an area of nearly one square mile; there, the early city was surrounded by rich, fertile farmland. The ruins of the old city cover a huge area; a surviving (3rd Century AD) Oxyrhynchus Papyrus indicates that high-rise buildings with seven stories existed in the old ancient town. A wide elevated canal connected the ancient city with the western branch of the *Nile* that formed the island; via an alcove on the island's southwestern coast, which sufficed as a small harbor serving the city.

It was here that Ausar's three-ship *Armada* dropped anchor just before sunset, having made the voyage from *Henen-nesut* (Hēráclĕŏpŏlis) to *Khmunu* (Hermopolis) in less than a day; upon securing the flagship anchor, *Ausar* and the most trusted of his entourage ferried into the city, via the canal. With word of his impending arrival having long preceded him, as *Ausar* (Osiris, Kush, Zeus, Dionysus) and his trusted entourage entered the city, they were promptly received and greeted by a host of dignitaries and officials of the city, led by his son *Thoth* (Djehuty, Hermes), the *Anu* High Priest *Tera-Neter*, and *Governor Busiris*, who had delayed his return to the *Delta* for the opportunity to welcome and perhaps meet with *Ausar* (Osiris, Kush, Zeus, Dionysus). The planned celebration of *Ausar*'s return arranged by *Thoth* (Djehuty, Hermes) far exceeded the impromptu affair arranged by *General Sia* at *Henen-nesut* (Hēráclĕŏpŏlis), with diverse processions of Neophytes, Initiates and Adepts from the great ecclesiastical college at *Khmunu* (Hermopolis), accompanying *Ausar*, his entourage, and *Governor Busiris* and *Thoth* as the group made their way toward the *Old Castle*, to the south of the city.

Throngs of citizenry crowded along the path to the old citadel as the group made their way to the front of the Castle, where the festivities of the evening were well underway. *Thoth* (Djehuty, Hermes) arranged a more quiet and intimate setting for *Ausar* and his entourage, along with *Governor Busiris* and a select group of priests and dignitaries from the city, a fest secreted away from the noise of the broader festivities, in a large room of the citadel overlooking the city's main harbor, on the eastern bank of *Nile*. The diverse peoples of *Khemet* and greater *Kush* had long been enthralled by tales of the exotic *Kushite* expedition and migrations told by its earlier returning participants. First had been those who returned from the unknown lands of the east, followed later by those who returned by way of the *Land of Kanaan;* as they returned to their home provinces, cities and villages, they brought with them tales of their exotic exploits, capturing and focusing the imagination of the people.

And now, alas, the return of *Kush* (Ausar, Osiris, Zeus, Dionysus) himself, who, bestowing honor upon his entourage, deferred to the best story tellers amongst them to relate their most memorable experiences during the great expedition. *Anu* mariners of the entourage told of guiding the first Armada across the Straits of the *Red Sea* from the *Horn of Africa* to arrive upon the shores of the land that would later be called *Ancient Yemen* (on the present-day southern Arabian Peninsula). They told of navigating along the coast guided by ancient legends of the old Anu migrations and of the discovery of new sources of aromatics, such as myrrh and frankincense, in the land that would later be called *Southern Oman* ("Magan"). The *Anu* mariners told of sailing just off the eastern coast of the peninsula, ahead of the overland migrations, and of encountering the *Nagas* in the *Isles of Dilmun* ('Bahrain').

According to legends of the ancient 'Anu Empire' of the earliest antiquity, the *Anu* was the first to have settled in this region; they were the only people at the earliest stages of the world in possession of the arts of civilization.[mxiii] So it was no doubt with some trepidation that they found the *Nagas* having encroached, if not usurped, the prominence of their old empire and influence, even in this remote area of the world. By all appearances, the *Nagas* had unchallenged control of large parts of the eastern lands; however, rather than *Sethians* (followers of Set) of *Nagau-Punt*, the *Nagas* of the eastern lands were *Shivites* (followers of Shiva) of *Naga-Mandala'*. Elders of the *Kushite* tribes, in turn, told of settlements established in the eastern lands that would become ancient *Yemen* (at Hawagir), *Oman* (at Dhofar), and *Sumer* (at Eridu). *Kushite-Dasas* elders told of *Dasas* in the huge *Susiana Plain*, east of *Sumer*, and of the *Kushite-Dasas* settlement established at 'Shoosh' ('Susa'), in the earliest *Elam*.[mxiv]

Kushite-Si, in turn, told of the migrations over the *Hindu Kush Mountains* and settlements established in the fertile lands that would become ancient *Bactra*. Others told of the grand expedition into *Indus* (the Indian Sub-Continent), with part of the *Kushites* entering the northwest through the *Khyber Pass*, under the leadership of *Ausar,* while others entered in the southwest through the *Bolan Pass*, under the guidance of *Apollo*. While still others told of the rondevu in the *Saraswati River Delta* and of *Dasas* villages and settlements in the river valley*;* while still others told of *Kususthali*, the 'Port City of Kush,' in the Gulf of Kutch (Kush), and of rumors of a mighty *Naga* capital city in the heart of the *Dekkan,* in the southern part of the sub-continent. Merchants told of the coastal *Naga* kingdom of *Goa, the* epicenter of the spice trade of early antiquity, noting that they, the *Kushites*, were advised that the relationship between *Nagu-Punt* and *Naga-Mandala,* in no way precluded *Naga-Mandala* from establishing a mutually beneficial relationship with emergent *Kusha Dwipa* (Kush).

Merchants and traders amongst the entourage told of exotic herbs and spices brought back from the east, and of valuable commodities such as marble and emery brought back from the isle of *Naxos,* and the high-quality obsidian brought back from the isle of *Milos* in the Northern Seas. With all immersed in lively discourse, celebration and the elaborate feast prepared for the occasion, at the behest of *Ausar* (Osiris, Kush, Zeus, Dionysus), he, *Thoth, Tera-Neter* and *Governor Busiris* took leave of the boisterous festivities, retiring instead to a smaller, somewhat more private and quieter chamber, in order that the *Vizier* (Thoth), *Tera-Neter* and *Governor* (Busiris) might apprise him of the state-of-affairs in the lands, since his departure. Looking to the *Vizier* for the broadest assessment, *Thoth* (Djehuty, Hermes) affirmed that at the behest of *Governor Antee,' Hercules* (Herakles, Heryshaf, Alcides) was indeed on campaign with *General Hu,* reinsuring security along the frontier in the southern highlands, where the creeping influence of the *Naga* had gradually spread beyond the borderlands of *Nagu-Punt*, into the highlands of *Kush*.

The *Vizier* noted that 'though many of those who rallied to the aid of *Kush* during the conflict with *Nagu-Punt* had since the return to their kingdoms within the (Maa) Confederation, many of the *Anu* and *Anu-bians* in the southern highlands had gravitated to *Kush*... moreover, their strong affinities and alliances with the fervent *Kushite-Anu-bians* of the lowlands, in the heart *Kush*, had served to maintenance the balance of power'. The *Vizier* (Thoth, Djehuty, Hermes) noted that the 'return of the first *Kushite Armada*, with its exotic herbs and spices, and new sources of frankincense and myrrh from the mysterious lands of the east, had served to both invigorate and attract trade from across the extent of greater *Kush* (ancient Sudan)*;* from as far as the walled cities of the *Sao* in the central Sahel, and the *Holly City of Igbo Ukwu,* in the forest of north-eastern Nigeria,' he reported.

Return to Ancient Ṭhebes

The *Queen* ('Auset, Isis') holds court in the *Thebaid*, in the *City of Thebes;* the *Vizier* (Thoth, Djehuty, Hermes) continued, 'where she awaits the return of her *King* (Ausar, Osiris, Kush, Zeus, Dionysus), and presides over *Upper Khemet* and the heart of *Kush*'... '*Governor Antee* and *Governor Busiris* extend the weight of her rule and authority to the southern and northern provinces of the land, where each holds court in her honor,' *Thoth* concluded. To which *Ausar* noted that 'while in *Hērāclĕŏpŏlis* (Henen-nesut) *General Sia* informed of discord in *Lower Khemet* and the *Delta;* a restiveness prompted by a newly anointed provincial city, the *City of Bousiris* (Busiris), in the heart of the *Delta*'; with both the *Vizier* (Thoth) and *Governor (*Busiris) affirming that much of the rumored discord emanated from *Shedet* (the latter day 'The *City of Krocodilopolis*').

'The fledgling *City of Bousiris* (Djedu, Βούσιρις, Bousiris, Busiris) poses no issue of usurpation for the esteemed royal house of the reverent *City of Onu*,' Governor *Busiris* asserted, explaining that 'by long tradition, the *Kana-An*u and *Deltic-Anu* of the old *City of the Sun* have traded and intermediated commerce between the *Kana-An*u (Kanaanites) of *Kanaan* to their east, and the *Anu* kingdoms in the *Lower River Valley* to their immediate south and west. Particularly the prosperous kingdoms around the shores of *Mr-wr* (Paleo-Lake Moeris), circumventing the heart of the delta over which the new provincial *City of Bousiris* shall preside as the customs hub through which maritime trade from the great *Mediterranean Sea* shall enter *Khemet*'.

'A defiance broods among certain of the elders and priest of *Shedet* ("Krocodilopolis"),' *Thoth* (Djehuty, Hermes) observed, explaining it as a recalcitrance rooted in the long memory and oral history of the (Faiyum) basin.' 'The traditions of their oral histories, ' he continued, 'recite a time when *Shedet* and the kingdoms around the shores of *Mr-wr* (Paleo-Lake Moeris) amassed their armies and defended against the aggressions of the kings of latter-day *Atlatia*... whose incursions brought Atlatian armies to the frontier lands of *Mr-wr*... and beyond this into the *Lower River Valley*.' *Thoth* (Djehuty, Hermes) explained that 'the poems of their oral histories tell of the plight and despair of their struggles, and of a time when their spirits were sustained only by their tenuous vassalage under *Nagu-Punt,*' and their belief in the age-old preeminence of the *Naga*.'

'In aligning with *Kush* against *Nagu-Punt,*' *Thoth* (Djehuty, Hermes) explained that 'the objective of the royal house of *Shedet* ('Krocodilopolis') and the allied kingdoms around the shores of *Mr-wr* (Paleo-Lake Moeris) was to gain greater (if not unfettered) autonomy for the kingdoms of the (Faiyum) basin.' 'An objective,' *Tera-Neter* interjected, that most, if not all the royal houses, agree has been largely achieved. 'The angst from *Shedet* ('Krocodilopolis') emanates from the influential elders and sects of the priesthood in the city,' the *Vizier* (Thoth, Djehuty, Hermes) reported, noting that; 'the elders who recite the poems of their histories chafe at the notion paying homage to an heir of *Atlatia*'...*Thoth* explained, a travesty, in their view, whilst *Nagu-Punt* is seemingly even more reviled'.

'The angst among the priesthood at *Shedet* ('Krocodilopolis'), or more aptly, certain sects of the priesthood, is somewhat less nuanced,' *Thoth* (Djehuty, Hermes) observed, 'they find greater affinity and comfort with the kindred *Naga*... than with the unfamiliar tenets of *Amun*'. 'The ancient priesthood at *Shedet* (Krocodilopolis) is quite influential, including those who find true affinity with the *Naga*,' *Tera-Neter* noted, adding that 'it is the strength of their influence that lends merit and impetus to the discord sewn by the elders who recite the poems telling of the oral history of the conflict between Altatia and the kingdoms around the shores of *Mr-wr* (Palaeo-Lake Moeris) and the great (Fayium) basin.'

Wisdoms of Isis

'Having advised *Queen Isis* of this, the *Vizier* (Thoth, Djehuty, Hermes) reported, at her behest, it was resolved that he visit *Shedet* (Krocodilopolis) and assess the level of discord.' 'Thoth noted that he 'requested an audience with the king of *Shedet*, not merely as *Vizier*, but as a *High Priest* of the *Oru*,' renowned adherents of the orthodoxy of the Hydra Priesthood, and were thus held in high esteem by priesthood at *Shedet*. 'In addition,' *Thoth* noted that he was accompanied to *Shedet* by the *Anu High Priests Tera-Neter*, of the *Lower River Valley*. '*Tera-Neter*, in turn, noted that upon their arrival, they 'were met, with some surprise, not by a representative of the Royal House, but by the *High Priestess Het-Heru* (Hathor, Aphrodite), who would in time explain the crux of the discord in the kingdoms of *Mr-wr* (Lake Moeris) and the *Delta*.'

Throughout much of antiquity, High Priests and High Priestesses often possessed powers that were hardly inferior to those of the sovereigns of the realms in which they resided. Such was the case with the beautiful and sultry High Priestess Het-Heru (Hathor, Aphrodite, Venus), who was, at times, seen as consort of Sobek Shedety, eponymous King of Shedet. As a High Priestess of the Hydra Cult ("Followers of Heru"), she was more broadly and reverently seen as the figurative Wife of Heru ("Horus the Elder") and bore the serpent insignia of the Prophetess and Visionary.

The High Priestess symbolized the inductive feminine force that balances the assertive masculine energy of the High Priests; in the orthodoxy of the *Hydra Priesthood*, this was symbolic of the importance of balance between feminine and masculine energy in maintaining order and harmony. *Thoth* confessed that "High Priestess Het-Heru (Hathor, Aphrodite, Venus) possesses a type of beauty and sensuality that enhance her powers of persuasion," observing that "she is also endowed with the art of eloquent speech, a talent on captivating exhibition as she recited the oral legends of their struggles against the unprovoked invasion by *Atlatia*. Het-Heru (Hathor, Aphrodite, Venus) told of *Sobek Shedety* imploring the kings of the (Faiyum) basin to raise armies in defense against the *Atlatian* invaders, invaders who sought to conquer the whole of the *Lower River Valley*.

Shadows of Atlatia

The huge (*Faiyum*) basin where *Paleo-Lake Moeris* (Mr-wr) was located was the most prosperous province of the *Lower River Valley*, and it was against this key province that the ever-astute *Atlatians* launched their overland invasion. [mxv] Coveting the rich kingdoms along the northern shore of *Mr-wr*, the *Atlatians* first seized villages in the northwest woodlands abutting *Mr-wr* as they advanced on the northern shore.[mxvi]

The Legends

The allied armies of the north shore kingdoms met and engaged the frontal forces of the invading armies before they could fully emerge from the thick forests, taking the *Atlatians* completely by surprise. The fledgling north shore alliance had early success, fighting on familiar terrain and pushing the invaders back into the thick woodlands. But as the full mass of the invading forces reached the battle lines, the armies of the northern alliance were soon overwhelmed and sent retreating in differing directions, emerging from the woodlands in all but a full flight with the invaders in distant but persistent pursuit.

The armies of the south shore kingdoms and the southern (Faiyum) basin were last to take the field, led by *Sobek* of *Shedet,* who, upon observation, rallied all the forces of the basin and met and fought the *Atlatians* to a standstill at the edge of the forest... halting their advance on the north shore kingdoms. In the ensuing battles and contests between the allied armies of the kingdoms around *Mr-wr* and the (Faiyum) basin and the vast armies assembled by the *Atlatian* invaders, each side suffered major military defeats and won major military victories. But none more prominent than the opening campaign led by *Sobek* of *Shedet* ... a hard-fought campaign that forced the invaders to retreat far back into the thick forest. A thick tropical coastal forest characterized the northwestern borderland of the *Faiyum* during this era of antiquity, a forest with thick vegetation, tall trees, large vines, mangroves, and patches of dense woodlands; terrain largely nullifying the superior weaponry and field tactics of the *Atlatians.*

The Generals of the invading forces fought mightily to push beyond the confines of the forest, only to have their spent armies drawn into and bogged down by hard-fought unconventional counter-offensives launched by the shrewd and wily *Sobek.* Though in later writings *Sobek* (also known as "Sebek") is deified, depicted and reverently referred to as a '*God,*' in earlier lore, he is appropriately described and referred to as simply a *"Great General"* and (eponymous) *"Pharaoh"*... the first *Sovereign of Shedet;* a ruler of great prowess and stature whom early legend has accorded great epithets, such as the *"Protector of Pharaohs"* and the *"Lord of Faiyum,"* [mxvii] With the *Atlatian* invasion bogged down in the coastal woodlands, the duration of the war slowly stretched from several months to several years, exhausting and expending much of the manpower, resources, and resolve of the kingdoms and peoples of the (Faiyum) basin... a time in which the population fell into deep despair ...their spirits sustained only by their tenuous vassalage and belief in the preeminence of *Nagu-Punt,* who nonetheless appeared hesitant to defend or rescue them from the attack.

The vast invasion forces assembled by the kings of latter-day *Atlatia* attacked the *Lower Nile River Valley* and the kingdoms about the shores of *Mr-wr* by both sea and land ... *Atlatian* ships entered the *Delta* by sea, sailing upriver to just south of *Giza*, where they seized the mouth of the outlet channel by which ships returned from *Mr-wr* to the main corridors of the *Lower Nile,* en route to the *Delta* and the open sea. By seizing the mouth of the canal, the *Atlatians* enforced a blockade of maritime trade and communication between the kingdoms around *Mr-wr* and those in the *Lower River Valley,* the *Delta* ...and in kindred *Kanaan*. Nonetheless, the *Atlatian* overland invasion was eventually repulsed by *Sobek* and the armies of the basin, who doggedly persisted, repelling and finally driving the exhausted *Atlatians* from the northwestern woodlands and the (Faiyum) basin.

Yet, with the *Atlatian* blockade still in place, the kingdoms around *Mr-wr* remained somewhat cut off from the *Lower River Valley* and *Delta...* with the area and villages around the mouth of the outlet channel (from *Mr-wr*) having succumbed to attack and occupation by the invaders. It was several weeks before *Sobek*, as recognized commander of the combined armies of the basin, could muster a sufficient force from the spent ranks of the allied armies... to attack the blockade, and liberate the mouth of the channel, to reconnect with the *Deltic-Anu* and kindred *Kana-An*u of *Kanaan.* However, hours before the arrival of *Sobek* and his ragtag army... the *Atlatians* inexplicably abandoned their occupation, lifting the blockade and hastily departing *Lower River Valley* and *Delta...* fleeing to the open seas.

Later legends report that the *Atlatians* retreated after a resounding defeat by *Cecrops* and the armies of *Athens*, *Thessaly* and *Thrace* in the distant realm of earliest ancient Greece. Yet ancient oral lore tells of the invaders taking flight at the sight of the fierce forces amassed by *Sobek*. It was thus that *Sobek* was bestowed the epithet "*God of the Nile*," It was also the course of these events that delivered the kingdoms about *Mr-wr* into the formal vassalage of *Nagau-Punt*, a submission they had long resisted and hoped their remoteness in the backwaters of the *Nile* would avoid. 'That they should now pay homage to *Kush* (Ausar, Osiris, Zeus, Dionysus), a lineal descendent of the *Atlatian* throne,' the *Hathor* opined, 'is a source of angst and distrust, not only in *Shedet* but in the Royal Houses of many of the kingdoms around *Mr-wr* (Paleo-Lake Moeris).' '

After the long struggle against *Atlatia*, the kingdoms around *Mr-wr* were exhausted and concerned about further attacks,' *Het-Heru* (Hathor, Aphrodite) continued, noting that 'it fell to *Sobek* (Sebek) to dispatch an emissary to meet with *Set*, the Grand Regent of *Nagau-Punt*, on behalf of the kingdoms around *Mr-wr* and the basin. An undertaking in which he essentially acquiesced to informal vassalage in exchange for military support should the *Atlatian* armies return. An act that still sears deeply within his soul,' noted *Het-Heru*, advising that 'in the conflict between *Kush* and *Nagau-Punt*, *Sobek* (Sebek) refrained from coming to the aid of the *Nagas*, just as the *Naga*s had refrained from coming to the aid of the (Faiyum) basin during the *Atlatian* invasion. He saw in it an opportunity to regain a measure of autonomy, rather than a new form of vassalage… under a descendent of the *Atlatian* throne,' she quipped.

'It would have been unwise to have taken the fervent perspectives of the *High Priestess Het-Heru* lightly,' cautioned *Tera-Neter*, apprising *Ausar* (Osiris, Kush, Zeus, Dionysus) that 'her influence extends well beyond provincial *Shedet* and the kingdoms about the shores of *Mr-wr* (Paleo-Lake Moeris). 'The influence and perspectives of the *High Priestess Het-Heru* are prominent throughout much of the Delta,' *Tera-Neter* advised, noting that '*Het-Heru* and her Order are also prominent in the *City of Onu* (Anu, On, Heliopolis) in the southern Delta, in the *City of Imu* (latter day 'Kom el-Hisn') in the western Delta, and well beyond the confines of the eastern Delta, into the land of *Kanaan*, where she is held in reverence by the kindred *Kana-Anu* of the southern provinces.'[mxviii]

'And yet,' continuing with his report, *Thoth* (Djehuty, Hermes) confessed that he 'could not resist but to inquire of her, was it not the very royal lineage of whom you now object that once granted the *Anu* safe province in the (Faiyum) basin as they sought sanctuary from intrusions of the *Nagas*?' 'I could not resist but to retort,' *Thoth* continued, 'that by the most ancient of legends was this not the *Land of Khronos* (Khem, Kham, Cham, Ham), and province allotted his son (Ausar, Osiris, Kush, Zeus, Dionysus) when apportioning his realm among his progeny? Was this not the ancient province that young *Ausar* availed to *Followers of Horus, the Elder*? 'This is his affinity for *Southern Atlatia*,' the land of his Grandmother, where *Ausar* became first acquainted with the *Oru*, in the lands south of *Southern Atlatia*.'

Encountering Het-Heru (Hathor, Aphrodite, Venus)

'As intoxicating as the *High Priestess* was,' *Thoth* confessed, seemingly reliving the moment, 'in a quite sober manner, he informed her that 'had *Sobek* granted him a due audience, it might have assuaged his angst to learn of *Ausar's* self-imposed exile …in opposition to the aggressions of latter-day *Atlatia*. That so distinguished was he, in contrast to the loathsome latter-day kings, he was bestowed the affectionate title of *'Kush'* (the "Perfect Black Sovereign"). Had *Sobek* granted us audience, *Thoth* continued, it would have assuaged his mistrust to learn that *Ausar* departed *Atlatia* well before the invasion of the (Faiyum) basin. That during those times, Ausar built a sacred city, below the southwestern shores of the *Atlantean Sea,* from where he launched the alliance that now spans from the (Atlantic) Ocean in the west to the (Red) Sea in the east (the *Sahel,* the *Ancient Sudan,* the eponymous *"Land of Kush")*. 'Would that the noble *Sobek* (Sebek) have granted us the audience,' persisted *Thoth* (Djehuty, Hermes), 'it would surely have assuaged his mistrust to learn that the *Maa Confederation* itself formed in confederacy against the very kings of (Latter-day) *Atlatia* whom he so reviles.' 'An argument which clearly penetrated *Het-Heru's* usually rather stern demeanor,' observed *Tera-Neter,* noting that at first he thought it simply the mutual attraction between *She* and the *Vizier,* but it later became clear that it was this and more.

'Having known *Het-Heru* since her childhood,' reflected *Tera-Neter*, 'he could attest to having never before witnessed such vulnerability, as when she sheepishly informed that… rather than grant our requested audience, in the absence of the King (of Khemet), *Sobek* instead insisted upon the direct audience with the *Queen* (Isis)'.'Regaining her composure,' *Tera-Neter* continued… 'the High Priestess advised there would be a feast at the Palace in honor of he Thoth, celebrating the union of Upper and Lower Khemet.' 'But the formalities of any such union, in *Sobek's* view,' she emphasized, 'have yet to be determined.' 'One could sense that more than her demeanor had softened towards us,' observed *Tera-Neter,* ', particularly towards the *Vizier*. Prompted by what appeared to be a sense of scorn*,* and perhaps equally by her apparent attraction to the Vizier (Thoth, Djehuty, Hermes)*,'* opined *Tera-Neter,* 'her usual intransigence gave way to a softer, subtly seductive demeanor.' According to legend, she was one of the most beautiful women of her era and was by no means a demure beauty; *Het-Heru* was well-aware of her sexuality and the power of her sexual appeal.

As the *Patron Goddess of Women,* she was symbolic of the seductive role of feminine energy, inducing masculine energy toward productive works. As *High Priestess,* she (and the high priestesses of her own Order) propagated the use of the regenerative power of passion and sexual rejuvenation to aid in transforming life so that it more accurately reflects the highest vision that aspirants had for themselves. *Hathor* was the archetype in the inner teachings of her cult, the embodiment of feminine sexuality, adept at using her beauty and seductive skills, granting her influence over those vulnerable to such persuasive powers. 'At my age,' admitted *Tera-Neter,* 'having watched her blossom from childhood, I am, for the most part, immune to the power she wields over most men …yet I could not avoid concern for the *Vizier,*' he confessed.

The Legends

Known in early ancient *Khemet* as *Het-Heru,* she became familiar to most as "Hathor," a *Primitive Greek* corruption of variants of the name Het-Heru, such as Het Heret and Hat Hor (the name "Hathor" deriving from the latter). While *Hathor* has become the name most commonly used, she was anciently known by *Classical Greeks* as *Aphrodite*, while the later *Romans* called her *Venus*.[mxix]

Though her contribution to *Khemet* was within its early formative period, by late antiquity, veneration of her legend had elevated her to the status of 'Goddesses.' As such, she is one of the oldest known 'Goddesses' of ancient *Khemet*.[mxx] *Het-heru* (Aphrodite, Venus) was easily one of the most recognizable and yet mysterious of Goddesses; so vast was her influence that her lore existed as a powerful and influential factor for the entire history of the ancient Khemet. None so fully embodied a woman's sexuality and femininity as *Hathor*; she is described as extremely feminine and exceptionally beautiful, with a soft, smooth, *seductive* voice and an affable disposition. Hers was a warm, sensual beauty, not aloof or remote but alluring and captivating. In many paintings, she is crowned with an arisen serpent; the symbol of an awakened kundalini; a source of vitality, energy, vibration, excitation and invigoration of one's life force.

That sexual arousal was considered arousal of one's life force was a major religious theme of the time, and the beautiful and alluring *Het-heru* (Hathor, Aphrodite, Venus) was deemed "Goddess of Sexuality and Fertility,' As Goddess of Sexuality, she was symbolic of the seductive role of (magnetic) feminine energy in stimulating and inducing (electric) masculine energy to produce; she was said to symbolize and embody the very feminine aspect of divinity. Ichnographically she was usually represented as a beautiful woman, swathed in turquoise (her sacred color) or red raiment, wearing a headdress of the sun disk surmounted between two elongated (cow) horns.[mxxi]

As the "Goddess of Love," *Het-heru* (Hathor, Aphrodite, Venus) was a quintessential Tantric Goddess whose priestesses were educated in the sacred feminine arts of adornment, seduction, passion, and lovemaking. Adept at the inducement of masculine energy, the priestesses of her order propagated that while it is the synthesis of the two great energies that *creates*, it is (magnetic) feminine energy first invigorates (electric) masculine energy, which in turn, stimulates (magnetic) feminine energy, bringing the two into harmony; with a concordance of the two energies needed to "pro-create,'

Masculine energy was characterized as assertive and aggressive, manifesting physically, emotionally, and mentally; spiritually, it was viewed as divine will, the outward-focused attributes of the *Amun* (the masculine aspect of the Creator). Yet devoid of balance with sacred feminine energy, it was seen as self-serving, in an aggressive quest for vaguely defined and transitory happiness. Feminine energy was characterized as receptive, intuitive and nurturing, and manifesting physically, emotionally, and mentally; spiritually, it was viewed as the inductive and receptive attributes of the procreative Cosmos.

Yet devoid of balance with divine masculine energy, sacred feminine energy was said to be inert, impassive, and barren. However, feminine energy always attracts and accommodates masculine energy; indeed, not merely accommodates, but inspires, influences, and enhances it. The balancing of feminine and masculine energy, in mutual respect and in harmony, was believed to invigorate the power of each life force …this as the energy of unconditional acceptance (love) was said to flow through the physical, emotional, mental, and spiritual bodies to the creator, permitting a direct experience of the selves, as pure energy, in union with the divine source. [mxxii]

As Goddess of Beauty, Sexuality and Creation, *Het Heru* (Hathor, Aphrodite, Venus) represented the universal flow of divine feminine energy. As High Priestess, she espoused that the paths of sensuality and spirituality not only cross, but merge …with frequencies of love resonating through the physical, emotional, mental, and spiritual bodies, and the transcendent function of passion inducing, enhancing and transmuting those vibrational energies; availing a gateway accessed only through divine perfect love. Women of the era were altogether greatly attracted and inspired by *Hathor* and aspired to embody her beliefs and her (earlier and later) conjoined roles as lover, wife, and mother.

As *Goddess of Women,* she presided over the sacred feminine arts of adornment, beauty rituals, enchantment, and lovemaking; in her role as Goddess, she was considered the very incarnation of feminine sexuality. As *High Priestess,* she was said to be extremely sexually confident and aware of her beauty and sexual desirability, with no qualms about using her power of feminine persuasion. To *Hathor,* feminine powers of persuasion were aspects of the transformative power of love. In her role, she encouraged females sexually and used feminine energy to induce and incline masculine energy to produce.[mxxiii]

"Feminine powers of inducement and persuasion are not be underestimated," admonished *Tera-Neter,* cautioning that 'the powers of persuasion of exceptionally beautiful women, such as *Het-Heru*, can be extremely compelling, particularly upon men of new acquaintance… such as the *Vizier*'.[mxxiv] Ancient legends report that "*Thoth* (Djehuty, Hermes) looked upon the face of *Het-Heru* and praised her according to her desire… and that she, in turn, was strengthened by his words." *Thoth* was deeply impressed with *Het-Heru's* beauty but, much like *Tera-Neter* …wary of her motivations. 'By what contrivance was she is seeking audience with *Queen Auset* (Isis), whose beauty is said to rival her own …and this on behalf of her consort, *Sobek Shedety*, famed sovereign of *Shedet*,' he pondered.

'At first,' *Tera-Neter* noted, 'he thought it simply the mutual attraction between her and the *Vizier* (Thoth, Djehuty, Hermes) that so softened her usually intractable demeanor …but it was more than this,' he explained, noting that '*Thoth* had subtly induced the usually intractable *High Priestess* to reassess her opinion of *Kush* and *Khemet.*' 'Astutely seeing that she and her cult, more so than *Sobek* (Sebek) and the royal houses of the realm, had been key to the dissemination and discord at *Heliopolis* and the *Delta* …and would thus be key to its amelioration'. 'As the evening wore on …in what appeared an obvious gesture to shift the subject from *Sobek,*' quipped *Tera-Neter,* 'the *High Priestess* inquired into rumors of the *Vizier's* famed enlightened teachings at the *School of the Mysteries,* here in *Khmunu* (early ancient Hermopolis).'

'The following evening, the *High Priestess* graciously met and accompanied us to the Palace and feast held in our honor,' reported *Thoth*. Admitting that 'after the formal introduction and the *High Priestess* took what was clearly her dutiful seat beside *Sobek,'* he wondered if perhaps the wily *Sobek* had averted their interposition by yet another clever counteroffensive, 'as he had done so successfully against *Atlatia* ...but this time in the form of the seductive *Hathor.'* 'A suspicion somewhat assuaged,' he then reported, 'when the *High Priestess* surprised all by announcing she would be returning with us to *Khmunu*, enroot to *Thebes,* where, as an emissary for *Sobek,* she shall seek audience with the *Queen* on his behalf'... 'Honoring the *Queen* as the *Vizier* has so honored *Sobek,* she whispered softly,' added *Tera-Neter,* 'leaving the noble *Sobek* little room to object.' 'Once in the island city *City of Khmunu* (Hermopolis), enthralled by teachings of the *School of the Mysteries,* as well as her tacit intrigue with the *Vizier,'* quipped *Tera-Neter,* 'the *High Priestess* graciously accepted our invitation to reside and study in the temple for a few days, before continuing her voyage onward to the royal *City of Thebes.'* 'Among the priests of the temple, *Thoth* propounded, 'the *High Priestess* was second only to the *High Priest Tera-Neter* himself in grasping the teachings of the *Mysteries.'*

Like the ever discerning and honorable *Tera-Neter,'* explained *Thoth,* 'the intuitive *High Priestess* gained new insight into precreation, *Amun,* and the origin of the *Hydra* (the "Cosmic Serpent") itself. 'By what canon does your *School of the Mysteries* reveal the mystical origin of the *Hydra,* inquired *Ausar* (Osiris, Kush, Zeus, Dionysus)'? Subtly unveiling his revelation to *Ausar* for the first time, *Thoth* alluded to 'a divine epiphany' arising within his meditations on the ontology of *Amun* (Amon) and the cosmology of the *Hydra.* Describing what he experienced as 'an enlightened flow of wisdom, bringing forth distinctively new perceptions ...and verily, new insight into the impetus, aspects, and mechanisms creation itself'.[mxxv] 'Creation,' he illuminated, 'is, in reality, an act of differentiation (and the transformation) of the primordial abyss, from its undifferentiated state, into differentiated energy (matter).' 'The primordial abyss is made up four elements, personified by an *Ogdoad* of four balanced male and female dualities of divine beings,' *Thoth* further elucidated, revealing '*Heh* and *Hauhet* as personifying the spatial infinity and formlessness of the abyss, and *Kek* and *Kauket* as personifying its darkness and obscurity. *Nun* (Nu) and *Nunet* (Neith, Nu, Nut) are revealed as personifying the ocean of primordial consciousness (awareness) and divine existence (being) within the abyss, and *Amun* and *Amaune*t personify the hidden power and the breath of life within *Nun*.

Though the *Nun* was credited with setting the process of creation in motion and thus being the foremost creative force, the very act of creation was considered a fundamentally feminine process of transmutation of primordial substance into the universal tapestry. The story of the unfolding of creation is fundamentally a story of movement from non-duality to duality, with polarity affected by (magnetic) feminine energy stimulating and inducing (electric) masculine energy. A relationship and role fundamental to the transmutation of undifferentiated energy to differentiated energy (matter) and an essential aspect of cohesive dispersion. The expansion of the cosmos is primarily a masculine process of dispersion, while the transmutation and formation of (differentiated energy) matter, through a process of contraction, densification and cohesion, is a purely feminine process. The first creative act was then the setting of differentiated energy (matter) into motion, an act brought about by the inducement of *Nun* (Chaos) by *Nunet* (Order), it's female counterpart'.[147]

---

[147] See the 'Metu Neter' (Volume Two, Page 44); by: Anuk Ausar, published (1994) by Khamit Corp, Btooklyn NY

Nunet (Order) was more of a representation of duality than a true deity, yet in the subjective realm, she is the purveyor and goddess of sacred ecstasy and heightening states of bliss and pleasure.[mxxvi] When the potentialities of *Nun* (Chaos) were stimulated and focused by the seduction of *Nunet* (Order), in the grasp of his pursuit, *Nun* entered into an emotional union with *Nunet* (also known as Neith, or Nut), evoking states of divine ecstasy. It was thus that *Nunet* gave birth to *Amun* …while she was still in the waters of *Nun* (Nu). The first transmutation from an undifferentiated state to differentiated energy (matter) was achieved by *Nunet's* projection of the sound 'Au' into *Nun*, creating the first manifestation, and it was thus that *Amun* arose from the primordial waters of consciousness. *Amun* arose from the primordial waters of consciousness in *divine duality*, existing in serene meditation and contemplation for eons, pondering pre-creation, nurturing and exponentiating the omniscience and omnipresence of *Nous* (the "*Divine Mind of Amun*").[mxxvii]

In his duality *Amun* is hidden and unknowable, with a soul-like quality (the "Ba") rendering him everywhere and nowhere; he is *Omniscience*, having infinite awareness and *Omnipresence*, being all-present. While his feminine counterpart, *Amunet*, is unhidden and knowable, with a soul-like quality (the "Ba") rendering her nowhere and everywhere, she is the essence of *Sentience*, the ability to experience sensations, and *Eros*, the personification of divine love, a most powerful spiritual force.[mxxviii] The act of creation involves releasing the forces of duality, with *Eros* as the primary force attracting *Amun* away from the state of non-duality to a state of duality, unity, and wholeness. It is through Eros that *Amunet* seduces and stimulates desire and passion within *Amun,* inculcating the life-instilling and preserving instincts of propagation and protection of the continuity of the spiritual mind and body. Eros is the inspiring force behind creation, awakening *Amun* from within and guiding and accompanying Nous. Eros is the cause of love and creation and, thus, all life.[mxxix]

Nous (the Divine Mind of Amun), stimulated by Eros (the Seduction of Amunet), gave parturition to *Logos* (the "Word"), a direct emanation of *Amun* manifested as the spiritual energy known as the "Ka,' It was the Ka, illuminated by Eros and Ma'at, direct emanations of *Amunet,* that was observed on earth as the great *Cosmic Serpent;* personified in the divine personage of "Heru" ('Horus the Elder'), the metaphorical *Hydra* (or 'Naga'). The *Hydra* circled within oceans of undifferentiated energy for eons, giving form and order to the temporal cosmos and ensouling the ordered elements …whereby they coalesced into forms. With Ma'at (Order) brought to Chaos, the cosmic elements spontaneously began to differentiate, constellating in myriad ways, giving shape to the complex dimensions and entities forming the cosmos. 'It is thus that *Amun* brought the states of being in the manifested cosmos into existence,' concluded *Thoth*, propounding that 'the Hydra is an instrument of *Amun* in the unfolding of creation …and in its administration'. 'A revelation of profound interest throughout the temples of the *Hydra Priesthood,'* interceded *Tera-Neter,* noting that 'for the "*Followers of Heru*" ('Horus the Elder'), the ontology of the *Hydra* has long been a mystery without hypotheses.

'And yet,' *Thoth* digressed*,* 'that what has captivated *Het-heru* (Hathor) as much, if not more, than any infatuation or intrigue between she and he is her realization that masculine and feminine energies are the most powerful forces of *Creation*, that indeed, the very unfolding of *Creation* itself is a phenomenon of the reflexive and reciprocal interplay between these great forces.' 'An awakening that has caused a perceivable change within her consciousness,' noted *Thoth,* observing that 'before one could sense an intransigence and strong-willed resistance, and afterward one could sense an uneasy ambivalence …a vacillation between acceptance and defiance, characterized by moments of acquiescence, contrasted with moments of hash regret'. 'It was a change further acknowledged by *Tera-Neter,* who explained it as a perceivable change that began in the *Temple of Khmunu* (Hermopolis) *and* reached culmination during her audience with the *Queen*.'

A transformation was observed when, at the behest of Thoth, *Tera-Neter* explained, he accompanied the High Priestess and her entourage on their voyage to *Thebes,* noting the voyage to have been 'uneventful, apart from *Het-heru's* insatiable inquiries regarding *Queen* Isis. In the ancient traditions of the *Amunite Priesthood,* a "Queen" such as Isis inherently ascended to *High Priesthood* by virtue of her royal status and was anointed "*High Priestess,*"; a carry-over from the *Atlatian* era. Conversely, under the protocol of the *Hydra Priesthood*, an aspirant, such as *Het-Heru* (Hathor), ascended through years of initiation and many levels of priesthood. *Het-heru* had been among a small core of superior priests, priestesses and adepts that served in their temples and studied for many years to achieve the highest level of spiritual accomplishment and personal attainment. Few High Priestesses attained *Het-heru's* exalted status within the priesthood, as she eventually attained a position equivalent to any (male) High Priest.
mxxx

Incredulous of the *Queen's* merit and true abilities as a "High Priestess," *Het-heru's* disposition during much of the voyage vacillated between disdain for 'royal assent to High Priesthood …on the mire basis of marriage,' and admiration for the grace and acuity with which the *Queen* has ruled and endeavored to bring the peoples of *Khemet* together.' 'Ambivalence such as this was an entirely new experience for one usually as certain and resolute as *Het-heru,*' opined *Tera-Neter,* connoting that 'surprisingly, at times, her uncertainty seemed to reveal unsettled insecurities.' 'All of which were drastically reshaped during the first of what became our two audiences with the Queen,' *Tera-Neter* recounted, recalling 'the initial meeting, with the two of us hastily ushered before the *Queen,* whose famed beauty, grace and eloquence, were all at once mesmerizing.'

'It was perhaps the first time *Het-heru* had encountered a beauty rivaling her own,' suggested *Tera-Neter,* adding that 'having made the *Queen's* prior acquaintance, *Her Majesty* requested he formally introduces *Het-heru.* He then introduced as the "*High Priestess Het-heru* of the provincial *City of Shedet*; the prosperous kingdoms around the shores of *Mr-wr*, and the reverent *City of Onu,* …in the eastern delta'.'To which *Queen Auset* (Aset, Iset, Isis), who accommodates everyone with such grace,' *Tera-Neter* recalled, 'listened intently and softly inquired, "and to what do I owe the pleasure of your acquaintance, *High Priestess Het-heru* (Hathor)?"' 'In near awe,' *Tera-Neter* observed, *Het-heru* found her usual feminine powers of seductive persuasion, the essence of her magic, all but nullified and rendered useless.

'Yet, recovering quickly,' *Tera-Neter* recalled, *Het-heru* explained she had "been sent as Royal Emissary of the *King of Shedet*, who has welcomed and received, yet deferred audience with the *Queen's* eminent *Vizier* …opting instead, in the absence of *Pharaoh* (Ausar) …that she request a direct audience with *Her Majesty* …on his behalf"'. 'After pondering for but a moment,' *Tera-Neter* recounted, '*Auset* (Isis) express curiosity 'as to why the honorable *King of Shedet* would so insolently decline audience with her esteemed *Vizier?*''A question which *Het-heru* answered by recounting the story told here today,' *Tera-Neter* recalled, 'the story of the history of *Shedet* and the kingdoms around the shores of *Mr-wr*; and their age-old alliance with *Nagu-Punt*, arranged in good faith by an emissary, that nonetheless eventually devolved into near vassalage.

'In accord with *Kush*,' *Het-heru* recounted, 'arranged again by "emissary," in the personage of his eminence *Tera-Neter;* the kingdoms of *Mr-wr* and those of the (Faiyum) basin sought and were promised a measure of autonomy ...an autonomy that again appears to be waning'. 'It is for this reason, Her Majesty,' *Het-heru* emphasized, 'that the pharaoh *Sobek of Shedet* seeks a direct audience rather than negotiation through an emissary.' 'And yet *Het-heru* (Hathor),' *Queen Auset* (Isis) interjected and observed, 'you are here as his *emissary*'; 'an observation leaving *Het-heru* momentarily speechless,' *Tera-Neter* noted. Recalling that 'she was again momentarily stunned when the *Queen* later stated that 'neither you nor your *Order* are unknown to us High Priestess Het-Heru...whose Temples adorn the cities of *Shedet* ("Krokodilópolis"), *Imu* (Kom el-Hisn) and *Onu* ("Heliopolis,")'.[mxxxi]

'Your *Order* brings *Ma'at* (form and structure) to the Priestesses of the *Hydra cult;* a testament to providence and your abiding prescience and influence *Het-heru* (Hathor),' *Auset* (Isis) proclaimed, describing her influence as 'radiating well beyond *Shedet* and the kingdoms around *Mr-wr* ...into the *Delta,* and far beyond'. 'Wherein lies an unavoidable irony,' *Auset* (Isis) opined; 'my *Vizier* went to *Shedet* to assess the discord spreading from that city into the *Delta* and beyond; ...evoking the question, is it fate or irony that brings you here *Het-heru*?'[mxxxii] By a knowing smile and the slightest gesture of her hand the *Queen* indicated her query to have been rhetorical, rather than literal, and she then instructed that we 'return in the morrow,' *Tera-Neter* recounted, 'when she would render her decision regarding *Sobek's* request for the audience.'

'This first encounter clearly reshaped *Hathor's* earlier opinion, and perhaps even her insecurities,' *Tera-Neter* mused, recalling that 'she later confessed to finding *Auset* (Isis) "mysteriously intuitive, with a kind of radiance that draws one toward enlightenment, and leaves one somehow changed by the encounter." Initiates and adepts at the temples of *Thebes* ('Waset') called her by the endearing epithet "Nebet Heka," the "Lady of Magic,' While to the laity, she was known as the "Great Enchantress," the "One Whose Words Come to Pass Without Fail"; epithets' not lost on Het-heru, who reassessed and dismissed her prior presumptions regarding the questionable merit of the *Queen. Auset* (Isis) embodied the very essence of a *Royal High Priestess,* gifted with prescient intuition and an innate sense of elegance and grace.

Cerebral, yet guided by a gifted sense of intuition, *Auset* (Isis) was known as a prescient visionary and healer with abilities to sense and cure illness (and imbalance) within the physical, emotional, and spiritual body. The combination of her cerebral and intuitive gifts enables her to discern between reality and delusion and truth and falsity, to see clearly, rather than be blinded or misled by illusions or figments of the imagination. 'A prescience duly sensed by *Het-heru*,' recalled *Tera-Neter,* observing that 'she was visibly unsettled at the prospect of *Auset* clairvoyantly discerning a fuller truth than she had presented.' Noting that 'she spent much of that evening pondering the riddle of the *Queen's* query (regarding "fate and irony") ...and more explicitly, what the answer to the riddle might imply'.

Finally, she deduced that if it is *"fate,"* then it is a providence beyond which she could verily attest, resolving that the answer to the riddle must surely then be in the *"irony"* to which the *Queen* alluded.' 'It is a query that honors you and yet, all at once, seeks to assess your integrity,' proffered *Tera-Neter*. Having been so advised, and after an evening of honest introspection, *Het-heru* emerged the following morning with a clear sense of mission ...and an aura of calm. *Tera-Neter* recounted that as they were again ushered into the throne room the following morning, though we were each admittedly less mesmerized by *Auset's* beauty, they were nonetheless unavoidably enchanted by her grace'.

Isis was so confident in the natural beauty that she found elaborate adornment unnecessary, giving her a casual and disarmingly alluring mystique. The *Queen* (Auset, Isis) at once set the tenor and tone of the second audience by immediately and rather succinctly inquiring if *Het-heru* had 'given consideration' to her query pertaining to "fate or irony,' To which the high-minded *High Priestess* (Het-heru, Hathor) self-assuredly replied that, 'in truth, I am before *Her Majesty* because *my* people, the *Anu* of the *Lower Valley,* seek to preserve our dignity and autonomy.' This evokes a word of prudence and a brief bit of history from *Auset*, who cautioned, 'let it not be lost on you, *Het-heru*, that *my* people, those who inhabit the lands of *Upper Khemet* and *Kush* to its immediate south, are *Anu-bian* descendants of *you* whom we honor as *Ancestors.* Know that we *Anuba* have not acceded to assimilation but assented to the alliance for greater security, autonomy, and prosperity of all.

Auset then told at length of having met and married *Ausar* shortly after the *Sahelian* tribes that then comprised the *Kushites* finally settled and expanded into what has since become the *Land of Kush*, immediately south of *Upper Khemet'*. She told of *Ausar's* 'prescience and grace in preserving the cultural inheritances of the diverse populous that are the *Kushites'*; advising that 'he governs by what he terms *"Immutable Laws,"* more anciently known as the *"Laws of Poseidon,"* as they have been handed down.' Although a term not commonly used for states outside latter-day Europe, the founding laws of *Khemet* were based on an archaic form of 'federalism' that had existed since the time of *Atlatia*.[mxxxiii]

The evolvement towards the system began as a form of cooperation inspired by ancestral descent and sentiments of ethnic comradery, with most early ancient polities built around regional ethnic identities. The emergent form of archaic federalism was a combination of self-rule and shared rule, a compound mode of governance combining a "central" (or "federal") government with ("provincial" or "territorial") regional governments united in a single political system. It was a system in which common policies were made (and implemented) through negotiation, enabling the regional (or provincial) rulers to share in the decision-making process.[mxxxiv]

This archaic form of federalism was the best system for integrating diverse regional and ethnic groups, particularly those cautious of control by an overly powerful central government. It represented a central pathway for regional integration, delimited on the less integrated side by "Confederalism" (where the central government is subordinate to regional governments) and on the more integrated side by the single Unitary State (where regional governments subordinate to the central government).[mxxxv] In terms of governance, the most important characteristics of archaic federalism were its adaptability and role in promoting cooperation and unity in diversity. It unified constituent polities together in critical ways for the interest of trade, communication, and other reasons while maintaining the respective integrities of all parties.

In terms of formal governance, early ancient *Khemet* was a theocracy, a form of government in which a deity is a source from which all authority derives, with the royal *City of Thebes* as its theological and political capital.[mxxxvi] Pharaoh (or the "King") was the figurative head of the society, in charge of its economy and army, and empowered, as *"Tutelary Priest,"* to act on behalf of the government and citizens of the country. As a theocracy, the Priests were one of the most important parts of the government and were given the utmost respect by the other classes, granting them a special status above the rest of the citizens, forming a kind of unique nobility. Religious exigencies guided statecraft to the extent that social and public policies were often guided or, at minimum, influenced by religious considerations.

Notions of "law" and "justice" were influenced by the concept of *Ma'at*, the inspiration of *Divine Order,* and the foundation and basis of ethical behavior, including that of Kings.[mxxxvii] Proper behavior was expected in all relationships, within the family, between neighbors, between officials, nobility, soldiers, the governed, and so on. Pharaoh held the balance of *Ma'at* and was charged with settling disputes and matters of discord, shifting the balance and influence of mundane daily power away from the Priests and onto Pharaoh. The social hierarchy started from the top, consisting of the Pharaoh, the Vizier, Nobles, Priests, Scribes, and Soldiers. Most of the people in early ancient Khemet were farmers, who tended fields, raised animals, and maintained irrigation canals and reservoirs.

Because grain was used as an early form of money, farmers played a uniquely important role in the society of the era; each farmer paid taxes in the form of grain, which was then stored in Pharaoh's warehouses and used to feed the people in times of famine. The physicians, craftsmen, merchants, artisans, traders, and storekeepers who made up the middle class, together with lower-class laborers such as the builders who made the mud bricks used in almost every building and the cobblers, potters, carpenters, and water carriers who brought water for washing and drinking, along with the brewers, fishermen and boat crews, each paid taxes in goods and services. Citizens were also drafted into the army and forced to labor for given periods of time to pay what was called a "corvée," essentially a labor tax.

Nonetheless, social mobility was possible in ancient *Kheme*t by acquiring valuable skillsets and capabilities, enabling those in the lower classes to move up the social hierarchy. For instance, a boy born on a farm who learned to read and write could become a scribe and gain employment in government and, in this manner, work his way up the ranks of the hierarchy. Contrary to conventional history and popular belief, there was no slave class in ancient *Khemet* (Egypt) until the time of the Greeks (after 332 BCE). However, there was involuntary servitude and forced labor, which became the fate of captured invaders and prisoners of war (and their descendants). In addition, to use as forced labor on building projects, such captives also worked in stone quarries and mineral mines alongside regular criminals.

Power in early ancient *Khemet* was a balanced affair between an executive branch, represented by *Pharaoh*, and a legislative branch, represented by the *Priesthood*. The guiding principle underpinning the governing of the country was the notion that *Amun* was an aspect of the *Ka* of each citizen of the land.[mxxxviii] A principle spawning the notion that due consideration be given to the laity in all policy deliberations, a concept based on the fundamental spiritual belief in the equality of all before *Amun*. This, together with the edict that all provinces of the polity be duly represented, added resilience to the fabric of nascent *Khemet*. A concomitance to which *Auset* in noting that '*Ausar* arranged governance in a way that equitably distributes power, and provides a means to peacefully resolve discord; governance with *Ma'at* as its basis.'

Auset (Aset, Iset, Isis) propounded that 'such governance confers equilibrium of power, with primacy in the royal house of *Thebes;* it proffers a destiny in which the fates of the royal houses (of the polity) are each in their own hands …and casts no constraints upon one's autonomy. It is governance under which each may blossom to the fullness of their potentiality; governance under which it may be destined that your lord *Sobek* gain provincial prominence over the whole of the (Faiyum) basin. Just as it may be destined *Het-heru* that the influence of your Order spread beyond the confines of the *Delta* and *Lower Valley* and gain prominence in the cities of the *Upper Valley*, and perhaps *Kush* itself'. *Auset* (Isis) explained that *Ausar* 'auspiciously placed *Khemet* ("House of Khronos") at the very heart of greater *Kush* (Kusha Dwipa).'

'This begins a new era,' *Auset* (Isis) proclaimed, noting it to be 'an era of boundless possibility and opportunity, particularly for one as gifted as thee *Het-heru* …let it not be constrained by bygone acrimony and petty antipathies of the past. 'This much is up to us,' asserted *Auset*, alluding to precepts of the *OGDOAD,* which infer masculine and feminine energies to be the most powerful forces of Creation …and the feminine aspect of being the vessel of that Creation. *Auset* (Isis) continued that, 'as propagated by your "Order" *Het-heru*, it is the way of things that feminine energy induces masculine energy to create. Thus, in the inheritance of *Ma'at,'* she then challenged, 'is it not within the evolving tasks of those who have attained the vaunted mantle of "Priestess" to nurture and strengthen, rather than weaken and abort, that that has been conceived?'

'With her new sense of resolve,' *Tera-Neter* noted, *Hathor* submitted that 'it is the way of things that, mutually invigorated, (magnetic) feminine energy focuses (electric) masculine energy toward divine will, strength, and purpose; the bestowed attributes of *Amun* (the masculine aspect of divinity).[mxxxix] In this manner, feminine energy does indeed induce masculine energy to create and simultaneously becomes the vessel through which such creation unfolds, the bestowed attributes of *Amunet* (the feminine aspect of divinity). Through divine and reciprocal interaction between these two great forces …that is worthy of creation is created and nurtured in divine and prescient design'.

'Creation is a discovery, not design *Het-heru* (Hathor),' *Auset* (Isis) retorted, illuminating that 'the future and the present are each fluid, with infinite possibilities, which is why fate is not predetermined.' 'After pausing to allow a moment of reflection, *Tera-Neter* recalled, 'the *Queen* (Auset, Isis) elucidated that 'that which is worthy of creation is created by impetus and intercourse of the two great forces, rendering creation both eternal and infinite.' She further explained that 'it is *Nous* (the "Divine Mind") that imbues prescience *Het-heru* …a prescience limited by the luminosity of individual enlightenment; an illumination that reveals only the margins of what it unveils'.[148] '

Our world is not predesigned, predestined, or predetermined *Het-heru,'* admonished *Auset*, advising that 'it is ever-changing and in many ways given actualization by our choices and decisions. 'Ever the Enchantress,' *Tera-Neter* noted, '*Auset* (Isis) proffered that 'it is *Reverence* that transforms us *Het-heru* (Hathor)'; alluding to the sanctifying role of *Reverence* in enlightening man, and the evolution of his societies. Early *Khemet* was a theocracy, implying "divinely guided" rule over society; it was governed by religious belief and moral and ethical codes embodying *Divine Law* and the *Law of Karma* (or "Natural Law").[mxl] It is a form of governing with no separation of church and state, with laws interpreted by religious leaders.

The argument in favor of this form of theocracy was that the presence of religious ethos in governance dissuaded discontent in the polity (it is difficult to argue with policies that are reputed to come from a higher power). 'Governance without *Reverence* is blind to the common good …and deaf to the needs of the powerless,' *Auset* proffered, propounding that a society without *Reverence* is brutish and selfish.[149] Such incipient power is aflame with arrogance, smoldering blindly toward discord and eventual rebellion.[150] A reverent society requires moral and ethical codes, with its rulers and citizenry living and practicing them as a basis of daily life.

---

[148] In paraphrase of 'Prescient' used In Dune' (see http://www.verbalworkout.com).
[149] American classical scholar, Paul Woodruff (b. 1943)
[150] In paraphrase of American classical scholar, Paul Woodruff (b. 1943)

Though intangible and unseen, societies are discreetly guided by *Virtues of Reverence* such as duty, devotion, responsibility, fairness, humility, tenacity, and fidelity, touchstones for vital virtues like respect, integrity, trustworthiness, ambitiousness, achievement, and social responsibility. 'Adherence to such transforms who we are into who we can become,' Isis illuminated, propounding that 'these are the basis of ethical codes like truth, justice, and reciprocity.'[mxli] With the latter of these, *Reciprocity,* a touchstone for *Virtues* like honesty, compassion and forbearance, alludes to an integral aspect of the trading system of antiquity (what present-day scholars call the "reciprocity system"), operated by time-delay exchanges, wherein goods were given, and at a later time, goods of relatively equal value were returned.

Goods thus given were tangible (gold, material goods) or intangible (public acclaim, authority), receipt of which inferred that an obligation existed to repay the favor owed; it was essentially an informal system of economics.[mxlii] 'Embryonic *Khemet* is at the very heart of nascent *Greater Kush* (Kusha Dwipa),' *Auset* (Isis) proclaimed, describing *Khemet* as 'auspiciously situated between the *Sahelian* kingdoms of the west, and the mysterious kingdoms given rise in the east.' 'No longer shall the *Nile Valley* and its provinces be viewed merely as the northern backwaters down river from southward and eastward facing *Nagu-Punt*.

This was the dawn of a new era, and each new era is born in the womb of the old, spawn of the inadequacies and constraints of the bygone era. Thus were *Kush* and *Khemet* spawned the vassalage and repression of the overlords of the bygone era; the rise of *Khemet* signifies the dawn of an era in which we of these lands shall decide our own destinies. Whether it was her mastery of the art of eloquent speech and subtle persuasion, or her innate ability to empower women, *Auset* (Isis) had clearly inspired and captured the admiration of *Hathor* (Het-heru), *Tera-Neter* reported; describing *Hathor* as all but entranced as the *Queen* pontificated on how, 'throughout the ages women have been the unseen nurturers of society, fulfilling common and often unique and in many ways defining roles within society.'

'So it shall be with *Khemet,*' she emphasized, 'yet with greater impetus and potentiality. Describing it as potentiality given greater scope and dimension by the constituent cultures of *Khemet,* each contributing its own unique strengths and traditions. Isis (Auset) proffered that 'for women of *Anuba* ...childbirth is completely up to them, giving rise to the development of techniques and (later) medical training in the practice of midwifery. However, *Kushite* women are homemakers and wives, skilled women of their communities work as weavers, spinning and weaving cloth and sewing clothing, activities that are important at all levels of society. Women of the *Anu* have gained specialized knowledge in collecting, preparing, and medicinally using herbs, giving rise to cultivation's processing and storage of dried herbs for medicinal uses.

In harmonizing this potentiality, we contribute to the greatness of *Khemet*, and to the greatness of greater *Kush* (Kusha Dwipa), *Auset* (Isis) asserted, proffering that she could 'think of none better to inspire and guide such an undertaking …than thee and thou Order *Het-heru'*. 'A proposal,' *Tera-Neter* mused 'that seemed to surprise and yet empower Het-heru; the latter more so than the former, he postulated, explaining that '*Auset* then imparted her vision of the crucial role of women in weaving the social fabric upon which the societies of Khemet and greater Kush shall be transformed.'[mxliii] A postulate that left Het-heru transfixed by its magnitude, *Tera-Neter* observed, describing it 'as if she and Isis had all at once become kindred spirits.'

'By challenging her integrity,' *Tara Neter* opined, Isis had stripped away her superficial façade, and by sharing her inner vision, she challenged Het-heru to extend the gaze and scope of her prescience to a grandeur destiny within Khemet.' Isis presented the vision of a destiny more reverential and far-reaching than any *Het-heru* (Hathor, Aphrodite, Venus) had theretofore envisioned. An integral, formative and indeed prominent role as '*Spiritual Mother*' ...perhaps second only to the *Queen Mother* herself in nurturing and inuring the veneration, virtue, and harmony *Auset* had so elegantly expressed ....and sought to instill within the heart and fabric of nascent *Khemet,* and by extension the greater *Kushite Empire* (Kusha Dwipa). 'Having so enlightened and challenged *Het-heru* (Hathor, Aphrodite, Venus),' *Tara Neter* continued, '*Auset* (Isis) then addressed her request for a direct audience on behalf of *Sobek*.

The *Queen* informed that should *Pharaoh* not return by the end of the year, she would invite *Sobek* to *Wep Renpet* (Wp Rnpt), the celebration of the 'Opening of the Year' ('New Year'), in the *Royal City of Thebes*. The *Queen* advised that it is then that she shall next convene her *Vizier* (Djehuty, Thoth, Hermes) and *Supreme Military Commander* (Hercules, Herakles, Alcides) in counsel regarding the affairs of the provinces'. 'An opportunity at first somewhat underappreciated by *Het-heru*,' mused *Tera-Neter*, admitting that 'she did not at first fully grasp the sanctity of *Wep Renpet*, nor the reverence with which the *Kushites* hold *Zep Tepi* (the "first time").'[151] *Kushites* believe the "first time" ("Zep Tepi") occurs again ...with each 'Opening of the Year' ("Wep Renpet") ...renewing and bringing renewal to the world. During the end of each year, the essence of this renewal diminishes, and order begins to unravel; the coming of *Zep Tepi* (the "first time") re-establishes *Ma'at* ("cosmic order").

The heliacal rising of the star *Sirius*, the brightest star in the ancient sky, signified the "Opening of the Year,"; an event that usually occurred and announced the beginning of each new year around June 21st..[152] Hidden for the previous seventy days, the heliacal rise of *Sirius* usually coincided with the rising of the waters of the *Ancient Nile River*, foreshadowing annual floods which brought renewal to the whole of the vast and fertile *Ancient Nile River Valley*.[mxliv] Heavy spring floodwaters from the southern and central highlands inundated the *Ancient Nile* with organic nutrients and sediments, around the same time each year, for thousands upon thousands of years. It is these sediments deposited along the valley that creates its renowned fertility. The *Nile River Valley* is a flat flood plain, following the river over the length of *Khemet* from north to south; often described as a 900-mile-long oasis. The river floods for about six months around the same time each year, and as it recedes, it deposits rich black sediments and a layer of silt suitable for growing wheat, beans, barley, and cotton. [153]

The secret of the *Nile Valley* is in the nature, composition, and depth of the ancient silt and sediments deposited in the river valley over thousands upon thousands of years. While the onset of the modern discharge regime of the river can be traced back to the beginning of the early Holocene wet phase (around 12 000 BC), over an earlier millennium, the river carved a deep, wide, "Grand Canyon" size gorge (the "Ancient Nile Valley Canyon") through the (mostly) hard granite bedrock tablelands of *Khemet* in its journey to the *Delta*.[mxlv] This while simultaneously depositing and infilling the *Ancient Nile Valley Canyon* with untold volumes of silt and sediments brought down from southern and central highlands, with the gradual build-up of silt and sediments eventually forming the ancient floor of the *Nile River Valley*. [mxlvi]

---

[151] Wep Renpet (wp rnpt) means "opener of the year".
[152] Sopdet is the ancient Khemetan name of the star Sirius.
[153] Herodotus (ca 485–425 BC) [1, pp. 104–106]

Reverence for the annual floods and renewal of fertility throughout the valley had long been an age-old but "unnamed tradition" celebrated along the shores, islands, and recesses of the river. Yet, it was during the rise of early *Ancient Khemet* that the unifying theology arising from the *Revelations of the Ogdoad* transformed it into a tradition of religious relevance. The revelation of the metaphorical *Hydra* (the "Cosmic Serpent") observable from the earth, as a personification of the *Divine Logos,* a direct emanation of *Amun,* both enlightened and attracted further investigation by the *Hydra Priesthood*. 'It is a revelation that shall redefine the ancient priesthood,' surmised *Tera-Neter*, predicting that the 'celebration of *Wep Renpet* will aid in this coalescence, with the annual floods seen as a manifestation of *Zep Tepi* …and the re-establishment of cosmic order'. *Wep Renpet* festivities began with the intercalary days, the five days in which *Sopde*t (Sirius) rises in the night sky, and the constellation of *Orion* becomes visible, announcing the re-occurring of *Zep Tepi* (the "first time").

These five sacred days are known as the *"Epagomenal Days,"*; a transition period between the end of the old year and the start of the new one. 'As discussed with *Het-heru* during our return voyage to *Khmunu* (Hermopolis),' *Tera-Neter* confessed, 'one of the most important rituals of *Pharaoh* is the "offering of *Ma'at,"*; essentially a royal guarantee of maintaining order, justice, and political stability. 'For *Sobek*,' *Tera-Neter* continued, 'I advised that there could be no better time for a direct audience with the *Queen* than *Wep Renpet*, advising further that by this, he had been extended a great honor.'[mxlvii] This was the message that the *High Priestess Het-heru* (Hathor, Aphrodite, Venus) dutifully delivered to *Sobek* …upon her return to the *City of Shedet* (Krocodilopolis)' *Tera-Neter* recounted. Conceding that 'she later confessed it to have been a message warily received by *Sobek* and the Ambassadors from around the shores of *Mr-wr* (Paleo-Lake Moeris).'

Nonetheless, at the behest of his Eminence, the *High Priest Thoth* (Djehuty, Hermes), *High Priestess Het-heru* immediately returned to the island *City of Khmunu* (Hermopolis) …to complete her initiation into the *School of the Mysteries,* with much of her tutelage under the close and direct auspice of his *Eminence*, *the High Priest* (Thoth, Djehuty, Hermes) himself'. *Tera-Neter* recounted that 'the *High Priest* (Thoth, Djehuty, Hermes) and *High Priestess* (Het-heru, Hathor, Aphrodite) resided in near recluse in the deepest confines of the *Temple,'* noting that 'they were thus unseen by the uninitiated for several weeks.' 'Her initiation ceremony also took place deep within the temple, *Tera-Neter* noted, recalling that 'when the *High Priest* and *Priestess* finally emerged, their mutual affection was so apparent that *Het-heru* had become viewed by the laity of *Khmunu* as a concubine and intimate confidant of the *High Priest.'* 'However, to the Initiates and Priests of the Temple,' *Tera-Neter* revealed, 'she is reverently accepted as an admirable (feminine) counterpart, uniquely postured to bring the *"Revelations of Ogdoad"* to the *Anu* priesthood in the figurative heart of the *Lower Valley.'*

His eminence, the venerable *High Priest* and *Vizier* (Thoth, Djehuty, Hermes),' has indeed affirmed that cessation of the discord plaguing the *Delta*, particularly that beleaguering the *Delta* from the *City of Onu* (Heliopolis) shall be a slow process,' mused the theretofore-quite patient *Governor Busiris*. ' 'The *Vizie*r predicts,' the *Governor* continued, 'that as word of the *Revelations* spread, the *Temples* will begin to first look inward …which will give pause and eventually bring an end to the discord emanating from the priesthood. The *Vizier* instructs that, although *Sobek* and the *Royal Houses* about the shores of *Mr-wr* will surely remain wary …to better align the key cities of *Shedet* (Krocodilopolis) and *Onu* (Heliopolis), the kings of those provincial cities are to be empowered to collect, retain and remit taxes …directly to the royal *City of Thebes*.'

Thebes is actually the ancient Greek name for the ancient royal city originally known as "*Waset,*" which meant "city of the scepter," a name more worthy and reflective of the city's royal stature during the rise of the earliest ancient *Khemet*.[mxlviii] Thebes was located along the banks of the *Nile River* in the middle part of *Upper Khemet*, about 800 km from the *Delta*, built largely on the alluvial plains of the valley that follows the great bend of the *Nile River*. As a natural consequence, the city was laid in a northeast-southwest axis parallel to the river channel, from where it maintained and played an integral role in the economic, political and cultural affairs of *Khemet* during the earliest antiquity.[mxlix] At her behest, it was *Heracles* who secured *Waset* (Thebes) as the capital from where the *Queen* (Auset, Isis) would rein until the return of *Pharaoh* (Ausar, Osiris, Zeus, Kush, Dionysus). *Governor Busiris* opined that 'the *Vizier's* edict instructing that the royal cities of *Shedet* (Krocodilopolis) and *Onu* (Heliopolis) be empowered to collect and remit provincial taxes to *Thebes,* should, at the least, assuage the abiding recalcitrance of these Royal Houses; this while simultaneously strengthening the authority of the newly anointed *City of Bousiris* (Djedu, Busiris) over the greater Delta.'

The Governor explained that 'the larger Central and Western Delta, well beyond the influence of *Onu,* shall remain firmly under the administrative authority of the Governorship, at *Bousiris*'; call it 'an edict that will grant sufficient time for the "change" that the *Vizier* (Thoth, Djehuty, Hermes) alluded to …to indeed spread and gain a definitive measure of acceptance'. 'It is "change" that shall spread faster than first alluded,' predicted *Thoth,* explaining that 'it is hastened by the return of *Het-heru* to her temple in *Shedet,* where she instructs in the *Revelations of the Ogdoad,* and oversees changes within her own Order.' *Het-heru* then plans to depart *Shedet* during "*Akhet"* (the floods), together with *Adepths* of her Order to join in the annual pilgrimage to her temples in the City of *Imu* (Kom el-Hisn), in the western Delta, and *Onu* ("Heliopolis") in the eastern Delta. Het-heru will provide insight into the *Revelations* at each temple during her pilgrimage. Her plans are to depart *Onu* during *Proyet* (Summer) when the *Nile* is most favorable for a voyage to *Khmunu* (Hermopolis). Once here, her *Adepths* will seek initiation at the *School of the Mysteries.'*

The annual seasons in the *Nile Valley* of the era were defined within the framework of an ancient *Khemetic* calendar so unique that its very conceptualization of "time" was based on the evolution of the cosmos and thus was measured by its cycles. It was for this reason that astronomy played such a major role in the *Khemetic* perception of the "passage of time" and that the *Priest of Amun* (the "time watchers") were so keenly aware of the *Precession of the Equinoxes*. They focused on the stars to ensure precision in telling time, and thus the "*Opening of the Year"* was determined by the appearance of the star *Sirius* in the constellation of *Canis Major,* with *Wep Renpet* (New Year) celebrated on the morning of the visible rise of *Sirius,* just prior to sunrise. An advent anciently viewed as the re-occurrence of *Zep Tepi* (the "first time"), the continuation of Order (*Ma'at*) and the creation of Life (*Ankh*).

Because they lived an agrarian lifestyle in *Ancient Khemet,* the seasons of the year were named after events significant to farming. Summertime, the dry season (from March to July), was known as "*Shumo,"* when crops were harvested, often the busiest time of the year. The Nile floods began each year around the end of June, with the season of "*Akhet,"* a name literally meaning "inundation," signifying the flooding of the valley (from July to December), when irrigation canals were used to redirect water to more arid areas for farming. The following season was "*Proyet,"* when the river receded, and temperatures were cooler; the perfect time of year for *Nile Valley* farmers to sow their crops (from December to March) …and for the planned voyage by *Het-heru* (Hathor, Aphrodite) and her followers …from *Onu* ("Heliopolis") to *Khmunu* (Hermopolis).

The currents of the *Nile River* always flow from south to north, while the currents of the wind always blow from north to south, with the slow flowing currents during *Proyet* (Summertime), when the river recedes, generally ideal for faster, less eventful voyages upriver; from the *City of Onu* ("Heliopolis") in the eastern delta to the island *City of Khmunu* (Hermopolis) near the middle of the *Lower River Valley*. The High Priest Thoth (Djehuty, Hermes) predicted that proselytization by Het-heru (Hathor, Aphrodite) during her pilgrimage would hasten cessation of the discord plaguing the Lower Valley and Delta, in particular, that emanating from the temples of *Shedet* (Krocodilopolis) and *Onu* ("Heliopolis"). "With the spread of the "Revelations" among the priesthood, and through them to the laity,' *Thoth* explained that, 'as High Priest of the Royal Cities in which each resides, the Pharaoh of *Shedet* (Krocodilopolis) on the shores of *Mr-wr* (Paleo-Lake Moeris) and the Pharaoh of *Imu* (Kom el-Hisn) in the western Delta, like the Pharaoh *Onu* ("Heliopolis") in the eastern Delta, will each thus be compelled to grasp the precepts presented before them.

For the true Seeker among them, the Revelations will perhaps illuminate greater enlightenment, while for those for whom the power of the throne is its own end, a rudimentary mastery of the precepts will, at minimum, be required to foment their discernments and formulate their objections; the latter will distract, while the former will aid in quieting and transforming the discord that plagues the *Delta'*. 'And what manner of discord attracts *Hercules'* (Herakles, Heryshaf, Alcides) to the frontier lands,' *Ausar* (Osiris, Kush, Zeus, Dionysus) inquired of *Thoth* (Djehuty, Hermes), alluding to the frontier southern borderlands between *Kush* and *Nagu-Punt,* in the highlands of present-day Ethiopia and Somalia. 'It is more affinity than discord,' replied *Thoth*, elaborating that 'the highlands of the Horn (of Africa) have long been at the heartland of *Nagu-Punt;* the peoples who inhabit those highlands share age-old affinities with the *Nagas* …enabling the ancient influence of *Nagu-Punt* to extend deep into the southern borderlands of *Kush'*.

Finally, *Thoth* continued, with the concurrence of the *Queen* and *Governor Antee, Hercules* launched a joint campaign with *General Hu* to reinforce and insure security in the southern highlands. 'And what of *Apollo*?' inquired *Thoth* (Djehuty, Hermes) of *Ausar* (Osiris, Kush, Zeus, Dionysus), alluding to his oldest brother and the only of *Ausar's* sons to have aided him in the eastern (Kushite) migrations. '*Apollo* has chosen to make his destiny in the lands of *Anatolia*,' replied *Ausar*, describing the *Anatolian Peninsula* as 'the lands between the upper ("Proto-Black Sea") and lower ("Mediterranean Sea") northern seas. There he dwells among the descendants of *Ōkeanós*, a renowned king of early *Atlatia* who led his subjects into self-exile after the unification of *Atlatia* under *Khronos*. At length, they re-settled in the old colonies along the southwestern coast, and in the adjacent northwestern mountains, from where they built an empire embracing the length of the Upper Northern Sea.

But alas, it has been a fragmenting empire since the death of *Ōkeanós,* its founder …a renowned early *Atlatian* king who sought to rival even *Khronos* (Khem, Kham, Ham) himself, explained *Ausar* (Osiris, Kush, Zeus, Dionysus). In emulation of Khronos, whose empire spanned the length of the Lower Northern Sea (the "Mediterranean Sea'), *Ōkeanós* aspired that his empire span beyond the length of the Upper Northern Sea (the "Proto-Black Sea"); from the coastal ports of *Thrace* in the west, beyond the coastal ports of *Aea* (Kolchis) to the frontier lands where *Ōkeanós's* grandson, *Prometheus,* still toils in repentance for his betrayal of the Oath of the Sacred Mysteries …in the east. A betrayal with which the inheritors of the *House of Ōkeanós* must now contend.

The autochthones tribes for whom *Prometheus* betrayed his oath have, alas, betrayed his trust; the resettlements of their highland kingdoms now encroach upon the periphery of the fragmenting old empire. It is an irony of fate that the remnants of the proud empire of *Ōkeanós* must now look to the *House of Khronos* for its salvation. As *Apollo* aided Kush in fomenting the (Maa) Confederation, the House of *Ōkeanós* seeks his aid in fomenting such a league among the provincial kingdoms of the old empire that they might be more secure and prosperous …and aptly contend with the rising threat of the autochthone kingdoms. In compensation, they have allotted and granted *Apollo* sovereignty over a kingdom on the coast of the Lower Northern Sea that will itself be part of the league he endeavors to organize. The royal houses of the league will each be represented along the corridor of the *Scamandrus River Valley* approaching the old inland colonial city of *Troy;* by this, *Apollo* brings together the vast resources and armies of the seven kingdoms …to both buttress regional security and facilitate trade.

The three ships anchored in your harbor are each heavily ladened with rare and valuable goods from merely two small former colonial islands of the region; the seven kingdoms forming the league are vastly larger, each with unique mineral wealth. As *Troy* is situated at the nexus between the Upper ("Proto-Black Sea") and Lower ("Mediterranean Sea") Northern Seas, this and far, far more will be accessible for barter and exchange ("trade") along the inner corridors of the *Scamandrus River Valley.* 'However, it is trade for which we must contend against the formidable fleets of neighboring *Kanaan;* fleets from the city of *Old Byblos* in the north and fleets from the cities of *Tyre* and *Sidon,* led by *Agenor,* son of *Poseidon* and *Eurynome,* daughter of *Ōkeanós. Agenor* is aided by close relations with his half-brother *Kelainos,* (eponymous) king of Kelainai ("Celænæ"), one of the founding royal houses of the League.

Yet we are better aided by close relations with *Apollo*, appointed Viceroy of the League …but were being hampered by *Khemet's* lack of adequate seaports …and vessels of sufficient seaworthiness'. The evolution of early Khemet's Mediterranean maritime trade is underappreciated and little understood, in large part due to the ultimately transitory nature of even those that are deemed to be permanent islands in the Delta. During the annual Nile inundations, villages and towns located along the riverside often became separated from the banks and transformed into one of the many islands scattered along the course of the Upper and Lower Valleys and, most significantly, in the Nile Delta. During the rise of Khemet, the Nile of the era served as a natural link between the villages, townships, cities and many islands along its corridors and as a natural conduit for communication and trade with the regions bordering the Upper Valley to the south, the Red and Mediterranean Seas to the east and north, and the Ennedi Highlands to the west.

To the south, the route led to Nagu-Punt on the horn of Africa, while to the north, it led downriver to one of the then seven branches of the ancient Nile that traversed the Delta and emptied into the Eastern Mediterranean Sea. 'Sire,' interrupted the erudite yet always polite and politically astute *Governor Busiris,* 'if I might,' he proposed, 'the admixture of *Delta-Anu* and *Kana-An*u (Kanaanites) inhabiting the old provincial *City of Onu* provide a compelling if the somewhat asymmetrical opportunity of potentially vast benefit for *Kanaan* and *Khemet.* 'Opportunity,' he propounded, 'that will enable immediate trade with *Troy* and the kingdoms of the (nascent) *Phrygian* league *and* will enable immediate support of *Apollo.'* 'Sire, let us employ,' the *Governor* proposed, 'rather than contend with the sizeable and formidable fleets of *Kanaan*,' adding that, 'such a strategy will aid in quailing dissension in the old city, while the spread of the "Revelations" among the priesthood, and ultimately the laity, gradually dampens the discord of our discontent in the delta.'

'It is a strategy,' *Governor Busiris* further added, 'that will aid in both granting sufficient time and prompting well-situated cities in the Delta to build seaworthy vessels and seaports for direct trade.' Having listened intently, *Tera-Neter* dutifully interceded, cautioning, 'be not deluded *Governor*, the inhabitants of whom you allude, like the ancient *Oru* in the ancient heritage of the *High Priest* and *Vizier* (Thoth, Djehuty, Hermes) are among the purest and most learned descendants of the ancestral *Anu* (the "Annu")*;* the first to have pondered the heavens and received revelation. It is they who first perceived the rotation of the stars and organized them into the constellations, and it is their ancestral lineage that first tracked the precession of the equinoxes, foretold the changing of the ages …and first revealed such divine wisdom to humanity. 'Theirs was amongst the most prominent of the ancient kingdoms of the legendary *Lands of Yam*,' boasted *Tera-Neter,* recounting the early ancient kingdoms at the base of the *Mountains of the Moon* (the Ruwenzoris), the first of the three pillars, from where they spread over the eastern highlands (of present-day Kenya and Somalia) to be among the first to traverse the Red Sea (at the Gulf of Aden), and spread into the mysterious lands of the east.[ml]

These were the *Annu* of the "Old Race" (the "Twa"), among the earliest inhabitants of the Arabian peninsula, the landmass bounded by the Red Sea, the Gulf of Aden and the Arabian Sea, the Indian Ocean, the Gulf of Oman, and the Persian Gulf. The Arabian peninsula of the era abounded in riches, especially spices, and the *Annu* settlements anciently spread along the then-broad peninsular coastal plains. The present-day Red Sea is about twelve miles wide. However, during the Ice Age, sea levels were over two over hundred feet lower, and the straits were much narrower.[mli] The Arabian peninsula coastline at the glacial maximum was accentuated by broad southern coastal plains; at the lower sea level, the exposed shelf of the peninsula is relatively shallow and extensive, anciently forming a broad, fertile coastal plain bordered by the distinctive coastal wetlands, of the era. The *Annu* who settled in the coastal plains spread generation by generation around the southern coastal strip of the peninsula until they reached the then far broader and more varied, fertile, and well-watered lands of the southern Mesopotamian alluvial plains.[mlii]

Sumerian text record that they arrived in the "valley between the two rivers" in reverence of a prominent king under whose auspice they had extended their dominion eastward: the eponymous king known as "An," the "king-of-kings," whom ancient Annu lore calls "the ultimate source of authority, responsible for conferring power on other (Annu) kings," and Sumerian mythology calls "the progenitor of the oldest generations of Mesopotamia,'[mliii] After the conquest of Sumer (Lower Mesopotamia) by the Akkadians in 2,334 B.C., legendary king "An" became revered as a godlike figure they then called "Anu."[mliv] In his mythical form and prominence, "An" became devoutly revered throughout the neighboring ancient nations, emergent nations, and growing diaspora of the early Anu (the "Annu"); under his auspice, they built and inhabited mound settlements around the ancient southern Arabian coastal plains, and across the broad and varied alluvial plains of early ancient Mesopotamia.

The broad and fertile lands of the gulf floor during the Palaeolithic, Mesolithic and Early Neolithic provided a natural route for those spreading eastward, with the *Annu* building a network of mound-top villages as they spread eastward across the ancient alluvial plains.[mlv] The first long-distance trade occurred between the East African Highlands, the Southern Arabian coastal plains, and the Mesopotamian alluvial plains. The *Anu* of Old Punt, the second pillar, became the source of goods that could be found nowhere else other than Africa; goods not only from the width and breadth of the ancient *Lands of Yam* but goods from elsewhere in Africa, transforming the highlands into an early economic center with profound effect on surrounding peoples and cultures. Indeed, this is what first attracted the *Naga* to the highlands (of Punt), an advent that eventually prompted the *Annu* to migrate northward.

The proximity of the *Mountains of the Moon* to Lake Victoria and Lake Albert, between which flows the *Nile* facilitated their northward migrations, with the most fervent devoutly following the instruction of *An*, the "King of kings," in the building of the second eponymous "City of An" (On, Onu, Anu, Heliopolis) in the Lower Nile Valley. [mlvi] In early *Anu* (Annu) lore, the name of the ancient city became 'Iunu,' meaning 'pillar' (or "pillar city"), as it was the third of the three great pillars of the emergent empire of the *Annu* (written with three pillars); with the second pillar in the *Eastern Highlands* (of present-day Somalia) all but fully lost to the *Naga*, and the first pillar at the base of the *Mountains of the Moon* all but fully cut-off from direct trade with the old *Annu* colonies and kingdoms of the east. Since its inception, the *City of Onu* (On, Onu, Anu, Heliopolis) has been a symbol of the old empire and the last bastion of direct trade with the old (Annu) kingdoms of the east. The city's influence as a commercial center thus still radiates throughout the delta and the lower river valley; it would be naive to believe that they would remain unaware of a shift in a major trade concession, once granted.'

'In many ways, the *Annu* were forebears of *Kusha Dwipa*,' interjected a weary but ever discerning *Ausar* (Osiris, Kush, Zeus, Dionysus), 'the reciting of their ancient legends inspired and guided early Kushite exploration and expeditions into the mysterious lands of the east.' 'We must thus guard against the perception of betraying the trust we seek to instill in them,' cautioned *Thoth* (Djehuty, Hermes), advising that 'the High Priest of *Onu* is revered as the "Greatest of Seers"; his temple attracts and influences neophytes, initiates and initiate-adepts from throughout the Delta.' 'Though more significant spiritually than politically,' *Tera-Neter* elaborated, '*Onu* is a vital commercial center; the last bastion of direct trade with kingdoms of the east, like the *Kena-Anu* of *Kanaan*, and the *Annu* kingdoms of the *Sinai* and *Northern Arabian Peninsulas*.' 'As he who arrested the advance of the *Nagas* and reopened the highland trade routes to the lands of *Yam* and the lands of the east,' *Thoth* (Djehuty, Hermes) interjected, propounding that 'despite the dissension emanating from *Shednet* and around *Mr-wr* (Paleo-Lake Moeris), the royal house of *Onu* (Anu, Heliopolis, On) holds *Pharaoh* (Ausar, Osiris, Kush, Zeus, Dionysus) in the highest esteem,' to which the *Vizier* added 'beyond bridging and bonding Upper and Lower Khemet, it is Pharaoh's decided purview to open gateways into new lands to accommodate the necessities and luxuries of the kingdoms of *Khemet*.'[mlvii]

Though early *Khemet* was rich in natural resources, it was not fully self-sufficient and had to rely on foreign trade, the exclusive province of *Pharaoh*, which held all rights regarding who could engage in trade and with whom.[mlviii] It was *Pharaoh's* responsibility to care for both the people and the land, and under this construct, if the land produced sufficiently and there was a surplus, *Pharaoh* was regarded as successful; if not, the *Priests* would intervene to determine what steps were needed to regain the goodwill of *God*. Trade was deemed important because it provided the citizenry with the resources they needed to live and prosper, and equally important, it fostered a sense of cohesion and national identity. The kingdoms of early ancient *Khemet* produced excess grains, mined precious metals and valuable stones and minerals, and gathered natron (a valuable salt) to trade for needed and desired foreign goods. Khemet's inherent demand for such goods, and ability to produce commodities to barter, in time, gave rise to prosperity.

A prospect grasped by *Thoth* (Djehuty, Hermes), the venerable *Vizier*, who foresaw that at length, the appetites of the provincial kingdoms (the later "Nomes") across the length and breadth of *Khemet* will alas surely exceed even the renowned capabilities of the adroit merchants and traders of ancient *Onu*.' During this time (and throughout most of antiquity), much of the trade beyond local exchanges were handled by wholesale merchants, acting on behalf of the kings (or "minor pharaohs") of each city or on behalf of the great temple estates of the priesthood.[mlix] Nonetheless, it was only upon the authority and behest of the *Pharaoh* that kings ("minor pharaohs") and merchants so sanctioned would organize and launch expeditions to barter, trade, and cultivate trade relations with foreign countries.

Trade was used to gain access to needed foreign goods and commodities and promote alliances between countries; key trade relationships thus became important sources of wealth and power. 'Trade networks between the *Kingdoms of Khemet* and the maritime *Cities of Kanaan* will be valuable sources of wealth for the royal house and temple of *Onu,*' concluded *Thoth* (Djehuty, Hermes) in his role as *Vizier,* foreseeing it as 'an opportunity that will surely be seized upon by the great Seers of the *Temple of Onu*'; adding that 'the inevitable prospect of emergent cities in the *Delta* emulating the prosperity they witnessed in *Onu*, is an eventuality that will hardly be found surprising to the adept *Initiates* of the old priesthood of Onu (Anu, On, Heliopolis), the "pillar city"; last bastion and symbol of the old empire of the *Annu.*' 'Theirs is the lineage of legendary King *An*, whose second oldest son Enlil anciently led the Annu down the river, through the Nile Valley, where, under his auspice, they founded the ancient cities of *Anu Tseni* (later called "Esneh" or "Esna"), *Anu Shemo, Aunu Menti,* and *Aunti;* beyond which, in the far fertile north they founded the second (eponymous) *City of An* (On, Onu, Heliopolis),' recounted *Thoth* (Djehuty, Hermes).

The *Annu* were the first people of this epoch of man's ascendance to build diverse societies, and it was they who built the oldest cities and trade networks in the Nile Valley. 'Had they abandoned this treasured aspect of their heritage,' queried *Thoth*. 'It is not loss of the trade concession that would most betray,' acknowledged *Tera-Neter*, 'it is loss of the perception of preeminence, as the last bastion of the old empire, in the Delta.' 'The hulls of the ships of the *Armada* are ladened with rare and highly valued goods and resources from the emergent kingdoms of the isles and vast lands of the great northern seas,' interceded *Ausar* (Osiris, Kush, Zeus, Dionysus), recounting that 'beyond the exotic herbs, spices and incense of *Kusha Dwipa* …the merchants aboard the *Armada* bring back high-quality obsidian and rare minerals from the *Isle of Milos,* brilliant white marble and sought after emery from the *Isle of Naxos;* this together with highly-valued gold and silver from *Mount Pangaion,* near old colonial *Kavala City,* in the budding land of *Thrace'*.

'Once the merchants aboard the *Armada* return to their kingdoms with such highly prized commodities, the zeal for such luxuries and wares will surely increase,' *Ausar* (Osiris, Kush, Zeus, Dionysus) predicted, envisioning that 'the kingdoms and cities of *Khemet* will readily barter for items they don't have at hand from cities and kingdoms in faraway lands,' where the climate and natural resources produce different things. *Ausar* opined that 'the cities and kingdoms of *Khemet* will barter highly valued commodities such as wheat and other grains, to obtain minerals and resources not found here; using *Khemet's* many ports to grow its economy. 'Cities active in such trade will become prosperous and influential,' *Ausar* predicted, noting that 'such cities will augment the strength and prominence of all *Khemet.*'[mlx]

'It is fitting,' asserted *Ausar* (Osiris, Kush, Zeus, Dionysus), 'that the reverent *City of Onu* (An, Anu, Heliopolis, On), provincial capital of the eastern *Delta*, duly broaden its traditional role as intermediary between the (Annu) kingdoms of *Yam* and the *Lower River Valley*, and the old (Annu) kingdoms of *Kanaan, Sinai,* and *Northern Arabia* (Arabia Petraea); adding to this intermediation of maritime trade between the kingdoms of *Khemet, via* the fleets of the southern cities of *Kanaan,* and the kingdoms of the nascent *Phrygian League.*' 'Reopening of the direct highland trade route between *Yam* and the remnants of the old *Annu* empire along the coast of the *Southern Arabian Peninsula* has, at length, dampened the erstwhile prominence and heralded preeminence of *Onu,*' observed and advised *Thoth* (Djehuty, Hermes), again in his role as *Vizier*.

'The *Royal House of Onu* is cognizant of its waning commercial influence and fading preeminence in the eastern *Delta,* conceded *Tera-Neter*, noting that 'nonetheless the *Royal House* does not fault, but extols and holds *Pharaoh* (Ausar, Osiris, Kush, Zeus, Dionysus) in highest esteem for the reopening of the old southern (highland) trade route between the kingdoms of *Yam,* and the remnants of the old *Annu* kingdoms along the coastal plains of the *Arabian Peninsula,* and the alluvial plains of (Mesopotamia) the land between two rivers.' 'The royal house of *Onu,*' *Thoth* connoted, 'must assuredly recognize that "perception of preeminence," and indeed preeminence itself, emanates not merely from inured tradition, but inspired leadership manifested by decisiveness, rather than recoil, in the face of the formidable challenges we confront.'

'Sire, if I might,' interceded *Governor Busiris*, directly addressing *Ausar* (Osiris, Kush, Zeus, Dionysus) 'given that the issue at hand is essential that the *House of Onu* retains its "perception of preeminence" in the eastern *Delta* …while the proposed trade concession for the city can only be bonded by royal edict of *Pharaoh;* in resolution might I suggest a "Compact" by *Pharaoh* on behalf of *Khemet* via the *City of Onu* (Anu, On, Heliopolis)*,* and *Apollo* on behalf of the kingdoms of the (nascent) *Phrygian League.* A royal pronouncement inaugurating the (maritime and transshipment) intermediary of the *House of Onu* on behalf of *Khemet* and *Apollo* as *Viceroy* on behalf of the *Phrygian League*'. 'A compact sanctioning *Onu* as the "*City of Apollo*" …anointing it as nexus of (triangulated) maritime trade between *Khemet*, *Kanaan* and the *Phrygian League,*' mused *Tera-Neter,* a gesture that would both honor the *House of Onu* …and reinvigorate the old trade network between the *Kana* and *Delta Anu* of *Onu*, and the *Anu* of the *Valley* and *Mr-wr* (Paleo-Lake Moeris)'.

'Such a *Compact* would inure an aura of stature in its association with the *House of Khem* (Kham, Ham, Khronos), and primacy in its trade position between *Khemet* and the old (Atlatian) colonies and emergent kingdoms of the northern seas,' concurred *Thoth* (Djehuty, Hermes). 'This' agreed on *Governor Busiris,* 'while inspiring other cities in the Delta to build reliable seaports and seaworthy vessels for ultimate direct trade.''Let it be so ordained,' resolved a now quite weary *Ausar* (Osiris, Kush, Zeus, Dionysus), instructing that *Thoth* (Djehuty, Hermes), in his role as *Vizier,* 'coordinate and attend all necessary affairs and requisites …to be reviewed and discussed' when he and *Alcides* (Herakles, Hercules), in his role as *Supreme Military Commander,* attend *Wep Renpet* (Wp Rnpt), "New Year" in the Royal *City of Thebes.*' Indeed Sire responded Thoth, advising that he would begin forthwith, with the pending return of *Governor Busiris* to the Delta and his newly anointed capital *City of Bousiris* (Busiris), from where he shall advisably coordinate his dispatch to the *City of Onu* (On, Anu, Heliopolis), with that of *Het-heru* (Hathor, Aphrodite, Venus) …for optimal effect.

'As the *Governor* apprises of the anointment of *Onu* as "The City of Apollo, and the related trade concession, and further advises the *House of Onu* of their empowerment to collect and directly remit taxes to *Thebes,*' *Thoth* propounded, 'the *High Priestess Het-heru* will be proselytizing *Revelations of the Ogdoad* before the priesthood of *Onu*. A convergence of incentive and enlightenment,' *Thoth* surmised, 'that surely will aid in bonding the *Upper Valley* (Upper Khemet), *Lower Valley* and *Delta* (Lower Khemet).' To seal the bond, *Ausar* would later be "enthroned" in the *City of Khmunu* ("Hermopolis," the "City of Hermes"), "crowned" in the *City of Neni-nesu* ("Herakleopolis," the "City of Hercules"), and receive the royal Sekhem and Heqa Scepters in the *City of Onu* ("Heliopolis," the "City of Apollo"); gestures honoring the Anu of *Lower Khemet.* [mlxi]

The royal "Heqa Scepter" was a "Staff of Authority," symbolizing Pharaoh's kingship and governance, while the "Sekhem-Scepter" was a "Spiritual Symbol," symbolizing his spiritual power and authority. Of all the different versions of ancient Khemetan scepters, the Sekhem-Scepter was the most widely revered and used. To the ancient priesthood of *Onu,* the Sekhem-Scepter was seen as a physical representation of Pharaoh's earthly power, and Ausar's later assent, at the behest of *Tera-Neter,* to receive the scepter in the eponymous city of the last great (Anu) "king of kings," the ancient *City of An* (Anu, Onu, On, Heliopolis), symbolized his ascendance to the mantle of "high king,' An attainment prompting the priesthood to anoint *Ausar* (Osiris, Kush, Zeus, Dionysus) "the Great Sekhem" ...the "Foremost of Powers,' Before *Ausar* (Osiris, Kush, Zeus, Dionysus), the inhabitants of the Upper and Lower Valleys lived under the rule of one of several early kingdoms along the Nile, around the shores of *Mr-wr* (Paleo-Lake Moeris), or in the *Delta*. Unification of these kingdoms marked the true birth of early ancient *Khemet*, with *Ausar* assuming the *Nile Valley* title for "king" among the *Anu*, "Pharaoh,'

Notwithstanding the war between *Kush* and *Nagu-Punt*, which necessarily preceded unification, and coalescence among the early provincial kingdoms in the valley, unity was largely achieved by peaceful means, though intermittently tenuous. An emissary was accordingly dispatched to *Shedet* to inform of Pharaoh's return and apprise of the empowerment of the *House of Shedet* to directly collect and remit (provincial) taxes to *Thebes* (Waset)Just before dawn over the ancient island *City of Khmunu* (Hermopolis), having reached resolution on the major issues of the day, and having taken notice of Pharaoh's obstinate weariness, this time more in his role as dutiful *Son* than as *Vizier* or *High Priest*, *Thoth* (Djehuty, Thoth, Hermes) requested deferral of further discussion 'until the upcoming convening and celebration of *Wep Renpet* (New Year) at *Thebes* (Waset).'

'For now,' *Thoth* (Djehuty, Hermes) implored of Ausar, 'let us join the *Priests of Amun* in ascending atop the *Temple of the School of the Mysteries* to greet the rising sun with prayers and witness the majestic glow from its rays expand across the horizon. After this, let us adjourn,' *Thoth* advised, 'that *Pharaoh* may rest, and *Governor Busiris* may prepare for the return voyage to the *Delta*, and his new capital *city of Bousiris* (Busiris).'It was thus that early the next morning, after a full day of rest, the three-ship *Armada* lifted anchor in the harbor of *Khmunu* (Hermopolis), and with *Ausar* and the captain of the flagship at the bow of the leading vessel, hoisted their sails and departed southward, upriver to the *City of Asyut,* the final port of the expedition. *Asyut* was on the west bank of the *Nile*, at the border of *Upper* and *Lower Khemet*; in antiquity, it was not only the last city on the river en route from *Lower* to *Upper Khemet* but also sat on the crossroads of key trade routes into the Western Desert. Trade routes of the era extended between *Asyut* and the heavily populated oases of the ancient Western Desert; the *Kharga Oasis, Dakhla Oasis, Farafra Oasis, Bahariya Oasis, Qattara Oasis, Siwa Oasis,* and the *Fayum*.

A key ancient trade route extended southeast from ancient *Asyūt* to *Kharga,* the largest of the Oasis in the *Western Desert*; another route extended west into the eastern frontier lands of the *Maa Confederation,* first to the *Farafra Oasis,* from there the route extended northwestward to the *Bahariya Oasis*, and from there still further northwestward to the *Siwa Oasis.* The *City of Asyūt* (known as 'Syūt' in ancient Khemet) was ideally situated just above the mouth of the *Great Canal,* whose waters flowed northward (west of and parallel to the main corridor of the Nile) until veering westward into the *Fayoum*, and through the *City of Shedet* (Krocodilopolis), to empty into (Mr-wr) *Paleo-Lake Moeris*. [mlxii]*Asyūt's* location at the entrance to prosperous kingdoms around (Mr-wr) *Paleo-Lake Moeris* further heightened its strategic significance as a trade center.

Early ancient *Asyūt* ("Syūt") was thus a place of considerable importance in antiquity, not only as a busy river port at the crossroads of major ancient overland and maritime trade routes but as a strategic political and market center. Except for occasional storms, or lack of wind, the slow-flowing Nile was ideal for transport and trade between Upper and Lower Khemet; with its winds always blowing from north to south and its current always flowing from south to north, two-way transport along the river was, for the most part, predictable. The *Armada's* five-day voyage from the *City of Khmunu* (Hermopolis) to the *City of Asyūt* ("Syūt") was fairly uneventful, except for the final day when a weakening of the southerly winds forced the still heavily laden vessels to deploy oars, at times, to maintain speed and momentum. By decree of *Ausar* (Osiris, Kush, Zeus, Dionysus), once at *Asyūt* ("Syūt"), the merchants aboard each vessel of the Armada were allotted and apportioned one-half of the trade cargoes carried by their respective ships; valuable trade goods with which to return to their home regions.

Accordingly, each, in turn, made necessary arrangements for the transport of their allotted merchandise to their disparate areas of the land. *Anu* merchants, priests, and mariners from the area of *Paleo-Lake Moeris* (Mr-wr) obtained boats and availed themselves of the entrance and northward flowing current of the *Great Canal* to return to *Shednet* and the other kingdoms, while the merchants, traders, and others from the eastern frontier lands of the *Maa Confederation* availed themselves of the trade routes leading to major oases in the Western Desert. The disembarking of roughly two-thirds of the crew and ship's company, with the off-loading of fully one-half of each ship's trade cargoes, served to necessarily lighten each vessel's load and draft for the final leg of their voyage from *Asyūt* ("Syūt") to the royal *City of Thebes* (Waset). The voyage from *Asyūt* ("Syūt") to *Thebes* (Waset), a distance of 119 nautical miles, though once again fairly uneventful, nonetheless took the three ships *Armada* nearly three full days, arriving in port just after midday (noon) the third day.

The *Holocene* era *Nile River* was far deeper, broader and more robust than its present-day iteration, allowing vessels of significant size and draft to sail freely up-river, southward along the main corridor, through and beyond the six cataracts that watermark the heartland of early ancient *Kush*.[mlxiii] *Thebes* was located along the banks of the Nile, in the middle part of *Upper Khemet*, built largely on the alluvial plains north of the *"Great Bend"* of the Nile. The six groups of cataracts were just south of the *Royal City,* with the first (northernmost) at Aswan and the sixth (southernmost) just north of *Khartoum*. The heartland of the early ancient *Kingdom of Kush* began at the first cataract, announced by the rocky part of the river, known anciently as the *"Stony Nile,'* Contrary to common reports, the cataracts are seldom rapids, with few "white water" characteristics. They are simply stretches of the river where water flow becomes rough because it is broken among islands and, in some areas, runs shallow over hazardous rocks. These are areas anciently left to the experienced hands of river pilots knowledgeable of the contours, currents, and hazards of the *Stony Nile*.

Ancient *Thebes* was originally known as "Wo'se," "Wase," or more commonly "Waset," after the "was" scepter of Pharaoh. [mlxiv] The city was known as "Thebes" by the Greeks and as the "City of No" (or "No'we") in the Old Testament; the Hebrews simply called it "No-Amon," the "City of Amun,'[mlxv] The ancient priests of *Amun* claim that as the first city in the world, *Wo'se* (the oldest name) became a model for all others to build their cities in its emulation.[mlxvi] The royal city held an area of 36 sq miles, including parts of the Theban Hills in the west, while to the east was the mountainous Eastern Desert, where *Wadi Hammamat* drained into the valley near the city and was used as a trade route to the Red Sea coast.To the south, near the southern point of the "Great Bend," the ancient *Yellow Nile* (also known as "Wadi Howar") joined the main corridor of the Nile, just south of the third cataract in the ancient *Kingdom of Kush* (present-day Sudan).

The *Yellow Nile* descended from the highlands of the southern Ennedi, rising in the mountainous area of the highlands, from where the river descended and traversed the southern fringe of the Sahara for nearly four hundred miles, to become one of the largest Nile tributaries of the era; connecting the highlands of the *Ennedi* and eastern *Chad*, to the very heart of the early ancient *Kingdom of Kush*, and the *Upper Nile River Valley*. Like at *Asyūt*, once at *Thebes* (Waset), the remaining merchant and traders aboard each vessel availed themselves of the ancient trade routes to return home. The *Kush-Shi* from the *Ennedi* highlands and *Lake Yoa*, the *Shi* (Si) from the *Tadrart Acacus* highlands and *Paleo-Lake Fezzan*, and the *Manding-Shi,* also from *Paleo-Lake Fezzan,* availed themselves of the *Yellow Nile*, and like the *Anu* at *Asyūt,* obtained several boats for their voyage and trek to the *Ennedi* and *Tadrart Acacus.*

The *Anu* from the interior of the *Eastern Sudan,* availed themselves of overland trade routes leading to their home regions, while those of the *Tribes of Kush* from central and western *Ancient Sudan*, the *Sao* from *Paleo-Lake Chad*, and the *Igbo* from the *Holly City of Igbo Ukwu,* at the western extent of *Ancient Kush*, in northern *Nigeria*, availed themselves of the *Yellow Nile* to reach the central *Sahe*l (in Central Sudan), from where they made way to their respective kingdoms. This broad dissemination of trade and commerce brought prosperity and prominence to the kingdoms of the *Sahel*, a region synonymous with the ancient *Land of Kush*. Theirs was a prominence that resonated northward, influencing trade and commerce from the theretofore waning kingdoms of the Maa Confederation …along the southern shores and isles of the fragmenting *Ancient Atlantean Sea*. All of which, over time, aided in the ever-heightening prominence and growth of *Thebes* ("Waset"), the first metropolis, which later generations would call the "*City of a Hundred Gates*"; Capital of the "Crown Jewel" of early ancient *Kush*.

Having instructed that one-half the trade cargoes aboard each ship of the *Armada* be off-loaded as property of *Pharaoh*, and the remaining cargoes returned with the vessels to *Agenor* at *Sidon,* as compensation for their consignment; *Ausar* (Osiris, Kush, Zeus, Dionysus), at long last, reunited with his *Queen* (Auset, Aset, Iset, Isis), at the *Grand Temple*. In very ancient times, though still confined to the west bank, a vast city of temples and palaces grew to cover the western shore as far back as the desert hills. Nonetheless, the most prominent structure remained the *Grand Temple,* famous for its size and two golden chapels, and adjoining palace, situated at the very heart of earliest *Thebes* ("Waset"), built by *Ausar* (Osiris, Kush, Zeus, Dionysus) after the founding of the city and dedicated to(Khronos and Rhea) his parents.

Reunion and Solace with Ausar

Here, in the confines of their private chamber in the *Palace*, like his reclusive father Khem, *Ausar* (Osiris, Kush, Zeus, Dionysus) caste himself into extended semi-isolation with his *Queen* (Auset, Aset, Iset, Isis). A semi-isolation characterized by periods of deep, reflective meditation, the in-depth conversation regarding all that had transpired since his parting, and long periods of heightened passion and intercourse, punctuated by long periods of rest followed by feast-like meals. During the days and weeks following his return, it was *Isis* who asserted the voice of *Pharaoh*, with *Ausar* leaving day-to-day affairs in the capable hands of his sons, the Vizier *Thoth* (Djehuty, Hermes) and Supreme Military Commander *Hercules* (Herakles, Heryshaf, Alcides).

Like *Rhea* with *Khronos*, it was *Auset* (Aset, Iset, Isis) who best gave rest, regenerative energy, and inspirational impetus to his being, a reciprocation in which each was somehow made stronger. In their recluse, *Ausar* (Osiris) told of northern city-states and kingdoms such as Athens and Thrace, which arose from the old Atlatian colonies along the coasts of southern Europe, and of the incessant wars plaguing their lands; war led by none other than his misguided eldest brother, *Haides* who has become mired in avarice, and a lust for material wealth and power. *Ausar* (Osiris) told of how *Haides* continued to launch wars of aggression across *Europe,* taking captives into slavery to work mines in the captured territories, and how he promised the *Thracians* he would dispatch *Hercules* to aid in their efforts against *Haides*.

Ausar (Osiris, Kush, Zeus, Dionysus) then told of the plight of *Prometheus,* of the emergent kingdoms of the northern sea (the present-day "Black Sea"), and of the appointment of *Apollo* as Viceroy of the nascent *Phrygian League*. Of his earlier sojourn in the east, he told of the formation of *Kusha Dwipa*, from his encounter with remnants of the old *Anu* empire, in the alluvial plains they would become earliest *Sumer*, to his awareness of the constant, watchful presence of the *Nagas*. 'Not the *Sethians* of *Nagu-Punt*,' clarified *Ausar* (Osiris, Kush, Zeus, Dionysus), 'but an empire reverently known as *Naga-Mandela*, led by an enlightened *Grand Regent* known as *Shiva* (Siva, Shambo).'

Ausar (Osiris, Kush, Zeus, Dionysus) recalled the stories imparted about the mystical island *City of Shambhala* amidst a sapphire blue inland sea anciently known as the *"Sea of Knowledge"* in the Tarim basin of the central Asian highlands. *Ausar* told of the legends that report "adepts from every race gathered within the island sanctum, and that from among them, great Sages were said to be in perpetual residence, forming a continuous inner circle of human wisdom,"; noting the great Sages of the *Nagas* were among those in residence, yet missing, he noted 'are the great *Sages of Amun.'* With several peaceful and promising encounters between *Kusha Dwipa* and *Naga Mandela*, and with a broader understanding of the ethos of the Nagas*, Ausar* surmised that the *Revelations of the Ogdoad* might truly serve as a catalyst for greater understanding and peaceful dialog and relations with *Nagu-Punt*.

Ausar (Osiris, Kush, Zeus, Dionysus) illuminated the revelation of the origin and relation of the *Hydra* to *Amun* and opined that 'it is a revelation that will not only serve to demystify the Amunite Priesthood but may indeed be the basis for a broader mutual, ontological understanding …and unification theology'. *Ausar* shared with his queen his desire to craft a lasting peace with Nagu-Punt, and his intention to meet forthwith with their Grand Regent Setekh (Set). To which the affable Isis responded by advising that the Anuba in the highlands of *Old Punt* informed that Setekh (Set) had traveled southward to the City of Nagu-Naro, eponymous capital of the great southern empire of the Nagas, where the regents of all the royal houses were gathering to honor of the death of the last of the lineage of the city's founding "House of Noura,'

With the passing of the last of the great Grand Regents of the lineage of Noura, *Auset* (Aset, Iset, Isis) explained, the relentless prowess of Setekh (Set) and the prominence of the Grand Regency of Nagu-Punt will most certainly usurp the past stature of Nagu-Naro; what this portends for the peace you desire is unclear, Isis propounded. To which *Ausar* (Osiris, Kush, Zeus, Dionysus) resolved that 'what is clear …is that there is that the Nagas are far more extensive in Abukulan (ancient Africa of the era) than first surmised. With the impending consolidation of their power, *Ausar* (Osiris, Kush, Zeus, Dionysus) surmised it would be important for the forces of Upper and Lower Khemet to be well aligned.

Grasping the moment and unaware of his earlier discourse with Thoth on the Subject, *Isis* then made mention of the dissension and discord in the *Lower River Valley,* specifically amongst the kingdoms around the shores of *Mr-wr* (Palaeo-Lake Moeris), and certain of the influential cities in the Delta beyond the Lower Valley. Isis recounted the tale of the overland invasion by which the *Atlatians* seized villages in the northwestern woodlands abutting *Mr-wr* as they advanced on the prosperous kingdoms along the northern shore; she told of how it was *Sobek* of the City of Shedet (Krokodilópolis) who organized the armies of the kingdoms around *Mr-wr* to repel the invading armies of the *Atlatians*. In the ensuing battles, she continued, each side suffered defeats and victories before the bogged-down, exhausted armies of the *Atlatians* were eventually repulsed.

As *Ausar* (Osiris, Kush, Zeus, Dionysus) patiently listened, the Queen recounted the tale of how, during their despair, the spirits of the embattled kingdoms around *Mr-wr* (Palaeo-Lake Moeris) were sustained only by their tenuous vassalage and belief in the preeminence of *Nagu-Punt,* who nonetheless were hesitant to defend or rescue them from the *Atlatian* invasion. It was nonetheless the course of these events that delivered the kingdoms about *Mr-wr* into the formal vassalage of *Nagau-Punt,* a submission they had long resisted and hoped their remoteness in the backwaters of the *Nile* would avoid. 'That they should now pay homage to a lineal descendent of the *Atlatian* throne' is a source of angst and distrust among the kingdoms around the shore of *Mr-wr* (Paleo-Lake Moeris) and certain of the cities in the Delta.

It was after due consideration that *Ausar* (Osiris, Kush, Zeus, Dionysus) informed that he should grant direct audience to *Sobek Sheddy* and the royal houses around the shores of *Mr-wr* (Palaeo-Lake Moeris); this at the royal house of the City of Shedet ((Krokodilópolis). Thus, it was that the kings and queens of the royal house around the shores of *Mr-wr* came to gather at the royal house of Shedet (Krokodilópolis), where each, individually and collectively, gained assurance and confidence in the ancient federation that was earliest Khemet under *Ausar*. That being achieved and having been advised of the return of Setekh (Set) to the City of Berbera, *Ausar* (Osiris, Kush, Zeus, Dionysus) sent a personal emissary to arrange a meeting between the two leaders.

Endeavor for Accord with Seteth (Set)

Nowhere is the true site of their meeting disclosed; the ancient legend only holds that the two formidable leaders at first found one another affable and forthcoming, far from what each had separately expected. *Seteth* (Set) told *Ausar* (Osiris) of the ancient rise of Nagu-Nora under the regal Noura and of the eastward spread of the ethos of the Nagas into the lands of Sunda and present-day southern and southeastern Asia, while *Ausar* (Osiris), in turn, told *Seteth* (Set) of the rise of ancient Atlatia under his father Khem and of the northern spread of the ethos of the Atlatians into the lands of Europe and the eastern lands of Anatolia, and Kannan. This a tale by which *Seteth* (Set) came to realize that before he sat his own half-brother, a favored son of the father for which held a lifetime of hatred and scorn.

Though the most ancient of legends profess a premeditated intent and plan by *Seteth* (Set) to assassinate *Ausar* (Osiris) in an endeavor to take over his throne, the greater context of the rage that led to *Ausar's* infamous dismemberment …was *Setekh's* thirst for vengeance against their father. By both prudence and tradition, seasoned wartime leaders such as *Ausar* (Osiris) and *Setekh* (Set) were accompanied by what they deemed adequate security forces. However, in this instance, the insidious contrivance by *Seteth* (Set) led *Ausar* (Osiris) to underestimate the true peril. Thus his forces were badly outnumbered. Nonetheless, when the Nagas beset *Ausar* (Osiris), the Kushite warriors responded with a valiant fight, befalling many Naga warriors before they themselves were overcome, with many Kushites falling before *Ausar* (Osiris) was slain.

Assassination of Ausar (Osiris, Kush, Zeus, Dionysus)

No more than three or four besieged Kushite warriors survived to flee to the north, where they apprised of the death of *Ausar* (Osiris) and warned the Kushite generals of an impending onslaught. Drunken and sullen *Seteth* (Set), no longer enraged but now full of remorse and regret, having realized the murder of his half-brother ended his only and last connection to the familial lineage of his father. But as *Seteth* (Set) sunk into deeper remorse and regret, but when he recalled being told that Ausar's wife Isis was pregnant with child, a surviving connection to his familial lineage, *Seteth* (Set) moved to protect Isis and the child from the carnage to come. *Seteth* (Set) enlisted the aid of the Anuba from Nagu-Punt to travel to Thebes and spirit the Queen away to safety. But Auset (Isis) would have none of it, believing *Seteth* (Set) to be a threat to her unborn child, the Queen fled northward to *Mr-wr* (Palaeo-Lake Moeris) and the protection of Sobek and the cult of Het-Heru at Krokodilópolis.[mlxvii]

The seasoned Kushite Generals arose to the occasion, forever forestalling the impending Naga invasion, indeed the Kushites, under a hastily arranged war council led by *Hercules* (Herakles, Heryshaf, Alcides), held fast to all their lands, including the highlands of *Old Punt,* and the *Port of Berbera* near the capital of *Nagu-Punt*. Thus, it was that for more than a generation, an uneasy peace blanketed Khemet, with Queen Isis as its tutelary head and the Vizier *Thoth* (Djehuty, Hermes) administrating the affairs of state on her behalf. Isis gave birth to Horus, the eighth son of *Ausar* (Osiris, Kush, Zeus, Dionysus) at the onset of this era, and it was during this time that he was raised to majority, educated by his brother Thoth (Djehuty, Hermes), and trained in martial skills and adeptness by his brother *Hercules* (Herakles, Heryshaf, Alcides). Though Isis had early on told *Hercules* of *Ausar's* promise to dispatch him to aid the Thracians in defense of their lands against the aggression of *Haides, Hercules* committed to remainin Khemet and train Horus until he attained acuity and reached majority; that being done, *Hercules* (Herakles, Heryshaf, Alcides) and what could best be described as a ragtag band of mercenaries set sail for Thrace.

The tacit understanding existing for more than a generation between *Hercules, Thoth,* and *Horus* was that *Horus* would avenge the death of their father, *Ausar* (Osiris, Zeus, Kush, Dionysus), and duly assume the throne of Khemet from his mother, Queen *Auset* (Aset, Iset, Isis). And so, after an early lifetime defined and driven by the cruel assassination of his father, an early lifetime of training and planning, an adept, focused and well-prepared Horus gathered his forces and, alas, launched a campaign of revenge against *Seteth* (Set) that set-in motion and began the long era of Tribulation.

[i] In paraphrase of Professor Ira Berlin
[ii] Dr. John Henrik Clarke, African Historian
[iii] THE FUTURE OF AFRICAN GODS THE CLASH OF CIVILIZATIONS (ACCRA - W.E.B. DU BOIS CENTER - JULY 10, 1998), by Professor Molefi Kete Asante Temple University
[iv] African-Centered scholars engaging in what Dr. Jacob H. Carruthers called "Intellectual Warfare" are struggling against well-financed and organized European intellectual armiespreparing to do battle with us to the end. In order to combat these challenges Africana scholarsmust be grounded in African-Centered theory, methodology and pedagogy.

Europeans have had a monopoly on the construction of historiography relative to Kemet and Kush since the Napoleonic invasions of Egypt in 1798. From that point on there was a conscious and systematic effort to remove Egypt from Africa and consequently Africans from Egypt, replacing them, in the minds of naïve observers from afar, with an Arab population that did not arrive until 639 C.E. In Europe's haste to whitewash classical African history through the use of curricular and pedagogical planning, whole generations of African people were deprived of their rightful place in the history of humanity.

Many of these ideas go back to the so-called Curse of Ham mythos perpetuated by Judeo-Talmudic literature and continued through Christian and Islamic discourses. First, starting with the collection of Jewish oral traditions called the Babylonian Talmud from the 2nd to the 6th century C.E. (Goldenberg, 2003; Harris, 1972) and later the works of Arab writers such as Muhammad ibn Abdullah al-Kisai in his book "Tales of the Prophets" written in the 6th century (Al-Haqq, 2006). Later European thinkers such as David Hume, Charles Montesquieu, George W.F. Hegel, Thomas Jefferson, John Calhoun, Immanuel Kant, Jean Jacque Rousseau and others supported these false notions about African people and their supposed inferiority.

We have a long and storied tradition of African scholars who have fought to keep the importance of our link to Nile Valley civilizations alive. These include such people as Martin Robeson Delany, Antonir Firmin, William Wells Brown, David Walker, Edward Wilmot Blyden, Henry Highland Garnet, George Washington Williams, Drusilla Dunjee Huston, and Hosea Easton, just to mention a few from the 19th century. In more contemporary times we have William Leo Hansberry, John G. Jackson, Willis N. Huggins, Chancellor Williams, John Henrik Clarke, Yosef Ben Jochannan, Ivan Van Sertima, Joel Augustus Rogers, Arthur Schomburg, are still groping in darkness with tools to re Carter G. Woodson, Charles Wesley, W.E.B. DuBois, and J.C. DeGraft-Johnson. These pioneers of what has come to be known as Africana Studies served as forerunners to the contemporary greats such as Cheikh Anta Diop, Theophile Obenga, Molefi Asante, Maulana Karenga, Asa G. Hilliard, Dr. Jacob H. Carruthers, and countless unnamed others.

The fact that ancient Khemetans / Egyptians and Nubians came from one essential African genus was completely unthinkable to most Europeans, then as well as now. The discovery of Nubian culture in 1907 so close on the heels of the development of Egyptology and the period of the European colonial and imperialist enterprise, must certainly have confounded their predisposition

However, while some of them conducted very honorable work, in some cases European scholars intentionally and completely misrepresented key particular aspect of African antiquity. How on earth were they to justify the enslavement and colonization of millions of Africans they considered to be wretched and savages

To complete this justification they had to take Khemet /Egypt out of Africa and thereby take the Africans out of Khemet / Egypt. Once Khemet /Egypt was removed from the African continent and placed in the mysterious Middle East, a term that was invented by Europeans at the beginning of the 20th century (Lewis, 1998, p. 3), or the Near East, thanks to the development of the Suez Canal by the French in 1865, the geographical and paradigmatic shift was simultaneously accomplished. It is time for willing and courageous Africana scholars to reclaim this ancient past.
We must have what Dr. Cheikh Anta Diop called the necessary pluridisciplinary skills. These have to be supported with what he described as three factors: Historical, Linguistic, and Psychological (Diop, 1974, p. xiii). Without them Africana scholars will be looking down the barrels of powerful, well financed and well organized European intellectual armies preparing to do battle with us to the end (D'Souza, 1995; Lefkowitz, 1996; Schlesinger, Jr., 1992).

[v] Much of this is corroborated by archaeology, which is often more objective, credible, and eloquent than mainstream chroniclers. The marvelous discoveries of archaeology have already served the purposes of African historical research well. The language of archaeological excavation has, by nature, something objective and irrefutable about it. Living ties of the past are revived, beyond the modern landscape, through studies of the typology of pottery and ancient artifacts; engravings uncovered demonstrate links between the past, present and future. Archaeology is the study of the physical traces left by people of the past, and as such, it is a major source of information about how ancient Africans lived at various times in the course of their long history.

[vi] Modern archeological studies emphasize paleoclimatic or paleoenvironmental history as a triggering (or a very important) cause of past human development (e.g. Weiss et al., 1993; Verschuren et al., 2000; Lamb et al., 2003; Weninger et al., 2006; Zielhofer and Linsta¨dter, 2006). Nevertheless, a correlation of archeological data with paleoenvironmental findings often remains unsatisfactory due to a lack of well-dated and continuous sequences.

[vii] Historical linguistics, another tool, concerns the relationships among languages and how they have changed over time. It provides clues about the past migrations and relationships of ethnic groups. Ethnography, the study of present-day ethnic groups and their immediate ancestors, helps archaeologists trace connections between the past and the present.

The entire concept of the "Afro-Asiatic" language and migration for example is nothing more than a revamped "Hamitic Hypothesis" by so-called experts such as American linguist Christopher Ehret, who specializes in promoting the existence of this fake language family, which means that he specializes in the denial of the relationship between Niger-Congo speakers to ancient Northern and Eastern Africa. Here is a piece that he wrote in which he acknowledges the undeniable fact that Niger-Congo originated in Northeast Africa (Nubia) due to the fact that it is the sibling of Cushitic languages (which he considers "Afro-Asiatic") which is undeniably East African in origin, but attributes the absence of Niger-Congo in the region's history to do an undisclosed yet major migration from Nubia into West Africa (which was uninhabitable swamp land until the 3rd millennium BC).

[viii] The disappearance of the vast sacred and literature; the loss of those keys which alone could solve the thousand riddles of the hieroglyphic records. Simply brand them all as purveyors of wildly fantastic and unproveable hypotheses of nonsense; this includes even those modern alternative free-thinkers who delve in fields, such as the Hollow Earth and Planets-Inside Earth Cosmogony theory. They can all be lumped together as a bunch of poor demented self-deluding, self-righteous intellectuals who haven't bothered to seriously consider anything other than their own spoon-fed concepts.

These patronizingly omniscient and patently dishonest attitudes and conclusions on the part of the so-called 'Orthodox Scientific Establishment' are all founded very largely upon pure speculation, hypothesis and theory. But these insubstantial *concepts* have somehow miraculously evolved into "Factual Truth and Affirmated Knowledge" simply by means of their substantiated proclamations

[ix] Drusilla D. Houston, historian, Wonderful Ethiopians of the Ancient Cushite Empire, Chapter XI: The Strange Races of Chaldea (1926). Myths have often proven themselves to be fact…"Men once claimed that ancient Troy was a myth and that the Labyrinth of Minos was fiction; but archaeologists have unearthed the Troy of Greek legends and the Labyrinth of Crete."

[x] And thus, because truth has been sacrificed and lost to the predilections and hubris of the victors of mankind's incessant wars and conquest, who, in turn, violated, disgarded, distorted and readily recast it in their own images. An advent that has, in effect, dispersed the unity of knowledge over time and space, burying it within the reinterpretations, half truths and repositories of past regimes, sometimes one has to make choices between the historical interpretations propounded by the powers of the day, and alternative interpretations that can be supported by cooroberating historical and archaeological literature, reference and evidentiary materials. If the available evidence seems to favor one interpretation over another, that interpretation became part of the narrative. Where the evidence is lacking or hard to evaluate, suitable hedging accompanies any descriptive generalizations that are advanced.

[xi] Over the ages, the hubris of a long parade of conquerors wishing to usurp the heritage of those they viewed as their enemies have led to the destruction and burning of many ancient and sacred scrolls and books. Endeavors are intent on distorting history in favor of the "conquerors", yet, tellingly, these corruptions make themselves obvious by their lack of comportment with surrounding and juxtaposing histories. Over the passage of time, repeating patterns of distortions by the usurpers has created a confounding of global history that has led to the notion that a vital missing aspect of history is needed to reconcile truth..

[xii] What the Ancient Wisdom Expects of Its Disciples, by: M. Hall
[xiii] Significant portions of the information underlying the early sections, applies to the period before historical documentation begins to become available (roughly before the 3rdmillennium) when the clues are even more few and far between than after actual trade records begin to be preserved for posterity. The fact that there are sources for these myths, ledgend and oral histories does not render them carved in stone in terms of their indisputable accuracy. The reader must keep in mind that this interpretation is not fully based on corroboration or substantiation from a multi-disciplinarial perspective.
[xiv] The Pygmies were a nation of dwarfs. Ptah was the great icon of these so-called "Little People"; Ptah is represented in the form of a pygmy, and his Ari are seven little pygmies
[xv] The Eemian interglacial
[xvi] Climate records derived from ice cores taken through the Greenland ice cap suggested the warm climate of the Eemian might have been punctuated by many sudden but relatively short cold phases, and at least one major cold and dry event in Europe and China during period seems to corroborate the Greenland ice cores; the terrestrial pollen record during the Eemian interglacial period in Asia and Eurasia (Zhisheng & Porter 1997).
[xvii] High-resolution Atlantic sediment records (Adkins et al 1997) suggests the move from interglacial to severely colder conditions occurred over a period of less than 400 four
[xviii] Even the mountain ranges of Central Africa were covered by ice flow during the "Younger Dryas". However, the roughly 1,300 year cold and aridity phase, which defined the era, ended when a sudden warming period ensued, resulting in a global climate as warm as today. During the long build-up phase of the Glaciers, surviving plants, animals and humans were able to do so only by learning to adapt to the slowly changing environment and terrain. A great portion of the northern continents, and a significant portion of the south (extending from the polar region), were blanketed and covered by compounding thick sheets of ice, for thousands of years

[xix] For thousands of years during the glacial period, enormous volumes of water were withdrawn from the oceans and locked up in the

enlarged ice caps of both poles of the globe. However, the great sheets of ice never covered more than a third of the earth's land surface, even at the greatest extent of the glaciation.

xx The African glaciers left behind deep deposits of rock formed from sediments deposited in the northwestern Sahara and the Congo River Basin. Geomorphological and biological evidence indicates that, during the Pleistocene Epoch, glaciers extended across several hundred square miles of the African mountains.

xxi The separation of the plates caused violent earthquakes, volcanic activity, and upheavals in central and eastern Africa until, ultimately, the Arabian plate pulled away from the rest of the continent, leaving behind a very long, steep-sided, Y-shaped valley, six thousand miles in length, from south to north. The Eastern arm of the valley stretches from Lebanon and North Syria, through the Red Sea, through Eritrea, Ethiopia, Kenya, Tanzania, Malawi, to Mozambique. The western arm of the Rift extends through Congo, Uganda, Urwanda, Urundi, and Tanzania, where it links up with the eastern arm.

xxii The Rift Valley enters Africa on the coast of present day Eritrea; winding over 3,500 miles southward to the coast of southern Mozambique, and varies in width from twenty to sixty miles, and in depth from a few hundred to several thousand meters

xxiii A "Major Ice Age" is defined as a period of time, maximum peak to peak temperatures of the order of 115 kiloyears, during which the Earth's mean atmospheric temperature is 4Co to 9Co colder than at present, and ice sheets and glaciers extend much beyond their present boundaries. [Ref. : Major Ice Ages Earth-States Transitions, by L. David Roper, Professor Emeritus of Physics, Department of Physics, Virginia Polytechnic Institute and State University, Blacksburg, Virginia 24061, USA]. In this work the term 'Last Major Ice Age' shalll refer to the Major Ice Age that the Earth just experienced. "Major Interglacials", in turn, are warm periods of 5-10,000 years duration at the boundaries between the Major Ice Ages. Similarly, the term 'Last Major Interglacial' refers to the Major Interglacial at the beginning of the Last Major Ice Age, traditionally called the 'Emian Interglacial', at about 120,000 years ago [Ref. : Major Ice Ages Earth-States Transitions, by L. David Roper, Professor Emeritus of Physics, Department of Physics, Virginia Polytechnic Institute and State University, Blacksburg, Virginia 24061, USA].

xxiv Tools enabled them to broaden the range of food available to them, for instance, to cut meat from animal carcasses, and enabled materials such as wood, bark reeds and hides to be cut and fashioned into useful everyday items. The evolution of the nascent cultures afforded the *Ancestral Alkebu* broader ranges of habitation and settlement throughout the region. Ancient settlement areas have been found in what would have then been channels of the highland rivers and streams flowing into the Gorge during the wetter periods, causing many of the sites to be displaced by overflowing waters. (Preservation of surviving sites around the lake was made possible by ash falls from nearby volcanoes and the inconsistency of the lake's depth.)

xxv During last ice age, temperatures over tropical Africa were 21C, about 4C lower than today.

xxvi The leading theories on the evolution of "straight hair" focus on the relationship between ultraviolet radiation [or "UV light"] and the cold climate of the highlands and the northern hemisphere; based primarily on the principle that straight fibers better facilitate the passage of UV light into the body relative to curly hair. It is substantiated by Iyengar's (1998) findings that UV light can pass through straight human hair roots in a manner similar to the way that light passes through fiber optic tubes (Iyengar, 1998)."

xxvii The oldest known fossil remains, according to Dr. Louis Leakey, were found in the Olduvai Gorge in Kenya, Uganda and Tanzania; these first "small" people were the "Ba-Twa" (also simply known as the "(Twa"). Over time the *Ba-Twa* expanded into and became mostly based in the forested foothills around Lake Kivu, in the Great Lakes region of the Rift Valley, from where they spread into the forested foothills of the *Rwenzori* mountains. They were equatorial forest-dwelling *Negriods* of diminutive stature, with deep dark brown skin, tight curly hair, broad faces, flat noses, deeply set eyes, and full lips; it was they who first populated the forest of the hot interior lowlands. The major difference between them and the *Vedda* of the cooler forested coastal plains was the tightly curled hair of the *Ba-Twa,* in contrast to the curled to wavy hair of the *Veddas*.

xxviii Scientific DNA gene tracing has revealed that the first human were pygmyoid BaTwa (Twe) or Sarwa (San) in Africa.Scientific genetic studies have shown that the African Pygmy tribes have the oldest living DNA on planet earth. Namely, the San, Twa, Mbuti, Aka, and Bayaka tribes of Southern and Central Africa.

xxix Psilocybin users may experience audio visual and tactile hallucinations, a sense of euphoria and feeling of interconnectedness with the environment

xxx An aurora (plural: auroras), sometimes referred to as polar lights, northern lights (aurora borealis) or southern lights (aurora australis), is a natural light display in the Earth's sky, predominantly seen in the high-latitude regions (around the Arctic and Antarctic).

xxxi The "Southern Lights" phenomenon occurred then as it does now, when charged particles from the Sun's solar winds bombard and interact with the Earth's magnetosphere

xxxii The magnetosphere is a region of space that surrounds the Earth's magnetic field and has a primary purpose of preventing cosmic rays, such as solar winds from entering Earth's atmosphere. However, occasionally, at particular times of the year, a few charged particles from solar winds make their way through the magnetosphere into our atmosphere. The charged particles move along the Earth's magnetic field lines towards the south and north pole. When they reach the each pole, they collide with atoms in the atmosphere, particularly nitrogen and oxygen, and become increasingly charged. Once the electrons settle back down to their normal level of excitement they glow, creating the magnificent light display, we know as an Aurora.

[xxxiii] The recent discovery of an assemblage of chipped-stone artifacts characteristic of an Acheulean industry at an open-air site near Mpala in the central Kenya highlands expands the regional sample of Acheulean sites beyond the Rift Valley. An archaeological reconnaissance of the site in February 2005 mapped 69 surface artifact locations concentrated along seasonal stream channels. This poster presents some initial analyses of the surface distribution of artifact classes, artifact condition, and depositional context and integrity of the deposits for future fieldwork.

[xxxiv] The Middle Wisconsin interstadial period is said to have been characterized by pluvial conditions in the Kalahari (30-19 000 yr BP), while the last glacial maximum climatic conditions are said to have prevailed between ca.19 000 and 13 000 yr BP. The period between 13,000 and 10 000 yr BP presents the transition from glacial climatic conditions to the post-glacial climatic optimum. During the Holocene temperature maximum around 9500 yr BP geomorphic and palaeopedologic features indicate wetter conditions in the Kalahari.

[xxxv] Before formation of the Okavango Delta the Okavango River flowed right through Botswana and drained into a massive lake in the region of the Makgadikgadi pans in Botswana. Rivers like the Okavango are hard-coded to flow towards large low-lying bodies of water, like lakes; but then about 50 000 years ago, there was a massive earthquake in Southern Africa, near the present day border between Botswana and Namibia. The huge earthquake shifted and interrupted the Okavango River's theretofore usual flow, with a 11 trillion litres of water flooding the basins of the vast low-lying area; creating the Okavango Delta. The Delta consists of a multitude of main channels, smaller tributaries and lagoons as well as floodplains, islands and large mainland areas.

[xxxvi] Researchers have documented thousands of stone tools on the lake bed, which shed light on how early ancient *San* and *Khoi* in Southern Africa adapted to several substantial climate change events during the *Ice Age*. Researchers from the School of Geography and the Environment at the University of Oxford Their research was prompted by the discovery of the first of what are believed to be the world's largest stone tools on the bed of the lake. Equally remarkable is that the dry lake floor where they were found is also littered with tens of thousands of other smaller stone-age tools and flakes, suggesting that clans from both core groups, the ancient *Khoi* and *San*, each liberally used the lake basin when it had evaporated, or was at least seasonally dry. Professor David Thomas, Head of the School of Geography and the Environment at the University of Oxford, said: 'Many of the tools were found on the dry lake floor, not around its edge, which challenges the view that big lakes were only attractive to humans when they were full of water.

[xxxvii] Archeologists in Zambia, to the north of the modern Khoisan range, have in uncovered skulls of people resembling the modern Khoisan, as well as stone tools resembling those of the San.

[xxxviii] Hypotheses about further encursions of the Khoisan into the Eastern African Highlands have been made on the basis of Khoisan-like skeletal materials found on the East African Plateau; archeologists in Zambia, to the north of the modern Khoisan range, have in fact found skulls of people resembling the modern Khoisan, as well as stone tools resembling those the Khoisan peoples were making in southern Africa during the era in the region.

[xxxix] The term "San" is interpreted as "outsider" in the language of the *Khoi* and was at first considered derogatory in the way it distinguished the indigenous San from the *Khoikhoi*, whose name means the "Men of Men" or the "First People".[xxxix]

[xl] According to a study on San culture by the Kalahari People's Fund

[xli] Like the San, the Khoi people also had a yellowish complexion but they were bigger in size.

[xlii] The Myths of the Milky Way have long be forgotten, which is remarkable as having the most important connection to the basically Story of Creation

[xliii] The flow of cosmic energy from the Rainbow Serpent was considered the source of the regenerative and reproductive power in nature and human beings

[xliv] The oldest rock paintings they created are in Namibia and have been radiocarbon-dated to be 26 000 years old

[xlv] The Mountain of the Gods is the only uplifted hill like area for over a 100 kilometres in all directions. These hills are of great cultural and spiritual significance to the peoples of the Kalahari, who believe Tsodilo is the birthplace of all life, and that mankind was descended from the serpent, and it was the descendants of the first people who created the rock art found there. The association of serpent deities with the creation myth, or our beginnings, is a constantly reoccuring theme across many different cultures. As is the case with most churches, temples and other sacred places of worship, the San believe that the Tsodilo Hills are a resting place for spirits of the deceased, and that these spirits will cause misfortune and bad luck if anyone hunts or causes death near the hills. This place if revered and treated with the respect given to sacred ground.

[xlvi] The San identify the hills as "Male Hill," "Female Hill" and "Child," according to their respective sizes; the fourth is the "First Wife" (the "Female Hill" being the male's second wife). At the top of the Male Hill, the most sacred spot for the San, deep impressions in the rock are regarded as where the first spirit knelt to pray after creating the earth

[xlvii] Some ancient rock art in the Kalahari shows women clapping and people dancing as in the trance dance ritual.

[xlviii] In paraphrase and partial reference to a fictional depiction used in the text of the 'Eightfold Path: Chanting' (see www.earthspirit.com/eightfold-path-part-twochanting)

[xlix] Regarding repeditive use of sound in chanting, it has been noted that while sound created can vary from a single note or word, to elaborate verse, the simpler the chant, the easier it is to achieve deep trance. If the words are too complicated to remember, the mind feels it must stay in control, must remember what words go in what order, and never really turns itself off to allow an altered state of consciousness to

occur. Regarding the use of "drumming", according to Andrew Neher, a researcher who investigated the effects of drumming on EEG patterns, the rhythmic pounding dramatically alters brain wave activity. In his research the point is made that multiple frequencies of drums activates multiple neural pathways, similar to light frequencies. Rhythmic light induces similar brain patterns to drumming, where brain waves respond to amplitude and frequency of the stimulus (aka visual/auditory driving). Brain wave frequency is noted to be in between 8 and 13 cycles per second, varying between individuals, but stays constant in the individual himself.

[l] Psychoactive plants and southern African hunter-gatherers: a review of the evidence; by Peter Mitchell and Andrew Hudson. Katz's (1982) extensive study of the Ju/'hoãn (!Kung) trance dance in the Dobe area of northwestern Botswana provides more detailed information on one of the plants in Lee's list, Ferraria glutinosa. Known to the Ju/'hoãnsi as !kaishe or gaise noru noru, this is listed by Lee (1979: 469) as a hallucinogen, although without further discussion. Katz (1982: 281–294) discusses at length its employment as an apparently mind-altering drug once used in teaching people how to handle the experience of trance, although this practice had apparently ceased many years before his fieldwork in the mid-1960s. Katz's principal informant, Kinachau, indicated that the plant's root was used to make a drink which everyone drank, although those who had not previously succeeded in reaching a state of trance drank more of it

[li] Marriage among the Khoikhoi was more complex. It was only after initiation (boys underwent initiation where their hunting skills were tested, which prepared them for adulthood. Initiation was mainly performed at puberty) and marriage within the same clan was forbidden. The young couple stayed with the bride's parents until the birth of their first-born child.

[lii] Evidence of serpent worship ritual sites and temples are scattered all over the ancient world, but the Tsodilo Hills Serpent Cave is the oldest such site that has ever been found. The practice of worship of or attribution of divine or sacred nature to serpents, simply referenced as Ophiolatry, is a practice that can be found all over the world, including China, India, Cambodia, Thailand, Japan, Indonesia, Ancient Greece and Rome, Egypt, United Kingdom, Scandinavia and the Americas, North, Central and South

[liii] , The two off-shore islands just off the coast of Tanzania (Zanzibar and Pemba) are believed to have once formed part of the African continent; the separation of Pemba having occurred during the Miocene epoch (23.7 million to 5.3 million years ago) while Zanzibar dates from the Pliocene epoch (5.3 million to 1.6 million years ago) or even later.

[liv] The Indo-Aryan is thus very similar to the European, possessing a fine nose, while the Sudroid is related to the Africans -

[lv] Kilimanjaro is the tallest free-standing mountain on the Earth's land surface, rising about 15,000 feet above the surrounding plain; its great size and height strongly influence the climate, vegetation, animal life and variability for habitation in the region.

[lvi] The phrase 'Kilema Kyaro' literally means 'that which cannot be conquered', or 'that which makes a journey impossible' or 'completely inaccessible' or 'where a traveller can disappear or be completely lost'.

[lvii] Recent advances in genetics has shed some light on their common ancient lineage, and subsequent divergence of the so-called "Black Pygmies" .

[lviii] The present-day islands of the Indonesian archipelago were then merely the mountain heights of the huge Ice Age era sub-continent known as "Sunda,"; a landmass twice the size of the present-day Indian Sub-Continent.

[lix] The Celebes was then also a more prominent landmass, with mountains extending northeast from the highland's north-south backbone, and three fertile low land regions extending to the north, east, and south. The Celebes had of ranges of mountains cut by deep rift valleys, many of which contained rivers and lakes; the Celebes was bordered by oceanic troughs in the south, separating the Sunda and Sahul Shelfs.

[lx] Geographically the Mountains of the Moon, which are now known as the Rwenzori Mountains, the spelling having been changed from Ruwenzori in about 1980 to conform more closely with the local name 'Rwenjura', lie slightly north of the Equator on the western edge of Uganda bordering the Democratic Republic of the Congo. The range is up to 30 miles (50 km) wide and extends south-north for 80 miles (130 km). The highest point is Mt Stanley's Margherita Peak at 16,763 feet (5,109 m), the higher peaks are permanently snow-capped and often hidden by clouds, and the higher valleys are glaciated

[lxi,lxi] Lake Tanganyika is the second deepest lake in the world after ancient Lake Baikal in present day Russia. It is also the second oldest freshwater lake in the world, the second largest by volume, and the second deepest, in all cases after Lake Baikal in Siberia. Lake Tanganyika (Surface elevation, 2,536 ft)) is located in the Albertine Rift, the western branch of the Great East African Rift Valley, and is confined by the mountainous walls of the valley

[lxii] Recent studies of ancient and modern human DNA provide strong support for the common use of fishing or aquatic foraging in human evolution; a notion that was generally dismissed. In the East African rift zone, ancient peoples appear to have consumed a regular diet of fish. In the Kenya rift valley the main stage of Leakey's 'Kenya Capsian' culture was essentially the local manifestation of this far-flung 'aquatic culture'. Freshwater crabs are among the most important invertebrates inhabiting african inland waters, and these large and conspicuous crustaceans are present in almost all freshwater habitats, from mountain streams to large lowland rivers and smaller water bodies (rathbun 1921; Balss 1936; Bott 1955; Cumberlidge 1999; yeo et al. 2008). The african continent is, for the purposes of this project, subdivided into the fi ve main regions, and each of these has a distinct freshwater crab faunal composition, with only a few species (14 out of 120) found in more than one region. for example, the most diverse regions are eastern africa (44 species, three genera), central africa (33 species, three genera), and western africa (24 species, six genera), while southern africa (20 species, one genus) and northern africa (four species, two genera) each have a less diverse regional fauna (Bott 1955; Cumberlidge 1997, 1998, 1999, 2009a,b; Cumberlidge and Boyko 2000; Corace et al. 2001; Cumberlidge et al. 2002; Cumberlidge and Vanini 2004; Cumberlidge and reed 2004, 2006; Cumberlidge and Tavares 2006; Cumberlidge and dobson 2008; Cumberlidge et al. 2009)

lxiii The exploitation of fish and other marine resources is usually a far more reliable and productive form of foraging than the diversified hunting and gathering of most foragers

lxiv Ancient art verifies that honey consumption is not a recent phenomenon. Rock art depicting honeycombs, swarms of bees and honey collecting date to as many as 40,000 years ago. Such art has been found in Africa

lxv . Early settled "kingdoms" in East Africa began to first emerge by 20,000 B.C

lxvi Complex Hunter-Gatherer societies have been widely referenced in evolutionist literature as providing a bridge between simple HG societies and agrarian societies (see e.g. Finlayson, 2009 Finlayson, B. (2009). The 'complex hunter-gatherer' and the transition to farming. In N. Finlay, S. McCartan, N.Milner, & C. Wickham-Jones (Eds.), From Bran Flakes to Bushmills: Papers in honour of Professor Peter Woodman(Vol. 1 Prehistoric Society Research Papers, pp. 175–188). Oxford: Oxbow Books.

lxvii Sources for Africa's forest history are found in the literature of physical and biological science, anthropology, history, religion, literature, and philosophy. Each discipline casts forest history in a different light. The natural history favored by science renders the past in millions of years, time scales that dwarf human history. In this history, dynamism describes forest expansion, contraction, migration, and ecological change. To the natural historian, then, human alteration of forest environments is both very recent and extraordinarily jarring. *Homo sapiens* has clearly and indelibly marked Africa's forests.

lxviii . Ptah's original name in Ancient Khemetan / Egyptian is reconstructed to have been pronounced as *Pitáḥ based on the occurrence of his name in hieroglyphics, *ptḥ*, surviving into Coptic as *Ptah*, just as it is now written in English

lxix Ptah was depicted as a dwarf (a sacred dwarf *Ptah*-Partakos), as Herodotus claimed to see statues in this form in the temple of Hephaistos (Ptah) at Memphis.

lxx This everbecoming is a total cosmic process, involving everything from sub-atomic particles to planetary globes, and even suns and galaxies.

lxxi The ancient Art of Magick encompassed many things: science, art, philosophy, metaphysics, psychology and religion; it was an adventure at the borderlands of the unknown, but most of all it was an expression of the true Will of the individual

lxxii Nature is the totality of all things (space, matter and energy) in the universe and its boundaries (if it has one although implausible) that are either visible, detectable or invisible, non detectable with our senses and their behaviors, properties and above all, the ultimate laws of all laws that govern these properties and behaviors.

lxxiii The observed celestial energies of the "Southern Lights" were symbolically referred anciently to as the Cosmic Serpent (the mythological "Hydra")), which, like electromagnetism and all energy fields, exists as a spectrum of various colors, frequencies, or powers. Their activities resonate in the shapes and energies that bathe the earth and all life processes.

lxxiv At least forty thousand years ago, and possibly as long as two hundred thousand years ago, human social life in and around forests complicated natural history.

lxxv Temperatures during the last glacial maximum are estimated to have been 4–7°C lower than today, and they were coupled with intensive aridity and regression of lakes throughout the African continent, resulting from reduced precipitation as a consequence of weaker monsoons, stronger dry trade winds, and lowered SST (Coetzee, 1967; Flenley, 1979; COHMAP Members, 1988; Bonnefille et al., 1990; Vincens et al., 1993).

lxxvi de Monocal, 2001

lxxvii The Rwenzori are the site of 30 named lakes, all located in the highlands. Nine of which are located in the D. R. Congo and 21 in Uganda. The lakes are all of glacial origin, with the exception of Lake Bujuku which formed within the last millennium behind a landslide from the slope of Mt. Baker(Livingstone 1967). The Ruwenzoris Mountains Range is dotted with numerous lakes, mainly occupying glacially-excavated and moraine-dammed basins formed after the last glacial period (Osmaston, 1989; Section 4).

lxxviii Natural levees commonly form around highland rivers and tributaries without human intervention. Such natural levees are embankments created by deposited river sediments as a river floods. They are asymmetrical structures with almost vertical walls adjacent to the river while tapering landwards along a gentle slope.

lxxix Ptah in Egypt was one of the earliest gods of Creation. Ptah was sometimes none other than the great hill, which rose from the waters of Creation. He was called the "Father of the Gods." And more importantly to these discussions, he was "The Keeper of Sacred Geometry," "Grand Master Architect" and "Creator of the Universe." And with Egypt's vast dedication to sacred geometry in its temples and pyramids, one can see that Ptah was probably the most revered god of all. Pictured above are two depictions of the god Ptah. The picture on the right is Ptah in the geometric "Magic 3-4-5" position. What is displayed here is none other than the famed geometric theorem identified with Pythagoras. This theorem was known in Egypt for several thousand years before the birth of the Greek mathematician to whom it is commonly attributed.

lxxx Credited to Ptah, Man understands Engineering and the nature of advanced skills like Electromagnetism, Ohms Law, and Thermodynamics: the branch of physical science that deals with the relations between heat and other forms of energy (such as mechanical, electrical, or chemical energy), and, by extension, of the relationships between all forms of energy.

lxxxi . Ptah is the root of many schools of thought, including the philosophies of the Greeks, the Cathars, the Templars and the freemasons. His energy is very much that of the prime architect, and he carries the compass and square familiar to many and having great esoteric significance

lxxxii Credited to Ptah, Man understands Engineering and the nature of advanced skills like Electromagnetism, Ohms Law, and Thermodynamics: the branch of physical science that deals with the relations between heat and other forms of energy (such as mechanical,

[lxxxii] electrical, or chemical energy), and, by extension, of the relationships between all forms of energy.
[lxxxiii] Ptah was seen as progenitor of the pataikoi, a race of dwarf craftsmen. (Pinch, 181; Wilkinson, 124; Erman, 77)
[lxxxiv] A demographic approach to defining cities can be ethnocentric in that it assumes cities in all cultures will resemble the large and densely settled cities of the modem United States and Europe (see Sjoberg, this volume, for a critique of this notion).

[lxxxv] The development of states—large-scale, populous, politically centralized, and socially stratified polities governed by powerful rulers—marks one of the major milestones in the evolution of human societies. Archaeologists often distinguish between primary (or pristine) states and secondary states. Primary states evolved independently through largely internal developmental processes rather than through the influence of any other preexisting state. Understanding Ancient State Societies in the Old World.

[lxxxvi] Henry Morton Stanley's last expedition in Africa was for the relief of Mehmed Emin Paşa, governor of the Equatorial Province of Egypt, who had been cut off by the Mahdist revolt of 1882 in the environs of Lake Albert. Stanley was appointed to lead a relief expedition and decided to approach Lake Albert by way of the Congo River, counting on Tippu Tib to supply porters. Stanley left England in January 1887 and arrived at the mouth of the Congo in March. The expedition reached the navigable head of the river in June, and there, at Yambuya, Stanley left a rear column with orders to await Tippu Tib's porters. The failure of the rear column to rejoin the main body later gave rise to controversy harmful to Stanley's reputation. Eventually the expedition was assembled at Lake Albert, and, despite Emin's initial reluctance to leave his province, some 1,500 persons set out for the east coast on April 10, 1889, and arrived at Bagamoyo on December 4. On the way, the Ruwenzori Range (the legendary 'Mountains of the Moon') was revealed to European explorers for the first time. Stanley's original birth name was John Rowlands, (born January 28, 1841, Denbigh, Denbighshire, Wales—died May 10, 1904, London, England); he gained fame for his rescue of the Scottish missionary and explorer David Livingstone in the Congo region. He was knighted in 1899.

[lxxxvii] In the far later mythology and descendent culture of ancient Khemet (Egypt) they recognized Sekhmet's ability to attract celestial energy and precipitate this energy into form (a function of the celestial æthereals).

[lxxxviii] An aurora is a natural electric phenomenon that creates bright and colorful light displays in the sky, and are most common at higher latitudes. These dramatic and colorful lights are created when electrically charged particles from solar winds enter the Earth's atmosphere and interact with the atmosphere. When the solar cycle is at its optimum, the southern lights can be seen from anywhere in the southern hemisphere.

[lxxxix] The Congo-Nile Divide is the area where the sources of the Congo and Nile Rivers both are found within the present day Nyungwe and Kibira National Parks of Rwanda and Burundi; the parks, are contiguous at the international border between Rwanda and urundi

[xc] The Congo-Nile divide starts where the Congo, Chad and Nile basins meet, and runs southeast and then south along the border between South Sudan and Uganda to the east and the Central African Republic and Democratic Republic of the Congo (DRC) to the west

[xci] The culture of the emergent western *Twa* were verily effected by that of the eastern Twa (the "Early Anu"), the Twa of central Congo and the Zaire river basin, the Baka, BaAka (also Bayaka, also known as Babinga or Bambenga, and BaMbenzele) (Bahuchet 1972, 1985; Demesse 1978, 1980; Hewlett 1991; Kitanishi 1995; Lewis 2002); the BaMbuti Northeastern Congo (DRC, formerly Zaire), a group actually divided into at least three ethnic groups: Efe, Asua, and BaSua (Bailey 1991; Demolin 1993; Harako 1976, 1981; Ichikawa 1978, 1981, 1983; Peacock 1984, 1985; Schebesta 1941; Tanno 1976, 1981; Terashima 1983, 1985, 1998; Turnbull 1965a, 1965b, 1983).

[xcii] In the late 1950s, a Belgian archaeologist named Jean de Heinzelin conducted an archaeological excavation in the Ishango District of Congo, Central Africa. De Heinzelin found many interesting harpoon heads and a bone that captured his attention immediately because it contained groups of peculiar markings. This bone would become known as the Ishango bone. Originally, de Heinzelin dated the bone via a carbon-dating process to be from 8500 BCE. Later dating with more sensitive radiocarbon instruments found that the Ishango bone dates to 25,000 BCE

[xciii] The smallest of the two bones carries several incisions organized in three columns; the left column can be divided into 4 groups, with each possessing 19, 17, 13, and 11 notches. The sum of these being 60. Those are the four successive prime numbers between 10 and 20, constituting what mathematician call a "quad of prime numbers"

[xciv] The Ishango was discovered in the area of Ishango near the Semliki River, near where. Lake Edwarde empties into the Semliki, forming part of the headwaters of the Nile River (on the border between modern-day Uganda and Congo). The bones were found among the remains of a small community that fished and gathered in this area of Africa. The settlement had been buried in a volcanic eruption.Named after the place where it was found in the Democratic Republic of Congo, the Ishango bone is what is called a bone tool or the cradle of mathematics."

[xcv] Since historical records are relatively recent, it goes without saying that archaeology is indispensable for the reconstruction of Central Africa's past. With its wide diversity of pre-colonial political systems, ranging from 'acephalous' societies to highly centralized kingdoms, the archaeology of Central Africa provides an important input to recent theories on the growth of social and political complexity. Volumetric estimates on extracted iron-ore and associated slag mounds from prehistoric sites in the southern Central African Republic suggest large-scale iron production.

[xcvi] The Twa had already been throughout "Ta Neteru" (throughout the Tropics) from much earlier migrations (also into northern Asia establishing the Ainu cultures of proto Japan) out of Africa that placed them throughout Asia, the Pacific Islands, and the Americas (where the so called "good hair" seen in us - via our "Native American ancestry" really comes from).

[xcvii] Amélineau, is credited with the discovery of the Anu and their contribution to Egyptian civilization. It was Amélineau who designated the first black race to occupy Egypt as the Anu. He showed how they came slowly down the Nile and founded the cities of Esneh, Erment, Qouch and Heliopolis

xcviii Sources for Africa's forest history are found in the literature of physical and biological science, anthropology, history, religion, literature, and philosophy. Each discipline casts forest history in a different light. The natural history favored by science renders the past in millions of years, time scales that dwarf human history. In this history, dynamism describes forest expansion, contraction, migration, and ecological change. To the natural historian, then, human alteration of forest environments is both very recent and extraordinarily jarring. *Homo sapiens* has clearly and indelibly marked Africa's forests

xcix The three "Dryas" periods (younger, older, oldest) are named for a marker species," Dryas octopetala", detected in core samples of glacial ice and peat bogs

c Stadials and interstadials are phases dividing the Quaternary period (or the last 2.6 million years); stadials are periods of colder climate while interstadials are periods of warmer climate. The Younger, Older, and Oldest Dryases cold periods have been recognized in sequence and relative magnitude in paleoclimatic records from Greenland ice cores, European lacustrine sediments, Atlantic Ocean sediments, and the Cariaco Basin, Venezuela.

ci A calibrated range between 14,700 and 14,100 BP has been assigned to the Bølling layer of the excavation at Lake Neuchatel, Switzerland, 1992-1993

cii The date of the Older Dryas are not well defined, with estimates varying by 400 years, but its duration is agreed to have been around 200 years

ciii The Younger Dryas is the youngest and longest of three stadials, the Younger, Older, and Oldest Dryases, which resulted from typically abrupt climatic changes that took place over the last 16,000 calendar years; the prefix "Younger" refers to the recognition that this original "Dryas" cold period was preceded by a warmer stage, the Allerød oscillation, which, in turn, was preceded by the Older Dryas cold period, around 14,000 calendar years BP. That is not securely dated, and estimates vary by 400 years, but it is generally accepted that it lasted around 200 years.

civ The Ethiopian Highlands formed over 75 million years ago with the rift that separates the sections occurring around 30 million years ago.

cv Bes was sometimes depicted with feline or leonine features and often sports a long tail prompting the speculation that in earlier times, he was not in fact a dwarf but a lion or cat rearing up on his hind legs. Furthermore, his name may be derived from the Nubian word for cat ("besa") and is written using the determinative for a mammal rather than the determinative of a god or a man (the cow skin). It is equally likely that he was always seen as a dwarf with the strength and power of a cat.

cvi In his own inimitable fashion, Bes (Bisu, Aha) propounded that the most ascendant warrior is the warrior who has come to terms with his most predominant fear, that of death', adding that 'when a warrior no longer fears his own own death, anything becomes possible. From the perspective of the ancients', death was seen as a natural transition from the visible to the invisible, where the spirit, the essence of the person, is not destroyed lives in the spiritual realm, in a state of personal immortality. This form of fearlessness, Bes (Bisu, Aha) exposed, was attainable through recognition and possession of the transcendent-self; denoting the ability of human beings to go beyond themselves, attaining a sense of 'being above and beyond' the mire body.

cvii The Abyssinian Catbird - one of the finest, if not the finest singer of all the birds of Africa - is frequent to common in the western and southern highlands between 1800 and 3500 meters (600-11,500 feet) in giant heath, St. John's wort, highland bamboo, juniper, podocarpus and olive forests. It lives singly, in pairs or in parties up to eight often in thickets and vines that fringe these forests. Typically found in Ethiopia's western and southern highlands at elevations of up to 11,500 feet, this endemic Ethiopian bird isn't much to look at. With its gray body, white forehead, and chestnut belly, it can appear somewhat drab (if you see it at all, given its preference for dense thickets). But many bird-lovers consider it the finest avian singer in Africa, with the loud ringing song of the male offset by the purring response of the female. Look for them in forests with giant heath, highland bamboo, juniper, or olive trees.

cviii Traditional healers and diviners of omens in earliest ancient African clan societies were often essentially known as "Shamanic Priest". In some discendent cultures separate terms were in common use, such as "shaman", referring to a religious official leading sacrificial rites, while others refer this official as a "priest"; there is clear an overlap in functions between Priests and Shaman. In the context of earliest ancient African clannic society this overlap was essentislly seen as the seamless connective tissue between the functions of the "Shamn" and the "Shamanic Priest". The ancient name "Apu-t', or Apt, Áp-t, and Ápu-t, may refer to the ancient Khemetian (Egyptian) word for 'messenger, wpwtj or jpwtj; translated as "message, task".

cix The word "Anointed" is used under the present day urban definition, meaning: Blessed and called to be great, made with a purpose, honest and pure, set aside for a unique reason; Unshakable and strong. In the context used, the word "Archon" means both "to be first, to rule; and "to stand between the people and a transcendent Netjer (Neter), that can only be reached through spiritual transcendence.

cx Metes-ab was later deified as an ibis headed god in ancient Khemetan (Egyptian) mythology; see Budge, Sir Ernest A. Wallis (2010). An Egyptian hieroglyphic dictionary : (in two volumes, with an index of English words, king list and geographical list with indexes, list of hieroglyphic characters. New York: Cosimo Classics. p. 336. ISBN 978-1-61640-460-4.)

cxi Abu was later deified as a god of light: see Coulter, Charles Russell; Turner, Patricia (2000). Encyclopedia of ancient deities. Chicago: Fitzroy Dearborn. ISBN 1-57958-270

cxii The Laas Gaal's cave paintings are estimated to date back to the early Holocene; even under the scorching sun, the paintings have retained their strong, vibrant colors and stark outlines, showing the ancient inhabitants of the area with their cattle.

cxiii The Lass Geel complex contains approximately 20 shelters or rock caves made of naturally occurring rock formations of different size, the largest being ten meters long having a depth of about 5 meters. These shelters have multi-colored painted panels that are one of the oldest known rock art in the Horn of Africa. It is estimated that there are approximately 350 animal and human representations, as well as frequent tribal marks among the rock art at Laas Geel. Some of the cave paintings are strikingly well preserved as they have been protected from the elements by the granite projections. Others have faded due to rock degradation and the effects of weathering and erosion.

cxiv Cave paintings are notoriously hard to date, and the scatter of lithics found in one shelter may or may not date from the time of the paintings. Some archaeologists estimate they're up to 15,000 years old, while others say they're more recent, being "only" 5,000 years old. Either way, they're an evocative link to the past

cxv Hundreds of rock art sites have been found throughout Somaliland, thanks to the tireless efforts of Dr. Sada Mire. She's currently the only Somali with a PhD in archaeology and she's devoted her career to documenting and preserving her culture's past

cxvi Professor Ahmad Dughleh Jameh, Head of the Archaeology Research Unit associated with the Ministry of Commerce, Industry and Tourism in Hargeisa (Somaliland), concurs the affirms that Laas Geel was a permanent settlement; the "people who created this art were not nomads," he told Gulf News. Professor Jameh added: "The high quality of material that was used to create this art is still a mystery for us. It is so unique that we are still not able to tell what kind of leaves they used to make that paint. Laas Geel is a true treasure trove. We are trying to get it recognized as a Unesco Heritage Site."

cxvii The Law of Sympathy informs that if two beings or entities are sufficiently similar, they may be linked with each other; under the Law of Similarity if a being or entity is similar to another, one can attract or affect the other.

cxviii A "Prelate" in this this context is a high-ranking member of the clergy who either is an ordinary or ranks in precedence with ordinaries, such as clergy holding a higher rank

cxix Biologically, the forests of Daallo represents the most reachable and largest semi-original relic of early civilisations of Somaliland, confined to the 300km-long ridge running inland from the northern Somali coast.

cxx Many plants create this fragrance, such as Pistacia aethiopica and others, but, by far, the best known fragrant tree in this area is the legendary Coptic Frankincense (Boswellia frereana). Locals sometimes call this tree – "king of all frankincense" and consider this to be the best frankincense in the world. Frankincense was given to baby Jesus as a gift and used in the rituals of Ancient Egypt.

cxxi See study entitled the "Medicinal Properties of Frankincense", by Akhtar J Khan; Department of Crop Sciences, College of Agricultural and Marine Sciences, Sultan Qaboos University, P.O. Box-34, Al-Khod 123, Oman (9-May-2012)

cxxii Bulhar (Somali: Bulaxaar) is a historic port situated near Berbera, with routes dating back to antiquity; the site is believed to correspond with the ancient commercial Port of Isis described by the Roman scholar Pliny the Elder

cxxiii The remains of ancient Karinhegane now comprise an archaeological site in the northern Sanaag region of present day Somalia; it contains some unique polychrome rock art. It is the site of numerous cave paintings of real and mythical animals. Each painting has an inscription below it,

cxxiv Dhambalin, a sandstone rock shelter, was discovered in autumn 2007. Dhambalin, meaning "half, vertically cut mountain" is an archaeological site in the northwestern Togdheer, a province in Somaliland. This unique site possesses some of the best polychrome paintings in Africa

cxxv The sites of Laas Geel, Dhagah Kure, Karin Hagane, Dhagah Nabi Gallay, Haadh, Jilib Rihin and Dhambalin depict paintings that are generally of the same style as that of the bovine rock-art sites of northeast Africa and Proto-historic, Ethio-Sabaean style (Červiček 1971, 1979). Most of the rock-art sites are on the plateau and concentrated in the natural shelters of the mountain chains, a roughly east–west belt in the middle of Somaliland. Hunt (1951) and Pallister (1963) have outlined the topography of this region. However, it will suffice to say that painted or engraved rocks are mostly of granite and limestone, but also sandstone like at Dhambalin (Mire 2008).

cxxvi These early ancient clans were often composed of over thirty generations, deriving their identity in part from their common sense of territorial belonging

cxxvii Ancient Doolow sits on the Jubba River near the Somali Region in Ethiopia, just 31 miles north of Luuq, on the main border crossing for Somali s entering Ethiopia; over the border towns of Dolo, Ethiopia and Doolow, Somalia.

cxxviii Southwestern Somalia is dominated by the country's only two permanent rivers, the Jubba and the Shabeelle. With their sources in the Ethiopian highlands, these rivers flow in a generally southerly direction, cutting wide valleys in the Somali Plateau as it descends toward the sea; the plateau's elevation falls off rapidly in this area. Baidoa, locally known as Baydhabo, is a strategic town in south-central Somalia, situated approximately 240 kilometers west of Mogadishu, on an ancient trade corridors, connecting the seaport of Mogadishu and the productive region of the Lower Shabelle with Ethiopia and Kenya

cxxix Ancient Mandera is situated near the borders of Kenya, Somalia and Ethiopia, in the Mandera triangle. The Mandera triangle is a geographical region in Eastern Africa where the countries of Kenya, Ethiopia, and Somalia meet. The tri-border region is centered on the city of Mandera and corresponds with the Juba and Shabelle river basins. Beled Hawo is situated strategically where Kenya, Ethiopia and Somalia where three borders meet together. The border with the Ogaden as well as its close proximity to Kismaayo brought wealth into the city, which made it grow dramatically. Beled Hawo was founded in 1910 by Xaawo Cismaan Gurey, a woman from whom the town's name is ultimately derived. Beled Hawo literally means "City of Xawo" in Somali.

cxxx Baidoa and the broader Bay region is home to a number of such ancient sites; it was on the outskirts of the present day city that archaeologists first found the pre-historic rock art of Buur Heybe. Pre-historic archaeological sites have been discovered in the area in the form of cemeteries, rock paintings and remnants of prehistoric settlements from the middle and late stone age. Skeletal remains of 14 people have been found at Buur Hebye ("Buur", meaning "Granite hills", and "Hebye" translated as "Potter's sand"), which constitute the earliest burials in the Horn of Africa having the earliest grave artefacts. These burial sites sit on top of the mountain's peak and are a centre of annual pilgrimage. A channel is present near these holy places and is said to serve as a passage toward heaven. These burial sites were later made into Muslim holy sites in the subsequent Islamic period, including the tomb of Owol Qaasing (derived from the Arabic "Abdul Qaasim") and Sheikh Abdulqadir al-Jilaani.

cxxxi An inselberg or monadnock is an isolated rock hill, knob, ridge, or small mountain that rises abruptly from a gently sloping or virtually level surrounding plain. The presence of an inselberg typically indicates the existence of a nearby plateau or highland, or their remnants.

cxxxii Mer-wer (or Nem-wer), although initially a separate god, it was later assimilated to the syncretized god Mnevis, often depicted as a black bull wearing a solar disk and uraeus

cxxxiii **Sed** was an ancient jackal deity who name first appears on the Palermo Stone from the Fifth Dynasty (2498-2345 BCE) but who was most likely much older. He was the protector of kingship and the individual king. He presided over the Sed Festival (also known as the Heb-Sed Festival) which was held every thirty years of a king's rule to rejuvenate him. He was eventually absorbed by Wepwawet or it could be that Wepwawet (whose name means "Opener of the Ways") was simply one of Sed's epithets which became more popular. As protector of the divine king, Sed was associated with justice and so linked to the goddess Ma'at. Wepwawet (Wepiu or Wepuaut) - One of the most ancient gods of Egypt and the oldest depiction of a jackal god, pre-dating Anubis, with whom he is often confused. His name means "Opener of the Ways" and this has been interpreted as opening the way for king in battle, opening the way to the afterlife, and opening the way at one's birth.

[cxxxiv] Anhur was later deemed and deified a god of war; his name means "He Who Brings Back The Distant One"

[cxxxv] Pakhet the Great, whose eyes are keen and whose claws are sharp, the lioness who sees and catches at night"; whose name means "the one who tears" or "the scratcher"

[cxxxvi] The eland is an incredibly large and powerful animal. It is the biggest species of antelope found in Africa. A fully grown adult can stand as high as two meters and weigh as much as 700kg. From the stationary position they can jump to a height of 8 feet and it has been suggested that, if motivated, they can push over trees to get to the green shoots on the top branches

[cxxxvii] Thmei was later deified as the "Goddess of Truth" (See 'Durdin-Robertson (1979). Communion With The Goddes,' p. 38.)

[cxxxviii] Science now recognizes the role of great catastrophes in the history of the Earth, and, evidence is accumulating for the existence of periodicity within the processes of global change. To what extent modern scientific findings can be reconciled with ancient mythic or religious traditions remains to be seen, yet the more we learn the more it seems likely that some degree of reconciliation is likely.

[cxxxix] The origin of African astrology can be traced back to the development of the ancient African civilization. It is believed that the Africans were the most primitive civilization to have given birth to the science of stars, invented names of planets and discovered the study of astrology. Though in African astrology there are twelve signs yet the African astrological signs are quite different from the other Western and Indian astrology. The African people believed that the man started his life in African so they considered that the African civilization is one of the oldest forms of civilization ever known to man which gave birth to the science of stars, invented names of planets and even discovered the study of ancient African astrology. The African Zodiac signs are based upon the ancestral symbols honoring the twelve Neteru. According to present day scientists, the Earth enters a new Zodiacal Age approximately every 2160 years, and these ages are called the Great Ages. The generally excepted number of 2160 years for the length of each Great Age, is derived by using 72 degrees, in which the Earth moves throughout the constellations, multiplied by 30 degrees in a Zodiacal sign – assuming one is using twelve signs per cycle. 2160 years multiplied by 12 (signs) makes the 'full cycle' of all Great Ages to be 25,920 years. However, the Earth today moves through thirteen signs in the Mazzaroth Trail [the constellations], so the set number of 2160 years per Great Age is no longer correct. Each Age would be somewhat different in duration one from the other, and from earlier Ages past the length of Earth time was anywhere from 1994 years [13 signs] to 2520 years [ten signs], in difference. Scientists use an average of 2160 years now, but during ancient Biblical times the sum of 2520 years was mentioned - perhaps if incorporating the entire twelve Great Ages the first Great Age was 2520 years. Today, the actual count would in reality, be approximately 1994 years for the duration of the Great Age of Aquarius.

[cxl] Many consider the entrance into each Great Age a gradual transition that does not begin at an exact day or year; accordingly, the beginning of any age cannot be defined to a single year or a decade but blend its influences with the previous age for a period of time until the new age can stand in its own right.

[cxli] The head of the Hydra is configured by fives stars, located south of the faint constellation Cancer; the northernmost of these stars, Epsilon, which is actually a multiple star system with at least five members. The primary is a yellow-white giant star with a white sub-giant star orbiting so close that it is considered a spectroscopic binary star. A bit further away is another binary pair, and further away yet is a dwarf star

[cxlii] The spiral galaxy NGC 3312 is located 140 million light-years away and is part of the Hydra Galaxy Cluster (Abell 1060). Abell 1060 contains 157 bright galaxies and is part of the Hydra-Centaurus Supercluster; M83 (NGC 5236), the Southern Pinwheel Galaxy, is an 8th magnitude face-on spiral galaxy.

[cxliii] Present day astronomers have designated the two elliptical galaxies NGC 3309 and NGC 3311, and designated the spiral galaxy NGC 3312. These galaxies are all about 150,000 light years in diameter

[cxliv] The "Ghost of Jupiter" is a planetary nebula (NGC 3242) discovered by William Herschel that bears a resemblance to our solar system's largest planet.

[cxlv] Present day astronomers have cataloged the central white dwarf star within the Ghost of Jupiter as HD 90255.

[cxlvi] ." Due to the precession of the Earth's axis, it takes approximately 26,000 years for the pole to precess through all 12 signs, a period which the ancients referred to as a Cosmic Year. The pointer on this giant clock is identified with the vernal equinox, the ecliptic direction where the sun rises on the first day of spring, when day and night are of exactly equal length. (Again, here we are reminded of the aker sphinx symbology of the Sun, and its day and night passage.).

[cxlvii] The Pleiades cluster actually contains hundreds of stars, of which only a handful are commonly visible to the unaided eye; the brightest stars in the cluster represent the Pleiades, the Seven Sisters.

[cxlviii] For many the (historic) heliacal rising of the Pleiades marked the new year and the beginning of the spring planting season; for others this time was marked by the period when the Pleiades were conjunct with the sun and invisible in the sky (Maunder, 1906; Sparavigna, 2008; White, 2016)

[cxlix] Metni - A hippopotamus god: Budge, Sir Ernest A. Wallis (2010). An Egyptian hieroglyphic dictionary : (in two volumes, with an index of English words, king list and geographical list with indexes, list of hieroglyphic characters, Coptic and Semitic alphabets. New York: Cosimo Classics. p. 336. ISBN 978-1-61640-460-4

[cl] One of the largest networks of caves in the East African region is the Amboni caves (Mapango ya Amboni) near Tanga in Tanzania, which has tunnels as long as 166 km at the Kenya-Tanzania border.

[cli] Ahti was later deified as a malevolent hippopotamus goddess.

[clii] One of the ancient traditions found in Kenya is red geometric art made by early ancient Twa hunter-gatherers (Batwa); some red, infilled animal paintings are also ascribed to the Twa, the ancestral Anu. The geometric paintings appeared reminiscent of similar patterns in paintings and engravings recorded elsewhere in East Africa and referred to there as Twa art

[cliii] The timberline forest is usually found between 9,800 ft and 11,500 ft, although it extends to lower altitudes on the drier slopes. Smaller trees dominate in the timberline forest, and the characteristic trees are African Rosewood and Giant St. John's Wort.

[cliv] The entire mountain is deeply dissected by valleys which diverge from its peaks. The highest peaks are Batian at 5,199 m and Nelion at 5,188 m with its base stretching approximately 96 km wide. There are about twenty glacial tarns of varying sizes and numerous glacial moraine features between 3,950 m and 4,800 m. There are four secondary peaks and about a dozen other remnant glaciers on the mountain that are all receding rapidly.

[clv] Correspondingly, the Ancient Egyptian refers to a group of nine divinities as one unit—being an Ennead

[clvi] Earth's vortexes or vortices are points where energy spirals and flows in and out; they connect with Earth's chakra points, working together as an energetic grid around the planet. The Earth's "Chakra points" are where energy spirals and flows down like a faucet, whereas Vortices are clarifying amplifiers; the two balance and regulate the electromagnetheric field of Earth to stabilize the planet's energy, working together as a sort of crystalline grid around the planet. Chakra points are often Volcanoes or other Earth active areas, due to the rich crystal deposits, electromagnetic volcanic material and increased ormus from Inner Earth. All of Earth's chakra points and vortices are connected in an energy grid around the planet.

[clvii] Maunder, 1906; Sparavigna, 2008 Thousands of years ago the Pleiades were conjunct with the sun at the vernal equinox; the heliacal rising would occur roughly six weeks later, and the acronychal rising at the autumnal equinox. There have been times, where the Pleiades processions and equinoxes lined up exactly, but that timing is fluid

[clviii] Seshat - (a.k.a. Sesat, Seshet, Sesheta, Seshata, Safkhet) Her name means "She Who Is A Scribe." This goddess of knowledge, wisdom, and writing is the record keeper of the gods

[clix] The spiritual idea of the Cosmic dialectic is really an essential feature of the transcendent idea and underdstanding of the ongoing unfolding of creation.

[clx] Vega was the northern pole star around 14,000 BC.

[clxi] Our Solar System is located at a radius of 26,490 (± 100) light-years from the Galactic Center (the "Central Sun"), on the inner edge of the Orion Arm, one of the spiral-shaped concentrations of gas and dust.

[clxii] The system of Sirius contains two known stars, the first binary star system discovered. The larger and brighter of the two, Sirius A, is three times the mass of our sun, and over ten times as bright. Shining with a brilliant blue-white radiance, Sirius A easily overshadows her darker companion star. Sirius B is a "white dwarf" star, invisible to the naked eye and packing the equivalent mass of our sun into an incredibly dense globe only 4 times the diameter of our Earth

[clxiii] Just as the Earth goes around the Sun, the Sun goes around the center of the Milky Way. It takes 250 million years for our Sun and the solar system to go all the way around the center of the Milky Way.

[clxiv] The "Void", known by present day Astronomers as "Sagittarius A", a supermassive black hole located in the constellation Sagittarius, was located at the very center of our Galaxy, despite being some 32 degrees south-west of the conjectured galactic center. Astronomers now purport to have evidence of the supermassive black hole at the center of the galaxy. Sagittarius A* (abbreviated Sgr A*) is agreed to be the most plausible candidate for the location of this supermassive black hole. The Very Large Telescope and Keck Telescope detected stars orbiting Sgr A* at speeds greater than that of any other stars in the galaxy. One star, designated S2, was calculated to orbit Sgr A* at speeds of over 5,000 kilometers per second at its closest approach

[clxv] The constellation, Virgo, is extra large and covers double the area the other 11 signs cover. The Virgo Cluster is a large, extended, and complex structure of over 1300 galaxies and represents the major feature of the Local Supercluster. Two separate subclumps, each dominated by a giant elliptical galaxy, i.e., M87 and M86 (see Binggeli) The precise distance to the Virgo cluster or, more generally, a good understanding of its three-dimensional structure plays an important role in many research areas of extragalactic astronomy. However, despite concerted efforts to resolve these issues over the past decades, the spatial extension of the Virgo cluster remained highly uncertain. Virgo means virgin and might imply it was never touched or was "skipped" in our history.

[clxvi] Antares, also known as Alpha Scorpii or Cor Scorpii, is the brightest star in Scorpius and the 15th brightest star in the night sky. Antares is a class M red supergiant marking the heart of the celestial scorpion. Antares was named for its resemblance to Mars, as they both appear reddish in color; a comparison that may have originated with Sumarian astronomers

[clxvii] Albert Einstein provided the first hint of the dark universe exactly 100 years ago, when he discovered a parameter in his equations known as the 'cosmological constant," which we now know to be synonymous with dark energy. Einstein famously called the cosmological constant his 'biggest blunder," although modern astrophysical observations prove that it is a real phenomenon. In notes dating back to 1918, Einstein described his cosmological constant, writing that 'a modification of the theory is required such that "empty space" takes the role of gravitating negative masses which are distributed all over the interstellar space." It is therefore possible that Einstein himself predicted a negative-mass-filled universe

[clxviii] Antares is moving through the Milky Way Galaxy at a speed of 20.7 km/s relative to our Sun. The star's projected galactic orbit takes it between 20,400 and 23,900 light years from the Milky Way's centre.

[clxix] The star's visual luminosity is roughly 10,000 times that of the Sun. However, as Antares radiates a lot of its energy in the infrared part of the spectrum, the star's bolometric luminosity is considerably greater, about 65,000 times that of the Sun

[clxx] Alcyone is the third brightest star in its home constellation and also the brightest star of the Pleiades or Seven Sisters. In fact, it's name means "the Central One." "The Pleiades group is an open star cluster in the constellation of Taurus, existing approximately [400 to] 500 light years from Earth. There are 250-500 stars within the cluster, although only nine have been named. Most ancient cultures claim seven stars. These include China, who called them 'The Seven sisters of Industry,' and Greece, who referred to them as the 'seven daughters of Atlas.' More than any other star system, the Pleiades has captured the attention of both ancient and modern civilization." The names of the main stars are: Alcyone, Celaeano, Electra, Atlas, Merope, Sterope I & II, Taygeta, Maia and Pleione. Alcyone is the third brightest star in its home constellation and also the brightest star of the Pleiades or Seven Sisters. In fact, it's name means "the Central One." "The Pleiades group is an open star cluster in the constellation of Taurus, existing approximately [400 to] 500 light years from Earth

[clxxi] Sirius designated α Canis Majoris (Latinized to Alpha Canis Majoris, abbreviated Alpha CMa, α CMa)) is the brightest star in the night sky. Sirius A is orbited by a small white dwarf, Sirius B, some ten magnitudes fainter than Sirius itself; the period of the orbit is very close to 50 years

[clxxii] Observations made with ESO's Very Large Telescope (VLT) have revealed for the first time that a star orbiting the super massive black hole at the center of the Milky Way moves just as predicted by Einstein's theory of general relativity. Not only does the research further confirm Einstein's theory, it also provides crucial information about the area surrounding Sagittarius A*.

[clxxiii] The understanding that all creatures are ontologically interrelated and interdependent in the web of life through a common denominator that is mediated by the vital force, sums up the basis of African ontological thought; a view engendering positive attitudes towards nature.

[clxxiv] According to the ancient texts, the home of Bes was Punt. Bes is also described in ancient inscriptions as "Coming from the Divine Land" and was known as the "Lord of Punt."

[clxxv] Bes has anciently been described as 'Coming from the Divine Land' and 'Lord of Punt' (in present day Somalia - see Hatshepsut's Expedition to Punt).

[clxxvi] Bes, many scholars believe, sits at the door of the beginnings of human involvement with carving images that reflected the most intense desires of the human community for communication with the mysterious.

[clxxvii] The Great East African Rift Valley has two arms or branches; the Western (or "Albertine") Rift Valley, and the Eastern Rift Valley. The Western Rift (the Albertine Rift) is bordered by some of the highest mountains in Africa, with the Rwenzoris towering above like a natural promontory of the Albertine Rift

[clxxviii] The Congo-Nile Divide is the area where the sources of the Congo and Nile Rivers. Streams and rivers flowing west end up in the Congo river while those flowing east end up in the Nile. The Virunga Mountains separate the basins of the Nile and the Congo rivers and are the only East African mountains to form a divide of continental stature. The Ruwenzori Range stretches between Lakes Edward and Albert on the Uganda-Congo border, and farther south the Virunga Mountains extend along the contiguous borders of Uganda, Rwanda, and Congo. The entire system of the Ruwenzori Range drains into the Semliki River, a tributary of the Nile.

[clxxix] Extensive study of humanity's ancient theological culture and ancestry has confirmed that many of the forerunners of our planet had established a sacramental relationship with the power of this mystical fungus.

[clxxx] The psilocybin mushrooms of our world exist in a wide array of shapes sizes, potency, and characteristics. Each species of these mystical mushrooms – over 180 known – have their own unique growing conditions and environments depending entirely on their region of origin. While some strains have made an appearance in a plethora of locations on our planet, other strains have proven themselves more rare and exotic with unique conditions necessary for growth. In our search for the "holy grail" of mushrooms, we narrowed our sights to only the rarest, most potent, and primordial of the known species

[clxxxi] The Roan is the largest African antelope after the eland; they are mainly found in the tropical and subtropical grasslands, savannas, and shrublands. Their habitats range in tree density from the forest with a grass cover to grasslands scattered with few trees

[clxxxii] Considering that some types of mushrooms have only ever been found in the wild once, perhaps the most exotic, mythical, or most potent strains have yet to be stumbled across and documented by science

[clxxxiii] The Rwenzori form an extremely steep and rugged mountain range including the third highest mountain in Africa, Mount Stanley, reaching an altitude of 5,109 m. The range is about 120 kilometres (75 mi) long and 65 kilometres (40 mi) wide

[clxxxiv] The name Virunga is derived from the Kinyarwanda word "ibirunga", which means "volcanoes." They are also known as the Mufumbiro ranges, which means "mountains that cook" due to the active volcanoes in D.R. Congo.

[clxxxv] The Virungas form a barrier between the Nile Basin to the north and east and the Congo Basin to the west and south. Lake Rutenzige is fed by several large rivers, the Rutshuru River being one, and drains to the north through the Semliki River into Lake Albert, the Victoria Nile flows from Lake Victoria into the northern end of Lake Albert and exits as the White Nile from a point slightly to the west, flowing north to the Mediterranean.

[clxxxvi] The region between the Rwenzoris and the Virungas was an early frontier area where ancient interlacustrine peoples and cultures met and interacted with peoples and cultures from west of the continental divide. The ancient "watershed" that crosses the Rwenzoris represents the northern-most part of this frontier area, where the basins of Lake Rutanzige and Lake Dweru (formerly Lake George) lie between the Ruwenzoris and Virungas, and Lake Mwitanzige (formerly Lake Albert) and the Albert Nile River lie to the north.

[clxxxvii] The name "Virunga" is an English version of the Kinyarwanda word ibirunga, which means "volcanoes."

[clxxxviii] Nomadism does not imply undirected wandering, but rather, during the predawn of the Neolithic, it was based on temporary centres whose stability depends on the availability of food supply and / or trade. The term nomad encompasses three general types: nomadic hunters and gatherers, pastoral nomads, and craft or trader nomads. Some nomadic peoples move among densely populated areas to offer specialized services (crafts or trades).

[clxxxix] In cultural anthropology, sedentism (sometimes called sedentariness; compare sedentarism) is the practice of living in one place for a long time. In evolutionary anthropology and archaeology, sedentism takes on a slightly different sub-meaning, often applying to the transition from nomadic society to a lifestyle that involves remaining in one place permanently. Essentially, sedentism means living in groups permanently in one place

[cxc] South of the Virungas, Lake Kivu drains to the southward into Lake Tanganyika, through the Ruzizi River; Lake Tanganyika then drains into the Congo via the Lukuga River.

[cxci] Ethnohistoric and ethnographic data aided interpretation of archaeological evidence suggest that people seasonally gathered at resource-rich locations, exchanged commodities and reinforced social relationships, and later dispersed returning to their home ranges

[cxcii] Mt Muhabura is 13,540 ft (4127m) and is shared between Uganda and Rwanda. "Muhabura" is a derived from the Rufumbira language which means "guide" because the locals could see it regardless of where they were acting as a guide for them on the way home

[cxciii] The East African Rift System is one of the most outstanding and significant rift systems on Earth and transects the high-elevation Ethiopian and East African plateaux.

[cxciv] The Virunga ecosystem is composed of four major vegetation zones: bamboo (base altitude), hagenia and hypericum forest (8,500-10,800 feet), sub-alpine (10,800-13,000 feet) and afro-alpine (above 13,000 feet). Gorillas here live on the slopes of ancient volcanoes in high elevation forests. During the rainy season when new bamboo shoots are growing, the gorillas spend more time foraging in the bamboo forests at base altitude

[cxcv] Ala (also known as Ani, Ana, Ale, and Ali in varying Igbo dialects) is the Earth Mother Goddess; female Alusi (deity) of the earth, morality. Her name literally translates to 'Ground' in the Igbo language, denoting her powers over the earth and her status as the ground itself.

[cxcvi] As the Goddess of morality, Ala is involved in judging human actions and is in charge of Igbo law and customs known as 'Omenala'. Taboos and crimes among Igbo communities that are against the standard of Ala are called nsọ Ala.

[cxcvii] Endemic species in this region may have evolved due to glacial cycles that compressed these montane populations and then expanded allowing speciation to occur.

[cxcviii] Terence McKenna argues that psilocybin (magic mushrooms) were responsible for the transformation of Homo erectus into Homo sapiens. And it actually makes quite a bit of sense. He claims that psilocybin in the hominid diet would have led to enhanced eyesight, sexual enjoyment, and language ability and would have thereby placed the mushroom-eaters in the front lines of genetic evolution. Contemporary ethnobotanists Terence McKenna (1946-2000) and Clark Heinrich (1945-), the former a psychonaut and broadly accepted "religious mystic", the latter specializing in comparative religion and ethno-botany, appear to concur that the human species has a symbiotic relationship with certain psychoactive plants, propounding that it is no mere coincidence that our neuronal receptors match with a wide variety of psychoactive alkaloids found in nature.

[cxcix] As the years went by, chemical and physical alchemy became exclusive of each other. Chemical scientists chose to focus only on the physical one. The key to alchemy is found in the word *transmutation*, a word that in its original Latin meaning refers to *total change*. Physically this denotes a change of the properties of matter, and thus of substance; psycho-spiritually, it refers to inner transformation

[cc] In the past, there wasn't any clear demarcation between religion and science. Both elemental and spiritual alchemy used the same symbols. The ancient practice of alchemy and its closely guarded secrets were enshrined in the symbolism and mythology of the philosopher's stone. The mystical "stone of the wise", believed to be the key to immortality. The philosopher's stone is also referred to as the "stone of projection" as it is said to facilitate a bodily liberation of consciousness to explore and roam astral planes understood in alchemy as methods of spiritual travel.

[cci] The Oxford English Dictionary states that the first record of the use of this term was in 1718, in Francis Hutchinson's work An Historical Essay concerning Witchcraft, with Observations upon Matters of Fact; Tending to Clear the Texts of the Sacred Scriptures, and Confute the Vulgar Errors about that Point. Hutchinson used the phrase in a chapter defending a prisoner who was charged with witchcraft, by asserting that the "Witch-Doctor" himself was the one using sorcery

[ccii] This rebirth is what the earliest Gnosic Priest reproted Yeshua (the Biblical Jesus) did in his lifetime. He departed his body for a day or two and then returned to it as planned. Meanwhile, his body was clinically dead. This was not an uncommon feat in those days as shared by Paul Brunton in his book. Yeshua's disciples had taken care of his body while he was in another dimension. The Romans, of course, believed he was completely dead (common sense of course!) and released his body to his disciples. Later Yeshua (Jesus) awoke from this sleep as planned, performing the resurrection. He was then twice-born.

[cciii] Their temples had private sections built for these secret initiations and the persons going to be initiated took an oath of secrecy. And this secrecy has continued to our day and time, the sacred knowledge has been kept in secret, and it is only now the veils of secrecy are slowly being lifted.

[cciv] This is a major aspect initiation ino ultimate initiation the sacred "Mystery Schools", and the information around this has been kept very secret until our times.

[ccv] African meditation techniques are focused on the attainment of divinity and true selfhood through an active, focused and determined connection with the divine forces that exist both inside and outside of the self.

[ccvi] During the so-called "Middle Ages", due to the great repression of the Inquisition, the conscious projection was practiced, studied, and known only within certain schools or secret societies. Likewise, after the end of the Inquisition, these esoteric and occult movements continued to hide information from the population, inclusively creating the basis for current myths and lies about the dangers of astral projections (out-of-body experiences), maintaining the old structure of power and hierarchy.

[ccvii] Spiritual belief during antiquity was very much like religion during modern times; not everyone worshiped in the same way.

ccviii "Ascension" is the belief in some religions that some individuals have ascended into Heaven without dying first; accounts of such Astral projection date all the way back to earliest Ancient Khemet (Egypt). The Ancient Khemetans used hieroglyphics as a record/depiction of how the Astral Body (Kha) leaves the physical body.

ccix Early ancient Fetish Priest believed that when we ascend ("astrally project"), we send our consciousness to another place, but like any other muscle, if it's unused, it begins to atrophy — so learning to astral project is about strengthening this ability through practice and visualization."

ccx The Mysteries, as they were called in later Khemetan (Egyptian) tradition, are transcendent experiences where the spirit of the initiate consciously leaves the physical body, and travels to the Aethereal Plane. Ancient Khemetan (Egyptian) teachings present the soul (*ba*) as having the ability to hover outside the physical body via the _ka_, or subtle body. Nowadays this type of experience is called either astral projection or OBE (Out of Body Experience).

ccxi Transmutation is the act of changing a substance, tangible or intangible, from one form or state into another. To the alchemists of old, this meant the conversion of one physical substance into another, particularly base metals such as lead into valuable silver and gold. To the modern scientists, this means the transformation of one element into another

ccxii Netjer means Nature, simply put that before vowels(the corruption) existed it was Ntr. The Khemetan word 'neter' (or nature or 'netjer') means a power that is able to generate life and to maintain it when generated.

ccxiii Khonsu has a single occurrence in the Pyramid Texts which is nevertheless notable insofar as it is said here (utterances 273-4) that "It is Khonsu who slew the lords, who strangles them for the King and extracts for him what is in their bodies, for he is the envoy who is sent to punish," [trans. mod. in accord with Lichtheim, vol. 1, p. 37] The violent side of Khonsu's nature in the passage from the Pyramid Texts is reinforced in later texts. Hence in CT spell 945 the operator affirms that "My striking-power is Khonsu," and spell 310 calls Khonsu "the raging one." Some of Khonsu's belligerence is to be attributed to his observations and study of Amadioha who resulted to violence when provoked (he was also reputed to be a king of great military might and acumen; often described as an astute military tactician, engineer and armiger).

ccxiv Amélineau, is credited with the discovery of the Anu and their contribution to Egyptian civilization. It was Amélineau who designated the first black race to occupy Egypt as the Anu. He showed how they came slowly down the Nile and founded the cities of Esneh, Erment, Qouch and Heliopolis

ccxv The later Khemetans (Egyptians) would occasionally refer to the Land of as Ta-Netjeru, which meant the"Land of Gods.." Khemetan (Egyptian) myth from around 15,000 BC told of a southern land of gods called Ta Neteru, where the three main Egyptian Gods lived before travelling north at the dawn of man.

ccxvi Lake Victoria has dried up completely at least three times since it formed. These drying cycles are probably related to past ice ages, which were times when precipitation declined globally. Lake Victoria last dried out about 17,300 years ago, and it refilled 12,600 years ago as the African humid period began.

ccxvii The distance from Rwenzori to Kampala Mountains is 187 miles, and the distance from Kampala Mountains to Mt Elgon is 146 miles, respectively

ccxviii An interesting irony is how Eurocentric historians and purported experts and authorities still strenuously insist that farming didn't develop in Sub-Saharan Africa until after 500 BC, while simulteanously asserting that ancient farmers in central Africa may have played a role in the disappearance of rainforests. Popular Archaeology reporte: "Scientists have long held that some of the rainforests of Central Africa disappeared about 3,000 years ago, abruptly replaced by savannas due to a dramatic shift in the regional climate. However, the conclusions of a recent study now suggest that it was not climate change alone that may have been responsible for the shift -- that humans may have had a big hand, as well. [Source: Popular Archaeology, February 9, 2012] Over recent millennia, human populations have regularly reconstructed their subsistence niches, changing both how they obtain food and the conditions in which they live. For example, over the last 12,000 years the vast majority of human populations shifted from foraging to practicing different forms of agriculture.

ccxix In 1959 biologist Louis Kervran successfully demonstrated the natural spontaneous transmutation of certain elements within living organisms. This confirmed, to some degree, the earlier findings of scientists Baron von Herzeele and Rudolf Steiner. And while scientists do not as yet understand the transmutation process in biological terms, the primary fact remains that transmutation does exist and can no longer be denied by scientists. An ongoing question in paleoenvironmental reconstructions of the central African rainforest concerns the role that prehistoric metallurgy played in shaping forest vegetation; archeologist report evidence of intensive iron-ore mining and smelting in forested regions of the northern Congo Basin dating to the late Holocene. The "Hapi Valley" was an ancient region of untold early innovations and advances of civilization, such as the inception of mathematics and what is believed to be the first primitive form of calculator; the early ancient Ishango Bone, dated to 25,000 BCE, considered to be the first evidence of a calculator in the world. The fabled "Hapi Valley" was along central Congo-Nile Divide was an interlacustrine area mixed with clans and divergent groups interconnecting the clans and cultures in the Nile and Congo basins

ccxx Long-distance trade as primary cause of State formation and growth in central Africa is shared by many historians and archaeologists Oliver Page 1962 Vansina 1966 Wilson 1972 Huffman 1970 Summers 1969

ccxxi The Imatong Mountains mark the edge of the Ugandan plateau to the north at the country's borders with South Sudan. The average elevation here is 1,800 m. To the northeast, the plateau ends in a string of volcanic mountains with Mount Elgon being the highest at 4,321 m The mountain range rises steeply from the surrounding plains, which slope gradually down from about 1,000 metres (3,300 ft) on the South Sudan-Uganda border The mountains are highest in the southeast where a group of peaks reach about 3,000 metres (9,800 ft), and the tallest, Mount Kinyeti, reaches 3,187 metres (10,456 ft). This central block group of high mountains around Mount Kinyeti are sometimes called the Lomariti or Lolibai mountains, and the high central part on the Uganda side is sometimes called the Lomwaga Mountains. There has been little exploration of the Imatong Mountains for over 40 years, due to long running conflict in the region. The ccxxi first map to show the mountains and give them the name of the Imatong Mountains was published in the Geographical Journal in May 1929, prepared from a compilation of the Sudan Government Survey Department.

ccxxii Thomson, the European explorer, believed the caves were of artificial origin, and was inclined to the belief that the excavations were the work of ancient miners.

ccxxiii The lower elevation caves are not lava tubes, since Elgon had few suitable lava flows, but were instead eroded from the volcanic tuff (welded ash flows) which make up the bulk of Elgon's volume (digging by elephants may also contribute to the enlargement of the caves).

ccxxiv The occupation of caves by ancient humans on Mount Elgon had, hitherto, attracted little archaeological research compared to the rest of East Africa. A series of excavations at Chepnyalil Cave have yielded a large sample of artefacts and faunal remains that shed light on the potential of the Mount Elgon region as an important location for understanding human adaptive strategies for East African populations during the terminal stages of the Pleistocene. This is because there have been so few studies carried out on archaeological assemblages from such high altitude settings. The excavated assemblage from Chepnyalil Cave provides a rare insight into subsistence behaviour throughout continuous history probably stretching back to the Middle Stone Age and through to recent historical times. Another key site is the Kakapel monument – a rock shelter on the southern lower flank of Mount Elgon in Kenya close to the border with Uganda. It is at a dramatic granite outcrop and exhibits a succession of rock art paintings often superimposed in different styles. This reflects the fact that the site was frequented by a series of different people from late Holocene hunter-gatherers, early Iron Age farmers and other people who were probably livestock keepers.

ccxxv In ancient Sumerian mythology An had but one wife, Uraš, but she is later referred to as the goddess Ki and, in Akkadian texts, the goddess Antu. According to the Eridu Model, Enlil is the first of the young gods to be born, was slightly older than Enki. Bau (or Baba) was daughter to An & Uraš in most ancient texts Bau, (Sumerian), also called Nininsina, Akkadian Gula or Ninkarrak, in Mesopotamian religion, city goddess of Urukug in the Lagash region of Sumer and, under the name Nininsina, the Queen of Isin, city goddess of Isin, south of Nippur. In Nippur she was called Ninnibru, Queen of Nippur

ccxxvi The *Vela X Supernova* was seen around 14,000 years ago (about 13,000 radiocarbon years ago), coinciding with the onset of the Holocene era, and the first of three global super floods. After sighting of the supernova there was a rapid global warming and moistening of climates, occurring within the space of only a few centuries, causing enormous ice sheets and gigantic glaciers to withdraw as global temperatures rose, bringing a close end to the *Great Ice Age* and marking the beginning of the *Holocene* period of warmer climate.

ccxxvii The Younger Dryas (around 12,900 to 11,700 years BP) was a return to glacial conditions after the Late Glacial Interstadial, which temporarily reversed the gradual climatic warming after the Last Glacial Maximum (LGM) started receding around 20,000 BP.

ccxxviii Controversial from the time it was proposed, the hypothesis even now continues to be contested by those who prefer to attribute the end-Pleistocene reversal in warming entirely to terrestrial causes. But Kennett and fellow stalwarts of the Younger Dryas Boundary (YDB) Impact Hypothesis, as it is also known, have recently received a major boost: the discovery of a very young, 31-kilometer-wide impact crater beneath the Greenland ice sheet, which they believe may have been one of the many comet fragments that impacted Earth at the onset of the Younger Dryas. Now, in a paper(link is external) published in the journal Nature Scientific Reports, Kennett and colleagues, led by Chilean paleontologist Mario Pino, present further evidence of a cosmic impact, this time far south of the equator, that likely led to biomass burning, climate change and megafaunal extinctions nearly 13,000 years ago. "We have identified the YDB layer at high latitudes in the Southern Hemisphere at near 41 degrees south, close to the tip of South America," Kennett said. This is a major expansion of the extent of the YDB event." The vast majority of evidence to date, he added, has been found in the Northern Hemisphere. "This is further evidence that the Younger Dryas climatic onset is an extreme global event, with major consequences on the animal life and the human life at the time," Kennett said. "And this Pilauco section is consistent with that." Research on this study was also conducted by Ana Abarzúa, Giselle Astorga, Alejandra Martel-Cea, Nathalie Cossio, Maria Paz Lira and Rafael Labarca of Universidad Austral de Chile; R. Ximena Navarro of Universidad Católica de Temuco; and Malcolm A. LeCompte and Victor Adedeji of Elizabeth City State University. Christopher Moore of University of South Carolina; Ted E. Bunch and Charles Mooney of Northern Arizona University; and Wendy S. Wolbach of DePaul University contributed research, as did Allen West of Comet Research Group.

ccxxix During phases of very high Nile flow, clastic muds rich in continental organic matter and highly organic sapropels accumulated on the floor of the Nile Valley; very recent flood sediments have been found to contain reworked charcoal fragments several thousand years older than the actual sediment.

ccxxccxxx Today it is well known for the finds of great, ancient whales.

ccxxxi The ancient lake evaporated to approximate its present day diminished incarnation as *Lake Qārūn* during the most recent desertification of the Sahara. Researches on the margin of the depression indicate that the waters of ancient *Lake Moeris* once stood over 100 feet above sea level, and probably filled the whole of the *Fayoum* depression.[ccxxxi]

ccxxxii Ancient deltic marine deposits have been identified as far south as the ancient city of *El Minya*, which is roughly at the border of Upper and Lower *Khemet*, 130 miles above the apex of the present Delta. At the onset of the late Paleolithic period, and the northern migrations, the delta and much of lower *Khemet* was still covered with water.

ccxxxiii Arithmetic, geometry, esoteric proportions and symbology, numerology, astrology and astronomy, geology, philosophy, chemistry, medicine, and other physical, social and metaphysical sciences were the gifts of the Anu to an unfolding world

ccxxxiv To the Anu, we can attribute, without fear of error, the most ancient Egyptian books, The Book of the Dead and the Texts of the Pyramids, consequently, all the myths or religious teachings. I would add almost all the philosophical systems then known and still called Egyptian

[ccxxxv] Two sphinxes existed on the Pyramids Plateau, according to a study which was published in 2007 by Egyptologist Bassam El Shammaa. The sphinxes were in line with ancient Anu beliefs, which were mainly based on duality. Researchers cited Ancient Khemetan (Egyptian) records and mythology saying that lightening had destroyed part of the Sphinx. The demolished temple in front of the Sphinx's paws and the Valley Temple that stands next to the site of what we assume to be the second sphinx is proof that the two statues once stood side by side.

[ccxxxvi] Millions of years ago, the Giza Plateau was under water. Sea creatures and plants died, falling to the bottom. Over time, their remains were compressed to form limestone. But not all limestone is created equal. Some limestone is formed from the soft sea bottom and some from hard coral reefs. Together they form a kind of layer cake of hard and soft limestone. The Sphinx is composed out of several different limestone layers. So it's as though you carved the Sphinx out of a layer cake. And there are gooey layers of soft frosting, and then there are intervening harder layers. The harder layers of rock have held up better than the softer layers. Today it looks a lot different from when it was first built. Its original smooth surface has been eaten away by over 4,000 years of wind, water and sand.

[ccxxxvii] Paraphrasing Graham Hancock, "the Great Sphinxes were an equinoctial marker, with its gaze directed precisely at the point of sunrise on the vernal equinox."

[ccxxxviii] In a series of expeditions between 1991 and 1993 led by John Anthony West, and independent Egyptologist, scientific investigators conducted geological and seismic surveys around the Great Sphinx of Egypt. The chief geologist was Dr. Robert Schoch, Professor of Geology at Boston University, and the chief seismologist was Thomas Dobecki from the highly-respected Houston consulting firm, McBride-Ratclif & Associates. The team's conclusions were as follows: A. Geology, The pattern of erosion on the Sphinx indicates that it was carved at the end of the last Ice Age, when heavy rains fell in the eastern Sahara - perhaps more than 12,000 years ago. This contrasts starkly with the 'orthodox' Egyptological dating for the Sphinx of around 4,500 years ago. In 1993 John West and his team were physically expelled from the site by Dr. Zahi Hawass then (and now) the Egyptian government's Chief Inspector of Antiquities for the Pyramids and Sphinx. He appeared to be angered by the suggestion that the Sphinx might be far older than the civilization of Egypt itself - and thus the work of a lost civilization - and was particularly incensed by an NBC television film that was made about the team's work

Researcher and noted author, Graham Hancock gave a very insightful explanation regarding the huge disparities between timeline assertions of the so-called "Egyptologists", and the timelines proven by actual scientic investigation, by simply asking the question "What would most of the Egyptologists think (about the scientifically proven timelines)? Probably the same information that has made them famous and has paid for their grants. Mr. Hancock pointed out that some of what Egyptologists hold as solid fact has little solid scientific evidence to back it." As an example, "that the Sphinx is really a representation of Chephren because of the heiroglpyhic inscription of one letter of Chephren's name in the stone tablet in the front of the Sphinx. Egyptologists inserted the second syllable in the translation of the ancient texts without really knowing what it is supposed to mean." Graham Hancock's explanation of the Sphinx and the pyramids make the orthodox Egyptologists look like fools and pseudo-archaeologists. In a way, the so-called "Egyptologists" have lost their scientific validity, Mr. Hancock noted, saying "Egyptologists find facts to fit their theories when they should be making theories based on the facts." In 1992, the American scholar John Anthony West (1932 - 2018) observed that the sides of the Sphinx showed a type of erosion different from that caused by sand and wind. The type of erosion West observed was caused by prolonged and extensive exposure to rainfall, but that area of the Sahara Desert has been dry for millennia. West's hypothesis was taken up by Robert M. Schoch, a geologist and associate professor of natural science at the College of General Studies at Boston University. Schoch traveled to Egypt and examined the erosion at the Great Sphinx. He presented his findings at the 1992 convention of the Geological Society of America. West and Schock reasoned that if the sides of the Sphinx were eroded by water, then the Sphinx must have been carved at a time when the the Sahara was wet. Geological records showed that the last time the Sahara was wet was around 10,500 years ago.

[ccxxxix] During phases of very high Nile flow, clastic muds rich in continental organic matter and highly organic sapropels accumulated on the floor of the Nile Valley; very recent flood sediments have been found to contain reworked charcoal fragments several thousand years older than the actual sediment.

The massive outflow and build-up of sands, soils and sediments pouring from the Nile into the Delta, over the long millennia, pushed the bay northward from its ancient shores at *Waset* (Thebes), to the present day Delta where the Nile empties into the Mediterranean Sea. During early antiquity more people lived in the *Fayoum* than in the *Nile Valley*; the land there was lush, with an abundance of fresh water. The *Fayoum* is a six hundred ninety square mile depression, where, during early antiquity, the waters of *Paleo-Lake Moeris* transformed the surrounding lands into an abundant paradise. It's water level was eighty-five meters higher than today, and the Nile regularly flooded through the low mountains separating it from the Fayoum.

The lands amenable to agriculture surrounded *Lake Moeris* to the south, and the Anu soon developed the fertile lands south of the Fayoum into one of the earliest agricultural areas in the world, where fences were erected and guarded warehouses built. However, because of the rise in the water table, it is more difficult to ascertain where the settlements and villages of earliest antiquity arose and existed in the present day delta. The early areas inhabited included a fertle strip of land bordering the Nile up to the first cataract at Aswan, a fertile valley to the east of the delta, apart from the marshes, and to the west, the *Fayum* around *Lake Moeris*. It was here that they were united into a somewhat loose federaton. The chronology provided by the last student of the *Ancient Mystery School of the Anu* places the formal beginnings of anu civilization in the Nile Valley around 17,000 BC[ccxxxix], from the fertile shores and islands of the *Proto-Nile* corridor to the rich grass lands around ancient *Lake Moeris*.

[ccxl] . It is Enki who receives credit as the great civilizer of mankind; he is also credited with agriculture into the northern river valley, and it is he who gave laws to mankind establishing the tradition of hereditary kingship.

[ccxli] "The common ancestor of the Annu settled along the Nile was Ani or An, a name determined by the word (khet) and which, dating from the earliest versions of the `Book of the Dead' --Cheikh Anta Diop, Origin of The Ancient Egyptians, 1981

[ccxlii] Khonsu was broadly seen as a magician credited with powers of healing, divination, and protection; an intermediary (go-between) between the living and the spirit world.'

ccxliii Contrary winds, coastal waters, and the currents of what was then termed the "Eastern Sea" (where the present-day Arabian Sea and northwestern Indian Ocean were partially cordoned from the greater Indian Ocean by the existence of the ancient Kumari peninsula, which then extended southward from the Indian Sub-Continent to just beyond the present day Chagos Archipelago, then the southern mountain range of the peninsula) permitted multiple trips each year

ccxliv The meaning of the name Ta-Nehisi (pronounced Tah-Nuh-Hah-See) is 'Land of The Black' and it is of earliest ancient Khemetan/Egyptian origin, derived from the Ancient Anu; in it's earliest iteration Ta-Nehisi encompassed the whole of Sudan,as far south as Imatong Mountains. It was only later that the term became somewhat confused and mis-associated exclusively with later Nubia

ccxlv The view used to be that people did not settle in large numbers in Arabia until the development of agriculture. Now, the findings by members of the University of Huddersfield's Archaeogenetics Research Group demonstrate that modern humans have dwelt in this territory for far longer than previously thought. The new genetic data and analysis bolsters a theory that has long been held by archaeologists, although they had little evidence to support it until now. The new argument for an Ice Age refugium in Arabia - perhaps on the Red Sea plains - is put forward in a new article published in the journal Scientific Reports. Its principal author is Dr Francesca Gandini, who was based at the University of Pavia in Italy before relocating in early 2015 to the University of Huddersfield, where she is a Research Fellow in Archaeogenetics and a member of the group headed by Professor Martin Richards. The name '"Ubaid" derives from Tell al-'Ubaid where the earliest excavation of Ubaid period material was conducted initially.

ccxlvi The Gulf of Aden is a gulf located in the Arabian Sea between Yemen, on the south coast of the Arabian Peninsula, Djibouti, Somalia and Somaliland in the Horn of Africa. In the northwest, it connects with the Red Sea through the Bab-el-Mandeb strait, which is more than 20 miles (32 kilometres) wide.

ccxlvii The last 150.000 years represent a full glacial and interglacial cycle The period from 20,000-10,000 yrs BP, is traditionally referred to as the terminal phase of the last ice age with its culmination around 18,000 yrs BP (LGM).

ccxlviii We know the first people to settle in the region were the 'Anu', because the Sumerian texts claim that the original people in the area were Anu

ccxlix More ancient agricultural plains must lie in 100metres of water on the continental shelf around India, unfortunately this can only be surmised by circumstantial evidence.

ccl American anthropologist Robert McCormick Adams says that irrigation development was associated with urbanization, and that 89% of the population lived in the cities. Sumerian agriculture depended heavily on irrigation, which was accomplished by use of canals, channels, dykes, and reservoirs. The Sumerians developed core agricultural techniques including large-scale intensive cultivation of land, mono-cropping, organized irrigation, and the use of a specialized labour force, particularly along the waterways, from its Persian Gulf delta to the confluence of the Tigris and Euphrates. The surplus of storable food created by this economy allowed the population to settle in one place instead of migrating after crops and grazing land. Consistent with Anu spiritual belief, early Sumerian religion had its roots in the worship of nature, which werey worshipped, as entities onto themselves. The false assertion that agriculture began in Sumer is no doubt the reason Enlil is credited with creating the hoe, the earliest tool used in farming.

ccli The cult center of Enlil was located in the holy city of Nippur, which was never a political capital and does not appear as a capital city on the Sumerian King List. Nippur was instead a sort of religious capital where the kings of Sumer went to receive Enlil's approval and to honor the mightiest and most-feared of the Sumerian gods

cclii The ruins of Nippur, among the largest in southern Mesopotamia, cover approximately 180 acres. They are divided into two well-nigh equal parts by the now dry bed of the Shatt-en-Nil, a canal which at one time branched off from the Euphrates and watered the otherwise barren territory through which it flowed. The eastern half contains the temple structures, including the ziggurat and the group of buildings which must have formed the scribal school and library; it is in this part of the mound that the "tablet house" was excavated. The western half seems to mark the remains of the city proper. The Sumerian ideogram for Enlil or Ellil was formerly incorrectly read as Bel by scholars, but in fact Enlil was not especially given the title Bel 'Lord' more than many other gods.

ccliii Excavations also occurred at smaller Ubaid sites in Bahrain and Qatar (Roaf 1976; de Cardi 1978), with Masry concluding that this part of Arabia had enjoyed a close and integral relationship with Southern Mesopotamia. More controversially, he suggested that the Mesopotamian and Ubaid-related Arabian sites should be regarded as part of the same social and economic system, and that the origins of Mesopotamian civilization lie as much in the Arabian Peninsula as in Mesopotamia.

ccliv The Bak were 'dimunitive' or small-stature Blacks. The Bak came first from Central Africa. The first was about 10,000 BC. The last was about 2800 BC when Hu Na Kunte settled the Loh River Valley with a number of Black Mesopotamian families The Diminutive ('Ba-Twa") Negroids called the 'Bak' in Asia aided in the development of Mesopotamian civilization, and settled from India to Melanesia; they were the progenitors of earliest civilization in ancient Asia. (see "African Presence in Early Asia," pub. by www.AuthorHouse.com also see www.stewartsynopsis.com).

cclv "The Rig Veda is a collection of more than a thousand hymns written between 1200 and 900 B.C. by people known as Aryans, who came to Afghanistan, Pakistan, and India from the Eurasian steppes to the north. "The name Anu or Ânava for the Iranians appears to have survived even in later times: the country and the people in the very heart of Avesta land, to the immediate north of Hâmûn-i Hilmand, were known as late as Greek times as the Anauon or Anauoi.

Several waves of Anu people migrated into India. Anu is a Vedic Sanskrit term for one of the five major tribes in the Rigveda, RV 1.108.8, RV 8.10.5 (both times listed together with the Druhvu). Notwithstanding, the Anu were not Vedic Aryans, but a black tribe who were actually enemies of the Vedic Aryans in the only non-enumerational references to them in the old books: VI.62.9; VII.18.13,14. In The

Rigveda,the Druhyu and Anu, outside references enumerating tribes, are mentioned only a few times: in all the references in the old books(VI.62.9; VII.18.6,12,13,14) they figure as enemies of the Vedic Aryans. Therefore itis clear that the Anu and Druhyu are not the Vedic Aryans. Their geographical location to the west of the Vedic Aryans indicates that they were the descendents of the ancient Anu of Sumer

The Puranas describe the original location of these three tribes as follows:the Puru were located in the centra lregion (Haryana and bordering areas of U.P.), the Anu in the lands to their north (Kashmir and surrounding areas),the Druhyu to the west (the areas of present day northern Pakistan). The Puranas further describe early historical events(wars between expansionist Druhyu tribes and the tribes to their east) which led to a change of area: the Anu expanded southwards and occupied the original areas of the Druhyu, pushing the Druhyu further west into Afghanistan.

In the most important Vedic historical event described in the old books of the Rigveda, the expansionist activities of the Bharata king Sudas in the Punjab led to an alliance of all the Anu subtribes (and the residual, and probably Anu-ized, Druhyus) againstthe Bharatas in the "Battle of the ten kings" described in a few hymns in book 7.

[cclvi] The East Anu culture in the land that would become ancient was a Late Epipaleolithic archaeological culture dating from around 13,000 BC.

[cclvii] Cisterns have been traced back to the Neolithic time period over 12,000 years ago give or take a little. Cisterns are about 4,000 years older than wells.

[cclviii] Until recently, the first consistent evidence of symbolic communication came from the geometric shapes that appear alongside rock art all over the world, which date to 40,000 years ago (*New Scientist*, 20 February, p 30). Older finds, like the 75,000-year-old engraved ochre chunks from the Blombos cave in South Africa.

[cclix] In a landmark study, it was demonstrated, for the first time, that there are seeming tradition in the production of geometric engraved representations, includes the production of a number of different patterns and this set of evolving traditions have roots that go back in time to at least 100,000 years ago (around a time I say Animism begins in Africa). The fact that they were created, that most of them are deliberate and were made with representational intent, strongly suggests they functioned as artifacts within a society by symbols with meaning. Here we see the tracings of the engraved ochres from the Blombos cave site's in South Africa, from its Middle Stone Age layers and their stratigraphic locations where they were found in the dirt and the years they relate too. M1 dates to around 73,000 years ago, M2 around 85,000 to 77,000 years ago, and M3 dates to around 100,000 to 99,000 years ago. Middle Stone Age generally started around 280,000 years ago and ended around 25,000 years ago or so. Therefore, amazing as it is, here we have proof that "Symbolic Meaning," seems to be clear at the beginning of Animism, as seen in Africa 100,000 years ago

[cclx] Pieces of ochre engraved with abstract designs have been found at the site of the Blombos Cave in South Africa, dated to around 75,000 years ago

[cclxi] The name Kenya means 'God's resting place' in all three of the original languages of the indigenous people of the area. The country of Kenya, got its name from the mountain. Not the other way around.

[cclxii] The twelve seers who entreaty in favor of the ancient Gikuyu who inhabit present day Mt. Kenya, who operate in secrecy to guard their wisdom, have a very interesting fashion of the formation of Mount Kenya, They say Mount Kenya was formed after a "Star" known as riuki (literally meaning –the stone that came from outer space) hit the earth's surface. The impact created a huge explosion followed by an earthquake and outward symmetrical waves. The depression created by riuki extruded magma- gicurucuru, volcanic ashes- umbi and debris of disintegrated riuki to the surface. Riuki became an embeddedment of Mount Occasionally, very rare events like a massive asteroid impact can cause the rocks of the Earth's crust to melt and cause volcanoes and magma bodies to form that may have lasted over 50,000 years. Two processes -- decompression and flux melting -- are the main modes of generating the magma that drives volcanoes. A volcanic cone is or mountain formed by the accumulation of volcanic material where magma reaches the surface. A batholiths, a great mass of igneous rock, extending to great depths, is formed from the extensive magmatic intrusions over a long period of time, an advent typically associated with volcanic arcs. The size and shape of the volcanic mountain depends on the volume of material ejected over time, the composition and temperature of the material (lava, rock and gases) vented from the volcano, and the nature of the eruption (explosive or otherwise).

[cclxiii] Spiritual vortexes are said to be cross-points between energy fields in the earth's grid system, or intersecting ley lines. ... In the same way, a vortex is said to assist in aligning spiritual properties, bringing together the pieces and parts of our spiritual make up to create balance and harmony in the body.

[cclxiv] The early ancient concept "twice-born" comes from this clinical death experience; when an initiate adept successfully leave his or her physical body consciously, and then returns, the initiate essentially perform a rebirth.

[cclxv] Urit would later be deified as "Urit-en-kru," a lioness headed hippopatomus goddess

[cclxvi] The ancient Anu and later the early Khemetans (Egyptians) believed in a resurrection after ascending the physical body; these original ideas of resurrection and renewal informed and influenced the far later Abrahamic traditions in their concepts of resurrection, judgment, and eternal life

[cclxvii] The exact significance of the ka remains a matter of controversy, chiefly for lack of an Khemetan (Egyptian) definition; the usual translation, "double," is incorrect. Written by a hieroglyph of uplifted arms, it seemed originally to have designated the protecting divine spirit of a person. The ka survived the death of the body. See: The Ancient Khemetan (Egyptian) Doctrine of the Immortality of the Soul.

[cclxviii] Humming creates vibrations within the body, vibrations that stimulate the vagus nerve, which in turn reduces your heart rate, lowers your blood pressure, oxygenates your cells, reduces your stress response, and releases neurochemicals like endorphins and oxytocin.

[cclxix] The term "Dividual" is an Archaic adjective meaning (and defined) as separate, distinct, divisible (or divided), distributed, and shared. The term "Creator" is the context ued is deemed to mean the sole "Supreme Being," eternal, spiritual, and transcendent Creator of all, and infinite in all attributes.

[cclxx] Etymology of the word "Zion": The etymology of the word Zion is uncertain. Mentioned in the Bible in the Book of Samuel (Samuel 5:7) as the name of the Jebusite fortress conquered by King David, its origin likely predates the Israelites. If Semitic, it may be associated with the Hebrew root "ṣiyyôn ("castle"). Though not spoken in Jerusalem until hundreds of years later, the name is similar in Arabic and may be connected to the root ṣiyya ("dry land") or the Arabic šanā ("protect" or "citadel"). It might also be related to the Arabic root ṣahî ("ascend to the top") or ṣuhhay ("tower" or "the top of the mountain"). A non-Semitic relationship to the Hurrian word šeya ("river" or "brook") has also been suggested.

[cclxxi] THERE IS NO MOUNT ZION IN JERUSALEM. That's why till this very day most still disagree about it's true location. Only in the South western hill known as the "temple Mt and Mt Moriah." That location has only been been labelled as "Mt Zion" since the 12th century by the "Byzantine pilgrims." However archaeological evidence has proved otherwise

[cclxxii] Psalm: For the LORD has chosen Zion; He has desired it for His habitation. "This is My resting place forever; Here I will dwell, for I have desired it Mount Kenya was held sacred by all ancient Nile Valley civilizations, including Egyptians who referred to it as the mountain of Heru (Huru/Noble Ancestors), sitting directly on the East African Equator in a region known as "Ta Neteru (Ntore) meaning the Land of the Gods. Much later in history, the Kabiru (Hebrew) Council of Prophets would simply refer to the mountain as "Peace" in their language, Thaio/Thayu/Sio/Sayu. This word ultimately became "Zion" repeated in biblical scriptures.

[cclxxiii] The word Zion occurs over 150 times in the Bible. It essentially means "fortification" and has the idea of being "raised up" as a "monument."

[cclxxiv] The strength of the monsoon intensity at this time was similar to what it had been during the general period of the Last Glacial Maximum, but not as low as it had reached during the weakest phase between 14,000 and 12,500 14C years ago. In Malawi, a river channel cutting stage that is interpreted as the result of moister conditions begins around 12,000 14C y.a. (work by Meadows 1985, cited in Thomas & Thorp 1992). Rainfall in the watersheds of the White Nile seems to have been particularly high about 11,500-11,000 ^{14}C y.a., resulting in high river discharge (Williams 1995).

[cclxxv] Although direct evidence for agriculture and animal herding has not yet been found for this early period, grinding stones, usually associated with grain production, and hence farming, were discovered. Unable to credit agriculture at this date some archeologists presume that the people ground harvested wild plants

[cclxxvi] On November 7, 1885, a report on his discovery to the members of the Berlin Geographical Society was made by Jelarmi Farini. On March 8, 1886, he repeated the same report before the Royal Geographical Society of Great Britain. In the same year in London, Farini published his book "Through the Kalahari Desert," in which, in particular, he described the find of the lost city.

[cclxxvii] An unprecedented archaeological discovery that reframes the origins of the Sahara and Kalahari "deserts" in the North and South of Africa as the result of humongous tsunami activity in the North Atlantic resulting from a solar system catastrophe that destroyed a great ancient maritime civilization that Plato described as "Atlantis."

[cclxxviii] Not surprisingly the world's greatest repository of gold, caught the attention of ancient prospectors; it was with the discovery of gold, that ancient man moved from the age of stone to the age of metals, a transition which clearly occurred first in southern Africa, the world's greatest repository of gold. Researchers hypothesize that a vanished civilization from the distant past lived in that part of the world while mining gold.

[cclxxix] A distinct series of beach ridges marking the former shorelines of large inter-connected lacustrine basins in the Kalahari can be clearly identified from Landsat imagery and Shuttle Radar Topography Mission (SRTM) data. These basins, which form the terminal sump of the Okavango system in northern Botswana, are now almost completely dry.

[cclxxx] Koisan settlements have been discovered at the *Klasies River* mouth, at a bluff overlooking the Indian Ocean at the southern tip of the continent

[cclxxxi] One theory is that this 300-mile -long agricultural smart grid was apparently powered by an array of crop circle-like spirals clearly visible on Google Earth that generate a "Tesla-like" Crop Circle science energy as a multiplier effect amplifying the nutritional value of the food produced by this giant agricultural technology grid such that it can produce sufficient food to feed the people throughout and beyond the region

[cclxxxii] According to researcher and author, Michael Tellinger, in his association with Johan Heine, a local pilot who had the unique opportunity to see these incredible structures from the air for meny years, and realizing their significance was not appreciated, these discoveries are so incredible that It will need a complete paradigm shift in how we view our human history.
According to Tellinger, the photographs, artifacts and evidence we accumulated, point towards a lost civilization that has never before been and precedes all others – not for a few hundred years, or a few thousand years ... but many thousands of years."

[cclxxxiii] The extensive ruins are found at map co-ordinates -30° 0' 21.64", +21° 6' 21.69 and can be viewed on Google Earth or Google Maps.

[cclxxxiv] Palaeolake Makgadikgadi seems to have made regular appearances in the Kalahari, driven by vastly increased discharge in the Okavango and the Zambezi, the latter backflooding into the basin via the Mababe depression.

[cclxxxv] Equally remarkable is that the dry lake floor where they were found is also littered with tens of thousands of other smaller stone-age tools and flakes, the researchers report. They have documented thousands of stone tools on the lake bed, which sheds new light on how Africans adapted to several substantial climate change events during the period that coincided with the last Ice

[cclxxxvi] The Pseudohistoric and Pseudoscientific claims about "Bakoni Ruins": The Bakoni ruins are located in the province of Mpumalanga in present day South Africa. They refer to the many, complex hills that people terraced with stone to create walls for the sake of improving agricultural practices If you were to fly over the area in a small plane you would be amazed by the endless stone circles, set in bewildering mazes and linked by long stone passages, that cover the landscape below.

In some places the coverage is quite sparse and intermittent but in others it is dense, continuous and intricate. If you study the views provided by Google Earth and focus on the ghostly circles that cover the landscape you may get a sense of the extent of the heartland of this world, which stretched from Ohrigstad to Carolina and connected over 10,000 square kilometers of the Mpumalanga escarpment into a complex web of walled structures (Schoeman).

There are many disputes regarding the age of these structures, ranging from 25,000 to 250,000 years old. Needless to say, the Bakoni ruins have never been excavated to date—yet alone thoroughly researched. Nonetheless, Eurocentric Archaeologists, in collaboration with Eurocentric historians, relying on untenable and unreliable dating tachniques, have reached the dubious and ludicrous conclusion that the ruins date to the 19th century

[cclxxxvii] Research indicates that climatic changes and earth movements over thousands and thousands of years caused this dramatic change to take place.

[cclxxxviii] Previous research has suggested that Khoisan people may be directly descended from mankind's oldest common paternal ancestors. DNA studies in the 1990s, found that the Y chromosome of San men, one of the indigenous populations making up the Khoisan, share certain patterns of genetic variation that are different from those of all other populations. It was theorized that the San are one of the first populations to have differentiated from the most recent common paternal ancestor of all extant humans, estimated to have lived 90,000 years ago

[cclxxxix] The Khoikhoi were originally located above modern Botswana. The people began to migrate into Southern Africa. A new life was taken into Southern Africa and to the San.Once the migration started the Khoikhoi traveled west through the Kalahari desert, down to the Cape. Another route the same group took was going south east into Highveld and toward the southern coast. (rivers,mountains, etc.) In the Cape, the KhoiKhoi were limited the land because the rocky cliffs and mountains made it difficult for survival. The land was limited to the KhoiKhoi because they needed a good secure place to have their homes, and food for the animals.

[ccxc] The huge stone concentricly circled walls of the southern city are best seen from the air. They are estimated to be 1500 square kilometers, although each wall is only 3,5meters high in places. The walls would have been far taller before the 200,000 years of weather erosion. The surrounding geology is interesting due to numerous gold mines located in the vicinity. Researchers have proposed that a missing civilization from the distant past, could have lived and proposed in that part of the world while mining gold.

[ccxci] Naro was spoken in the central Kalahari and western Botswana to the borderlands of present day Namibia. While there was and is no one 'official' San language, meny ancient San spoke a dialect called "Naro"; other San groups in Botswana speak variations of it (these groups are the Naro, Anikhwe, the Bugakhwe, Haillom, Kua and the !Xun), and among them they speak some 30 variations of the language.

[ccxcii] The Tsodilo Hills are of great cultural and spiritual significance to the local San peoples of the Kalahari, who believe Tsodilo is the birthplace of all life, and that mankind was descended from the serpent, and it was the descendants of the first people who created the rock art found there.

[ccxciii] The recent archaeological findings in Tsodilo indicate that the earliest man worshipped a snake-like thing as god as far back as 70 000 years ago

[ccxciv] Evidence of serpent worship ritual sites and temples are scattered all over the ancient world, but the Tsodilo Hills Serpent Cave is the oldest such site that has ever been found. The practice of worship of or attribution of divine or sacred nature to serpents, simply referenced as Ophiolatry, is a practice that can be found all over the world, including China, India, Cambodia, Thailand, Japan, Indonesia, Ancient Greece and Rome, Egypt, United Kingdom, Scandinavia and the Americas, North, Central and South

[ccxcv] Koisan settlements have been discovered at the *Klasies River* mouth, at a bluff overlooking the Indian Ocean at the southern tip of the continent.

[ccxcvi] Located in Mpumalanga, South Africa Adam's Calendar is a standing stone circle about 30 meters in diameter and has been estimated by some accounts to be more than 75,000 years old

[ccxcvii] The site is aptly named Adam's Calendar because the stones are placed to track the movement of the sun, which casts shadows on the rock. It still works perfectly as a calendar today by following the shadow of the setting sun, which is cast by the taller central monolith onto the flat stone beside it. This remarkable calendar was originally a large circular stone structure resembling Stonehenge and in the center of the 'circle' are two upright stones which are said to have been carved. Its original shape is still clearly visible from satellite images. The stones are all dolomite, weighing up to 5 tons each, and are said to have been transported from a distant site. It should be noted that the area surrounding Adam's Calendar is extremely rich in gold. Several mining shafts have been reported in the area with one of the richest working mines in the world today being the Sheba Gold Mine, located in Mpumalanga.

The first calculations of the age of the calendar were made based on the rise of Orion, a constellation known for its three bright stars forming the "belt" of the mythical hunter. The Earth wobbles on its axis, so the stars and constellations change their angle of presentation in the night sky on a cyclical basis. This rotation, called the precession completes a cycle about every 26,000 years. By determining when the three stars of Orion's belt were positioned flat (horizontal) against the horizon, it is possible to estimate the time when the three stones in the calendar were in alignment with these stars. According to Tellinger, a calculation done by astronomer Bill Hollenbach based on the rise of Orion suggested an age of the site of at least 75,000 years.

The latest and most interesting discovery of the stone circles and Adam's Calendar is the sound frequencies of the rock formations from the earth below them. With modern technology, Tellinger and scientists have been able to detect and measure sound frequencies with acoustic properties made from the earth inside the circles which conduct electricity. These sound frequencies of the earth under the stones are shaped as flowers of sacred geometry as they surface to the ground.

There is still much about Adam's calendar that is yet to be understood, including who built them, what their civilization was like, and how they constructed it with such precise measurements. Perhaps in time, more research will piece together this prehistoric mystery.

ccxcviii The pyramids are in the Kruger Park about a 150 km to the North of the Barberton Valley Pyramids and probably on the same longitudinal line.

ccxcix The Ridge called the 'Ninetyeast Ridge' because the linear chain is located at 90° East longitude; the ridge stretches about 5000 km north to south, and is one of the longest chains of volcanoes in the world

ccc The west coast was affected by the cold currents of the Atlantic Ocean, which gave rise to dense ocean fogs when the warm winds from the interior hit the cold waters of the Atlantic; a dense fog visible for much of the year. Further southward, down the western coast, to where the cold Atlantic Ocean currents meet the warmer current of the Indian Ocean, at the Cape of Good Hope, the very southern tip of the African continent, the clashing currents create continous stormy unpredictable weather and ocean waters, discurraging and thus foreclosing explorations or migrations to the southeast..

ccci There is little consensus on what forced the climate of southern Africa to change during the Last Glacial Maximum (LGM). Because of southern Africa's latitudinal position, changes in seasonal precipitation can help resolve the influence of internal climate factors such as groundwater and external climate forcers such as large scale atmospheric circulation patterns

cccii In Botswana the Kalahari forms a broad watershed between the Okwa and Mmone dry river systems (Bakalahari-Schwelle), which are directed towards the Makgadikgadi depression (Okwa), nd the Nossob and Molopo, both of them dry rivers, which form the southern border of Botswana.

ccciii Researchers have documented thousands of stone tools on the lake bed, which sheds new light on how humans in Africa adapted to several substantial climate change events during the period that coincided with the last Ice Age in Europe.

ccciv At Makgadikgadi Pan (P3), lacustrine sediments show that paleo-Lake Makgadikgadi was in a high-stand phase and connected to Lake Ngami and the Zambezi and Okavango Rivers between 20 ka and 15 ka, meaning it was wetter than present (Shaw and Thomas, 1996; Shaw et al., 1997). At Lake Nagami (P4), deeper lake levels are also found at the end of the LGM (19-17 ka). The authors attribute this to higher riverine input (Hunstman-Mapila et al., 2006).

cccv A distinct series of beach ridges marking the former shorelines of large inter-connected lacustrine basins in the Kalahari can be clearly identified from Landsat imagery and Shuttle Radar Topography Mission (SRTM) data. These basins, which form the terminal sump of the Okavango system in northern Botswana, are now almost completely dry.

cccvi Most of the scholars accepted that genetic, climatic and archaeological evidence suggests a single southern exit from Africa to Sunda: however, recent evidence has shown that the migration out of Africa happened in multiple waves. All non-African ancient groups in the region are descended from these waves of migration.Human presence in Southeast Asia dates back to at least 40,000 years ago, when the current islands formed a continental shelf called Sundaland. There are several human populations scattered throughout Southeast Asia that are descendants of the people collectively known as Negritos, who are the indigenous groups currently found in the Andaman Islands, Malay Peninsula, the Andaman Islands, and several islands in the Philippines, whose ancestry can be traced to Africa

cccvii It is worth noting that it is now generally accepted that South East Asia was probably the entry point of modern humans from Africa, facilitating intercontinental transfer. A largely accepted theory argues that every living human being is descended from a small group in Africa, who then dispersed into the wider world.

cccviii The vast majority of scholars accept that every living human being is descended from a small group in Africa, who then dispersed into the wider world.Archaeological and fossil evidence support an early migration of modern humans left Africa and followed the coastlines of Africa, Arabia, India and Sunda.

cccix In 2012, Stephen Oppenheimer pointed out that the genetic, climatic and archaeological evidence logically suggests a single southern exit of modern human from Africa to Sundaland.

cccx .Khoisan people of South Africa were once the most populous humans on Earth

cccxi According to statments from Geologist Dr Danny Hilman the site could hide the remains of a lost temple that could date back at least 20,000 years. Hilman believes that the site (Gunug Padang) is of great cultural and historical importance since it contains the remains of a huge Pyramid that was built some 20,000 years ago, by a lost civilization, adding that it may have been built for worship or as a giant astronomical instrument

cccxii Genetic studies have concluded that the Dravidian people are not a distinct race but, rather, a common genetic pool within the Sudra

cccxiii Many of them have almost completely eroded or have been covered by the movement of soil, while some have survived and still display the great sizes of the original walls that stand 2,5 metres high and over a metre wide in places. Prof Guy Charlesworth of Wits University concurs that if these were the original heights of some of the walls, it would have taken thousands of years to erode to knee-height through the effects of nature alone.

cccxiv The country which is now known as Zimbabwe does not have one single history, nor was it a single geographical entity; the earliest settlement in the region goes back about 100.000 years. Though many different peoples and polities have come to inhabit the land throughout history, the Khiosan were amongst the first to settle in Zimbabwe cccxv . Until about 1966 the **Zambezi** was called the "Balovale" after the dominant chief (and his village within the town is still known by that name) but the name was changed in an attempt to defuse tensions between the main groups and the government of the newly independent country

cccxvi For the next 500 km the river serves as the border between Zambia and Zimbabwe. Below the Falls the river continues to flow due east for about 200 km (120miles), cutting through gorges of basalt rock between 200 to 250 metres (660 to 820ft) high

cccxvii The Zambezi's most noted feature is Victoria Falls. Other notable falls include the Chavuma Falls at the border between Zambia and Angola, and Ngonye Falls, near Sioma in Western Zambia. Up to the Late Pliocene or Pleistocene (more than two million years ago), the Upper Zambezi river used to flow south through what is now the Makgadikgadi Pan to the Limpopo River. The change of the river course is the result of epeirogenic movements that uplifted the surface at the present-day water divide between both rivers.

cccxviii Mãna (in this context) anciently described the spiritual life force energy or healing power that permeates the universe. It was anciently viewed as a cultivation or possession of energy and power, rather than being a source of power; it was viewed as an intentional force.

cccxix See: Settlement and Subsistence of Prehistoric Farming Communities in the Mid-Zambezi Valley, Northern Zimbabwe By: Gilbert Pwiti, published in The South African Archaeological Bulletin Vol. 51, No. 163 (Jun., 1996), pp. 3-6 (4 pages). Published By: South African Archaeological Society

cccxx Buddhist tenets included the 'Golden Rule' ..."Do unto others as you would have them do unto you.."

cccxxi Buddhism is a very ancient and prehistoric religion whose roots and tenets can be traced back to Africa in those days when Africa was speading the earliest forms of civilization around world Original Buddhism, also called early Buddhism, earliest Buddhism, and Pre-Buddhism is the Buddhism that existed before the various subsects came into being. Some of the contents and teachings of this Pre-Buddhism may be deduced from the earliest Buddhist texts, which by themselves are already sectarian. Pre-Buddhism refers to the earliest Buddhism, the ideas and practices that were foundational to the Gotama- Buddha himself.

cccxxii Intense debate persists about the climatic mechanisms governing hydrologic changes in tropical and subtropical southeast Africa since the Last Glacial Maximum, about 20,000 years ago.

cccxxiii Draco was a constellation formerly at the very heart of the heavens, and was so extensive, that it was called the Great Dragon

cccxxiv The name drakensberg, which means dragon mountain in afrikaans, is traditionally said to be named that because of the fact that its ragged peaks resemble the back of a dragon, another story says that the white settlers heard legends of a dragon that lived within the massif, in reality the local had been calling it the mountain of the dragon for thousands of years.

cccxxv The Younger Dryas was first recognized in 1901, at Allerød in Denmark, where it was discovered that lake sediments showed a pattern of organic mud with birch remains sandwiched by lower and upper clay layers containing the remains of cold-adapted plants (Joosten 1995). This suggested that the warming following the end of the last glacial was interrupted by a shift back to cold conditions before the full interglacial conditions of the Holocene became established.

cccxxvi Tamil historians have discussed this land mass in detail throughout history; eg. Ariyarkkunallar in the 12th century. Linguistic evidence indicates that the Dravidians are related to the C-group Nubians of the Western Sahara who built the Kerma empire. Since Egypt was often at war with Kerma, the connection across Lemuria seems more plausible. [Winters:Agri]

cccxxvii Where the Indian Ocean, the Bay of Bengal and the Arabian sea mate together

cccxxviii Some anthropologists tried to identify the Dravidians with what was known as "the Mediterranean race'. It has been noted that such a general label (which conceals gaps in our knowledge of pertinent anthropology) is more than a little confusing; since it purports a concept of race stripped of credible origin and details. This is the sense in which we generally speak of and refer to the 'black race', 'white race' or 'yellow race'. It might have been less ambiguous to call that 'Mediterranean race' the "Negroid race" (as some experts have done), since its espoused characteristics are precisely those of "blacks" in general: an elongated skull, dark or brown skin, and these two adjectives being quite often euphemisms for 'black'. It is significant to note that the ancient Greeks did not label as white the former inhabitants of North-West Africa, that is to say, of the present Maghreb, Morocco, Algeria and Tunisia -- since they called the inhabitants Mauroi or 'moors', meaning men with ' a dark skin'

cccxxix Archaeological discoveries, including small stone tools, have been uncovered at many sites in East African highlands. Near Lake Nakuru in Kenya archaeologists have found blades, scrapers, and other tools crafted from obsidian between 13,000 and 9,000 years ago. Settlemeent sites of the era have also been discovered on the shores of Lake Turkana in Kenya, and around Lake Victoria. Among the artifacts found are pieces of highly decorated pottery with stamped decorations.

cccxxx The world's earliest known mass-homicide grave of 27 adults and children shot with arrows and bludgeoned to death about 10,000 years ago has been found west of Lake Nataruk in Kenya. The authors of a study say the broken skeletons of the hunter-gatherers provide evidence that there was inter-group violence among prehistoric hunter-gatherers, but add that such conflict was extremely rare at that time. A team of many researchers, from Kenyan institutions and from Cambridge University in England and other institutions, published a closed-access paper about the astounding find in the journal Nature.

cccxxxi These four new weapons, together with the much older spear, were the principal weapons of all armies until around 1000 AD. Among fire weapons, arrows can kill at maximum distances of from 50 to 200 meters depending on their weight, their point type, and the power of the bow. The rate of fire of bows is potentially high, approximately five to ten aimed shots per minute.

cccxxxii Violence was clearly a fact of life in the Pleistocene, and people apparently got very, very good at it. Most of the injuries evident on the Jebel Sahaba skeletons came from projectiles, ranging from light arrows to heavy spears. It's easy to underrate how sophisticated and deadly these stone-tipped weapons really were. Based on the damage to the bones, combined with the points and chips mingled with the bodies, most of these projectiles involved a carefully-shaped stone point at the end of a wooden shaft, with sharp pieces of stone sticking out from the sides of the shaft for added damage.

[cccxxxiii] Mt. Meru, is a conical shaped volcanic mountain, 4,566 m high, located in Tanzania at the border of Kenya, Africa. It is located on the equator, which compares well with the Indian descriptions of 'centre of the Jambu-dwipa'!. Even though now it is considered as the fourth highest mountain in Africa geological studies have shown that it was about 6000m during the ice ages (period of glaciation) and the height was reduced subsequently on account of erosion. Volcanic mountains are generally conical in shape being wide at base with a narrow summit. Indian texts describe the Meru mountain precisely as wide at base and narrow at top. The word 'Meru' in Sanskrit means 'high', possibly after the Meru mountain.

[cccxxxiv] The archipelago consists of four large islands: Socotra, Abd al Kuri, Samhah, and Darsah, as well as 3 small islets to the north of the archipelago

[cccxxxv] Initially a lifeless basin, the Faiyum was transformed into a fertile garden by the natural silting of the Nile which diverted a significant branch of freshwater in its direction. The flow of the water carried with it the rich soil of the Nile River bed which settled in and around the newly-created lake and sprouted vegetation along its banks. Research on the desert margin of the Lake Moeris depression indicate that in early Paleolithic times the lake's waters stood about 120 feet (37 m) above sea level and probably filled the depression; the lake's level gradually fell until about 10,000 BC, when it was about 15 feet (4 1/2 m) below sea level, perhaps because its connection with the Nile River was temporarily cut off. Early in the Neolithic Period (nearly 4,000–11,000 years ago), the lake rose again and then gradually subsided. Neolithic and Early Dynastic people made their homes on the slowly shrinking shores.

[cccxxxvi] Once established the Dragon Culture engendered a brotherhood of priest kings and spiritual masters called the Djedhi whose definitive symbol was Uadjet, the Ureaus, a golden likeness of the indigenous desert asp. The roots of Djedhi and Uadjet, "Dj" and "Djed," denoted serpent and column respectively, and thus designated a Djedhi as one who had raised the inner serpent (the kundalini) up the human vertebral column to the spiritual centers within the head and thus become a Serpent of Wisdom. The mark of such an evolved Djedhi was the golden asp or golden band which was honorably worn over the seat of wisdom, the third eye. As Isa Shwaller de Lubicz, one of the foremost authorities on Egyptian mysticism, informs us: "... the victorious rising of this fire (the serpent fire) to the frontal lobe is symbolized by the Ureaus (the golden serpent) on the forehead of the Pharaoh."

[cccxxxvii] John Milton's book 'Paradise Lost', advises that the towns of *Mombasa* and *Malindi* were in existence before 4000 BC; according to Milton, 'the port of Mombasa has existed since shortly after the creation of the world' (paraphrase).

[cccxxxviii] Deva refers to a class of beings or a path of the six paths of the incarnation cycle. It includes some very different types of beings which can be ranked hierarchically according to the merits they have accumulated over lifetimes. The lowest classes of these beings are closer in their nature to human beings than to the higher classes of deva. Devas can be degraded to humans or the beings in the three evil paths once they have consumed their merits.

[cccxxxix] The Anu word 'neter' (or nature or 'netjer') means a power that is able to generate life and to maintain it when generated. As all parts of creation go through the cycle of birth-life-death-rebirth, so do the driving energies, during the stages of this cycle. It is therefore that the Ancient Anu neteru, being divine energies, went (and continue to go) through the same cycle of birth-growth-death and renewal.

[cccxl] This energy was considered to be the sacred energy of Creation – something each of us is born with, but most must work to "uncoil," and in so doing, awaken our Higher Self and come into direct contact with the Divine.

[cccxli] . Kundalini-type descriptions or experiences are found in esoteric teachings of the Khoisan.

[cccxlii] " the immanence of the gods in nature, far from diminishing their significance for the Animists, enabled a correlation of human and natural life which was an inexhaustible source of strength; the life of man was integrated with the life of nature ..." - Frankfort, 1948, p.29.

[cccxliii] The self-contemplation by each stage of existence brings into being each lower stage; as such, the hierarchy of energies is interrelated, and each level is sustained by the level below it. This hierarchy of energies was believed to be set neatly into a vast matrix of deeply interfaced natural laws, both physical and metaphysical

[cccxliv] When the *kundalini* touches and opens the heart centre, the forces of the *Buddhic* or Christ-consciousness in man resident in the vehicle of intuition, if sufficiently unfolded, begin to flow through the neophyte at the physical level and the "mystic rose"—the heart*chakra*—"blooms" upon his breast. For thousands of years, the science of Kundalini was kept hidden, passed on in secret from master to a chosen disciple who was considered worthy. The exact origin of Kundalini Yoga is unknown, but it is thought by many to be the Mother of all Yogas. The earliest known written mention of Kundalini is in the Vedic texts (c. 1,000 B.C. – 500 B.C.)., which indicate that Kundalini was actually a science of energy and spiritual philosophy before the physical practice was developed. For thousands of years, the science of Kundalini was actually kept hidden, and the sharing of Kundalini outside an elite community.

[cccxlv] The Dravidian classic, the Chilappathikaran made it clear that the first great kingdom of India was Naganadu. The Naga people were one of the early ancient peoples on isle of present day Sri Lanka; anciently concentrated in the Jaffna Peninsula. The Jaffna peninsula was known as late as the pre-mediaval era as "Naga Nadu," which means "Land of the Nagas" as mentioned in the twin epics of ancient Tamilakam, the Silappatikaram and Manimekalai.

[cccxlvi] The plane of our Milky Way Galaxy runs through this complex and beautiful skyscape. At the northwestern edge of the constellation Vela (the Sails) the four frame mosaic is over 10 degrees wide, centered on the glowing filaments of the Vela Supernova

Remnant, the expanding debris cloud from the death explosion of a massive star. Light from the supernova explosion that created the Vela remnant reached Earth about 11,000 years ago. In addition to the shocked filaments of glowing gas, the cosmic catastrophe also left behind an incredibly dense, rotating stellar core, the Vela Pulsar. Some 800 light-years distant, the Vela remnant is likely embedded in a larger and older supernova remnant, the Gum Nebula

[cccxlvii] Notable deep sky objects in Vela are the Eight-burst Nebula (NGC 3132), the Vela Supernova Remnant and the Gum Nebula. The Eight-burst Nebula (NGC 3132), also known as the Southern Ring Nebula, is a bright planetary nebula approximately 2,000 light-years from Earth. It contains two faint stars lying close together. The central one is a hot white dwarf that emits the ultraviolet radiation that illuminates the nebula. The Vela Supernova Remnant is a remnant of a star that exploded between 11,000 and 12,300 years ago approximately 800 light-years from Earth. Studies suggest correlations between the Younger Dryas and a supernova that exploded within the constellation of Vela approximately around the same time, leaving behind what is now known as the Vela Supernova Remnant. Researchers that studied effects of close-by supernovae on earth and uncovered suggestive correlating evidence during the Younger Dryas, including depletion of the ozone layer, increased UV exposure, nitrogen changes on the Earth's surface and troposphere, evidence of global cooling, changes in 14C and 10Be in ice cores, a thin layer (approximately 30 centimeters) of "black mats," and many extinctions that may have been caused by the explosion of the Vela Supernova.

[cccxlviii] The smaller islands include Madura, Lombok, Sumbawa, Flores, Bali and Timor. A stretch of mostly open water consisting of the Java, Flores, and Banda seas divides the major islands of into two unequal strings; in the south, the long, narrow islands of Sumatra, Java, Timor, and others. Several of the Greater Sunda Islands, including Java, Madura, Sumatra, and Kalimantan, form part of the Sunda Shelf, an extension of the coastal shelves of Malaysia, Thailand, Cambodia, and Vietnam, in the north.

[cccxlix] According to M. Gopinath of Dalit Sahitya Sangathane, in ancient times, a race of people related to Africans, Blacks called Naga, were spread from South Asia (also found from the South Pacific, through Indo-China to South India to the west to Cape Verde in Africa) all the way to West Africa.

[cccl] The French derived the name "Cambodia" from "Kampuchea," the country they colonized in the 1800's. "Khmer" is the French spelling for "K'mai," the ethnicity of many Cambodians and how most refer to themselves. Ancient stories tell how Khmer people are descended from the Naga.

[cccli] Carbon 14 dating of a cave at Laang Spean in northwest Cambodia reveals stone tools from 6000-7000 BCE

[ccclii]. The Earth's elliptical orbit around the sun and the degree of the 'angle' of the planet's axis, with respect to its path around the sun, define its orbital or rotational 'tilt'. The rotation axis of the Earth is inclined with respect to its orbital plane by 23.5 degrees; this 23.5 degree 'tilt' of the earth's rotational axis is manifest by the position of the sun in the sky. The direction of tilt traces a full circle about every 22,000 years; last polar shift occurred about 12,500 years ago, approximately 8,500 BC

[cccliii] The remnants of Kumari have been rediscovered across an enormous area of sunken islands by the vessel Vityaz (Knight Errant), which explored the Indian Ocean region between Asia and Africa for seven months in during 1961. The results of which gave witness to the ancient peninsula and the surrounding seabed. Many areas, which appeared on maps as deep blue spots, were found to contain extensive elevations and mountains, with great accumulations of ancient animal remains.

[cccliv] During and after the polar shift the land rearranges and the oceans eventually settle into the newly defined lower areas. Coastal spots that had formerly been above the water line may then be submerged and plates that may have supported areas of dry land may be undermined, with vast regions submerged under the seas. How much land remains above the waves depends on how deep and wide the ocean rifts are, however, tectonic plates supporting the land mass may rise and fall, depending on the interaction and pressure place upon the plates; these tectonic interactions often give rise to extended periods of violent volcanic eruptions, earthquakes, and upheavals, as the land mass settles into its new disposition.

[ccclv] Afro-Australoids constituted a significant factor also in the initial peopling of South Arabia; with their skeletal remains also having been exhumed from sites in Iraq. THE AFRICAN PRESENCE IN ASIA, By: RUNOKO RASHIDI

[ccclvi] The Saharan pump was invoked to explain three waves of human migrations outside Africa, namely: Homo Erectus to Southeast Asia, perhaps twice, once as far as China and India, once again to Pakistan. Homo heidelbergensis to the Middle East and Western Europe. Homo Sapiens Sapiens towards the Middle East and Western Europe, the so-called "out of Africa" The Sahara has expanded and contracted, changing the course of civilizations, with human communities

[ccclvii] Ancient lake deposits in the region have been dated to provide a chronology of climate change in the Central Sahara over the last 750,000 years.

[ccclviii] European Journal of Human Genetics advance online publication, 6 January 2010; doi:10.1038/ejhg.2009.231

[ccclix] R-V88 presents a paternal genetic record of the migration of Proto-Chadic speakers through the Central Sahara; recent geomorphological evidence fully supports this view

[ccclx] Present-day Geneticists maintain that the Dravidian speakers originated in India (Rajkumar et al. 2005; Thangaraj et al. 2006). They support this view by showing how the Indian mtDNA belonging to the M haplomacrogroup must have developed in situ in India, and the only location of M1 haplogroup among Africans is in East Africa (Thangaraj et al. 2006). Using the same molecular evidence these researchers make it clear that although Dravidians are phenotypically Africans, they are probably more related to Eurasians than Africans. Although this is the view of the molecular anthropologists, the anthropological and linguistic data tells a different story (Winters 2007).

The most frequent haploids in India belong to L3M and L3N lineages. An estimated 60% of Indian DNA consists of haplogroup (hg) M. The Dravidian speakers do not carry any ancient M lineages associated with the first exit of anatomically modern humans (AMH) from Africa. Indians bearing these genes live on the Andaman and Nicobar Islands. The most frequent M clade found in India is hg M2 which has transitions at nps 477G-1780-8502-16329. The defining HVS-I mutations of haplogroups M3, M4 and M5 include 16126, 16311, and 16129 (Metspalu et al. 2004).

These HVS-I mutations for M3, M4 and M5 are common to hg M1. Sun et al. (2005) believe that the presence of these M1 transitions in Indian M haplogroups is the result of parallel mutation. This view is disputed by the fact that the distribution of M1 mutations in the Indian M haplogroups is incongruent with the normal distribution of parallel mutations (Winters 2008). The anthropological and archaeological evidence makes it clear that the M1 haplogroup is spread throughout Africa (Gonzalez et al. 2007) The researchers who hold this view claim that hg M1 must be the result of back flow and the M macro-haplogroup developed in situ in India because hg M1 is only found in East Africa. This view is not supported by the molecular evidence of hgs M* and M1 among sub-Saharan populations across the continent (Gonzalez et al. 2007).

The HVSI transitions defining M1 are 16129-16223-16249-16278-16311-16362; 16129-16223-16234-16249-16211-16362. Haplogroup M1 has four transitions in the coding region (6446, 6680, 12403 and 14110) and five transition motifs in the noncoding region (195, 16129.16189,16249 and 16311) (Sun et al. 2005). The RFLP of M1 is diagnosed by MnlI site loss at 12402. The molecular evidence makes it clear that haplogroup M1 is not confined solely to Ethiopia. This haplogroup along with HGs N and M, are also found in Tanzania, Uganda, Egypt and the Senegambian region (Gonzalez et al. 2006; Gonder et al. 2006; Winters 2007). In addition to M1, M* and N1 in Senegambia we also find among the Senegambians haplotype AF24, which is delineated by a DdeI site at 10394 and AluI site of np 10397. This haplotype is a branch of the African subhaplogroup L3a.

This makes it clear that the M1, M and N haplogroups are found not only in Northeast Africa, but across Africa from East to West (Winters 2007) The M1 haplogroup is also found in India. Gonzalez et al. (2006) reported the presence of M1 in India. Kivisild et al. (1999) noted that 26 of the subjects in his study belonged to the M1 haplogroup. These researchers reported that the Indian subcluster M1 was found mainly in Kerala and Karnataka among high caste individuals. Chaubey et al. (2007) argues that the Indian hg M1 in Kivisild et al. (1999) was changed into hg M3 to avoid parallel nomenclatures. This seems unlikely because Kivisild et al. (1999) already had a nomenclature hg M3, in addition to hg M1. Moreover, a cursory examination of the Indian hg M1 of Kivisild et al. (1999) indicates that this subcluster had transitions at 16311, 16129 and 16189, the same as Ethiopian hg M1.

There are other genetic markers which point to a relationship between South Indians and Africans. Cordaux et al. (2003) during a study of 370bp of the HVS-I control region found that although Indians were closely related to the east Eurasian gene pool, it was noted in Figure 5,that clusters I,II, VII,IX, X, XI,XII,and XIV are found in Africa and India. B.B. Lal (1963) proved conclusively that the Dravidians were genetically related to the C group of Nubia, given the fact that both groups used 1) a common black-and-red ware (BRW), 2) a common burial complex incorporating megaliths and circular rock enclosures and 3) a common type of rock cut sepulchre. The BRW industry diffused from Nubia, across West Asia into Rajastan, and thence to East Central and South India. (Rao 1972) This explanation has some merit given the anthropological (Lahavory 1963; Sistri 1966), and osteological (Lahovary 1963; Sastri 1966; Sjoberg 1971) evidence of an African origin of the Dravidian speakers (Aravanan 1980; Sergent 1992; Winters 2007). Lal's (1963) research suggests that the Dravidian speaking people may have belonged to the C-Group.

The C-Group people spread culture from Nubia into Arabia, Iran and India as evidenced by the presence of BRW. Although the Egyptians preferred the cultivation of wheat, many ancient C-Group people were agro-pastoral people who cultivated Millet/Sorghum and raised cattle. It was the Dravidians who probably took this cultigen to India (Winters 2008b). The C-Group people used a common black and red ware that has been found from the Sudan, across Southwest Asia and the Indian Subcontinent all the way to China (Singh 1982). The earliest use of this BRW was during the Amratian period (c.4000 3500 BC). The users of the BRW were usually called Kushites.

In the controversy surrounds the origin of the Dravidian languages, Krishnamurti (2001) outlines the alleged relationship of Dravidian languages to Elamite, Sumerian and Japanese. Although the relationship of Dravidian languages to these languages is disputed, there is abundant evidence that Dravidian languages are genetically related

to the Niger-Congo group (Aravanan 1979, 1980 ; Homburger 1948, 1957; Upadhyaya and Upadhyaya, 1976, 1979; Winters 1985, 1988, 1989). The Proto-Dravidian speakers probably migrated across Arabia to reach India. The first civilization in Arabia was the Tihama culture. The Tihama civilization probably originated in Nubia (Fattovish 2008). It is characterized by the cheesecake or pillbox burial monuments which extend from Dhofar in Nubia, the Gara mountains to Adulis on the Gulf of Zula, to Hadramaut, Qataban, Ausan, Asir, the Main area and Tihama in Arabia. At Tihama and other sites in Arabia we find pottery related to the C-Group people of Nubia (Keall 2000; 2008; Fattovish 2008; Giumlia-Mair 2002).

East African hg M1 and Indian haplogroups are also found in Arabia and Yemen (Metspalu et al. 2004). On the Horn of Africa we find the Indian hg M3a and M3. In Yemen we have the Indian haplogroups M6, M6a, M3 and M4a. On the Horn of Africa and Yemen, no archaic M haplogroups have been found (Abu Amero et al. 2008). The archaeological and molecular evidence provides footprints of a recent hg M ancestral migration from Nubia to India. The existence of the L3a-M motif in the Senegambia characterized by the DdeI site np 10394 and AluI site np 10397 in haplotype AF24; the presence of the nucleotides characteristic of the Indian macrohaplogroup M in Africa and

Arabia; and the reality that M1 does not descend from an Asian M macrohaplogroup (Sun et al. 2005) make a 'back migration' of M1 to Africa highly unlikely.

The geographical distribution of the archaeological signature of the C-Group people from Nubia to India matches the location of populations carrying hg M. The presence of Indian M sequences in Africa, Arabia, Iran and Yemen (Gonzalez et al.. 2006) in conjunction with the linguistic (Aravanan 1976, 1979; Upadhyaya and Upadhyaya 1976, 1979), archaeological (Lal 1963; Lahovary 1963; Rao 1972) and anthropological (Nayar 1977; Sergent 1995; Sastri 1966) evidences suggest that the Dravidian speakers formerly lived in Nubia and migrated to India over 5000 years ago and the Indian M macrohaplogroups do not have an in situ origin. A recent origin for the Dravidian speakers would explain the absence of genetic material dating to the first out of Africa exit by AMH 60kya among Dravidian speaking Indians, and the numerous M1 transitions found in the Indian M haplogroups (Winters 2008). [See 'Origin and Spread of Dravidian Speakers; By Dr. Clyde Winters (Uthman dan Fodio Institute, Chicago, Illinois 60643, USA)]

[ccclxi] Lake Yoa is the most famous, and second largest of the Lakes of Ounianga, a series of Lakes in Borkou-Ennedi-Tibesti Region basin of northeastern Chad. It is located in the Ounianga Kebir about 40 km west of Ounianga Sarir. These lakes are remnants of a much larger lake which occupied this basin during the African Humid period which lasted from approximately 15,000 to 5,500 years before present. There are currently 15 lakes in the basin with a total surface area of approximately 20 kilometres (12 mi) square.

[ccclxii] Dravidian languages are spoken in the African nation of Cameroon. In relation to East African languages the Dravidian Family of languages are related to Egyptian, the Bantu Family of Languages. This is supported by the linguistic genetic relationship between Telugu and ancient Egyptian. Clyde Winters, Origin and Spread of the Dravidians, Int Jour of Hum genetics, 8(4) , 2008 https://www.academia.edu/1898555/Origin_and_Spread_of_Dravidian_Speakers Tamil Spoken in Cameroon. https://www.youtube.com/watch?v=vWyAYGlFZjk.

[ccclxiii] Several teams undertook excavations in the centre and the western border of the firki floodplains south of Lake Chad. New facts and new dates concerning the material culture of the inhabitants of the firki lands came to light. Historical research did not keep pace with these enormous advances (Borno Museum Society Newsletter nos. 72/73 & 74/75, 2008 84).

[ccclxiv] This is supported by and the ancient fertile expanse and tremendous productivity of stands of wild grasses still prevalent in the southern regions adjacent to and surrounding Lake Chad.

[ccclxv] Proto-ancestors of the Ijos

[ccclxvi] Middle Stone Age sites indicate that by then people butchered rhinoceroses, antelopes, and gazelles; a few sites also contain stones used to grind wild plant foods. The Late Stone Age, which began about 45,000 years ago, marked the appearance of stone blades and tools that people attached to handles of wood or bone; they made beads, painted pictures on rock walls, formally buried their dead, and produced many artifacts which have survived at a few sites

[ccclxvii] The Mousterian Pluvial was an extended wet and rainy period in the climate history of North Africa. It occurred during the Upper Paleolithic era, beginning around 50,000 years before the present (ybp), lasting 20,000 years, and ending around 30,000 bp.

[ccclxviii] These are the same Africans, the 'Manding-Shi (Niger-Bantu) and Manding-Kush (Niger-Kordofan) who entered the Americas with Emperor Ci before 3000 BC (Popul Vuh as translated by Sahagun) up to the 1400's. Another group of Africans from the Nubia-Egypt region entered into the Americas, according to (Zacharia Sitchin) excavations done by Mexican, American and other archeologists, who discovered an Egyptian-Nubian calender in use in ancient Mexico; that calendar is said to have been brought to Mexico by Tehuti Mez (Thoth).

[ccclxix] Ma'at uses a Scale. A dead person's Heart was placed on the scale, balanced by the Feather of Ma'at. If the Heart weighed the same as the Feather of Ma'at, the deceased was allowed to go on to the Eternal Afterlife and gained Immortality (Heaven). If the deceased had been found not to have followed the concept of Ma'at during his life (if he had lied or cheated or killed or revenged) his heart was devoured by a demon and he died the final death and was Reincarnated

[ccclxx] The geological changes which have taken place in the Niger basin are imperfectly known. The French scientists E. F. Gautier and R. Chudeau, summing up the evidence available in 1909, set forth the hypothesis that the xisting upper Niger and the existing lower Niger were distinct streams. According to this theory the upper Niger, somewhat above where Timbuktu now stands, went north and north-west and emptied into the Juf, which in the beginning of the quaternary age was a salt-water lake, the remnant of an arm of the sea which in the tertiary age covered the northern Sudan and southern Sahara as far east as Bilma. Lake Fagubini is regarded as a remnant of the ancient course of the upper river. When the upper Niger had this direction, the Wadi Taffassassent, now a dried-up river of the central Sahara, which rose in the Ahaggar mountains, is believed to have formed the upper course of the existing lower Niger. While the upper and lower parts of the Niger have all the appearance of ancient streams, the middle Niger is the result of a "recent" capture; "it has no past, it scarcely has a present" (see R. Chudeau, *Sahara soudanais,* Paris, 1909).

[ccclxxi] Referred to as 'Aterian' tools, after the so-called 'Bir el Ater' site, south of Annaba.

[ccclxxii] Discovered at a site in the Atlas Mountains, of Morroco, Africa, Aterian tanged points/tools represent a milestone in early human cognitive thinking as well as Paleolithic history. The man-made protruding process on Aterian tools is the first evidence of a tang on a projectile point, proof that the points were hafted on shafts and eventually developed into arrowheads.

[ccclxxiii] A reconstruction of the historical dynamics can be elicited by an archaeological analysis of the settlement and economic strategies adopted across the region during the era. Archaeologists believe that constraints on food sources led to more settled communities. The Earth's climate entered another big freeze-up following the brief but protracted rainey period. Temperatures fell abruptly, deserts expanded and ice sheets spread across the northern latitudes, much as they had done 40,000 years prior.

[ccclxxiv] An ethnonym (from the Greek: ἔθνος, éthnos, "nation" and ὄνομα, ónoma, "name") is the name applied to a given ethnic group.

[ccclxxv] Chott is an Arabic term for dry, salt depression

[ccclxxvi] The huge endorheic salt lake is famous for its position below the sea level; it acts as the country's lowest point since it lies almost entirely below the sea level.

ccclxxvii As was shown by the May 21, 2003 Zemmouri Earthquake (Mw=6.8) (Meghraoui et al., 2004), and the October 10, 1980 El Asnam Earthquake (Mw=7.3) (Ouyed et al.,1981).

ccclxxviii Few studies were dedicated to these faults (Aoudia & Meghraoui, 1995; Chiabbara et al., 1996; Meghraoui, 1988; Phillip & Meghraoui, 1983), consequently the timing and amount of displacement of these faults, as well as their relationship with the basin development, are still a matter of debate (Thomas, 1985; Neurdin-Trescartes, 1992; Belkebir et al., 1996; Bessedik et al., 2002).

ccclxxix The term Triton is associated with Poseidon, the Trident symbol and the planet Neptune which are all ssociated with the control and navigation of the sea and also with the esoteric symbology of the fish. In mythical lore Triton was the son of Poseidon, and was represented as a man above the waist and a dolphin below the waist; a symbol that was placed into the constellations as the sea-goat: Capricorn.

Triton, the son of Poseidon, is represented as a man above the waist and a dolphin below the waist. This symbol was placed into the constellations as the sea-goat: Capricorn. The identification of Poseidon, with a boat (i.e., a boat on the ocean is like a mountain on the sea) suggest that Poseidon, is another name for the Fish, that showed Maa the boat that saved mankind from the ancient great flood

ccclxxx According to Herodotus the *Triton Sea* was bordered on the west by the *Atlas Mountains*,[ccclxxx] and a study in 1883 cooroberates that the large Northern Inland Sea stretched eastward fully to the Gulf of Gabes, on the Mediterranean coast.

ccclxxxi Aound 70,000 years BP Africa suffered an extinction of 30% of its wildlife species; according to the theory by which the world is said to have entered the last major ice age around 30,000 years BP. In consequence, the greatly expanded Sahara Desert extended nearly to the Ethiopian Highlands, and the mountain ranges as far south as Central Africa were covered by ice

ccclxxxii Generally speaking there are two kinds of history: the popular history written by the invaders, and the suppressed history preserved by the natives. For example, most Arab historians in writing Libya's history fail to mention the Berbers (direct descendents of the ancestral Xi (Si) or Shi people) and their influence on the Egyptian and Sumerian civilisations, and instead use the phrase "ancient Libyans."

Eurasians generally purport that the ancient Libyans came from Asia; Eurocentrics say they came from Europe during the Ice Age, or they purport that they were descendents of an early ancient Greek invasion. To deny the Black origin of the Xi (Si) and indeed early civilization, Euro-centric theorists created the Hamitic myth, that black skinned whites were the founders of early ancient civilization; a major component of the myth is that the Xi (Si) Shi people, ancestors of the present-day Berbers and Tuaregs, were remnants of this ancient white population that lived in Africa during antiquity. They created this myth even though the Greco-Romans claimed the Berbers were negroes (blacks) from the Atlas mountains across west Africa (Diop,pg.66). The Greco-Roman writers make it clear that the original Berbers were Black Africans. Nonetheless, another self serving version of the origin of the so-called "ancient Libyans" is expounded by Arab theorists and sympathizers, who purport that the Xi (Si) or Shi people (ancestors of the present-day Berbers and Tuaregs) came from Southern Arabia (Yemen)

The truth is that the whole of the North African littoral was originally inhabited by an indigenous group of Black Berber tribes (the ancestral Xi (Si) or Shi people) whose linguistic unity proves an ethnic sub-stratum of autochthons single race that existed in North Africa from the Mediterranean to the Sudan and from the Atlantic Ocean to the Red Sea; occupying nearly half of Africa and comprising Libya, Algeria, Egypt, Tunisia, Morocco, Mauritania, Niger, Mali, Burkina Faso, the conquered Canary Islands, and of course the Sahara herself – the Mother of Human Civilization.

ccclxxxiii From 75,000 to 35,000 years BP, the Aterian Tool Tradition develops concurrent with and later, supersedes the Mousterian Tool Industry in Northwest Africa as well as in several other regions of the continent. The exact dating of the beginning and ending of this technology is unclear and it varies with different regions of Africa. It is believed that the Aterian Tradition dates back to a time in excess of 80,000 years ago but it is widely accepted that by 30,0000 years ago, the Aterian sites were abandoned and the period came to an end. The Aterian tradition tool-makers derived their technology from the Mousterian Tradition tools and flakes.

ccclxxxiv Some of the dating techniques were Thermoluminescence (TL) which proved successful in dating several types of sediments including "desert loss" sand dunes. This method can date organic materials that are older then 50,000 years old. Another technique used in dating Aterian tools was the optically stimulated lumininscence (OSL) which uses optical instead of thermal excitation sources to stimulate remission of light. The third used was radiocarbon dating for the Aterian tool aging.

ccclxxxv Between 50,000 and 30,000 B.C., the Aterian tool culture is known to have spread fully across the region

ccclxxxvi While there is no clear dating for this rock art, the age of these artefacts extend over many thousands of years, and the effect of recent radiocarbon dates from North Africa has largely been to extend the principal phases of prehistory to which they relate further back in time.

ccclxxxvii By analogy with recently dated Upper Acheulian occupation sites at Kalambo Falls and elsewhere, the Upper Acheulian stone assemblages at Adrar Bous are probably at least 60,000 years old (Clark, 1971; and *in litt.*, 1971).

ccclxxxviii Very little in the way of excavation has been carried out in the region due to the difficult working conditions in the desert as well as the problematic politics associated with different universities and national permissions. Thus, there is no clear dating for this rock art, nor has it been reliably associated with a stratified material culture. This negative picture is compounded by key sites being divided between different colonial spheres of influence, namely French and Italian, with little collaboration between respective scholars. Post-colonial research has been similarly hampered in both countries, worsened by little or no interest on the part of the Algerian and Libyan academics.

The situation is further complicated by the fact that over the millennia the aeolian erosion in this dry environment has completely removed the prehistoric soil deposition in many places, thus mixing the stratigraphic record. This has resulted in an enormous quantity of lithics and pottery being dispersed and exposed on these palaeo-surfaces. The dates of these artefacts extend over many thousands of years, so that Acheulean lithics are lying, on the same level, next to Epipalaeolithic microliths and Neolithic ceramics (Barich 1987; Cremaschi & Di

Lernia 1998; Aumassip 2004). However, many rock shelters with intact stratigraphic archaeological deposits offer significant potential for information about the past. [Round Heads: The Earliest Rock Paintings in the Sahara By Jitka Soukopova; Cambridge Scholars Publishing, 12 Back Chapman Street, Newcastle upon Tyne, NE6 2XX, UK (2012)]

ccclxxxix Until a few years ago, the Aterian was considered a subsequent *fades* of the Mousterian, even on the basis of stratigraphic contexts where such a succession appeared to be preserved (e.g., Tixier, 1967; Petit-Maire, 1982; Tillet, 1987; Raimbault, 1988), and radiocarbon dated from 47,000 ± 3200 years BP at Haua Fteah (McBurney, 1967) to 24,500 ± 600 years BP at Grotte des Contrebandiers (Delibrias *et al.*, 1982) (Table I). Such an attribution seems to be based on two main elements: radiometric datings, with their intrinsic technical problems, and the (not explicitly) expected equation between wet phases and human occupations in the prehistoric Sahara [see also Wendorf and Schild (1992) for a thorough reexamination of the matter].

Based on radiocarbon datings, the Aterian was thought to have an age greater than 40,000 and to last until 20,000 years BP (Table I). However, it has been observed recently that not only was this method inappropriate, but also the dated materials were of questionable reliability and/or from uncertain contexts (Wendorf and Schild, 1992). Radiocarbon dates on Late Pleistocene organic sediments run the risk of being biased by the recycling of old carbon or by detrital carbonates or recrystallization (Fontes and Gasse, 1991). In addition, many deposits with Aterian lithics contained no organic matter that could be dated by 14C methods. Uranium-series technique provided more reliable results than radiocarbon and it actually revised the Late Pleistocene chronology of North Africa acquired by 14C. A large number of Th/U dates from the Northern and Central Sahara collected in the PALHYDAF program (Fontes and Gasse, 1991) indicated a humid phase between 150,000 and 75,000 and, possibly, another one at 45,000 years BR.: African Archaeological Review, Vol. 15, No. 4, 1998: Some Insights on the Aterian in the Libyan Sahara: Chronology, Environment, and Archaeology, By Mauro Cremaschi, Savino Di Lernia, and Elena A. A. Garcea.

cccxc It is evident, that in lower paleolithic times (150,000 – 100,000 years b.p.) the whole of North Africa was populated, as the characteristic pear shaped Acheulean hand axes may be found in the whole region.

cccxci Prior to about 4200 years ago, Lake Yoa was a freshwater lake; over the next several centuries the lake became more saline until becoming a salt lake about 3900 years ago.

cccxcii Palinological data indicate a longer occupation of these settlement sites than once assumed

cccxciii The effect of recent radiocarbon dates from North Africa has largely been to extend the principal phases of prehistory back in time. The Middle Palaeolithic now seems to be essentially beyond the range of the radiocarbon technique, at least in North Africa

cccxciv Rock art (engravings and paintings) have made Tassili world famous [from 1933 the date of its first discovery by Europeans explorers]. 15,000 petroglyphs have been identified to date, while cave paintings found in the Tassili depict a separate group of over 30,000 petroglyphs (primarily of large river animals such as crocodiles).

cccxcv The leading theories on the evolution of "straight hair" focus on the relationship between ultraviolet radiation [or "UV light"] and the cold climate of the highlands and the northern hemisphere; based primarily on the principle that straight fibers better facilitate the passage of UV light into the body relative to curly hair. It is substantiated by Iyengar's (1998) findings that UV light can pass through straight human hair roots in a manner similar to the way that light passes through fiber optic tubes (Iyengar, 1998)."

cccxcvi In many respects the Mousterian Pluvial resembled the earlier Abbassia Pluvial; the later Neolithic Subpluvial was a weaker re-iteration of the same pattern.

cccxcvii At site BT-14

cccxcviii The Aterian Industry improved spear and projectile points by adding a notch on the bottom of the stone point, so it could be more securely fastened to the wooden shaft. The other breakthrough in this period is the invention of the spear-thrower, which allowed for more striking power and better accuracy. The spear-thrower consisted of a wooden shaft with a notch on one end where the spear rested. The development of the spear-thrower allowed for increased efficiency in hunting large animals. They hunted a wide variety of animals such as the white rhinoceros, camel, gazelles, warthogs, ostriches, and various types of antelopes.

cccxcix The Fezzan is a large closed basin that contains a wealth of ancient lake deposits that can be dated using modern techniques to produce a chronology of climate change in the central Sahara; a chronology that demonstrates evidence of relatively humid conditions during interglacial periods, when planetary ice cover was at a minimum, spanning the last 750,000 years. From 750,000 to 420,000 years ago rainfall was high enough to produce a giant lake rough'y the size of England, that has been termed 'Lake Megafezzan'.

cd The main river systems that fed the giant lake were the Tasilli N'Ajjer and Hamada Mangueni. The locations of the current Ubari lakes are situated near the middle of the lake; left over as the mother-lake slowly evaporated away into thin air.

cdi Though not as big as Lake Megachad (3 million km2), Lake Megafazzan is the second largest Pleistocene lake in the Sahara so far reported. In general terms it appears that the lake had one arm in the Wadi al-Ajal that went from Sabha, terminating to the west of Ubari. Other arms of this lake would have stretched from Sabha along Wadi ash-Shati and Wadi Barjuj

cdii The bottom of that basin is today a great sand sediment, the eastern Grand Erg [part of the ancient 'Igharghar River Valley'].

cdiii This scene would thus be the representation of a Holy Trinity, illustrated by a precise iconography; with the upper part of one of the three figures - a kind of mushroom-shaped "primordial deity."

cdiv This double line could signify an indirect association or non-material fluid passing from the object held in the right hand and the mind. This interpretation would coincide with the mushroom interpretation if we bear in mind the universal mental value induced by hallucinogenic mushrooms and vegetals, which is often of a mystical and spiritual nature (Dobkin de Rios, 1984:194).

cdv By Barth in 1850

cdvi Chemical analysis of the artefacts affirms they were dairy farming in the valley when the region was humid and 'green

cdvii Preliminary analyses ultizing several methods of chronometric dating suggests almost all the sites fall firmly within the Middle Pleistocene period.

cdviii The Triton Sea is documented in the book entitled, " The Chotts of Tunis, Or, The Great Inland Sea of North Africa in Ancient Times."

cdix Tectonic subsidence or uplift of a basement datum, sediment compaction involving subsidence of a datum within the sediment pile, and vertical eustatic movements of the seasurface all contribute to relative sea-level changes.

cdx The mean sea level in the proximity of a coast is defined as the height of sea surface referred to a local terrestrial benchmark and averaged over a period of time long enough to remove high–frequency oscillations. However, given the high space–and time–variability of the physical processes perturbing sea surface, the definition of true mean sea level becomes extremely difficult, or even impossible, and puts on the characteristics of an elusive concept (Daly, 2002). Given the low tidal excursion and the presence of geological indicators and archaeological remains, the Mediterranean coasts are particularly suitable for the reconstruction of past sea levels (Flemming, 1972, 1978).

cdxi While the Mediterranean region is sufficiently remote from the North European centre of glaciations, the tectonic mobility of the active basins of the northern Mediterranean, verses the proximity of the North African centre of glaciations and the tectonically stable vestiges of the Tethyan passive margin of the south; manifested in differing Isostatic responses to Glacial Loading during the last ice age, culminating in subsidence at amenable delta such as the Gulf of Gabes

cdxii Starting from the ideas of Strabo who ruled out the existence of slopes on the ocean surface, Suess introduced the concept of "eustatic" changes in sea level, that is, since the oceans are interconnected, the vertical displacements of the ocean surface would follow a uniform pattern throughout the world. Despite the strong influence of this concept over the sea level research, the observed evidences of the Holocene relative sea level (RSL) variations collected around the world during the XX century indicated a strong influence of local to regional scale factors.

The post–glacial global sea level variation could not be explained by a single sea level curve as stated by Suess. During the first decades of the XX century Daly (1920, 1940, and 1943) stressed the importance of the glacio–isostatic effects accompanying the lasts deglaciation phase, with uplift movements in areas of ice melting and subsidence movements in a wide peripheral belt. It soon became clear that during the last glaciation the huge ice sheets isostatically deformed the surface of the Earth as a consequence of their load. While the regions covered by the ice caps were depressed below the level prior to the glaciation, the surrounding peripheral regions were raised up above.

Following the subsequent melting phase, the depressed regions started uplifting, thus locally reducing the entity of the sea level rise, while, at the same time, the peripheral forebulges started subsiding and therefore accelerating the rate of sea level rise. [This geophysical phenomenon is called Post–Glacial Rebound (PGR) or even Glacio Isostatic Adjustment] Vertical movements of the solid surface are driven by the isostatic adjustment which results from the slow viscoelastic response of the Earth to the melting of the ice loads and to the contemporaneous addition of meltwater into the ocean. Furthermore, variations in the distribution of the surface loads [both in the cryosphere and in the hydrosphere] induce an interior redistribution of mass which in turn affects the equipotential surface of the terrestrial gravity field (geoid), and therefore modifies sea level

cdxiii The Mediterranean basin has experienced major sealevel change during glacial cycles, evidence for which occurs in both the geological and archaeological records, of decreasing resolution with time, throughout the last glacial cycle. Sea-level change in the Mediterranean Sea during glacial cycles is determined by the temporally variable eustatic change and by the spatially variable glacio-hydro-isostatic response of the earth and ocean to the growth and decay of ice sheets. Superimposed upon this are the relative changes from any vertical tectonic movement of the land. A principal process contributing to sea-level change on glacial time scales is the exchange of water between the continental ice sheets and the oceans, upon which may be superimposedvertical land movements driven by active tectonic processes. The growth and decay of the ice sheets change the ocean volume, deform the ocean basins and their margins, and modify the gravitational field, or geoid, of the planet. All three effects modify sea level.

cdxiv Tectonic subsidence or uplift of a basement datum, sediment compaction involving subsidence of a datum within the sediment pile, and vertical eustatic movements of the seasurface all contribute to relative sea-level changes.

cdxv The mean sea level in the proximity of a coast is defined as the height of sea surface referred to a local terrestrial benchmark and averaged over a period of time long enough to remove high–frequency oscillations. However, given the high space–and time–variability of the physical processes perturbing sea surface, the definition of true mean sea level becomes extremely difficult, or even impossible, and puts on the characteristics of an elusive concept (Daly, 2002). Given the low tidal excursion and the presence of geological indicators and archaeological remains, the Mediterranean coasts are particularly suitable for the reconstruction of past sea levels (Flemming, 1972, 1978).

cdxvi Bas Saharan Artesian Basin; enclosing the northeastern extremity of a huge basin underlying the Eastern Erg in the present-day Tunisian and Algerian Sahara

cdxvii Substantiating the antiquity of the ancient waters discovered and investigated in the basins of the Sahara, where the IAEA has carried out a number of hydrological investigations with isotope techniques under contract from other UN organizations (FAO, UNESCO, UNDP), the deep groundwater is generally found to be extremely old. The carbon-14 content is frequently at or below 2% of the modern content, thus indicating an age greater than 20 000 years (taking into account the errors and the uncertainties inherent in the method). This would indicate that recharge probably occurred during the Pluvial period of the Upper Pleistocene (10 000 to 65 000 years ago).

cdxviii Otherwise known as sand seas, the present-day ergs are the Saharan dunes of popular imagination. They cover about 20 percent of the Sahara and can stretch for hundreds of miles at heights of up to 1,000 feet. The basins of the Great Western Erg and Eastern Erg cover most of Algeria, while the basin of the Selima Erg blankets more than 3,000 square miles underlying Libya, and the basin of the Erg Cherch cdxviii stretches for 600 miles across Mali and Algeria. Formed in basins and low-lying depressions, the present-day ergs also contain large quantities of salt from the dried-up ancient Saharan Inland Sea (the "*Atlanean Sea*"); deposits that later fueled the Sahara's ancient salt trade.

cdxix Observations similar to those described have also been made for the so-called "Continental Intercalaire" aquifer, the major water-bearing formation in the western Sahara: extending mostly in Algeria from the Atlas to the Ahaggar mountains, in the north-south direction; and from Tunisia and western Libya to the Wadi Saura valley, in the east-west direction. The total area is some 600 000 km2, about 10% larger than that of France and seven times that of Austria. The amount of water stored in such an aquifer is enormous, in the order of thousands of cubic kilometers.

cdxx Before the world was formed, there was said to be a watery mass of dark, directionless chaos; the celestial waters of "Nun." Nun was older than all the other gods and was thus was considered the masculine aspect of the creator god. Nun's qualities were believed to include boundless potentiality, limitless unformed matter, darkness and turbulence. Neith (or "Neter"), the feminine aspect of the creator god, is said to have emerged from the primeval waters of Nun, and is often referred to in ancient texts as the "eldest," and even as the "first" deity.

cdxxi In the Ennead cosmogony Nun is perceived as transcendent at the point of creation alongside Atum the creator god.

cdxxii Neith never engaged in any kind of sexual union; that is, she was eternally a virgin. Yet, as the primordial Being, she was also generative. Thus, in Neith we have one of the earliest appearances of the archetype of the Virgin Mother, the Holy Parthenos, in her original, unadulterated form."

cdxxiii She is said to have floated upon the waters of Nun and, in parse representation of her function as creator, was the first primordial mound.

cdxxiv There are much earlier references to Neith 's association with the primordial flood-waters and to her demiurge

cdxxv The forest has been exploited sustainably by man tor thousands of years, but modern developments have destroyed or damaged much of it, especiallyin the lowlands.

cdxxvi Argan oil helps in increasing the body's immunity against diseases and infections because of its high antioxidant levels. It has the ability to reduce triglyceride levels in men, thus preventing the development of cardiovascular disease. Though not proven, it is believed to be able to prevent the development of breast, prostate, colorectal, and endometrial cancer. Argan oil is also known to soothe and give relief from pain due to rheumatism and arthritis.

cdxxvii From all main periods of the prehistory of the Sahara rock-engravings and rock-paintings have been found. Foum Chenna (Tinzouline), Aït Ouaazik (Asguine Tarna, Tazzarine) Tiouririne e Tisguinine (Zagora) are amongst the best known sites in the Draa region. At Ighir N'tidri between Tagunit and Mhamid al-Ghizlane there is the necropolis of Foum Larjam. The necropolis is the largest of North Africa and consists of several kilometers of tumuli and dates back to prehistoric times. It is one of the few sites where not just rock-drawings but also rock-paintings were found..

cdxxviii Palaeolithic tools have been discovered all around Ouarzazate

cdxxix These engravings were noted and reported by the officers and doctors of the French Colonial Army during operations against the Southern Ouranais ksours. Thus, in 1847 Dr F. Jacquot and Captain Koch made known the engravings at Thyout and Moghar-et-Tahtani (Flamand 1921: 14). In 1881 Captains Boucher and Tournier noted the site of El Haj Mimoun, which was studied and published by Dr E.-T. Hamy in 1882. The Col de Zenaga site was discovered in 1902 by Captain Normand. Between 1890 and 1904, G.–B.–M. Flamand, while carrying out missions for the Geological Department of the Algerian Government-General, copied and studied numerous rock art sites in the region of Figuig and In Salah (Flamand 1921). Our first heritage inventory field work, including rock art, was carried out in the Figuig district in 1999. This was followed by two more expeditions in 2002 and 2005. During these inventories we examined several rock art sites, including a painted cave. This article is limited to the study of four representative sites of the region.

cdxxx The Saharan Atlas includes a series of shorter ranges: theAmour, Ksour and Ouled-Naïl Mountains.

cdxxxi Savannas are transitional areas of slightly higher precipitation that surround and lie between deserts and the highlands and forests.

cdxxxii The main effects of the most recent desertification event in the Sahara are assumed to have been the great contraction of species distribution ranges and the associated fragmentation of populations, constituting a great challenge for the survival and regeneration of species. Biodiversity declined massively, as evidenced by fish and crocodile populations surviving in widely scattered and constantly dwindling bodies of water in the Sahara. Plants suffered the same fate

cdxxxiii Human habitation in North Africa has been greatly influenced by the climate of the Sahara, which has undergone enormous variations between wet and dry over the last few hundred thousand years. This is due to a 41,000 year cycle in which the tilt of the earth changes between 22° and 24.5°.[1] At present (2000 AD), we are in a dry period, but it is expected that the Sahara will become green again in 15000 years (17000 AD).

cdxxxiv The Canary Islands are a volcanic group of islands that includes the Azores, Madeira and the Cape Verde Islands, lying off the coast of Morocco.

cdxxxv The monuments include tumuli with long 'arms' often curving out over 300 feet, stone platforms, flat circular areas defined by small smooth stones placed side by side with a loose infilling of pebbles, crescents, circular or ellipic stone-bordered enclosures with a central corridor leading to a tumulus, and variations on all these themes. However, without excavation, it is impossible to date them, though they are clearly prehistoric.

cdxxxvi Researchers have carried out molecular genetic analysis of the Y chromosome (transmitted only by males) of the aboriginal population of the Canary Islands to determine their origin and the extent to which they have survived in the current population. The results suggest a North African origin for these paternal lineages which, unlike maternal lineages, have declined to the point of being practically replaced today by European lineages

Researchers from the University of La Laguna (ULL), the Institute of Pathology and Molecular Immunology from the University of Porto (Portugal) and the Institute of Legal Medicine from the University of Santiago de Compostela (USC) have studied the Y chromosome from human dental remains from the Canary Islands, and have determined the origin and evolution of paternal lineages from the pre-Hispanic era to the present-day.

[cdxxxvii] The situation in the Canaries is unfortunately one where ethnographic data has progressively disappeared as a consequence of the conquest and colonization of the island archipelago in the 15th century, making the interpretive study of the corpus of Canarian rock art an all the more complex and challenging undertaking. In other words, the study or approach to uncovering the meaning and or function that the engraved panels and art work held for the society that produced them, has been rendered a daunting and challenging task, always open to obfuscation and dubious interpretive reconstruction

In a thinly veiled attempt to conflate African early settlement of the Canary islands to the so-called late stage 'horse period' of rock art, eurocentric 'historians' have sought to deny the antiquity of African incursions into north isles, and most significantly (to them) the European peninsula itself – a feat generally attempted by presumptively authoritarian proclamations such as, "The Canary Islands can only be related to the African frame of reference from the *Horse* period onwards." A particularly absurd proclamation given that, for the most part, there is a virtual lack of representations of horses among the corpus of Canarian rock art. Indeed the most ancient evidence of the production of the art significantly predates the generally accepted dates for the so-called 'Saharan Horsemen Cycle', by many, many of thousands of years

[cdxxxviii] Sahara (18/2007), Farrujia de la Rosa - García Marín [Tracing of panel II.].

[cdxxxix] Aripe I and Aripe II in the Canaries and Leyuad in the South-western Sahara. Nontheless, once the groups were settled in the Canary Islands, there are several factors that not only explain the differences between Canarian and Mainland African cultures, but also those within the Canarian scenario which is, in fact, defined by the variety of its rock art, with clearly-documented differences existing between some islands.

[cdxl] The schematic anthropomorphs of panels II and III enable direct parallels to be established with those of Leyuad site (site I) in southwestern Sahara

[cdxli] The Gleib Qetba and Uad Bomba sites

[cdxlii] The geometric motifs of panels I, II, IV and V bear a clear likeness to those documented at sites located in the south of the Western Sahara

[cdxliii] Pellicer et al., 1973-1974: 28-29

[cdxliv] At Temara are a collection of prehistoric settlement sites spanning some 125 000 years, with traces of many successive settlements at the site over long periods of time. This includes a deposit base surmounted by Mousterian levels containing lithic Aterian assemblages, with many caves also occupied by the first farmers, suggesting a close relationship between the first farmers, marine resources, and the fishing clans. Next are deposits containing Ibero-Maurusian artifacts

[cdxlv] Among these sites, the smugglers cave offers a unique opportunity to study the behavior of the Aterian by combining the results of studies of their lithic industries, faunal remains and their skeletal material. Moreover, this cave offers the opportunity to date the occupation of the site using different dating techniques. More importantly, the *Smugglers Cave* offers Archaeological Ibero-Maurusians remains directly superimposed over Aterian deposits, providing opportunity to examine the much debated question of which came first. The Smugglers cave site allows us to directly compare the two industries, and examine carefully the transition within the same framework. First of all, unlike the Aterian, Ibero-Maurusians distribution appears to have been confined to a large coastal part of Morocco, Algeria and Tunisia.

[cdxlvi] It is now known that there was at least a three hundred foot rise in ocean levels at the end of the last Ice Age, suggesting the caves were carved hundreds of thousands, and perhaps a million years before the time of man.

[cdxlvii] North Africans of the era must be seriously reconsidered in the debate about the earliest occupations of the Iberian Peninsula; especially in earnest assessments of the "Out of Africa" hypotheses through the Mediterranean straits and isthmus. No truly rational argument can firmly exclude their ability to cross the waters of the narrow strait of Gibraltar.

[cdxlviii] The Iberian Peninsula is located in the extreme southwest of the European-Sub-Continent and includes modern-day states Portugal, Spain, Andorra and Gibraltar and a very small area of France. It is the westernmost of the three major southern European peninsulas—the Iberian, Italian, and Balkan peninsulas. It is bordered on the southeast and east by the Mediterranean Sea, and on the north, west and southwest by the Atlantic Ocean. The Pyrenees form the northeast edge of the peninsula, separating it from the rest of the European-Sub-Continent. In the south, it approaches the northern coast of Africa. The coast is a drowned one, with sea levels having risen from a minimum of 115 metres (377 ft) to 120 metres (390 ft) lower than today at the Last Glacial Maximum (LGM) to its current level at 4000 years BP.

[cdxlix] Journal of Archaeological Research, December 2001, Volume 9, Issue 4, pp 287-350, The Archaeology of Aquatic Adaptations: Paradigms for a New Millennium (article by Jon M. Erlandson)

[cdl] In the past it was common to think that Paleolithic developements in Iberia were influenced or caused by North African arrivals; later the opposite position became preferable to Eurocentric Historians, and thus overwhelmingly dominant, and the Gibraltar Strait was percieved more as a barrier than anything else. Today we witness some review of this paradigm, because some elements appear to exist at both sides of the strait forcing researchers and thus historians to admit some sort of contact; these include the:

- Taforalt harpoon (Magdalenian- Camps, 1974)
- Revisions of Rock Art interpretations at both sides of the straits (Balbin & Alcolea, 2005; Huyge et al, 2007)

cdli DNA evidence suggests that during the Last Glacial Maximum there was distinct gene flow from Africa into Iberia; when the Eurasian climate warmed up, the refuges of the era are thought to have been the source from which 'Europe' was repopulated. African lineages that had been introduced into the Iberian refuge would have then dispersed all over Europe with the Northward expansion of humans. This could explain the presence of genetic lineages in Eastern Europe and as far North as Russia, that appear to have prehistoric links to Northwest and West Africa. The expansion of human populations from Iberian refuges is also believed to have moved back to Northwest Africa.

cdlii However, "development" on the peninsula has destroyed many of the most ancient sites – leaving little if any record.

cdliii The North African clans practiced specialized hunting and collected local wild cereals, which led them to adopt a sedentary lifestyle.

cdliv There is a group of over 700 sites of prehistoric Rock art of the Iberian Mediterranean Basin, also known as Levantine art, were collectively declared a World Heritage Site by Unesco in 1998. The sites are in the eastern part of Spain and contain rock art dating to the Upper Paleolithic or (more likely) Mesolithic periods of the Stone Age.

cdlv Neanderthals were prehistoric humans, named after the Neander Valley not far from Dusseldorf in Germany. This area is where the first remains of an ancient humanlike skeleton were discovered in 1856. Since then more remains have been found in Europe and Asia,

cdlvi The Cave of Salemas, located in Loures Municipality, was inhabited in the Paleolithic; archaeological industries of the Middle Paleolithic in Iberia lasted until about 26,000 BC.

cdlvii Neanderthals are said to have first entered the Iberian Peninsula around 200,000 BC, during the Lower Paleolithic period. Around 70,000 BC, during the Middle Paleolithic and the last ice age the Neanderthal Mousterian culture is said to have been established in the peninsula.

cdlviii In Zafarraya a Neanderthal mandible and Mousterian tools, associated with the Neanderthal culture, were found in 1995. The mandible was dated to about 28,000 BC and the tools to about 25,000 BC. These dates make the Zafarraya remains the youngest evidence of Neanderthals and have expanded the timeline of Neanderthal existence. The more recent dating of the remains also provides the first evidence for prolonged co-existence between Neanderthals and modern man. L'Arbreda Cave in Catalonia contains Aurignacian cave paintings, as well as earlier remains from Neanderthals. Some have also suggested that the newer remains in Iberia suggest Neanderthals were driven out of Central Europe to the Iberian peninsula where they sought refuge.

cdlix Neanderthals were deemed to be a separate species after the discovery of their remains in Neandertal, Germany in 1856, though their classification as a separate species has recently been called into question

cdlx Jonathan Haws, Associate Professor with the Department of Anthropology, University of Louisville; the 2011 recipient of the Archaeology of Portugal Fellowship. His project, "The Middle-Upper Paleolithic transition in Portugal: the view from Lapa do Picareiro" examined the transition marked by Neanderthal extinction and anatomically modern human colonization of Southern Iberia, and involved excavating the cave site at *Lapa do Picareiro*. This site in central *Portugal* has intact deposits dated 10,000-45,000 years ago that encompass the transition period and allow for study of *Neanderthal* and modern human socio-ecology

cdlxi Together with France, the Iberian peninsula is one of the prime areas of Paleolithic cave paintings; found most importantly in the northern Cantabrian area

cdlxii The history of rock art on the Iberian Peninsula dates back over 32,000 years ago when the first modern humans arrived on the Peninsula.

cdlxiii The Aterian is a distinctive North African culture, which seems to have developed among these early hunter-gatherers locked into the Algerian and Moroccan Maghreb. The earliest dates for it - 120-110 thousand years ago - come from Dar es-Soltan I on the Atlantic coast of Morocco.6 In 2010 a team of archaeologists from the University of Pennsylvania discovered the skeleton of an Aterian child from 108,000 years ago in Smuggler's Cave, Temara, Morocco. The child could have been as young as six when he died. The project leader named him Bouchra, meaning good news in Arabic. Artist Viktor Deak almost seems to have brought this unique discovery back to life in his reconstruction.

cdlxiv The Côa engravings represent a fully outdoor art (with the exception of those in the Faia rock shelters).

cdlxv DNA evidence suggests that during the Last Glacial Maximum there was distinct gene flow from Africa into Iberia; when the Eurasian climate warmed up, the refuges of the era are thought to have been the source from which 'Europe' was repopulated. African lineages that had been introduced into the Iberian refuge would have then dispersed all over Europe with the Northward expansion of humans. This could explain the presence of genetic lineages in Eastern Europe and as far North as Russia, that appear to have prehistoric links to Northwest and West Africa. The expansion of human populations from Iberian refuges is also believed to have moved back to Northwest Africa.

cdlxvi A team of researchers from Harvard analyzed genetic variants in 846 people of non-African heritage, 176 people from sub-Saharan Africa, and a 50,000-year-old Neanderthal whose genome sequence the team had earlier published in 2013. Genetic variations occur when mutation causes a permanent change in the chemical structure of a gene. After carrying out their study, the Harvard team concluded that there were certain areas within the modern non-African human genome that were rich in Neanderthal DNA, while other areas were "barren."

The team found that Neanderthal ancestry was nearly absent in genes most active in the testes and genes on the X chromosome. "This suggests that when ancient humans met and mixed with Neanderthals, the two species were at the edge of biological incompatibility," said David Reich professor of genetics at HMS and senior author of the paper. Earlier research shows that Neanderthals and humans started interbreeding thousands of years ago.

cdlxvii Erik Trinkaus, Ph.D., professor of anthropology in Arts and Sciences; Trinkaus was the principal paleontologist examining the 4-year-old child's skeleton that was excavated from the Abrigo do Lagar Velho, near Leiria, Portugal, about 90 miles north of Lisbon. Trinkaus is a renowned paleontologist who has written several books and numerous articles on Neandertals and early modern humans.

cdlxviii The skeleton is the first archaeological find demonstrating characteristics of both Neandertals and early modern humans. The child's stocky trunk and short leg bones are similar to those of the Neandertals, while its prominent chin and modest-sized front teeth are similar to those of early modern humans. Other aspects of the skull and features of the arms and pelvis show a mosaic or blend of Neandertal and early modern human features, the pattern seen in individual hybrids between modern species.

cdlxix Referred to as the "Würm glaciation" in Europe

cdlxx The present-day precipitation gradient mirrors the former Pleistocene snowline gradient with precipitation levels of over 2000 mm in the Algerian Tell (Vita-Finzi, 1969, p.54), over 1000 mm at Ifrane in the Middle Atlas (Griffiths, 1972) and c. 800 mm in the High Atlas (Messerli, 1967). This is related to the effect of cool north-western air brought from eastwards-moving cyclones in the western Mediterranean; penetrating into the Atlas region where it encounters warmer air, resulting in vertical instability and the development of active depressions. This presently occurs mainly during the cool season and thus most precipitation falls during winter months (Griffiths, 1972).

cdlxxi During this period, the lower temperatures reduced the strength of the *Hadley Cell* whereby the rising tropical air of the Inter-Tropical Convergence Zone brought rain to the tropics; while dry descending air about 20 degrees north flowed back to the equator, bringing desert conditions to the Sahara.

cdlxxii The general circulation model of CLIMAP (1976) showed the Polar Front as low as northern Portugal (42°N) during the Last Glacial Maximum (LGM), remaining there until approximately 12,000 bp (Ruddiman and McIntyre, 1981; COHMAP, 1988). The occurrence of cold temperatures below 42° was also attributed by Bard et al. (1987) to the southward movement of the Polar Front

cdlxxiii The sand-dunes, salt efflorescence and deposits, and the occurrence of certain marine mollusks across the present-day terrain of the basins of the Sahara all support and give witness to the presence of a huge inland sea covering large portions of the Sahara before and during earliest antiquity.

cdlxxiv To synchronize the thirteen moons cycles of twenty-eight days (totaling 364 days), one day had to be added to synchronize to the 365 days known to comprise one year. The missing day was usually dedicated as a day for renewal and preparation for the New Year.

cdlxxv The *Boulaq Papyrus* describes him as "Lord of all, who is in all things

cdlxxvi In paraphrase of an excerpt of 'The Shape of Ancient Seas', from the 'The Sea Around Us'; by Rachel Carson [Jan. 1951]

cdlxxvii The time span of the last 130,000 years has seen the global climate system switch from warm interglacial to cold glacial conditions, and back again. This broad interglacial-glacial-interglacial climate oscillation has been recurring on a similar periodicity for about the last 900,000 years, though each individual cycle has had its own idiosyncrasies in terms of the timing and magnitude of changes

cdlxxviii The outcrops of the whole Saharan basin explain the structure of this entity, composed of two basins, namely the basin of the Western Big Erg (in Algeria) and the basin of the Eastern Big Erg (in Algeria and in Tunisia), and of a shelf called "Hamada El Hamra" (in Libya). The outcrops of the older formations can be seen on the southern and western borderlines of the basin [The secondary and tertiary sedimentation series are subject to a thickening in the middle of the two basins and on the borderline of the South – Atlas flexure].

cdlxxix Marine fossils have been found in southern Morocco and Mauritania

cdlxxx Facts suggest certain items of obsidian came via maritime trade across the inland sea and portage and barter near the *Central Highlands*.

cdlxxxi Today, some surgeons prefer to use Obsidian scalpel blades as well crafted Obsidian blades have a cutting edge that is many times sharper than the best steel surgical scalpels.

cdlxxxii Obsidian is a very, very special stone. It is not a true mineral. It is actually a volcanic glass that forms when molten lava cools too rapidly to crystallize. It consists mostly of Silicon Dioxide.

cdlxxxiii A new technique which dates obsidian suggests that people were mining for obsidian and shipping the once valuable rocks as far back as 20,000 years ago. If you wanted to have sharp tools and weapons in the days before bronze, you needed to import from regions like the Atlas.

cdlxxxiv There are deposits of gold, silver, lead, zinc, iron, manganese, antimony, phosphates and oil found throughout the Atlas mountains; some of these many deposits have been worked since earliest antiquity.

cdlxxxv Ham, also known, as Cham, Chem, Kem, Chronus, and Chronos, was reputed by the Greeks to have overseen the building of the ancient megalithc cites of North Africa, ruins of which can be found both on and offshore at Syrtis, Cyrene, and just east of Gibraltar, and some of his progeny, through a son of Posidon, Euennor, were the ancestors of the present day Tuareg tribes who now live in the mountainous desert regions of the northwest Sahara. The *Tuaregs* call their ancient ancestor Uenur, which is Euenor, son of Posidon, according to Plato.

cdlxxxvi Ruins of the ancient megalithc North African cites constructed under Khem (the legendary and fabled Ham) can be found both on and offshore at Syrtis, Cyrene, and just east of Gibraltar

cdlxxxvii Morocco, Tunis, Algeria, and Tripoli all abound in such megalithcs.

cdlxxxviii Prehistoric Desert Town Found In Western Sahara (15,000 Years Old) - RABAT (Reuters) - Thu Aug 19, 2004 (01:52 PM ET): Moroccan state media [reported that] a team of Moroccan scientists stumbled across the sand-covered ruins of the town *Arghilas* deep in the desert of the Morocco-administered territory.

cdlxxxix The transition from last glacial to Holocene in the Southern Hemisphere began before the Younger Dryas, and the maximum warmth flowed south to north from 11,000 to 7,000 years ago. An advent which appears to have been influenced by the residual glacial ice remaining in the Northern Hemisphere.

cdxc The Sub-pluvial was the most recent of the Saharan wet phases, a period during which the Sahara was moist and supported a richer biota; sometimes called the Holocene, it began immediately following the close of the last Ice Age. It is accepted by the International Commission on Stratigraphy that the period and era of the Holocene started approximately 11,700 years BP (before present); roughly 12,000 BCE.

cdxci Aside from contributing to direct sea level rise, melting (especially along the coast) can speed up glaciers, since the melt-water can percolate down to the ice-bedrock interface, acting as a lubricant between the ice and the bedrock. The faster glaciers flow, the more water enters the ocean and the greater the potential for sea level rise.

[cdxcii] The sculpturing of the earth's surface to its present form was completed during the Holocene epoch.

[cdxciii] Culmination of orbitally induced insolation maxima of the era

[cdxciv] The period referred to as the Sub-Pluvial, sometimes called the Holocene. The term Holocene means "completely recent"; referencing the present geological era. The beginning of the Holocene marked the boundary between the Pleistocene (the last Ice Age) and the recent or current era, approximately 14,000 years ago (about 12,000 BCE), and represented a distinct climatic warming phase.

[cdxcv] The satellite photos of Sahara seem to affirm the thesis that there was a gigantic inland sea in the present day central and western desert.

[cdxcvi] The most prominent feature in the recorded history of Lake Yoa is its relatively rapid transition from a seemingly stable freshwater habitat to a true salt lake in which only specialized fauna and flora can survive. Prior to about 4200 years ago, Lake Yoa was a freshwater lake. Over the next several hundred years, the lake became rapidly more saline until becoming a salt lake about 3900 years ago.

[cdxcvii] The *Tibesti* highlands contain significant quantities of Gold and Diamonds, with Emeralds found in lesser quantities. But most significantly during and after the *Sub-Pluvial*, the highly valued mineral *Natron* was extracted from geothermal pools on the westernmost volcanic mountain of the *Massif*, the *Trou au Natron*, in the northern *Chad*. This was and is the location of the *Soborom* geothermal field, a name of which means "water cure," known for its medicinal qualities, and the pools were known to cure dermatitis and rheumatism after several days of soaking. The *Natron* found in the pools is a naturally occurring mixture of sodium carbonate decahydrate, a kind of soda ash, and sodium bicarbonate,[cdxcvii] along with small quantities of sodium chloride and sodium sulfate.

Natron was harvested directly as a salt mixture from dry lake beds in the geothermal fields, and was used as a cleansing and purification product for the body. The mineral was used as an early antiseptic for wounds and minor cuts, as a cleanser for the teeth,an early mouthwash, and an ancient household insecticide. The valuable and multifaceted mineral was also used to dry and preserve fish and meat, and was used for making leather, and as a bleach for clothing. Moreover, when exposed to moisture, the carbonate in natron increases, which creates a hostile environment for bacteria, and was thought to enhance spiritual safety for both the living and the dead. The multifaceted mineral was also added to oil made from castor beans ('castor oil') to make a smokeless fuel, and thus became a valuable commodity traded and exchange along with *Obsidian* from the *Tibesti* highlands.

[cdxcviii] Tin Tartaït pottery has provided the opportunity to date the shift in pottery decoration from a rocker comb pattern, predominant among broadly contemporaneous contextsdating to the early Holocene, to the rocker bifid comb pattern, prevalent since the beginning of pastoralism (Caneva 1987)

[cdxcix] Vandals have destroyed prehistoric rock art in lawless southern Libya, endangering a sprawling tableau of paintings and carvings classified by UNESCO as of "outstanding universal value."

[d] These are an archaic tradition depicting wild animals whose antiquity is unknown but certainly goes back well before 10,000 B.C.; engravings of animals such as the extinct giant buffalo are among the earliest works, followed later by paintings in which color is used to depict humans and animals with striking naturalism

[di] Like many other areas of the Sahara, the large flagship antelopes of the Ahaggar, notably Addax and Dama Gazelle, are believed to have become extinct. Important species such as Dorcas Gazelle, Barbary Sheep and particularly the elusive Saharan Cheetah are still present, and although seldom seen, are attracting renewed interest (Hamdine et al. 2003).

[dii] Ancient writers, such as Diodorus Siculus, who mentions the tribes of "Atlantis" are clearly referring to the native tribes of North-West Africa, in the vicinity of the Atlas mountain range. Some ancient Greek and Roman writers describe this continental region as the largest of the "islands."

[diii] Tree-dominated vegetation types on the Canary Islands include Canarian pine woodland, thermophilous forest, Canarian palm, Canarian willow and monteverde forest (del Arco *et al.* 2010): the latter being one of the most biologically distinct ecosystems in Macaronesia.

[div] Four major rivers are evident which once flowed across the *Saharan-Atlas Steppes*, visibly prominent though now extinct, these rivers are seen on most maps, referred to as present day '*Oued Namous*', '*Oued Rharbi*', '*Oued Seggur*', and '*Oued Mehaiguene*'.

[dv] Atlantis (1st Edition); Circumstantial evidence by Michael Hubner Published 2008 by antimony Publisher [ISBN-13: 978-3-9812150-0-7, ISBN: 3-9812150-0-1]

[dvi] The legendary Zingh Empire which, according to historians and anthropologists, was centered in present day Mauritania, and covered much of West Africa, the Southern Sahara, the Sahel and the bordering tropics, and was the first culture and civilization to build an international empire. The Zingh Empire is also said to have established the red, black and green flag, which are still the colors of Africa and many Middle Eastern nations. (Blisshords Communications, Zingh Empire, "Mobetter News," The History of the African Standard, South Holland, Illinois.).

[dvii] The Pitt Rivers Museum (PRM) holds an assorted range of post-Stone Age and Holocene era archaeological materials from the Cape Verde Islands.

[dviii] The Buache map of 1737 said to be the result of copying an ancient Greek map, which in turn is believed to have been copied from a map originating in the library in ancient Alexandria.

[dix] The name "Ham" orignated as a Hebrew name. The name first occurs in Genesis 5:32, where, as in 6:10 and elsewhere, it occupies the second place. The name has been translated to mean "to be black," supported by evidence of the Hebrew (and Arabic) word "chamam"

which means "to be hot" and "to be black,"

Since Noach's curse of the "dark" Cham was often used to justify the chattel slavery of blacks, it is not surprising that many modern scholars and writers have challenged the proposition inferred by this literal translation, including the etymology. For example, in the 2003 book "The Curse of Ham" by David M. Goldenberg, in which he dedicataes a large number of pages discussing and attempting to dissuade the issue.

Wherein he notes: "A derivation of Ham (ham) from kmt 'Egypt', also seemed like a good choice despite the differences between the first and last letters of the two words, and scholars until about a generation ago entertained the notion that Ham was a Hebraized form of this Egyptian word for "Egypt..".Not only Coptic documents provide us this information, but Plutarch (d. after 120 CE) does too. He noted that the Egyptians called Egypt "Chemia." With the loss of the final t and the realization of k as kh or the Greek [chi], the word looked very much like the biblical Ham. This theory too had more than phonology on its side. First, from a political-geographic perspective, the extent of Egypt's rule during the New Kingdom is neatly circumscribed by the four areas that the Bible allocates to Ham's sons..."

However, he clearly rejects the theory: "Despite the attractions of the various theories, however, not one of these etymological suggestions is acceptable." He goes on to advance an argument which includes the fact that the Hebrew letter chet "is not transliterated at all or is transliterated by a vowel" in Greek - as in Noach נח becoming "Noah."

He concludes: "One thing is, however, absolutely clear. The name Ham is not related to the Hebrew or to any Semitic word meaning "dark," "black," or "heat" or to the Egyptian word meaning "Egypt." To the Early Hebrews, then, Ham did not represent the father of hot, black Africa and there is no indication from the biblical story that God intended to condemn black-skinned people to eternal slavery."

However, one person who noted that there might be a connection between "Cham" and "Khemia" was Yitzhak Avineri. In a 1945 article published in Yad HaLashon (page 202), he complains about how recently the spelling of the Hebrew word for chemistry - chimiya - has changed from חימיה (with a chet) to כימיה (with a kaf). While the linguist pushing for the change base it on the Arabic cognate al-kimiya, he gives two proofs: 1) that chimiya might originate either in the chum (dark) color of the Nile soil, or be related to Cham, and 2) everyone pronounces the word chimiya, not kimiya. If it was to be spelled with a kaf, it would require a dagesh in the beginning, making it kimiya (my guess is the pronunciation is influenced by those of European languages, such as the Russian khimiya.) Avineri quotes a couple of dictionaries that still spell the word with a chet, but the new spelling won out, and only כימיה is found today.

Goldenberg's argument that "the Hebrew letter "chet" 'is not transliterated at all or is transliterated by a vowel' in Greek" appears to clearly fail on the facts. Sometimes that it is true, as with נח (νωε) and יצחק (Ισαακ); but other times it is indeed transliterated with a "chi," as in רחל

[dx] See the present day archaeological site known as "Baalbek"

[dxi] Mainstream archaeology has different points of view when it comes to the exact age of the site. The truth is, the exact age remains a mystery, but some researchers consider this ancient megalithic site as being at least 12.000 years old but could be over 20,000 years old.

[dxii] The Greeks, too young to have shared in the religion of Atlantis, but preserving some memory of that great country, proceeded to convert its kings into gods, and to depict Atlantis as the heaven of the human race." "It is not necessary to pursue the study of the gods of Greece any farther. They were simply barbarian recollections of the rulers of a great civilized people who in early days visited their shores and brought with them the arts of peace. (Excerpted from: Atlantis, the Antediluvian World" by Ignatius Donnelly; Harper. New York, 1882)

[dxiii] Diodorus tells how a great king there, renowned as an astrologer, called Atlas, named the whole region and the sea. Diodorus Siculus (c. 90-21 BC) was born in Agyrium, Sicily; he travelled extensively through Europe and Asia gathering information that was incorporated in his *Bibliotheca Historica*, a work of forty books divided into three parts; unfortunately, only the first five books are extant. He quotes extensively from an earlier historian *Skytobrachion*. Nonetheless in the surviving remnants of his work Diodorus makes a number of references to 'Atlantis'; he calls the land bordered by the Atlantic and surrounded by the Atlas Mountains, 'Atlantis', which would be modern Morocco.

[dxiv] It is at least worth noting that the very names of Khem, Poseidon, Atlas, even the mythical name "Atlantis" itself, have no etymology in the Indo-European languages

[dxv] The "Atlantis" legend was originally translated from ancient Khemetian texts by *Sonchis,* an aging priest of ancient Khemet, to Solon an ancient Greek statesman, in the ancient sacred city of Sais (in the Nile delta) at a temple dedicated to the goddess Neith

[dxvi] It was from Ausar ("Kush") that the land of *Kush* derived its name. This ancient land ultimately came to apply to the full west-east extent of the Ancient Sudan (encompassing the present day Sahel, from the coast of the Atlantic Ocean in the west, to the coast of the Red Sea the east); and was also generally associated with Saba (in Ancient Yemen), Sumer (where Ausar ("Kush") fathered Nimrod (Gen. 10:8; 1 Chr. 1:10)), and Elam (Ancient Persia).

[dxvii] Osiris also left writings on bronze and copper, which were excavated in the 1950s by a young British archaeologist, called Thurstan Shaw. But Shaw, either not perhaps know what he had or because of the colonial conspiracy to keep Africans backward, did not reveal that Igbo Ukwu was in fact a prehistoric a city of the Atlatian age.

[dxviii] New Evidence for a Large Prehistoric Settlement in a Caldera-Like Geomorphological Structure in Southwest Morocco; by Michael and Sebastian Huebner (Version 6, February 1, 2012); The expeditions took place 10-16 September 2008, 19-29 May 2010 and 22 November - 2 December 2011.

[dxix] The reason being that the stone grinding mill companies had just started to demolish the large detached debris field which this ruin was part of.

[dxx] According to Edwards (2007) incised Wavy Line pottery is "'found across much of Sudanic and Saharan Africa (Sutton (1977)) and is some of the oldest pottery in the world, with radiocarbon dates as early as 8000 BC.

[dxxi] Many have obvious attributes of prehistory, but only after a thorough archaeological investigation can we be sure of their age.

[dxxii] For example, in September 2008, the researchers could photograph the remains of an unusual large circular stone construction in the

central area of the settlement. In May 2010, none of the large stone plates that once formed this monument were left over.

dxxiii Unfortunately, the entire site is subject to massive destruction. The authors spotted illicitexcavations and two large hydrotechnical constructions that date back to the 1960s. Moreover,the area is used as quarry by the local building industry which every day is carryingaway hundreds of large stones. In fact, the area is exploited because there are so many nicelarge stone slabs to be found. [Excerpted from: New Evidence for a Large Prehistoric Settlement in a Caldera-Like Geomorphological Structure in Southwest Morocco; by Michael and Sebastian Huebner (Version 6, February 1, 2012)]

dxxiv The Carthaginians, built on top of these ancient megalithic walls and foundations of the prehistoric city, and occupied the ancient port around 800 B.C. Serious work needs to be done to date the prehistoric ruins and culture which initially built here; yet even today the prehistoric ruins of Lixus remain to be examined.

dxxv Much of the damage was done by excavations undertaken in 1935-6 by César Luis de Montalban

dxxvi The only professional survey of the site was conducted in the 1970s by James Watt Mavor, Junior of the Woods Hole Oceanographic Institute in Massachusetts, USA. It is this survey that revealed Mzora to be not only remarkable in its own right but to have implications for the history of megalithic sites in Britain. Mzora, incredibly, appears to have been constructed either by the same culture that erected the megalithic sites in France, Britain and Ireland or by one that was intimately connected with them. The ellipse is constructed using a Pythagorean right angled triangle of the ratio 12, 35, 37. This same technique was used in the construction of British stone ellipses of which 30 good examples survive including the Sands of Forvie and Daviot rings. Of the use of Pythagorean triangles in British sites Professor Alexander Thom remarked: "The remarkable thing is that the largest, the 12, 35, 37, was known and exploited more than any other with the exception of the 3, 4, 5." Thom, Alexander (1967). Megalithic Sites in Britain.[dxxvi]

dxxvii Balbín & Tejera, 1983

dxxviii Farrujia & García, 2005

dxxix Muñoz, 1994; González et al., 1995

dxxx The president of the Portuguese Association of Archeological Research (APIA), Nuno Ribeiro, revealed having found rock art on the island of Terceira, supporting his belief that human occupation of the Azores predates the arrival of the Portuguese by many thousands of years, Lusa reported. "We have found a rock art site with representations we believe can be dated back to the Bronze Age," Ribeiro told Lusa in Ponta Delgada, at a presentation in University of the Azores on the topic of early human occupation of the Azores.

"In some cases, we believe that there are temples and hypogea. We have no doubt that there are sanctuaries," he said, remarking that data still needs to be dated. Ribeiro also said that the archeological research findings in the Azores have been published in scientific articles and presented at international conferences on archeology, and have received "great acceptance among the international scientific community." Ribeiro has alleged before that the time of human settlement in the Azores may not be what history says, but a different one based on the archeological evidence found on the archipelago recently.

dxxxi Given the situation in the Canaries, where ethnographic data progressively disappears as a consequence of the conquest and colonization of the archipelago in the 15th century, it is possible to understand how complex the interpretive study of Canarian rock art becomes. In other words, the study or approach to the meaning or function that the engraved panels contained for the society that generated them is certainly a daunting task

In a thinly vailed attempt to conflate the African settlement of the Canary islands to the late stage 'horse period' of rock art, eurocentic 'historians' seek to deny the antiquity of African incursions into the north isles, and most significantly (to them) eurasia itself – this is attempted by 'authoritarian proclimations such as "The Canary Islands can only be related to the African frame of reference from the (late) Horse period onwards"; particularly given that, to a great extent, there is a the virtual non-existence of representations of horses in the Canarian rock engravings

They state or further infer that the' rock art sites of Risco Blanco, Aripe I and Aripe II documented inTenerife are related to the so-called Saharan Horsemen Cycle and can(only) be related to the rock art sites documented for this period in the south-west of Morocco, Western Sahara and the north of present-day Mauritania, that is to say, in the Saharan area closest to the Canaries. TheRisco Blanco site. Nonetheless, the most ancient evidence of the production of the rock art in the Canaries clearly and conclusively predates their generally accepted "earliest dates" for the appearance of both the subject art, and "modern humans."

dxxxii The northwest end is affected by rockslides, and from the point of view of conservation, the site is not well-preserved due to local environmental conditions; the fracture and falling of large rocks, as a result of changes in humidity, temperature, intense exposure to the sun and precipitation has meant that some panels are partially covered by rockslides

dxxxiii In 1991, the Archaeology Department of La Laguna University carried out the first excavations and the Canary Islands' Astrophysical Institute looked into possible ancient astronomical relationships. These studies revealed that the pyramids were aligned to the winter and summer solstices. Carefully built stairways on the west side of each pyramid lead up to the summit, which is not a pile of stones, but a perfectly flat platform covered with gravel, as though for ceremonial performances and/or sun worship. The stones were not weather-worn, rounded boulders, but sharp fragments of lava, and some of the corner stones had been trimmed. Despite many archaeological excavations on the pyramids, their age has never been determined.

dxxxiv Referencing a relatively recent presentation by Nuno Ribeiro at the University of the Azores, on the topic of early human occupation of the Azores. Ribeiro also said that the archeological research findings in the Azores have been published in scientific articles and presented at international conferences on archeology, and have received "great acceptance among the international scientific community." Ribeiro has alleged before that the time of human settlement in the Azores may not be what history says, but a different one based on the archeological evidence found on the archipelago recently.

dxxxv Archaeologists from the Portuguese Association of Archaeological Research (APIA) have identified new archaeological evidence on Pico island that supports their belief that human occupation of the Azores predates the arrival of the Portuguese by many thousands of years.

dxxxvi   Portuguese news sites are reporting on the discovery of a man-made (sub-aquatic) pyramid between the islands of São Miguel and Terceira in the Azores. The underwater pyramidal structure was found by a private yacht owner, Diocleiano Silva, who spotted the strange shaped object on sonar at a depth of 40 metres while sailing in the area; He says his find may be a remnant of the legendary lost world of Atlantis, which sank into the ocean. Silva found the pyramid around five months ago while fishing on his yacht in the area. He discovered the structure through bathymetric navigation and its tip is submerged around 40ft. The Portuguese Hydrographic Institute of the Navy is currently analysing the data to determine whether it is in fact man-made or not.

dxxxvii   A Russian submarine under the command of Nikolai Seleznev

dxxxviii   The wall was first discovered in 1974 by a diver while he was spearfishing; the wall has since been photographed and further investigated.

dxxxix   Dr. J. Thorne, a marine archaeologist observed and investigated the wall.

dxl   The name Mogador appeared for the first time in the world map of Medici in 1357 (a name originating from the Phoenician word 'Migdol', meaning a 'small fortress'), and later on a map designed by Pizzigani in 1367, when the Portuguese called it "Mogadouro" and the Spanish called it "Mogadour" (Mogador). The name Essaouira originated from when the Sultan Sidi Mohammed Ben Abdallah renewed the on the island city and called it Souira (Souera) in 1767.

dxli   A Greek term meaning "large stone"

dxlii   These megaliths come in several forms, most of them originally tombs that were once covered in earthen mounds that have eroded over time to leave stone.

dxliii   The presence of the megaliths greatly influenced the native hunting and fishing tribes in north-central Europe, such as the Ertebølle-Ellerbek of Scandinavia and Germany, who, in turn, developed the "*Corded Ware*" culture, often mistakenly associated with Indo-European tribes (whose earliest arrivals didn't reach the area until over six thousand years later).

dxliv   In the North-West of the *Souss-Massa* plain a large circular caldera-like geomorphologic structure has been discovered that is of major archaeological interest. This structure fits the dimensions of Plato's capital of Atlantis and is covered with hundreds of large and small prehistoric ruins of different types. The caldera-like annular geomorphological structure is located 8 km east of Agadir in a landscape called Tagragra. It is situated between the shore of the Atlantic Ocean, the Souss River and the western Atlas Mountains.

Inside the annular geomorphological structure and on the surrounding hills, hundreds of stone constructions of different types are present. We found large numbers of ruined buildings, caverns, cisterns, paths, stone heaps and traces of agricultural landscaping.

For the most part, the buildings were found in the central area of the annular structure. In many cases, the researchers observed that on top of solid, thick and accurately formed foundation walls, new walls were built; usually, the new walls were very inaccurately made and stones of the old walls were recycled to built them.

Basic features of ruined buildings are: (1) Foundation walls were accurately manufactured and very solid; (2) Foundation walls are covered by large amounts of debris; (3) Both large and small stones were used; (4) Oval, circular and triangular ground plans are present; (5) Fewer rectangular ground plans are present (some of these seem to be recent, but may have been built on top of earlier walls). A remarkable stone circle complex was once located in the very center of the central area. The complex has been entirely destroyed by stone grinding mills, however historical images could still be seen on (before 2009).

The central circular structure A has had a diameter of about 50m and the entire complex measured 130m x 110m. Inside the central circular structure, several caverns and stone heaps are situated. In 2008, we were able to photograph some of the last large stone plates of the central circular structure still present at that time. In May 2010, none of these plates were leftover.

dxlv   This is the same approximate time Plato suggests a "bountiful plains of a garden island paradise" fitting the description of the high plateau between the Saharan Atlas and the Tell Atlas was ruled by the offspring of Poseidon, the mythical first king of Atlatia. These four rivers descending the highland which Plato describes were connected by a perimeter canal near the sea surrounding the rectangular and oblong plain.

dxlvi   In recent years what has previously been known as " Oranian" has been increasingyy referred to as ¨Ibero-Maurusian"; a term that clearly does not follow the standard practice of naming an archaeological industry after a site at which it has been recognized and described, and it carries the undue and unwarranted implication of connection between Africa and the Iberian peninsula. The original terminology and term 'Eastern Oranian' (herein referred to as 'Northern Oran'), known also at other Libyan sites such as Hagfet et Tera, takes its name from its apparent close similarity to the industry of the present day Maghreb, farther to the west. This 'Oranian' industry was widespread in the North African coastland and hinterland from south of Rabat, as far east as Tunis (Camps 1974, 1975).

Oranian occurrences are those located in Morocco and Algeria; at Tamar Hat on the coast of eastern Algeria (an occupation dated as early as 20,000 to 16,000 years ago), and is attributed to this industry (Saxon et al. 1974; see also J. Roche 1971). The industries designated Oranian and Eastern Oranian (the latter herein referred to as 'Northern Oran') are restricted to zones of Mediterranean vegetation along the North African littoral, in the present day Maghreb and Cyrenaica; being interrupted only at the Gulf of Sirte, where desert conditions extend almost to the shore. At the time when these industries were active sea levels were significantly lower than at present, and their distribution may have been continuous across the coastal plain that was then exposed.

dxlvii   The ancient Libya known to Plato was a separate entity to Atlatia.

dxlviii   In Critias, Plato claims that his accounts of ancient Athens and "Atlantis" stem from a visit to Egypt by the legendary Athenian lawgiver Solon in the 6th century BC. In Egypt, Solon met a priest of Sais, who translated the history of ancient Athens and "Atlantis," recorded on papyri in Egyptian hieroglyphs, into Greek.

dxlix   Compared with the history of Khemet (Egypt), historians know little about the history of ancient Cyrenaica (Libya), as there are few surviving written records. The name Libya has been in use since 1934, prior to which the region was known as "Tripolitania" and "Barca," the Latin designation(s) for the region of Northwest Africa, from the Greek (Ancient Greek: Λιβύē Libúē, Λιβΰā Libúā, in the Attic and Doric dialects respectively). The Greek name is based on the ethnonym Libu (Ancient Greek: Λίβυες Líbues, Latin: Libyes). The land of the Libu was Λιβύη (Libúē) andΛιβΰā (Libúā) in the Attic and Doric dialects, respectively. The people they referred to as the "Libu" (descendents of the ancient Atlatians; ancestors of the present day Black Berbers) have been attested (by the late arriving Europeans) as inhabiting the region since the Late Bronze Age.

Homer referred to the region in the Odyssey (IX.95; XXIII.311); Homer used the name in a geographic sense, while he called its inhabitants "Lotophag," meaning "Lotus-eaters." After Homer, Aeschylus, Pindar, and other Ancient Greek writers use the old name when the Greeks settled in the region; the old name, "Cyrenaica" was taken from the Egyptians by the Greeks when they co-existed in the region with those referred to as the "Libu." The oldest historical references to the" Libu" dates to Ramesses II and his successor Merneptah, Egyptian rulers of the nineteenth dynasty, during the 13th century BCE. ("Libu" appears as an ethnic name on the Merneptah Stele). Cyrene was colonized by ancient Greeks from the island of Therea around 630 B.C

[dl] A recent tact of Eurocentric theorists is to conflate latter stage mitochondrial DNA occurrences on the isle of Crete with earlier, founder stage DNA, essentially to assert that the founders of Crete were "Proto-European"; or, more aptly, "Neolithic humans from the regions of Anatolia that today comprise parts of Turkey" (with the inference that they were progenitors of modern Europeans). Purporting that recent mitochondrial DNA analysis shows that the Minoans' strongest genetic relationships are with these Neolithic humans, as well as with ancient and modern Europeans, and further that these results suggest that Minoan civilization arose 5,000 years ago in Crete, from an ancestral Neolithic population that arrived in the region about 4,000 years earlier (approximately 7,000 BC).

Though the author of this treatise is admittedly not an expert on the subject, researched and available informed analysis of mitochondrial DNA occurrences on Crete reveals that of the 57 J2-DYS413 chromosomes on the island, a total of nine chromosomes are derived at J2a1h-M319. A mutation that has been discovered in two Moroccan (ancient Atlatia) chromosomes, and one Iraqi (ancient Sumer (founded / inhabited by descendent Kushites; ancestors of "Nimrod" who "was the son of Kush")) chromosomes, and has not been reported in any other population. The analysis notes that seven out of the nine Cretan M319-derived chromosomes have the (CA)16-(CA)18 genotype at the DYS413 microsatellite marker, a pattern that was not observed in any other DYS413-derived lineage. A prominent frequency of DYS413 (CA)16-(CA)18 chromosomes in Crete, particularly in the prefecture of Chania, was detected in the past, and attributed to a founder effect on the island.

It appears from this analysis and results that the "founder effect" is associated with the introduction or origin in Crete of the J2a1h-M319 mutation, and it significantly notes that J2a-M410 was scarce. And further, alternatively, that Crete, like Anatolia shows a high frequency of J2a-M410, and a low frequency of J2b-M12, and that both are YDNA, which, in essence, discloses the inherent flaw in the premise presented by the Eurocentric theorist: Jumping back and forth between MtDNA and YDNA to support a predisposed and errant conclusion; which suggest, if not proves, that each incremental part of their entire argument is similarly flawed.

In addition, there are several other serious objections that can be raised to their hypothesis. Among the most noteworthy being that the DNA tests were performed on "Lasithi Minoans"; it is pertinent to note that following the founding and habitation of the (original) Neolithic and descendent Atlatians, referred to as "Minoans" (a term coined by 19th century British archaeologist, Arthur Evans (after King Minos of Knossos)), the Dorians, one of four major ancient Greek tribes, later inhabited the Lasithi Plateau; which has been continuously inhabited (by non-North Africans) since that time. Further underscoring the point, the DNA testing itself showed that the inhabitants of the graves (tested) were "very closely related" to the "current inhabitants" of the Lasithi Plateau. Based on this inherent flaw in this methodology (i.e., testing clearly latter stage Lasithi Cretan populations), attempts to purport ancient ancestry of the Bronze Age Cretans on said basis, quite frankly, lacks merit, and derives conclusions that are clearly fallacious.

Further underscoring the point is the notion advanced by the theorist that "the first Neolithic inhabitants reached Crete from regions of Anatolia" (Asia Minor of the era), "about 9,000 years ago." This would be approximately 7,000 BCE, at least 2,000 years after the established date of the remains of the settlement found under the Bronze Age palace at the ancient city of Knossos (layer X); which dates to before 9,000 B.C. Additionally confounding is absence of the development or use of Neolithic boats, ships, or anything resembling a contemporary maritime reservoir of experience, or navigational history to infer sufficient knowledge to ply the open seas from Asia Minor to the island of Crete; a distance of hundreds of nautical miles on the open seas.

And finally, at ancient Çatalhöyük, reputedly the most advanced of the Neolithic sites in Anatolia, existing from approximately 7,500 BC to 5,700 BC, and flourishing around 7,000BC; according to a recent Executive Summary by the Republic of Turkey, Çatalhöyük was composed of mudbrick houses, densely packed together, where all walls were "constructed of unbaked mud-brick." Further noting that "generally every building had its own four walls, although during the early sequences there was more use of party walls between buildings." And "the feeling is of an organic, cellular agglomeration of buildings over time, rather than a unified planned layout." A more than significant distinction (notwithstanding the fraudulent mythological stories presented by James Mellaart, who first excavated the site in 1958), when compared to the level of contemporary architectural planning and development at the City of Knossos, on Crete. Given the foregoing, the notion that "the first Neolithic inhabitants reached Crete from Anatolia about 9,000 years ago," seems purely untenable and borders on the absurd.

[dli] Referencing the book "Myths of Crete & Pre-Hellenic Europe," By Donald A. Mackenzie (1917); however, it should be noted that in excerpts and paraphrases taken from the book by Dr.. Mackenzie, like all Eurocentric writers of history, he struggles to tell Black history, without actually mentioning Black people. As an example "Pre-Hellenic" actually means "Pre-Whites" as the Hellenes were the first of the White Central Asians to reach Western Europe. But since many of his factual observations are accurate, these excerpts from his book have been included.

[dlii] Arthur Evans, a 19th century British archaeologist, named the people who built this civilization 'Minoans' after the legendary Minos, the King of Knossos. Evans also suggested that the founders of the Minoan civilization were refugees from the Delta region of Egypt when North Egypt was conquered by the Southern king Narmer (Menes of ancient historians) at about 5,000 YBP, ; his evidence were the similarities between Minoan and Egyptian art and elements he was considering Libyan in origin, such as the cod piece worn by Bronze Age Cretans and the circular tombs of the early inhabitants of Southern Crete that were similar to tombs built by the Libyans.

dliii   Long after the Atlatians, their descendents (and eventually others from diverse areas of North Africa) reached the shores of the Southern European mainland, the later arriving Pagan-Greeks came to referr to them (collectively) as "Pelasgians". According to the mythology of these early Greeks, the first man was Pelasgus--ancestor of the Pelasgians. Though in actuality the so-called "Pelasgians" were a combination of different Black tribes (the Greeks called Achaeans, Cadmeans, Leleges, and Carians or Garamantes); the earlier arriving North Africans, or "Pelasgians" had theretofore occupied all the Aegean Islands and much of the mainland

dliv   Historical traditions of these and earlier time are shrouded in mystery, because they have in large measure been redacted by the purportedly priestly colleges of ancient Europe, where they were, in effect, changed into miraculous legends, in which the historical figures from antiquity were dogmatically defined as "Gods." In this way their history became mythical, and theological; thus those looking in the ancient legends for symbolisms, or personifications of the elementary forces, are deluded. In pre-historical antiquity, the thoughts and acts of humankind were dominated by real facts, not all of these "mythologies"

It was in this way that the kings of antiquity, who had lived mortal lives, began to be called "Gods," and they became the heads of ancient religion As soon as the "divine nature" of these kings – who had put the first foundations of human civilization in place – had been proclaimed, their epoch began to darken. Historical traditions were thus redacted by the so-called "priestly colleges" of ancient Europe, and, in effect, changed into "miraculous legends."

dlv   In the absence of written historical records, evidence of the proto-Thracians in the prehistoric period depends on remains of material culture. If, as some scholars believe, they were intermingling with the people who inhabited Bulgarian lands since the most ancient of times, they presumably exchanged knowledge, and their wisdom swelled as they incorporated the skills, practices, and information of other cultures.

Bulgarian archaeology has thus played a major role in the effort to uncover and preserve Thracian heritage; these efforts are unfortunately in constant competition with looters and the traffic in historical artifacts. "Bulgarian Scholars (Alexander Fol, Ivan Marazov, Elka Penkova) suggest that the Thracians were part of the larger Pelasgian' group of peoples, due, primarily, to observed parallels between ancient Thracian and Minoan cultures." The Bulgarians retain many remnants from Thracian time, and have a significant Thracian heritage. Thracian civilization geographically coincides predominantly with modern Bulgaria and it's quite popular to hold that Bulgarians are the overwhelming descendants of the Thracians.

In archaeological terms, evidence of civilization in Bulgarian lands date back thousands of years. - "The history of Bulgaria spans from the first settlements on the lands of modern Bulgaria to its formation as a nation-state and includes the history of the Bulgarian people and their origin. The earliest human remains discovered on what is today Bulgaria date from 44,000 BC. Around 5000 BC, a sophisticated civilization already existed and produced some of the first pottery and jewelry in the world. In Provadia (Bulgaria) the oldest prehistoric city in Europe, dated between 4,700 BC and 4,200 BC, a fortified settlement of 350 inhabitants.

According to a foremost authority in Romanian early history, namely the professor Nicolae Densusianu, an ancient Pelasgian population once "constructed" what is considered as pre-historical Europe's largest and strongest Empire, by enlarging its boundaries to as far as Norway's mountains. They didn't leave, unfortunately, anything behind in written form, in order to prove their glorious past, with the exception of some ruins and stones full of weird scribbles, about which nobody has ever thought to see whether any of these might actually bear a hidden meaning, or not.

One fact remains, yet, for sure: through centuries of running across the vast European plains, until their culture and language became, finally, widespread, the Pelasgians or Thracians, you choose to name them, were too slowly generate afterwards "Latin culture and civilization," a fundamental basis for the upcoming expansion of the Roman Empire... As always, behind an universally-acknowledged great historic culture is to be found another one, going usually unobserved or in the former's shadow, becoming forgotten, neglected or simply ignored.

dlvi   Around 9,000 BC the Black Sea was not the sea we know today; it was then a substantially smaller fresh-water lake, and the surrounding land areas was much broader

dlvii   Europe was inhabited by indigenous peoples during distant ancient ages when the region passed through several stages of climatic oscillations of such pronounced character that the remains of these peoples are found in strata yielding alternately tropical, temperate, and arctic flora and fauna. The period in question, the lengthiest in the history of the region, is the archaeological Paleolithic (or Early Stone Age). Towards its close, for which the minimum dating is 20,000 B.C., there existed in Europe at least two indigenous groups of people, whose cultures are referred to as Aurignacian and Magdalenian.

A stage called Azilian links this period with the Neolithic Age, and the continuity of these ancient cultures, from the earliest times, is now generally regarded as an established fact. The links with Crete are so close and suggestive that writers like Angelo Mosso have expressed the belief in the Neolithic and Cretan origin of Aurignacian and Magdalenian art. "The resemblances," writes Mosso, "between the most ancient female figures in France and the Neolithic figures of Crete are very striking." He also comments in another instance on the skirts, which were also characteristic of Crete.

Use by the expeditions from Crete of the discussed river valley and overland trade routes through the regions occupied by these cultures significantly pre-date the so-called "Aryan invasions" (which should more aptly be termed the "Caucasian invasions") of Europe. The Danube Valley Civilization, which arose along and in the wake of these remote Neolithic trade routes was, essentially, populated by the pre-invasion indigenous peoples inhabiting the confines of Southeastern Europe (and surrounding areas); with said Civilization beginning somewhere between 7,000 – 6,200 BC, and reaching its peak was between 3,500BC and 3,000 BC; the civilization fell into decline with the arrival of the Indo European speaking people from Eastern Europe.

dlviii   The resemblance of the idols of Crete and those of Europe is a well established fact; the evolution of art in Southern France and in Spain also went on during this era of the Neolithic, and we know that navigation was general on the Mediterranean in the times preceding the introduction of copper

dlix   Quoted in the book 'Myths of Crete & Pre-Hellenic Europe'; By Donald A. Mackenzie (1917) It should be noted that Angelo

Mosso also favoured the hypothesis that Crete's early supplies came from England; "We know the road," he says, "followed by the caravans bringing English tin through France to the mouth of the Rhone at the end of the Neolithic period"

[dlx] Referring to the Book of Going Forth by Day (commonly known as the 'Egyptian Book of the Dead') and the Pyramid Texts (among others)

[dlxi] See "Atlantis: the Myth, by Alan G. Hefner

[dlxii] A growing number of enterprising geologists are beginning to embrace analytical mythology as a tool in their search for field evidence of natural cataclysmic events that may have occurred in ancient history and prehistory. This fledgling field is called geomythology, in which comprehensive research and investigations begin by asking and seeking plausible answers to provocative questions concerning common interpretation of the most popular and well known of myths; such as the myth of a sunken island transcribed by Plato. The Greek to English translations of Plato's Critias and Timaeus dialogues used in the subject study are those of Benjamin Jowett (1871).

To answer the pertinent questions the researchers' first look at a geophysics model of the general area Plato described, to gain an understanding of the tectonic forces that could have been the source of the seismic action associated with the catastrophe. And, with this geophysics model as a template, they then followed the virtual map Plato left behind (in similar fashion to the method in which Homer's descriptions were followed by Heinrich Schliemann for Troy, and Robert Bittlestone for Ithaca) to locate the site known to the Greeks as "Atlantis" and to the early Pre-Dynastic Egyptians as "Bakhu of Zep Tepi." [see Atlantis: the Myth, by Alan G. Hefner]

Fortuitously, according to a study, released January 3, 2014 by the Earth Sciences Department at the University of Southern California (USC), a team of scientists researched and eventually created a new model revealing that the Atlas Mountains are actually floating on a layer of hot molten rock flowing beneath the lithosphere, the Earth's most rigid outer layer. The study, published in Geology and highlighted in Nature Geoscience, shows that the molten rock might encompassed an area as far away as the volcanic Canary Islands, just off the coast of Northwestern Africa. "Our findings confirm that mountain structures and their formation are far more complex than previously believed," said Meghan Miller, assistant professor of Earth sciences at the USC Dornsife College of Letters, Arts and Sciences.

In much the same way a tall iceberg doesn't simply float on the surface of the water, but is supported by a large submerged mass of ice, a well-established model of the lithosphere suggests that the height of the Earth's crust must be supported by a commensurate depth. Earth scientists call this property "istostacy." "The Atlas Mountains are at present out of balance, likely due to a confluence of existing lithospheric strength anomalies and deep mantle dynamics," Thorsten Becker, professor of Earth sciences at USC Dornsife, said.

To measure the thickness of the lithosphere beneath the Atlas Mountains in Morocco, the scientists used 15 seismometers to analyze 67 distinct seismic events. This allowed the team to use the Earth's vibrations to "see" into the deep subsurface. Miller and Becker found that while the Atlas Mountains reach heights of over 13,000 feet, the crust beneath only reaches a depth of around 22 miles. This is about 9 miles shy of traditional model predictions. "This study shows that deformation can be observed through the entire lithosphere and contributes to mountain building even far away from plate boundaries" Miller said.

The timing and effects of the mountain building on other geological processes will now be the focus of further research in Miller's lab. Moroccan mountains float on superhot rock, study finds by Robert Perkins (January 2, 2014). The Atlas Mountains defy the standard model for mountain structure in which high topography must have deep roots for support, according to a new study from USC scientists. In a new model, the researchers show that the mountains are floating on a layer of hot molten rock that flows beneath the region's lithosphere, perhaps all the way from the volcanic Canary Islands, just offshore northwestern Africa.

"Our findings confirm that mountain structures and their formation are far more complex than previously believed," said lead author Meghan Miller, assistant professor of Earth sciences at the USC Dornsife College of Letters, Arts and Sciences. The study, co-authored by Thorsten Becker, professor of Earth sciences at USC Dornsife, was published by Geology on Jan. 1 and highlighted by Nature Geoscience. A well-established model for the Earth's lithosphere suggests that the height of the Earth's crust must be supported by a commensurate depth, much like how a tall iceberg doesn't simply float on the surface of the water but instead rests on a large submerged mass of ice. This property is known as "Isostasy."

" "The Atlas Mountains are at present out of balance, likely due to a confluence of existing lithospheric strength anomalies and deep mantle dynamics," Becker said. Miller and Becker used seismometers to measure the thickness of the lithosphere — that is, the Earth's rigid outermost layer — beneath the Atlas Mountains in Morocco. By analyzing 67 distant seismic events with 15 seismometers, the team was able to use the Earth's vibrations to "see" into the deep subsurface. The researchers found that the crust beneath the Atlas Mountains, which rise to an elevation of more than 4,000 meters, reaches a depth of only about 35 kilometers — about 15 km shy of what the traditional model predicts.

"This study shows that deformation can be observed through the entire lithosphere and contributes to mountain building even far away from plate boundaries," said Miller, whose lab is currently conducting further research into the timing and effects of the mountain building on other geological processes.

[dlxiii] Time-dependent subsidence

[dlxiv] With a need to define this dynamic, researchers in the field of geophysics have found that there is a relatively slow tectonic process known as epeirogenesis, whereby large areas of the Earth's crust gradually heave and subside more or less as a uniform body; imperceptibly floating on the Earth's hot and viscous mantle, which is much like very dense clay in slow-motion. Although a rather slow process, this phenomenon was the framework of the sudden unprecedented upheavals and convulsions suggested by Plato; a diastrophic dynamic sufficient in magnitude and proportion.

A review of geologic data in this area has in fact identified several tectonic studies that are investigating stretching, tearing and uplift anomalies on the seafloor approaching and along the western most extension of the northern aspects of the African Plate. The first two of these anomalies are Atlantic Transform and Non-Transform Fault movements (which precipitate uplifting).

dlxv   Referring to the ancient city founded by the Atlatians (during their Bronze Age) on the coast of southern Europe; there are no archaeological remains of the city at the site of present day Athens

dlxvi   Cape Spartel is the point at which the Atlantic and the Mediterranean meet; a promontory off the Morocco coast, about 1,000 feet (300 m) above sea level at the entrance to the Strait of Gibraltar, 12 km West of Tangier. Africa's most northwesterly promontory, Cape Spartel, is a dramatic and fertile point; known to the Greeks and Romans as the "Cape of the Vines."

dlxvii . Plato described it as being buried under a flood of water about 9,000 BC. Modern archeologists suggest that the 9,000 years may have been mistranslated from earlier Khemetian (Egyptian) accounts.

dlxviii British nautical archaeologist Nic Flemming reported submerged bronze age ruins off the coasts of at Gigthis, Al Jezirah, Thaene, Achulla, Sullectum, Thapsus, Horrea Cahelia, Neopolis, Mour, and Carpis, and off Sleima, Malta; Plato described "Atlantis" with attributes that clearly classify it as an empire of the Bronze Age.

dlxix   Over time, it was the faint recollection of the histories and events centered upon the legendary ancient straits, that later civilizations interpreted and attributed to the entrance to the still surviving sea (the "Atlantic Ocean"), at the Straits Gibraltar, situated farther to the west.

dlxx   The Adrar mountain range in (present day) northern Mauritania

dlxxi   The Richat Structure (also known as the Eye of the Sahara) is a prominent circular feature in the Sahara desert of west – central Mauritania near Ouadane. This structure is a deeply eroded, with sedimentary rocks comprising a structural dip outward at 10°-20°. Differential erosion of resistant layers of quartzite has created high-relief circular cuestas; its center consists of a siliceous breccia covering an area that is at least 3 km in diameter. Exposed within the interior of the Richat structure are a variety of intrusive and extrusive igneous rocks, including rhyolitic volcanic rocks. The rhyolitic rocks consist of lava flows and hydrothermally altered tuffaceous rocks that are part of two distinct two eruptive centers, which are interpreted to be the eroded remains of two maars.
Several competing theories exist as to the exact mechanism of formation. The most common is the theory of explosive thermal contraction of particles under rapid cooling from contact with water. The other competing theory is based on fuel-coolant reactions, which have been modeled for the nuclear industry. Under this theory the fuel (in this case, the magma) fragments upon contact with a coolant (the ocean, or an inland sea). The propagating stress waves and thermal contraction widen cracks and increase the interaction surface area, leading to explosively rapid cooling rates. The two mechanisms are very similar and the reality is most likely a combination of both. Both mechanisms are widely recognized in the geological record, and are generally accepted by modern Geology

dlxxii Unlike other physical examples of catastrophic water flows, such as the inflows and outflows of the Black Sea through the Bosporus strait, the strong forces released by the draining waters of the Atlantean into the Mediterranean and Atlantic were dampened by the existing sea and ocean themselves.

dlxxiii The Igbo (part of the *KWA*) called him *Eshi,* from the root of the word Sirius. Most scholars have argued that Igbo society was "stateless" and that the Igbo did not evolve centralized political institutions. This primarily because the relatively egalitarian Igbo lived in small, self contained groups of villages, organized according to a lineal system that did not allow social stratification. Despite the absence of chiefs, the Igbo relied on an order of priests, chosen from outsiders on the northern fringe of Igbo land, to ensure impartiality in settling disputes between communities. An individual's fitness to lead and govern was determined by his wisdom and his wisdom by his age and experience.

dlxxiv Its tilt lessened from 24.14 degrees off vertical to its present 23.45 degrees, while the time when the planet is closest to the Sun shifted gradually from July to January. Nobody knows what triggered the changes, but geologists think they were probably caused by shifts of material deep inside the Earth's molten core. They altered the pattern of sunshine on the Earth, with profound effects on many weather systems.

dlxxv   The Western Sahara's position at the fringe of the Sahara means that research in this area may yield important results concerning the timing, extent and nature of past climatic variations. Climatic variation, as a tool of serious investigation is gaining fundamental importance, with informed interest and research conducted by meteorologists, geologists and geographers. Heretofore, common references made to climatic changes (particularly during in the "classical period") have generally been eluded to in the writings of Greek and Arab historians and theorists; with the speculations propounded by these authors broadly adapted by "conventional historians" and propagated and continued throughout the twentieth century, and well into the twenty-first century. To the originated authors climatic variation was only considered as a means to an end, to either refute or support the generally accepted theories of the time

dlxxvi It wasn't just down to the sun, the so-called 'African Humid Period' of the greater Sub-Pluvial had theretofore been reinforced by newly grown vegetation that absorbed the sun's energy, which strengthened the monsoon system; rather than reflecting the sun's energy back into space. Increased surface inland sea and ocean temperatures supported stronger monsoons, as well as numerous permanent lakes such as Mega-Lake Chad. Peter De Menocal, a researcher at Columbia University's Lamont-Doherty Earth Observatory, argues that the climate change started and ended rather abruptly, within a few decades to centuries, triggered largely by summer insolation crossing a threshold of 470 Watts per meter squared (4.2 percent higher than the prevailing present day temperatures across the region). He speculates that there could be an insolation tipping point "whereby subtropical African climate flips abruptly between humid and arid conditions. However, he notes, other evidence suggests a more gradual transition (layers of sediment drilled from the bottom of Lake Yoa in northeastern Chad hint that the environment changed occurred in phases from trees and bushes to shrubs and grasses and finally to nothing but sand).

dlxxvii Atlatian Script in this context refers to 'Proto-Saharan Script'. The 'Proto-Saharans' engraved their syllabic script in rocks, or used a stylus to engrave wet clay. Their script was the model script for the ancient Mande script, Proto-Elamite, Indus Valley writing and Linear A. The Proto-Saharan writing was first used to write characters on pottery, to give the ceramics a talismanic quality. Thus we find Proto-Saharans characters on ancient Chinese, Egyptian, Linear A and the Indus Valley. (Winters 1985).

dlxxviii There is evidence that the ancestors of the Igbo people and most of their neighbors were the proto-Kwa group, before settling at the old Sahara grasslands. The Igbo are the second largest group of people living in southern Nigeria. They are socially and culturally diverse, consisting of many subgroups; they live in scattered groups of villages, and all speak one language. Although the Igbo have no common traditional story of their origins.

The Ogam Inscriptions of the Igbo, depicting among the earliest forms of writing, baffled anthropologists and historians since they were discovered in the turn of the 20th century by British colonial officials Charles Partridge (1903), P.A. Talbot (1926) and Philip Allison (1963). (Philip Allison, Cross River Monoliths, 1967) It was researcher Don Luke in an article titled "African Presence in the Early History of the British Isles and Scandinavia" (*African Presence in Early Europe*, ed. Ivan Van Sertima, 1985) that first pointed out that *Ogam* might be a West African language and not the North African Basque language suggested by Barry Fell. Luke argued that (Ogam) script may have originated in Africa and been taken northward by early adventurers…(for) this same script can be found along the Niger in West Africa because there appears to be a possible West African Scandinavian link in our findings.

Further investigation confirmed that there was a similar kind of writing along the Niger area and found that indeed the column writing existed among the Igbo of Southern Nigeria, which had literally been lost. *Ogam* was written in the form of strokes or lines, originally on sticks and later on rock. Other examples of the use of the column writing by Igbo elders as recorded in Achebe's *Things Fall Apart* confirm that the writing was essentially a sacred activity employed by the initiates of the *ozo*, the cult of holy men/senators/judges as a demonstration of their holiness and their title each time they were about to embark upon the most sacred act of sharing communion which was done through the ritual breaking, sharing and eating of the kola nut: the seed of the *cola acuminata* tree.

Igbo translations of *Ogam* inscriptions reveal them to be proverbs and wise sayings that not only have their roots in Igbo language, but also in the current Igbo geographical environment. Frequent references to Imo, the longest River in Igbo land, and the recurrence of the Igbo word *ete* (palm-tree-climbing rope) lend further credence to an Igbo origin of this ancient orthography whose major distinguishing attribute, according to its ancient users, is that "*Ogam* is climbed as a tree is climbed."

Ogam inscriptions are statements of ageless philosophies that teach universal truths and lessons of everyday life. Their metaphors, drawn from the rustic environment, emphasize the importance of hard work, patience, perseverance, sharing, giving, tolerance, and service, condemning acquisitiveness, greed and excessive self-gratification. They emphasize the need to place more premium on eternal values and less on material acquisitions; the superiority of collective good over individual comfort; the imperative power of the Eternal over the transient; natural wisdom over bookish knowledge, and above all, the indispensability of Eternal Being (God) in the affairs of man. In *Ogam* and in Igbo worldview the metaphor for God or Eternity is the sea or the river.

These Scriptures on stone are the same philosophies and morals for which the Holy Bible, the Koran, the I-Ching and other Scriptures of other civilizations were later to be written. No wonder the Benedictine Christian monks of Ireland adopted *Ogam* philosophy and codes for their early missionary work. *Ogam* writings were transliterations (literal translations) of a West African language: a language still spoken today in Nigeria.

[dlxxix] Shaw's dating of the bronze artefacts had suggested they belonged to a period dating from 800 to 900 AD. However, given his seemingly cognitive and volitional failure to tell the world of the magnitude of what he found when he excavated the prehistoric city of Igbo Ukwu – that an ancient city and link to the emergence of earliest civilization lay buried in the forests of Nigeria; whether a mistake or a cover-up, in view of Professor Acholonu's subsequent research and analysis, Shaw's dating could no longer be deemed reliable (or trusted). Shaw's dating, whether mistake or intentional, created distinct problems for the study of Igbo antiquity, because the artefacts discovered at Igbo Ukwu had no relationship with any known Igbo historical experience; nonetheless Shaw's dating placed it within bounds contemporary history, thus discouraging pre-historical and mythological research and analysis.

[dlxxx] Wrong and false dating of Nigerian artifacts and omission of historical discoveries have been the norm since the dawn of Eurocentric Archaeology in Nigeria. Nonetheless, since news of the discovery of the Nsude pyramids, black and Afro-centric scholars all over the world have seen them as the long sought-after missing link to a Black African origin of Egyptian civilization. It further informs that present day Igbo ritual attests to a time when the Igbo practiced elaborate burial ceremonies in which the king is buried with his earthly possessions in readiness for life after death, as practiced by Pharisaic Egypt.

[dlxxxi] The mythologies maintained that after the world dried up, it was repopulated from this Holy City, from where groups of colonists were sent forth by the resident gods to repopulate the earth. When the founding god travelled around the world bringing writing and civilization [dlxxxi]. The name of this world hero was Kush. Kush was the founder of both the Nubian civilization, the Egyptian civilization and the Hindu Kush civilization of India. Later civilizations called him Rama, but the word Kush actually emanated from an ancient Nigerian word Akwa Nshi/Kwa Nshi. Akwa nshi was the name of the monoliths of Ikom and of the dwarfs (Igbo Nwa Nshi) who wrote them[dlxxxi].

[dlxxxii] The Kumoni-Oru who settled the Niger Delta with the most ancient inhabitants also known as ORU (TOBU OTU) gave birth to the Ijos. The original settlements were in the western & central delta, from where they spread out to people the whole Niger Delta. These original ancestors were spiritual initiates of the ancient African spiritual initiation system.

Those that remained behind at Benin intermarried with Efa women, and the offspring's of this intermarriage referred to themselves as "ORU-

BO" meaning "AN ORU PERSON." It was from the term ORU-BO, that URHOBO was derived. As a people they slowly lost the use of the original language through taking on their mother tongue. This language was common to them and the Ijos (Orus) who were established in the main central delta. These people left Benin for the western delta uplands during the second period of Benin Kingdom. Furthermore Ijo men, who have fled the upheavals of communities in the central delta and elsewhere during the epoch of the slave trade, also intermarried with Efa women.

The offspring of this intermarriage referred to themselves as "UJO-BO" or "UZO-BO" meaning "AN UJO PERSON." It was from the term UZO-BO, that UZOBO OR SOBO was derived. Hence the term SOBO also refers to the Urhobo people. In their isolation from the main body of Ijo people, they intermarried more and more with Efa people. In so doing they lost their Ijo culture and adopted the culture of the Efas. Traditional history maintains that at a point in time a common language existed between, not only the Ijos and Urhobos, but also the Benis (Benin Kingdom of the 1st Ogiso period). This language was a proto-Ijo language, which is now only spoken by the Ijos.

[dlxxxiii] Because of the obliteration caused by the volcanic eruption and implosion in the Adrar Mountains, the destruction of and consequential absence of the remains of the early settlement groups of antiquity, and the concomitant lack of evidence of earlier stone-age and subsequent bronze age cultures in the region, has frustrated research into the ancient peoples inhabiting West Africa before the eruption.

[dlxxxiv] While the upper and lower parts of the Niger have all the appearance of ancient rivers, the middle Niger is the result of a "recent" capture; "it has no past, it scarcely has a present."[dlxxxiv] Though, as stated previously, the geological changes that have taken place are imperfectly known, it is theorized that climatic conditions and shifts in the topography over the millennium have caused the river to assume its present course.

[dlxxxv] Illustrated in the Kannada, Telugu and Tulu, Dravidian tribes, that use the terms 'Mande' or 'Mandi' to denote "people or persons"), who stringent ascribed to th tenets of "Ma"

[dlxxxvi] The latest genetic research has conclusively proven that Sudroids (the "Sudra") are of Africoid stock. The word 'Sudra' is attested from the Vedic Dark Ages, and is of African origin (the 'Dravidians' are a Sudroid subset (or tribal group), and the Dravidian word 'Sudra' is essentially derived from the word 'Sudan'). The related terms 'Dravida' and 'Dalit' are much later innovations; the word 'Dravida' is of Sanskrit origin, and the term 'Sudra' and 'Adi-Sudra' are now more in vogue for this reason. While the ancient division between 'Dravidian' and 'Adi-Dravidian' is an artificial construct resulting from the Aryan invasions of the Indus Valley; with the former succumbing to Aryan aggressions and slavery, and the latter battling against the savage Aryan onslaught to retain their freedom in the margins of the jungle (Adi-Dravida means 'Original Dravidian').

The Sudroids (or "Sudra") are today an considered an 'Indo-African Race', with the greater preponderance of them continuing to primarily inhabit the Indian Sub-Continent. The Sudra originally entered the Indian Sub-Continent (and Indus Valley) at difference stages of prehistory; first from the south, after the series of inundations of *Kumari,* and later from north, as attested to by the noted Indian historian and anthropologist Bharatiya Vidya Bhavan, who noted: "We have to begin with the Negroid or Negrito people of prehistoric India who were the first human inhabitants. Originally they would appear to have come from Africa through Arabia and the coastlands of Iran and Baluchistan."

There is evidence to suggest that the Dravidian priest-scribes were linked to Kushite religion which reflects Proto-Saharan beliefs and practices.

[dlxxxvii] The middle Nile Valley is characterized by the presence of six main cataracts, the great bend, the islands, the Sudd and the big Wadis. The cataracts are distinctive features of the River between Aswan and Khartoum and it has led to this stretch often being referred to as the Cataract Nile, while the downstream portion is occasionally referred to as the Egyptian Nile.

[dlxxxviii] Thus it is suggested that recent uplift of the Nubian swell diverted the Nile, forming the "Great Bend."

[dlxxxix] 11,000 - 9300 years ago

[dxc] 11,000BC – 5500 B.C.

[dxci] Around 12,000 B.C.

[dxcii] Ceramics found from this period are considered to be some of the oldest identified in Africa

[dxciii] Neolithic Warfare, By: Arther Ferrill (Re the article that was published in MHQ: The Quarterly Journal of Military History)

[dxciv] Neolithic Warefare, By: Arther Ferrill (an article that was published in MHQ: The Quarterly Journal of Military History)

[dxcv] Horses are depicted in the rock art of Nubian, and horses were also well known to the Proto-Saharans. This view is supported by the archaeological evidence which indicates the remains of a small stature horse in North Africa, and its presence in Egyptian hieroglyph. In the hieroglyph the large Egyptian horse was called sesem, while the small Egyptian horse was called nefer. The term nefer, is analogous to PS *par. The horse was just as common to Upper Egypt as in Nubia. This is further supported, though somewhat later, by the fact the Thebans (of ancient Thebes) rode horses bareback as early as the 18th Dynasty. (The Thebens could not have inherited the horse from the Hyksos (as propose by Eurocentrics) because the Hyksos never conquered Thebes). Moreover, the appearance of Egyptians on horseback on the paintings found in the tomb of Menena, and the horse and rider in painted wood, dating to the early 18th Dynasty, testify to the existence of earlier traditions of horsemanship throughout the region. [The Proto-Saharan Homeland of the Dravidian, African, Sumerian and Elamite People: FERTILE AFRICAN CRESCENT, By Dr. Clyde A. Winters]

[dxcvi] The Naga presence in the east African highlands and great lakes areas (and points further north), has been reported in a number of archeological studies of the region; several point to the Khiosan as original carriers of ethos into the east African highlands. One notes fossils uncovered in the highlands with features that might be termed 'Proto-Khoisan', and others make reference to anatomically modern Khoisan presences as far north as the Upper Nile Valley and Eastern Sudan. Unfortunately, many of the most ancient sites, such as Naga-ed-Der opposite Girga , have been plundered by the long succession of invaders.

dxcvii   Archaeologists have discovered one of the two oldest cemeteries ever found in Kerma (dating back to around 8,000 B.C); the economic basis of both of the pre-urban and urban cultures of ancient Kerma was cattle; the people during the latter period seem to have come from two distinct groups. Excavations have revealed how, for the first 100 years of Kerma's existence, these two peoples continued to preserve their distinct cultural traditions while living in the same city. Although the distinctions may have been tribal in origin, they also reflected differences in wealth and possibly social status.

French archaeologists have found exquisite ceramic figurines, bowls and funerary objects at sites that date from at least 8000 B.C. They are as old as any Neolithic sites in Africa and predate prehistoric finds in Egypt by a staggering 3,000 years

dxcviii   An ancient document with a portrait of Tera-Neter (roughly modeled in relief in green glazed faience) has been uncovered in the early temple at Abydos. Preceding his name, his address is given - at the Palace of the Aunu in Hermopolis.

dxcix   The Proto-historic figure of Tera-Neter, a nobleman of the Anu who were the first inhabitants of the ancient Nile River Valley (Khemet). The "Tera-neter" tile is pre-dynastic being found by British Egyptologist W.M. Flinders Petrie (1853-1942) in 1939 the early temple at Abydos underneath the dynastic temple

dc   Diospolis to the later Greeks

dci   According to the biographical note at Dendara, Osiris, crowned in Herakleopolis, chose the god Thoth as vizier and appointed two generals, Hu (language) for Upper Egypt, and Sia (intellect) for Lower Egypt (Dend. II, 101, 6-7). Diodore echoes a similar tradition: Osiris chooses Hermes (Thoth) as counselor, Heracles as strategist of the whole country

dcii   Dend. II, 101, 6-7; Dend. I,17,3. According to Diodorus (i. 17), Busiris was the governor whom Osiris, on setting out on his expedition through the world, appointed over the north eastern portion of Egypt, which bordered on the sea and Phoenicia.

dciii   The profusion of Stone Age tools and cave paintings hint at the industriousness and vibrancy of the lifestyles of the earliest Ethiopians and attests to the country's antiquity.

dciv   As noted by the archaeologist David Phillipson

dcv   This name 'Arabia Felix' is a Latin translation from Periplus of the Erythraean Sea, a 1st century AD book by an anonymous Greek writer, who coined the original phrase "Eudaemon Arabia" when describing the port of Aden. The expression Arabia Felix was used in the ancient world, in the time of the Queen of Sheba (10 centuries BC) which was surrounded by a sense of mystery and the air of unimaginable wealth and luxury. Her country on the shores of the Red Sea was fortunate not only because of the trade route passing through it, but also because of the climate considered favorable by the standards of Arabian Peninsula – the "green Yemen".

The classical Greek (and Roman) writers commonly accepted the division of Arabia into Deserta (desert), Felix (happy), and Petraea (stony). Not much is known today about the exact configuration of those divisions. Later day Islamic Arabic geographers know nothing of this division, and this is not surprising since many of those later day Arabs are actually immigrants that later acculturated and assimilated into the culture of the original Black Arabs.

Arab geographers of the Islamic period divided Arabia generally into five provinces: The first is Yemen, embracing the whole south of the peninsula and including Hadramaut, Mahra, Oman, Shehr, and Nejran. The second is Hijaz, on the west coast and including Mecca and Medina, the two famous centres of Islam. The third is Tehama, along the same coast between Yemen and Hijaz. The fourth is Nejd, which includes most of the central table-land, and the fifth is Yamama, extending all the wide way between Yemen and Nejd. This division is also inadequate, for it omits the greater part of North and East Arabia.

A more recent division of Arabia, according to politico-geographical principles, is into seven provinces: Hijaz, Yemen, Hadramaut, Oman, Hasa, Irak, and Nejd. It has always been the assertion of experts that certain tribes that lived on the coast of Yemen and on the coast of Ethiopia and Eriteria were almost identical. The linkages between Ethiopia Kush and Arabia must be considered in the context of any discourse on Arab people, or more precisely stated the Black Africans of Arabia.

dcvi   Arabia Petra to the north spread between African Kushitic Egypt and Mesopotamia (another African kushitic area in the ancient times) (Josephus). It was originally settled by an early branch of the Cushitic Ethiopian people who spoke a proto-type semitic dialect.

dcvii   According to older versions of the Encyclopedia Britannica "The institutions of Yemen bear a close resemblance to African types". The inhabitants of Yemen, Hadramaut, Oman and the adjoining districts, in the shape of the head, color, length and slenderness of limbs and scantiness of hair, point to an African origin." Even in these modern times, these Himyarites (Yemenites) still identify culturally with the Black (so-called sub-Saharan) people of African Ethiopia. Arabia Kush and Arabia Musri

dcviii   Given the historical, genetic, physical and geographical proximity between Ethiopia and Arabia Felix and the similarity of the cultural expression of both land, it is not a wonder why the ancient Greek writers swore that the Ethiopians ruled the whole of Arabia. It was clear to the sophisticated Greeks and the worldly Romans that Black Africans settled and developed this portion of Arabia.

dcix   Sir Arthur Keith and Dr. Wilton Marion Krogan, in their discussion of "The Racial Characteristic of the Southern Arabs," opined that "the Arabian Peninsula was at one time occupied by a people intermediate to the Somalis on the one hand and to the Dravidian peoples of India on the other."

In other words, the original Arabs looked more like the Dravidians (or Sudroids) of today. Carlton Coon suggested the same: "It's easy enough to account for the southern Arabian Bedawi of the course type. He is obviously related to the Veddas of Ceylon, and to the most important element in the Dravidian-speaking population of India. His hair form, his facial features, his pigmentation, and his general size and proportions confirm this relationship."

dcx   Sites occupied are extremely common on these well-watered highlands (elevation ca. 2,000-3,000 m above sea level; rainfall: 200-700 mm per annum).

dcxi   These were the first inhabitants (the Sudra followed by the Kushites) of Arabia; those whom became known (at first) as the 'tawny Arabs' didn't migrate into the peninsula until many thousands of years later; when they did, they were first known as the 'Adites' (from their progenitor, who was called Ad). Prior to this (for thousands of years) "the south(ern) Arabs represent(ed) a residue of 'Hamitic' populations which at one time occupied the whole of Arabia." John D. Baldwin from Pre-historic Nations: Concerning some of the Great peoples and Civilizations of Antiquity. Harpers 1869

dcxii Today the lands of Ancient Yemen lie at the edge of the great sand seas, but the region still bears the unmistakable imprint of past flowing streams and rivers. The dry gullies or wadis appear to pose a paradox in an area that is exceptionally arid desert, with no vestige of plant life. But the answer to the paradox lies in the centuries over which numerous rainstorms and flash floods in the region gradually deepened and extend the gullies; the drainage pattern is clearly a fossil.

dcxiii *Easton's Bible Dictionary* puts the descendants of Raamah in Yemen rather than neighbouring Oman.

dcxiv While Sumer's many cultural and technical achievements are much celebrated, the important question of her ethnic composition is frequently either glossed over or left out of the discussion altogether. Independent and objective study of the available data however, reveals the very real question of whether the so-called "problem of Sumerian origins" is actual or artificial. The Sumerians did, after all, refer to themselves as "the Blackheaded people," and their most powerful and pious leaders, such as Gudea, consistently chose very dark (and preferably black) stone for their statuary representations. There is also no doubt that the oldest and most exalted deity of the Sumerians was Anu, a name that loudly recalls the thriving and widely-spread Black civilizers found at history's dawn in Africa, Asia and even Europe. Eye-witness accounts, religious similarities, linguistic affinities, skeletal evidence, Biblical references, architectural patterns, and oral traditions all point to an early African origin for the Sumerians of Iraq.

dcxv While Sumer's many cultural and technical achievements are much celebrated, the important question of her ethnic composition is frequently either glossed over or left out of the discussion altogether. Independent and objective study of the available data however, reveals the very real question of whether the so-called "problem of Sumerian origins" is actual or artificial. The Sumerians did, after all, refer to themselves as "the Blackheaded people," and their most powerful and pious leaders, such as Gudea, consistently chose very dark (and preferably black) stone for their statuary representations. There is also no doubt that the oldest and most exalted deity of the Sumerians was Anu, a name that loudly recalls the thriving and widely-spread Black civilizers found at history's dawn in Africa, Asia and even Europe. Eye-witness accounts, religious similarities, linguistic affinities, skeletal evidence, Biblical references, architectural patterns, and oral traditions all point to an early African origin for the Sumerians of Iraq.

dcxvi Controversy surrounding the Kushite/African/Black origins of the Elamites, Sumerians, Akkadians and "Assyrians" is simple and yet complicated. It involves both the racism exhibited toward the African slaves in the Western Hemisphere and Africans generally which led to the idea that Africans had no history ; and the need of Julius Oppert to make Semites white, to accommodate the "white" ancestry of European Jews.

To understand this dichotomy we have to look at the history of scholarship surrounding the rise of Sumero-Akkadian studies. The study of the Sumerians, Akkadians. Assyrians and Elamites began with the decipherment of the cuneiform script by Henry Rawlinson. Henry Rawlinson had spent most of his career in the Orient. This appears to have given him an open mind in regards to history. He recognized the Ancient Model of History, the idea that civilization was founded by the Kushite or Hamitic people of the Bible.

As result, Rawlinson was surprised during his research to discover that the founders of the Mesopotamian civilization were of Kushite origin. He made it clear that the Semitic speakers of Akkad and the non-Semitic speakers of Sumer were both Black or Negro people who called themselves sag-gig-ga "Black Heads". In Rawlinson's day the Sumerian people were recognized as Akkadian or Chaldean, while the Semitic speaking blacks were called Assyrians.

Rawlinson identified these Akkadians as Turanian or Scythic people. But he made it clear that these ancient Scythic or Turanian speaking people were Kushites or Blacks.

A major supporter of Rawlinson was Edward Hincks. Hincks continued Rawlinson's work and identified the ancient group as Chaldeans, and also called them Turanian speakers. Hincks, though, never dicussed their ethnic origin.

A late comer to the study of the Sumerians and the Akkadians was Julius Oppert. Oppert was a German born of Jewish parents. He made it clear that the Chaldean and Akkadian people spoke different languages. He noted that the original founders of Mesopotamia civilization called themselves Ki-en-gi "land of the true lords" . It was the Semitic speakers who called themselves Akkadians.

Assyrians called the Ki-en-gi people Sumiritu "the sacred language". Oppert popularized the Assyrian name Sumer, for the original founders of the civilization. Thus we have today the Akkadians and Sumerians of ancient Mesopotamia.

Oppert began to popularize the idea that the Sumerians were related to the contemporary Altaic and Turanian speaking people, e.g., Turks and Magyar (Hungarian) speaking people. He made it clear that the Akkadians were Semites like himself . To support this idea Oppert pointed out that typological features between Sumerian and Altaic languages existed. This feature was agglutination.

The problem with identifying the Sumerians as descendants from contemporary Turanian speakers resulted from the fact that Sumerian and the Turkish languages are not genetically related. As a result Oppert began to criticize the work of Hincks (who was dead at the time) in relation to the identification of the Sumerian people as Turanian following the research of Rawlinson.

Oppert knew Rawlinson had used African languages to decipher cuneiform writing. But he did not compare the Sumerian to African languages, probably, due to the fact that he knew they were related given Rawlinson's earlier research.

It is strange to some observers that Oppert,never criticized Rawlinson who had proposed the Turanian origin of the Ki-en-gi (Sumerians). But this was not strange at all. Oppert did not attack Rawlinson who was still alive at the time because he knew that Rawlinson said the Sumerians were the original Scythic and Turanian people he called Kushites. Moreover, Rawlinson made it clear that both the Akkadians and Sumerians were Blacks. For Oppert to have debated this issue with Rawlinson, who deciphered the cuneiform script, would have meant that he would have had to accept the fact that Semites were Black. There was no way Oppert would have wanted to acknowledge his African heritage, given the Anti-Semitism experienced by Jews living in Europe.

Although Oppert successfully hid the recognition that the Akkadians and the Sumerians both referred to themselves as sag-gig-ga "black heads" , some researchers were unable to follow the status quo and ignore this reality. For example, Francois Lenormant, made it clear, following the research of Rawlinson, that the Elamite and Sumerians spoke genetically related languages.

This idea was hard to reconcile with the depiction of people on the monuments of Iran, especially the Behistun monument, which depicted Negroes (with curly hair and beards) representing the Assyrians, Jews and Elamites who ruled the area. As a result, Oppert began the myth that the Sumerian languages were isolated from other languages spoken in the world even though it shared typological features with the Altaic languages. Oppert taught Akkadian-Sumerian in many of the leading Universities in France and Germany. Many of his students soon began to dominate the Academe, or held chairs in Sumerian and Akkadian studies these researchers continued to perpetuate the myth that the Elamite and Sumerian languages were not related.

Francois Lenormant, made it clear, following the research of Rawlinson, that the Elamite and Sumerians spoke genetically related languages.

This idea was hard to reconcile with the depiction of people on the monuments of Iran, especially the Behistun monument, which depicted Negroes (with curly hair and beards) representing the Assyrians, Jews and Elamites who ruled the area. As a result, Oppert began the myth that the Sumerian languages were isolated from other languages spoken in the world even though it shared typological features with the Altaic languages. Oppert taught Akkadian-Sumerian in many of the leading Universities in France and Germany. Many of his students soon began to dominate the Academe, or held chairs in Sumerian and Akkadian studies these researchers continued to perpetuate the myth that the Elamite and Sumerian languages were not related.

There was no way to keep from researchers who read the original Sumerian, Akkadian and Assyrian text that these people recognized that they were ethnically Blacks. This fact was made clear by Albert Terrien de LaCouperie. Born in France, de LaCouperie was a well known linguist and China expert. Although native of France most of his writings are in English. In the journal he published called the Babylonian and Oriental Record, he outlined many aspects of ancient history. In these pages he made it clear that the Sumerians, Akkadians and even the Assyrians who called themselves salmat kakkadi â€˜black headed peopleâ€•, were all Blacks of Kushite origin.

Even though de LaCouperie taught at the University of London, the prestige of Oppert, and the fact that the main centers for Sumero-Akkadian studies in France and Germany were founded by Oppert and or his students led to researchers ignoring the evidence that the Sumerians, Akkadians and Assyrians were Black.

In summary, the cuneiform evidence makes it clear that the Sumerians, Akkadians and Assyrians recognized themselves as Negroes: â€œblack headsâ€•. This fact was supported by the statues of Gudea, the Akkadians and Assyrians. Plus the Behistun monument made it clear that the Elamites were also Blacks.

The textual evidence also makes it clear that Oppert began the discussion of a typological relationship between Sumerian and Turkic languages. He also manufactured the idea that the Semites of Mesopotamia and Iran, the Assyrians and Akkadians were â€œwhitesâ€•, like himself. Due to this brain washing, and whitening out of Blacks in history, many people today can look at depictions of Assyrians, Achaemenians, and Akkadians and fail to see the Negro origin of these people.

To make the Sumerians â€œwhiteâ€• textbooks print pictures of artifacts dating to the Gutian rule of Lagash, to pass them off as the true originators of Sumerian civilization. No Gutian rulers of Lagash are recognized in the Sumerian King List.

Tamil Dravidians, Australoids and ancient Sumerians: Quote: "The second study concerns physical examination of Sumerian skulls. Buxton and Rice have found that of 26 Sumerian crania they examined 22 were Australoid or Austrics. Further According to Penniman who studied skulls from other Sumerian sites, the Australoid Eurafrican, Austric and Armenoid were the "racial" types associated with the Sumerians. Here is Penniman's description of the Austric type. [Black Kushites of Sumer and Akkad By: Clyde Winters Ph.D]

dcxvii That Babylonian civilization and culture originated with the Sumerians is no longer in dispute; the point upon which difference of opinion now centres concerns the period at which Sumerians and Semites first came into contact.

dcxviii The name "An" wa changed to "Anu" by the much later during Assyrian and Babylonian times.

dcxix Anu's original name in Sumerian is *An*; *Anu* is a Semiticized form of it.

dcxx The earliest Sumerian texts make no mention of where Anu came from or how he came to be the ruler of the gods; instead, his preeminence is simply assumed.

dcxxi Anu was a very important deity, his nature was often ambiguous and ill-defined; he almost never appears in Mesopotamian artwork[15] and has no known anthropomorphic iconography

dcxxii Although it is sometimes unclear which deities were considered members of the Anunnaki, the group probably included the "seven gods who decree":] Anu, Enlil, Enki, Ninhursag, Nanna, Utu, and Inanna.

dcxxiii The main source of information about the Sumerian creation myth is found in the prologue to the epic poem Gilgamesh, Enkidu, which says of the process of creation: originally, there was only Nammu, the Primordial Waters or Sea. According to the poem, Nammu, the Goddess of the Primordial Waters or Sea, was the first to exist and hence, the creator of all things. She began by giving birth to Anshar (all-father) and Kishar (all-mother), who, in turn, gave birth to An (the "sky father") and Ki (the "earth mother"). Though not well attested in Sumerian mythology, Nammu was the Goddess of the primeval waters or sea, the goddess of the watery deep and the womb of human consciousness.

Despite her extremely important role, much of her story is wrapped in mystery. Nammu (also transliterated as Namma) does not appear as a main character in any of the known Sumerian myths, though she is referred to briefly in several of them.dcxxiii In the Nibiru myth, Nibiru, which is said to have occupied the passageways of heaven and earth, is said to cross the middle of Nammu, the "primordial waters", with the myth further instructing that "the path of the stars of the sky should be kept unchanged", presumably guiding followers from earth (the "Land of Man") to heaven (the "Land of the Gods") .

dcxxiv The tradition of a Kushite migration from Africa to Asia recorded in the classical literature is supported by the clinal biological pattern of y-chromosome lineages in Africa and Eurasia. The presence of R1*-M173 among Anatolians and Iranians supports a Neolithic demic diffusion of Kushite agro-pastoral populations into this region. The cranial discrete traits, y-chromosome haplogroups and linguistic affiliations shared between Sub-Saharan Africans, the ancient Mesopotamian, Anatolian and Iranian populations can only be the result of a human migration from Africa to Eurasia in ancient times as noted by the Classical writers of Greece and Rome.

See 'The Kushite Spread of Haplogroup R1*-M173 from Africa to Eurasia', by: Dr. Clyde A. W inters; Uthman dan Fodio Institute, Chicago, 60643, United States of America Current Research Journal of Biological Sciences 2(5): 294-299, 2010 ISSN: 2041-0778 Submitted Date: April 14, 2010 Accepted Date: April 27, 2010 Published Date: September 15, 2010

dcxxv Diop points to the Africoid presence in early Elam, focusing especially on the region's artistic and sculptural remains identified by Marcel Dieulafoy from his late nineteenth century excavations at Susa

dcxxvi Strabo in Book 15, Chapter 3,728 wrote that in fact it is claimed that Susa was founded by Tithonus (Memnon's father), and his citadel bore the name Memnonium

dcxxvii The Dieulafoy and de Morgan Missions (with French archaeologist Dieulafoy and Jacques de Morgan (1896:175))

dcxxviii The Elamites and Sumerians were pretty much the same ethnically, as attested to by later Assyrian reliefs of the two peoples, in appearance and dress; they are indistinguishable one from the other.

dcxxix During the earliest eras of Sumer and Elam the rivers central to each were those which exist today; however, their courses were different and each reached the Persian Gulf independently, by one or more mouths.

dcxxx The transition to the Neolithic is characterised by changes in subsistence behaviour, as well as other social, technological and economic factors (Bar-Yosef 1998: 143). These changes occurred at sites across the Near East during the ninth millennium BC.

dcxxxi The ancient name of 'Shoosh' was 'Soos' (or 'Dasht-e-Soosiana'), and later on was changed to Shoosh. Archeologists divide time periods & discoveries of Shoosh, into two periods: Period One & Period Two. These periods are based on Geological Layers which the fossils & other material has been found in them, layer one & two which are on top of one another. Archeologists were digging in Shoosh since 1897 by 'Jan Morgan' the French Archeologist, all the way until the present-day. Dr. Scheil was also another valuable archeologist who dedicated a lot on uncovering the secrets of Shoosh.

dcxxxii The rapid growth of Anshan (in the highlands), coincided with the decline of population in Susiana; J. R. Alden (1982, p. 620; 1987, pp. 159, 164)

dcxxxiii The ancient Sudra of earliest antiquity inhabited a significant portion of western Asia, from the present republic of Turkestan to the Mediterranean.

dcxxxiv According to crude, racist, but still regarded by many as eminent, anthropologist Harry Johnston, "The Elamites of Mesopotamia appear to have been a Negro people with kinky hair, and to have transmitted this racial type to the Jews and Assyrians." Completing this short 1st of· authorities is anthropologist A. C. Haddon who remarks, "There is one portrait of an Elamite (Kushite) king on a vase found at Susa; he is painted black and thus belongs to the Kushite race."

dcxxxv The Kushite origin of this people is supported by Strabo in BK. 15. 3. 728, a Greek geographer who noted that the Kushites founded the civilization of Iran.[Proto-Dravidians, Dravidian Encyclopedia, by: Dr. Clyde Winter]

dcxxxvi . Proto-Elamite presence is reflected in well-built rectangular-roomed complexes intruded into local settlements of different form and cultural features.

dcxxxvii The Iranian Plateau, is a geological formation in Western Asia and Central Asia. It is the part of theEurasian Plate wedged between the Arabian and Indian plates, situated between the Zagros Mountains to the west, the Caspian Sea and the Kopet Dag to the north, the Hormuz Strait and Persian gulf to the south and the Indus River to the east in Pakistan. The plateau encompasses the greater part of present-day Iran, Afghanistan and Pakistan west of the Indus River. In geological terms, the Iranian plateau is defined as the geographical area north of the great folded mountain belts resulting from the collision of the Arabian plate with the Eurasian plate. In this definition, the Iranian plateau does not cover southwestern Iran. It extends from Eastern Azerbaijan, northwest of Iran, all the way to Pakistan west of the Indus River

dcxxxviii The sources for the prehistoric period in Iran are entirely archaeological. Early excavation in Iran was limited to a few sites. In the 1930s archaeological exploration increased rapidly, but work was abruptly halted by the outbreak of World War II. After the war ended, interest in Iranian archaeology revived quickly, and since 1950 numerous excavations have revolutionized the study of prehistoric Iran. For the proto-historic period the historian is still forced to rely primarily on archaeological evidence, but much information comes from written sources as well. None of these sources, however, is both local to and contemporary with the events described. Some sources are contemporary but belong to neighboring civilizations that are only tangentially involved in events in the Iranian Plateau; for example, the Assyrian and Babylonian cuneiform records from lowland Mesopotamia. Some sources are neither contemporary nor local but are nevertheless valuable in reconstructing events in the proto-historic period

dcxxxix The word Hindu does not mean Indus or Sindhu but 'black'. Notwithstanding that the term was probably derogatory, it meant to refer to the generally darker indigenous peoples of the Indus valley, as compared the invaders from the north. The word 'Kush' does not mean to kill or slaughter but simply 'side' as in left or right. Kush is also referred to in Jewish texts. Moreover the original inhabitants of this area were not of the Sanathana-dharma tradition. The word Hindu did not (and actually still should not) refer to a religion; the name 'Hindu Kush' has absolutely nothing to do with a "massacre of Hindus". It simply means the 'Hindu side', or more aptly, the 'black side' (referring to the inhabitants) of the mountains.

dcxl The Neolithic began in Iran about 10,000 years before the present (B.P.) and ended about 7,500 B.P. All known Neolithic sites in Iran were situated in regions where rain-fed agriculture was possible. Settlements were few and often widely separated, usually in locales with a good source of water, arable land, fuel, as well as wild plant and animal foods, which people continued to gather and hunt (Bernbeck, 2001; Hole, 1987a; 1987b).

Because of its size and geographic diversity, when viewing the ancient history of Iran, it is useful to divide it into its primary regions, each of which is large enough to have fostered distinct and thriving societies throughout the Neolithic (and beyond). The principal regions are the northern, the central, and the southern Zagros, the Khuzestan lowland, southern Iran, and the northeastern Kopet Dag region. Most of southern Iran, which is likely to have been important in the Neolithic, has not been sufficiently investigated, a situation that also pertains to much of the northeast. Iran's history as a nation of people speaking an Indo-European language did not begin until the middle of the second millennium BC. Before then Iran was occupied by peoples with a variety of cultures. There are numerous artifacts attesting to settled agriculture; permanent sun-dried brick dwellings and pottery making from the sixth millennium BC. The most advanced culture and civilization was in ancient Khuzestan.

dcxli   Artificial hills or mounds on the ancient Iranian plains are called a 'tepes' (also spelt depes, tapes, tappehs, tappas, teppeh and tappes).

dcxlii   The 'Čoḡā Bonut' (Chogha Bonut), archaeological site in lowland Susiana, in the present-day province of Ḵuzestān in southwestern Iran, is located at 32°13′20″ N, 48°30′18″ E; the site is about 20 km southeast of the city of Dezful and 5 km west of Čoḡā Miš.

dcxliii   *Čoḡā Bonut* is a small mound; in its truncated state it has an artificially rounded diameter of about 50 m, and rises just over 5 m above the surrounding plain.

dcxliv   The pre-pottery phase was excavated over only a very small area, and exposed a series of fire pits or hearths, but no houses. The Archaic 0 Phase, with pottery, had small mud brick houses, typical of the era. In all respects the material culture, from flint to figurines and grinding stones, resembles that from Tula'i. At the present, however, Aceramic at Chogha Bonut is the oldest site known on the Khuzestan plain.

dcxlv   Archaeological excavations at Čoḡā Bonut began in 1976 as a salvage project (Kantor, 1976-77). After the political upheavals of 1978, excavations resumed in 1996 for one season, and the combined results were published in 2003 (Alizadeh). Five phases of occupation were documented at the site: 1) the Aceramic phase, 2) the Formative Ceramic phase, 3) the Archaic Susiana 0 phase, 4) the Late Middle Susiana phase, and 5) the Late Susiana 2 phase

dcxlvi Ancient Crops such as barley, various kinds of wheat, lentils and peas. 'Weed seeds' were also helpful - the presence of the sort of weeds found in farmers' fields is good evidence that crops were being deliberately sown

dcxlvii   Radiocarbon dating of the archaeological deposits, some 8 meters in depth, showed that Chogha Golan had been occupied continuously between about 12,000 and 9,700 years ago.

dcxlviii   The work by archaeologists from the University of Tübingen at Chogha Golan since 2009 shows that its inhabitants were not only growing wild plants but also beginning to domesticate emmer wheat during their period of occupation from 12,000 to 9,800 years ago. People there were cultivating wild cereals, including barley and wheat, and progenitors of other modern crops, including lentils and peas, at the same time as inhabitants of settlements farther west in Mesopotamia and the Levant.

dcxlix According to Simone Riehl, an archaeologists from the University of Tübingen "mortars and grinding stones may have been used for turning the grain into some kind of bulgur or flour, which may have been further processed either by cooking or roasting." "Findings of chaff remains of the cereals indicate that people processed their harvest within the sites they were living in"

dcl Qora-Kottal and Dandan-Shikan

dcli Bactria would play a major role in Central Asia during both antiquity and the historical age, and at times stretched its political influence far beyond the geographic frame of the Bactrian plain

dclii The Hindu Ḵush Mountains are also known as the 'Pāriyātra Parvata' and 'Caucasus Indicus'

dcliii The ancient name of the region has survived to present time in the name of the Afghan province of "Balkh".

dcliv Regarding the Kushite migrations into Indus, Dr. Herman Hoeh noted "to the plains of India moved tens of thousands of Ethiopians, thousands of Egyptians and multitudes from the region of the Hindu-Kush Mountains in early Ancient *Bactra*."

dclv The Karakoram Pass is a hill pass in the middle of India and China, lying in the Karakoram Mountain Range. It is the tallest pass on the very old caravan path in the midst of Leh in Ladakh and Yarkand in the Tarim Valley. The Karakoram Pass rises to an elevation of 5,540 m (18,176 ft). The towering altitude and deficiency of food grains were the principal causes for the losses of numerous pack animals. The course through the pass was disreputable for the trace of bones sprinkled adjacent to the itinerary. There is virtually no presence of flora on the entry routes to the pass. The southern segment of the pass is more barren than the north.

dclvi   Kashgar borders present-day Kyrgyzstan, Tajikistan, Afghanistan, Pakistan and India to its west and southwest respectively.

The Takla Makan extends over 1,000 km from west to east and has a maximum width of 400 km, with a sandy area of more than 300,000 sq km. The relief is flat. Elevations gradually decrease to the north and east from 1,200–1,300 m to 800– 900 m. There is a gradual transition to the Lop Nur basin in the east.

The Takla Makan is an interior desert basin, enclosed by high ranges and therefore isolated from the influences of the west wind of the general circulation and of the southerly monsoon. The vast depression runs nearly 1,200 km from west to east, and is 400 km wide from north to south. It forms an elliptical, semi-open basin in the Lop Nur marsh, at an altitude between 1,450 m in the west to 771 m in the east. The desert is open to the east through the Hexi Corridor, while on the other three sides its borders are high relief mountain ranges: the Kunlun to the south, the Karakorum and Pamir to the west, and Tien Shan to the north

dclvii   An immense fresh water lake formed in the interior of the Taklamakan during the Quaternary (Norin, 1932): this was based on observations of lacustrine sediments along the rivers flowing into the desert and on the western margin of the basin. Norin (1932) noted and reported Quaternary age erosion forms due to waves and residues of lacustrine sediments on the southern slope of the Mazhatage Mountains, in the southwestern part of the Tarim Basin. A great lake appeared in the Tarim Basin during the Early Pleistocene (A Russian expert named Shumef, originally written in Russian, cited from Zhu et al., 1981) : the lake level was supposed to be as high as 1250 m asl. and extended to the Turpan-Hami depression. Much of the Taklamakan Desert is assumed to have been later inundated by the expanse of the large palaeo-lake (*Palaeo-Lake Lop Nuer*), with its highest lake level then reportedly approaching ± 1000 m asl. (Jäkel, 1991). The Lop Nuer is seen as the final residue of this formerly large lake.

dclviii The latest iteration of the Takla Makan was shaped by a large inland sea that transformed the depression in which it is located into a huge shallow inland sea (or lake) just after 10,000 BC. Researchers suggest that a series (or "storms") of earthquakes over periods of fifty to one hundred years aided bring the ancient inland sea to an end. Four millennia ago a series of quakes appear to have resulted in a shift and slight rise in the western floor of the depression, causing a gradual transition along the seabed towards the Lop Nur basin in the east. In consequence, the waters of the ancient inland sea appear to have gradually drained south-eastward, over thousands of years, leaving first a dwindling remnant of its former prominence as it slowly discharged, followed by fragmented interior lakes and salt marshes, until finally reaching the present-day desolate desert conditions. The sand seas that now define ancient Takla Makan are thought to have originally formed as dunes along the shorelines of the old inland sea, mobilized by shifts in the seasonal winds.

dclix The lowest elevation point in the Tarim Basin is over five hundred feet (154 metres) below sea level. Rosstagh Mountain, also known as Tokhtakaz Mountain, reaches an elevation of 5,117 feet, and rise from 600 to 800 feet (180 to 240 meters) above the plain. The arc-shaped Mazartag Mountains rise from the floor of the Tarim Basin and arch toward the southwest, some ninety miles long and two to three miles wide, at a maximum height of roughly 5,363 feet; they once rose nearly two thousand feet above the surface of the ancient Sea of Knowledge. [The Mazartag are susceptible to low impact (5 or less) earthquakes (on average one every 50 years), with occurrences at <5 Richter; an advent that has served to reconfigure and disguise the once prominent geographical features of the heights of the range (and the yet to be discovered remnants of the fabled islands in the ancient Sea of Knowledge]

dclx In the ancient records of China, from Lao-tze down to Hiouen-Thsang, the literature is filled with allusions and references to that island and the wisdom of the Himalayan adepts. With respect to the traditions concerning the island, and apart from the historical records of it preserved in the ancient Chinese and Tibetan texts, the legend is alive (to this day) among the people of Tibet.

Precious ancient relics are hidden deep under the ancient Taklamakan basin, an area that is larger than Poland. Present-day archaeologists are beginning to discover some of the secrets that have been hidden in this ancient desert basin, however, it seems that they are barely scratching the surface; only time will tell what more secrets and wonders are waiting to be unraveled.

dclxi In the Eastern legends, Shamballa is said to exist somewhere between the Himalayas and the Gobi desert. By definition the fabled city is 'hidden', with its precise location protected by allegory, obfuscation, and ancient routes described in terms so vague and obtuse that only the truly initiated arrive at its gates. The location of Shambhala has thus been both in the eye of the beholder, and a moving target; the Hindus thought it was up toward Nepal, the Nepalis in Tibet, the Tibetans in the northern deserts; always somewhere farther than the known. Many learned occidental Orientalists have endeavored to identify this mystical and unknown locality with some well-known modern district or town, but unsuccessfully.

At the beginning of this century, some new lakes unexpectedly appeared in the Taklamakan Desert; like Shamballa itself, the origin of the water in the new lakes, has been a matter of debate.

dclxii Stretching over 1800 km east to west the Tien Shan mountain range extens from the Xinjiang province of Western China across southern Kazakhstan and the entire country of Kyrgyzstan to the border of Uzbekistan. North-south the Tien Shan are as wide as 500 km in some locations

dclxiii The extensive mountains of the Tien Shan can be geographically organized in many different fashions. Generally, references are made of five main orographic areas. It is important to note that the Tien Shan hold a total of 88 constituents chains with fourteen peaks towering over 6000m. The five main areas of the Tien Shan with their most prominent ranges are: the Central Tien Shan (Kakshal-Too, Sary Djaz, Koolyu-Too), Northern Tien Shan (Kyrgyzskii, Talasskii, Kungei Ala-Too), Internal Tien Shan (Susamyr-Too, Naryn-Too, At-Bashy), Western Tien Shan (Ferganskii, Chatkalskii) and South Tien Shan (Alaiskii, Turkestanskii) (Azykova, 2002). The ranges of the Tien Shan culminate at the Central Tien Shan, which the locals refer to as Muztag meaning "Ice Mountain". Within the Central Tien Shan is Kokshal-Tau which contains the highest mountains of the Tien Shan and the most extensive network of glaciers. The present-day Tien Shan are still home to thousands of glacier ranging from sprawling dendritic valley glaciers such as the Inylchek Glacier to numerous small hanging glaciers.

dclxiv Herbal medicine was essentially restricted by the establishment of the type of medicine the Shamen practised.

dclxv Mongolia before the 'present-day Mongolians' was inhabited by autochthonous (if not ancestral) proto-Mongolians, since before the dawn earliest antiquity.

There are rock-art concentrations found in present-day in China (Chen Zhaofu 1990; 1991) along the northern and western frontier (Xinjiang, Gansu, Ningxia, Inner Mongolia) that are particularly significant in understanding inter-actions, prompts to mobility, and migrations across greater Mongolia during the prehistoric era. The rock-art sites in south-central Inner Mongolia and nearby Ningxia Province (which share a cultural unity) are the richest and best-documented on the Chinese northern frontier (Gai Shanlin 1985; 1986; 1989; Xu Cheng & Wei Zhong 1993).

Rock-art sites are also found in the west-central area (the Alashan desert and the Yinshan, or Yin Mountains, and to a lesser degree in the

Wulanchabu grassland to the north of the Yinshan). Petroglyph sites in the Yinshan and Helanshan ranges were documented during recent surveys, in which archaeological remains indicate the areas have been both borders and trading zones, connecting the peoples of Northern Asia, for thousands of years. The petroglyphs formed a significant part of the material and symbolic culture of this transitional zone, beginning in the Neolithic era

[dclxvi] For that reason also, for the many thousands of years that man has lived in Siberia there was minimal negative impact on the environment until the current time. This is a way of life which is radically different from that of European peoples, whose philosophy considers most of the world to be lacking sentience and useful only for exploitation

[dclxvii] Shamanism´ implies that a religious specialist is needed and central to it's faith and practices. Central in this belief is the worship of the Blue, Mighty, Eternal Heaven (köke tngri, erketü tngri, möngke tngri) (Heissig 1980: 6, 47-8). There is a total of 99 tngri or heavenly creatures of which Köke Möngke Tngri (Eternal Blue Heaven) is the chief. According to European sources from the thirteenth century this would be one god, from whom it is believed he is the creator of the visible and invisible (Heissig 1980: 48). In Asian Mythologies it is referred to as monotheistic with multiple gods.

[dclxviii] In later legends of the broader region (from Samarkand to Kashgar) the word 'Naga' was transformed into a 'collective name' used for 'many tribes', descended from a common ancestor.

[dclxix] The Hotan and Keriya river valleys have survived up to the present-day, but most of the shallower rivers have been lost in the sands, after which their empty valleys were filled by wind-borne sand

[dclxx] The highlands around Mt. Kailash are the source of four life-giving rivers; the Indus, Brahmaputra, Surlej and the Karnali (the last a major tributary of the Ganges); its solitary location, free of neighboring mountains that might dwarf or obscure it, give effect to its prominence and grandeur. To further enhance the symbolic mysticism of the mountain as a sacred place, two lakes are situated along its base; the higher lake, Lake Manasarovar (one of the highest freshwater lakes in the world), is the considered a sacred lake, and is round like the sun. The lower lake, Lake Rakhast Tal (one of the highest salt-water lakes), is considered a lake of darkness, and has the shape of the crescent moon. The two lakes represent solar and lunar forces, good and negative energies respectively. Mt. Kailash rises from the shores of the Lake Mansarovar, reaching heights exceeding 20,000 feet in elevation

[dclxxi] It is said that Shiva first imparted his knowledge to Parvati, his spouse. And, for the good of mankind, he taught the science of Yoga to the ancient rishis, who then passed on this knowledge to the rest of humanity. (Parvati was a native daughter of the Nagas of the Himalaya; deemed by the later followers of Shiva to be a deity of strength.)

[dclxxii] These teachings have come down to us in the form of Agama Sastras. These techniques have been refined over the centuries through masters who perfected the art, and then taught it their disciples. Thus the Guru-disciple tradition was developed and the wisdom of yoga was passed on through the ages. Siva Sutrasand Vighyana Bhairava Tantra are popular texts that contain specific techniques to liberate the embodied soul from the limitations of the body and mind and experience his true blissful nature.

[dclxxiii] Sanskrit is a language given to the Vedic rishis by Lord Shiva.

[dclxxiv] The hidden meaning of the word "Tantra"is said to derive from the combination of two words "tattva" and "mantra". "Tattva" means the science of cosmic principles, while "mantra" refers to the science of mystic sound and vibrations. Tantra, therefore, is the application of cosmic sciences with a view to attain spiritual ascendancy

[dclxxv] Because Tantra is a mystical subject, it is nearly impossible to define. Even eminent scholars have had a hard time explaining what Tantra actually is. The different explanations of Tantra indicate its multifaceted nature.

Tantra, in essence, is a body of beliefs and practices which, working from the principle that the universe we experience is nothing other than the concrete manifestation of the divine energy of the godhead that creates and maintains that universe, seeks to ritually appropriate and channel that energy, within the human microcosm, in creative and emancipatory ways.

Tantric visualizations are said to bring the meditator to the core of their humanity and unity with transcendence. Tantric meditations do not serve as training, extraneous beliefs or unnatural practices. On the contrary, the transcendence reached by such meditative work does not construct anything in the mind of the practitioner; instead, it deconstructs all preconceived notions of the human condition. The limits on thought (cultural and linguistic frameworks) are removed. This allows the person to experience liberation, followed by unity with reality

The word "tantra" is derived from the combination of two words "tattva" and "mantra". "Tattva" means the science of cosmic principles, while "mantra" refers to the science of mystic sound and vibrations. Tantra therefore is the application of cosmic sciences with a view to attain spiritual ascendancy. In another sense, tantra also means the scripture by which the light of knowledge is spread:Tanyate vistaryate jnanam anemna iti tantram.

Tantra is different from other traditions because it takes the whole person, and his/her worldly desires into account. Other spiritual traditions ordinarily teach that desire for material pleasures and spiritual aspirations are mutually exclusive, setting the stage for an endless internal struggle. Although most people are drawn into spiritual beliefs and practices, they have a natural urge to fulfill their desires. With no way to reconcile these two impulses, they fall prey to guilt and self-condemnation or become hypocritical. Tantra offers an alternative path.

The tantrik approach to life avoids this pitfall. Tantra itself means "to weave, to expand, and to spread", and according to tantrik masters, the fabric of life can provide true and ever-lasting fulfillment only when all the threads are woven according to the pattern designated by nature.

When we are born, life naturally forms itself around that pattern. But as we grow, our ignorance, desire, attachment, fear, and false images of others and ourselves tangle and tear the threads, disfiguring the fabric. Tantra "sadhana" or practice reweaves the fabric, and restores the original pattern. This path is systematic and comprehensive. The profound science and practices pertaining to hatha yoga, pranayama, mudras, rituals, kundalini yoga, nada yoga, mantra, mandala, visualization of dieties, alchemy, ayurveda, astrology, and hundreds of esoteric practices for generating worldly and spiritual prosperity blend perfectly in the tantrik disciplines.

[dclxxvi] By contrast, there was no mystic tradition during the Brahmanic Dark Ages (1500 BC - 1000 AD), since the Brahmins maintained India in a period of enforced illiteracy and darkness.

[dclxxvii] The source of Tantrism is given by the Tantric texts themselves as being Mahacina or Cina, ie. Tibet and the surrounding regions. However, the study of the Tantric tradition is very deep and complex; many scholars question whether there really is such a thing as a unitary Tantric tradition, or if it is a sloppy term for covering a range of traditions, like the term Hinduism.

[dclxxviii] Tantra" means liberation from darkness, the root "tan" meaning darkness, and "tra" liberation. Sensual or erotic tantra, as the term "tantra" is often mistakenly associated to in the West, is not a part of the original tantra nor of the Shaivita or Shakta tantra tradition. In the tantric tradition of Himalayas the spiritual aspirant is called a sadhaka, and he practices sadhana. Sadhana signifies the effort through which a person becomes completely realized.

[dclxxix] Through the use of visualization, meditation, and mantra recitation, ordinary perception is transformed into "pure perception" or a sacred outlook

[dclxxx] Tantra is a process of subjective transformation, which may be practiced by anyone irrespective of gender, cultural background, education, social status or intellectual evolution, as an adequate system of spiritual endeavor is the birthright of all.

[dclxxxi] Because the Tantric path may be specially challenging in the beginning, often requiring changes of lifestyle habits and mental breakthroughs that supersede dogmas and ingrained irrational beliefs, many people stray temporarily from the path when not able to succeed in triumphing over the initial difficulties.

[dclxxxii] When the aspirant decides to follow the path of bliss, he or she is initiated by a qualified meditation teacher called acarya; Sanskrit for "one who teaches through example" (most commonly a monk or nun); each aspirant is required to keep their individual lessons personal.

[dclxxxiii] All of the practices known to be Yogic in nature—asanas (physical yoga exercises), pranayama (breathing exercises), mantra meditation, kundalini awakening, samadhi (spiritual ecstasy), are Tantric (not vedic); hence, Tantra and Yoga are synonymous paths

Tantra Yoga is a system of techniques that links several systems of yoga together in order to create a potent form of yoga that specialize in raising the power of Kundalini. Tantra means to "Loom" or interlace. Yoga means a system of techniques that bring about union with God. Therefore Tantra Yoga is a Yoga system that interlaces several Yoga Techniques together in order to bring about a greater rise of consciousness under intense pressures of practice.

The Kundalini objective is to ascend the Kundalini from the base of the spine through all seven major chakras. In order to Do This Safely, All Seven Chakras Should Be Open and Balanced First. This Is Because In Order To Handle The Amount Of Energy The Kundalini Generates, Your Body Must Be Strong And All Seven Of Your Chakras Must Be Fully Open.

Yoga Can Help in Stimulating and Opening the Chakras by increasing ones Level of Flexibility, allowing one's Life Force to Flows Easier. There Are Also Other Methods Of Awakening Kundalini. Some Of These Include

Chanting. The Vibrations From Chanting Cause The Cause The Chakras To Open And Stimulate The Kundalini At The Base Of The Spine; Pranayama (Yogic Breathing), Paraná (Breath) Is Life; Visualization And Concentration, and Drawing In Spiritual Energy Daily.

[dclxxxiv] Tantra chakras use the seven chakra (chakras) levels (six in the body) of energy to raise and allow our energy to flow upwards in the body and spirit. Chakra is a concept referring to wheel-like vortices which, according to traditional Indian medicine, are believed to exist in the surface of the etheric double of man. The Chakras are said to be "force centers" or whorls of energy permeating, from a point on the physical body, the layers of the subtle bodies in an ever-increasing fan-shaped formation. Rotating vortices of subtle matter, they are considered the focal points for the reception and transmission of energies.

[dclxxxv] Tantra is said to be a spiritual science, mystical in its interconnectedness between ourselves, and the universe we inhabit.

[dclxxxvi] Professor James Liu argues that the Kunlun were all Negritos, Prof. Liu's book says "Kun-lun" is the Chinese term for Negrito.

[dclxxxvii] At this early stage the great trans-Asian overland route that would become eventually become the Silk Road was either in its infancy, or had not yet come into being.

[dclxxxviii] According to Eastern tradition, around the Isle of Shambhala, where now are found only salt lakes and sands, there was once a huge ancient inland sea (in Central Asia). This sea surrounded the island of which nothing now remains but mountains, where in a desolate mountainous region, in a hidden valley protected from the severe northern winds, thus enjoying a much warmer climate than the surrounding territory, is to be found the buried remains and remnants of the once great island city.

[dclxxxix] According to some scholars, Vedic God Rudra was evolved in Shiv. But this theory is not accepted by other scholars.

dcxc   Mount Kailash (Also known as Mount Kailas; Tibetan: གངས་རིན་པོ་ཆེ Kangrinboqê or Gang Rinpoche; simplified Chinese: 冈仁波齐峰, Gāngrénbōqí fēng, Sanskrit: कैलाश Kailāśa) is a peak in the Kailash Range (Gangdisê Mountains), which forms part of the Transhimalaya in Tibet, China

dcxci   The metabolic energy called Kundalini is symbolized as Parvati. Kundalini when properly quickened, unfolds her vibrating hoods and by an upward sweep enters the spinal cord and then the brain, and finally unites above the head with Shiva. In mythology, Shiva's wedding with Parvati is the entrance of this serpent power into the Higher Mind which is compared to the snowy mountains of Kailash.

dcxcii   The Kol belonged to the Australoid ethnic stratum; according to anthropology they are a Kolarian (or Munda) aboriginal tribe of Austro-Asiatics which are considered a primitive group. Most primitive tribes who spoke the Austro-Asiatic language (like the Santal, Munda, Ho, Bhumji, Kharia, Khairwar, Korwa and the Oraon tribes) were labeled as the Kol. Likewise, their languages were placed in same family of languages, better known as the Mundari or Austro-Asiatic language group. The term "Kol" means human, and despite their depiction as 'primitive', they were said to be experts in metal smelting during early civilization. Once upon a time they were so influential and their biological spread was so wide that group of many sub-tribes originated from them were named as Munda or Kolarian by anthropologists.

dcxciii   There are very few traces of the Kols today, except in the Kol tribes who live in the hilly parts of the present states of West Bengal, Chota Nagpur (in the present Jharkand State), Orrissa and Madhya Pradesh. See 'A History of the People of the Subcontinent of India In a Nutshell', By, Rajeswari Chatterjee; sponsored by the University of Nevada Department of English, the Washoe County Library System, and the Nevada Humanities Committee (Copyright © 2003 by Rajeswari Chatterjee)

dcxciv   The city lies between two streams, the Varana (to the north) and the Asi (to the south); together they make the name Varanasi. Present-day Varanasi (also known as Banaras) is situated on the left bank of the river Ganges, in the state of Uttar Pradesh.

dcxcv   Shiva's first wife was Sati. After the death of Sati, Shiva lost all interest in the world. He withdrew to his mountain top, Mount Kailash, and took residence in a cave where he immersed himself in intense meditation. Before the death of his beloved Sati,

When Sati died, Shiva also lost all his powers. The reason given for this in one of the stories of the sacred texts is that Sati is a reincarnation of Shakti, and Shakti means power. So when Sati died Shiva lost his Shakti. He was powerless.

In their desperation, the Gods turned to the goddess Shakti, imploring her to be of help. Shakti agreed to help and took the form of the goddess Parvati. *Parvati* was born to *Himavan*, the king of the mountains. Ever since she was a young girl, *Parvati* knew that she had been born so she could wed the great *Shiva*. From the time she could speak, she would sing all the songs dedicated to Shiva in a melodious voice. Soon, she knew them by heart. As she grew older, Parvati blossomed into a stunning woman filled with grace and beauty.

While she captured the hearts of many kings and princes, she only had eyes for Shiva. There is a story that mentions Parvati going to Shiva's cave every day, cleaning it out and decorating it with flowers. She would offer the ascetic Shiva freshly picked fruits and nuts. But Shiva was not to be shaken from his asceticism. Not once did he open his eyes or acknowledge the presence of Parvati. It is said that Parvati then turned to the Goddesses of Love and Longing, Priti and Rati the consorts of Kama, the God of love and passion. They turned the cave that Shiva meditated in, into a garden of pleasure, filled with flowers, trees, birds and bees.

Once the cave was packed with enchantments and wonders, they called upon Lord Kama. Upon his arrival *Kama* wasted no time in shooting *Shiva* with the arrow of desire. The arrow had no effect on Shiva, he was however intensely angered at being disturbed. Enraged, he opened his third eye and reduced Kama to ashes. With the destruction of *Kama*, *Parvati* lamented to the others Gods that love has been lost to the world. She reassured them however that when Shiva accepts Parvati as his wife, Kama will be reborn.

Parvati had tried everything in her power to make Shiva notice her, but nothing worked. Finally she decided to do what *Sati* had done to win over *Shiva*. Parvati left all the riches and comfort of her father's palace and went to live in the forest as an ascetic. It is said that in her trials, Parvati surpassed even the greatest ascetics. What she went through was even greater than what Sati, *Shiva's* first consort, had endured. She went through the most rigorous self-mortifications from walking in the winter snow without clothing to sitting under the hot summer sun for days, to standing on one foot motionless for long hours to eating nothing for days and surviving on the suns nourishment.

In fact her asceticism was so intense that it is said to have been equal to that of the great Shiva. Following in his footsteps, Parvati soon had utter control over her body and her mind. Parvati's Tapasya generated great amounts of energy and heat. This heat and energy finally reached Shiva who was shaken out of his meditation. When he was finally back in the world, Shiva wondered what or who it was that had wrenched him out of his intense tapasya. He then heard the story of how Parvati in order to have Shiva as her husband went through much rigorous self-mortification and achieved a state of asceticism almost akin to that of himself.

So impressed was he by her self-sacrifice that he immediately agreed to make Parvati his consort. Shiva and Parvati were married in great pomp and celebration. The gods rejoiced to have Shiva back and married at the same time and the heavens blessed their union. After they were married Shiva and Parvati went back to *Mount Kailash* and made it their abode.

dcxcvi   On the one hand Shiva is an ascetic who disappears from the mortal world, into Mount Kailash and meditates there. On the other hand, he is a fierce and angry god whose temper knows no bounds. He will destroy everything in his path. Through all this, Parvati brings him back to balance by pulling him towards the role of husband and householder.

dcxcvii The metabolic energy called Kundalini is symbolized as Parvati. She is conceived as the serpent power which lies coiled in the lowest chambers of the human body. Kundalini when properly quickened, unfolds her vibrating hoods and by an upward sweep enters the spinal cord and then the brain, and finally unites above the head with Shiva. In mythology, Shiva's wedding with Parvati is the entrance of this serpent power into the Higher Mind which is compared to the snowy mountains of Kailash. Kailash is the symbol of the highest mind and Shiva has his abode on this mountain where silence reigns eternally.

dcxcviii It can be appropriately asserted that Shiva-worship began among the ancient Nagas in the mountainous regions of the Himalaya, in pre-Vedic times; well before the advent and arrival of the Aryans. Too young to have shared in preserving some memory of the great leaders of early antiquity, the Aryans proceeded to convert the prescient leaders of earlier antiquity, such as Shiva, into gods. Nonetheless, it is beyond doubt that Shiva was clearly not Aryan. The Hindu myth about Daksha Yagya (assailed by Dr Ambedkar) exposes the clear manipulation of history and religious script. It is clear that Kali was also not Aryan, as noted by close examination and pre-historical analysis of the Satipeetha myth, which appears to have been created to conflate Kali with the Aryan goddess Chandi (the husband wife story which is the central theme of the myth appears baseless). Racially Shiva and Kali were each Negroid-Naga, non Aryan (Rastafarians with dreads closely resemble the appearance of the ancient (and not-so-ancient) Naga; a resemblance of the dreadlocks reported worn by Shiva himself)

Shiva can be traced to the pre-Aryan period, he was a non Aryan king who, in Aryan mythology, is reported to have fought against the Aryans; often against the Aryan god, Indra. The Aryans later co opted the worship Shiva in their pantheon gods to defeat the Non-Aryan culture of the Naga. (Similarly, were the indigenous gods of others, such as the Dasas, made Aryan.

The fusions of Shiva and the Nagas into the Hindu pantheon symbolize the cultural assimilation that had been happening over millennia. The figure of Shiva as we know him today was built up over time, with the ideas of many regional sects being amalgamated into a single figure. Whatever today we know about Shaivism, comes from the Puranik literature, which were written much later, and so are unauthentic and non-reliable.

dcxcix The 'Kailash' mountain range is also called the 'Ladakh ' mountain range

dcc The *Himalayas* reach heights at which the snow never melts, and nothing living can survive, forming a formidable barrier between northern and eastern Asia, and the plains and basins of the subcontinent to the south. While in the north, the mountain chains of the Himalayas enclose the Kashmir valley to the north-west, along with the group of valleys forming *Bactra, Kabul and Kandahar*, in Afghanistan.

dcci The Karakoram Pass is a hill pass in the middle of India and China, lying in the Karakoram Mountain Range. It is the tallest pass on the very old caravan path in the midst of Leh in Ladakh and Yarkand in the Tarim Valley. The Karakoram Pass rises to an elevation of 5,540 m (18,176 ft). The towering altitude and deficiency of food grains were the principal causes for the losses of numerous pack animals. The course through the pass was disreputable for the trace of bones sprinkled adjacent to the itinerary. There is virtually no presence of flora on the entry routes to the pass. The southern segment of the pass is more barren than the north.

dccii The present-day Karakoram Pass is situated on the border of areas under the dominance of India (the territory of Jammu and Kashmir) and China (Xinxiang Autonomous Territory)

dcciii Though close encounters with Nagas have been regularly mentioned in the ancient texts like Nilmat purana and Nagas have been credited with having established laws and regulations regarding religious worship even having recognized Neela Naga as the 'supremo', no mention is made of their origins.

dcciv The origins of the strong belief in Shaivism of ancient Kashmiris was inherited from the Nagas; it is only now that several inquisitive anthropologists are making efforts to unearth background of the Nagas that the true ancient history and antiquity of Kashmir is being brought into focus. Scattered pieces of information when painstakingly collected from extremely diverse sources, after being compiled into a cohesive mosaic, discloses a meaningful picture, revealing the habitation of a people who settled in the marshy surroundings and mountain top caves even before the Lake Satisar (now Valley of Kashmir) was drained, many thousands of years prior to the arrival and settlement of the nomadic Aryan tribes.

The origins of Kashmiris and their distinctive Shaivism, even their antiquity, as proven by their Saptrishi calendar, which is nearly 3,000 years older than the oldest calendar of Aryan origins practiced in the plains of Hindustan, corroborate their ancient historical records about the roots of Kashmiris, and their earliest religious beliefs. Though the contribution of the Nagas of Kashmir to the earliest prevalent religion and culture has been portrayed as semi- mythological, many Kashmiri festivals (still) relate to Naga worship (for example during the first snowfall, Nila, the Lord of Nagas, is worshipped).

In the language of Kashmir, the word for "a spring" is naga and, in fact, Nagas are indeed considered the earliest inhabitants of that region (the Nilamatapurana listed 527 Nagas that were worshipped in Kashmir) The Rajatarangini of Kalhana mentions Sushravas and Padma Nagas, who were tutelary deities connected with the Wular lake. The Dikpalas of Kashmir are believed to be four nagas, viz. Bindusara in the east, Srimadaka in the south, Elapatra in the west and Uttarmansa in the north. In Kalhana's Rajatarangini, the Nagas are described as the civilized humans. The persistent references to the 'Nagas' in the ancient Kashmiri scriptures like Nilmat Purana, and the super human qualities attributed to them are all indicative of the high degree of culture and civilization inculcated by the Nagas of early Kashmir

dccv The term Saka, now used to describe a late Indo-European group that conquered Central Asia formerly was used to refer to the Kushites / Proto-Saharans of ancient Central Asia.

dccvi Later evidence of extensive trade between Elam and the Indus Valley Civilization supports the notion that there was extensive and ongoing links between the two regions

dccvii At present it appears that India was settled later than Africa, although the lithic technology of the subcontinent broadly evolved in the same manner as it did in Africa. The early man in India used these tools of stone roughly dressed by crude chipping, which have been discovered throughout the country except the alluvial plains of Indus, Ganga and Yamuna rivers. They served as weapons for hunting wild animals, and could also be used as hammers or for purposes of cutting and boring. Palaeolithic man barely managed to gather his food and lived on hunting. He had no knowledge of cultivation and house-building. This phase generally continued till 9000 B.C.

With the end of the Ice Age and the Upper Paleolithic Age around 9000 B.C., the climate became warm and dry. Climatic changes brought about changes in flora and fauna and made it possible for human beings to move to new areas. In 9000 B.C. began an intermediate stage in Stone Age culture, which is called the Mesolithic Age. It intervened as a transitional phase between the Paleolithic Age and the Neolithic or New Stone Age. The Mesolithic People lived on hunting, fishing and food gathering; at a later stage they also domesticated animals and practiced some sort of primitive agriculture.

dccviii Described in appearance as 'Negroids and all those belonging to the Negroid-Australoid Black race, as well as pure Negritic racial types'

dccix In ancient India the 'mythological Nagas' were regarded as demi-gods, whose 'kings' were said to lived in magnificent palaces in the depths of the sea or at the bottom of inland lakes. They were said to inhabit an underworld, and were believed to control the clouds, produce thunderstorms, guard treasures, and do marvelous things in general.

Many feats were attributed to them which could be performed only by beings having human powers and faculties, whence they were said to assume human form from time to time; and stories are told in the writings of 'Naga-people' appearing mysteriously and then escaping to the depths of the ocean--probably developed from incidents in which wild strangers had raided the coast and when discovered had fled over the horizon in their boats.

dccx The major gift of the Naga to India was the writing system: Nagari. Nagari is the name for the Sanskrit script. Over a hundred years ago Sir William Jones, pointed out that the ancient Ethiopic and Sanskrit writing are one and the same. William Jones, explained that the Ethiopian origin of Sanskrit was supported by the fact that both writing systems the writing went from left to right and the vowels were annexed to the consonants.

Today Eurocentric scholars teach that Indians taught writing to the Ethiopians, yet the name *Nagari* for Sanskrit betrays the Ethiopia origin of this form of writing. Moreover, it is interesting to note that Sanskrit vowels: a,aa,',I,u,e,o, virama etc., are in the same order as Geez. The Ethiopian script has influenced many other writing systems. Y.M. Kobishnor, in the Unesco History of Africa, maintains that Ethiopic was used as the model for Armenian writing, as was many of the Transcaucasian scripts.

dccxi Dravidian is the name given by the British, however to the Greeks, they were Eastern Kushites and "like the Ethiopians." who were called Western Kushites

dccxii Tribals of India are composed a very large number of Anu' ethnic groups such as the Anuak (with curly to kinky hair as well as straight to wavy hair, but black skin and Negro features as well as blood type), the Tibbou and others

dccxiii The wide river bed (paleo-channel) of the Ghaggar river suggest that the river once flowed full of water during the great meltdown of the Himalayan Ice Age glaciers, some 10,000 years ago, and that it then continued through the entire region, in the presently dry channel of the Hakra River, possibly emptying into the Rann of Kutch.

dccxiv The unity between the Sumerian, Elamite and Dravidian languages all support the common origin of these Proto-Saharan people.

dccxv Glaciological record indicates that more than 12000-10000 years back there were glaciers all around in Himalayas which began to melt due to the warming of climate. The melting of glaciers released the pent up waters that flowed into mighty river channels, which included the Sarasvati and its tributaries.

dccxvi Sites have been found dating from 6,500-7,000 BC.

dccxvii Excavations at Harappa have uncovered skeletons belonging to members of various racial groups, which are all still present in India today.

dccxviii One of the reasons the Indus-Sarasvati culture was labelled non-Vedic was the absence of horses and chariots, which are prominently mentioned in the Vedas. However, evidence for the presence of horses has now been found at a number of Harappan and pre-Harappan sites, along with wheeled toys suggesting the use of carts and chariots. In the Rig-Veda, the enemies of the Vedic peoples are also said to have horses. Moreover, chariots are not the vehicles of nomadic people, and it is hard to imagine anyone using chariots to cross the rocky passes of Afghanistan

dccxix More than two decades ago archaeologists and earth scientists discovered primarily through satellite photography, the pale channels of a mighty river that originated in the Himalaya and ran its full course to the sea, the Rann of Cutch in the Arabian Sea.

dccxx The ancient Bay of Kutch (Kush) is presently represented by the Great Rann of Kutch, which covers an area of about 7,000 square miles and lies almost entirely within Gujarat state, India (along the border with Pakistan). Originally an extension of the Arabian Sea, the ancient Bay of Kutch was closed off and transformed into the present-day Great and Little Ranns by centuries of silting.

dccxxi   The Rig-Veda is a 'samhita' or collection of mantras consists of 1,017 hymns ('suktas'), covering about 10,600 stanzas, divided into eight 'astakas' each having eight 'adhayayas' (chapters), which are again sub-divided into various groups.

dccxxii   The word Rishi (Sage) means the person who is traveling towards the ultimate truth ("Rutham"). Rishis are always in search Truth. The toils, efforts, penances, researches and austerities of the Rishis are to unfold the ultimate truth. The knowledge obtained in that process, is conveyed the humanity at large for its well-being and happiness. It is said that the Sciences, Arts and every branch of learning owe their allegiance these great souls. They dedicated themselves to the pursuit of inner bless and divine light; they are known as "seers" as they are said to possess perfect knowledge about the past, present & future of humanity.

dccxxiii   Vega is one of the brightest stars in the sky, the 5th brightest in the whole sky; around 12,000 BCE, it was Earth's pole star. And such cycles being what they are, it will be Earth's pole star yet again – just prior to the year 14,000 CE

dccxxiv   The date of the Rig Veda has always been controversial, as it is one of the oldest surviving literary works. The debate is in part political, given that much of the foundational information on the Prehistoric Indian history comes from (i) the corpus of Vedic texts, headed by the Rig Veda (Griffith 1896; Macdonell and Keith 1912), and (ii) archaeological excavation of Neolithic sites such as Mehrgarh and the various phases of the Harappa (Agrawal 1982; Shaffer 1992).

At the current level of scholarship the Rig Vedic and the pre-Iron Age archaeological traditions remain mutually exclusive. In archaeological parlance there has been nothing in the material remains unearthed so far which could positively associate any of the Aryan tribes with those of the early Vedic people; the Vedic text composed and added to by the Brahmins after the Aryan incursions and eventual supplanting of the original *Vedic* and *Saraswati- Indus Valley Civilizations*

The Sama Veda, Yajur Veda and Atharva Veda were compiled after the age of the Rig Veda, and are thus 'Post-Vedic' text ascribed to the Vedic period. The Sama Veda is purely a liturgical collection of melodies ('saman'). The hymns in the Sama Veda, used as musical notes, were almost completely drawn from the Rig Veda and have no distinctive lessons of their own. Hence, its text is a reduced version of the Rig Veda.

The Yajur Veda is a liturgical collection and was made to meet the demands of a ceremonial religion. The Yajur Veda practically served as a guidebook for the priests who execute sacrificial acts muttering simultaneously the prose prayers and the sacrificial formulae ('yajus').

The last of the Vedas, the Atharva Veda, is completely different from the other three Vedas and is next in importance to Rig-Veda with regard to history. A different spirit pervades this Veda. Its hymns are of a more diverse character than the Rig Veda and are also simpler in language. In fact, many scholars do not consider it part of the Vedas at all. The Atharva Veda consists of spells and charms prevalent at its time

The bulk of the Atharva Veda text dates between c. 1500 BC to- 1000 BC – far younger than the Rig-Veda, and roughly contemporary with the Yajurveda mantras, the Rig-Veda Khilani, and the Sāmaveda. The Atharvaveda is also the first Indic text to mention iron (as krsna ayas, literally "black metal"), so the scholarly consensus dates the bulk of the Atharvaveda hymns to the early Indian Iron Age, c. 1200 or 1000 BC, corresponding to the early Kuru Kingdo.

Atharvan (अथर्वन्, atharvan-; an n-stem with nominative singular अथर्वा atharvā) was a legendary Vedic sage (rishi) of Hinduism who along with Angiras is supposed to have authored ("heard") the Atharvaveda. He is also said to have first instituted the fire-sacrifice or yagna. Sometimes he is also reckoned among the seven seers or Saptarishi. His clan is known as the Atharvanas.

Tradition holds that Atharvan is the person (man) who discovered the fire. Rishis Atharvan is said to have been the discoverer of fire (among the Aryan tribes of early antiquity. Legends hold that he found the way by which fire could be produced with sticks and systematized it in a way that the other (Arya) rishis could easily replicate this process.

In old Sanskrit, lightning is called Atharvan. In ancient Persia Arthvan meant a priest and this word evolved to become Brahmin. There are clear indications in the Avesta that the religion of the Medes and Persians before Zoroaster's time agreed in most respects with that of the Indian Aryans, and in a less degree with the beliefs of the Aryans in general. Substantiating the little told history of the Aryans coming from Persia and conquering the Indus Valley civilization; the Rig Veda gives pinpoint details on the movement of Persian from India in this regard

It shows that the original religion of the Iranians and of the Indian Aryans agreed very closely; many of the names of supernatural beings are practically the same; e.g. Indra (Indra, Andra), Mitra (Mithra), Aryaman (Airyaman), Asura (Ahura), Apam Napat (Apam Napat), Tvashtri (? Tishtrya), Rama (Raman), Vayu (Vayu), Vata (Vata). So are many words of religious import, as Soma (Haoma), Mantra (Mathra), Hotra (Zaotar). The Yama of India is the Yima of Persia, and the father of the one is Vivasvat and that of the other Vivanhat, which is the same word with dialectic change.

As time went on Brahmins added to and corrupted the Vedas to confirm their excessive pretentions. There are several 'post-Vedic' texts such as Puranas, which is said to contain a complete narrative of the history of the Universe from creation to destruction, genealogies of the kings, heroes and demigods, and descriptions of Hindu cosmology and geography. There are 17 or 18 canonical Puranas, divided into three categories, each named after a deity: Brahma, Vishnu and Shiva. There are also many other works termed Purana, known as 'Upapuranas.'

Puranas describe penance for several years without food, which are only a description of such divine power. That divine power is revealed to mankind through some sages, who propagate the truths and tenets recorded in the eternal Vedas. The Upanishads, another 'post-Vedic' work, are a continuation of the Vedic philosophy, and were written between 800 and 400 B.C. They elaborate on how the soul (*Atman*) can be united with the ultimate truth (*Brahman*) through contemplation and mediation, as well as the doctrine of *Karma*-- the cumulative effects of persons' actions.

Upanishad means Brahma-knowledge by which ignorance is loosened or destroyed. The Upanishads are found in the concluding sections of the Vedas and are classified as Vedanta, or the end of the Vedas. In addition to the 'post-Vedic' text, are the 'post-Vedic' epics, such as the Mahabharata and Ramayana. The Mahabharata was written from 540 to 300 B.C., and tells the legends of the Bharatas, a Vedic Aryan group. The Ramayana was written during the first century A.D., although it is said to be based on oral traditions that go back six or seven centuries earlier. The Bhagavad Gita, usually considered part of the sixth book of the Mahabharata (dating from about 400 or 300 B.C.)

dccxxv   Out of the seven only five exist now; the remaining two, the Saraswati and Drishadwati have disappeared.

dccxxvi   The Vedic people were certainly not a primitive culture; Vedic astronomy and mathematics were well-developed sciences, and the Rig-Veda shows an advanced level of cultural and philosophical sophistication, attesting to an advanced civilization.

dccxxvii   Geologists report that at one time the Sarasvati River had at least three tributaries, the Shatadru originating from Mt Kailas, the Drishadvati from the Shiwalik Hills and the old Yamuna. They flowed together along a channel, presently known as Ghaggar in Punjab, Hakra and Nara. Research reports by geologists have revealed that the drainage systems/ pale channels of this area came into existence more than 8,000 years back as is indicated by the age of waters trapped beneath the desert in Jaisalmer of west Rajasthan

dccxxviii   The Rig Veda is essentially a composition of hymns, and the term "rishi" originally denoted the composers and singers of the Vedic hymns.

dccxxix   The geographical data of the Rig-Veda clearly indicate that the Punjab and its neighboring region constituted the homeland of early northern Vedic people, known as the Sapta-Sindhu region; which the Vedic people called Devakrita Yoni or Devanirmita Desha.

dccxxx   The Rig-Vedic 'samhita' or collection of mantras consists of 1,017 hymns or 'suktas', covering about 10,600 stanzas, divided into eight 'astakas' each having eight 'adhayayas' or chapters, which are sub-divided into various groups.

dccxxxi   In Vedic ontology when Lord Brahma decided to create the universe he created Seven Sages out of his thoughts; they were called as Saptha Rishi or Manasa Putra (created out of mental thoughts).

dccxxxii   The astronomical identity of these stars is very easy to establish due to explicit definitions given by Varaha Mihira in his Brihat Samhita (circa 550 AD).
Varaaha Mihira explicitly identifies the Ursa Major and provides the proper names of seven dominant stars, and attributes the origin of these names to sage 'Vruddha Garga'.

dccxxxiii   Sapta Rishis are two Sanskrit words meaning "Seven Sages". Sapta Rishis

dccxxxiv   Rig Veda 8/58/2: Only One is the Fire, enkindled in numerous ways; only One is the Sun, pervading this whole universe; only One is the Dawn, illuminating all things. In very truth, the One has become the whole world.

dccxxxv   The ancient Vedic rishis in all their wisdom said as early as 9000 B C, that our universe is not woven from matter but consciousness. These seers and channels said, that the universal laws are clear, your attitude about your life will shape it; that Matter, energy and consciousness are interchangeable.

dccxxxvi   The Institute of Scientific Research on Vedas (I-SERVE), established in 2004, undertook research on the Scientific Dating of Ancient Events from Rig-Veda to Aryabhatiam, which had two parts: (i) to ascertain astronomical dating of planetary references in ancient Sanskrit manuscripts by making use of planetarium software. (ii) To correlate such astronomical dates with corroborating archaeological, anthropological, pale botanical, geological, ecological, oceanographic and remote sensing evidences.

Astronomical dates, calculated so far, indicate the development of indigenous civilization in India from the dates even prior to 6000 BC. Astronomical references in Rig-Veda represent the sky view of dates belonging to the period 8000 BC to 4000 BC and those mentioned in Valmiki Ramayana refer to sky views seen sequentially on dates around 5000 BC. Astronomical dates of some of the planetary references in Mahabharata on planetarium software work out to be around 3000 BC. Many archaeological, anthropological, pale botanical, geological, ecological, oceanographic and remote sensing evidences have been found which corroborate the astronomically calculated dates giving evidence that Indian civilization could be much older than what is normally believed.

dccxxxvii   The names of the ethnicities constituting these 'five tribes' is not explicitly stated in the Rig-Veda, resulting in certain wild speculations by some ancient and medieval authorities (Cf, Aitareya Brahmana, 3.31; Yaska, Nirukta, 3.8; Sayana on RV 1.7.9, etc.)

dccxxxviii   The Iravati River (the Ravi River in Punjab province of Pakistan) is mentioned along with other rivers like the Vipasa, the Satadru, the Chandrabhaga, the Saraswati, the Vitasta, the Sindhu etc at (2,9). It is also mentioned at (3,12), (6,9), (8,44) and (13,146).

dccxxxix   The languages spoken by Dravidians such as Telegu, Malayalam, Kanada and others are related to the Kushite languages of East Africa, such as Gala and those spoken by the Nilotic peoples.

dccxl   It is important to note that people from south like the Yadus are mentioned in the Rig Veda as the Purus of North India.

dccxli   Rig-Veda 6.61.12: From one of the earliest of the family Mandala

dccxlii   Dating of the Rig Veda has always been controversial as it is the oldest surviving literary work. Surprisingly, the accepted dating of ancient text is 1900BC; formulated by a German-born "Orientalist" who lived and studied in Britain (for most of his life). Friedrich Max Müller, generally known as Max Müller, assigned the period 1500 BCE to 500 BCE for Rig-Veda Samhita. One of the reasons given is that beginnings of human kind cannot be earlier to 4000 B.C.E. Muller took particular care to ensure that the hypothetical Aryan invasion took place after the Biblical flood (Biblical Creation Theory states that the world was created with all its life forms at 9.00 AM, October 23, 4004 BC.) and he arbitrarily assigned a date of 1200 B.C to the Rig Veda, which is considered as the oldest among the four Vedas. Since the evidence was flimsy, he recanted his earlier assignment near the end of his life.

Friedrich Max Müller (1823-1900), was said to be a Sanskrit scholar and philologist and pioneer in the fields of Vedic studies, comparative philosophy, comparative mythology and comparative religion. He was one of the founders of the western academic field of Indian studies and the discipline of comparative religion. Max Muller, it is said, was also an agent of the British Colonialists, and was funded by them to write, rewrite and distort the history of Asia so as to establish Christian history as superior to that of the Asians (for purposes of creating an inferiority complex among the Indians by proving to them that their history, traditions, culture, philosophy, religion etc. had no value before the history and culture of Europe).

Müller's connections with the East India Company and with Sanskritists based at Oxford University led to a career in Britain, where he eventually became the leading intellectual commentator on the culture of India, which Britain controlled as part of its Empire. Müller's Sanskrit studies came at a time when scholars had started to see language development in relation to cultural development. The recent discovery of the Indo-European language group had started to lead to much speculation about the relationship between Greco-Roman cultures and those of more ancient peoples. In particular the Vedic culture of India was thought to have been the ancestor of European Classical cultures, and scholars sought to compare the genetically related European and Asian languages to reconstruct the earliest form of the root-language.

Müller believed that the earliest documents of Vedic culture should be studied to provide the key to the development of pagan European religions, and of religious belief in general. To this end, Müller sought to understand the most ancient of Vedic scriptures, the Rig-Veda. Müller was greatly impressed by Ramakrishna Paramhansa, his contemporary and proponent of Vedantic philosophy, and authored several essays and books on him. Muller once wrote that "the translation of the Veda will hereafter tell to a great extent on the fate of India, and on the growth of millions of souls in that country. It is the root of their religion, and to show them what the root is, is, I feel sure, is the only way of uprooting all that has sprung from it during the last 3,000 years."

In 1868 he wrote to George Campbell, the newly appointed Secretary of State for India: India has been conquered once, but India must be conquered again, and that second conquest should be a conquest by education. Much has been done for education of late, but if the funds were tripled and quadrupled, that would hardly be enough (...) By encouraging a study of their own ancient literature, as part of their education, a national feeling of pride and self-respect will be reawakened among those who influence the large masses of the people. A new national literature may spring up, impregnated with Western ideas, yet retaining its native spirit and character (...) A new national literature will bring with it a new national life, and new moral vigor. As to religion, that will take care of itself. The missionaries have done far more than they themselves seem to be aware of, nay, much of the work which is theirs they would probably disclaim. The Christianity of our nineteenth century will hardly be the Christianity of India. But the ancient religion of India is doomed—and if Christianity does not step in, whose fault will it be?

—Max Müller, (1868)

Müller's work contributed to the developing interest in Aryan culture which set Indo-European ('Aryan') traditions in opposition to Semitic religions. He was purportedly saddened by the fact that these later came to be expressed in racist terms, as this was far from his intention. Friedrich Max Muller was a colonial Orientologist who, embarked on the study of comparative religion and hastily misread the Veda to accord with his own Eurocentric perspective, ideas, principles and pre-determined objectives, and, accordingly his dating or opinion of the dating of the Rig Veda is clearly less than objective and falls decidedly short of the time frame and eras suggested by the material contained in the Vedas and supporting documents, scriptures and archeological artifacts.

dccxliii   Houston states that Brahmanism (from the God Brahma, the first person in the trinity), "claims to be founded upon the Vedas, the sacred books of India, taken over by the Brahmins. They were not the creators of the writings, although today they are the custodians, interpreters and priests.

They only attained this place after a bloody struggle with the native races. Upon the suppression of Buddhism, a line of apostles of Brahmanism appeared, with a philosophy built upon the peculiar mystic, ascetic, teachings of Buddha. A mass of Hindu legends sprang up around them".

Drucilla Dunjee Houston explains that many of India's ancient books were of Black Kushite origins, however the religious writings were corrupted by the invaders(or infiltrators, since they most likely they did not invade India but took advantage of weaknesses and calamities in order to infiltrate and occupy).

dccxliv Vedas make no mention of the Indus (Sindhu) River, but instead are full of praise for the Saraswati River; identifying the Saraswati River Valley as a settlement area and corridor of early civilization during the contemporary period of the Vedas

dccxlv The rivers Hakra (in Pakistan) and the Ghaggar (in India) have been identified as the lost Saraswati that once flowed through the plains of Punjab in Pakistan and India.

dccxlvi This is confirmed by Indian historian R. C. Majumdar, who stated that the people of the Sarasvati-Indus Civilization engaged in trade with centers of culture in western Asia and as far away as Crete.

dccxlvii According to the Matsya, an ancient book from India, the world belonged to the Kushites or the "Saka" (as they were sometimes called) for 7000 years.

dccxlviii The name of the city was 'Kususthali', not 'Krishnathali', after Kusu ("Kush"), not Krishna

dccxlix The great nautical archaeologist and linguist of the ancient history of India, academic pioneer S. R. Rao, rightly posited that the script of ancient Vedic Sanskrit writings was of the so-called Semitic alphabet having been applied to the language of the symbols of the Indus Valley Script.

But Rao has said the Hebrews learned the alphabet from the refugees of the Indus Valley Civilization, not the other way around, seemingly ignoring the history in the Word confirmed with India's patriarchs such as Manu (Noah), Prajapati (Japheth), Kush, Rama, and Seba (Shiva), the Indus Valley symbols Hamitic, the Semitic alphabet having been brought later by Canaanites and/or Hebrews then applied to that Indo European (Japhetic) language Sanskrit.[see http://dancingfromgenesis.com/]

dccl The Indus symbol for 'thala' having been much like a triton-shaped figure; the 'U' shape meaning 'tha', and the 'I' shape within the 'U' shape meaning 'la', for 'Kususthali', as said in ancient Sanskrit; the same as the *Saraswati-Indus Valley* language of eight-thousand years ago.

dccli Kush (Ausar, Osiris, and Zeus) namesake of the Hindu Kush Mountains was the original builder of Kususthali, the first city of Dwaraka now submerged in the Gulf of Kutch/Kush. The very name of the 'Kususthali', which means thalassocracy (port city) of Kush, firmly substantiates Kush as the founder and original builder of the first city.

After so many years it turned out that the legendary city was not a myth at all, but a real place that existed in the distant past. Carbon-dating estimates the site to be a whopping 9,500 years old. The discovery astounded scientists because it predates all other finds in the area by 5,000 years, suggesting a much longer history of the civilization than was first assumed. More amazingly, the ruins contain architecture, pottery and human remains which are still intact. This forces historians to reevaluate their understanding of the history of civilization in the region.

The Cambay Ruins the Cambay Ruins, found off the coast of India in the bay of Cambay is one of many ancient sunken cities we currently know about. The vast city lies 120 feet below the ocean's surface, it is 5 miles long and 3 miles wide, it predates the oldest known civilizations by around 5,000 years. It was discovered in 2001 on accident by India's National Institute of Ocean Technology as they where testing pollution levels. Found within the ancient sunken city is pottery, human remains, and a structure resembling that of the early pyramids, keep in mind that this city sank 5,000 years before any other known civilization, but it is believed to have lived in prosperity for 4,000 years before that.

This sunken city lies 120 feet below sea level and is 5 miles long and 3 miles wide. It was discovered by accident in 2002 by India's National Institute of Ocean Technology as they where testing pollution levels. The discovery is more significant for Indians because Hindu Epics such as Mahabharata which are often considered as myths have often mentioned this city. The ancient book says "On the same day that Lord Krishna departed from the earth the powerful dark-bodied Kali Age descended. The oceans rose and submerged the whole of Dwaraka. "[Kali -Usage: Hindu Mythology -Pronounced: KAH-lee means "The Black One" in Sanskrit. In Hindu mythology Kali is the fierce destructive form of the wife of Shiva. She is also known as Kalikamata ("black earth-mother") and Kalaratri ("black night"). Among the Tamils she is known as Kottavei. Kali is worshipped particularly in Bengal. Her best known temples are in Kalighat and Dakshineshvara. Black: Black in the ancient Hindu language of Sanskrit is kaala. The feminine form is Kali. Black is a symbol of The Infinite and the seed stage of all colors.]

Dwarka also known as Dwarawati in Sanskrit literature is rated as one of the seven most ancient cities in the country. The legendary city of Dvaraka was the dwelling place of Lord Krishna. It is believed that due to damage and destruction by the sea, Dvaraka has submerged six times and modern day Dwarka is the 7th such city to be built in the area. Now archaeologists and Indian Navy divers are investigating underwater ruins at Dwarka on India's western coast, said to be Krishna's city. The new efforts, it is hoped, will settle the debate currently raging over the age and authenticity of the site near the Samudranaraya temple.

Divers have collected blocks and samples which will now be dated. Traditional Hindu scholars referencing ancient Hindu scriptures believe the location to be very ancient, originally built many thousands of years ago. Such notions are, of course, vehemently rejected by "establishment scientists" though they are willing to concede that there is evidence indicating an age of as much as 3500 years. Of course the date when the city was destroyed would be long after the date of its inception, so a definitive maximum date has not been established. The new study is expected to resolve some of the issues. Archaeologists will now use the carbon dating technique to determine the exact age of the ruins. The earlier excavations, that first began about 40 years ago, had only revealed stones, beads, glass and terracotta pieces.

Marine archaeologists have used a technique known as sub-bottom profiling to show that the buildings remains stand on enormous foundations.Also see: https: // dancingfromgenesis.wordpress.com/2010/03/24/submerged-underwater-cities-ham-kush-india-kususthali-dwarka-key-solution-james-i-nienhuis-dancing-from-genesis-origin-development-vedic-sanskrit-language-biblical-tongue-proto-canaanite-semitic-alph/

dcclii "According to the theory of Elamite origin for the Dravidian races, India was originally occupied by two batches of Elamite invaders, one taking the sea-route by the Persian Gulf and settling on the west coast of India, and the {p.28} other choosing the land-route through the Bolan Pass and occupying North India. The theory is based on the Puranic myths of the deluge and the Ark common to India and Elam, and on the so-called philological identity of words in Tamil and Accadian tongues." (Iyengar 1925 p.27-28).

dccliii Goa's history stretches back to 8000-6000 BC. Early Paleolithic and Mesolithic rock art engravings have been found on the bank of river Kushavati at Usgalimal. Petroglyphs,cones,stone-axe,choppers dating back 10,000 years back have been found in many places in Goa like Kazur,Mauxim and the Mandovi-Zuari basin.Palaeolithic cave existence is seen at Dabolim, Adkon, Shigao, Fatorpa, Arli, Maulinguinim, Diwar, Sanguem, Pilerne, Aquem-Margaon etc. Difficulty in carbon dating the laterite rock compounds poses problems in determination of exact time period. These discoveries have shed light on Goa's prehistory

dccliv Traces of Negroid physical characteristics are found in parts of Goa, at least upto the middle of the first millennium. The proto-Australoid tribe known as the Konkas, from whom is derived the name of the region, Kongvan or Konkan with the other mentioned tribes formed reportedly the earliest settlers in the territory, followed by the negritic tribes known the Naga.

dcclv Dr Nandkumar Kamat(University of Goa),made a discovery of the prehistoric petroglyphs of Goa

dcclvi There is a scientific explanation of the fertility aspect of the termite hills which are built by worker termites over a period of 2-3 years. Termites are social insects having different classes and a system of division of labour. Only the termites of Macrotermitinae sub-family build massive over ground mounds/hills. These have compartments where the termites store their food. This food is composed of finely divided and regurgitated dead plant matter. The termites grow a type of fungus called Termitomyces over this food-pile. The fungus grows on the pile and makes its digestion easier for the termites

dcclvii The site was discovered by Dr P.P.Shirodkar.Exploration of several Mesolithic sites of the Mandovi-Zuari basin. Difficulty in carbon dating the laterite rock compounds poses problems in determination of exact time period.

dcclviii Dr Nandkumar Kamat(University of Goa),made a discovery of the prehistoric petroglyphs of Goa.

dcclix The Holy Spirit Is Kundalini: The Great Naga Force; by: Khadirah El-Bey [also see: http://www.dralimelbey.com/blog-of-enlightenment/category/the-holy-spirit-is-kundalini-the-great-naga-force]

dcclx The practice of Yoga aims at awakening this overwhelming force of spiritual experience. For this reason some yoga scholars say Naga Yoga is the highest form of Yoga. Yoga derives from a Sanskrit word which means to bind, join, attach and yoke; it also means union or communion. It is surrendering all the powers of body, mind and soul to God. In Yoga practice one is seeking communion with God.

dcclxi When that Kundalini awakes, it tries to force a passage through this hollow canal, and as it rises step by step, as it were, layer after layer of the mind becomes open and all the different visions and wonderful powers come to the Yogi. When it reaches the brain, the Yogi is perfectly detached from the body and mind; the soul finds itself free. In other words, the Kundalini energy enables the brain cells to register spiritual or "higher" experiences and stimuli.

A mental slave uses less than 10% of his/her entire brain. The other 90% remains undeveloped and unconscious. A Master uses the undeveloped sense receptors, the physical sense receptor activation ranges are expanded and undeveloped brain cells are developed. In other words, the quality of the physical body, especially the brain and the nervous system, is improved or upgraded. Here is another way of saying it, "After a certain period of time, a person whose Kundalini is highly awakened may become a genius, a great charismatic leader or a great spiritual teacher." THE HOLY SPIRIT IS KUNDALINI: THE GREAT NAGA FORCE, by: Khadirah El-Bey [see: http://www.dralimelbey.com/blog-of-enlightenment/category/the-holy-spirit-is-kundalini-the-great-naga-force]

dcclxii By Prof. P.C. Jain and Dr Daljeet. Prof. Jain specializes on the aesthetics of ancient Indian literature. Dr Daljeet is the chief curator of the Visual Arts Gallery at the National Museum of India, New Delhi.

dcclxiii Naga scholars strongly deny any link between the ancient Naga and the present Nagas of Nagaland and Burma (due to a paucity of evidence).

dcclxiv Termite-hill thus became a cult-symbol and the serpent-like forms, white at the top and black underneath, the immature or pseudorhizal stage of Termitomyces mushrooms were transformed into Kshetrapala gods -the consorts of Santeri, Renuka andYellamma. The 'Nagakashtha' is one of the chief emblems of cult of Santeri, Renuka and Yellamma. It is carried by the Matangis in Karnataka and by the Guravas in Goa. The 'tarangas' are 'Nagakashtas' of Santeri and Ravalnatha, which are taken in a procession. The origin of 'Nagakashtha' could be traced to the snake-like objects emerging from the womb of the earth-goddess the Roen/Santeri.

dcclxv The Kebra Nagast identification of an eastern Indian empire ruled by the Naga, corresponds to the Naga colonies in the Dekkan, and on the East coast between the Kaviri and Vaigai rivers

dcclxvi In one such study, the scientists at National Institute of Oceanography have developed sea level variation history of the last ~14,500 years B.P., for the western Indian continental margin. To generate the sea level variation curve for the west coast of India, they compiled all the dates of past shore line indicator features available between 21°N to 14°N latitude (till south of Saurashtra Peninsula). These dates ranging from 1,500 to 14,500 yr B.P. were then plotted against height/depth from which the dated material was recovered. The sea level curve was then drawn based on geological reasoning and supporting evidences such as presence of terraces, nature of samples dated and inferences of sea level rise from similar stable areas elsewhere.

The curve shows that the sea level along the west coast of India was about 100m lower as compared to present, around 14,500 years before and rose to 80m depth around 12,500 years before with a rate of ~10m/1,000 years. It was followed by a quiet period when the sea level remained unchanged for about 2,500 years. From 10,000 to 7,000 years sea level rose at a very high rate (~20m/1000 years). After 7,000 years B.P. it fluctuated to more or less the present level

The potential application as well as validity of this sea level variation curve was established when ~7500 BC old Neolithic settlements were discovered from Gulf of Khambat from a seawater depth of 30-40m. Plotting the age of discovered settlement over the sea level variation curve generated by NIO scientists gives a water depth of 30-40m, exactly matching with the depth zone from which the new findings of ancient civilization were reported. Further observation of the curve indicates that the sea came to a standstill at that level for some time, thus providing time for civilization to flourish before being engulfed by the sea again, thus providing scientific proof for the possible ancient Neolithic settlements off Gujarat.

See 'Changing sea level and ancient civilization along west coast of India' article published by The National Institute of Oceanography (NIO)[at: http://www.nio.org/index/option/com_nomenu/task/show/tid/85/sid/92/id/74]; for original article refer to 'Holocene sea level fluctuations on western Indian continental margin: An update'. J. Geol. Soc. India. 46; 1995; 157-162.; by Hashimi, N.H.; Nigam, R.; Nair, R.R.; Rajagopalan, G., Nigam, R.; Hashimi, N.H. Has sea level fluctuations modulated human settlements in Gulf of Khambhat (Cambay)? J. Geol. Soc. India. 59; 2002; 583-584.

dcclxvii In 2005 the remains of what could possibly have been an 'ancient sea wall' (dated to about 8,000 BC) was discovered off the western coast of India. In what could be a huge archaeological discovery, researchers have found a uniform wall, running a distance of approximately fifteen miles below the sea waters of Konkan coast, along the western coast of India. In what could turn out to be a major discovery, researchers have found a wall-like structure, which is 24km long, 2.7m in height, and around 2.5m in width. The structure shows uniformity in construction. "The structure is not continuous from Shrivardhan to Raigad, but it is uniform. It has been found 3m below the present sea level. Considering the uniformity of the structure, it is obvious that the structure is man-made," said Dr Ashok Marathe, department of archaeology, Deccan College Postgraduate and Research Institute, Pune.

While the structure, discovered while studying the effects of tsunamis, is currently 10 feet below sea level, it is this uniformity that has lead researchers to believe that it is man-made. This joint expedition, carried out by Deccan College, Pune and Department of Science and Technology, Central Government, has been in progress since 2005. "We were actually studying the impacts of tsunami and earthquake on western coast when we first found this structure in Valneshwar," said Marathe.

dcclxviii Considering the uniformity of the structure, it is obvious that the structure is man-made," said Dr Ashok Marathe, department of archaeology, Deccan College Postgraduate and Research Institute, Pune.

dcclxix See the Aitareya Aranyaka

dcclxx The natural habitat, climate, available minerals, presence of other plants and trees, etc have influence on the medicinal properties of plants

dcclxxi The exact location of Muziris is still not known to historians and archaeologists; it is generally speculated to be situated around present-day Kodungallur.

dcclxxii Baluchistan is bordered by Iran (west), by Afghanistan (northwest), by North-West Frontier and Punjab provinces (northeast and east), by Sindh province (southeast), and by the Arabian Sea (south). There are four major physical regions in Baluchistan, the upper highlands of the central and northeast, bounded by the Sulaiman Mountains to the east and the Toba Kakar Range to the northwest. The lower highlands include the eastern slopes of the Sulaiman Range; the lower ranges of the Makran, Kharan, and Chagai on the west; and the Pab and Kirthar ranges on the southeast. The upper highlands drain into the Indus River, while the lower highlands drain northward into the swamps or southward into the Arabian Sea.

dcclxxiii From the (Kushite and Proto-Elamite) 'Kash' or 'Kach' of ancient Baluchistan derived the great Kashwaha or Kachwaha (Kushwaha or Kuchwaha) of the Rajput genealogies. The later Assyrians called the Kushites *Kashshi* (or *Kusu*)

dcclxxiv Situated roughly fourteen (14) miles west of the present-day city of Mazar-i Sharif, ancient Baktra is situated amid extensive ruins, chief among them are the outer walls of the ancient city, which are more than 7 miles in circumference.

dcclxxv The ancient Naga northwestern capital city known as 'Oudh' (or 'Ancient Oudh') should not to be confused with present-day Oudh (or Ayodhya) in the Indian state of Uttar Pradesh. The Naga of Ancient Oudh were called 'Oudh-Am' and 'Otia-Am' (Am = "People" in Sanskrit)

dcclxxvi According to Abu Haukal "The Afghans are the descendants of the Avagana, the serpent tribe (Naga) of the Apivansa region of ancient India." According to him, the city of Herat is also called "Heri" or "Hari"

dcclxxvii In Rigvedic accounts, there is mention of Nagas or Ahi (serpent) race, Naga warriors or Naga kings. The Nagas were not only a civilized people, but a maritime power (and in the Mahabharata, where the ocean is described as their habitation, an ancient legend is preserved of how 'Kadru', the mother of serpents, compelled 'Garuda' (the Eagle or Hawk) to serve her sons by transporting them across the sea to a beautiful country in a distant land, which was inhabited by Nagas). The Nagas were expert navigators, possessed of very considerable naval resources, and had founded colonies upon distant coasts." (The Encircled Serpent, by M. Oldfield, p. 47.)

dcclxxviii Shiva (or Siva) means gracious, auspicious. In Tamil, it means 'the Supreme One', 'the Purest'. Shiva was an enemy of Vedics, they referred to him as a 'destroyer'.

dcclxxix The ancient city of Bactra stood at the crossroads of east and west since the earliest Kushite habitation in the region; earlier archaeological research and evidence revealed that the ancient city and the surrounding territories had been occupied since the Neolithic Era. The ruined walls and ruins of Bactra are situated just over seven miles from the right bank of the Balkh River, at an elevation of about 1,200 ft, where the remnants of the splendor of the ancient city lay largely in ruins (present-day professional archaeologists are generally unable to properly excavate the site, due to war in the region during the early 21st century).

Most of the city was destroyed during an invasion by Genghis Khan in the 13th century. It lay in ruins until the early 15th century, and the city is more of a village today, with a population of only a few thousand. But a handful of the original buildings have survived, including a number of ancient Buddhist reliquary mounds and the outer walls of the city.

dcclxxx Over time the early Kushite settlers at ancient Bactra would also gain prominence and wealthy off the lapis lazuli they found along riverbeds, which they traded to early city sites to the west, across the Iranian plateau and Mesopotamia. Researchers have also noted the existence of strong Elamite affinities among the later Bactrian aristocracy.

dcclxxxi The first kingdom of ancient Sumeria and Sumerians called themselves Kishites/Kish or Kush.

dcclxxxii Sir Henry Rawlinson, who was an army officer for the British East India Company and translator of the first cuneiform scripts in the 19th century, said that the language of the early Babylonians "was undoubtedly Kushite or Ethiopian." At this time there was actually an informal consensus among historians and archaeologistse, that the Sumerians originally came from Africa.

dcclxxxiii Rawlinson concurred that the race of Nimrod passed from east Africa by way of Arabia to the valley of the Euphrates before the beginning of history. Arab myths also agree that the Kushitic King Nimrod crossed from beyond the waters of Ethiopia in the earliest times with a fine crop of soldiers and established what was to become the world's oldest civilization. Many existing sites in Iraq are still named after Nimrod.

dcclxxxiv A spiritual achievement that was once the ultimate goal of all religions.

dcclxxxv Innumerable evidence from various cranial, skeletal, archaeological, sculptural and textual sources has confirmed the racial origins of the Sumerians as Nile valley Africans that migrated to Mesopotamia.

dcclxxxvi The Mesopotamian kingdoms of Sumer, Babylon, Erech and Elam which thrived in the regions where modern Iraq covers today were thus black civilizations

dcclxxxvii The Sumerians called themselves sag-giga, meaning "the black-headed people" (W. Hallo, W. Simpson. *The Ancient Near East*. New York: Harcourt, Brace, Jovanovich, 1971, 28.) In numerous inscribed tablets, the Sumerians refer to themselves in this fashion. Not black-haired, but black-headed. A few of the numerous references of this sort include: "May Ur-Ninurta, the king in whom Enlil trusts, open up your house of wisdom in which you have gathered knowledge in plenty, and then be the great ruler of the black-headed" (A tigi to Enki for Ur-Ninurta, Black 272). "Great lord...Suen...light of heaven, whose majestic radiance is visible even at mid-day, light who illuminates the black-headed people" (An ululumama to Suen for Ibbi-Suen, Black 273).

The goddess Ninisinna..."the great physician of the black-headed people (the Sumerians)" (Kramer, *History Begins at Sumer*, 64). "go to your brothers, the blackheaded people" ("Inanna and Shukallituda: The Gardner's Mortal Sin", in Kramer, *History Begins at Sumer*, 74). "Lipit-Es^tar, son of Enlil, may you shine as brilliantly as the sunlight!...May the black-headed people, numerous as flocks, follow the right path under you!" (Black et al., *The Literature of Ancient Sumer*, 53). "To the lady [Nisaba], the celestial star...who rules the black-headed, who posesses the tablet with all the names (?)" ("Nergal, Numus^da, and Ninurta," in Black et al., *The Literature of Ancient Sumer*, 180). "I, S^ulgi, am the herdsman and shepherd of the black-headed people" (A praise poem of S^ulgi, Black et al., *The Literature of Ancient Sumer*, 305). "I am the good shepherd of the black-headed...I am a human god, the lord of the numerous people. I am the strong heir of kingship" ("A praise poem of Lipit-Es^tar" in Black et al., *The Literature of Ancient Sumer*, 309).

"[The god] Utu, shepherd of the land, father of the black-headed" (Black et al. 17). "To the lady [Nisaba], the celestial star...who rules the black-headed, who posesses the tablet with all the names (?)" (from the composition "Nergal, Numus^da, and Ninurta," Black 180).

dcclxxxviii There is a concept called "Maat" from the ancient Kushites (and Khemetans) that permeated the way they lived and related to the world. Maat, simply translated, means living, creating and reasoning in adherence to the natural structures of the universe as created by God.

dcclxxxix Rawlinson says that the race of Nimrod passed from east Africa by way of Arabia to the valley of the Euphrates before the beginning of history.

dccxc The sons of Ausar (Osiris, Zeus, Kush, Dionysus) were: First,when *Ausar* married his first wife, *Hera,* at the height of *Atlatia,* and through this union had his first son, *Are;*then *Ausar* and Leto from their union bore twins, a beautiful daughter, *Artemis*, and a second son, *Apollo;* His third son, *Herakles* (also known as Hercules), was by *Alkmene*, his third wife, a woman considered a "commoner; *Thoth* was the fourth son of *Ausar* (Osiris, Kush, Zeus) by his third wife Maia who gave birth to his son *Thoth* (Hermes) in the *Holly City.* Ausar's fifth son, *Raama(h)* or *Regma*, who began the ancient lineage of S(h)eba and Dedan, was fathered in what would later become the ancient eponymous village of *Regma* (or "Raamah"), just beyond the northern borderlands of present-day Yemen in southern Oman. Ausar's fifth son was Raama(h), who was the father of S(h)eba and Dedan (1Chr. 1:9). The RSV uses both spellings in the same verse for Raama(h; in the LXX it is given as *Regma*, which also happens to be the capital city of a people known as the Rhammanitae in southern Oman. The *ISBE* gives a brief description of Raama. Ausar's sixth son, Nimrod**,** was born through his union with Semiramis in ancient Sumer. Ausar (Osiris, Kush, Zeus, Dionysus)'s seventh son, *Macedon* (Makedon), was born through his union with *Thyia,* daughter of *Deucalion*, in *Old Kavalla City.* Ausar's (Osiris, Kush, Zeus, Dionysus) eighth son Horus, was born of his union with his wife Isis in earliest Khemet

dccxci In Persian legend of the very early (pre Arian) period when Iran was civilized by a western Mesopotamian ruler, Takma Urupi (Tana=Takma) whose wife was also Eneth. Nimrod later had other wives and from them were born other sons and daughters.

dccxcii Archaeologists have found that this city was one of the oldest of Babylonia, founded before 4000 B.C. One of the earliest dynasties of the Sumerians ruled from Erech, it boasted the first ziggurat, or temple tower, and began the use of clay cylinder seals

dccxciii This is consistent with the development of the written Sumerian language where the more explicit orthography of the later texts painstakingly includes all the amissable consonants of a name which would not have been expressed in the older texts. ... one copy of the Sumerian King List, found at Nippur and published by Arno Poebel in 1914, gives En-me-er-ru-kar. We might, therefore, justifiably vocalise the name as Enmerukar. Next we come to a crucial point. The four syllables En-me-er-ru-kar can be understood as a name plus an epithet -- once realised that *kar* is the Sumerian word for 'hunter' (Akk. *habilu*). Thus we have King 'En-me-ru, the hunter'.

dccxciv . Nimrod was also said to be a great builder, who constructed the cities of Uruk, Akkad and Babel. Both Nimrod and Enmerkar were renowned for their huntsmanship. Nimrod, as the grandson of Ham, belongs to the second 'generation' after the flood ... and this is also true of Enmerkar who is recorded in the Sumerian King List as the second ruler of Uruk after the flood (Ubartutu -- (Utnapishtim) -- Flood -- Meskiagkasher -- Enmerkar). Both ruled over their empires in the land of Shinar/Sumer. In the epic literature of Mesopotamia, Nimrod is variously referred to as Enmerkar, Ninurta and Ninus, while in Phoenicia, Aram and Egypt he was known as Reshep or Reshpu, and to the Greeks, Orion, *the mighty hunter.*

dccxcv Also attributed to Nimrod are the founding and building of the cities of: Nineveh (Heb. nineweh) is one of the most ancient cities of the world, founded by Nimrod. It is on the banks of the Tigris opposite the site of the modern Mosul in Iraq; Nimrud (Gen. 10:6-12) is ancient Calah (Heb. Calneh) in Assyria, founded by Nimrod but possibly built by Asshur and is famous for its immense statuary in the form of winged lions and winged bulls; Akkad (Heb. 'akkadh), whose location is unknown, but thought to be identified with Agade, which Sargon I, the Semitic conqueror of the Sumerian Akkadians, made his capital in c.2350 B.C; Shinar (Heb. shin'ar) or the region that contained the cities of Babel, Erech, Akkad, and Caleh. Genesis 11:1-9 on the plain of Shinar, they started to build a tower. Amraphel, king of Shinar, invaded Canaan in the days of Abram (Gen. 14:1). Nebuchadnezzar was ruler of the land of Shinar (Dan. 1:20); Resen (Heb. resen, fortified place), as Xenophon reports that Larissa was a strongly fortified city in this section between Nineveh and Calah, and Rehoboth (Heb. rehovoth, broad places).

dccxcvi (Justin, Hist. Rom. Script., Vol. ii, p. 615; Diodorus, Bibliotheca, lib. ii, p. 63) Ninus was said to be the husband, of Semiramis. According to Eusebius these two reigned as king and queen in the time of Abraham; but the great chronologist Clinton, and the celebrated Excavator and Linguist Layard, both assign an earlier date to the reign of Ninus and Semiramis.

The study of the Sumerians, Akkadians. Assyrians and Elamites began with the decipherment of the cuneiform script by Henry Rawlinson. Henry Rawlinson had spent most of his career in the Orient. This appears to have given him an open mind in regards to history. He recognized the Ancient Model of History, the idea that civilization was founded by the Kushite or Hamitic people of the Bible.

As result, Rawlinson was surprised during his research to discover that the founders of the Mesopotamian civilization were of Kushite origin. He made it clear that the Semitic speakers of Akkad and the non-Semitic speakers of Sumer were both Black or Negro people who called themselves sag-ga-ga "Black Heads" . In Rawlinson's day the Sumerian people were recognized as Akkadian or Chaldean, while the Semitic speaking blacks were called Assyrians.

Rawlinson identified these Akkadians as Turanian or Scythic people. But he made it clear that these ancient Scythic or Turanian speaking people were Kushites or Blacks.

A major supporter of Rawlinson was Edward Hincks. Hincks continued Rawlinson's work and identified the ancient group as Chaldeans, and also called them Turanian speakers. Hincks, though, never dicussed much about their ethnic origin.

A late comer to the study of the Sumerians and the Akkadians was Julius Oppert. Oppert was a German born of Jewish parents. He made it clear that the Chaldean and Akkadian people spoke different languages. He noted that the original founders of Mesopotamia civilization called themselves Ki-en-gi "land of the true lords" . It was the Semitic speakers who called themselves Akkadians.

Assyrians called the Ki-en-gi people Sumiritu "the sacred language" . Oppert popularized the Assyrian name Sumer, for the original founders of the civilization.

Oppert began to popularize the idea that the Sumerians were related to the contemporary Altaic and Turanian speaking people, e.g., Turks and Magyar (Hungarian) speaking people. He made it clear that the Akkadians were Semites like himself . To support this idea Oppert pointed out that typological features between Sumerian and Altaic languages existed. This feature was agglutination.

The problem with identifying the Sumerians as descendants from contemporary Turanian speakers resulted from the fact that Sumerian and the Turkish languages are not genetically related. As a result Oppert began to criticize the work of Hincks (who was dead at the time) in relation to the identification of the Sumerian people as Turanian following the research of Rawlinson.

Oppert knew Rawlinson had used African languages to decipher cuneiform writing. But he did not compare the Sumerian to African languages, probably, due to the fact that he knew they were related given Rawlinson's earlier research.

It is strange to some observers that Oppert,never criticized Rawlinson who had proposed the Turanian origin of the Ki-en-gi (Sumerians). But this was not strange at all. Oppert did not attack Rawlinson who was still alive at the time because he knew that Rawlinson said the Sumerians were the original Scythic and Turanian people he called Kushites. Moreover, Rawlinson made it clear that both the Akkadians and Sumerians were Blacks. For Oppert to have debated this issue with Rawlinson, who deciphered the cuneiform script, would have meant that he would have had to accept the fact that Semites were Black. There was no way Oppert would have wanted to acknowledge this African heritage.

Although Oppert successfully hid the recognition that the Akkadians and the Sumerians both referred to themselves as sag-gig-ga "black heads"• , some researchers were unable to follow the status quo and ignore this reality. For example, Francois Lenormant, made it clear, following the research of Rawlinson, that the Elamite and Sumerians spoke genetically related languages. This idea was hard to reconcile with the depiction of people on the monuments of Iran, especially the Behistun monument, which depicted Negroes (with curly hair and beards) representing the Assyrians, Jews and Elamites who ruled the area.

As a result, Oppert began the myth that the Sumerian languages was isolated from other languages spoken in the world evethough it shared typological features with the Altaic languages. Oppert taught Akkadian-Sumerian in many of the leading Universities in France and Germany. Many of his students soon began to dominate the Academe, or held chairs in Sumerian and Akkadian studies these researchers continued to perpetuate the myth that the Elamite and Sumerian languages were not related.

There was no way to keep from researchers who read the original Sumerian, Akkadian and Assyrian text that these people recognized that they were ethnically Blacks. This fact was made clear by Albert Terrien de LaCouperie. Born in France, de LaCouperie was a well known linguist and China expert. Although native of France most of his writings are in English. In the journal he published called the Babylonian and Oriental Record, he outlined many aspects of ancient history. In these pages he made it clear that the Sumerians, Akkadians and even the Assyrians who called themselves salmat kakkadi â€˜black headed peopleâ€• , were all Blacks of Kushite origin. Eventhough de LaCouperie taught at the University of London, the prestige of Oppert, and the fact that the main centers for Sumero-Akkadian studies in France and Germany were founded by Oppert and or his students led to researchers ignoring the evidence that the Sumerians , Akkadians and Assyrians were Black.

In summary, the cuneiform evidence makes it clear that the Sumerians, Akkadians and Assyrians recognized themselves as Negroes: black heads. This fact was supported by the statues of Gudea, the Akkadians and Assyrians. Plus the Behistun monument made it clear that the Elamites were also Blacks.

The textual evidence also makes it clear that Oppert began the discussion of a typological relationship between Sumerian and Turkic languages. He also manufactured the idea that the Semites of Mesopotamia and Iran, the Assyrians and Akkadians were whites, like himself. Due to this brain washing, and whitening out of Blacks in history, many people today can look at depictions of Assyrians, Achamenians, and Akkadians and fail to see the Negro origin of these people.

To make the Sumerians white textbooks print pictures of artifacts dating to the Gutian rule of Lagash, to pass them off as the true originators of Sumerian civilization. No Gutian rulers of Lagash are recognized in the Sumerian King List.

Kohl did not mention the red-and-black ware. This ceramic style was found at NKSD sites and is discussed by Singh and Andersson.

Rawlinson was convinced that there was a relationship between the Sumerians and Africans. As a result he used two African languages: one Semitic and the other Kushitic to decipher the cuneiform writing. Rawlinson was sure that the ancient Nubians and Puntites founded Mesopotamian civilization. The Sumerians came from the Sahara before it became a desert. Affinities exist between Nubia ware and pottery from Ennedi and Tibesti.

This would explain why the Sumerians and Elamites often referred to themselves as "ksh." For example the ancient Sumerians called their dynasty "Kish." The words "kish", "kesh" and "kush" were also names for ancient Nubia-Sudan. The Elamites also came from Kush. According to the classical writer Strabo, Susa the centre of the Elamite civilization was founded by Tithonus, king of Kush.

Sumer's greatness and grandeur was both alluring and a magnate to the Aryan-Semites and the Aryan-Europeans who began to invade its territory and society until they finally conquered, dominated and destroyed it greatness. At the hands of the nomadic-barbarians the Sumerians (Africans) experienced invasions of their homeland, pillage of their resources, genocide, rape, slavery, exile, colonization, cultural theft, barbarism, and racism (in its beginning stages). From as early as 2,200 BCE Sumer, including its African neighbor Susa/Elam, endured the invasions of one increasingly brutal nomadic-barbaric 'White' people after another.

Under the invasions of the Martu, also called the Assyrians, the strength of the African population known as Sumerian in Mesopotamia was defeated resulting in complete and utter domination at the hand of barbaric warring populations set on plunder and exploitation.

[dccxcvii] Many authorities translate Genesis X, 2, to read, "Out of that land, he (Nimrod) went forth into Assur or Assyria, and builded Nineveh." This is the proper translation of the passage and not that "Asher went forth and builded Ninevah," the connection is broken and destroyed by the latter mode of rendering. Asher a son of Shem being inserted among the descendants of Ham, and an event of his history narrated before his birth, first mentioned in verse 22. Mic. V, 6, calls Assyria, the land of Nimrod. Diod. Sic. II, 1., calls the founder of the kingdom Ninus.

Where the Genesis stories really came from: Not surprisingly, it seems the Genesis stories really came from the same place that the Jewish people said they really came from– the much, much more ancient civilization of Sumer (in the region later known as Babylon). This no doubt explains the reason why all the major stories of "Jewish" history prior to the beginning of Abraham's story in Genesis 11 are nearly identical to tales written first in Sumer.

There is, however, one very important difference between the Jewish (later to become Christian) version of these stories and those of the the far more ancient Sumerian culture: In the Biblical creation narrative the gender of the Creator of Heaven and Earth has been switched from female to male and the Goddess erased from the tale. Unless, that is, you know where to look

According to the Sumerians, Nammu, the Primordial Sea Goddess, was the first to exist and hence, the creator of all things. She began by giving birth to the Sky GodThe disappearance of Nammu: Yahweh of the Israelites was not the first Sky God to usurp Nammu's position. Around the same century that Abraham allegedly skipped town (whether before, during, or after depends on which scholar's estimate of his century is correct), the city-state of Babylon took over Ur and the rest of the country of Sumer. Under the much more patriarchal influence of the Babylonian Empire the Creator Goddess lost her position to the Sky God Marduk.

The Babylonians said Marduk created the heavens and earth by murdering Tiamat (Nammu's Babylonian name) and forming the universe from her body. Eventually, when the priests of Judah rewrote the tale, the Goddess would disappear altogether from the narrative . Well, almost disappear. She is traceable still by linguistics, for when God hovers over "the deep" in the opening scene of Genesis (Chapter 1, Verse 2), the word translated here is tehom, meaning the deeps, the abyss, and linguistically the Semitic form of Tiamat, the name of the Babylonian Goddess.

In time, Nammu would be forgotten, but now, thanks to archaeologists, we can remember the Goddess who came before Heaven and Earth, before the sky gods ascended the throne of history, before even the Bible, before ever the priest put pen to scroll to write the words "In the Beginning…."

[dccxcviii] The fundamental difference between Assyrian and Syria is that one is a civilization; the other is a relatively modern social construct based on the European concept of a Nation-State.

[dccxcix] The Epic of Gilgamesh has been of interest to Christians ever since its discovery in the mid-nineteenth century in the ruins of the great library at Nineveh, with its account of a universal flood. The Epic was composed in the form of a poem. The main figure is Gilgamesh, who actually may have been an historical person. The Sumerian King List shows Gilgamesh in the first dynasty of Uruk reigning for 126 years.[11] This length of time is not a problem when compared with the age of the pre-flood patriarchs of the Bible. Indeed, after Gilgamesh, the kings lived a normal life span as compared with today. The King List is also of interest as it mentions the flood specifically—"the

deluge overthrew the land." The story starts by introducing the deeds of the hero Gilgamesh. He was one who had great knowledge and wisdom, and preserved information of the days before the flood. Gilgamesh wrote on tablets of stone all that he had done, including building the city walls of Uruk and its temple for Eanna.

There have been numerous flood stories identified from ancient sources scattered around the world. The stories that were discovered on cuneiform tablets (cuneiform writing was invented by the Sumerians), which comprise some of the earliest surviving writing, have obvious similarities. Which begs the question, how should one relate to the Noah story, given that it clearly couldn't have happened as related in Genesis? For one thing, there is no geological or archaeological evidence that a flood covered the world's landmasses up to Mount Ararat in the mountains of Armenia. Also the notion that each animal species in the world, or even a fraction of them, could be housed within an ark strains credibility.

[dccc] Ashur (or A$\underline{s}$sur) was a deified form of the city of Assur, and as such, Ashur did not originally have a family, but as the cult came under southern Mesopotamian influence, he later came to be regarded as the Assyrian equivalent of Enlil, the chief god of Nippur. Enlil was the most important god of the southern pantheon

[dccci] Rawlinson anticipated Perry by tracing the Sumerians back to Ethiopia" (Jackson 246). Note that the descend of Sumerians from Ethiopia (Cush) fits precisely with the scriptural statement that Nimrod was son of Cush, father of the Ethiopians

[dcccii] This reference is perpetuated in Akkadian literature. The Semitic king Sargon of Akkad describes his conquest and rule over the Sumerians of Mesopotamia as recorded in Akkadian cuneiform: "The black headed peoples I ruled, I governed" (Rogers, Robert W. *Cuneiform Parallels to the Old Testament*. New York: Eaton & Mains, 1912, 136). "They are described in the Assyrio-Babylonian inscriptions as a black-faced people" (Jackson, John G. *Man, God, and Civilization* 242). For an example, see "Erra and Ishum" in Dalley's *Myths from Mesopotamia* 290. Most Sumerian depictions of themselves are distinctly non-Semitic with shaved heads, broad noses, and negroid-appearing features (See Kramer, History, 203, 207-209, 217). Black and colleagues wrote, "Semites supposedly had long hair and beards; Sumerians wore their heads and faces shaved" (Black et al., *The Literature of Ancient Sumer*, lvi). Sumerians "are shown on the monuments as beardless and with shaven heads, whereas Semitic and later Babylonian figures are represented with sharp facial features and long beards (Jackson 242).

Thus we have the Sumerians' own description of themselves as black, others' description of them as black, and their own depictions of themselves which demonstrate predominately negroid-appearing features and which, when colored, are typically dark or black. The evidence suggests that the Sumerians were prominently black, the kinsmen of Nimrod as scripture suggests

[dccciii] In this classic essay entitled "Nimrod A Mighty Hunter," Rowlands does not come down firmly on the side of a heroic Nimrod, he thoroughly debunks the ignorant, lying notion that the scriptures say Nimrod was evil. Rowlands wrote: "If we study what the scriptures say in Hebrew, many people will be surprised. We need to remember that in Hebrew, the nuances of English grammar and punctuation do not appear. This is word for word what the Hebrew Scriptures say about Nimrod written in Hebrew; "Cush he generated Nimrud ... He started to become of masterful in the earth. He became masterful hunter to faces of YHVH ... on so he is being said as Nimrud masterful hunter to faces of YHVH." That verse is very surprising. Nimrod was closer than just being before the Lord, he was literally face to face with God. To be face to face with someone means to be close enough to be within visual range. Could a wicked man be face to face with God?"

[dccciv] But, what accounts of Nimrod came first? Mighty Hunter, Fool, Rebel? History is written by the victors and to him goes the spoils. It came from a long line of those who wanted to *control* History and put fear in the hearts of men toward those who had the keys to all religions, the African. Rabbinic as well as Catholic and later Christian and Arabic leaders redesigned the nature of Nimrod to suit their racist paradigm. Some Rabbinical scholars have identified Nimrod as part of the first of a family (Cush) and ignorantly cast him as the first Homosexual who was licentious and practiced bestiality. It is also said that Noah wife was of the offspring of Cain (another biblical sinner) who transferred all of those hateful characteristics to her son Ham [but not Shem and Japheth?] and from this evil hatred of God and disobedience to his word was transferred from the line that was considered African.

[dcccv] In Truth, this once revered figure from the bible has been unjustly maligned by a few liars who have gotten away with it by playing on the "emotional nature" of the masses. In this case the "emotional nature" is racism against black people, which has kept the masses from questioning the liars even when it is clear that what they are saying goes against the biblical teachings. For centuries this combination of a lying tradition, scholarly deceit and institutional racism has kept the information that I shall reveal below about Nimrod from the public. And that is a shame, because these lies have had a tremendously detrimental effect upon the study of history and the standing of people of African descent in the world. Along with the so called "Curse Of Ham," this lying lore about Nimrod has been used to justify all manner of prejudice, oppression and genocide.

These same sources claim he was the builder of the Tower of Babel and because of his desire to 'Reach God' the languages of the world were confused, but the Bible does not exactly say that (See Genesis 10), no! It says "men." What men? The men migrating in the East that came to the Valley of Shinar and settled there. But where was Nimrod? We are told he taught the people to rebel, but where is that story within the Bible? Nowhere! That came from extra-biblical non-canonized writings from the 1st and 6th century AD after the death of Christ. Ask yourself: Why during those centuries after Christ were they trying to re-write the story of Nimrod? Cain, Ham an all the rest of the so-called black folks in the Bible?

Without any extra-Biblical information Nimrod was just a powerful leader and the son of Cush. We need to sift through the extra-Biblical information The Talmud is not helpful when it comes to the truth, it cast the same shadow on the Nimrod. The Talmud is a record of rabbinic discussions pertaining to the law, ethics, customs and history. The Talmud has two components: the Mishnah (c. 200 CE), the first written compendium of Judaism's Oral Law; and the Gemara (c. 500 CE). The Talmud - The Talmud gets its name from the word Lamud - taught, and means "The Teaching." By metonymy it is taken to mean the book which contains the Teaching, which is called

Talmud, that is, the doctrinal book which alone fully expounds and explains all the knowledge and teaching of the European Jews..

The Midrash - The collection of mostly halakic Jewish traditions compiled about 200 AD and made the basic part of Talmud. Mishnah means "teaching." It is the compilation of "unwritten" or "oral laws" which were passed down the centuries by the word of mouth. The compilation of the discussions on the articles of Mishnah is called the Gemara (which means complementary) The explanations in the Gemara have further explanations called Midrashim (exposition, explanation - A haggadic or halakic exposition of the underlying significance of a Bible text).

"But Midrashim are not considered a part of The Talmud. Mishnah had taken its final form as a result of 50 years of study by Judah Ha Nasi in Beth Shearim in Galilee . Judah Ha Nasi ("The Prince"-135-220 AD.) was a Palestinian Patriarch, a disciple of the school of Rabbi Akiba . Judah Ha Nasi went through the "Oral Law" and organized it in six sections as established by Rabbi Akiba and his student Rabbi Meir. This work of Judah Ha Nasi became the foundation of the Talmud.

Nasi or Nesi mean BLACK!!!! But, why would black man use Talmudical writing to disrespect black people? Did he or was his work was added to and rewritten over the years to reflect a negative African view-point? The Mishnah - The Mischnah is the foundation and the principal part of the whole Talmud. This book was accepted by the Jews everywhere and was recognized as their authentic code of law. It was expounded in their Academies in Babylon

It has been a rough historical ride for this Kushite hero and for the depiction of ancient Kushite culture, but the time of the lies is now over; let us never again allow Nimrod to be taken from us by such liars.

[dcccvi] See the '*African Presence in Early Asia*', edited by Runoko Rashidi and Ivan Van Sertima; REFERENCES: *Analcalypsis*, by Godfrey Higgins; *A Tropical Dependency*, by Lady Lugard.

[dcccvii] The original homeland of all ancient Semitic peoples, including Hebrews, was not northern Arabia, as is currently believed, but northwestern Mesopotamia. An ecological catastrophe that impacted the area around the Black Sea forced Indo-European tribes inhabiting the surrounding coast of the former inland lake to migrate outward in all directions. On their way to the south and the south-east, the Indo-Arians displaced and partially mingled with the Hurrians of Eastern Anatolia. In turn, arianized Hurrians first displaced the Eastern Semites from the upper courses of Tigris, and then, at the end of the 3rd millennium B.C., occupied the land of Western Semites (Amorites) in the upper courses of Euphrates. The referencing by the Bible of Harran as the original birthplace of Abraham is the indirect evidence of these ethnic changes. The last wave of Western Semites (Arameans) in 12-11 centuries B.C. was also caused by the movements of Hurrians and Indo-Europeans in northwestern Mesopotamia.

At the end of the 3rd millennium BC, large groups of Western Semitic peoples, specifically the Amorites, began settling in mass in Mesopotamia, Syria and Canaan and took control over the majority of the cities, forming their own Amorite countries. One of these, for example, was Babylon – during the reign of the infamous ruler Hammurapi in the 18th century BC. This written and material evidence gathered in the last decades speaks in favor of the fact that the Amorites did not come from northern Arabia or the Syrian Desert region, as had previously been thought, but instead from the north, from northwestern Mesopotamia. The second mass wave of Western Semites, known as the Aramaens, came to Syria, central and southern Mesopotamia much later in the 12-11th centuries BC. Judging from the directions of their migrations, their place of exodus was again northwestern Mesopotamia. (Based in the Abstract 'Where did the Ancient Semites come from ?' (by Igor Lipovsky))

Ancient written and archeological sources confirm that the Semites came to central Mesopotamia, Syria and Palestine not from the south (Arabia), but from the north (northwestern Mesopotamia) and from the upper courses of the two large-scale rivers in Western Asia, the Tigris and the Euphrates. The Bible concretely designates the fatherland of the Jewish patriarchs, specifying the region surrounding the city of Haran which was situated approximately 30 km to the southwest of today's Turkish city Sanliurfa (ancient Edessa), not far from the border with Syria. Biblical texts unambiguously show that the city of Ur in Sumer, from which Abraham came into Canaan (present-day Palestine), was never his place of birth. Moreover, on the way to Canaan, the family of Abraham and his father Terah, stopped for a long time in the place of their birth, Haran.3 This is where Terah died and the clan leadership was transferred to his son – Abraham. Archeological excavations in Palestine have unearthed sufficient proof that the Western Semitic peoples also came from the north.

The Chaldean country, in the strict sense, lay in southern Babylonia, on the lower Euphrates and Tigris. But the name was extended by the Biblical writers to include the whole of Babylonia, after the Chaldean Nebuchadnezzar had established the new Babylonian empire and brought his people to world-wide fame. Indeed, it is doubtful whether the Biblical "Chaldea" and "Chaldeans" ever connoted the ancient country and people; these terms, until the eighth century B.C., were restricted to the region along the head of the Persian gulf.

It is impossible to define narrowly the boundaries of this early land of Chaldea, and one may only locate it generally in the low, marshy, alluvial land about the estuaries of the Tigris and Euphrates, which then discharged their waters through separate mouths into the sea. In a later time, when the Chaldean people had burst their narrow bonds and obtained the ascendency over all Babylonia, they gave their name to the whole land of Babylonia, which then was called Chaldea.

On the whole the Bible agrees with the inscriptions in making the Chaldeans of history a comparatively modern race, and in excluding them from all association with the ancient dynasties of Babylonia (The only doubtful passages are those in which "Ur of the Chaldees" is spoken of (Gen. xi. 28 *et seq.*).

[dcccviii] Early Chaldean tribal regions were ill-defined and the political strength of each individual shaikh was said to be largely a matter of personal ability and prestige.

[dcccix] See "Ancient Assyria", by: C.H.W. Johns

[dcccx] See the "The Conquest of Civilization", by James Henry Breasted

[dcccxi] According to "The Penguin Encyclopedia of Ancient Civilization" / Arthur Cotterell "Throughout the remainder of the 8th century BC Babylonian Political life was disturbed by the Chaldeans, a Semitic speaking group of people who had entered the plain earlier and who were now settled along the coast of the Persian Gulf. One tribe of Chaldeans, Yakin, produced an eminently capable leader called Merodach-baladan, who with Elamite support made numerous attempts to seize the Babylonian crown…"

dcccxii   Berossus was born during or before Alexander the Great's reign over Babylon (330-323 BC), with the earliest date suggested as 340 BC. It is significant to note that Berossus published his 'Babyloniaca' ('History of Babylonia') by the patronage of the Macedonian-Seleucid king, Antiochus I Soter (during the third year of Antiochus I, according to Diodorus Siculus). It is suggested that it was commissioned by Antiochus I, perhaps desiring a history of one of his newly acquired lands, or by the Great Temple priests, seeking justification for the worship of Marduk in Seleucid lands. Pure history writing per se was not a Babylonian concern, and none other than the equally suspect Josephus testifies to Berossus' reputation.

dcccxiii   Later adopted by Eusebius, a scribe of the early chiristian church). In his Ecclesiastical History (written about A.D. 324)) Eusebius indirectly confesses that he has related whatever might redound to the glory, and that he has suppressed all that could tend to the disgrace, of religion. An acknowledgement that naturally elicits the suspicion that a writer who has so openly violated one of the fundamental tenets and laws of all credible historians. See Gibbon, Edward, The Decline and Fall of the Roman Empire, Encyclopedia Britannica reprint, 1990, ISBN 0-85229-531-6. Volume I, chapter 16, p.232. In the introduction to the 1965 Williamson edition of the 'Eusebius' Historia Ecclesiastica' (Penguin Classics, p.27): "He indirectly confesses that he has related whatever might redound to the glory, and has suppressed all that could tend to the disgrace, of religion"

dcccxiv The etymology of the name Babel in the Bible means "confused" (Gen 11:9) and throughout the Bible, Babylon was a symbol of the confusion caused by godlessness. The name Babylon is the Greek form of the Hebrew name Babel.

dcccxv   Special interest attaches to this reference, since Berosus is now supposed to have drawn his material from Babylonian sources. ("Histor. Graec. Fragm.", ed. Didot, II, 512; IV, 282; Euseb., "Chron.", I, 18, in P.G., XIX, 123; "Praep. Evang.", IX, 14, in P.G., XXI, 705).

dcccxvi   Authorities like George Smith, Chad Boscawen, and Sayce believed they had discovered a reference to the Tower of Babel; but Frd. Delitzsch pointed out that the translation of the precise words which determine the meaning of the text is most uncertain (Smith-Delitzsch. "Chaldaische Genesis", 1876, 120-124; Anmerk., p. 310).

dcccxvii Among the reasons for this association are the larger size of the ruins, the older age of the ruins, and the fact that one epithet of Eridu was "NUN.KI" (the "mighty place"), which later became the title of Babylon.

dcccxviii They're the most damaging accusation, the supposed rebellious activity of Nimrod against God, has been booted from the court of history because no credible evidence has ever been reported or witnessed by those who were around during his time; in fact they reported just the opposite and the false evidence of the Hebrew has been proven linguistically impossible. This phony charge has been replaced by proof that Nimrod's activities were actually done on behalf of God, whom he has been notoriously and falsely accused of rebelling against.

dcccxix   On one hand some Jewish traditions claimed the Kemetians and other Kushites were devil worshippers, enslavers and sinners, which is partly why the lies about Nimrod have gone unquestioned for so long and why the "Curse of Ham" garbage has been so effective. On the other hand the Greeks said the Kushites were the most advanced and just people who communed face to face with divinity.

dcccxx The first century Roman-Jewish author Flavius Josephus similarly explained that the name was derived from the Hebrew word Babel (βαβὲλ), meaning "confusion." The Greek form of the name in the Septuagint, Babylon (Βαβυλὼν), was from the Akkadian Bāb-ilim, "Gate of the gods", in reference to the great temple-towers (the ziggurats) of ancient Sumer (Biblical Shinar).

dcccxxi   The Tanakh (or Mikra) is the canon of the Hebrew Bible; the body of scripture known to non-Jews as the Old Testament, and to Jews as the Tanakh or Written Torah.

dcccxxii   The Yahweh cult began for all intents and purposes with the rise of John Hyrancus as ruler of a backwater place in the land of Canaan called Judea, which appeared after Alexander; officially in the history with Pompey.

The Septuagint stories shed light on John Hyrancus in the three books of Maccabes (the fourth book of which clearly dates from the 1st century AD.), which recount a civil war in the region between the Yahweh cult leader, Judah Maccabe, and the locals who had adopted Greek culture

We have to move to Flavius Josephus to pick up the story after Judah Maccabe. We read his son and grandson spread their Yahweh cult by military force, successfully imposing it upon the Iodumeans (from whom Herod arose), the Galileans and the Itureans. They were forced to circumcise and adopt Judean worship customs and practices.

Viewing the Septuagint stories against the rise of a Yahweh cult in a region around Jerusalem (which would be named after the cult leader, Judah Maccabe) clarifies the mounting influence and power of the cult.

The nature of the Yahweh cult was not like religion as we recognize it today. In the 1st century AD it was a savage and primitive cult in a culture which abjured any kind of body mutilation.

The cult was vehemently opposed to that of the cults of other Canaanite and Mesopotamian deities and belief systems. Nonetheless, there are some who purport the evolution of Yahweh through his encounters with Canaanite deities on his way to becoming the "One God" of post-exhilic Judaism.

dcccxxiii   Nimrod was purportedly murdered during the chaos that followed the "confusion of tongues.

dcccxxiv   Josephus, the Jewish historian, quoting from an ancient source, records these words: When all men were of one language, some of them built a tower, as if they would thereby ascend up to heaven, but the gods sent storms of wind and overthrew the tower, and gave everyone his peculiar language; and for this reason it was that the city was called Babylon (Antiquities of the Jews, 1.4.3)..

dcccxxv   Higgins then added that: "The same myths are found in India. The ancient peoples of India were Asiatic Kushites and it should not surprise us that they shared common traditions with their brothers in Africa. [See: *African Presence in Early Asia*, edited by Runoko Rashidi and Ivan Van Sertima; REFERENCES: *Analcalypsis*, by Godfrey Higgins; *A Tropical Dependency*, by Lady Lugard].

dcccxxvi   The fact that this is not commonly known is example of both sloppy scholarship, a campaign of distortion and outright lies by latter era Hebrew scribes to destroy the reputation and personage of Nimrod. A mighty man can be a simple bully, but a masterful hero is always a learned person who has risen up as a part of a highly respected masterful tradition. In this case it would have been a Kushite, or African tradition, and this is a part of what the liars have been trying to conceal.

dcccxxvii These were the Kushite people whom the Hebrews knew all too well, having sojourned in their lands for a long time as documented in the Old Testament.

dcccxxviii There is a pre-dynastic artifact called the Gebel el-Arak Knife found in southern Egypt that depicts one of the earliest representations of Nimrod from around 3,300 BC; scholars point to it as proof positive that people from Mesopotamia interacted with people from the Nile Valley because the figure in the middle is dressed like an Elamite/Sumerian, not a person from the Nile Valley. Other representations of this multinational Kushite heroic tradition from the Sahara desert, Mesopotamia and Sudan are even older.

dcccxxix (The root word from which leviathan is derived is , "lavah," with means in ancient Hebrew "to join." Leviathan in Hebrew is , "livyathan" which means "twisted."

dcccxxx See Benno Landsberger's book, "The Beginning of Civilization in Mesopotamia", VOL 1, pp. 8-9, and Stephanie Dalley, in the book "Myths from Mesopotamia: Creation

dcccxxxi The Bible, Genesis says that the ancient Kush was between the rivers of Euphrates and Tigris (Iraq), Gihon (Egypt, Nile), Pishon (Indus, India), and the land of Havilah (Arabia).

dcccxxxii Mesopotamia is Greek for "between the rivers."

dcccxxxiii The Fertile Crescent is region of fertile irrigated land that stretched across Mesopotamia and reached down the Mediterranean coast and included present-day Iran, Syria, southeastern Turkey, Lebanon, Israel and Palestine.

dcccxxxiv The area referred to as 'Canaan' in the Bible is today known as the southern half of the Levant, a region in the Middle East that is bounded by the Taurus Mountains in the north, the Mediterranean Sea in the west and the north Arabian Desert to the east. The exact borders of early Kanaan are unknown, but it is thought to be the footprint of modern-day Israel, Jordan, Lebanon and Syria. In Greek history, Canaan is Phoenicia.

dcccxxxv The "Natufians," as they are call, is a name of convenience, from the name of the place in present-day Israel where the archeological site was uncovered, and has no historical significance. The British archaeologist Dorothy Gerrod coined the term "Natufian" because she was studying remains from the Shuqba cave at Wadi an-Natuf in Palestine. The term is derived from the place, but Natufianceramics and stone work has been found in other locations as well.

dcccxxxvi There is, of course, a long-standing disagreement regarding evolution (of all things) and early migration into the Levant; the point of contention (or more aptly 'obfuscation') is that 'there were two different populations, perhaps different species, of Upper Pleistocene Levantine hominids'. The first, from the Israeli sites of Qafzeh and Skhul, is anatomically modern with "African-like affinities"; the second (and this is truly reaching), from sites such as Amud, Kebara, and Tabun, is archaic, or "Neandertal" in morphology.

Others argue that this is nothing more than a false dichotomy derived from the opportunity presented by a single but highly variable early ancient population. A tactic which seeks creates distractive debate around issues such as 'the dimensions of the Natufians heads compared to those of the pre-dynastic Egyptians', or the purported size and shape of their faces, and the prominence of their chins, etc

From a genetic point of view, several recent genetic studies have shown that Sub-Saharan genetic lineages (affiliated with the Y-chromosome PN2 clade; Underhill et al. 2001) have spread through Egypt into the Near East, the Mediterranean area, and, for some lineages, as far north as Turkey (E3b-M35 Y lineage; Cinniogclu et al. 2004; Luis et al. 2004), probably during several dispersal episodes since the Mesolithic. "From the Mesolithic to the early Neolithic period different lines of evidence support an out-of-Africa Mesolithic migration to the Levant by northeastern African groups that had biological affinities with sub-Saharan populations. (Cinniogelu et al. 2004; King et al. 2008; Lucotte and Mercier 2003; Luis et al. 2004; Quintana-Murci et al. 1999; Semino et al. 2004; Underhill et al. 2001).

This finding is in agreement with morphological data that suggest that populations with sub-Saharan morphological elements were present in northeastern Africa, from the Paleolithic to at least the early Holocene, and diffused northward to the Levant and Anatolia beginning in the Mesolithic. This northward migration of northeastern African populations carrying sub-Saharan biological elements is concordant with the morphological homogeneity of the Natufian populations (Bocquentin 2003), which present morphological affinity with sub-Saharan populations (Angel 1972; Brace et al. 2005).

In addition, the Neolithic revolution was assumed to arise in the late Pleistocene Natufians and subsequently spread into Anatolia and Europe (Bar-Yosef 2002), and the first Anatolian farmers, Neolithic to Bronze Age Mediterraneans and to some degree other Neolithic-Bronze Age Europeans, show morphological affinities with the Natufians (and indirectly with sub-Saharan populations; Angel 1972; Brace et al. 2005), in concordance with a process of demie diffusion accompanying the extension of the Neolithic revolution (Cavalli-Sforza et al. 1994)." -- Ricaut et al 2008. Cranial Discrete Traits in a Byzantine Popion Hum Bio 80:5 535-64 .."one can identify Negroid traits of nose and prognathism appearing in Natufian latest hunters (McCown, 1939) and in Anatolian and Macedonian first farmers, probably from Nubia via the unknown predecessors of the Badarians and Asians....." (Angel 1972. Biological Relations of Egyptians and Eastern Mediterranean Populations.. JrnHumEvo 1:1, p307 "Analyses showed that the Natufian dentition was much like the more recent Southern Levant people as well as Holocene Nubians." -- Turner (2008) "A dental anthropological hypothesis relating to the ethno genesis. p. 21-25. "A late Pleistocene-early Holocene northward migration (from Africa to the Levant and to Anatolia) of these populations has been hypothesized from skeletal data (Angel 1972, 1973; Brace 2005) and from archaeological data, as indicated by the probable Nile Valley origin of the "Mesolithic" (epi-Paleolithic) Mushabi culture found in the Levant (Bar Yosef 1987).

According to Graeme William Walter Barker, CBE, FBA, a British archaeologist and Professor of Archaeology in the Department of Archaeology at the University of Leicester (which became the School of Archaeological Studies in 1990 and the School of Archaeology and Ancient History in 2001, there are distinct "similarities in the respective archaeological records of the Natufian culture of the Levant, and of contemporary foragers in coastal North Africa, across the late Pleistocene and early Holocene boundary"

Ofer Bar-Yosef further cites that the microburin technique and "microlithic forms such as arched backed bladelets and La Mouillah points" as well as the parthenocarpic figs found in Natufian territory originated in the Sudan. [Ofer Bar-Yosef (born 1937) is an Israeli archaeologist whose main field of study is the Palaeolithic period.] Ofer Bar-Yosef was Professor of Prehistoric Archaeology at Hebrew University in Jerusalem, the institution where he originally studied archaeology at undergraduate and post-graduate levels in the 1960s. In 1988, he moved to the United States of America where he became Professor of Prehistoric Archaeology at Harvard University as well as Curator of Palaeolithic Archaeology at the Peabody Museum of Archaeology and Ethnology. He has excavated widely on prehistoric Levantine sites including Kebara Cave, the early Neolithic village of Netiv HaGdud, as well as on Palaeolithic and Neolithic sites in China and the Republic of Georgia]

In further support, Christopher Ehret noted that the intensive use of plants among the Natufians was first found in Africa, as a precursor to the development of farming in the Fertile Crescent. [Christopher Ehret (born July 27, 1941) currently holds the position of Distinguished Research Professor at the University of California at Los Angeles, is an American scholar of African history and African historical linguistics particularly known for his efforts to correlate linguistic taxonomy and reconstruction with the archeological record. He has published ten books, most recently History and the Testimony of Language (2011) and A Dictionary of Sandawe (2012), the latter co-edited with his wife, Patricia Ehret. He has written around seventy scholarly articles on a wide range of historical, linguistic, and anthropological subjects. These works include monographic articles on Bantu sub classification; on internal reconstruction in Semitic; on the reconstruction of proto-Cushitic and proto-Eastern Cushitic; and, with Mohamed Nuuh Ali, on the classification of the Somali languages. He has also contributed to a number of encyclopedias on African topics and on world history.]

Lastly, shortly after their discovery, it was noted in the 1932 article that "They were clearly a Negroid people, said Sir Arthur, and with wide faces flat- noses and long large heads." And the archeological artifacts from as late as biblical times still show that the population in the Levant/Arabia/Mesopotamia/Canaan area looked like people of African descent today. More recently, according to Larry Angel (1972) "one can identify Negroid traits of nose and prognathism appearing in Natufian latest hunters"(McCown, 1939)

dcccxxxvii See Christopher Ehret "On the antiquity of agriculture in Ethiopia", Jour. of African History 20, [1979], p.161

dcccxxxviii According to J.D. Clark in "The origins of domestication in Ethiopia" (Fifth Pan-African Congress of prehistory and quaternary Studies, Nairobi,1977), by 13,000 BC, the Natufians were collecting grasses which later became domesticated crops in Southwest Asia.

dcccxxxix See F. Wendorf, The History f Nubia, Dallas,1968, pp.941-46

dcccxl In the Bible, Kanaanites are clearly identified as belonging to the group of 'Ethiopic' or black skinned nations: the so-called children of Ham (Kham).

dcccxli Before Byblos was excavated, the ruins of successive cities had formed a mound about 12 meters high covered with houses and gardens. The ancient cite was discovered in 1860 by the French writer and savant Ernest Renan, who made a survey of the area.

dcccxlii Virgil the Aeneid Harlan Hoge Ballard trans. (New York: Charles Scribner's Sons, 1930), 1.335-1.368, refers to these legends.

dcccxliii Agenor was said to have founded Tyre. Vid. Roscher, Ausfiihrliches Lexikon Griech. und Rom. Mythologie, s. v. Kadmos.

dcccxliv Fleming, p. 4.

dcccxlv See 'Evidence of late Holocene Sea-Level' as recorded by Morhange et al. (2006)

dcccxlvi The sea wall in the ancient harbor of Byblos is believed to be at least 5000 years old (situated at the site of the harbor of ancient Byblos, north of present-day Beirut, Lebanon).

dcccxlvii Herodotus says: "these Phoenicians anciently dwelt upon the Erythrian Sea; and having crossed over thence, they inhabited the sea-coast of Syria" This tradition was held by the Persians. "The learned among the Persians allege that the Phoenicians . . . coming from the sea called Erythria to this sea (Mediterranean) and having settled in the country which they now occupy, immediately undertook distant voyages; and carrying cargoes both of Egyptian and Assyrian goods, visited among other places, Argos,"

dcccxlviii Two bronze serpents were excavated in the Holy of Holies of Temple H at Hazor (Tell el-Qedah). The first one belongs to Stratum I B (LB II), dated to 1400–1300 B.C.E. (Locus 2147). It is approximately 11 cm long and very likely to be an image of a cobra (fig. 4).8 The second serpent belongs to Stratum I A (also LB II), dated to 1300–1200 B.C.E. It is shorter than the first one (only approximately 7 cm long) and has a handle at the end, which suggests that the serpent was worn as a pendant amulet

The date of the artifacts discovered is uncertain, however, because distinguishing the strata in this place is difficult. There were two terracotta figures of birds (pigeons?) in the same locus. It is suggested that the room was associated with temple 2048. The temple's foundations are almost 5 m from the room where the serpent was found. The oldest bronze serpent was excavated at Megiddo (Tell el-Mutesellim). There is no doubt, however, that the model of serpent was found in a sacral area. The other serpent from Megiddo (approximately 10 cm long) was found in Stratum VII B, dated by the excavator to 1250–1150 B.C.E. (Locus 3187, Square K 6, Area AA; see fig. 2).3 Perhaps Stratum VII B should be dated earlier or later, to either approximately 1300 B.C.E.4 or to 1150–1100 B.C.E.5 The room where the serpent was found can be associated with palace 2041, which is about 10 m away. 1 2 G. Loud, Megiddo II: Seasons of 1935–1939 (Oriental Institute Publications 62; Chicago: University of Chicago Press, 1948), fig. 400, and pl. 240:1. The date of this temple is problematic. Initially it was associated with Stratum VIII, but later Stratum IX was suggested (K. R. Joines, Serpent Symbolism in the Old Testament: A Linguistic, Archaeological, and Literary Study [Haddonfield, N.J.: Haddonfield House, 1974], 75 n. 5), or even Strata XI–X (A. Kempinski, Megiddo: A City State and Royal Centre in North Israel [Materialien zur Allgemeinen und Vergleichenden Archäologie 40; Munich: Beck, 1989], 181]. Loud, Megiddo II, pl. 240:4. Joines, Serpent Symbolism, 75 n. 6. O. Keel, Das Recht der Bilder gesehen zu werden: Drei Fallstudien zur Methode der Interpretation altorientalischer Bilder (OBO 122; Freiburg: Universitätsverlag, 1992), 195. 3 4 5 Macie Ma Maclej A third bronze serpent is from Tel Mevorakh (Tell Mubarak). It is about 20 cm long and dated to LB III (1500–1300 B.C.E.; see fig. 3).6 It was excavated on the platform on the west side of a sanctuary (Locus 185).

dcccxlix It is generally taken for granted that the Bible (really there are many bibles for there are many versions) is the basis of Western religious doctrine.

The various versions of the Bible have layers and layers of additions and corrections and they have been perverted throughout the ages in order to serve the function of those who dared alter scripture. The Hebrews rewrote their version to present themselves in the most favorable light, in spite of the facts, and the later Catholic Church rewrote its version to give it the power and authority which it did not really have or deserve.

Unfortunately a number of the self-serving biblical myths have done much to confuse, slander and pervert the history and reputation of Kanaan and the Kanaanites — myths that, while designed to assassinate the character, morality and ethnicity of the Kanaanites, when taken in context (and full perspective), are more revealing about the depravity and covetous nature of their authors, than they purport to be about the spirituality and beliefs of the Kanaanites.

In the Bible, the Kanaanites are clearly identified as belonging to the group of 'Ethiopic' or black skinned nations: the so-called children of Ham (Khem, Kham); yet at the same time they were ancient inhabitants of a much-coveted area, and they are thus portrayed in the Bible as being a great hindrance to the territorial aspirations of the landless Hebrews. Consequently throughout the Old Testament, the Kanaanites are denounced, demonized and marked for ethnic cleansing from the 'promised' land. Ironically, although the Hebrew Bible (and thus the Old Testament) contain numerous polemics against the Kanaan and the Kanaanites; elements and practices of the religion and religious beliefs of the Hebrews are best understood within the context of the Kanaanite history and mythology they so condemn.

[dccccl] The Amorites were members of an ancient Semitic-speaking people who actively invaded Kanaan and Mesopotamia from about 2,100 to about 1,500 BC.

[dcccli] The Egyptian historian Manetho, and the traitor Hebrew, Josephus Flavius, both wrote of the Amorite coup as an invasion, but there is no evidence of an invasion, apparently it was a gradual takeover. In Egyptian history, the Hyksos comprise the 15th. Dynasty

[dccclii] Many of these Amorites/Semitics, such as the Biblical Abraham, continued on to Khemet (Egypt).

[dcccliii] That the Hyksos were indeed driven out of Khemet (Egypt) by the army of Ahmose I, and were allowed to settle in Kanaan, is the only known event in Khemetian (Egyptian) history similar to the Biblical Exodus' of the Hebrews (Jews) out of Khemet (Egypt) ,and into Southern Kanaan

[dcccliv] A unique example is the letters of Tell el-Amarna, sent by the kings of Palestine to the Pharaoh in Khemet (Egypt)

[dccclv] The main source of knowledge about Kanaanite religion before the new sources became available after 1930 (primarily the Ugaritic materials) was Philo of Byblos. Philo lived around 100 AD. He was a native Phoenician scholar and gathered data for a historical work called Phoenicia or "Phoenician Matters", designated "Phoenician History" by later Greek scholars. According to Porphyry and Eusebius, Philo translated the writings of an earlier Phoenician named Sanchuniathon, who was supposed to have lived at a very remote age.

[dccclvi] Found among the texts of Ugarit are the typical Ancient Near Eastern texts such as the Epic of Gilgamesh which is the Mesopotamian version of the Flood Story – not the flood story that contains the biblical Noah, but it instead features, Gilgamesh. The Ugaritic texts are may be considered "cosmopolitan" because the writings were found in seven different languages: English Egyptian, Cypriot-Minoan Linear B, Hittites, Hurrian, Sumerian, Akadian, and Ugarit. So, plates Ugarit contains forms of hieroglyphics (Egypt), cuneiform (Sumer), and linear (five other languages).

[dccclvii] Abram (Abraham) the Hebrew (Habiru) reckoned Amorite groups as his confederates. Without regard to the date reflected in this tradition we may be justified in concluding that it reveals conditions of times long since passed when there existed friendly relations between the Habiru/Hebrews and the Amorites. This is by no means astonishing for there is also in late tradition a clear consciousness of the fact that the Amorites were an important ethnic group merging into the Israelite people once upon a time (Ezekiel 16:1-3).

[dccclviii] The word Amorite is used first in the Bible in Genesis ten, where it is stated that Canaan, son of Ham, begat Sidon and Heth. Then follows a list of tribes who sprang from Canaan: Jebusites, Amorites, Girgasites, Hivites, Arkites, Sinites, Arvadites, Zemarites and Hamathites.

[dccclix] (Gen. 15:16; Dt. 20:17; Jgs. 6:10; 1 S. 7:14; 1 K. 21:26; 2 K. 21:11); the older population of Judah is called Amorite (in Josh. 10:5f), in conformity with which Ezk. states that Jerusalem had an Amorite father; and the Gibeonites are said to have been "of the remnant of the Amorites" (Ezk.16:3) (2 S. 21:2).

[dccclx] Despite the paramount import of Kanaanite morality and religion in the realm of theology and general Biblical studies, little was known about the subject seventy years ago except that which, on the one hand, could be gleaned from the Bible, which, however, was ample enough for faith and on the other hand, that which was preserved in the Greco-Roman authors, which was meager enough from the scholar's viewpoint.

[dccclxi] Throughout the history of Kush, Amun (Amon) remained the chief deity, which greatly shaped the order in which the Kushite pharaohs ruled.

[dccclxii] The ancient 'Leontes River' (at this writing) is known as the 'Litani River'

[dccclxiii] Sometime after the founding of the island city of Tyre, the mainland city of Tyre was founded (in the Plain of Tyre); originally called Ushu in cuneiform texts (Ward 1997:247) and later Palaetyrus ("old Tyre") in Greek texts (Jidejian 1996:19).

[dccclxiv] Although there is general agreement about the attribution of numerous moles and seawalls to the Phoenicians (Haggai, 2006), very few can be unequivocally constrained to the Bronze Age, due to the difficulties in dating rock-cut structures.

[dccclxv] Two harbors hewn out of the natural rock of Tyre were protected by a wide breakwater in a feat of engineering beyond compare and lasting for many centuries. Ancient sources state that there were two harbors at Tyre, one facing north and the other south. The function of these was to allow ships to navigate in to port safely regardless of the direction of the winds. As early as the nineteenth century, travelers mentioned both harbors at Tyre. The location and even the existence of the southern harbor is still a matter of discussion, but the existence of the northern harbor is not controversial, since it was documented by several travelers, such as Jules de Bertou (1843), John Kendrick (1855), Ernest Renan (1864), and Poidebard (1939).

The pioneering aerial photographer and archaeologist Fr. Antoine Poidebard focused his efforts mainly on finding the so-called "Egyptian," or southern, harbor, albeit with mixed results. As for the northern harbor, his contribution was limited to the detection of a submerged jetty located on the northern side of Tyre, which appears in one of his aerial photographs. Based on this evidence, he confirmed the existence of Tire's northern harbor and pointed to the need for further studies of this area. See 'New Light on the Phoenician Harbor at Tyre', by Ibrahim Noureddine (Ibrahim Noureddine holds a M.A. degree in Archaeology from the Lebanese University and is preparinghis Ph.D.

dissertation on costal and submerged harbors in the eastern Mediterranean during the Bronze Age). Underwater surveys undertaken by a team from the University of Perpignan (programme ARESMAR) have relocated remains of a late construction, submerged underwater, consistent with the ancient mole of Tyre's northern harbor.

dccclxvi For many scholars, the ancient Near East is the cradle of coastal harbor development, logically adapted from the del-taic contexts of Mesopotamia and Egypt (Fabre, 2004/2005). However, the presence of urban structures, walls and drowned quarries within the southern basin at Tyre called into question its use as a seaport during antiquity.

After extensive research spanning 1934-1936, Poidebard eventually diagnosed what he believed to be an artificial harbor basin enclosed by an imposing 670 m long mole. For many scholars Tyre's southern seaport had been rediscovered and, despite reanalysis by Frost (1971) during the 1960s and 1970s, archaeologists and historians continue to promulgate Poidebard's (mis)interpretations to this day (Bikai, 1979; Bi-kai and Bikai, 1987; Jidejian, 1996; Kassis and Tyr, 2005; Kat-zenstein, 1997). Building on Frost's partial reinterpretation of Poidebard's southern harbor, new underwater research undertaken in 2002 has confirmed that this locale is in fact a drowned quarter of the ancient city (El Amouri et al., 2005).

Work undertaken in the southern harbor has clearly shown that the drowned area, called the "southern harbor" was not a harbor complex. The presence of numerous land-based structures (walls, quarries) suggests that this area corresponds to an urban quarter of the ancient city, protected from the sea by a mole (presently submerged underwater) extending across the mouth of the basin.

dccclxvii Previous studies of some of this evidence for the past 8000 years have shown that the sea level along the Mediterranean coast of Israel (Fig. 2), rose rapidly until about 7500 BP (Galili and Nir, 1993) and perhaps up to 6000 BP (Galili et al., 1988), followed by a less rapid rise up to the present. However, some studies suggest that at about 3500 years ago sea level may have been higher than today (Sneh and Klein, 1984; Raban and Galili, 1985; Raban, 1995). This is consistent with archeological discoveries of the era made in and around the northern (harbor) and southern (urban quarter) basins of Tyre, where submergence is recorded since late antiquity by coastal stratigraphy, and the submerged urban quarters and harbor works

dccclxviii The Nile being 5 meters higher during the flood implied that the floodplain was around 6 km wider in the eastern area (the plain slopes slightly higher eastwards) (Haaland, 1981: 46). In general, this Early Holocene Wet Phase set in during the second half of the ninth millennium BC (after 9500 bp) with peaks in rainfall at 7000 BC and 6000 BC (Wickens 1982; Hassan 1988; Haynes et al 1989; Muzzolini 1993; Grove 1993). The early to middle Holocene (c. 10500 - 6000 years B.P.) was wet and warm in central Sudan and the present savanna zone of western Sudan. Late Pleistocene dunes became submerged beneath White Nile alluvium in central Sudan, and further west small lakes and swamps occupied the depressions between the now vegetated and stabilized dunes.

dccclxix The later Greeks named this city Thebes, Thebai, Thisbe and Thespai but the early Kushites called their city Waset. Later, seeking to establish a place for their 'Greek Heracles', the Greeks then took the name they assigned to Waset, the original 'Thebes", and gave it to one of their own cities; thus the Greek city of 'Thebes'.

dccclxx According to Plutarch, who wrote a work on the cult of Isis and Osiris, when "Ra departed to the heavens and Osiris became pharaoh of Egypt with Isis, they built Thebes [present-day Luxor]"

dccclxxi Sidon is located in modern Lebanon, about 40km (25 miles) north of Tyre, and is now its third-largest city, a busy port called Saydah. For the reason that it is still occupied, archaeological research of the Canaanite city is very difficult, so its history is pieced together from what records remain, plus what digs can be carried out during any rebuilding or construction projects. A whole suite of harbor works, including seawalls, quays and mooring bits have been dug into the Quaternary sandstone, rendering Zire an integral component of Sidon's port system. The study of Zire has detailed the island's use as a sandstone quarry and outer harbor. A prominent "sea wall" has been fashioned into part of the quarry, in addition to an artificial quay and two jetties built during Persian times.

dccclxxii Geoarchaeology of Sidon's ancient harbors, Phoenicia; by Nick Marriner, Christophe Morhange and, Claude Doumet-Serhal Universite´ Aix-Marseille, BP 80 Europo^le de l'Arbois, 13545 Aix-en-Provence, France b British Museum, LBFNM, 11 Canning Place, London W85 AD, UK (February 2006)

dccclxxiii The (1st Century A.D.) Greek geographer Strabo wrote that Sidon rivaled Tyre not only in size, but also in antiquity.

dccclxxiv Neolithic remains are prolific throughout Crete in general, and *Knossos* in particular; Knossos has a thick Neolithic layer indicating the site was continually inhabited, by a sequence of settlements.

dccclxxv *Plato, Laws 713a (trans. Bury):* "[Plato employs the myth of the Golden Age of Khronos in his description of an ideal state ruled by a philosopher-elite:] Long ages before even cities existed . . . there existed in the time of Khronos, it is said, a most prosperous government and settlement . . . Well, then, tradition tells us how blissful was the life of men in that age, furnished with everything in abundance, and of spontaneous growth. And the cause thereof is said to have been this: Khronos was aware of the fact that no human being is capable of having irresponsible control of all human affairs without becoming filled with pride and injustice; so, pondering this fact, he then appointed as kings and rulers for our cities, not men, but beings of a race that was nobler and more divine, namely, Daimones (Spirits). He acted just as we now do in the case of sheep and herds of tame animals: we do not set oxen as rulers over oxen, or goats over goats, but we, who are of a nobler race, ourselves rule over them. In like manner the god, in his love for humanity, set over us at that time the nobler race of Daimones who, with much comfort to themselves and much to us, took charge of us and furnished peace and modesty and orderliness and justice without stint, and thus made the tribes of men free from feud and happy. And even today this tale has a truth to tell, namely, that wherever a State has a mortal, and no god, for ruler, the people have no rest from ills and toils; and it deems that we ought by every means to imitate the life of the age of Khronos, as tradition paints it." [Cf. The Daimones of Hesiod's *Works and Days* above.]

dccclxxvi Collectively referred to as *"Minoans"*; a term coined by a 19th century British archaeologist, notably after King Minos of Knossos

dccclxxvii Excavations at Trapeza cave (cave of Khronos (Khem, Ham), at Karfi and Plati, indicate that the area has been inhabited ever since the Neolithic Period

dccclxxviii Also referred to as the 'Mount Dikti Range'

dccclxxix Far later Iconic images of Khronos depicted two wings upon his head, one representing the all-ruling mind.

dccclxxx Enlightenment is a continuous realization that you are an eternal being who will never die. It comes from a deeper knowing that YOU are beyond body and behind the mind. Ascension represents the complete transcendence of the human condition.

dccclxxxi The ancient literary texts relating to the port of early archaic Knossos bring another site into focus: Amnisos, the region at the mouth of the homonymous river that is called Karteros today.

dccclxxxii The earliest seaworthy ships may have been developed as early as 45,000 years ago, a type of manpowered sailing vessel

dccclxxxiii Described by later Latin classical writers as black; see perusti (Lucan 4.679),furvi (Arnoloius, Adversus Nationes , 6.5) and nigri (Anthologia Latina, 155,no.183)

dccclxxxiv The colonists at Milos became specialist in making tools, and weapons. Obsidian tools have been found in Crete, Cyprus, in areas of Peloponnese and Khemet (Egypt). Since the Neolithic Age Knifes, blades, chisels, spear edges and arrows were constructed in the very old times and before the discovery of metals, from this black stone that looks quite similar to a glass. Tools from volcanic glass of Milos were found in prehistoric facilities in Peloponnesus and this proved that Milos and the mainland Greece were in contact through the sea some 9,000 years ago B.C.

dccclxxxv The word myth derives from the Greek mythos, signifying "word" or "story." A myth has different meanings for the believer, the anthropologist, the folklorist, the psychologist, the literary critic. That is one of myth's functions—to celebrate ambiguity and contradiction. It has been said that there is no more point expecting a myth to offer a single, clear, consistent message than there is in trying to turn one of Shakespeare's sonnets into plain prose.

That being said, the history of Atlatia (or 'Atlantis') is clearly the key to Greek mythology; there can be no question that the so-called 'Gods' of Greece were actual human beings. The tendency to attach divine attributes to great earthly rulers is one deeply implanted in human nature. We find the barbarians of the coast of the Mediterranean regarding the civilized people of Atlantis with awe and wonder: "Their physical strength was extraordinary, the earth shaking sometimes under their tread. Whatever they did was done speedily. They moved through space almost without the loss of a moment of time." This probably alluded to the rapid motion of their sailing-vessels. "They were wise, and communicated their wisdom to men."

That is to say, they civilized the people they came in contact with. 'They had a strict sense of justice, and punished crime rigorously, and rewarded noble actions, though it is true they were less conspicuous for the latter." (Murray's "Mythology" (p. 4.); we should understand this to mean that where they colonized they established a government of law, as contradistinguished from the anarchy of barbarism.

"There were tales of personal visits and adventures of the gods among men, taking part in battles and appearing in dreams. They were conceived to possess the form of human beings, and to be, like men, subject to love and pain, but always characterized by the highest qualities and grandest forms that could be imagined." (Ibid.) Another proof that the gods of the Greeks were but the deified kings of Atlantis is found in the fact that "the gods were not looked upon as having created the world." They succeeded to the management of a world already in existence.

Nearly all the gods of Greece are connected with Atlantis; we have seen the twelve principal gods all dwell on the mountain of Olympus, in the midst of an island in the ocean in the far west, which was subsequently destroyed by a deluge. And when we turn to Plato's description of Atlantis (p. 13, ante) we find that Poseidon and Atlas dwelt upon a mountain in the midst of the island; and on this mountain were their magnificent temples and palaces, where they lived, separated by great walls from their subjects.

The mythology of Greece is really a history of the kings of Atlatia (Atlantis). The Greek heaven was Atlantis. Hence the references to statues, swords (etc.), that fell from heaven and were preserved in the temples of the different states along the shores of the Mediterranean from a vast antiquity, and which were regarded as the most precious possessions of the people. They were relics of the lost race received in the early ages.

According to the English philosopher, statesman, scientist, and author Sir Francis Bacon, "the mythology of the Greeks, which their oldest writers do not pretend to have invented, was no more than a light air, which had passed from a more ancient people into the flutes of the Greeks, which they modulated to such descants as best suited their fancies."

The modern theory that the gods of Greece never had any personal existence, but represented atmospheric and meteorological myths, the movements of clouds, planets, and the sun, is absurd. Rude nations repeat, they do not invent; to suppose a barbarous people creating their deities out of clouds and sunsets is to reverse nature. Men first worship stones, then other men, then spirits. Resemblances of names prove nothing; it is as if one would show that the name of 'Napoleon' meant "the lion of the desert" (Napoleon), and should thence argue that Napoleon never existed, that he was a myth, that he represented power in solitude, or some such stuff.

dccclxxxvi There are many known and unknown earth energies, the most commonly talked about, however, is 'magnetic field'. The electromagnetic radiations are emitted due to rotation of the earth around its axis. This is a well-established phenomenon. These currents are deemed to the flowing from north towards south. Interestingly, in the human body they flow from the head downwards to the feet. See 'The Electromagnetic Field, by Rakeesh Chawla (2004.

dccclxxxvii As we drift into slumber, our brains gradually step down into drowsiness by graduated steps. Each of these steps corresponds to different levels of consciousness, and each level can be measured by brain wave measuring devices called electroencephalographs.

dccclxxxviii The human energy field is interacting and influencing the quantum field all around us at all times and the energy of our beliefs and intentions are infused into our energy field because they are defined by the energy of our thoughts and emotions.

Vortexes are areas of high energy concentrations, originating from magnetic, spiritual, or sometimes unknown sources, and typically exist where there are strong concentrations of gravitational anomalies. They were anciently considered to be gateways or portals to other realms, both spiritual and dimensional.

According to Pete A. Sanders Jr. and Richard Dannelley in their works Scientific Vortex Information and Sedona Power Spot Vortex respectively, vortexes are labeled according to the direction of their energy flow. Up-flow Vortexes, where energy is flowing upward out of the earth; and Inflow Vortexes, where energy is flowing inward, toward the earth; Up-flow Vortexes are said to boost spiritual skills associated with going to a higher level. They are said to stretch or expand consciousness.

Places labeled as a 'magnetic vortex' are areas of inflow energy, and places labeled as an 'electric vortex' is an area of up-flow energy. Sometimes vortexes are referred to as 'positive' or 'negative.' The terms are intended to be used more in a yin/yang fashion, meaning neither good nor bad, just being opposite. However, there are those that feel there actually are 'negative vortexes' in the sense of meaning bad or evil. Such a conception is not true. It is thought the misconception originated when Up-flow Vortexes were labeled 'positive' because of the tremendous exhilaration they generated. While an experience at an Up-flow Vortex is exhilarating, an inflow area generates a much more pensive feeling. Because the power of the vortex is flowing down rather than up, the energy at an inflow site feels heavier.

dccclxxxix Before reaching the summit, at an altitude of approximately 630 meters, you will find the caves of Zas.

dcccxc Archaeological finds indicate that the cave was inhabited during the Neolithic; prehistoric artifacts have been found inside, including stone objects from Milos, and copper objects including a dagger and gold sheet. The presence of gold and other objects within the cave indicated to researchers the status of the inhabitant.

dcccxci The cave would accordingly become known as the 'Cave of Zeus'. The cave was first explored in 1962 and the excavations carried out in 1985-1986 and 1994 brought to light artifacts dating from the Neolithic Era.

dcccxcii Ancient quarries have been found in different parts of the island. Emery is found mostly on the eastern side of the island, in the areas of Apeiranthos and Koronos. It was the material out of which temples and sculptures were made, creations which decorated two of ancient Greece's most holy places, Delos and Delphi, both dedicated to Apollo.

dcccxciii Modern-day Thrace consists of the southeastern regions of Bulgaria, northeastern Greece, and the parts of Turkey that separate the Black Sea from the Sea of Marmara. But the antiquity of Thrace dates back to ancient Greek legends and the geographical boundaries of the Kingdom of Thrace were the Bosporus Strait, the Balkan Mountains, and the Rhodope Mountains

dcccxciv Such a wind, whether blowing directly over the stern or over the quarters (i.e., from a point on either side of the stern) is a favorable wind.

dcccxcv Thasos or Thassos (Greek: Θάσος) is a Greek island in the northern Aegean Sea, close to the coast of Thrace and the plain of the Nestos River, but is geographically part of Macedonia..

dcccxcvi Before the arrival of the Greeks, the island had been called Odonis and was occupied by a Thracian tribe (the 'Sintes'). Nothing had been known archaeologically about prehistoric Thasos until two sites were discovered in the S part of the island, a cave on the W coast near Maries with Neolithic and Early Bronze Age sherds, and an inland site at Kastri with a settlement that has Neolithic and perhaps later sherds and an extensive cemetery of the Late Bronze and Early Iron Ages.

dcccxcvii The Neolithic era was once thought to have lasted from the 5th up to the 6th millennium in coastal Thrace; however radiocarbon dating from recent excavations has proved that it lasted during the 6th millennium B.C. (5500-3000); notwithstanding the archeological gap between 10,000 BCE and 6,000 BCE.

dcccxcviii The history of Kavala city is rooted back in prehistoric times and runs until today. The city of Kavala was built on the following two prehistoric sites; Antissara (today Kalamitsa) where its history is rooted in the Homeric epics and Sidiros settlement (today Perigiali) that was located in the east side of the city. However, only a part of Antissara wall has been survived which stands among the city's modern buildings. The oldest findings of Kavala came into light in Tzines region (Thasos) around 50s. These referred to mining tools of the late Paleolithic Era 20,300 BC. At that time, the sea levels were much lower than today, resulting to the connection of Thassos island to Kavala mainland. However, during the Mesolithic period where the environmental temperature rose and glaciers melted, sea water flooded the valley.

dcccxcix Present day knowledge about the port of Kavala is fragmentary, at best, and mainly based on written sources; such as Bakalakis who indicates certainty that the ancient port of Kavala was much greater than the gulf preserved in its place today. Lichounas and Tsouris report the existence of two ports, with two respective shipyards; whose functioning's through the centuries, however, were reportedly somewhat inconsistent.

cm Extraction of mineral ores and its associated metal production has been a persistent element of the ancient economy of Thassos since as early as the Upper Paleolithic, around 20,000 years ago, when ochre was mined on the former peninsula (See 'Reassessment and new data on the diachronic relationship of Thassos Island with its indigenous metal resources: a review'; by N. Nerantzis and S. Papadopoulos; Archaeological and Anthropological Sciences September 2013, Volume 5, Issue 3, pp 183-196)

Mount Pangaion (also spelled Pangeon, Pangaeum, Pangaeos, or Pangaios, and in Modern Greek Pangaíon) is situated on the present-day mainland at the mouth of the Struma (Modern Greek: Strymónas) River, in present day northeastern Kaválla nomós (department), Macedonia (Makedonía), Greece.

It was during the late Neolithic that *Thassos* gradually became an island, separating from the Thracian mainland as sea levels rose between 7000 B.C.E. to 5000 B.C.E.

cmi Attica is the historical region centered on the Attic peninsula, which projects into the Aegean Sea. Lavrion (Λαύριον, Λαύριο, Lavrio, Laurio, Laurium), in eastern Attica, is a rugged area near Athens, where the ancient silver mines were (and are) located; Lavrion's history has been tightly bound to the history of Greece since prehistoric times.

cmii According to Plato, the war between Atlantis and Athens burst out in the times before Theseus. Setting something before the time of Theseus would simply be placing it in a time before Athens became the Athens of memory. Cecrops is listed as the founder of Athens, while Theseus is the king credited with giving the ancient Athenians their traditions; it was Cecrops who united the former colonists and led the fight against the invaders.

cmiii   Descendent Indo-European / Eurocentric versions of the victory by Athens, portraying themselves as the 'Athenians', erroneously overstate the victory by indicating that Athens actually 'drove the Atlatians out of Europe and North Africa altogether', while in the same paragraph stating that "badly beaten, the Atlatian Navy limped back to their home ports", which, of course, were in North Africa. These were accounts written thousands of years after an event in which the Indo-Europeans (and their descendents) were not yet inhabitants of Athens, and simply could not have participated in the war; Indo-Europeans did not migrate into Europe until around 1,800 BCE (by Plato's account, over 7,000 years after the event).

Plato placed the war conflict between Atlantis and Athens to the time when the area of the later Athens was inhabited by the original Pelasgians; an epithet referring to colonists from North Africa (Atlatians) and their descendants.

According to Herodotus "The Athenians, while the Pelasgians ruled what is now called Hellas, were Pelasgians". "When Kekrops was their king they were called Kekropidai (sons of Kekrops), and when Erekhtheus succeeded to the rule, they changed their name and became Athenians". "When, however, Ion son of Xouthos was commander of the Athenian army, they were called after him Ionians." Herodotus, Histories 8. 44. 2 (trans. Godley) (Greek historian C5th B.C.)

cmiv   North African colonist (those from the Atlas and the Sahara (the "Atlatians")) who migrated to and populated Southern Europe during antiquity were referred to and recorded in the pre-histories and mythologies of Ancient Greece as "Pelasgians"; a term also reserved for later arriving East African colonists (those from Khemet and Kush), and those of African descent arriving from Kanaan.

The Greeks have made it clear in their histories that the founders of Ancient Greece were Pelasgians or Blacks; Blacks who founded Athens, Thebes Thera and Attica; the Greeks' own mythology states that these cities were founded by Hamites (descendents of Ham (Kham, Khem, Khronos)). For a more detailed discussion regarding Pelasgian Civilization, see Parker (1917, 1918).

Cecrops and other heroes named by Plato lived at the same time within the range of one or two generations, according to Geek myths. These heroes were considered the original inhabitants of Attica by the Ancient Greeks, and they were believed to have lived in this area for thousands of years before the first Indo-European tribes came to Greece (1850-1600 B.C.), and gradually assimilated with the pre-Greek population of Pelasgians.

cmv   Archaeologist Manfred Bietak conducted extensive research on ancient Greek civilizations and their connections to ancient Egypt. Bietak unearthed evidence from artwork as early as 7000 B.C. that depicts the early people inhabiting Greece were of African descent

cmvi   The Pelasgians were described as dolichocephalic (long-headed) people who were short, black, dark haired, and dark eyed. (See, 'Celtic Myth and Legend' by Charles Squire. London: The Gresham Publishing Company, LTD, 1905, pp 19-20.) Dolichocephalicism is a characteristic of the Black race. They spoke a non-Indo-European language. Herodotus confirmed that it was not Greek. They are identified as a "pre-Greek", "pre-Hellenic" people. The Pelasgians were also described as "highly intellectual, receptive, active and simple people, chiefly occupied with agriculture; war like when necessary, though preferring peace. It is reported that they built canals, subterranean water-works, dams, and walls of astounding strength and most excellent construction." (Five Years of Theosophy Edited by George Robert Stow Mead. London: Reeves and Turner, 1885, pg. 417)

cmvii   There are good reasons to believe that Greek Mythology is an embellished version of real history, and the so-called 'gods' were just ordinary men and women whose deeds have been exaggerated so that they could be made into gods. Solid ancient Greek history is said to have begun with the Heroic Age Pelasgian writings of Homer and Hesiod. They all say the Pelasgians dominated the scene in most ancient times, back before the Flood of Ogyges which was the end of the Ice Age. The five centuries or so before that was peaceful and pastoral, when Greece had vast dense forests and rich crops twice per year, where now maybe twenty of inches of rain falls per year, back then was closer to forty inches per year.

cmviii   Autochthonous: indigenous, native; formed or originating in the place where found; autochthones: from Ancient Greek αὐτός autos "self," and χθών khthon "soil"; i.e. "people sprung from earth itself"

cmix   Dionysus in Greek mythology is a god of foreign origin; while born at Mount Nysa, a mythological location, it is invariably set far away to the east or to the south. The Homeric hymn to Dionysus places it "far from Phoenicia, near to the Egyptian stream."

cmx   See 'Persian War, II, 144', by *Herodotus*. Herodotus insisted that Dionysos and his worship had been brought from Egypt (Khemet) into Greece, and claimed that (in his time) the people of Meroe, in Ethiopia, "worship no other Gods but Zeus and Dionysos".

According to the testimony of other ancient authors, "Osiris is he who is called Dionysos in the Greek tongue"(Herodotus 2.144); "Dionysos and Osiris are the same… "(Mnaseas); "Osiris is identical with Dionysos… " (Plutarch, On Isis and Osiris, 35,) and "it is proper to identify Osiris with Dionysos", (Plutarch, On Isis and Osiris, 28); even Cicero equated Osiris with Dionysos (De Natura Deorum 3.21), and finally, under the entry for 'Osiris' in Suidas' Lexicon is the following: "Some say he was Dionysos, others say another - who was dismembered by the daimon Typhon (Set) and became a great sorrow for the Egyptians (Khemetians); they kept the memory of his dismemberment for all time."

cmxi   Mount Pangaion (also spelled Pangeon, Pangaeum, Pangaeos, or Pangaios, Modern Greek Pangaíon Óros) sits at the mouth of the Strymónas (or 'Strymon') River, which flows into the Aegean from the interior of Thrace.

cmxii   A prehistoric marsh that would later become known as the Plains of Drama (and much later become known as the 'Plains of Kaválla' and the 'plains of Philippi',). During the Holocene the Plain of Drama was characterized by marshes and alluvial depositions. Since the seventh millennium BC, the climate in the region has remained stable, and pollen and pedological analyses prove that the area was covered by woodland (Davidson & Thomas 1986).

cmxiii The mines of Mount Pangaion were the richest source of gold in ancient Thrace of the era (a region which later became northern Greece)

cmxiv When sea levels were over four hundred feet (130 meters) lower than at present there were large coastal plains along most of the northern Aegean

cmxv Participants in the International Underwater Photography Competition, hosted on the north Aegean island of Thasos by the Greek marine photography center (PKYFET) recently discovered the sunken city about five (5) miles south of Thasos, at a depth of 328feet (100 meters); the ruins they discovered and photographed at the bottom of the sea (at this writing unstudied by archaeologists) are likely to change to both extend and change the notion of island's earliest ancient history.

cmxvi Participants in an International Underwater Photography Competition hosted on the island of Thassos (by the Greek marine photography center (PKYFET)) were astonished by the ancient ruins they discovered and photographed at the bottom of the *Thasos Strait*. Neolithic age ruins that are likely to change the island's history; archaeologists have yet to begin to study the ancient submerged city discovered, which is at a depth of 328 feet (100 meters).

cmxvii Paus. i. 2. § 4; Diod. i. 97 The myths concerning Dionysus do not agree in every land; therein underlying the reason that classical historians found it impossible to convey a clear-cut view of either the antiquity or era in which he lived

cmxviii Greek poet Hesiod

cmxix The term Euxinus Pontus is the Latinized version of the Greek εὔξεινος πόντος 'Euxinos Pontos' and is the historical name commonly used to describe the body of water presently known as the Black Sea. The Euxinus 'εὔξεινος' part of the term which means 'hospitable' is believed to be a euphemism of aksenos (Grk: άξενος). Aksenos means inhospitable and is believed to describe the difficulty in navigating the water and also the savage tribes that historically surrounded it. The name later changed to Euxinus after the Miletians colonized it and made it part of Greek civilization.

The word Pontos 'πόντος' was first used by Homer (circa 850 BC) in the context of describing the sea. It was also used with other words to describe certain bodies of water, eg Icarios Pontos, Thrikios Pontos etc.

The north-eastern region of Asia Minor starts being termed Pontus during the time of Alexander the Great and onwards. Up until then the region was usually referred to as Cappadocia or 'to the Pontus'. The use of the term became general after the foundation of the Kingdom of Mithradates (the word with its modern meaning was in use from the 3rd century BC onwards by many writers such as Strabo, Appiano and others) The poet Strabo (64BC-24AD) mentions Euxinos Pontos when referring to Jason, Medea, Aiti, the Colchians (see Geographica).

cmxx Its ancient name Propontis describes it as "the sea before the entrance of the Pontus" or Euxine; while its modern name is derived from the island of Marmora, the ancient Proconnesus, near the western entrance of the sea. (Appul. de Mund.p. 6; Steph. B. sub voce Προποντίς)

cmxxi Water flows in both directions along the straits via surface currents, and in the opposite direction via undercurrents

cmxxii Apollonius Rhodius, Argonautica 2. 1231 ff (trans. Rieu) (Greek epic C3rd B.C.): "The Isle of Philyra [at the eastern end of the southern Black Sea coast]. This was where Kronos son of Ouranos, deceiving his consort Rhea, lay with Philyra daughter of Okeanos in the days when he ruled the Titanes in Olympos and Zeus was still a child, tended in the Kretan cave by the Kouretes of Ida. But Kronos and Philyra were surprised in the very act by the goddess Rhea. Whereupon Kronos leapt out of bed and galloped off in the form of a long-maned stallion."

Virgil, Georgics 3. 92 ff (trans. Fairclough) (Roman bucolic C1st B.C.) : "Such, too [i.e. in the form of a fine stallion], was Saturnus [Kronos] himself, when at his wife's [Rhea's] coming he fled swiftly, flinging his horse's mane over his shoulders, and with shrill neigh filled the heights of Pelion." [The Theoi Project http://www.theoi.com/]

cmxxiii Apollod. iii. 5. § 1

cmxxiv The Gallipoli peninsula is located in the European part of present day Turkey, to the west, with the *Hellespont* to the east. The peninsula runs in a south-westerly direction into the Aegean Sea, between the Hellespont and the bay of Melas (present day 'Saros Bay'); Gallipoli derives its name from the Greek "Καλλίπολις" (Kallipolis), meaning "Beautiful City". In antiquity, it was known as the Thracian Chersonese, from Greek: Θρακική Χερσόνησος (Latin:Chersonesus Thracica). According to Herodotus, the Thracian tribe of *Dolonci* held possession of the *Gallipoli Peninsula* before Greek colonization. Geography of Thrace [http://www.thracian.info/thrace_geography.htm]

cmxxv According to Homer (and Hesiodus), the country of the first deified kings of the ancient world had been in the extreme parts of the Greek horizon, at north of Thrace or Istru, called in Greek legends Oceanos potamos, the father of gods (Homer, Iliad, XIV, v. 201. 227).

In regard to the ancient geographical meanings of the word *Ōkeanós* (or 'Oceanos'), three periods have been distinguished; in the first period, or ante-Homeric, under the name of "Oceanos" was understood the *Pontus Euxinus*, or the *Black Sea*, a name from which the epithet axeinos had been preserved until late, but with an entirely different meaning in Greek language than the original one, and the Istru was considered in those times only as a gulf of the Ocean (Strabo, I. 1. 7). In the second geographical period, or the Homeric and Hesiodic times, the Black Sea is *Pontus Euxinus*, and the Istru appears under the name 'Ocheanos potamos and roos 'Ocheanoio. Finally, in the third period, the names "Oceanos" and "Oceanos potamos" are a merge and the term "Oceanos" is applied only to the external seas.

Homer does not say anywhere that Oceanos had been an external sea. In fact, the Greeks did not know in those times either the western

Ocean, nor the northern one.

cmxxvi The most ancient tribes of Asia Minor are usually designated by the name Pelasgians; the whole of the western part of the peninsula was once inhabited by a variety of tribes all belonging to the same family. This was a time when the race of the *Pelasgians* formed, if not the sole population of *Asia Minor*, at least by far the most important. This conclusion is supported by many facts derived from ancient writers; independently of several Greek and Trojan legends referring to the southern coasts of Asia.

Autochthones (Proto-European) settlements expanded along the northern, eastern, and western coasts of the Pontus Euxinus by as early as 8,500 BC, with most living on the northern shores, and a few living along the narrow southern coast, which were much more mountainous. Geographical barriers such as the mountains, forests and swamplands served to preserve the early territorial ranges and separation of the early major tribal groups in the region, having kept most geographically isolated for thousands of years.

cmxxvii Parthenope, the wife of Oceanus, by whom she became the mother of Europa and Thrace (Tzetz. Ad Lyc. 894; comp. Schol. Ad Aeschyl, Pers. 183.); daughter of Ancaeus and Samia , became by Apollo the mother of Lycomedes . (Paus. Vii. 4, § 2)

cmxxviii Ancient Greek myth was in reality not 'Greek' but 'Pelasgic, as noted by the eminent German philosopher Schelling, who defined the Pelasgic period in the development of Greece as Sabism (i.e. the period of clairvoyant wisdom). From Greek mythology of the subsequent period we learn that Perseus and other heroes transferred the clairvoyant, Pelasgic culture to Greek culture.

cmxxix According to historical traditions, the great empire of the Pelasgian race had its beginnings near the high Atlas Mountain, situated in the geographical region Gaea or Terra (Hesiodus, Theog. v. 517-8; Diod. Siculus, lib II. 60).

cmxxx Hesiod (*Theogony*) Pelasgians included: a. Ionians b. Athenians c. Aeolians d. Islanders Argeoi, Pelasgjoi, Danaidai, Mykenaoi, Argives, Pelasgos, Pelasgjikos, Pelasgjia, Argolis.

cmxxxi Phrygian texts appear to carry a language similar to the Lydian language, both of which are close to the Etruscan language, based upon data developed so far. It appears we are dealing with a common language base (of which Latin appears to be a derivative), being represented in the Lydian, Phrygian and Etruscan scripts. See 'The Phrygian language, Translation of Phrygian scripts, by Mel Copeland (Based on a related work, Etruscan Phrases, first published in 1981)

cmxxxii Some regard the *Phrygians* as a Thracian tribe (Briges or Bryges), who had immigrated into Asia; this account of their migrations has been reversed, a distortion found in many other cases; the Phrygians were a predominantly *Pelasgian* people , and as such, among the most ancient peoples of Asia minor. Racial affinities between Thracians and Phyrgians are that each were predominantly of *Pelasgian* derivation.

cmxxxiii The ancient Greeks used to change very often the sound b with ph, especially in words spoken by the Pelasgians from the northern parts of Hellada. They said therefore Phryges instead of Bryges (Herodotus, lib. VII. 73), Philippos instead of Bilippos, Phalacros instead of Balacros, and Pherenice instead of Berenice, as pronounced in fact by the Macedonians (Plutarc, Oeuvres, Ed. 1784, Tome XIII. p. 105).

cmxxxiv Paphlagonia was located in Asia Minor, lying along the Euxine (Black) Sea between Bithynia and Pontus, its borders delimited according to Strabo's Geography by the river Parthenius in the west and by the Halys in the east.

The origins of the Paphlagonians are unclear. In the Illiad, Homer refers to the Paphlagonians as one of the most ancient nations of Asia Minor. Others admit that the Paphlagonians have common roots with the Phrygians; each being descendent Pelasgians. The Paphlagonians were also anciently recognized as related to the Thracians, tracing common roots to the Phrygians and ancestral Pelasgians.

Ancient Paphlagonia emerged at the end of the second millennium BC during the Bronze Age collapse. A distinct similarity between the apparel of the Phrygians and Paphlagonians was recorded by Herodotus: "The dress of the Phrygians closely resembled the Paphlagonian, only in a very few points differing from it"

In 'classical times' Paphlagonia was located between Bithynia to the west and Pontus to the east. Phrygia lay to the south-west but was separated from it by a mountain range called the Bithynian Olympus.

Philotas, the eldest son of Parmenion, one of Alexander the Great's most experienced and talented Generals equated the terms 'Phrygians' and 'Paphlagonians'.

cmxxxv The present day city of Çankırı is the remnant of the old capital city known in antiquity as Gangra; the city has also been known as Changra, Kandari or Kanghari, and later Germanicopolis. Although the city has been continuously inhabited since Neolithic times, numerous earthquakes have inflicted heavy damage on historical remnants.

Archeological information about Gangra (Çankiri) is derived from tumuli and river banks, since no extensive excavations have been done. Settlement dates to the Neolithic Age (7000-5000 BC).

cmxxxvi Ancient historians and poets, including Virgil, referred to the Troad and the sea off its coast as "Phrygian."

cmxxxvii Before the arrival of Dardanus, the land that would eventually be called Dardania was known as 'Teucria' (and the inhabitants as Teucrians), after Teucer.

cmxxxviii Teucer was the first king of Troy, whence the Trojans are sometimes called Teukroi. (Herod. vii. 122.)

cmxxxix Mt. Ida is the name of two mountain ranges, one in Crete where Zeus was fed as a babe, and the other southeast of Troy.

cmxl Sangas was the husband of Metope, by whom he became the father of the Trojan queen Hecuba (known in Greek as Hekabe); he was also the father of Nana, and therefore the grandfather of Attis

cmxli The ancient city of Gordium is situated on the place where the ancient Royal road between Lydia and Babylon crosses the river Sangarius, which flows from central Anatolia to the Black Sea. Remains of the road are still visible. The Ancient Roman historian, Quintus Curtius Rufus described Gordium as being 'on the banks of the river 'Sangarius, equidistant from the Pontic and Cilician Seas'; the Pontic was the ancient Black Sea and Cilician was that part of the Mediterranean that touches Cilicia in the south-east of Asia Minor.

cmxlii Research suggests that permanent settlement within the river's catchment began by the Late Neolithic. The limited amount of archaeological research conducted in the region has restricted our understanding of the inhabitants' settlement histories and intra- and inter-regional cultural contacts during prehistory.

cmxliii It was only later that geographers applied this name to the continent. According to some traditions the continent of Asia derived its name from her. (Herod. iv. 45.)

cmxliv A legend depicted in Ovid's 'Metamorphoses' wherein he writes "His [Epaphos, prince of Egypt] peer in pride and years was Phaethon, child of Phoebus [i.e. Helios], whose arrogance one day and boasts of his high parentage were more than Inachides [Epaphos] could bear. 'You fool,' he said, 'To credit all your mother [Klymene] says; that birth you boast about is false.' Then Phaethon flushed, though shame checked his rage, and took those taunts to Clymene, his mother. 'And to grieve you more, dear mother, I so frank,' he said, 'So fiery, stood there silent. I'm ashamed that he could so insult me and that I could not repulse him. But, if I indeed am sprung from heavenly stock, give me sure proof of my high birth, confirm my claim to heaven.'

He threw his arms around his mother's neck, and begged her by his own and Merops' [i.e. Clymene's mortal husband] life, his sisters' hopes of marriage, to provide some token that that parentage was true. And Clymene, moved whether by his words or anger at the insult to herself, held out her arms to heaven and faced Sol [Helios the Sun] and cried, 'By this great glorious radiance, this beaming blaze, that hears and sees us now, I swear, dear child, that he, Sol [Helios the Sun], on whom you gaze, Sol who governs all the globe, he is your father. If I lie, let him deny his beams, let this light be the last my eyes shall ever see! And you may find your father's home with no long toil. The place from which he rises borders our own land [of Egypt]. Go, make the journey if your heart is set, and put your question to Sol [Helios] himself.'

Then up flashed Phaethon at his mother's words [to seek out his father] . . . [Phaethon finds Helios and asks him:] 'Phoebus, my father, if to use that name thou givest me leave, and Clymene spoke truth and hides no guilt, give proof that all may know I am thy son indeed, and forever end the doubt that grieves me.'

Then his father laid aside the dazzling beams that crowned his head and bade him come and held him to his heart: 'Well you deserve to be my son,' he said, 'Truly your mother named your lineage; and to dispel all doubt, ask what you will that I may satisfy your heart's desire; and that dark marsh [the river Styx] by which the gods make oath, though to my eyes unknown, shall seal my troth.'

He scarce had ended when the boy declared his wish--his father's chariot for one day with license to control the soaring steeds. Grief and remorse flooded his father's soul."

Ovid, Metamorphoses 2. 333 & 355 ff : "[Phaethon fell to his death from the chariot of the sun:] Clymene, distraught with sorrow, said whatever could be said in woes so terrible and beat her breast, and roamed the world to find his lifeless limbs and then his bones, and found his bones at last buried beside a foreign river-bank. And, prostrate there, she drenched in tears his name carved in the marble and hugged it to her breast . . . (trans. Melville) (Roman epic C1st B.C. to C1st A.D.)

cmxlv Oceanus was the oldest of the Titans, a son of Gaia and Uranus.

cmxlvi The word 'Prometheus' in its original form had only the meaning of: the first in mind, brainy man, wise, with deep understanding. The origin of the word is northern Pelasgian. "Preminte Solomon", meaning Solomon the most wise (Sezatoarea, Flaticeni, An. III. 84. 110; V. 4. 49).

cmxlvii Prometheus [Pro-metheia, pro-metheo] in Greek means prophetic thinking, foresight, forethought. In Greek language the words Prometheus and Prometheus had the primary meaning of clear sighted, or seeing in advance (providus) and only its secondary meaning was that of "wise man" (Fulgentius, Myth. II. 9). The Greek form of Prometheus (Lat. Providus) appears only as a modification of the primitive Pelasgian word "Preminte", having preserved nevertheless a similar meaning, although somewhat different.

cmxlviii Promêtheus is sometimes called a 'Titan', though in reality he did not belong to the Titans, but was only a son of the Titan Iapetus (whence he is designated by the patronymic Iapetionidês, Hes.Theog. 528; Apollon Rhod. iii. 1087), by Clymene

cmxlix For the quote "know yourself and adapt yourself to new ways", see, Oceanus to Prometheus: Aeschylus, Prometheus Bound (310)

cml Paraphrasing Apollonius Rhodes who wrote that "Kolchian Aia lies at the furthest limits of sea and earth"

cmli Prometheus vinctus, v. 443 seqq

cmlii Aeschyl, Prometheus vinctus, v. 447 seqq

cmliii According to the North Caucasus myths, Prometheus was chained either to Elbrus or to Kazbek - two of the highest mountains in Caucasus.

The four most ancient historical sources for the Prometheus myth are Hesiod, Homer, Pindar, and Pythagoras; the four most ancient sources for understanding the origin of the myths and legends all rely on the images represented in the 'Titanomachy' (the cosmological struggle between the God and their parents, the Titans, in Greek mythology).

cmliv About 5000 BC, in the Balkans, Europe's earliest Metal-smiths produced beads & awls by beating (naturally occurring*) copper & gold. By about 4500 BC, these Metal-smiths started Smelting these metals from their ore forms, using high-temperature Kilns originally designed for firing fine pottery

The several sources inform to us that the Greeks learned from the Pelasgians not only the art of the working of the metals, of the construction of wall, but they learned, perfecting it, their way to write and made their divinities their own

cmlv   Cilicia as a whole consists of two parts: the inaccessible western area of the Taurus mountains, also known as "rough Cilicia"; the Taurus is the region's northern border. Here, we find the Cilician Gate, a pass that connects the plain with Cappadocia in the north. To the south is the Mediterranean Sea, and the region knew (and knows) close contacts with Cyprus. In the east the Syrian gates are the connection with Syria and Mesopotamia.

Cappadocia is defined as the ancient land (and later country) between the Black Sea, the Upper Euphrates, the Taurus Mountains, and the river Halys. East of the Euphrates is Armenia;

cmlvi   Legend suggests that Poseidon was in earliest Phrygia because of the frequent earthquakes throughout the country (Strabo, Geography 12. 8. 18 (trans. Jones) (Greek geographer C1st B.C. to C1st A.D.)

cmlvii A Kingdom known to later antiquity as ancient *Karia* (Caria)

cmlviii Phoroneus, king of what later was named the Peloponnesus, and said (by the later Indo-European Greeks) to be the first man, was the father of Kar (Car), who built the citadel of Megara, calling it Karia (Caria). Some say that Kar's mother was Cerdo, others say Teledice, and still others say Cinna. The Megarians themselves affirm that it was during Kar's times that the city got its name.

cmlix   Ancient Caria (spelled Karia or Karya in Turkish) was a civilization that took root and sprouted in western Anatolia. Its second capital was Bodrum (Halicarnassus) in southwest Anatolia, where at 55 meters tall blossomed one of the seven wonders of the ancient world: the mausoleum of the powerful governor of Caria, Mausolos. British archaeologist C.T. Newton, however, carried the ruins of this site to the British Museum in the 19th century.

So many people have written about Caria, but the primary source is indeed Herodotus. Regarded as the father of history with his nine-volume masterpiece called the "History of Herodotus," in fact, Herodotus, himself, was a true Karian that was born in Halicarnassus. His father Lykses (Karca Lukshu) bore a Karian name and was a member of a rich dynasty. Even though Herodotus left Karia in resentment both because of his political stances and because the cruel Governor Lygdamis killed his uncle, Herodotus always maintained the Karian spirit. The best descriptions of the long-forgotten Anatolian populations are found in his history.

The tomb of Kar was in the Karian city Souangela, giving that city its name— according to Stephanus, "Souangela" meant "tomb of the king" in Karian. (Stephanus of Byzantium v Souaggela) Twelve generations after Kar, Lelex arrived from Khemet (Egypt) and made himself the ruler of vast territories both in Megara and Peloponnesus. Some have called Lelex an autochthon, but others call him a son of Poseidon and Libya.

cmlx   On the north side of the peninsula of Miletus was the bay of Latmus, so called from the neighboring range of Latmnus, but the bay has disappeared, and a large tract of sea has been filled up by the alluvium of the Maeander, which once entered the sea on the north side of the bay of Latmus. South of the bay of Latmus was the bay of Iasus, also called Sinus Bargylieticus, the northern side of which terminated in the promontory Posidium, and the southern side was the. north coast of the peninsula of Halicarinassus.

Mitchell & McNicoll 1978-1979, p. 79 under Caria: "There has been much archaeological activity in Caria, and there is little doubt that the discoveries made in the last decade, when fully published, will provoke a reappraisal of Carian history at all periods.

Drews 2001, p. 260: "That Neolithic Caria was uninhabited is quite incredible. Hacilar directly east of Caria, was a Neolithic settlement already in 8000 B.C."

cmlxi   Homer records that Miletus (later an Ionian city), together with the mountain of Phthries, the river Maeander and the crests of Mount Mycale were held by the Carians. In what is now Aydin Province, in present day Turkey

cmlxii Only one road leads into Hisarlik, true cities have roads radiating out from them – it really isn't a city. Google Translate translates Hisarlik as 'fort' and 'of', hisar meaning, fort, fortress, citadel, castle or tower but certainly not a city. (Reference 'The Real Troy Discovered', by John Chaple [john@johnchaple.co.uk])

cmlxiii Sea-level rise during the Holocene brought about a ria-type bay (Troian Bay) in the lower part of the Karamenderes (Scamander) valley which intruded approx. 17 km up to the south of the present plain about 7000-6000 years ago. Since then, alluviation and deltaic progradation has moved the shoreline north of the Canakkale Strait (Dardanelles)

cmlxiv There was no port, wharfs or sheltered anchorage at Hisarlik.

cmlxv   The Troad (or Troas) is the historical name of the Biga peninsula in the northwestern part of the Anatolian peninsula. The Troad has not always been the same, geographically and geologically. There has been a change of the sea-level since the last glacial age.

Archaeological excavations in 2004 and 2005 at Gulpinar, located on the southern coast of the Troad, shed new light on Late Neolithic life in the eastern Aegean world. The cultural horizon to which the assemblages from Gulpinar, Kumtepe (and Besik-Sivritepe) were assigned dates to the first half of the 5th millennium B.C., corresponding to the poorly understood early or middle stages of the Late Chalcolithic in western Anatolia and the Late Neolithic (LN) I in Greece.

Despite this difference in chronological terminology, archaeologists investigating the pre-Bronze Age Troad have generally favored the term Neolithic over Chalcolithic when referring to the 5th-millennium sequences revealed at Kumtepe and Besik-Sivritepe in the 1980s and 1990s.

The fact that the Troad is geographically situated within a liminal zone surrounded by western Anatolia, the Aegean islands, and the Balkans has further confused archaeologists attempting to establish the cultural and chronological affiliations of the region. Indeed, the material remains from this coastal Troadic cultural horizon exhibit more links to the Aegean and Balkans than they do to Anatolia.

The picture for western Anatolia is far from complete. In addition to the excavations carried out at Kumtepe and Besik-Sivritepe, geomorphological investigations in the plain of Troy recently identified a new site at Alacaligol, which also belongs to this 5th-millennium Troadic horizon.

In particular, the pottery from Gulpinar finds parallels among the repertoires of sites in the Cyclades (e.g., Saliagos, Ftelia on Mykonos, Zas and Grotta on Naxos) and the eastern Aegean islands (e.g., Tigani I-II on Samos, Emporio X-VIII on Chios). This Troadic horizon also shows some links to the sites of Dikili Tash I, Sitagroi I-II, and Dimitra I-II in eastern Macedonia, and Paradimi I-II and parts of Karanovo III-IV in Bulgaria. See 'The late Neolithic in the Eastern Aegean: Excavations at Gulpinar in the Troad./ Hesperia'; June 22, 2006 [Takaoglu, Turan; Copyright]

cmlxvi   The outline of this promontory is no longer visible due to the alluvial activity of the Karamenderes which has filled in the embayment east of Yenişehir. The name Sigeion means silent place and is derived from Ancient Greek, silence; in Classical Antiquity, the name was assumed to be antiphrastic, i.e. indicating a characteristic of the place contrary to reality, since the seas in this region are known for their fierce storms.

cmlxvii   During the Holocene (10,000 yr BC to present), which corresponds also with the prehistoric periods, rapid geomorphological changes occurred in Anatolia. It has been accepted that from the beginning of the Holocene, the climatic conditions of Anatolia have explicitly changed and the present climatic conditions have started to occur. In the period of 9000–6000 years BP, hot climatic conditions had an influence in Anatolia in general. The melting of glaciers due to humid and warm-hot climatic conditions resulted in a rise of +2m from -40m in sea level compared to the existing level (Flandrian transgression). This hot period has been determined by names such as "Climatic Optimum, Holocene Optimum, and Holocene Thermal Maximum". Although this period was a hot period in general, in some time spans such as 8200–8100 years BP, cold conditions were effective.

cmlxviii   The former harbor, consisting of two bays, is now completely silted up. Archaeological work has recently been conducted on its territory.

cmlxix   It is supposed that the ancient name of Ezine was Eolya.

cmlxx   According to Strabo the site was first called Sigeia, until around 306 BC when Antigonus, one of the commanders of Alexander III of Macedon ("Alexander the Great"), refounded the city as the much-expanded *Antigonia Troas* by settling the people of five other towns in Sigeia, including the once influential city of Neandreia. Pliny however advises that the name was subsequently changed from Antigonia to Alexandria in memory of Alexander; it then continued to be known as *Alexandria-Troas* until as recently as the time of St. Paul. The life of St Paul and the early Church was set within the context of the Roman Empire, which in turn succeeded the ancient Greek Empire. Present day Ezine is not just a town but an administrative district in the province of Çanakkale, in present day Turkey (which occupies the Anatolian Peninsula).

cmlxxi   Herodotus tells us that the Lycians called themselves the Trmmili and claimed to come from Crete. The Dodecanese Isles have been inhabited since prehistoric times; the island group generally defines the eastern limit of the Sea of Crete. The most historically important and well-known island in the group is the Isle of Rhodes (Rodos), which, for millennia, has been the island from which the region is controlled; of the others, the Isle of Kos and the isle of Patmos are historically more important.

cmlxxii   The ruins of Neandria are at a height of 500 m on the granite crest of Cgri Dag, to the South of the river Skamandros and of Troy. The ruins of the ancient city of Neandreia are located at the highest point of the Çığrı Dağ (Cıgrı mountain) southwest of Ezine (archaeologists have identified this site with the ancient city). The walls of the city enclose an irregular polygon; w within the walls, on an esplanade in the center of the city, a Temple to Apollo has been found. Kolonia is now called Axara

cmlxxiii   The tribes of Asia Minor, which are usually designated by the name Phrygians were unquestionably of Pelasgian stock

cmlxxiv   Arzawa, a region and a political entity (a "kingdom" or a federation of local powers) in Western Anatolia, formed in the second half of the 2nd millennium BCE as the successor of the Assuwa league, but was later conquered by the Hittites in c. 1400 BCE. Some scholars have identified Phrygia with the Assuwa league

cmlxxv   The city of Sminthe in Troas was where Apollo was worshipped in pre-Hellenic times; thus the use of the ancient epithet 'Apollo Smintheus' found in Homer's Ilias (I, 39) essentially meant 'Apollo from Sminthe'. The ruins of the Apollo Smintheus temple have been excavated in the southwest corner of the Biga Peninsula; the temple is located in an area, which was rich in water in ancient times, and it is believed that this may be the reason why a large temple was erected on the site.

Strabo, Geography 13. 1. 13 (trans. Jones) (Greek geographer C1st B.C. to C1st A.D.) : "The city [of Adrasteia in the Troad] is situated between Priapos and Parion; and it has below it a plain that is named after it, in which there was an oracle of Apollon Aktaios (of the Shore) and Artemis ((lacuna)) . . But when the temple [of Apollon] was torn down, the whole of its furnishings and stonework were transported to Parion, where was built an altar the work of Hermokreon, very remarkable for its size and beauty; but the oracle was abolished like that at Zeleia [in the Troad]."

Strabo, Geography 13. 1. 35: "The plain of Thymbra . . . and the Thymbrios River [in the Troad], which flows through the plain and empties into the River Skamandros at the temple of Apollon Thymbraios."

In Lycia, Leto, Apollo and Artemis (Apollo's twin sister) were worshiped above all other deities; the existence of an Apollon temple at the Lycian site of Patara has been indicated by the discovery of a large bust of Apollo. Many temples have been found at Patara, but the whereabouts of the Apollon temple is unknown. Excavators have found the remains of a temple under a harbor basilica and hope that this is not the temple of Apollo, since it has been largely destroyed and is underwater.

[cmlxxvi] Xen. Cyneg. 1; Philostr. Her. 9, Icon. ii. 2; Pind. Pyth. ix. 65.

[cmlxxvii] Hughes and Hughes (1992) Over 8,000 years ago, a slowing down in sea-level rise prompted the development of the modern Nile Delta (Said, 1990, 1993). In ancient times the Nile Delta was recorded as having seven tributaries; however the flow has been controlled so that now there are only two main branches, the Damietta and Rosetta

[cmlxxviii] The landscape of the Nile Delta underwent extensive changes throughout the course of history. The most profound of these changes occurred more recently after the construction of the two dams at Aswan in 1964 and several barrages on the Nile. One of the most devastating results of the dam has been the departure of the annual Nile flood. The majority (98%) of the flood discharge and suspended sediments are no longer distributed across the Delta, causing extensive coastal erosion and increased salinization of the groundwater. Consequently, the dynamic landscape of the ancient Nile Delta is no longer evident.

[cmlxxix] During the early and mid-Pleistocene, forceful Nile floods created sand mounds, also known as geziras ('islands') or turtle-backs.70 Originally these geziras stood above the alluvial plain and often provided havens for settlement within the Nile Delta. Most of these sand mounds were eventually buried by the continuous deposit of alluvial sediments. Today, the only viable means for determining whether a settlement was established upon a levee or a sand gezira is through coring. See 'Islands In The Nile Sea', a (Master of Arts) Thesis by Veronica Marie Morriss; Submitted to the Office of Graduate Studies of Texas A&M University (May 2012)

[cmlxxx] According to Herodotus "when the waters peaked, the Nile Delta was transformed into an inland sea'. See 'Islands In The Nile Sea', a (Master of Arts) Thesis by Veronica Marie Morriss; the Office of Graduate Studies of Texas A&M University (May 2012)

[cmlxxxi] Tanis's creation was most likely due to the silting up of the Nile branch on which it was located Tanis has been known by different names across ages, Djane by the Egyptians, theZoan of the Hebrews, the Coptic Tani or Athenniks, and the modern Arabic San ElHagar, an allusion to the monumental remains of the site

[cmlxxxii] The oldest remains in Tanis manifest the existence of the city of earlier time in old kingdom particularly the Fifth Dynasty (2392-2282 B.C.).

[cmlxxxiii] The Nile Delta was once known for large papyrus (Cyperus papyrus) swamps, but papyrus is now largely absent from the delta. Vegetation consists of Phragmites australis, Typha capensis, and Juncus maritimus, with some small sedges

[cmlxxxiv] The huge Fayoum depression is renown today for archeological finds of ancient whale skeletons and bones.

[cmlxxxv] The Fayoum takes its name from the Coptic word, Phiom or Payomj, meaning lake or sea. Researches on the desert margin of the depression indicate that in early Paleolithic times the lake's waters stood about 120 feet (37 m) above sea level and probably filled the depression; the lake's level gradually fell until about 10,000 BC, when it was about 15 feet (4 1/2 m) below sea level, perhaps because its connection with the Nile River was temporarily cut off.
According to James Trifil, some 243 fossilized whale skeletons and loose bones were discovered in a large valley 150 miles southwest of Cairo (100 miles inland from the Mediterranean Sea and more than 200 miles from the Red Sea). These skeletons are of Zeuglodon whales, like those found all over the southeastern United States. The Egyptian whale bones were scattered among the sand dunes; when the wind exposed them, the paleontologists rapidly dug out as much of the fossilized whale as possible because windborne sand erodes exposed bones

[cmlxxxvi] The Fayoum at that time was about five miles from the mainstream of the Nile, separated by a low ridge. The Fayoum, also spelled Faiyum, or Fayum, occupies a great depression of the Western Desert, not too far south of Cairo; it is sometimes referred to as the Fayoum Oasis, although it has clearly been far more than a mere Oasis.

[cmlxxxvii] Shedet is one of Egypt's oldest cities, due to its strategic location; in its most ancient form the city was originally called Shedet in Ancient Khemet; the later Greeks called it Krocodilopolis or Crocodilopolis, and the even later Romans called it 'Arsinoë'.

[cmlxxxviii] Shedet was one of Ancient Khemet's oldest cities due to its strategic location; in its most ancient form the city was originally called Shedet; the later Greeks called it Krocodilopolis or Crocodilopolis, and the even later Romans called it 'Arsinoë'. The city is now called Medinet el Fayum (the 'City of Faiyum').

[cmlxxxix] The present day Egyptian city of Asyūt was known as "Sauti" ("the Guardian" or "place of the Guardian") in Neolithic Khemet; the Arabic form Asyut (or Siuti) is derived from the Egyptian derivative of the ancient Khemetian name.

[cmxc] Today the canal is known as the 'Bahr Yussef' (Arabic for "the waterway of Joseph"); in ancient times the channel was known as Mer-Wer (the Great Canal), which paralleled the Nile for about 200 miles (320 km) to the north, irrigating much of Middle Egypt

[cmxci] The Kharga Oasis is the southernmost of Egypt's five western oases. It is located in the Libyan Desert, about 200 km to the west of the Nile valley; it is the closest of the oases to the Nile Valley.

cmxcii . Distance between Asyut and Giza is (195.48 miles) 169.75 nautical miles; the Nile Delta covers an area stretching about 100 miles from north to south and about 150 miles from east to west. In antiquity, the average speed sailing up-river was between 40 kms (24.9 miles) and 70 kms (43.5 miles) per day.

cmxciii This distinction is even reflected in the Egyptian hieroglyphs for travelling south (a boat with a sail up) and travelling north (a boat being rowed). The Egyptians, with access to the Mediterranean, also use larger seagoing vessels. The earliest documentary evidence of a sailing craft is a crude painting on an Egyptian vase that dates back to 6000 B.C. The mast, the square sail, the high bow and the curve of the hull depict the first beginnings of the modern full-rigged ship or yacht; this was discovered on an amphora found in Upper Egypt (and now in the British Museum). The date ascribed to it by the ablest 'Egyptologists' is that of the Pre-Dynastic period, which for the sake of clearness we may regard as about 6000 B.C.

cmxciv See 'Islands In The Nile Sea', a (Master of Arts) Thesis by Veronica Marie Morriss; Submitted to the Office of Graduate Studies of Texas A&M University (May 2012)

cmxcv In the beginning of the Early Holocene, the Sahara went from being a hyperarid desert to savannah-type vegetation (Brooks, 2006). In 8500 BC, the onset of semi-arid conditions in the north, and semi-humid conditions in the south, has been found in the geological and archeological archives of the Eastern Sahara (Kuper & Kröpelin, 2006). The climate was monsoon-controlled with short but violent summer rains, and because of the monsoonal rains, the desert margin shifted up to 800 km north to latitude 24°N within only a few centuries. The region, today covered by desert, was well vegetated (Brooks, 2006)! Lakes and temporary rivers were formed because of rising water tables (Nicoll, 2004; Kuper & Kröpelin, 2006).

cmxcvi Heracleopolis (hərăk‚lēŏp′əlĭs) is an ancient city in Northern Khemet (Egypt), just south of the Fayum. It is one of the oldest cities ancient Khemet; the Greek name for the city came from the identification with Heracles, the principal deity of the early fortress-city.

cmxcvii Remains of ancient Heracleopolis were first excavated by Edouard Naville for the 'Egypt Exploration Fund' in 1890-1891. He found a rectangular hall with six fallen granite columns at it's front. It was thought that this was all that remained of the temple of Herishef. The six columns were given to the BM, Boston, Adelaide, Manchester, Bolton and Philadelphia. The two fragments of a column that Bolton received weighed about 1½ tons each and are displayed in two pieces; originally the columns were each 17 feet tall.

cmxcviii Overtime the harbor along with the very branch of the Nile that formed the Isle of Hērăclĕŏpŏlis finally silted up, eventually culminating in a shift og the Nile and the island of Hērăclĕŏpŏlis becoming part of its western bank (Mart. Cap. 6, 676.).

cmxcix Unlike the permanent and often monumental facilities found at seaports, Nilotic harbors were constructed under entirely different parameters. Fluctuating conditions, dictated by the flow of the Nile, influenced the construction of riverine harbors. As a result, transitory facilities were often adopted in lieu of more permanent designs using stone-works.

m In Diodorus Siculus, Busiris appears as the founder of the line of kings at Thebes. In Greek mythology, Isocrates, in his witty declamation Busiris recounts "the false tale of Heracles and Busiris" (11.30 11.40), which was a comic subject represented almost entirely in the repertory of early 5th century BC Athenian vase-painters: the theme has a narrow narrative range, according to Niall Livingstone: Heracles being led to sacrifice; his escape; the killing of Busiris; the rout of his entourage. In Isocrates' rhetorical use of the theme (that he himself purportedly considered unworthy of serious treatment) the villainous king named Busiris was the ancient founder of Egyptian civilization, with an imagined "model constitution" that Isocrates sets up as a parodic contrast to the Republic by Plato. The monstrous Busiris sacrificed all visitors to his gods. Heracles defied him, broke his shackles at the last minute and killed Busiris. This part of the mythology concerning Herakles appears to have origins in a corruption of an Egyptian myth concerning Osiris' sacrifice by Set, and subsequent resurrection

mi The sites of Abu Sir Bana and Beheyt were never been excavated; the site continues to decline year after year, bringing into question the choices of archaeological priorities in present day Egypt

mii The ancient city is known today as 'Heliopolis' or 'Ain-Shams', and was considered the first capital of the Lower River Valley during the predynastic period

miii The seven depressions in the western desert – Siwa, Qattara, Fayum, Bahariya, Farafra, Dakhla, and Kharga – (which once constituted the eastern frontier of the *Maa Confederation*) may represent parts of old drainage systems with deflation, extensive erosion, and possibly, some tectonic activity. Oases with freshwater exist in these depressions. Geological and geophysical investigations in the Qattara Depression indicate the presence of buried fluvial channels with southeast to northwest flow directions from the highland areas. The origin of these fluvial systems, as well as the origin of the depressions themselves, is still unresolved.

miv Hermopolis was founded on an island where Thoth was worshipped in the form of the ibis. He was Hermes to the Greeks and Trismegistus, the scribe who presided over all forms of knowledge. The modern city of El Ashmunein, the Coptic "Shmounein", located in Middle Egypt, 300 km south of Cairo, far from the Nile, near the canal called Bahr el Yusuf, is considered to be one of the many cities with the name of Khemenu, the city of eight, called Hermopolis by the Greeks who have recognized their god Hermes in Thoth.

mv Thoth, is actually a Greek name derived from the Khemetan (ancient Egyptian) 'Dḥwty' or 'Dihauti' (djih-how-tee); however, many write "Djehuty", inserting the letter 'e' automatically between consonants in Egyptian words, and writing 'w' as 'u', as a convention of convenience for English speakers, not the transliteration employed by Egyptologists. Djehuty is sometimes alternatively rendered as Tahuti, Tehuti, Zehuti, Techu, or Tetu. Thoth (also Thot or Thout) is the Greek version derived from the letters ḏhwty.

mvi . Nun is a threatening state of affairs into which order could relapse at any moment. It is the opposite of order, light and life. In fact, the cosmos, or ordered natural whole, is constantly balancing "on the edge" of this abyss of chaos, although periods of extended peace are possible.

[mvii] The 'Ogdoad' from Khmwnw, dates back well before the Old Kingdom although names do not appear in writing until the Late Period. It also appears that, in the case of this particular grouping, the term Ogdoad ties back to the name of the city itself – City of Eight – and so it is postulated that although the concept existed throughout Ancient Egypt, the exact term didn't come into common use for all such groups until Egyptologists started looking at the pattern.

[mviii] The ancient Khemetians gave discriptive rather than denominative qualifications, in which Nun is conceived as an inchoate, nonexistent state-of-no-state. The 'virtual' state is not 'actual', but confirms possibility, latency and potentiality. As a potency anterior to creation, it was conceived as a nonexistent object, before "form", i.e. anterior to space and time, and before the creation of the temporal Universe and its natural dynamics.

[mix] Although ontologically, precreation is isomorphic, homogeneous, unknown, insubstantial, void, undifferentiated and without organization, the need to characterize it is already felt in the Pyramid Texts.

The creation myth promulgated in the city of Hermopolis focused on the nature of the Universe before the creation of the world. The Hermopolitans claimed that their theory of creation was older than any other in Khemet; they believed in a system of eight ancestors of creation arranged in four male-female pairs: Nu and Naunet, Amun and Amaunet, Kuk and Kauket, Huh and Hauhet.

Essentially, each pair represents the male and female aspect of one of the four concepts of primordial chaos, namely the primordial waters (Nu and Naunet), air, invisibility, and hidden powers (Amun and Amaunet), darkness and obscurity (Kuk and Kauket), and eternity or infinity (Huh and Hauhet). The two that became the most prominent in later times were Nun and Amun. Nun was respected in many parts of Khemet as the primordial waters from which everything emerged during creation.

As might be suspected, these qualities of the primordial state have often been compared with the shadowy waters of the Biblical Genesis, when 'the earth was without form and void, and darkness was upon the face of the deep'. But rather than regard the Nun as an initial or primal chaos, in the Biblical mode, it seems more fruitful to see it as indefinable substance, the eternal and infinite source of the Universe. The lotus, which has its roots in mud, its stem in water and its leaves and flowers opening out into air, receiving the celestial dew and the sun's rays, has always been a symbol of the four elements

[mx] According to Watterson, the soul of Amun was represented by a coiled serpent, the Cosmic Serpent, and went by the name of Kematef, or "He Who has Finished His Moment." The Hydra (Naga) Wisdom in Africa, was the first truth to be revealed, that's why, when you read the Sutra (The Large Sutra on Perfect Wisdom) you can find all the religions in it, it is the (Genetrix of the Beginning), the Mother of the Law

[mxi] Hermopolis was founded on an island and it was subsequently moved to the location at which Antinoopolis was founded. The large collection of documents that bear on the puzzling relationship between the two cities of Hermopolis and Antinoopolis generally come from the main papyrusyielding areas of Oxyrhynchus and the Fayum and several other quite distant locations. The texts that refer to both cities however mostly originated from one of the two, predominantly Hermopolis.

[mxii] See Ἑρμοπολιτάνη φυλακή, Strabo xvii. p. 813; Ptol. loc. cit.; theBahr Jusuf in Arabic. The first archaeological map with a detailed description of Hermopolis is found in the French Description de l'Egypte by Jornard, a member of Napoleon's Egyptian Expedition during 1798-1799.

[mxiii] The founders of civilization in South West Asia were the Anu people, archaeologists call Natufians. Founded along the Tigris and Euphrates Rivers, in Asia-Mino (Mesopotamia) We know the first people to settle in the region were called 'Anu', because the Sumerian texts claim that the original people in the area were Anu (or Anunaki). In India, the Veda (Vedic people or tribes) were also known as the Anu; in Hebrew texts from which the old testament was wriiten, Lord Anu was the culture bringer to the Sumerians, this occurred 10,000 years ago.

[mxiv] *Elam* was the first civilization in the area of ancient Persia (present day Iran); sharing *Sumer's* eastern border. The first *Kushite* settlements in *Elam* were part of the expansion of their permanent settlement range in *Sumer*. Several ancient scholars have noted that the first rulers of *Elam* were *Kushite*; according to *Strabo*, the first *Elamite* colony (at *Susa*) was founded by *Tithnus*, a "King of Kush". Ancient historians have identified vestiges of *Proto-Elamites* in the highlands of *East Africa* and the *Sahara*. The earliest of the *Proto-Elamites* emerged as an admixture of *Dasas, Negrito* and *Kushite;* archeologists have compared pottery uncovered from prehistoric *Elam* with similar ware found in *Kush*, and found the fragments at earliest *Susa* to be similar in dating and other aspects.

[mxv] The Fayum is a natural depression, separated from the Nile Valley by a ridge known as the Nile-Fayum divide (Sandford & Arkell 1929).

[mxvi] The Jebel Qatrani Formation, the northwestern borderland of the Faiyum basin, was then a tropical lowland coastal plain with damp soils and seasonal rainfall that supported an abundance and variety of vegetation, including large vines, tall trees, mangroves, a large and varied variety of fauna and patches of forest and woodlands.

[mxvii] Sobek became known as an ancient god of strength and power; the god who protected the Egyptian army, the pharaohs, and the ancient Egyptian people. His strength and courage allowed the Pharaoh to overcome obstacles and also protected him.

[mxviii] The City of Imu (latter day 'Kom el-Hisn') is one of the most ancient and important towns in the western Delta region of the Nile. In antiquity it was situated near a branch of the Nile which has since shifted eastward, and it was also near the desert edge on the route to the Libyan frontier. The ancient site was called Imu, or "imAw," meaning the plural of a type of tree in the Kemetic language. The site was

initially uncovered by Flinders Petrie during his excavation at Naukratis in 1881. It was then surveyed by Francis Llewellyn Griffith from 1885 to 1887; this survey captured the remains of a mudbrick temple, enclosure wall, and four statues of Ramesses II. Two of these statues had inscriptions dedicating them to Sekhmet-Hathor, "Mistress of Imu". The temple and enclosure wall have since been destroyed.

[mxix] Oshun (Osun) by the Yoruba of Nigeria, and Sarasvati in the Vedic tradition. Also known as Hathor, Nephthys and Neb-t Het.,Het Heru may be found throughout other cultures under, Kamalatmika, Hana-El, etc. In addition to native variations by locality or over time, there are often several possible transliterations into the Roman alphabet used for English.) Greek names: Hat Hor, Hathor, Athyr; Semitic name: Baalat

[mxx] The religious origins of Hathor are uncertain among Egyptologists.

[mxxi] The horns of sacred cow signifying the crescent moon, the chalice and the boat in which the goddess ferries souls across the ocean of existence; and the sun, symbol of essence, source, warmth, heat, vitality, energy, vibration, excitation and power.

[mxxii] It was believed that when the two are brought into balance within our own bodies, we are balancing the electric (male) principle and the magnetic (female) principle; a balancing of electromagnetics. Which has less to do with sexuality, and more to do with the subtle energies within the nervous system.

[mxxiii] It is unclear how common this type of sexual confidence was in Anu women, but since Khemet was a patriarchal society, we may assume that it was not too common amongst married or marriageable women.

[mxxiv] Intiates to Hathor's Order were bound to lives of reverence and dedication, though not strictly lives of celibacy and deprivation of their feminine needs (as is the case of a present day nun).

[mxxv] "Ontology" is the philosophical study of the nature of being, becoming, existence or reality as well as the basic categories of being and their relations; "Cosmology" (from the Greek κόσμος, kosmos "world" and -λογία, -logia "study of") is the study of the origin, evolution, and eventual fate of the universe.

[mxxvi] This refers to a form of ecstasy anciently described as the vision of, or union with, some otherworldly entity; a form of ecstasy that pertains to an individual trancelike experience of the sacred or of God.

[mxxvii] Exponentiation in this sense is defined as the act of raising a quantity to a power. Omniscience means "all-knowing", in the sense that he is aware of past, present, and future. Nothing takes him by surprise. His knowledge is total. He knows all that there is to know and all that can be known The *Nous* (Greek: "mind" or "intellect") is defined as divine intellect; most anciently applying to *Amun's* apprehension of eternal intelligible substances and first principles.

[mxxviii] Sentience in this sense is the capacity to feel, perceive, or experience subjectively. Eighteenth-century philosophers used the concept to distinguish the ability to think (reason) from the ability to feel (sentience). In modern Western philosophy, sentience is the ability to experience sensations (known in philosophy of mind as "qualia"). In the philosophy of consciousness, sentience can refer to the ability of any entity to have subjective perceptual experiences, hence sentience is the only aspect of consciousness that can't be explained

[mxxix] The term "erotic" is derived from Eros; Eros has also been used in philosophy and psychology in a much wider sense, almost as an equivalent to "life energy".

[mxxx] There were prominent early ancient temples under the auspices of *Hathor* in the *City of Shedet* on the shores of *Mr-wr* (Paleo-Lake Moeris); the *City of Imu* (latter day 'Kom el-Hisn') in the *Western Delta;* and the *City of Heliopolis* (the ancient "City of the Sun") in the *Southern Delta*.

[mxxxi] The epithet "Het-heru of the Three Cities", refere to the predynastic Temples of the Hathor Sect (or Order) of the early priesthood in the ancient cities of Shedet, Onu, and Imu.

[mxxxii] The term "irony" is from the Ancient Greek "εἰρωνεία eirōneía", meaning hypocrisy, deception, or feigned ignorance. The contemporary term "irony" can best be defined as that middle ground between what is said and what is meant (or more precisely, others' interpreration and understanding of what was said and what was meant).

[mxxxiii] Theoretically, the concept of federalism, according to Mogi (1931 cited in Ifesinachi, 2007) can be said to have originated from ideas on intergovernmental relations which dates back to Greek civilization, when efforts were made to describe the legal relationships between the leagues and the city states.

[mxxxiv] Federalism is a political system in which several states or regions defer some powers to a central government, while retaining a measure of self-government. It differs from "Confederalism", which is a political system in which the central of government is subordinate to the regional governments; and is also different from a "Unitary State", which is a political system in which the regional government is subordinate to the central government. The terms 'Federalism' and 'Confederalism' both have a root in the Latin word "Foedus", meaning "Treaty, Pact or Covenant." Their common meaning until the late eighteenth century was a simple "League" or inter-governmental relationship among Sovereign States based upon a Treaty. They were therefore initially synonyms

[mxxxv] It was in this sense that James Madison in Federalist 39 had referred to the new United States as 'neither a national nor a federal Constitution, but a composition of both' (i.e. neither a single large unitary state nor a league/confederation among several small states, but a hybrid of the two).

[mxxxvi] Theocracy is a form of government in which a deity is the source from which all authority derives. (The Oxford English Dictionary)

[mxxxvii] Manning, J.G. (2012) "The Representation of Justice in Ancient Egypt," *Yale Journal of Law & the Humanities*: Vol. 24: Iss. 1, Article 4.

mxxxviii See 'The African Origins of the Athenian Democracy' (NCOBPS 2012 Annual Meeting Paper), by Narcisse Tiky University of Connecticut, Department of Political Science.

mxxxix Masculine energy is that which is active, which manifests on all levels-- physically, emotionally, and mentally. Spiritually it is divine will, power, purpose and outward focused attributes of the Creator." (Ronna Herman).

mxl The word theocracy originates from the Greek theokratia; the components of the word are theos, "god," and kratein, "to rule," hence "rule by god" or "government by god."

mxli In ancient Khemet, there were seven cardinal virtues (or principles) of Ma'at to achieve human perfectibility; Truth, Justice, Balance, Order, Compassion, Harmony, and Reciprocity.

mxlii See 'Grace', a mistranslated word and misunderstood concept (at http://theogeek.com) Kushites and Khemetans did not see trade as a legitimate way to get rich; merchants were simply servants employed to find and deliver merchandise. They were paid for their labor, but did not expect any additional profit; temples and wealthy noblemen had them scour the known world for whatever was needed.

mxliii Cultural fusion theory describes how newcomers acculturate into the dominant culture and maintain aspects of their minority culture, while at the same time the dominant or host culture also fuses aspects off the newcomer's culture into the dominant culture to create a fused intercultural identity. Cultural Fusion Theory: An Alternative to Acculturation, by Stephen M. Croucher & Eric Kramer (Pages 97-114; Published Sep 2016

mxliv The heliacal rising of a star occurs annually when it first becomes visible above the eastern horizon for a brief moment just before sunrise, after a period of time when it had not been visible

mxlv Toward the mouth of the River the ancient Nile Valley Canyon underlyinh the valley floor reaches depths simular to that of the Grand Canyon (in Arizona), and as one travels southward, upstream on the Nile. the canyon becomes less entrenched.

mxlvi During phases of very high Nile flow, clastic muds rich in continental organic matter and highly organic sapropels accumulated on the floor of the Nile Valley; very recent flood sediments have been found to contain reworked charcoal fragments several thousand years older than the actual sediment.

mxlvii The heliacal rising of Sirius marks the start of the agricultural year, when the innundation of the Nile is about to commence. When Sirius rises, the New Year officially begins with the festival known as the "Opening of the Year". The Feast of Sopdet was celebrated in every temple in Khemet; the priests and priestesses dressed in ritual clothing and would gather within the temples before dawn. They climbed up to the rooftops before dawn and turned to face the rising sun in the east so that they could watch and bathe in the first light of the New Year as the sun rose. Despite the erratic timing of the flood from year to year, and the slow procession of Sirius within the solar year, Sopdet continued to remain central to cultural depictions of the year and to celebrations of Wep Renpet (Wp Rnpt)

mxlviii Thebes is the Latinized form of the Greek Thebai. The ancient royal City of Thebes was known as "Wase" during the rise of early ancient Khemet, and it was actually during later antiquity (through early ancient times) that it became known as "Waset", a derivative name also indicative of its royal power. A *"was"* was the ancient *"scepter"* of the *Pharaohs,* the so-called "was scepter", which were used as symbols of power or dominion. The "was scepter" is a symbol that appears often in ancient relics, art, and hieroglyphics

mxlix Historian Ian Morris postulated that by 1500 BC, Thebes may have grown to be the largest city in the world, with a population of about 75,000, a position which it held until about 900 BC.

ml The first migration of modern humans began over 100,000 years ago; these Africans included the four branches of the Black race who live intact in Africa today, and with members found from South Arabia to India all the way to the Philippines, the Mountains of Vietnam, Australia, Melanesia and parts of SE Asia.

mli The straits were narrow, but never completely closed between Yemen on the south coast of the Arabian Peninsula, and Somalia on the Horn of Africa.

mlii Some genetic evidence points to migrations along two routes, however, nost other studies corroborate the single migration route.

mliii Another group who migrated to from the central African lowlands to Asia were the Bak tribes, 'dimunitive' or small-stature Blacks (compared to most American and West African, East African Blacks who average five feet, eight inches to six feet two inches). The Bak came first from Central Africa, from where they migrated to Sudan, across the Gulf and around the coastal pinensula to Mesopotamia. From Mesopotamia, the Bak made a number of migrations to East Asia. The first was about 10,000 BC About 3000 BC and specifically in the period of about 2800 BC, Hu-Na-Kunte, a Black Mesopotamian of the Bak Tribes (who settled Mesopotamia) settled in the Loh River Valley region of China. About 3000 BC and specifically in the period of about 2800 BC, Hu-Na-Kunte, a Black Mesopotamian of the Bak Tribes (who settled Mesopotamia) settled in the Loh River Valley region of China.

mliv An is most often represented in iconography simply by a crown or crown on a throne symbolizing his status as King of Kings. "An" can be translated from the Sumerian as "high one", a name that later became synonymous with "god". Over time An became known as "lord of the heavens" above the sky and the "god" who ordered and maintained all aspects of existence. The doctrine of Anu's kingship and his place in a triad of primary male deities, once established, remained an inherent part of Babylonian-Assyrian religion. It also led to the universalization of the three gods constituting the triad, disassociating them from their original local limitations. After Hammurabi, Anu retained his identity as the god of heaven, but was replaced as the chief god by Marduk, his grandson.

mlv Sea levels were lower during the Palaeolithic, Mesolithic, and Early Neolithic, but gradually rising due to massive distant glacial unloading, and meltwater that ultimately flowed into the Gulf and adjacent Indian Ocean. By 14000 yr BP the Strait of Hormuz had opened up as a narrow waterway and by about 12500 years ago the marine incursion into the Central Basin had 99started. The Western Basin flooded about 1000 years later. Momentary stillstands may have occurred during the Gulf flooding phase at about 11300 and 10500 yr BP.

The present shorelines were reached shortly before 6,000 BCE, as sea levels rose inundating the low-lying areas of the Gulf; leaving the settlements and civilizations of the earlier era in the Gulf obscured under water and alluvium. Much of the Gulf floor was exposed during the Palaeolithic, Mesolithic and Early Neolithic, with broad alluvial plains and lakes and marshes forming in the flatter regions, providing a natural migration route for those spreading eastwards into the regions that would become earliest Elam (Persia, Iran) enroute to India

[mlvi] The Anu or Annu (written with three pillars), were the "Twa" (now errioniously labled "pygmies") who built the holy City of An, known as Anu or Onu by the Kushites, Heliopolis by the Greeks, and the biblical City of On by the Hebrews.

[mlvii] In antiquity, markets were typically situated in the town's centre. The market was surrounded by alleyways inhabited by skilled artisans, such as metal-workers, leather workers and carpenters. These artisans may have sold wares directly from their premises, but also prepared goods for sale on market days. Bintliff, J., "Going to Market in Antiquity," In Stuttgarter Kolloquium zur Historischen Geographie des Altertums, Eckart Olshausen and Holger Sonnabend (eds), Stuttgart, Franz Steiner, 2002, pp 209-25 Across the Mediterranean and Aegean, a network of markets emerged from the early Bronze Age. A vast array of goods were traded including: salt, lapiz-lazuli, dyes, cloth, metals, pots, ceramics, statues, spears and other implements. Archaeological evidence suggests that Bronze Age traders segmented trade routes according to geographical circuits

[mlviii] Foreign trade in ancient Khemet was not like the free trade of modern society, as it was predominantly a royal liberty; the right to trade for profit was granted by selectively granted by Pharaoh.

[mlix] Since there was no law prohibiting priests from engaging in trade, and all profit went to the temple instead of the crown, these priests often lived as comfortably as royalty.

[mlx] Inter-regional trade occurred before and during the Predynastic period. The presence of Syrian pottery imported stone tools and metals, and the remains of Lebanese cedar confirm the existence of maritime trade links between Khemet and the region of present day Syrias well before the conventionally recognized formation of Khemet. Though the advent of international trade advantaged all social classes of early ancient Khemet, trade affected differing social classes in different ways; the lower classes (predominantly farmers) had fewer material goods and traded for items needed to survive, while Artisans used ebony and copper for crafts, and Scribes traded for leather from other places to be made into carrying bags by artisans. Priests bought incense and linen, while Pharoah and the upper echelon traded for luxury goods and resources. Throughout its long history, Ancient Khemet enjoyed the benefits of international trade, which became more abundant, luxurious, and exotic as transportation technologies improved or were expanded.

[mlxi] The Greek god "Helios" was identified with Apollo: "Different names may refer to the same being," Walter Burkert observes, "or else they may be consciously equated, as in the case of Apollo and Helios. The earliest certain reference to Apollo identified with Helios appears in the surviving fragments of Euripides' play Phaethon in a speech near the end (fr 781 N²), Clymene, Phaethon's mother, laments that Helios has destroyed her child, that Helios whom men rightly call Apollo.

[mlxii] Asyut was the birthplace of the Neoplatonist philosopher Plotinus (c. 205–269/270 ce). The ancient city and its temples have been almost completely buried and lost under the strata of the alluvial plain and especially the rapidly growing modern city. Despite this difficult situation of the archaeological inaccessibility of the city itself, the exploration of the mountain situated to the west of Asyut provides plenty of information.

[mlxiii] During the Holocene the climate was marked by monsoonal rains, and short but violent summer rains; Nile was more rebust because of rising water tables in the great lake region of the highlands. Archeological excavations in the upper nile river valley reveal that the Nile flood levels during antiquity were far higher than at present. The Nile valley from Aswan down, which looks to be a flat-floored valley just a few hundred feet below the surrounding desert, is a canyon filled up to that level with silt. The canyon begins at Aswan, gets deeper as it goes north, till at Cairo it is eight thousand feet deep. Stated differently, Cairo is eight thousand feet above the real bottom of the canyon. Over time the ancient Egyptian canyon became a long inlet, which the Nile gradually silted up; during the earlier part of the era the floor of the canyon was far deeper than at present.

[mlxiv] The name "Thebes" was given by the ancient Greeks, for unknown reasons; there is no known connection with the famous Greek city of Thebes.

[mlxv] "Wo'se" is the Ta'Nehisi'an (Nubian) name of Waset, which is why it predates all other names of the city. Further proof of this is found in the fact that, not only did the name "Wo'se" originate in the South, but the name itself also equates to the imperial scepter of Ethiopia. (See 'Williams, Destruction..(pg. 89))

[mlxvi] This was the original ancient *Thebes* (Waset) of which the later Greek legends speak when they recount the early feats of Heracles (Hercules).

[mlxvii] In Khemetan / Egyptian accounts, the pregnant Isis hides from Set, to whom the unborn child is a threat, in a thicket of papyrus in the Nile Delta.